T0189691

Lecture Notes in Artificial Intelligence 13501

Subseries of Lecture Notes in Computer Science

More information about this subseries at https://link.springer.com/bookseries/1244

Ngoc Thanh Nguyen · Yannis Manolopoulos ·
Richard Chbeir · Adrianna Kozierkiewicz ·
Bogdan Trawiński (Eds.)

Computational Collective Intelligence

14th International Conference, ICCCI 2022
Hammamet, Tunisia, September 28–30, 2022
Proceedings

Springer

Editors
Ngoc Thanh Nguyen (iD)
Wrocław University of Science
and Technology
Wrocław, Poland

Richard Chbeir (iD)
University of Pau and Pays de l'Adour
Anglet, France

Bogdan Trawiński (iD)
Wrocław University of Science
and Technology
Wrocław, Poland

Yannis Manolopoulos (iD)
Open University of Cyprus
Nicosia, Cyprus

Adrianna Kozierkiewicz (iD)
Wrocław University of Science
and Technology
Wrocław, Poland

ISSN 0302-9743   ISSN 1611-3349 (electronic)
Lecture Notes in Artificial Intelligence
ISBN 978-3-031-16013-4   ISBN 978-3-031-16014-1 (eBook)
https://doi.org/10.1007/978-3-031-16014-1

LNCS Sublibrary: SL7 – Artificial Intelligence

This Springer imprint is published by the registered company Springer Nature Switzerland AG
The registered company address is: Gewerbestrasse 11, 6330 Cham, Switzerland

Preface

This volume contains the first part of the proceedings of the 14th International Conference on Computational Collective Intelligence (ICCCI 2022), held in Hammamet, Tunisia, during 28–30 September, 2022. Due to the COVID-19 pandemic, the conference was organized in a hybrid mode which allowed for both on-site and online paper presentations. The conference was hosted by the French SIGAPP Chapter (ACM Special Interest Group on Applied Computing), France, and organized by Wrocław University of Science and Technology, Poland, in cooperation with the IEEE SMC Technical Committee on Computational Collective Intelligence, the European Research Center for Information Systems (ERCIS), the Université de Pau et des Pays de l'Adour, France, the Université de Jendouba, Tunisia, and the International University, VNU-HCM, Vietnam.

Following the successes of the previous conferences held in Wrocław, Poland (2009), Kaohsiung, Taiwan (2010), Gdynia, Poland (2011), Ho Chi Minh City, Vietnam (2012), Craiova, Romania (2013), Seoul, South Korea (2014), Madrid, Spain (2015), Halkidiki, Greece (2016), Nicosia, Cyprus (2017), Bristol, UK (2018), Hendaye, France (2019), Da Nang, Vietnam (2020), and Rhodes, Greece (2021), this conference continued to provide an internationally respected forum for scientific research in the computer-based methods of collective intelligence and their applications.

Computational collective intelligence (CCI) is most often understood as a subfield of artificial intelligence (AI) dealing with soft computing methods that facilitate group decisions or processing knowledge among autonomous units acting in distributed environments. Methodological, theoretical, and practical aspects of CCI are considered as the form of intelligence that emerges from the collaboration and competition of many individuals (artificial and/or natural). The application of multiple computational intelligence technologies such as fuzzy systems, evolutionary computation, neural systems, consensus theory, etc., can support human and other collective intelligence, and create new forms of CCI in natural and/or artificial systems. Three subfields of the application of computational intelligence technologies to support various forms of collective intelligence are of special interest but are not exclusive: the Semantic Web (as an advanced tool for increasing collective intelligence), social network analysis (as a field targeted at the emergence of new forms of CCI), and multi-agent systems (as a computational and modeling paradigm especially tailored to capture the nature of CCI emergence in populations of autonomous individuals).

The ICCCI 2022 conference featured a number of keynote talks and oral presentations, closely aligned to the theme of the conference. The conference attracted a substantial number of researchers and practitioners from all over the world, who submitted their papers for the main track and 11 special sessions.

The main track, covering the methodology and applications of CCI, included knowledge engineering and the Semantic Web, recommender systems, collective decision-making, data mining and machine learning, computer vision techniques, and natural language processing, as well as the Internet of Things (IoT) technologies and applications. The special sessions, covering some specific topics of particular interest, included cooperative strategies for decision making and optimization, optimization approaches of production systems in Industries 4.0 and 5.0, collective intelligence in medical applications, IoT, deep learning and natural language processing, computational collective intelligence, computational intelligence for multimedia understanding, machine learning for social data analytics, malware analytics in smart environment, big text mining searching, and artificial intelligence.

We received over 420 papers submitted by authors coming from 46 countries around the world. Each paper was reviewed by at least three members of the international Program Committee (PC) of either the main track or one of the special sessions. Finally, we selected 66 papers for oral presentation and publication in one volume of the Lecture Notes in Artificial Intelligence series and 58 papers for oral presentation and publication in one volume of the Communications in Computer and Information Science series.

We would like to express our thanks to the keynote speakers: Grigorios Tsoumakas from the Aristotle University of Thessaloniki, Greece; Sören Auer, Director and Head of the research group Data Science and Digital Libraries at the TIB – Leibniz Information Centre for Science and Technology and University Library, Germany; Jahna Otterbacher from the Open University of Cyprus and CYENS Centre of Excellence, Cyprus; and Grzegorz J. Nalepa from Jagiellonian University, Poland, for their world-class plenary speeches.

Many people contributed toward the success of the conference. First, we would like to recognize the work of the PC co-chairs and special sessions organizers for taking good care of the organization of the reviewing process, an essential stage in ensuring the high quality of the accepted papers. The workshop and special session chairs deserve a special mention for the evaluation of the proposals and the organization and coordination of 11 special sessions. In addition, we would like to thank the PC members, of the main track and of the special sessions, for performing their reviewing work with diligence. We thank the Local Organizing Committee chairs, publicity chair, Web chair, and technical support chair for their fantastic work before and during the conference. Finally, we cordially thank all the authors, presenters, and delegates for their valuable contributions to this successful event. The conference would not have been possible without their support.

Our special thanks are also due to Springer for publishing the proceedings and to all the other sponsors for their kind support.

It is our pleasure to announce that the ICCCI conference series continues to have a close cooperation with the Springer journal Transactions on Computational Collective Intelligence and the IEEE SMC Technical Committee on Transactions on Computational Collective Intelligence.

Finally, we hope that ICCCI 2022 contributed significantly to the academic excellence of the field and will lead to the even greater success of ICCCI events in the future.

September 2022

Ngoc Thanh Nguyen
Yannis Manolopoulos
Richard Chbeir
Adrianna Kozierkiewicz
Bogdan Trawiński

Organization

Organizing Committee

Honorary Chair

Arkadiusz Wójs — Wroclaw University of Science and Technology, Poland

General Chairs

Ngoc Thanh Nguyen — Wroclaw University of Science and Technology, Poland

Yannis Manolopoulos — Open University of Cyprus, Cyprus

Program Chairs

Richard Chbeir — University of Pau and Adour Countries, France

Costin Badica — University of Craiova, Romania

Jan Treur — Vrije Universiteit Amsterdam, The Netherlands

Djamal Benslimane — University of Lyon, France

Steering Committee

Ngoc Thanh Nguyen — Wroclaw University of Science and Technology, Poland

Piotr Jędrzejowicz — Gdynia Maritime University, Poland

Shyi-Ming Chen — National Taiwan University of Science and Technology, Taiwan

Kiem Hoang — University of Information Technology, VNU-HCM, Vietnam

Dosam Hwang — Yeungnam University, South Korea

Lakhmi C. Jain — University of South Australia, Australia

Geun-Sik Jo — Inha University, South Korea

Janusz Kacprzyk — Systems Research Institute, Polish Academy of Sciences, Poland

Ryszard Kowalczyk — Swinburne University of Technology, Australia

Yannis Manolopoulos — Open University of Cyprus, Cyprus

Toyoaki Nishida — Kyoto University, Japan

Manuel Núñez — Universidad Complutense de Madrid, Spain

Klaus Sölien — Halmstad University, Sweden

Khoa Tien Tran — International University, VNU-HCM, Vietnam

Special Session Chairs

Bogdan Trawiński	Wroclaw University of Science and Technology, Poland
Salma Sassi	Université de Jendouba, Tunisia
Bogumiła Hnatkowska	Wroclaw University of Science and Technology, Poland
Adrianna Kozierkiewicz	Wroclaw University of Science and Technology, Poland

Doctoral Track Chairs

Marek Krótkiewicz	Wroclaw University of Science and Technology, Poland
Elio Mansour	University of Pau and Adour Countries, France

Organizing Chairs

Krystian Wojtkiewicz	Wroclaw University of Science and Technology, Poland
Anis Tassaoui	Université de Jendouba, Tunisia
Abderrazek Jemai	Université de Jendouba, Tunisia
Adrianna Kozierkiewicz	Wroclaw University of Science and Technology, Poland

Publicity Chairs

Karam Bou Chaaya	University of Pau and Adour Countries, France
Farouzi Mhamdi	Université de Jendouba, Tunisia

Webmaster

Marek Kopel	Wroclaw University of Science and Technology, Poland

Local Organizing Committee

Ahmed Dridi	Université de Jendouba, Tunisia
Sami Zghal	Université de Jendouba, Tunisia
Ahmed Khemiri	Université de Jendouba, Tunisia
Amani Drissi	Université de Jendouba, Tunisia
Marcin Jodłowiec	Wroclaw University of Science and Technology, Poland

Rafal Palak   Wroclaw University of Science and Technology,
                                   Poland
Patient Zihisire Muke   Wroclaw University of Science and Technology,
                                   Poland

Keynote Speakers

Grigorios Tsoumakas   Aristotle University of Thessaloniki, Greece
Sören Auer   Leibniz University of Hannover, Germany
Jahna Otterbacher   Open University of Cyprus and CYENS Centre of
                                   Excellence, Cyprus
Grzegorz J. Nalepa   Jagiellonian University, Poland

Special Session Organizers

BDAIH 2022: Special Session on Big Data and Artificial Intelligence in Healthcare

Sami Naouali   Military Academy, Tunisia
Chihebeddine Romdhani   University of Tunis El Manar, Tunisia
Semeh Ben Salem   Military Academy, Tunisia

BigTMS&AI 2022: Special Session on Big Text Mining Searching and Artificial Intelligence

Rim Faiz   University of Carthage, Tunisia
Seifeddine Mechti   University of Sfax, Tunsia

CCINLP 2022: Special Session on Computational Collective Intelligence and Natural Language Processing

Ismaïl Biskri   University of Québec à Trois-Rivières, Canada
Nadia Ghazzali   University of Québec à Trois-Rivières, Canada

CSDMO 2022: Special Session on Cooperative Strategies for Decision Making and Optimization

Piotr Jędrzejowicz   Gdynia Maritime University, Poland
Dariusz Barbucha   Gdynia Maritime University, Poland
Ireneusz Czarnowski   Gdynia Maritime University, Poland

DLANLP 2022: Special Session on Deep Learning for Arabic Natural Language Processing

Mounir Zrigui   University of Monastir, Tunisia
Sadek Mansouri   University of Monastir, Tunisia

FAITSIT 2022: Special Session on Formal and Artificial Intelligence Techniques for Service and Internet of Things

Mohamed Graiet   University of Monastir, Tunisia
Mohamed Tahar Bhiri   University of Sfax, Tunisia
Lazhar Hamel   University of Monastir, Tunisia

Innov-Healthcare 2022: Special Session on Innovative Use of Machine Learning and Deep Learning for Healthcare Empowerment

Yassine Ben Ayed   University of Sfax, Tunisia
Wael Ouarda   Ministry of Higher Education and Scientific
                          Research, Tunisia

IWCIM 2022: International Workshop on Computational Intelligence for Multimedia Understanding

Davide Moroni   National Research Council of Italy, Italy
Maria Trocan   Institut Supérieur d'Électronique de Paris, France
Behçet Uğur Töreyin   Istanbul Technical University, Turkey

MASE 2022: Special Session on Malware Analytics in Smart Environments

Maha Driss   University of Manouba, Tunisia
Iman Almomani   Prince Sultan University, Saudi Arabia
Wadii Boulila   Prince Sultan University, Saudi Arabia
Anis Koubaa   Prince Sultan University, Saudi Arabia

ML-SDA 2022: Special Session on Machine Learning for Social Data Analytics

Salma Jamoussi   University of Sfax, Tunisia
Hanen Ameur   University of Sfax, Tunisia
Hasna Njah   University of Gabes, Tunisia

OAPSI 2022: Special Session on Optimization Approaches of Production Systems in Industries 4.0 and 5.0

Olfa Belkahla Driss   University of Manouba, Tunisia
Houssem Eddine Nouri   University of Gabes, Tunisia
Ouajdi Korbaa   University of Sousse, Tunisia

Senior Program Committee

Plamen Angelov   Lancaster University, UK
Costin Badica   University of Craiova, Romania
Nick Bassiliades   Aristotle University of Thessaloniki, Greece

Maria Bielikova	Slovak University of Technology in Bratislava, Slovakia
Abdelhamid Bouchachia	Bournemouth University, UK
David Camacho	Universidad Autonoma de Madrid, Spain
Richard Chbeir	University of Pau and Pays de l'Adour, France
Shyi-Ming Chen	National Taiwan University of Science and Technology, Taiwan
Paul Davidsson	Malmo University, Sweden
Mohamed Gaber	Birmingham City University, UK
Daniela Godoy	ISISTAN Research Institute, Argentina
Manuel Grana	University of the Basque Country, Spain
William Grosky	University of Michigan, USA
Francisco Herrera	University of Granada, Spain
Tzung-Pei Hong	National University of Kaohsiung, Taiwan
Dosam Hwang	Yeungnam University, South Korea
Lazaros Iliadis	Democritus University of Thrace, Greece
Mirjana Ivanovic	University of Novi Sad, Serbia
Piotr Jedrzejowicz	Gdynia Maritime University, Poland
Geun-Sik Jo	Inha University, South Korea
Kang-Hyun Jo	University of Ulsan, South Korea
Janusz Kacprzyk	Systems Research Institute, Polish Academy of Sciences, Poland
Ryszard Kowalczyk	Swinburne University of Technology, Australia
Ondrej Krejcar	University of Hradec Kralove, Czech Republic
Hoai An Le Thi	University of Lorraine, France
Edwin Lughofer	Johannes Kepler University Linz, Austria
Yannis Manolopoulos	Aristotle University of Thessaloniki, Greece
Grzegorz J. Nalepa	AGH University of Science and Technology, Poland
Toyoaki Nishida	Kyoto University, Japan
Manuel Núñez	Universidad Complutense de Madrid, Spain
George A. Papadopoulos	University of Cyprus, Cyprus
Radu-Emil Precup	Politehnica University of Timisoara, Romania
Leszek Rutkowski	Częstochowa University of Technology, Poland
Tomasz M. Rutkowski	University of Tokyo, Japan
Ali Selamat	Universiti Teknologi Malaysia, Malaysia
Edward Szczerbicki	University of Newcastle, Australia
Ryszard Tadeusiewicz	AGH University of Science and Technology, Poland
Muhammad Atif Tahir	National University of Computer and Emerging Sciences, Pakistan
Jan Treur	Vrije Universiteit Amsterdam, The Netherlands

Serestina Viriri	University of KwaZulu-Natal, South Africa
Bay Vo	Ho Chi Minh City University of Technology, Vietnam
Gottfried Vossen	University of Münster, Germany
Lipo Wang	Nanyang Technological University, Singapore
Michał Woźniak	Wrocław University of Science and Technology, Poland
Farouk Yalaoui	University of Technology of Troyes, France
Slawomir Zadrozny	Systems Research Institute, Polish Academy of Sciences, Poland

Program Committee

Muhammad Abulaish	South Asian University, India
Sharat Akhoury	University of Cape Town, South Africa
Bashar Al-Shboul	University of Jordan, Jordan
Stuart Allen	Cardiff University, UK
Adel Alti	University of Setif, Algeria
Taha Arbaoui	University of Technology of Troyes, France
Mehmet Emin Aydin	University of the West of England, UK
Thierry Badard	Laval University, Canada
Amelia Badica	University of Craiova, Romania
Paulo Batista	Universidade de Évora, Portugal
Khalid Benali	University of Lorraine, France
Szymon Bobek	Jagiellonian University, Poland
Leon Bobrowski	Bialystok University of Technology, Poland
Grzegorz Bocewicz	Koszalin University of Technology, Poland
Peter Brida	University of Zilina, Slovakia
Ivana Bridova	University of Zilina, Slovakia
Krisztian Buza	Budapest University of Technology and Economics, Hungary
Aleksander Byrski	AGH University of Science and Technology, Poland
Alberto Cano	Virginia Commonwealth University, USA
Frantisek Capkovic	Institute of Informatics, Slovak Academy of Sciences, Slovakia
Amine Chohra	Paris-East Créteil University, France
Kazimierz Choroś	Wrocław University of Science and Technology, Poland
Robert Cierniak	Częstochowa University of Technology, Poland
Mihaela Colhon	University of Craiova, Romania
Antonio Corral	University of Almeria, Spain

Jose Alfredo Ferreira Costa	Universidade Federal do Rio Grande do Norte, Brazil
Rafal Cupek	Silesian University of Technology, Poland
Ireneusz Czarnowski	Gdynia Maritime University, Poland
Camelia Delcea	Bucharest University of Economic Studies, Romania
Konstantinos Demertzis	Democritus University of Thrace, Greece
Shridhar Devamane	Global Academy of Technology, India
Muthusamy Dharmalingam	Bharathiar University, India
Tien V. Do	Budapest University of Technology and Economics, Hungary
Abdellatif El Afia	Mohammed V University in Rabat, Morocco
Nadia Essoussi	University of Tunis, Tunisia
Marcin Fojcik	Western Norway University of Applied Sciences, Norway
Anna Formica	IASI-CNR, Italy
Dariusz Frejlichowski	West Pomeranian University of Technology in Szczecin, Poland
Naoki Fukuta	Shizuoka University, Japan
Faiez Gargouri	University of Sfax, Tunisia
Mauro Gaspari	University of Bologna, Italy
K. M. George	Oklahoma State University, USA
Janusz Getta	University of Wollongong, Australia
Chirine Ghedira	University of Lyon 3, France
Daniela Gifu	Romanian Academy - Iasi Branch, Romania
Barbara Gładysz	Wrocław University of Science and Technology, Poland
Arkadiusz Gola	Lublin University of Technology, Poland
Petr Hajek	University of Pardubice, Czech Republic
Kenji Hatano	Doshisha University, Japan
Marcin Hernes	Wrocław University of Economics, Poland
Huu Hanh Hoang	Hue University, Vietnam
Frédéric Hubert	Laval University, Canada
Zbigniew Huzar	Wrocław University of Science and Technology, Poland
Agnieszka Indyka-Piasecka	Wrocław University of Science and Technology, Poland
Dan Istrate	Université de Technologie de Compiègne, France
Joanna Jedrzejowicz	University of Gdańsk, Poland
Gordan Jezic	University of Zagreb, Croatia
Christophe Jouis	Université de la Sorbonne Nouvelle, France
Ireneusz Jóźwiak	Wroclaw University of Science and Technology, Poland

Przemysław Juszczuk	University of Economics in Katowice, Poland
Arkadiusz Kawa	Poznań School of Logistics, Poland
Petros Kefalas	University of Sheffield, Greece
Zaheer Khan	University of the West of England, UK
Attila Kiss	Eotvos Lorand University, Hungary
Marek Kopel	Wroclaw University of Science and Technology, Poland
Petia Koprinkova-Hristova	Bulgarian Academy of Sciences, Bulgaria
Janusz Kowalski-Stankiewicz	Pomeranian Medical University in Szczecin, Poland
Ivan Koychev	University of Sofia "St. Kliment Ohridski", Bulgaria
Jan Kozak	University of Economics in Katowice, Poland
Adrianna Kozierkiewicz	Wrocław University of Science and Technology, Poland
Dalia Kriksciuniene	Vilnius University, Lithuania
Stelios Krinidis	Centre for Research and Technology Hellas (CERTH), Greece
Dariusz Król	Wrocław University of Science and Technology, Poland
Marek Krótkiewicz	Wrocław University of Science and Technology, Poland
Jan Kubicek	VSB - Technical University of Ostrava, Czech Republic
Elzbieta Kukla	Wrocław University of Science and Technology, Poland
Marek Kulbacki	Polish-Japanese Academy of Information Technology, Poland
Piotr Kulczycki	Systems Research Institute, Polish Academy of Science, Poland
Kazuhiro Kuwabara	Ritsumeikan University, Japan
Mark Last	Ben-Gurion University of the Negev, Israel
Florin Leon	"Gheorghe Asachi" Technical University of Iasi, Romania
Doina Logofătu	Frankfurt University of Applied Sciences, Germany
Juraj Machaj	University of Žilina, Slovakia
George Magoulas	Birkbeck, University of London, UK
Bernadetta Maleszka	Wrocław University of Science and Technology, Poland
Marcin Maleszka	Wrocław University of Science and Technology, Poland
Adam Meissner	Poznań University of Technology, Poland

Héctor Menéndez	University College London, UK
Mercedes Merayo	Universidad Complutense de Madrid, Spain
Jacek Mercik	WSB University in Wrocław, Poland
Radosław Michalski	Wrocław University of Science and Technology, Poland
Peter Mikulecký	University of Hradec Králové, Czech Republic
Miroslava Mikušová	University of Žilina, Slovakia
Jean-Luc Minel	Université Paris Ouest Nanterre La Défense, France
Javier Montero	Universidad Complutense de Madrid, Spain
Anna Motylska-Kuźma	WSB University in Wrocław, Poland
Dariusz Mrozek	Silesian University of Technology, Poland
Manuel Munier	University of Pau and Pays de l'Adour, France
Phivos Mylonas	Ionian University, Greece
Laurent Nana	University of Brest, France
Anand Nayyar	Duy Tan University, Vietnam
Filippo Neri	University of Napoli Federico II, Italy
Loan T. T. Nguyen	International University, VNU-HCMC, Vietnam
Sinh Van Nguyen	International University, VNU-HCMC, Vietnam
Linh Anh Nguyen	University of Warsaw, Poland
Adam Niewiadomski	Łódź University of Technology, Poland
Adel Noureddine	University of Pau and Pays de l'Adour, France
Alberto Núñez	Universidad Complutense de Madrid, Spain
Tarkko Oksala	Aalto University, Finland
Mieczysław Owoc	Wrocław University of Economics, Poland
Marcin Paprzycki	Systems Research Institute, Polish Academy of Sciences, Poland
Marek Penhaker	VSB - Technical University of Ostrava, Czech Republic
Isidoros Perikos	University of Patras, Greece
Maciej Piasecki	Wrocław University of Science and Technology, Poland
Bartłomiej Pierański	Poznań University of Economics and Business, Poland
Marcin Pietranik	Wrocław University of Science and Technology, Poland
Nikolaos Polatidis	University of Brighton, UK
Piotr Porwik	University of Silesia, Poland
Paulo Quaresma	Universidade de Évora, Portugal
David Ramsey	Wrocław University of Science and Technology, Poland
Mohammad Rashedur Rahman	North South University, Bangladesh
Ewa Ratajczak-Ropel	Gdynia Maritime University, Poland

Katerina Zdravkova	Ss. Cyril and Methodius University of Skopje, Macedonia
Aleksander Zgrzywa	Wrocław University of Science and Technology, Poland
Haoxi Zhang	Chengdu University of Information Technology, China
Jianlei Zhang	Nankai University, China
Adam Ziębiński	Silesian University of Technology, Poland

Contents

Natural Language Processing

Data Mining and Machine Learning

Knowledge Engineering and Semantic Web

Computer Vision Techniques

Social Networks and Intelligent Systems

Cybersecurity and Internet of Things

Cooperative Strategies for Decision Making and Optimization

Computational Intelligence for Digital Content Understanding

Applications for Industry 4.0

Collective Intelligence and Collective Decision-Making

Inferring Event Causality in Films via Common Knowledge Corpora

Ben Aidlin, Armin Shmilovici, and Mark Last[✉]

Department of Software and Information Systems Engineering,
Ben-Gurion University of the Negev, Be'er Sheva, Israel
benaid@post.bgu.ac.il, {armin,mlast}@bgu.ac.il

Abstract. Human understanding of a movie plot is partially driven by our ability to reason about the causal relations between events. Thus, recognizing causal chains of events is a key requirement for computational models of movie understanding. In this paper, we propose to use available corpora of common-sense knowledge about human behavior for automatically inferring event causality in movie scenes.

Our initial experiments with a dataset of annotated movie events and a corpus of human commonsense reasoning demonstrate that a) for 86% of movie events, there exist relevant commonsense rules and those rules can be used for predicting other movie events. b) in 70% of the cases, the consequences of the rules triggered by movie events can accurately or semi-accurately predict subsequent movie events.

These preliminary results indicate the potential of automated commonsense reasoning to detect the narrative structure in movies. Hence, the proposed method can contribute to the development of story-related video analytics tools, such as automatic video summarization and movie editing systems.

Keywords: Automated reasoning · Computational narrative understanding · Movie analytics · Event causality identification

1 Introduction

1.1 Background

Popular movies convey stories in an audio-visual manner. In a typical movie, there are about 40–60 scenes – film segments that happen in a specific time and place, involving a specific set of characters. A scene is a plot device used to advance the story, convey new information, presents the characters and their traits, and amuse the audience. The scenes develop and connect through short-term chains of cause and effect. Movie characters formulate specific plans, react to changing circumstances, gain or lose allies, and otherwise take specific steps toward or away from their goals [1, 4, 7]. Sometimes a film puzzles or frustrates us, when we can't identify character goals or clear-cut lines of cause and effect [5, 6].

N. T. Nguyen et al. (Eds.): ICCCI 2022, LNAI 13501, pp. 3–15, 2022.
https://doi.org/10.1007/978-3-031-16014-1_1

Movie viewers are expected to use their common sense to understand simple scenes such as the one depicted in Fig. 1 from the movie *Chasing Amy*: Person X accuses Person Y of being insecure. As a consequence, Person Y gets angry and fights Person X. This insight is essential for grasping the future relation between those two story characters. Current computer vision technology is far from being there yet: it may recognize actions and relations between visual objects [2] (e.g., Person X fights Person Y), However, it cannot infer why the fight happened, or what will be its consequences – an essential element in story understanding.

Recent progress in the understanding of event causality in a story is being made for text [9–11, 14, 32] and for video [12, 13, 24, 26]. However, these studies attempt to learn the event causality from sequences of event-result examples, therefore, critically depend on the availability of large sets of labeled examples. Current training sets of examples are neither sufficiently large to span many types of common events, nor sufficiently detailed to consider the existence of latent intermediate states such as human emotions (e.g., anger, fear) that often drive human behavior.

The huge gap between the state-of-the-art computer vision algorithms and story analytics seems hard to bridge, therefore, novel approaches to understanding the video stories are needed. **The main contribution of this paper is the use of common-sense knowledge corpora** [17, 18] **for automatically inferring event causality in movie scenes.** To this end, we assembled a new corpus of common-sense knowledge. As a complement to the learned event-causality methods, features from the latent states (e.g., emotions) can be utilized to enhance applications such as movie search engines, Video Question Answering [21] and movie recommendation [28].

Fig. 1. "PersonX accuses PersonY of being insecure". The reaction predicted is for PersonY to get angry and fight PersonX, which actually happened. From *Chasing Amy*.

Fig. 2. Kevin asked Jane if she thinks he is attractive. We can infer that he is attracted to her, and since it is a romantic comedy, that she will be attracted to him, which is not her immediate reaction. From *27 dresses*

1.2 Research Objectives and Contributions

Event Causality Identification (ECI) aims to identify causal relations between events in a story [10, 32]. Our first objective is to infer causality between movie events, thus advancing automatic movie understanding. Current research, either focus on acquiring a knowledge base of common causal relations between events (from movies and text), or by attempting to understand a particular story or macro-event (in a movie). For that purpose, they annotate datasets of events, or use unsupervised learning methods, that may not distinguish between temporal relations (e.g., event A precedes event B) and causal relations (e.g., event A enables event B).

Human understanding of narrative is mainly driven by reasoning about causal relations between events and thus recognizing them is a key capability for computational models of movie understanding. Cognitive theory of narrative posit that humans can distinguish between four types of narrative causality: Physical, Psychological, Motivational, and Enabling [12]. Most previous work focus on the Physical event causality, e..g, a gunshot can wound. Our second objective is to identify non-physical causations as well. For example, consider Fig. 2, which depicts a scene from a romantic comedy, we expect that if a man reveals his positive interest in a woman – then she will (eventually) reciprocate: PersonX demonstrates appreciation to PersonY because he likes her, the appreciation causes PersonY to like PersonX.

The original contributions of our paper to the domain of computational narrative understanding in movies are two-fold: a) to the best of our knowledge we are the first to demonstrate that without any training, existing corpora of explicit common-sense knowledge can excel at event casualty identification in movies. b) We demonstrate that common-sense knowledge can identify even non-physical event causalities, e.g., events that cause emotions (a fire can cause fear). Integrating the proposed method with supervised learning from annotated examples can enhance the understanding of narratives in movies.

The rest of the paper is organized as follows: Sect. 2 presents some background and some related work; Sect. 3 describes the system construction; Sect. 4 describes the experiments; Sect. 5 concludes with a discussion.

2 Background and Related Work

2.1 Event Causality in Films

Human engagement in movies is partially driven by reasoning about the relations between narrative events, and the expectations about what is likely to happen next that results from such reasoning [26]. Movies' plots tend to be told in temporal order, which makes them a good resource for learning about contingencies between events. In addition, scenes in film represent many typical sequences from real life, while providing a rich source of event clusters related to battles, love and mystery [26].

Narratology frameworks labels a *chronological sequence* of events as *fabula* or story and a *logically ordered sequence* of events as *plot* [11]. Plots make explicit "why" things happen, rather than just telling "how" and "when". The focus is on connecting relevant event sequences in terms of explanatory relations, rather than simply chronological ones (the fabula). Human understanding of narrative is mainly driven by reasoning about causal relations between events and thus recognizing them is a key capability for computational models of movie understanding. Computational work in this area has approached this via two different routes: by focusing on acquiring a knowledge base of common causal relations between events, or by attempting to understand a particular story or macro-event, along with its storyline [8, 13].

Stories as they are commonly understood are the combination of chronologically and logically ordered sequence of events. In a story, we typically select certain events, not others. One factor that determines this selection is the *casual relation* that we focus onto explain why things happened. Causelines address a specific type of explanatory relations in narratives, namely reasons why events happened. However, causality is also a debated relation, and causes often remain vague or implicit in stories. *Circumstantiality* [11] captures a broad range of weak and strong relations including causality, enablement, prevention, and entailment. Circumstantial relations make explicit why one event enabled the next event to facilitate the understanding of a narrative [11]. These relations differ from strict casual relations in that the sequence is not logically necessary but (culturally or empirically) expected, made possible or explained by backward presupposing. e.g., you crossed the street and thercfor you were hit by a truck [11].

Causelines are then simply sequences of event mentions connected by circumstantial relations [11]. A Crucial aspect of understanding and reconstructing narratives is identifying casual chains, which explain why certain things happen and make a coherent story [9]. Circumstantial events surrounding the casual complex are rarely expressed with language as they are part of human common sense. *Therefore, discovering casual common sense is also important to fill the gaps in the casual chains* [9].

To understand narrative, humans draw inferences about the underlying relations between narrative events. Cognitive theories of narrative understanding posit four different relations that underlie narrative coherence [12]: *Physical*: Event A physically causes event B to happen; *Motivational*: Event A happens with B as a motivation; *Psychological*: Event A brings about emotions (expressed in event B); *Enabling*: Event A creates a state or condition for B to happen (i.e., A enables B). We posit that film scene descriptions are a good resource for learning all types narrative causality because they are: (1) action rich; (2) about everyday events; and (3) told in temporal order, providing a primary cue to causality [26].

Previous work on video understanding has largely treated video clips as independent entities, divorced from their context [22]. However, this is not how movies are understood: the meaning and significance of a scene depends on its relationship to previous scenes [1, 5, 30]. Previous work on learning causal relations has primarily focused on Physical causality [12], to be able to reason about emotions invoked at various clips of the movie, it is important to develop a causal understanding of the story. [30] aligns with the psychological theory of *Emotional Causality* [15] to better model the emotions evoked by each clip of a movie. The theory of emotion causality consists of the following main events:

1. Identifying *Outer Event*: This stage refers to a stimulus that is contained in the multimedia content that causes an emotion in the movie viewer. For the movie character, the outer event is typically a physical one, or an observation of a physical one (e.g., PersonX hits PersonY).
2. Perceiving the *Emotional State*: This event refers to the formation of an emotional state in the movie viewer (or the movie character) upon receiving the stimuli (e.g., PersonY felt fear).

Lastly, the theory assumes a notion of causality between the two events. That is, the "outer event" causes the "perceived emotional state".

2.2 Computational Methods

The paper [26] implement and evaluate various unsupervised methods for learning event pairs (from a corpus of film scene descriptions which comprises of 123,869 unique event pairs) that are likely to be *Contingent* on one another. Their definition of the Contingent relation encapsulates relations elsewhere called *Cause, Condition* and *Enablement* [26]. The accuracy of their best method is 75.15%. They used web-search counts to further improve the accuracy to 85.64%.

The papers [12, 13] learned the four different types of narrative causality from causal pairs in a corpus of 955 films. The accuracy computed per 11 different movie genres with more than 100 films from each genre is in the range of 82.6% (for the Drama genre) to 90.7% (for the Fantasy genre).

The authors of [10] suggest integrating causal knowledge from four datasets of common-sense knowledge into an unsupervised learning framework for learning new casual dependencies. One of the four datasets is the ATOMIC dataset [18]. They outperformed other methods and obtained the F1 measure in the range of 51.1% to 53.2% for event causality identification on two benchmarks datasets derived from *textual documents*.

The paper [30] attempts to learn emotion causality from the same dataset of movies we use here – the MovieGraphs of [16]. They obtain a validation accuracy of 39.8% and test accuracy of 30.58%. On the same dataset, [24] predicted human interactions with an accuracy of 26.1%.

3 Event Causality Inference System

We extract textual descriptions of scene events from the MovieGraphs [16] dataset, which contains graph information about 7,637 manually annotated scenes of 51 full movies. Each scene graph contains information about the characters involved; and every character's node is marked by attributes (e.g., kid) including the relations with other characters. (e.g., parent), the interactions it involves in and so on. Most interactions are associated with topics, that provide further information about the interaction, and reasons, that explain why the interaction occurred. In addition, most interactions are provided with a time stamp indicating when it took place inside the bounds of the scene. For example, consider the 22 s scene from the romantic movie *Sleepless in Seattle* depicted in Fig. 3. The right panel in Fig. 3 demonstrates the micro events that can be extracted from the scene graph. For example, at seconds 0–4 Sam Baldwin orders Jona Baldwin (his kid) not to touch food. This may be the cause why Sam is annoyed. Jona does not like Victoria (his dad's date). This may be the cause that Victoria feels offended. Later in the movie, Jona arranges that his father (a widower) will date another woman – another likely cause of not liking his father current date.

In this research, we would like to predict casual effects in movies by utilizing common sense knowledge about events. For this purpose, we decided to use two recently published corpora of everyday commonsense reasoning: Event2Mind [17], and Atomic [18]. Atomic contains about 60,000 entries, one for each possible event. Consider Figs. 4 and 5: each event is represented by the commonsense attributes, effects, intents, needs, desires, and reactions of the active person ("PersonX" in the event described above)

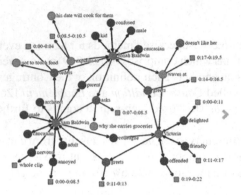

0-4: Sam B. orders Jona B. not to touch food
0-8.5: Sam B. is annoyed
7-8.5: Jona B. asks Sam B. why she carries groceries
8.5-10.5: Sam B. explains to Jona B. his date will cook for them
0-11: Victoria is delighted
11-13: Victoria greets Sam B.
14-16.5: Victoria greets Jona B.
11-17: Victoria is friendly
17-19.5: Jona B. waves at Victoria
19-22: Victoria is offended

Fig. 3. A MovieGraphs [16] analysis of a 22 s scene from the movie *Sleepless in Seattle*. Green nodes represent the characters, red nodes represent attributes, blue nodes stand for relationships, orange for interactions, pink for summary, yellow for topic and purple for reason. Gray nodes indicate the relevant timestamp. The right panel presents the micro-event times.

along with the desires, reactions, and effects of the passive person ("PersonY"). There are three possible relations: *If-Event-Then-Persona*; *If-Event-Then-Event*; and If-Event-Then-Mental-State. The Event2Mind dataset has about 55,000 entries which are less elaborate (Fig. 5 right) providing only the intent and emotion of the active person and the emotion of the passive person.

To extract events from the scene graphs in the MovieGraphs dataset, we applied a procedure that finds all node triplets, where two character-related nodes are either connected by one of three types of nodes: Interactions (e.g., gives), Relations (e.g., parent), Summaries (descriptions of a long video-clip e.g., listens to), or pointed by their Attributes (e.g., curious). Figure 6 presents examples for event extraction from a scene: the two characters (PersonX and PersonY), the type of connection, and the Topic, Reasons, or Time frame (when available). The existence of a timeframe marks that the line describes a strict event.

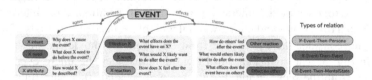

Fig. 4. The If–then module used by Atomic [18]

We merged the two commonsense corpora (Atomic and Event2Mind) together – one line per each rule. However, repeating rules (e.g., gives gift), which cause different effects, were not merged. Atomic has 9 categories of effect types (e.g., what the two interacting persons want), while Event2Mind has only three. Therefore, in the combined dataset, commonsense rules originating from the Event2Mind dataset had some null effect types.

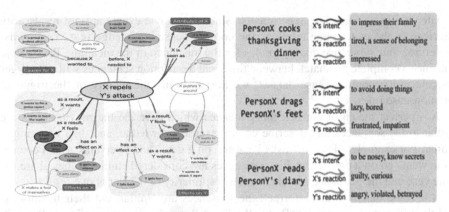

Fig. 5. Left, An example of an Atomic event [18] and its commonsense reasoning: Right: Examples of Event2Mind events [17] and their reasoning

For each extracted movie event, we looked for matching commonsense rules in the merged corpus, and for each matched movie event, we counted the number of expected effects from the respective commonsense rules that were actually observed in the movie storyline. Sentence similarity between event and rule descriptions was measured with Python's Sequence Matcher function [20]. It uses a pattern matching algorithm that compares pairs of sequences of any type.

	PersonX	Interaction	PersonY	Topic	Reason	Time
0	Helen St.	gives	Don Birnar	N/A	N/A	0:00-0:06
1	Helen St.	suggests	Don Birnar	how to tak	N/A	0:08-0:10.5
2	Helen St.	kisses	Don Birnar	N/A	N/A	0:17-0:20.5

interactions	summaries	attributes	relationships	⊕

	PersonX	relationshi	PersonY	Topic	Reason	Time
0	Don Birnar	lover	Helen St.	N/A	N/A	N/A
1	Don Birnar	sibling	Wick Birna	N/A	N/A	N/A

interactions	summaries	attributes	relationships	⊕

	PersonX	Summary	PersonY	Topic	Reason	Time
0	Helen St.	cares for	Don Birnar	N/A	N/A	N/A
1	Wick Birna	listens to	Helen St.	N/A	N/A	N/A

interactions	summaries	attributes	relationships	⊕

	Person	Attribute	Topic	Reason	Time
0	Helen St.	caring	N/A	N/A	0:00-0:13
1	Helen St.	excited	N/A	N/A	0:26.5-0:28.5
2	Don Birnar	curious	N/A	N/A	0:28-0:30.5

interactions	summaries	attributes	relationships

Fig. 6. Example of the results for extracting the events from the MovieGraphs representation of the 3rd scene of *The lost weekend*.

4 Evaluation Experiments

The following experiments intend to measure how well commonsense knowledge can be used to predict movie events. First, we need to define some quality measures, which we later use to evaluate our experiments. Since the movie events are not necessarily described in the exact same terms as the commonsense knowledge (e.g., synonyms) we defined four subjective quality grades for the mismatch in the meaning. Please note that since a complete mismatch between the event description sentences will not trigger any rule in the commonsense dataset, we measure only the quality of the triggered commonsense rules.

A – perfect match or correct: the sentences which describe the movie events are similar to the sentences that describe commonsense knowledge, and their meaning is similar. For example: "PersonX asks PersonY on a date" and "PersonX asks PersonY if she wants go on a date". Matching sentences are considered similar if they share the same verb and the Sequence Matcher scores a similarity of 0.72 or above.

B – some match or semi-correct: the sentences are similar, but their meaning is slightly different. For example: "PersonX talks to PersonY on the phone" and "PersonX talks to PersonY about their business".

C – completely false; the sentences are similar, but their meaning is completely different, for example: "PersonX asks PersonY on a date" and "PersonX asks PersonY for explanation". The similarity in the verb *asks* triggered a sentence with a different meaning.

D – missing or irrelevant information; the sentences have different meanings. For example: "PersonX walks with PersonY" and "PersonX walks his dog on a trip". The similarity in the verb *walks* triggered an irrelevant (prediction-wise) commonsense event.

We used the following definitions for the Precision, Recall, and F1 quality measures, where the A grades are regarded as True-Positives, the C grades are regarded as False-Positives, the B grades are counted both as True-Positives and False-Positives, and the D grades are either (context dependent) addressed as false positives, or not considered at all since they are irrelevant to generating the predictions.

Precision = True Positives/(True Positives + False Positives)
Recall = True Positives/(True Positives + False Negatives)
F1 Measure = (2*Precision*Recall)/(Precision + Recall)

Experiment 1: Do the Events Extracted from the MovieGraphs Match the Film Scenes?. The purpose of this experiment is to test the quality of the information in the MovieGraphs dataset. The accuracy of the MovieGraphs scene descriptions will have a direct effect on the accuracy of our event predictions based on that information source. The first author watched 20 scenes from the movie "27 dresses" and graded manually the correctness of the corresponding 377 events described in the MovieGraphs. Of the 377 entries evaluated, there were 337 entries marked as correct, 11 marked as semi correct, 14 marked as wrong, 12 marked as missing info, and only 3 marked as irrelevant. We also noticed that some entries described correct details related to a different scene. If the related scene was the previous or the next scene, we marked the event as correct. If the related scene was chronologically distant, we labeled the event as irrelevant (case D). Semi-correct entries (case B) were marked when the description was correct, yet, lacking important details regarding the situation. Mostly because "topic" or "reason" were missing attributes.

The second line in Table 1 presents the quality measures for this experiment. Though the evaluation was performed on a single movie, the superior results (e.g., Accuracy =

96.5%) indicated the high quality of the MovieGraphs descriptions. Hence, we could continue with our experiments.

Experiment 2: Do the Events Extracted from the MovieGraphs Match the Commonsense Rules? In this experiment, we wrote a Python script that traversed the events in each scene, focusing on interaction and summary attributes and searching for matching rules from the commonsense ruleset. To facilitate the rule matching process, the character names were replaced by PersonX for the active character and PersonY for the other character.

For the 3 scenes in the movie *27 Dresses* we intended to inspect, there were about 3,000 matches between the scene's events and events in the ruleset. Manual inspection detected many similarities in the triggered commonsense rules, (e.g., because of slightly different word order), therefore, we decide that we will consider for evaluation only the *unique matchings* (e.g., each event will appear only once), though repeating events may also be significant for story understanding. Eventually, there were only 114 unique matches. For each one of those unique matches, we manually graded the similarity between MovieGraphs description and commonsense rule description. The results are presented in the third line of Table 1.

Table 1. Summary of the experiments' results

	#Scenes (#films)	#Events	A	B	C	D	Precision	Recall	F1
Exp.1	20 (1)	377	337	11	14	12/3	0.965	0.961	0.962
Exp.2	3 (1)	114	66	32	13	3	0.859	0.882	0.871
Exp.3	30 (10)	5498	2739	1123	1056	541	0.5867	0.5858	0.5863

Though the evaluation was performed on 3 scenes from a single movie, the encouraging results (e.g., Accuracy = 85.9%) indicate that when we apply a ruleset to a film event, with a high probability, some rules will resemble the event occurring in the film. This accuracy is on par with the results presented in [12, 13, 26] that were obtained via a machine learning process.

Please note that on average, there were 6.6 correct matches for each unique movie event, which indicates redundancy in the rules, or that we need to enhance the similarity function. We also noticed that film events where the verb is rather common (e.g., *talks*, *asks*) were involved in more false matchings, since those kinds of verbs blend in more sentences with different meanings, unlike less common verbs such as *declines*, for example.

Experiment 3: Do the Predictions from the Commonsense Dataset Match the Events in the Movies? The first experiment indicated that the MovieGraphs dataset contains accurate de-scriptions of events. The second experiment indicated that those events likely have a matching rule in our commonsense rule base. In this experiment, we evaluate the quality of the prediction given by the consequence part of the triggered rules. The consequence part of many rules is rather rich with assumptions about the intentions, emotions, desires, reactions, needs, effects and even attributes of the characters involved in triggering the rule. We will focus on the emotions, reactions, and effect categories predicted for each event.

In the first step of the experiment, we repeated the algorithm [23] developed for experiment 2 on 30 scenes taken from 10 MovieGraph films. To capture more types of events, for each movie we selected a scene from the initial part, a scene from the middle part, and a scene from the final part. The events in those 30 scenes triggered 5,498 rules. 5,459 of those rules have consequences for which we can easily describe an event. For example, consider the rules demonstrated in Fig. 5 right: *PersonX reads PersonY 's diary*. One possible predicted consequence is *PersonY feels angry*. Now, we measure the similarity of this consequence sentence with all the MovieGraphs event descriptions (such as Fig. 3 on the right) that follow that event looking for an event similar to *PersonY feels angry*. Following experiment 2, a sequence similarity of above 0.72 scored quality grade A for the prediction. Figure 1 presents a grade A example, where an accusation triggered a fight. B grades were given when a prediction semi happened, meaning it happened to a certain degree. For example, "PersonX got excited" was predicted, when in reality the character was affected positively but not as far as excited. We believe the cause for many predictions being graded B is that the rule-sets auto reasoning is very concrete, it does not suggest a wide range of feelings or reactions when indeed that is what happens in real life and in films. Figure 2 presents a grade B example, where the predicted attraction happened much later in the movie. Predictions were graded as C in cases when the predicted event did not happen in the film. It does not necessary mean that the prediction rule was defective. It could be the cause of a movie's specific genre (e.g., no violence in romantic comedies) or the specific individual's character traits. An example for grade C from the movie *Pulp Fiction* is when the first character drives the second character home. The prediction is that the second character will be happy and appreciative. However, in the previous scene, the second character almost died and is still in a state of shock. D grades were given mostly because of false matches between events, and not because of actual wrong predictions.

The fourth line in Table 1 presents the quality measures in the third experiment. The bottom line of this experiment is that the commonsense rules generated correct or semi-correct predictions for $(2739 + 1123)/5498 \sim 70\%$ of the movie events. This is a step towards movie narrative understanding – it demonstrates that reasoning with commonsense knowledge provides better results than the machine learning methods such as [30].

5   Discussion

In this paper, we are the first to demonstrate that with an existing corpus of common sense knowledge we can infer event causality in movies with an accuracy of 58.7%. Using the proposed approach, we can detect nonphysical causality chains, such as evolving human emotions. The results are on par with supervised learning methods of [30] that attempt to infer the emotional causality from movie examples with an accuracy less than

40%. Integrating common sense knowledge with learning from example methods will potentially boost the accuracy. This is an important step towards computational models for movie understanding and story analytics.

Future research can naturally follow our results by (1) fully automating the inference process via semantic similarity matching (e.g., BERT[31]); (2) Improving the prediction accuracy via integration with machine learning methods (supervised [12] or unsupervised [10]) and more event causality datasets [10]; (3) adding cinematic cue events such as shots and camera angle, illumination, music and voice [19, 27]; (4) generating an event-cause chain summary (in a video or text format) of a given narrative video, hopefully detecting the most important story elements and scenes, (e.g., following the work in [3, 25, 29]); (5) Studying genre specific event causations [12, 13] (such as horror or romantic comedy) and the effect of the accumulations of similar events and emotions; (6) utilizing story-related scene classification to boost the performance of other story-related tasks, such as movie question-answering [21]; (7) constructing a fully automated pipeline that can process a video from start (e.g., scene splitting) to the detected casual chain of events and using it to annotate a large dataset such as [18]; (8) consider more complex dependencies between a sequence of events, such that an event is triggered by a sequence of preceding events and not by just one previous event.

To obtain the code and/or the data used in this paper, please refer to [23].

Acknowledgement. This research was partially supported by the Israeli Council for Higher Education (CHE) via the Data Science Research Center, Ben-Gurion University of the Negev, Israel.

References

1. Kristin T.: Storytelling in the New Hollywood: Understanding Classical Narrative Technique, Paperback (1999)
2. Ji, J., Krishna, R., Fei-Fei, L., Niebles, J.C.: Action genome: Actions as compositions of spatio-temporal scene graphs. In: Proceedings of the IEEE/CVF Conference on Computer Vision and Pattern Recognition (CVPR) (2020)
3. Evangelopoulos, G., Zlatintsi, A., Potamianos, A., Maragos, P., Rapantzikos, K., Skoumas, G., et al.: Multimodal saliency and fusion for movie summarization based on aural, visual, and textual attention. IEEE Trans. Multimedia **15**(7), 1553–1568 (2013)
4. Bordwell, D., Staiger, J., Thompson, K.: The Classical Hollywood Cinema. Columbia University Press, New York (1985)
5. Iglesias, K.: 8 Ways to hook the reader. Creative Screenwriting **13**(4), 48–49 (2006)
6. Iglesias K.: Writing for Emotional Impact. Wingspan, Livermore, CA (2005)
7. Bordwell, D., Thompson, K.: Film Art: An Introduction. McGraw-Hill (2010)
8. Piper, A., Jean So, R., Bamman, D.: Narrative Theory for Computational Narrative Understanding. In: Proceedings of the 2021 Conference on Empirical Methods in Natural Language Processing (EMNLP) (2021)
9. Mirza, P.: Event Causality. Computational Analysis of Storylines: Making Sense of Events, 106. In: Caselli, T., Hovy, E., Martha: (editors), Computational Analysis of Storylines: Making Sense of Events (2021)

10. Zuo, X., et al.: Improving event causality identification via self-supervised representation learning on external causal statement. In: Findings of the Association for Computational Linguistics: ACL-IJCNLP 2021, pp. 2162-2172 (2021)
11. Vossen, P., Caselli, T., Segers, R.: A Narratology-Based Framework for Storyline Extraction. Computational Analysis of Storylines: Making Sense of Events, 125 (2021)
12. Hu, Z., Walker, M.A.: Inferring narrative causality between event pairs in films. In: Proceedings of the 18th Annual SIGdial Meeting on Discourse and Dialogue, pp. 342–351 (2017)
13. Hu, Z., Rahimtoroghi, E., Walker, M.A.: Inference of fine-grained event causality from blogs and films. EventStory **2017**, 52 (2017)
14. Droog-Hayes, M., Wiggins, G., Purver, M.: Automatic detection of narrative structure for high-level story representation. In: The 5th AISB Computational Creativity Symposium, pp. 26–33 (2018)
15. Coegnarts, M., Kravanja, P.: Perceiving causality in character perception: a metaphorical study of causation in film. Metaphor. Symb. **31**(2), 91–107 (2016)
16. Vicol, P., Tapaswi, M., Castrejón, L., Fidler, S.: MovieGraphs: towards understanding human-centric situations from videos. In: Proceedings of the IEEE Computer Society Conference on Computer Vision and Pattern Recognition, ISBN 9781538664209 (2018)
17. Rashkin, H., Sap, M., Allaway, E., Smith, N.A., Choi, Y., Paul, G.: Event2Mind: commonsense inference on events, intents, and reactions, Allen School of Computer Science & Engineering, University of Washington, Allen Institute for Artificial Intelligence (2019). https://www.aclweb.org/anthology/P18-1043/
18. Sap, M., et al.: ATOMIC: An Atlas of Machine Commonsense for If-Then Reasoning. Allen School of Computer Science & Engineering, University of Washington, Allen Institute for Artificial Intelligence, Seattle, USA (2019). https://ojs.aaai.org//index.php/AAAI/article/view/4160
19. Avgerinos, C., Nikolaidis, N., Mygdalis, V., Pitas, I.: Feature extraction and statistical analysis of videos for cinemetric applications. 2016 Digital Media Industry and Academic Forum, DMIAF 2016 - Proceedings, pp. 172–175 (2016)
20. Sequence Matcher https://www.kite.com/python/docs/difflib.SequenceMatcher
21. Garcia, N., Nakashima, Y.: Knowledge-based video question answering with unsupervised scene descriptions. In: Vedaldi, A., Bischof, H., Brox, T., Frahm, J.-M. (eds.) ECCV 2020. LNCS, vol. 12363, pp. 581–598. Springer, Cham (2020). https://doi.org/10.1007/978-3-030-58523-5_34
22. Zhong, Y., Wang, L., Chen, J., Yu, D., Li, Y.: Comprehensive image captioning via scene graph decomposition. In: Vedaldi, A., Bischof, H., Brox, T., Frahm, J.-M. (eds.) ECCV 2020. LNCS, vol. 12359, pp. 211–229. Springer, Cham (2020). https://doi.org/10.1007/978-3-030-58568-6_13
23. GitHub project link, including all the computational procedures discussed in this paper: https://github.com/BenAidlin/DescriptionWork, Note: the data files can be obtained by emailing the first author: benaid@bgu.ac.il
24. Kukleva, A., Tapaswi, M., Laptev, I.: Learning interactions and relationships between movie characters. In: Proceedings of the IEEE/CVF Conference on Computer Vision and Pattern Recognition, pp. 9849–9858 (2020)
25. Liu, C., Shmilovici, A., Last, M.: Towards story-based classification of movie scenes. PLoS ONE, ISSN 19326203 (2020). https://doi.org/10.1371/journal.pone.0228579
26. Hu, Z., Rahimtoroghi, E., Munishkina, L., Swanson, R., Walker, M.A.: Unsupervised Induction of Contingent Event Pairs from Film Scenes. In: Proceedings of the 2013 Conference on Empirical Methods in Natural Language Processing, pages 369–379, Seattle, Washington, USA, 18–21 (2013)

27. Cascante-Bonilla, P., Sitaraman, K., Luo, M., Ordonez, V.: Moviescope: Large-scale Analysis of Movies using Multiple Modalities https://doi.org/10.48550/arXiv.1908.03180
28. Gomez-Uribe, C.A., Hunt, N.: The netflix recommender system: Algorithms, business value, and innovation. ACM Trans. Manage. Inf. Syst. 6(4),. ISSN 2158–656X. (2016). https://doi.org/10.1145/2843948. URL https://doi.org/10.1145/2843948
29. Liu, C., Last, M., Shmilovici, A.: Identifying Turning Points in Animated Cartoons. Expert Systems with Appl. 123, 246–255 (2019). ISSN 09574174. URL https://linkinghub.elsevier.com/retrieve/pii/S0957417419300041. https://doi.org/10.1016/j.eswa.2019.01.003
30. Mitta, T.l., Mathur, P., Bera, A., Manocha, D.: Affect2mm: Affective analysis of multimedia content using emotion causality. In: Proceedings of the IEEE/CVF Conference on Computer Vision and Pattern Recognition, pp. 5661–5671 (2021)
31. Kenton, J.D.M.W.C., Toutanova, L.K.: BERT: Pre-training of deep bidirectional transformers for language understanding. In: Proceedings of NAACL-HLT, pp. 4171–4186 (2019)
32. Keith, K., Jensen, D., O'Connor, B.: Text and causal inference: a review of using text to remove confounding from causal estimates. In: Proceedings of the 58th Annual Meeting of the Association for Computational Linguistics) (2020). https://doi.org/10.18653/v1/2020.acl-main.474

Cooperation Game on Communication Multigraph with Fuzzy Parameters

Barbara Gładysz[1] and Jacek Mercik[2]([✉])

[1] Faculty of Management, Wroclaw University of Science and Technology, Wybrzeże
Wyspiańskiego 27, 50-370 Wrocław, Poland
barbara.gladysz@pwr.edu.pl
[2] Faculty of Finance and Management, WSB University in Wroclaw, Fabryczna 29/31,
53-609 Wrocław, Poland
jacek.mercik@wsb.wroclaw.pl

Abstract. In this paper, we derive the Mean Value for nodes in Fuzzy Communication Structure (FCS). The novel solution is proposed for a class of cooperative games over FCS with a sub-additive characteristic function. We propose two cooperative game concepts over communication multigraph with fuzzy parameters. We also introduce how the fuzzy characteristic function is calculated via maximal flow. In the first model, parameters (arc capacities) of FCS are given by fuzzy numbers. In the second model, parameters (arc capacities) of FCS are given by fuzzy numbers, too, and there is also given fuzzy goal determining the degree of satisfaction with the flow value that can be transmitted in the network between each pair of network vertices. In order to compare nodes' Mean Values, we use the possibility measure and expected fuzzy number value. Obtained results may be useful for managing of development of a network of communication nature. Illustrating examples are presented.

Keywords: Fuzzy communication structure · Maximal flow · Fuzzy cooperative game · Sub-additive characteristic function

1 Introduction

Fuzzy Communication Structure is a multigraph in which the parameters of signal transmission of different nature (e.g., material, information in a company, or signal in a computer network) through a given structure are fuzzy. In our paper, in the game theory-based language (cooperative games), the players, as in many other publications (e.g., Reijnierse et al. 1996; Basallote et al. 2019; Kumar and Kaur 2012), are the vertices (nodes) of the multigraph. The existing connections (graph structure) determine possible coalitions and define the value of a given coalition as a function of possible transfers between players (nodes) in this coalition. Multigraph is a graph where multiple (also called parallel edges) arcs and loops (arcs ending at the same nodes) can occur (Forlicz et al. 2018).

The work of von Neumann and Morgenstern (1944) is considered the beginning of modeling various real phenomena using the theory of cooperative games. On its

© The Author(s), under exclusive license to Springer Nature Switzerland AG 2022
N. T. Nguyen et al. (Eds.): ICCCI 2022, LNAI 13501, pp. 16–28, 2022.
https://doi.org/10.1007/978-3-031-16014-1_2

basis, Shapley (1953) introduced the so-called Shapley value as the only (under certain assumptions) solution to the distribution of profit (or costs) of participants in such a game. Since then, there have been proposals for modifications of the assumptions of the game, allowing for the modification of the payment proposals for its participants (a priori solutions). In the original axiomatization of the Shapley Value (efficient value, i. e. the payoff vector exactly splits the total value), we find three basic axioms: dummy axioms (the player that contributes nothing to any coalition has zero value), permutation axiom, also known as equal treatment or symmetry axiom, and additivity axiom. There are many different Shapley value modifications related to the modification of these axioms. For example, by introducing the gain-loss axiom (Einy and Haimanko 2011), (the total worth generated does not change, a player can only gain at the expense of another one) or by replacing Additivity and the equal treatment axiom by fairness (van den Brink 2001) or differential marginality (Casajus 2011), where the latter requires equal productivity differentials of two players to translate into equal payoff differentials. Similarly, (Roth 1977) and (Chun 1989), for example, suggest alternative foundations of the Shapley value without Additivity.

Galindo et al. (2021) propose, in the process of defuzzification, a real number Shapley value for cooperative games with fuzzy characteristic function. Gładysz and Mercik (2018) and Gładysz et al. (2019) propose fuzzy Shapley value for simple cooperative games with fuzzy characteristic function, and Gladysz et al. (2020) propose a number of applications of the fuzzy set theory for modeling various optimization problems modeled by cooperative games. Mercik (2015) and Mercik et al. (2021) use this approach to valuate elements of a network of companies.

For issues related to cooperative games on graphs, the basic set of axioms is the set introduced by (Myerson 1977; Owen 1995): monotonicity (strong) axiom and independence axiom. Moreover, the communication graph determines the different probability of coalitions, which changes the mean value in a priori attempt into weighted mean value. This significantly complicates the calculation of such Shapley-like values. All the above sets of axioms were created to find an effective solution equivalent to Shapley values. The basis of this value is the assumption that we are dealing with a cooperative game defined by a super-additive characteristic function (Owen 1995). Consequently, we expect the so-called Individual rationality: No player receives less than what he could get on his own. In the proposed estimation of the value of the node of the communication multigraph, we depart from this assumption, which means that the characteristic function of such a game may be a sub-additive function. Based on management theory, it can be assumed that, in some cases, a given player is ready to "pay extra" just to become a member of a given coalition. This may lead to the conclusion that a coalition containing such a member does not increase its value (side payment is only a matter of the player-payer) or reduces its value (side payment is then a matter for all members of this coalition). We consider both such cases.

The concept of subadditivity is, in certain sense, an opposite one to the super-additivity concept. Its special cases for the classical cooperative games, namely for the games with side payments, contradict the usual interpretation of the game model and the von Neumann-Morgenstern (1944) characteristic function of the coalition game. It is the cause why it was not considered and investigated in the classical theory of cooperative games. However, the notion of subadditivity has its sense in the case of some special cooperative games, namely the market games (Mareš 1976, 1978).

The subadditivity assumption essentially simplifies some properties of stability in general cooperative games. The game is called sub-additive if its general characteristic function is sub-additive.

The article is set up as follows. The next section outlines the concept of a cooperative game over communication multigraph with fuzzy parameters. We also introduce how the fuzzy characteristic function is calculated via maximum flow between any two nodes of a multigraph. Section 3 presents a concept of the value of the sub-additive cooperative game and the average a priori value of the players (nodes of FCS). Section 4 presents the model where parameters (arc capacities) of FCS are given by fuzzy numbers. In Sect. 5, according with Chanas and Kołodziejczyk (1984), we propose a model where parameters (arc capacities) of FCS are given by fuzzy numbers, and there is given goal determining the degree of satisfaction with the flow value that can be transmitted in the network between each pair of network vertices. Finally, there are some conclusions and suggestions for future research.

2 Preliminaries

A game on N is given by a map $v : 2^N \rightarrow \mathbb{X}$ with $v(\varnothing) = 0$. A game on N is called a fuzzy game on N if $\mathbb{X}$ is a fuzzy space $\mathbb{F}$. The space of all fuzzy games on N is denoted by $\bar{\mathbb{N}}$. A subset of players from N is called a coalition. The coordinates of the payoff vector describe the payoff of players.

Let's consider (a multigraph) FCS = $(N, E, \tilde{c})$ with node set N and arc set E. There could be two distinguished nodes: the source $s \in N$ and the sink $t \in N$. Arcs can be directed or undirected. An arc $e \in E$ has a fuzzy capacity $\tilde{c}_e \in \mathbb{F}$.

For nodes N from FCS we propose to define the mapping as follows

$$\tilde{v}(T) = \begin{cases} \min_{s,t \in T; s \neq t} \max \tilde{v}_{T,s,t}, & \text{for} \quad \text{connected graph} \\ 0 & \text{for inconsistent graph } T \\ 0 & \text{for} \quad T : |T| = 1 \end{cases} \tag{1}$$

where: $\tilde{v}_{T,s,t}$, - flow from node s (sink) to node t (sink) for multigraph FTS expended over T: FCS = $(T, ET, \tilde{c})$; $T \subseteq N$, $s, t \in T$; $s \neq t$, $ET \subseteq E$ – the set of all edges connecting nodes of the subset $T \subseteq N$.

In order to estimate characteristic functions for coalitions $T \subseteq N$ we will use the modified multigraph FCS. Each undirected edge e connected $i, j \in E$ we will replace by two directed edges e and e'': e' - edge directed from node i to node j ($e' \in \overrightarrow{i}$ and $e' \in \overleftarrow{j}$), e'' – edge directed from node j to node i $\left(e'' \in \overrightarrow{j} \text{ and } e'' \in \overleftarrow{i}\right)$, where: $\overleftarrow{i}$ - set of arcs incoming into node i, and $\overrightarrow{i}$ - set of arcs outcoming from node i.

Due to sub-additivity, we do not expect a fuzzy game on N to fulfill efficiency and individual rationality. Therefore, the eventual payoff of some coordinates may be negative.

We assume the fuzzy game G on FCS fulfills the following axioms (von Neumann and Morgenstern 1944; Chun 1989):

- Existence: The solution concept exists for any fuzzy game G (including a fuzzy game on FCS).
- Uniqueness: The solution concept is unique for any game G.
- Marginality: The player's payoff depends only on the marginal contribution of this player, i.e., if these marginal contributions are the same in two different games, then the payoff is the same.
- Monotonicity: A player's payoff increases if the marginal contribution of this player increases.

Computational ease: From the theoretical point of view, it is not necessary that computational ease exists (the solution concept can be calculated efficiently, i.e., in polynomial time with respect to the number of players), but we also have it in mind when proposing a new solution.

Less Equal Zero Allocation to Null Players: The allocation to a null player is less than or equal to zero. In economic terms, a null player's marginal value to any coalition that does not contain him is less than or equal to zero.

Definition 1. The marginal a priori value of a player i under the assumption all coalitions are equally likely is defined as follows:

$$\varphi_i(\tilde{v}) = \left(\sum_{T \subseteq N, i \in T} \frac{(|T| - 1)!(|N| - |T|)!}{|N|!} (\tilde{v}(T) - \tilde{v}(T \setminus \{i\})) \right) \tag{2}$$

Definition 2. The expected marginal value of player i is equal to

$$E(\varphi_i(\tilde{v})) \tag{3}$$

Zadeh (1965) introduced the concept of a fuzzy set. Fuzzy set $\tilde{A}$ in space X is a set of ordered pairs : $\{(x, \mu_A(x) : x \in X)$ where $\mu_A : X \to [0, 1]$ is a function of belonging to a fuzzy set. We will represent the fuzzy set as $\tilde{A} = x_1/\mu_1 + \cdots + x_n/\mu_n$, where μ_i – denotes the possibility of the event that the fuzzy variable $\tilde{X}$ takes the value of x, $i = 1, \ldots, n$.

According to the fuzzy logic proposed by Zadeh (1965) membership function of the logic operator $\tilde{A}$ and $\tilde{B}$ takes the following form:

$$\mu_{A \text{ and } B}(x) = min\{\mu_A(x), \mu_B(x)\} \tag{4}$$

Let $\tilde{X}$ be a single-valued variable whose value is not precisely known. The membership for $\tilde{X}$ is a normal, quasi concave and upper semicontinuous function $\mu_X : \mathcal{R} \to [0, 1]$. The value $\mu_X(x)$ for $x \in \mathcal{R}$ denotes the possibility of the event that the fuzzy variable $\tilde{X}$ takes the value of x.

For a given fuzzy number $\tilde{X}$ and a given λ, the λ-level is defined to be the closed interval $\left[\tilde{X} \right]_\lambda = \{x : \mu(x) \geq \lambda\} = \left[\underline{x}(\lambda), \overline{x}(\lambda) \right]$. An interval-valued fuzzy number $\tilde{X}$ is called an $L - R$ fuzzy number if its membership function takes the form of (Dubois and Prade 1978):

$$\mu_X(x) = \begin{cases} L\left(\frac{m-x}{\alpha}\right) & for \quad x < \underline{m} \\ 1 & for \ \underline{m} \le x \le \overline{m} \\ R\left(\frac{x-\overline{m}}{\beta}\right) & for \quad x > \overline{m} \end{cases} \tag{5}$$

where: $L(x), R(x)$ - continuous non-increasing functions x; $\alpha, \beta > 0$.

The functions $L(x), R(x)$ are called the fuzzy number shape functions. The most common shape functions are: $\max\{0, 1 - x^p\}$ and $\exp(-x^p)$, $x \in [0, +\infty)$, $p \ge 1$. Interval fuzzy number for which $L(x), R(x) = \max\{0, 1 - x^p\}$ and $\underline{m} = \overline{m} = m, p = 1$ is called a trapezoidal fuzzy number; we will mark it as $(m - \alpha, \underline{m}, \overline{m}, m + \beta)$.

Let $\tilde{X}, \tilde{Y}$ be two fuzzy numbers with membership functions, respectively $\mu_X(x)$, $\mu_Y(y)$ and let $z = f(x, y)$ be a real function. Then, according to Zadeh's extension principle (1965), the function of belonging to a fuzzy number $\tilde{Z} = f\left(\tilde{X}, \tilde{Y}\right)$ takes the form:

$$\mu_Z(z) = sup_{z=f(x,y)}(min(\mu_X(x), \mu_Y(y))) \tag{6}$$

If we want to compare two fuzzy sets, that is, to determine the possibility that the realization $\tilde{X}$ is greater than the realization $\tilde{Y}$, then we can use the index proposed by Dubois and Prade (1988):

$$Pos(X > Y) = sup_{x \ge y}(min(\mu_X(x), 1 - \mu_Y(y))) \tag{7}$$

Carlsson and Füllér (2001) proposed a possibilistic generative expected value of a fuzzy number $\tilde{X}$:

$$E\left(\tilde{X}\right) = \frac{\int_0^1 \frac{(\underline{x}(\lambda) + \overline{x}(\lambda))}{2} \lambda d\lambda}{\int_0^1 \lambda d\lambda} \tag{8}$$

If $\tilde{X}$ is trapezoid fuzzy number $(m - \alpha, \underline{m}, \overline{m}, m + \beta)$ then its expected value is equal to

$$E\left(\tilde{X}\right) = \frac{\underline{m} + \overline{m}}{2} + \frac{\beta - \alpha}{4} \tag{9}$$

Expected value of sum of fuzzy numbers $\tilde{X}, \tilde{Y}$ is a sum of expected values of these numbers

$$E\left(\tilde{X} + \tilde{Y}\right) = E\left(\tilde{X}\right) + E\left(\tilde{Y}\right) \tag{10}$$

Expected value of the fuzzy number $\tilde{Y} = a\tilde{X}$, where a is a real number $a \in \mathcal{R}$, is equal to $E\left(a\tilde{X}\right) = aE\left(\tilde{X}\right)$.

The conditional expected value for fuzzy number is equal to

$$E\left(\tilde{X}\right) = \frac{\int_0^{\lambda_0} \frac{(\underline{x}(\lambda) + \overline{x}(\lambda))}{2} \lambda d\lambda}{\int_0^{\lambda_0} \lambda d\lambda} \tag{11}$$

3 Concept of the FUZZY Value of the Sub-additive Cooperative Game on Communication Multigraph with Fuzzy Capacities

Now, we introduce the fuzzy maximal flow problem discussed in (Diamond, 2001). Fuzzy maximal s-t flow in FCS is a feasible flow from source s to sink t; $s, t \in N \ s \neq t$:

$$max(\tilde{v})$$

subject to:

$$\tilde{v} \cong \sum_{e \in \overleftarrow{t}} \tilde{x}_e \cong \sum_{e \in \overrightarrow{s}} \tilde{x}_e$$

$$\sum_{e \in \overleftarrow{i}} \tilde{x}_e \cong \sum_{e \in \overrightarrow{i}} \tilde{x}_e \text{ for } i \in N, \tag{12}$$

$$0 \leq \tilde{x}_e \widetilde{\leq} \tilde{c}_e \text{ for } e \in E,$$

where: $\overleftarrow{i}$, set of arcs incoming into node i, and $\overrightarrow{i}$ - set of arcs outcoming from node i.

An s-t cut $CUT(NS, NT)$ is a partition of set N such that $s \in NS$ and $t \in NT$. That is, s-t cut is a division of the vertices of the network into two parts, with the source in one part and the sink in the other. The cut-set X_C of a cut C is the set of edges that connect the source part of the cut to the sink part. Thus, if all the edges in the cut-set of C are removed, then no positive flow is possible because there is no path in the resulting graph from the source to the sink.

The capacity of an s-t cut is the total capacities of its edges

$$\tilde{c}(CUT(NS, NT)) = \sum_{e \in X_C} \tilde{c}_e y_e \tag{13}$$

where $y_e = 1$ if $e \in X_C$, otherwise $y_e = 0$.

A minimum cut is a cut with minimal capacity. The maximum value of an s-t flow is equal to the minimum capacity over all s-t cuts (Guha et al. 2019; Diamond, 2001; Mabela Makengo Matendo 2020).

Example 1. Suppose there is a network with 4 nodes: A, B, C and D and connections between them: $AB1, AB2, BC1, CD1$ and $CD2$ as presented on Fig. 1.

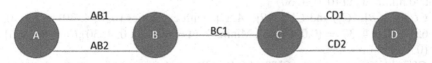

Fig.1. Multigraph with four nodes: A, B, C, D and five connections (edges).

Fuzzy capacities of edges from the example are presented in Table 1.

Table 1. Fuzzy capacities of edges from Fig. 1.

Edge	Capacity
AB1	(0, 0, 4, 20)
AB2	(0, 0, 5, 45)
BC1	(0, 0, 4, 30)
CD1	(0, 0, 7.5, 9)
CD2	(0, 0, 8.5, 12.5)

A membership function for maximal flow for coalition $\{ABCD\}$ equals:

$$\mu_{v_{ABCD}}(x) = \begin{cases} 1 & for \quad 0 \le x < 4 \\ R\left(\frac{x-4}{30-4}\right) & for \quad 4 \le x \le 19.2 \\ R\left(\frac{x-16}{215-16}\right) & for \ 19.2 \le x \le 21.5 \end{cases}$$

where: $R(x) = \max\{0, 1 - x\}$.

Let consider the coalition $\{ABCD\}$. Value for coalition $\{A\}$ is $\tilde{v}(A) = (0,0,0,0)$. In the subgraph $FCS = ((\{A, B\}, \{AB1, AB2\}, \tilde{c})$ there are two cuts with the same capacity $\tilde{c}(CUT(\{A\}, \{B\})) = \tilde{c}(CUT(\{B\}, \{A\})) = \tilde{c}(AB1) + \tilde{c}(AB2) = (0,0,4,20) + (0,0,5,45) = (0,0,9,65)$. Therefore, $\tilde{v}(\{A, B\}) = (0,0,9,65)$ and $E(\tilde{v}(\{A, B\})) = 18.5$. Analogically, for $FCS = ((\{C, D\}, \{CD1, CD2\}, \tilde{c})$, $\tilde{c}(CUT(\{C\}, \{D\})) = \tilde{c}(CUT(\{D\}, \{C\})) = \tilde{c}(CD1) + \tilde{c}(CD2) = (0,0,7.5,9) + (0,0,8.5,12.5) = (0,0,16,21.5)$. So the fuzzy value of this coalition $\{C, D\}$ is equal to $\tilde{v}(\{C, D\}) = (0,0,16,21.5)$. From Eq. (3) expected value $E(\tilde{v}(\{C, D\})) = 9.375$.

For $FCS = (\{A, B, C\}, \{AB1, AB2, BC1\}, \tilde{c})$ there are the following combinations of sources and sinks: 1) $s = A$ and $t = C$, 2) $s = B$ and $t = C$,3)$s = A$ and $t = B$ and the minimal cuts (maximal flows) respectively:

1) $CUT(\{A, B\}, \{C\})$ and $CUT(\{A\}, \{B, C\})$ with capacities (0,0,4,30) and (0,0,9,65) and minimal cut $(0, 0, 4, 30)$.
2) $CUT(\{A, B\}, \{C\})$ and $CUT(\{B\}, \{A, C\})$ with capacities $(0, 0, 4, 30)$ and $(0, 0, 9, 65) + (0,0,4,30) = (0,0,13,95)$. Minimal cut $= \min\{(0, 0, 4, 30),(0, 0, 13, 95)\} = (0, 0, 4, 30)$.
3) $CUT(\{A, C\}, \{B\})$ and $CUT(\{A\}, \{B, C\})$ with capacities $(0, 0, 13, 95)$ and $(0, 0, 9, 65)$ respectively.

Therefor the fuzzy value of the coalition $\{ABC\}$ equals $\tilde{v}(A, B, C) = (0,0,4,30)$ with expected value equals 8.5.

Finally, for $FCS = (\{A, B, C, D\}, \{AB1, AB2, BC1, CD1, CD2\}, \tilde{v})$ membership function for the value of coalition $\{A, B, C, D\}$ takes the following form:

$$\mu_{v_{ABCD}}(x) = \begin{cases} 1 & for \quad 0 \leq x < 4 \\ L\left(\frac{x-4}{30-4}\right) & for \quad 4 \leq x \leq 19.2 \\ R\left(\frac{x-16}{215-16}\right) & for \ 19.2 \leq x \leq 21.5 \end{cases}$$

where: $R(x) = L(x) = \max\{0, 1 - x\}$ and expected value for this FCS is equal to $E(\tilde{v}(\{A, B, C, D\})) = 7.42$.

Values of characteristic functions for the pre-coalition $T \subseteq N$ are as follows (see Fig. 2): $\tilde{v}(\{A, B\}) = (0, 0, 9, 65), \tilde{v}(\{B, C\}) = v(\{A, B, C\}) = (0, 0, 4, 30), \tilde{v}(\{C, D\}) = (0, 0, 16, 21.5), \tilde{v}(\{B, C, D\}) = \tilde{v}(\{A, B, C, D\}) = min\{(0, 0, 4, 30), (0, 0, 16, 21.5)\}$, for the other coalitions T: $\tilde{v}(T) = 0$.

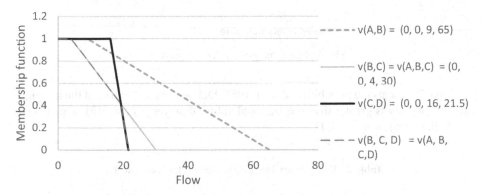

Fig. 2. Fuzzy characteristic functions for Example 1.

From above calculations for the line of coalitions: $\{A\}$, $\{A, B\}$, $\{A, B, C\}$ and $\{A, B, C, D\}$, on the base of Eqs. (2) and (3) one may evaluate apports (marginal values) of a given players (respectively for A, B and C): $(0, 0, 0, 0)$, $(0, 0, 9, 65) - (0, 0, 0, 0) = (0, 0, 9, 65)$ with expected value $E(0, 0, 9, 65) = 18.5$, $(0, 0, 4, 30) - (0, 0, 9, 65) = (-65, -9, 4, 30)$ with expected value $E(-65, -9, 4, 30) = -10$. Apport of player D to coalition $\{A, B, C, D\}$ is given as follows:

$$\mu_{v_{ABCD}}(x) = \begin{cases} 1 & for\ 0 \leq x < 4 \\ R\left(\frac{x-4}{30-4}\right) & for\ 4 \leq x \leq 19.2 \\ R\left(\frac{x-16}{215-16}\right) & for\ 19.2 \leq x \leq 21.5 \\ L\left(\frac{-4-x}{26}\right) & for -30 \leq x < -4 \\ 1 & for -4 \leq x \leq 4 \\ R\left(\frac{x-4}{26}\right) & for\ 4 \leq x \leq 19.2 \end{cases} - (0, 0, 4, 30) =$$

where: $R(x) = L(x) = \max\{0, 1 - x\}$, with expected value $E = -0.88$.

Figure 3 shows membership functions of marginal values of players for all possible permutations of players $\{A, B, C, D\}$. In this example, expected values of marginal values $E(\varphi_i(\tilde{v}))$ for all possible permutations of $\{A, B, C, D\}$, for all players ($i = A, B, C, D$) are equals to 0.76, 4.52, 3.20 and -1.05 respectively.

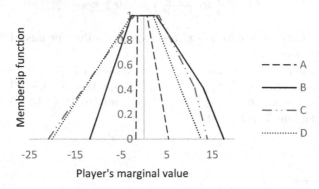

Fig. 3. Fuzzy marginal values of players.

Table 2 presents the possibility (Zadeh, 1965, Dubois, Prade, 1988) that the marginal value of player i is greater than the marginal value of player j: $\text{Pos}(\varphi_i(\tilde{v}) > \varphi_j(\tilde{v}))$ for $i = A, B, C, D; j = A, B, C, D$.

Table 2. Fuzzy index $\text{Pos}(\varphi_i(\tilde{v}) > \varphi_j(\tilde{v}))$ for Example 1.

$\text{Pos}(\varphi_i(\tilde{v}) > \varphi_j(\tilde{v}))$	A	B	C	D
A		0,14	0,14	0,31
B	0,86		0,56	0,75
C	0,86	0,44		0,72
D	0,69	0,25	0,28	

According to Eq. (7), we have:

$Pos(SV(A) > SV(B))$ AND $POS(MV(A) > SV(C))$ AND $POS(SV(A) > MV(D)) = 0.14$

$Pos(SV(B) > SV(A))$ AND $POS(MV(B) > SV(C))$ AND $POS(SV(B) > MV(D)) = 0.56$

$Pos(SV(C) > SV(A))$ AND $POS(MV(C) > SV(B))$ AND $POS(SV(C) > MV(D)) = 0.44$

$Pos(SV(A) > SV(B))$ AND $POS(MV(A) > SV(C))$ AND $POS(SV(A) > MV(D)) = 0.25$

Therefore, it is the most possible (at degree 0.56), player B is a winning player. Player B is also a winning player when we compare the marginal values using the expected fuzzy number value.

4   Concept of the FUZZY Value of the Sub-additive Cooperative Game on Communication Multigraph with Fuzzy Capacities and Fuzzy Goal

Let's consider (a multigraph) $FCS = (N, E, \tilde{c})$ with node set N and arc set E. We have two distinguished nodes: the source $s \in N$ and the sink $t \in N$. Arcs can be directed or undirected.

Let us assume that a decision-maker defines a fuzzy goal $\tilde{G} = \{(v, \mu_G(v) : v \epsilon X)$ where $\mu_A : X \rightarrow [0, 1]$ determining the degree of satisfaction with the flow value v that can be transmitted in the network between each pair of network vertices. We define the maximum s-t flow as the solution of the following decision problem (Chanas and Kołodziejczyk (1984), Hernandes et al. (2007)):

$$\max \lambda$$

$$\sum_{e \in \overleftarrow{t}; e \in T} x_e = v \text{ for } s \in N, \ s \neq t$$

$$\sum_{e \in \overrightarrow{s}; e \in T} x_e = v \text{ for } t \in N, \ s \neq t \tag{14}$$

$$\sum_{e \in \overleftarrow{t}} x_e = \sum_{e \in \overrightarrow{s};} x_e \text{ for } e \in N$$

$$L_e^{-1}(\lambda) \leq x_e \leq R_e^{-1}(\lambda) \text{ for } e \in N$$

$$\lambda = \mu_G(v)$$

where: $\overleftarrow{i}$, set of arcs incoming into node i, and $\overrightarrow{i}$ - set of arcs outcoming from node i.
    For nodes/players N from FCS, we define the mapping as there is proposed in Eq. (1).

Example 2. Let us consider data from Example 1. Let us assume further that the decision-maker define the following fuzzy goal $\mu_G(v) = (8, 25, +\infty, +\infty)$, see Fig. 4.

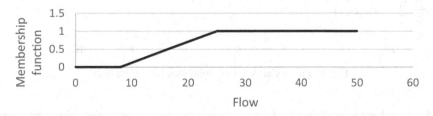

Fig. 4. Fuzzy goal.

Using formulas (1) and (14), we can find the characteristic functions for pre-coalitions. For example, for pre-coalition {A,B} the solution of fuzzy maximal flow problem (14) for the multigraph $FCS = (\{A, B\}, \{AB1, AB2\}, \tilde{c})$ takes the form: $v = 21.3$ and $\lambda = 0.78$. So we can say that possibility that maximal flow equals 21.3 is 0.78.

The characteristic function of precoalition {A,B} is equal to $\tilde{v}\{A, B\} = 21.3/0.78$. By analogy, we can find characteristic functions for remaining pre-coalitions:

$\tilde{v}(B, C) = 16.7/0.51$, $\tilde{v}\{C, D\} = 18.2/0.6$, $\tilde{v}\{A, B, C\} = 16.7/0.51$,

$\tilde{v}\{B, C, D\} = 16.7/0.51$, $\tilde{v}\{A, B, C, D\} = 16.7/0.51$,

and for the remaining pre-coalitions $\tilde{v} = 0/1$.

Using formulas (2) and (6), we can calculate fuzzy marginal values for the players A, B, C, D, see Table 3 and Fig. 5.

Table 3. Fuzzy marginal values for players.

Player/Node	A	B	C	D
Fuzzy Shapley value	0.26/0.51	8.61/0.51	8.09/0.51	-0.26/0.51

Now we can calculate the possibility (Zadeh, 1965; Dubois and Prade 1988) that the marginal value of player i is greater than the marginal value of player j: $Pos(\varphi_i(\tilde{v}) > \varphi_j(\tilde{v}))$ for $i = A, B, C, D$; $j = A, B, C, D$, see Table 4.

According to Eq. (7), we have:

$$Pos(SV(A) > SV(B)) \text{ AND } POS(MV(A) > SV(C)) \text{ AND } POS(SV(A) > MV(D)) = 0$$

$$Pos(SV(B) > SV(A)) \text{ AND } POS(MV(B) > SV(C)) \text{ AND } POS(SV(B) > MV(D)) = 0.51$$

$$Pos(SV(C) > SV(A)) \text{ AND } POS(MV(C) > SV(B)) \text{ AND } POS(SV(C) > MV(D)) = 0$$

$$Pos(SV(A) > SV(B)) \text{ AND } POS(MV(A) > SV(C)) \text{ AND } POS(SV(A) > MV(D)) = 0$$

Therefore, player B is, most possibly (at degree 0.51), the winning player.

Fig. 5. Fuzzy characteristic functions for Example 2.

So in both measures (possibility measure and conditional expected value) the winner is player B.

Table. 4. Fuzzy relation $\mathrm{Pos}(\varphi_i(\tilde{v}) > \varphi_j(\tilde{v}))$ for Example 2.

$\mathrm{Pos}(\varphi_i(\tilde{v}) > \varphi_j(\tilde{v}))$	A	B	C	D
A		0	0	0,51
B	0,51		0,51	0,51
C	0,51	0		0,51
D	0	0	0	

5 Conclusions and Future Works

In a priori analysis of the importance of individual nodes of a fuzzy communication net-work (FCS), it is necessary to solve two practical problems: the occurrence of different measures assigned to successive permutations of network nodes and the possibility of occurrence of sub-additive values assigned to individual coalitions. We analyzed games for two different fuzzy maximal flow models. Both problems can generate significant computational complexity associated with determining the maximum flow in a network with fuzzy parameters. This flow's fuzzy characteristics can be determined in polyno-mial time. The problem, however, remains an NP-hard problem due to the number of nodes permutations. It seems that the only solution will be to use an approximate algo-rithm in the future, similar to the asymptotic calculation algorithm of Shapley values. The presence of sub-additivity should not, in our opinion, hinder the application of the proposed approach.

Additionally, it will be necessary to establish the interpretation of the negative mean values of the evaluation of a given vertex. The existing interpretation related to the possibility of "payment" for participation in the communication network should be extended and tested on real examples.

References

Basallote, M., Hernandez-Mancera, C., Jimenez-Losada, A.: A new Shapley value for games with fuzzy coalitions. Fuzzy Sets and Systems **383**, 51–67 (2019)

van den Brink, R.: An axiomatization of the Shapley value using a fairness property. Internat. J. Game Theory **30**, 309–319 (2001)

Carlsson, C., Fullér, R.: On possibilistic mean value and variance of fuzzy numbers. Fuzzy Sets Syst. **122**, 315–326 (2001)

Chanas, S., Kołodziejczyk, W.: Real-valued flows in a network with fuzzy arc capacities. Fuzzy Sets Syst. **13**, 139–151 (1984)

Chun, Y.: A new axiomatization of the Shapley value. Games Econom. Behav. **1**, 119–130 (1989)

Casajus, A.: Differential marginality, van den Brink fairness, and the Shapley value. Theor. Decis. **71**(2), 163–174 (2011)

Diamond, P.: Fuzzy max-flow min-cut theorem. Fuzzy Sets Syst. **119**, 139–148 (2001)

Dubois, D., Prade, H.: Operations on fuzzy numbers. Int. J. Syst. Sci. **9**(6), 613–626 (1978)

Einy, E., Haimanko, O.: Characterization of the Shapley-Shubik power index without the efficiency axiom. Games Econom. Behav. **73**(2), 615–621 (2011)

Dubois, D., Prade, H.: Possibility Theory: An Approach to Computerized Processing of Uncertainty. Plenum Press, New York (1988)

Forlicz, S., Mercik, J., Stach, I., Ramsey, D.: The Shapley Value for Multigraphs. In: Nguyen, N.T., Pimenidis, E., Khan, Z., Trawiński, B. (eds.) ICCCI 2018. LNCS (LNAI), vol. 11056, pp. 213–221. Springer, Cham (2018). https://doi.org/10.1007/978-3-319-98446-9_20

Galindo, H., Gallardo, J.M., Jiménez-Losada, A.: A real Shapley value for cooperative games with fuzzy characteristic function. Fuzzy Sets Syst. **409**, 1–14 (2021)

Gładysz, B., Mercik, J.: The Shapley value in fuzzy simple cooperative game. In: Nguyen, N.T., et al.: (eds.) Intelligent Information and Database Systems. 10th Asian Conference on Intelligent Information and Database Systems ACIIDS 2018, LNAI, vol. 10751, pp. 410–418. Springer Cham (2018) https://doi.org/10.1007/978-3-319-75417-8_39

Gładysz, B., Mercik, J., Stach, I.: Fuzzy shapley value-based solution for communication network. In: Nguyen, N.T., Chbeir, R., Exposito, E., Aniorté, P., Trawiński, B. (eds.) ICCCI 2019. LNCS (LNAI), vol. 11683, pp. 535–544. Springer, Cham (2019). https://doi.org/10.1007/978-3-030-28377-3_44

Guha, S., Kupferman, O., Vardi, G.: Multi-player flow games. Auton. Agent. Multi-Agent Syst. **33**(6), 798–820 (2019)

Hernandes, F., Lamata, M.T., Takahashi, M.T., Yamakami, A., Verdegay, J.L.: An algorithm for fuzzy maximal flow problem. In: 2007 IEEE International Fuzzy Systems Conference, IEEE, London, UK (2007)

Kumar, A., Kaur, M.: An improved algorithm for solving fuzzy maximal flow problems. Int. J. Applied Sci. **10**(1), 19–27 (2012)

Mabela Makengo Matendo, R., Mamanya Tapasa, F., Mukeba Kanyinda, J.P.: The problem of fuzzy maximal flow - fuzzy minimal cut. Int. J. Scientific Innovative Mathematical Res. **8**(3), 9–17 (2020)

Mareš, M.: On cooperative games connected with markets. Kybernetika **12**(6), 451–461 (1976)

Mareš, M.: Additivity in general coalition-games. Kybernetika **14**(5), 350–368 (1978)

Mercik, J.: Classification of committees with vetoes and conditions for the stability of power indices. Neurocomputing **149**(Part C), 1143–1148 (2015)

Mercik, J., Gładysz, B., Stach, I., Staudacher, J.: Shapley-based estimation of company value— concept. Algorithms and Parameters. Entropy **23**(12), 1598 (2021)

Myerson, R.: B: Graphs and cooperation in games. Math. Oper. Res. **2**, 225–229 (1977)

von Neumann, J., Morgenstern, O.: Theory of Games and Economic Behavior. Princeton University Press, Princeton (1944)

Owen, G.: Game Theory. 3rd edn. Academic Press, San Diego (1995)

Reijnierse, H., Maschler, M., Potters, J., Tijs, S.: Simple flow games. Games Econom. Behav. **16**(2), 238–260 (1996)

Roth, A.E.: The Shapley value as a von Neumann-Morgenstern utility. Econometrica **45**, 657–664 (1977)

Shapley, L.S.: A value for n-person games. In: Kuhn, H.W., Tucker, A.W.: (eds) Contributions to the Theory of Games, vol. II. Annals of Mathematical Studies **28**, 307–317 (1953)

Zadeh, L.A.: Fuzzy sets. Inf. Control **8**, 338–353 (1965)

Impact of Similarity Measure on the Quality of Communities Detected in Social Network by Hierarchical Clustering

Paweł Szyman⬤ and Dariusz Barbucha$^{(\boxtimes)}$⬤

Department of Information Systems, Gdynia Maritime University,
Morska 83, 81-225 Gdynia, Poland
p.szyman@wznj.umg.edu.pl, d.barbucha@umg.edu.pl

Abstract. The starting point of any hierarchical clustering method is the definition of the similarity measure between objects. In case of a social network the similarity must be inferred from the adjacency relationships between vertices. The main contribution of the paper is to investigate the impact of similarity measure on the quality of clusters (communities) detected in an organizational social network by agglomerative hierarchical clustering method. Three different similarity measures have been considered in the computational experiment. The quality of communities generated by the proposed method has been compared with the quality of clusters generated by the Louvain algorithm using modularity. Because of the fact that the computational experiment has been carried out on the network referring to real public organization, the results of the experiment have been also compared with the structure of the investigated organization.

Keywords: Organizational network analysis · Community detection · Similarity · Hierarchical clustering

1 Introduction

One of the most known and important problem in social network analysis (SNA) is a problem of community detection. It focuses on discovering the cohesive groups (called communities, clusters or modules) of vertices (nodes), where vertices belonging to the same group are similar to each other. Depending on the area a social network refers to, the communities may refer to a group of people which play similar roles within the network and/or share common properties, for example common research area in collaboration networks of scientists.

Last years one can observe a growing interest of researchers in social networks referring to organizations and different relations between employees and/or units

© The Author(s), under exclusive license to Springer Nature Switzerland AG 2022
N. T. Nguyen et al. (Eds.): ICCCI 2022, LNAI 13501, pp. 29–42, 2022.
https://doi.org/10.1007/978-3-031-16014-1_3

of them [4]. It is expected that analysis of an organizational social network may bring interesting observations about several aspects of real organizations.

Because of the fact that the problem of finding communities in a network is intended as a data clustering problem, a natural way to solve it is to use methods which divide graph or cluster the nodes into groups. The main difference is that, while communities in graphs are related, explicitly or implicitly, to the concept of edge density (inside versus outside the community), in data clustering communities are sets of points which are 'close' to each other, with respect to a measure of distance or similarity, defined for each pair of points. Some classical techniques for data clustering, like hierarchical, partitional and spectral clustering may be sometimes adopted to network clustering too [6].

The paper aims at answering the question whether hierarchical clustering methods can be used with success to solve the problem of detecting communities in a social network. Because of the fact that the quality of clustering often depends on the way of measuring the similarity between objects, the main contribution of the paper is to investigate the impact of similarity measure on the quality of clusters (communities) detected in a social network by hierarchical clustering. The organizational network investigated in the paper refers to a middle-sized public organization located in Poland, where the structure of the network is based on digital form of communication (electronic mail) between employees. Three different similarity measures have been considered in the computational experiment. The quality of communities generated by the proposed method has been compared with the quality of clusters generated by the Louvain algorithm using modularity. The results of the computational experiment have been also compared with the structure of the investigated organization.

The rest of the paper is divided into five sections. Section 2 defines an organizational social network and presents main topics of interests of researchers referring to this type of networks. Section 3 formally defines the problem of community detection in social networks. Section 4 presents main assumptions of the hierarchical method and describes different measures of similarity between vertices. Section 5 presents results of computational experiment, and Sect. 6 concludes the paper and points directions of future work.

2 Organizational Social Networks

Research on organizational social networks has achieved a significant position in the analysis of social networks. Organizational social network (OSN) is meant as a network, where people or units of the organization are represented in the form of nodes in the network, and relationships or information flow between these people or units are represented in the form of edges between the nodes. One of the form of an OSN is a network built on various digital forms of communication between employees or units within an organization. They may refer to direct e-mail communication or to activities performed by them in social media. The analysis of social networks in the organizational aspect and comparing the results of the analysis with an organization itself allow one to gain significant knowledge about an organization and its environment.

Focusing on OSN, a lot of research have been done to solve theoretically and practically important problems. Wright and Hinson presented an extensive report in which they included the results of their twelve-year analysis of how social technologies and other emerging technologies can be used in public relations practice based on the analysis of data from Facebook and Twitter [21]. Creamer et al. [5] attempted to align social networks and corporate hierarchy in organizations. Nguyen and Zheng investigated the correlation between the influence of a given person in the organization and his position [12]. Raut et al. investigated how the interactions between two persons show the power relations between them [18]. Kolli and Narayanaswamy used the community discovery problem in organizational networks to detect crisis situations in a large organization [9]. A social network based on e-mail communication in a public organization was also investigated by Authors in their earlier works. They made an attempt to identify the most important actors in the network [1] and to detect potential communities using modularity-based algorithms [2].

3   Community Detection Problem

Let $G = (V, E)$ be an undirected graph, representing a social network, where V represents a set of n vertices, and E - set of edges between vertices. Let A be an adjacency matrix of G, where each element $a_{ij} \in A$ is equal to 1 if vertices i and j are neighbors, otherwise it is equal to 0. Let we also assume that for each $i \in V$, $\Gamma(i)$ denotes the set of neighbors of i, $deg(i)$ be the degree of the node i, which in terms of the adjacency matrix A of the network G, can be defined as $deg(i) = \sum_j a_{ij}$.

Let C be a subset of G. Less formally, it can be defined as a *community* if connections between the vertices belonging to C are denser than connections with the rest of the network. Some researches proposed more formal view on a community in a social network, for example Radicci et al. [17] distinguishes two kinds of communities: strong communities and weak communities. The subgraph C is a community in a *strong* sense if $\forall_{i \in C} deg^{in}(i) > deg^{out}(i)$, and the subgraph C is a community in a *weak* sense if $\sum_{i \in C} deg^{in}(i) > \sum_{i \in C} deg^{out}(i)$, where $deg^{in}(i) = \sum_{j \in C} a_{ij}$ is the number of edges connecting node i to other nodes belonging to C, and $deg^{out}(i) = \sum_{j \notin C} a_{ij}$ is the number of connections toward nodes in the rest of the network $(deg(i) = deg^{in}(i) + deg^{out}(i))$. It means that in a strong community each node has more connections within the community than with the rest of the graph, and in a weak community the sum of all degrees within C is larger than the sum of all degrees toward the rest of the network.

The problem of *community detection* focuses on dividing the vertices of a network into some number k of groups, while maximizing the number of edges inside these groups and minimizing the number of edges established between vertices in different groups. The problem has been studied by many authors who proposed various methods to solve it. A comprehensive review of the methods used to solve the problem, the reader can find for example in [6].

4 Hierarchical Clustering Approach to the Community Detection

If we assume that communities are groups of vertices similar to each other, the natural way of detecting communities in a social network seems to be finding an effective way to cluster a set of vertices into groups with high similarity between vertices belonging to the same group. It means that the community detection problem can be considered as a clustering problem. This section focuses on hierarchical clustering to solve the problem of community detection in the social network.

4.1 Hierarchical Clustering

Clustering is one of the most important data mining problem. Having a set of objects (observations, instances), clustering aims at organizing them into a set of groups (clusters), where each group contains objects which are 'similar'. In other words, any cluster is a subset of objects such that the distance between any two objects in the cluster is less than the distance between any object in the cluster and any object not located inside it. The number of clusters is known in advance [22].

There is a lot of methods dedicated to solve clustering methods, starting from 'classical' methods like k-means, and ending at metaheuristics or hybrid approaches. It is expected that a good clustering method will produce high quality clusters in which the intra-class (that is, intra-cluster) similarity is high and the inter-class similarity is low [22]. Because of the fact that the quality of clustering results depends not only on a method used to solve it but also on similarity measure chosen, the next section presents a few representative similarity measures are presented.

4.2 Similarity Measures in Social Networks

The concept of similarity plays an important role in information processing. In case of social networks they could help to answer the questions: how similar are two vertices or which vertices are most similar to some vertex. Similarity measure could be based on the information stored in nodes and/or structure of connections between the nodes. In the first case it has assumed that vertices have their own attributes. Whereas in classic social networks, it can be assumed that the vertex can be described with attributes such as age, name or education, in networks based on email communication, the attribute can be the user's email address or domain. This type of similarity is called *semantic similarity*. In case of similarity measure based on links between nodes (called *structural similarity*), the link pattern of the network is taken into account. This paper focuses on structural similarity.

The first natural way of thinking about similarity in the network is to assume that two vertices are similar to each other if there exists direct connection between them. Another view on similarity takes into account the neighborhood of the vertices: two vertices in the network are similar to each other if they have common neighbors [8]. On the other hand, some similarity measures allow nodes to be similar even when they do not have common neighbors [10]. Generally one can say that similarity between each pair of vertices may be considered with respect to some reference property, local or global, no matter whether they are connected by an edge or not. What is important, it is natural to assume that communities are groups of vertices similar to each other and each vertex in the network ends up in the cluster whose vertices are most similar to it [6].

The simple form of similarity may arise when it is possible to embed the network vertices in an n-dimensional Euclidean space. By assigning a position to the vertices, one could use the *distance* between a pair of vertices as a measure of their similarity (in fact it is a measure of dissimilarity because similar vertices are expected to be close to each other). Given the two data points $X = (x_1, x_2, ..., x_n)$ and $Y = (y_1, y_2, ..., y_n)$, one could use for example the *Euclidean* (Eq. (1)) or *Manhattan distance* (Eq. (2)).

$$d_{XY}^E = \sum_{k=1}^{n} \sqrt{(x_k - y_k)^2} \tag{1}$$

$$d_{XY}^M = \sum_{k=1}^{n} |x_k - y_k| \tag{2}$$

If it is impossible to embed the network in a space, the similarity must be inferred from the adjacency relationships between vertices. One of the most representative measure belonging to this group is for example the *Pearson correlation* between columns or rows of the adjacency matrix A (Eq. 3).

$$C_{ij} = \frac{\sum_k (A_{ik} - \mu_i)(A_{jk} - \mu_j)}{\sigma_i \sigma_j} \tag{3}$$

where the averages $\mu_i = (\sum_j A_{ij})/n$ and the variances $\sigma_i = \sqrt{\sum_j (A_{ij} - \mu_i)^2/n}$.

Another broad class of similarity measures between two vertices i and j referring to the common neighbors of them and degree of each vertex includes for example: Jaccard index - $SJ(i, j)$ (Eq. (4)), Salton index - $SC(i, j)$ (Eq. (5)), and Sörensen index (also known as Sörensen-Dice index or Dice coefficient) - $SS(i, j)$ (Eq. (6)). In case of Jaccard index [7] similarity score between each pair of nodes is calculated as the ratio between the intersection (the number of common neighbors between each pair of nodes) and the union of the neighborhoods. It reaches its maximum if all neighbors are common to both vertices. Salton index (also called cosine similarity) [19] measures the cosine of the angle between columns of the adjacency matrix, corresponding to given vertices. Sörensen index [20] is similar to the Jaccard index, it measures the relative size of an intersection of neighbors' sets.

$$SJ(i, j) = \frac{|\Gamma(i) \cap \Gamma(j)|}{|\Gamma(j) \cup \Gamma(j)|} \tag{4}$$

$$SC(i,j) = \frac{|\Gamma(i) \cap \Gamma(j)|}{\sqrt{deg(i)deg(j)}} \qquad (5)$$

$$SS(i,j) = \frac{2|\Gamma(i) \cap \Gamma(j)|}{deg(i) + deg(j)} \qquad (6)$$

In context of SNA, an interesting important class of measures of vertex similarity is a class based on properties of random walks on graphs. For instance, in the popular Walktrap method the similarity between vertices i and j is given by the probability that a random walker moves from i to j in a fixed number of steps [13]. If there is a pronounced community structure, pairs of vertices in the same cluster are much more easily reachable by a random walk than pairs of vertices in different clusters, so the vertex similarity is expected to be considerably higher within groups than between groups [6].

4.3 Hierarchical Clustering Approach to the Community Detection in Organizational Social Network

The proposed approach (AHC) to solve the community detection problem is based on agglomerative hierarchical clustering. It means that the process of identifying groups of vertices is organized in bottom-up direction: it starts from the vertices as separate clusters, iteratively merges clusters if their similarity is sufficiently high and ends up with the whole network as a unique cluster.

As it was stated, the starting point of any hierarchical clustering method is to define the similarity measure between vertices s_{ij} $(i, j = 1, ..., N)$, no matter if they are connected or not, and calculate value of similarity for each pair of vertices. Having the similarity calculated for each pair of vertices, a similarity matrix S is created. In the proposed approach three similarity measures have been considered and implemented (Jaccard, Sörensen, and Pearson correlation).

Taking into account that in each iteration of the agglomerative algorithm the process of merging clusters is performed, it is necessary to define also a measure that estimates how similar clusters are, out of the similarity matrix S. Three methods of linkage of clusters have been defined: single, complete, and average linkage. In single linkage clustering, the similarity between two groups is the minimum element x_{ij}, with i in one group and j in the other. On the contrary, the maximum element x_{ij} for vertices of different groups is used in the procedure of complete linkage clustering. In average linkage clustering one has to compute the average of the x_{ij} [6].

5   Computational Experiment

In order to check to what extent, if any, the agglomerative hierarchical clustering method with different similarity measures can be used to discover communities in the social network, a computational experiment has been carried out. The network investigated in the paper refers to middle-sized public organization located in Poland, where the structure of the network is based on digital forms of communication (electronic mail) between people within the organization. Three above-mentioned different measures of similarity between vertices (Jaccard, Sörensen and Pearson correlation), and three methods of linkage of clusters (single, complete and average) have been considered and and their influence on the behavior of the algorithm was observed. The quality of communities generated by the proposed method has been compared with the quality of clusters generated by the Louvain algorithm [3] using modularity proposed by Newman and Girvan [11]. The results of the computational experiment have been also compared with the structure of the investigated organization and allowed one to check whether detected communities refer to the real structure of the institution.

The experiment was divided into several steps. The first step was to select the observation period, to select investigated departments and then extraction and collection of the data from organization's e-mail server logs referring to selected period and departments to analyze. For the purpose of the experiment it has been decided to select six months (January to June 2020) as observation period and a single department with the biggest number of employees (91 persons) has been selected for observation. Total number of identified messages between the employees within the whole organization was equal to 251 129, and the number of messages related to internal communication between the employees of the selected department was equal to 10 364. The density of the network was equal to 0.1094.

In the second step of the experiment the organizational network of the department has been built basing on cleaned data from organization's e-mail server logs referring to digital communications between employees. Employees were represented by vertices and communication between employees - by edges linking respective vertices. It has been assumed that an edge between two vertices exists if two employees represented by these vertices exchanged at least a single message within observed period without considering roles of employees (sender or receiver). An important aspect of this step was to ensure the security of employees' personal data. For this purpose, each e-mail address was anonymized by assigning it an individual number from 1 to 91.

The third step focused on applying AHC algorithm to discover communities in the social network built in the previous step. The proposed algorithm has been implemented using R software environment [14] with the *iGraph* [15] and *LSA* [16] packages. And in the last step, the obtained results were analyzed.

Main results of the broad experiment are presented in Tables 1, 2 and 3, and Fig. 1, 2 and 3. Tables 1 and 2 present the results of the experiment in the form of a set of clusters (with their sizes) detected by proposed algorithm with considered three similarity measures between vertices and for each form of linkage between clusters, respectively. Because of the fact, that the results obtained by the algorithm with Jaccard and Sörensen indexes used as similarity measure are the same (first observation from the experiment), they are presented in the same Table 1. Additionally, Fig. 1 and 2 present two groups of dendrograms based

Table 1. Results of the computational experiment obtained by AHC algorithm used to detection of communities with Jaccard/Sörensen similarity measure

Linkage		Members
Single	C1 (87)	1 2 3 4 5 6 7 8 9 10 11 12 13 14 15 16 17 18 19 20 21 22 23 24 25 26 27 28 29 30 31 32 33 34 35 36 37 38 39 40 41 42 43 44 45 47 48 49 50 51 52 53 55 56 57 58 61 62 63 64 65 66 67 68 69 70 71 72 73 74 75 76 77 78 79 80 81 82 83 84 85 86 87 88 89 90 91
	C2 (1)	60
	C3 (1)	46
	C4 (1)	54
	C5 (1)	59
Complete	C1 (63)	1 2 3 4 5 6 7 8 9 10 11 12 13 14 15 16 17 18 19 20 21 22 23 24 25 26 27 28 29 30 31 32 33 34 35 36 37 38 39 40 41 42 43 44 45 46 47 48 49 50 51 52 53 54 55 56 57 58 59 60 61 62 63 64 65 66 67
	C2 (5)	71 74 86 88 91
	C3 (7)	68 69 79 81 85 87 90
	C4 (6)	70 73 76 77 82 84
	C5 (6)	72 75 78 80 83 89
Average	C1 (15)	1 2 3 4 5 6 7 8 9 10 11 12 13 14 15
	C2 (10)	16 17 18 19 20 21 23 24 25 26
	C3 (15)	27 28 29 30 31 32 33 34 35 36 37 38 39 49 65
	C4 (27)	22 40 41 42 43 44 45 46 47 48 50 51 52 53 54 55 56 57 58 59 60 61 62 63 64 66 67
	C5 (24)	68 69 70 71 72 73 74 75 76 77 78 79 80 81 82 83 84 85 86 87 88 89 90 91

on the results obtained by AHC algorithm with Jaccard/Sörensen indexes and Pearson correlation and for each form of linkage between clusters, respectively.

Figure 3 and Table 3 focuses on the quality of the communities generated by AHC algorithm and its comparison to the results of Louvain algorithm. They present modularity values calculated for AHC algorithm with different similarity measures and different form of linkage between clusters, and the results obtained by Louvain algorithm, which has been used by Authors in their last paper [1], respectively. An interesting observation at this point is that communities with their members obtained by Louvain algorithm exactly correspond to the structure of investigated organization.

By analysis of the results one can conclude that the proposed AHC algorithm has divided the network into five clusters (regardless the similarity measure used), which correspond to the number of units of investigated organization, however the number of vertices belonging to each cluster and the content of each

Table 2. Results of the computational experiment obtained by AHC algorithm used to detection of communities with Pearson correlation as a similarity measure

Linkage		Members
Single	C1 (15)	1 2 3 4 5 6 7 8 9 10 11 12 13 14 15
	C2 (73)	16 17 18 19 20 21 22 23 24 25 26 27 28 29 30 31 32 33 34 35 36 37 38 39 40 41 42 43 44 45 47 48 49 50 51 52 53 55 56 57 58 60 61 62 63 64 65 66 67 68 69 70 71 72 73 74 75 76 77 78 79 80 81 82 83 84 85 86 87 88 89 90 91
	C3 (1)	46
	C4 (1)	54
	C5 (1)	59
Complete	C1 (17)	1 2 3 4 5 6 7 8 9 10 11 12 13 14 15 45 47
	C2 (10)	16 17 18 19 20 21 23 24 25 26
	C3 (14)	27 28 29 30 31 32 33 34 35 36 37 38 39 77
	C4 (27)	22 40 41 42 43 44 46 48 49 50 51 52 53 54 55 56 57 58 59 60 61 62 63 64 65 66 67
	C5 (23)	68 69 70 71 72 73 74 75 76 78 79 80 81 82 83 84 85 86 87 88 89 90 91
Average	C1 (15)	1 2 3 4 5 6 7 8 9 10 11 12 13 14 15
	C2 (11)	16 17 18 19 20 21 22 23 24 25 26
	C3 (17)	27 28 29 30 31 32 33 34 35 36 37 38 39 49 65 77 78
	C4 (28)	40 41 42 43 44 45 46 47 48 50 51 52 53 54 55 56 57 58 59 60 61 62 63 64 66 67 68 79
	C5 (20)	69 70 71 72 73 74 75 76 80 81 82 83 84 85 86 87 88 89 90 91

Table 3. Results of the computational experiment (communities and modularity) obtained by Louvain algorithm used to detection of communities

	Members	Modularity
C1 (15)	1 2 3 4 5 6 7 8 9 10 11 12 13 14 15	0.504965
C2 (11)	16 17 18 19 20 21 22 23 24 25 26	
C3 (13)	27 28 29 30 31 32 33 34 35 36 37 38 39	
C4 (29)	40 41 42 43 44 45 46 47 48 49 50 51 52 53 54 55 56 57 58 59 60 61 62 63 64 65 66 67 68	
C5 (23)	69 70 71 72 73 74 75 76 77 78 79 80 81 82 83 84 85 86 87 88 89 90 91	

cluster are different, they depend on the methods of linking clusters during the process of solving the problem by the algorithm. Whereas AHC with average and complete linkage provide a balanced division of the network into communities, AHC with single linkage detects a subset of communities with only a single node.

Deeper analysis of the content of obtained communities by AHC with average linkage (with both similarity measures: Jaccard/Sörensen and Pearson correlation) provide an observation that they mostly refer to real structure of the

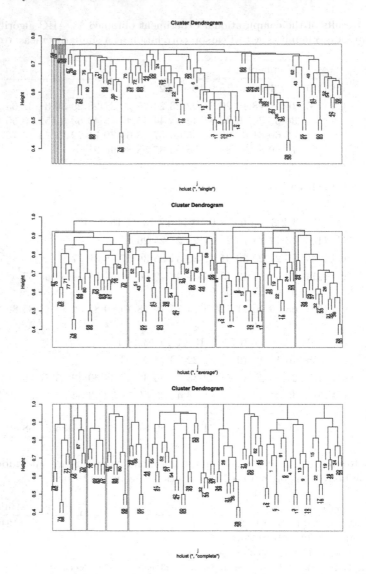

Fig. 1. Results of the computational experiment (dendrograms) obtained by AHC algorithm used to detection of communities with Jaccard/Sörensen similarity measure

organization. In case of AHC with Jaccard/Sörensen similarity measure, a single community (C1) has been detected correctly when compare to the structure of the organization, and rest of them differ by one vertex from the real structure (vertex 65 should belong to C4 instead of C3, vertex 22 should belong to C2 instead of C4, and vertex 68 should belong to C4 instead of C3). In case of AHC with Pearson correlation, two communities (C1 and C2) have been detected correctly when compare to the structure of the organization. The community C3

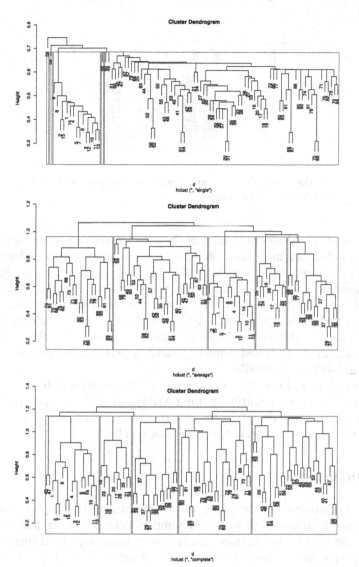

Fig. 2. Results of the computational experiment (dendrograms) obtained by AHC algorithm used to detection of communities with Pearson correlation as a similarity measure

contains four vertices which should belong to other communities (49 and 65 - to C4, 77 and 78 - to C5). Also the community C4 contains a single incorrectly assigned node (79), which should belong to C5. Promising results have been also obtained for AHC with Pearson correlation and with complete linkage. The difference between two structures (AHC vs. Louvain) refers only to five incorrectly assigned nodes to communities.

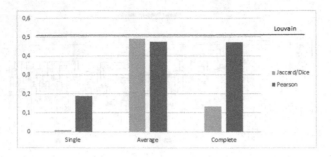

Fig. 3. Results of the computational experiment (modularity) obtained by AHC algorithm used to detection of communities

Analysis of the results presented in the Fig. 3 allow one to see that the best values of modularity have been observed for two abovementioned cases (Jaccard/Sörensen, average linkage: 0.491054, Pearson, average linkage: 0.475245). A slightly worse value of modularity has been obtained for AHC with Pearson correlation and complete linkage (0.471304). It is also easy to see that values of modularity is definitely worse for AHC with single linkage (Jaccard/Sörensen: 009016, Pearson: 0.188604). Of course, values of modularity obtained by proposed algorithm for all tested similarity metrics were worse that value obtained by Louvain method (0.504965).

At the end, it is also worth to mention that the experiment has been also carried out to discover communities by using AHC with original adjacency matrix as similarity matrix. Unfortunately, the way of merging clusters, regardless linkage methods used, has not guaranteed promising results.

6   Conclusions

The main contribution of the paper was to investigate the impact of similarity measure on the quality of clusters/communities detected by agglomerative hierarchical clustering in the organizational network based on e-mail communication between people within the organization. Three similarity measures between vertices have been inferred from the adjacency relationships between vertices and tested in the experiment. The quality of communities detected by the proposed method has been compared with the quality of clusters generated by the Louvain algorithm using modularity. The results of the computational experiment have been also compared with the structure of the investigated organization.

The main conclusion from the research is that hierarchical methods can be used with success to detect communities, however it requires a good measure of similarity between vertices. Communities detected by proposed algorithm with different similarity measures and average linkage in most cases correctly assigns vertices to communities, when compare to real structure of the organization.

Future work will aim at considering a weighted social network and finding new similarity measures which will better refer to the structure of the network.

An interesting direction is to solve other network problems, e.g. link prediction, which may allow to pose a new knowledge about the investigated organization.

References

1. Barbucha, D., Szyman, P.: Detecting communities in organizational social network based on e-mail communication. In: Czarnowski, I., Howlett, R.J., Jain, L.C. (eds.) Intelligent Decision Technologies. SIST, vol. 238, pp. 15–24. Springer, Singapore (2021). https://doi.org/10.1007/978-981-16-2765-1_2
2. Barbucha, D., Szyman, P.: Identifying key actors in organizational social network based on e-mail communication. In: Wojtkiewicz, K., Treur, J., Pimenidis, E., Maleszka, M. (eds.) ICCCI 2021. CCIS, vol. 1463, pp. 3–14. Springer, Cham (2021). https://doi.org/10.1007/978-3-030-88113-9_1
3. Blondel, D.V., Guillaume, J.-L., Lambiotte, R., Lefebvre, E.: Fast unfolding of communities in large networks. J. Stat. Mech. Theory Exp. **10**, 10008 (2008)
4. Christidis, P., Losada, A.G.: Email based institutional network analysis: applications and risks. Social Sci. **8**, 306 (2019)
5. Creamer, G.G., Stolfo, J.S., Creamer, M., Hershkop, S., Rowe R.: Discovering Organizational Hierarchy through a Corporate Ranking Algorithm: The Enron Case, Complexity, vol. 2022, Article ID 8154476, 18 pages (2022)
6. Fortunato, S.: Community detection in graphs. Phys. Rep. **486**, 75–174 (2010)
7. Jaccard, P.: The distribution of the flora in the alpine zone. New Phytologist **11**(2), 37–50 (1912)
8. Jeh, G., Widom, J.: Simrank: a measure of structural-context similarity. In: Proceedings of the 8th ACM SIGKDD International Conference on Knowledge Discovery and Data Mining, pp. 538–543. ACM (2002)
9. Kolli, N., Narayanaswamy, B.: Analysis of e-mail communication using a social network framework for crisis detection in an organization. Procedia-Social Behav. Sci. **100**, 57–67 (2013)
10. Leicht, E., Holme, P., Newman, M.E.: Vertex similarity in networks. Phys. Rev. E **73**(2), 026120 (2006)
11. Newman, M.E.J., Girvan, M.: Finding and evaluating community structure in networks. Phys. Rev. E **69**(2), 026113 (2004)
12. Nguyen H., Zheng, R.: A data-driven study of influences in Twitter communities. In: Proceedings of the IEEE International Conference on Communications, pp. 3938–3944. IEEE, Sydney (2014)
13. Pons, P., Latapy, M.: Computing communities in large networks using random walks. J. Graph Algor. Appl. **10**(2), 191–218 (2006)
14. R software environment. https://www.r-project.org/
15. R iGraph. https://igraph.org/r/
16. R LSA. https://cran.r-project.org/web/packages/lsa/
17. Radicchi, F., Castellano, C., Cecconi, F., Loreto, V., Parisi, D.: Defining and identifying communities in networks. PNAS **101**(9), 2658–2663 (2004)
18. Raut, P., Chawhan, R., Joshi, T., Kasle, P.: Classification of power relations based on email exchange. In: Proceedings of the IEEE International Conference on Computing, Power and Communication Technologies, New Delhi, India, pp. 486–489 (2020)
19. Salton, G., McGill, M.J.: Introduction to Modern Information Retrieval. McGraw-Hill Inc., New York (1986)

20. Sörensen, T.: A method of establishing groups of equal amplitude in plant sociology based on similarity of species content and its application to analyses of the vegetation on danish commons. Biologiske Skrifter **5**, 1–34 (1948)
21. Wright, D.K., Hinson, M.: Tracking how social and other digital media are being used in public relations practice: a twelve-year study. Public Relat. J. **11**(1), 1–30 (2017)
22. Xu, R., Wunsch, D.: Clustering. John Wiley & Sons, Piscataway (2008)

An Approach to Modeling a Real-Time Updated Environment Based on Messages from Agents

Marek Krótkiewicz[1] , Krystian Wojtkiewicz[1] , Marcin Jodłowiec[1(✉)] ,
Rafał Palak[1] , Mikołaj Szczerbicki[2], and Piotr Nawrocki[2]

[1] Faculty of Information and Communication Technology,
Wrocław University of Science and Technology, Wrocław, Poland
{marek.krotkiewicz,krystian.wojtkiewicz,marcin.jodlowiec,
rafal.palak}@pwr.edu.pl
[2] Trackimo CEE Ltd., New York, USA
mikolaj@trackimo.eu, piotr@trackimo.com

Abstract. Agent-based systems follow similar rules as object-oriented models. However, they distinguish agents as entities that can perceive their environment, process information about it, change it via actions, and interact with other agents. In this paper, the authors proposed some solutions coupled to creating models of such environments on a high level of abstraction, considering the applicability of these models in real-world projects. As a result, a conceptual environment model has been elaborated and proposed. The presented case study of the AriaDNA Life system verifies the model.

Keywords: Conceptual modeling · Agent-based modeling · Agent systems metamodeling

1 Introduction

Agent-based solutions are a trending approach aiming to solve complex problems. The usage of agents of various sorts is expanding quickly across computer science, particularly artificial intelligence fields. That is partly owing to their broad application. The word agent *"concerns the meaning of autonomy which means self-activity for the achievement of its objectives"* [3]. The issues of real-time systems modeling are crucial from the real-world systems point of view. An example of such a system can be the *AriaDNA Life* project. In this project, the phase of conceptual design had to consider a relatively complex model of the environment, in which the system operates.

The contribution of this paper is a conceptual model containing both syntax and semantics of real-time updated environments. Moreover, the case study has been presented as the evaluation of the proposed solution.

N. T. Nguyen et al. (Eds.): ICCCI 2022, LNAI 13501, pp. 43–50, 2022.
https://doi.org/10.1007/978-3-031-16014-1_4

This paper is structured as follows. The next section contains an elaboration on the related works. In the subsequent section, we have described and exemplified the most crucial concepts within the model. This section also contains the model, which is described using a UML class diagram (Fig. 1). Thereafter, we describe a case study. This case study introduces a model of an agent-based environment, which has been conceptualized and implemented within the *AriaDNA Life* system. The last section contains a summary and conclusions.

2   Related Work

Typically, the approaches to agent-based modeling rarely focus on modeling agent environment and mostly use mathematical models to describe agents and agent's behavior [2,5]. Some approaches try to use neural network models [7] to capture agents' knowledge upon environment [1].

We can find examples in literature of approaches focused on modeling environment for agent systems. However, there is no common approach. There are researchers that use foundational ontologies, like Unified Foundational Ontology (UFO) [4] or Bunge-Wand-Weber ontology [9], to express vocabulary and concepts and to build an agent-based ontology. Alternatively, authors of [4] distinguish (among others) the following issues in agent modeling: agents and their roles, events, mental moments (beliefs and perceptions), and social moments. While ontological definitions proposed in [9] cover perceptions, learning, beliefs, resources, actions, procedures, goals, and capabilities.

Some approaches propose a semi-formal manner to model agents and their environments. In [8], the authors have proposed a formal model of collective supplemented with a UML class diagram, which further was used to model a collective intelligence system [11]. Authors of [10] define environment as a pair of values (which describe the environment) and self-executing mapping which makes alternations within this environment. Such high-level definitions are very broad, although convenient in terms of conformance of agent-based solutions within this formalism. Authors of [6] focus on environmental dynamism aspects and provide formal apparatus to make statements about agents and the environment.

3   Proposed Approach

3.1   Environment Model Assumptions

To deliver a domain model, we have proposed a few interconnected fragments which carry the semantics of specific parts of modeled reality. Our approach is quite general, i.e., our model is highly abstract in terms of its domain application and the level of its description. In the following section, we briefly describe the main assumptions and concepts used in the model.

Structural, Behavioral and Temporal Aspects. The proposed model is stateless and holds the structure of the environment. The model can change over time. However, it represents current values only, i.e., at a particular time instant. The intensional structure is static and is not supposed to change over time.

Spaces and Dimensions. We define Environment as a set of spaces, where each space consists of an ordered set of dimensions. A dimension is an abstract notion described by a set of a comparable value. We consider two types of dimensions: enumerated dimensions and numerical dimensions. The first type is denoted by the finite set of distinct values. While the latter is a finite or infinite set of numerical values, with optional bounds. Numerical dimensions can be either continuous or discrete, containing integer or real values respectively.

Example 1. Euclidean 3D space is a space with three dimensions: *width*, *height*, *depth*. Each of the dimensions is linear, continuous, and infinite.

Spaces can have regions. Regions are named derived subspaces which are computed by an expression. We have identified three kinds of relationships between spaces and regions: Labeling – the region exists in space, its expression is defined by the use of its dimensions. Extension – the region extends the space, expression can add additional subspaces to the linked space. Subtraction – the region constraints the space, expression uses space's dimensions and computed region is interpreted as excluded from space.

Agents and Other Entities. An entity is anything what can be perceived as a separate being in the environment. The main distinction of entities covers their behavioral aspect. The agents (actors) are able to interact with the environment and communicate with other actors, while other entities are passive and can exclusively be objects of the interaction.

We use object-oriented paradigm to perceive the structure of entities. Thus, entities are classified by their types, which define the schema with the set of attributes. Technically, the most crucial information about the entity is the set of values for each entity type's attribute. Attributes in entity types may be visible or not. If attributes are visible they might be objects of interaction with other entities. Otherwise, they might be accessed by the entity only. The entities can be collective, what means that the group of entities is perceived as a separate entity within the model.

The entities exist in spaces. In each of the spaces entity exists, we need to specify its position. The position is tuple of values corresponding to the consecutive dimension in the space.

Example 2. An oak `tree` is an entity type. It has the following visible attributes: height, number of branches and planting year. "Bartek" is an entity defined as oak `tree`. It has the value 33,5m for the height attribute, number of branches equal to 8 and value 1330 for the attribute defining planting year.

Interaction Traits. The traits are inherent features of the environmental elements. Their role is to characterize entities by the way how they can interact with the environment. We have distinguished the following traits:

Existential trait – this trait gives the entity the ability to be responsible for the existence management of the other types. In the other words, a specific entity can create and destroy other entities if needed.

Example 3. The entities of human type can create and destroy other entities of human type. However, the entities of human type cannot create the entities of leopard type. But they can surely destroy them.

Self-existential Trait – this trait gives entities the ability to be responsible for their own existence management in terms of breaking their lifeline.

Example 4. The entities of the human type can commit suicide and end their life intentionally. However, cucumbers cannot do so.

Mutability Trait – trait for alternation of attributes' or dimensions' values. The trait consists of two flags: internal and external. The external flag is responsible for information, whether other entities are capable of transforming an entity's state. On the contrary, the internal flag determines if the entity can transform its state. Mutability traits describe also the relationship between entity types and their attributes. Each of the attributes in type might be mutable or not.

Example 5. The planting year of an oak tree is immutable, thus cannot be changed in the environment. However, number of its branches is mutable (branches decay over time).

Interactions and Messages. Interactions are events which can happen due to the contact between exactly two entities. These interactions may be of various kinds. Each interaction has exactly one entity playing the role of subject and one playing the object. Before the interaction can occur, there is a need to check whether all the rules enforced by the model traits are fulfilled. E.g., if the interaction is alternating the object state, we need to check whether the subject has specific mutability trait to mutate the object's value. Otherwise we need to cancel the interaction.

Messages are interactions which contain a payload. Entities can exchange their information by messages. The message has a payload which can be interpreted by the entity and possibly lead to its state mutation. The payload in the model is abstract. Thus, its syntax and semantics is defined beyond the model. The model's structure only carries the information upon the message's author and receivers.

Example 6. Let us consider two entities of the soldier type that are inside the trench. The first one sends the other message in the natural language with the following payload: "*get down*". On this command, the second one falls on the ground immediately, updating its position in the vertical dimension.

3.2   Environment Model

The proposed model has been presented in the Fig. 1 utilizing a UML notation.

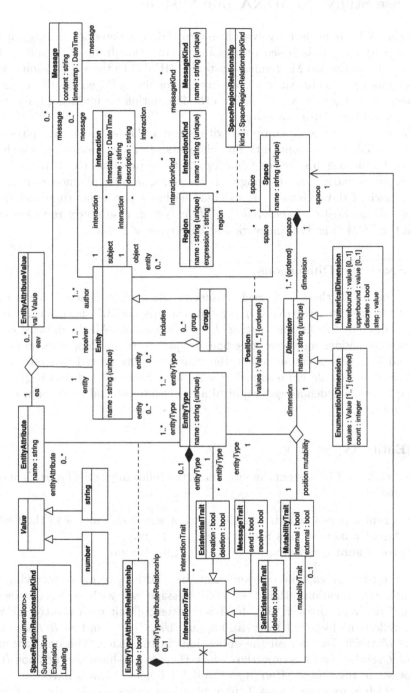

Fig. 1. UML diagram class of *Environment Conceptual Model* (ECM)

4   Case Study: AriaDNA Life System

The *AriaDNA Life* project involves the issues of danger detection during outdoor physical activities. It is based on passing information from GPS and motion sensors – Micro Electro Mechanical Systems (MEMS) to the supervision center. The signals are monitored, analyzed, and recognized. Based on those signals the messages are generated, which form the foundation for updating the current state of agents and their environment.

The agents are people equipped with sensors. Those agents are physically present within the environment. The elements of the environment, which are reflected by the systems are the following: static terrain map (background) with such elements marked on it: dangerous elements, agents, planned routes, and events. Each of those elements is specified within a particular time and space. A short characteristic of the *AriaDNA Life* system case study representation within the ECM (Fig. 1) framework will be presented below.

4.1   Space and Dimensions

To use the ECM, there is a need to specify the environment's Space and its Dimensions first. In *AriaDNA Life* system there is one 3D space with the following indiscrete dimensions: *latitude, longitude, altitude*. All the dimensions are NumericalDimensions and have lowerbound equal to 0. The upperbound of *latitude* and *longitude* is equal to 360, the values are interpreted as degrees. The upperbound of *altitude* is undefined. Spaces have been divided into Regions via Labeling, the labels denote geographical areas of interest and expressions consist of polygons.

4.2   Entity Types

In the *AriaDNA Life* system's environment the following EntityTypes have been distinguished:

User Agent a person who is equipped with a sensor and moves in the field.
SAR Agent a member of a Search & Rescue Team,
Operator Agent a coordinating and integrating person.

All the entities are capable of communicating (both in terms of receiving and sending communication), thus they hold MessageTrait with positive values of send and receive. Moreover, they hold SelfExistentialTrait with positive deletion flag to reflect the fact that they can log out. *User Agent* and *SAR Agent* hold internal MutabilityTrait for all the dimensions in the space. The position mutability of *Operator Agent* is objectless, since they do not have any Position (they are not set in the Space). *User Agent* and *SAR Agent* always have Position in Space, which is expressed as a 3-tuple of values corresponding to the Dimensions of Space. Each of the agents has several EntityAttributes. However, they are irrelevant to the case study understanding. The other, non-agent type of entity types are *Points of Interest* (e.g. mountain shelters, signposts, waterholes, etc.). They hold fixed Position, and they do not have position mutability. All remaining InteractionTraits comprise the false flags.

4.3 Messages

The Messages are crucial to model communication between the agents. The *AriaDNA Life* system proposed a collection of environment-related messages. The most important messages involve the information about environmental danger (such as *Avalanche* or *Dangerous Animal*), which are sent by *Operator Agent* to the *User Agents* which are in specific Region.

4.4 Interactions

An example of interaction is a state of affairs when *User Agent* approaches the *Point of Interest*. *User Agent* is a subject of such an interaction, and *Point of Interest* is the object. The InteractionKind can be defined as *approaches*.

5 Summary

In this paper, we have presented the approach to modeling real-time updated environments. The proposed model is very general and relatively concise. It contains all crucial categories needed to express necessary information. Moreover, we presented the case study involving the project comprising a commercial application. The model has been successfully utilized and implemented in this project. Despite many simplifications, the model turned out to be successfully modeling the problem domain. The limitation of this paper did not allow to present the extent of the model utilization. However, future work focuses on broadening the expressiveness and semantic capacity of the model to cover as many issues as possible.

Acknowledgment. The research and this paper was supported by the National Centre for Research and Development through the project name *"Active Search and Rescue System (AS&RS) - AriaDNA Life"* under POIR.01.01.01-00-1081/18-00 number.

References

1. Akintunde, M.E., Kevorchian, A., Lomuscio, A., Pirovano, E.: Verification of RNN-based neural agent-environment systems. In: Proceedings of the AAAI Conference on Artificial Intelligence, vol. 33, pp. 6006–6013 (2019). https://doi.org/10.1609/aaai.v33i01.33016006
2. DeGroot, M.H.: Reaching a consensus. J. Am. Stat. Assoc. **69**(345), 118–121 (1974)
3. Durfee, E.H., Lesser, V.R., Corkill, D.D.: Trends in cooperative distributed problem solving. IEEE Trans. Knowl. Data Eng. (1989)

4. Guizzardi, G., Wagner, G.: Towards ontological foundations for agent modelling concepts using the unified fundational ontology (UFO). In: Bresciani, P., Giorgini, P., Henderson-Sellers, B., Low, G., Winikoff, M. (eds.) AOIS -2004. LNCS (LNAI), vol. 3508, pp. 110–124. Springer, Heidelberg (2005). https://doi.org/10.1007/11426714_8
5. Helbing, D.: Agent-Based Modeling, pp. 25–70. Springer, Heidelberg (2012)
6. Helleboogh, A., Vizzari, G., Uhrmacher, A., Michel, F.: Modeling dynamic environments in multi-agent simulation. Auton. Agent. Multi. Agent. Syst. **14**(1), 87–116 (2006)
7. Huk, M.: Non-uniform initialization of inputs groupings in contextual neural networks. In: Nguyen, N.T., Gaol, F.L., Hong, T.-P., Trawiński, B. (eds.) ACIIDS 2019. LNCS (LNAI), vol. 11432, pp. 420–428. Springer, Cham (2019). https://doi.org/10.1007/978-3-030-14802-7_36
8. Jodłowiec, M., Krótkiewicz, M., Palak, R., Wojtkiewicz, K.: Graph-based crowd definition for assessing wise crowd measures. In: Nguyen, N.T., Chbeir, R., Exposito, E., Aniorté, P., Trawiński, B. (eds.) ICCCI 2019. LNCS (LNAI), vol. 11683, pp. 66–78. Springer, Cham (2019). https://doi.org/10.1007/978-3-030-28377-3_6
9. Monu, K.: Intelligent agents as a modelling paradigm. Ph.D. thesis, University of British Columbia (2005). https://open.library.ubc.ca/collections/ubctheses/831/items/1.0092420
10. Odell, J.J., Van Dyke Parunak, H., Fleischer, M., Brueckner, S.: Modeling agents and their environment. In: Giunchiglia, F., Odell, J., Weiß, G. (eds.) AOSE 2002. LNCS, vol. 2585, pp. 16–31. Springer, Heidelberg (2003). https://doi.org/10.1007/3-540-36540-0_2
11. Palak, R., Wojtkiewicz, K.: The formal framework for collective systems. Axioms **10**(2), 91 (2021)

Updating the Result Ontology Integration at the Concept Level in the Event of the Evolution of Their Components

Adrianna Kozierkiewicz[1] (ID), Marcin Pietranik[1(✉)] (ID), Mateusz Olsztyński[1], and Loan T. T. Nguyen[2,3]

[1] Faculty of Information and Communication Technology, Wroclaw University of Science and Technology, Wybrzeze Wyspianskiego, 2750-370 Wroclaw, Poland
{adrianna.kozierkiewicz,marcin.pietranik}@pwr.edu.pl,
mateusz.olsztynski@student.pwr.edu.pl
[2] School of Computer Science and Engineering, International University, Ho Chi Minh City, Vietnam
nttloan@hcmiu.edu.vn
[3] Vietnam National University, Ho Chi Minh City, Vietnam

Abstract. Ontology integration is the task of combining a set of ontologies into a single ontology. Such ontology should contain all the knowledge expressed in the partial ontologies, without all the potential conflicts between them being resolved. In the literature, one may find several approaches to this problem, however, to the best of our knowledge most of them assume that the input ontologies remain static in time, therefore there is no risk of the outcome of integration becoming stale. If one of the partial ontologies changes over time (evolve) then the outcome of its integration may become obsolete. Therefore, a necessity of performing ontology integration once again appears. However, such a procedure may be very time and resource consuming. In this paper, we propose a solution for this issue. We claim that it is possible to update the integrated ontology based solely on a description of changes applied to the input ontologies, acquiring a similar quality as if the ontology integration be conducted from scratch.

Keywords: Ontology integration · Ontology evolution · Knowledge management

1 Introduction

Ontology integration [10] is a straightforward task of combining two (or more) ontologies into one, unified ontology, which contains the knowledge expressed in all input ontologies. The task, although very simple to explain and understand, entails several issues which, if not addressed, result in a final ontology consisting of conflicting information. For example, a method of ontology integration should cope with a problem of different concept hierarchies, contradicting relations among concept, different naming

© The Author(s), under exclusive license to Springer Nature Switzerland AG 2022
N. T. Nguyen et al. (Eds.): ICCCI 2022, LNAI 13501, pp. 51–64, 2022.
https://doi.org/10.1007/978-3-031-16014-1_5

conventions etc. In other words, it is not possible to simply merge several ontologies expecting that the output of such operation will preserve the quality of its input.

In the literature it is possible to find a plethora of different solutions of this task, which usually yield good results. However, to the best of our knowledge, none of these solutions include the aspect of ontology evolution. Consider a situation in which two ontologies (namely $O^{(m-1)}$ and $O'^{(n)}$) created in two moments in time $(m-1)$ and (n) have been properly integrated. Then, in some further moment in time (m) one of these ontologies has changed (e.g., new concepts have been added, some concepts have been changed, some have been deleted). Obviously, if such a situation occurs, the integrated ontology no longer carries the expected knowledge and need to be revalidated and eventually updated.

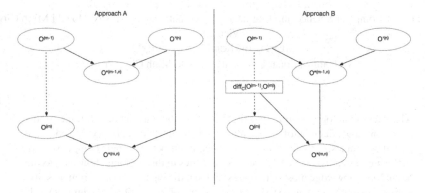

Fig. 1. Different approach to integrating evolved ontologies

The naive approach to the described situation (presented as Approach A on the left side of Fig. 1) could involve performing the base integration algorithm once again for the changed ontology in its newer state $(O^{(m)})$ and the unchanged ontology $(O'^{(n)})$. Obviously, such an approach would render good results, however, depending on the size and complexity of input ontologies it can be very time or resource consuming.

In this paper we propose a different route. We claim that it is possible to update the result of the initial integration of two source ontologies based only a description of changes applied to the evolving ontology (on the concept level an output of a function $diff_C$ which compares two states of the selected ontology), acquiring a comparable quality to the basic naive approach described earlier. Due to the limited space, this paper addresses only ontology integration on the concept level. The proposed idea is illustrated as Approach B on the right side of Fig. 1.

The remaining part of the article is structured as follows. Section 2 contains an overview of related works done in the field. Section 3 presents mathematical definitions which serve as a foundation for the rest of the paper. Section 4 provides a core contribution, which is a set of algorithms for updating the result ontology integration at the concept level in the event of the evolution of their components. Section 5 contains results of experimental verification of developed ideas. The last section is a summary and sheds some light on our upcoming research plans.

2 Related Works

Ontology evolution is a widely known topic [4] which lends a lot from a similar topic related to the evolution of relational database schema evolution [9]. A comprehensive approach to this issue can be found in [6]. Authors provide a method for automatic detection of ontology modifications and a method for rewriting queries to assert their compatibility with evolving ontologies. This approach tackles an important issue when ontologies evolve, all the tools related to such ontologies need to be at least revalidated and, if required, updated to the new structure.

Ontology alignment is probably the most prominent issue which entails the necessity of checking if the mapping between two ontologies needs to be updated if one of them has changed. This topic is widely discussed [2, 14], and there exists a plethora of tools that can be used to assert that mappings between two ontologies remain sound.

One of such solutions is the one presented in [7]. The authors of this research proposed an approach that initially detects changes in ontologies on the schema and instance level, which may potentially entail inconsistencies in alignments. These inconsistencies are then addressed by using a set of recovery and roll-back mapping reconciliation algorithms. All the provided procedures are based on the notion of the change history log, like the one proposed in the following paper and some of our previous works [12].

A different approach can be found in [1] where authors reject analyzing the change history of maintained ontologies. They propose using a Historical Knowledge Graph which contains knowledge from all versions of the ontology. That way all the knowledge is freely available at any time, which simplifies any kind of inference or querying processes.

Beyond research presented in the following section, there exist multiple issues related to ontology evolution that are addressed in the literature (e.g., creating a graph of change relevance in [13] or preserving the inner consistency of altered ontologies [5]. However, to the best of our knowledge, there exist no solution devoted solely to applying consequences of ontology evolution in the context of ontology integration, which is the main topic of the following paper.

3 Basic Notions

A pair (A, V), where A is a finite set of attributes describing objects from given domain of discourse and V is a set of these attributes domains is called "a real world". Assuming that V_a is a domain of some attribute a, the following statement is true $V = \bigcup_{a \in A} V_a$. Following our work [11], ontology is defined as a quintuple:

$$O = \left(C, H, R^C, I, R^I \right) \tag{1}$$

C is a finite set of concepts. H denotes a hierarchy of concepts. A pair of concepts (c_1, c_2) belonging to this set can be interpreted that a concept c_1 is more general than a concept c_2. R^C is a finite set of relations between concepts $R^C = \{r_1^C, r_2^C, \dots, r_n^C\}$, $n \in N$, where $r_i^C \in R^C$ ($i \in [1, n]$) is a subset of Cartesian product $r_i^C \subset C \times C$. I is a finite set of concept instance identifiers. $R^I = \{r_1^I, r_2^I, \dots, r_n^I\}$ is a finite set of relations between instances of concepts.

Every concept c taken from the set C is defined as:

$$c = \left(id^c, A^c, V^c, I^c\right) \tag{2}$$

id^c is an identifier of c. A^c denotes a set of concept's attributes ($A^c \subseteq A$). V^c is a set of domains of concept's attributes ($V^c = \bigcup_{a \in A^c} V_a$ where V_a is a domain of an attribute a taken from the set V). I^c denotes a set of concept's instances. A pair (A^c, V^c) will be further called a structure of concept's c. The ontology O can be balled the *(A,V)-based ontology* if the following conditions are met: (i) $\forall_{c \in C} A^c \subseteq A$, (ii) $\forall_{c \in C} V^c \subseteq V$.

To define the semantics of the attributes from the set A^c, it is assumed that there is a sub-language of the sentence calculus L_s^A and the function $S_A : A \times C \to L_s^A$, which assigns logic sentences to the attributes of the concept c. This function allows to distinguish attributes with the same names between different concepts due to the differences in their semantics. The overall meaning of a concept is given by its context, which can be defined as a conjunction of the semantics of each of its attributes. Formally, for any concept of c, where $A^c = \{a_1, a_2, \ldots, a_n\}$, its context is given as:

$$ctx(c) = S_A(a_1, c) \wedge S_A(a_2, c) \wedge \cdots \wedge S_A(a_n, c) \tag{3}$$

Such approach allows to define formal criteria for three relations between two attributes a and b and two concepts c and c':

- equivalency (denoted with $\equiv$) if the following condition is met $S_A(a, c) \Leftrightarrow S_A\left(b, c'\right)$,
- generalization (denoted with $\uparrow$) if $S_A(a, c) \Rightarrow S_A\left(b, c'\right)$,
- contradiction (denote with $\downarrow$) if $\neg\left(S_A(a, c) \wedge S_A\left(b, c'\right)\right)$,

Assuming the existence of two *(A,V)*-based ontologies O and O', and the existence of two concepts c and c' (such that $c \in C$ and $c' \in C'$) a degree to which these two concepts can be aligned is denotes as $\lambda_C\left(c, c'\right)$. The method of calculating the value of this degree can be freely choses from the plethora of approaches available in the literature. In our previous works we have proposed a solution based on an analysis of attributes semantics. For details, please refer to [1]. Based on the accepted method we can define the alignment of ontologies O and O' as a set containing tuples:

$$Align_C\left(O, O'\right) = \left\{\left(c, c', \lambda_C\left(c, c'\right), r\right) | c \in C, c' \in C', \lambda_C\left(c, c'\right) \geq TC\right\} \tag{4}$$

The value of TC is an arbitrarily chosen threshold value, and the r is the type of relationship connecting two concepts. The most used one is the equivalency relationship denoted with the symbol $\equiv$.

Let $\overline{TL}$ denote a universal timeline which include all valid moments is time in which some ontology from the set of maintained ontologies has changed. Such structure can be defined as an ordered set of elements representing the discrete moments in time $\overline{TL} = \{t_n | n \in \mathbb{N}\}$. A pair $\langle \overline{TL}, \prec \rangle$ (where $\prec$ is an ordering relation, which can be identified with a time sequence) forms a strict partial order (irreflexive, transitive and antisymmetric). By *TL(O)* we will denote a subset of $\overline{TL}$ containing only moments in time in which the selected ontology O has changed ($TL(O) \subseteq \overline{TL}$). The above definitions allow us to define the ontology repository $Rep(O) = \{O^{(m)} | \forall m \in TL(O)\}$, where $O^{(m)} = (C^{(m)}, H^{(m)}, R^{C(m)}, I^m, R^{I(m)})$ denotes the ontology O in certain moment in time t_m. By $O^{(m-1)} \prec O^{(m)}$ we will denote the fact that $O^{(m-1)}$ is the version of ontology O earlier than $O^{(m)}$. Such notion can be easily extended to all the elements of ontologies (e.g. $c^{(m-1)} \prec c^{(m)}$).

A function that can be used to designate concepts from the given ontology O which changed in time has the signature: $diff_C : Rep(O) \times Rep(O) \rightarrow Rep(O) \times Rep(O) \times Rep(0)$. . As input, this function receives two different versions of the ontology (denoted as $O^{(m-1)}$ and $O^{(m)}$) and returns a 3-element tuple of sets containing concepts added to the ontology, concepts delete from the ontology and concepts which were altered. Formally, the function $diff_C$ can be defined as follows:

$$diff_C\left(O^{(m-1)}, O^{(m)}\right) = \langle new_C(C^{(m-1)}, C^{(m)}), \left(C^{(m-1)}, C^{(m)}\right), alt_C\left(C^{(m-1)}, C^{(m)}\right)\rangle$$

(5)

where:

- $new_C\left(C^{(m-1)}, C^{(m)}\right) = \{c | c \in C^{(m)} \wedge c \notin C^{(m-1)}\}$
- $del_C\left(C^{(m-1)}, C^{(m)}\right) = \{c | c \in C^{(m-1)} \wedge c \notin C^{(m)}\}$
- $alt_C\left(C^{(m-1)}, C^{(m)}\right) = \{(c^{(m-1)}, c^{(m)}) | c^{(m-1)} \in C^{(m-1)} \wedge c^{(m)} \in C^{(m)} \wedge c^{(m-1)} \prec c^{(m)} \wedge \left(A^{c^{(m-1)}} \neq A^{c^{(m)}} \vee V^{c^{(m-1)}} \neq V^{c^{(m)}} \vee I^{c^{(m-1)}} \neq I^{c^{(m)}}\right) \vee ctx(c^{(m-1)}) \neq ctx(c^{(m)})\}$

The definitions for the first two functions are self-explanatory and do not require any additional commentary. The third describes the changes made to the ontology by returning a set of pairs containing different versions of the concept c, which has not been added or removed from the ontology, but its structure has changed.

4 Methods of Updating Integrated Ontologies

This chapter is devoted to the presentation of the method of updating integrated ontologies at the concept level in the event of the evolution of their components. The backbone of the proposed framework is based on $diff_C$ - a function, which output describes the changes at the concept level between different versions of a selected ontology.

The second foundation is the base algorithm for concept integration is taken from [8]. It takes as an input a set of concepts to be integrated denoted as $X = \{c_1, \ldots, c_m\}$. Initially it sums sets of their attributes. Then it iterates over its cartesian product and for each pair it is checked whether two attributes are in generalization relationship and if so, then the more general attribute it removed. Finally, for each remaining attribute its domain is designated. Due to the limited space available for this article it is not possible to include it in its full form, therefore for details please refer to [8]. In the further sections of the following article, we will refer to it as the Base Algorithm.

The actual integration update framework consists of three heuristic algorithms. Each of the algorithms deals with a different aspect of evolution: concept removal (Algorithm 1), adding new concepts (Algorithm 2) and concept modification (Algorithm 3). The input of all algorithms is the result of the function $diff_C(O^{(m-1)}, O^{(m)})$, the set of mappings $Align_C(O^{(m-1)}, O'^{(n)})$ determined in the previous integration process and the output of the integration of earlier version of the considered ontology $\widetilde{O^*}$.

As mentioned in Sect. 4 the concept mappings used during the ontology integration process should be valid. For this reason, apart from updating the integration result, the task of the algorithms presented in the subsequent parts of the following section, is also to update the considered alignments.

4.1 Updating Results of Ontology Integration After Concept Removal

The algorithm presented in the current updates the result of the integration in case some concepts have been removed from the ontology. For each deleted concept $c^{(m-1)} \in del_C(C^{(m-1)}, C^{(m)})$ an auxiliary set del (line 4) is created containing all mappings in which the concept occurs. As the concept has been removed, these mappings are no longer correct and must be also removed (line 5).

Algorithm 1. Updating results of ontology integration after concept removal

Input: $diff_c(O^{(m-1)}, O^{(m)}), Align_c(O^{(m-1)}, O'^{(n)}), \widetilde{O^*}$

1    $O^* = \widetilde{O^*}$

2    $Align_C(O^{(m)}, O'^{(n)}) = Align_C(O^{(m-1)}, O'^{(n)})$

3   **for** $c^{(m-1)} \in del_C(C^{(m-1)}, C^{(m)})$ **do**

4        $del = \{(c^{(m-1)}, c'^{(n)}, \lambda_C(c^{(m-1)}, c'^{(n)}), r) \in Align_C(O^{(m-1)}, O'^{(n)})\}$

5        $Align_C(O^{(m)}, O'^{(n)}) = Align_C(O^{(m)}, O'^{(n)}) \setminus del$

6   **if** $\exists (c^{(m-1)}, c'^{(n)}, \lambda_C(c^{(m-1)}, c'^{(n)}), r) \in del \wedge r = " \equiv "$ **then**

7            $C^* = C^* \setminus \{c^*: c^*$ is an integrated concept previously
                created from $c^{(m-1)}$ i $c'^{(n)}\}$

8            $C^* = C^* \cup \{c'^{(n)}\}$

9   **end**

10   **else**

11           $C^* = C^* \setminus \{c^{(m-1)}\}$

12   **end**

13       $H^* = H^* \setminus \{(b, c^{(m-1)}) \in H^{(m-1)}\}$

14   **end**

15   **return** $O^*, Align_C(O^{(m)}, O'^{(n)})$

The integration result should also be updated accordingly. In Line 6, the algorithm checks if the previous integration result has a mapping linking $c^{(m-1)}$ to some other concept $c^{'(n)}$. If such mapping existed, it means that on this basis the integrated concept $c^* \in C^*$ was determined, which should eventually be removed (Line 7).

Since the mapping connecting $c^{(m-1)}$ to $c^{'(n)}$ is no longer correct, thus the integrated concept has been removed. Therefore, it is necessary to add $c^{'(n)}$ to the integration result (Line 8). Otherwise, the algorithm removes the concept $c^{(m-1)}$ (Line 11) from the integration result. The last steps of the procedure update the concept hierarchy (line 13) by removing all pairs of the form $\left(b, c^{(m-1)}\right)$.

4.2 Updating Results of Ontology Integration After Adding New Concepts

The goal of Algorithm 2 presented in the following section is to update the integration result when some new concepts have been added to the input ontology. For each added concept $c^{(m)} \in new_C\left(C^{(m-1)}, C^{(m)}\right)$, the procedure checks if it can be mapped with any concepts from the second ontology. If the calculate mapping degree λ_C is higher than the assumed threshold value τ, the alignment is kept (Lines 6–7), otherwise nothing as added.

Additionally, an auxiliary variable *aligned* is introduced, which tells whether the new concept was successfully combined by mapping connecting it with any concept $c^{'(n)}$ from the target ontology. If such a mapping exists, the integration result must be updated accordingly (Lines 8–14):

- using the Base Algorithm, the structure $\left(A^{c^*}, V^{c^*}\right)$ of the concept c^* is determined, where the input X is the set containing the concept structures $X = \{c^{(m)}, c^{'(n)}\}$,
- the concept $c^{'(n)}$ is removed from the integration,
- the concept c^* is added to the integration.

In case the new concept has not been integrated with any other concept from the second ontology, it can be added to the integration result (Line 15–17) directly. The last step (Line 18) adds to the resulting hierarchy of concepts all pairs of the form $\left(b, c^{(m)}\right)$, which appeared in the source ontology in consequence of the addition of the concept $c^{(m)}$.

Algorithm 2. Updating results of ontology integration after adding new concepts

Input: $diff_C\left(O^{(m-1)}, O^{(m)}\right), Align_C\left(O^{(m-1)}, O'^{(n)}\right), \widetilde{O^*}$

1   $O^* = \widetilde{O^*}$

2   $Align_C\left(O^{(m)}, O'^{(n)}\right) = Align_C\left(O^{(m-1)}, O'^{(n)}\right)$

3   **for** $c^{(m)} \in new_C\left(C^{(m-1)}, C^{(m)}\right)$ **do**

4        $aligned = 0$

5   **for** $c'^{(n)} \in C'^{(n)}$ **do**

6   **if** $\lambda_C\left(c^{(m)}, c'^{(n)}\right) \geq \tau$ **then**

7                  $Align_C\left(O^{(m)}, O'^{(n)}\right) = Align_C\left(O^{(m)}, O'^{(n)}\right)$
                  $\cup \left\{\left(c^{(m)}, c'^{(n)}, \lambda_C\left(c^{(m)}, c'^{(n)}\right), r\right)\right\}$

8   **if** $r = " \equiv "$ **then**

9                       $aligned = 1$

10                      $Create\ c^* = \left(A^{c^*}, V^{c^*}\right) using\ Base\ Algorithm\ with\ input:$
                       $X = \left\{\left(A^{c^{(m)}}, V^{c^{(m)}}\right), \left(A^{c'^{(n)}}, V^{c'^{(n)}}\right)\right\}$

11                      $C^* = C^* \setminus \left\{c'^{(n)}\right\} \cup \{c^*\}$

12   **end**

13   **end**

14   **end**

15   **if** $aligned = 0$ **then**

16            $C^* = C^* \cup \left\{c^{(m)}\right\}$

17   **end**

18       $H^* = H^* \cup \left\{\left(b, c^{(m)}\right) \in H^{(m)}\right\}$

19   **end**

20   **return** $O^*, Align_C\left(O^{(m)}, O'^{(n)}\right)$

4.3   Updating Results of Ontology Integration After Concepts Modification

The most complex scenario of the considered problem is addressed by Algorithm 3 presented in the following section. Its purpose is to update the integration result in case some concepts taken from the source ontologies have been modified. The algorithm iterates over the elements of the set $alt_C\left(C^{(m-1)}, C^{(m)}\right)$ and for each modified concept, the procedure checks whether the mappings determined in the previous integration process are still correct. If the mapping degree λ_C has changed significantly from the previous value, then such mapping should be removed. For this purpose, an auxiliary set del (Line 4) is created, the elements of which are eventually removed from the set of mappings (Line 5).

If in the set of previous mappings there is a mapping connecting $c^{(m-1)}$ with some other concept $c'^{(n)}$, it means that on this basis the integrated concept $c^* \in C^*$ was determined. It needs to be removed (Line 7) and additionally, the concept $c'^{(n)}$ (Line 8)

can be added to the integration result. Otherwise, the previous version of the modified concept (Line 11) should be removed from the integration result.

The next aspect which needs to be considered is concept hierarchy. The procedure should check whether the modified concept has received any new ancestors (Line 13). All pairs in the form $(b, c^{(m)})$ that appeared in the source ontology in consequence of the modification of the concept $c^{(m)}$ must be added to the resulting hierarchy of concepts. The procedure also checks whether there are mappings that need to be updated (Lines 15–17). The opposite situation is checked on Lines 19–24. If the modified concept has lost its ancestors, then the pair $(b^{(m-1)}, c^{(m-1)})$ can be removed from the resulting hierarchy of concepts. In addition, any redundant concept mappings with no taxonomic link between them can also be discarded.

Algorithm 3. Updating results of ontology integration after concepts modification

Input: $diff_C(O^{(m-1)}, O^{(m)}), Align_C(O^{(m-1)}, O'^{(n)}), \overline{O^*}$

1   $O^* = \overline{O^*}$

2   $Align_C(O^{(m)}, O'^{(n)}) = Align_C(O^{(m-1)}, O'^{(n)})$

3   **for** $(c^{(m-1)}, c^{(m)}) \in alt_C(C^{(m-1)}, C^{(m)})$ **do**

4       $del = \{(c^{(m-1)}, c'^{(n)}, \lambda_C(c^{(m-1)}, c'^{(n)}), r) \in Align_C(O^{(m-1)}, O'^{(n)}):$
        $|\lambda_C(c^{(m-1)}, c'^{(n)}) - \lambda_C(c^{(m)}, c'^{(n)})| \geq \epsilon \}$

5       $Align_C(O^{(m)}, O'^{(n)}) = Align_C(O^{(m)}, O'^{(n)}) \setminus del$

6   **if** $\exists (c^{(m-1)}, c'^{(n)}, \lambda_C(c^{(m-1)}, c'^{(n)}), r) \in Align_C(O^{(m-1)}, O'^{(n)}) \wedge r = " \equiv "$
        then

7           $C^* = C^* \setminus \{c^*: c^* \text{ is the intergration of } c^{(m-1)} \text{ and } c'^{(n)}\}$

8           $C^* = C^* \cup \{c'^{(n)}\}$

9   **end**

10   **else**

11          $C^* = C^* \setminus \{c^{(m-1)}\}$

12   **end**

13   **if** $\exists (b^{(m)}, c^{(m)}) \in H^{(m)} \wedge \neg \exists (b^{(m-1)}, c^{(m-1)}) \in H^{(m-1)}$ **then**

14          $H^* = H^* \cup \{(b^{(m)}, c^{(m)})\}$

15   **if** $\exists (c^{(m)}, c'^{(n)}) \in Align_C(O^{(m)}, O'^{(n)})$ **then**

16              $Align_C\left(O^{(m)}, O'^{(n)}\right) = Align_C\left(O^{(m)}, O'^{(n)}\right)$
                $\cup \{(b^{(m)}, c'^{(n)}, \lambda_C(b^{(m)}, c'^{(n)}), r)\}$

17   **end**

18   **end**

19   **if** $\exists (b^{(m-1)}, c^{(m-1)}) \in H^{(m-1)} \wedge \neg \exists (b^{(m)}, c^{(m)}) \in H^{(m)}$ **then**

20          $H^* = H^* \setminus \{(b^{(m-1)}, c^{(m-1)})\}$

21   **if** $\exists (b^{(m-1)}, c'^{(n)}, \lambda_C(b^{(m-1)}, c'^{(n)}), r) \in Align_C(O^{(m)}, O'^{(n)})$ **then**

22              $Align_C\left(O^{(m)}, O'^{(n)}\right) = Align_C\left(O^{(m)}, O'^{(n)}\right)$
                $\setminus \{(b^{(m)}, c'^{(n)}, \lambda_C(b^{(m)}, c'^{(n)}), r)\}$

23   **end**

```
24      end
25      aligned = 0
26      for c'^(n) ∈ C'^(n)
27          if λ_C(c^(m), c'^(n)) ≥ τ then
28              Align_C(O^(m), O'^(n)) = Align_C(O^(m), O'^(n))
                    ∪ {(c^(m), c'^(n), λ_C(c^(m), c'^(n)), r)}
29              if r = " ≡ " then
30                  aligned = 1
31                  Create c* = (A^{c*}, V^{c*}) using Base Algorithm with input:
                        X = {(A^{c^(m)}, V^{c^(m)}), (A^{c'^(n)}, V^{c'^(n)})}
32                  C* = C* \ {c'^(n)} ∪ {c*}
33              end
34          end
35      end
36      if aligned = 0 then
37          C* = C* ∪ {c^(m)}
38      end
39  end
40  return O*, Align_C(O^(m), O'^(n))
```

Modifying a concept may lead to a situation in which it can be connected with concepts with which it could not be previously connected. The algorithm checks all the concepts of $c'^{(n)} \in C'^{(n)}$ for possible new mappings (Lines 26–29). An auxiliary variable *aligned* is introduced, which tells whether the modified concept was successfully merged with any concept $c'^{(n)}$. If such mapping exists, then the integration result should be updated accordingly (lines 29–35), by analogy to Algorithm 2 for newly added concepts (Lines 8–14). If such mapping does not exist, the current version of the modified concept (Lines 38–40) is added to the integration result.

5 Experimental Evaluation

The main experiment of the research is the comparison of the effectiveness of algorithms updating the result ontology integration presented in the previous section with the vanilla algorithm (integrating ontologies from scratch) in the case of the evolution of ontology components. The benchmark dataset provided by the Ontology Alignment Evaluation Initiative (OEAI) [15] called Conference Track has been chosen. It contains ontologies related to the organization of conferences with reference alignments.

We assumed that one of the input ontologies (called a source ontology) has evolved. The same ontologies shared in different years by OAEI do not differ in structure. There-fore, to adapt the data for the study, random changes to the source ontology have been introduced to obtain a new version. For the determination a new alignment between ontologies the LogMap tool [3] has been used.

In our first step we would like to verify the hypothesis that the updated integration result obtained using the developed method is identical (or almost identical) to the inte-gration result obtained using an algorithm integrating ontologies from scratch. Let $O^* = (C^*, H^*, R^{C^*}, I^*, R^{I^*})$ and $O^*_{van} = \left(C^*_{van}, H^*_{van}, R^{C^*}_{van}, I^*_{van}, R^{I^*}_{van}\right)$ denotes the updated integration result obtained with the developed and vanilla method, respectively.

For experimental purpose, accuracy metrics have been used: $Acurracy_C = \frac{C^* \cap C^*_{van}}{C^* \cup C^*_{van}}$, $Accuracy_H = \frac{H^* \cap H^*_{van}}{H^* \cup H^*_{van}}$, $Accuracy_A = \frac{A^* \cap A^*_{van}}{A^* \cup A^*_{van}}$. For each test case, the $Accuracy_C$, $Accuracy_H$, $Accuracy_A$ were 1.0.

The second part of the experiment allows us to verify the hypothesis, that the time needed to update the integration result using the developed method is shorter than the determination of the integration result using the vanilla algorithm, in the case of the evolution of the source ontology components.

The research has been carried out in terms of the different type of changes introduced, their number, and the different source ontologies that were evolved. *Cmt* has been chosen as a source ontology and *confOf* as a target ontology. Table 1 contains the results of experiments where random changes of a given type (adding, removing, modifying concepts) to the source ontology are introduced.

Table 1. Different scenarios for a single pair of ontologies, 39 concepts in the source ontology *confOf*

Type of the applied modification	Execution time of the vanilla algorithm [ms]	Execution time of the developed algorithm [ms]
Removing 5 concepts	56	25
Adding 5 related concepts	56	24
Modifying 5 concepts	57	37
Adding and removing 5 concepts	54	31
Adding, removing, and modifying 5 concepts	56	36
Removing 20 concepts	50	33
Adding 20 related concepts	58	29
Modifying 20 concepts	55	48

Table 2 presents the results of algorithms examinations in terms of the number of changes introduced. The studies included cases that reflect both small changes (from 10%) and complete remodeling of the ontology (up to 100%).

Table 2. Different number of modifications in a source ontology

Number of changes	Execution time of the vanilla algorithm [ms]	Execution time of the developed algorithm [ms]
10%	54	26
20%	53	30

(continued)

Table 2. (*continued*)

Number of changes	Execution time of the vanilla algorithm [ms]	Execution time of the developed algorithm [ms]
30%	54	33
40%	53	31
50%	55	32
60%	54	35
70%	56	38
80%	56	37
90%	57	43
100%	58	43

Table 3 allows us to check that the change of the source ontology influence on algorithms' execution time. The following ontologies have been selected as the source ontology: *cmt, conference, confious, crs, edas, ekaw, iasted, linklings, micro, MyReview, OpenConf, paperdyne, pcs, sigkdd.*

Table 3. Different source ontologies

Source ontology	Execution time of the vanilla algorithm [ms]	Execution time of the developed algorithm [ms]
cmt	52	27
conference	60	25
confious	61	27
crs	48	22
edas	76	36
ekaw	56	26
iasted	57	31
linklings	51	27
micro	49	30
MyReview	59	31
OpenConf	55	28
paperdyne	60	33
pcs	50	25
sigkdd	47	21

As easily seen both approaches yield similar results in terms of the accuracy of the final ontologies. The execution time of the methods proposed in the following paper is always significantly shorter that the time required to integrate a pair of ontologies from scratch. The first experiment additionally confirmed rather obvious observation that the higher the number of changes applied to ontologies the longer it takes to create a unified ontology. However, the considered time increases linearly to the amount of introduced changes.

According to the research assumptions, the time needed to determine the mappings between input ontologies was not taken into consideration. It should be noted, however, that the developed algorithms can also be used to update mappings between ontologies during the integration result update process.

6 Summary

In this paper we presented a framework for updating the result ontology integration at the concept level in the event of the evolution of their components. Three algorithms have been proposed, each addressing different scenarios of ontology evolution. All have been experimentally verified using widely accepted OAEI datasets, yielding promising results.

The computational complexity of the proposed method is lower than the computational complexity of determining mappings from scratch and integrating them on their basis. This occurs because the developed algorithms process only those parts of the ontology that have changed. This is especially important when integrating large ontologies, where the mapping process can be very time-consuming.

References

1. Cardoso, S.D., Da Silveira, M., Pruski, C.: Construction and exploitation of an historical knowledge graph to deal with the evolution of ontologies. Knowl.-Based Syst. **194**, 105508 (2020)
2. Dos Reis, J.C., Pruski, C., Da Silveira, M., Reynaud-Delaître, C.: Understanding semantic mapping evolution by observing changes in biomedical ontologies. J. Biomed. Inform. **47**, 71–82 (2014)
3. Jiménez-Ruiz, E., Cuenca Grau, B.: LogMap: logic-based and scalable ontology matching. In: Aroyo, L., et al. (eds.) ISWC 2011. LNCS, vol. 7031, pp. 273–288. Springer, Heidelberg (2011). https://doi.org/10.1007/978-3-642-25073-6_18
4. Khattak, A.M., Batool, R., Pervez, Z., Khan, A.M., Lee, S.: Ontology evolution and challenges. J. Inf. Sci. Eng. **29**(5), 851–871 (2013)
5. Khattak, A.M., Pervez, Z., Khan, W.A., Khan, A.M., Latif, K., Lee, S.Y.: Mapping evolution of dynamic web ontologies. Inf. Sci. **303**, 101–119 (2015)
6. Kondylakis, H., Plexousakis, D.: Ontology evolution without tears. J. Web Semantics **19**, 42–58 (2013)
7. Kozierkiewicz, A., Pietranik, M.: Updating ontology alignment on the concept level based on ontology evolution. In European Conference on Advances in Databases and Information Systems, pp. 201–214. Springer, Cham (2019). https://doi.org/10.1007/978-3-030-28730-6_13

8. Nguyen, N.T.: Advanced methods for inconsistent knowledge management. Springer Science & Business Media (2007). https://doi.org/10.1007/978-1-84628-889-0
9. Noy, N.F., Klein, M.: Ontology evolution: not the same as schema evolution. Knowl. Inf. Syst. **6**(4), 428–440 (2004)
10. Osman, I., Yahia, S., Diallo, G.: Ontology integration: approaches and challenging issues. Information Fusion **71**, 38–63 (2021)
11. Pietranik, M., Nguyen, N.T.: A multi-attribute based framework for ontology aligning. Neurocomputing **146**, 276–290 (2014)
12. Sassi, N., Jaziri, W., Alharbi, S.: Supporting ontology adaptation and versioning based on a graph of relevance. J. Exp. Theor. Artif. Intell. **28**(6), 1035–1059 (2016). https://doi.org/10.1080/0952813X.2015.1056239
13. Tomczak, A., et al.: Interpretation of biological experiments changes with evolution of the gene ontology and its annotations. Sci. Rep. **8**(1), 1–10 (2018)
14. Yamamoto, V.E., dos Reis, J.C.: Updating Ontology Alignments in Life Sciences based on New Concepts and their Context. In: SeWeBMeDa@ ISWC, pp. 16–30 (2019)
15. http://oaei.ontologymatching.org/, [Online]

Integrating Machine Learning into Learner Profiling for Adaptive and Gamified Learning System

Souha Bennani[1]([⊠]) [iD], Ahmed Maalel[1,2] [iD], Henda Ben Ghezala[1] [iD], and Achref Daouahi[3]

[1] RIADI Laboratory, National School of Computer Sciences, University of Manouba, 2010 Manouba, Tunisia
`souha.bennani@ensi.rnu.tn`
[2] Higher Institute of Applied Science and Technology, University of Sousse, 4003 Sousse, Tunisia
[3] Envast, Technopôle de Sousse, Cité Hammam Maarouf, Route Ceinture de Sahloul Sousse, 4000 Sousse, Tunisia

Abstract. The success of an adaptive learning system depends on the learning content. Each student seeks an environment that is suitable for his needs, with personalized and adaptable content that allows him to have a more successful and meaningful learning experience. Learner profile is a structure comprising direct and indirect information of learner's background, objectives, interest and preferences. Taking a leaner's profile into account while designing courses is beneficial, and profile modeling is an essential method that seeks to provide a comprehensive representation of all factors linked to the user's attributes. In this paper we propose a machine learning model for predicting learner profile. It serves as a basis to a suitable user-centered adaptation of gamification and content. The potential of our model is considering both the player and learner contexts by integrating learners' interactions, preferences, troubles and cognitive capacities. We tested the efficiency of our contribution in a gamified learning environment called "Class Quiz". We used a dataset of 1000 examples to develop classification models by combining several techniques.

Keywords: E-learning · Adaptive learning · Adaptive Gamification · Machine Learning · Learner Profile

1 Introduction

Online learning environments have gotten a lot of attention in the previous decade and during the Covid-19 time, when in-person learning was not possible, the learning process was replaced with e-learning. But the main problem that e-learners have is that they are unable to receive relevant information depending on their needs, which leads to ennui and reluctance among learners, as well as a loss in their sense of motivation and engagement. Educational progress is recently made as a result of gamification, which generated

© The Author(s), under exclusive license to Springer Nature Switzerland AG 2022
N. T. Nguyen et al. (Eds.): ICCCI 2022, LNAI 13501, pp. 65–71, 2022.
https://doi.org/10.1007/978-3-031-16014-1_6

excitement and positively influenced the desire to achieve the best educational results. Gamification, frequently employed in e-learning platforms, is advantageous since it aids students in concentrating on their studies, enriching their education experiences, and increasing motivation and engagement. Combining creative and enhanced gamification experiences leads to the acquisition of knowledge and allows student to develop important skills [1]. However, in most cases, the design of gamified experiences adopts a one-size-fits-all approach. These approach uses the same gamification elements for all people. Thus, adaptive gamification is an alternative that takes into account the fact that learners have different playing preferences. Adaptive gamification aims to maximize gamification effects by providing personalized incentives tailored to the specific attributes of distinct learners and environments [2–4, 7].

There is no perfect adaptive gamification system that incorporates game elements while also taking into account the learner's profile, player type, feedback, interactions and previous experiences, abilities and preferences, and the calculation of his commitment and motivation. The basis of an adaptive gamification approach applied in e-learning shows that it is critical to dynamically capture data from an individual's interaction with e-learning applications in order to detect several aspects [7, 8, 10]. Dealing with the variety of student profiles in many aspects is a hard challenge among the solutions related with content personalization in learning systems [5, 6, 9].

A student profile classification allows for the creation of an adaptive gamified learning environment that is tailored to the student's needs and is depends on a set of important characteristics (academic, personal, and gamification) in order to motivate and engage students while also improving learning quality [7–9, 11].

This article highlights our contribution to the development of a gamified learning environment called "Class Quiz," which is a Web/mobile application produced by the ENVAST startup, as well as the evaluation of its effectiveness. Section 2 describes the architecture of our proposed method. The implementation of our profiling model, the experimentation, and the results are presented in Sect. 3. Section 4 concluded the paper.

2 Proposed Method

2.1 Functional Architecture

Our proposed Approach presented in Fig. 1 is composed of two parts: Data collection and User Profiling.

- *Data collection.* Our process begins with the collecting of static and dynamic data from the students.
- *Student Profiler.* Dynamically capturing data from learner's interaction with e-learning applications, including: Learner's profile and Learner's interactions with the learning environment.

Learner Profiling as presented in our previous works [7–11] and Fig. 1 are based on interactions data and data collected from test described below:

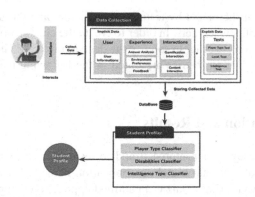

Fig. 1. Architecture of the proposed approach

- *Player Type Test:* We offer a Hexad questionary. Gamification data includes information such as player types and preferences for game aspects.
- *Intelligence Type Test:* to find out what kind of intelligence users have and whether you have any disabilities: through a self-developed questionnaire based on Gardner's Multiple Intelligence Theory and Gardner's original test.
- *Level Test:* Bloom's taxonomy, which is employed in Tunisian institutions, is adopted. It is a classification system for cognitive learning that ranges from basic knowledge and norms to advanced learning level.

   Based on those tests and learner's interactions and experience, we employed machine learning techniques to identify the user profile in this phase. Using the classification technique, the captured data is used to predict the profile. There are two types of data in this collection:

- *Gamification data.* The Player Type and their preferences for gamification elements are examples of gamification data. We employed not only a questionnaire, but also the users' experiences in the learning system to establish the player type [8].
- *Learning Data.* We've given some data from the academic data, such as intelligence type and learning disabilities, in this subsection. We developed a learning disability machine learning model and questionnaire that was approved by a psychiatrist from the Sousse regional delegation's psychology department.
- *Classification Model.* The user profiling phase is based on the machine learning technique of classifying learners using the data presented in the preceding section. The user profile is made up of numerous features, and these individuals are classified according to each category of data, therefore we'll get multiple classification models, one for each category. The purpose of classification is to determine which class each profile belongs to. The classification method applies to two forms of training data: training data, which explains a group of instances that have been divided into classes, and test data, which represents new examples that users have acquired. To complete this classification of a learner's profile, several steps must be completed, including data collection, data cleaning, data engineering and the construction of classification

models. The use of the model by testing its precision, and the use of the model in the classification of new learners. In order to create the classification model, we must test several algorithms in order to solidify the decision we made in our approach, and we can use the evaluation metrics presented in the following part to compare these algorithms.

3 Experimentation and Results

To evaluate the efficacy of our approach and to test our contribution with real data, we integrated our solution into a mobile application named "Class Quiz,"[1] which is developed by ENVAST[2]. Class Quiz is a gamified application that provides interactive exercises for revision and academic excellence in primary school courses. Class Quiz, on the other hand, does not focus on the student's profile and instead gives typical learning scenarios that ignore cognitive level variation as well as differences in learners' needs and preferences.

3.1 Used Method

Data collection. We carried out experiments using 1000 lines extracted from the database of the Class Quiz application which includes information about Class Quiz effective learners.

Data preprocessing, cleaning and feature engineering. After collecting the data and before building our models, it is important first to perform the data preprocessing and cleaning steps and we tried to create new features that help us to evaluate student learning results and to measure his engagement like total time spent on the application, average score, average time for answers.

First, we divided our dataset into 3 data subsets, and we created a classification model for each set to predict the profile by testing several algorithms, as shown in Fig. 2.

3.2 Results

To measure the performance of our classification model, for each tested algorithm, we calculated the accuracy for our three models. The accuracy (A) appears to be a useful synthetic indicator; it represents the percentage of correct predictions for a given dataset. In addition, to better understand and compare our classifiers' performances, we specified the scores of Precision (P), Recall (R) and the Score (F1) for each category in all the classification models for Player Type and Intelligence Type.

---

[1] https://classquiz.tn/, Class Quiz won the first prize among 481 competitors from all Arab countries, during its participation in the "Mada - ALECSO" Competition for mobile applications for the year 2019 as the best Arabic mobile application.

[2] ENVAST is a Startup founded in 2016 by young engineers, provides innovative digital educational products by mixing new technologies with creative design (https://envast.tn/). Among its projects, the mobile application "Class Quiz" (https://classquiz.tn/).

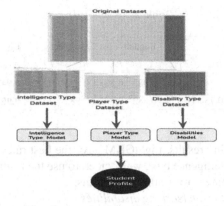

Fig. 2. Proposed classification model

- *Classification model for the player type*
  For the features, and the split was 80% for training and 20% for testing. The first model used is Random Forest Classifier, and no hyper-parameters were used. Then we trained the LGBM Classifier, in this model some parameters were used to improve the results (Table 1).

Table 1. Comparison of the performance of the classifiers tested with the Player type dataset

	Accuracy (A)	Precision (P)	Recall (R)	Score (F1)
Random Forest Classifier	87.05%	82.96%	96.51%	84.17%
Light GBM Classifier	99.99%	99.85%	99.99%	99.87%

LGBM Classifier gave the best possible result no need to experiment with more models and it will be selected as the main model for the next work.

- *Classification model for the intelligence type*
  We used Cross-validation method which is a statistical method to estimate the skill of our machine learning models (Table 2).

Table 2. Comparison of the performance of the classifiers tested with the Intelligence type dataset

Model	SVM Classifier				Random Forest classifier				Light GBM Classifier			
Evaluation	A	P	R	F1	A	P	R	F1	A	P	R	F1
Fold1	0.729	0.729	0.729	0.792	0.889	0.889	0.889	0.889	**0.949**	**0.949**	**0.949**	**0.949**
Fold2	0.75	0.75	0.75	0.75	0.906	0.906	0.906	0.906	**0.964**	**0.964**	**0.964**	**0.964**
Fold3	0.744	0.744	0.744	0.744	0.884	0.884	0.884	0.884	**0.957**	**0.957**	**0.957**	**0.957**

(*continued*)

Table 2. (*continued*)

Model	SVM Classifier				Random Forest classifier				Light GBM Classifier			
Evaluation	A	P	R	F1	A	P	R	F1	A	P	R	F1
Fold4	0.741	0.741	0.741	0.741	0.883	0.883	0.883	0.883	**0.947**	**0.947**	**0.947**	**0.947**
Fold5	0.754	0.754	0.754	0.754	0.882	0.882	0.882	0.882	**0.951**	**0.951**	**0.951**	**0.951**

Based on our testing results, LightGBM gave the best rates of correct classifications. Thus, for the intelligence type, we decided to use the LightGBM algorithm due to its superior performance over other algorithms.

- *Classification model for the learning disabilities*
  For this classification, we tried to extract labels from the datasets of Trouble using mathematical equations to make new features (Table 3).

Table 3. Comparison of the performance of the classifiers tested with the Disability type dataset

Model	ACCURACY
Random forest classif*ier*	0.749
XGBOOT	0.889
Light GBM classifier	0.910

The LightGBM algorithm has the superior performance over other algorithms. So, we decided to use it disability type model.

4   Conclusion

Adaptive learning and adaptive gamification supply teachers and students with useful information. Machine learning algorithms are used to create a system that can learn from the users' experiences and adapt to varied learning scenarios. In this paper we propose a machine learning model for predicting learner profile. Our classification model serves as a basis to a suitable user-centered adaptation of gamification and content based. Our model's strengths is considering both the player and learner contexts by integrating learners' interactions, preferences, troubles and cognitive capacities. To test our contribution's efficiency, we integrated our model in a gamified learning environment called "Class Quiz." We used a dataset of 1000 examples to develop classification models by combining several techniques. Our future work is to create and test learning adaption scenarios. More statistics and correlations between features could be added to the feedback system, which could effect learning scenario personalization.

Acknowledgement. This project is carried out under the MOBIDOC scheme, funded by The Ministry of Higher Education and Scientific Research in Tunisia through the PromEssE project and managed by the ANPR (National agency for the Promotion of Scientific Research of Tunisia).

We would also like to thank ENVAST company and Association of Scientific Research and Innovation in Computer Science (ARSII).

References

1. Moseikina, M., Toktamysov, S.: Danshina, S.: Modern Technologies and Gamification in Historical Education. Simulation Gaming **53**(2), 135–156 (2022)
2. Böckle, M., Novak, J., Bick, M.: Towards adaptive Gamification: a synthesis of current developments. ECIS. (2017)
3. Nicholson, S., Fuchs, M., Fizek, S., Ruffino, P., Schrape, N., (Eds.): Exploring the endgame of gamification Rethink gamification, pp. 289–303. Lueneburg, Germany (2015)
4. Hallifax, S.: Adaptive gamification of digital learning environments, Doctoral dissertation, Université Jean Moulin Lyon (2020)
5. López, C., Tucker, C.: Toward personalized adaptive gamification: a machine learning model for predicting performance. IEEE Trans. Games **12**(2), 155–168 (2018)
6. Pliakos, K., Joo, S.H., Park, J.Y., Cornillie, F., Vens, C., Van den Noortgate, W.: Integrating machine learning into item response theory for addressing the cold start problem in adaptive learning systems. Computers & Education, pp. 91–103 (2019)
7. Bennani, S., Maalel, A., Ghezala, H.: Adaptive gamification in E-learning: A literature review and future challenges. Computer Applications in Engineering Education (2021)
8. Bennani, S., Maalel, A., Ghezala, H.: Towards an adaptive gamification model based on ontologies. In: 2021 IEEE/ACS 18th International Conference on Computer Systems and Applications (AICCSA), pp. 1–8. IEEE (2021)
9. Bennani, S., Maalel, A., Ghezala, H.: AGE-Learn: Ontology-based representation of personalized gamification in E-learning. Procedia Computer Science (176), 1005–1014 (2020)
10. Missaoui, S., Bennani, S., Maalel, A.: Towards an Ontology for Representng a Student's Profile in Adaptive Gamified Learning System. In: KEOD, pp. 149–156 (2020)
11. Missaoui, S., Maalel, A.: Student's profile modeling in an adaptive gamified learning environment. Educ. Inf. Technol. **26**(5), 6367–6381 (2021)

Deep Learning Techniques

A New Deep Learning Fusion Approach for Emotion Recognition Based on Face and Text

Nouha Khediri[1,2]([⊠]) , Mohammed Ben Ammar[2] , and Monji Kherallah[3]

[1] Faculty of Sciences of Tunis, University of Tunis El Manar, Tunis, Tunisia
Nouhakhediri@gmail.com, Nouha.khediri@fst.utm.tn
[2] Faculty of Computing and IT, Northern Border University,
Rafha, Kingdom of Saudi Arabia
{Nuha.khediri,Mohammed.Ammar}@nbu.edu.sa
[3] Faculty of Sciences, University of Sfax, Sfax, Tunisia
Monji.kherallah@fss.usf.tn

Abstract. Automatic emotion recognition has attracted much interest in the last years and is becoming a challenging task. One modality by itself does not carry all the information to convey and perceive human emotions. Also, sometimes, it isn't easy to choose between several affective states. To remove these ambiguities, we propose a deep learning-based decision-level fusion approach for Facial Textual Emotion Recognition (FTxER) to classify emotions into discrete emotion classes. Our approach is based on Deep Convolution Neural Network (DCNN) and Bidirectional Long Short Term Memory (BiLSTM). We use the latter to improve the correlation of the time dimension of DCNN face data. Our experiments on the CK+ dataset show that the weighted average of F1-score of the FTxER model is about 79%.

Keywords: Bi-modal system · Deep learning · Facial emotion recognition · Text emotion recognition · Decision-level fusion

1 Introduction

Emotion recognition (ER) is the ability to recognize emotion, and it is a valuable asset in many fields like medical sciences, e-learning, etc. The literature [1–3] shows that most emotion recognition studies are carried out using the facial modality. However, another aspect of human communication is that humans do not rely on visual information alone to display emotion. Text, verbal context, speech, and body gestures contribute more to emotion than facial expression alone. This study is limited to recognizing emotions from both facial and textual features in a bi-modal system. For more details about the methods used for uni-modal emotion recognition, the readers can refer to [4]. Compared to single modal fusion, multi-modal fusion does not only increase performance but

© The Author(s), under exclusive license to Springer Nature Switzerland AG 2022
N. T. Nguyen et al. (Eds.): ICCCI 2022, LNAI 13501, pp. 75–81, 2022.
https://doi.org/10.1007/978-3-031-16014-1_7

it is also more robust when one of the modalities is disturbed by noise or has missing data. In recent years, deep learning has been used with great success in determining emotional states. Inspired by this success and in order to improve the accuracy of emotion recognition, we intend to add additional information from another modality because one modality alone does not provide the necessary information to convey the user's emotion. Despite the available range of communication modalities, the mainstream research on emotion recognition has mostly focused on dual modalities; facial expression (video) and speech (audio) [5–7]. Hence, it is observed that the combination of face and text is not yet used enough. In this regard, Lee et al. [8] try to classify textual information as well as the facial images of the characters in a Korean series TV into seven emotions (angry, disgust, fear, happy, neutral, sad, and surprise). The image processing is based on the sequential fully-CNN, and they use ELMo as a word embedding method for text processing to obtain an f1-score equal to 0.69. In [9], they propose a multi-modal emotion recognition based on the LSTM network applied with text modality and based on the ResNet network applied with image modality. Then they merge the two networks with the shallow feature vectors of ResNet and LSTM in the decision fusion layer. This multi-modal macro f1-score is 73.54 obtained with their own dataset and 5 emotion classes (angry, sad, normal, happy, and surprised). Another work done by Kumar et al. [10] takes as modalities image and text. This paper proposes their dataset, which treats four emotion labels: happy, sad, anger, and hate. For Textual Emotion Recognition (TER), they start pre-processing by making all letters lowercase, removing punctuation and stop-words from it. Then, they use BalanceNet [11], which takes GloVe representation as input. For Image Emotion Recognition (IER), they use the VGG16 model [12]. The outputs of these two models with intermediate fusion, which takes the combined information from text and image, were all fed as input to the late fusion phase. This fusion uses the weighted average to find the final emotion labels. The authors in [13] combine an early and late fusion. In early fusion, they concatenate the visual regions and the global sentence representation. In late fusion, the original image is fed to visual encoder, and the textual features are fed into the textual encoder. The work [14] proposes the Bayesian Model Averaging (BMA) method that combines five classifiers as independent models. These classifiers are Naive Bayes (NB), Bayesian Network (BN), Nearest Neighbor (NN), Decision Tree (DT), and linear Support Vector Machine (SVM). The execution of this method on DATA345 dataset gives a performance equal to 76% and generates heightened emotions: amusement, awe, contentment, excitement, anger, disgust, fear, and sadness.

The goal of this paper is to automatically classify user's emotion using a deep learning-based late fusion approach from two modalities. The first one is face image since it is the earliest and most common technique to perceive emotions and the second modality is text since the amount of text data available is huge due to the emergence of social media and Web2.0.

The rest of the paper is organized as follows. We first start by explaining our Facial Textual Emotion Recognition (FTxER) Architecture in Sect. 2. Thereafter, we report the obtained results in Sect. 3. Finally, in Sect. 4, we conclude and outline future work.

2   Facial-Textual Emotion Recognition (FTxER) Architecture

Because one modality is still poor in robustness and gives inaccurate emotion recognition, and does not carry all the information to convey the human affective state, our bi-modal system considers face and text information. Our Facial Emotion Recognition (FER) approach, which is shown in Fig. 1a), based on the combination of Deep Convolution Neural Network (DCNN) and Bidirectional Long Short Term Memory (BiLSTM). We use the latter to improve the correlation of the time dimension of DCNN face data. The BiLSTM uses 2 LSTM networks and combines the past and future information from forward and backward calculations. DCNN is an improved CNN. Deep means many intermediate layers between input and output, wherein each node in hidden layers represents a different configuration of inputs through feature identification and processing. The model's input was in CSV format, and each element on the table was converted to a vector which will be converted in turn to an image. Then the image is converted using Hue Saturation Value (HSV) color space because it separates luma (the image intensity) from chroma (the color information). Additionally, the HSV color model is more correlated to how humans perceive color as compared to Red Green Blue (RGB) in our previous work [15]. We start with the pre-processing and apply rotation to some images with a range equal to 10. Then, we flip the image to the horizontal direction, and we shift the image to the left

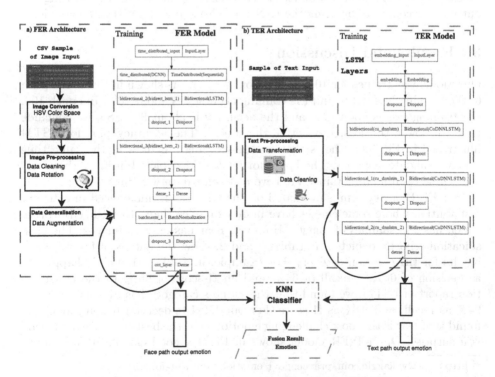

Fig. 1. Decision level fusion architecture for FTxER

or right with a width and height range equal to 0.1, and we choose the nearest as fill-mode. Then, we proceed to data augmentation to feed into the network with a more significant number of images. After data generation, we define our FER model, which contains 2 parts. The first part is the DCNN which is based on VGG16 model [12] and includes 8 convolution layers and 3 max-pooling layers (with a 2×2 pool size), all of them wrapped by time-distributed layers (see Fig. 1a). The activation function used in the convolution layers was the Rectified Linear Unit (ReLU) [16] that gives the optimal result. The second part takes the result of the first part and applies the bidirectional LSTM. We trained, tested, and validated our FER model using the extended Cohn Kanade (CK+) dataset [17] to track how much improvement the DCNN-BiLSTM provides in classifying the emotion. For processing textual data, we propose a deep learning based on LSTM architecture. Our TER system is evaluated on the dataset named Emotions dataset for NLP[2]. It contains text documents with an emotion flag. As depicted in Fig. 1b), we start our approach with Pandas to load the CSV files of the dataset. Then, we proceed to data cleaning by applying lowercase and removing all of the e-mails, spatial characters, accent characters, and stop-words. At that time, we transform data into a categorical form to facilitate the word tokenization task that means splitting sentences or text documents into smaller units called tokens. After that, the TER model is applied as shown in Fig. 1b). Our models FER and TER use respectively a separate classifier as a pre-classification for a decision level fusion. We were able to determine the combination of features which produce the highest recognition rate when fusing the output of recognizers by using the K-Nearest Neighbors (KNN) as a classifier.

3   Results and Discussion

Our model was trained for 100 epochs from scratch. As shown in Fig. 2, in epoch 0, the training loss is 1.9, and the training accuracy is about 20%. In epoch 100, the training loss is about 0.2, and the accuracy is about 92%. So, we conclude that the lower the loss, the better the model. The accuracy plot for LSTM illustrated in Fig. 3.(a) shows that we are training our data at the same time that we validate accuracy. The Loss plot for LSTM depicted in Fig. 3.(b) assert that these results are obtained after we test some data without training.

For FER, our system is evaluated on the CK+. It is imbalanced in category distribution where some classes have more examples than others, like Surprise, which has 249 samples of images. However, Fear has only 75 images. The classification reports, depicted in Tables 1 and 2, show the details of the obtained results for the emotion category. For example, in Table 1, the class happy has a precision of 66%, a recall of 64%, and an f1-score of 65%. In the classification report of LSTM, we found that the sadness category has 91% as precision, 94% as recall, and 93% as f1-score. For our FTxER decision fusion model, we found that fear is the most challenging emotion, and the best-recognized emotion is a surprise. Our FTxER model shows in Fig. 4 a good classification on both

---

[2] https://www.kaggle.com/praveengovi/emotions-dataset-for-nlp.

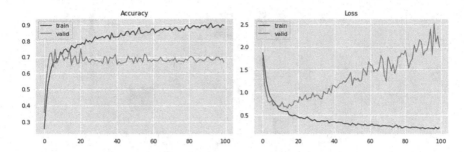

Fig. 2. Accuracy and loss plots for DCNN-BiLSTM.

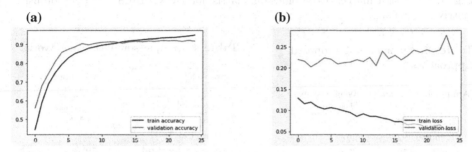

Fig. 3. LSTM results: (a): accuracy plot for LSTM, (b): loss plot for LSTM.

classes "happy" (named also "joy" on NLP Emotions dataset) and "Surprise" for both image face and text. Contrary, FTxER model performed poorly for "sadness" and "fear" categories. On the first hand, Table 3 compares the proposed bi-modal fusion method FTxER with the proposed uni-modal approaches. We

Table 1. Classification report of DCNN-BiLSTM

	Pr.	Rec.	f1-sc.	Sup.
Anger	0.64	0.51	0.57	35
Contempt	0.23	0.23	0.23	13
Disgust	0.67	0.56	0.61	55
Fear	0.16	0.40	0.23	10
Happy	0.66	0.64	0.65	45
Sadness	0.38	0.43	0.40	14
Surprise	1.00	1.00	1.00	74
Accuracy			0.67	
Macro avg.	0.53	0.54	0.53	246
Weighted avg.	0.70	0.67	0.68	246

Pr.: Precision, **Rec.**: Recall, **f1-sc.**: f1-score, **Sup.**: Support

Table 2. Classification report of LSTM

	Pr.	Rec.	f1-sc.	Sup.
Sadness	0.91	0.94	0.93	674
Joy	0.93	0.88	0.90	292
Surprise	0.85	0.73	0.79	184
Love	0.94	0.95	0.95	575
Anger	0.84	0.93	0.88	202
Fear	0.76	0.68	0.72	73
Accuracy			0.91	2000
Macro avg	0.87	0.85	0.86	2000
Weighted avg	0.90	0.91	0.90	2000

Pr.: Precision, **Rec.**: Recall, **f1-sc.**: f1-score, **Sup.**: Support

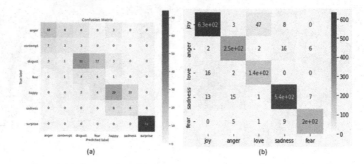

Fig. 4. Confusion matrix: (a): confusion matrix for DCNN-BiLSTM, (b): confusion matrix for LSTM.

Table 3. Summary of proposed Approaches

Approach	Accuracy	Weighted Avg. f1-score
FER model	67%	68%
TER model	91%	90%
FTxER	79%	79%

Table 4. Comparison with other Works

Approach	Weighted Avg. f1-score
Lee et al. [8]	69%
Li et al. [9]	73.54%
Corchs et al. [14]	76%
Proposed method (FTxER)	**79%**

observe that using text modality enhances the recognition performance significantly. On the other hand, Table 4 compares the performance of the proposed approach FTxER with the state-of-the-art and shows that FTxER has outperformed the other Works with weighted average *f1-score* of 79%.

4   Conclusion and Future Work

In this work, we propose a new FER model based on DCNN-BiLSTM architecture, and we achieved a good result of around 67%. Another contribution of this study was the use of the LSTM model to recognize emotion from the text channel (TER), which gives a better performance of 91%. Otherwise, one modality by itself is still poor in robustness and gives inaccurate emotion recognition. Besides, when textual modality improves the classification performance, this observation led us to present a description of a new bi-modal decision fusion emotion recognition system (FTxER) that uses face and text through the combination of FER and TER models. In future work, we will move from the bi-modalities to the multi-modalities by adding voice and video emotion recognition in future work. Additionally, we will try to apply a new fusion method. Finally, we plan to move to the real-time dimension to get more efficient and real results.

References

1. Saroop, A., Ghugare, P., Mathamsetty, S., Vasani, V.: Facial emotion recognition: a multi-task approach using deep learning (2021)
2. Minaee, S., and Abdolrashidi, A.: Deep-emotion: facial expression recognition using attentional convolutional network. Sensors (Basel, Switzerland) **21**, 3046 (2021)
3. Mukhopadhyay, M., Dey, A., Shaw, R.N., Ghosh, A.: Facial emotion recognition based on Textural pattern and Convolutional Neural Network. In: 2021 IEEE 4th International Conference on Computing, Power and Communication Technologies (GUCON), pp. 1–6 (2021)
4. Khediri, N., Ben Ammar, M., Kherallah, M.: Towards an online emotional recognition system for intelligent tutoring environment. In: The International Arab Conference on Information Technology, Yassmine, Hammamet, Tunisia, 22–24 December 2017 (2017)
5. Manisha, S., Saida H.N., Gopal, N., Anand, R.P.: Bimodal emotion recognition using machine learning. Int. J. Eng. Adv. Technol. (IJEAT) **10**(4) (2021)
6. Bahreini, K., Nadolski, R., Westera, W.: Data fusion for real-time multimodal emotion recognition through webcams and microphones in e-learning. Int. J. Human-Comput. Interact. **32**(5), 415–430 (2016)
7. Handa, A., Agarwal, R., Kohli, N.: Audio-visual emotion recognition system using multi-modal features. Int. J. Cogn. Inf. Nat. Intell. **15**(4), 1–14 (2021)
8. Lee, J., Kim, H., Cheong, Y.: A multi-modal approach for emotion recognition of TV drama characters using image and text. In: IEEE International Conference on Big Data and Smart Computing (BigComp), pp. 420–424 (2020)
9. Li, W., Hirota, K, Lui, X., Dai, Y., Jia, Z.: The multi-modal emotion recognition based on text and image. In: The 9th International Symposium on Computational Intelligence and Industrial Applications, Beijing, China, 31 October–3 November 2020 (2020)
10. P. Kumar, V. Khokher, Y. Gupta and B. Raman: "Hybrid Fusion Based Approach for Multimodal Emotion Recognition with Insufficient Labeled Data," 2021 IEEE International Conference on Image Processing (ICIP), pp. 314–318, (2021)
11. Sosa, P.M.: Twitter sentiment analysis using combined LSTM-CNN models. ACADEMIA, CS291, University of California, Santa Barbara (2017)
12. Simonyan, K., Zisserman, A.: Very deep convolutional networks for large-scale image recognition. In: 3rd International Conference on Learning Representations, ICLR, San Diego, CA, USA, 7–9 May 2015, Conference Track Proceedings (2015)
13. Wang, L., He, Z., Meng, B., Liu, K., Dou, Q., Yang, X.: Two-pathway attention network for real-time facial expression recognition. J. Real-Time Image Process. **18**(4), 1173–1182 (2021). https://doi.org/10.1007/s11554-021-01123-w
14. Corchs, S., Fersini, E., Gasparini, F.: Ensemble learning on visual and textual data for social image emotion classification. Int. J. Mach. Learn. Cybern. **10**(8), 2057–2070 (2017). https://doi.org/10.1007/s13042-017-0734-0
15. Khediri, N., Ben Ammar, M., Kherallah, M.: Comparison of image segmentation using different color spaces. In: 2021 IEEE 21st International Conference on Communication Technology, ICCT2021, Tianjin, China, 13–16 October 2021 (2021)
16. Nair, V., Hinton, G.E.: Rectified linear units improve restricted boltzmann machines. In: ICML, pp. 807–814 (2010)
17. Lucey, P., Cohn, J.F., Kanade, T., Saragih, J., Ambadar, Z., Matthews, I.: The extended cohn-kanade dataset (ck+): a complete dataset for action unit and emotion-specified expression. In: 2010 IEEE Computer Society Conference on Computer Vision and Pattern Recognition-Workshops, pp. 94–101. IEEE (2010)

Cycle Route Signs Detection Using Deep Learning

Lukas Kopecky[1], Michal Dobrovolny[1(✉)] [iD], Antonin Fuchs[2], Ali Selamat[1,3,4] [iD], and Ondrej Krejcar[1] [iD]

[1] Faculty of Informatics and Management, Center for Basic and Applied Research, University of Hradec Kralove, Hradec Kralove, Czech Republic
`{lukas.kopecky,michal.dobrovolny,ondrej.krejcar}@uhk.cz`
[2] Rubi Consulting s.r.o., Zámocká 3, Bratislava, Slovakia
[3] Malaysia Japan International Institute of Technology (MJIIT), Universiti Teknologi Malaysia Kuala Lumpur, Jalan Sultan Yahya Petra, 54100 Kuala Lumpur, Malaysia
`aselamat@utm.my`
[4] School of Computing, Faculty of Engineering, Universiti Teknologi Malaysia (UTM), 81310 Skudai, Malaysia

Abstract. This article addresses the issue of detecting traffic signs signalling cycle routes. It is also necessary to read the number or text of the cycle route from the given image. These tags are kept under the identifier IS21 and have a defined, uniform design with text in the middle of the tag. The detection was solved using the You Look Only Once (YOLO) model, which works on the principle of a convolutional neural network. The OCR tool PythonOCR was used to read characters from tags. The success rate of IS21 tag detection is 93.4%, and the success rate of reading text from tags is equal to 85.9%. The architecture described in the article is suitable for solving the defined problem.

Keywords: YOLOv5 · YOLO · OCR · Object detection · Machine learning · Computer vision

1 Introduction

Humanity is now dependent on automation and robotic technologies. Computer vision is the most widespread issue of artificial intelligence today. Artificial intelligence is widely used in medicine, helping to detect and distinguish, for example, brain cancer. Magnetic resonance imaging is used, on which abnormalities are subsequently detected using neural networks [3]. Surveys among radiology oncologists have found that the majority (69%) use or are about to use machine learning in the clinic. The great advantage of using machine learning in medicine is the large number of high-quality images of patients, so it is possible to compile a learning dataset very effectively [8]. Another use of computer vision is to

N. T. Nguyen et al. (Eds.): ICCCI 2022, LNAI 13501, pp. 82–94, 2022.
https://doi.org/10.1007/978-3-031-16014-1_8

count and plot the gathering density of people at mass events. They are used mainly in security monitoring services, such as sports stadiums, shopping malls, and airports. This method can prevent tragic scenarios where people could lose their lives. The tool can be very useful in building and designing spaces with a high density of people to avoid tragic scenarios in evacuation [19]. Machine learning did not escape space exploration either. It can allow greater autonomy to improve space missions' time, reliability and cost. Space missions operate in extreme and dangerous conditions for humans and machines. Due to the risk, the price, and the distance, the survey is most often conducted remotely. Some locations can be hazardous, inhospitable, or remote for posting people. In all these cases, such a role could be represented by autonomous robots. Autonomous operations allow remote space stations to observe the environment and decide independently what action to take, what data to collect, and what data to send back to Earth. In space, there is already an autonomous station. Autonomous off-road navigation has improved the capabilities of the 2003 Exploration Rover on Mars, which has made it possible to overcome significantly larger terrain [14]. One of the main goals of machine vision is to create autonomous cars. The aim is for vehicles to recognize other means of transport and for driving the car to be possible without interaction with the driver. The pixels of the video from the front camera are converted into control instructions with the help of neural networks. Autonomous management is predicted as the most developing area of application of artificial intelligence. It is being developed with the promise of reducing the number of accidents, reducing emissions, etc. According to the NHTSA (National Highway Traffic Safety Administration), up to 90% of accidents are caused by human error. Autonomous driving advantages of safety, time savings, avoiding rush hour traffic, and parking [16]. This article also focuses on brand recognition, where the brand to be recognized will be the brand-defining the cycle route. For example, IS21 is the identifier of the bicycle brand. This tag contains the text or the number of the bike path that will need to be detected and then read.

Previous results [13] shows, as well as employing deep convolutional networks to upscale medical images [6], demonstrate possible uses of object detection architectures.

Khazaee et al. wrote in the article that they use YOLO for licence plate detection. A similar approach to our own. Experimental results showed the system's high performance with a precision of 0.979 and recall of 0.972 [11].

Bensouilah et al. have created a new dataset of licence plates among with Automatic license plate reading (ALPR) system. The best approach had a 92% recognition rate [4].

In the article Chen DJ. et al. was YOLO used for High-speed Railway Real-time Localization. This localization was able to work on up to 50 fps. They proposed YOLO-toc as an end-to-end multi-target detection framework [5].

Upadhyay et al. proposed a methodology utilizing specific information enlargement instances. The proposed strategy and deployment architecture perform exceptionally well on data collected dynamically from a video using a Raspberry Pi. With no parameter adjustments, and has been successful in identifying multiple license plates and extracting the characters; however, the process is time-consuming [20].

2   Problem Definition

The main goal of the experiment was to find a solution for reading text from bicycle signs (IS21). The problem deals with object detection and text reading from images (OCR). The method of recognizing traffic signs is a current problem in machine learning, and countless solutions exist. At the same time, the issue is very similar to identifying license plates of cars and automatic reading of license plates. This issue is used in almost every shopping centre which has an adjacent shopping centre parking lot. The entrance gates automatically detect the license plate of the car, automatically read it and print a ticket where the read license plate appears. This task is straightforward to solve thanks to OCR and object detection using a neural network. Another very similar issue is the recognition and detection of traffic signs. In modern IT technology, it is normal for autonomous vehicles to appear globally. Cars are self-driving without the intervention of a driver. An example is now the best-known car manufacturer Tesla, which produces fully autonomous cars. This is associated with recognizing and reading traffic signs in front of the car. It is now routine for a regular vehicle to have road sign reading assistants to help the driver acknowledge the road signs.

2.1   Car License Plate Recognition and Reading

One of the solutions described above was developed by the Department of Communication and IT Engineering at the University of Vellore in India. The group of developers dealt with the issue of ALPR (Automatic License Plate Recognition). The development team used YOLO version 4 technology, which is based on convolutional neural network technology, learned to detect license plates on cars. The success rate of the neural network was 98%. They also used preprocessing of cropped license plate images. The technique, image conversion to grayscale, Gaussian blurring and the Otsu binarization method were used. This resulted in marked and easy-to-read numbers and letters on the license plates. This preprocessing was achieved using the OpenCV library. It was then possible to use the TesseractOCR library to read letters and numbers from a preprocessed image [1,10,17].

2.2   Real-time Traffic Sign Detection Using CNN

An article by Alexander Shustanov and Pavel Yakimov, deals with real-time road sign recognition and detection. The authors used the method of convolutional neural networks to solve the problem. The main difference between this article and the previous ones is the design and testing of the convolutional neural network architecture design and testing. The solution used the TensorFlow library to design CNN, which offers the possibility of building your neural network. The solution used convolution layers, fully connected layers and the Softmax layer to create a neural network.

Furthermore, the neural network was tested on Nvidia GeForce GTX 650, GT650M and Intel Core i7 processor graphics cards. The fastest training was on the Nvidia GeForce GTX 650 graphics card. In the end, this neural network architecture achieved a detection success of 99.89% was achieved [18].

3 Solution

The IS21 mark recognition solution will be solved with the latest version YOLO, version 5. More about the YOLO model can be found in the Sect. 3.1. The PyTorch library, which should now support compatible simple model loading, including trained scales, will be used. In addition, image preprocessing methods will be used to achieve the best possible result of reading text using OCR tools.

3.1 YOLO

YOLO (You Only Look Once) is a new approach to detecting objects in a picture or video. Previous object detection approaches used classifiers to perform detection. In this case, a bounding box (Bounding box) with a probability of a related class will be assigned to the detected objects. Thus, a single neural network can predict a bounding box and an associated class in a single step. This high-speed method can process video at up to 45 frames per second. With the Fast YOLO version, it's even up to 155 frames per second. Before the invention of the YOLO architecture, R-CNN (Region Convolution Neural Network) convolutional neural networks were used to detect objects. They used methods that first generated potential frames and then ran a classifier over them. After classification, the frames were improved, duplications were eliminated, and the frames in the image were recalculated. This approach is prolonged and difficult to optimize. So YOLO combines these two steps of frame detection and classification into one problem. Therefore, the name: "Look only once" means that only one step is needed for frame detection and classification. Thus, the advantage of the YOLO architecture is high speed. When streaming video, the latency is only 25 ms. The second advantage is that YOLO looks at the image as a whole and thus sees a context between classes over regional methods [15].

Detection. The system divides the input image into a grid of size $S * S$. If the centre of an object falls into a grid cell, that cell is responsible for detecting that object. Each of these cells detects B frames and scores. The score reflects how the model predicts that the box contains an object with a probability of inclusion. If there is no object in the cell, the score is 0. Otherwise, the score is expressed as the intersection of the predicted and actual frames. This method is explained in Subsect. 3.1. Each predicted frame consists of five values: x, y, w, h and a value calculated based on the Intersection over Union (IOU) method. (x, y) are coordinates that express the centre of the frame relative to the grid cell. (w, h) express width and height relative to the whole image. Each cell can predict C classes. These predictions are coded as a $S * S * (B * 5 + C)$ tensor. For example, the parameters $S = 7$, $B = 2$ were used to evaluate the YOLO model on the PASCAL Visual Object Classes (VOC) dataset. Since PASCAL has a VOC, 20 distinguishing classes, so: $C = 20$. The resulting prediction is the tensor $7 * 7 * 30$ [15].

IOU. This method of calculating the score is called IOU. It is calculated as the intersection area of the predicted frame and the given frame, which is, for example, manually entered in the dataset, to the unified area of the predicted and given frame. The value indicates how well the position of the predicted frame was calculated. If coordinates predict the frame exactly at the location of the given frame, the IOU value is equal to 1. The IOU value is related to the position of the predicted and given frames [2].

Neural Network Design. The YOLO model is designed as a convolutional neural network and trained on the VOC dataset. Initial convolution layers extract image properties, while fully interconnected layers predict output probabilities and frame coordinates. The GoogleNet image classification network inspires the network. The network has 24 convolution layers followed by two fully interconnected layers. The Fast YOLO model uses nine convolution layers instead of 24 [15].

3.2 OCR

OCR (Optical Character Recognition) are models for obtaining the text from images. Efficiency and accuracy depend greatly on quality, brightness value, noise level, background contrast and many other attributes. Many models have been developed that improve text reading. The most famous model is Tesseract. OCR works best when there is pure segmentation between the text and the background so that the text can be easily distinguished from the background. These segmentations require high image resolution. If an image is forwarded or printed in any way, it immediately loses quality, making segmentation more difficult. An important step is image preprocessing. This will help separate the text from the background. The image is converted to grayscale, which reduces the size of the image and works only with a shade of black [12]. It is also necessary to emphasize the text in the background as much as possible. Binarization is used for this. Usually, two classes, such as text and background, are unbalanced. One of the binarization methods is the Ōtsu Nobuyuki Method (Otsu) method, which automatically determines the optimal threshold that divides pixels into two classes based on the histogram. The output is an image in binary colours. If the pixel intensity exceeds the threshold, the pixel is marked as forward and coloured white. If the intensity is below the threshold, the pixel is coloured black. Today, many methods extend the Otsu method [7]. The main disadvantage of the Otsu method is the manual setting of the threshold. The OpenCV library offered the implementation solution; it is possible to use Otsu method. Both with a manually adjustable threshold parameter and with automatic threshold detection. Figure 1 shows the use of the Ostu method and other binarization methods on the issue of reading text from IS21 tags.

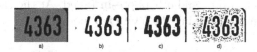

Fig. 1. (a) Ground truth (b) Otsu method (c) binary thresholding (d) adaptive thresholding with averaging of neighboring areas

It is possible to clearly show from the actual implementation what effect the use of image preprocessing with text has on the result of text reading using OCR. The Table 1 shows the results when using the Otsu method and without using the method. Prior to the implementation of the Otsu method in the project, the reading success rate for some brands was 0%. The Otsu method was always used only on the cropped image, where the text was on the markers according to the predicted coordinates of the frames from the output of the YOLO model. The first two rows in the table increased by 100%, and the text was finally read correctly. The experiment was performed with the same OCR model as PyOCR.

Table 1. Result achieved with and without Otsu method

Text on the sign	Otsu	Accuracy %	Without Otsu	Accuracy %
4363	4363	100%	LAGS	0%
4363	4363	100%	AY	0%
A 244	A264	75%	A2L	50%
4367	4367	100%	4362	75%

4   Implementation

The dataset was created using the Mapy.cz and Google Maps servers, were using the panorama and Street view, IS21 signs were searched, selected and cropped from the panorama. The dataset size of the collected images was 260 images. Image tagging and labelling were done in the Roboflow cloud solution. The IS21 signs and the adjacent text sections with the cycle path number were interactively marked here. The tag was tagged with the "IS21" class, and the tag number was kept under the "text" class. Data Augmentation was applied to the dataset so that the dataset was expanded with additional images. Extensions included image rotation, colour and contrast adjustment, and image skew. In this way, the dataset size was tripled from the original size of 250 images.

4.1   Technologies Used

External libraries and cloud solutions were used for training learning the YOLO model.

Google Colab. Google Colab is a hosted Jupyter laptop environment that is available for free. It is a free cloud service and supports the use of GPUs for free, where users can quickly write programs in Python, with libraries such as OpenCV, Keras, Tensorflow and others pre-installed. At the same time, there is a ready environment for training the YOLOv5 model.

Python. Python is a high-level language that supports dynamic type checking, object-oriented programming, imperative approaches, or the procedural and functional paradigm. It is the most widely used programming language in the world.

PyTorch. It is an optimized library that primarily uses GPU and CPU for in-depth learning. It is an open-source library for the Python programming language, which was created by the Facebook AI team. Tensorflow and Keras are the most widely used libraries to support machine learning. The main advantage and reason for using PyTorch is easy uploading and working with the YOLOv5 model.

PyOCR. It is an OCR tool for the Python programming language. The main advantage is that it can work directly with the Pillow library (PIL), primarily used to work with images. It can output text or, for example, bounding boxes for each letter. It can easily set the library to work with numbers only.

PIL. PIL is a library for working with images in the Python programming language.

Flask. Flask is a micro-web framework written in the Python programming language. It is a micro-framework because it does not require any added libraries and tools to run. Suitable for quick creation of REST APIs for applications.

4.2   Data Training

The created and tagged dataset was trained using the online Jupyter laptop Google Colab, where the laptop is directly prepared for working with the YOLO5 architecture. Google Colab already fully supports automatic uploading of a dataset from Roboflow, where only an authorization token is required so that the dataset can be downloaded from the server and automatically ready for use. The YOLO5 model was set to an image size of 416px and a batch size of 16 images. The number of epochs was set to 100 repetitions. Data was delivered automatically from Roboflow. Pre-trained YOLO5 scales on a COCO dataset were used for the model. The - *cache* parameter was used for faster training.

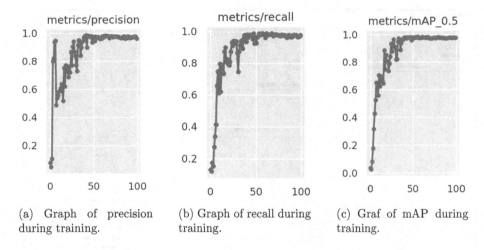

(a) Graph of precision during training.

(b) Graph of recall during training.

(c) Graf of mAP during training.

Fig. 2. Graph of precision during training.

The output of the model's training is detailed training statistics, and the main output of the training is the trained weights on this model. Output scales are two files with the extension *.pt*. The first, named *best.pt*, are the scales that correspond to the greatest success of the model. The *last.pt* file is the last run weight of the model training (Fig. 2).

Summary of Training Results. The file training results are best visible on the **mAP** (Mean Average Precision) metric. It is calculated on the basis of two metrics: precision (*precision*) and sensitivity (*recall*). Sensitivity is calculated as positive to all positive and false negative elements in the model [9].

The primary monitored metric of the model is mAP (*Mean Average Precision*). It is calculated as an integral from 0 to 1 below the graph curve, where the x-axis expresses the sensitivity variable and the y-axis expresses the precision variable. In this case, the model is trained to 0.973%.

4.3   Applications

The application is written in the Python programming language. It uses essential libraries such as Pytorch, which can load and work with YOLO5 scales, which are the learning output. The Tesseract library was used to read text from text snippets, but PyOCR replaced it. Tesseract could not read the font correctly from the tags even in the basic form, so it was replaced by PyOCR, which had significantly better results in reading the text on the tags. In addition, libraries such as PIL for working with images, Pandas for working with CSV and frames, and the Flask library were used to allow the user to use public REST API libraries to detect objects and generate call results (Fig. 3).

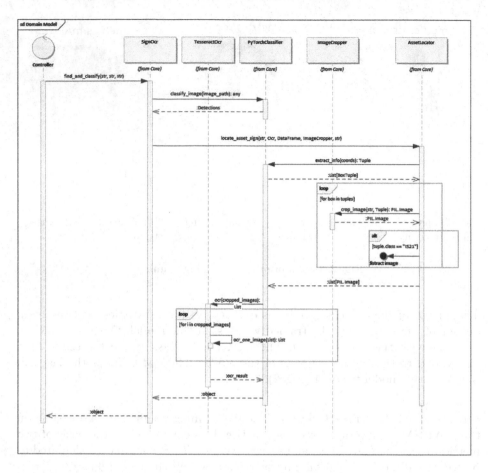

Fig. 3. Sequential diagram of solution.

SignOcr. The main class, SignOCR, contains instances of the ImageCropper, PyTorchClassifier, PyOCR, and AssetLocator classes. This class handles requests from the public API via Flask and uses class instances to detect and read the text in an incoming image sequentially.

ImageCropper. As the name suggests, this class has the task of cropping the image according to the incoming bounding frames, which the YOLO5 model generated. At the same time, it stores these images on a server so that the clippings can be accessed later, and it is easier to analyze how the YOLO5 model detects the required objects.

PyTorchClassifier. PyTorchClassifier is the main class for working with the YOLO5 architecture. It can detect markers and text objects on markers according to the set model. The output of model detection is Pandas Frame, which contains the coordinates of the bounding frame, class identification and other auxiliary information. ImageCropper and AssetLocator further use this information. AssetLocator A class that uses ImageCropper and that other filters only images that contain only a cropped image with a "text" class. It stores these in a separate field, to which the OCR tool is then applied.

PyOCR. It is a class that provides reading and text on the cropped image, where the text of the IS21 tag is located.

5   Testing of Developed Application

The application was tested on a set of images that will be uploaded to the sports application. The main goal is to find the IS21 mark so that it can be verified that the activities in the application are not falsified, and it is confirmed that there is a mark in the photo marking the cycle path. Because the application has a public REST API, the application was tested through the REST API to check if the tag had been found and the text on the tag was read correctly. Thanks to reading and getting the text from the brand, it is then straightforward to find out which athlete chose the bike path for his training and verify the route or part of the route during the sports activity. The pictures were diverse, both from a distance and at close range, and the marks behind the athlete if the athlete's face is photographed. All of these image variations are shown in Fig. 4.

Fig. 4. Example images from our dataset.

Thirteen different images, different qualities, and sizes were tested. The results are recorded in the Table 2. Associated thumbnails with tag and text detection results are shown in Fig. 4. In all test images, the text on the mark was read with a success rate of 100%. The average detection certainty of the IS21 brand was 93.42%. Here it was essential how the brand was photographed. The biggest influence on the detection certainty was the rotation of the mark

Table 2. Table to test captions and labels.

Image	Confidence IS21 (%)	Confidence text (%)	On sign	Predicted	Accuracy (%)
a)	94.9%	48.1%	303	303	100%
b)	94.9%	90.9%	2055	2055	100%
c)	95.5%	**93.5%**	6134	6134	100%
d)	89.8%	85.1%	31	31	100%
e)	94.9%	92.2%	8129	8129	100%
f)	**96.7%**	89.6%	6078	6078	100%
g)	93.2%	88.1%	26	26	100%
h)	93.9%	90.2%	1070	1070	100%

to the camera. If the mark was photographed rotated or bevelled, this significantly affected the certainty of detection. The average text detection certainty was 85.9%. In this case, the text was read very well by OCR. However, problems occurred if the mark was photographed from an angle, so the text was cropped at an angle. OCR was unable to deal with the rotated text several times. If there were more marks in the image, these marks were also detected correctly. Sometimes the texts were incorrectly detected, as in the case of the image h)., where text with kilometres that were never marked as a "text" class in the dataset was marked as tag text. The same thing happened with the image b), where the icon was marked as text. However, the neural network was taught to detect these very places, as they are identical to the direction sign, and in these places, there is usually a text with the number of the cycle path, as in the picture h).

6   Conclusion

The experiment proved the suitability of using the YOLO5 model for detecting IS21 traffic signs. At the same time, the effect of image preprocessing before the application of OCR tools was shown. The marks were detected very well. The text from the marks was read very well, but only if the mark was photographed in good conditions, in high resolution and photographed without considerable rotation. If the mark was filmed in some specific angles, the OCR tools had a problem reading the text well. Nevertheless, the proposed model is of high quality and will continue to be used to detect IS21 marks.

Acknowledgements. The work and the contribution were supported by the SPEV project "Smart Solutions in Ubiquitous Computing Environments", University of Hradec Kralove, Faculty of Informatics and Management, Czech Republic (under ID: UHK-FIM-SPEV-2022-2102).

References

1. Agbemenu, A., Yankey, J., O., E.: An Automatic Number Plate Recognition System using OpenCV and Tesseract OCR Engine. International Journal of Computer Applications 180, 1–5 (May 2018). https://doi.org/10.5120/ijca2018917150

2. Bao, J., Wang, H., Lv, C., Luo, K., Shen, X.: IOU-guided Siamese tracking. Math. Probl. Eng. **2021**, 1–10 (2021). https://doi.org/10.1155/2021/9127092
3. Basheera, S., Ram, M.: Classification of brain tumors using deep features extracted using CNN. J. Phys: Conf. Ser. **1172**, 012016 (2019). https://doi.org/10.1088/1742-6596/1172/1/012016
4. Bensouilah, M., Zennir, M.N., Taffar, M.: An ALPR system-based deep networks for the detection and recognition. In: DeMarsico, M., DiBaja, G.S., Fred, A. (eds.) Proceedings of the 10th International Conference on Pattern Recognition Applications and Methods (ICPRAM), pp. 204–211. Scitepress. https://doi.org/10.5220/0010229202040211, https://www.webofscience.com/wos/woscc/full-record/WOS:000662835900022, WOS:000662835900022
5. Chen, D., Zhang, W., Yang, Y.: High-speed railway real-time localization auxiliary method based on deep neural network. In: Simos, T.E., Kalogiratou, Z., Monovasilis, T. (eds.) Proceedings of the International Conference of Computational Methods in Sciences and Engineering 2017 (iccmse-2017). vol. 1906, p. 200019. Amer Inst Physics. https://doi.org/10.1063/1.5012495,https://www.webofscience.com/wos/woscc/full-record/WOS:000419835900200, ISSN 0094-243X WOS:000419835900200
6. Dobrovolny, M., Mls, K., Krejcar, O., Mambou, S., Selamat, A.: Medical image data upscaling with generative adversarial networks. In: Rojas, I., Valenzuela, O., Rojas, F., Herrera, L.J., Ortuño, F. (eds.) IWBBIO 2020. LNCS, vol. 12108, pp. 739–749. Springer, Cham (2020). https://doi.org/10.1007/978-3-030-45385-5_66
7. Ershov, E., Korchagin, S., Kokhan, V., Bezmaternykh, P.: A generalization of Otsu method for linear separation of two unbalanced classes in document image binarization. Comput. Opt. **45**, 66–76 (2021). https://doi.org/10.18287/2412-6179-CO-752
8. Field, M., Hardcastle, N., Jameson, M., Aherne, N., Holloway, L.: Machine learning applications in radiation oncology. Phys. Imaging Radiat. Oncology **19**, 13–24 (2021). Elsevier, Amsterdam. https://doi.org/10.1016/j.phro.2021.05.007, https://www.webofscience.com/wos/woscc/full-record/WOS:000694711800003, WOS:000694711800003
9. Henderson, P., Ferrari, V.: End-to-end training of object class detectors for mean average precision. arXiv:1607.03476 [cs], March 2017. http://arxiv.org/abs/1607.03476
10. Jain, A., Gupta, J., Khandelwal, S., Kaur, S.: Vehicle license plate recognition, **4**, 15–21 (2021). https://doi.org/10.5281/zenodo.5171216
11. Khazaee, S., Tourani, A., Soroori, S., Shahbahrami, A., Suen, C.Y.: An accurate real-time license plate detection method based on deep learning approaches, **35**(12), 2160008. World Scientific Publ. C.o Pte Ltd., Singapore. https://doi.org/10.1142/S0218001421600089, https://www.webofscience.com/wos/woscc/full-record/WOS:000714085600003, WOS:000714085600003
12. Kshetry, R.: Image preprocessing and modified adaptive thresholding for improving OCR, November 2021
13. Mambou, S., Krejcar, O., Selamat, A., Dobrovolny, M., Maresova, P., Kuca, K.: Novel thermal image classification based on techniques derived from mathematical morphology: case of breast cancer. In: Rojas, I., Valenzuela, O., Rojas, F., Herrera, L.J., Ortuño, F. (eds.) IWBBIO 2020. LNCS, vol. 12108, pp. 683–694. Springer, Cham (2020). https://doi.org/10.1007/978-3-030-45385-5_61
14. McGovern, A., Wagstaff, K.L.: Machine learning in space: extending our reach. Mach. Learn. **84**(3), 335–340 (2011). https://doi.org/10.1007/s10994-011-5249-4

15. Redmon, J., Divvala, S., Girshick, R., Farhadi, A.: You only look once: unified, real-time object detection, pp. 779–788, June 2016. https://doi.org/10.1109/CVPR.2016.91
16. Amar, V.S., et al.: Autonomous driving using CNN. Int. J. Res. Appl. Sci. Eng. Technol. **9**, 3633–3636 (2021). https://doi.org/10.22214/ijraset.2021.35771
17. Sham, A.S.D., Pandey, P., Jain, S., Kalaivani, S.: Automatic license plate recognition using YOLOV4 and tesseract OCR. Int. J. Electr. Eng. Technol. **12**(5) (2021). https://www.academia.edu/49045889/AUTOMATIC_LICENSE_PLATE_RECOGNITION_USING_YOLOV4_AND_TESSERACT_OCR
18. Shustanov, A., Yakimov, P.: CNN design for real-time traffic sign recognition. Procedia Eng. **201**, 718–725 (2017). https://doi.org/10.1016/j.proeng.2017.09.594, https://www.sciencedirect.com/science/article/pii/S1877705817341231
19. Sindagi, V., Patel, V.: A survey of recent advances in CNN-based single image crowd counting and density estimation. Pattern Recogn. Lett. **107** (2017). https://doi.org/10.1016/j.patrec.2017.07.007
20. Upadhyay, U., Mehfuz, F., Mediratta, A., Aijaz, A.: Analysis and architecture for the deployment of dynamic license plate recognition using YOLO darknet. In: 2019 International Conference on Power Electronics, Control and Automation (ICPECA-2019), pp. 111–116. IEEE. https://www.webofscience.com/wos/woscc/full-record/WOS:000540004400022, WOS:000540004400022

Data Augmentation for Morphological Analysis of Histopathological Images Using Deep Learning

Martin Tabakov$^{(\boxtimes)}$ [iD], Konrad Karanowski, Adam R. Chlopowiec,
Adrian B. Chlopowiec, and Mikolaj Kasperek

Department of Artificial Intelligence, Wroclaw University of Science and Technology, Wroclaw,
Poland
martin.tabakow@pwr.edu.pl, {254533,254518,254517,
242433}@student.pwr.edu.pl

Abstract. In this study, we introduce a data augmentation procedure for
histopathology image classification. This is an extension to our previous research,
in which we showed the possibility to apply deep learning for morphological analysis of tumour cells. The research problem considered, aimed to distinguish how
many cells are located in a structure composed of overlapping cells. We proved
that the calculation of the tumour cell number is possible with convolutional neural networks. In this research, we examined the possibility to generate synthetic
training data set and to use it for the same purpose. The lack of large data sets is a
critical problem in medical image classification and classical augmentation procedures are not sufficient. Therefore, we introduce completely new augmentation
approach for histopathology images and we prove the possibility to apply it for a
cell-counting problem.

Keywords: Data augmentation · Convolutional neural networks · Image
morphing · Digital histopathology · Morphological image processing · Medical
images · Histopathology images

1 Introduction

Data augmentation is very important step in medical image classification. It is because
often machine learning models or other classifiers have to deal with small data sets
and limited annotations [7, 15, 18, 19]. This is a challenging issue especially in case
of supervised learning. Additionally, the annotation process of medical data is time
consuming and expensive [3] and Experts often disagree with each other.

Majority of standard augmentation techniques for medical imaging in deep learning
still consist of noise injections or simple geometric and color transformations of input
images [1]. Often this type of data extension is not sufficient for medical problems.

One very interesting solution to the above-mentioned problems is a generation of
synthetic data. A popular solution here is the use of generative adversarial networks
(GANs), which is also applied for medical data. Mixing synthetic data with real training

© The Author(s), under exclusive license to Springer Nature Switzerland AG 2022
N. T. Nguyen et al. (Eds.): ICCCI 2022, LNAI 13501, pp. 95–105, 2022.
https://doi.org/10.1007/978-3-031-16014-1_9

data leads to better classification performance. Recently, such a concept was used for improvement of histopathology image classification [23]. Many other applications are using this concept and increasing the performance of the applied deep learning models - for example: liver lesion classification [6], detection of pneumonia and COVID-19 in chest X-ray images [16], bone age assessment [11] and other.

In our research, we approach the problem of histopathology data augmentation with a new concept. The GAN concept is very promising for medical data, but it still needs annotated real data to train. Our augmentation method and the contribution of this research, is the application of image morphing of tumour cells and geometric transformations to generate synthetic images with overlapping cells. The whole training data applied for morphological analysis of cell structures is synthetic. This approach gives a possibility to generate data, which we know that may occur in the considered histopathology classification problem, but are not available.

This research is an extension of our previous publication [24], in which we proved that the calculation of the tumour cell number in cell conglomerations (histopathology image regions with cell overlapping) is possible with convolutional neural networks. The rest of the paper is organized as follows: in Sect. 2, the medical data used is described and the methodology applied is explained, in Sect. 3 the research experiment and the achieved results are presented, and Sects. 4 and 5 draw discussion and conclusions.

2   Materials and Methods

2.1   Materials

In this research as previously we worked on the SHIDC-BC-Ki-67 (Shiraz Histopathological Imaging Data Center) histopathology image dataset introduced in [14]. It consists of 2357 microscopic tru-cut biopsy images of malignant breast tumours of the invasive ductal carcinoma type. Each histopathology image contains 69 cells on average and approximately, there are 162 998 cells in total. As the data was prepared and labelled in order to use it for Ki-67 index proliferation calculation, the cell types which determine the recognition problem are Ki-67$^+$ and Ki-67$^-$. Some examples are given in Fig. 1 below.

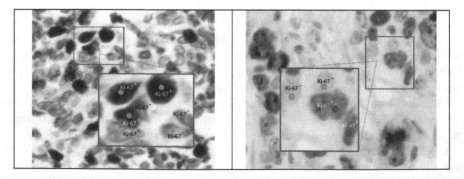

Fig. 1. Examples of Ki-67 positive and negative tumour cells.

We focused our research on the problem of cell overlapping. It is natural that histopathology preparations cannot guarantee cell separation. Therefore, exact cell number recognition is a critical issue in accurate Ki-67 index calculation problem. Often algorithms applied in this research domain approximate the number of cells if overlapping occurs. Below, we show some examples of 'two' and 'three' cell overlapping regions (Fig. 2).

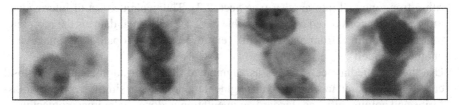

Fig. 2. 'Two' and 'three' cell overlapping regions.

2.2 Methods

In our proposal, first we applied convolutional neural networks models with known medical applications, in the problem of recognition of number of cells in cell conglomerations (cell overlapping image regions) [24]. We have tested the following deep learning models: *ResNet-18* [8], *DenseNet* [10], *EfficientNet* [22], *GoogLeNet* [21], *MobileNetV2* [17] and *VGG-11* [20] achieving best results with the EfficientNet: F1-score ≈ **0.88**. The deep learning models acted as morphology operators, classifying images presenting overlapping cells into '*one*', '*two*' or '*three*' cell classes, as such a training data was prepared. Nevertheless, only three classes are not sufficient as the number of cells in a cell conglomeration region varies a lot (see Fig. 3).

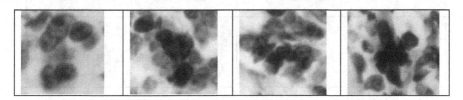

Fig. 3. Various types of cell conglomerations.

Unfortunately, preparation of corresponding training sets is very hard, as medical data are usually limited. Therefore, we came up with the idea to generate synthetic data for this purpose, according to the following procedure:

1. Extract single cancer cells of the target type from histopathology images. It can be done manually by domain expert,
2. As the above set of cells will be limited, provide a transform using morphing algorithm from one cell into another (see Sect. 2.3). The generated set of intermediate images can be considered as cells possible to occur in the real data, as the morphing transform is defined from one 'real cell' (extracted from histopathology image) into another 'real cell',
3. Use the intermediate cell images as augmented data. Our augmentation proposal cannot be compared to standard data augmentation based on simple geometry transforms and colour shifts, as standard augmentation is done to the image/object itself with no relation to other images/objects. This procedure can produce unlimited data of potential cancer cells,
4. Applying simple affine geometric transformations, such as scaling, rotation and translations over the above augmented data set of tumour cells, we are able to generate any cell conglomeration image. Thus, we are able to generate synthetic training images (see Fig. 4).
5. The synthetic training data can be additionally extended with additional augmentation procedures (see Table 1). Finally, we can achieve unlimited training sets of images representing cell conglomerations.

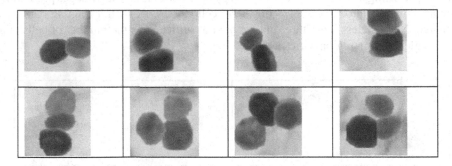

Fig. 4. Synthetic cell data – 'two' and 'three' cell overlaps

We present our research concept as a pipeline in Fig. 5 below.

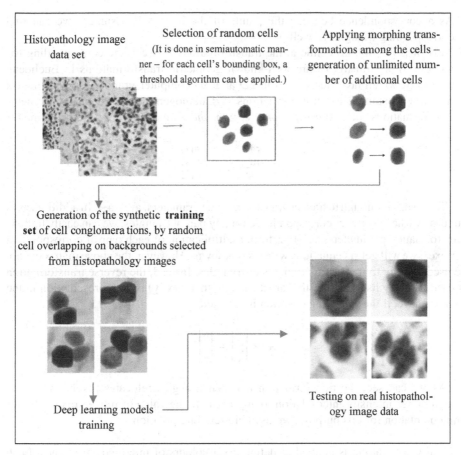

Fig. 5. Our research pipeline.

2.3 Morphing Concept

We have applied a morphing algorithm, available online[1] as a proof of concept, which was sufficient for our experiments. The idea of the morphing algorithm used, consists of the following steps:

– Load images (*input image* and *target image*). The algorithm will transform, in terms of morphing transformation, the input image into the target image,
– Define a set of points of the input image and the corresponding set of points of the target image. The cardinality of the sets should be equal – i.e. for each point in the input image, there is a corresponding point in the target image.
– Apply a Delaunay triangulation (well-known triangulation method with many applications in computer graphics) over the set of points of the input image.

---

[1] https://github.com/ddowd97/Python-Image-Morpher.

– As a correspondence between the points of the images is assumed, we can find corresponding triangles as well.
– Next, it is possible to define affine transformations between the corresponding triangles. Affine transforms are well-known geometric transformations in Euclidean geometry, which are widely used in 2D and 3D computer graphics. By the matrix A below (assuming 2D transformations and homogenous coordinates), geometry transformations such as: *translation*, *rotation*, *shearing* and *scaling* can be defined.

$$A = \begin{bmatrix} a_{11} & a_{12} & a_{13} \\ a_{21} & a_{22} & a_{23} \\ 0 & 0 & 1 \end{bmatrix}$$

To do so, it is enough to find the transformation parameters: $a_{11} - a_{23}$. In addition, as in our case we have vertexes correspondence for any pair of triangles, we can easily find the transformation parameters, i.e. if preform multiplication of each pair of corresponding vertexes, we will get six equations with six unknowns. However, the above matrix cannot be used directly to transform all pixels of triangles. Instead, the reverse transformation is used. If $P(x',y')$ is a pixel of the target triangle then $P(x, y)$ is its representation in the source image, if the following equation is satisfied:

$$A^{-1} * \begin{bmatrix} x' \\ y' \\ 1 \end{bmatrix} = \begin{bmatrix} x \\ y \\ 1 \end{bmatrix}$$

As we can see, the transformation between triangles relocates pixels and therefore, requires intensity interpolation to approximate the value of moved pixels. In our implementation for this purpose, we used bilinear interpolation.

– Finally, α-blending is applied to define pixel colours of intermediate images. Each intermediate image, after being generated, becomes the new input image and the procedure is repeated. For every cycle, new α value is considered, reducing the 'importance' of the input image and transferring it into the target image.

For better explanation of the morphing algorithm used, see Fig. 6.

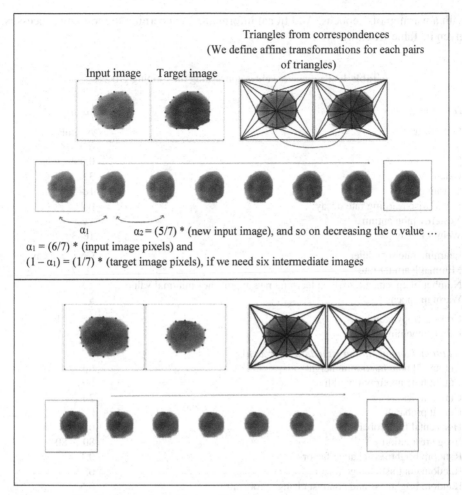

Fig. 6. Generation of intermediate images used for augmentation.

We can notice that it is possible to define infinite number of intermediate images (tumour cells), which can be used for augmentation. The number of images corresponds to the set of α values ($\alpha \in [0, 1]$). In the discrete domain, we are limited to corresponding computational precision.

3 Results

Our strong assumption was to initiate training on synthetic data only. We trained the same deep learning models as in our previous research [24] using AdamP [9] with a learning rate of 1e-5, Nesterov momentum, layer-wise learning rate decay [2, 4, 25], default betas and a batch size of 32. For regularization, we apply label smoothing [13] and weight decay of 1e-3.The networks' learning rate follows the cosine decay [12] with a warmup of 5 epochs. Additional information, concerning the training process is given in Table 1 below.

Table 1. Parameters values concerning the training process

Hyperparameter	Value
Optimizer	AdamP
β_1	0.9
β_2	0.999
Batch size	32
Learning rate	1e–5
Layer-wise learning rate decay	0.4
Nesterov momentum	Yes
Weight Decay	1e–3
Learning rate scheduler	Cosine decay
Minimal learning rate	1e–7
Number of epochs after which learning rate approaches minimal value	10
Warmup epochs	5
Cross entropy weights	0.5, 1, 1
Label smoothing	0.1
Additional augmentation (standard approach):	.
Cutout [5] hole maximum height	6px
Cutout hole maximum width	6px
Cutout holes	20
Cutout probability	0.5
Horizontal flip probability	0.5
Image resolution	80×80
Random brightness change factor	0.1
Random contrast change factor	0.15
Random brightness and contrast change probability	0.5
Rotate angle	$< -45, 45 >$
Rotate probability	0.8
Translation	3px
Translation probability	0.5
Vertical flip probability	0.5
Early stopping patience	3

The achieved classification results are given in Table 2 below. We report mean and standard deviation over 5 runs. Without loss of generality, we limited our data sets to Ki-67 positive cells. Additionally, we show only the best three models. The number of synthetic training data for each class ('*one*', '*two*' and '*three*' cell conglomerations) $\approx$ 20 000. The test set consists of real histopathology images of '*one*', '*two*' and '*three*' cell conglomerations with number of images $\approx$ 804, 138 and 100 respectively.

Table 2. Classification results – whether image presents single cell, 'two cell overlap' or 'three cell overlap'.

	MobileNetV2 (mean ± std)	ResNet18 (mean ± std)	VGG11 (mean ± std)
F1 score macro	**72.56 ± 1.54**	69.74 ± 1.15	69.18 ± 1.13
F1 score single cell	93.83 ± 1.50	94.14 ± 0.58	**94.28 ± 0.74**
F1 score double cell	**50.82 ± 2.29**	45.85 ± 1.45	40.75 ± 3.51
F1 score triple cell	**73.04 ± 2.31**	69.14 ± 2.41	72.51 ± 1.45
Sensitivity mean	**69.45 ± 1.29**	67.86 ± 1.65	67.02 ± 0.72
Sensitivity single cell	**95.77 ± 3.49**	95.49 ± 1.94	97.23 ± 1.07
Sensitivity double cell	**49.82 ± 4.93**	45.09 ± 5.47	35.09 ± 6.16
Sensitivity triple cell	62.75 ± 3.10	63.00 ± 4.65	**68.75 ± 5.76**
Specificity mean	87.93 ± 0.59	**88.41 ± 0.79**	87.26 ± 0.71
Specificity single cell	71.89 ± 3.29	**75.05 ± 3.97**	69.47 ± 2.08
Specificity double cell	92.86 ± 3.10	92.20 ± 2.14	**94.55 ± 1.53**
Specificity triple cell	**99.04 ± 0.18**	97.98 ± 0.31	97.77 ± 1.19
AUC mean	86.11 ± 0.90	**86.12 ± 1.69**	85.29 ± 0.78
AUC single cell	**94.06 ± 1.76**	93.84 ± 0.79	93.44 ± 0.7
AUC double cell	**84.84 ± 2.40**	81.01 ± 1.15	79.75 ± 1.44
AUC triple cell	79.44 ± 2.19	**83.51 ± 3.67**	82.57 ± 1.05
Accuracy	**86.53 ± 2.17**	85.71 ± 1.10	86.29 ± 0.58

4 Discussion

The achieved results show the potential of the augmentation method proposed. Moreover, the results could be improved by initial selection of larger number of cells or presenting more cell diversity as well. Additionally, better cell overlapping technique could be used. By our experience, we see that cells does not literally overlap, but rather penetrate into each other. Nevertheless, even with such rough assumptions, the achieved results show potential. With this kind of augmentation, we can define completely random cell conglomerations in terms of cell number. Therefore, as further research, in order to count the accurate Ki-67 proliferation index, it is possible to apply well-known image segmentation techniques (for example, by clustering) and to define the corresponding segments (image sub-regions with cell conglomerations) as inputs for deep models trained on synthetic data. This kind of data can be produced without any labeled real data, except few single cells, which are easy to select. This states our research contribution. What more, the augmentation process proposed can be applied in any medical problem which requires cell counting, as we proved that deep CNN models can be trained for this purpose.

5 Conclusions

In this paper, we showed the possibility of medical data augmentation with morphing algorithms. We used the generated intermediate images as tumour cell candidates and next, we generated synthetic data of cell conglomerations. We confirmed the possibility of recognizing the number of cells in a cell conglomeration, concerning one, two and three cell overlapping, with deep convolutional models. Moreover, the training process was applied only on synthetic data, but testing was provided on real data. We achieved promising results, which justify further development of our proposal.

References

1. Anaya-Isaza, A., Mera-Jiménez, L.: Data augmentation and transfer learning for brain tumor detection in magnetic resonance imaging. IEEE Access **10**, 23217–23233 (2022). https://doi.org/10.1109/ACCESS.2022.3154061
2. Bao, H., Dong, L. Wei., F.: BEiT: BERT Pretraining of Image Transformers. arXiv:2106.08254 (2021)
3. Chaitanya, K., et al.: Semi-supervised task-driven data augmentation for medical image segmentation. Med Image Anal. **68**, 101934 (2021). https://doi.org/10.1016/j.media.2020.101934. Epub 2020 Dec 9 PMID: 33385699
4. Clark, K., Luong, M.-T., Le, V.Q., Manning, D.: ELECTRA: Pre-training text encoders as discriminators rather than generators. In: ICLR (2020)
5. DeVries, T., Taylor. W.G.: Improved regularization of convolutional neural networks with cutout. arXiv preprint arXiv:1708.04552 (2017)
6. Frid-Adar, M., Diamant, I., Klang, E., Amitai, M., Goldberger, J., Greenspan, H.: GAN-based synthetic medical image augmentation for increased CNN performance in liver lesion classification. Neurocomputing **321**, 321–331 (2018)
7. Greenspan, H., van Ginneken, B., Summers, R.M.: Guest editorial deep learning in medical imaging: overview and future promise of an exciting new technique. IEEE Trans. Med. Imaging **35**(5), 1153–1159 (2016). https://doi.org/10.1109/TMI.2016.2553401
8. He, K., Zhang, X., Ren, S., Sun, J.: Identity mappings in deep residual networks. European conference on computer vision. Springer, Cham, (2016). https://doi.org/10.1007/978-3-319-46493-0_38
9. Heo, B., et al.: Slowing Down the Slowdown for Momentum Optimizers on Scale-invariant Weights. arXiv: Learning (2021)
10. Huang, G., Liu, Z., Van Der Maaten, L., Weinberger, K.Q.: Densely Connected Convolutional Networks. In: 2017 IEEE Conference on Computer Vision and Pattern Recognition (CVPR), pp. 2261–2269 (2017). https://doi.org/10.1109/CVPR.2017.243
11. Liyilei, S., Xianjun, F., Qingmao, H.: Generative adversarial network based data augmentation and gender-last training strategy with application to bone age assessment. Computer Methods and Programs in Biomedicine **212**, 106456 (2021)
12. Loshchilov I., Hutter, F.: Sgdr: Stochastic gradient descent with warm restarts. In: International Conference on Learning Representations (2017)
13. Müller, R., Kornblith, S., Hinton. E.G., When does label smoothing help?. Advances in neural information processing systems **32** (2019)
14. Negahbani, F., Sabzi, R., Pakniyat Jahromi, B., et al.: PathoNet introduced as a deep neural network backend for evaluation of Ki-67 and tumor-infiltrating lymphocytes in breast cancer. Sci Rep **11**, 8489 (2021)

15. Roth, R.H., et al.: Improving computer-aided detection using convolutional neural networks and random view aggregation. IEEE Trans. Med. Imaging **35**(5), 1170–1181 (2016). https://doi.org/10.1109/TMI.2015.2482920
16. Saman, M., Rogalla, P., Khalvati, F.: Data augmentation using Generative Adversarial Networks (GANs) for GAN-based detection of Pneumonia and COVID-19 in chest X-ray images. Informatics in Medicine Unlocked **27**, 100779 (2021)
17. Sandler, M., Howard, A., Zhu, M., Zhmoginov, A., Chen, L.-C.: MobileNetV2: inverted residuals and linear bottlenecks. In: Proceedings of the IEEE Conference on Computer Vision and Pattern Recognition (CVPR), pp. 4510–4520 (2018)
18. Shi, J., Zhou, S., Liu, X., Zhang, Q., Lu, M., Wang, T.: Stacked deep polynomial network based representation learning for tumor classification with small ultrasound image dataset. Neurocomputing **194**, 87–94 (2016)
19. Shorten, C., Khoshgoftaar, T.M.: A survey on image data augmentation for deep learning. Journal of Big Data **6**(1), 1–48 (2019). https://doi.org/10.1186/s40537-019-0197-0
20. Simonyan, K., Zisserman, A.: Very deep convolutional networks for large-scale image recognition. In: 3rd International Conference on Learning Representations (ICLR) (2015)
21. Szegedy, C., Liu, W., Jia, Y., et al.: Going deeper with convolutions, In: Proceedings of the IEEE Conference on Computer Vision and Pattern Recognition (2015)
22. Tan, M., Quoc, L., Efficientnet: Rethinking model scaling for convolutional neural networks, International Conference on Machine Learning. PMLR, (2019)
23. Xue, Y., et al.: Selective synthetic augmentation with HistoGAN for improved histopathology image classification. Medical Image Analysis **67**, 101816, ISSN 1361-8415 (2021). https://doi.org/10.1016/j.media.2020.101816
24. Zawisza, A., Tabakov, M., Karanowski, K., Galus, K.: Morphological analysis of histopathological images using deep learning. In: Wojtkiewicz, K., Treur, J., Pimenidis, E., Maleszka, M. (eds.) ICCCI 2021. CCIS, vol. 1463, pp. 134–145. Springer, Cham (2021). https://doi.org/10.1007/978-3-030-88113-9_11
25. Zhuang, L., et al.: A ConvNet for the 2020s, arXiv preprint arXiv:2201.03545 (2022)

An End-to-End Framework for Evaluating Explainable Deep Models: Application to Historical Document Image Segmentation

Iheb Brini[1]([✉])[iD], Maroua Mehri[1][iD], Rolf Ingold[2][iD],
and Najoua Essoukri Ben Amara[1][iD]

[1] LATIS-Laboratory of Advanced Technology and Intelligent Systems,
Université de Sousse, Ecole Nationale d'Ingénieurs de Sousse, 4023 Sousse, Tunisie
{brini.iheb,maroua.mehri,najoua.benamara}@eniso.rnu.tn
[2] DIVA Group, University of Fribourg, 1700 Fribourg, Switzerland
rolf.ingold@unifr.ch

Abstract. Recently, researchers have raised several questions related to the explainability of deep learning (DL) model predictions. Indeed, the inherent and undeniable risk remains the abandonment of human control and monitoring in favor of these DL models. Thus, many tools that allow humans to verify the agreement between the DL model predictions and ground truth have been explored. These tools fall into the field of explainable artificial intelligence (XAI) which focuses on proposing methods to explain how the AI-based systems generate their decisions. To contribute to this purpose, we propose in this paper a framework, called DocSeg-Exp, for explaining the decisions of DL models applied for historical document image segmentation (HDIS). The proposed framework is evaluated using three XAI attribution methods on two DL architectures that are performed on a large-scale synthetic dataset having 12K pixel-wise annotated images. Besides, we propose an adaptation of four state-of-the-art metrics (that were previously introduced in the context of object classification) in order to evaluate the generated explanations in the case of a pixel-wise segmentation task.

Keywords: Historical document images · Pixel-wise segmentation · Deep learning · Explainable artificial intelligence

1 Introduction

Since 1990, researchers and archivists have become increasingly interested in the questions related to the sustainable preservation and open access of documentary heritage on the one hand, and to the use and analysis of archival materials on the other hand. In order to process a huge amount of these printed

N. T. Nguyen et al. (Eds.): ICCCI 2022, LNAI 13501, pp. 106–119, 2022.
https://doi.org/10.1007/978-3-031-16014-1_10

and handwritten manuscripts, archivists and historians require human-aided systems that automate document analysis and speed up the transcription process. Nevertheless, the existing systems carry several issues with them, including the poor performance of the optical character recognition (OCR) tools they rely on. This is mainly due to the particularities of the digitized documents, such as the superposition of several layers of information (e.g. stamps, handwritten notes, noise) and the high variability and the complexity of the content and/or layout. Moreover, analyzing archival document images without prior knowledge of their layouts and contents is complex and tedious. Besides, the OCR tools are usually used by archivists without going through the image segmentation stage. However, it is often agreed that it is critical to verify that the analyzed documents have been accurately segmented at some certain degree by distinguishing the textual and graphical components in order to obtain a high accuracy rate of text recognition [15].

In this context, we are working on a collaborative research project with the "National Archives of Tunisia" (ANT)[1]. This project aims at developing a novel AI-powered platform for multilingual text transcription in archival handwritten document images. Indeed, the commercial OCR tools currently used by the ANT are hindered by many issues related to the performance of their different preprocessing modules (e.g. text and graphic separation). Since the recent DL based solutions are showing significantly more efficient results in this research field, we rely on DL architectures to built our solutions. However, the DL models tend to outperform the classical ad-hoc solutions at the cost of increasing system complexity. The so called black-boxes used to extract DL representations from input features loose the ability to provide simple reasoning to support their predictions, and this would result in a lack of trust of end-users. For instance, a system may learn misleading artifacts during the training phase, and project that knowledge in the form of misclassified predictions or by making correct predictions based on false cues, a phenomenon known as "clever hans effect", contributing more in favor of uncontrollable and unreliable systems. In our work, we mainly focus on solving this issue by removing the barrier of distrust and expanding our work in the field of XAI. XAI is a subfield of AI, created to expose complex DL models to humans in a systematic and interpretable way. The goal of XAI is to propose methods to "understand" and "explain" or "interpret" how these AI-powered systems generate their decisions.

To contribute to this purpose, we present in this paper, a framework called DocSegExp, for explaining the decisions of DL models applied for HDIS. More specifically, we are targeting the task of layout analysis which is commonly framed as a pixel-wise segmentation problem, with the goal of dividing a document image into separate regions, such as text, text-outline, paragraph, background, graphic, table, figure caption [14]. The proposed framework currently supports three XAI methods: GradCAM [27], "Gradient × Input" (G × I) [29] and DeepLIFT [28], which are evaluated using the prediction outputs of the two following deep architectures: FCN_101 [13] and ResUNet [17]. These two DL

---

[1] http://www.archives.nat.tn/.

architectures are trained and tested on a large-scale synthetic dataset. We also propose an adaptation of four state-of-the-art metrics which were introduced and used to evaluate the produced explanations of an image classification task on the ImageNet dataset [21]). This adaptation is proposed to fit with the context of our work, a pixel-wise HDIS task. Furthermore, to show quantitatively the appropriateness of the adaptive four XAI evaluation metrics, an in-depth comparative study has been conducted.

The remainder of this paper is structured as follows. Section 2 reviews the main stat-of-the-art methods related to HDIS and XAI. Section 3 details the proposed framework and the four adapted XAI evaluation metrics. Section 4 presents the experimental protocol and the achieved results. Finally, the conclusions and the further work are given in Sect. 5.

2   Related Work

In this section, we firstly report a review of the main stat-of-the-art methods related to HDIS and XAI including the evaluation metrics, frameworks, toolboxes and libraries.

The HDIS task is primarily used to determine the physical structure of a document and extract the various components contained within it (e.g. text or graphic). HDIS is usually based on a pixel-wise segmentation which involves dividing an image into several segments or objects each of which refers to a specific class [16]. Since the last two decades, many state-of-the-art solutions proposed to tackle the HDIS task have been centered almost around the deep neural networks (DNN) [5,12]. For instance, Oliveira et al. [20] presented a generic framework, called dhSegment, that handles multiple tasks at the same time, such as page extraction, baseline extraction, layout analysis or multiple typologies of illustrations and photograph extraction. The convolutional neural networks (CNN) were firstly used in the dhSegment framework as a result of the computational complexity of predicting pixel-wise characteristics. Following that, simple image processing techniques were applied to extract the components of interest (e.g. boxes, polygons, lines, masks). The dhSegment model has an encoder-decoder architecture composed of an encoder which follows the ResNet-50 architecture [7], and a decoder which maps the low resolution encoder feature maps to full input resolution feature maps. The DIVA-HisDB dataset [30] was used to evaluate the dhSegment model for the document layout analysis task. Monnier and Aubry [17] proposed an encoder-decoder architecture, called ResUNet, that combines the descriptive power of ResNet [7] with the localization recovery capacity of U-Net [24] for extracting different historical document contents (e.g. text line, caption, title, image drawing, glyph, table, background). To evaluate their architecture, Monnier and Aubry [17] generated a dataset of 10k synthetic images.

To explain the AI-based model predictions, the XAI methods are recently deployed. A number of XAI techniques have been proposed, such as the layer-wise relevance propagation (LRP) [25], local interpretable model-agnostic explanations (LIME) [23], and generalized additive model (GAM) [6]. Some of them have already proved useful in detecting certain flaws in the architectures of the evaluated DL models [3]. These techniques have made it possible to verify whether the decisional behavior is based on relevant features or rather on spurious correlations or artifacts. An XAI method (e.g. GradCAM) takes into account the input image, the model parameters and the output predictions in case of an attribution-based method. It is mainly composed of an explainer block that aims at generating an explanation map in a form of heatmap. The explanation map highlights the most relevant pixels contributing to the predictions given a class of interest. The XAI methods have a large variety of options and multiple taxonomies and approaches have been used to explore and evaluate different state-of-the-art XAI-based solutions. As detailed in [31], XAI methods could be model-agnostic (i.e. work on different model architectures) or model-specific (i.e. bound to one type of models). Explanations could be global that are based on detailing the working mechanism of the model (e.g. using mathematical equations imitating the model behavior) or local by referring to the resulting predictions. The state-of-the-art methods addressing the XAI issues can be categorized into two classes: mathematical and gradient-based. Among the well-known mathematical approaches of XAI, we state: LIME [23] which is an optimization algorithm that approximates the predictions locally with an interpretable model, and TCAV [8] which is based on the concept activation vectors to explain a prediction. Among the gradient-based approaches are, for example, the gradient-based methods that include guided backpropagation and GradCAM [27]. GradCAM is an XAI attribution method employing the gradients of model outputs with respect to a specific layer. The XAI methods proposed in the literature are mainly applicable to the classification task. However, in our work we are dealing with the segmentation task since we focus on assigning a specific class (e.g. text or graphic) to each pixel in the image. Recently, the evaluation approaches of the generated explanations have been explored in order to assess the XAI methods in terms of interpretability, fidelity [33], class discriminability and sensitivity [2]. For instance, the image occlusion [35] are among the widely used XAI evaluation methods. It is based on covering certain patches from the input image and then measuring the difference between the initial and the predicted scores of the DL model or by referring to domain experts [18,36]. Being a visual metric image occlusion often fails to satisfy the objective characteristic of the evaluation explanations unlike relying on quantified measured metrics. Newer idea was introduced by Leila et al. [4] to built a benchmark dataset of the ground truth evaluation of DNN explanations using VQA system to assess the performance of XAI methods. Another common approach is to design a set of objective metrics in order to mathematically interpret the resulting explanation maps. For example, Lin et al. [10] used three evaluation metrics in their analysis through neural backdoors: intersection over union, recovering rate and recovering difference. Muddamsetty et al. [19] used three different evaluation metrics: area under ROC curve, Kullback-Leibler divergence and Spearmans correlation coefficient. Poppi et al. [21] evaluated the class activation maps (CAM) on the classification task by defining four XAI evaluation metrics: average drop, complexity, coherency, and the combination of these three metrics (called ADCC in [21]). CAM represents an illustration of the discriminating image regions used by the model to identify the target class [27]. It is presented in a form of heatmap showcasing salient regions in the input image.

The majority of the state-of-the-art frameworks, toolboxes and libraries related to XAI only support the classification task [1,11,22,34]. Nevertheless, the neuroscope toolbox [26] tackles two tasks: classification and semantic segmentation dedicated solely for scene segmentation. To the best of our knowledge, no research work has reported results related to explaining the decisions of DL models applied for pixel-wise semantic segmentation in historical document images (HDI). Hence, in our work, we present a novel XAI framework, called DocSegExp, able to explain the decisions of DL models applied for the pixel-wise HDIS task. Besides, we adapt the four state-of-the-art metrics which were previously introduced by Poppi et al. [21] in the context of object classification, in order to evaluate the generated explanations on pixel-wise segmentation and added it to our framework.

3   Proposed Framework

In this work, we propose a novel XAI framework, called DocSegExp, for explaining the decisions of DL models. To adequately use the DocSegExp framework, a DL model should be firstly loaded. Then, an available XAI method should be selected. Third, an input image (I), a target class (cl) and a layer to interpret (l) should be specified (by default, the last convolutional layer is picked). The generated output corresponds to a heatmap highlighting the contribution of each specific input feature to the output prediction for the chosen class. Finally, the option to run the evaluation of the generated explanations can be enabled using our adapted XAI evaluation metrics. DocSegExp is composed of three stages (cf. Fig. 1). The first stage covers the standard DL model predicting process of an input image into a segmentation map. The second stage is the explanation of the segmentation map using the XAI methods, resulting an attribution map for a specific target class. The final stage is the evaluation of the attribution map using a set of evaluation metrics. All DocSegExp stages share the same resources (e.g. compute the attribution map in the second stage requires one forward pass of the model to be computed, also some evaluation metrics rely on the attribution map).

Two DL models are used in our framework. The first DL model is FCN_101 [13], a traditional fully CNN based on ResNet101 architecture with ResNet18 backbone [7]. The second one is ResUnet, a variant of U-Net architecture [24], that was introduced in Monnier and Aubry' [17] framework. In this work, we evaluate the following XAI methods: GradCAM [27], G × I [29] and DeepLIFT [28]. Since both GradCAM and DeepLIFT operate on gradient propagation to a target layer, which is usually the last convolutional layer for CNN-based architectures, we opted for a different implementation of G × I that only requires computing the gradient of the output to a target layer instead of reaching to

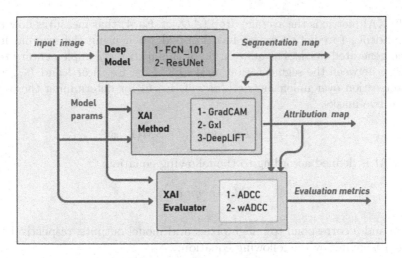

Fig. 1. Pipeline overview of DocSegExp.

the input layer. Hence, we are using the Activation × Gradient as an attribution. This ensures that we can safely compare the results of the three mentioned methods on the same target layer.

An adaptation of the four state-of-the-art metrics (that were introduced by Poppi et al. [21] in the context of object classification) is proposed in this paper in order to evaluate the generated explanations in the case of a pixel-wise segmentation task. In Poppi et al.' [21] work, the first evaluation metric is the complexity which favors the smallest value of pixel intensities to explain a prediction. The second metric is the coherency which measures the correlation between the original CAM of the input image with a class of interest (cl) and the CAM of the input image multiplied by the CAM itself.

In our work, we first normalize respectively each resulting CAM pixel (α_i) in the complexity measure (C_m, cf. Eq. 1) and the input image masked by the attribution map (I_{cam}, cf. Eq. 2) in the coherency measure (C_h, cf. Eq. 3). This normalization is added since the original metrics only consider a probability distribution vector of size N (where N denotes total number of classes) as an output of the model, compared to our segmentation mask (SM, cf. Eq. 5) for a pixel-wise segmentation task which has different shape of $N \times H \times W$, where W and H denote the input image dimensions. SM corresponds to an output matrix of the same size as the input image, in which each pixel represents the corresponding target class prediction in the input image.

$$C_m = \frac{1}{W \times H} \sum_{\alpha_i \in CAM_{cl}} \alpha_i \tag{1}$$

$$I_{cam} = I \odot CAM_{cl} \tag{2}$$

$$C_h = \frac{Cov(CAM_{cl}(I_{cam}), CAM_{cl}(I))}{\sigma_{CAM_{cl}(I_{cam})} \sigma_{CAM_{cl}(I)}} \tag{3}$$

The 3ʳᵈ XAI metric is the average drop (AD, cf. Eq. 4) that measures how much the confidence (prediction score) has dropped when using the original image and the generated mask. The adaptation of this metric is complementary to the similarity between the segmentation masks (SM, cf. Eq. 5) of I and I_{cam} using the intersection over union metric (IoU, cf. Eq. 6) for determining the overlap between two masks.

$$AD = 1 - IoU_{cl}\left(SM(I), SM(I_{cam})\right) \tag{4}$$

where SM is defined according to the following equation:

$$SM = \underset{p \in y}{argmax}\ y \tag{5}$$

where p and y correspond to image pixels and model outputs, respectively. IoU_{cl} is giving by the following equation:

$$IoU_{cl} = \frac{A_{cl} \cap B_{cl}}{A_{cl} \cup B_{cl}} \tag{6}$$

where A_{cl} and B_{cl} denote the spatial mapping of an object with class cl of two vectors A and B, respectively.

The 4ᵗʰ XAI metric, that is computed similarly to Poppi et al. [21]' work, corresponds to a combination score of the first three aforementioned metrics ($ADCC$, cf. Eq. 7). The higher the $ADCC$ values, the better the results.

$$ADCC_{cl} = 3\ (\ \frac{1}{C_h} + \frac{1}{1 - C_m} + \frac{1}{1 - AD}\ )^{-1} \tag{7}$$

4   Experiments and Results

In order to evaluate the performance of the proposed framework, a set of experiments is outlined below.

4.1   Experimental Corpus

In our work, docExtractor[2] which is a fast and scalable synthetic document generation engine, is used to create a large-scale synthetic annotated dataset of HDI [17]. The docExtractor engine also provides accurate pixel-wise annotations. The generated dataset, called in this paper SynDoc12K, is composed of 12K annotated images of historical documents (one-page and double pages).

---

[2] https://github.com/monniert/docExtractor.

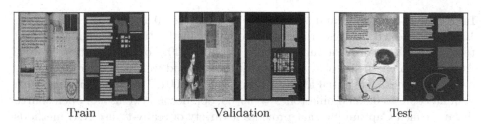

Train   Validation   Test

Fig. 2. SynDoc12K examples with ground truth (Background , graphic , text and text-outline). (Color figure online)

The SynDoc12K dataset is characterized by strong heterogeneity (e.g. varying text column widths), complex layouts, etc. The resolutions of the SynDoc12K images range from 1192×1192 to 2384×2175 pixels. Figure 2 illustrates few examples of document images of the SynDoc12K dataset with their corresponding ground truth. The SynDoc12k dataset contains four distinct classes: background (cl_b), graphic (cl_g), text (cl_t) and text-outline (cl_{to}). The graphic class represents the pixels of visual images or drawings. The text class represents the pixels of handwritten or printed text. The text-outline class represents the rectangular bounding boxes drawn around the borders of text lines. The background class represents the remainder pixels in the input image.

The ground truth annotation of the SynDoc12K dataset contains more than 31 billion annotated pixels. Table 1 details the distribution of the annotation classes (background, graphic, text and text-outline) of the SynDoc12K dataset in terms of the number of annotated pixels. 73.1% of the total number of the annotated pixels represent the background, while 14.1%, 6.3% and 6.5% represent the graphic, text and text-outline contents, respectively. 83.4%, 8.1% and 8.5% of the total number of the annotated pixels represent those of the train, validation and test subsets, respectively.

Table 1. Ground truth statistics of the SynDoc12K dataset in terms of the number of annotated pixels, where B denotes billion.

	Train	Validation	Test	Total
Background (cl_b)	19,018B (73.1%)	1,870B (73.6%)	1,923B (72.8%)	**22,811B (73.1%)**
Graphic (cl_g)	3,693B (14.2%)	0,343B (13.5%)	0,376B (14.2%)	**4,412B (14.1%)**
Text (cl_t)	1,629B (06.3%)	0,161B (06.3%)	0,168B (06.4%)	**1,958B (06.3%)**
Text-outline (cl_{to})	1,679B (06.5%)	0,166B (06.5%)	0,173B (06.6%)	**2,018B (06.5%)**
Total	**26,019B (83.4%)**	**2,540B (08.1%)**	**2,640B (08.5%)**	31,199B

4.2   Implementation Details

Our experiments have been conducted using the PyTorch framework. First, FCN_101 and ResUnet models are trained and tested on a machine with an

Intel Core i7-8700 CPU and a single GeForce RTX 2080 Ti with 12 GB memory. $10K$, $1K$ and $1K$ images are used respectively in the training, validation and test phases. We resize the input images to 640×640. For optimization, we use Adam with a batch size of 1, a momentum of 0.1, and weight decay of 0.000001, over 100 epochs. The initial learning rate is set to 0.001. We use a scheduler with gamma equal to 0.5 and milestones $= [30, 60, 80]$. Second, we use an open source library, called Captum [9], that provides a variety of ready-to-use XAI methods and support both the classification and segmentation tasks using the same API. Usually, an XAI method considers an input vector, an AI-based model and a vector containing the prediction scores for each class. In our work context (i.e. pixel-wise segmentation), the output predictions have the same 2D-representation as the input image. Hence, to use the same XAI method signatures, we propose a computation adaptation of the output vector. This adaptation is performed by summing the scores corresponding to pixels predicted to a specific class across each channel. The XAI method attributes then the summed scores to a target class. The generated heatmap is later upsampled and overlaid on the input image. Hence, each spatial location of the upsampled heatmap corresponds to the spatial coordinate pixel in the input image. Third, the following XAI methods: GradCAM, $G \times I$ and DeepLIFT have been used in DocSegExp to explain the obtained predictions of the FCN_101 and ResUNet models. Following the work of Poppi et al. [21], we replicate the fake XAI method, named fakeCAM, in which weights k are not dependent on the confidence scores. This is achieved by generating a weighted k for each activation map with all pixels set to $1/M$, where M is the number of activation maps, except for the top-left pixel, which is set to 0. This results in a class activation map of all pixels equal to 1 except for the top-left pixel, which is set to 0.

4.3   Results

In this paper, we focus on the semantic segmentation task which consists in predicting the class of each pixel in a document image, and afterward explaining the obtained predictions. First, to evaluate and compare the performance of the FCN_101 and ResUNet models, we compute the overall accuracy (A), mean accuracy (mA), mean intersection over union $(mIoU)$ and weighted mean intersection over union $(wmIoU)$ scores which are the main common evaluation metrics used for assessing the pixel-wise semantic segmentation methods [32]. These metrics are computed on the validation subset of the SynDoc12K dataset (cf. Table 2). We note significant gains of $21.65\%\,(A)$, $17.94\%\,(mA)$, $36.15\%(mIoU)$ and $30.05\%(mIoU))$ for the ResUNet model thanks to the high complexity of its network architecture. ResUNet has the particularities to have in its architecture both the residual blocks and connections between its different layers that contribute to have a deeper network and avoid the gradient vanishing issues.

Table 2. FCN_101 and ResUNet performances.

	A ↑	mA ↑	$mIoU$ ↑	$wmIoU$ ↑
FCN_101	75.05	74.49	49.93	63.95
ResUNet	**96.70**	**92.43**	**86.08**	**94.00**

Second, the fake method (fakeCAM) and the three following state-of-the-art XAI methods: GradCAM, G × I and DeepLIFT have been used in DocSegExp to explain the obtained predictions of the FCN_101 and ResUNet models. Figure 3 illustrates the qualitative results of the pixel-wise segmentation task using a pretrained ResUNet model and the explanation of graphic class cl_g using the three explored XAI methods. Compared to DeepLIFT, GradCAM and G × I have similar visual results. Indeed, more attribution has been assigned on specific parts of target objects on the image (the highest pixel intensity in green). Unlike DeepLIFT which tends to provide more uniform distribution of attribution across the pixels of the target class.

Third, to evaluate the explications of FCN_101 and ResUnet predictions obtained by using the fake method (fakeCAM) and the three following state-of-the-art XAI methods: GradCAM, G × I and DeepLIFT, we compute the four following evaluation metrics: average drop (AD, cf. Eq. 4), maximum coherency (C_h, cf. Eq. 3), minimum complexity (C_m, cf. Eq. 1) and their combination ($ADCC$, cf. Eq. 7) on the validation subset of the SynDoc12K dataset. Indeed, the validation set is commonly used in the literature (e.g. the validation subset of the ImageNet dataset was used in [19,21]). Table 3 reports the obtained values of the four adapted XAI metrics and the explication evaluation in terms of the ADCC metric of each class separately. First, we note that GradCAM has better score of $ADCC$ for the graphic class with 70.66% on ResUNet model compared to G × I with 67.53% though the two attributions are very visually similar (cf. Fig. 3). This confirms the need to perform a quantitative evaluation after generating explanations. Second, we observe that in the G × I and DeepLIFT methods, the background class has scored the highest, while the text-outline one has scored the lowest performance. This could be explained by the fact that the background class appears in large proportions throughout the evaluated dataset.

Furthermore, based on the evaluation results of the $ADCC$ metric, we observe that some target classes are performing poorly and favor class discrimination like in the case of the graphic class which contradicts the visual nature of XAI methods. Hence, we compute the weighted ADCC ($wADCC$) by applying classes weights on the computed $ADCC$ scores (cf. Table 4). Indeed, we multiply the $ADCC$ score by the frequency of the target class in an image (i.e. how much the class covers pixels in the input image). We note a considerable drop in the $wADCC$ score in DeepLIFT for the text-outline class. We note that fakeCAM has the lowest $wADCC$ values, while GradCAM scores the highest $wADCC$ results. Besides, ResUNet scores also better $wmADCC$ for the three evaluated XAI methods. This can be justified by the fact that measuring $wmADCC$ takes

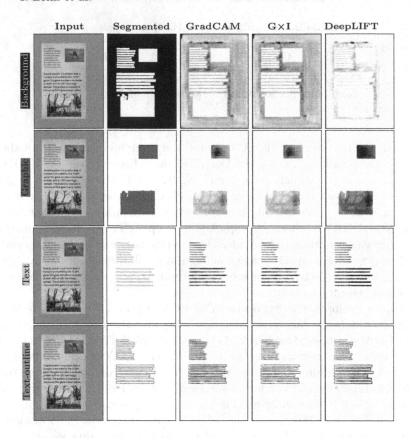

Fig. 3. Image segmentation and explanation outputs. From top to bottom, each row corresponds to the attribution of the four classes: background, graphic, text and text-outline, respectively using the three XAI methods: GradCAM, G × I and DeepLIFT.

into account the model performance more directly in the AD metric (cf. Eq. 4), where the better IoU score the model should generate the less AD it would generate. Finally, we conclude that the proposed $wADCC$ scores are more uniform for each class. On the other side, we note that GradCAM scores the highest $wADCC$ for the graphic, text and text-outline classes for the two evaluated DL, while DeepLIFT shows better results to explain the background class in the ResUNet model. Hence, we conclude that the GradCAM method scored pertinent explication performance to the foreground classes. This could be explained by the fact that GradCAM has the advantage to generate more class discriminatory explanations (i.e. the resulting attribution maps visually differ from one another when picking a different target class).

Table 3. Explication evaluation of DL predictions using the fakeCAM method and the three XAI methods: GradCAM, G × I and DeepLIFT.

					$ADCC$ ↑				
DL model	XAI method	AD ↓	C_h ↑	C_m ↓	cl_b	cl_g	cl_t	cl_{to}	$mADCC$ ↑
FCN_101	FakeCAM	**6.48**	**100.00**	99.96	0.12	0.11	0.11	0.11	0.11
ResUNet	FakeCAM	12.04	**100.00**	100.00	0.00	0.00	0.00	0.00	0.00
FCN_101	GradCAM	23.17	86.20	**9.38**	90.94	**74.85**	**84.03**	80.91	**82.89**
ResUNet	GradCAM	15.70	85.99	21.86	94.84	70.66	82.28	**81.76**	82.39
FCN_101	G × I	42.69	78.31	11.84	82.15	68.31	68.79	52.23	68.10
ResUNet	G × I	38.90	74.35	17.05	93.59	67.53	73.21	28.25	66.13
FCN_101	DeepLIFT	42.77	82.19	13.87	83.57	63.31	67.66	46.26	65.20
ResUNet	DeepLIFT	42.94	74.56	17.22	**98.27**	65.98	67.61	7.67	59.88

Table 4. Explication evaluation of DL predictions using the weighted ADCC.

		$wADCC$ ↑				
DL model	XAI method	cl_b	cl_g	cl_t	cl_{to}	$wmADCC$ ↑
FCN_101	FakeCAM	0.12	0.12	0.12	0.12	0.12
ResUNet	FakeCAM	0.00	0.00	0.00	0.00	0.00
FCN_101	GradCAM	88.64	90.67	92.70	90.99	89.40
ResUNet	GradCAM	95.13	**96.31**	**94.56**	**94.46**	**95.22**
FCN_101	G × I	80.98	83.66	78.58	62.73	79.88
ResUNet	G × I	93.98	90.30	87.07	37.99	88.86
FCN_101	DeepLIFT	82.69	82.72	80.85	59.26	80.85
ResUNet	DeepLIFT	**98.16**	88.22	84.06	10.96	89.32

5   Conclusions and Further Work

In this paper, we propose DocSegExp, an extensible framework allowing the "documents community" to assess their DL models using a variety of XAI methods. The proposed framework is dedicated to a pixel-wise segmentation application since the majority of published XAI methods work on the classification approach. We propose an adaptation of the existing XAI evaluation metrics to work on pixel-wise segmentation. We present thorough evaluation experiments on two different deep architectures applied on a large-scale synthetic dataset for document layout analysis with a variety of XAI methods.

As future work, there are essentially two main streams. On the one hand, we will evaluate the proposed framework on other public pixel-wise annotated datasets. On the other hand, we will test different DNN, as well as more state-of-the-art XAI methods.

References

1. Alber, M.: Software and application patterns for explanation methods. In: Explainable AI: Interpreting, Explaining and Visualizing Deep Learning, pp. 399–433 (2019)
2. Ancona, M., Ceolini, E., Öztireli, C., Gross, M.: Towards better understanding of gradient-based attribution methods for deep neural networks. arXiv:1711.06104 (2017)
3. Anders, C., Weber, L., Neumann, D., Samek, W., Müller, K., Lapuschkin, S.: Finding and removing Clever Hans: using explanation methods to debug and improve deep models. Inf. Fusion, 261–295 (2022)
4. Arras, L., Osman, A., Samek, W.: CLEVR-XAI: a benchmark dataset for the ground truth evaluation of neural network explanations. Inf. Fusion, 14–40 (2022)
5. Aubry, M.: Deep learning for historical data analysis. In: SUMAC (2021)
6. Hastie, T., Tibshirani, R.: Generalized additive models. Statis. Sci. 297–310 (1986)
7. He, K., Zhang, X., Ren, S., Sun, J.: Deep residual learning for image recognition. In: CVPR, pp. 770–778 (2016)
8. Kim, B., et al.: Interpretability beyond feature attribution: quantitative testing with concept activation vectors (TCAV). In: ICML, pp. 2668–2677 (2018)
9. Kokhlikyan, N., et al.: Captum: a unified and generic model interpretability library for PyTorch. arXiv:2009.07896 (2020)
10. Lin, Y., Lee, W., Celik, Z.: What do you see? Evaluation of explainable artificial intelligence (XAI) interpretability through neural backdoors. arXiv:2009.10639 (2020)
11. Linardatos, P., Papastefanopoulos, V., Kotsiantis, S.: Explainable AI: a review of machine learning interpretability methods. Entropy (2021)
12. Lombardi, F., Marinai, S.: Deep learning for historical document analysis and recognition - a survey. J. Imaging (2020)
13. Long, J., Shelhamer, E., Darrell, T.: Fully convolutional networks for semantic segmentation. In: CVPR, pp. 3431–3440 (2015)
14. Markewich, L., et al.: Segmentation for document layout analysis: not dead yet. Int. J. Doc. Anal. Recogn. (2022)
15. Mechi, O., Mehri, M., Ingold, R., Amara, N.E.B.: A two-step framework for text line segmentation in historical Arabic and Latin document images. Int. J. Doc. Anal. Recogn. 197–218 (2021)
16. Mehri, M., Héroux, P., Mullot, R., Moreux, J., Coüasnon, B., Barrett, B.: ICDAR2019 competition on historical book analysis - HBA2019. In: ICDAR, pp. 1488–1493 (2019)
17. Monnier, T., Aubry, M.: docExtractor: an off-the-shelf historical document element extraction. In: ICFHR, pp. 91–96 (2020)
18. Montavon, G.: Gradient-based vs. propagation-based explanations: an axiomatic comparison. In: Explainable AI: Interpreting, Explaining and Visualizing Deep Learning, pp. 253–265 (2019)
19. Muddamsetty, S., Jahromi, M., Ciontos, A., Fenoy, L., Moeslund, T.: Visual explanation of black-box model: similarity difference and uniqueness (SIDU) method. Pattern Recogn. (2022)
20. Oliveira, S., Seguin, B., Kaplan, F.: dhSegment: a generic deep-learning approach for document segmentation. In: ICFHR, pp. 7–12 (2018)
21. Poppi, S., Cornia, M., Baraldi, L., Cucchiara, R.: Revisiting the evaluation of class activation mapping for explainability: a novel metric and experimental analysis. In: CVPR, pp. 2299–2304 (2021)

22. Rauber, P., Fadel, S., Falcao, A., Telea, A.: Visualizing the hidden activity of artificial neural networks. IEEE Trans. Visual. Comput. Graph. 101–110 (2016)
23. Ribeiro, M., Singh, S., Guestrin, C.: Why should I trust you? Explaining the predictions of any classifier. In: SIGKDD, pp. 1135–1144 (2016)
24. Ronneberger, O., Fischer, P., Brox, T.: U-net: convolutional networks for biomedical image segmentation. In: Navab, N., Hornegger, J., Wells, W.M., Frangi, A.F. (eds.) MICCAI 2015. LNCS, vol. 9351, pp. 234–241. Springer, Cham (2015). https://doi.org/10.1007/978-3-319-24574-4_28
25. Samek, W., Montavon, G., Lapuschkin, S., Anders, C., Müller, K.: Explaining deep neural networks and beyond: a review of methods and applications. IEEE, 247–278 (2021)
26. Schorr, C., Goodarzi, P., Chen, F., Dahmen, T.: Neuroscope: an explainable AI toolbox for semantic segmentation and image classification of convolutional neural nets. Appl. Sci. (2021)
27. Selvaraju, R., Cogswell, M., Das, A., Vedantam, R., Parikh, D., Batra, D.: Grad-CAM: visual explanations from deep networks via gradient-based localization. In: ICCV, pp. 618–626 (2017)
28. Shrikumar, A., Greenside, P., Kundaje, A.: Learning important features through propagating activation differences. arXiv:1704.02685 (2017)
29. Shrikumar, A., Greenside, P., Shcherbina, A., Kundaje, A.: Not just a black box: Learning important features through propagating activation differences. arXiv:1605.01713 (2016)
30. Simistira, F., Seuret, M., Eichenberger, N., Garz, A., Liwicki, M., Ingold, R.: DIVA-HisDB: a precisely annotated large dataset of challenging Medieval manuscripts. In: ICFHR, pp. 471–476 (2016)
31. Singh, A., Sengupta, S., Lakshminarayanan, V.: Explainable deep learning models in medical image analysis. J. Imaging (2020)
32. Sokolova, M., Lapalme, G.: A systematic analysis of performance measures for classification tasks. Inf. Process. Manag. 427–437 (2009)
33. Yeh, C., Hsieh, C., Suggala, A., Inouye, D., Ravikumar, P.: On the (in) fidelity and sensitivity of explanations. Adv. Neural Information Processing Systems (2019)
34. Yosinski, J., Clune, J., Nguyen, A., Fuchs, T., Lipson, H.: Understanding neural networks through deep visualization. arXiv:1506.06579 (2015)
35. Zeiler, M.D., Fergus, R.: Visualizing and understanding convolutional networks. In: Fleet, D., Pajdla, T., Schiele, B., Tuytelaars, T. (eds.) ECCV 2014. LNCS, vol. 8689, pp. 818–833. Springer, Cham (2014). https://doi.org/10.1007/978-3-319-10590-1_53
36. Zhou, B., Bau, D., Oliva, A., Torralba, A.: Comparing the interpretability of deep networks via network dissection. In: Explainable AI: Interpreting, Explaining and Visualizing Deep Learning, pp. 243–252 (2019)

Deep Convolutional Neural Network for Arabic Speech Recognition

Rafik Amari[1,2(✉)], Zouhaira Noubigh[2], Salah Zrigui[4],
Dhaou Berchech[5], Henri Nicolas[3], and Mounir Zrigui[1,2]

[1] Faculty of Science of Monastir, University of Monastir, Monastir, Tunisia
{Rafik.amari,Mounir.zrigui}@fsm.rnu.tn
[2] Research Laboratory in Algebra, Numbers Theory and Intelligent Systems
RLANTIS, Monastir, Tunisia
[3] University of Bordeaux, Bordeaux, France
Henri.nicolas@u-bordeaux.fr
[4] Laboratoire LIG, Université Grenoble-Alpes, Grenoble, France
[5] 5DS 38 rue de la Glacière, 75013 Paris, France
dhaou.b@db-consulting-group.com

Abstract. Deep neural networks (DNNs) have made remarkable achievements in acoustic modeling for speech recognition. In this paper, we compare the performance of two proposed models based on Convolutional neural network (CNN). In the first model, CNN is used for features extraction and Long Short- Term Memory (LSTM) is used for recognition. In the second model, CNN with deep architecture is mainly used to execute feature learning and recognition process. This work is focused on single word Arabic automatic speech recognition. We explore the optimal network structure and training strategy for the proposed models. All experiments are conducted using the Arabic Isolated Words Corpus (ASD) database. The results demonstrate the performance and advantages of using the deep CNN for both features extraction and recognition steps.

Keywords: Deep learning · CNN · LSTM · Arabic speech · Single word recognition

1 Introduction

Humans communicate preferably through speech using the same language. Speech recognition can be defined as the ability to understand the spoken words of the person speaking [1–3].

Automatic speech recognition (ASR) refers to the task of recognizing human speech and translating it into text. The main goal of an ASR system is to transform an audio input into a sequence of words or characters. The labels might be character-level labels (letters) or word-level labels (words) [4, 5]. A major challenge in the field of automated voice recognition (ASR) existed in the vision systems. These systems are crucial for real-world applications where high levels of noise are frequently present.

N. T. Nguyen et al. (Eds.): ICCCI 2022, LNAI 13501, pp. 120–134, 2022.
https://doi.org/10.1007/978-3-031-16014-1_11

This research field has gained a lot of focus over the last decades. It is an important research area for human-to-machine communication [6]. Early methods focused on manual feature extraction and conventional techniques such as Gaussian Mixture Models (GMM), the Dynamic Time Warping (DTW) algorithm and Hidden Markov Models (HMM) [7, 8].

More recently, deep neural networks such as recurrent neural networks (RNNs), convolutional neural networks (CNNs) and in the last years Transformers, have been applied on ASR and have achieved great performance [9, 10].

Deep learning is a branch of machine learning that inspired by the act of the human brain in processing data based on learning data by using multiple processing layers that has a complex structure or otherwise. Their industrial application is now possible with the landing of powerful matrix computing machines [11]. Machine learning requires extensive databases and their processing also benefits from technological advances in both physical media and software [12]. Access to massive data is now possible with their systematic virtualization in digital format although their use depends on legal permissions. Scientific research in deep learning is advancing. All fields of science are involved and these new methods are compared with the more traditional machine learning methods already in use [13, 14] However, the decision-making mechanism of prediction by deep neural networks remains largely misunderstood [15–18]. However, in the context of their large-scale industrialization, it is not preferable and preferable to use algorithmic tools of which one is unaware to explain the reason of such or such prediction [19–22]. In recent years, various deep models have been used for improving Automatic Speech Recognition (ASR) [23–26]. Between these advanced models, Convolutional Neural Net- works (CNNs) and Long-Short-Term-Memory (LSTM) networks attain state-of-the- art recognition accuracy, which generally surpass feed-forward Deep Neural Net- works (DNNs). In this paper, CNN and LSTM networks were explored as ASR acoustic models. The results show that CNN and LSTM remarkably improves ASR accuracy for different tasks [27, 28].

The document is organized as follows. A brief review of convex work is presented in Sect. 2. The proposed system is presented in Sect. 3. Section 4 contains, in first part, a detailed report of the experiments and in second part, a discussion of the recorded results. We conclude the document and list some future works in Sect. 5.

2 Related Works

Work on Arabic automatic speech recognition has focused on Standard Arabic recognition. Among them we find the work of El Ani [29], which deals with the acoustic and structural exploration of Arabic sounds, and the work of Mrayati [30], which is more interested in syntactic aspects. M. Djoudi [31] implemented the work on the MARS detection system at the University of Poitiers. The system consists of two parts, an acoustic-speech decoder (SAPHA) and a linguistic decoder (SALAM), the last linguistic decoder handles prosody, morphological aspects and syntactic semantics specific to Arabic.

Convolutional Neural Networks (CNNs) have proven successful in modeling the local structure of input data. In recent years, some CNN models have been propagated from computer vision tasks to ASR systems [32, 33]. The early CNN acoustic model, proposed in [34] uses simple one-dimensional convolution along the frequency dimension of speech spectrum, and outperforms DNNs. Eventually, very deeper CNN models with carefully designed network structures, such as the VGG network [35], Residual Network (ResNet) [36] highly advancing the cutting-edge ASR acoustic modelling. Today, deep CNN models are hard used in state-of-the-art ASR, such as in the Microsoft 2016 evaluation [37]. In insertion to recognition for clean speech, CNNs significantly boost the noise robustness of ASR as well compared with DNN [38] Speech is sequence data, in which the identity of the HMM state given a frame at time t is dependent on both the previous and future frames. Recurrent Neural Networks (RNNs) and their advanced LSTM version are able to exploit long historical information to predict the current class label. Deep RNN and LSTM have been powerful sequence acoustic models. Recently, few works use recurrent neural networks (RNNs) [39, 40] to capture the longer context and report better performance than feedforward DNNs. On the other hand, the temporal dependencies learned by standard RNNs are still limited by reason of the fact that of the gradient problem that disappears and explodes [41, 42]. Acoustic modeling is now exploring the use of long-term memory RNNs (LSTMs) [43]. The recurrent cells of the LSTM NRNs are connected linearly to address the evanescent gradient problem. Input, recurrent and output signals from LSTM NRNs are controlled by door signals to obtain accurate timing.

Then LSTM-based systems realized interesting results in the TIMIT phone recognition task in 2013 [44]. Then, the hybrid LSTM RNN-HMM models are applied to extend vocabulary tasks [45], and then Google researchers extend the acoustic LSTM RNN model to big data and achieve impressive results in speech search tasks [46, 47]. The excellent results of LSTMs on various tasks show their capacity to learn long-term dependencies from original data.

3 Proposed System

In this section, we describe different architectures tested and compared in this work. The first is based on two CNN layers, each followed by a max-pooling layer, a flattening layer, and two dense layers. The second model is based on a combination of CNN and LSTM. The CNN layer is followed by two LSTM layers, a dropout layer and a softmax layer, as shown in Table 1. The third proposed model is based on a deep CNN architecture with 5 convolutional layers. For the first and third models, CNN is used in two steps: feature extraction and classification. In the second model, CNN is used for feature extraction and LSTM is used for classification. Figure 1 shows the difference between the two proposed strategies. In the following subsections, we present the definitions and mathematical formulations of the used techniques (Table 2).

Table 1. 5 CNN architecture and parameters

Layer	Type	Output shape
0	Input	(None, 32, 32, 1)
1	Conv2d	(None, 32, 32, 64)
2	Batch_normalization	(None, 32, 32, 64)
3	Max_pooling	(None, 16,16,64)
4	Conv2d	(None, 16,16,128)
5	Batch_normalization	(None, 16,16,128)
6	Max_pooling	(None, 8,8,128)
7	Conv2d	(None, 8,8,265)
8	Batch_normalization	(None, 8,8,265)
9	Max_pooling	(None, 4,4,265)
10	Conv2d	(None, 4,4,265)
11	Batch_normalization	(None, 4,4,265)
12	Max_pooling	(None, 2,4,265)
13	Conv2d	(None, 2,4,265)
14	Batch_normalization	(None, 2,4,512)
15	Max_pooling	(None, 1,4,512)
16	Lambda	(None,4,512)
17	Flatten	(None, 2048)
18	Dense	(None, 128)
19	Dense	(None, 20)

Table 2. CNN-LSTM architecture

Layer	Type	Output shape
0	Input	(None, 20, 11)
1	Conv1d	(None, 3,128)
2	Batch_normalization	(None, 3,128)
3	Activation	(None, 3,128)
4	Dropout1	(None, 3,128)
5	LSTM1	(None, 3,128)
6	LSTM2	(None, 256)
7	FC	(None, 64)
8	Droupout2	(None, 64)
9	softmax	(None, 20)

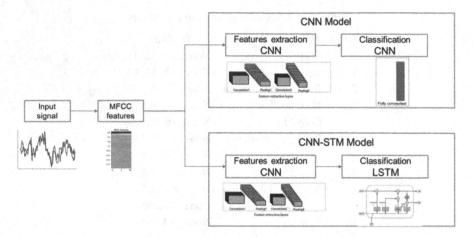

Fig 1. Model overview

3.1 Convolutional Neural Network (CNN)

CNN also known as ConvNet is a feedforward deep neural network. The CNN can get input as an image in two dimensions. This greatly diminishing the number of parameters to be tuned in a network. The idea was proposed in 1998 by LeCun et al. [48]. Then, a new era of artificial intelligence started when Krizhevsky et al. [49] won the ILSVRC-2012 competition, with the architecture popularly known as AlexNet. In the years after, various inspired architectures have been developed. They have proven excellent performance in several machine learning applications [50–52]. Although, it was used oftentimes for classification, CNNs are particularly useful in extracting image descriptors using local spatial information. With CNNs, the neurons can be aligned in a three-dimensional structure using length, height and depth and these attributes can be mapped with the dimension of the input signal. CNNs transform the input signal through several connected layers and output a set of class probabilities. Its basic architecture contains convolution layers, ReLU layers, pooling layers and fully connected layer at the end.

Convolutional Layers. Convolutional layers are the core components of CNN architectures. The convolution operation simply consists on passing a filter over the image [53, 54]. The layer per- forms dot product between the region of the neurons in the input layer and the filters to generate the Convolved layer (Feature map). Filters differ in shapes and in values to get different features. The filter matrix is a weight matrix for which values are initialized with random small numbers and need to be trained using backpropagation [55, 56].

The result of feature map depends on four parameters need to be defined before the convolution is performed:

- The depth of the output represents the number of layers. This value depends on the number of filters used.
- Filter size represents the height and width of the filters.

- Stride represents the number of pixels by which the filter matrix is slid
- over the input matrix. Smaller feature maps are produced if a larger stride is used.
- Padding: helps to retain the height and width of the input image. In padding, we add various rows and columns about the image.

Batch Normalization. Batch normalization (BN) [50] is a regularization method which allows for much faster training of neural networks because it can allow the optimization algorithm to even work with slightly higher learning rates and to converge in fewer epochs. Batch normalization addresses the so-called problem of internal covariate shift [49], which can be defined as the changing (shifting) of the input distribution when training a classifier. A deep neural network can be seen as a composition of stacked layers, each taking as input the output of previous layers. In this paper, we use Batch normalization between convolution and activation.

Activations ReLU. ReLU [57] is widely used in deep learning. For value that is greater than 0, it produc- es the value itself, for the other values it produces 0. In short, given an input matrix X, the output matrix of ReLU is defined by Eq. (1):

$$ReLU(X) = Max\{0, X\} \qquad (1)$$

Pooling Layer. The second construction element of CNNs are pooling layers, which perform sub- sampling of the feature maps by simple operations like maximum or mean. The pooling layer reduces the input size for the next layer and allows learning more mappings instead. And second, it helps combining the output from the previous layer on a coarser scale. Pooling layers reduce data representation and help control overfitting. Each pooling summarizes the area they cover. Average pooling and max pooling are the most commonly used strategies.

Fully-Connected. This layer is used to calculate the probabilities of the output classes for the input data. The output is a vector with N numbers representing the probability of each of the N output classes. In fully connected layer, each neuron from previous layer (convolution layer or pooling layer or fully connected layer) is connected to every neuron in the next layer and every value contributes in predicting how strongly a value matches a particular class.

3.2   LSTM

The most successful Recurrent Neural Network architectures for sequence learning stem from two papers published in 1997. The first paper, Long Short-Term Memory by Hochreiter and Schmidhuber [58], introduces the memory cell, a unit of computation that replaces traditional nodes in the hidden layer of a network. With these memory cells, networks are able to overcome difficulties with training encountered by earlier recurrent networks. The second paper, Bidirectional Recurrent Neural Net- works by

Schuster and Paliwal [57], introduces an architecture in which information from both future and past are used to determine the output at any point in the sequence. Long Short-Term Memory (LSTM) network is a RNN introduced to over- come the vanishing gradient problem of RNN [59]. LSTM is able to learn long-term dependencies. It has appeared as the most competent classifier for handwriting and speech recognition [60].

The amount of information to be retained from previous time steps is controlled by a sigmoid layer known as 'forget' gate whereas the sigmoid activated 'input gate' decides upon the new information to be stored in the cell followed by a hyperbolic tangent activated layer to produce new candidate values which are updated taking forget gate coefficient weighted old state's candidate value. Finally, the output is produced controlled by output gate and hyperbolic tangent activated candidate value of the state.

The LSTM cell is defined mathematically as follows in Eqs. 2, 3, 4, 5, 6, 7. We have the hidden state f_t, $\overline{C_t}$, I_t and O_t

$$f_t = \sigma\left(X_t * U_f + H_{t-1} * W_f\right) \tag{2}$$

$$\overline{C}_t = tanh(X_t * U_c + H_{t-1} * W_c) \tag{3}$$

$$I_t = \sigma(X_t * U_i + H_{t-1} * W_i) \tag{4}$$

$$O_t = \sigma(X_t * U_o + H_{t-1} * W_o) \tag{5}$$

The outputs C_t and H_t are calculated as:

$$C_t = f_t * C_{t-1} + I_t * \overline{C}_t \tag{6}$$

$$H_t = O_t * tanh(C||t) \tag{7}$$

With X_t is the input vector, H_t and $H_t - 1$ are the current and previous cell outputs respectively and C_t and $C_t - 1$ are respectively the current and the previous cell memory.

4   Experimental Results and Discussion

4.1   Datasets and Input Features

Arabic Speech Data Set (ASD). The corpus used in the experiments was developed by the Management Information Systems Department of King Faisal University. It is an Arabic speech corpus for isolated words [61].

This corpus uses in the raw format (.wav files). It consists of 9018 recorded statements from 50 speakers speaking 20 words presented in Table 3 with its equivalent word in English. Each word was labelled using the following coding scheme: S (Number of speakers) (Number of repetitions) (Number of words) and the recordings are sampled at 44100 Hz with a precision of 16 bits. Statistics of the dataset are presented in Table 4.

Table 3. Word classes of the dataset

Arabic word	English translation	Arabic word	English translation
صفر	Zero	التنشيط	Activation
واحد	One	التحويل	Transfer
اثنان	Two	الرصيد	Balance
ثالثة	Three	التسديد	Payment
اربعة	Four	نعم	Yes
خمسة	Five	ال	No
ستة	Six	التمويل	Funding
سبعة	Seven	البيانات	Data
ثمانية	Eight	الحساب	Account
تسعة	Nine	انهاء	End

Table 4. Dataset statistics

Training statements	Testing statements	Speakers	Words
7212	1806	50	20

Data Augmentation. Machine learning models can do wonderful things if they have enough training data. Unfortunately, for many applications, access to quality data remains a barrier. An interesting solution to this problem is "data augmentation," a technique that generates new training examples from existing ones. Data augmentation is an inexpensive and effective method for improving the performance and accuracy of machine learning models in data-constrained environments. Due to limited input sample sizes, CNN training is subject to overfitting resulting in low detection rates [62]. One solution to mitigate this problem is the data augmentation technique in which the goal is to generate more training data from the existing training set [63]. Data augmentation can be performed in data space or feature space. Experimentally, we have found that it is preferable to perform data augmentation in the data space as long as the label-preserving transformations are known. Different data augmentation techniques, such noise injection, shifting time and changing speed are applied to datasets in order to create more training samples.

Input Features. An example of the input signals is presented in Fig. 2. It is not possible to com- pare different characteristic extraction methods or evaluate the performance of the proposed model in the presence of different types of noise. However, in the Arabic speech corpus for Isolated Words, dataset and extraction of various features of the methods were considered.

After having unified the duration of the raw signals, several works proposed to use acoustic parameters at the entrance of a network of convolutive neurons, such as MFCC, PLP, etc. In the ASD dataset, we used the MFCC functions. An example of the MFCC features is shown in Fig. 2.

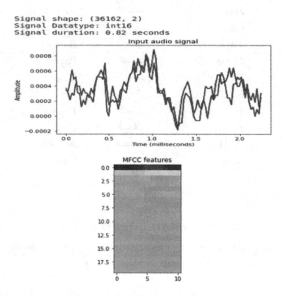

Fig. 2. Input audio signal (left) and its MFCC features (right)

4.2   Results and Discussion

Experiments are performed on the ASD corpus where the training set contains 7212 audio files and the test set have 1806 audio files. The inputs were MFCC file extracted from this database.

In these experiments, we compare the performance of three models, the first based on CNN with one convolutional layer, the second combine CNN with the LSTM network and the last based on deep CNN model with 5 convolutional layers.

In this work, we report the recognition accuracy of the proposed model as presented in Table 5. We have used two deep neural networks, namely Convolutional Neural Network and Recurrent Neural Networks.

The obtained accuracy, using the CNN-LSTM model significantly exceeds that based on one CNN layer. These shows the benefit of combining the two networks. The experimental results show that the combination of CNN and LSTM model provides a large improvement compared to the model using only CNN. The word error rate increased from 80% to 87%. This can be explained by the fact that the recurrent structure of LSTMs is better suited for classifying long-term sequences (one word). Furthermore, CNN models have proven themselves to be a feature extraction method.

We tested convolutional neural networks with different depths, and we have shown that deeper neural network achieves significantly better results when we compared with other models. It should be noted that increasing the depth of neural networks also increases the number of parameters in the models, and therefore their capacity. Figure 3 shows the word error rate evolution using the training and test sets 5CNN model that recorded the best results.

Table 5. Recorded recognition accuracy with the two models

Model	Accuracy
CNN	80%
CNN + LSTM	88%
5CNN	98,39%
5CNN + D-Aug	98,42%

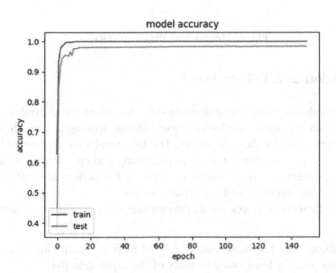

Fig. 3. Results with deep CNN model

Data augmentation is useful to improve performance and outcomes of the proposed model by forming new and different examples to train datasets. It improve the performance of the model and assure the fast convergence of results as it is give more training examples, the model performs better and more accurately. In Fig. 4, we illustrate the accuracy evolution using data augmentation. We can note the improvement in the training step that become equal to 1 from the fifth epoch and in the testing set where results are improved and the overfitting was resolved.

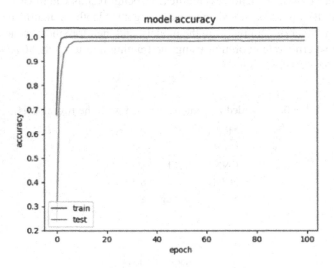

Fig. 4. Results with data augmentation

5   Conclusion and Future Works

This paper introduces a new recognition model for discontinuous Arabic speech. We compare three architectures based on the word model approach. The ASD data set is used in experience for training and testing. The best results are performed by the deep CNN model. The results obtained are very promising and encouraging to improve the quality of the system. It will be useful to improve the performance of the proposed model with a large corpus of isolated Arabic words.

Although our work achieves good performance, there is still some further work to do.

- Using Bidirectional LSTM instead of LSTM help to ameliorate the results as we will get information from two directions of the input data [64].
- Language models are crucial for ASR, and shows that with enough speech transcripts, end-to-end ASR can learn the language model implicitly. There- fore, another future work is to explore the language model and develop an end-to-end ASR for Arabic language on larger databases. We will explore KALDI toolbox or other techniques to replace our system.

References

1. Terbeh, N., Trigui, A., Maraoui, M., Zrigui, M.: Arabic speech analysis to identify factors posing pronunciation disorders and to assist learners with vocal disabilities. In: 2016 International Conference on Engineering & MIS (ICEMIS) (2016)
2. Bsir, B., Zrigui, M.: Bidirectional LSTM for author gender identification .In: International Conference on Computational Collective Intelligence, 393–402
3. Slimi, A., Hamroun, M., Zrigui, M., Nicolas, H.: Emotion recognition from speech using spectrograms and shallow neural networks. In: MoMM '20: Proceedings of the 18th International Conference on Advances in Mobile Computing & Multimedia (2020)
4. Merhben, L., Zouaghi, A., Zrigui, M.: Lexical disambiguation of arabic language: an experimental study. Polibits **46**, 49–54 (2012)
5. Métais, E., Meziane, F., Vadera, S., Sugumaran, V., Saraee, M. (eds.): NLDB 2019. LNCS, vol. 11608. Springer, Cham (2019). https://doi.org/10.1007/978-3-030-23281-8
6. Mohamed, M.A.B., Mallat, S., Nahdi, M.A., Zrigui, M.: Exploring the potential of schemes in building NLP tools for Arabic language. Int. Arab J. Information Technol. (IAJIT), **12**(6) (2015)
7. Merhbene, L., Zouaghi, A., Zrigui, M.: A semi-supervised method for Arabic word sense disambiguation using a weighted directed graph. In: Proceedings of the Sixth International Joint Conference on Natural Language Processing, pp. 1027–1031 (2013)
8. Maraoui, M., Antoniadis, G., Zrigui, M. : CALL System for Arabic Based on Natural Language Processing Tools. In: IICAI, pp. 2249–2258 (2009)
9. Hkiri, E., Mallat, S., Zrigui, M.: Events automatic extraction from Arabic texts. In: Natural Language Processing: Concepts, Methodologies, Tools, and Applications, pp. 1686–1704. IGI Global (2020)
10. Ayadi, R., Maraoui, M., Zrigui, M. : LDA and LSI as a dimensionality reduction method in arabic document classification. In: International Conference on Information and Software Technologies, pp. 491–502. Springer, Cham (2015) https://doi.org/10.1007/978-3-319-24770-0_42
11. Noubigh, Z., Mezghani, A., Kherallah, M.: Densely Connected Layer to Improve VGGnet-based CRNN for Arabic Handwriting Text Line Recognition, pp. 113 – 127 (2021)
12. Terbeh, N., Labidi, M., Zrigui, M.: Automatic speech correction: A step to speech recognition for people with disabilities. In Fourth International Conference on Information and Communication Technology and Accessibility (ICTA), pp. 1–6. IEEE (2013)
13. Batita, M.A., Zrigui, M.: The enrichment of arabic wordnet antonym relations. In: International Conference on Computational Linguistics and Intelligent Text Processing, pp. 342–353. Springer, Cham (2017). https://doi.org/10.1007/978-3-319-77113-7_27
14. Bacha, K., Zrigui, M.: Machine Translation System on the Pair of Arabic/English. In: KEOD, pp. 347–351 (2012)
15. Zouaghi, A., Zrigui, M., Antoniadis, G. : Compréhension automatique de la parole arabe spontanée. In : Traitement Automatique des Langues **49**(1), 141–166
16. Zouaghi, A., Zrigui, M., Antoniadis, G., Merhbene, L.: Contribution to semantic analysis of Arabic language. In: Advances in Artificial Intelligence (2012)
17. Terbeh, N., Zrigui, M.: Vocal pathologies detection and mispronounced phonemes identification: case of arabic continuous speech. In: Proceedings of the Tenth International Conference on Language Resources and Evaluation (LREC'16) (2016)
18. Ghazali, S., Habaili, H., Zrigui, M. : Correspondance graphème-phonème pour la synthèse de la parole arabe à partir du texte. In : IRSIT, Actes du Congrès dialogue homme ma chine, Tunis

19. Noubigh, Z., Mezghani, A., Kherallah, M.: Open vocabulary recognition of offline Arabic handwriting text based on deep learning. In: International Conference on Intelligent Systems Design and Applications, pp. 92–106. Springer, Cham (2020) https://doi.org/10.1007/978-3-030-71187-0_9

20. Maraoui, M., Zrigui, M., Antoniadis, G.: Use of NLP Tools in CALL System for Arabic. In: Intertional Journal of Computer Processing Of Languages 23(04), 427–439

21. Mars, M., Antoniadis, G., Zrigui , M.: Statistical part of speech tagger for Arabic language. In: ICAI 2010: Proceedings of the 2010 International Conference on Artificial Intelligence

22. Terbeh, N., Zrigui, M.: Vers la correction automatique de la Parole Arabe. In: Citala (2014)

23. Trigui, A., Maraoui, M., Zrigui, M.: The gemination effect on consonant and vowel durtion in stan dardArabic speech. In: 2010 international conference on image processing, computer vision, & pattern recognition

24. Bassem, B., Zrigui, M.: An empirical method for evaluation of author profiling frame work. In: PACLIC- (2017)

25. Mahmoud, A., Zrigui, M.: Sentence embedding and convolutional neural network for semantic textual similarity detection in Arabic language. Arabian Journal for Science Eng. 44(11), 9263–1090,9274 (2019)

26. Mallat, S., Zouaghi, A., Hkiri, E., Zrigui, M.: Method of lexical enrichment in information retrieval system in Arabic. Int. J. Information Retrieval Research (IJIRR) 3(4), 35–51 (2013)

27. Zrigui, M., Charhad, M., Zouaghi, A.: A framework of indexation and document video retrieval based on the conceptual graphs. J. Comput. Inf. Technol. 18(3), 245–256 (2010)

28. Mahmoud, A., Zrigui, M.: Semantic similarity analysis for corpus development and paraphrase detection in Arabic. Int. Arab J. Inf. Technol. 18(1), 1–7 (2021)

29. Al-Ani, S.: Abstract and concrete interaction in the arabic sound system, Islamic and middle eastern societies. Oslan, R., Al-Ani, S.: Amana Books (1987)

30. Mrayati, M., Makhoul, J.: Man-machine communication and the arabic language, Lecture notes, Applied Arabic linguistics and signal and information processing, pp. 133–145 (1984)

31. Djoudi, M.: Contribution a etude et la reconnaissance de la parole en arabe standard. Thèse de l'Université de Nancy I (1991)

32. Hkiri, E., Mallat, S., Zrigui, M. : Arabic-English text translation leveraging hybrid NER. In: Proceedings of the 31st Pacific Asia Conference on Language, Information and Computation, pp. 124–131 (2017)

33. Hkiri, E., Mallat, S., Zrigui, M., Mars, M.: Constructing a Lexicon of Arabic-English named entity using SMT and semantic linked data. Int. Arab J. Information Technol. (IAJIT) 14(6) (2017)

34. LeCun, Y., Bottou, L., Bengio, Y., Haffner, P.: Gradient-based learning applied to document recognition. In: Proceedings of the IEEE, pp. 2278–2324 (1998)

35. Simonyan, K., Zisserman, A.: Very deep convolutional networks for large-scale image recognition. In: ICLR (2015)

36. He, K., Zhang, X., Ren, S., Sun, J.: Deep residual learning for image recognition. In: CVPR (2016)

37. Xiong, W., et al.: The Microsoft 2016 conversational speech recognition system. preprint at https://arxiv.org/abs/1609.03528

38. Qian, Y., Bi, M., Tan, T., Yu, K.: Very deep convolutional neural networks for noise ro bust speech recognition. In: IEEE/ACM Trans. Audio Speech Language Process. 24(12), 2263–2276 (2016)

39. Graves, A., Mohamed, A., Hinton, G.: Speech recognition with deep recurrent neural networks. In: Acoustics, Speech and Signal Processing (ICASSP), 2013 IEEE International Conference on, pp. 6645–6649. IEEE (2013)

40. Vinyals, O., Ravuri, S.V., Povey, D.: Revisiting recurrent neural networks for robust ASR. In: Proceedings of International Conference on Acoustics, Speech and signal Processing. ICASSP. Kyoto, Japan, pp. 4085–4088 (2012)

41. Saon, G., Soltau, H., Emami, A., Pichen, M.: Unfolded recurrent neural networks for speech recognition. In: Proceedings of Interspeech. Singapore pp. 343–347 (2014)

42. Y Bengi., P Simard, P Frasconi.: Learning long-term dependencies with gradient descent is difficult. IEEE Trans. Neural Netw. **5**(2), 157–166 (1994)

43. F A Gers., N N Schraudolph., J Schmidhuber.,: Learning precise timing with LSTM recurrent networks. J. Mach. Learn. Res. **3**, 115–143 (2002)

44. Grave, A., AMohamed, G.E.H.: Speech recognition with deep recurrent neural networks. In: Proceedings of International Conference on Acoustics, Speech and Signal Pro- cessing. ICASSP. Vancouver, Canada, pp. 6645–6649 (2013a)

45. Graves, A., Jaitly, N., Mohamed, A.: Hybrid speech recognition with deep bidirectional LSTM. In: Proceedings of Automatic Speech Recognition and Understanding. ASRU. Olomouc, Czech Republic, pp. 273–278 (2013b)

46. Sak, H., Senior, A., Beaufays, F.: Long short-term memory recurrent neural network architectures for large scale acoustic modeling. In: Proceedings of Inter speech. Singapore, pp. 338–342 (2014a)

47. Sak, H., et al.: Sequence discriminative distributed training of long short- term memory recurrent neural networks. In: Proceedings of Inter speech. Singapore, pp. 1209–1213 (2014)

48. LeCun, Y., et al.: Backpropagation applied to handwritten zip code recognition. In: Neural Computation (1989)

49. Krizhevsky, A., Sutskever, I., Hinton, G.E.: Imagenet classification with deep convolution-al neural networks. In: Proceedings of the 25th International Conference on Neural In-formation Processing Systems (2012)

50. Ioffe, S., Szegedy, C.: Batch normalization: accelerating deep network training by re- ducing internal covariate shift. In: ICML'15: Proceedings of the 32nd International Conference on International Conference on Machine Learning (2015)

51. Mansouri, S., Charhad, M., Zrigui, M.: A heuristic approach to detect and localize text in Arabic news video. In: Computación y Sistemas **22**(1), 75–82 (2018)

52. Mahmoud, A., Zrigui, M.: BLSTM-API: Bi-LSTM recurrent neural network-based approach for Arabic Paraphrase identification. In: Arabian Journal for Science and Engineering (2021)

53. Aziz, I.: Deep learning: an overview of Convolutional Neural Network (CNN). In: Faculty of Information Technology and Communication Sciences M.Sc. Thesis (2020)

54. LeCun, Y., Bengio, Y., Hinton, G.E.: Deep learning. In: Nature (2015)

55. ArifWani, M., Bhat, F.A., Afzal, S., Khan, A.I.: Advances in Deep Learning. In: Book, JanuszKacprzyk, Polish Academy of Sciences, Warsaw, Poland (2020)

56. Voulodimos, A., Doulamis, N., Doulamis, A., Protopapadakis, E.: Deep learning for computer vision: a brief review. In: Comput. Intell. Neurosci. (2018)

57. Schuster, M., Paliwal, K.K.: Bidirectional recurrent neural networks. Signal Processing, IEEE Transactions (1997)

58. Hochreiter, S., Schmidhuber, J.: Long short-term memory. Neural computation (1997)

59. Balaha, H., Ali, H., Badawy, M.: Automatic recognition of handwritten Arabic characters: a comprehensive review. Neural Computing and Applications (2021)

60. Garcia, C.: Deep Neural Networks for Large Vocabulary Handwritten Text recognition. Paris-Sud University, Thesis (2016)

61. Alalshekmubarak, A., Smith, L.S.: On improving the classification capability of reservoir computing for arabic speech recognition. In: Wermter, S., et al. (eds.) ICANN 2014. LNCS, vol. 8681, pp. 225–232. Springer, Cham (2014). https://doi.org/10.1007/978-3-319-11179-7_29

62. Kassani, S.H., Kassani, P.H.: A comparative study of deep learning architectures on melanoma detection. Tissue and Cell 58 (2019)
63. Li, C., Wang, X., Liu, W., Latecki, L.J., Wang, B., Huang, J.: Weakly supervised mitosis detection in breast histopathology images using concentric loss. Medical Image Analysis **53** (2019)
64. Amari, R., Mares, A., Zrigui, M.: Arabic Speech Recognition Based on CNN-BLSTM Combination. SETIT (2022)

RingNet: Geometric Deep Representation Learning for 3D Multi-domain Protein Shape Retrieval

Hela Haj Mohamed[1]([✉])[iD], Samir Belaid[1], and Wady Naanaa[2]

[1] MARS Research Laboratory, DM Research Group, University of Sousse, Tunis, Tunisia
hajmohamedhela@yahoo.fr
[2] University of Tunis El Manar, Tunis, Tunisia

Abstract. Many applications use three-dimensional polygon meshes as geometric representation to achieve central tasks, such as 3D object retrieval and classification. However, implementing a deep learning approach dedicated to 3D meshes is a bit hard due to the complexity and irregularity of the mesh surface representation. In this paper, we propose a new geometric deep learning approach dedicated to representation learning, which applies convolutional operations on 3D meshes. In particular, we introduce a ring-unit convolutional operator that aggregates two graphs deduced from the mesh surface. Our network can learn highly discriminating features by avoiding complexity and irregularity problems.

We experimentally validated our approach on 3D shape classification tasks and the multi-domain protein shape retrieval challenge. A comparison with the state-of-the-art approaches proved the relevance of the learned features to the accuracy of 3D object classification and retrieval.

Keywords: 3D multi-domain protein shape retrieval · Geometric deep learning · Deep representation learning · Neural network

1 Introduction

Over the last decade, deep learning methods have achieved much success in several domains, such as natural language processing and computer vision. The basic idea is to apply several convolutions and pooling operations on an Euclidean plane with a regular grid-like image and video data. Thus, all these models cannot be directly applied to the non-Euclidean domain. Recently, many researchers have attempted to generalise these models from 2D to 3D Data, mainly through the development of 3D sensors and the construction of large-scale 3D models databases [3]. This new area, which is called *geometric deep learning*, has great potential in several applications. However, the main challenge is the 3D representation, which makes traditional deep learning operators impossible to be

N. T. Nguyen et al. (Eds.): ICCCI 2022, LNAI 13501, pp. 135–147, 2022.
https://doi.org/10.1007/978-3-031-16014-1_12

directly applied, essentially on the 3D non-Euclidean-structured data such as point clouds, graphs, and meshes. This type of data neither preserves the properties of the grid-structured data nor has a global parameterization or a common system of coordinates [1]. Despite the fact that point clouds are easy to be capture using any of the available technologies, their lack of structure makes the processing task a major challenge. In contrast, 3D meshes are one of the most popular representations for 3D shapes. This representation is comprised of a set of polygons called faces and a set of vertices associated with a connectivity list which describe how these vertices are connected to each other. Globally, meshes are non-Euclidean geometric data representations. Furthermore, a surface mesh contains important geometric shape features that are sensitive to the deformation, unlike a structural graph. Thus, in order to facilitate the 3D shape analysis, a deep learning model is required in order to enable learning invariant geometric features beyond the graph topology, as well as global and local geometric features.

Therefore, in this study, we propose an innovative graph neural network model called RingNet, to learn a mesh representation. RingNet integrates mesh-specific multi-modal features, such as a vertex-vertex relations, face-face relations, and other heterogeneous information, into mesh embedding. Hence, 1-Ring neighbourhood is regarded as the unit and two types of graph connections are defined, to solve the problem of complexity. These graphs have an inherent duality between topology and geometry in meshes. Moreover, multimodal features are used, depending on the graph type, convolution and aggregation of mesh. The proposed neural network is used in the tasks of multi-domain protein shape retrieval challenge on the Shrec database [15]. Our model successfully learns the final embedding of a 3D shape by training the graph convolution neural network and a max pooling layer is used to decode the protein embedding and predict class. Furthermore, it shows comparable results or superior to state-of-the-art approaches. Our contributions can be summarised as follows:

- We propose a new geometric deep learning model called RingNet that integrates mesh-specific multi-modal features with graph neural networks.
- In the model, we construct two types of graphs from a mesh surface to cope with topological and geometric features. Then, we build two graph convolutional operators to propagate these features along with the mesh data.
- We conduct extensive experiments to evaluate the performance of the proposed method, and compare the model results with several state-of-the-art methods.

2   Related Works

Learning a 3D shape representation, from a collection of 3D mesh data, as hand-craft descriptors, has been extensively studied [9,11]. Other works, fed these extracted shape features into traditional machine learning, or deep learning [1,12]. Recently, the geometric deep learning approach has attempted to propose deep descriptors of 3D shapes by generalizing deep neural networks. These works can be summarised according to the nature of the data and on how to perform the main DL operations, such as convolutions. Essentially, we distinguish three categories of methods:

Point-Based Methods: The well-known method that uses the point cloud as an input is *PointNet* [20], where each point is represented using the (x, y, z) coordinates. The model solves data irregularity thanks to three main modules: an STN module (Spatial Transformer Network), an RNN module and a simple symmetric function that aggregates all the information from each point in the point cloud. While it ignores the local information of points, PointNet proved to be robust against partial data and input perturbation. Despite the competitive results, many models are proposed to address its weakness in capturing the detailed fine-grained patterns. Among these methods, we cite PointNet++ [21] that successfully captures more features. However, this method requires a high computational time.

Graph-Based Methods: Among these methods, we cite the Spectral CNN (SCNN) that introduces the notion of spectral convolution on graph-structured data [4]. Despite its innovation aspect, SCNN model has serious limitations due to being basis dependent and computationally expensive. Several works proposed to solve these issues by proposing new filters [6]. Otherwise, GNNs [22] is first proposed to generalise the notion of spatial filtering on graphs. GNNs are composed of multiple layers where each layer is a linear combination of graphs. Also, a nonlinear function, applied to all the nodes of the graph, and a pooling operation can be employed on graph-structured data. Several GNN based methods have been proposed, where the difference resides in how the convolution and the aggregation of the learned features are performed.

Mesh-Based Methods: The first method that opened the door for innovation in extending CNN paradigm to triangular meshes is Geodesic CNN [16]. The main idea of this approach is to construct local patches in local polar coordinates and apply geodesic convolution. However, this framework suffers from multiple drawbacks, such as its sensitivity to the irregularity of triangulated mesh, its radius measure and its long computational time. To overcome some of these limitations, several methods are proposed such as Anisotropic CNN (ACNN) and MoNet [18]. Recently, PD-MeshNet [17] performs attention-based feature aggregation and implementing a task-driven pooling operation specific to 3D mesh. While, CurvaNet [13] integrates differential geometry with graph neural networks to learn direction sensitive geometric shape features at each vertex on a mesh surface.

Obviously, all these methods consider the input mesh as a point set or a simple graph and ignore its specific geometric properties. Other methods are applied to deep learning approaches on mesh structures independently of their local topology. In this paper, we propose a method that benefits from the stengths of all types of approaches. In fact, we extend a primal framework drawn from the graph-neural-network literature to triangle meshes, and define convolutions on two types of graph constructed from an input mesh. Our method can learn highly discriminating features for the ring-unit structure (points and faces) of a 3D mesh as input, and dynamically aggregates them using a convexity aware mechanism.

3   RingNet Neural Network

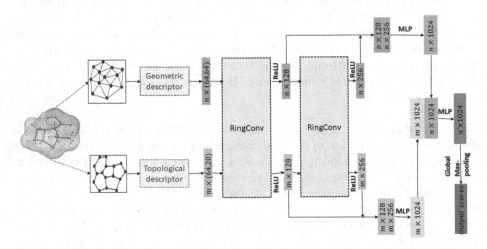

Fig. 1. The overall pipeline of our model. The input is a graph built from the target mesh surface.

In this section, we proceed by introducing our proposed approach, where an overview of the model architecture is depicted in Fig. 1. Our contribution is a novel geometric deep learning network called RingNet to address the challenge posed by the 3D mesh surface. Our model consists of two graph convolution layers and a fusion layer. Each convolution layer aims to learn the deep representation associated with each graph unit. While the fusion layer integrates geometry and topological features with a graph neural network and calculates the final mesh representation.

Given an input 3D mesh $\mathcal{M}$, our model builds a primal and a dual graph, denoted by $\mathcal{G}$ and $\mathcal{T}$ respectively. The mesh $\mathcal{M}$ is comprised of a set $\mathcal{V}$ of vertices that represent points in $\mathbb{R}^3$ together with a set $\mathcal{F}$ of faces, each defined by three vertices at its corners.

Many related works proceed to build a graph $\mathcal{G}$ over the mesh by omitting the coordinates of the vertices while preserving the edges [17]. In a different way, we consider $\mathcal{G}$ as **the Geometric-primal Graph** of the input mesh. It is a weighted and undirected graph having a node for each vertex $v_i \in \mathcal{V}$, defined by their corresponding coordinates, and an edge between two adjacent vertices if they belong to the same face. Let us denote by $\mathcal{N}_i$ the neighbours of vertex v_i. For each mesh vertices, we assign, to the corresponding vertex, the feature defined as its unit normal vector. Each edge e_{ij} is weighted by the distance between incident vertices v_i and v_j. Formally, we define the primal graph $\mathcal{G} = (V, E, W)$ as follows:

- $V \in \mathbb{R}^3$ is the vertices set where each vertex v_i is defined by its spatial coordinates (x, y, z).
- $E \in V \times V$ is the edge set.
- $X \in \mathbb{R}^{n \times |V|}$ is a matrix of node features defined by the unit normal vector of each vertex.
- $W = \in \mathbb{R}^{n \times |n|}$ is the adjacency matrix where $W_{i,j} = \|v_i - v_j\|$ if $(v_i, v_j) \in E$.

Furthermore, we define **the Signed-dual Graph** of a mesh as a graph having a node for each face $f_i \in \mathcal{M}$, and an edge connecting two nodes, where the corresponding mesh faces share a common edge face in $\mathcal{M}$. We assign to each node of the dual graph the same type of geometric features as in [10]. In particular, we use the spatial features defined by the unit normal vector at the centre of the corresponding face and the corner vectors. In addition, each edge shared by two adjacent faces is weighted by the dihedral angle between their associated normal vectors.

Formally, we define the dual graph $\mathcal{T} = (F, E', W')$ as follows:

- $F \subseteq \mathbb{R}^3$, where each face $f_i \in F$ is defined by its geometric centre.
- $E' \in F \times F$ is the edge set.
- $X \in \mathbb{R}^{m \times |F|}$ is a matrix of node features defined by the unit normal vector of each face and its corner vectors.
- $W' \in \mathbb{R}^{m \times |m|}$ is the adjacency matrix, where $W'_{i,j}$ is set to $\theta_{i,j}$, the dihedral angle if $(f_i, fj) \in E'$.

By construction, $\mathcal{T}$ is topologically the dual of $\mathcal{G}$. The advantage of the dual graph is that it allows defining a convexity aware model by using dihedral angle as hand-craft features for convolution operations. This can be easily interpreted in terms of deep representation learning of the mesh faces.

3.1 Descriptors Calculation

After building the pair of primal and dual graphs from the input 3D mesh, outputs are fed into two blocks, called "Geometric descriptor" and "Topological descriptor", to generate their initial geometric and topological features. As the geometric descriptor is expected to be relevant to the spatial and local geometric information of the primal graph, the topological one is relevant to the spatial and local information of the dual graph. Initially, a simple linear layer, similar to the methods based on point cloud, is applied. We define the geometric descriptor as a pair of spatial and geometric features of primal graph nodes. Therefore, the descriptor can be written equivalently as:

$$\mathbf{X}_v^{(0)} = (h_\Theta (V), h_\Theta (\mathbf{X})),\tag{1}$$

where $\mathbf{V}$ and $\mathbf{X}$ are respectively the node set and the node features of the primal graph $\mathcal{G}$, and h_Θ is a multilayer perceptron.

Since node features in the dual graph are defined by the unit normal vector of each face and its corner vectors, we propose to combine these features in a single matrix and then extract meaningful features. In this block, we simply perform data clustering by using a semi non-negative matrix factorisation method. Our choice is based on the fact that $Semi-$NMF offers a low-dimensional represen-tation of data points which leads itself to a convenient clustering interpretation. In fact, given the dual graph features $X \in \mathbb{R}^{m \times |F|}$, with m being the dimension of the data and $|F|$ being the number of nodes, the objective of $Semi-$NMF is to learn powerful new data representation by the following matrix factorisation

$$X \approx UH$$

where $U \in \mathbb{R}^{m \times k}$ is a matrix whose columns form a basis of $\mathbb{R}^k$ and $H \in \mathbb{R}^{k \times |F|}$ are the new representations of the data in the new basis. Then, we use matrix H as the new topological features. We define, therefore, the topological descriptor of $\mathcal{T}$ as a pair of spatial features calculated by a simple linear layer and H. The descriptor is defined as follows:

$$\mathbf{X}_f^{(0)} = (h_\Theta(F), H(X)), \tag{2}$$

where F and X are respectively nodes set and node features of the dual graph $\mathcal{T}$, and h_Θ is a multilayer perceptron.

3.2 RingNet Layer

After calculation the topological and geometric descriptors, we perform the con-volution operation by using the method of [7] and [8], which were previously applied only to graphs from standard graph benchmark datasets. Figure 2 illus-trates the design of the convolution layer that consists in applying two convolu-tion operations simultaneously on the dual and on the primal graph.

Geometric Aware Topology Adaptive Graph Convolutional Operator: In particular, the primal convolutional layer is a modified version of the topology adaptive graph convolutional network (TAGCN) consistent with convolution as defined in the graph signal processing. TAGCN offers implement in the spec-trum domain unifying the graph CNN in both the spectrum and the vertex domain. In fact, it rearchitects the classic CNN by designing a set of fixed-size learnable filters and shows that these filters are adaptive to the topology of the graph. The topology adaptive graph convolution network (TAGCN) uses the definition of graph convolution to form a graph convolutional layer for the classification of graph signals [8]. This method only requires finding the coeffi-cients of a polynomial in A and the adjacency matrix of the underlying graph.

Through experiments, it has been shown that the needed K for good performances is low at around $K = 2$. The TAGConv operator is defined by:

$$\mathbf{X}_v^{(l+1)} = \sum_{k=0}^{K} \left(\mathbf{D}^{-1/2}\mathbf{A}\mathbf{D}^{-1/2}\right)^k \mathbf{X}_v^{(l)}\mathbf{\Theta}_k^{(l)}, \tag{3}$$

where $\mathbf{A}$ is the normalised adjacency matrix representing edge weights, $\mathbf{D} = diag(d)$, with the ith components being $d(i) = \sum_j A_{i,j}$, $\mathbf{\Theta}^{(l)}$ is the trainable weight matrix and K is the degree of the graph polynomial filter and a hyperparameter of the model.

To make the operator (3) geometric aware, we adopt the Multi-layer perceptron (MLP) to combine the TAGConv output features with the spatial features of the primal graph $\mathcal{G}$. Our idea is to define the convolution by a geometric features propagation in the vertex domain as well as in the spectral domain. The modified operator is defined by the following equation:

$$\mathbf{X}_v^{(l+1)} = h_{\mathbf{\Theta}}\left(\sum_{k=0}^{K} \left(\mathbf{D}^{-1/2}\mathbf{A}\mathbf{D}^{-1/2}\right)^k \mathbf{X}_v^{(l)}\mathbf{\Theta}_k^{(l)}, \mathbf{P}_v^{(l)}\right), \tag{4}$$

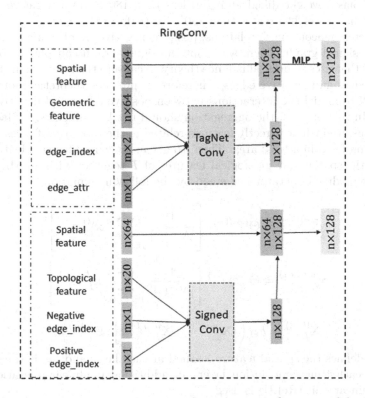

Fig. 2. The inner structure of the RingConv layer: inputs and outputs of the geometric aware topology adaptive graph convolutional operator are coloured in red, while inputs and outputs of the convexity aware Signed Graph Convolutional operator are coloured in blue. (Color figure online)

where P defines the spatial feature learned at each layer and h_Θ is the MLP.

Our propagate operator is adaptive to the graph topology thanks to the TAGCN filter that scans the graph. These properties lead to a noticeable performance advantage on local feature extraction, weight sharing as well as for classification accuracy.

Convexity Aware Signed Graph Convolutional Operator: Similarly, the dual convolution consists of a graph convolution operator designed to expand the receptive face features by aggregating information of neighbouring faces. In fact, this block contains two parts: aggregation of topological features and combination of spatial and topological features. The key property of the approach is that the aggregation is further weighted through attention coefficients defined on the edges as the convexity information. For this reason, we suppose that our dual graph can be represented as a signed graph having both positive and negative links. The semantic meaning of these links are defined based on the edges weights. By definition a polygon is convex if all the interior angles are less than 180°, while a concave polygon is a polygon that has at least one interior angle greater than 180°. Therefore, we define a positive link between two faces as the edge that has a weight(dihedral angle) less than 180°, and a negative link the edge that has a weight greater than 180°. To perform the aggregation, we first use the heterogeneous mesh relations, positive/negative, to obtain a face-to-face convexity signed graph. Then, we adopt the signed graph convolution operator SGCN [7] that uses structural balance theory to capture the interactions between positive edges and negative edges. Therefore, it provides theoretical foundation for SGCN to model the interactions between positive edges and negative edges (Fig. 3). In this process, the aggregation should not be influenced by face locations. Thus, we include directly features related to the topology of faces because we focus on faces in a local area. Then, to get more comprehensive features, we combine the spatial and topological features of $\mathcal{T}$ together with an MLP layer. Thus, the modified operator is defined by the following equation:

$$
\begin{aligned}
\mathbf{x}_i^{\mathrm{pos}(l+1)} &= \Theta^{\mathrm{pos}(l+1)} \left[\frac{1}{|\mathcal{N}^+(i)|} \sum_{j \in \mathcal{N}^+(i)} \mathbf{x}_j^{(l)}, \mathbf{x}_i^{(l)} \right] \\
\mathbf{x}_i^{\mathrm{neg}(l+1)} &= \Theta^{\mathrm{neg}(l+1)} \left[\frac{1}{|\mathcal{N}^-(i)|} \sum_{j \in \mathcal{N}^-(i)} \mathbf{x}_j^{(l)}, \mathbf{x}_i^{(l)} \right]
\end{aligned}
\tag{5}
$$

$$
\mathbf{X}_f^{(l+1)} = h_\Theta \left(\left[\mathbf{X}_f^{pos(l+1)}, \mathbf{X}_f^{neg(l+1)} \right], \mathbf{P}_f^{(l+1)} \right),
\tag{6}
$$

where P defines the spatial feature learned at each layer and h_Θ is the MLP.

After each Ring convolution layer, an additional nonlinear operation, e.g., rectified linear unit (ReLU) is used.

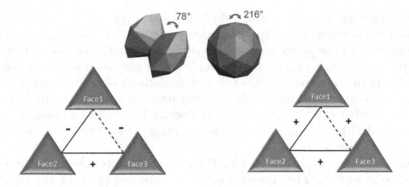

Fig. 3. Face-face convexity signed relations.

3.3 Fusion Layer

The final mesh representation is obtained in the last layer of our neural network, by aggregating topological and geometric features. In fact, in the fusion layer, we concatenate all output feature channels. Then, another MLP is applied to further fuse the neighbouring nodes and generate global feature, which is used for further tasks. Formally, we define the fusion operator as:

$$\mathbf{Z} = h_{\Theta}\left(\mathbf{X}_v, \mathbf{X}_f\right), \tag{7}$$

where $\mathbf{X}_v$ is the final geometric feature for the primal graph $\mathcal{G}$ and $\mathbf{X}_f$ is the final geometric feature for the dual graph $\mathcal{T}$ defined respectively as:
$\mathbf{X}_v = \gamma_{\Theta}\left[\mathbf{X}_v^{(1)} \cdots \mathbf{X}_v^{(L)}\right]$ and $\mathbf{X}_f = \gamma_{\Theta}\left[\mathbf{X}_f^{(1)} \cdots \mathbf{X}_f^{(L)}\right]$. We denote by h_{Θ} and γ_{Θ} neural networks (MLP) and L is the final layer.

The key property of our approach is that it allows to capture structures of a wider field around each ring unit (vertex and face neighbourhoods).

4 Experimental Results

4.1 Dataset and Metrics

We evaluated our model on the SHREC 2020 (Track on multi-domain protein shape retrieval) [15]. The aim of this track is to assess the performance of shape retrieval algorithms on a dataset of related multi-domain protein surfaces. Proteins are complex macro-molecular molecules constituted of hundreds to millions of atoms. They are usually classified according to their function in the cellular environment. Otherwise, they can be described as non-rigid surfaces representing their solvent-excluded surface as defined by Connoly [5]. Detecting partial similarities and/or dissimilarities between a large number of related protein surfaces is of main importance in drug discovery pipelines, diverse drug event prediction and in the characterisation of molecular processes and diseases.

The Shrec database is a set of 588 mesh surfaces (provided as off files) representing the conformational space of seven proteins. The contest is focused on the evaluation of the performance in the retrieval of multi-domain protein surfaces from 26 orthologous proteins in addition to the usual evaluation of the performance in the retrieval of the different conformers of a given protein.

For fair comparisons, we use the common retrieval evaluation criteria as the Nearest Neighbour (NN), First Tier (T1), Second Tier (T2), and Mean average Precision (MAP). The value of these metrics ranges from 0 to 1, and the higher value means good performance.

Our model was implemented with Python and PyTorch-geometric and was trained from scratch. The cross-entropy was minimised by using the standard SGD with a momentum 0.9 and a weight decay 1e−4. The model was trained with a GeForce GTX1070 GPU with batch size 6 and initial learning rate 0.005. The training time was about 1 h while the calculation of descriptors took on average 45 ms per mesh sample. The average comparison time between two descriptors was negligible (0.001 ms on an Intel Core i7- 6700 K CPU).

4.2 3D Protein Shape Classification

The proposed neural network was trained on a classification task aiming to assign each 3D protein to each corresponding class. In fact, the latent representation of the mesh was passed to a readout operation with learnable parameters to perform graph-level predictions. This is similar to the conventional CNN where we applied max-pooling to reduce the spatial resolution. In this context, we apply a max-pooling layer to the global features (see Sect. 3.3) as the classifier, and add a dropout layer with drop probability of 0.5 before the last fully-connected layer.

To analyse the design of our model layers and prove their effectiveness, we conducted several experiments, which compare the classification results while varying architecture. For the first experiment, we just used the primal graph G as input and then we maintained just the convolution and aggregation of geometric features. The modified version is labelled as "VertexNet" in Table 1, since $\mathcal{G}$ is constructed based on the vertex unit. In the same way, we conducted the second experiment based on the dual graph $\mathcal{T}$ and its topological features learned throughout all layers. Since $\mathcal{T}$ is constructed based on the face unit, we labelled this model as "FaceNet" in Table 1. Finally, we compare accuracy results of these networks with the RingNet accuracy in both protein level classification and species level classification.

Table 1 shows the experimental results of classification on the Shrec database. It is shown that our RingNet achieved satisfying performance and improved compared with its altered versions.

We also explored the effectiveness of different readout layers in this approach, and compared them in Table 2. The experimental results showed that the global max-pooling layers perform better for features aggregating.

Table 1. Classification results with primal graph features (VertexNet), dual graph features (FaceNet) and fusion model(RingNet) on Shrec.

Network	Species-level accuracy (%)	Protein-level accuracy (%)
VertexNet	0.356	0.518
FaceNet	0.298	0.493
RingNet	**0.880**	**1.000**

Table 2. Classification results with different readout layer on Shrec.

Readout layer	Species-level accuracy (%)	Protein-level accuracy (%)
Global AveragePool	0.691	0.722
Global MaxPool	**0.880**	**1.000**

4.3 3D Protein Shape Retrieval

In the retrieval task, the global features of each 3D protein shape are used to measure their dissimilarity using the L2 distance metric. Small distance values indicate that these latter are in the same class. Then, we evaluated the result with mean average precision (mAP)metric. The results are reported in Tables 3 and 4, respectively. For comparison, we take the evaluations directly from [15], who compare against: WKS [2] (The wave kernel signature), GraphCNN [23] (A graph-cnn for 3d point cloud classification), 3DZD/3DZM [14] (The 3D Zernike descriptors) and finally HAPPS [19] (A novel hybrid augmented point pair signature). It is obvious that our method significantly outperforms other methods essentially the WKS [15] and GraphCNN [15] in the overall metrics (MAP) at the protein level.

The higher accuracy of our model comes from the power of its RingConv layers to learn the geometric and topological features of the input mesh structure. Therefore, it can capture detailed features of each corresponding graph and conduct the 3D protein shape representation well.

Table 3. Evaluation metrics at the protein level. NN, T1, T2, MAP. For each metric, the highest value is in bold.

Method	NN	T1	T2	MAP
WKS/SGWKS	0.985	**0.818**	0.438	0.848
3DZD/3DZM	0.980	0.789	0.436	0.823
GraphCNN	0.770	0.310	0.243	0.339
HAPPS	0.983	0.746	0.420	0.779
RingNet	**1.000**	0.816	**0.468**	**0.868**

Table 4. Evaluation metrics at the species level. NN, T2, MAP. For each metric, the highest value is in bold.

Method	NN	T1	T2	MAP
WKS/SGWKS	0.844	0.460	0.298	0.508
3DZD/3DZM	0.825	0.419	0.277	0.470
GraphCNN	0.499	0.181	0.122	0.186
HAPPS	0.768	0.400	0.269	0.430
RingNet	**0.961**	**0.540**	**0.355**	**0.650**

5   Conclusion

This paper proposes a geometric deep learning model named RingNet, which can learn 3D shape representation directly from the mesh data and solve its complexity and irregularity problem. The model is novel over existing works in integrating multi-modal features with graph neural networks by considering the Ring structure as the unit and splitting features into geometric and topological features. We have designed two novel convolutional operators: geometric aware topology adaptive graph convolutional operator and Convexity Aware Signed Graph Convolutional operator, to propagate features along the mesh surface. We have also designed a fusion operator to learn the high-level features of the input 3D mesh. Preliminary results showed that the RingNet model is promising and achieves state-of-the-art results approaches in 3D protein shape classification and retrieval tasks. We believe that further exploring other features, associated with physio-chemical properties of protein surfaces, is interesting for future work.

References

1. Ahmed, E., et al.: A survey on deep learning advances on different 3D data representations. arXiv preprint arXiv:1808.01462 (2018)
2. Aubry, M., Schlickewei, U., Cremers, D.: The wave kernel signature: a quantum mechanical approach to shape analysis. In: 2011 IEEE International Conference on Computer Vision Workshops (ICCV workshops), pp. 1626–1633. IEEE (2011)
3. Bronstein, M.M., Bruna, J., Cohen, T., Veličković, P.: Geometric deep learning: Grids, groups, graphs, geodesics, and gauges. arXiv preprint arXiv:2104.13478 (2021)
4. Bruna, J., Zaremba, W., Szlam, A., LeCun, Y.: Spectral networks and locally connected networks on graphs. arXiv preprint arXiv:1312.6203 (2013)
5. Connolly, M.L.: Solvent-accessible surfaces of proteins and nucleic acids. Science **221**(4612), 709–713 (1983)
6. Defferrard, M., Bresson, X., Vandergheynst, P.: Convolutional neural networks on graphs with fast localized spectral filtering. Adv. Neural. Inf. Process. Syst. **29**, 3844–3852 (2016)
7. Derr, T., Ma, Y., Tang, J.: Signed graph convolutional networks. In: 2018 IEEE International Conference on Data Mining (ICDM), pp. 929–934. IEEE (2018)

8. Du, J., Zhang, S., Wu, G., Moura, J.M., Kar, S.: Topology adaptive graph convolutional networks. arXiv preprint arXiv:1710.10370 (2017)
9. Fang, Y., et al.: 3D deep shape descriptor. In: Proceedings of the IEEE Conference on Computer Vision and Pattern Recognition, pp. 2319–2328 (2015)
10. Feng, Y., Feng, Y., You, H., Zhao, X., Gao, Y.: MeshNet: mesh neural network for 3D shape representation. In: Proceedings of the AAAI Conference on Artificial Intelligence, vol. 33, pp. 8279–8286 (2019)
11. HajMohamed, H., Belaid, S., Naanaa, W., Romdhane, L.B.: Local commute-time guided MDS for 3D non-rigid object retrieval. Appl. Intell. **48**(9), 2873–2883 (2018)
12. HajMohamed, H., Belaid, S., Naanaa, W., Romdhane, L.B.: Deep sparse dictionary-based representation for 3D non-rigid shape retrieval. In: Proceedings of the 36th Annual ACM Symposium on Applied Computing, pp. 1070–1077 (2021)
13. He, W., Jiang, Z., Zhang, C., Sainju, A.M.: CurvaNet: geometric deep learning based on directional curvature for 3D shape analysis. In: Proceedings of the 26th ACM SIGKDD International Conference on Knowledge Discovery and Data Mining, pp. 2214–2224 (2020)
14. Kihara, D., Sael, L., Chikhi, R., Esquivel-Rodriguez, J.: Molecular surface representation using 3D Zernike descriptors for protein shape comparison and docking. Curr. Protein Pept. Sci. **12**(6), 520–530 (2011)
15. Langenfeld, F., et al.: Shrec 2020: multi-domain protein shape retrieval challenge. Comput. Graph. **91**, 189–198 (2020)
16. Masci, J., Boscaini, D., Bronstein, M., Vandergheynst, P.: Geodesic convolutional neural networks on Riemannian manifolds. In: Proceedings of the IEEE International Conference on Computer Vision Workshops, pp. 37–45 (2015)
17. Milano, F., Loquercio, A., Rosinol, A., Scaramuzza, D., Carlone, L.: Primal-dual mesh convolutional neural networks. arXiv preprint arXiv:2010.12455 (2020)
18. Monti, F., Boscaini, D., Masci, J., Rodola, E., Svoboda, J., Bronstein, M.M.: Geometric deep learning on graphs and manifolds using mixture model CNNs. In: Proceedings of the IEEE Conference on Computer Vision and Pattern Recognition, pp. 5115–5124 (2017)
19. Otu, E., Zwiggelaar, R., Hunter, D., Liu, Y.: Nonrigid 3D shape retrieval with HAPPS: a novel hybrid augmented point pair signature. In: 2019 International Conference on Computational Science and Computational Intelligence (CSCI), pp. 662–668. IEEE (2019)
20. Qi, C.R., Su, H., Mo, K., Guibas, L.J.: PointNet: deep learning on point sets for 3D classification and segmentation. In: Proceedings of the IEEE Conference on Computer Vision and Pattern Recognition, pp. 652–660 (2017)
21. Qi, C.R., Yi, L., Su, H., Guibas, L.J.: Pointnet++: deep hierarchical feature learning on point sets in a metric space. arXiv preprint arXiv:1706.02413 (2017)
22. Scarselli, F., Gori, M., Tsoi, A.C., Hagenbuchner, M., Monfardini, G.: The graph neural network model. IEEE Trans. Neural Netw. **20**(1), 61–80 (2008)
23. Zhang, Y., Rabbat, M.: A graph-CNN for 3D point cloud classification. In: 2018 IEEE International Conference on Acoustics, Speech and Signal Processing (ICASSP), pp. 6279–6283. IEEE (2018)

Patch Selection for Melanoma Classification

Guillaume Lachaud$^{(\boxtimes)}$, Patricia Conde-Cespedes, and Maria Trocan

ISEP - Institut Supérieur d'Électronique de Paris.,
10 rue de Vanves, Issy les Moulineaux 92130, France
{glachaud,pconde,maria.trocan}@isep.fr

Abstract. In medical image processing, the most important information is often located on small parts of the image. Patch-based approaches aim at using only the most relevant parts of the image. Finding ways to automatically select the patches is a challenge. In this paper, we investigate two criteria to choose patches: entropy and a spectral similarity criterion. We perform experiments at different levels of patch size. We train a Convolutional Neural Network on the subsets of patches and analyze the training time. We find that, in addition to requiring less preprocessing time, the classifiers trained on the datasets of patches selected based on entropy converge faster than on those selected based on the spectral similarity criterion and, furthermore, lead to higher accuracy. Moreover, patches of high entropy lead to faster convergence and better accuracy than patches of low entropy.

Keywords: Entropy · Texture spectral similarity criterion ·
Melanoma · Patch-based classification · ResNet

1 Introduction

With the development of better machine learning methods driven by deep learning, there have been many successful applications of neural networks in medical image processing, such as biomedical image segmentation or cancer diagnosis [1]. This is the case in cancer diagnosis and prognosis, with applications in breast cancer [22], lung cancer [14] and skin cancer [2].

Medical images can be widely different depending on their source, such as CT (Computed Tomography) scans, MRI (Magnetic Resonance Imaging) images, dermoscopy, etc. While classification is usually performed on the whole images, medical images can have extremely high resolution, e.g. gigapixels for skin tissue images, which makes it more time efficient to train on subsets or patches of images. Additionally, it can enhance a classifier performance in some settings. For example, in [11], the authors argue that cancer subtypes are distinguished at the image patch scale. Patch-based classification is also used in [18] for breast histology. More applications of patch-based applications are introduced in [17,25].

N. T. Nguyen et al. (Eds.): ICCCI 2022, LNAI 13501, pp. 148–159, 2022.
https://doi.org/10.1007/978-3-031-16014-1_13

A judicious choice of patches reduces the importance of noise and focuses on the most important parts of the image. Two approaches of selecting the patches used for classification are to score the patches individually based on a given metric, or to compare each patch with the other patches of an image and rank the similarity between the patches. In the first approach, the patches can be scored using entropy, while the second approach relies on a similarity measure between images.

On one hand, entropy is used in information theory as a way to quantify the level of information of an object. Higher entropy means that there is more information in the object. For instance, a random noise image has high entropy while a unicolored one has very low entropy. Entropy plays an important role in data compression where it provides the lower bound on the storage required to compress an object without loss of information [19]. Entropy can also be used for object reconstruction using the principle of maximum entropy, which aims at selecting the most uniform probability distribution amongst multiple candidate distributions. It can be used for image reconstruction where the candidates are the set of missing pixels [20]. It applies to text data as well [15]. Entropy can also be used in image texture analysis [26] and texture synthesis. Selecting patches using entropy was explored in [13].

On the other hand, the Mean Exhaustive Minimum Distance (MEMD) is a criterion that was introduced in [8] to compare two images by trying to find the best pairing of pixels from the first and the second image; the criterion score then indicates how similar the images are. A low score indicates that the images are similar, and a high score that the image are different. This can be extended to comparison between a patch and several patches by averaging the scores.

In this paper we study the training time and the accuracy of these two criteria for patch-based binary classification. The data we use comes from the ISIC (International Skin Imaging Collaboration) archive. [1] This consortium was created to improve the fight against skin melanoma cancer by improving computer-aided diagnosis. The consortium has held an annual challenge since 2016 [6]. Starting from 2019, the challenges are centered around dermoscopic image multi-class classification. The best team on the 2019 challenge [4], investigated patch-based classification on the HAM10000 dataset [21], where information from several patches is combined via an attention-based mechanism.

The paper is divided as follows. In Sect. 2 we present the dataset and the preprocessing we perform on the data. We also introduce the entropy and MEMD criterion that we use in our experiments. In Sect. 3 we present the results of our experiments and we conclude the paper in Sect. 4.

2 Materials and Methods

In this section we describe the dataset, the criteria of entropy and Mean-Exhaustive Minimum Distance (MEMD) we use, and the network architecture that is trained on the data.

---

[1] The data is publicly available at https://www.isic-archive.com.

2.1 Dataset Description and Preprocessing

The ISIC archive database comprises skin lesion images associated with a label indicating the status of the lesion. The image resolution is arbitrary. The archive provides an API to retrieve the images and their metadata, as well as the mask of the region of interest when an expert has created one. The total number of patches created is presented in Table 1. We perform binary classification on patches of the images. Our target variable is a categorical variable with two possible values: *benign*, or *malignant*.

The preprocessing steps are:

1. We download images from the ISIC archive, as well as the masks that are annotations from experts and indicate the lesion location.
2. All the malignant images with a mask are selected. The same number of benign images is sampled out of all the benign images.
3. The region of interest is divided in square patches of width 32, 64, 128 and 256. The region of interest is defined by the downloaded masks.
4. The entropy of each patch is computed, and we use these values to extract a subset of patches. This is explained in Sect. 2.2.
5. For each image, we compute a spectral measure of similarity between a patch and all the other patches of the image; we use this measure to extract a subset of patches. The details are in Sect. 2.3.
6. Finally, a classifier is trained on all the datasets we have created in the two previous steps.

Table 1. Number of patches for each patch size

Patch size	Number of patches
32×32	$4,889,969$
64×64	$1,173,052$
128×128	$270,821$
256×256	$58,253$

We divide the images in three groups: 90% of the images are in the train set, with 20% of the train set reserved for validation; the remaining 10% constitutes the test set.

2.2 Entropy

We use the Shannon entropy [19]. It is defined by the formula

$$H = \sum_{k=1}^{M} p_k \log(p_k) \tag{1}$$

where we sum across all the pixel intensities, i.e. from 0 to $M = 255$. p_k is the probability a pixel in the image is at intensity k. The entropy ranges from 0 to $\log_2(255) \approx 8$. Because there is no consensus on how to compute the entropy for multi channel images, we convert our RGB images to grayscale. The conversion process is defined in the ITU-R Recommendation BT.601-2.

Using the entropy, we extract two datasets for each patch size:

- a *low* dataset, whose patches are all the patches that rank below the 15-th and the 30-th quantile of entropy with respect to the other patches of the same image.
- a *high* dataset, with entropy above the 85-th · and the 70-th quantile.

2.3   Mean Exhaustive Minimum Distance (MEMD) Criterion

The first methods of similarity measure usually consisted in computing certain features on a given image, such as the Haralick features [7], and then comparing the features obtained for different images. More recent techniques dealing with the structural similarity in textures have been proposed in [27] and [16]. Handling color or hyperspectral images is often done using histograms [24], but histograms require a large amount of data to get good estimates of the spectral distribution. A new criterion to evaluate the similarity of two images was proposed in [8]. This approach does not require histograms and generalizes to any number of channels.

Following the notation from [9], let A and B be two images, which can have multiple channels. Let $M = \min(\#A, \#B)$, with $\#A$ and $\#B$ the number of pixels in A and B. Let $\langle A \rangle$ be the set of pairs of coordinates for the pixels of A, and U the unprocessed pairs of coordinates of pixels of B. Let ρ be the distance induced by a vector metric. $A_{i,j}$ denotes the pixel of A at coordinates (i, j); the channels dimension is implied. Similarly, $B_{k,l}$ is the pixel of B at coordinates (k, l). The MEMD criterion ζ is defined by Eq. 2.

$$\zeta(A, B) = \frac{1}{M} \sum_{(i,j) \in \langle A \rangle} \min_{(k,l) \in U} \{\rho(A_{i,j}, B_{k,l})\} \tag{2}$$

The lower the score is, the more similar images A and B are. Inversely, the higher the score, the higher the difference between the two images. The score can take values between 0 and 255. A score of 0 happens when we compare one image to itself; a score of 255 happens when we compare a white image with a black one.

To improve the computation time, [9] suggested that the pixels of both the images be sorted with respect to the chosen norm. Finding the minimum distance between the pixels of the two images then comes down to choosing the closest unprocessed neighbour in the sorted array. In the special case where A and B are of the same size, we can simply match the first element of the sorted pixels of A with the first of element of the sorted pixels of B, and so on.

We compute the MEMD score of each patch with respect to all the other patches of the same image, and we average the scores. Figure 1 shows the distribution of the MEMD score at varying patch sizes. We observe two peaks.

The peak on the left corresponds to the patches that are representative of the overall image, and the peak on the right corresponds to the patches that are more unique. The reason why we only have two peaks is that the images of the lesion all share similar elements: a little bit of skin, the lesion, and some noise such as hair, a ruler, etc. The distinction between the lesion and the skin is quite drastic, meaning that few patches are going to be equally similar to skin and lesion. The variation in scores is in part due to the different number of patches per image. The more patches an image has, the less extreme the MEMD score of the patches will be. The patches with a score of 0 are from images that have only one patch. This happens for big patch sizes where the region of interest is too small to get more patches.

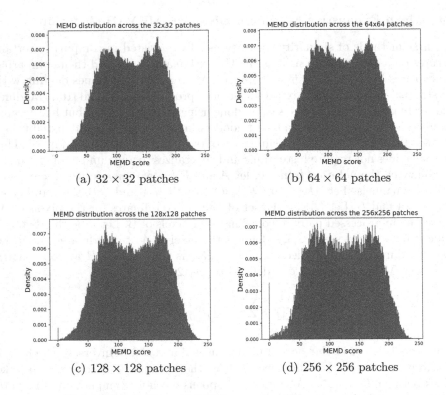

(a) 32 × 32 patches

(b) 64 × 64 patches

(c) 128 × 128 patches

(d) 256 × 256 patches

Fig. 1. Distribution of MEMD score for different patch sizes

Similarly to what was done in Sect. 2.2, we create datasets using the same quantiles for the MEMD score.

In the rest of the paper, we use the max norm for ρ, i.e. $\rho : x \mapsto \|x\|_\infty = \max_i |x_i|$, where x_i are the coordinates of x. The distance induced by the max norm is $(x, y) \mapsto \|x - y\|_\infty$. Because the sorting of the pixels is done based on the norm of a single pixel, and the min is computed using the distance between two pixels, the optimization via sorting is not compatible with pixels with multiple channels. Indeed, let $p_1 = [135, 18, 89]$, $p_2 = [130, 16, 86]$ and $p_3 = [12, 134, 1]$. If we sort the pixels by the max norm, we get $P = [p_2, p_3, p_1]$. Selecting the closest matching pixel using the proposed method in [9] would make us pair p_2 with p_3, which leads to $\zeta(p_2, p_3) = 118$. But p_2 and p_1 are clearly a better match, with $\zeta(p_2, p_1) = 5$. To alleviate the complications imposed by the multiple channels, we convert the images to grayscale before computing the MEMD score. Since the grayscale image has only one channel, the optimization via sorting works.

The computation of the average MEMD of all the patches of an image has $O(m^2)$ with respect to m, the number of patches in the image. There is a trade-off between space and time complexity, where vectorizing part of the process using higher order tensors allows for faster computation but requires more space.

2.4   Network Architecture

For the choice of classifier, we follow [23] and [3] who found that ResNet50 achieved the best results for the same task and dataset. ResNet50 [10] is a 50-layer convolutional neural network (CNN) that was proposed to alleviate the problem of vanishing and exploding gradients [5] by introducing the notion of *residual units*.

With enough computing resources, ResNets can have as many layers as we want, e.g. 101 or 152 layers. We use the 50-layer version, which we adapt to binary classification by removing the last layer and replacing it with a max pooling layer followed by a Dense layer and a *sigmoid* activation.

We use the Adam optimizer [12]. We set the learning rate to 0.001 and we use a *binary cross-entropy loss* for training.

We train the model for 10 epochs, each epoch representing a full pass through the train set. To mitigate overfitting, the training stops if the validation loss does not decrease after 3 consecutive epochs.

Additionally, we investigate combining predictions from several patches of an image to classify the image. We train a Resnet for 10 epochs and choose the weights that result in the best validation loss. To classify an image from the test set, we individually classify its patches and aggregate the results. Let $\mathcal{P}_i$ be the set of patches from an image I_i, $|\mathcal{P}_i|$ the number of patches selected from the image, f be the classifier that maps a patch to 0 for a benign patch and 1 for a malignant one. The prediction $\hat{y}$ is given by the Eq. 3.

$$\hat{y}_i = \begin{cases} 0 & \text{if } \left(\frac{1}{|\mathcal{P}|} \sum_{p \in \mathcal{P}_i} f(p) \right) < 0.5 \\ 1 & \text{otherwise} \end{cases} \tag{3}$$

3   Experimental Results

The experiments were performed with an Nvidia Titan XP GPU. The code is written in Python and Tensorflow. The Pillow library was used for computing the entropy.

To make our results robust against the random initialization of the model parameters, we train 10 instances of a ResNet50 per dataset. Results of the experiments with the entropy datasets are presented in Table 2, and those performed on the MEMD datasets are presented in Table 3. The low entropy dataset contains the 15% patches with the lowest entropy, and the high entropy dataset contains the 15% patches with the highest entropy. Correspondingly, the low MEMD dataset contains the 15% patches with the lowest MEMD score, and the high MEMD dataset contains the 15% patches with the highest MEMD score. Additional results for datasets with intermediate entropy are presented in [13].

Table 2. Quantiles of training time for datasets of different entropy and patch size

Patch size	Entropy	Quantile of training time (in seconds)		
		30	50 (median)	70
32	High	1350.7	2013.2	2781.4
32	Low	1534.9	2906.7	3078.5
64	High	291.0	382.9	441.9
64	Low	290.6	338.3	414.2
128	High	155.0	204.6	220.0
128	Low	204.8	255.0	255.4
256	High	142.4	152.2	189.7
256	Low	189.6	226.4	226.5

Regarding the entropy datasets, we observe a tendency of faster convergence for datasets with higher entropy compared to datasets with lower entropy. Lower entropy means that the distribution of pixel intensity concentrates on fewer pixels than it does for higher entropy. This concentration makes for smoother textures, which might be harder for the classifier to learn. Higher entropy datasets have more salient features that more discernible and thus more easily learnable by the network.

As for the MEMD datasets, the dataset composed of patches with higher score tends to converge faster than the dataset with lower score. This might be explainable by the fact that a low MEMD score means a high similarity of the patch with the rest of the image, while a high score indicates a distinctive spectral texture compared with the other patches of the same image. Thus, the higher score patches capture the more unique features of the lesion, while the lower score patches are more representative of the overall texture of the lesion. The high representativeness of a patch might extend to patches of low score from another image, while the unique features are probably different between images. Therefore, the dataset with high score is richer in more unique patches, which provide more information than the similar patches contained in the lower score dataset. This, in turn, makes the network training converge faster for the dataset with higher score patches.

Table 3. Quantiles of training time for datasets of varying MEMD score and patch size

patch_size	memd_score	Quantile of training time (in seconds)		
		30	50 (median)	70
32	High	3150.4	3254.8	3258.9
	Low	3256.4	3260.0	3260.9
64	High	465.3	495.1	527.0
	Low	564.4	691.9	986.3
128	High	241.5	281.9	387.9
	Low	256.6	357.7	373.1
256	High	189.7	245.2	264.4
	Low	215.4	226.7	275.2

These interpretations are borne out by the results of the experiments presented in Table 4. For the 128×128 patches, the accuracy does not improve when we select more patches: it stagnates around 50%. This indicates that this patch size is too small to properly discriminate the lesions. The problem is not about the number of patches but about the fact that small patches do not contain enough information to determine the status of the lesion. We believe that this situation holds also for even smaller patches, e.g. 32×32 or 64×64 patches. Conversely, for the case of 256×256 patches, we remark that using too few patches results in very low accuracy (around 25%); however, the accuracy increases considerably when we select more patches (30% of 15%), achieving 71% accuracy for patches of high entropy. This accuracy is similar to the 74% accuracy obtained by the authors of [3] when training on the whole region of interest with a ResNet50.

The lower accuracy for the low MEMD and low entropy datasets, compared with the high MEMD and entropy datasets, suggests that it is not sufficient to select more patches to reach a higher level of accuracy; it is also important to select appropriate patches (Fig. 3).

Figures 3 and 4 illustrate the role of MEMD and entropy in patch selection. The patch on the left of Fig. 3 is one of the patches with the lowest MEMD score for the image, while the patch on the right has one of the highest scores. Due to the fact that the masks cannot perfectly capture the lesion, there will always be some part of the skin that will be present in the mask. Since the skin has more uniform texture than the lesion, it is likely that patches of skin will have the lowest score. Similarly, the patches with low entropy will have more uniform features, while the patches with higher entropy will have more salient ones, as in Fig. 4.

Table 4. Test accuracy (in percentage) for the different datasets. For a given patch size, the test images are the same for each method.

Dataset	Low MEMD	High MEMD	Low entropy	High entropy
128 × 128, 15% patches	46.7	50.5	46.2	52.7
128 × 128, 30% patches	43.9	51.6	39.6	52.7
256 × 256, 15% patches	27.2	26.3	25.1	32.0
256 × 256, 30% patches	45.5	57.2	52.7	**71.0**

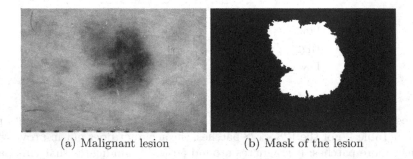

(a) Malignant lesion   (b) Mask of the lesion

Fig. 2. A malignant image and its mask

(a) Patch with low MEMD score   (b) Patch with high MEMD score

Fig. 3. Two different MEMD patches

The datasets extracted using the entropy converge faster than the datasets extracted with the MEMD criterion. We hypothesize that a likely explanation is that patches extracted with the entropy share similar distributions of pixels, albeit sometimes shifted. The entropy quantifies the distribution of pixel intensity: the higher the entropy, the closer the pixel distribution will be to the uniform distribution. Thus, the patches from entropy extracted datasets are sim-

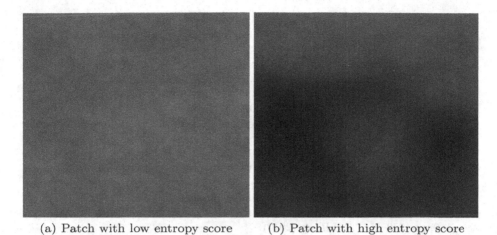

(a) Patch with low entropy score   (b) Patch with high entropy score

Fig. 4. Two different entropy patches

ilar across the images, and this similarity is learnable by the network. On the other hand, datasets extracted using the MEMD criterion do not provide any quantifiable information about the pixel distribution. Their score is only indicative of how representative the patch is with respect to the image. The network might thus be confronted with a wider variety of patches which lead to a longer training time.

4   Conclusion

We examined the role of entropy and the MEMD criteria on both CNN training time and classification efficiency for patch-based melanoma detection. The preprocessing is longer with the MEMD criterion because we have to compare patches two by two, whereas entropy requires a single computation per patch. We found that higher entropy leads to faster convergence than lower entropy; similarly, a higher MEMD score, which indicates that the patch does not resemble other patches from the same image, also leads to faster convergence. In terms of accuracy, the models trained on the higher entropy dataset or the higher MEMD are more performant than the models trained on the lower entropy or lower MEMD datasets. We also found that creating patch datasets using an absolute measure of information, such as entropy, makes the network train faster than when the datasets were created using a similarity measure. We also observed that patch size plays a significant role in the classifier accuracy, with small patches leading to poor results, regardless of the percentage of patches used.

References

1. Anwar, S.M., Majid, M., Qayyum, A., Awais, M., Alnowami, M., Khan, M.K.: Medical image analysis using convolutional neural networks: a review. J. Med. Syst. **42**(11), 1–13 (2018). https://doi.org/10.1007/s10916-018-1088-1

2. Esteva, A., et al.: Dermatologist-level classification of skin cancer with deep neural networks. Nature **542**(7639), 115–118 (2017). https://doi.org/10.1038/nature21056

3. Favole, F., Trocan, M., Yilmaz, E.: Melanoma detection using deep learning. In: Nguyen, N.T., Hoang, B.H., Huynh, C.P., Hwang, D., Trawiński, B., Vossen, G. (eds.) ICCCI 2020. LNCS (LNAI), vol. 12496, pp. 816–824. Springer, Cham (2020). https://doi.org/10.1007/978-3-030-63007-2_64

4. Gessert, N., Nielsen, M., Shaikh, M., Werner, R., Schlaefer, A.: Skin lesion classification using ensembles of multi-resolution EfficientNets with meta data. MethodsX **7**, 100864 (2020). https://doi.org/10.1016/j.mex.2020.100864

5. Glorot, X., Bengio, Y.: Understanding the difficulty of training deep feedforward neural networks. In: Teh, Y.W., Titterington, D.M. (eds.) Proceedings of the Thirteenth International Conference on Artificial Intelligence and Statistics, AISTATS 2010, Chia Laguna Resort, Sardinia, Italy, 13–15 May 2010. JMLR Proceedings, vol. 9, pp. 249–256. JMLR.org (2010)

6. Gutman, D., et al.: Skin Lesion Analysis toward Melanoma Detection: A Challenge at the International Symposium on Biomedical Imaging (ISBI) 2016, hosted by the International Skin Imaging Collaboration (ISIC). arXiv:1605.01397 [cs], May 2016

7. Haralick, R.M., Shanmugam, K., Dinstein, I.: Textural features for image classification. IEEE Trans. Syst. Man Cybern. **SMC-3**(6), 610–621 (1973). https://doi.org/10.1109/TSMC.1973.4309314

8. Havlíček, M., Haindl, M.: Texture spectral similarity criteria. IET Image Proc. **13**(11), 1998–2007 (2019). https://doi.org/10.1049/iet-ipr.2019.0250

9. Havlíček, M., Haindl, M.: Optimized texture spectral similarity criteria. In: Wojtkiewicz, K., Treur, J., Pimenidis, E., Maleszka, M. (eds.) ICCCI 2021. CCIS, vol. 1463, pp. 644–655. Springer, Cham (2021). https://doi.org/10.1007/978-3-030-88113-9_52

10. He, K., Zhang, X., Ren, S., Sun, J.: Deep residual learning for image recognition. In: 2016 IEEE Conference on Computer Vision and Pattern Recognition (CVPR), pp. 770–778. IEEE, Las Vegas (2016). https://doi.org/10.1109/CVPR.2016.90

11. Hou, L., Samaras, D., Kurc, T.M., Gao, Y., Davis, J.E., Saltz, J.H.: Patch-based convolutional neural network for whole slide tissue image classification. In: 2016 IEEE Conference on Computer Vision and Pattern Recognition (CVPR), pp. 2424–2433 (2016). https://doi.org/10.1109/CVPR.2016.266

12. Kingma, D.P., Ba, J.: Adam: a method for stochastic optimization. CoRR abs/1412.6980 (2015)

13. Lachaud, G., Conde-Cespedes, P., Trocan, M.: Entropy role on patch-based binary classification for skin melanoma. In: Wojtkiewicz, K., Treur, J., Pimenidis, E., Maleszka, M. (eds.) ICCCI 2021. CCIS, vol. 1463, pp. 324–333. Springer, Cham (2021). https://doi.org/10.1007/978-3-030-88113-9_26

14. Marentakis, P., et al.: Lung cancer histology classification from CT images based on radiomics and deep learning models. Med. Biol. Eng. Comput. **59**(1), 215–226 (2021). https://doi.org/10.1007/s11517-020-02302-w

15. Nigam, K., Lafferty, J., McCallum, A.: Using maximum entropy for text classification. In: IJCAI-99 Workshop on Machine Learning for Information Filtering, vol. 1, pp. 61–67. Stockholom, Sweden (1999)

16. Qin, X., Yang, Y.H.: Similarity measure and learning with gray level aura matrices (GLAM) for texture image retrieval. In: Proceedings of the 2004 IEEE Computer Society Conference on Computer Vision and Pattern Recognition, CVPR 2004, vol. 1, pp. I-I, June 2004. https://doi.org/10.1109/CVPR.2004.1315050

17. Rousseau, F., Habas, P.A., Studholme, C.: A supervised patch-based approach for human brain labeling. IEEE Trans. Med. Imaging **30**(10), 1852–1862 (2011). https://doi.org/10.1109/TMI.2011.2156806

18. Roy, K., Banik, D., Bhattacharjee, D., Nasipuri, M.: Patch-based system for classification of breast histology images using deep learning. Comput. Med. Imaging Graph. **71**, 90–103 (2019). https://doi.org/10.1016/j.compmedimag.2018.11.003

19. Shannon, C.E.: A mathematical theory of communication. Bell Syst. Tech. J. **27**(3), 379–423 (1948). https://doi.org/10.1002/j.1538-7305.1948.tb01338.x

20. Skilling, J., Bryan, R.: Maximum entropy image reconstruction-general algorithm. Mon. Not. R. Astron. Soc. **211**, 111 (1984)

21. Tschandl, P., Rosendahl, C., Kittler, H.: The HAM10000 dataset, a large collection of multi-source dermatoscopic images of common pigmented skin lesions. Sci. Data **5**(1), 180161 (2018). https://doi.org/10.1038/sdata.2018.161

22. Yala, A., Lehman, C., Schuster, T., Portnoi, T., Barzilay, R.: A deep learning mammography-based model for improved breast cancer risk prediction. Radiology **292**(1), 60–66 (2019). https://doi.org/10.1148/radiol.2019182716

23. Yilmaz, E., Trocan, M.: Benign and malignant skin lesion classification comparison for three deep-learning architectures. In: Nguyen, N.T., Jearanaitanakij, K., Selamat, A., Trawiński, B., Chittayasothorn, S. (eds.) ACIIDS 2020. LNCS (LNAI), vol. 12033, pp. 514–524. Springer, Cham (2020). https://doi.org/10.1007/978-3-030-41964-6_44

24. Yuan, J., Wang, D., Cheriyadat, A.M.: Factorization-based texture segmentation. IEEE Trans. Image Process. **24**(11), 3488–3497 (2015). https://doi.org/10.1109/TIP.2015.2446948

25. Zhang, F., et al.: Lung nodule classification with multilevel patch-based context analysis. IEEE Trans. Biomed. Eng. **61**(4), 1155–1166 (2014). https://doi.org/10.1109/TBME.2013.2295593

26. Zhu, S.C., Wu, Y.N., Mumford, D.: Minimax entropy principle and its application to texture modeling. Neural Comput. **9**(8), 1627–1660 (1997). https://doi.org/10.1162/neco.1997.9.8.1627

27. Zujovic, J., Pappas, T.N., Neuhoff, D.L.: Structural similarity metrics for texture analysis and retrieval. In: 2009 16th IEEE International Conference on Image Processing (ICIP), pp. 2225–2228. IEEE, Cairo, November 2009. https://doi.org/10.1109/ICIP.2009.5413897

Natural Language Processing

Multi-model Analysis
of Language-Agnostic Sentiment
Classification on MultiEmo Data

Piotr Miłkowski$^{(\boxtimes)}$ ⓘ, Marcin Gruza ⓘ, Przemysław Kazienko ⓘ,
Joanna Szołomicka ⓘ, Stanisław Woźniak ⓘ, and Jan Kocoń ⓘ

Department of Artificial Intelligence, Wrocław University of Science and Technology,
Wrocław, Poland
piotr.milkowski@pwr.edu.pl

Abstract. We carried out extensive experiments on the MultiEmo
dataset for sentiment analysis with texts in eleven languages. Two
adapted versions of the LaBSE deep architecture were confronted against
the LASER model. That allowed us to conduct cross-language validation of these language agnostic methods. The achieved results proved
that LaBSE embeddings with an additional attention layer within the
biLSTM architecture commonly outperformed other methods.

Keywords: Cross-language NLP · Sentiment analysis ·
Language-agnostic representation · LaBSE · BiLSTM · LASER ·
Opinion mining · MultiEmo

1 Introduction

There are two extensively explored topics in natural language processing (NLP)
related to opinion mining: sentiment analysis [1–3] and emotion recognition
[4,5]. We can observe that comments published on the Internet are becoming
increasingly expressed in different natural languages. Therefore, scientists have
focused their interest on new solutions for language-agnostic sentiment analysis.
It appears that suitable embeddings, i.e. language-independent models, may be
very efficient for that purpose.

Here, we designed, implemented, and tested three language-agnostic
approaches to sentiment analysis. One is based on the LASER model [6], while
the other two are based on LaBSE [7]. The LaBSE model was implemented
in both its primary version ($LaBSE_b$) and also with an additional attention

This work was partially supported by the National Science Centre, Poland, project
no. 2020/37/B/ST6/03806; by the statutory funds of the Department of Artificial
Intelligence, Wrocław University of Science and Technology; by the European Regional
Development Fund as a part of the 2014–2020 Smart Growth Operational Programme,
CLARIN - Common Language Resources and Technology Infrastructure, project no.
POIR.04.02.00-00C002/19.

N. T. Nguyen et al. (Eds.): ICCCI 2022, LNAI 13501, pp. 163–175, 2022.
https://doi.org/10.1007/978-3-031-16014-1_14

layer ($LaBSE_a$). All of them were used within the biLSTM architecture (bidirectional LSTM). Experimental studies were carried out on our new MultiEmo benchmark dataset [8], which is an extension of MultiEmo-Test 1.0 [9]. In the latter, only test texts were translated into other languages. The MultiEmo data proposed and exploited here is fully multilingual. Since our experiments showed that LaBSE with the additional attention layer ($LaBSE_a$) performs best (see Sect. 4), this model was utilized in the MultiEmo online service with language-agnostic sentiment analysis: https://ws.clarin-pl.eu/multiemo, Fig. 1. All data related to this article can be downloaded: the MultiEmo dataset at https://clarin-pl.eu/dspace/handle/11321/798 and the source codes at https://github.com/CLARIN-PL/multiemo.

The preliminary results of our studies were published in our short article [8]. Here, we present more in-depth, comprehensive, and mature analyses.

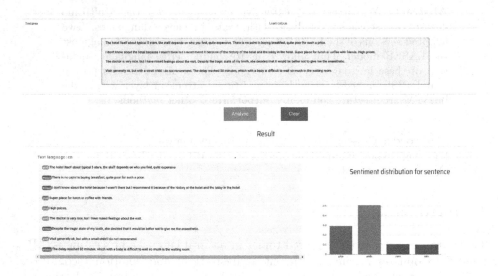

Fig. 1. Screenshot of the MultiEmo webservice working in the mode of analysis of individual sentences, https://ws.clarin-pl.eu/multiemo. A chart presents model's confidence for the first sentence and each sentiment class.

2   Related Work

Recently, most of the research in the field of sentiment analysis has relied on effective solutions based on deep neural networks. The current state-of-the-art applies Recurrent Neural Networks and Transformers, such as BiLSTM/CNN [10,11], BERT [11,12], or RoBERTa [13,14]. The concept of knowledge transfer between domains, document types, and user biases within social networks has been discussed in [15]. However, *Language-agnostic Sentiment Analysis* is a less considered issue. This problem goes beyond the classic approach, which relies exclusively on one resource-rich language, typically English, and does not emphasize other languages.

In our previous work [9], we analyzed the task of cross-language sentiment analysis. In particular, we implemented vector representations that do not directly depend on a given language [6], therefore, transferring knowledge from one language to another seems to be quite effective. We also proposed a benchmark dataset containing test files translated into 8 different languages. However, we have not exploited state-of-the-art methods. Therefore, the dataset published in this study served as a basis for our subsequent experiments.

Another interesting approach is zero-shot learning, explored by the Slovenian CLARIN-SI team in [16]. They used it for news sentiment classification. Given the annotated dataset of positive, neutral, and negative news in Slovenia, their goal was to develop a news classification system that not only assigns sentiment categories to Slovenian news, but also to news in another language, without any additional training data. Their system was based on the multilingual BERT model [12]. At the same time, they tested different methods of processing long documents and proposed a new BERT model that uses emotional enrichment technology as an intermediate training step. They also evaluated the zero-sample cross-language ability of their system on the new news sentiment test set in Croatian. Due to their work, their cross-language approach is also superior to most classifiers to a large extent, and to all settings without emotional richness in pretraining.

Most of the most advanced sentiment classification methods are based on supervised learning algorithms that require large amounts of manually labeled data. However, annotated resources are often unbalanced differently and of little quantity among different languages. Cross-lingual sentiment classification solves this problem by using knowledge from high-resource languages to low-resource ones. In [17], an attention-based bilingual representation learning model was proposed. It can learn the distributed semantics of documents in source and target languages. In each language, the authors use long-short-term memory (LSTM) networks to model documents, which have proven to be very effective for word sequences. At the same time, the hierarchical attention mechanism of the bilingual LSTM network (BiLSTM) was proposed. The sentence-level attention model learns which sentences are more important in a document to determine overall sentiment, while the word-level attention model learns which words are decisive in each sentence. The proposed model showed good results on the benchmark dataset, while being trained in English and assessed in Chinese.

We tested LASER and LaBSE embeddings on multiple NLP tasks, including primarily sentiment studies. In this paper, however, we go further and investigate them in a multiple-language environment.

3   Experimental Setup

3.1   Pipeline

Model training and evaluation were carried out in the following stages: (1) train on 80% data and validate on 10%; (2) train the model until the loss function value stops decreasing for 25 epochs; keep the lowest achieved value of loss; (3) evaluate the trained model using the test part of the data – the remaining 10%. All experiments were repeated 30 times to perform robust statistical tests. This eliminated the level of uncertainty caused by the randomness of the learning process of neural network models. If the difference between the results in our statistical tests was $p < 5\%$, they were treated as insignificantly different.

3.2 MultiEmo Dataset

We created a new kind of dataset for sentiment analysis tasks – PolEmo 2.0 [11]. Each sentence, as well as the entire document, is labeled with one of the four following sentiment classes: (1) P: positive; (2) O: neutral; (3) N: negative; (4) AMB: ambivalent, that is, there are positive and negative aspects in the text that are balanced in terms of relevance. In all subsequent experiments, we exploited only the labels assigned to the entire text – the document level processing. The entire MultiEmo corpus in Polish contains more than 40K sentences. Since each text and sentence was manually annotated with sentiment in the 2+1 scheme, we received in total over 150K annotations. A high value of Positive Specific Agreement (PSA) [18] equals 0.91 for texts and 0.88 for sentences.

We also considered the MultiEmo dataset in Polish labeled with 6 sentiment classes: strong positive, weak positive, neutral, strong negative, weak negative, and ambivalent. The cartography data map method [19] has been used to check how well the $LaBSE_a$ model learns in instances from the data set with 4 and 6 sentiment classes, Table 1. The cases from the training set with 4 sentiment classes: easy, ambiguous, and hard-to-learn are shown in Fig. 2. The learning difficulty of the model depends on its confidence, variability, and correctness over epochs. Confidence is the mean probability of the true label among epochs. The variability determines how decisive the model is between epochs: the higher the value, the more inconsistent the model in assigning the same label. The correctness $corr \in [0, 1]$ indicates the fraction of times that the model predicts the ground truth label. The mean values of confidence, variability and correctness for the models trained on data with 4 and 6 sentiment classes are depicted in Table 1. The mean confidence and correctness of *weak positive*, *weak negative* and *ambivalent* sentiments in 6 classes dataset increases significantly after merging them into one *ambivalent* sentiment in the 4-classes dataset. It confirms the findings obtained in [11] where PSA increased from 83% to 91% for texts after merging. The results for *strong positive/positive*, *strong negative/negative* and *neutral* classes are comparable for both datasets.

Furthermore, the entire corpus was machine translated into different languages using DeepL (https://www.deepl.com/translator), resulting in a new MultiEmo dataset. It provides an opportunity to train and test the model in any out of 11 languages: Polish (origin), English, Chinese, Italian, Japanese, Russian, German, Spanish, French, Dutch, and Portuguese. The comprehensive profile of the MultiEmo dataset is presented in Table 2. Only the mixed-domain corpus was exploited in the experiments described in Sects. 3.3 and 4, see the last row in Table 2.

Table 1. Mean confidence, variability and correctness values of $LaBSE_b$ in the Polish MultiEmo dataset labeled with 4 and 6 sentiment classes.

		Confidence	Variability	Correctness
6 sentiments	Strong positive	0.9	0.12	0.94
	Strong negative	0.9	0.11	0.95
	Neutral	0.97	0.05	0.98
	Ambivalent	**0.68**	**0.32**	**0.75**
	Weak positive	**0.73**	**0.27**	**0.82**
	Weak negative	**0.62**	**0.34**	**0.68**
4 sent.	Positive	0.92	0.11	0.94
	Negative	0.93	0.1	0.95
	Neutral	0.97	0.05	0.98
	Ambivalent	**0.82**	**0.2**	**0.86**

Table 2. The number of texts in the train/dev/test set of the MultiEmo corpus. The average length is calculated for the entire set (SUM).

Type	Domain	Train	Dev	Test	SUM	Average length [chars]
Mixed-domain texts (all domains)	Class P – positive	1,824	236	227	2,287	648
	Class 0 – neutral	971	128	118	1,217	854
	Class N – negative	2,469	304	339	3,112	817
	Class AMB - ambivalent	1,309	155	136	1,600	707
	All classes	**6,573**	**823**	**820**	**8,216**	**754**

3.3 Scenarios

To validate the quality of the models, we used three research scenarios, differing in the language of the texts used to train and test the models:

- **Any->Same** – the model is both trained and tested on texts in one chosen language (e.g. Polish-Polish, English-English).
- **PL->Any** – the model is trained only on Polish texts and tested on docs translated to any other language (e.g. Polish-English, Polish-Chinese).
- **Any->PL** - the model is trained on texts in any language and tested only on Polish texts (e.g. English-Polish, Chinese-Polish, Dutch-Polish).

All scenarios use the same train-validation-test split, Table 2, which ensures that the model will not be trained and tested on the same translated texts.

4   Experimental Results

The results of the same language training and testing on the MultiEmo dataset (all domains mixed) are presented in Table 4. It is the first scenario described in Sect. 3.3. We can observe that $LaBSE_a$ is better in almost all cases. There are 5 situations where $LaBSE_b$ was not significantly better than $LaBSE_a$. It happened in English (positive and negative labels), French (positive and neutral), and Italian (neutral). In the second scenario, training was carried out on Polish data and testing on other languages. The results are depicted in Table 5. Moreover, $LaBSE_a$ is almost always statistically better than the other models. There are only eight cases out of all 88, in which $LaBSE_b$ was insignificantly better than $LaBSE_a$. There is also a situation (Portuguese: $F1_{samples}$) where $LaBSE_b$ is not significantly worse than $LaBSE_a$. The results aggregated in all languages separately for each of the three considered models are shown in Fig. 3a for the LASER language model, in Fig. 3b for basic LaBSE ($LaBSE_b$), and in Fig. 3c for LaBSE with custom mean pooling ($LaBSE_a$).

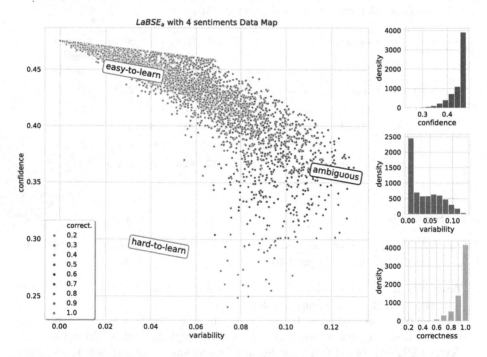

Fig. 2. Data map [19] for the $LaBSE_a$ model and MultiEmo dataset with 4 sentiment classes. Easy-to-learn texts demonstrate low variability and high confidence and hard-to-learn cases have low variability and low confidence. hard-to-learn texts are a minority in the dataset considered.

The learning difficulty distribution of the model trained in the second scenario for individual sentiment classes is shown in Table 3. It has been calculated using cartography data map method [19]. Almost one fifth of the instances belonging to *ambivalent* sentiment class are ambiguous-to-learn, whereas cases with other sentiment classes are mostly easy-to-learn by the model.

Table 3. Distribution of learning difficulty of the $LaBSE_a$ model trained on Polish texts for individual sentiment classes obtained using the data map method [19].

	Sentiment			
	Positive	Negative	Neutral	Ambivalent
Easy-to-learn	93.97%	95.67%	98.04%	81.21%
Hard-to-learn	0.27%	0.2%	0.51%	0.31%
Ambiguous-to-learn	5.76%	4.13%	1.44%	**18.49%**

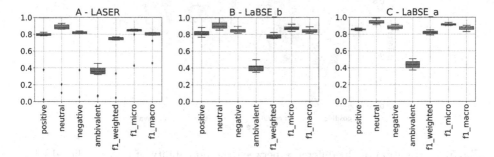

Fig. 3. Distribution of F1 scores for models learned on Polish texts and evaluated on all languages from the MultiEmo dataset (PL->Any scenario) aggregated over all test languages. (**A**) – for the LASER embeddings; (**B**) – for the basic $LaBSE_b$ embeddings; (**C**) – for the LaBSE with attention, i.e. $LaBSE_a$ embeddings

In the third scenario, the classifier was trained in different languages, but testing was carried out on Polish texts only, Table 6. Similarly to the previous scenarios, $LaBSE_a$ outperforms the $LaBSE_b$ and LASER language models. In all scenarios, the results for the *ambivalent* class are worse by about 40%–50% than for the *negative* or *positive* class, meaning that some documents are more controversial than others. Rather, we should consider applying personalized rea-

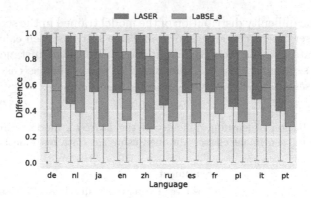

Fig. 4. Distribution of the difference between the probability of a wrongly predicted label (indicated as the highest) and probability of a true label for various languages.

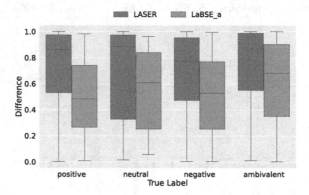

Fig. 5. Distribution of the difference between the probability of a mispredicted label (indicated as the highest) and the probability of a true label for various classes and both models aggregated over all languages.

soning to them [4, 5, 20, 21]. In addition, the *neutral* class is poorly classified, especially for LASER and non-Latin languages (Chinese, Japanese, Russian). $LaBSE_a$ in the second scenario overcomes this problem, revealing the superiority of language-agnostic solutions over language-specific ones. Languages using the Latin alphabet perform almost the same.

Table 4. F1 scores of multilingual models evaluated on the same language for all languages from the MultiEmo dataset: Any->Same scenario. The best model for a specified language (rows) is marked in **bold**. Underlined value means statistical insignificance between the underlined value and the best value.

Embeddings	Language	Positive	Neutral	Negatives	Ambivalent	$F1_{samples}$	$F1_{weighted}$	$F1_{micro}$	$F1_{macro}$
LASER	Chinese	21.35 ±0.59	0.0 ±0.0	26.3 ±0.73	0.0 ±0.0	13.9 ±0.39	20.09 ±0.56	64.74 ±1.8	54.47 ±1.51
$LaBSE_b$	Chinese	68.09 ±1.67	2.08 ±0.05	78.27 ±1.93	57.15 ±1.41	66.7 ±1.64	59.7 ±1.47	77.66 ±1.91	72.83 ±1.79
$LaBSE_a$	Chinese	**71.13 ±1.31**	**5.69 ±0.1**	**83.91 ±1.54**	**58.14 ±1.07**	**72.74 ±1.34**	**63.84 ±1.17**	**82.23 ±1.51**	**74.23 ±1.37**
LASER	Dutch	15.38 ±0.43	73.12 ±2.03	68.42 ±1.9	23.74 ±0.66	55.0 ±1.53	47.01 ±1.31	70.0 ±1.95	63.96 ±1.78
$LaBSE_b$	Dutch	17.88 ±0.44	76.74 ±1.89	73.55 ±1.81	26.0 ±0.64	61.53 ±1.51	49.35 ±1.21	72.35 ±1.78	69.76 ±1.72
$LaBSE_a$	Dutch	**23.34 ±0.43**	**81.84 ±1.51**	**74.82 ±1.38**	**29.47 ±0.54**	**62.2 ±1.14**	**51.69 ±0.95**	**75.85 ±1.4**	**72.24 ±1.33**
LASER	English	71.54 ±1.99	64.37 ±1.79	77.16 ±2.14	21.8 ±0.61	67.32 ±1.87	64.58 ±1.8	78.21 ±2.17	71.64 ±1.99
$LaBSE_b$	English	**74.92 ±1.84**	67.84 ±1.67	**81.88 ±2.01**	24.65 ±0.61	68.01 ±1.67	65.83 ±1.62	79.69 ±1.96	73.42 ±1.81
$LaBSE_a$	English	74.14 ±1.36	**69.1 ±1.27**	81.84 ±1.51	**25.35 ±0.47**	**70.2 ±1.29**	**68.19 ±1.25**	**81.1 ±1.49**	**78.91 ±1.45**
LASER	French	76.24 ±2.12	93.67 ±2.6	82.35 ±2.29	42.05 ±1.17	77.56 ±2.16	75.6 ±2.1	85.09 ±2.37	81.96 ±2.28
$LaBSE_b$	French	**82.01 ±2.02**	**98.8 ±2.43**	85.65 ±2.11	43.3 ±1.07	79.48 ±1.96	78.9 ±1.94	90.53 ±2.23	85.71 ±2.11
$LaBSE_a$	French	80.75 ±1.49	97.39 ±1.79	**86.6 ±1.59**	**49.68 ±0.91**	**82.16 ±1.51**	**80.62 ±1.48**	**92.79 ±1.71**	**86.73 ±1.6**
LASER	German	61.41 ±1.71	4.96 ±0.14	82.14 ±2.28	1.42 ±0.04	60.37 ±1.68	51.91 ±1.44	73.58 ±2.05	65.48 ±1.82
$LaBSE_b$	German	61.38 ±1.51	4.15 ±0.1	81.12 ±2.0	1.36 ±0.03	60.95 ±1.5	53.06 ±1.31	71.68 ±1.76	63.83 ±1.57
$LaBSE_a$	German	**66.84 ±1.23**	**11.82 ±0.22**	**88.06 ±1.62**	**10.16 ±0.19**	**69.84 ±1.28**	**60.61 ±1.12**	**83.42 ±1.53**	**75.32 ±1.39**
LASER	Italian	65.71 ±1.83	0.0 ±0.0	74.68 ±2.08	52.2 ±1.45	63.05 ±1.75	57.72 ±1.6	75.37 ±2.1	68.62 ±1.91
$LaBSE_b$	Italian	68.55 ±1.69	**4.96 ±0.12**	77.97 ±1.92	54.4 ±1.34	68.52 ±1.69	62.14 ±1.53	77.18 ±1.9	70.89 ±1.74
$LaBSE_a$	Italian	**72.44 ±1.33**	4.37 ±0.08	**79.29 ±1.46**	**56.75 ±1.04**	**70.59 ±1.3**	**64.03 ±1.18**	**81.64 ±1.5**	**73.9 ±1.36**
LASER	Japanese	0.0 ±0.0	0.0 ±0.0	21.16 ±0.59	0.0 ±0.0	11.83 ±0.33	9.41 ±0.26	60.44 ±1.68	50.0 ±1.39
$LaBSE_b$	Japanese	65.05 ±1.6	1.77 ±0.04	73.82 ±1.82	49.91 ±1.23	62.82 ±1.55	55.45 ±1.36	73.54 ±1.81	67.15 ±1.65
$LaBSE_a$	Japanese	**73.03 ±1.34**	**4.87 ±0.09**	**80.45 ±1.48**	**58.83 ±1.08**	**70.39 ±1.3**	**62.57 ±1.15**	**81.01 ±1.49**	**77.19 ±1.42**
LASER	Polish	78.04 ±2.17	85.99 ±2.39	80.44 ±2.24	35.16 ±0.98	75.49 ±2.1	73.06 ±2.03	83.66 ±2.33	78.82 ±2.19
$LaBSE_b$	Polish	80.02 ±1.97	89.7 ±2.21	81.93 ±2.02	37.99 ±0.93	78.56 ±1.93	76.89 ±1.89	85.59 ±2.11	80.7 ±1.99
$LaBSE_a$	Polish	**87.53 ±1.61**	**94.37 ±1.74**	**88.65 ±1.63**	**43.87 ±0.81**	**83.93 ±1.54**	**82.83 ±1.52**	**92.52 ±1.7**	**88.34 ±1.63**
LASER	Portuguese	72.94 ±2.03	89.2 ±2.48	86.13 ±2.39	54.19 ±1.51	77.07 ±2.14	77.62 ±2.16	84.72 ±2.36	83.33 ±2.32
$LaBSE_b$	Portuguese	72.97 ±1.8	91.25 ±2.24	84.41 ±2.08	55.13 ±1.36	74.83 ±1.84	79.53 ±1.96	83.36 ±2.05	85.5 ±2.1
$LaBSE_a$	Portuguese	**79.28 ±1.46**	**97.1 ±1.79**	**90.5 ±1.67**	**59.66 ±1.1**	**83.95 ±1.54**	**81.7 ±1.5**	**89.53 ±1.65**	**91.6 ±1.69**
LASER	Russian	52.23 ±1.45	0.0 ±0.0	67.74 ±1.88	31.92 ±0.89	55.24 ±1.54	47.76 ±1.33	70.16 ±1.95	60.89 ±1.69
$LaBSE_b$	Russian	54.51 ±1.34	1.31 ±0.03	70.74 ±1.74	30.66 ±0.75	58.25 ±1.43	46.86 ±1.15	71.87 ±1.77	61.83 ±1.52
$LaBSE_a$	Russian	**60.81 ±1.12**	**9.7 ±0.18**	**73.33 ±1.35**	**39.74 ±0.73**	**62.54 ±1.15**	**55.46 ±1.02**	**77.33 ±1.42**	**68.01 ±1.25**
LASER	Spanish	61.75 ±1.72	93.33 ±2.59	68.65 ±1.91	6.94 ±0.19	63.54 ±1.77	60.06 ±1.67	75.69 ±2.1	74.49 ±2.07
$LaBSE_b$	Spanish	63.86 ±1.57	98.29 ±2.42	69.15 ±1.7	9.89 ±0.24	68.55 ±1.69	64.62 ±1.59	80.15 ±1.97	76.73 ±1.89
$LaBSE_a$	Spanish	**70.92 ±1.3**	**99.22 ±1.83**	**74.83 ±1.38**	**13.99 ±0.26**	**71.94 ±1.32**	**69.19 ±1.27**	**85.24 ±1.57**	**84.19 ±1.55**

To compare the $LaBSE_a$ and $LASER$ models, we also analyzed their wrong predictions. Therefore, we calculate the differences between the probability of a wrong decision and the probability of a correct label. This indicates how the model was convinced to provide an incorrect answer. These distributions for different languages are shown in Fig. 4 and for different classes in Fig. 5.

Table 5. F1 scores of models trained on Polish texts and evaluated on other languages represented in the MultiEmo dataset: PL->Any scenario. The best model for a given language (row) is marked in **bold**. <u>Underlined</u> values are statistically insignificant compared to the best one.

Embeddings	Language	Positive	Neutral	Negatives	Ambivalent	$F1_{samples}$	$F1_{weighted}$	$F1_{micro}$	$F1_{macro}$
LASER	Chinese	2.27 ±0.06	10.26 ±0.29	5.29 ±0.15	6.25 ±0.17	2.93 ±0.08	4.56 ±0.13	42.54 ±1.18	45.59 ±1.27
$LaBSE_b$	Chinese	79.5 ±1.96	86.17 ±2.12	81.21 ±2.0	41.68 ±1.03	79.91 ±1.97	74.96 ±1.84	85.28 ±2.1	83.23 ±2.05
$LaBSE_a$	Chinese	**84.29 ±1.55**	**95.01 ±1.75**	**87.5 ±1.61**	**47.13 ±0.87**	**84.8 ±1.56**	**85.15 ±1.57**	**90.94 ±1.67**	**88.08 ±1.62**
LASER	Dutch	79.11 ±2.2	88.68 ±2.47	81.99 ±2.28	45.13 ±1.25	77.68 ±2.16	76.04 ±2.11	85.12 ±2.37	81.22 ±2.26
$LaBSE_b$	Dutch	79.32 ±1.95	89.89 ±2.21	83.54 ±2.06	48.45 ±1.19	78.7 ±1.94	76.77 ±1.89	85.2 ±2.1	81.34 ±2.0
$LaBSE_a$	Dutch	**85.71 ±1.58**	**92.15 ±1.7**	**85.88 ±1.58**	**49.94 ±0.92**	**84.22 ±1.55**	**81.56 ±1.5**	**91.15 ±1.68**	**88.17 ±1.62**
LASER	English	80.0 ±2.22	91.74 ±2.55	82.44 ±2.29	44.66 ±1.24	78.29 ±2.18	76.84 ±2.14	85.53 ±2.38	81.95 ±2.28
$LaBSE_b$	English	82.15 ±2.02	94.56 ±2.33	86.02 ±2.12	49.63 ±1.22	79.74 ±1.96	80.1 ±1.97	89.47 ±2.2	83.5 ±2.05
$LaBSE_a$	English	**85.72 ±1.58**	**99.3 ±1.83**	**90.22 ±1.66**	**50.63 ±0.93**	**87.09 ±1.6**	**84.91 ±1.56**	**93.94 ±1.73**	**90.42 ±1.66**
LASER	French	81.36 ±2.26	92.73 ±2.58	82.92 ±2.31	35.56 ±0.99	78.54 ±2.18	76.03 ±2.11	85.74 ±2.38	81.86 ±2.28
$LaBSE_b$	French	84.58 ±2.08	<u>97.21 ±2.39</u>	84.5 ±2.08	37.4 ±0.92	83.58 ±2.06	79.43 ±1.95	91.74 ±2.26	**86.94 ±2.14**
$LaBSE_a$	French	**85.01 ±1.56**	<u>96.85 ±1.78</u>	**91.23 ±1.68**	**43.45 ±0.8**	**85.45 ±1.57**	**80.06 ±1.47**	**92.88 ±1.71**	<u>86.6 ±1.59</u>
LASER	German	79.45 ±2.21	86.54 ±2.41	81.13 ±2.26	33.88 ±0.94	76.1 ±2.12	73.6 ±2.05	84.07 ±2.34	79.26 ±2.2
$LaBSE_b$	German	77.51 ±1.91	87.72 ±2.16	82.08 ±2.02	35.5 ±0.87	74.9 ±1.84	75.04 ±1.85	83.38 ±2.05	80.99 ±1.99
$LaBSE_a$	German	**85.32 ±1.57**	**95.08 ±1.75**	**90.34 ±1.66**	**38.94 ±0.72**	**84.42 ±1.55**	**83.04 ±1.53**	**90.81 ±1.67**	**88.6 ±1.63**
LASER	Italian	79.0 ±2.2	87.08 ±2.42	82.64 ±2.3	42.16 ±1.17	77.2 ±2.15	75.55 ±2.1	84.8 ±2.36	80.66 ±2.24
$LaBSE_b$	Italian	79.54 ±1.96	85.08 ±2.09	83.37 ±2.05	41.77 ±1.03	79.37 ±1.95	75.84 ±1.87	87.42 ±2.15	83.17 ±2.05
$LaBSE_a$	Italian	**85.61 ±1.58**	**93.92 ±1.73**	**88.45 ±1.63**	**47.27 ±0.87**	**84.24 ±1.55**	**83.58 ±1.54**	**91.67 ±1.69**	**89.06 ±1.64**
LASER	Japanese	37.53 ±1.04	20.34 ±0.57	37.18 ±1.03	6.9 ±0.19	21.34 ±0.59	33.16 ±0.92	79.61 ±2.21	72.09 ±2.0
$LaBSE_b$	Japanese	81.15 ±2.0	88.25 ±2.17	84.33 ±2.07	42.27 ±1.04	77.4 ±1.9	75.53 ±1.86	85.93 ±2.11	83.5 ±2.05
$LaBSE_a$	Japanese	**86.19 ±1.59**	**93.51 ±1.72**	**88.01 ±1.62**	**45.59 ±0.84**	**80.13 ±1.47**	**82.81 ±1.52**	**90.33 ±1.66**	**84.65 ±1.56**
LASER	Polish	78.04 ±2.17	85.99 ±2.39	80.44 ±2.24	35.16 ±0.98	75.49 ±2.1	73.06 ±2.03	83.66 ±2.33	78.82 ±2.19
$LaBSE_b$	Polish	76.59 ±1.88	87.43 ±2.15	81.69 ±2.01	34.59 ±0.85	76.45 ±1.88	75.16 ±1.85	86.19 ±2.12	80.99 ±1.99
$LaBSE_a$	Polish	**84.36 ±1.55**	**91.97 ±1.69**	**85.45 ±1.57**	**40.56 ±0.75**	**81.04 ±1.49**	**80.19 ±1.48**	**90.34 ±1.66**	**82.9 ±1.53**
LASER	Portuguese	81.15 ±2.26	90.23 ±2.51	83.71 ±2.33	37.36 ±1.04	78.66 ±2.19	76.25 ±2.12	85.77 ±2.38	81.81 ±2.27
$LaBSE_b$	Portuguese	85.81 ±2.11	92.44 ±2.27	85.85 ±2.11	**41.21 ±1.01**	85.27 ±2.1	**82.07 ±2.02**	87.7 ±2.16	86.86 ±2.14
$LaBSE_a$	Portuguese	**86.86 ±1.6**	**93.57 ±1.72**	**88.11 ±1.62**	40.74 ±0.75	**85.69 ±1.58**	81.79 ±1.5	**91.51 ±1.68**	**87.62 ±1.61**
LASER	Russian	82.33 ±2.29	92.73 ±2.58	83.49 ±2.32	31.76 ±0.88	79.02 ±2.2	75.92 ±2.11	86.02 ±2.39	81.89 ±2.28
$LaBSE_b$	Russian	**88.21 ±2.17**	99.98 ±2.46	89.43 ±2.2	35.33 ±0.87	**85.5 ±2.1**	79.28 ±1.95	91.66 ±2.25	88.88 ±2.19
$LaBSE_a$	Russian	86.47 ±1.59	**99.27 ±1.86**	**91.57 ±1.68**	**37.2 ±0.68**	83.85 ±1.54	**80.01 ±1.47**	**93.44 ±1.72**	**89.95 ±1.66**
LASER	Spanish	79.63 ±2.21	88.15 ±2.45	80.69 ±2.24	34.78 ±0.97	76.22 ±2.12	73.86 ±2.05	84.15 ±2.34	79.63 ±2.21
$LaBSE_b$	Spanish	80.3 ±1.98	89.43 ±2.2	<u>85.46 ±2.1</u>	38.36 ±0.94	81.25 ±2.0	77.54 ±1.91	86.37 ±2.12	**83.67 ±2.06**
$LaBSE_a$	Spanish	**87.31 ±1.61**	**92.85 ±1.71**	<u>85.44 ±1.57</u>	**39.21 ±0.72**	**82.73 ±1.52**	**78.98 ±1.45**	**90.61 ±1.67**	<u>83.63 ±1.54</u>

It is visible that the *LASER* model was more convinced of its wrong predictions than $LaBSE_a$. In addition, all languages have a similar level of confidence in the case of a wrong prediction. Figure 5 reveals that the greatest difference between both models was due to wrong predictions in the *positive* class. The $LaBSE_a$ model was the least confident when making mistakes with this label.

Table 6. F1 scores of models trained on documents in different languages from the MultiEmo dataset (the second column – *language*) evaluated on Polish test data: Any->PL scenario. The best model for a specified language (row) is marked in **bold**. The underlined value means statistical insignificance between it and the best value.

Embeddings	Language	Positive	Neutral	Negatives	Ambivalent	F1_{samples}	F1_{weighted}	F1_{micro}	F1_{macro}
LASER	Chinese	29.17 ±0.81	0.0 ±0.0	16.14 ±0.45	0.0 ±0.0	20.12 ±0.56	16.53 ±0.46	46.75 ±1.3	41.36 ±1.15
LaBSE_b	Chinese	73.27 ±1.8	1.87 ±0.05	74.81 ±1.84	**56.63 ±1.39**	**68.78 ±1.69**	60.11 ±1.48	76.76 ±1.89	70.4 ±1.73
LaBSE_a	Chinese	**75.63 ±1.39**	**8.21 ±0.15**	**81.28 ±1.5**	56.11 ±1.03	67.7 ±1.25	**65.04 ±1.2**	**81.83 ±1.51**	**73.47 ±1.35**
LASER	Dutch	9.21 ±0.26	64.37 ±1.79	66.54 ±1.85	21.8 ±0.61	52.2 ±1.45	42.93 ±1.19	68.13 ±1.89	61.33 ±1.71
LaBSE_b	Dutch	8.8 ±0.22	64.67 ±1.59	68.87 ±1.69	20.68 ±0.51	52.96 ±1.3	41.93 ±1.03	71.51 ±1.76	61.3 ±1.51
LaBSE_a	Dutch	**13.73 ±0.25**	**72.34 ±1.33**	**73.9 ±1.36**	**25.85 ±0.48**	**58.71 ±1.08**	**48.43 ±0.89**	**73.47 ±1.35**	**68.89 ±1.27**
LASER	English	73.66 ±2.05	60.36 ±1.68	76.55 ±2.13	23.53 ±0.65	67.56 ±1.88	64.62 ±1.8	78.37 ±2.18	71.6 ±1.99
LaBSE_b	English	74.24 ±1.83	64.64 ±1.59	77.68 ±1.91	24.73 ±0.61	68.96 ±1.7	66.4 ±1.63	79.14 ±1.95	72.84 ±1.79
LaBSE_a	English	**79.02 ±1.45**	**65.84 ±1.21**	**81.98 ±1.51**	**29.94 ±0.55**	**74.07 ±1.36**	**71.45 ±1.31**	**87.91 ±1.62**	**81.5 ±1.5**
LASER	French	79.61 ±2.21	94.64 ±2.63	83.72 ±2.33	42.2 ±1.17	78.66 ±2.19	77.27 ±2.15	85.77 ±2.38	82.45 ±2.29
LaBSE_b	French	82.81 ±2.04	**99.21 ±2.44**	86.35 ±2.12	42.41 ±1.04	79.64 ±1.96	80.17 ±1.97	89.31 ±2.2	82.59 ±2.03
LaBSE_a	French	**86.79 ±1.6**	98.62 ±1.81	**87.34 ±1.61**	**48.42 ±0.89**	**85.29 ±1.57**	**84.61 ±1.56**	**90.87 ±1.67**	**89.49 ±1.65**
LASER	German	62.3 ±1.73	21.21 ±0.59	79.57 ±2.21	1.34 ±0.04	60.37 ±1.68	53.42 ±1.49	73.58 ±2.05	66.17 ±1.84
LaBSE_b	German	63.96 ±1.57	21.94 ±0.54	82.16 ±2.02	2.17 ±0.05	61.45 ±1.51	56.78 ±1.4	76.26 ±1.88	69.36 ±1.71
LaBSE_a	German	**67.22 ±1.24**	**27.59 ±0.51**	**88.01 ±1.62**	**6.16 ±0.11**	**66.53 ±1.22**	**58.57 ±1.08**	**78.79 ±1.45**	**72.68 ±1.34**
LASER	Italian	68.72 ±1.91	0.0 ±0.0	73.79 ±2.05	51.7 ±1.44	63.41 ±1.76	58.1 ±1.62	75.61 ±2.1	68.47 ±1.9
LaBSE_b	Italian	69.23 ±1.7	2.56 ±0.06	75.53 ±1.86	52.61 ±1.29	64.09 ±1.58	58.55 ±1.44	73.78 ±1.82	67.25 ±1.65
LaBSE_a	Italian	**76.16 ±1.4**	**6.48 ±0.12**	**82.17 ±1.51**	**60.24 ±1.11**	**68.85 ±1.27**	**65.94 ±1.21**	**84.21 ±1.55**	**73.58 ±1.35**
LASER	Japanese	0.0 ±0.0	0.0 ±0.0	58.5 ±1.63	0.0 ±0.0	41.34 ±1.15	24.18 ±0.67	60.89 ±1.69	50.0 ±1.39
LaBSE_b	Japanese	70.88 ±1.74	4.55 ±0.11	75.95 ±1.87	55.91 ±1.38	65.53 ±1.61	60.45 ±1.49	78.29 ±1.93	72.3 ±1.78
LaBSE_a	Japanese	**77.37 ±1.42**	**7.21 ±0.13**	**79.66 ±1.47**	**59.48 ±1.09**	**71.52 ±1.32**	**64.16 ±1.18**	**82.75 ±1.52**	**75.91 ±1.4**
LASER	Polish	78.04 ±2.17	85.99 ±2.39	80.44 ±2.24	35.16 ±0.98	75.49 ±2.1	73.06 ±2.03	83.66 ±2.33	78.82 ±2.19
LaBSE_b	Polish	**83.35 ±2.05**	89.89 ±2.21	84.08 ±2.07	39.98 ±0.98	79.02 ±1.94	76.78 ±1.89	85.14 ±2.09	**85.0 ±2.09**
LaBSE_a	Polish	83.12 ±1.53	**93.12 ±1.71**	**84.6 ±1.56**	**42.72 ±0.79**	**79.47 ±1.46**	**79.87 ±1.47**	**89.11 ±1.64**	83.97 ±1.54
LASER	Portuguese	56.55 ±1.57	89.91 ±2.5	75.66 ±2.1	25.59 ±0.71	67.2 ±1.87	64.11 ±1.78	78.13 ±2.17	73.76 ±2.05
LaBSE_b	Portuguese	56.85 ±1.4	90.25 ±2.22	78.87 ±1.94	26.59 ±0.65	67.25 ±1.65	67.81 ±1.67	77.98 ±1.92	77.52 ±1.91
LaBSE_a	Portuguese	**60.53 ±1.11**	**97.05 ±1.79**	**81.02 ±1.49**	**29.73 ±0.55**	**71.63 ±1.32**	**69.03 ±1.27**	**84.25 ±1.55**	**80.04 ±1.47**
LASER	Russian	52.23 ±1.45	0.0 ±0.0	66.93 ±1.86	28.57 ±0.79	54.39 ±1.51	46.87 ±1.3	69.59 ±1.93	60.43 ±1.67
LaBSE_b	Russian	54.26 ±1.33	1.38 ±0.03	72.44 ±1.78	33.04 ±0.81	55.68 ±1.37	52.2 ±1.28	74.66 ±1.84	63.32 ±1.56
LaBSE_a	Russian	**56.56 ±1.04**	**5.01 ±0.09**	70.8 ±1.3	**34.03 ±0.63**	**62.21 ±1.14**	**53.74 ±0.99**	**77.01 ±1.42**	**64.71 ±1.19**
LASER	Spanish	59.32 ±1.65	92.31 ±2.57	62.26 ±1.73	6.99 ±0.19	60.12 ±1.67	56.6 ±1.57	73.41 ±2.04	72.65 ±2.02
LaBSE_b	Spanish	61.19 ±1.51	93.8 ±2.31	68.05 ±1.67	9.0 ±0.22	62.7 ±1.54	60.51 ±1.49	74.39 ±1.83	75.28 ±1.85
LaBSE_a	Spanish	**65.22 ±1.2**	**99.6 ±1.83**	66.95 ±1.23	**11.49 ±0.21**	**66.71 ±1.23**	**62.09 ±1.14**	**78.3 ±1.44**	**78.76 ±1.45**

5 Conclusion and Future Work

The pre-trained models that capture general knowledge about multiple natural languages at ones, i.e. language-agnostic representation models, can provide worthwhile information that facilitates prediction of sentiment polarization. In our experiments that validated the performance of the LaBSE and LASER models, a new multilingual MultiEmo dataset was exploited. The results proved that language-agnostic embeddings are commonly very efficient. The best result was provided by the LaBSE model enhanced with an additional attention layer ($LaBSE_a$). Therefore, this method was utilized in our open web service.

At the same time, we found that the sentiment prediction for ambiguous texts cannot be satisfactory enough. It seems that such documents require other, for example, personalized methods. This will be the subject of our future work, making sentiment analysis similar to other subjective NLP tasks such as hate speech and offensiveness [20,21] or the perception of emotional content [4,5]. The application of multi-task approaches will be another direction of research for further investigation [22].

References

1. Hemmatian, F., Sohrabi, M.K.: A survey on classification techniques for opinion mining and sentiment analysis. Artif. Intell. Rev. **52**(3), 1495–1545 (2017). https://doi.org/10.1007/s10462-017-9599-6
2. Augustyniak, Ł, Szymański, P., Kajdanowicz, T., Kazienko, P.: Fast and accurate - improving lexicon-based sentiment classification with an ensemble methods. In: Nguyen, N.T., Trawiński, B., Fujita, H., Hong, T.-P. (eds.) ACIIDS 2016. LNCS (LNAI), vol. 9622, pp. 108–116. Springer, Heidelberg (2016). https://doi.org/10.1007/978-3-662-49390-8_10
3. Bartusiak, R., Augustyniak, L., Kajdanowicz, T., Kazienko, P.: Sentiment analysis for polish using transfer learning approach. In: Second European Network Intelligence Conference 2015, pp. 53–59 (2015)
4. Miłkowski, P., Gruza, M., Kanclerz, K., Kazienko, P., Grimling, D., Kocon, J.: Personal bias in prediction of emotions elicited by textual opinions. In: ACL-IJCNLP 2021: Student Research Workshop, pp. 248–259. ACL (2021)
5. Kocoń, J., et al.: Learning personal human biases and representations for subjective tasks in natural language processing. In: ICDM, pp. 1168–1173. IEEE (2021)
6. Artetxe, M., Schwenk, H.: Massively multilingual sentence embeddings for zero-shot cross-lingual transfer and beyond. Trans. Assoc. Comput. Linguist. **7**, 597–610 (2019)
7. Feng, F., Yang, Y., Cer, D., Arivazhagan, N., Wang, W.: Language-agnostic BERT sentence embedding. arXiv preprint arXiv:2007.01852 (2020)
8. Miłkowski, P., Gruza, M., Kazienko, P., Szołomicka, J., Woźniak, S., Kocoń, J.: Multiemo: language-agnostic sentiment analysis. In: Proceedings of the 2022 International Conference on Computational Science (ICCS 2022). IEEE (2022)
9. Kanclerz, K., Miłkowski, P., Kocoń, J.: Cross-lingual deep neural transfer learning in sentiment analysis. Procedia Comput. Sci. **176**, 128–137 (2020)
10. Chen, T., Xu, R., He, Y., Wang, X.: Improving sentiment analysis via sentence type classification using BILSTM-CRF and CNN. Expert Syst. Appl. **72**, 221–230 (2017)
11. Kocoń, J., Miłkowski, P., Zaśko-Zielińska, M.: Multi-level sentiment analysis of Polemo 2.0: extended corpus of multi-domain consumer reviews. In: CoNLL 2019, pp. 980–991 (2019)
12. Devlin, J., Chang, M.-W., Lee, K., Toutanova, K.: BERT: pre-training of deep bidirectional transformers for language understanding. arXiv preprint arXiv:1810.04805 (2018)
13. Liu, Y., et al.: Roberta: a robustly optimized BERT pretraining approach. arXiv preprint arXiv:1907.11692 (2019)
14. Rybak, P., Mroczkowski, R., Tracz, J., Gawlik, I.: Klej: comprehensive benchmark for polish language understanding. arXiv preprint arXiv:2005.00630 (2020)
15. Calais Guerra, P.H., Veloso, A., Meira Jr., W., Almeida, V.: From bias to opinion: a transfer-learning approach to real-time sentiment analysis. In: ACM SIGKDD'2011, pp. 150–158 (2011)
16. Pelicon, A., Pranjić, M., Miljković, D., Škrlj, B., Pollak, S.: Zero-shot learning for cross-lingual news sentiment classif. Appl. Sci. **10**(17), 5993 (2020)
17. Zhou, X., Wan, X., Xiao, J.: Attention-based LSTM network for cross-lingual sentiment classification. In: EMNLP'16, pp. 247–256 (2016)
18. Hripcsak, G., Rothschild, A.S.: Agreement, the f-measure, and reliability in information retrieval. J. Am. Med. Inform. Assoc. **12**(3), 296–298 (2005)

19. Swayamdipta, S., et al.: Dataset cartography: mapping and diagnosing datasets with training dynamics. In: EMNLP 2020, pp. 9275–9293. ACL (2020)
20. Kocoń, J., Figas, A., Gruza, M., Puchalska, D., Kajdanowicz, T., Kazienko, P.: Offensive, aggressive, and hate speech analysis: from data-centric to human-centered approach. Inf. Process. Manag. **58**(5), 102643 (2021)
21. Kanclerz, K., et al.: Controversy and conformity: from generalized to personalized aggressiveness detection. In: ACL-IJCNLP 2021, pp. 5915–5926. ACL (2021)
22. Miłkowski, P., Saganowski, S., Gruza, M., Kazienko, P., Piasecki, M., Kocoń, J.: Multitask personalized recognition of emotions evoked by textual content. In: EmotionAware 2022: Sixth International Workshop on Emotion Awareness for Pervasive Computing Beyond Traditional Approaches at PerCom 2022, pp. 347–352, March 2022

Sentiment Analysis of Tunisian Users on Social Networks: Overcoming the Challenge of Multilingual Comments in the Tunisian Dialect

Samawel Jaballi[1,2(✉)], Salah Zrigui[3], Mohamed Ali Sghaier[1,2], Dhaou Berchech[4], and Mounir Zrigui[1,2]

[1] Department of Computer Science, Faculty of Sciences of Monastir, University of Monastir, Monastir, Tunisia
jaballisamawel7@gmail.com
[2] Research Laboratory in Algebra Numbers Theory and Intelligent Systems, Monastir, Tunisia
[3] Institute of Research in Computer Science of Toulouse (IRIT), 31400 Toulouse, France
[4] DB Consulting, 4 rue Simone de Beauvoir Alfortville, 94140 Paris, France

Abstract. The presence of the dialect in the Arabic texts made Arabic sentiment analysis (ASA) a challenging issue, owing to it usually does not follow specific rules in writing systems, especially Tunisian Dialectical (TD) which presents an undertaking challenge due to its complexity, ambiguity, the morphological richness of the language, the absence of contextual information, the code-switching (CS) and mostly the multilingualism phenomena in textual productions. Recently, deep learning models have clearly demonstrated a great success in the field of sentiment analysis (SA). Although, the state-of-the-art accuracy for dialectical sentiment analysis (DSA) still needs improvements regarding contextual information and implicit sentiment expressed in different real cases. To address this challenge, we propose, an efficient Bidirectional LSTM network preceded by a preprocessing stage in order to enhance Tunisian SA, by applying Forward-Backward encapsulate contextual information from multilingual feature sequences. To evaluate our model, and due to the lack of publicly available multilingual resources associated with the TD, we collect different datasets available with different variants of TD to create our own multilingual corpus for sentiment classification. The experimental results based on the evaluation standards "Accuracy", "Recall" and "F1-score" demonstrate that our model achieves significant improvements over the state-of-art deep learning models and the baseline traditional machine learning methods.

Keywords: Social networks · Sentiment analysis · Multilingual text classification · Tunisian dialect · Deep learning · Bi-LSTM · Text preprocessing · Word embeddings

© The Author(s), under exclusive license to Springer Nature Switzerland AG 2022
N. T. Nguyen et al. (Eds.): ICCCI 2022, LNAI 13501, pp. 176–192, 2022.
https://doi.org/10.1007/978-3-031-16014-1_15

1   Introduction

Recently, SA has received special attention in several research laboratories on the one hand. On the other hand, the great benefit that it may grant to the industrial, advertising, marketing and production fields encourages large corporations of the globe to invest there. In the same context, the amount of research work on ASA has been growing explosively. However, most of the researchers were contributed to SA in Modern Standard Arabic (MSA), but few of them focus on dialectical Arabic [1].

SA is one of the leading research fields that attempts to automatically or semi-automatically determine attitude polarity of phrases embedded in comments. In general, there are three approaches for SA. First, unsupervised learning approaches that rely on sentiment lexicons such as the work reported in [2–4]. Second supervised learning approaches that rely on classification such as the work reported in [5–8]. Finally, semi-supervised learning approaches that combine the two previous approaches such as the work reported in [9].

Sentiment is language and culture dependent. Any successful SA system should take language aspects and culture into consideration. Arabic language comes in three varieties: MSA used in formal events, Traditional Arabic found in religious scripts and Dialectical Arabic, which is typically region dependent [10]. A close examination of the posts or comments posted on social media channels will reveal that dialectical Arabic is present in these written comments, particularly TD Language which presents a challenge undertaking due to its ambiguity, complex nature and rich morphological system [11].

In this paper, we address the classification challenges of SA of multilingual comments in the TD. We also tackle the complexity and the CS in Tunisian users comments by taking into account the improvement of our preprocessing method.

The rest of this paper is organized as follows: In Sect. 2, we present specificities of Tunisian dialect SA. In Sect. 3, we present the recent trend in research on Arabic language and the domain of DSA. Section 4 is dedicated to a detailed presentation of our proposed method for multilingual SA in the Tunisian dialect. Section 5 is reserved for the presentation of the results and experiments. Lastly, Sect. 6 summarizes the conclusions of this paper and highlights future work.

2   Specificities of Tunisian Dialect Sentiment Analysis

In Tunisia, MSA is the official language taught in education and used in business communication, administration and state media, while in the social networks, Tunisian users resort to the informal Tunisian language also called Tunisian dialect in their written exchanges. They often include language loans, especially from French and English. Posts and written comments on Tunisian social networks are indeed strongly characterized by the CS and the multilingualism phenomena [12].

The next subsection briefly highlights the features and the properties of textual productions on Tunisian social networks.

2.1   The Use of Multilingual Vocabulary

The diversity that Tunisia witnessed especially historically and culturally, favored the emergence of multilingualism. Indeed, Tunisians use more than one language in their daily social exchanges (MSA, TD, French, English, etc.). In the same context, according to the statements of the Digital discovery[1] platform, active Tunisian internet users who are reached more than 7 million by January 2020, trend to use dialectical words attached with multilingual vocabulary to express their opinions about services, products, events, political parties, etc., in website comment, social media and blogs.

Table 1 shows some examples of multilingual comments used on Tunisian social networks translated to MSA and English.

Table 1. Examples of multilingual comments used by tunisian on social networks translated to MSA and English

Tunisian comments	Corresponding language	MSA translation	English translation
chna7welk	Arabizi[a]	كيف حالك	How are you
الخدمة سريعة	MSA	----	The service is fast
Magnifique	French	رائـع	Wonderful
finally	English	أخـيرا	----

[a] Arabizi: Arabizi refers to Arabic written using the Roman script.

2.2   The Phenomenon of Linguistic Code-switching

Many Tunisian Internet users use CS and code-mixing in their daily conversations and informal writing such as posts and comments on on-line social media such as Facebook. According to the Cambridge Dictionary[2], CS refers to the act of changing between two distinct languages or more in the same discourse. Moreover, we distinguish two types of CS:

- Inter-sentential CS: defined as switching languages from one sentence to another [13], e.g., "Je t'aime Ons Jabeur. بوحة إنشـاء الله مربوحـة" (I love you Ons Jabeur. God Willing, you are the winner.)
- Intra-sentential CS: defined as using multiple languages within the same sentence [13], e.g., "les sallons de thé هو في تـونس projet rentable أحسن" (The best profitable project in Tunisia is the tea rooms.)

---

[1] https://www.digital-discovery.tn.
[2] https://dictionary.cambridge.org/dictionary/english/code-switching.

3 Background and Related Work

This section describes related research which addressed SA in Arabic reviews. We also present the recent trend in research related to SA of TD textual content, in order to study how the multilingualism phenomena have been treated so far.

3.1 Arabic Dialects Sentiment Analysis

Shoukry et al. [14] have proposed a corpus for Egyptian dialect. The corpus contains 500 positive and 500 negative tweets. The performance of proposed corpus is evaluated using NB classifier and SVM. The Findings showed that SVM model (72%) outperformed as compared to NB classifier (65%).

Abdulla et al. [15] have proposed a corpus-based and lexicon-based for Jordanian dialect and MSA. The corpus contains 1000 positive and 1000 negative tweets. The performance of the proposed corpus is evaluated using Decision Tree (DT), NB, SVM, KNN classifiers. The experimental results showed that SVM and NB (80%) outperformed as compared to other classifiers.

Salamah et al. [16] have proposed a corpus for Kuwaiti dialect. The corpus contains 340K tweets. The performance of proposed corpus is evaluated using SVM J48, DT, and Random Forests (RF) classifiers. The results showed that SVM (76%) outperformed as compared to others.

In [17], Abdelli et al. have collected two corpora for Algerian dialect, the final corpus contains more than 100K comments from popular Algerian Facebook pages. To evaluate the performance of proposed corpus, they have used the SVM classifier compared to the LSTM model. Both of them are trained using two different word embedding methods: TF-IDF and Word2vec. The experimental results showed that the SVM Model outperform the LSTM model in terms of accuracy.

3.2 Tunisian Dialect Sentiment Analysis

Masmoudi et al. [18] have proposed a corpus for TD, contains more than 43K comments from official Facebook pages of Tunisian supermarkets. To evaluate the performance of proposed corpus, they have used three deep learning models: Convolution Neural Networks (CNN), Long Short-Term Memory (LSTM), and Bi-directional LSTM (Bi-LSTM). Findings show that LSTM and Bi-LSTM achieved the best performance with an F-Measure value of 87%.

In [19], the authors have presented the Tunisian Sentiment Analysis Corpus (TSAC), which mainly focused on the TD. They have collected 17k users comments from the official Facebook pages of Tunisian radios and TV channels. To evaluate the performance of proposed corpus, they have used three classifiers, namely Multilayer Perceptron (MLP), Multinomial NB and SVM. Both of them are trained using doc2vec method. The results showed that MLP and SVM outperformed about 22% and 23% error rate as compared to Multinomial NB classifier (42%).

On the flip side, some corpora have been developed for targeting specific variant of TD such as the work reported in [20] where the authors introduce TUNIZI as a SA Tunisian Arabizi dataset, collected from comments on YouTube social network. The datasets include than 17K Tunisian comments written using Latin characters and numerals rather than Arabic letters. The collected corpus is balanced, containing 47% of positive comments and 53% negative comments and preprocessed for NLP tasks and analytical studies.

Mulki et al. [21] have proposed to study the impact of several preprocessing methods on TD SA. They have experimented two SA models: a supervised machine learning based model (NB and SVM) and a lexicon-based model. They have showed the improvement of the negation tagging preprocessing, emoji and stemming tasks for the TD SA.

For their part, Jerbi et al. [22] have proposed an approach based on deep learning techniques for the SA of code-switched TD. For the experiment, they have highlighted the performance of four variants of RNNs, namely: LSTM, Bi-LSTM, deep LSTM and deep Bi-LSTM. The experiments performed on TSAC corpus [19] showed that the high performance with an accuracy of 90% is obtained by using a deep LSTM model (two-layers), as compared to other classifiers.

3.3 Discussion

According to this state-of-the-art review on SA of dialectical Arabic social media content, works fall into three major approaches, namely a linguistic based approach, a machine learning based approach and deep learning approach. It seems that approaches integrating deep learning models are leading to better performance and they are considering as the state-of-the-art model in Arabic SA. We can also deduct that the preferred approach in several research works, which seems to be the most effective, is that which considers the monolingual text in its entirety, without going through multilingual corpora.

As for the challenge of multilingual comments in the TD which is our goal in this work, we can notice that there is very little research that addresses this problem. Among the five surveyed works, four of them (Masmoudi et al. [18], Mdhaffar et al. [19], Fourati et al. [20] and Mulki et al. [21]) have had as objective, to classify TD writings comments by sentiment and they have had only dealt with monolingual text. While we notice that only, Jerbi et al. [22] considered a multilingual corpus enclosing both Arabic and Latin scripts. As for the explored approaches, we can see that deep learning approach have been practically not explored with the TD language. We however notice that the TD SA has been approached, mainly by experiencing classical machine learning classifiers. For this reason, our work is part of the automatic analysis of Tunisian multilingual comments that are posted on social networks. In addition, we propose to study and evaluate some machine learning and deep learning techniques applied with multilingual textual productions. We focus in particular on using Bi-LSTM model.

4 Proposed Methodology

Basically, our approach consists of three major phases: Firstly, the data collection phase, where we collect and develop a corpus of multilingual comments. Secondly, the data preprocessing phase, where we preprocess the collected data. Finally, the model training phase where we train and test our Bi-LSTM model and evaluate it as compared to several machine learning classifiers (e.g., SVM, DT, NB, etc.) and deep learning models (e.g., LSTM, CNN, etc.). Figure 1 below shows the overall architecture of our SA system in which we have explained a process from the data collection, preprocessing, feature extraction and comments classification.

4.1 Data Collection

First of all, we will start by presenting the first phase "Data Collection" as shown with the block No.1 in Fig. 1.

Multilingual Tunisian Dialect Corpus

As a seed for our data collection process, we started by collecting data from the available Arabic and TD dataset that were used in classification tasks. We have collected four corpora, the first is the ASTD corpus; Arabic Sentiment Tweets Dataset, made available[3] by the authors [23]. The second corpus is TUNIZI [20]: A Tunisian Arabizi SA dataset, publicly available[4] for TD tasks and analytical studies. The third namely TSAC corpus: Tunisian Sentiment Analysis Corpus, TSAC is restricted to the TD and did include the Arabizi, Arabic and Latin texts. The authors [19] made the dataset publicly available[5] to the research community. Additionally, the CTSA dataset: Corona Tunisian Sentiment Analysis, freely available[6] for research. Finally, we have added more than 5K comments written using Latin and Arabic language extracted from Tunisian users from Twitter. Hence, the process of gathering data is inspired by the work of Abdellaoui et al. [24].

---

[3] https://github.com/mahmoudnabil/ASTD.

[4] https://github.com/chaymafourati/TUNIZI-Sentiment-Analysis-Tunisian-Arabizi-Dataset.

[5] https://github.com/fbougares/TSAC.

[6] https://www.kaggle.com/naim99/tsnaimmhedhbiv2.

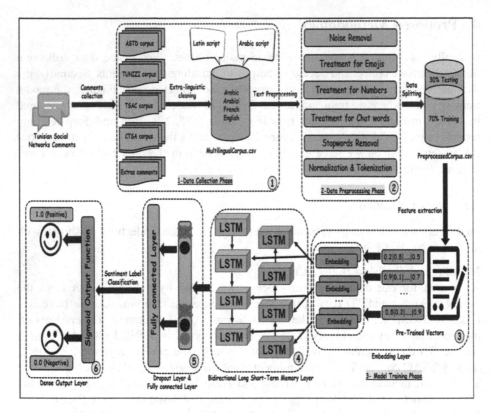

Fig. 1. The general architecture of the proposed sentiments analysis system

Extra-linguistic Cleaning

Once we combined all these sources, and randomly shuffled the data, an extra-linguistic cleaning step is necessary: Firstly, we have removed duplicated comments because repeated comments don't add an extra value to the SA, therefore, we have kept only one occurrence of each comment. Then, we have deleted duplicated words from the collected corpus comments. Subsequently, we have deleted comments that contain less than 10 characters. Finally, we have removed rows that contain empty comments. For the data manipulation, we have used the pandas[7] tool.

Table 2 shows some examples of comments extracted from the resultant corpus ("MultilingualCorpus.csv[8]" as illustrated in Fig. 2) after the extra-linguistic cleaning step.

---

[7] https://pandas.pydata.org.

[8] https://github.com/SAMAWELJABALLI/MultilingualDataset_TD.

Table 2. Sentiment classes with examples of Tunisian comments from the resultant corpus

Comments	Language	Sentiment
No comment 😒 😒 😒 😒	English	Negative
Mr le ministre donnez l'exemple et mettez une bavette svp 😊	French	Negative
N7ebkom barcha ya twensa ♡ ♡ البلاء عنكم يرفع ربي الله شاء إن و	Arabizi + Arabic	Positive
Au moins howa sre9 men dowal okhra w jabha ltounes mouch kima…	Arabizi	Negative
تونس في متضررة المناطق أكثر هي الحامة 😒😒	Arabic	Negative
Site arnaqueur de lux !!!!! Rodbelkom ya twensa 😨	French+ Arabizi	Negative

4.2 Data Preprocessing

The available collected corpus must go through a data preprocessing stage in order to create a usable corpus. To preprocess our data simply means to bring our multilingual text into a form that is predictable and analyzable for our classification task. The pipeline of data pre-processing is shown with the block No.2 in Fig. 1.

Noise Removal

As the comments of our corpus are web scrapped, chances are they contain some HTML tags, URLs, and links. Since these tags are not useful for our classification tasks, it is better to remove them. In addition, noise removal refers to removing special characters, hashtags, mentions and multiple whitespaces.

Treatment for Emojis

In social media networks, Tunisian users often use emoji and emoticon in a sentence to describe object instead of writing a word. Both emoji and emoticon give strong informations about a text such as feeling and emotional expression. The better approach to deal with emoji is to convert emoji to word so that it's being helpful to preserve information. For this reason, we have developed a small emoji to word converter that works as shown in the Table 3.

Table 3. Examples of conversions from an Emoji to a word

Emoji	Comment	Comment after the conversion
☹	Very bad service ☹ ☹الخدمة سيئة للغاية	Very bad service **sad** **حزين** الخدمة سيئة للغاية
😨	Site arnaqueur de lux 😨 😨موقع احتيال بامتياز	Site arnaqueur de lux **scared** موقع احتيال بامتياز **خائف**

Treatment for Numbers

There are two steps in our treatment of numbers. One of the steps involves the removal of numbers out-of-word. This step may make sense for SA since numbers contain no information about sentiments. While the other step refers to replace numbers concatenated with letters by their substitute letters (e.g., 7 = > h, 5 = > kh) such as the case of the Arabizi words as shown in the Table 4.

Table 4. Examples of comments after the treatment for numbers

Comment	Comment after the Treatment for numbers
5amsa w 5miss 3lik bent o5ty	Khamsa w khmis alik bent okhty
1000 Mabrouk 3zizty fra7tlek barcha	Mabrouk azizty frahtlek barcha

Treatment for Chat Words

Treatment for chat words refers to eliminate the characters redundancy while keeping the meaning of the words (e.g., رائععع <= رائع, veryyyyy helpful => very helpful). Frequent chat words also will be converted to their original words (e.g., slm => alem, lbs => abes). To extract the frequent chat words, we use the Unigram model.

Stopwords Removal

Recall that in our work, we are interested in the SA of multilingual comments and since publicly available stopwords extraction tools work only with monolingual corpora such as the example of NLTK[9] library, that's why we have developed a multilingual extractor stopwords. To do this, we used two N-grams models (Unigrams and Bigrams) and then we manually check the extracted words in such a way as the words which do not carry important meaning are removed. We cite as an example of stopwords (e.g., 'wiw', 'inty', 'na', 'je', 'wé', 'cete', 'بعد', 'eni', 'انت', 'ben', 'عن', 'al', 'mes', 'و'…).

Normalization & Tokenization

The final step in our preprocessing pipeline is the application of the normalization and the tokenization. Firstly, the normalization step which refers simply to lower casing all the words to reduce the vector dimensions. Secondly, we applied the tokenization step. To tokenize our text simply means to split the given text into smaller pieces called tokens. We have used the Keras Tokenizer[10] tool for tokenization. Thus, statistics, after preprocessing are stated in Table 5.

Table 5. Corpus statistics after preprocessing

Characteristic	#Comments	#Positive comments	#Negative comments	#Words	#Unique words
Number	199097	136821 (69%)	62276 (31%)	1583826	198994

---

[9] https://www.nltk.org.

[10] https://keras.io/api/preprocessing/text.

4.3   Model Training

At the beginning, we perform feature extraction for multilingual comments by using the Keras Embedding layer[11] which is defined as the first hidden layer of our proposed network. Firstly, the keras Embedding layer, requires that the input data should be integer encoded, so that each word is represented by a unique integer, i.e., a 2D input of shape (samples, indices). The next step refers to padding all the individual comments to be of the same length, accordingly, we will pad the shortest comments with 0 by using 'pad_sequences' function[12] from the Keras library.

Therefore, the 'input_length' will be equal to the length of the comment with maximum length or maximum number of words. Once all the comments are of the same length, we are ready to create and use our own embeddings. The following table shows the parameters used to create this layer (Table 6).

Table 6. Parameters used in the embedding layer

Input_dim[13]	Output_dim[14]	Input_length[15]
174834	148	50

Secondly, the vectors generated by the embedding layer will go through the next Bidirectional LSTM (Bi-LSTM) layer. A bidirectional LSTM which is variant of LSTM capable of capturing long-range dependencies on sequential data, it relies on the connection of two LSTMs layers from opposite directions (forward and backward) on the input sequence. Whereas in unidirectional LSTM, information flows from the backward to forward i.e., the LSTM networks reads the input sequence from one direction left to right. Thus, Bi-LSTM were used to escalate the chunk of input

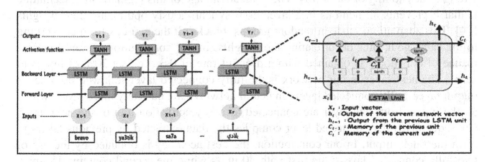

Fig. 2. The workflow of Bidirectional LSTM layer

---

[11] https://keras.io/api/layers/core_layers/embedding.

[12] https://keras.io/api/preprocessing/timeseries.

[13] input_dim: The vocabulary size that we will choose.

[14] output_dim: The number of dimensions we wish to embed into.

[15] input_length: The length of input sequences.

information usable to the network. The workflow of Bidirectional LSTM layer and the structure of one unit LSTM are shown in the following figure.

As shown in the Fig. 2, the outputs of the Bi-LSTM layer are determined by combining the outputs of the forward layer and backward layer by receiving both status information from the previous sequence (backward) and the next sequence (forward). Hence, outputs are activated by an activation function which is used to introduce a non-linearity in the functioning of the neurons. The default activation function of LSTM is the TANH which helps to normalize the output of any input by producing outputs in scale of [−1, 1].

LSTM unit, is generally composed of 4 layers, interacting and controlling the information to forget or to pass on to the next time step [25]. The right block in Fig. 2 illustrates the interaction between the layers in an LSTM unit. These layers can be summarized as follows, where f_t, i_t, o_t and C_t represent respectively the forget, input, output gates and cell state. As well, δ is the sigmoid function.

$$f_t = \delta\left(W_f[h_{t-1}, x_t] + b_f\right) \tag{1}$$

$$\tilde{C} = tanh(W_c[h_{t-1}, x_t] + b_c \tag{2}$$

$$i_t = \delta(W_i[h_{t-1}, x_t] + b_i) \tag{3}$$

$$C_t = f_t C_{t-1} + i_t \tilde{C}_t \tag{4}$$

$$o_t = \delta(W_o[h_{t-1}, x_t] + b_o) \tag{5}$$

$$h_t = o_t tanh(C_t) \tag{6}$$

Afterwards, we apply the dropout layer to avoid overfitting or even to avoid the wrong dimensioning of the words. The main advantage of this regularization technique is that it prevents all neurons in a layer from synchronously optimizing their weights [24]. This adaptation, made in random groups, blocks all the neurons from converging to the same goal, thus decorrelating the weights. In our contribution, the best performance of our model is obtained with a dropout rate of 0.3 (i.e., set 30% of inputs to zero). The next layer in our network is the fully connected layer followed by a dense output layer. Fully connected layers in neural networks are basically those layers where all the inputs from one layer are connected to every activation unit of the next layer. Consequently, fully connected layer compiles the data extracted by previous layers to form the final output. In our contribution, the best accuracy is obtained by the use of two fully connected layers: the first with 30 units while the second contains 15 units.

Lastly, the output dense layer (as shown with the block No.6 in Fig. 1) receiving the last hidden layer output to merge and produce the final result which means to generate the polarity of each input comment. In this context, a sigmoid activation function with 2 output units is used to predict the correct label, this function takes any real value as input and produces outputs values in scale of [0, 1]. The larger the input (more positive), the closer the output value will be to 1.0, while the smaller the input (more negative), the closer the output will be to 0.0.

5 Experiments and Results

5.1 Baseline

In the experiment, we have performed our experiments with several types of classification algorithms. The first set of experiments is performed to measure the performance of traditional machine learning method. We cite as an example the NB, SVM, and Logistic Regression (LR) classifiers, and these are applied on different combination of preprocessed data. At the feature extraction level, we have used three embedding models, namely the Bag Of Words (BOW), Term Frequency-Inverse Document Frequency (TF-IDF) and the Average Word2vec model (avg-word2vec).

The second set of experiments is performed to evaluate the performance of the state-of-art deep learning models (CNN, LSTM and Bi-LSTM). The performances of those models are represented by testing different configurations and hyper-parameters during the training phase. Notice, we have used the most widely popular measures retrieval namely, Accuracy, Recall and F1 score.

5.2 Dataset

With the object of presenting our multilingual corpus used for sentiment classification, we have divided randomly our collected data into two corpora. The first is the training corpus which represents 70% of the total size, while the second constitutes 30% of the corpus used for the test. Table 7 reports the corpus size followed by the vocabulary size for the training and test corpus.

Table 7. The Corpus size followed by the vocabulary size

	#Comments	Vocabulary size
Training corpus	139 k	1109 k
Test corpus	60 k	475 k

5.3 Experimental Results

In the experiment, deep learning models were performed using Keras library, while machine learning models were performed using Scikit-Learn[16] library. During training, the hyperparameters that resulted in the best performance are shown in the Table 8.

---

[16] https://scikit-learn.org.

Table 8. Hyperparameters that resulted in the best performance during training phase

Hyperparameter	Value	Hyperparameter	Value
Epochs	4	Maxlen	50
Learning rate	0.2	Dropout	0.3
Optimization function	Adam	BatchSize	128
Loss Function	BinaryCrossentropy	VectorSize	148

Table 9. Experimental results obtained with machine learning classifiers on our multilingual test corpus

Label prediction after preprocessing					
Classifier + Embedding	Label	Recall	F1 score	Accuracy	Preprocessing Improvement
SVM + BOW	POS	0.96	0.88	**0.82**	**+ 0.018**
	NEG	0.5	0.63		
SVM + TF-IDF	POS	0.96	0.85	**0.77**	**+ 0.012**
	NEG	0.36	0.5		
SVM + Avg-Word2vec	POS	0.95	0.82	**0.72**	**+ 0.012**
	NEG	0.21	0.32		
NB + BOW	POS	0.9	0.88	**0.84**	**+ 0.02**
	NEG	0.74	0.76		
NB + TF-IDF	POS	0.93	0.9	**0.85**	**+ 0.013**
	NEG	0.7	0.75		
LR + BOW	POS	0.94	0.88	**0.84**	**+ 0.027**
	NEG	0.68	0.73		
LR + TF-IDF	POS	0.93	0.89	**0.85**	**+ 0.029**
	NEG	0.71	0.75		
LR + Avg-Word2vec	POS	0.91	0.82	**0.73**	**−0.013**
	NEG	0.34	0.44		
DT + BOW	POS	0.89	0.86	**0.8**	**+ 0.01**
	NEG	0.58	0.64		
DT + TF-IDF	POS	0.9	0.86	**0.79**	**+ 0.009**
	NEG	0.56	0.63		
DT + Avg-Word2vec	POS	0.86	0.82	**0.74**	**−0.002**
	NEG	0.49	0.54		
RF + TF-IDF	POS	0.85	0.84	**0.78**	**+ 0.01**
	NEG	0.62	0.64		
RF + Avg-Word2vec	POS	0.89	0.86	**0.81**	**+ 0.012**
	NEG	0.63	0.67		
XGBoost + TF-IDF	POS	0.96	0.86	**0.79**	**+ 0.012**
	NEG	0.42	0.56		
XGBoost + Avg-Word2vec	POS	0.89	0.87	**0.81**	**+ 0.016**
	NEG	0.63	0.68		

Table 9 above shows the experimental results obtained with machine learning classifiers by taking into account the improvement of our preprocessing method. The following table (see Table 10) summarizes the second set of experiments obtained with deep learning models (CNN, LSTM and Bi-LSTM) by testing different configurations during the training phase.

Table 10. Experimental results obtained with deep learning models on our multilingual test corpus

Model Configuration	Label	Recall	F1 score	Accuracy
Embedding Layer + RNN layer	POS	0.93	0.89	**0.84**
	NEG	0.68	0.73	
Embedding Layer + LSTM Layer + Fully Connected Layer	POS	0.91	0.89	**0.85**
	NEG	0.71	0.75	
Embedding Layer + LSTM Layer + Dropout Layer + Fully Connected Layer	POS	0.93	0.9	**0.86**
	NEG	0.72	0.77	
Embedding Layer + Bi-LSTM Layer + Fully Connected Layer	POS	0.93	0.91	**0.87**
	NEG	0.73	0.78	
Embedding Layer + Bi-LSTM Layer + Fully Connected Layer	POS	0.92	0.88	**0.85**
	NEG	0.73	0.73	
Embedding Layer + CNN Layer + Fully Connected Layer	POS	0.92	0.86	**0.84**
	NEG	0.67	0.74	
Embedding Layer + CNN Layer + 2 Dropout Layer + 2 Fully Connected Layer	POS	0.93	0.9	**0.85**
	NEG	0.7	0.75	
Embedding Layer + Bi-LSTM Layer + 2 Dropout Layer + 2 Fully Connected Layer	POS	0.95	0.93	**0.88**
	NEG	0.76	0.8	

The Models' Parameters Were Tuned as follows[17]

5.4   Discussion

According to Table 9, in which we have performed six machine learning algorithms applied with three embeddings models (BOW, TF-IDF, Avg-Word2vec), we can clearly see that the NB and the LR were the only classifiers obtaining above 84% of accuracy. We note also That the TF-IDF features model performed slightly better with these two classifiers. For the same table, the experimental results clearly indicate that our preprocessing approach has improved the prediction performance of our SA system (i.e., + 0.029 improvement with the LR classifier). Otherwise, we note that the Recall values of the negative class (varies from 0.21 to 0.74) are very low compared to the positive classes (varies from 0.85 to 0.96). We can conclude here that both LR and NB classifiers did a great job in correctly classifying true comments or examples of the positive class (High Recall) but they did less in eliminating the false examples of the

---

[17] Epoch = 4 (all models); Batch size = 128 and LSTM/CNN Units = 100.

negative class (Relatively low Recall). This problem is solved later thanks to sequential deep learning models (see Table 10).

Table 10 shows the second set of experiments performed with deep learning models by testing different configurations during the training phase. The experimental results clearly indicate that the Bi-LSTM and the LSTM model can obtain a good performance of the multilingual sentiment classification. The two best performances are underlined. We note that Bi-LSTM outperforms both of LSTM and CNN in terms of accuracy and F1 score whatever the configuration. Recall is significantly improved for the negative class, reaching around 68% in the worst cases. Additionally, we notice that the use of dropout layer decreases the overfitting problem as a result it improves the performance of proposed deep learning models.

The best performance (about 88% accuracy) is obtained with embedding layer, Bi-LSTM layer and two dropout layers followed by two fully connected layers. The architecture proposed in this paper introduces Bi-LSTM network, which can capture the semantic information of the context more effectively, so the SA system works better. Therefore, we can consider the Bidirectional LSTM network as a good solution for extracting semantic information from multilingual corpora.

6 Conclusion

We tackled in this paper, the issue of multilingual comments in Tunisian dialect textual productions that are generated on social networks. This type of data still presents a number of challenges, due to its complexity, unformal, and code-switched nature. We consider our work as a preliminary study that aimed to propose sentiment classification approach based on Bidirectional LSTM for multilingual comments.

Due to the lack of publicly available multilingual resources associated with the TD, we collected different datasets available with different variants of TD to create our own multilingual corpus for sentiment classification. Notice, that our dataset is publicly[18] available to the research community. The comparison experiments demonstrate that our model achieves significant improvements over the state-of-art deep learning models and the baseline traditional machine learning methods.

Our future works will focus on exploring other word embeddings models specifically trained for the multilingual SA task, for example, those that use an attention mechanism. In addition, we will try to increase the corpus size by using data augmentation techniques.

Acknowledgment. The authors would like to express their greatest gratitude to other members of the Research Laboratory in Algebra, Numbers theory and Intelligent Systems (RLANTIS) for their support and help to realize this paper.

---

[18] https://github.com/SAMAWELJABALLI/MultilingualDataset_TD/.

References

1. Ayadi, R., Maraoui, M., Zrigui, M.: Latent topic model for indexing Arabic documents. In: International Journal of Information Retrieval Res. **4**(2), 57–72 (2014)
2. Merhben, L., Zouaghi, A., Zrigui, M.: Lexical disambiguation of arabic language: an experimental study. In: Polibits **46**, 49–54 (2012)
3. Batita, M.A., Ayadi, R., Zrigui, M.: Reasoning over Arabic wordnet relations with neural tensor network. In: Computación y Sistemas **23**(3), 935–942 (2019)
4. Haffar, N., Hkiri, E., Zrigui, M.: TimeML annotation of events and temporal expressions in Arabic texts. In: Nguyen, N.T., Chbeir, R., Exposito, E., Aniorté, P., Trawiński, B. (eds.) ICCCI 2019. LNCS (LNAI), vol. 11683, pp. 207–218. Springer, Cham (2019). https://doi.org/10.1007/978-3-030-28377-3_17
5. Bsir, B., Zrigui, M.: Enhancing deep learning gender identification with gated recurrent units architecture in social text. In: Computación y Sistemas **22**(3), 757–766 (2018)
6. Mahmoud, A., Zrigui, M.: Deep neural network models for paraphrased text classification in the Arabic language. Natural Language Processing and Information Systems. Springer Cham (2019) https://doi.org/10.1007/978-3-030-23281-8_1
7. Zrigui, S., Ayadi, R., Zouaghi, A., Zrigui, S.: Isao: An intelligent system of opinions analysis. In: Research in Computing Science **110**(1), 21–30 (2016)
8. Sghaier, M.A., Zrigui, M.: Sentiment analysis for Arabic e-commerce websites. In: International Conference on Engineering & MIS (ICEMIS), pp. 1–7 (2016)
9. Merhbene, L., Zouaghi, A., Zrigui, M.: A semi-supervised method for Arabic word sense disambiguation using a weighted directed graph. In: Proceedings of the Sixth International Joint Conference on Natural Language Processing, pp. 1027–1031 (2013)
10. Bellagha, M.L., Zrigui, M.: Using the MGB-2 challenge data for creating a new multimodal Dataset for speaker role recognition in Arabic TV Broadcasts In: Procedia Computer Science **192**, 59–68 (2021)
11. Legrand, A., Trystram, D., Zrigui, S.: Adapting batch scheduling to workload characteristics: What can we expect from online learning? In: IEEE International Parallel and Distributed processing symposium (IPDPS), pp. 686–685. (2019)
12. Sghaier, M.A., Zrigui, M.: Rule-Based Machine Translation from Tunisian Dialect to Modern Standard Arabic. In: Procedia Computer Science **176**, pp. 310–319 (2020)
13. Merhben, L., Zouaghi, A., Zrigui, M.: Disambiguation of Arabic language: an experimental study. In: Polibits **46**, pp. 49–54 (2012)
14. Shoukry, A., Rafea, A.: Sentence-level arabic sentiment analysis. In: 2012 International Conference on Collaboration Technologies and Systems (CTS), pp. 546–550 (2012)
15. Abdul-Mageed, M., Diab, M., Kübler, S.: SAMAR: subjectivity and sentiment analysis for Arabic social media. In: Computer Speech Language **28**(1), 20–37 (2014)
16. Salamah, J.B., Elkhlifi, A.: Microblogging opinion mining approach for Kuwaiti Dialect. In: Proceedings of the International Conference on Computing Technology and Information Management, pp. 388–396 (2014)
17. Abdelli, A., Guerrouf, F., Tibermacine, O., Abdelli, B.: Sentiment analysis of Arabic algerian dialect using a supervised method. In: 2019 International Conference on Intelligent Systems and Advanced Computing Sciences (ISACS), pp. 1–6 (2019)
18. Masmoudi, A., Hamdi, J., Belguith, L.H.: Deep learning for sentiment analysis of Tunisian Dialect. In: Computación y Sistemas **25**(1), 129–148 (2021)
19. Medhaffar, S., Bougares, F., Esteve, Y., Hadrich-Belguith, L.: Sentiment analysis of tunisian dialects: Linguistic ressources and experiments. In: Proceedings of the third Arabic natural language processing workshop (WANLP), Valencia, Spain, pp. 55–61 (2017)

20. Fourati, C., Messaoudi, A., Haddad, H.: TUNIZI: a Tunisian Arabizi sentiment analysis Dataset. In: The International Conference on Learning Representations (ICLR) (2020)
21. Mulki, H., Haddad, H., Ali, C.B., Babaoğlu, I.: Tunisian dialect sentiment analysis: a natural language processing-based approach. In: Computación y Sistemas **22**(4), 1223–1232 (2018)
22. Jerbi, M.A., Achour, H., Souissi, E.: Sentiment analysis of code-switched tunisian dialect: exploring RNN-based techniques. In: Smaïli, K. (ed.) ICALP 2019. CCIS, vol. 1108, pp. 122–131. Springer, Cham (2019). https://doi.org/10.1007/978-3-030-32959-4_9
23. Nabil, M., Aly, M., Atiya, A.: ASTD: Arabic Sentiment Tweets Dataset. In: Proceedings of the 2015 Conference on Empirical Methods in Natural Language Processing, pp. 2515–2519 (2015)
24. Abdellaoui, H., Zrigui, M.: Using tweets and emojis to build TEAD: an arabic dataset for sentiment analysis. In: Computación y Sistemas **22**(3), 777–786 (2018)
25. Haffar, N., Hkiri, E., Zrigui, M.: Using bidirectional LSTM and shortest dependency path for classifying arabic temporal relations. KES **2020**, 370–379 (2020)
26. Bsir, B., Zrigui, M.: Bidirectional LSTM for author gender identification. In: International Conference on Computational Collective Intelligence, pp. 393–402 (2018)

Non-Contextual vs Contextual Word Embeddings in Multiword Expressions Detection

Maciej Piasecki[✉][iD] and Kamil Kanclerz[iD]

Department of Artificial Intelligence, Wrocław University of Science and Technology,
Wrocław, Poland
{maciej.piasecki,kamil.kanclerz}@pwr.edu.pl

Abstract. Multiword Expression (MWE) detection is a crucial problem
for many NLP applications. Recent methods approach it as a sequence
labeling task and require manually annotated corpus. Traditional methods are based on statistical association measures and express limited
accuracy, especially on smaller corpora. In this paper, we propose a novel
weakly supervised method for extracting MWEs which concentrates on
differences between interactions with context between the whole MWE
and its component words. The interactions are represented by contextual
embeddings (neural language models) and the observations are collected
from various occurrence contexts of both the whole MWEs and their
single word components. Our method uses a MWE lexicon as the sole
knowledge base, and extracts training samples by matching the lexicon
against a corpus to build classifiers for MWE recognition by Machine
Learning. Thus, our approach does not require a corpus annotated with
MWE occurrences, and also works with a limited corpus and a MWE
list (≈1400 MWEs in this work). It uses a general contextual embeddings model, HerBERTa, a kind of BERT model for Polish. The proposed
method was evaluated on the Polish part of the PARSEME corpus and
expressed very significant gain in comparison to the top methods from
the PARSEME competition. The proposed method can be quite easily
applied to other languages.

Keywords: Natural language processing · Multiword expressions ·
Detection of multiword expressions · Contextual embeddings

1 Introduction

Multiword expressions (henceforth MWEs) are defined in different ways with
different scope, e.g. see the overview in [26]. In our work, we lean towards lexi-
cographic perspective on MWEs, i.e. considered as lexical units that "has to be
listed in a lexicon" [12] and focus on automated extraction of MWEs from text
corpora to include them in a lexicon as multi-word lexical units. Summarising

© The Author(s), under exclusive license to Springer Nature Switzerland AG 2022
N. T. Nguyen et al. (Eds.): ICCCI 2022, LNAI 13501, pp. 193–206, 2022.
https://doi.org/10.1007/978-3-031-16014-1_16

a bit the definition of [26], MWEs are "lexical items that decomposable into multiple lexemes", "present idiomatic behaviour at some level of linguistic analysis" and "must be treated as a unit" from the computational point of view and thus should be described in a semantic lexicon. A similar definition was adopted in the PARSEME Shared Task resource [27,28]. Several MWE properties are postulated that can guide the extraction process, like arbitrariness, institutionalisation, limited semantic variability (especially non-compositionality and non-substitutability), domain-specificity and limited syntactic variability [26]. Description of MWEs in a semantic lexicon is important for many NLP applications like semantic indexing, knowledge graph extraction, vector models, topic modelling etc. Due to specific properties of MWEs as whole units their good description by distributional semantics, e.g. embeddings, is not guaranteed by default, especially in the case of low frequency MWEs.

Traditionally, MWEs extraction is performed by recognition of significant collocations by statistical association measures combined with different forms of filtering, e.g. by syntactic patterns. Recently sequence labelling scheme started to dominate in MWE extraction, in which MWEs are language expressions of specific behaviour recognised by deep learning. However, such approaches require a corpus manually annotated with MWEs that is always a limited resource.

We propose a new weakly supervised method for MWE extraction from large text corpora that takes into account their peculiar properties and behaviour as elements of language structures in various contexts. The proposed method combines neural language modelling with machine learning and a lexicon of MWES as the sole knowledge base. We assume that most MWEs are monosemous, see Sect. 2, and having a list of correct MWEs and incorrect 'MWEs' (i.e. language expressions that should not be included in a lexicon), we can find their occurrences in a corpus and learn from them properties that distinguish genuine MWEs from mere language expression. In contrast to most recent methods, we neither need a corpus laboriously annotated with MWE occurrences, nor language models specially trained for this task. We have investigated and combined non-contextual representation of MWEs as a lexical units and their contextual representation as elements of sentence structure (language structures). For the latter purpose, we leverage deep neural contextual embeddings to describe peculiarities of the semantic but also syntactic behaviour of MWEs in contrast to the behaviour of their components in the same contexts. What is more, the evidence for the whole MWEs and their components can be collected from across the whole corpus, not only the actual MWE occurrences. Our method can be relatively easy applied to any language, as the only required elements are: a text corpus, an initial lexicon of MWEs and a general contextual embeddings model.

In Sect. 3 we present the key element of the approach: two ways of representing MWEs and their occurrences with the help of non-contextual and contextual embeddings. Section 4 presents ML methods applied to the proposed representation. In the rest of the paper we discuss and compare the obtained very good results, as well as ways to expand the proposed approach to the whole spectrum of MWEs.

2   Related Work

Initially MWE recognition was based on statistical association measures applied to MWE statistics calculated on corpora to rank collocations as potential MWEs, e.g. [12]. Individual measures were also combined into complex ones, e.g. by a neural network [24]. Syntactic information from parsing, e.g. [33], or morpho-syntactic tagging and lexico-syntactic constraints, e.g. [7], was used in counting statistics, pre-filtering (detecting candidates), e.g. [2], or post-filtering extracted collocations. MWE detection was also leveraged by tree substitution grammar formalism [13] or a finite state transducer combined with a part of speech tagger [15]. In the case of Polish, [25] combined several association measures by a genetic algorithm and added filtering based on lexico-syntactic constraints. Several systems for MWE extraction combining different techniques were also proposed, e.g. *mwetoolkit* of [26], which also offers a possibility to describe collocations with feature vectors for supervised ML-based filtering.

ML-based MWE extraction use lexico-syntactic patterns, different properties (e.g. length, frequency, specificity) or association measure values to represent training/testing samples (mostly MWE as types, not occurrences), e.g. [34].

Recently, MWE extraction started to be treated as a sequence labelling problem. A corpus is annotated at the level of single words (BIO format [29]: B – a word begins a MWE occurrence, I – its component, and O – falls outside any MWE) and supervised ML-based methods are applied to label word sequences, e.g. [9].

Sequence labelling approaches can also be combined with heuristic rules [32] or supersenses of nouns or verbs [17] to detect MWEs characterised by language-specific structures. Heuristics are also applied to extraction of linguistic features from texts for training Bayesian network model [8]. Thus, convolutional graph networks and self-attention mechanisms can be used to extract additional features characterising language expressions [30]. There are many challenges related to the nature of the MWEs detection task, like discontinuity (O tokens occur inside an MWE sequences) or overlapping (a special case of discontinuity, components of two MWE are intermingled). To counteract this, a model based on the LSTM network expanded with CRF layer was developed [4]. The model of [35] proposes learning of the two tasks: MWE recognition and dependency parsing in parallel. The approach presented in [20] leverages feature-independent model with standard contextual embeddings obtained via BERT model. The mBERT model was also tested, but with lower results.

Morpho-syntactic information can be also an input to recurrent neural networks [18]. In [36] a bidirectional LSTM-CRF architecture was applied to a rich set of word features: word embedding, POS tag, dependency relation, and its head word. Sentences containing MWEs were also represented as subgraphs enriched with morphological features [6]. Graphs were expanded with *word2vec* [21] embeddings to describe word relations and predict the corresponding linguistic functions [3]. [31] compared two approaches to MWE recognition within a transition system (the problem: "a sequence of local transition predictions"): the first based on a multi-layer perceptron and the second on linear SVM. Both utilise only lemmas and morpho-syntactic annotations from the corpus and were trained and tested on PARSEME Shared Task 1.1 data [27].

Sequence labeling approaches brought relatively good results. However, they focus mainly on the position and order of words within a sentence, and seem to pay less attention to semantic incompatibility or relations between MWE components. Furthermore, sequence labeling methods do not emphasize the semantic diversity of contexts in which MWEs occur – each MWE occurrence is treated separately. In addition, it allows to distinguish a true MWE from a mere collocation. To the best of our knowledge, the concept of using deep neural contextual embeddings to describe the semantics of the MWEs components and the internal relationship between their meanings in the MWE detection task has not yet been sufficiently studied. Moreover, due to the sparsity of the MWEs occurrences in the corpus, the process of annotating each word in a corpus is very time consuming and can lead to many errors and low agreement level among the annotators. For this reason, we propose a lexicon-based corpus annotation method. Assuming that the vast majority of MWE are monosemous, e.g. the set of more than 50 k MWEs in plWordNet [11], we perform an automated extraction of sentences containing the MWE occurrences and treat all sentences including a given MWE as representing the same multiword lexical unit.

3   Dataset

In order to facilitate comparison with other approaches, we used the PARSEME corpus [28] manually annotated with MWE occurrences as the data source. In all experiments we focused only on two-word continuous MWE[1] and the Polish subcorpus of PARSEME. Two separate datasets to test the two different MWE representations were extracted from the corpus. The first one was based on *noncontextual* word embeddings: all expressions marked as MWEs were collected to form a list of correct samples. To obtain the learning samples of incorrect MWEs, we extracted all two-word expressions that were marked as MWE in PARSEME but which matched MWE structural patterns observed for correct MWEs. Furthermore, we used dependency graphs to verify if in each of the expressions the two words are syntactically related.

The second set includes MWE occurrences represented by contextual embeddings. The extracted sentences contain both: correct or incorrect MWEs that were found by matching the elements of the first set with the corpus sentences on the level of lemmas, see the extraction procedure in Algorithm 1.

3.1   Non-Contextual Dataset

The non-contextual dataset contains 1,481 correct and 28,917 incorrect MWEs from the PARSEME dataset. In order to generate the embeddings of MWE

---

[1] Such MWEs form the vast majority of cases, both in PARSEME (only 111 out of 1,481 total correct MWE are longer) and plWordNet.

Algorithm 1. Extraction of sentences (s) from corpus (C) if they contain MWEs or their components on the basis of comparing sentence word lemmas $(l_i \in [l_0, l_1, \ldots, l_n])$ to the list (M) of lemmatized MWEs $(m_j \in [m_0, m_1, \ldots, m_k])$

 1: *sentence_list* ← [ ]
 2: **for** $s \in C$ **do**
 3:    **for** $l_i \in s$ **do**
 4:       **for** $m_j \in M$ **do**
 5:          **if** $l_i \in m_j$ **then**
 6:             *sentence_list*.insert(s)
 7:          **end if**
 8:       **end for**
 9:    **end for**
10: **end for**
11: **return** *sentence_list*

---

components we leveraged the SkipGram model variant from the *fastText* library [5]. The final vector representation consists of five major components: (1) x – first multiword unit component embedding, (2) y – second multiword component embedding, (3) $x_i - y_i$ – the vector of differences between the embeddings , (4) $|x_i - y_i|$ – the vector of absolute values of differences, and (5) $x \circ y$ – the vector of Hadamard products based on component embeddings. The SkipGram model was trained on the KGR10 [19] – a very large corpus of general Polish. The procedure of generating non-contextual embeddings is shown in Fig. 1.

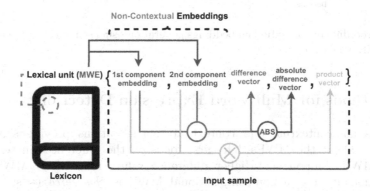

Fig. 1. Non-contextual embeddings generation using lexicon obtained from the PARSEME dataset.

3.2   Contextual Dataset

MWEs from the first set (Sect. 3.1), both correct and incorrect, were used to collect 47,695 sentences from PARSEME as examples of their use. In this way we simulated a situation in which the only description of MWEs is a lexicon, not an annotated corpus. MWE occurrences were detected by simply comparing their lemmas with sentence lemmas (sub-sequences). If multiple MWEs were detected in a single sentence, then each of them was associated with that sentence and stored as a separate samples. The process starts with generating the contextual embeddings of the whole MWEs and their components in sentence contexts. Firstly an embedding of a single MWE component is an average of the vectors of its subtokens. Next, a component in a sentence is replaced by the complete MWE and its vector representation is also generated as the average. The final sample representation consists of 5 parts: (1) x – the component contextual embedding, (2) m – the whole MWE embedding, (3) $x_i - m_i$ – the vector of element-wise differences between the component and MWE, (4) $|x_i - m_i|$ – the absolute values of the differences, (5) $x \circ y$ – the Hadamard product of both vectors. The complete procedure is presented in Fig. 2.

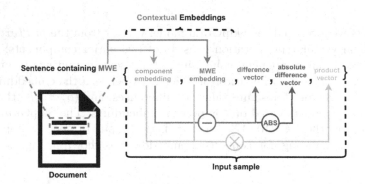

Fig. 2. Procedure of contextual embeddings generation using sentences extracted from the PARSEME dataset.

4   Methods for Multiword Expression Detection

Both the non-contextual and contextual representations provide significant knowledge about the MWEs. The first focus on the differences in semantics of the MWE components. Higher difference values may signal MWE non-compositionality, e.g. a non-compositional MWE is *głos serca* (≈'strong self persuasion'), whose meaning is a simple function of the component meanings, in contrast to a compositional and an incorrect MWE (in PARSEME) *materiał opatrunkowy* ('bandage cloth'), whose meaning can be easily deduced. Moreover, the contextual embeddings express the MWE interaction with the context and, *vice versa*, the influence of the context on the MWE semantics, e.g. a correct MWE *ojciec chrzestny* ('a godfather') occurs in many different contexts, but its non-compositional meaning is not affected by them, contrary to compositional *barwnik naturalny* ('a natural pigment') which may be modified in many ways in different contexts.

In order to verify the role of contextual knowledge in the MWEs detection task we used three different classifiers:

- **Logistic Regression (LR)** – a low complexity model, leveraging the logistic function to model the probability distribution of class occurrence,
- **Random Forest (RF)** – an ensemble model, using predictions of multiple decision trees to calculate the mode of their predictions as the final output,
- **Convolutional Neural Network (CNN)** – using convolution kernels to extract additional knowledge from the input data.

In selecting of classifier settings, we focused on the specificity of our datasets. We decided to use logistic regression (LR), random forest (RF), and convolutional neural network (CNN) architectures, i.e. following a completely different scheme than the sequence labelling methods.

5   Experiments

For the contextual embeddings, we used the HerBERT model [22], built on a very large corpus and expressing good performance for Polish texts. We used the LR and RF implementations from the scikit-learn library [23], and TensorFlow framework [1] for CNN. The selected CNN architecture contains three convolutional hidden layers each followed by pooling and dropout layers. Due to the high class imbalance in both datasets, we focused on the F1-macro measure during evaluation. We also used a modified variant of the loss function, including the knowledge about the class imbalance and applying weights to compensate the differences between the number of samples for each class in the training set.

In order to cope with the class imbalance, we generated additional synthetic samples with the use of the four different SMOTE methods: (1) SMOTE [10], (2) SVM-SMOTE [10], (3) Borderline SMOTE [14], and (4) ADASYN [16]. The 10-fold cross-validation scheme was applied during evaluation. Statistical tests verified the significance of differences between method variants. Firstly, we checked the assumptions of the t-test for independent samples and conducted it if they were met. Otherwise the Mann-Whitney U test was used.

6   Results

The evaluation results with comparison between the non-contextual and contextual approaches are shown in Table 1. The contextual embeddings turned out to provide more in-depth information that resulted in higher F1-score values. Figure 3 shows the gain in the macro F1-score resulting from contextual embeddings. The LR model achieved the highest gain (10%) that may be caused by the low complexity of this model, preventing overfitting to the long input vectors which potentially contain noise. On the other hand, the low F1-score measure of the CNN model may be caused by the small size of the dataset. Such a complex deep neural architecture requires large datasets to propagate the knowledge across all of its layers. The high imbalance between classes caused the CNN model to overfit only to the majority class. The increase in the F1-score for the incorrect MWEs is shown in the Fig. 4. The highest gains were observed for RF and CNN.

Table 1. F1-score values for incorrect MWEs (Inc F1), correct MWEs (Cor F1) and macro F1-score (F1) for non-contextual (N-C) and contextual (C) embeddings of the PARSEME dataset. Models: logistic regression (LR), random forest (RF), convolutional neural network (CNN). Values in **bold** are statistically significantly better.

Model	Embedding	Inc F1	Cor F1	F1
LR	N-C	0.83	0.80	0.81
	C	**0.98**	**0.85**	**0.91**
RF	N-C	0.81	0.67	0.74
	C	**0.97**	**0.69**	**0.83**
CNN	N-C	0.78	0.00	0.39
	C	**0.94**	0.00	**0.47**

Table 2 presents the application of different SMOTE methods, see Sect. 5, for generation of additional synthetic samples in the non-contextual embeddings dataset. Every SMOTE method provided a significant improvement in the performance of the RF and CNN models. The highest gains were observed for Borderline SMOTE in the case of CNN model – 34% for correct MWEs and 12% points for the overall F1-score.

Table 2. F1-score values for incorrect MWEs (Inc F1), correct MWEs (Cor F1) and macro F1-score (F1) for logistic regression (LR), random forest (RF), and convolutional neural network (CNN) models trained on the non-contextual embeddings of the PARSEME dataset with the use of four different SMOTE methods: SMOTE, SVM-SMOTE, Borderline SMOTE, and ADASYN in comparison to not using any SMOTE method (None). Values in **bold** are statistically significantly better.

SMOTE Method	LR			RF			CNN		
	Inc F1	Cor F1	F1	Inc F1	Cor F1	F1	Inc F1	Cor F1	F1
None	0.83	0.80	0.81	0.81	0.67	0.74	**0.78**	0.00	0.39
SMOTE	0.83	0.80	0.81	0.81	**0.72**	**0.76**	0.76	0.25	0.50
SVM-SMOTE	0.83	0.80	0.81	0.81	**0.72**	**0.76**	0.76	0.16	0.46
Borderline SMOTE	0.83	0.80	0.81	0.81	**0.72**	**0.76**	0.68	**0.34**	**0.51**
ADASYN	0.83	0.80	0.81	0.81	0.71	**0.76**	0.72	0.28	0.50

The results for the application of the SMOTE methods for the contextual embeddings are presented in Table 3. The highest increase brought Borderline SMOTE combined with CNN in the case of correct MWEs both for correct MWEs and macro F1-score – 41% and 15%, respectively.

Table 3. F1-score values for incorrect MWEs (Inc F1), correct MWEs (Cor F1) and macro F1-score (F1) for logistic regression (LR), random forest (RF), and convolutional neural network (CNN) models trained on the contextual embeddings of the PARSEME dataset with the use of four different SMOTE methods: SMOTE, SVM-SMOTE, Borderline SMOTE, and ADASYN in comparison to not using any SMOTE method (None). Values in **bold** are statistically significantly better.

SMOTE Method	LR			RF			CNN		
	Inc F1	Cor F1	F1	Inc F1	Cor F1	F1	Inc F1	Cor F1	F1
None	0.98	**0.85**	0.91	0.97	0.69	0.83	**0.94**	0.00	0.47
SMOTE	0.98	0.84	0.91	0.97	**0.76**	**0.86**	0.91	0.30	0.60
SVM-SMOTE	0.98	0.84	0.91	0.97	**0.76**	**0.86**	0.91	0.22	0.56
Borderline SMOTE	0.98	0.84	0.91	0.97	0.75	**0.86**	0.82	**0.41**	**0.62**
ADASYN	0.98	0.84	0.91	0.97	0.75	**0.86**	0.88	0.32	0.60

The LR model trained on the contextual embeddings (LR-C) achieved the best results in total. Therefore, the comparison of its performance with the methods presented during the PARSEME Shared Task on Semi-supervised Identification of Verbal Multiword Expressions for incorrect MWEs [28]. The LR-C model achieved better results than all methods – 21% gain for the F1-score in comparison to the next best method (Table 4).

Table 4. Results of our best model – LR trained on the contextual embeddings (LR-C) in comparison to the approaches presented during Edition 1.2 of the PARSEME Shared Task on Semi-supervised Identification of Verbal Multiword Expressions for incorrect MWEs [28]. Metrics: precision (P), recall (R), F1-score (F1). The results, which are statistically better than others are set in **bold**.

Model	P	R	F1
LR-C	**0.90**	**0.93**	**0.91**
MTLB-STRUCT	0.71	0.69	0.70
Seen2Seen	0.76	0.59	0.66
Seen2Unseen	0.63	0.63	0.63
TRAVIS-multi	0.61	0.58	0.59
ERMI	0.65	0.53	0.58
TRAVIS-mono	0.50	0.44	0.47
FlipsCo	0.12	0.03	0.10
HMSid	0.05	0.05	0.05

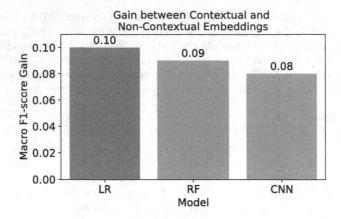

Fig. 3. The increase of F1-score between the evaluation results for models trained on contextual embeddings and the one trained on the non-contextual embeddings.

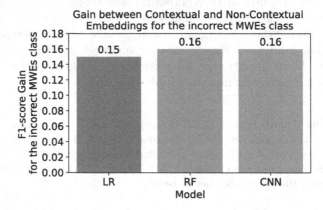

Fig. 4. F1-score gain between the performance of models trained on contextual and non-contextual MWE embeddings measured only on incorrect MWEs.

7   Discussion

Our method of generating contextual embeddings can be applied to any collection of documents in order to transform it into a fully fledged, annotated corpus. The only necessary element is the lexicon containing example MWEs for a given language. In comparison to the standard annotation process, our procedure is less time-consuming and requires less resources. The lexicon is also easier to maintain and keep in high quality than annotations in a corpus. Moreover, the example lexicon can be acquired from already existing resources. Our method can be also used to prepare a very large, automatically annotated corpus, which is required for training complex deep neural network architectures.

Our contextual embeddings dataset also allows for training models faster than the sequence labeling methods. We include the complete representation of the training samples in the input of the model in one step. This way, the inference time is shorter than in the case of methods focused on the analysis of the subsequent sample elements. On the other hand, the non-contextual dataset size is much smaller than the contextual one. This results in a shorter training time and may allow for training a classifier on the multilingual model in similar time as training the same model on the contextual dataset for a specific language.

Using the full vector, representing a training sample as the model input in one step allowed also for leveraging the SMOTE methods. Enriching the dataset with synthetic samples can cause too much deviation in comparison to the original data. This can be especially risky in the case of the sequence labeling methods, which are much more susceptible to outliers.

8 Conclusions and Future Work

Our research shows that knowledge about the context is an essential aspect in multiword expressions detection task. Representation based on contextual embeddings improved significantly performance in the case of every classifier in comparison to the non-contextual embeddings setup. The best performance expressed the linear regression classifier. It was also significantly better than the results of the PARSEME shared task. The higher relevancy of information extracted from the contextual embeddings may be related to the non-compositionality of MWEs – their semantics cannot be derived from their component meanings, that is especially visible when they are used in contexts.

The use of non-contextual embeddings forced the model to predict on the basis of the component semantics only. However, this approach reduced the training time significantly, which makes it more applicable in business cases, when the prediction quality is not as important as training time. This approach is also based solely on the lexicon itself, so it needs no annotated corpus at start.

On the other hand, the contextual embeddings approach allows transforming any collection of texts into a corpus with annotations for MWE occurrences, a kind of silver standard, but the achieved results prove its high potential. The only required resource is a MWE lexicon, whose preparation is easier than a manually annotated corpus. The classifiers had to analyse the semantic differences between the component and the entire expression. This way the models focused on the variability of the sentence context and detect MWEs using the assumption of their monosemous nature.

Providing a complete sample representation at the input of the model in one step allowed us to use the SMOTE methods. Those techniques carry the risk of producing noisy data, which can be especially important in the case of sequence labelling methods. However, in our approach, using SMOTE methods improved the performance of our models and helped to cope with the natural imbalance of the dataset.

In the future work, we want to focus on the multilingual aspect of our methods, which can be used with a multilingual MWE lexicon consisting of multiple monolingual ones. This can be applied both in non-contextual and contextual scenarios. Moreover, we can combine this multilingual resource with transfer learning techniques to obtain the language-agnostic MWEs detection method.

Acknowledgements. This work was partially supported by the National Science Centre, Poland, project no. 2019/33/B/HS2/02814; the statutory funds of the Department of Computational Intelligence, Wroclaw University of Science and Technology; the Polish Ministry of Education and Science, CLARIN-PL Project.

References

1. Abadi, M., Agarwal, A., Barham, P., et al.: TensorFlow: large-scale machine learning on heterogeneous systems (2015). software available from tensorflow.org
2. Agrawal, S., Sanyal, R., Sanyal, S.: Hybrid method for automatic extraction of multiword expressions. Int. J. Eng. Technol. **7** (2018)
3. Anke, L.E., Schockaert, S., Wanner, L.: Collocation classification with unsupervised relation vectors. In: Proceedings of the 57th Annual Meeting of ACL, pp. 5765–5772 (2019)
4. Berk, G., Erden, B., Güngör, T.: Deep-BGT at PARSEME shared task 2018: bidirectional LSTM-CRF model for verbal multiword expression identification. In: LAW-MWE-CxG-2018, pp. 248–253. ACL (2018)
5. Bojanowski, P., Grave, E., Joulin, A., Mikolov, T.: Enriching word vectors with subword information. Trans. ACL **5**, 135–146 (2017)
6. Boros, T., Burtica, R.: GBD-NER at PARSEME shared task 2018: multi-word expression detection using bidirectional long-short-term memory networks and graph-based decoding. In: Proceedings of the Joint Workshop on Linguistic Annotation, Multiword Expressions and Constructions, pp. 254–260. ACL (2018)
7. Broda, B., Derwojedowa, M., Piasecki, M.: Recognition of structured collocations in an inflective language. Syst. Sci. **34**(4), 27–36 (2008)
8. Buljan, M., et al.: Combining linguistic features for the detection of Croatian multiword expressions. In: Proceedings of the 13th Workshop on MWE, pp. 194–199 (2017)
9. Chakraborty, S., Cougias, D., Piliero, S.: Identification of multiword expressions using transformers (2020). https://doi.org/10.13140/RG.2.2.31047.32169
10. Chawla, N.V., Bowyer, K.W., Hall, L.O., Kegelmeyer, W.P.: Smote: synthetic minority over-sampling technique. J. AI Res. **16**, 321–357 (2002)
11. Dziob, A., et al.: plWordNet 4.1-a linguistically motivated, corpus-based bilingual resource. In: Proceedings of the Tenth Global Wordnet Conference, pp. 353–362 (2019)
12. Evert, S.: The statistics of word cooccurrences: word pairs and collocations. Ph.D. thesis, Institut für maschinelle Sprachverarbeitung, Univ. of Stuttgart (2004)
13. Green, S., de Marneffe, M.C., Manning, C.D.: Parsing models for identifying multiword expressions. Comput. Linguist. **39**(1), 195–227 (2013)
14. Han, H., et al.: Borderline-smote: a new over-sampling method in imbalanced data sets learning. In: International Conference on Intelligent Computing, pp. 878–887 (2005)
15. Handler, A., Denny, M., Wallach, H., O'Connor, B.T.: Bag of what? simple noun phrase extraction for text analysis. In: NLP+CSS@EMNLP (2016)
16. He, H., Bai, Y., Garcia, E.A., Li, S.: ADASYN: adaptive synthetic sampling approach for imbalanced learning. In: 2008 IEEE International Joint Conference on Neural Networks, pp. 1322–1328. IEEE (2008)

17. Hosseini, M.J., et al.: UW-CSE at SemEval-2016 task 10: detecting multiword expressions and supersenses using double-chained conditional random fields. In: Proceedings of the 10th International Workshop on Semantic Evaluation, pp. 931–936 (2016)
18. Klyueva, N., Doucet, A., Straka, M.: Neural networks for multi-word expression detection. In: Proceedings of the 13th Workshop on MWE, pp. 60–65. ACL (2017)
19. Kocoń, J., Gawor, M.: Evaluating kgr10 polish word embeddings in the recognition of temporal expressions using bilstm-crf. Schedae Informaticae **27** (2018)
20. Kurfalı, M.: TRAVIS at PARSEME shared task 2020: how good is (m)BERT at seeing the unseen? In: Proceedings of the Joint Workshop on Multiword Expressions and Electronic Lexicons, pp. 136–141. ACL (2020)
21. Mikolov, T., Chen, K., Corrado, G., Dean, J.: Efficient estimation of word representations in vector space. In: Bengio, Y., LeCun, Y. (eds.) 1st International Conference on Learning Representations (2013)
22. Mroczkowski, R., Rybak, P., Wróblewska, A., Gawlik, I.: HerBERT: efficiently pretrained transformer-based language model for Polish. In: Proceedings of the 8th Workshop on Balto-Slavic Natural Language Processing, pp. 1–10. ACL (2021)
23. Pedregosa, F., Varoquaux, G., Gramfort, A., et al.: Scikit-learn: machine learning in python. J. Mach. Learn. Res. **12**, 2825–2830 (2011)
24. Pečina, P.: Lexical association measures and collocation extraction. Lang. Resour. Eval. **44**, 137–158 (2010)
25. Piasecki, M., Wendelberger, M., Maziarz, M.: Extraction of the multi-word lexical units in the perspective of the wordnet expansion. In: Proceedings of the International Conference Recent Advances in Natural Language Processing, pp. 512–520 (2015)
26. Ramisch, C.: Conclusions. In: Multiword Expressions Acquisition. TANLP, pp. 201–205. Springer, Cham (2015). https://doi.org/10.1007/978-3-319-09207-2_8
27. Ramisch, C., et al.: Edition 1.1 of the PARSEME shared task on automatic identification of verbal multiword expressions. In: Proceedings of the LAW-MWE-CxG-2018, pp. 222–240. ACL (2018)
28. Ramisch, C., et al.: Edition 1.2 of the PARSEME shared task on semi-supervised identification of verbal multiword expressions. In: Proceedings of the Joint Workshop on Multiword Expressions and Electronic Lexicons, pp. 107–118. ACL (2020)
29. Ramshaw, L., Marcus, M.: Text chunking using transformation-based learning. In: Third Workshop on Very Large Corpora (1995)
30. Rohanian, O., Taslimipoor, S., Kouchaki, S., Ha, L.A., Mitkov, R.: Bridging the gap: attending to discontinuity in identification of multiword expressions. In: Proceedings of the 2019 Conference of the North American Chapter of the ACL: Human Language Technologies, vol. 1, pp. 2692–2698. ACL (2019)
31. Saied, H.A., Candito, M., Constant, M.: Comparing linear and neural models for competitive MWE identification. In: Proceedings of the 22nd Nordic Conference on Computational Linguistics, pp. 86–96. Linköping University Electronic Press (2019)
32. Scholivet, M., Ramisch, C.: Identification of ambiguous multiword expressions using sequence models and lexical resources. In: Proceedings of the 13th Workshop on MWE, pp. 167–175 (2017)
33. Seretan, V.: Syntax-Based Collocation Extraction, Text, Speech and Language Technology, vol. 44. Springer, Netherlands (2011). https://doi.org/10.1007/978-94-007-0134-2
34. Spasić, I., et al.: Unsupervised multi-word term recognition in Welsh. In: Proceedings of the Celtic Language Technology Workshop, pp. 1–6. EAMT (2019)

35. Taslimipoor, S., et al.: MTLB-STRUCT @parseme 2020: capturing unseen multi-word expressions using multi-task learning and pre-trained masked language models. In: Proceedings of the Joint Workshop on Multiword Expressions and Electronic Lexicons, pp. 142–148 (2020)
36. Yirmibeşoğlu, Z., Güngör, T.: ERMI at PARSEME shared task 2020: embedding-rich multiword expression identification. In: Proceedings of the Joint Workshop on Multiword Expressions and Electronic Lexicons, pp. 130–135. ACL (2020)

Context-free Transformer-based Generative Lemmatiser for Polish

Wiktor Walentynowicz[✉][iD], Maciej Piasecki[iD], and Artur Kot

Wrocław University of Science and Technology, Wrocław, Poland
{wiktor.walentynowicz,maciej.piasecki,artur.kot}@pwr.edu.pl

Abstract. In this paper we present a new approach to the problem of lemmatisation in inflectional languages on the example of Polish. We made an introduction to the problem domain, described the solution used – the Transformer architecture and learning process on lexical data – and presented experimental results showing a high degree of generalization of the new solution. At the very end, we presented conclusions and plans for future research.

Keywords: Lemmatization · Character-based generation · Transformer

1 Introduction

Morphological analysis of inflectional languages, like the Polish language and other Slavic languages, is a very well studied problem and solved on a very practical scale, but only when it comes to the standard language. That is, for most such languages, if not all, there are comprehensive morphological dictionaries, as well as morphological analyzers based on them, that provide for every word form a set of morpho-syntactic tags which describe *lemmas* and values of grammatical categories (like case, number, person, etc.) as potential interpretations of a word form. *A lemma* is a technical term for a basic morphological form, i.e. an arbitrarily (but also traditionally) selected word form which represents a whole set of word forms that differ in values of grammatical categories, but share the same meaning. For instance the SGJP dictionary [6] includes description of 455830 Polish word lexemes and the morphological analyzer Morfeusz2 [7] recognizes 5001961 word forms, including many proper names.

However, even resources and tools of so large coverage still miss many words that may be found in practice in processing texts. Such OOV (Out of Vocabulary) words are the more frequent, the less carefully a text is edited, e.g. letters, notes, texts from Internet, especially from social media. In the context of large coverage dictionaries, OOV words, originate from errors, foreign words, proper names (often of foreign origin), very specific domain terms or just neologisms. In all such cases, most OOV words are inflected and a native speaker can guess their morphological properties on the basis of their morphological structure and

N. T. Nguyen et al. (Eds.): ICCCI 2022, LNAI 13501, pp. 207–219, 2022.
https://doi.org/10.1007/978-3-031-16014-1_17

context of use. The structure corresponds first all to affixes (i.e. especially suffixes, but also prefixes), but also inter-stem transformations can be spotted, e.g. in the case of typos and neologisms. The context comprises morfo-syntactic dependencies in an expression.

Context plays a very important role in recognizing morphological properties of OOV word forms, or, more precisely, potential word forms, that is shown by good results in lemmatization obtained by morpho-syntactic taggers, e.g. MorphoDiTa [18] for Czech and Polish, and COMBO [15] for Polish. However, not in all applications such a contextual information is available, e.g. single words or short expressions put in queries or forms. Some taggers depend also on morphological information to filter their decisions. A context-less morphological guesser may also be a way to discovery of the whole sets of forms, including the lemma, given a few examples. Moreover, a guesser may also allow for predicting forms that have not yet been observed. Finally, a good guesser embodies to some extent knowledge about the morphological paradigms linking word forms and allows for exploring it.

Thus, our goal is to construct a lemmatization procedure which for a word form generates its lemma. We assume that its input is a single word out of the context. Thus it can explore only the morphological structure of a word. It should express good generalization going beyond the largest known morphological dictionaries, as well as misspelled forms and inflected foreign words. The procedure should facilitate analysis of single OOVs as potential word forms for the needs of matching them against dictionaries collected from textual datasets. It should also provide support for lemmatisation of multi-word expressions, and linguistically sensitive indexing of documents. The procedure should facilitate studying word formation process by means of higher fidelity and precision.

2   Related Works

2.1   Contextual Lemmatisation

Multitasking architecture presented in [17] describes an architecture for tagging, lemmatisation, and dependency parsing. The lemmatisation module is separate from the tagging one and relies on lemmatisation rules and lemmas stored in a dictionary.

In turn [1] describes a multipurpose architecture for tagging and lemmatisation based on a LSTM (Long Short-term Memory) network, while the lemmatisation module itself is based on a GRU (Gated recurrent unit) decoder. The decoder receives consists of a vector representation of the word to be lemmatised, after it has been processed by the feature extractor, consisting of a character vector representation of the word form, positional embeddings, and information about the previous character in the lemma generation process.

A similar mechanism was used in the work [11] which presents an architecture aimed at tagging and lemmatisation of morphologically rich languages that is constructed on top of bidirectional recurrent neural networks. Lemmatisation is based on a decoder similar to those known from sequence-to-sequence architectures. The LSTM layer receives as an initial state information from the internal feature extractor. In addition to this, the decoder has an attached multiplicative attentional mechanism described in [12]. The decoder also receives information about the context of a word, its embedding vector, and the tagging result.

COMBO [15] is a multitasking architecture for tagging, lemmatisation and parsing. It is based on a shared feature extraction layer that provides information to the classifiers responsible for each task. The lemmatiser uses the information from the extractor and the character embedding for the word. Then dilated convolutional neural network transforms the input character sequence into a new character sequence which is intended to be a lemma.

Another approach is [10] – a tagging and lemmatisation system participating in the SIGMORPHON 2019 competition [13]. It uses BERT [4] contextual embedding vectors and character embedding vectors as input representations. Parallel LSTM networks make tag and lemma decisions. The lemmatisation is based on previously prepared lemma generation rules. As implemented in [16], the existing rules for transforming a word form into a lemma are first generated from the learning set, and then during the learning process, the classifier points to a given rule as the answer.

An architecture targeting tagging, lemmatisation, and diactrisation in Arabic is presented in [22]. It is based on combined recurrent neural networks. The lemmatisation module is based on a sequence-to-sequence architecture. The encoder processes information consisting of a combination of embedding vectors for characters and word pretrained embeddings with FastText [2], which is passed to the decoder along with Luong's attention [12]. Two separate decoders, based on LSTM, handle the lemmatisation and diactrisation of a word.

Contextual lemmatisation is frequently applied due to its natural integration within tagging tools. However, the drawback of such a solution is the need to have access to a large manually annotated corpus of texts where the lemmatisation layer has also been annotated.

2.2 Context-free Lemmatisation

In addition to learning from manually annotated corpora, context-free lemmatisation can also utilise information from grammar dictionaries, which are sources of a large number of training examples.

Nefnir [5] is a context-free trained lemmatiser that relies on rule extraction (learning) for lemma generation. Nefnir is trained on a dictionary of suffix transformations using also information about the given morphological tag. A lexical basis for training Nefnir contains only inflected forms, so in order to learn all lemmatisation cases it has been manually expanded to include non-convertible forms. The learning process involves generating new rules as long as these rules reduce the number of errors that occur.

Statistical guesser from MorphoDiTa [18] generates not only possible tags during analysis, but also suggests lemmas. It is based on statistical learning of rules, that rely mainly on prefix and suffix analysis, that are aimed at performing transformation of a word form into its lemma.

2.3   Lemmatisation for the Polish Language

The KRNNT [21] tagger simplifies the lemmatisation process to only selecting the statistically most frequent possible response for a word form and morphological tag pair. For word forms for which there are no morphological analyses proposed (e.g. by a morphological analyser), the entire word form is simply copied as a lemma. The CMC [20] tagger also simulates lemmatisation in a similar way. Thus, lemmatisation in the Polish taggers is therefore directly integrated with a morphological analyser which makes it insensitive to cases outside of the analyser coverage.

A morphological guesser for Polish based on A Tergo index [14] uses a slightly different method. The entire guesser is based on constructing a tree for identifying endings in words. First, a full a tergo tree is built for word forms, which is then pruned to not contain branches representing only one path. Morphological tags are then added to the leaves at the end of the branches representing the word. Finally, a rule is added to each such marker to edit the end of the word to obtain its base form. Thus, at prediction time, a lemma is obtained from the word form.

Our solution focuses on using the character information and discarding the dependence on analyzer's proposition to get word base form. In addition to exchanges occurring in endings, it also supports character exchanges in the word core or prefixes.

3   Problem Description

The goal of lemmatisation is to derive a basic morphological form – with morphological properties fundamental to its grammatical class – from a word form. We represent word forms as character sequences, which reduces the lemmatisation process to transforming a character sequence into a character sequence. For most word forms, this process is regular – some fixed word stem remains intact, while the suffix or prefix of the word form changes. In inflectional languages, however, there are also changes to single characters or character sequences inside word stems that depend on inflectional paradigms. However, much lower degree of regularity of these varieties causes problems when rule-based systems are used. In extreme cases, there is a complete change of a word stem and several different stem-internal exchanges within one inflectional paradigm. For instance, the plural word form for the lemma "pies" ('a dog') is inflected into the form "psy" ('dogs':plur. & nominal case). So the change is done by attaching the suffix "y", but also by reducing in parallel the sequence "ie" to null (i.e. by removing) in the stem. In the case of the verb "być" almost every its form has a different stem, but this is an extreme case.

4   Architecture

Recently, deep-learning models are state-of-the-art solutions for most of the NLP problems. Progress in general-purpose GPUs technology coupled with creation of large datasets both automatically scraped from the Internet and prepared by linguists opened ways to building larger models with greater generalisation and feature extracting capabilities. Currently, the go-to architectures for most natural language understanding models are variants of RNN (Recurrent neural network) – with the most prominent being LSTM and its bidirectional equivalent Bi-LSTM. GRU and bidirectional – Bi-GRU are often mentioned as alternatives for LSTM and Bi-LSTM, respectively.

However, since RNN based solutions have well documented problems with vanishing gradients, mechanism of attention was added. Attention allows the model to remember features after each sequential step. In most cases, empirical evidence shows improvement in the quality of results. Unfortunately, attention mechanism comes with drawbacks. The largest one is computational complexity of pairing attention with sequential models – the increasing time and resources required to successfully train the model. The other non-exclusionary approach for vanishing gradient problem is using force-teaching with some probability. Force-teaching is a model training technique based upon simple principle: $N + 1$-th token prediction uses initial N tokens of the expected sequence instead of the previously predicted tokens. This results in early prediction errors not propagating forward – the classification error for every token should be similarly affecting the loss. However, it could be rather important for a real-world sequentially predicting network to put more importance on errors that propagate throughout sequence. Nowadays, Transformers are becoming more and more popular. In the original Transformer architecture [19], the authors backed out from any type of RNN and solely focused on using attention mechanism. They claimed that following their modifications, a new Multi-Head Self-Attention is all one needed to correctly embed a given sequence. An neural architecture based on encoder-decoder principle and Multi-Head Self-Attention layers only is called *Transformer*. The largest benefit of using a transformer in contrast to the RNN+Attention network is the scale of possible parallelisation during the training process. This alone allows for reducing the training time and training larger models within the same time-frame. As more and more state-of-the-art solutions are based on the Transformer architecture or already large pre-trained Language Models like BERT or GPT-3 [3], we decided to use this architecture for the lemmatisation problem. It is hard to find any prior research on training a Transformer-based solution for the morphological analysis. On the basis of substantial benefits from application of transformers in other NLP tasks, we would like to investigate how would Transformer affect processing of inflectional morphology. We chose the Polish language as the main focus for its rich morphology and existing public morphological resources.

4.1 Transformer-based Lemmatiser

The construction of our lemmatiser is based on the classic Transformer architecture from [19], which we have expanded with a morphological knowledge injection module. The proposed architecture consists of the three main components:

Table 1. Hyperparameters of transformer-based lemmatiser model

Hyperparameter	Value	Hyperparameter	Value
Character embedding dim	256	Transformer hidden dim	256
# of transformer layers	4	Feedforward hidden dim	1024
# of attention heads	4	Dropout	0.3
# of epochs	100	Label smoothing ratio	0.1

1. an input characters embedding,
2. an input sequence encoder,
3. and an output sequence decoder.

The obtaining embedding vectors for the characters from the input sequence consists of two components – a character embedding model trained during the task and an additive sinusoidal positional embedding. The two vectors are added together to give the final embedding vector for a character in the sequence. The input sequence encoder consists of stacked multi-head attention layers. Both the embedding module for the characters and the encoder module do not change from the solution proposed in [19].

We enhanced the output sequence decoder module by injecting morphological knowledge related to a word form being processed. Knowledge injection requires knowledge representation to be encoded as a vector – in this case a positional morpho-syntactic tag. For this purpose, we concatenated the vectors for a grammar class (e.g. noun, finite verb, adjectival participle, etc.) and the corresponding attributes (representing values of grammatical categories like number, gender, case etc.) into a single vector. It is a binary vector with bits representing to the different classes and values for categories. The vector is next processed by a non linear layer to bring the vector to the dimension of the internal encoding in the transformer. Thus, in a result, the morphological information in a vector form is presented to the decoder as the first token of the output sequence.

Since the decoding process must be done in the autoregressive mode, we chose a greedy method for generating the final sequence. As a correct character in the sequence the method selects the one that receives the highest probability from the classifier in a given step, without changing the previous decisions in the successive steps.

In addition, an element of randomness to the learning process was applied in a form of an output function generation. With the equal probability, it is randomly chosen for the whole learning batch between force-teaching and traditional autoregressive output sequence generation known from recurrent networks. Such a process increases the learning time of a single epoch, but facilitates faster convergence of the solution to the space where the model learns correctly.

The hyperparameters of the final model are presented in Table 1. The model was trained using the Adam optimizer [8] with default parameter values and using a Noam learning rate scheduler [19].

5   Experiments

Table 2. Lemmatiser results on a test set from the lexicon.

Test data	SGJP
Baseline (A Tergo [14])	85.05%
Whole dataset	97.96%
Unique samples	97.96%
Known forms	92.10%
Unique known forms	87.27%
Unknown forms	98.02%
Unique unknown forms	96.83%
Known lemmas	90.02%
Unique known lemmas	85.21%
Unknown lemmas	98.05%
Unique unknown lemmas	96.89%

The SGJP dictionary was used as a gold standard, training-testing data source for the lemmatiser. For the sake of compatibility with the exiting corpus-based datasets for Polish, we restricted its tags to the information compatible with the NKJP tagset – we removed examples with grammar classes that are not described in the NKJP tagset and cannot be directly mapped (for example, the grammar class *cond*), and we removed from the tagset the values for the subgender attribute, which is only found in the Morpheus tagset.

The entire set has been randomly divided into training, validation, and test sets according to the numerical ratio of 8:1:1. The division was also intended to maintain lemma-wise separation between the subsets as far going as possible, i.e. in the idea case there should not be word forms of the same lemmas shared between the test subset and the other two. In practice, we managed to achieve a state in which the test set shares only 2.09% of word forms (not necessarily with the same morphological tag) and 2.62% of lemmas (word forms derived from a particular lemma) with the training subset. We cannot completely separate the training and test sets for word forms (not samples) or lemmas occurring in the training set, preserving the number ratio. For example, the word form "miałem" (ang. *had* or plural *dust*) can be a derivative of the verb lemma "mieć" (ang. *have*) or a derivative of the noun lemma "miał" (ang. *dust*) – are not counted as the same training example, but as the same word form. The rest are word forms and lemmas that the model did not see during the training process.

The validation set was created for hyper-parameter optimisation and final epoch selection. In addition, it was drawn in a way to reflect the distribution of the training set to a large extent. As a result, the validation set shared 88.32%

Table 3. Lemmatiser results on a test set from the PolEval2017 Task 1B.

Test Data	PolEval 2017 Task B Gold Standard Tags	PolEval 2017 Task B CMC Tagger Tags
Whole dataset	64.35%	63.13%
Unique samples	87.44%	84.31%
Known forms	91.27%	89.59%
Unique known forms	95.35%	92.27%
Unknown forms	32.23%	31.61%
Unique unknown forms	69.78%	67.02%
Known lemmas	86.31%	84.74%
Unique known lemmas	91.34%	88.42%
Unknown lemmas	32.56%	31.92%
Unique unknown lemmas	77.86%	74.56%
	PolEval 2017 Task B Gold Standard Tags Inflectional Only	PolEval 2017 Task B CMC Tagger Tags Inflectional Only
Whole dataset	92.61%	90.51%
Unique samples	94.53%	91.56%
Known forms	93.38%	91.44%
Unique known forms	95.91%	92.91%
Unknown forms	89.53%	86.81%
Unique unknown forms	90.50%	86.81%
Known lemmas	93.23%	91.29%
Unique known lemmas	95.77%	92.78%
Unknown lemmas	89.71%	86.86%
Unique unknown lemmas	90.38%	86.54%

of the occurrences of the word form and 99.84% of the lemmas with those that occur in the training set.

The tables representing the results include the following rows:

- *whole dataset* – all samples (word form & morphological tag pairs) in the test set
- *unique samples* – repeated samples are reduced to a single occurrence (in the case of lexicon data this situation does not occur)
- *known forms* – results for the samples with word forms present in the training set
- *unique known forms* – as above except that the results for all occurrences of a given word form derived from the same lemma are averaged
- *unknown forms* – results for samples with word forms not present in the training set

– *unique unknown forms* – as above except that the results for all occurrences of a given word form derived from the same lemma are averaged
– *known lemmas* – results for the samples with word forms derived from the lemma present in the training set
– *unique known lemmas* – as above except that the results for all occurrences of word forms derived from the same lemma are averaged
– *unknown lemmas* – results for the samples with word forms derived from the lemma not present in the training set
– *unique unknown lemmas* – as above except that the results for all occurrences of word forms derived from the same lemma are averaged

The evaluation results of the constructed lemmatiser are presented in Table 2. A specific case can be noted where word forms known from the learning set are less lemmatized than word forms unknown. This result is affected by the fact that word forms shared between sets are not identical in lemma or morphology, so they cannot be treated as the same training example. As a baseline of context-free lemmatization for Polish, we chose A Tergo's guesser. Since this solution did

Table 4. Lemmatiser results on a test set from the PolEval2017 Task 1C.

Test Data	PolEval 2017 Task C Gold Standard Tags	PolEval 2017 Task C CMC Tagger Tags
Whole dataset	63.60%	62.26%
Unique samples	87.01%	83.52%
Known forms	90.43%	88.41%
Unique known forms	95.09%	91.40%
Unknown forms	31.53%	31.00%
Unique unknown forms	68.78%	65.93%
Known lemmas	85.34%	83.41%
Unique known lemmas	90.95%	87.41%
Unknown lemmas	31.74%	31.25%
Unique unknown lemmas	77.40%	74.22%
	PolEval 2017 Task C Gold Standard Tags Inflectional Only	PolEval 2017 Task C CMC Tagger Tags Inflectional Only
Whole dataset	91.89%	89.56%
Unique samples	93.96%	90.51%
Known forms	93.04%	90.71%
Unique known forms	95.66%	92.09%
Unknown forms	87.20%	84.89%
Unique unknown forms	89.23%	85.38%
Known lemmas	92.87%	90.46%
Unique known lemmas	95.55%	91.92%
Unknown lemmas	87.23%	85.29%
Unique unknown lemmas	88.79%	85.23%

not split the lexical data between training and test data, a comparison of the performance of the two solutions must be made on the value concerning the recognition of known forms.

We also performed tests on the corpus data that were distributed as a part of Task 1 during the PolEval 2017 shared task in morpho-syntactic tagging [9]. When evaluating the lemmatiser on these data, we applied the same setting and terms as during the experiments on the SGJP dictionary data. Thus, known and unknown forms refer to the training data from the dictionary, not to the training data from the corpus – which in fact was not used for training at all, only for testing a lemmatiser. The results on the test set from the subtask B are shown in Table 3, and the results on the test set from the subtask C are presented in Table 4. In both cases, we performed evaluations on the full set and a subset containing examples only from those that have a different inflectional paradigm for word forms – where there are letter changes due to morphological variation, and does not contain closed grammatical classes (fully covered by the morphological analyzer i.e. pronouns).

Table 5. Lemmatiser results on the NKJP 1M corpus.

Test data	NKJP Gold Standard Tags	NKJP CMC Tagger Tags
Whole dataset	63.02%	63.82%
Unique samples	90.12%	88.73%
Known forms	90.66%	90.38%
Unique known forms	97.59%	95.99%
Unknown forms	30.73%	30.62%
Unique unknown forms	75.83%	74.56%
Known lemmas	85.46%	85.20%
Unique known lemmas	93.46%	91.93%
Unknown lemmas	31.02%	30.91%
Unique unknown lemmas	82.70%	81.33%
	NKJP Gold Standard Tags Inflectional Only	NKJP CMC Tagger Tags Inflectional Only
Whole dataset	92.17%	91.78%
Unique samples	95.09%	93.62%
Known forms	93.23%	92.91%
Unique known forms	97.77%	96.15%
Unknown forms	87.64%	87.15%
Unique unknown forms	87.50%	85.89%
Known lemmas	92.89%	92.52%
Unique known lemmas	96.83%	95.21%
Unknown lemmas	88.69%	88.22%
Unique unknown lemmas	88.97%	87.37%

As a final experiment, we performed lemmatisation on a manually annotated one million word subcorpus of NKJP. The obtained results, divided in way similar to the previous ones, are presented in Table 5.

We frame the reason for the sizeable difference in performance between lexical and corpus data in the influence of data distribution on the learning process. First, the difference in the morphological distribution of the lexical data, which is much more uniform than the corpus data, where the large concentration is around noun and adjective forms. Besides, the corpus data also contain many occurrences of irregular forms (for example, derivatives of the verb "być" 'to be' or pronouns). This is evidenced by the large difference in the results when only inflected forms differing from the character representation are taken into account in the tests.

6   Conclusions

The presented lemmatization method expressed ability to generalizing the acquired inflectional patterns very well, that makes it a valuable complement to the dictionary-based lemmatization method. High sensitivity to the distribution of the dataset, which is processed, can be a problem if it differs from the distribution of lexical data. However, the distribution of corpus data over dictionary data can be modelled – for example, by maintaining the same distribution over morphological classes in lexicon examples. We see the usefulness of this method as a complement to the analyzer-based method where the analyzer does not recognize a given word form. This would result in a hybrid method that has full coverage regardless of the size of the dictionary in the analyzer.

Since this method is based on transforming character strings rather than pseudo-morphemes, we plan to perform experiments with pre-trained character-based language models. We also look for ways to reduce the size of the model without significant loss of quality.

Acknowledgements. This work has been carried out as part of the Project "SentiCognitiveServices - next generation service for automating voice of customer and social media support based on artificial intelligence methods" (POIR.01.01.01-00-0806/16), cofinanced by the European Regional Development Fund under the Smart Growth Programme 2014–2020.

References

1. Arakelyan, G., Hambardzumyan, K., Khachatrian, H.: Towards JointUD: part-of-speech tagging and lemmatization using recurrent neural networks. In: Proceedings of the CoNLL 2018 Shared Task: Multilingual Parsing from Raw Text to Universal Dependencies, pp. 180–186. Association for Computational Linguistics, Brussels, Belgium, October 2018. https://doi.org/10.18653/v1/K18-2018, https://www.aclweb.org/anthology/K18-2018
2. Bojanowski, P., Grave, E., Joulin, A., Mikolov, T.: Enriching word vectors with subword information. Trans. Assoc. Comput. Linguist. **5**, 135–146 (2017)

3. Brown, T.B., et al.: Language models are few-shot learners. arXiv preprint arXiv:2005.14165 (2020)
4. Devlin, J., Chang, M.W., Lee, K., Toutanova, K.: BERT: pre-training of deep bidirectional transformers for language understanding. In: Proceedings of the 2019 Conference of the North American Chapter of the Association for Computational Linguistics: Human Language Technologies, vol. 1 (Long and Short Papers), pp. 4171–4186. Association for Computational Linguistics, Minneapolis, Minnesota, June 2019. https://doi.org/10.18653/v1/N19-1423, https://aclanthology.org/N19-1423
5. Ingólfsdóttir, S.L., Loftsson, H., Daðason, J.F., Bjarnadóttir, K.: Nefnir: a high accuracy lemmatizer for Icelandic. In: Proceedings of the 22nd Nordic Conference on Computational Linguistics, pp. 310–315. Linköping University Electronic Press, Turku, Finland, Sep-Oct 2019. https://www.aclweb.org/anthology/W19-6133
6. Kieraś, W., Woliński, M.: słownik gramatyczny języka polskiego -wersja internetowa. Język Polski 97(1), 84–93 (2017)
7. Kieraś, W., Woliński, M.: Morfeusz 2–analizator i generator fleksyjny dla języka polskiego. Język Polski XCVI I(1), 75–83 (2017)
8. Kingma, D.P., Ba, J.: Adam: A method for stochastic optimization. arXiv preprint arXiv:1412.6980 (2014)
9. Kobyliński, Ł., Ogrodniczuk, M.: Results of the PolEval 2017 competition: part-of-speech tagging shared task. In: Proceedings of the 8th Language and Technology Conference: Human Language Technologies as a Challenge for Computer Science and Linguistics, pp. 362–366 (2017)
10. Kondratyuk, D.: Cross-lingual lemmatization and morphology tagging with two-stage multilingual BERT fine-tuning. In: Proceedings of the 16th Workshop on Computational Research in Phonetics, Phonology, and Morphology, pp. 12–18. Association for Computational Linguistics, Florence, Italy, August 2019. https://doi.org/10.18653/v1/W19-4203, https://www.aclweb.org/anthology/W19-4203
11. Kondratyuk, D., Gavenčiak, T., Straka, M., Hajič, J.: LemmaTag: jointly tagging and lemmatizing for morphologically rich languages with BRNNs. In: Proceedings of the 2018 Conference on Empirical Methods in Natural Language Processing, pp. 4921–4928. Association for Computational Linguistics, Brussels, Belgium, Oct-Nov 2018. https://doi.org/10.18653/v1/D18-1532, https://www.aclweb.org/anthology/D18-1532
12. Luong, T., Pham, H., Manning, C.D.: Effective approaches to attention-based neural machine translation. In: Proceedings of the 2015 Conference on Empirical Methods in Natural Language Processing, pp. 1412–1421. Association for Computational Linguistics, Lisbon, Portugal, September 2015. https://doi.org/10.18653/v1/D15-1166, https://www.aclweb.org/anthology/D15-1166
13. McCarthy, A.D., et al.: The SIGMORPHON 2019 shared task: morphological analysis in context and cross-lingual transfer for inflection. In: Proceedings of the 16th Workshop on Computational Research in Phonetics, Phonology, and Morphology, pp. 229–244. Association for Computational Linguistics, Florence, Italy, August 2019. https://doi.org/10.18653/v1/W19-4226, https://aclanthology.org/W19-4226
14. Piasecki, M., Radziszewski, A.: Morphological prediction for polish by a statistical a Tergo index. Syst. Sci. 34(4), 7–17 (2008)

15. Rybak, P., Wróblewska, A.: Semi-supervised neural system for tagging, parsing and lematization. In: Proceedings of the CoNLL 2018 Shared Task: Multilingual Parsing from Raw Text to Universal Dependencies, pp. 45–54. Association for Computational Linguistics, Brussels, Belgium, October 2018. https://doi.org/10.18653/v1/K18-2004, https://www.aclweb.org/anthology/K18-2004

16. Straka, M.: UDPipe 2.0 prototype at CoNLL 2018 UD shared task. In: Proceedings of the CoNLL 2018 Shared Task: Multilingual Parsing from Raw Text to Universal Dependencies, pp. 197–207. Association for Computational Linguistics, Brussels, Belgium, October 2018. https://doi.org/10.18653/v1/K18-2020, https://www.aclweb.org/anthology/K18-2020

17. Straka, M., Straková, J.: Tokenizing, POS tagging, lemmatizing and parsing UD 2.0 with UDPipe. In: Proceedings of the CoNLL 2017 Shared Task: Multilingual Parsing from Raw Text to Universal Dependencies, pp. 88–99. Association for Computational Linguistics, Vancouver, Canada, August 2017. https://doi.org/10.18653/v1/K17-3009, https://www.aclweb.org/anthology/K17-3009

18. Straková, J., Straka, M., Hajič, J.: Open-source tools for morphology, lemmatization, POS tagging and named entity recognition. In: Proceedings of 52nd Annual Meeting of the Association for Computational Linguistics: System Demonstrations, pp. 13–18. Association for Computational Linguistics, Baltimore, Maryland, June 2014. https://doi.org/10.3115/v1/P14-5003, https://www.aclweb.org/anthology/P14-5003

19. Vaswani, A., et al.: Attention is all you need. In: Advances in Neural Information Processing Systems, pp. 5998–6008 (2017)

20. Walentynowicz, W., Piasecki, M., Oleksy, M.: Tagger for polish computer mediated communication texts. In: Proceedings of the International Conference on Recent Advances in Natural Language Processing (RANLP 2019), pp. 1295–1303. INCOMA Ltd., Varna, Bulgaria, September 2019. https://doi.org/10.26615/978-954-452-056-4_148, https://www.aclweb.org/anthology/R19-1148

21. Wróbel, K.: KRNNT: polish recurrent neural network tagger. In: Proceedings of the 8th Language & Technology Conference: Human Language Technologies as a Challenge for Computer Science and Linguistics, pp. 386–391. Fundacja Uniwersytetu im. Adama Mickiewicza w Poznaniu (2017)

22. Zalmout, N., Habash, N.: Joint diacritization, lemmatization, normalization, and fine-grained morphological tagging. In: Proceedings of the 58th Annual Meeting of the Association for Computational Linguistics, pp. 8297–8307. Association for Computational Linguistics, Online, July 2020. https://doi.org/10.18653/v1/2020.acl-main.736, https://www.aclweb.org/anthology/2020.acl-main.736

French Object Clitics in the Interlanguage: A Linguistic Description and a Formal Analysis in the ACCG Framework

Amina Affes[1,2], Ismaïl Biskri[2(✉)], and Adel Jebali[1,2]

[1] Concordia University, Montreal, Canada
adel.jebali@concordia.ca
[2] LI2A, Université du Québec à Trois-Rivières, Trois-Rivières, Canada
ismail.biskri@uqtr.ca

Abstract. The interlanguage of second language French learners presents certain regularities that provides a formal framework within the context of the Applicative Combinatory Categorical Grammar. To illustrate an example, we examined the object clitic pronouns that appeared in a corpus of texts by scrutinizing the different facets of these pronouns. A formal analysis was then proposed. The ultimate goal of this research is to establish an automated system for processing learners' interlanguage in terms of the Applicative Combinatory Categorial Grammar.

Keywords: L2 · Interlanguage · ACCG · French object clitics

1 Introduction

Research examining the object clitic (OC) in Roman languages in general, and French language in particular, constitute an inexhaustible source of information for linguists, as they are studied in terms of various aspects of language such as in syntax, phonology, morphology, semantics and in pragmatics. While the mastery of the OCs does not imply significant difficulties for native speakers, their assimilation by French L2 learners represents several challenges as it requires a mental effort before selecting and placing the appropriate OC in a sentence. Some learners, in some cases, try to determine the accurate place of the clitic in a sentence before selecting the appropriate clitic. Some others use avoidance, a technique that French second language (L2) learners use when facing clitics that enables them to avoid the target language feature when they have difficulty with it.

To assist L2 learners in mastering these complex language units, some researchers propose using action-oriented didactic tasks [1], while others believe that ICT and remote communication, among other action-oriented tasks, enable learners to perform better in this specific language field. (see [2]).

We believe that, in addition to these strategies which have been proven to be effective, we can offer a computerized tool based on a formal analysis of the productions of learners. This tool will allow learners to detect the most typical errors and propose

N. T. Nguyen et al. (Eds.): ICCCI 2022, LNAI 13501, pp. 220–231, 2022.
https://doi.org/10.1007/978-3-031-16014-1_18

relevant corrections and feedback. To this end, we will start by examining the use of OCs in the productions of French L2 learners. These productions will allow us to discover the regularities that characterize the linguistic system of the learners, known as the interlanguage. Once the analysis is completed, the different realizations of the OCs will then be formalized.

The following section presents learner interlanguage while the third section discusses the formalization in the context of Applicative and Combinatory Categorial Grammar.

2 Interlanguage

2.1 The Concept

[3] proposed the concept of interlanguage by identifying three systems that are linked to the process of L2 learning: the first language (L1, also called mother tongue or native language), the second language (L2, also called target language) and interlanguage. Interlanguage is defined as the language system that is used by the language learners that holds features from learner's L1 and the target language. This language "system" is dynamic as it evolves during the process of learning and is susceptible to external changes (social, psychological, etc.).

Despite its dynamic features, the interlanguage has common spheres that overlap regardless learners' individual differences, L1 or the target language. In fact, the assessment of the various interlanguages revealed the presence of certain properties that are common and shared between L2 learners. Among the most noteworthy properties, according to [3], the omission of functional categories (including OC pronouns) and the grammatical morphemes.

In addition, several researchers found that some L2 appropriation sequences can be classified as universal (see [4] and [5]). When it comes to the acquisition of OC pronouns, the following order was proposed: the production of the clitic in a position that the object phrase would occupy (example: J'ai vu le médecin -- > *J'ai vu le), the omission of the object (*J'ai vu), the production of the clitic in an inappropriate position in relation to the auxiliary (*J'ai le vu), and then the production of the expected correct form (Je l'ai vu). This universal appropriation allows us to locate the regularities and to transcribe the grammar of the interlanguage of French L2 learners.

2.2 French Object Clitics in the Interlanguage

Corpus. CEFLE (Corpus Écrit de Français Langue Étrangère) is a corpus of 460 texts written in French by Swedish learners of French L2. This corpus was developed by Ågren Malin at Lund University, Sweden, during the 2003/04 academic year for her PhD dissertation. The dissertation examined French L2 number and gender. It was published online in 2009 at the following URL: https://projekt.ht.lu.se/cefle/.

For the purpose of our research, 400 texts were used from the transversal and longitudinal sub-corpuses. The texts were written by 110 high school French L2 learners with four proficiency levels: beginners, elementary, intermediate, and low-advanced. 60 additional texts in the corpus produced by a control group were not used in our study because they were written by French native speakers. The 400 texts emerged from two main tasks:

1. A narration task in which students were asked to narrate two essays on their lives: *Me, my family and friends*; and *A trip memory.*
2. A picture description in which students described two sets of pictures created to elicit narratives: *The man on the island* and *The trip to Italy.*

All of the measures taken to ensure that learners were in a stress-free environment while performing the tasks were described in detail by [6].

Although this corpus was not originally designed to elicit OCs, it was considered as a valuable source for French L2 learners' interlanguage. In fact, the researcher did not target OC in her original study which ensures that these productions were not controlled. Thus, this corpus will allow us to have an authentic picture about the spontaneous use of OCs. [7] confirms that:

> Patterns based on elicited data may differ from those based on the production of spontaneous utterances, because careful elicitation generally compels the learner to commit to a response type, often prematurely.

Object Clitics in CEFLE. The properties of OCs in the interlanguage of participants in the CEFLE corpus will be presented in this section. As a reminder, the interlanguage is a language system that combines elements from several sources, including L1, L2 and the interlanguage itself. Therefore, we anticipate that learners will produce both correct and incorrect OCs (regardless of the origin of errors).

In CEFLE corpus, OCs were not frequently used, which reflects the typical behavior of learners towards these pronouns (i.e., the avoidance technique). Furthermore, and as expected, some participants succeeded to accurately use the OC while others did not. The following sentence presents an example where the OC respects the rules of the target language:

– (1) Ils voyagent en car et un guide leur donne des explications sur plusieurs monuments. (English: They travel by coach and the guide gave them information about the numerous monuments.)

OCs were also misused in several contexts by the participants in this corpus. These mistakes can be classified into two types:

1. The absence of the OC pronoun: occurs when participants avoided using the OC by repeating the noun phrase or by omitting the object with a verb that usually requires it.
2. The inappropriate placement of the OC according to its host: occurs when misinterpreting the case (accusative / dative / subject / object / strong pronoun), the morphosyntactic (the gender, the number, person) or the semantic (animate vs inanimate) features.

The following sentence presents an example where the OC that was avoided by using repetition:

– (2) *Elle a deux chiens, un noir et un blanc. Elle aimes les chiens. (Meaning: She has two dogs; one black and the other is white. She likes dogs.)

Example (3) demonstrates an example where OC was avoided by omitting the object:

– (3) *Autres hommes construent autres maisons et fabriques. (Meaning: Other men build other houses and make them.)

Example (4) illustrates an example where the OC is misplaced according to its host:

– (4) *Ils disent que ils veulent faire un usine à l'île de Pierre et ils le vont donner beaucup des argent. (Meaning: They say that they want to make a factory on Pierre's island and that they will give him a lot of money.)

Example (5) exemplifies the use of an OC pronoun where the gender / number traits were inconsistent with their antecedent:

– (5) *Ils y rencontrent deux jeunes garcons qui viennent le voir. (Meaning: There, they met two young boys who came to see them.)

As presented in examples (2) to (5), the errors made with OCs were almost always accompanied by other types of errors. For instance, in example (2), the verb "aimes" is not accurately conjugated. In example (3), the determinant is omitted twice and the verbs "construire" and "fabriques " are not properly conjugated. Therefore, multiple errors in the same sentence are detected and although the meaning conveyed by these statements is understood, these structures represent a real challenge to the formalization and to the automatic language processing systems.

The following section presents a formal framework for OCs in the interlanguage in the context of the Applicative Combinatory Categorial Grammar.

3 Applicative Combinatory Categorical Grammar

Within the model of Applicative Combinatory Categorial Grammar (ACCG), we distinguish two levels of language representation. The first level is the level of observable statements where syntagmatic organization, word order and morphology are taken into consideration. The second level is the level of applicative representations underlying the first level where the units of the language directly apply to each other through the operation of application, independently of any morphosyntactic constraint. ACCG allows encoding the procedures to validate the morphosyntactic correctness of statements; and to construct their applicative representation.

Like the entirety of categorial models [8], ACCG conceptualizes languages as organized linear systems of linguistic units, some of which function as operators and others as operands. To achieve this, each lexical token is assigned to one (or more) category that expresses how it functions. These categories are types recursively developed from the basic types (N for noun, S for sentence, N* for noun phrase, etc.) by using two constructive operators '/' and '\' according to:

1. Basic types are types.
2. If X and Y are types, then X/Y (the type of an operator whose typed operand Y is positioned on the right) and X\Y (whose typed operand Y is positioned on the left) are types.

Rules of ACCG canonically associate categorial combinatory rules with combinators of combinatory logic. Categorial combinatory rules ensure to validate the syntactic correctness of sentences, whereas combinators allow the construction of the applicative expressions underlying the sentences.

Combinatory logic is a variable-free logic. It uses abstract operators known as combinators to enable the construction of more complex operators from simpler one. Each combinator is provided with a β-reduction rule to express how it applies to its operands.

Table 1 represents some combinators and their β-reduction rules (For more combinators, the reader might read ([9] and [10]).

Table 1. Combinators and β-reduction rules

Combinator	Role	β-Reduction
B	Composition	**B** x y z → x (y z)
C	Permutation	**C** x z y → x y z
Φ	Distribution	Φ x y z u → x (y u) (z u)
C*	Type raising	**C*** x y → y x

The composition combinator **B** combines two operators x and y together and constructs the complex operator **B** x y that acts on an operand z, z being the operand of y and the result of the application of y to z being the operand of x.

The permutation combinator **C** uses an operator x in order to build the complex operator **C** x that acts on the same two operands as x but in reverse order.

The distribution combinator Φ distributes an operand u to two operators y and z. The results (y u) and (z u) become the first and second operands of x.

The type raising combinator **C*** takes an operand x and constructs the complex operator **C*** x that acts on the operator y.

All β-reduction rules are independent of the meaning of the arguments. They establish a relationship between an expression with combinators and a possible expression without combinators called the normal form. In the ACCG model, normal forms represent functional semantic interpretation or simply the applicative representation of sentences. This normal form is unique, according to the Church-Rosser Theorem.

Elementary combinators can be combined to construct a more complex combinator. Its global action is determined by the successive application of its elementary combinators taken from left to right. For instance, in the combinatory expression $\mathbf{B}\,\mathbf{C}\,x\,y\,z\,u\,v$, the combinator $\mathbf{B}$ is applied first, then $\mathbf{C}$. The obtained expression $(x\,y)\,u\,z\,v$ is the normal form of the expression $\mathbf{B}\,\mathbf{C}\,x\,y\,z\,u\,v$.

$$\mathbf{B}\,\mathbf{C}\,x\,y\,z\,u\,v$$
$$\mathbf{C}\,(x\,y)\,z\,u\,v$$
$$(x\,y)\,u\,z\,v$$

Two other types of complex combinators exist: the power of a combinator X, noted by X^n, and the distance of a combinatory X, noted by X_n.

The power of a combinator X is recursively defined by these two rules:

$$X^1 = X \text{ and } X^n = \mathbf{B}\,X\,X^{n-1}$$

For instance, the steps of the reduction of $\mathbf{B}^3\,x\,y\,z\,u\,v$ are:

$$\mathbf{B}^3\,x\,y\,z\,u\,v$$
$$\mathbf{B}\,\mathbf{B}\,\mathbf{B}^2\,x\,y\,z\,u\,v$$
$$\mathbf{B}\,\mathbf{B}\,(\mathbf{B}\,\mathbf{B}\,\mathbf{B}^1)\,x\,y\,z\,u\,v$$
$$\mathbf{B}\,\mathbf{B}\,(\mathbf{B}\,\mathbf{B}\,\mathbf{B})\,x\,y\,z\,u\,v$$
$$\mathbf{B}\,((\mathbf{B}\,\mathbf{B}\,\mathbf{B})\,x)\,y\,z\,u\,v$$
$$((\mathbf{B}\,\mathbf{B}\,\mathbf{B})\,x)\,(y\,z)\,u\,v$$
$$\mathbf{B}\,\mathbf{B}\,\mathbf{B}\,x\,(y\,z)\,u\,v$$
$$\mathbf{B}\,(\mathbf{B}\,x)\,(y\,z)\,u\,v$$
$$(\mathbf{B}\,x)\,((y\,z)\,u)\,v$$
$$\mathbf{B}\,x\,((y\,z)\,u)\,v$$
$$x\,(((y\,z)\,u)\,v)$$
$$x\,(y\,z\,u\,v)$$

The distance of a combinator X is recursively defined by these two rules:

$$X_0 = X \text{ and } X_n = \mathbf{B}\,X_{n-1}$$

For instance, the steps of the reduction of $\mathbf{B}_3\,x\,y\,z\,u\,v$ are:

$$\mathbf{B_3}\, x\, y\, z\, u\, v\, t$$
$$\mathbf{B}\, \mathbf{B_2}\, x\, y\, z\, u\, v\, t$$
$$\mathbf{B}\, (\mathbf{B}\, \mathbf{B_1})\, x\, y\, z\, u\, v\, t$$
$$\mathbf{B}\, (\mathbf{B}\, (\mathbf{B}\, \mathbf{B_0}))\, x\, y\, z\, u\, v\, t$$
$$\mathbf{B}\, (\mathbf{B}\, (\mathbf{B}\, \mathbf{B}))\, x\, y\, z\, u\, v\, t$$
$$(\mathbf{B}\, (\mathbf{B}\, \mathbf{B}))\, (x\, y)\, z\, u\, v\, t$$
$$\mathbf{B}\, (\mathbf{B}\, \mathbf{B})\, (x\, y)\, z\, u\, v\, t$$
$$(\mathbf{B}\, \mathbf{B})\, ((x\, y)\, z)\, u\, v\, t$$
$$\mathbf{B}\, \mathbf{B}\, ((x\, y)\, z)\, u\, v\, t$$
$$\mathbf{B}\, (((x\, y)\, z)\, u)\, v\, t$$
$$(((x\, y)\, z)\, u)\, (v\, t)$$
$$x\, y\, z\, u\, (v\, t)$$

As shown with these two examples, X^n applies the action of X n times, whereas X_n postpones the action of X by a distance of n.

Let us now go through the rules of the ACCG model that will be used in this paper (for the whole model, the reader might read [11]). The premises in each rule is the linear concatenation of linguistic units, whereas the consequence in each rule is the application of one linguistic unit to another with the introduction of one combinator. Let us assume that u, u1 and u2 are linguistic units.

Application rules:

$$\frac{[X/Y : u_1] - [Y : u_2]}{[X : (u_1\ u_2)]} >; \qquad \frac{[Y : u_1] - [X\backslash Y : u_2]}{[X : (u_2\ u_1)]} <$$

Type raising rules:

$$\frac{[X : u]}{[Y/(Y\backslash X) : (\mathbf{C_*}\ u)]} >\mathbf{T}$$

Functional composition rules:

$$\frac{[X/Y : u_1] - [Y/Z : u_2]}{[X/Z : (\mathbf{B}\ u_1\ u_2)]} >\mathbf{B}$$

We proved in our previous works that applicative approaches, combinatory logic (combinators and their β- reduction rules) and ACCG are concrete, flexible and sufficiently powerful concepts that precisely formulate the assumptions on the nature of most of linguistic markers. We have analyzed, for instance, various complex linguistic cases in (i) French: coordination of constituents, coordination of non-constituents, correlative coordination, non-distributive coordination, relative subordination, completive subordination, interrogative subordination, topicalization, etc… [12]; (ii) Arabic: verbal phrases, noun phrases, markers of subject, markers of object, morphological agreements (rich and poor), etc… [13].

In the light of our previous results, we believe that this approach is a viable option that is in accordance with empirical evidence and especially with the requirements of the formalization of the analysis of clitics in the interlanguage of L2.

4   Object Clitics by Means of ACCG

Before analyzing some of the aforementioned ungrammatical sentences, let us first demonstrate how ACCG analyzes the valid sentence with object clitics (1).

```
Ils      voyagent   et      un        guide   leur                          donne des
         en car                                                             explications
                                                                            sur plusieurs
                                                                            monuments

------   ---------   ----   ---------   -----   ----------------------       --------------
N*_3PM   (S\N*_3PM)  (X\X)/X  N*_3SM/N_3SM  N_3SM  (S\N*_3SM)/((S\N*_3SM)/N*_3SM)  (S\N*_3SM)/N*_3SM
-----------------                --------------------->
S                      N*_3SM
                      ------------->T
                      S/(S\N*_3SM)
                      ----------------------------------------------->B
                      S/((S\N*_3SM)/N*_3SM)
                      --------------------------------------------------------------------->
                      S
                   ------------->
                   S\S     {X = S}
-----------------------------<
S
```

By getting the type S at the end of the analysis, the sentence is considered correct. In this example, we established morphological agreement between nouns and their determinants and verbs and their subjects in their assigned types (as a reminder, there are no morphological agreements between verbs and objects in French). We assign to *ils* (*they*) the type N^*_{3PM} (N^* for noun phrase, 3 for third person, P for plural and M for masculine), since it is a noun phrase of 3rd person plural masculine. We assign to the intransitive verb *voyagent en car* (*travel by coach*) the type $(S\backslash N^*_{3PM})$. This is to express that this verb is an operator whose operand is a noun phrase of 3rd person plural masculine positioned on its left.

The object clitic *leur* (*them*) in this sentence is not a noun phrase. It is an operator whose operand is the transitive verb *donne des explications sur plusieurs monuments* (*gives information about several monuments*) whose type is $(S\backslash N^*_{3SM})/N^*_{3SM}$. Consequently, we assign it the type $(S\backslash N^*_{3SM})/((S\backslash N^*_{3SM})/N^*_{3SM})$. Just as a reminder, the verb *donner* (*to give*) is considered as a verb with two objects. The first one in this case is *des explications sur plusieurs monuments* (*information about several monuments*) and the second one is replaced by the clitic *leur*. Since *leur* is an anaphora of *ils*, they must agree morphologically on person, number and gender.

Let us now have a look at the analysis of the ungrammatical sentence in example (3) "Autres hommes construent autres maisons et fabriques". There are four errors in this sentence. *Construent* (*build*) should have been conjugated in the 3rd person plural of the verb *construire* (*to build*). The right word should have been *construisent*. The word *construent* will therefore not be included in the dictionary entry for the categorial types, and should appear as an error. To explain the detection of other errors, we will assume that *construent* is replaced with *construisent*.

Autres	hommes		construisent	autres	maisons	et	fabriques
----------	------------		--------------	--------	-----------	------	-----------
N_P/N_P	N_{3PM}		$(S\backslash N^*_{3PM})/N^*$	N_P/N_P	N_{3PM}	$(X\backslash X)/X$	$(S\backslash N^*_{2S})/N^*$

$$\text{----------------------->}$$
$$N_{3PM} : (\text{autres maisons})$$
$$\text{---}$$
$$\text{fail}$$

In French *autres hommes* (*other men*) and *autres maisons* (*other houses*) must be used with their determinants. This kind of error can be easily detected by the analyzer. The analysis fails since, for instance, the operator *construisent*, as clearly shown by its type, needs a noun phrase as a first operand, whereas *autres maisons* is a noun. It needs a determinant to be a noun phrase. It is, exactly, the same situation with *autres hommes*. *Construisent* needs a noun phrase as a second operand, not a noun. To present the detection of the other two errors, we must assume that the first ones have been corrected.

D'	autres	hommes	construisent	d'	autres	maisons	et	fabriques
---	-------	----------	--------	-----	--------	-----------	------	------------
N^*/N	N_P/N_P	N_{3PM}	$(S\backslash N^*_{3PM})/N^*$	N^*/N	N_P/N_P	N_{3PM}	$(X\backslash X)/X$	$(S\backslash N^*_{2S})/N^*$

$$\text{------------------>}\mathbf{B}$$
$$N^*_P/N_P : (\mathbf{B}\ \text{d'autres})$$
$$\text{----------------------------------->}$$
$$N^*_{3PM} : ((\mathbf{B}\ \text{d'autres})\ \text{maisons})$$
$$\text{-->}\mathbf{B}$$
$$S\backslash N^*_{3PM} : (\text{construisent}\ ((\mathbf{B}\ \text{d'autres})\text{maisons}))$$
$$\text{---}$$
$$\text{Fail}$$

There are two members of coordination: *construisent d'autres maisons* (*build other houses*) and *fabriques* (*make*). The derived type of *construisent d'autres maisons* is $S\backslash N^*_{3PM}$ whereas the type of fabriques is $(S\backslash N^*_{2S})/N^*$. The two members of coordination are supposed to have the same type according to the type $(X\backslash X)/X$ of the conjunction.

Therefore, the analysis fails at this stage. There are two reasons for this. First, *fabriques* is conjugated at the 2nd person of singular whereas *construisent* is conjugated at the 3rd person of plural. Second, *fabriques* needs a noun phrase object complement positioned to its right or an object clitic preceding it, whereas *construisent d'autres maisons* has the behavior of an intransitive verb. The correct sentence should have been: *d'autres hommes construisent d'autres maisons et les fabriquent*. It would have been analysed as follows:

d'	autr es	homm es	cons- truisent	d'	autr es	mai- sons	et	les	fabri- quent
---	-----	-------	--------	---	-----	----	---	----	------
$N^*/$ N	N_P/N $_P$	N_{3PM}	$(S\backslash N^*_{3P})/$ N^*	$N^*/$ N	$N_P/$ N_P	N_{3PM}	$(X\backslash X)$ $/X$	$(S\backslash N^*_{3P})/(S\backslash N^*$ $_{3P})/N^*$	$(S\backslash N^*_{3P})/$ N^*

```
                      ---------->B
                      N*_P/N_P : (B d'autres
                      ------------------------->
                      N*_3P : ((B d'autres) maisons)
          ----------------------------------->B
          S\N*_3P : (construisent ((B d'autres) maisons))
                                         ----------------------->
                                         (S\N*_3P) : (les fabriquent)
                                         -------------------------------------------
                                         >  (S\N*_3P)\(S\N*_3P))  :  (et (les fabri-
                                            quent))
          ------------------------------------------------------------------------<
          S\N*_3P : ((et (les fabriquent)) (construisent ((B d'autres) maisons)))
---------->B
N*_P/N_P : (B d'autres)
------------------------->
N*_3P : ((B d'autres) hommes)
--------------------------------------------------------------------------------<
S : (((et (les fabriquent)) (construisent ((B d'autres) maisons))) ((B d'autres) hommes))
```

By getting the type S the sentence is considered as syntactically correct. (((et (les fabriquent)) (construisent ((**B** D'AUtres) maisons))) ((**B** D'AUtres) Hommes)) is the Combinatory Applicative Representation of the Sentence. Replacing the Conjunction *et* by the logical operator $\Phi \wedge$ according to [12] and reducing combinators will allow to construct the expression in which the order of linguistic units represents is the one in which an operator applies to its operands. steps of combinators' reductions phase are given below.

(((et (les fabriquent)) (construisent ((**B** d'autres) maisons))) ((**B** d'autres) hommes))

(((Φ $\wedge$ (les fabriquent)) (construisent ((**B** d'autres) maisons))) ((**B** d'autres) hommes))

Φ $\wedge$ (les fabriquent) (construisent ((**B** d'autres) maisons)) ((**B** d'autres) hommes)

$\wedge$ ((les fabriquent) ((**B** d'autres) hommes)) ((construisent ((**B** d'autres) maisons)) ((**B** d'autres) hommes))

$\wedge$ ((les fabriquent) (**B** d'autres hommes)) ((construisent ((**B** d'autres) maisons)) ((**B** d'autres) hommes))

$\wedge$ ((les fabriquent) (d' (autres hommes))) ((construisent ((**B** d'autres) maisons)) ((**B** d'autres) hommes))

$\wedge$ ((les fabriquent) (d' (autres hommes))) ((construisent (**B** d'autres maisons)) ((**B** d'autres) hommes))

$\wedge$ ((les fabriquent) (d' (autres hommes))) ((construisent (d' (autres maisons))) ((**B** d'autres) hommes))

$\wedge$ ((les fabriquent) (d' (autres hommes))) ((construisent (d' (autres maisons))) (**B** d'autres hommes))

$\wedge$ ((les fabriquent) (d' (autres hommes))) ((construisent (d' (autres maisons))) (d' (autres hommes)))

5 Conclusion

The purpose of this study is to provide an automated system for processing learners' interlanguage in terms of the Applicative Combinatory Categorial Grammar. The suggested system allows the comprehension of the difficulties that L2 learners of French experience when using OC pronouns and allows the automatic correction as well.

We believe that the ACCG framework is flexible and adaptable to analyze the interlanguage of the L2. Conceptualizing the sentences as sequences of linguistic units in terms of operators and operands provides a formal framework for conducting a formal analysis. Through this study, we have shown how errors related to the use of OC pronouns and the morphological agreements can be detected. This research has demonstrated as well that extending the categorial types by integrating morphological knowledge about the person, the gender and the number is crucial.

References

1. Privulescu, M., Hill, V.: Object clitic omission in french-speaking children: effects of the elicitation task. Lang. Acquis. **19**, 73–81 (2012)
2. Jebali, A. : Anxiété langagière, communication médiée par les technologies et élicitation des clitiques objets du français L2. Alsic 21 (2018)
3. Selinker, L.: Interlanguage. IRAL-International Review of Applied Linguistics in Language Teaching **10**(1–4), 209–232 (1972)
4. Herschensohn, I.: Functional categories and the acquisition of object clitics in L2 French. In: Prévost, P., Paradis, J. (eds.): The Acquisition of French in Different Contexts: Focus on functional categories, pp. 207-242. John Benjamins Publishing Company (2004)
5. Jasmin, L.: Acquisition des pronoms clitiques objets par des apprenants adultes du français langue seconde. Thesis University of Ottawa (1994)

6. Ågren, M.: À la recherche de la morphologie silencieuse. PhD Thesis. Department of French studies, Lund University, Sweden (2008)
7. Helms-Park, R.: Evidence of lexical transfer in learner syntax. Studies in Second-Language Acquisition. **23**, 71–102 (2001)
8. Steedman, M.: The syntactic process. MIT Press (2000)
9. Desclés, J.P., Guibert, G., Sauzay, B. : Logique Combinatoire et (Lambda)-Calcul : des logiques d'opérateurs. Cépaduès Éditions (2016)
10. Curry, B.H., Feys, R.: Combinatory Logic. North-Holland, Amsterdam (1958)
11. Biskri, I., Desclés, J.P.: Applicative and combinatiry categorical grammar (from syntax to functional semantics). In: Recent Advances in Natural Language Processing, pp. 71–84. John Benjamins Publishing Company (1997)
12. Biskri, I.: La coordination et la subordination en français et les systèmes applicatifs typés. Revue VERBUM, pp. 173–198 (2018)
13. Biskri, I., Jebali, A.: Categorial Analysis of Agreement Asymmetries in Arabic. In: Shaalan, K., El-Beltagy, S. R. (eds.): Procedia Computer Science, **142**, pp. 278–285. Elsevier (2018)

Contradiction Detection Approach Based on Semantic Relations and Evidence of Uncertainty

Ala Eddine Kharrat[(✉)], Lobna Hlaoua, and Lotfi Ben Romdhane

Mars Research Lab, Isitcom, University of Sousse, Hammam Sousse, Tunisia
alaeddinekharrat@gmail.com

Abstract. The automatic detection of contradictions or the detection of contradictory statements consists in identifying the discrepancies, inconsistencies, conflicts and disagreement in a given text. This technique has several applications in the real world; as in question-and-answer systems, multi-document synthesis, and contradictions of opinions analysis in social networks. The automatic detection of contradictions is a technically difficult natural language processing problem, given the variety of ways in which contradictions occur between texts. Indeed, even if brutal negations, antonyms and numerical mismatches are obvious characteristics to diffuse contradictions, there can be a contradiction which also comes from an inconsistent domain knowledge, from uncertain coreferences or from differences in the structures of the assertions.

In this paper, we address the problem of detecting contradictions for uncertain statements when the user (author) not only provides factual information, but also clues about its plausibility. Therefore, we propose a contradiction detection approach which introduces additional criteria for detecting linguistic semantic features due to natural language ambiguity and evidence of uncertainty. The idea is to build a model to detect contradictions using a joint analysis of semantic relations and evaluations of uncertainties. In order to validate our proposed approach, we are carrying out experiments on four data sets. The results based on the experiments indicate the effectiveness of our approach.

Keywords: Contradiction detection · Semantic relations extraction · Uncertainty assessment · Word embedding

1   Introduction

Contradiction is a type of semantic relationship between sentences. It occurs when the sentences in a text are unlikely to be correct at the same time [1]. According to this context, the automatic detection of contradictions or contradictory statements consists in detecting and identifying the discrepancies, inconsistencies and mistrust in a text in natural language. In other words, the detection of contradictions is the task of identifying from a text information about

N. T. Nguyen et al. (Eds.): ICCCI 2022, LNAI 13501, pp. 232–245, 2022.
https://doi.org/10.1007/978-3-031-16014-1_19

events or actions that cannot hold simultaneously. According to the literature, there are several real applications of contradiction detection. In fact, contradiction detection has attracted the attention of several researchers in many areas of natural language processing, such as information integration, inconsistency discovery, sarcasm detection, false information detection, and information retrieval [2,4–6]. For example, Harabagiu et al. [9] (who are among the first researchers to deal with the problem of contradiction detection) have given examples of applications such as question-and-answer and multi-document summary systems that use contradiction detection as one of the word processing steps. For example, if there are conflicting answers to a question in a question-and-answer system, a contradiction detection application can help identify such instances of user intervention requiring resolution of the contradiction between two answers.

Due to the ambiguity of the natural language, it is technically almost difficult to detect the contradiction. Indeed, there are various characteristics that are relatively obvious to the detection of contradicting sentences. Among these characteristics we can cite negation, antonyms and numerical shift (numerical mismatch). Identifying these characteristics may seem easy and simple, but in practice it can be much more complex and require deeper understanding and inference about the text in order to analyze the consistency of the information as well as its implication. Taking as an example the following couple of sentences:

– In a hotel with a hundred residents, the police arrested a terrorist and neutralized the explosion of the bomb.
– In a hotel, 100 people were injured.

This couple of sentences is contradictory, since the bomb is neutralized and cannot explode. So, it cannot hurt anyone. This example tells us that detecting implications in a sentence is very important in detecting contradiction. Actually, it is relatively easy to identify the lack of implication: the first sentence involves no injury, so the second is unlikely to be implied by the first. In the literature, most systems of implication function as a weak proof theory [3,9,13], but the detection of contradictions requires semantically more indepth inferences. According to this goal, the detection of contradictions can be considered as a classification problem. Indeed, traditional approaches create classifiers and design efficient features to improve classification accuracy. However, feature design relies on professional knowledge and barely captures latent semantic features. For the contradiction detection task, an effective feature learning approach is to learn the representation of the semantic relation from the input texts. This explains why the detection of contradictions in the text is still not a fully resolved problem and there are several limitations and research gaps in the existing work.

In this paper, we tackle the problem of detecting contradictions in pairs of sentences with uncertain statements. We propose a new system of contradiction detection based on the relations between the statements in the sentences allowing to present a sentence in a fairly thorough semantic way, while using a combination of lexical and syntactic models. This semantic representation helps our system to better understand the contradiction. According to this goal, we attempt, to understand the ways in which the contradictions occur between the texts.

This document is organized as follows. Section 2 presents the related work on the detection of contradictions. In Sects. 3, 4 and 5 we present our motivation and the description of our approach. The experimental results are presented in Sect. 6. Finally, Sect. 7 concludes this paper and highlights our future work.

2   Related Work

Much of the previous research on contradiction detection has been done in the field of natural language processing. Among the first results on the detection of contradictions, we cite the work of Harabagiu et al. [9] which exposed a system making it possible to identify the existence of contradictions between a pair of texts, based on the presence of negation, of antonyms and of semantic and pragmatic information characterizing the contrasted speeches. The proposed approach requires the adaptation of various modules such as linguistic preprocessing, lexical alignment, feature extraction and classification. Harabagiu et al., evaluated their approach on two data sets (one based on contradictions conveyed by negations and the other based on paraphrases), and revealed good results. However, the contradictions should not be limited to these characteristics only; in fact, a contradiction detection system must provide more coverage in order to be more effective in practice.

To go beyond negation and antonymy, De Marneffe et al. [13] proposed another concept based on a block of functionalities making it possible to acquire diagrams of contradiction. These functionalities include: the characteristics of date and time, the polarity of feelings and opinions, numbers, and the consistency of related facts and sentences as well as their structure and relational characteristics. According to the results obtained, the major problem with their approach is the lack of generalization of characteristics.

To improve the work of De Marneffe et al., Alan Ritter [3] analyzed the problem of detecting contradictions from a functional relationship matching point of view while presenting indepth knowledge of these relationships. A functional relationship assigns a unique unchangeable value to a specific argument (for example "was born in", relates a person to their unique place of birth). The results obtained by their proposed system (called "AUCONTRAIRE"), on data collected from the web, revealed that the main factors of error are synonymy, meronymy, errors from the data extraction step and ambiguity from natural language. This explains why a thorough basic knowledge is very important to improve the accuracy of contradiction detection.

From another perspective, several researchers have focused their work on developing techniques and tools for detecting disparities or inadequacies in the various information disseminated on the Web. Among these tools we cite "DisputeFinder" by Ennals et al. [7], "NewCube" by Souneil Park, Seungwoo [14] and "WikiTrust". All of these tools are built as an extension to a web browser. "DisputeFinder" is used, based on reliable sources, to alert the user with complaints in the event that he encounters a contradiction in the text which is being consulted. "NewCube" searches for articles presenting different aspects of the same news. And "WikiTrust" detects useless sections from Wikipedia articles based on statistics on when they were recently written.

Based on sentiments in a text, Tsytsarau et al. [18] present an approach to detecting contradictions based on the analysis of user opinions on the web. Their idea is to apply thematic analysis to estimate a statistical score capable of detecting conflicting opinions that overlap at different points in time. The score obtained helps to detect not only contradictions but also to detect significant changes in opinions over time.

To solve the problem of the lack of specific basic knowledge in contradiction detection, Shih et al. [17] proposed a new contradiction detection approach based on the distribution of a Web query composed of critical mismatch combinations on the Internet. Their approach aims to measure the availability of conjunction sentences (MCP) that do not match. On the same basis Lendvai [11] created a textual implication recognition (TEN) dataset based on a natural contradiction in tweets posted during crisis events on Twitter. They created the dataset that allows researchers in the natural language processing and information retrieval field to build statistical models to rely on semantic inferences through microblogging articles and text.

According to a new principle, Lingam et al. [12] proposed to derive several linguistic characteristics of the text and use it in a classification framework to detect contradictions. The novelty of their approach lies in the application of artificial neural networks and deep learning. They run a series of experiments on various datasets while measuring their system's performance using a confusion and error matrix.

Unlike previous work, Pham et al. [15] explore the use of shallow semantic representations for the detection of contradictions in a rulebased framework. In their approach, they tackle the problem of low coverage of superficial semantic representations by using a backup module which relies on binary relations extracted from sentences for the detection of contradictions. Their system achieves better recall and accuracy in detecting contradictions than most basic methods.

In the context of existing work, our approach is based on previous solutions based precisely on the analysis of relations like the work of Pham et al. [15], extended with additional processing to treat the semantics in a more in-depth way between pairs of sentences, and also to process and evaluate the uncertainty assigned to each sentence. Indeed, unlike previous work, which relies on derived information from predicate-argument structures, our proposed system explores the use of shallow semantic representations making it possible to detect sentences with an incompatible meaning or information concerning events which cannot be held simultaneously. The whole idea is mainly based on the detection of linguistic clues caused by natural language ambiguity, and clues of evidence of uncertainty in a sentence. This in turn explains why the study presented in this paper makes new and unique research contributions.

3 Motivation and Proposed Model

3.1 Motivation

The main objective of our approach is to detect and identify discrepancies, inconsistencies and mistrust in a natural language text, relying on the semantic understanding of words. That is, to develop a contradiction detection system that builds on previous solutions based on relationship analysis, extended with additional procedures to deal with sentences conveying facts and uncertainty assessments that assigned to them. Indeed, detecting the contradiction in the statements requires methods capable of taking into account both factual information and the subjective dimension which often integrates clues on the strength of the authors to support the content conveyed. Therefore, we propose an approach that introduces additional criteria to detect linguistic cues due to natural language ambiguity and uncertainty cues, and provides mechanisms to detect sentences with incompatible meaning, or information concerning events or actions which cannot be held simultaneously. This explains why our approach requires specific steps to understand the semantics of sentences in depth; such as advanced lexical and grammatical analyses with detailed concept extraction to understand the exact meaning of each word, and the extraction of binary relations.

3.2 Description of the Approach

In this section we present our model of contradiction detection by taking into account the semantic aspect of the factual information conveyed by the sentences, and the degree of uncertainty of the latter. The advantage behind this tactic is to better separate the contradictions resulting from a disagreement on the certainty of the facts and those related to more conflicting views on the reported facts. In order not to do a direct analysis on sentences, our model relies on a chain of preprocessing blocks which semantically extracts the facts and recovers the characteristics of uncertainty around these facts. According to this goal, we define below a typology of relations which characterizes the sentences of a text in the form of semantic relations: $s = (c, i, u, t)$. where s is the sentence, c the set of concepts in the sentence, i the information conveyed, u the uncertainty, and t the time. This description leads us to obtain four types of relations between the sentences: *conformity*, *opposition*, *inconsistency* and *conflict*. Each category is explained with a detailed example below.

Conformity. Conformity between two sentences is the fact of having a semantic relation in which these two sentences have common concepts, identical information, the same degree of uncertainty, similar implications, and approaching moments (time). According to this context, two sentences in conformity are not contradictory. We can formally express the conformity between two sentences $s_1 = (c_1, i_1, u_1, t_1)$ and $s_2 = (c_2, i_2, u_2, t_2)$ as follows: $c_1 \cap c_2 \neq \emptyset, i_1 \doteq i_2, u_1 \doteq u_2, t_1 \doteq t_2$. Example:

– It is possible that there will be an earthquake tomorrow morning.
– Tomorrow, in the morning, we are likely to have an earthquake.

There may be the case where the time is missing in the two sentences. In this case, to prove the conformity of two sentences, one must obligatorily concentrate on all the other elements (c, i, u). Example:

– Apples can help prevent high blood pressure.
– You can eat apples to prevent high blood pressure.

Opposition or Disagreement. The opposition or disagreement between two sentences is the fact of having a semantic relation in which these two sentences have concepts in common, but they have only one different element in their relation. According to this context, two opposing sentences are necessarily contradictory. We can formally express the opposition between two sentences $s_1 = (c_1, i_1, u_1, t_1)$ and $s_2 = (c_2, i_2, u_2, t_2)$ according to 3 different cases:

Case 1: The two sentences contain two opposite pieces of information:

$$c_1 \bigcap c_2 \neq \emptyset, i_1 \neq i_2, u_1 \doteq u_2, t_1 \doteq t_2$$

– People are **looking forward** to be vaccinated against COVID-19.
– People **don't want** to be vaccinated against COVID-19.

Case 2: The two sentences have different uncertainties:

$$c_1 \bigcap c_2 \neq \emptyset, i_1 \doteq i_2, u_1 \neq u_2, t_1 \doteq t_2$$

– Tunisia will **possibly** be in quarantine for 14 days
– It seems **unlikely** for Tunisia to have quarantine for 14 days

Case 3: The two sentences discuss two different tenses:

$$c_1 \bigcap c_2 \neq \emptyset, i_1 \doteq i_2, u_1 \doteq u_2, t_1 \neq t_2$$

– It is possible that there will be an earthquake **this Monday**.
– This **Tuesday**, we are likely to have an earthquake.

Inconsistency. The inconsistency between two sentences is the fact of having a semantic relation-ship in which these two sentences have no concept in common. We can formally express the incompatibility between two sentences $s_1 = (c_1, i_1, u_1, t_1)$ and $s_2 = (c_2, i_2, u_2, t_2)$ as follows: $c_1 \bigcap c_2 \doteq \emptyset$. Example:

– Abou el Kacem Chebbi is a Tunisian poet.
– Apples can help prevent high blood pressure.

In this example, we notice that each sentence relates to a unique subject and is totally different than the subject of the other sentence. In this case, one cannot state the existence of the obvious contradiction. In fact, the evaluation of the contradiction depends on the objective of the system to be built for the detection of the contradictions. For example, for multi-document synthesis systems, these two sentences are contradictory since they do not share the same subject. However, for systems for detecting contradictions in opinions and feelings, these two sentences are not contradictory since they are not in opposition on a specific subject.

Conflict. The conflict between two sentences is the fact of having a semantic relation in which these two sentences have concepts in common, but not identical information, or they do not relate to the same implications. We can formally express the conflict between two sentences $s_1 = (c_1, i_1, u_1, t_1)$ and $s_2 = (c_2, i_2, u_2, t_2)$ according to two different cases:

Case 1: The two sentences contain non-identical information:

$$c_1 \bigcap c_2 \neq \emptyset, i_1 \neq i_2$$

– SNCFT connects Sousse to Tunis.
– SNCFT connects Sousse to Sfax.

In this case of conflict, one cannot speak of an obvious contradiction. Indeed, Sousse can connect to Tunis and Sfax at the same time. Therefore, the evaluation of the contradiction depends on the purpose of the system to be built for the detection of the contradictions.

Case 2: The two sentences relate to two different implications:

$$c_1 \bigcap c_2 \neq \emptyset, i_1 \neq i_2$$

– Physical activity and sport have many benefits for the body.
– The Minister of Sports obliges sports activities in their establishments.

In this case of conflict, the two sentences have concepts in common like "sport", but they do not share the same implication. That is, these two sentences give two pieces of information with totally different results. Thus, the evaluation of the contradiction also depends on the objective of the system to be built for the detection of the contradictions. In what follows, we describe in detail the process of our model which is defined on two important stages: "Semantic construction of a sentence" and "Contradiction assessment". Figure 1 clarifies the general organization of the different stages of our approach.

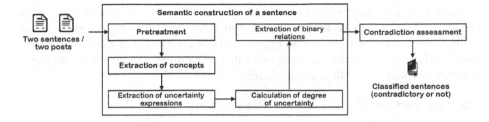

Fig. 1. General process of the proposed approach.

4   Semantic Construction of a Sentence

This step takes as input a natural language sentence (in English) in order to obtain a semantic relationship at the output: $s = (c, i, u, t)$. This step takes the form of a chain of fundamental sub-steps. Each sub-step is explained below.

4.1   Pretreatment

In this step, we start with a lexical analysis that converts a text into a set of terms. Then, we move on to the grammatical analysis which allows to associate for each word of a sentence the corresponding grammatical information such as part of speech, gender, number, etc. In this regard, we use the *"Tree Tagger"* tool by Schmid [16]. After applying the grammar analysis, it is important to proceed with the normalization. Lexical normalization identifies and removes lexical heterogeneities, which appear when the same type of information is provided by different lexical forms, and concerns in particular: the expression of the date and time (exp. *"Mars 21, 1995"* versus *"03/21/1995"*), currencies, geographic coordinates, metric units (*"Meter"* versus *"Inch"*), and expressions of quantifiers (exp. *"three pounds"* versus *"3 pounds"*). The idea of lexical normalization is to remove these heterogeneities to obtain a unique format that facilitates the linguistic analysis performed in the following steps.

4.2   Concept Extraction

A concept is an idea that applies to all the objects in a group. It is the way people can see or understand something. Taking for example the word *"book"*: the latter is a term used to characterize the concept of what a book is. Anything that can be understood in our mind, from experiences or imaginations, about a book is the concept of the term book. To apply the extraction of concepts belonging to a sentence, we used the semantic resource *"WordNet"*[1] The latter is structured in a network of nodes and links. A node, also called a *"synset"*, is a set of synonymous terms that are interchangeable in a context. In WordNet, a *"synset"* thus represents a *"concept"* which is related to other concepts according

---

[1] WordNet is an electronic lexical database that covers the majority of nouns, verbs, adjectives and adverbs in the English language.

to semantic relationships. To determine the most exact concepts or the close ones compared to the general idea of the sentence, we applied the idea of Kharrat et al. [10]. They proposed a new approach of semantic indexation allowing to lead to the exact meaning of each term in a document or query undergoing a contextual analysis at the sentence level.

4.3   Extraction of Uncertainty Expressions

Expressing uncertainty in a couple of two sentences plays a very important role in detecting the contradiction. Effectively, two sentences which discuss the same subject in the same way, but with a completely excluded degree of uncertainty, are said to be contradictory. According to this purpose, this step takes as input, a structured sentence, such that each term in the sentence is labeled by the concepts to which it belongs. Then, we get as output, the list of terms that share a common concept with the concept of uncertainty *"uncertainty"* in WordNet.

4.4   Calculation of Degree of Uncertainty

This step makes it possible to give a degree of uncertainty for each term expressing the uncertainty between 0 and 1. The higher the value, the greater the uncertainty. That is, the fact is almost impossible. The lower the value, the lower the uncertainty. That is, the fact is practically possible. To calculate the degree of uncertainty, we collected from WordNet the words expressing the uncertainty and added other words, resulting in exactly 42 words. Then, we gave each word a degree of uncertainty (0, 0.25, 0.5, 0.75 and 1). In the case where a term does not express uncertainty its degree of uncertainty is equal to -1.

4.5   Extraction of Binary Relations

In this step, our goal is to transform a given sentence into binary relations. These relations will be in the form of a triplet (a_1, R, a_2). With a_1 and a_2 are two arguments of the sentence, and R describes the relationship between a_1 and a_2. For example, the binary relation of the following sentence: *"Bananas are an excellent source of potassium"* is the following triplet: (*"bananas"*, *"be source of"*, *"potassium"*). To apply the extraction of binary relations, we used the *"ReVerb"* tool developed by Anthony Fader. [8]. ReVerb is a program that automatically identifies and extracts binary relations from sentences in English. In our case, we give it as input a POS-tagged and NP-chunked sentence in order to obtain a set of triples. Unfortunately, the ReVerb tool cannot extract all the equivalence relations *"isA"*. For example, the triplet (*"Adam"*, *"isA"*, *"his friend"*) is obtained from the following sentence: *"His friend Adam"*. To solve this problem case, we lead to the following idea: we extract all the entities named in the sentence S into a set $E1$. And we also extract the set of remaining mentions in an $E2$ set. For each element $e1$ of $E1$ and $e2$ of $E2$, we will construct the following equivalence relation $(e1, isA, e2)$. Another problem is getting a triplet with an incorrect equivalence relation. For example, the triplet (*"Adam and"*, *"isA"*, *"Yassine"*) is obtained from the following sentence: *"Adam and Yassine"*. To solve this problem, we must respect the following three constraints:

- The first argument must be an entity (a person, an organization, a product),
- The second argument must contain at least one name,
- The last word of the second argument must not be a conjunction word.

5 Contradiction Assessment

After obtaining a very in-depth semantic representation of the sentences, this step aims to detect and describe the contradiction between them in the form of two sub-steps; The first step is to determine if there is opposition or disagreement between the sentences. And the second step is to analyze this opposition in order to get a detailed statement about the sentences (contradictory or not).

5.1 Detection of Opposing Information

In order to determine the opposition or disagreement between two pieces of information, we propose to define an opposition function $f_{opposition}(R_1, R_2)$ which evaluates the degree of opposition between two binary relations R_1 and R_2 represented in the form of a triplet $(a1, r, a2)$. With $a1$ and $a2$ are two arguments of the sentence, and r is the verb that describes the relationship between $a1$ and $a2$. The function $f_{opposition}(R_1, R_2)$ gives the value 1 if R_1 and R_2 are opposite and 0 if they are similar. We also define a function $f_{similarity}(w_1, w_2)$ which evaluates the degree of similarity between two elements w_1 and w_2 of the triples of binary relations. The function $f_{similarity}$ gives the value 1 if w_1 and w_2 are two similar elements and 0 if otherwise. To calculate the similarity, we use WordNet and VerbOceas. Given two binary relations R1 and R2 such that: $R1 = (a_1, r_1, b_1)$ and $R2 = (a_2, r_2, b_2)$, the opposition function is calculated as follows:

$$f_{opposition}(R_1, R_2) = $$
$$max(f_{similarity}(r_1, r_2), min(f_{similarity}(a_1, a_2), f_{similarity}(b_1, b_2))) \tag{1}$$

5.2 Detection of Contradiction

This last step makes it possible to analyze the contradiction between two sentences by classifying them according to 4 different categories: *"Conformity"*, *"In opposition"*, *"Inconsistent"* and *"Conflictual"*. Algorithm 1 describes this step.

6 Experimental Evaluation

6.1 Test Environment

In order to be able to perform the evaluation of our contradiction detection approach in a fairly reliable and correct manner, and to increase the consistency of our results, we applied experiments on 4 sets of data. All of this data is publicly available which allows our results to be used in other work for benchmarking. At

---

Algorithm 1: Contradiction Detection Algorithm

---

1 **Input:** Two sentences of words(sentence1 and sentence2)
2 **Output:** C: Classified sentences (contradictory or not)
3 $S1 \leftarrow Semantic\_construction(sentence1)$
4 $S2 \leftarrow Semantic\_construction(sentence2)$
5 **if** $S1.c_1 \cap S2.c_2 \doteq \emptyset$ **then**
6 $\quad \lfloor\ C \leftarrow "Conflict"$
7 **else if** $S1.u_1 \neq S2.u_2$ or $S1.t_1 \neq S2.t_2$ **then**
8 $\quad \lfloor\ C \leftarrow "Opposition"$
9 **else if** $f_{opposition}(S1.R_1, S2.R_2) \doteq 1$ **then**
10 $\quad \lfloor\ C \leftarrow "Inconsistency"$
11 **else**
12 $\quad \lfloor\ C \leftarrow "Conformity"$

---

first, we applied our experiments to the standard collection of tests: *"SemEval"*[2]. This collection is of high quality and highly recommended in the literature. This collection contains pairs of labeled sentences (contradictory or not). Then, with the intention of testing the reliability of our approach on special or rare cases, we used the three test collections: *"RTE-3"*, *"RTE-4"* and *"RTE-5"* from the treatment group *"Stanford natural language"*[3] . These collections are used by Marneffe et al. [5] for their work. They are created as challenges of recognizing textual entailment (*"RTE"*). They contain texts so complicated, that even humans are not able to detect the contradiction easily. According to this context, testing our approach on these types of collections is a big challenge for us. These datasets are marked for a 3-way decision in terms of implication: *"YES"* (implies), *"NO"* (contradicts) and *"UNKNOWN"* (does not imply but it is not a contradiction). Table 1 presents the number of sentence pairs for each collection.

Table 1. The number of sentence pairs for each collection used in this work.

Data set	Number of sentence pairs			Total
	Implication	Unknown	Contradiction	
SemEval	2793	0	720	**3513**
RTE-3	800	0	800	**1600**
RTE-4	500	350	150	**1000**
RTE-5	600	420	180	**1200**
				7313

---

[2] http://alt.qcri.org/semeval2014/.
[3] https://nlp.stanford.edu/projects/contradiction/.

6.2   Experiments and Results

To evaluate our contradiction detection system, we used two performance measures: recall and precision. These two measurements are calculated as follows:

$$Recall = \frac{Number\ of\ contradictory\ sentences\ detected\ correctly}{Total\ number\ of\ contradictory\ sentences\ in\ the\ collection} \quad (2)$$

$$Precision = \frac{Number\ of\ contradictory\ sentences\ detected\ correctly}{Total\ number\ of\ contradictory\ sentences\ detected} \quad (3)$$

We compared the results obtained using our system for each data collection against three different works: De Marneffe [5], Pham [15] and Lingam [12]. All the results of our experiments obtained are shown in Table 2. From this table, we can observe that for the SemEval collection our system presents better precision as well as a better recall compared to the work of Lingam [12]. Compared to the other three collections: RTE-3, RTE-4, and RTE-5, even though the recall and precision values are not too high, our system still shows better values against all other works (even for the work of De Marneffe [5]). The experimental results presented in Table 2 have shown very well that our approach works perfectly. Especially since our system was able to have very reasonable results for the three collections: RTE-3, RET-4 and RTE-5 which are considered as a challenge for the contradiction detection systems. One possible explanation is that our system takes into consideration additional semantic criteria to detect linguistic cues due to natural language ambiguity and uncertainty cues. These two details are very important for the detection of pairs of sentences having incompatible meaning or information concerning events which cannot hold simultaneously. It is therefore obvious to say that our system is able to correctly detect and identify discrepancies, inconsistencies and mistrust in a natural language text.

Table 2. The obtained results of our experiments.

Method	SemEval		RTE-3		RTE-4		RTE-5	
	Recall	Precision	Recall	Precision	Recall	Precision	Recall	Precision
De Marneffe	-	-	19.44	22.95	-	-	-	-
Pham	-	-	19.44	14.00	22.67	23.00	28.89	21.14
Lingam	73.14	83.68	18.72	16.33	24.17	18.92	23.36	24.5
Our approach	**82.43**	**91.20**	**53.20**	**59.45**	**58.92**	**63.14**	**71.35**	**68.84**

7   Conclusion

In this paper, we have proposed a new approach to detect contradictions based on a joint analysis of semantic relations and assessments of uncertainties due to natural language ambiguity. Therefore, we have used some specific steps to understand the semantics of sentences in depth; such as advanced lexical and grammatical analyses with detailed concept extraction to understand the exact meaning of each word in sentences, and the extraction of binary and uncertainty relations. Our experimental results have clearly shown that this new contradiction detection approach works perfectly and provides good quality results.

It is true that our proposed model has successfully proven its efficiency, we might as well, in our future work, include improvements of contradiction detection measures by applying artificial neural networks and deep learning methods. As a matter of fact, we believe that more experiments are required to investigate if the study results and approach is applicable to other types of contradictions.

References

1. Adler, B.T., et al.: Assigning trust to Wikipedia content. In: Proceedings of the 4th International Symposium on Wikisym, pp. 1–12 (2008)
2. Asif, I., et al.: Using nanopublications to detect and explain contradictory research claims. In: 2021 IEEE 17th International Conference on eScience (eScience), pp. 1–10. IEEE (2021)
3. Best, E.C., Fellowship, N.: Alan Ritter: Software EngineerBest, vol. 2007 (2007).
4. Chklovski, T., Pantel, P.: VerbOcean: mining the web for fine-grained semantic verb relations. In: Proceedings of the 2004 Conference on Empirical Methods in Natural Language Processing, pp. 33–40 (2004)
5. de Marneffe, M.-C., Rafferty, A.N., Manning, C.D.: Finding contradictions in text. In: Proceedings of ACL-08: HLT, pp. 1039–1047 (2008)
6. Diao, Y., et al.: A multi-dimension question answering network for sarcasm detection. In: IEEE Access, vol. 8, pp. 135152–135161 (2020)
7. Ennals, R., Trushkowsky, B., Agosta, J.M.: Highlighting disputed claims on the web. In: Proceedings of the 19th International Conference on World Wide Web, pp. 341–350 (2010)
8. Fader, A., Soderland, S., Etzioni, O.: Identifying relations for open information extraction. In: Proceedings of the 2011 Conference on Empirical Methods in Natural Language Processing, pp. 1535–1545 (2011)
9. Harabagiu, S.M., Hickl, A., Lacatusu, V.F.: Negation, contrast and contradiction in text processing. In: AAAI, pp. 755–762 (2006)
10. Kharrat, A.E., Hlaoua, L.: New information retrieval approach based on semantic indexing by meaning (2019)
11. Lendvai, P., Reichel, U.: Contradiction detection for rumorous claims. arXiv preprint arXiv:1611.02588 (2016)
12. Lingam, V., et al.: Deep learning for conflicting statements detection in text. PeerJ Prepint(2018)
13. Padó, S., et al.: Deciding entailment and contradiction with stochastic and edit distance-based alignment. In: TAC (2008)
14. Park, S., et al.: NewsCube: delivering multiple aspects of news to mitigate media bias. In: Proceedings of the SIGCHI Conference on Human Factors in Computing Systems, pp. 443–452 (2009)
15. Pham, M.Q.N., Le Nguyen, M., Shimazu, A.: Using shallow semantic parsing and relation extraction for finding contradiction in text (2013)

16. Schmid, H.: Treetagger (1996)
17. Shih, C., et al.: Validating contradiction in texts using online co-mention pattern checking. In: ACM Transactions on Asian Language Information Processing (TALIP), vol. 11, no. 4, pp. 1–21 (2012)
18. Tsytsarau, M., Palpanas, T., Denecke, K.: Scalable detection of sentiment-based contradictions. DiversiWeb, WWW 2011, vol. 1, pp. 9–16 (2011)

C-DESERT Score for Arabic Text Summary Evaluation

Samira Ellouze[1](✉), Maher Jaoua[1], and Arem Atoui[2]

[1] ANLP Research Group, MIRACL Lab., University of Sfax, Sfax, Tunisia
ellouze.samira@gmail.com, maher.jaoua@gmail.com
[2] University of Gabes, ISIM Gabes, Gabes, Tunisia
arem.atoui@isimg.tn

Abstract. Text summary evaluation represents an important step after building any summarization system. Despite the important number of metrics that have been developed, there are a few metrics that evaluate Arabic text summary. In this paper, we present a new automatic metric for Arabic text summary evaluation. This metric combines ROUGE scores with documents embedding-based scores to build a regression model that predicts the manual score of an Arabic summary. First, we have constructed document embedding models with different vector sizes then, we have used these models to present each candidate and model summary as a document embedding vector. After that, a similarity score between the two document embedding vectors was calculated. Finally, we have combined several similarity scores based on the document embedding representation and the ROUGE scores to predict a manual score. Furthermore, in the combination phase, we have tried multiple regression models to obtain the most optimal predictive model. The obtained result showed that the proposed method outperforms all baseline metrics in the task of text summary evaluation and the task of the summarization system evaluation.

Keywords: Evaluation of text summary · Arabic summary · Document embedding · Machine learning · Regression model

1 Introduction

The text summary evaluation is indispensable as it can reveal its quality and compare it to other summaries obtained from the same input documents. Therefore, to verify the quality of the obtained summary, we should consider two aspects: the content and the linguistic quality. The former seeks to verify if the summary to be evaluated conveys the relevant information from the source document(s) while the latter focuses on the readability of the summary, such as grammaticality, cohesion, coherence, etc. The first evaluation of these two aspects can be produced manually. Moreover, manually evaluating summaries gives meaningful and reliable results however, this evaluation is costly and not reproducible. For this reason, many re-searchers undertook an automatic evaluation, which made the evaluation of summarization systems cheaper and can be carried out at any time given that this evaluation is reproducible. In fact, nowadays, this type of evaluation has a direct consequence on the summarizing systems as it is

N. T. Nguyen et al. (Eds.): ICCCI 2022, LNAI 13501, pp. 246–258, 2022.
https://doi.org/10.1007/978-3-031-16014-1_20

affordable and can be carried out at any time. However, until now most automatic evaluation metrics have been designed for the English language, whereas other languages have been neglected. Moreover, due to their dependency attachment to the lexical level, some metrics, such as ROUGE (Lin, 2004), and AutoSummENG (Giannakopoulos et al. 2008), can be used to evaluate the summaries in any other language. However, it is not enough to evaluate a summary only at the lexical level. Hence, the idea of creating an evaluation metric that takes into account several levels of evaluation by including lexical, syntactic and/or semantic levels, which help improve the evaluation of the text summary content. In fact, such an evaluation metric can correlate better with the human evaluation metrics, such as "Overall responsiveness", which evaluates both the content and the linguistic quality. However, the lack of efficient metrics that can evaluate Arabic text summaries has led us to propose a new method that enables us to assess automatic summaries written in Arabic so as to reach production of scores much closer to those found by human experts. In addition, with this proposed method, we can assess an Arabic text summary by taking into account the lexical and semantic levels of the evaluation.

Therefore, our three main contributions in this paper are as follows:

- Building several Arabic Doc2Vec (Le and Mikolov, 2014) models with different sizes, using the two Doc2Vec model versions (i.e. the distributed memory model or the distributed bags of words model) to learn document embedding.
- Presenting a summary as a Doc2Vec vector, and then calculating the cosine similarity or the Euclidean distance between two Doc2Vec vectors, where the first is for the candidate summary and the second is for the reference summary. As a matter of fact, we found that some works (Zhang et al. 2020) have used cosine similarity to detect similarity between two embedding representations, while some others have used Euclidean distance (Mrabet and Demner-Fushman 2020). For this reason, we have decided to try the cosine similarity and the Euclidean distance.
- Joining the lexical and semantic match between candidate and reference summaries by combining semantic similarity based on Doc2Vec vectors with various ROUGE scores to predict "Overall responsiveness" score.

The rest of this paper is organized in the following way. First, in Sect. 2, we introduce the main prior work studies on the evaluation of the text summarization systems. Then, in Sect. 3, we explain the adopted method first, by presenting the different steps of building our Doc2Vec models and then, by combining the schemes of different features to predict the human score. After that, in Sect. 4, we describe the used dataset, present the experiments and the results obtained through the summary level evaluation and the system level evaluations. Finally, the conclusion and the possible future research avenues are outlined in section.

2 Related works

To evaluate a text summary, several metrics have been introduced during the last two decades. In fact, to manually evaluate a summary, the TAC conference has mainly used two manual metrics: the PYRAMID (Nenkova and Passonneau 2004) and the Overall responsiveness. The first one evaluates the content of a text summary, while the second represents a combination of content and linguistic quality evaluation. Because of the complexity of manual evaluation, multiple automatic metrics have been developed, the most known of which is the ROUGE metric (Lin 2004), which detects common word n-grams between the system and the model summary (manually constructed summary). Then, a recall, precision, or f-measure score is calculated based on n-grams overlap. After the ROUGE metric, several other n-grams based metrics have appeared some of which are based on word n-grams (Lin 2004, He et al. 2008, Zhou et al. 2006) and the others are based on character n-grams (i.e. AutoSummENG (Giannakopoulos et al. 2008), MeMoG (Giannakopoulos and Karkaletsis 2011), BEER (Stanojevic and Sima'an 2014).

Besides, other than the n-grams-based metrics, several metrics were trained to optimize the correlation with the human scores. In fact, the first work that has adopted this approach to evaluate the text summary was that of (Conroy and Dang 2008) with the ROSE metric. This metric, which combines multiple ROUGE scores and BE score to predict the human judgment of the content and Overall Responsiveness. After that, Conroy et al. (2011) proposed Nouveau-ROUGE metric that combines the ROUGE variants to predict the PYRAMID and the Overall Responsiveness score for updating summaries. In the same context, Pitler et al. (2010) evaluated the five linguistic properties, such as grammaticality, non-redundancy, structure and coherence, focus and referential clarity, which were defined in the TAC conference by combining different types of linguistic quality features to predict each linguistic property. In the same regard, Ellouze et al. (2016) combined the "Adapted ROUGE" scores and several linguistic quality features to assess the linguistic quality. In fact, this "adapted ROUGE", which is devoted to the evaluation of the linguistic quality instead of the content summary, is based on the overlap between the candidate summary and the source documents. Another work related to this approach is that of Ellouze et al. (2017a), which evaluated the text summary content using the regression model by combining multiple evaluation metrics and linguistic quality features. In fact, Ellouze et al. (2017a) assumed that, since it is difficult to assess the content with a poor linguistic quality summary, it is recommended to add some linguistic quality features.

Moreover, in the last few years, some evaluation metrics have integrated the concept of the word embedding representation to measure the content overlap. In this context, Ng and Abrecht (2015) proposed the ROUGE-WE measure, which uses the Word2Vec model (Mikolov et al. 2013), to match the n-grams in the candidate summary with those of the model summary. The similarity score between two n-grams is the product of the Word2Vec vector of each n-gram. More recently, Sun and Nenkova (2019) have conducted an evaluation based on the overlap between the word embedding representation of words in the candidate summary and the reference summaries. In this work, the authors tested seven embedding variants, some of which are contextualized word embeddings, such as ELMo (Peters et al. 2018) and others, which are uncontextualized word embeddings, such as Word2Vec. Moreover, another similar work introduced by (Zhang et al. 2020), proposed the Bidirectional Encoder Representations from Transformers (BERT) score metric for the content evaluation, which uses a contextualized embedding named the BERT (Devlin et al. 2018) to represent the words of the candidate summary and the model summary. Then their compute the matching between contextual words embedding representations, using the cosine similarity. In addition, (Mrabet and Demner-Fushman 2020) have introduced a new summary evaluation metric named HOLMS. This metric is based on computing the distance between two embedding n-gram vectors, one from candidate summary and the other from reference summary. To obtain an embedding n-gram vector, the authors try three embedding models: BERT (Devlin et al. 2018), universal sentence encoder (Cer et al. 2018) and Glove (Pennington et al. 2014).

However, in a recent work presented by (Xenouleas et al. 2019), there has been an evaluation of the five linguistic qualities of a text summary that were introduced by (Dang 2006) (i.e. Grammaticality, Non-redundancy, Referential Clarity, Focus and Structure & Coherence) based on the BERT word embedding model.

Moreover, we mention two research studies that dealt only with the Arabic text summary evaluation. The first research has developed the KpEval metric (Elghannam and El-Shishtawy 2015), which is based on keyphrase overlap. In fact, keyphrases express the most relevant concepts of a summary. Therefore, the main idea of the KpEval metric is to calculate the matched keyphrases between the system summary and one or more reference summaries (manual summaries). After, a second reseach is proposed by (Ellouze et al. 2017b) and is based on merging lexical and syntactic features. Many existing lexical scores are used as features, such as ROUGE scores, AutoSummENG scores, NPowER scores and SIMetrix scores. In this work, the authors combine lexical overlap features with multiple linguistic quality features using the regression model to predict Overall Responsiveness.

However, these two research studies rely only on lexical similarity to evaluate the content of a summary. To address these issues, we have proposed a metric that include both lexical and semantic similarity measures. In fact, semantic similarity measures take into consideration the relations of synonymy, hypernymy, polysemyor homonymy between words.

3 Proposed method

To address the limitations of using only lexical similarity, we proposed an evaluation method based on both lexical and semantic similarity levels. In fact, we combine the lexical features with the semantic similarity features to predict Overall Responsiveness manual score. Therefore, to treat the lexical similarity level, we use multiple variants of the ROUGE score. Moreover, to deal with the semantic similarity, we built several Doc2Vec models then, we used each one to make a comparison between the candidate and the reference summaries. In the following section, we begin by presenting the document embedding technique that we used in the semantic level evaluation.

3.1 Document Embedding Model

The Doc2Vec (Le and Mikolov 2014) model, which is one of the documents embedding modeling approaches, is based on the Word2Vec model. In fact, it is used to represent the variable-length pieces of texts, such as the sentences, paragraphs, and documents, as a vector. Furthermore, the Doc2Vec vector preserves an important property of a word, which is its semantic.

Besides, the Doc2Vec models have two variants: the distributed memory model and the distributed bags of word model. The first model takes into consideration the word order, at least in a small context while the second does not take in consideration the word order. As it is mentioned in the work of Le and Mikolov (2014), it is recommended to combine distributed memory models with distributed bag of words models because it is usually more consistent. For this reason, we combine in our work several Doc2vec models, based on both the distributed memory model and the distributed bag of words model.

3.2 Building the Doc2Vec Model

In fact, the construction of a Doc2vec model for Arabic language requires three main phases, notably, preprocessing the input corpus, generating vocabularies that represent the training data and then, training the Doc2Vec model. However, before starting the construction of our model, we have built a corpus from multiple available Arabic corpora, such as (watan-2004 (Abbas et al. 2011), Khaleej-2004 (Abbas and Smaili 2005), etc.) but because of the small size of the collected documents, we have collected other news documents from various Arabic news web sites, namely the CNN, France 24, DW, the BBC, Al-Arabiya and Wikinews.

Preprocessing Phase: Pre-processing is an important phase that has a big influence on the vocabulary content and size. Since it has an evident impact on the final obtained model. Moreover, the input of this phase is a corpus that contains more than 145 k of newspaper documents and 41983609 tokens. First, we have removed the non-Arabic characters from the documents then, we have normalized some Arabic characters by replacing the same set of letters with more precise letters, such as the letters "إ" ('i), "أ" ('a) and "آ"('ā), which are now replaced with "ا" (ā), which are now replaced with "ا". After that, we have removed the stop-words since they do not add much meaning to a text, mainly when comparing the similarity between two texts (such as text summaries, in our case). In fact, by removing the stop-words we eliminate the unnecessary vocabularies from the input of the training Doc2vec model.

Finally, we have lemmatized all the documents in our corpus by using the FARASA system (Darwish and Mubarak 2016). In fact, the Arabic language is an agglutinative language. This means that the words can have some affixes (suffixes, prefixes, postfixes, antefixes) to a verb or a noun. For example, in some articles, prepositions and conjunctions can be attached to the beginning of words (noun or verb) and some pronouns can be attached to the end of the words. Therefore, the agglutination phenomenon can affect the size of the vocabularies and therefore, alter the quality of the vectors produced by the training Doc2Vec model. For instance, the three words, "دراجة" (daraǧat, bicycle), "دراجتنا" (daraǧatunā, our bicycle), "الدراجة" (āldaraǧat, the bicycle) have the same semantic meaning and also the same lemma. However, without lemmatization, these three words have three different vector representations, which increases the number of output vectors. Then, through the dissimulation of the meaning of words, we found it necessary to lemmatize all the documents in the corpus.

Generate the Training Data: Before training the model, we have first built a corpus vocabulary then, converted each document into a matrix that represents words by vector of numbers (digits) (i.e. "vectorize" the text) using a one-hot encoding.

Training the Doc2Vec Model: To benefit from the advantages of the two variants of the Doc2Vec model, we have built 6 models with the distributed memory (DM) model and 6 models with the distributed bags of words (DBOW) model. For each model, we have chosen multiple dimensions of the output vector: 100, 120, 150, 170, 200 and 250.

Computation of "Document Embedding for Summary Evaluation (DESE)" Score: Then, after training our models, we calculated the DESE score, which is a similarity score between the candidates and reference summary using a built model of the Doc2Vec. Therefore, given a candidate summary C and a set of three reference summaries, r_1, r_2 and r_3, first, for each summary, we began by the same pre-processing phase, as realized in the first phase of building the Doc2Vec model. After that, we used the Doc2Vec model to represent each summary by a Doc2Vec vector then, we have firstly computed the cosine similarity between the vector presenting the summary V_c and each vector representing a reference summary V_{ri}. Next, we have calculated the Euclidian distance and the cosine similarity between a candidate summary vector V_c and each reference summary vector. Finally, we took four scores: the maximum and the average cosine similarity[1] (CS) between the two Doc2Vec representations and the minimum and the average Euclidian distance[2] (ED) between the two Doc2Vec representations.

$$DESE_{AVG\_cos} = \frac{\sum_i^3 CS(V_c, V_{ri})}{3}$$

$$DESE_{MAX\_cos} = \text{Max}\{CS(V_c, V_{r1}), CS(V_c, V_{r2}), CS(V_c, V_{r3})\}$$

$$DESE_{AVG\_euc} = \frac{\sum_i^3 ED(V_c, V_{ri})}{3}$$

$$DESE_{Min\_euc} = \text{Min}\{ED(V_c, V_{r1}), ED(V_c, V_{r2}), ED(V_c, V_{r3})\}$$

3.3   Features

DESE Scores: for each model of the 12 Doc2Vec trained models, we have calculated the maximum and the average cosine similarity (CS) and the minimum and the average Euclidean distance for each candidate summary in our dataset. As a result, we obtained 24 DESE scores using cosine similarity and 24 DESE scores using Euclidean distance.

---

[1] The most closely related vectors will obtain the highest cosine similarity.

[2] The most closely related vectors will obtain the lowest Euclidean distance.

Next, for the maximum and the average cosine similarity or the minimum and the average Euclidean distance, we have measured, the Pearson correlation between the obtained cosine similarity or Euclidean distance and the human grade score (Overall Responsiveness). Therefore, from 48 DESE scores, we maintained as features, 21 DESE scores.

The ROUGE Scores. Actually, the ROUGE metric represents a standard in the summary evaluation task, because of its simplicity and its high correlation with the human judgment scores. In our work, we have added multiple variants of the ROUGE scores: ROUGE-1, ROUGE-2, ROUGE-3, ROUGE-L, ROUGE-SU4, ROUGE-S and ROUGE-W. Then, for each variant of the ROUGE metric, we have calculated the recall, the precision, and the F-measure. Therefore, we have obtained 21 ROUGE scores.

3.4 Combination Scheme

In this stage, we will use several regression models to find the model that correlates the best with the human judgment score. "Overall Responsiveness". However, sometimes, when combining all the features to train a model, the obtained model receives a less correlation with the human judgment than when combining a selection of features. For this reason, we used the Recursive Feature Elimination (RFE) (Guyon et al. 2002) algorithm to select the features. In fact, this algorithm has proven its efficiency in selecting adequate features to predict the targeted variable.

Moreover, after selecting the relevant features, we tested many regression classifiers included in "sklearn" python module like the HuberRegressor the Linear Regression, the Poisson Regressor, the Ridge, the SMR, etc.... In fact, to select some of these classifiers, we have tested them for linear and non-linear regression. In addition, we have used the deep learning algorithm LSTM implemented by the "Keras" python module. To test previously cited classifiers, we have divided our dataset into a training data set and a testing data set. Then, we adopted the one that best correlates with the "Overall responsiveness" in our test set. Finally, the score produced by the selected model is named C-DESERT, which stands for Combining Document Embedding for Summary Evaluation with ROUGE metric Tool.

4   Experiments

4.1   Data Sets

The Arabic part of two Multiling summarization task corpus constitutes our data set: TAC 2011 MultiLing Pilot, 2011 data set (Giannakopoulos and Karkaletsis 2011) and the MultiLing 2013 data set (Giannakopoulos 2013). MultiLing Pilot 2011 and MultiLing 2013 data set, contain 10 and 15 collections of newspaper articles, respectively, each one broach a topic such as natural disasters, terrorist explosions, sports, politics, etc. Each topic contains 10 newspaper articles. As well, for both data sets 10 summarization systems have participated. In addition, the two data sets involve system summaries (candidate summaries) and three model summaries for each collection. Then, each system summary takes three manual scores, each one is given by an evaluator. In our experiments, we used the average of the three manual scores given for each candidate summary. This average score will be used to calculate the correlation with the human score in all experimentations.

4.2   Result

We tested our method at the summary evaluation level (Micro-evaluation) and in a system evaluation level (Macro-evaluation). At the summary level, we took for each Summarizer system and each produced summary, a separate entry, which means, that at this level, each score calculated by our obtained model is the final score for a summary. However, at the system evaluation level, the average quality of a summarizing system is determined, by calculating the average scores produced by the C-DESERT metric for all the summaries that a system has produced.

As previously stated, we assess our model using test sets. We randomly divided the data set into training and testing sets, while making sure that the training set represent the two thirds of the data set and the rest represent the test set. Therefore, to evaluate the proposed method, we studied the correlation of Pearson, Spearman and Kendall between the manual scores "Overall Responsiveness" and the produced scores named "C-DESERT". Furthermore, we reported the "Root Mean Squared Error" (RMSE) measure generated by each model. This measure is based on the difference between the actual scores (in our case manual scores) and the predicted ones.

Summary Evaluation Level. We begin with the experiments performed with the summary evaluation level. The 8 selected features for building models are presented in Table 1.

Table 1. List of the selected features to predict the "Overall Responsiveness" score for Arabic text Summaries

Type	Features
ROUGE scores	rouge-1-precision, rouge-2-precision, rouge-S-precision, rouge-SU- precision
DESE scores	DESE-Max-Cos-Vec170-DBOW, DESE-Max-Cos-Vec150-DBOW, DESE-Avg-Cos-Vec100-DM, DESE-Avg-Euc-Vec120-DBOW

Table 1 shows that the selected features include features from both scores: ROUGE and DESE. We noticed the presence of ROUGE-SU, which can capture the lexical similarity by matching unigrams and the local context by matching Skipgrams. We also noticed the presence of the four DESE scores where one of which is based on the distributed memory variant of the Doc2Vec model that takes into account the semantic of words with the caption of small context for each word. This context is helpful with the evaluation of the local coherence. On the other hand, Pearson, Spearman and Kendall's correlations and the root mean square error (RMSE) generated by each classifier are presented in Table 2. Each correlation measure is used to determine the strength of the relationship between manual scores and predicted scores. Its value is a number between −1 and 1. The best classifier is the one that has the great correlation and the less RMSE.

Table 2. Correlations (p-value is between brackets) with the overall responsiveness and the RMSE for machine learning Classifiers

	Correlation			RMSE
Classifiers	Pearson	Spearman	Kendall	
PoissonRegressor	0.3817(0.0004)	0.3361(0.0022)	0.2379(0.0026)	0.6917
LinearRegression	**0.4276(7.58e-5)**	**0.3637(0.0009)**	**0.2564(0.0011)**	**0.6786**
SMR (linear kernel)	0.3315(0.0026)	0.2971(0.0074)	0.2022(0.0105)	0.7150
SVR (non-linear Kernel)	0.3686(0.0007)	0.3471(0.0016)	0.2504(0.0015)	0.7015
Ridge (linear kernel)	**0.4276 (7.59e-5)**	**0.3637(0.0009)**	**0.2564(0.0012)**	**0.6786**
Ridge (non-linear kernel)	0.3971(0.0002)	0.3515(0.0013)	0.2491(0.0016)	0.6883
ARDRegression	0.3384(0.0021)	0.2916(0.0086)	0.2062(0.0091)	0.7056
RandomForestRegressor	0.2721(0.0145)	0.2528(0.0236)	0.1678(0.0337)	0.7198
Bagging	0.3617(0.0009)	0.2932(0.0082)	0.2015(0.0107)	0.6964
LSTM	0.2723(0.0145)	0.2285(0.0414)	0.2025(0.0122)	0.6800

The performance of each classifier in building the predictive model is summarized in Table 2. As previously shown, the two classifiers that have the least RMSE and the best Pearson's correlation (0.4276) with the human judgment are the linear regressions and the Ridge classifier with linear kernel. Unexpectedly, the obtained result showed that the correlation obtained by the LSTM classifier which is a deep learning classifier is weak (0.2723). However, despite the use of deep learning in most NLP tasks gave the best results; the obtained correlations were lower than those of the majority of the other classifiers, which may be due to the small size of the used data set.

We will select the model obtained by combining the selected features using the Ridge classifier with linear kernel. We are going to call this selected model the C-DESERT metric. Then, we will compare the performance of the C-DESERT with several baseline metrics used in Multiling workshops, such as ROUGE-1, ROUGE-2, MeMoG (Giannakopoulos and Karkaletsis 2011), etc.

On the other hand, the correlation between the Overall Responsiveness and each baseline is calculated for the whole data set. Moreover, we will add the correlation of the best variant of two other famous metrics: the AutoSummENG and NPoWER (Giannakopoulos and Karkaletsis, 2013). Furthermore, we will compare our metric to various variants of the SIMetrix metric. Then we will compare C-DESERT with a combination of the selected ROUGE scores (that appeared in Table 1) and a combination of the selected DESE scores (that appeared in Table 1), to check the impact of each class of scores on the C-DESERT ones. The combination of the selected ROUGE scores is performed using a Ridge classifier with a linear kernel. While, the Ridge classifier with a non-linear Kernel is used to combine the selected DESE scores. Table 3 details the different correlations and RMSEs between overall responsiveness and the baseline metrics or our different experimentations.

Table 3. Pearson, Spearman and Kendall Correlations (p-value is between brackets) with Overall Responsiveness Score and RMSE at the Summary Evaluation Level

Correlation measures	Pearson	Spearman	Kendall
Baseline scores			
ROUGE-1	−0.1072(0.0975)	−0.1016(0.1164)	−0.0714(0.1145)
ROUGE-2	−0.0995(0.1243)	−0.1141(0.0775)	−0.0811(0.0732)
AutoSummENG	−0.0211(0.7448)	−0.0216(0.7382)	−0.0157(0.7277)
MeMoG	−0.0123(0.8498)	0.0141(0.8275)	0.0103(0.8194)
NPowER	−0.0175(0.7864)	−0.0159(0.8061)	−0.0122(0.7869)
SIMetrix unigramProb	0.2025(0.0016)	0.23975(0.0002)	0.1660(0.0002)
SIMetrix smoothedJSD	0.1158(0.0734)	0.1305(0.0434)	0.0884(0.0510)
SIMetrix unsmoothedJSD	0.1369(0.0340)	0.1539(0.0171)	0.1041(0.0215)
SIMetrix multinomialProb	0.0971(0.1337)	0.1459(0.0237)	0.1010(0.0256)
Our experimentations			
C-DESERT	**0.4276(7.59e-5)**	**0.3637(0.0009)**	**0.2564(0.0012)**
Combining ROUGE scores	0.3390(0.0020)	0.3110(0.0049)	0.2194(0.0055)
Combining DESE scores	0.3276(0.0030)	0.3135(0.0046)	0.2233(0.0047)

Table 3 shows that no metric produces a high correlation with the Overall Responsiveness, including our C-DESERT metric. Besides, the baseline SIMetrix based on the unigram probability has the best correlation with the human judgment, which is about 0.2025. Nevertheless, the best correlation is achieved by our C-DESERT metric, which combines the features based on the Doc2Vec representation and the ROUGE metrics. In addition, we can notice that the combination of features based on the Doc2Vec features and the combination of the ROUGE metrics have roughly the same correlation. In general, the correlation between any metric and the human judgment at the summary level evaluation is not very high, neither for English nor for other languages. However, for the Arabic language, the correlation is lower than the one for English. This is perhaps due to the complexity of this language. Indeed, several phenomena can increase the complexity of processing Arabic texts, such as the frequent absence of short vowels (for instance "ُ" (u), "َ" (a),"ِ" (i)), the agglutination, and the homographic words such as the word "تدرس" (tadrusu) which can mean, "she studies" or "you study". Actually, short vowels in general, play an important role in Arabic words because they remove the ambiguity of the word meanings. Therefore, with the absence of short vowels, the homographic words will increase then, many words that have the same orthographic forms but with different pronunciations and meanings will have the same Doc2Vec vector. Moreover, those words will be matched when using the ROUGE score instead of their different meanings. Inversely, the agglutination will produce a different Doc2Vec vector for the same words because of some characters that can be attached to a word without adding a meaning, such as "ال" (al). In fact, all this will have an influence on the correlation between each metric and the human judgment.

System Evaluation Level. At the system evaluation level, we have tried to calculate the average scores of all the summaries that a system has produced. In fact, Table 4 shows the different correlations between the different scores and the "Overall Responsiveness" human score at the system evaluation level.

Table 4. Pearson, Spearman and Kendall Correlations with overall responsiveness score and RMSE, in system level evaluation

Correlation measures	Pearson	Spearman	Kendall
Baseline scores			
ROUGE-1	−0.3241	−0.2860	−0.2111
ROUGE-2	−0.2628	−0.3186	−0.2229
AutoSummENG	−0.2557	−0.2913	−0.1759
MeMoG	−0.1511	−0.1746	−0.0938
NPowER	−0.2072	−0.2317	−0.1408
SIMetrix unigramProb	0.0724	−0.0263	−0.0117
SIMetrix smoothedJSD	0.1815	0.2185	0.1056
SIMetrix unsmoothedJSD	0.2180	0.2282	0.1173
SIMetrix multinomialProb	−0.2233	−0.1983	−0.1525
Our experimentations			
C-DESERT	**0.7022**	**0.7213**	**0.5161**
Combining ROUGE scores	0.6794	0.6511	0.4809
Combining DESE scores	0.3891	0.4001	0.3167

In fact, the best Pearson (0.7022), Spearman (0.7213) and Kendall's correlation (0.5161) is achieved by our C-DESERT metric. In addition, we have noticed that the combination of the ROUGE scores has a better correlation than the combination of the DESE scores that are based on the Doc2Vec vector. Furthermore, by observing all the baselines, we noticed that ROUGE-1 is the best baseline in its correlation with the human judgment although it does not take into consideration any context or semantic similarity. On the other hand, we have remarked the huge gap between the baseline metrics and the score obtained using the C-DESERT metric. This shows the importance of the combination of the metrics based on the lexical similarity level with that of the metrics based on semantic similarity level.

5 Conclusion

In fact, in this work, we have proposed two new evaluation metrics; the DESE and the C-DESERT. The first is based on the cosine similarity or Euclidean distance between two Doc2Vec vectors, one for the candidate summary and the other for the model summary. On the other hand, the second is a combination of the DESE and the ROUGE scores using regression models. We have experimented with the DESE and the C-DESERT metrics, which are the two metrics that outperform all the baseline metrics. However, the C-DESERT has demonstrated a better correlation with the Overall responsiveness. In addition, the constructed Doc2Vec models can be used for various Arabic NLP tasks, such as, the evaluation of question answering, the evaluation of machine translation, etc. Therefore, in future research, we plan to test other documents or word embedding models that take into consideration the semantic similarity and the word context, such as the Glove and ELMo, to measure the semantic similarity between summaries. Moreover, we project to add some linguistic features to our predictive model.

References

Lin, C.Y.: Rouge: a package for automatic evaluation of summaries. In: Proceedings of ACL-04 Workshop: Text Summarization Branches Out, pp. 74–81 (2004)

Giannakopoulos, G., Vangelis, K., George, V., Panagiotis, S.: Summarization system evaluation revisited: N-gram graphs. TSLP 5(3), 1–39 (2008)

Le, Q., Mikolov, T.: Distributed representations of sentences and documents. In: Proceedings of ICML - Volume 32, pp. II–1188–II–1196 (2014)

Mrabet, Y., Demner-Fushman, D.: HOLMS: Alternative Summary Evaluation with Large Language Models. In: Proceedings of the International Conference on Computational Linguistics, pp. 5679–5688 (2020)

Cer, D., et al.: Universal sentence encoder. In: arXiv preprint arXiv:1803.11175 (2018)

Pennington, J., Socher, R., Manning, C.: Glove: Global vectors for word representation. In: Proceedings of EMNLP, pp. 1532–1543 (2014)

Nenkova, A., Passonneau, R.: Evaluating content selection in summarization: The pyramid method. En Proceedings of the Human Language Technology Conference of the North American Chapter of the Association for Computational Linguistics: HLT-NAACL 2004, pp. 145–152 (2004)

He, T., et al.: ROUGE-C: A Fully Automated Evaluation Method for Multi-document Summarization. In: IEEE International Conference on Granular Computing, pp. 269–274 (2008)

Zhou, L., Lin, C.-Y., Munteanu, D.S., Hovy, E.: ParaEval: Using Paraphrases to Evaluate Summaries Automatically. In: Proceedings of NAACL, pp. 447–454 (2006)

Giannakopoulos, G., Karkaletsis, V.: Autosummeng and memog in evaluating guided summaries. In: TAC conference. NIST (2011)

Stanojević, M., Sima'an, K.: BEER: BEtter Evaluation as Ranking. In: Proceedings of the Workshop on Statistical Machine Translation, pp. 414–419 (2014)

Conroy, J.M., Dang, H.T.: Mind the Gap: Dangers of Divorcing Evaluations of Summary Content from Linguistic Quality. In: Proceedings of the International Conference on Computational Linguistics, pp. 145–152 (2008)

Conroy, J.M., Schlesinger, J.D., OLeary, D.P.: Nouveau-ROUGE: a novelty metric for update summarization. Computational Linguistics 37(1), 1–8 (2011)

Pitler, E., Louis, A., Nenkova, A.: Automatic evaluation of linguistic quality in multi-document summarization. In: Proceedings of the Annual Meeting of the Association for Computational Linguistics, pp. 544–554 (2010)

Ellouze, S., Jaoua, M., Belguith, L.H.: Automatic evaluation of a summary's linguistic quality. In: Métais, E., Meziane, F., Saraee, M., Sugumaran, V., Vadera, S. (eds.) NLDB 2016. LNCS, vol. 9612, pp. 392–400. Springer, Cham (2016). https://doi.org/10.1007/978-3-319-41754-7_39

Ellouze, S., Jaoua, M., Hadrich Belguith, L.: Merging multiple features to evaluate the content of text summary. In Procesamiento del Lenguaje Natural **58**, 69–76 (2017a)

Ng, J.-P., Abrecht, V.: Better Summarization Evaluation with Word Embeddings for ROUGE. In: Proceedings of the 2015 Conference on Empirical Methods in Natural Language Processing, pp. 1925–1930 (2015)

Mikolov, T., Chen, K., Corrado, G., Dean, J.: Efficient estimation of word representations in vector space. In: ICLR Workshop Poster, (2013)

Sun, S., Nenkova, A.: The feasibility of embedding based automatic evaluation for single document summarization. In: Proceedings of Empirical Methods in Natural Language Processing and International Joint Conference on Natural Language Processing (EMNLP-IJCNLP), pp. 1216–1221 (2019)

Peters, M., et al.: Deep contextualized word representations. In: Proceedings of the 2018 Conference of the North American Chapter of the Association for Computational Linguistics: Human Language Technologies, **1**, pp. 2227– 2237 (2018)

Zhang, T., Varsha, K., Felix, W., Kilian, Q.W., Yoav A.: BERT score: evaluating text generation with BERT. In: Proceedings of the International Conference on Learning Representations (2020)

Devlin, J., Ming-Wei, C., Kenton, L., Kristina, T.: BERT: pre-training of deep bidirectional transformers for language understanding. In: Proceedings of NAACL-HLT, pp. 4171–4186 (2018)

Xenouleas, S., Malakasiotis, P., Apidianaki, M., Androutsopoulos,I. : Sum-QE: a bert-based summary quality estimation model. In: EMNLP-IJCNLP, pp. 6004–6010 (2019)

Dang, H.T.: Overview of DUC 2006. In: Document Understanding Conference (DUC) (2006)

Elghannam, F., El-Shishtawy, T.: Keyphrase based evaluation of automatic text summarization. Int. J. Computer Appl. **117**(7), 5–8 (2015)

Ellouze. S., Jaoua, M., Hadrich Belguith, L.: Arabic text summary evaluation method. In: Proceedings of the International Business Information Management Association Conference - Education Excellence and Innovation Management through Vision 2020: From Regional Development Sustainability to Global Economic Growth, pp. 3532–3541 (2017b)

Abbas, M., Smaïli, K., Berkani, D.: Evaluation of topic identification methods on arabic corpora. J. Digital Inf. Manage. **9**(5), 185–192 (2011)

Abbas, M., Smaili, K.: Comparison of topic identification methods for Arabic language. In: Recent Advances in Natural Language Processing, pp. 14–17 (2005)

Darwish, K., Mubarak, H.: Farasa: a new fast and accurate Arabic word segmenter. In: Proceedings of LREC, pp. 1070–1074 (2016)

Guyon, I., Weston, J., Barnhill, S., et al.: Gene selection for cancer classification using support vector machines. Mach. Learn. **46**, 389–422 (2002)

Giannakopoulos, G., El-Haj, M., Favre, B., Litvak, M., Steinberger, J., Varma, V.: Tac 2011 multiling pilot overview. In: Proceedings of the Fourth Text Analysis Conference (2011)

Giannakopoulos, G.: Multi-document multi-lingual summarization and evaluation tracks in ACL'acl 2013 multiling workshop. In: Proceedings of the MultiLing 2013 Workshop on, pp. 20–28 (2013)

Giannakopoulos, G., Karkaletsis, V.: Summary evaluation: Together we stand NPowER-ed. In: Proceedings of international conference on Computational Linguistics and Intelligent Text Processing - **2**, pp. 436–450 (2013)

Data Mining and Machine Learning

Proficiency Level Classification of Foreign Language Learners Using Machine Learning Algorithms and Multilingual Models

Bogumila Hnatkowska(✉) [ID] and Damian Wawrzyniak

Wroclaw University of Science and Technology, Wroclaw, Poland
bogumila.hnatkowska@pwr.edu.pl

Abstract. This paper addresses the problem of classifying the proficiency of second language learners using multilingual models. Such models can be extremely useful in applications supporting the learning of multiple, even rare languages. Experiments based on Czech, German and Italian languages have been reported in the literature. This dataset was extended with texts in English. SVM, random forest, and logistic regression methods were used to train the model with different sets of language features. For the monolingual models – which served as benchmarks – the best results were observed for the random forest and SVM methods. For multilingual models, in contrast to other studies, the best results were obtained using the SVM algorithm. Models trained on a feature set containing n-grams of POS, n-grams of dependencies, and POS distribution performed better than models trained only on n-grams of POS, used in other works on multilingual models. The experiments confirmed the feasibility of using multilingual models in place of monolingual ones. Multilingual models were also able to classify texts in a language that was not involved in model learning.

Keywords: Classification · Language proficiency · CEFR

1 Introduction

The paper addresses the problem of automatic assessment of language proficiency based on students' written texts according to the Common European Framework of Reference for Languages (CEFR). The CEFR is a standard commissioned by the Council of Europe and published in [1]. It specifies six language levels: A1, A2, B1, B2, C1 and C2. Description of the levels and the requirements to be met by the learner are available on the Council of Europe website [2].

Automated assessment of proficiency level can find many applications including, for example, selection of content difficulty in language learning software, assessment of students' progress and achievements at a given stage.

Automation can also affect the process objectivity. According to the experiment described in [7], conducted for English learners, the full concordance of three experts in the evaluation of texts occurred only in 43.8% of cases.

© The Author(s), under exclusive license to Springer Nature Switzerland AG 2022
N. T. Nguyen et al. (Eds.): ICCCI 2022, LNAI 13501, pp. 261–271, 2022.
https://doi.org/10.1007/978-3-031-16014-1_21

Researchers try to evaluate different machine learning methods and different sets of text features to maximize the effectiveness of predicting the text author's language proficiency level. The tests are usually conducted on a single dataset for a given language, e.g. [3, 4, 8]. Thus, they answer the question of which AI method for automatic assessment of proficiency level is the best for a particular language. It remains an open problem to find a universal solution, effective in assessing the language level of a text, regardless of the language in which the text was written.

To address the problem, the authors propose to use a multilingual model trained using the most effective machine learning methods and text features found in the literature (see Sect. 2). They work on the Merlin dataset [6], which contains texts in German, Czech and Italian. The innovative elements (contribution) of this research are: (a) extended number of datasets used for training (English is added), (b) extended list of text features used in the experiments, (c) cross-lingual classification run on the model trained for many languages and verified for the language not included in the training process.

Section 3 describes the experiments and analyzes the results. The conclusions are presented in Sect. 4.

2 Related Works

The primary goal of the literature review was to identify the most effective machine learning methods for the problem under consideration, and to identify those language features that have the greatest impact on classification performance (see Sect. 3).

The secondary purpose was to review research on models trained for multiple languages and their applications.

The paper [4] compared regression and classification models in the problem of automatic assessment of language proficiency of Estonian learners. The study showed higher accuracy of the Sequential Minimal Optimization (79% accuracy) over the Linear Regression (76% accuracy).

The authors of [3] presented a comparative analysis of ten machine learning algorithms for assessing the language proficiency of Italian learners. The Random Forest and Support Vector Machine (SVM) achieved the best results of 74.1% and 72.7%, respectively. In contrast, the Quadratic Discriminant Analysis and Naive Bayes methods were the worst among the compared methods. Both achieved accuracy rates close to 63%.

The problem of automatic classification of text difficulty as teaching material for Portuguese language learners was addressed in [8]. The corpus on which the study was conducted consisted of texts from Portuguese language textbooks. This corpus was unbalanced, containing texts from levels A1-C1, of which up to 57% of the corpus were texts from level B1. In total, the corpus contained 237 texts. This is a small number compared to other works what should be taken into consideration when analyzing at the results. Two classifications were carried out: a five-level (A1, A2, B1, B2, C1) and three-level (A, B, C) classification. The best accuracy in the five-level classification achieved LogitBoost (75.11%), C4.5 grafted (72.57%) and C4.5 (71.31%). The Random Forest algorithm performed slightly worse (70.04%). In the three-level classification, the results were similar, with the C4.5 grafted algorithm being the most accurate (81.44%) and the Radom Forest on the fourth place (79.75%).

The authors of [5] conducted experiments on the Merlin corpus [6] containing the works of learners of Italian, Czech and German languages, evaluated according to the CEFR standard. The authors considered the following algorithms: Linear Regression, SVM, Random Forest and neural network model. For further experiments, they chose the Random Forest algorithm as the method that achieves the best results. The authors of [5] performed two experiments on multilingual models. In the first, they trained the model on all three languages and used it to classify texts in all languages. In the second, they trained the model on the language for which there was the most data in the corpus, and then assessed the effectiveness of the model for the other two languages. The same group of researchers continued similar experiments with the Merlin corpus with a pre-trained mBERT model [12, 13], obtaining slightly better average results for multilingual classification (f1 = 0.745) than for universal POS n-grams (the second place). In all cases, except Czech language, the multilingual classification worked worser compared to its monolingual version (German: 0.693 vs. 0.683, Italian: 0.829 vs. 0.826, Czech: 0.669 vs. 0.718).

The main differences between [5] and the present research are as follows:

(a) The English corpus was added,
(b) Extended number of language features was used for training multilingual models,
(c) Cross-lingual classification was run on the model trained for many languages and verified for the language not included in the training process.

The literature review shown that Random Forest and SVM are among the most effective algorithms in the problem of text-based language proficiency classification, e.g. [3–5, 9, 11]. In addition, the logistic regression algorithm has achieved promising results for multilingual models [5]. Therefore, these three algorithms were selected for further consideration.

3 Experiments

3.1 Datasets

Two datasets are used in experiments: Education First – Cambridge Open Language Database (EFCAMDAT) [20] and Merlin [6].

EFCAMDAT is a publicly accessible database developed by the University of Cambridge in partnership with Education First. The database contains texts by students of English (second language) from exams for each language level. The original dataset contains texts of one million exams written by 174,000 students. This study uses a pre-cleaned collection described in [20]. The collection is available as two Excel files, each containing 24 columns and 317220 records. Only three columns were used in experiments:

– Cefr – exam level (A1 – 341 155 tests, A2 – 215 344, B1 – 116 539, B2 – 40 238, C1 – 10 006)
– Grade – exam score (number from 0–100 range); in the experiment only those with the score above 90 were used

– Text – content of the exam (task)

The English corpus was truncated for the study to keep data more balanced. From the first data source of English texts (file engilish_1.xlsx), 1000 texts per level were randomly selected.

The second dataset is the Merlin corpus [6]. It contains 2286 texts of Italian, German and Czech language students. The texts were collected from language exams testing students' knowledge at A1 (De – 57 tests, It – 29 tests, Cz – 1 test), A2 (De – 306 tests, It – 381 tests, Cz – 188 tests), B1 (De – 331 tests, It – 394 tests, Cz – 165 tests), B2 (De – 293 tests, It – 2 tests, Cz – 81 tests) and C1 (De – 42 tests, It – 0 tests, Cz – 2 tests) levels of the CEFR standard. Due to the scope of the study, only information about the exam language, overall CEFR rating and text content were used. From the dataset were removed the levels with less than 5 instances. Table 1 presents the level distribution in the final corpus.

Table 1. Level distribution in the final corpus.

CEFR level	De	It	Cz	En
A1	57	29	–	1000
A2	306	381	188	1000
B1	331	394	165	1000
B2	293	–	81	1000
C1	42	–	–	1000

3.2 Features

There are many language features that can be used in solving the problem under consideration. Based on the literature, the following 16 features that have a significant impact on prediction and are language-independent were selected:

• Raw Text Features:

  – Number of sentences in the text [3, 8, 11]
  – Number of tokens per sentence [3, 8]
  – Number of unique tokens [3, 8, 11]
  – Document length [5, 8]

• Errors:

  – Total number of spelling errors [5]
  – Total number of style errors
  – Total number of grammar errors

- Lexical Richness Features [3, 5]:

  - Lexical diversity defined as the ratio between the number of types (unique tokens) and the number of tokens computed within n randomly selected tokens
  - Lexical variation defined as the ratio between content words (verbs, nouns, adjectives, or adverbs), and the total number of words

- Morpho-syntactic features:

  - Part of speech (POS) distribution [3, 5]
  - Word n-grams [5] (for n = 1 ... 3)
  - POS n-grams [5] (for n = 1 ... 3)
  - Dependency n-grams (unigrams are triplets consisting of dependency relation, POS tag of the dependent element and POS tag of the independent element) [5] (for n = 1 ... 3)

- Syntactic Features, e.g. [3, 10]:

  - Average depth of the dependency trees
  - Maximal depth of the dependency trees
  - Number of unique syntactic relations between tokens

3.3 Methods

Logistic Regression, Random Forest and SVM algorithms were used in this study. The selection was made based on the literature review. SVM and Random Forest have appeared in many works and have achieved satisfactory results ([3–5, 8]). The logistic regression, on the other hand, was mentioned and used in the paper on multilingual models ([5]), where it presented a promising level of performance.

Similarly to [5], due to the presence of unbalanced classes, F1 score was used to compare performance of the models.

3.4 Tool Implementation

Feature extraction was implemented in Python using spaCy, sklearn and language-check libraries.

Machine learning models were implemented using the scikit-learn library [14]. For natural language processing, the spaCy library [15] was used along with the spacy-udpipe [16], allowing the UDPipe [17] language processing models to be used in the spaCy library. This was necessary due to the lack of a Czech language processing model in the spaCy library. The following language processing models were used in this work [17]:

- English — english-ewt-ud-2.5–191206.udpipe
- Czech — czech-pdt-ud-2.5–191206.udpipe
- German — german-gsd-ud-2.5–191206.udpipe

– Italian – italian-isdt-ud-2.5–191206.udpipe

Additionally, the language-check library [18], which is an overlay on the Language-Tool [19], was used to extract errors from texts. Unfortunately, the library allowed the extraction of errors only from texts in English, German and Italian. No solution was found to find errors in the Czech language text.

3.5 Experiment Scenarios

The first experiment partially reproduced the research from [5] and [12] and aimed to identify features combinations that produce the best classification results for monolingual models. These serve as a benchmark for evaluating multilingual models. When examining the effectiveness of individual models in classifying language proficiency levels, models trained on a singular feature were examined first and then models trained on various features combinations. The models in the papers [5] and [12] were examined in the same way.

In the second experiment, the effectiveness of multilingual solutions was evaluated. The model was trained on the full dataset (see Table 1) and evaluated separately for each language. It was a reproduction of the experiment presented in [5], but with the extensions described in Sect. 2. The purpose of this experiment was to answer the question about the effect of the English dataset on the model performance. English belongs to the same language group as German, so a change would be expected.

The third experiment was designed to evaluate whether the multilingual model could classify a text written in a language that did not participate in the model training.

4   Results and Analysis

4.1 Experiment One

The main purpose of this experiment was to provide a baseline for further experiments. Table 2 shows the three best feature combinations for each language and each method. The best values for each language were written in bold. The underline results indicate the best algorithm for that feature combination. For example, the first combination (POS n-grams, and dependency n-grams) is the best for German, and the best results were produced by the Random Forest algorithm. For the same combination, SVM gives the best results for Italian and English. The results obtained are similar to those reported in [5], and [12] – see Table 3.

SVM is the best method with the highest number of underlined and/or bold elements.

For most languages, the feature set consisting of POS n-grams and dependency n-grams is good enough for the purpose of the proficiency level classification. An interesting observation is that the texts in Czech have distinct characteristics than the rest. In this case, the best results were obtained for a large set of language features (all minus word n-grams), which was probably caused by the fact that Czech is the only representative of Slavic languages.

Table 2. Top-3 results for monolingual models.

Features	Logistic regression				Random forest				SVM			
	It	De	En	Cz	It	De	En	Cz	It	De	En	Cz
POS n-grams Dep. n-grams	0.782		0.935		0.826	**0.696**	0.926		0.837	0.687	0.940	
POS n-grams Dep. n-grams Errors	0.786	0.599				0.691			0.841	0.688		
POS n-grams Dep. n-grams POS distribution			0.935				0.922	0.714			0.940	0.728
POS n-grams Dep. n-grams POS distribution Errors	0.788				0.824				**0.842**			
POS n-grams Dep. n-grams POS distribution Errors Raw text	0.788		0.942		0.827		0.923		0.841		0.940	
POS n-grams Dep. n-grams POS distribution Raw text			0.942				0.922				**0.943**	
All		0.617		0.700						0.690		
All except word n-grams		0.607		0.691	0.689	**0.735**						**0.733**
POS distribution Lexical Richness				0.714				0.698				0.728

Table 3. Comparison of monolingual model performance (f1) with [5] and [12].

Research	It	De	En	Cz
This work	**0.842**	**0.696**	0.943	0.735
[5]	0.837	0.686	–	**0.737**
[12]	0.829	0.693	–	0.669

4.2 Experiment Two

This experiment aimed in answer the question of whether the English dataset has any effect on the classifier. It also was used to identify the best combination of features, used later in the third experiment.

The results for the SVM (with the best results) and the top-3 feature combinations are shown in Table 4.

Table 4. Multilingual model performance (f1) for texts in specific language.

Features	It	De	En	Cz
POS n-grams	0.817	**0.677**	0.928	0.707
Dep. n-grams	**0.823**	0.670	0.918	0.703
POS n-grams Dep. n-grams	0.817	0.674	0.936	0.703
POS n-grams Dep. n-grams POS distribution	**0.823**	0.674	**0.937**	**0.717**

The fourth combination (POS n-grams, dependency n-grams, and POS distribution) scored highest and was used in the next experiment.

The model trained on all four languages achieved slightly worse performance than the monolingual models. The differences are shown in Table 5. They are compared with results reported in [12]. Unfortunately, detail results for these tests are not presented in [5].

Table 5. Comparison of monolingual and multilingual model performance (f1).

Id	Research	It	De	En	Cz
1	monolingual (this work)	0.842	0.696	0.943	0.735
2	multilingual (this work)	0.833	0.674	0.937	0.717
	Difference: (1) – (2)	0.009	0.022	0.006	0.018
3	monolingual [12]	0.829	0.693	–	0.669
4	multilingual [12]	0.826	0.683	–	0.718
	Difference: (3) – (4)	0.003	0.010	–	– 0.049

The new English dataset had no impact on the model performance. In [12] the multilingual model worked better than a monolingual one, but the multilingual version has equal results to this study. Please note that in [12] the multilingual model was prepared on a pre-trained model, therefore the results of this research and [12] are not fully comparable.

4.3 Experiment Three

The purpose of the experiment was to assess the effectiveness of a multilingual model in predicting student language proficiency for a language that did not participate in model training. Such multilingual model is marked with asterisk. The results are presented in Tables 6, 7.

Table 6. Multilingual* model performance (f1) for a language not used in the model training.

Features	It	De	En	Cz
POS n-grams Dep. n-grams POS distribution	0.824	0.678	0.938	0.723

Table 7. Performance comparison of monolingual, multilingual, and multilingual* models.

Research	It (De + En + Cz)	De (It + En + Cz)	En (De + It + Cz)	Cz (De + En + It)
monolingual	0.842	0.696	0.943	0.735
multilingual	**0.833**	0.674	0.937	0.717
multilingual*	0.824	**0.678**	**0.938**	**0.723**

The results are interesting. Still the results for the multilingual* models are worse than for monolinguals, but in many cases, they are slightly better than for multilinguals model. This is probably due to the introduction of the English dataset in the training process.

5 Conclusions

The main purpose of the research was to answer the question of whether multilingual models can be applied to classify the language proficiency of texts written in languages other than those used to train the model.

Three algorithms were investigated: Random Forest, Logistic Regression, and Support Vector Machine (SVM). On the full dataset containing texts in English, Czech, German, and Italian, the SVM performed best. The Random Forest algorithm performed slightly worse. It obtained the best results for the multilingual model trained only on the MERLIN corpus, what confirms findings described in [5]. However, according to the experiments results, the SVM algorithm was found to be more flexible, performing only slightly worse than the Random Forest in the case of the multilingual model trained on the MERLIN corpus, and achieving the best results in the individual tests where, in addition to the MERLIN corpus, data from the EFCAMDAT corpus containing English texts was used. Logistic Regression gained the worst results, which contradicts with findings in [12], where it achieved the best results for multilingual models.

The literature review allowed to select the promising language features used later in experiments. The results confirmed high effectiveness of the models trained using POS distribution, POS n-grams and n-grams of dependencies. Similar findings were presented in [5] and [12]. Other text features, e.g., lexical richness or syntactic features seem do not have critical impact on classification results.

The experiments confirmed that multilanguage models can effectively classify texts in languages not used during the training process even if they belong to different language groups. The loss of performance was less than 2.5 points.

References

1. Council of Europe: Common European framework of reference for languages: Learning, teaching, assessment, Cambridge. Press Syndicate of the University of Cambridge, U.K (2001)
2. Common European Framework of Reference for Languages: Learning, Teaching, Assessment (CEFR) (coe.int)
3. Santucci, V., Santarelli, F., Forti, L., Spina, S.: Automatic classification of text complexity. Appl. Sci. **10**(20), 7285 (2020)
4. Vajjala, S., Lõo, K.: Automatic CEFR Level Prediction for Estonian Learner Text, LiU Electronic Press, pp. 113–127 (2014)
5. Vajjala, S., Rama, T.: Experiments with Universal CEFR Classification, In: The 13th workshop on innovative Use of NLP for building educational applications, pp. 147–153, Association for Computational Linguistic, New Orleans, USA (2018)
6. Boyd, A., et al.: The MERLIN corpus: Learner language and the CEFR. In: 9th International Conference on Language Resources and Evaluation, pp. 1281–1288, European Language Resources Association (ELRA), Reykjavik, Iceland (2014)
7. Tack, A., François, T., Roekhaut, S., Fairon, C.: Human and automated CEFR-based grading of short answers, In: Proceedings of the 12th Workshop on Innovative Use of NLP for Building Educational Applications, pp. 169–179, Association for Computational Linguistics, Copenhagen, Denmark (2017)
8. Curto, P., Mamede, N.J., Baptista, J.: Automatic Text Difficulty Classifier. In: CSEDU 2015: Proceedings of the 7th International Conference on Computer Supported Education - **1**, pp. 77–87, SciTePress, Setubal, Portugalia (2015)
9. Rysová, K., Rysová, M., Mírovský, J.: Automatic evaluation of surface coherence in L2 texts in Czech, In: Proceedings of the 28th Conference on Computational Linguistics and Speech Processing (ROCLING 2016), pp. 214–228, The Association for Computational Linguistics and Chinese Language Processing (ACLCLP), Tainan, Taiwan (2016)
10. Pilán, I., Vajjala, S., Volodina, E.: A readable read: automatic assessment of language learning materials based on linguistic complexity. Int. J. Computational Linguistics Appl. **7**(1), 143–159 (2016)
11. Curto, P., Mamede, N.J., Baptista, J.: Automatic text difficulty classifier - assisting the selection of adequate reading materials For European Portuguese teaching, In: Proceedings of the 7th International Conference on Computer Supported Education - **1**, pp. 36–44, Lizbona, Portugalia (2015)
12. Rama, T., Vajjala, S.: Are pre-trained text representations useful for multilingual and multi-dimensional language proficiency modeling?. arXiv.org (2021)

13. Devlin, J., Chang, M.-W., Lee K., Toutanova, K.: BERT: Pre-training of deep bidirectional transformers for language understanding, In: In Proceedings of the 2019 Conference of the North American Chapter of the Association for Computational Linguistics: Human Language Technologies, Volume 1 (Long and Short Papers), pp. 4171–4186, Minneapolis, Minnesota. Association for Computational Linguistics (2019)
14. Pedregosa, F., et al.: Scikit-learn: machine learning in python. J. Machine Learning Res. tom **12**, 2825–2830 (2011)
15. Honnibal, M., Montani, I., Van Landeghem, S., Boyd, A.: spaCy: Industrial-strength Natural Language Processing in Python. Zenodo (2020)
16. TakeLab, spacy-udpipe https://pypi.org/project/spacy-udpipe/ Accessed 15 Apr 2022
17. Straka, M., Straková, J.: Universal Dependencies 2.5 Models for UDPipe, http://hdl.handle.net/11234/1-3131 Accessed 15 Apr 2022
18. Myint, S., language-check 1.1 https://pypi.org/project/language-check/ Accessed 15 Apr 2022
19. LanguageTool https://languagetool.org/ Accessed 15 Apr 2022
20. Shatz, I.: Refining and modifying the EFCAMDAT: Lessons from creating a new corpus from an existing large-scale English learner language database. International Journal of Learner Corpus Research, pp. 220–236 (2020)

Simulation System for Producing Real World Dataset to Predict the Covid-19 Contamination Process*

Bokri Ahmed(✉) (iD) and Naouali Sami (iD)

Laboratory of Science and Technology for Defense STD, Military Research Center, Tunis, Tunisia
Ahmed.Bokri.1994@outlook.fr

Abstract. The graph data modeling is the most convenient process to work with in order to answer almost all questions that came across our minds when it comes to covid-19 infection (when was I infected? where? and who gave it me ?). Most of us wonder when we enter a closed space if we are going to face someone who tested positive, but is there any way to predict that? Luckily yes! This could be done by streaming contact data of citizens to a server that looks for any contacts between infected people and non infected ones and sends back a notification for the purpose. The collection, management and exploitation of data in the field of health continues to require the attention of researchers in relation to confidentiality, security, privacy and protection of personal data. Research is active in this area and we are willing to use simulation technologies in order to anticipate the contamination area and predict the propagation due to lack of shared data for reasons listed above. These data flows also constitute a considerable input for the extraction of knowledge and the application of artificial intelligence algorithms and more precisely of machine learning to predict and prevent the evolution of the epidemic on the affected persons as well as its geographical spread, after correlating sensitive data securely from all users, the initial objective is to model the system in the form of a graph and apply graph flow algorithms to predict the propagation network and notify the users if contaminated.

Keywords: E health · Contact tracing · Graph mining · Simulation · Unity · 3D modelling · Ble · Neo4j · Kafka · IOT

1 Introduction

During the covid 19 pandemic, doctors and medical authorities were told questions confirmed cases in order to discover and anticipate the next contamination. This seems to be inefficient due to the exponential growth of the number of cases as shown in [1]. For this reason we started this research in order to refine as much as possible the tracking of the pandemic, the prediction of the spread and especially the prediction of the cases likely to be contaminated by combining IOT technologies like Bluetooth BLE, web 3.0, Blockchain, Data processing and cloud computing.

Supported by Military Research Center.

2   Contact Tracing

In order to collect persistent data from citizens, we started by thinking to modelise a complete pipeline that starts from the end-user and ends by notifying them whenever they contact an infected person with easy readable results. For this reason, we chose to combine two technologies: GPS as studied in [2] and Bluetooth LE [3]. These two technologies were used before to track people location. Our idea is to track each single user of the mobile application while ensuring the security of its personal data . For this purpose an android Application is being built and it's integrating several packages and technologies. Each user has his or her own account with some related information such as (Name, Date of birth and Age etc..). The location of the user is being stored in a JSON file each second while he or she is not in a fixed location . Another file ensure the collect of nearby users' phones (Their ID) when sensing the existence of another phone in a distance less than 2 m through RSSI signal [15] which is a hash of their Identity number (Identity number is not stored but only it's hash is kept in the phone when written once when creating the account). These files are for- warded to Firebase to be stored since it's a free tool that can help us develop our prototype. After that, this data is going to be retrieved and treated with Neo4j. Treating data in Neo4j implies that we are dealing with Graph Databases [4] The concept is to retrieve all the location data from GPS and all the contact traces via ID exchange between user-user using BLE Technology and that's due to the reasons listed below.

2.1   GPS Accuracy

The GPS system [5] is not an exact science. It is generally estimated that there is a 2 to 3 m error in a given position. This varies depending on the quality of the system, location, temperature, etc. This means that you may have a more accurate position than your GPS displays.

2.2   Bluetooth LE Distance Measurement

As mentioned in the paper [3] the distance between two smartphones can be measured through bluetooth LE signal RSSI. We can see obviously that the accuracy of distance measurements taken using a smartphone ranges from 0.79 m to 2.28 m which is almost the same distance recommended by doctors to keep from others in the covid context.

2.3   WiFi

Positioning is one of the potential WiFi [8] technology applications utilized in contact tracing. This is especially effective in an interior location, like train terminals and airports, where a throng is forming during a pandemic. The WiFi hardware capabilities are very handy to use because of their low cost of maintenance and ease of implementation (Fig. 1).

Fig. 1. Ble contact tracing

2.4 Zigbee

Zigbee is another technology that has the ability to preserve social distance. It is a wireless communication technology based on a standard that is used for low-cost and low-power wireless networks [6]. Zigbee-based devices can communicate with each other across a distance of 65 feet (20 m) and with an infinite number of hops. The user's location may be determined by the Zigbee control hub, which can be utilized for crowd control. As a result, the Zigbee communication technology may be used to track contacts and prevent the infection from spreading.

2.5 Comparing Technologies

As it is obvious in the figure below, we can see that bluetooth comes first for high precision followed by geolocation. Thus, the idea consists of combinig the two technologies to enhance the output and get more precious results with a minimum of wrong alerts (Fig. 2).

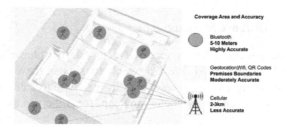

Fig. 2. Assessing the coverage area and accuracy of different sensing infrastructures

3 Dataset Collection

An application that concerns a whole country's population or at least 80% of them needs to pass several stages until it's ready and approved to be uploaded to the public. Meanwhile, our research didn't stop there so we need to get data for daily contacts of people. Downloading a dataset isn't possible in this context since no person or organisation would assume publishing user's private data. Therefore another solution took place **Simulating real world users behaviour** in order to generate a dataset.

3.1   Simulating Real World Scene

To get real data we need to modelise the real world! that's the idea so what we did is create a 3d map [14] of a region of Tunisia linked to all geolocation information in a 3d Engine after inspiring of the project of Design of Three- Dimensional Traction Substation Simulation System Based on Unity3D [7] (Fig. 3).

Fig. 3. Configuring real world terrain

After that the work was to create multiple entities in a given time and associate a random path to each one on the walkable area of the terrain with full respect to the colliders and collision avoidance. Each object will store its data in a file that's going to be treated later on, in order to look for intersections with others using gps stored locations and exchanged IDs when distance is smaller than 2 m which simulates Ble based contact tracing. So we started with 250 objects representing humans and this is the scene initially: After creating a navmesh [9] and preparing scripts for each object to randomise a path for it we launch our simulation for ten minutes and all data is stored in the streaming assets folder, this folder is the same as the collected data from users phones while storing GPS data of their movements and exchanged IDs with RSSI signal coming from BLE and which is going to be processed later to detect which of the users is contaminated or makes a probable infected node (Fig. 4).

The obtained data is real geographical data related to the simulated terrain and each position is labeled with time of acquisition following this form: when configuring characters we chose a speed of 1m per frame and the system executes n frame per update depending on the system performance. When calculating our performances it gives 64

Fig. 4. Preparing 3D scene

FPS given that we launched simulation for 30 min, an average walking speed for a human being varies between 4.8 and 6.4 km per hour which means 1.7 m per second. We calculate the real simulated time as follows :

$$Simulated\ time\ =\ nbr\ frames\ per\ second\ *\ time\ simulation \qquad (1)$$

In fact 30 mins of simulation represents 80 h of continoues movements in real life time. Now we have a dataset that mimics a community of people moving in a specific area randomly and we can search for probable contamination with constructing a graph database and querying it with specific ways (Fig. 5 and Fig. 6).

$$Travelled_d\ istance\ =\ walking\ speed\ per\ frame\ *\ simulated\ time \qquad (2)$$

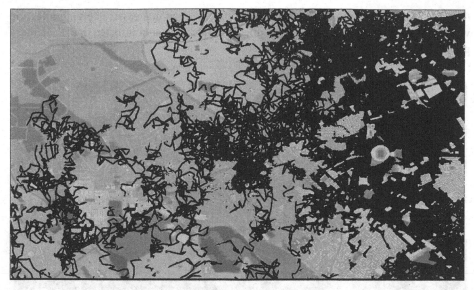

Fig. 5. Running simulation in unity

[truncated data listing]

Fig. 6. Stored data in each node on a single frame

4 Processing Data

After importing retrieved data into Neo4j [12] we create nodes that represent people and the edges that represent each stored contact between them. Properties allow us to store relevant data about the users and their possible relationship or interactions with the entity it describes. Additionally, and as mentioned before we are storing the users' data, hence when a new red node is mentioned we can launch a search process to look through its history location and look for any possible interactions and contamination and predict any possible link between them.

4.1 Graph Modeling

The most important process in this work is to construct a convenient model to the studied situation in order to obtained the desired results. In our case, graph is the based on users nodes that have links between them representing that they met within a distance smaller than 2 m and that last more than 10 min. Another relation that exists is giving infection which represents a meeting between an infected node and a non infected one. With these parameters we obtain the Graph Data Model shown in Fig. 7 (Fig. 8).

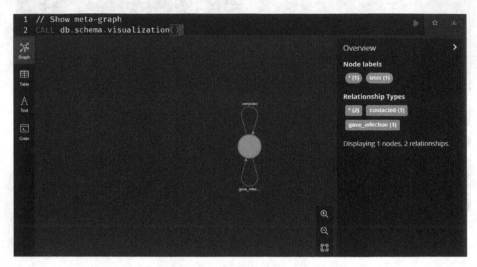

Fig. 7. Graph data model

4.2   Retrieving Basic Statistics

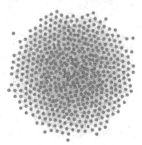

Fig. 8. Graph database

After importing data into neo4j, the graph now is constructed including all nodes with proprieties and relations between them. Starting from that we can initially extract some key values such as interactions based on the health situation of people as follows in these figures:

The query shown in Fig. 9 parses all graph nodes to look for the links between individuals infected with coronavirus who have met a no infected persons and the sum returned to reveal the probable number of contamination after a while of time.

The query shown in Fig. 10 parses all graph nodes to look for the links between uncontaminated individuals which reveal a huge number comparing to infection links

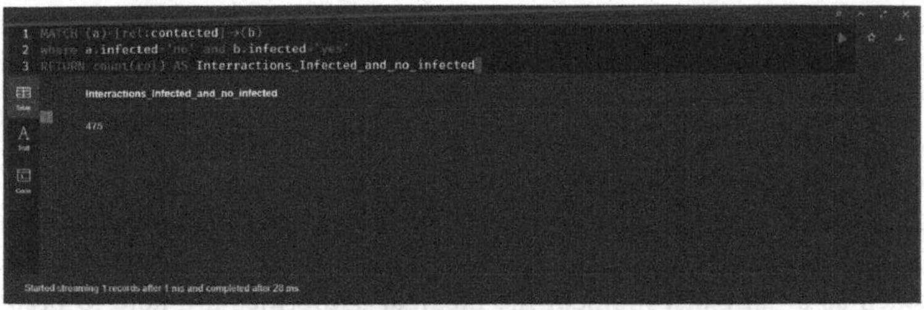

Fig. 9. Extracting links between infected and no infected persons

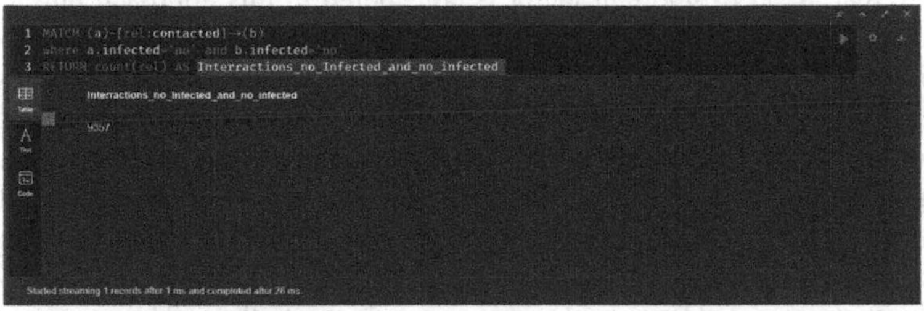

Fig. 10. Extracting links between no infected persons

and that's logically acceptable since human beings lives in groups and interacts with each other to survive.

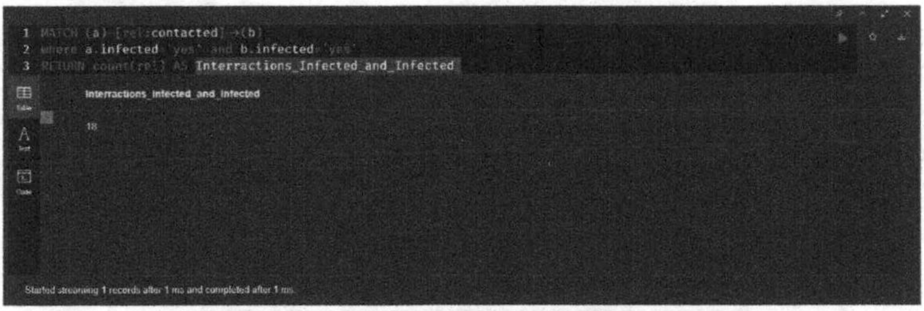

Fig. 11. Predicting possible links between infected persons

The query shown in Fig. 11 parses all graph nodes to look for the links between contaminated persons which reveal a very small number which may be explained with the isolating process once a person discovers his or her contamination; though, sometimes it may be a group (family) isolation.

4.3 Graph Data Science Algorithms

In this part, we are going to explain more the process that we talked about before: Those are coordinates retrieved from an "Infected" user and what is obvious is that he is roaming around far from his place which is represented by the node property user infected. The system is querying the streamed data from all the app's users and searching for a real time relation between new users and infected ones, and because the visited area is all the time busy with clients a group of users are having a new relationship called contacted that reveales a close contact between two users configured as vecor3 distance (user one, user two) is smaller then 1m since research shows that even a brief contact with or without a sanitary mask makes the person strongly suspected of contamination as Jones Coll [10] says. Besides, the anticipation of an epidemic situation was never easier before this approach as at an exact moment the medical authorities are able to predict what the situation could look like through a simple pattern matching of epidemic evolution which is easily retrieved through node's covid situation property variation pattern. In addition to that, a very important factor is considered in this approach but never was mentioned before which are relatives. Persons who take care of an ill person and move all around without being checked of how safe they are. Once applied in this system the epidemic situation could be controlled and hosts are dynamically updated and we no longer need to test for the inappropriate individuals, but we are anticipating the virus. Applying neighbours method on our graph model can be applied and gives authorities to encounter the circle of infection with n nodes travelling. The output of This model would extract the centrality of infected nodes around the infector node which didn't respect the confinement at home and to distance oneself of others. This representation is based on a graph algorithm known as spreading activation described by Fabio Crestani in its paper [11] which describes the continuous spreading of nodes activation through a constrained relationships. A later process consists at applying graph database science algorithms [13] in order to calculate several parameters for the graph obtained such as (Fig. 12, Fig. 13 and Fig. 14):

1. Centraliy
2. Community Detection
3. Page Rank
4. Closeness
5. Betweeness

Fig. 12. Same community algorithm

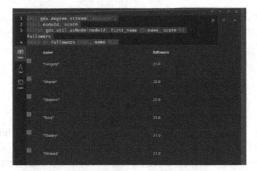

Fig. 13. Centrality algorithm

Fig. 14. Preferential attachment algorithm

5 Conclusion

As they prepare for future epidemic waves, nations must employ all available resources to stop the virus from spreading and minimize the physical, personal, economic, and societal harm it has inflicted since early 2020. The use of digital tools can help contain the tragedy. In the light of the emergency's severe measures and constraints on individual liberty, Following the COVID-19 epidemic, digital contact tracing applications have been widely used across the world. Digital contact tracing is more scalable than manual contact tracing, with the ability to identify contacts that would normally be impossible to track down manually. This paper presents a system that is able to simulate real world propagation of covid- 19 which is a simulation of collected flow during the pandemic combining GPS location of individuals and exchanged ID's through Ble when RSSI measures a distance less than 2 m. This step is a mandatory step since this type of data circumscribed by privacy challenges and lack of shared info. Although several research papers have examined contact tracing applications and techniques, we are trying to combine several technologies to reduce accuracy gaps and ensure an early alert extracted from graph predictions. Meanwhile a full pipeline is being developed to stream similar data extracted from individuals' phones in order to be processed and get early notifications as soon as possible.

Acknowledgements. The research leading to these results were in the context of cooperation between Tunisian Military Research Center and Euranova. (Euranova is a consulting firm with a private research center dedicated to data science and AI. Its mission is to promote a data-centric culture and help large companies and start-ups at every stage of their digital transformation. https:// euranova.eu/.)

References

1. Coronavirus Cases. Worldometer (2022). https://www.worldometers.info/coronavirus/
2. Soldano, G., et al.: On the effectiveness of digital contact tracing and contact prevention under varying COVID-19 infection detection rates . SSRN Electr. J. (2020). https://doi.org/10.2139/ssrn.3745828
3. Lee, Y.H., et al.: BLE beacon-based indoor distance measurement technique using outlier adjustment. J. Digit. Cont. Soc. **22**(5), 839–45 (2021). https://doi.org/10.9728/dcs.2021.22.5.839
4. Angles, R., Gutierrez, C.: Survey of graph database models. ACM Comput. Surv. **40**(1), 1–39 (2008). https://doi.org/10.1145/1322432.1322433
5. D'Eon, S.P.: Accuracy and signal reception of a hand-held global positioning system (GPS) receiver. For. Chron. **71**(2), 192–196 (1995). https://doi.org/10.5558/tfc71192-2
6. Luoh, L.: Zigbee-based intelligent indoor positioning system soft computing Soft Comput.**18**(3), 443–456 (2013). https://doi.org/10.1007/s00500-013-1067-x View PDF Google Scholar
7. Design of three-dimensional traction substation simulation system based on unity3D. J. Electr. Eng. **07**(02), 124–129 (2019). https://doi.org/10.12677/jee.2019.72015
8. Liao, L., Lin, K., Wang, X., Lai, X., Vuong, S.T.: WiFi positioning overview. Int. J. Commun. Netw. Distrib. Syst. **7**(3/4), 229 (2011). https://doi.org/10.1504/ijcnds.2011.042377
9. Brewer, D.: Tactical Pathfinding on a NavMesh — Daniel Brewer — Taylor Francis G. Taylor Francis. https://www.taylorfrancis.com/chapters/edit/https://doi.org/10.1201/9780429054969- 2/tactical-pathfinding-navmesh-daniel-brewer, 6 septembre 2019
10. https://www.inserm.fr/information-en-sante/dossiers- information/coronavirus-sars-cov-et-mers-cov
11. Crestani, F.: Application of spreading activation techniques in information retrieval. Artif. Intell. Rev. **11**(6), 453-482 (1997)
12. Babych, T., Gorokhovskyi, S.: Building and storing in graph database neo4j abstract symantic graph of PHP applications source code. NaUKMA research papers. Comput. Sci. **3**(0), 27–30 (2020). https://doi.org/10.18523/2617-3808.2020.3.27-30
13. Rao, B.: An approach to represent social graph as multi-layer graph using graph mining techniques. Int. J. Educ. Manag. Eng. **9**(1), 20–36 (2019). https://doi.org/10.5815/ijeme.2019.01.03
14. Ji, F., Deyong, W.: Design and implementation of 3- D terrain generation module in game. In: 2010 3rd International Conference on Advanced Computer Theory and Engineering (ICACTE) (2010), vol. 1, pp. 1-36 (2010). https://doi.org/10.1109/icacte.2010.5579067
15. Lin, Q., Son, J.: Analysis of bluetooth RSSI for proximity detection of ship passengers. Appl. Sci. **12**(1), 517 (2022). https://doi.org/10.3390/app12010517

Design and Compression Study
for Convolutional Neural Networks Based
on Evolutionary Optimization
for Thoracic X-Ray Image Classification

Hassen Louati[1]([⊠])[iD], Ali Louati[2][iD], Slim Bechikh[1][iD], and Lamjed Ben Said[1][iD]

[1] SMART Lab, University of Tunis, ISG, Tunis, Tunisia
`hassen.louati@stud.acs.upb.ro`, `slim.bechikh@fsegn.rnu.tn`,
`lamjed.bensaid@isg.rnu.tn`
[2] Department of Information Systems, College of Computer Engineering and
Sciences, Prince Sattam bin Abdulaziz University, Al-Kharj 11942, Saudi Arabia
`a.louati@psau.edu.sa`

Abstract. Computer Vision has lately shown progress in addressing a
variety of complex health care difficulties and has the potential to aid
in the battle against certain lung illnesses, including COVID-19. Indeed,
chest X-rays are one of the most commonly performed radiological techniques for diagnosing a range of lung diseases. Therefore, deep learning
researchers have suggested that computer-aided diagnostic systems be
built using deep learning methods. In fact, there are several CNN structures described in the literature. However, there are no guidelines for
designing and compressing a specific architecture for a specific purpose;
thus, such design remains highly subjective and heavily dependent on
data scientists' knowledge and expertise. While deep convolutional neural networks have lately shown their ability to perform well in classification and dimension reduction tasks, the challenge of parameter selection
is critical for these networks. However, since a CNN has a high number
of parameters, its implementation in storage devices is difficult. This is
due to the fact that the search space grows exponentially in size as the
number of layers increases, and the large number of parameters necessi-
tates extensive computation and storage, making it impractical for use
on low-capacity devices. Motivated by these observations, we propose an
automated method for CNN design and compression based on an evolutionary algorithm (EA) for X-Ray image classification that is capable
of classifying radiography images and detecting possible chest abnormalities and infections, including COVID-19.Our evolutionary method is
validated through a series of comparative experiments against relevant
state-of-the-art architectures.

Keywords: Deep CNN design · Deep CNN compression ·
Evolutionary algorithms · Thorax disease · Chest X-ray

© The Author(s), under exclusive license to Springer Nature Switzerland AG 2022
N. T. Nguyen et al. (Eds.): ICCCI 2022, LNAI 13501, pp. 283–296, 2022.
https://doi.org/10.1007/978-3-031-16014-1_23

1   Introduction

COVID-19, an infectious illness that causes severe acute respiratory syndrome, is also known as a coronavirus [27] due to its appearance. The fight against COVID-19 has pushed researchers worldwide to investigate, analyze, and develop novel diagnostic and treatment methods in order to eliminate this generation's greatest menace. Indeed, a chest X-ray is one of the most often used radiological procedures for diagnosing a range of lung diseases. Indeed, various X-ray imaging studies are archived and compiled in a variety of image archiving and communication systems in a large variety of recent hospitals. A question that remains unanswered is how a database containing critical image information may be used to assist data-starved deep learning models in the creation of computer-assisted diagnostic systems. There have been a few methods to detect the chest radiograph image view reported in the literature [23]. During the last decade, Deep convolution neural networks (DCNNs) has shown considerable progress in a variety of computer vision challenges. Several CNN designs have been developed and showed excellent accuracy in image identification and applications, such as AlexNet [1], VggNet [2], and ResNet [3]. Due to the fact that these architectures were created manually, researchers in the fields of optimization and machine learning hypothesized that better architectures could be discovered using automated methods [27]. They proposed modeling this task as an optimization problem and then solving it using an appropriate search algorithm. the designs are subjected to what is known as "the training process," which is a time-consuming procedure that considers suitable settings for the weights, activation functions, and kernels used. Based on previous works, there exists a topology of convolution within each block of a CNN that corresponds to an optimization problem with a large search space Unfortunately, there are no guidelines for designing an architecture appropriate to a specific task; consequently, such design remains highly subjective and heavily dependent on the expertise of data scientists.

In fact, CNN is composed of stacked convolution layers followed by a fully connected layer. Each convolutional layer is constructed using convolutional filters to identify features. Each filter is composed of stacked two-dimensional kernels in C channels that correspond to the image's depth. An RGB image has 3 channels, and the kernel is a two-dimensional structure that is applied to each input channel pixel to form the output.

A convolutional layer is composed of many filters applied to an input image. Each of these filters produces a feature map. The convolutional layer's output will take the form of a dimension (batch size (N), channel count (Cout), and the height and width of each output (Hout, Wout)). Convolution weights are four-dimensional (4D) $(F, C, K\ H, K\ W)$, with F representing the number of filters in the layer, C representing the number of channels, and $K\ H$ and $K\ W$ representing the kernel's height and width, respectively.

Deep network compression is a critical strategy for minimizing and resizing a deep learning model by removing ineffective and rudendent components. On the other hand, compressing deep models without significant loss of precision is a significant difficulty. Recent studies have focused on developing novel strategies for reducing the computational complexity of CNNs based on EAs while maintaining their performance.

Deep convolution neural networks have been successfully designed and compressed using evolutionary computing methodologies. However, these methods do not scale well to contemporary deep neural networks because of their complicated designs and large numbers of link weights.

Motivated by this observation, the proposed approach called **CNN-Xray-D-C**, combines the following CNN designing convolution layers and Compressing features to establish a trade-off between pruning the convolution layers with acceptable accuracy for categorizing X-ray images and recognizing probable thoracic anomalies and infections, including the COVID-19 case.

This work's primary contributions can be summarized as follows:

- Genetic algorithms are used to design CNN architectures that are dependent on the following: (1) hyperparameter settings; and (2) the graph topologies of convolution nodes.
- Genetic algorithms are used to compress CNN architectures that are dependent on convolution layer hyperparameters.
- quantization to the non-zero weights is applied. Quantization does not only help reduce the number of bits required to store the weights (instead of 32 bits for floating-point weights, an integer representation of 5 bits would be used); it also helps generate frequent duplicate weights, which aids in makinghe compression efficient to apply later.
- The Huffman compression approach will be employed, and it is an excellent option for lossless compression since it takes advantage of the statistical features obtained after compression to generate a CNN with the minimum complexity of complexity.
- Investigate the efficiency and adaptability of **CNN-Xray-D-C** in diagnosing COVID-19 patients using X-ray pictures.

2   Related Work

Over the last decades, **CNN for Xray images classification** has shown its effectiveness [34], outperformance, and importance in the field of medical diagnosis. Several computational approaches exist for diagnosing a variety of thoracic diseases using chest X-rays. Wang et al. [5] created a framework for semisupervised multi-label unified classification that incorporates a variety of DCNN multi-label loss and pooling methods. Islam et al. [6] developed a collection of several sophisticated network topologies to increase classification accuracy. Rajpurkar et al. [7] proved that a standard DenseNet architecture is more accurate than radiologists in detecting pneumonia. Yao et al. [8] developed a method for optimizing the use of statistic label dependencies and thus performance. Irvin et al. [9] developed CheXNet, a deep learning network that makes optimization manageable through dense connections and batch normalization. Prabira et al. [10] collected a set of deep features using nine pre-trained CNN models and then passed them to an SVM (Support Vector Machines) classifier.

In recent years, **Evolutionary optimization for CNN Design** has been successfully used for many machine learning tasks. According to previous research, this success can be attributed to population-based metaheuristics' global search capability, which allows them to avoid local optima while finding a near-globally optimal solution. Shinaozaki et al. [28] optimized a DNN's structure and parameters using GA. While GA works with binary vectors that reflect the structure of a DNN as a directed acyclic graph, CMA-ES, which is fundamentally a continuous optimizer, converts discrete structural variables to real values through an indirect encoding. Xie et al. [29] optimized the recognition accuracy by representing the network topology as a binary string. The primary constraint was the high computing cost, which compelled the authors to conduct the tests on small-scale data sets. Sun et al. [30] proposed an evolutionary method for optimizing the architectures and initializing the weights of convolutional neural networks (CNNs) for image classification applications. This objective was accomplished via the development of a novel weight initialization method, a novel encoding scheme for variable-length chromosomes, a slacked binary tournament selection technique, and an efficient fitness assessment technique. Lu et al. [31] proposed a multi-objective modeling of the architectural search issue by minimizing two potentially competing objectives: classification error rate and computational complexity, quantified by the number of floating-point operations (FLOPS). They used the NSGA-II as a multi-objective EA.

Channel Pruning. [11] is a different sort of weight pruning approach than neuron pruning. Channel pruning is a notion that refers to decreasing the number of channels in the input supplied to the CNN model's intermediate layers. The data fed into the CNN model is first channelized to produce an appropriate input. For example, an image has three channels (RGB). Each layer of the CNN model's output comprises a variety of channels that boost model efficiency while increasing storage and processing. So, it is desirable to remove unnecessary channels in order to reduce computation and storage needs.

Recently, various training-based channel pruning techniques [11,12] have been suggested, which include adding regularization terms to weights during the training stage. Many studies [13] are provided to conduct channel pruning on pre-trained models with varied pruning criteria, ignoring the pre-training procedure. Unfortunately, even existing techniques still have a lot of space for improvement when it comes to reducing model redundancy. Furthermore, most research [11–13] exclusively accelerates networks during the inference stage, with few focusing on off-line pruning efficiency. Following that, various inference-based channel pruning techniques [12,14] were presented, with the core of these methods defining selection criteria. Li et al. [13] argued that filters with lesser weights usually yield weaker activations and so may be eliminated. However, the criteria may exclude certain useful filters, particularly in shallow layers. Hu et al. [14] assessed the significance of each channel based on its sparsity and eliminated channels with more zero values in their output activations, indicating poor performance at convolution layers. Thinet [11] proposed using a greedy method to remove filters based on statistical information collected from its next layer. However, a greedy method would not be the ideal technique to solve the combinatorial optimization issue, especially if the solution space is very large. Furthermore, its off-line pruning procedure takes a long time since it must traverse the full training sets at each iteration step.

Weight Quantization. Decreases both the storage and computing requirements of the DCNNs model [15,16]. Han et al. [15] suggested a weight quantization approach for compressing deep neural networks by reducing the number of bits needed to encode weight matrices. The authors attempt to decrease the number of weights which should be stored in memory. The identical weights are removed as a result, and numerous connections are derived from a single remaining weight. During inference, the authors utilized integer arithmetic, while during training, they used floating-point operations. Jacob et al. [16] presented a quantization technique based on integer arithmetic for inference. Integer arithmetic is more efficient than floating-point arithmetic and requires fewer bits to represent. Additionally, the authors construct a training step that mitigates the accuracy penalty associated with the conversion of floating-point operations to integer operations. As a result, the suggested technique eliminates the trade-off between on-device latency and accuracy degradation caused by integer operations. The authors performed inference using integer arithmetic and training using floating-point operations. Quantization is a technique that creates an affine mapping between integers Q and real numbers R, i.e., of the type

$$R = W(Q - T) \tag{1}$$

where, Eq. (1) denotes the quantization method with the parameters W and T. For instance, Q is set to 8 for 8-bit quantization. W is an arbitrary positive real number, and T has the same type as variable Q. Existing work [15,16] explore quantization techniques for compressing DNN models. The approaches address model reduction by giving optimum weight matrix configurations.

A **Huffman code** is an efficient prefix code that is widely used for lossless data compression (Van Leeuwen, 1976) [17]. Schmidhuber et al. [18] compressed text files from a neural prediction network using Huffman coding. To encode the quantized weights, Han et al. [19] employed a three-stage compression approach consisting of pruning, quantization, and lastly, Huffman coding [17]. Ge et al. [20] presented a hybrid model compression method using Huffman coding to represent the trimmed weights' sparse nature. Among all variable length prefix codings, Huffman codes are the best. However, Elias [21] and Golomb encoding [22] can benefit from several intriguing features, such as the recurrent occurrence of specific sequences, to obtain superior average code-lengths.

3 Proposed Method

The following question inspires our approach:

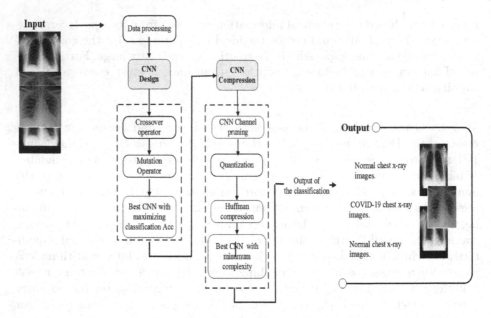

Fig. 1. The working principle of compression-CNN-XRAY on X-Ray images based on GA.

- There is an extremely huge variety of possible topologies for CNN convolution blocks' networks, each of which defines the interactions between nodes. How to determine the best block topology sequence for X-Ray images?
- How could we design a less complex effective CNN architecture with a minimum Number of convolution hyperparameters for X-Ray images?

To address this research question, we must first maximize accuracy by determining the optimal graph topology sequence for classifying X-Ray images and detecting possible thoracic anomalies and infections, such as COVID-19. Second, falling into very extremely high dimensional space, we must reduce the computational complexity of CNNs by optimizing the number of hyperparameters selected for the convolution layer through the use of a CNN architecture compressing process. We propose the **CNN-Xray-D-C** approach for designing an efficient architecture by defining the optimised sequence of block topologies for detecting various thoracic diseases evolutionary and compressing the CNN architecture by reducing model redundancy while improving or maintaining the Acc classification. Figure 1 illustrates our CNN-Xray-D-C approach, which will be discussed in the next subsections.

3.1 CNN Design

The solution encoding consists of a sequence of squared binary matrices, each representing a potential directed graph. A value of 1 indicates that the row node is the predecessor of the column node, but a value of 0 indicates that the two nodes are connected. The following constraints must be followed:

- Each active convolution node must have at least one preceding node. The latter could be either a previous or an input convolution node.
- Any active convolution node should have predecessors in its preceding layers. For example, node 4 may be preceded by nodes 3, 2, 1, and the input node.
- The initial convolutional node should have a single predecessor node, which serves as the input node.
- The output node of the last convolution node should have exactly one successor node.

The two-point crossover operator is utilized because it enables variation in all chromosomal parts. Each parent solution must be a set of binary strings . Two cutting points are applied to each parent and then the bits between the cuts are swapped to create two offspring solutions. Finally, infeasible solutions generated by the crossover are repaired through local adjustments that satisfy the five feasibility restrictions stated previously. Similarly to the crossover operator, the mutation operator's solution is converted to a binary string before the one-point mutation is applied.

3.2   CNN Compression

Each layer has i channels available to the i_{th} layer, however certain layers in AlexNet have 96 channels, which extends to 384 at the CONV-3 layer's output. Thus, determining which channels to prune at each layer in order to obtain the optimal solution is a challenging issue. This inspires the current technique, which use genetic algorithms to conduct heuristic search with the goal of discovering a solution that is near to optimal after a reasonable number of iterations. Each channel's genetic algorithms operate as follows:

- Only C chromosomes I $\{\theta_i, i = 1, 2, ..., c\}$) are used in the targeted layer of size L*L*C, therefore only C possibilities out of the 2^C possibilities are employed.
- Each chromosome M_i is encoded as a C length bit sequence of 0's and 1's, using Bernoulli probability density with mean = p, where p denotes the fraction of channels to be pruned.
- Therefore, if there are 3 channels, the possible initializations are $\{1, 1, 0\}$, $\{0, 1, 1\}$ and $\{1, 0, 1\}$, p = 0.666, the first chromosome $\{1, 1, 0\}$ results during the first kernel channel being pruned while the other two kernels are preserved.

We apply the two-point crossover operator to vary the population since it allows us to change all of the chromosomes at the same time. Each parent solution in this procedure is a set of binary strings. Two cutting points are used to make two of each parent. The bits between the cuts are then switched to provide two offspring solutions. Actually, we applied two-point crossover to maintain as much of the chromosome's local structure and solution feasibility as feasible. Similarly, with the crossover operator, the solution is binary string encoding followed by one-point mutation. The following Fitness Function:

Table 1. Summary of parameter Settings.

Categories	Parameters	Value
-	Batch size	128
gradient descent	Epochs	50/350
	SGD Learning rate	0.1
	Momentum	0.9
	Weight decay	0.0001
-	# Of generation	40
search strategy	Population size	60
	Crossover probability	0.9
	Mutation probability	0.1

- The error is represented by the layer wise - error difference, the primary aim is to find a pruned chromosome (Wp) that minimizes the term E(Yp), where the error is determined by an equation.

$$E(Y) = \frac{1}{N} \sum_{i=1}^{N} \|Y - Y_i\| \tag{2}$$

- However, after applying the Taylor expansion of the above equation and doing some approximation as detailed in Optimal Brain Damage (OBD), the goal function is reduced to a simpler version.

$$\delta E = \frac{1}{2} \delta W^T H \delta W \tag{3}$$

A quantization of 32-bit floating point values into 5-bit integer levels is used to further reduce the stored size of the weights file. The quantization part are spread linearly between Wmin and Wmax because it produces higher accuracy results than density-based quantization, thus even if a weight occurs with a low probability, it may have a high value and therefore a high influence, and if quantized to be less than its real value. This stage produces a compressed sparse row of quantized weights.

Due to the statistical characteristics of the quantization output, Huffman compression might be used to further reduce the weights file. However, this adds the additional hardware needs of a Huffman decompressor and a compressed sparse row to weights matrix converter.

4 Experiments

4.1 Expirement Configuration and Setup

The Chest X-Ray14 database contains 112,120 frontal-view radiographs and X-Ray images of 30,805 distinct patients. Natural language processing techniques were used to compile the database from associated radiological reports stored in hospital image archiving and communication systems. Each image may depict one or more common chest conditions (one or more common thoracic diseases), or it may simply be "Normal." Chest X-rays of COVID-19 patients were obtained from Dr. Joseph Cohen's opensource GitHub repository https://github.com/ieee8023/covid-chestxray-dataset. This repository contains chest X-ray images of a variety of patients who have been diagnosed with acute respiratory distress syndrome, severe acute respiratory syndrome, COVID-19, or pneumonia https://www.kaggle.com/paultimothymooney/chest-xray-pneumonia. To ensure the comparisons are fair, the parameters of the compared algorithms are set using the commonly used trial and error method. The following Table 1 outlines the parameter settings used in our experiments. The TensorFlow framework is implemented using the Python programming language (version 3.5). The tests used eight Nvidia 2080Ti GPU cards to analyze the CNN architectures generated from the test data. By randomly selecting 80% of the data records for training and 20% for testing, the holdout validation technique is used to establish the Accuracy.

4.2   Results and Discussion

Table 2. Obtained *AUROC and #Params*, results on ChestX-Ray14.

Method	Search Method	Test AUROC (%)	#Params
Yao et al. [8]	manual	79.8	-
Wang et al. [5]	manual	73.8	-
CheXNet [9]	manual	84.4	7.0M
Google AutoML [6]	RL	79.7	-
LEAF [25]	EA	84.3	-
NSGANet-X [26]	EA	84.6	2.2M
CNN-XRAY [27]	EA	87.12	5.1M
CNN-Xray-D-C	EA	86.98	1.1M

CNN-Xray-D-C is evaluated as the most significant work in each of the three main categories of methodologies for generating CNN architectures.

Table 2 illustrates the comparative findings obtained for the various architectures produced by the different CNN design approaches when applied to X-Ray images. Indeed, the AUROC for manual approaches ranges between 79.8 and 87.12%, and the #params lie between 2.2M and 7.0M. With an AUROC of 79.7%, Google AutoML is the worst approach among non-manual methods. In terms of classifying AUROC values, the evolutionary ones are 84.3% for LEAF (2019), 84.6% for NSGANet-X and 87.12% for CNN-XRAY. We observe that

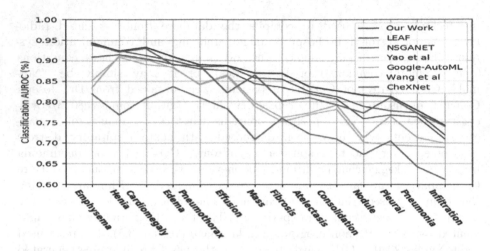

Fig. 2. CNN-Xray-D-C multi-label classification performance on ChestX-Ray14, the class-wise mean test AUROC comparison with peer works.

CNN-Xray-D-C is capable of automatically designing a CNN architecture that produces high AUROC values while using fewer parameters than the peer approaches studied. Furthermore, based on Table 3, **CNN-Xray-D-C** is capable of automatically designing a CNN architecture that produces good accuracy values compared with the peer approaches studied. There are more detailed results shown in Fig. 2. It shows the disease curve for the CNN-Xray-D-C method and the AUROC by disease compared to other methods. The following arguments could explain these findings. Concerning the design phase, manually designing CNNs is an extremely difficult and time-consuming operation that demands a high level of competence on the part of the user. Even with a high level of expertise, developing a suitable architecture is not easy due to the vast variety of alternative architectures. To automate this design effort, RL-based and evolutionary methods have been devised and have demonstrated superior performance to manual design due to their capacity to search automatically over the large search space of possible architectures. Evolutionary approaches demonstrated the best performance in this and previous studies because RL-based methods show greedy behavior that optimizes the AUROC across the search process. Indeed, evolutionary approaches are capable of escaping local optima and covering the whole search space due to their global search capabilities and the probability acceptance of less-performing individuals via the mating selection operator. To sum up, the optimization of the network topology has a significant impact on classification performance since each topology determines the interactions between the neural network nodes.

Concerning the compression phase, **CNN-Xray-D-C** has the potential to significantly decrease the number of parameters in CNN designs while maintaining acceptable Accuarcy. **CNN-Xray-D-C** provides better performance and accomplishes a reduction in design complexity by minimizing the number of

Table 3. Obtained *Acc* values on Chest X-Ray images.

Detection Method	Reference	Test Acc (%)	Sensitivity	Specificity
Deep features-based SVM	[10]	95.4	97.29	93.47
ResNet101		89.26	91.23	87.29
Inceptionv3		91.08	91.11	91.05
GoogleNet		91.44	89.82	93.05
VGG16		92.76	97.47	88.05
VGG19		92.91	95.11	90.70
XceptionNet		93.92	94.76	93.05
Inceptionresnetv2		93.32	94.76	93.05
AlexNet		93.32	93.41	93.23
DenseNet201		93.88	94.35	93.41
CNN-Xray-D-C	Our work	95.97	97.32	94.11

params. In fact, DCNNs must be trained using an approach that incorporates strong and specific regularization. Only the DCNN classification performance and computational complexity information are used to produce it. Thus, even without any regularization or other knowledge about the DCNN being pruned, **CNN-Xray-D-C** is capable of producing high-quality results. To conclude, the suggested **CNN-Xray-D-C** is capable of considerably reducing the number of parameters in DCNN architectures while maintaining acceptable Accuracy. **CNN-Xray-D-C** is the only EAs-based system that we are aware of that is capable of designing and compressing CNN architecture for detecting COVID-19 infection.

5 Conclusion

Designing or compressing an adequate Deep CNN architecture remains an extremely interesting, difficult, and current topic [32,33,35]. Numerous researchers have recently developed an interest in novel techniques for reducing the computational complexity of CNNs based on EAs. Following the channel pruning work, removing channels can also significantly reduce the computational requirements of the DCNN model, but this can result in a very high dimensional space.

In this work, we proposed an efficient evolutionary approach for designing the CNN architecture by searching for the optimal sequence of block topologies for detecting various thoracic diseases, including the COVID-19 data set. Then, by incorporating the following steps, we proposed a compression for the efficient generation of CNN architectures. channel Pruning is a technique that utilizes genetic algorithms to minimize the absolute error difference in the fitness function that has been derived and approximated. After that, quantization and various compression techniques are used to create a final model that is both faster to infer and smaller in size.

References

1. He, K., Zhang, X., Ren, S., Sun, J.: Deep residual learning for image recognition. In: IEEE Conference on Computer Vision and Pattern Recognition, pp. 770–778 (2016)
2. Simonyan, K., Zisserman, A.: Very deep convolutional networks for large-scale image recognition. CoRR, abs/1409.1556 (2014)
3. He, K., Zhang, X., Ren, S., Sun, J.: Deep residual learning for image recognition. In: IEEE Conference on Computer Vision and Pattern Recognition, pp. 770–778 (2016)
4. Kiranyaz, S., Ince, T., Gabbouj, M.: Real-time patient-specific ECG classification by 1-D convolutional neural networks. IEEE Trans. Biomed. Eng. **63**, 664–675 (2016). https://doi.org/10.1109/TBME.2015.2468589
5. Wang, X., Peng, Y., Lu, L., Lu, Z., Bagheri, M., Summers, R.M.: ChestX-ray8: hospital-scale chest X-ray database and benchmarks on weakly-supervised classification and localization of common thorax diseases. In: IEEE Conference on Computer Vision and Pattern Recognition, pp. 3462–3471 (2017)
6. Islam, M.T., Aowal, M.A., Minhaz, A.T., Ashraf, K.: Abnormality detection and localization in chest X-rays using deep convolutional neural networks. CoRR, vol. abs/1705.09850 (2017)
7. Rajpurkar, P., et al.: Deep learning for chest radiograph diagnosis: a retrospective comparison of the CheXNeXt algorithm to practicing radiologists. PLoS Med. **15**(11), 1–17 (2018)
8. Yao, L., Poblenz, E., Dagunts, D., Covington, B., Bernard, D., Lyman, K.: Learning to diagnose from scratch by exploiting dependencies among labels. CoRR, vol. abs/1710.1050 (2017)
9. Irvin, J., et al.: A large chest radiograph dataset with uncertainty labels and expert comparison. In: Thirty-Third AAAI Conference on Artificial Intelligence, pp. 590–597 (2019)
10. Sethy, P.K., Behera, S.K.: Detection of coronavirus disease (Covid-19) based on deep features. Int. J. Math. Eng. Manage. Sci. **5**(4), 643–651 (2020)
11. Luo, J., Wu, J., Lin, W.: ThiNet: a filter level pruning method for deep neural network compression. arXiv preprint arXiv: 1707.06342 (2017)
12. He, Y., Zhang, X., Sun, J.: Channel pruning for accelerating very deep neural networks. In: International Conference on Computer Vision (ICCV), vol. 2, p. 6 (2017)
13. Liu, Z., Li, J., Shen, Z., Huang, G., Yan, S., Zhang, C.: Learning efficient convolutional networks through network slimming. In: International Conference on Computer Vision (ICCV), pp. 2755–2763 (2017)
14. Hu, H., Peng, R., Tai, Y., Tang, C.: Network trimming: a datadriven neuron pruning approach towards efficient deep architectures. arXiv preprint arXiv: 1607.03250 (2016)
15. Han, S., Mao, H., Dally, W.J.: Deep compression: compressing deep neural networks with pruning, trained quantization and huffman coding. arXiv preprint arXiv:1510.00149 (2015)
16. Jacob, B., et al.: Quantization and training of neural networks for efficient integer-arithmetic-only inference. In: Proceedings CVPR, pp. 2704–2713 (2018)
17. Han, S., Mao, H., Dally, W.J.: Deep compression: compressing deep neural networks with pruning, trained quantization and Huffman coding. In: ICLR (2016)

18. Schmidhuber, J., Heil, S.: Predictive coding with neural nets: application to text compression. In: NeurIPS, pp. 1047–1054 (1995)
19. Han, S., Mao, H., Dally, W.J.: Deep compression: compressing deep neural network with pruning, trained quantization and Huffman coding. In 4th International Conference on Learning Representations, ICLR 2016, San Juan, Puerto Rico, 2–4 May 2016. Conference Track Proceedings (2016)
20. Ge, S., Luo, Z., Zhao, S., Jin, X., Zhang, X.-Y.: Compressing deep neural networks for efficient visual inference. In: IEEE International Conference on Multimedia and Expo (ICME), pp. 667–672. IEEE (2017)
21. Elias, P.: Universal codeword sets and representations of the integers. IEEE Trans. Inf. Theor. **21**(2), 194–203 (1975)
22. Gallager, R., van Voorhis, D.: Optimal source codes for geometrically distributed integer alphabets. IEEE Trans. Infor. Theor. **21**(2), 228–230 (1975). https://doi.org/10.1109/TIT.1975.1055357
23. Louati, H., Bechikh, S., Louati, A., Hung, C.-C., Said, L.B.: Deep convolutional neural network architecture design as a bi-level optimization problem. Neurocomputing **439**, 44–62 (2021)
24. Blog, G.R.: AutoML for large scale image classification and object detection. Google Research (2017). https://researchgoogleblog.com/2017/11/automl-for-large-scaleimage.html
25. Liang, J., Meyerson, E., Hodjat, B., Fink, D., Mutch, K., Miikkulainen, R.: Evolutionary neural AutoML for deep learning (2019). https://doi.org/10.1145/3321707.3321721
26. Lu, Z., et al.: Multi-criterion evolutionary design of deep convolutional neural networks. ArXiv, abs/1912.01369 (2019)
27. Louati, H., Bechikh, S., Louati, A., Aldaej, A., Said, L.B.: Evolutionary optimization of convolutional neural network architecture design for thoracic X-ray image classification. In: Fujita, H., Selamat, A., Lin, J.C.-W., Ali, M. (eds.) IEA/AIE 2021. LNCS (LNAI), vol. 12798, pp. 121–132. Springer, Cham (2021). https://doi.org/10.1007/978-3-030-79457-6_11
28. Shinozaki, T., Watanabe, S.: Structure discovery of deep neural network based on evolutionary algorithms. In: 2015 IEEE International Conference on Acoustics, Speech and Signal Processing, pp. 4979–4983 (2015)
29. Xie, S., Girshick, R., Dollar, P., Tu, Z., He, K.: Aggregated residual transformations for deep neural networks. In: IEEE conference on Computer Vision and Pattern Recognition, pp. 1492–1500 (2017)
30. Sun, Y., Xue, B., Zhang, M., Yen, G.G.: Completely automated CNN architecture design based on blocks. IEEE Trans. Neural Netw. Learn. Syst. **33**(2), 1242–1254 (2019)
31. Lu, Z., et al.: NSGA-Net: neural architecture search using multi-objective genetic algorithm. In: Genetic and Evolutionary Computation Conference, pp. 419–427 (2019)
32. Louati, A., Louati, H., Nusir, M., hardjono, B.: Multi-agent deep neural networks coupled with LQF-MWM algorithm for traffic control and emergency vehicles guidance. J. Ambient. Intell. Humaniz. Comput. **11**(11), 5611–5627 (2020). https://doi.org/10.1007/s12652-020-01921-3
33. Louati, A., Louati, H., Li, Z.: Deep learning and case-based reasoning for predictive and adaptive traffic emergency management. J. Supercomput. **77**(5), 4389–4418 (2020). https://doi.org/10.1007/s11227-020-03435-3

34. Louati, A.: A hybridization of deep learning techniques to predict and control traffic disturbances. Artif. Intell. Rev. **53**(8), 5675–5704 (2020). https://doi.org/10.1007/s10462-020-09831-8

35. Louati, H., et al.: Joint design and compression of convolutional neural networks as a Bi-level optimization problem. Neural Comput. Appl. **34**, 15007–15029 (2022). https://doi.org/10.1007/s00521-022-07331-0

TF-MOPNAS: Training-free Multi-objective Pruning-Based Neural Architecture Search

Quan Minh Phan[1,2] and Ngoc Hoang Luong[1,2(✉)]

[1] University of Information Technology, Ho Chi Minh City, Vietnam
`quanpm.16@grad.uit.edu.vn, hoangln@uit.edu.vn`
[2] Vietnam National University, Ho Chi Minh City, Vietnam

Abstract. Pruning-based neural architecture search (NAS) methods are effective approaches in finding network architectures that have high performance with low complexity. However, current methods only yield a single final architecture instead of an *approximation Pareto set*, which is typically the desirable result of solving multi-objective problems. Furthermore, the network performance evaluation in NAS involves the computationally expensive network training process, and the search cost thus considerably increases because numerous architectures are evaluated during an NAS run. Using computational resource efficiently, therefore, is an essential problem that needs to be considered. Recent studies have attempted to address this resource issue by replacing the network accuracy metric in NAS optimization objectives with so-called *training-free* performance metrics, which can be calculated without requiring any training epoch. In this paper, we propose a training-free multi-objective pruning-based neural architecture search (TF-MOPNAS) framework that produces competitive trade-off fronts for multi-objective NAS with a trivial cost by using the Synaptic Flow metric. We test our proposed method on multi-objective NAS problems created on a wide range of well-known NAS benchmarks, i.e., NAS-Bench-101, NAS-Bench-1shot1, and NAS-Bench-201. Experimental results indicate that our method can figure out trade-off fronts that have the equivalent quality to the ones found by state-of-the-art NAS methods but with much less computation resource. The code is available at: https://github.com/ELO-Lab/TF-MOPNAS.

Keywords: Pruning-based neural architecture search · AutoML · Multi-objective optimization · Training-free indicators

1 Introduction

Neural architecture search (NAS) is a subfield of automated machine learning (AutoML) that involves automating the design of high-performance deep neural networks (DNNs) on a specific task [21]. Nowadays, to employ DNNs on a particular platform (e.g., workstations, drones, mobile devices [8]), decision-makers

© The Author(s), under exclusive license to Springer Nature Switzerland AG 2022
N. T. Nguyen et al. (Eds.): ICCCI 2022, LNAI 13501, pp. 297–310, 2022.
https://doi.org/10.1007/978-3-031-16014-1_24

consider not only the prediction performance (i.e., the accuracy) but also other competing objectives such as the model size, latency, etc. It is thus more practical if we consider NAS as a multi-objective optimization problem rather than a single-objective one.

When solving a multi-objective NAS problem, it is impossible to find a *utopian* architecture (which is the one that achieves optimal values for all objectives) because it does not exist. A feasible aim is thus to obtain a *Pareto-optimal set* $\mathcal{P}_S$, which is a set of candidate solutions that yields a *Pareto-optimal front* $\mathcal{P}_F$ in the objective space. A characteristic of $\mathcal{P}_S$ is that all architectures in $\mathcal{P}_S$ are not Pareto dominated[1] by any other one in the search space and all architectures in $\mathcal{P}_S$ are thus considered equally good. Therefore, the Pareto-optimal set $\mathcal{P}_S$ is favored by decision-makers because they can consider many choices regarding different selection criteria.

It is ideal if we can figure out all architectures in $\mathcal{P}_S$ when solving a multi-objective NAS problem but it would be too costly if the size of $\mathcal{P}_S$ is large. A practical goal in solving multi-objective NAS is thus to find an *approximation set* S of non-dominated solutions which their objective value vectors $\boldsymbol{F}(S)$ approximate the Pareto-optimal front $\mathcal{P}_F$ in the objective space.

There are many approaches for solving a multi-objective NAS problem such as evolution-based NAS [11] or pruning-based NAS methods [4,16,17]. While the workflows of evolution-based NAS methods satisfy the required output of solving multi-objective NAS problems (i.e., returning an approximation set of non-dominated architectures), pruning-based NAS methods typically return a single network architecture after searching. With the insights of the Pareto-optimal set (or an approximation set) provided to decision-makers, designing NAS methods that can return a set of efficient trade-off architectures rather than a single network is more beneficial in solving NAS problems.

The exponential increasing of computational cost is also an issue that we face when approaching NAS. Earlier works on NAS show that hundreds to thousands of GPU days for an NAS run are required because of the enormous cost that comes from training a numerous number of architectures during the search [21]. Recently, a solution for this resource issue is to use some so-called *training-free* metrics, which can be computed without incurring any training epoch, as proxies for neural networks' performance [4,16]. Due to the time for computing these metrics being much smaller compared to the training time of architectures and the high correlation between them and the test accuracy, training-free metrics are utilized to design efficient NAS methods such as TE-NAS [4], Iterative Synaptic Flow Pruning [16], or evolutionary NAS with training-free initialization [14].

In this paper, we formulate multi-objective NAS as bi-objective minimization problems with the first objective being a training-based performance metric (e.g., the classification error rate) and the second objective being a complexity network metric (e.g., the number of trainable parameters, FLOPs). Motivated by the efficiency of training-free metrics and the functionality of approximation set,

---

[1] An architecture $\boldsymbol{x}$ is said to Pareto dominate another architecture $\boldsymbol{y}$ if $\boldsymbol{x}$ is not worse than $\boldsymbol{y}$ in any objective and $\boldsymbol{x}$ is strictly better than $\boldsymbol{y}$ in at least one objective [5].

we propose the *training-free multi-objective pruning-based NAS* (TF-MOPNAS) framework, which guides pruning-based NAS methods to produce an approximation set without incurring any training epoch by replacing training-based objectives with training-free ones when solving multi-objective NAS problems. Our contributions are summarized as below:

- We present a training-free multi-objective NAS framework, TF-MOPNAS, for pruning-based NAS methods that can provide an approximation front without incurring any training epoch.
- Our proposed method, TF-MOPNAS, can find out trade-off fronts that have the equivalent or better quality than the ones found by multi-objective evolution-based NAS methods but with less computation cost.
- In NAS-Bench-101 and NAS-Bench-201 search spaces, TF-MOPNAS can figure out architectures that outperform the ones found by all previous pruning-based NAS methods and almost other NAS methods with much lower costs of computational resources.

2 Background and Related Works

2.1 Progressive Search Space Shrinking and Architecture Selection

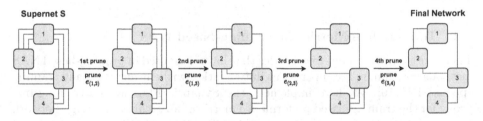

Fig. 1. Example of a progressive pruning process on a supernet.

Progressive search space shrinking is a pruning technique that reduces the cost of the search and the evaluation phase by pruning out weak operations (or edges) of a supernet *sequentially* during the search phase [4,9]. Figure 1 illustrates an example of the progressive pruning process on a supernet S that has four edges and three different operations on each edge. Operations (or edges) of a supernet are pruned based on the magnitudes of network parameters following DARTS [9,10] (see Algorithm 1). However, the magnitudes of architecture parameters do not reflect the importance of operations [17], and the resulting network based on the magnitude-based pruning might perform poorly after training at the evaluation phase. A perturbation-based architecture selection has been proposed in [17], in which an operation is kept if its contribution to the performance of the supernet is the largest when the other ones are pruned out (see Algorithm 2). The perturbation-based architecture selection can extract architectures that are better than the ones extracted by the magnitude-based method [17].

Our proposed TF-MOPNAS performs a sequential pruning procedure similarly to other progressive search space shrinking and architecture selection methods. We also evaluate the strength of each operation by considering its contribution to the performance of supernet as in [4,17]. However, instead of choosing the operation that has the largest contribution, we employ a different mechanism to decide which operations are kept or pruned (see Sect. 3).

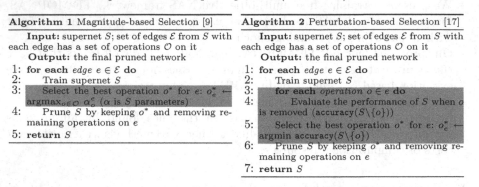

Algorithm 1 Magnitude-based Selection [9]

Input: supernet S; set of edges $\mathcal{E}$ from S with each edge has a set of operations $\mathcal{O}$ on it

Output: the final pruned network

1: **for each** $edge$ $e \in \mathcal{E}$ **do**
2:     Train supernet S
3:     Select the best operation o^* for e: $o_e^* \leftarrow \text{argmax}_{o \in \mathcal{O}} \, \alpha_o^e$ (α is S parameters)
4:     Prune S by keeping o^* and removing remaining operations on e
5: **return** S

Algorithm 2 Perturbation-based Selection [17]

Input: supernet S; set of edges $\mathcal{E}$ from S with each edge has a set of operations $\mathcal{O}$ on it

Output: the final pruned network

1: **for each** $edge$ $e \in \mathcal{E}$ **do**
2:     Train supernet S
3:     **for each** $operation$ $o \in e$ **do**
4:         Evaluate the performance of S when o is removed ($\text{accuracy}(S \backslash \{o\})$)
5:     Select the best operation o^* for e: $o_e^* \leftarrow \text{argmin accuracy}(S \backslash \{o\})$
6:     Prune S by keeping o^* and removing remaining operations on e
7: **return** S

Fig. 2. Pseudo-codes of magnitude-based and perturbation-based architecture selection. The yellow blocks represent the difference between the two mechanisms. (Color figure online)

2.2   Training-free Metrics in Pruning-based NAS

There are several training-free metrics that have been used in pruning-based NAS methods for pruning the supernet at initialization without incurring any training epochs [4,12,16]. We here implement the Synaptic Flow as the training-free proxy for the training-based performance metric of an architecture (e.g., network accuracy) when performing TF-MOPNAS. The Synaptic Flow was introduced by Tanaka et al. [16] to express the importance of each parameter in a network $\mathcal{N}$. The Synaptic Flow scores of all parameters in $\mathcal{N}$ are computed by taking the Hadamard product between the gradient of a loss function $\mathcal{L}$ (with respect to the network parameter θ) and the network parameter θ:

$$\text{Scores}_{SF}(\theta) = \frac{\partial \mathcal{L}}{\partial \theta} \odot \theta \tag{1}$$

Instead of the cross-entropy loss, Tanaka et al. [16] suggested that $\mathcal{L}$ can be computed as follows:

$$\mathcal{L} = \mathbb{1}^T \left(\prod_{l=1}^{L} |\theta^{[l]}| \right) \mathbb{1}, \tag{2}$$

Abdelfattah et al. [1] then proposed that the Synaptic Flow (`synflow`) of an entire network $\mathcal{N}$ with parameter vector θ can be computed by taking the sum of the Synaptic Flow score of each parameter in θ:

$$\text{synflow}(\mathcal{N}) = \sum_i \text{Scores}_{SF}(\theta)_i \tag{3}$$

Algorithm 3. Training-free Multi-objective Pruning-based NAS

    Input: supernet S; set of edges $\mathcal{E}$ from S; training-free metric θ
    Output: the final set of pruned networks P
1:   $P \leftarrow \{S\}$
2:   **for each** *edge* $e \in \mathcal{E}$ **do**
3:      $C \leftarrow \{\,\}$
4:      **for each** *parent network* $p \in P$ **do**
5:         **for each** *operation* $o \in e_p$ **do**
6:            Create *child network* c from p such that *edge* e_c only has *operation* o
7:            $C \leftarrow C + c$
8:      $F_C \leftarrow$ EVALUATE(C, θ) ▷ No training
9:      $P \leftarrow$ GETNONDOMINATEDNETWORKS(C, F_C)
10: **return** P

This `synflow` metric was reported in [1] to exhibit a high degree of correlation with network accuracy, i.e., Spearman's ρ 0.74, 0.76, and 0.75 for CIFAR-10, CIFAR-100, and ImageNet16-120, respectively, in NAS-Bench-201 search space.

3   Training-free Multi-objective Pruning-based Neural Architecture Search

The procedure of training-free multi-objective pruning-based neural architecture search (TF-MOPNAS) framework is outlined in Algorithm 3. Note that although the mechanism shown in Algorithm 3 is implemented for operation pruning, the cell topology selection (i.e., edges pruning) can be performed in the similar fashion. Similar to previous studies in progressive search space shrinking, a pruning process of TF-MOPNAS consists of $|\mathcal{E}|$ pruning times with $\mathcal{E}$ is the set of edges of the supernet S (Algorithm 3, line 2). In previous studies, the pruning at the i-th pruning is only performed on one *parent* network (which is the extracted network at the end of the $(i - 1)$-th pruning) and also yields one *child* network (which is the child network has the best performance out of $|\mathcal{O}|$ child networks ($\mathcal{O}$ is the set of operations in each edge)) at the end of the i-th pruning [4,9]. For TF-MOPNAS, we do not select the child network as the best performance one at the end of each pruning iteration. We instead employ the definition of Pareto dominance [5] to select non-dominated child networks and consider them as the parent networks for the next pruning (Algorithm 3, line 9). Consequently, the pruning is performed on one (or many) sub-networks instead of only one at each pruning of TF-MOPNAS. After performing $|\mathcal{E}|$ pruning times, last extracted child networks exhibit a non-dominated front in the objective space and are considered as the output result of TF-MOPNAS in an NAS run. Figure 3 shows an example of the pruning process of TF-MOPNAS on a supernet S having four edges and three different operations on each edge (i.e., $|\mathcal{E}| = 4$ and $|\mathcal{O}| = 3$). We here use the Synaptic Flow as the training-free proxy for the network performance (i.e., accuracy). The network evaluation process is

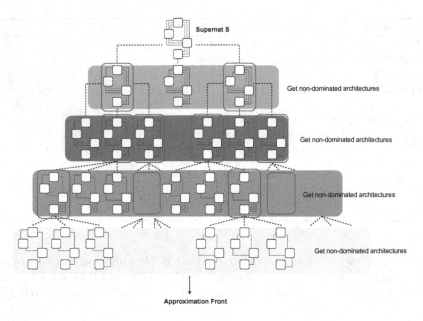

Fig. 3. Example of a TF-MOPNAS pruning process on an illustration supernet S has 4 edges and 3 different operations on each edge.

thus performed without any training epoch (Algorithm 3, line 8) and therefore, the cost of the whole pruning process of TF-MOPNAS is trivial. Our approach can be extended to other training-free proxy metrics (e.g., Jacov [12]) as well.

4   Experiments and Results

We evaluate our proposed method TF-MOPNAS on bi-objective NAS problems created on the basis of three NAS benchmarks: NAS-Bench-101 [18], NAS-Bench-1shot1 [20], and NAS-Bench-201 [7]. All NAS optimization objectives considered here are minimization. The first objective f_1 is one of the network complexity metrics (e.g., FLOPs, or #params) and the second one f_2 is the error rate.

We compare our method to two evolution-based NAS methods denoted as MOENAS and TF-MOENAS for all problems. Both methods employ the well-known multi-objective evolutionary algorithm (MOEA) NSGA-II [6] as the search algorithm. MOENAS employs the validation error rate (i.e., a training-based performance metric) while TF-MOENAS employs the Synaptic Flow (i.e., a training-free performance metric) as the objective f_2 during an NAS run.

For evolution-based NAS methods, the population size and the maximum number of evaluations (i.e., the total number of evaluated architectures) are set to 20 and 3000, respectively, for all problems. Variation operators are 2-point crossover with probability 0.9 and integer mutation with probability $1/l$.

We additionally implement an *elitist archive* $\mathcal{A}$, which is treated as an external secondary population, to preserve all non-dominated architectures found so far during an NAS run. When an architecture is evaluated, it is added to $\mathcal{A}$ if it is not Pareto dominated by any elite architectures currently existing in $\mathcal{A}$. Old members dominated by the newly-added architecture are then removed from the archive $\mathcal{A}$. At the end of each NAS run, architectures in the elitist archive $\mathcal{A}$ form an *approximation front* in the objective space, which can be considered as the optimization results obtained by MOEAs. The approximation fronts (obtained by MOENAS methods and TF-MOPNAS) are then used for evaluating their search performance via the Inverted Generational Distance (IGD [3]) indicator. The IGD value is computed as the average distance from each solution on the Pareto-optimal front $\mathcal{P}_F$ to its nearest solution on the approximation front $\mathcal{S}$:

$$IGD(\mathcal{S}, \mathcal{P}_F) = \frac{1}{|\mathcal{P}_F|} \sum_{f^0 \in \mathcal{P}_F} \min_{x \in \mathcal{S}} \|f(x) - f^0\|_2 \tag{4}$$

Note that $IGD(\mathcal{S}, \mathcal{P}_F) = 0$ if and only if all solutions on $\mathcal{P}_F$ are found. When comparing the performance of two algorithms in solving multi-objective NAS problems, the algorithm that has the smaller IGD value is the better one.

In our experiments, a Pareto-optimal front $\mathcal{P}_F$ is presented in terms of a network complexity metric (e.g., FLOPs, or #params) and a network performance metric (i.e., the test error rate). To ensure our experiments are similar to real-world NAS, in which the test performance are evaluated on unseen data finally, the performance metric objective of all algorithms during NAS runs are not the test one. We use the validation error rate for MOENAS and the Synaptic Flow metric for training-free NAS methods (TF-MOENAS and TF-MOPNAS). We thus cannot calculate the IGD value because the approximation fronts found by these algorithms are not presented in the same objective space as the Pareto-optimal fronts. We, therefore, need re-evaluate the architectures on the approximation fronts to get their test error rates (which can be easily done by querying the databases of NAS benchmarks) to obtain new approximation fronts that are in the same objective space as $\mathcal{P}_F$. The IGD values of these converted approximation fronts can then be computed following Eq. 4. Because the test performance information is only for the algorithm evaluation purpose, we do not count the costs incurred (e.g., the training time) in the process of evaluating the test performance toward the search cost.

We perform 31 independent runs for each algorithm for each problem. The obtained results are then run on statistical tests (i.e., Student's t-test) at the 99% confidence level (i.e., $\alpha = 0.01$) for assessing whether there are any significant differences in the performance between our proposed method and the other ones. After performing statistical tests, the best algorithms are presented with their performance results in bold format (e.g., the MOENAS and TF-MOPNAS algorithms in Table 1).

Along with the IGD indicator, the search time of an algorithm is also an aspect that we consider. The search time of TF-MOENAS and TF-MOPNAS are recorded on a single GeForce 940MX GPU for all search spaces (i.e., NAS-Bench-101, NAS-Bench-1shot1, and NAS-Bench-201). The search time of MOENAS is recorded on a TPU v2 accelerator (for NAS-Bench-101 and NAS-Bench-1shot1 search spaces) and on a GTX 1080Ti GPU (for NAS-Bench-201 search space).

4.1   Results on NAS-Bench-101

We firstly experiment TF-MOPNAS and its competitors (i.e., MOENAS, TF-MOENAS) on NAS-Bench-101 benchmark [18]. NAS-Bench-101 consists of about $423,000$ unique architectures and their performance (i.e., #params, the train time, the train/validation/test performance) at four different training epochs $\{4, 12, 36, 108\}$ on CIFAR-10 dataset [18]. In NAS-Bench-101 search space, each architecture is presented as a $7-$node directed acyclic graph (DAG) and each node represents one of three operations, i.e., conv1 × 1, conv3 × 3, and max pooling. For NAS-Bench-101 benchmark, we create a bi-objective NAS problem which minimizes the number of network parameters (#params) and the test error rate at the 108-th epoch. Because the cell topologies of DAGs in NAS-Bench-101 are not fixed (i.e., the number of edges in graphs can be different, or a node can receive data from one or many previous nodes), in addition to operations pruning, we also perform edges pruning to obtain cell topologies.

A straightforward approach is to prune the supernet for obtaining the cell topologies and then continue to prune each sub-network (corresponding to each cell topology) for operation selection on edges. A problem with this pruning approach is that we do not know when we can terminate the edge pruning process to obtain a suitable cell topology. NAS-Bench-101 benchmark only provides that the maximum number of edges for each architecture is set to 9 (i.e., $|\mathcal{E}| \leq 9$) and we thus cannot determine the reasonable number of edges that we can keep when performing edge pruning. We then refer to the approach which has been employed in [19] for single path one-shot NAS methods on NAS-Bench-101. Specifically, we randomly sample cell topologies and utilize TF-MOPNAS for pruning operations on the architectures created with those cell topologies. This process is repeated till the allowed budget (i.e., the maximum number of evaluated architectures) is exhausted. We set the maximum number of evaluated architectures equals to 3000 for ensuring the fairness between TF-MOPNAS and other candidate algorithms. As a result, we experiment on NAS-Bench-101 with three algorithms: MOENAS (with optimizing #params and the validation error rate at $12-$th epoch), TF-MOENAS and TF-MOPNAS (with optimizing #params and Synaptic Flow metric). At the end of NAS runs, we re-evaluate the architectures on approximation fronts to project them to the same objective space containing the Pareto-optimal fronts (#params and the test error rate at $108-$th epoch) and then calculate the IGD values for performance comparison.

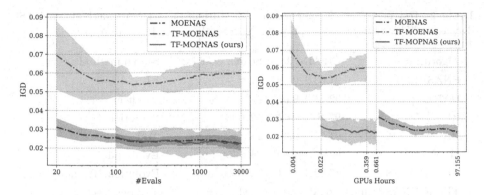

Fig. 4. Average IGD of algorithms on NAS-Bench-101. Horizontal axis (logarithm): the number of evaluations (Left); the search cost (GPUs hours) (Right).

Table 1. The search time and the final IGD of algorithms on NAS-Bench-101.

Algorithm	IGD (final)	Search cost (sec.)
MOENAS	**0.022 ± 0.004**	349, 759
TF-MOENAS	0.060 ± 0.008	1293
TF-MOPNAS (ours)	**0.022 ± 0.007**	2381

The results in Fig. 4 and Table 1 present the contrast in the performance of algorithms on NAS-Bench-101 when both MOENAS and TF-MOPNAS are effective in nearly finding the entire Pareto-optimal front but TF-MOENAS does not. These obtained results are interesting since both TF-MOENAS and TF-MOPNAS employ the Synaptic Flow metric as one optimization objective. The difference might be due to two following reasons. First, the Synaptic Flow metric has low correlation with network accuracy for the architectures in the NAS-Bench-101 search space (Spearman's ρ 0.37 [1]). Second, the variation operators (crossover and mutation) of TF-MOENAS are stochastic, and could thus be highly disruptive in the NAS-Bench-101 search space: e.g., recombining two parents having different cell topologies might yield two offspring that have another two different cell topologies. In contrast, the architecture selection operator of TF-MOPNAS performs on one cell topology at a time, ensuring the newly-pruned architecture has the same cell topology with the old one. Results in Table 1 additionally show that TF-MOPNAS has a search time of 140 times less than that of MOENAS ($2403 \ll 349,759$ seconds) but achieves a comparable performance to MOENAS (at the 99% confidence level). Moreover, architectures found by TF-MOPNAS are better than most architectures found by training-based approaches and are the best ones compared to architectures found by other training-free approaches (see Table 2).

Table 2. Test performance comparison with state-of-the-art NAS methods on NAS-Bench-101. The performance of previous NAS methods are taken from [19].

Algorithm	CIFAR-10	Search cost (sec.)	Search method
ENAS [13]	91.83 ± 0.59	-	RL
DARTS [10]	92.21 ± 0.61	-	Gradient
REA [15]	**93.87 ± 0.22**	12,000	Evolution
NASWOT [12]	91.77 ± 0.05	23	Training-free
MOENAS	93.44 ± 0.19	349,759	Evolution
TF-MOENAS	87.42 ± 1.01	1293	Evolution, Training-free
TF-MOPNAS (ours)	92.98 ± 0.95	2381	Training-free
Optimal	94.31	-	in the benchmark

4.2   Results on NAS-Bench-1shot1

NAS-Bench-1shot1 [20] is the sub-benchmark of NAS-Bench-101. Unlike NAS-Bench-101, the search space of NAS-Bench-1shot1 provides the total number of edges in a graph (i.e., $|\mathcal{E}| = 9$) and fixes the number of connections from the $(i-1)$ previous nodes to the i-th node. We can thus assess the performance of TF-MOPNAS in case of pruning both edges and operations. Specifically, we firstly prune the edges of the supernet to obtain the cell topologies. We then perform operation pruning on each network corresponding to each cell topology. The networks obtained after pruning edges and operations are then used for assessing the performance of TF-MOPNAS via the IGD indicator. Besides TF-MOPNAS (with pruning both edges and operations), we also implement three variants which we experimented on above NAS-Bench-101 experiments (i.e., MOENAS, TF-MOENAS, and TF-MOPNAS with randomly sampling the cell topology) for performance comparison. The experimental settings for algorithms (e.g., the variant operators, the maximum number or evaluations) on NAS-Bench-1shot1 are set up as in NAS-Bench-101.

Table 3. The search time and the final IGD of algorithms on NAS-Bench-1shot1.

Algorithm	IGD (final)	Search cost (sec.)
MOENAS	**0.034 ± 0.005**	302,407
TF-MOENAS	0.082 ± 0.008	2350
TF-MOPNAS (ours)[a]	**0.033 ± 0.011**	2630
TF-MOPNAS (ours)[b]	0.040 ± 0.002	395

[a] with sampling the cell topology and only pruning operations
[b] with pruning both edges and operations

For the algorithms experimented on NAS-Bench-101 (i.e., MOENAS, TF-MOENAS, and TF-MOPNAS with randomly sampling the cell topology), their performance ranking on NAS-Bench-1shot1 does not change. The performance of MOENAS and TF-MOPNAS (with randomly sampling the cell topology) are comparable and the performance of TF-MOENAS is worse than all the other competing methods. Pruning both edges and operations is not more effective than only pruning operations when Table 3 shows that the search performance of pruning both edges and operations is significantly worse than pruning operations.

4.3 Results on NAS-Bench-201

The search space of NAS-Bench-201 contains $15,625$ architectures with each architecture is also presented as a fully-connected DAG with 4 nodes and 6 edges [7]. Each edge in the graph represents one out of 5 operations (i.e., zeroize, skip connection, conv1 $\times$ 1, conv3 $\times$ 3, and average pooling). NAS-Bench-201 benchmark also provides logs of 200-epochs-training processes of architectures (e.g., the train/validation/test performance, FLOPs, the train time) on three different datasets, i.e., CIFAR-10, CIFAR-100, and ImageNet16-120. All bi-objective NAS problems we create on NAS-Bench-201 minimize simultaneously FLOPs and the test error rate (at the 200-th epoch) on CIFAR-10 dataset.

In NAS-Bench-201 search space, the cell topology of architectures (i.e., the connections between nodes) is fixed and we thus only search for the operation selection on each edge. We experiment with three algorithms on NAS-Bench-201: MOENAS (optimizing FLOPs and validation error rate at 12−th epoch), TF-MOENAS and TF-MOPNAS (optimizing FLOPs and the Synaptic Flow metric). At the end of NAS runs, we re-evaluate the architectures on the obtained approximation fronts to get their test error rates at the 200-th epoch and calculate the IGD values for performance comparison.

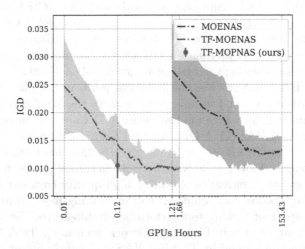

Fig. 5. Average IGD of algorithms on NAS-Bench-201 (CIFAR-10 dataset). Horizontal axis: the search cost (hours) (logarithm).

Table 4. The search time and the final IGD of algorithms on NAS-Bench-201.

Algorithm	CIFAR-10	CIFAR-100 (transfer)	ImageNet16-120 (transfer)	Search cost (sec.)
MOENAS	0.013 ± 0.003	0.025 ± 0.005	0.014 ± 0.003	$552,333$
TF-MOENAS	$\mathbf{0.010 \pm 0.002}$	$\mathbf{0.013 \pm 0.003}$	$\mathbf{0.010 \pm 0.002}$	5971
TF-MOPNAS (ours)	$\mathbf{0.011 \pm 0.002}$	0.017 ± 0.004	$\mathbf{0.011 \pm 0.002}$	427

Figure 5 and Table 4 exhibit that all algorithms are effective in figuring out almost the entire Pareto-optimal front when the final IGD values of algorithms are nearly 0. Statistical tests on results in Table 4 show that the trade-off fronts found by training-free methods (i.e., TF-MOENAS and TF-MOPNAS) are better than the ones found by the training-based method (i.e., MOENAS) and the total search time of both are much less compared to the total search time of MOENAS ($5970 \ll 552,331$ seconds; $427 \ll 552,331$ seconds). In other words, approximation fronts found by optimizing the Synaptic Flow and FLOPs are closer to Pareto-optimal fronts than the ones obtained by optimizing the validation accuracy (at the 12-th epoch) and FLOPs. Besides, Table 4 exhibits that TF-MOPNAS achieves comparable performance to TF-MOENAS but takes much less GPU times (approximately 14 times less). These results indicate the effectiveness of our approach in combining the training-free Synaptic Flow metric with (multi-objective) architecture selection methods to efficiently traverse the architecture search space, approximating the Pareto-optimal front.

4.4 Results on Architecture Transfer

Most studies conduct NAS runs on a small dataset (e.g., CIFAR-10) and then transfer found architectures on larger datasets (e.g., CIFAR-100, ImageNet). We evaluate the transferability of TF-MOPNAS by re-utilizing obtained architectures at the end of NAS runs on CIFAR-10 (in previous NAS-Bench-201 experiments) and evaluating their performance on CIFAR-100 and ImageNet16-120. NAS-Bench-201 also provides the networks' performance on CIFAR-100 and ImageNet16-120 datasets and we only need to query the benchmark database for their performance. Table 4 presents the mean IGD values of the approximation fronts found by MOENAS, TF-MOENAS, and TF-MOPNAS on CIFAR-10 when being transferred to CIFAR-100 and ImageNet16-120. Due to the high correlation of the Synaptic Flow metric with network accuracy [1], both training-free NAS methods are very efficient in obtaining high-quality transferred fronts with much lower computation cost compared to the training-based approach.

From the aspect of seeking top-performing architectures (i.e., disregarding network complexity and only focus on network accuracy), Table 5 shows that while the architectures found by TF-MOENAS are slightly better than the ones found by TF-MOPNAS, TF-MOENAS requires 10–15 times more computing time than TF-MOPNAS. There is no other method that costs less search time than TF-MOPNAS but can figure out architectures with higher performance.

Table 5. Test performance comparison with state-of-the-art NAS methods on NAS-Bench-201, of which the performance results are taken from [4,7,12].

Algorithm	CIFAR-10	CIFAR-100 (transfer)	ImageNet16-120 (transfer)	Search cost (sec.)	Search method
RS [2]	93.70 ± 0.36	71.04 ± 1.07	44.57 ± 1.25	12,000	Random
DARTS [10]	54.30 ± 0.00	15.61 ± 0.00	16.32 ± 0.00	10,890	Gradient
ENAS [13]	54.30 ± 0.00	15.61 ± 0.00	16.32 ± 0.00	13,315	RL
REA [15]	93.92 ± 0.30	71.84 ± 0.99	45.54 ± 1.03	12,000	Evolution
NASWOT [12]	92.96 ± 0.81	69.98 ± 1.22	44.44 ± 2.10	307	Training-free
TE-NAS [4]	93.90 ± 0.47	71.24 ± 0.56	42.38 ± 0.46	1558	Training-free
MOENAS	93.88 ± 0.20	71.17 ± 0.75	44.73 ± 0.77	552,333	Evolution
TF-MOENAS	$\mathbf{94.35 \pm 0.04}$	$\mathbf{73.42 \pm 0.28}$	$\mathbf{46.41 \pm 0.12}$	5971	Evolution, Training-free
TF-MOPNAS (ours)	94.21 ± 0.24	72.89 ± 0.73	46.24 ± 0.42	427	Training-free
Optimal	94.37	73.51	47.31	-	in the benchmark

5   Conclusion

In this paper, we presented TF-MOPNAS, a framework for training-free pruning-based NAS methods in solving multi-objective NAS problems. Instead of conducting pruning on a single network and extracting the best network at each pruning till the end, we performed pruning on one (or many) networks at the same time and employed the definition of Pareto dominance to extract a set of non-dominated networks, which represents an approximation front in the objective space after the pruning process is finished. We verified the performance of TF-MOPNAS by experimenting on multi-objective NAS problems created on different NAS benchmarks, i.e., NAS-Bench-101, NAS-Bench-1shot1, and NAS-Bench-201. The experimental results showed that our method was not only effective but also efficient in obtaining networks that form high-quality trade-off fronts with negligible costs. Validating our proposed methods on larger and more complex NAS search spaces is left for future work.

Acknowledgements. This research was supported by The VNUHCM–University of Information Technology's Scientific Research Support Fund.

References

1. Abdelfattah, M.S., Mehrotra, A., Dudziak, L., Lane, N.D.: Zero-cost proxies for lightweight NAS. In: ICLR 2021 (2021)
2. Bergstra, J., Bengio, Y.: Random search for hyper-parameter optimization. J. Mach. Learn. Res. **13**, 281–305 (2012)
3. Bosman, P.A.N., Thierens, D.: The balance between proximity and diversity in multi-objective evolutionary algorithms. IEEE Trans. Evol. Comput. **7**(2), 174–188 (2003)
4. Chen, W., Gong, X., Wang, Z.: Neural architecture search on imagenet in four GPU hours: a theoretically inspired perspective. In: ICLR 2021 (2021)
5. Deb, K.: Multi-objective optimization using evolutionary algorithms. Wiley-Interscience series in systems and optimization, Wiley (2001)
6. Deb, K., Agrawal, S., Pratap, A., Meyarivan, T.: A fast and elitist multi-objective genetic algorithm: NSGA-II. IEEE Trans. Evol. Comput. **6**(2), 182–197 (2002)

7. Dong, X., Yang, Y.: NAS-Bench-201: extending the scope of reproducible neural architecture search. In: ICLR 2020 (2020)
8. Howard, A.G., et al.: MobileNets: efficient convolutional neural networks for mobile vision applications. CoRR abs/1704.04861 (2017)
9. Li, G., Qian, G., Delgadillo, I.C., Müller, M., Thabet, A.K., Ghanem, B.: SGAS: sequential greedy architecture search. In: CVPR 2020, pp. 1617–1627 (2020)
10. Liu, H., Simonyan, K., Yang, Y.: DARTS: differentiable architecture search. In: ICLR 2019 (2019)
11. Lu, Z., et al.: NSGA-Net: neural architecture search using multi-objective genetic algorithm. In: GECCO 2019, pp. 419–427 (2019)
12. Mellor, J., Turner, J., Storkey, A.J., Crowley, E.J.: Neural architecture search without training. In: ICML 2021, pp. 7588–7598 (2021)
13. Pham, H., Guan, M.Y., Zoph, B., Le, Q.V., Dean, J.: Efficient neural architecture search via parameter sharing. In: ICML 2018, pp. 4092–4101 (2018)
14. Phan, Q.M., Luong, N.H.: Efficiency enhancement of evolutionary neural architecture search via training-free initialization. In: NICS 2021, pp. 138–143 (2021)
15. Real, E., Aggarwal, A., Huang, Y., Le, Q.V.: Regularized evolution for image classifier architecture search. In: AAAI 2019, pp. 4780–4789 (2019)
16. Tanaka, H., Kunin, D., Yamins, D.L., Ganguli, S.: Pruning neural networks without any data by iteratively conserving synaptic flow. In: NeurIPS 2020 (2020)
17. Wang, R., Cheng, M., Chen, X., Tang, X., Hsieh, C.: Rethinking architecture selection in differentiable NAS. In: ICLR 2021 (2021)
18. Ying, C., Klein, A., Christiansen, E., Real, E., Murphy, K., Hutter, F.: NAS-Bench-101: towards reproducible neural architecture search. In: ICML 2019 (2019)
19. Yu, K., Sciuto, C., Jaggi, M., Musat, C., Salzmann, M.: Evaluating the search phase of neural architecture search. In: ICLR 2020 (2020)
20. Zela, A., Siems, J., Hutter, F.: NAS-Bench-1Shot1: benchmarking and dissecting one-shot neural architecture search. In: ICLR 2020 (2020)
21. Zoph, B., Le, Q.V.: Neural architecture search with reinforcement learning. In: ICLR 2017 (2017)

Efficient Pneumonia Detection Method and Implementation in Chest X-ray Images Based on a Neuromorphic Spiking Neural Network

Tomohide Fukuchi⬤, Mark Ikechukwu Ogbodo⬤, Jiangkun Wang⬤, Khanh N. Dang⬤, and Abderazek Ben Abdallah$^{(\boxtimes)}$⬤

Adaptive Systems Laboratory, Graduate School of Computer Science and Engineering, The University of Aizu, Aizu-Wakamatsu, Fukushima 965-8580, Japan
{d8222111,mogbodo,d8222108,khanh,benab}@u-aizu.ac.jp

Abstract. Deep Learning has solved numerous problems in image recognition and information processing, and is currently being employed in tackling the coronavirus disease (COVID-19) which has become a pandemic. Incisively, deep learning models are utilized in diagnosis systems as a method to detect COVID-19 related pneumonia by analyzing lung X-ray images of patients. The accuracy of this method is in the range of 80–90%. However, it is computationally complex, requires high power, and has low energy efficiency. Consequently, it is not suitable a diagnosis/detection method to be deployed on the edge. In this paper, we propose an efficient pneumonia (COVID-19) detection method and implementation in chest x-ray images based on a neuromorphic spiking neural network. This method is implemented on our previously proposed AI-enabled real-time biomedical system AIRBiS (AIR-BiS project: u-aizu.ac.jp/misc/benablab/airbis.html) which is based on a high-performance low-power re-configurable AI-chip for inference, and an interactive user interface for effective operation and monitoring. The evaluation results show that the proposed method achieves 92.1%, and 80.7% detection accuracy of pneumonia (i.e., COVID-19) over-collected test data.

Keywords: Pneumonia detection · Spiking neural network · Edge computing

1 Introduction

The increasing relevance of Artificial intelligence in biomedicine driven by Neural networks facilitates the understanding of human health and diseases using biological and physiological data. Particularly, the COVID 19 pandemic has raged on for years, with over 539 million cumulative confirmed cases recorded by the world health organization (WHO) as of June 2022 [22], is progressively

N. T. Nguyen et al. (Eds.): ICCCI 2022, LNAI 13501, pp. 311–321, 2022.
https://doi.org/10.1007/978-3-031-16014-1_25

being tackled using deep learning among other approaches. Deep learning is a computational paradigm that is inspired by the computational principles of the brain's neural network, and several deep learning models have been proposed for solutions such as mobile contact tracing [9], social distance monitoring [3], and COVID-19 diagnosis/detection [2] in order to tackle the pandemic. For diagnosis/detection specifically, deep learning models have been proposed to comprehensively analyze lung x-ray images and CT scans of patients, in order to detect the infected [16,29]. Accelerated edge-based solutions [13,19,32] are equally being considered to achieve real-time decentralized detection/diagnosis and monitoring and to address patient data privacy concerns. Howbeit, these proposed deep learning systems employ conventional artificial neural networks (ANNs) which despite their successes, require huge amounts of computing power and energy due to their computational complexity [25], and this makes them a less suitable deep learning approach for COVID-19 detection/diagnosis and monitoring on the edge. Alternatively, spiking neural network (SNN), which has been demonstrated to be more energy-efficient can be employed to achieve energy-efficient real-time COVID-19 detection/diagnosis on the edge. The proposed system builds an automatic pneumonia detection and diagnosis system to achieve low power consumption and high-speed computation. In the detection process, SNN is used on chest X-ray images to predict whether a chest is "normal" or "abnormal". If the prediction result shows "abnormal", the diagnosis process gives a detailed analysis of the disease in hospitals.

1.1   Background

At the turn of the year 2020, the coronavirus disease (COVID-19) became a global pandemic, triggering a remarkable global health response that is focused on curbing its transmission and mortality rate. Nevertheless, the virus continues to spread and has evolved through 11 variants which are characterized by Specific genetic markers that define their transmission, diagnostics, therapeutics, or immune escape. The brisk transmission and mortality that occurred in the wake of the pandemic, made immense demand on medical resources which most health systems around the world could not meet. The shortage and reliability issues associated with early testing kits needed for precise diagnosis, and the lack of coordinated systems needed for quick response prompted the need for efficient approaches to combat the pandemic.

The nose swab polymerase chain reaction (PCR) test with sensitivity within the range of 60% to 97% [4] has become a classic way of detecting COVID-19. The test analyzes upper respiratory specimens obtained from patients for genetic materials of the SARS-CoV-2 virus. However, due to the substantial disparity in the advancement of the disease among different patients, the sensitivity of the detection decreases to the range of 60%–71% [11], resulting in the occurrence of results that are false-negative. Alternative methods are being explored to improve detection/diagnostic accuracy. One notable method is to analyze and detect COVID-19 in computed tomography (CT), radiograph X-rays, ultrasound, echocardiograms or magnetic resonance imaging (MRI) of patients. In this method, doctors are required to manually examine patients one at a time, and afterward, consider their findings and the physical condition of patients to finalize a diagnosis. This method, however, proved to be ineffective as the number of patients exponentially increased. To address this limitation, several conventional ANN-based deep learning models that detect COVID-19 pneumonia from subtle imaging features have been developed, and applied on the edge. Nevertheless, the computational complexity of conventional ANNs and their high power consumption make them less suitable for edge applications. SNN on the other hand is less computationally complex as can be seen in Fig. 1 where event-driven data is encoded as spikes in binary, and only accumulate and threshold operations are required to process them, while conventional ANN data are real static values, and a multiply accumulate (MAC) operation together with an activation function is required to process them. SNN is the third generation of ANNs, and

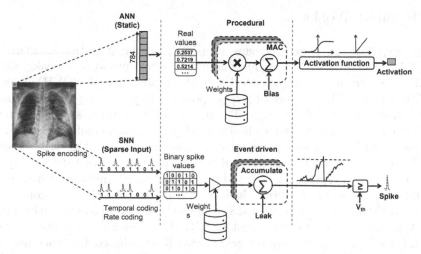

Fig. 1. Comparison of computational complexity between conventional ANN and SNN [15]

compared to conventional ANN, its computing principle is more analogous to the brain. Communication among neurons of an SNN is carried out in an event-driven manner using spikes. Operations of a simple integrate-and-fire (IF) spiking neuron model can be characterized by the accumulation of weighted input spikes at its membrane potential and the firing of an action potential which is triggered when the value of the membrane potential crosses a certain threshold. Given a sparse input spike train, the power consumption of SNN is significantly reduced when compared to ANN and when implemented in hardware (Neuromorphic) can exploit the parallelism and speed that hardware provides for rapid, low power [21] detection/diagnosis of COVID-19 on edge.

We previously proposed AIRBIS [29], an edge-based cyber-physical platform for pneumonia (i.e., COVID-19) detection and health monitoring. The platform is composed of a high-performance, re-configurable inference AI-chip based on conventional ANN, a robust collaborative-learning mechanism for privacy-preserving, and an interactive user interface for effective operation and monitoring. Although AIRBIS achieved impressive performance results with a COVID-19 detection accuracy of over 94%, we discovered that it is not suitable to be deployed for edge-based detection and monitoring due to the computational complexity and high power consumption of the conventional ANN on which it is based. To address this issue, we propose an efficient method of pneumonia detection in chest X-ray images based on SNN, towards energy-efficient neuromorphic COVID-19 detection on edge. We also present the design and evaluation of the system. The rest of this paper is organized as follows. Section 3 describes the architecture of the proposed system. In Sect. 4, we present a comprehensive evaluation of the proposed system, and discuss the results. Finally, in Sect. 5, we conclude the paper and present future works.

2   Related Works

Some deep learning based systems proposed for the detection/diagnosis of COVID-19 include the work in [30], where the authors proposed a weakly supervised deep learning framework to detect the probability of COVID-19 using 3D CT volumes. The authors in [17] proposed a deep learning-based prognosis model based on initial CT images. The model achieved impressive performance on the four-center dataset, which indicated that a CT scan combined with an AI method could be used as a powerful prognosis tool to alert high-risk patients. A CT-based COVID-19 diagnosis and monitoring framework called Compute-COVID19+ was proposed in [14], and was implemented and accelerated across several heterogeneous platforms, including multi-core CPU, many-core GPU, and even FPGA. The authors in [28] proposed a novel multi-task prior attention learning strategy to implement COVID-19 screening in volumetric chest CT images. Specifically, they integrated two ResNet-based branches into one model framework for end-to-end training by designing a prior-attention residual learning (PARL) block. The work in [1] proposed an effective software-hardware design framework for the development of CNN systems in hardware. A previous research [20] introduced the dataset collection and preprocessing, and evaluated several convolutional neural networks on diagnosis accuracy. [5] provided Generative Adversarial Network based synthetic data and four deep learning models for COVID-19 detection. They evaluated the performance of Chest Radiographs and the diagnosis of chest diseases including COVID-19. [27] proposed a method to generate synthetic chest X-ray (CXR) images in Auxiliary Classifier Generative Adversarial Network (ACGAN) based model. They achieved 85% accuracy for the classification using the back propagation learning algorithm. [10] proposed a convolutional neural network which is named COVID-Screen-Net for COVID-19 detection. They achieved an average accuracy of 97.71%. [26] proposed the EDL-COVID model, which is employing deep learning and ensemble learning. They achieved COVID-19 detection with an accuracy of 95%.

These works have in all, shown impressive results. Nevertheless, they are based on conventional ANN which makes them more computationally complex,

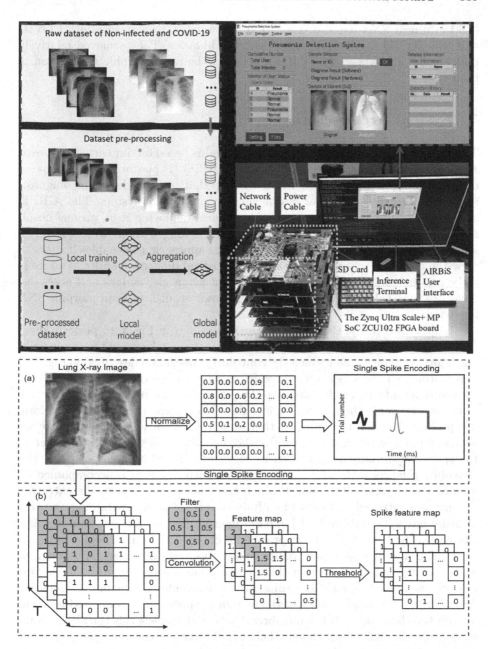

Fig. 2. High level view of the proposed pneumonia detection method in chest X-ray images based on a neuromorphic spiking neural network (AIRBIS) [29]

and less energy efficient compared to SNN, limiting their deployment for COVID-19 detection/diagnosis on edge. For SNN-based COVID-19 detection, very few works have been published. To the best of our knowledge, only the authors in

[12] performed SNN-based classification of chest CT scan images into COVID and non-COVID using various deep learning libraries. They achieved relatively high accuracy, however, they did not consider the neuromorphic application in their design.

3   System Architecture

The proposed system is described in Fig. 2, and is based on our earlier proposed AI-Enabled Realtime Biomedical System (AIRBiS) [1] platform, which is based on ANN, and provides a configurable AI chip that handles detection/diagnosis along with an interactive user interface and management system. The AIRBiS system target implementation approach requires deploying it at various hospitals/local areas, allowing patients to upload their lung x-ray images in a digital format to get the result of their diagnosis. This approach also enables doctors to view the diagnosis procedure and for the statistical diagnosis results of all users to be collated and reported to the government for proper actions and necessary measures to be taken. The proposed system however, utilizes neuromorphic SNN for diagnosis.

As described in the simulation scheme presented in Fig. 3, to perform diagnosis, the chest X-ray images are first encoded into a spike using the single spike encoding mechanism, after which the convolution operation described in Fig. 2(a) is performed on the single spike encoded tensor. Unlike the conventional ANN convolution that extracts feature maps by performing dot product as convolution filters stride over a chest X-ray image, the SNN convolution does not perform dot product. Instead, filter weights that match X-ray image pixel with spike are accumulated and taken through a threshold similar to [18] in order to generate the spike feature map as described in Fig. 2(b). The SNN model contains two convolution layers with a filter size of 3×3, each of which is accompanied by max-pooling layers. After going through the convolutions layers, the extracted features are flattened and fed to two fully connected layers containing an array of leaky-integrate-and-fire (LIF) spiking neuron models that perform the classification. The first step of spike processing on the LIF neuron begins with the accumulation of weighted presynaptic spikes received from presynaptic neurons as its membrane potential. After the accumulation is complete, a leak operation is performed which reduces the value of the accumulated membrane potential. Afterward, the remaining value of the membrane potential is compared with the neuron threshold value. If the membrane potential exceeds this threshold value, an output spike is fired, and none otherwise. If there is an output spike, the value of the membrane potential is reset to zero, and the neuron enters a refractory state that lasts a few time steps. While in the refractory period, the neuron cannot accumulate synaptic weights. The accumulation of weighted presynaptic spikes can be described as follows:

$$V_j^l(t) = V_j^l(t-1) + \sum_i w_{ij}^* x_i^{l-1}(t-1) - \lambda \qquad (1)$$

where V_j^l is the membrane potential of a LIF neuron j in layer l at a time-step t. w_{ij} is the synaptic weight from neuron i to j, λ is the leak and x_i^{l-1} is presynaptic spike from previous layer $l-1$. When the integration of input spikes is completed, the value of V_j^l at a time-step, is compared with the threshold value θ. If it exceeds, a spike is released and the neuron resets. This is mathematically expressed as:

$$\begin{cases} 1, \text{if } V_j^l > \theta \\ 0, \text{otherwise} \end{cases} \tag{2}$$

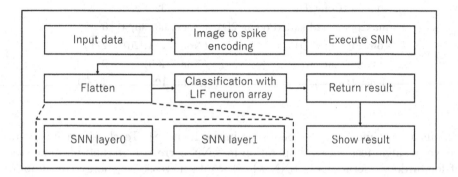

Fig. 3. Overview of the proposed neuromorphic SNN simulation scheme.

4   Evaluation Results

The proposed system was simulated on Spyketorch and Nengo [6] based on SNN simulation frameworks, using CNN. In spyketorch, the unsupervised spike timing dependent plasticity (STDP) learning algorithm is used for training, while the supervised backpropagation learning algorithm was used in Nengo. To evaluate the system in terms of accuracy and average classification time, we use a chest X-ray image dataset [7,23] from *Kaggle*, which is described in Table 1. The data set contains a total of 32,640 training images of which 50.25% is COVID positive, and a total of 1400 testing images which is 50% COVID positive. A comparison of the evaluation result with some existing work is also presented.

Table 2 describes the SNN structure of the proposed method which contains a total of 43,450 trainable parameters. The preliminary evaluation result shows that the proposed method achieves an accuracy of 92.1%, and 80.7% and a significantly low average classification time of 7.34×10^{-4} s and 2.14×10^{-6} s per lung X-ray image in Nengo [6] and Spyketorch [18] respectively, thanks to the binary spike representation, low complexity, and event-driven processing of SNN. The higher accuracy achieved by Nengo was due to the supervised learning algorithm. Another significant factor that contributed to achieving the low

Table 1. Attributes of chest x-ray images.

Label	Train dataset	Test dataset
COVID	16509	700
Non_COVID	16141	700
Sum	32,650	1400

Table 2. Structure of the proposed neuromorphic SNN with 64 × 64 Grayscale X-ray Images.

Layer	Output Shape	Param
conv2d (Conv2D)	(None, 62, 62, 4)	735
max_pooling2d (MaxPooling2D)	(None, 30, 30, 4)	0
conv2d (Conv2D)	(None, 1, 1, 20)	2715
flatten (Flatten)	(None, 400)	0
dense (Dense)	(None, 100)	40000

classification time is single spike encoding scheme [8]. To classify a lung x-ray image, a single feed-forward operation in ANN correlates to multiple time steps of forwarding operations in SNN which would increase its energy consumption and probably make it have the same average classification time or more compared to ANN. However, the single spike encoding scheme uses a direct encoding in its initial timestep where the single spike generated for each pixel is inversely proportional to the intensity of the pixel. This helps the SNN realize low classification time, while the temporal aspect of the single spike encoding increases spike sparsity. We also evaluated the sensitivity, specificity, and precision of the proposed method and achieved 85.3%, 99.8%, and 98.3%, respectively. Analyzing the proposed method further, we reached an F1 score of 91.3%. The sensitivity of the test ranges from 80%–90% due to differences in the disease of the different patient datasets.

4.1 Comparison with Existing Works

A comparison of the evaluation result of the proposed method and existing works is presented in Table 3. The work in [10] achieved the highest accuracy of 97.71%, however; the authors in this work trained a large model, and used the smallest evaluation dataset when compared to other works, which could lead to the problem of overfitting when evaluated with a generalized dataset, and high computation complexity. Its average classification time per image is next to the highest among the compared works at 1.75 s. The work in [26] achieved the second highest accuracy at 95%. Nevertheless, at 3.16 s per image, it has the highest average classification time when compared to other works. Compared to [12,31,33], the proposed method achieved a higher accuracy at 92.1% on

Nengo, and 80.7% on SpykeTorch. Similarly, when compared to other existing works, the proposed method achieved the smallest average classification time per image at 7.34×10^{-4} s and 2.14×10^{-6} s on Nengo and Spyketorch respectively. This is because SNN is less computationally complex than ANN, and requires fewer operations.

Table 3. Comparison with the Existing studies for the time cost

Works	Model	Dataset	Average classification time (s)	Data size	Platform	Accuracy (%)
Dhaka et al. [10]	ANN	X-ray images	< 1.75 s	570	Tesla K80	97.71
Tang et al. [26]	ANN	X-ray images	< 3.16 s	1579	Tesla P100	95
Zhang et al. [33]	ANN	X-ray images	-	-	-	78.52, 80.65
Wang et al. [31]	ANN	X-ray images	-	-	-	66.4
Garain et al. [12]	SNN	CT scan images	-	349	-	60
Proposed Work	SNN	X-ray images	7.34×10^{-4}, 2.14×10^{-6}	1400	x86-64 CPU	92.1, 80.7

5 Conclusion

In this paper, we proposed an efficient pneumonia (COVID-19) detection method and implementation in Chest X-ray images based on a neuromorphic spiking neural network. The proposed system leverages the information encoding and less complex event-driven spike processing in SNN to provide rapid energy-efficient COVID-19 diagnosis on the edge. The preliminary evaluation result presented that the proposed system achieved an accuracy of 92.1%, and 80.7% in Nengo and Spyketorch respectively. and the average classification time of 7.34×10^{-4} s and 2.14×10^{-6} s of the average classification time in Nengo and Spyketorch respectively. Although the energy merit cannot be clearly seen in this preliminary, evaluation because of the simulating software environment, the reduced complexity of spiking neuron operations has been shown to achieve significantly low power consumption compared to conventional artificial neurons [24]. In addition, the use of single spike encoding means that only at most a single spike will be fired by each neuron, which enables fast detection. In the future, we will develop our power-efficient and high-performance pneumonia detection neuromorphic system on hardware.

References

1. Abdallah, A.B., Huang, H., Dang, N.K., Song, J.: AI Processor: Japanese Patent Application Laid-Open No. 2020–194733 (2020)
2. Abdulkareem, M., Petersen, S.E.: The promise of AI in detection, diagnosis, and epidemiology for combating COVID-19: beyond the hype. Front. Artif. Intell. **14**(4), 652669 (2021). https://doi.org/10.3389/frai.2021.652669, www.frontiersin.org/article/10.3389/frai.2021.652669

3. Ahmed, I., Ahmad, M., Rodrigues, J.J., Jeon, G., Din, S.: A deep learning-based social distance monitoring framework for COVID-19. In: Sustainable Cities and Society, vol. 65, p. 102571 (2021)
4. Ai, T., et al.: Correlation of chest CT and RT-PCR testing for coronavirus disease 2019 (COVID-19) in china: a report of 1014 cases. Radiology **296**(2), 32–40 (2020)
5. Albahli, S.: Efficient GAN-based chest radiographs (CXR) augmentation to diagnose coronavirus disease pneumonia. Int. J. Med. Sci. **17**(10), 1439 (2020)
6. Bekolay, T., et al.: Nengo: a python tool for building large-scale functional brain models. Front. Neuroinform. **7**, 48 (2014)
7. Chowdhury, M.E.H., et al.: Can AI help in screening viral and COVID-19 pneumonia? IEEE Access **8**, 132665–132676 (2020). https://doi.org/10.1109/ACCESS. 2020.3010287
8. Datta, G., Kundu, S., Beerel, P.A.: Training energy-efficient deep spiking neural networks with single-spike hybrid input encoding. Computing Research Repository. CORR abs/2107.12374 (2021)
9. Dave, R., Gupta, R.: Data quality and network considerations for mobile contact tracing and health monitoring. Front. Digit. Health **3** (2021). https://doi.org/10. 3389/fdgth.2021.590194
10. Dhaka, V.S., Rani, G., Oza, M.G., Sharma, T., Misra, A.: A deep learning model for mass screening of COVID-19. Int. J. Imaging Syst. Technol. **31**(2), 483–498 (2021)
11. Fang, Y., et al.: Sensitivity of chest CT for COVID-19: comparison to RT-PCR. Radiology **296**(2), E115–E117 (2020)
12. Garain, A., Basu, A., Giampaolo, F., Velasquez, J.D., Sarkar, R.: Detection of COVID-19 from CT scan images: a spiking neural network-based approach. Neural Comput. Appl. **33**(19), 12591–12604 (2021). https://doi.org/10.1007/s00521-021-05910-1
13. Ghani, A., Aina, A., See, C.H., Yu, H., Keates, S.: Accelerated diagnosis of novel coronavirus (COVID-19)—computer vision with convolutional neural networks (CNNs). Electronics **11**(7), 1148 (2022). https://doi.org/10.3390/electronics11071148
14. Goel, G., Gondhalekar, A., Qi, J., Zhang, Z., Cao, G., Feng, W.: Computecovid19+: accelerating Covid-19 diagnosis and monitoring via high-performance deep learning on CT images. In: 50th International Conference on Parallel Processing, pp. 1–11 (2021)
15. Ikechukwu, O.M.: On the design of adaptive digital neuromorphic system, Ph. D. thesis, University of Aizu (2022)
16. Maghded, H.S., Ghafoor, K.Z., Sadiq, A.S., Curran, K., Rawat, D.B., Rabie, K.: A novel AI-enabled framework to diagnose coronavirus Covid-19 using smartphone embedded sensors: design study. In: 2020 IEEE 21st International Conference on Information Reuse and Integration for Data Science (IRI), pp. 180–187 (2020). https://doi.org/10.1109/IRI49571.2020.00033
17. Meng, L., et al.: A deep learning prognosis model help alert for Covid-19 patients at high-risk of death: a multi-center study. IEEE J. Biomed. Health Inform. **24**(12), 3576–3584 (2020). https://doi.org/10.1109/JBHI.2020.3034296
18. Mozafari, M., Ganjtabesh, M., Nowzari-Dalini, A., Masquelier, T.: SpykeTorch: efficient simulation of convolutional spiking neural networks with at most one spike per neuron. Front. Neurosci. **13**, 625 (2019)

19. Muhammad, G., Hossain, M.S.: A deep-learning-based edge-centric COVID-19-like pandemic screening and diagnosis system within a B5G framework using blockchain. IEEE Netw. **35**(2), 74–81 (2021). https://doi.org/10.1109/MNET.011.2000326

20. Nakamura, M., Wang, J., Phea, S., Abdallah, A.B.: Comprehensive study of coronavirus disease 2019 (COVID-19) classification based on deep convolution neural networks. In: SHS Web of Conferences, vol. 102, p. 04007. EDP Sciences (2021)

21. Ogbodo, M., Vu, T., Dang, K., Abdallah, A.: Light-weight spiking neuron processing core for large-scale 3D-NoC based spiking neural network processing systems. In: 2020 IEEE International Conference on Big Data and Smart Computing (BigComp), pp. 133–139. Institute of Electrical and Electronics Engineers (IEEE) (2020). https://doi.org/10.1109/BigComp48618.2020.00-86

22. WHO: Who coronavirus (COVID-19) dashboard – who coronavirus (COVID-19) dashboard with vaccination data. https://covid19.who.int/ (2022). Accessed on 05 Jun 2022

23. Rahman, T., et al.: Exploring the effect of image enhancement techniques on COVID-19 detection using chest X-ray images. Comput. Biol. Med. **132**, 104319 (2021)

24. Sorbaro, M., Liu, Q., Bortone, M., Sheik, S.: Optimizing the energy consumption of spiking neural networks for neuromorphic applications. Front. Neurosci. **14** (2020). https://doi.org/10.3389/fnins.2020.00662,

25. Strubell, E., Ganesh, A., McCallum, A.: Energy and policy considerations for deep learning in NLP. Computing Research Repository abs/1906.02243 (2019). https://arxiv.org/abs/1906.02243

26. Tang, S., et al.: EDL-COVID: ensemble deep learning for COVID-19 case detection from chest x-ray images. IEEE Trans. Industr. Inf. **17**(9), 6539–6549 (2021)

27. Waheed, A., Goyal, M., Gupta, D., Khanna, A., Al-Turjman, F., Pinheiro, P.R.: COVIDGAN: data augmentation using auxiliary classifier GAN for improved COVID-19 detection. IEEE Access **8**, 91916–91923 (2020)

28. Wang, J., et al.: Prior-attention residual learning for more discriminative COVID-19 screening in CT images. IEEE Trans. Med. Imaging **39**(8), 2572–2583 (2020). https://doi.org/10.1109/TMI.2020.2994908

29. Wang, J., Nakamura, M., Abdallah, A.B.: Efficient AI-enabled pneumonia detection in chest X-ray images. In: 2022 IEEE 4th Global Conference on Life Sciences and Technologies (LifeTech), pp. 470–474 (2022). https://doi.org/10.1109/LifeTech53646.2022.9754850

30. Wang, X., et al.: A weakly-supervised framework for COVID-19 classification and lesion localization from chest CT. IEEE Trans. Med. Imaging **39**(8), 2615–2625 (2020). https://doi.org/10.1109/TMI.2020.2995965

31. Wang, X., Peng, Y., Lu, L., Lu, Z., Bagheri, M., Summers, R.M.: ChestX-ray8: hospital-scale chest X-ray database and benchmarks on weakly-supervised classification and localization of common thorax diseases. In: 2017 IEEE Conference on Computer Vision and Pattern Recognition (CVPR), pp. 3462–3471 (2017). https://doi.org/10.1109/CVPR.2017.369

32. Yuuki, O., Wang, J., Ikechukwu, O.M., Abdallah, A.B.: Hardware acceleration of convolution neural network for AI-enabled realtime biomedical system. In: Roy, D., Fragulis, G., Campos, H.C. (eds.) The 4th ETLTC International Conference on Information and Communications Technology, vol. 102, p. 04019. EDP Sciences (2021). https://doi.org/10.1051/shsconf/202110204019,

33. Zhang, J., et al.: Viral pneumonia screening on chest X-rays using confidence-aware anomaly detection. IEEE Trans. Med. Imaging **40**(3), 879–890 (2020)

Oversampling for Mining Imbalanced Datasets: Taxonomy and Performance Evaluation

Piotr Jedrzejowicz[✉] [ID]

Gdynia Maritime University, Gdynia, Poland
p.jedrzejowicz@umg.edu.pl

Abstract. The paper focuses on methods and algorithms for oversampling two-classes imbalanced datasets. We propose a taxonomy for oversampling approaches and review state-of-the-art algorithms. The paper discusses also some strengths and weaknesses of the oversampling methods. A computational experiment aims at comparing the performance of several oversampling algorithms. Conclusions discuss possible directions for future developments in the field of balancing imbalanced datasets to achieve better performance when mining them.

Keywords: Imbalanced datasets · Data mining · Oversampling algorithms

1 Introduction

Mining imbalanced datasets remains a hot research topic. This can be attributed to several factors of which two are of the utmost importance. The first is the commonality of imbalanced datasets in real life. In the fields like medical diagnosis, fraud detection, fault diagnosis, intrusion detection, drift detection and many others where there are a lot of data on standard events and abnormal data is rare, decision-makers have to deal with imbalanced data on daily basis. To cope with the task, machine learning methods and tools supporting imbalanced data mining are required. Unfortunately, when traditional machine learning algorithms are used to mine imbalanced data the results tend to be more in favor of the majority class examples underestimating the importance of the minority class cases. Such limitation of traditional approaches stands, as the second important factor, behind the ongoing quest for machine learning methods able to deal effectively with imbalanced data.

Among methods used to cope with data imbalance oversampling and undersampling belong to the most often used. Both oversampling and undersampling involve changes in the data distribution by selecting more examples from one class than from another, to compensate for an imbalance. Over recent years numerous algorithms performing the oversampling and undersampling tasks have been proposed in the machine learning literature. Both approaches belong to the data-level methods (see (Krawczyk 2016; Guo et al. 2017), and both can be applied either as stand-alone methods or in a combined manner to produce balanced data.

N. T. Nguyen et al. (Eds.): ICCCI 2022, LNAI 13501, pp. 322–333, 2022.
https://doi.org/10.1007/978-3-031-16014-1_26

The paper focuses on oversampling methods for the two-classes classification problems involving imbalanced datasets. The goals of the paper include: proposing a taxonomy of the oversampling methods and algorithms, reviewing current approaches to oversampling task and commenting on their strengths and weaknesses, and, finally, evaluating their performance.

The paper was motivated, on one hand, by the continuing interest among the machine learning researchers in the imbalanced classification, and, on the other hand, by the lack in the literature of a coherent taxonomy for various approaches to oversampling techniques.

The rest of the paper is organized as follows: Sect. 2 contains a proposal for categorization of the oversampling methods and a review of best known and current solutions. Section 3 presents comments on the weaknesses and strengths of the oversampling methods, followed by results of the computational experiment, where the performance of different oversampling methods is compared. Conclusions contain ideas for future developments in constructing oversampling methods.

2 Taxonomy of the Oversampling Methods

Oversampling methods that increase the number of the minority class instances by producing synthetic examples are amongst the most popular techniques for dealing with class imbalance. In recent years numerous methods and algorithms performing oversampling tasks have been developed and published. In Fig. 1 categories of these approaches from the higher and lower levels perspectives are shown. Among the higher-level categories of the oversampling methods, we have identified three: approaches using minority class instances only, approaches using both – minority and majority classes instances, and hybrid techniques. The latter include techniques integrating oversampling with undersampling, and techniques integrating oversampling with the algorithm level solutions. Among the lower level categories we have identified neighborhood-based mathods, density and probability based methods, fuzzy and rough sets based approaches, and structure and feature based methods. In this paper, we do not cover approaches known as ensemble classifiers where construction of the so-called base classifiers may involve using oversampling methods.

2.1 Neighborhood-Based Oversampling

Among the most popular approaches to oversampling are SMOTE and its derivatives. In the Synthetic Minority Oversampling Technique (SMOTE) proposed in Chawla et al. (2002), the minority class is oversampled by introducing synthetic instances selected randomly and iteratively along the line segments joining some of the k minority class nearest neighbors until the balance between classes is achieved. SMOTE implicitly assumes that such locations are indeed suitable for the oversampling. This is not always the case, and generated locations can overlap with areas where the density of the majority class instances is high. This, in turn, may cause serious classification mistakes. In SMOTE only minority class instances are used, and the approach belongs to the neighborhood category. The main advantage of SMOTE is its simplicity and ease of use.

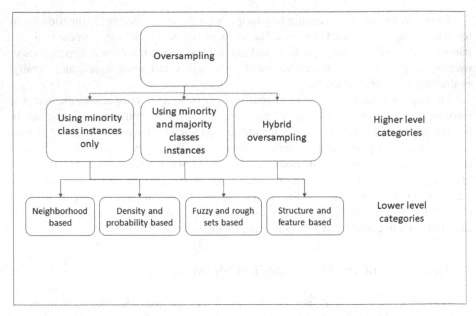

Fig. 1. Main categories of the oversampling methods and algorithms.

Among well-known derivatives of SMOTE one should mention Borderline-SMOTE (B-SMOTE), SL SMOTE, ASN SMOTE, and FW-SMOTE.

B-SMOTE proposed in Han et al. (2005) starts with dividing all minority class examples into three non-overlapping groups named safety, danger, and noise. Further steps involve only the danger group. Examples within this group serve as seeds for producing synthetic examples using the SMOTE algorithm. As expected, the resulting synthetic examples are, in a majority of cases, located in the vicinity of the borderline dividing the whole dataset into two classes. New instances are generated using only the borderline minority-class instances. Classes. The second variant of the Borderline SMOTE – B-SMOTE2 differs by producing synthetic instances by extending the neighborhood by closely located majority-class instances.

In Bunkhumpornpat et al. (2009) the Safe-Level-SMOTE (SL-SMOTE) algorithm, which closely resembles the Borderline SMOTE algorithm was proposed. In SL-SMOTE, each minority-class instance is assigned a safe level coefficient by checking the number of minority-class instances in its K nearest neighbors. Then according to the user-selected safe level coefficient, the algorithm is expected to filter noisy instances and generate the synthetic minority-class instances which are closer to the safe level location belonging to the minority class.

ASN-SMOTE (Yi et al. 2022), first filters noise in the minority class by determining whether the nearest neighbor of each minority instance belongs to the minority or majority class. After that, ASN-SMOTE uses the nearest majority instance of each minority instance to effectively perceive the decision boundary, inside which the qualified minority instances are selected adaptively for each minority instance by the proposed adaptive neighbor selection scheme to synthesize new minority instance. The key advantage of

ASN-SMOTE is that it performs the novel noise filtering and adaptive neighbor selection mechanisms before synthesizing minority instances. The former filters any minority instance whose nearest neighbor is a majority instance, and the latter only selects minority neighbors that are closer than the nearest majority instance for synthetic oversampling.

FW-SMOTE uses the weighted Minkowski distance for defining the neighborhood of each instance from the minority class. The authors Maldonado et al. (2022) claim that the approach assures a better definition of the neighborhood since it prioritizes those features that are more relevant for the classification task. As an additional advantage, the approach enables feature selection reducing the computation time. Reduction is based on discarding features with weights below some user-defined threshold.

ADASYN (ADAptive SYNthetic sampling) proposed in He et al. (2008) works by finding k-Nearest Neighbors of each minority example. It is assumed that neighborhoods containing more majority class examples are more difficult to learn. Hence, for neighborhoods dominated by majority class examples, more synthetic minority class examples will be generated. This feature gives the ADASYN ability to adapt using more synthetic data generated for difficult-to-learn neighborhoods. Within a neighborhood, examples are generated like in the SMOTE. The approach may suffer due to the necessity of increasing neighborhood size in case a neighborhood contains only one minority class example.

Clustering-based oversampling can be seen as a subcategory of neighborhood-based strategies. In MW- MOTE (Barus et al. 2014), the authors identify the boundary and interior of minority samples followed by clustering of the minority instances. Minority instances from the cluster are employed in adding the synthetic points.

The approach proposed in Nekooeimehr et al. (2015) is based on clustering the minority instances with the semi-unsupervised hierarchical clustering method. Next, using classification complexity and cross-validation the size of the oversample for each sub-cluster is determined. Then, the minority instances are oversampled depending on their Euclidean distance to the majority class. Adaptive semi-unsupervised weighted oversampling (A-SUWO) aims to identify hard-to-learn instances by considering minority instances from each sub-cluster that are closer to the borderline. It is expected to avoid generating synthetic minority instances that overlap with the majority class by considering the majority class in the clustering and oversampling stages.

Local distribution-based adaptive minority oversampling (LAMO) (Wang et al. 2021) works in two steps. In the first step so-called borderline instances are chosen from the minority class as seeds for generating synthetic instances. In the second step synthetic instances are generated using linear interpolation, similar to SMOTE and ADASYN. Two parameters $k1$ and $k2$ are used in the first step which starts with extracting those instances from the majority class which are in $k1$ neighborhoods of minority instances. Then those minority instances which are $k2$ neighbors of the extracted data are candidates for the borderline ones. Finally, some minority instances which might be noisy or redundant are removed from the borderline candidates.

2.2 Density and Probability-Based Oversampling

Density-based methods, opposite to neighborhood-based ones, concentrate on identifying regions of given density for the minority class. Density-based approaches focus only on density from the minority class, thus practically ignoring the role of the majority class and suffering from similar limitations as neighborhood-based approaches when facing difficult data distributions. Examples of the density-based approaches to oversampling include probability density function estimation (Gao et al. 2012), density-based SMOTE (DBSMOTE) (Bunkhumpornpat et al. 2012), and Gaussian-SMOTE (Pan et al. 2020).

Some limitations of the above approaches are alleviated in the SWIM algorithm (Sharma et al. 2018). Oversampling with the Majority (SWIM) is based on two intuitive findings. The first tells that synthetic minority instances should be generated in regions of the data space that have similar densities concerning the majority class as the real minority instances. The second tells that synthetic instances should be located in regions neighboring the real minority instances. SWIM uses a Mahalanobis distance (MD). The MD of each given minority class instance corresponds with a hyperelliptic density contour around the majority class. Synthetic minority class instances are generated along these contours. This, according to the authors, helps to overcome two well-known limitations of SMOTE-based methods which are generating synthetic samples outside of the convex hull formed by the minority class instances, and preventing them from being generated in higher probability areas of the majority class.

K-Nearest Neighbor Oversampling approach (KNNOR) proposed in (Islam et al. 2022) performs a three-step process to identify the critical and safe areas for augmentation and generate synthetic data points of the minority class. The relative density of the entire population is considered while generating artificial points. This enables the proposed KNNOR approach to oversample the minority class more reliably and at the same time stay resilient against noise.

Most oversampling techniques do not guarantee that the synthetic minority example indeed belongs to the minority class. In (Sadhukhan, Palit 2020) Adaptive Learning of Minority Class before Minority Oversampling (ALMCMO), is expected to alleviate this deficiency by estimating the minority set before oversampling the synthetic points. The idea is to estimate a varying and adaptive volume of minority space around the minority points. Minority points are then sampled from the estimated minority spaces to assure class membership of synthetic majority points. The novelty of the approach work lies with the method of estimating the minority set. ALMCMO tries to adaptively estimate the minority class by allowing a varying volume of estimated minority spaces around different minority instances. The relative distribution and densities of minority instances are taken into account while selecting the varying radii and volumes. This concept is an addition to what was proposed in the earlier version of the algorithm named LMCMO which was based on a constant estimated volume across all minority examples. The authors proposed also a simple and effective Relative Neighborhood Graph to get the neighborhood relations and configuration of the synthetic examples.

(Das et al. 2014) developed two probability-based oversampling methods, called RACOG and wRACOG, respectively. They all utilize the minority class to obtain the joint probability distribution of all attributes and then adopt the Markov chain-based Gibbs sampling algorithm to create new samples. However, RACOG is distinct from wRACOG in the selection method for new samples. That is, the former utilizes the predefined *lag-markers* to select new samples, while the latter uses the predicted probabilities of the existing classification models for choosing.

One of the disadvantages of SMOTE and similar algorithms is the potential risk of sample overlapping, noise introduction, and random neighbor selection. To address these problems (Jiang et al. 2021) presented a new oversampling method, OS-CCD, based on a concept of the classification contribution degree introduced by the authors. The classification contribution degree determines the number of synthetic samples generated by SMOTE for each positive sample. OS-CCD replicates the spatial distribution characteristics of original samples on the class boundary, as well as uses a simple mechanism for avoiding oversampling from noisy points.

2.3 Fuzzy and Rough Sets-Based Oversampling

Methods based on fuzzy and rough sets are well suited to deal with noisy data. Rough–granular computing approach (RGA) to oversampling was proposed in Borowska, Stepaniuk (2019). In their approach, synthetic instances are generated only in specific regions of the feature space found by the formation of information granules and an analysis of their degrees of inclusion in the minority class. The approach is expected to reduce the number of misclassified minority class instances.

In Chen et al. (2019) the authors proposed a method for feature selection for imbalanced datasets using the neighborhood rough set theory. The approach assumes that the imbalanced distribution of classes allows for identifying the significance of features. According to the authors, the neighborhood rough sets model can handle noisy data but cannot describe the fuzziness of the samples. A discernibility-matrix-based feature selection method is next proposed and used in the feature selection algorithm (RSF-SAID). Finally, a particle swarm optimization algorithm is suggested to optimize the parameters of the algorithm.

FCM-EBRB system based on fuzzy C-means clustering (FCM-EBRB) was proposed in Fu (2021). It adopts FCM clustering to oversample the positive samples and undersample the negative ones, to achieve a balance between them. Next, the construction method of the Extended Belief Rule-Based (EBRB) system is used to optimize the system through an efficient parameter learning strategy.

Deep Learning-Based Imbalanced Classification With Fuzzy Support Vector Machine (DFSVM) was proposed in Wang et al. (2022). DFSVM first uses a deep neural network to obtain an embedding representation of the data. This deep neural network is trained by using triplet loss to enhance similarities within classes and differences between classes. To alleviate the effects of imbalanced data distribution, oversampling is performed in the embedding space of the data. The oversampling is based on a random generation of features. This method can increase the diversity of the minority class samples and avoid overfitting. However, the method generates some outliers and noise, so a constraint-based on class center distance is used to filter the synthetic samples.

2.4 Structure and Feature-based Oversampling

Recently, several researchers have proposed kernel functions base oversampling method (see, for example, (Tang 2015; Perez-Ortiz et al. 2016; Mathew et al. 2018). The kernel-based approach requires a high-dimensional mapping into an artificial feature space leading to a better separation between classes. This makes oversampling easier and reduces the risk of producing synthetic examples that would add to increasing class overlapping. Kernel-based methods increase the dimensionality of the artificial feature space, which may, unfortunately, limit the access to minority class instances. Additionally, kernel-based approaches do not take into account individual difficulty of instances, thus allowing for outliers or noisy instances to strongly influence the mapping process.

The idea is to produce synthetic minority class instances in feature space to avoid generating minority samples falling into the majority class regions was proposed in Liang et al. (2018). The authors introduce a multi-linear feature space (MLFS) based on a quasi-linear kernel, which is constructed from a pre-trained neural network (NN). By using the quasi-linear kernel, the proposed MLFS oversampling method avoids computing directly the Euclidean distances among the samples when oversampling the minority class and mapping the samples to high-dimensional feature space. The feature makes it easier to mine high-dimensional datasets.

Another promising approach is using the concept of radial basis functions. Koziarski, et al. (2019), proposed the Radial-Based Oversampling (RBO) method, which can find regions in which the synthetic objects from the minority class should be generated based on the imbalance distribution estimation with radial basis functions. According to the authors, the idea is to use a real-valued potential surface, with potential at each point in space representing preferences towards that point belonging to either minority or majority class. To calculate that potential, a Gaussian radial basis function (RBF) is assigned to every example object in the training dataset, with the polarity dependent on its class. Based on a potential surface, various strategies of imbalanced data resampling can be designed. In their paper, the authors propose an oversampling algorithm that creates artificial objects as a product of an iterative optimization algorithm where the goal function is the absolute value of the potential. The result is placing the synthetic minority objects in regions of high uncertainty, close to the predicted decision border.

The approach proposed in Koziarski (2021) utilizes radial basis functions to preserve the original shape of the underlying class distributions during the resampling process. This is done by optimizing the positions of generated synthetic observations for the proposed potential resemblance loss. The final Potential Anchoring Algorithm combines over- and under-sampling within the proposed framework.

Oversampling tasks can be also performed using an incremental learning paradigm. In Ye (2020) the framework consisting of three stages: data mapping, oversampling, and classification was proposed. The testing data are merged with training to find a new dimensional space by Laplacian eigenmaps. Then, the training data in the new dimensional space are used to generate incrementally new points of minority class and used for classification model training.

In Jedrzejowicz and Jedrzejowicz (2021a) an incremental Gene Expression Programming based classifier (i-GEP) with reuse of the minority class instances was proposed. Another idea of the same authors is an approach named c-GEP integrating three techniques − oversampling, cellular Gene Expression Programming, and dynamic selection of classifiers (Jedrzejowicz 2021b). The oversampling algorithm is based on the Local Distribution-Based Adaptive Minority Oversampling technique. Cellular GEP is an extension of cellular genetic algorithms. In the first step of the approach, minority and majority datasets are balanced by replicating or synthesizing minority class examples.

Next, cellular GEP is used to produce a set of base classifiers in the form of expression trees. Finally, a dynamic selection of classifiers is used during testing.

3   Oversampling Algorithms Evaluation

It is well-known that oversampling techniques that inflate minority class instances without considering the structure and locations of the majority class ones are bound to introduce instances that overlap with areas where the density of the majority class instances is high. Other possible threats include overfitting and generating outliers and noisy examples. It is also clear that some datasets are better fitted than others for oversampling methods using only minority class instances. In the case of such datasets, advantages of the minority class-based approaches including their simplicity, low computational complexity, and availability in various software libraries should be fully exploited.

Some of the threats inherent to methods based on the minority class instances only can be alleviated by applying oversampling techniques using both – minority and majority datasets. Such techniques use majority information to generate new samples in minority areas thus avoiding new synthetic instances appearing in the majority class. There are, however, weaknesses that may limit the application of the discussed methods. Among them, typical are computational complexity, a high number of parameters, and the risk of overfitting.

Finally, hybrid oversampling offers, probably, the best performance at a cost of higher complexity, and a high number of parameters that need to be set using trials and errors procedures. Their application requires specialized knowledge which is not usually available at the industry level.

Validating the above observations is not an easy task. To obtain some answers concerning oversampling technique performance, we have carried out a computational experiment. In the experiment, 15 datasets from the Keel-Dataset Repository (Keel 2022) have been used. They include Abalone9–18, Cleveland0–4, Ecoli2, Ecoli3, Glass0, Glass1, Haberman, NewThyroid1, Page-blocks0, Pima, Vehicle1, Vowel1, Wisconsin, Yeast3, and Yeast5. Full details of these sets are available on the Keel-Dataset Repository homepage.

The experiment involved 18 oversampling algorithms, which, among others are reviewed in Sect. 2. To assure comparability we use the same Gene Expression Programming (GEP) classifier in all cases. GEP, introduced by Ferreira (2001). Combines the idea of genetic algorithms and genetic programming and makes use of a population of genes. More details on applying GEP and values of all settings can be found in Jedrzejowicz (2021a).

All algorithms have been implemented using settings as in the original papers. The experiment involved 10 runs of the 5 cross-validation scheme for each algorithm studied. Results in terms of F-measure averaged over all runs, and all algorithms are shown in Table 1. In Table 2 computational experiment results are sorted using two criteria. The first is the average value of the F-measure, and the second is the average value of ranks (18 – the best rank, 1 – the worst one). It is worth noting that the above two criteria produce slightly different orders of datasets.

To determine whether there are any significant differences among results from Table 1, produced by different classifiers we used the Friedman ANOVA by ranks test.

Table 1. Average F-measures obtained in the experiment.

Algorithm	F-measure	Algorithm	F-measure	Algorithm	F-measure
ALMCMO	0.815	i-GEP	0.901	DFSVM	0.842
LMCMO	0.814	c-GEP	0.905	FCM-EBRB	0.848
SMOTE	0.803	B-SMOTE	0.755	ASN-SMOTE	0.798
ADASYN	0.808	B-SMOTE2	0.741	SWIM	0.818
MWMOTE	0.797	A-SUVO	0.811	MLFS	0.805
DB SMOTE	0.784	SLSMOTE	0.741	ROS	0.709

Table 2. Oversampling methods used in the experiment ordered according to their performance.

Method	Av. F-m	Method	Av. Rank
ROS	0.709	ROS	4.367
SL SMOTE	0.741	SL-SMOTE	5.533
B-SMOTE2	0.741	B-SMOTE2	6.433
B-SMOTE	0.755	MWMOTE	6.700
DB SMOTE	0.784	B-SMOTE	7.133
MWMOTE	0.797	DB-SMOTE	7.967
ASN-SMOTE	0.798	ADASYN	8.767
SMOTE	0.803	SMOTE	8.867
MLFS	0.805	ASN-SMOTE	9.267
ADASYN	0.808	SWIM	9.700
A-SUVO	0.811	LMCMO	10.000
LMCMO	0.814	DFSVM	10.333
ALMCMO	0.815	MLFS	10.400
SWIM	0.818	A-SUVO	10.733
DFSVM	0.842	FCM-DBRB	11.500
FCM-EBRB	0.848	ALMCMO	12.000
i-GEP	0.901	i-GEP	15.133
c-GEP	0.905	c-GEP	16.167

The null hypothesis state that there are no such differences. With Friedman statistics equal to 83.346 and p-value equal to 0.00000 the null hypothesis should be rejected at the significance level of 0.05. Further insight can be gained using the Wilcoxon Rank-Sum test for pairwise comparisons. In Table 3 example results from several such comparisons are shown.

Table 3. Results from Wilcoxon Rank-Sum test for pairwise comparisons.

Methods	Z	p-value
i-GEP vs. FCM-EBRB	3,098387	0,001946
c-GEP vs. ALMCMO	1,870829	0,061369
c-GEP vs DFSVM	2,581989	0,009823
i-GEP vs. FCM-EBRB	3,098387	0,001946
FCM-ERB vs. ALMCMO	0,000000	1,000000
DFSVM vs. ADASYN	0,801784	0,422678
LMCMO vs. SMOTE	0,516398	0,605577
SWIM vs. B-SMOTE2	0,516398	0,605577
c-GEP vs. ROS	3,614784	0,000301
FCM-ERB vs. SMOTE	1,549193	0,121335

From Table 1, Table 2, and Table 3 the following observation can be drawn:

- Complex and hybrid oversampling algorithms tend to perform better than those simpler and less sophisticated ones.
- All methods studied perform better than random oversampling (ROS).
- Algorithms using both - minority and majority datasets tend to outperform oversampling algorithms using only minority datasets.
- The experiment does not allow the selection of a statistical winner among algorithms using only minority datasets.
- The experiment does not allow the selection of a statistical winner among algorithms using both - minority and majority datasets

4   Conclusions

The paper contributes by:

- Proposing a taxonomy for oversampling methods and algorithms.
- Reviewing the current research results in developing oversampling methods.
- Discussion of strengths and weaknesses of the main types of oversampling algorithms.
- Presenting results of the computational experiment illustrating the performance of several mainstream oversampling algorithms.

The presented computational experiment alone is by no means sufficient for thoroughly evaluating the performance of the oversampling techniques. However, its result, together with the review of current research allows for predicting future trends concerning directions of research on oversampling methods. In our view the promising approaches could include:

- Development of simple, yet stable, oversampling algorithms to be used as base classifiers in ensemble solutions.
- Construction of hybrid algorithms where hybridization involves the integration of oversampling with undersampling, as well as integration of the oversampling techniques with the algorithm level solutions.
- Searching for advanced methods of exploring minority and majority sets to obtain useful information on their structure and properties. Among such methods, an important role should play machine learning techniques.
- Identifying deeper properties of both minority and majority classes datasets, and using obtained information to guide the oversampling process.
- The Discovery of factors influencing the performance of classifiers used for mining imbalanced datasets leads to multi-criteria oversampling problems.

References

Guo, H., Li, Y., Jennifer Shang, G., Mingyun, H.Y., Bing, G.: Learning from class-imbalanced data: review of methods and applications. Expert Syst. Appl. **73**, 220–239 (2017)

Krawczyk, B.: Learning from imbalanced data: open challenges and future directions. Progr. Artif. Intell. **5**(4), 221–232 (2016). https://doi.org/10.1007/s13748-016-0094-0

Chawla, N.V., Bowyer, K.W., Hall, L.O., Kegelmeyer, W.P.: SMOTE: synthetic minority oversampling technique. J. Artif. Intell. Res. **16**, 321–357 (2002)

Han, H., Wang, W., Mao, B.: Borderline-SMOTE: A new oversampling method in imbalanced data sets learning. In: Advances in Intelligent Computing, International Conference on Intelligent Computing 2005, Hefei, China, Proceedings, Part I, pp. 878–887 (2005)

Bunkhumpornpat, C., Sinapiromsaran, K., Lursinsap, C.: Safe-level-smote: safe-level-synthetic minority over-sampling technique for handling the class imbalanced problem. In: Theeramunkong, T., Kijsirikul, B., Cercone, N., Ho, T.-B. (eds.) PAKDD 2009. LNCS (LNAI), vol. 5476, pp. 475–482. Springer, Heidelberg (2009). https://doi.org/10.1007/978-3-642-01307-2_43

Maldonado, S., Vairetti, C., Fernandez, A., Herrera, F.: FW-SMOTE: a feature-weighted oversampling approach for imbalanced classification. Pattern Recogn. **124**, 108511 (2022)

He, H., Bai, Y., Garcia, E.A., Li, S.: Adasyn: Adaptive synthetic sampling approach for imbalanced learning. In: Proceedings of the International Joint Conference on Neural Networks, part of the IEEE World Congress on Computational Intelligence. IEEE, Hong Kong, China, pp. 1322–1328 (2008)

Barus, S., Islam, M.M., Yao, X., Murase, K.: Mwmote–majority weighted minority oversampling technique for imbalanced data set learning. IEEE Trans. Knowl. Data Eng. **26**(2), 405–425 (2014)

Nekooeimehr, I., Lai-Yuen, S.K.: Adaptive semi-unsupervised weighted over-sampling (A-SUWO) for imbalanced datasets. Expert Syst. Appl. **46**, 405–416 (2016)

Gao, M., Hong, X., Chen, S., J. Harris, C.J.: Probability density function estimation based oversampling for imbalanced two class problems. In: The 2012 International Joint Conference on Neural Networks (IJCNN), Brisbane, Australia, pp. 1 – 8 (2012)

Bunkhumpornpat, C., Sinapiromsaran, K., Lursinsap, C.: DBSMOTE: Density-based synthetic minority over-sampling technique. Appl. Intell. **36**, 664–684 (2012)

Pan, T., Zhao, J., Wu, W., Yang, J.: Learning imbalanced datasets based on SMOTE and Gaussian distribution. Inf. Sci. **512**, 1214–1233 (2020)

Wang, X., Jian, X., Zeng, T., Jing, L.: Local distribution-based adaptive minority over-sampling for imbalanced data classification. Neurocomputing **422**, 200–213 (2021)

Sharma, S., Bellinger, C., Krawczyk, B., Zaiane, O., Japkowicz, N.: Synthetic over-sampling with the majority class: A new perspective on handling extreme imbalance. In: 2018 IEEE International Conference on Data Mining, pp. 448–456. IEEE, Singapore (2018)

Islam, A., Belhaouari, S.B., Rehman, A.U., Bensmail, H.: KNNOR: an oversampling technique for imbalanced datasets. Appl. Soft Comput. **115**, 108288 (2022)

Sadhukhan, P., Palit, S.: Adaptive learning of minority class prior to minority over-sampling. Pattern Recogn. Lett. **136**, 16–24 (2020)

Das, B., Krishnan, N.C., Cook, D.J.: Racog and wRacog: two probabilistic over-sampling techniques. IEEE Trans. Knowl. Data Eng. **27**(1), 222–234 (2014)

Jiang, Z., Pan, T., Zhang, C., Yang, J.: A new oversampling method based on the classification contribution degree. Symmetry **13**, 194 (2021)

Borowska, K., Stepaniuk, J.: A rough-granular approach to the imbalanced data classification problem. Appl. Soft Comput. J. **83**, 105607 (2019)

Chen, H., Li, T., Fan, X., Luo, C.: Feature selection for imbalanced data based on neighborhood rough sets. Inf. Sci. **483**, 1–20 (2019)

Fu, Y.-G., Ye, J.-F., Yin, Z.-F., Chen, L.-J., Wang, Y.-M., Liu, G.-G.: Construction of EBRB classifier for imbalanced data based on Fuzzy C-Means clustering. Knowl.-Based Syst. **234**, 107590 (2021)

Wang, K.-F., An J, Wei, Z., Cui, C., Ma, X.-H., Ma ,C., Bao, H.-Q.: Deep learning-based Imbalanced classification with fuzzy support vector machine. Front. Bioeng. Biotechnol. **9**, 802712 (2022)

Tang, B., He, H.: Kerneladasyn: kernel based adaptive synthetic data generation for imbalanced learning. In: IEEE Congress on Evolutionary Computation, CEC 2015, pp. 664 – 671. IEEE, Sendai, Japan (2015)

Perez-Ortiz, M., Gutierrez, P.A., Tino, P., Hervas-Martinez, C.: Oversampling the minority class in the feature space. IEEE Trans. Neural Netw. Learn. Syst. **27**(9), 1947–1961 (2016)

Mathew, J., Pang, C.K., Luo, M., Leong, W.H.: Classification of imbalanced data by oversampling in kernel space of support vector machines. IEEE Trans. Neural Netw. Learn. Syst. **29**, 4065–4076 (2018)

Liang, P., Li, W., Hu, J.: Oversampling the minority class in a multi-linear feature space for imbalanced data classification. IEEE J. Trans. Electr. Electr. Eng. **13**, 1483–1491 (2018)

Koziarski, M., Krawczyk, B., Woźniak, M.: Radial-based oversampling for noisy imbalanced data classification. Neurocomputing **343**, 19–33 (2019)

Koziarski, M.: Potential Anchoring for imbalanced data classification. Pattern Recogn. **120**, 108114 (2021)

Ye, X., Li, H., Imakura, A., Sakurai, T.: An oversampling framework for imbalanced classification based on Laplacian eigenmaps. Neurocomputing **399**, 107–116 (2020)

Jedrzejowicz, J., Jedrzejowicz, P.: GEP-based classifier for mining imbalanced data. Expert Syst. Appl. **164**, 114058 (2021)

Jedrzejowicz, J., Jedrzejowicz, P.: Imbalanced data mining using oversampling and cellular GEP ensemble. In: Nguyen, N.T., Iliadis, L., Maglogiannis, I., Trawiński, B. (eds.) ICCCI 2021. LNCS (LNAI), vol. 12876, pp. 360–372. Springer, Cham (2021). https://doi.org/10.1007/978-3-030-88081-1_27

Keel Dataset Repository. https://sci2s.ugr.es/keel/datasets.php. Accessed 07 Mar 2022

Ferreira, C.: Gene expression programming: a new adaptive algorithm for solving problems. Complex Syst. **13**(2), 87–129 (2001)

Yi, X., Xu, Y., Hu, Q., et al.: ASN-SMOTE: a synthetic minority oversampling method with adaptive qualified synthesizer selection. Complex Intell. Syst. **8**, 2247–2272 (2022). https://doi.org/10.1007/s40747-021-00638-w

A Block Coordinate DCA Approach for Large-Scale Kernel SVM

Van Tuan Pham[1]([✉]), Hoang Phuc Hau Luu[1], and Hoai An Le Thi[1,2][ID]

[1] LGIPM, Département IA, Université de Lorraine, 57000 Metz, France
{van-tuan.pham,hoang-phuc-hau.luu,hoai-an.le-thi}@univ-lorraine.fr
[2] Institut Universitaire de France (IUF), Paris, France

Abstract. In this study, we propose a novel block coordinate DCA based method for tackling the large-scale kernel SVM. The proposed method employs a unified scheme that is capable of handling almost all common losses in SVM. Owing to the block coordinate approach, the learning algorithm can deal with the high dimensionality of the optimization variables by updating one block of coordinates at a time to sufficiently decrease the objective value while keeping the other blocks fixed. As a result, calculation time can be significantly reduced while preventing the computer's memory from overflowing, which is crucial for computing in the context of big data. Numerical experiments are conducted intensively, which shows the algorithm's merits in both accuracy and computational cost.

Keywords: Block coordinate · DC programming · DCA · SVM

1 Introduction

Support vector machines (SVM) that were first proposed by Vapnik [1,4,22] have been shown to be a powerful machine learning method in the last two decades. Despite its advantageous properties, SVM is incapable of effectively dealing with large-scale datasets encountered in a variety of applications such as image classification, bioinformatics, or text classification, which are often in the millions in terms of data samples and features, rendering the computational and storage costs for training SVM prohibitively expensive or even infeasible.

The block coordinate (BC) approach has been widely studied to address this challenge. Thanks to their low iteration costs, low memory requirements, and the possibility of being implemented in parallel, block coordinate algorithms have evolved as essential tools for tackling some of the most challenging large-scale optimization issues. In principle, at each iteration, these methods choose a block of coordinates of the optimization variable to update while keeping the other variables fixed. As a result, the computation time is reduced while preventing the computer's memory from overflowing, which is crucial for big data computing.

N. T. Nguyen et al. (Eds.): ICCCI 2022, LNAI 13501, pp. 334–347, 2022.
https://doi.org/10.1007/978-3-031-16014-1_27

Related Works. Various block coordinate algorithms for machine learning, including SVM have been investigated in recent years. Hsieh et al. [5] introduced a dual coordinate descent approach for linear SVM with L1 and L2-loss functions. Chou et al. [3] proposed several coordinate descent approaches for linear one-class SVM and SVDD. Nutini et al. [14] proposed greedy block-selection strategies to make block coordinate faster on some classic machine learning problems. Numerous large-scale optimization problems have been successfully solved using block-coordinate approaches and their modifications [11,13,19].

Zhou and Zhou [24] proposed a unified SVM scheme using LS-DC loss for dealing with both the convex and nonconvex loss functions based on the difference of convex functions algorithms (DCA) [15,16]. This approach is promising since most loss functions of SVM are LS-DC or can be approximated by LS-DC. However, to address the large-scale problem, they employed low-rank approximation, which might be inefficient in some circumstances when dealing with the kernel matrix in SVM. For example, in natural language processing, image processing, or bioinformatics..., where data have a large number of attributes, there is little chance that the data will be strongly correlated. Due to the weak correlation in these cases, low-rank approximation algorithms are unable to efficiently reduce the rank of the kernel matrix. Additionally, it is possible to lose a considerable amount of information if the training data are not strongly correlated. This motivates us to use another approach for solving the large-scale problem. That is, instead of reducing the problem's size by approximation methods, we opt for customizing the DCA scheme in such a way that it can work in the large-scale context. Specifically, in this work we focus on applying the block coordinate technique to DCA in order to address the large-scale kernel SVM.

Our contributions

1. We propose a new block coordinate DCA based method for solving high dimensional DC programs. Then, the proposed method is specifically applied to the large-scale kernel SVM in a unified manner that is capable of handling almost all common losses used in SVM, including convex and nonconvex losses, as well as those for classification and regression. From the theoretical perspective, the proposed algorithm guarantees to find a weakly DC critical point (the precise definition is given later).
2. To further reduce the computational cost, we replace some large sums arising when applying the block coordinate DCA to the kernel SVM with their approximations based on the minibatch.
3. Finally, numerical experiments are carried out intensively for various datasets and loss functions. It is consistent that our proposed method outperforms existing algorithms in both solutions' quality and computational time.

2   Optimization Problems of Kernel SVM

Given a training dataset $\{(x_i, y_i)\}_{i=1}^m$ where x_i is a feature vector and y_i is the corresponding label, the kernel SVM that is based on structural risk minimization takes the following form

$$\min_{w \in \mathbb{H}} \frac{1}{m} \sum_{i=1}^{m} \ell(y_i, \langle w, \phi(x_i) \rangle) + \frac{\lambda}{2} \|w\|^2, \tag{1}$$

where $\mathbb{H}$ is a reproducible kernel Hilbert space induced by a kernel $\kappa(x, z) = \langle \phi(x), \phi(z) \rangle$ where ϕ is a feature map from $\mathbb{R}^d$ to $\mathbb{H}$, ℓ is a loss function measuring the fidelity of the prediction and the true label, $\lambda > 0$ is the regularization parameter. Once learned, the found w^* specifies a classifier $f(x) = \langle w^*, \phi(x) \rangle$ that is expected to separate two classes. Due to the high or even infinite dimension of $\mathbb{H}$, the problem (1) can not be solved efficiently. By applying the representor theorem [20, 21], we can substitute $w = \sum_{i=1}^{m} \alpha_i \phi(x_i)$ in (1) to have the finite dimensional optimization problem as follows:

$$\min_{\alpha \in \mathbb{R}^m} F(\alpha) = \lambda \alpha^\top K \alpha + \frac{1}{m} \sum_{i=1}^{m} \ell(y_i, K_i \alpha) \tag{2}$$

where K is the kernel matrix and K_i is the i-th row of K.

The problem (2) is an optimization problem in $\mathbb{R}^m$ space, whose properties (convex, nonconvex) depend on the structure of ℓ. For regression tasks, ℓ is usually of the form $\ell(y, t) = \psi(y - t)$, where ψ can be the least square loss, absolute loss, ϵ-insensitive loss, etc. For classification tasks, ℓ is usually given as $\ell(y, t) = \psi(1 - yt)$ where ψ can be the least square loss, hinge loss, ramp loss, etc. Each choice of ℓ leads to a different SVM problem for which an algorithm must be designed. This is extremely inconvenient when there are numerous loss functions, with each function having different merits. Therefore, Zhou and Zhou suggested a unified model to simultaneously enjoy the benefits of various losses while minimizing effort in designing algorithms, namely the least squares type DC loss (LS-DC). It is pointed out in [24] that most losses used in the literature are LS-DC or can be approximated by LS-DC losses. With ℓ being an LS-DC loss, the problem (2) is a DC program. However, the dimension of the optimization variable equals the number of data samples, posing a real scalability challenge.

3   A Block Coordinate DCA Based Method

3.1   An Overview of DC Programming and DCA

DC programming and DCA were introduced in a preliminary form by Pham Dinh Tao in 1985 and have been significantly improved since 1994 by Le Thi Hoai An and Pham Dinh Tao. DCA is a well-known technique for solving nonconvex problems (see, e.g., [9, 15, 17]). A standard DC program is as follows:

$$\inf \{ f(\alpha) := G(\alpha) - H(\alpha) : \alpha \in \mathbb{R}^p \}, (\mathrm{P}_{dc})$$

where the functions G and $H \in \Gamma_0(\mathbb{R}^p)$ are convex. Here $\Gamma_0(\mathbb{R}^p)$ denotes the set of proper lower-semicontinuous convex functions from a set $\mathbb{R}^p$ to $\mathbb{R} \cup \{+\infty\}$. Such a function f is called a DC function, and $G - H$ is called a DC decomposition of f, while G and H are DC components of f.

A point α^* is called a critical point of $G - H$ if it satisfies the generalized Kuhn-Tucker condition $\partial G(\alpha^*) \cap \partial H(\alpha^*) \neq \emptyset$, while it is called a strong DC critical point if $\emptyset \neq \partial H(\alpha^*) \subset \partial G(\alpha^*)$.

The standard DCA scheme is presented in the following algorithm.

Algorithm. Standard DCA scheme

Initialization: Let $\alpha^0 \in \mathbb{R}^p$ be a best guess. Set $k = 0$.
repeat
   1. Calculate $\beta^k \in \partial h(\alpha^k)$.
   2. Calculate $\alpha^{k+1} \in \operatorname{argmin}\left\{G(\alpha) - \langle \alpha, \beta^k \rangle : \alpha \in \mathbb{R}^p\right\}$.
   3. $k \leftarrow k + 1$.
until convergence of $\left\{\alpha^k\right\}$.

Convergence properties of the DCA and its theoretical basis are discussed in [10, 15]. For instance, it is worth mentioning the following properties:

1. DCA is a descent method *without linesearch* but with global convergence (i.e., it converges from an arbitrary starting point).
2. If $G(\alpha^{k+1}) - H(\alpha^{k+1}) = G(\alpha^k) - H(\alpha^k)$, then α^k is a critical point of $G - H$. In this case, DCA terminates at k-th iteration.
3. If the optimal value α of (P_{dc}) is finite, then every limit point of $\{\alpha^k\}$ is a critical point of $G - H$.

For decades, numerous DCA-based algorithms have been developed to efficiently solve a diverse number of large-scale problems in many application areas (see, e.g., [8,18]) and SVM, in particular [6,7]). A deeper insight into DCA has been given in [9,16].

3.2 Block Coordinate DCA

When dealing with large-scale problems, data appear with an enormous number of observations and/or features, which eventually results in high-dimensional optimization problems. Consequently, the standard DCA could be prohibitively expensive or even impossible. This motivates us to design and analyze a block coordinate DCA scheme to tackle a (high dimensional) DC program (P_{dc}) in general. Let us denote $\Omega = \{A : A \subset \{1, 2, \ldots, m\}, A \neq \emptyset\}$, which is the set of all non-empty subsets of $\{1, 2, \ldots, m\}$. A block of coordinates corresponds to an element of Ω. Now we prescribe a probability distribution $\mathcal{P}$ over Ω. This probability distribution represents a strategy on how likely a block is chosen at each iteration. In a certain strategy, one can simply assign a probability of 0 to blocks that are not supposed to be chosen. With a prescribed probability distribution over Ω, at each iteration, we randomly generate a set S with respect to the probability distribution $\mathcal{P}$ and perform one step of the DCA on the set S of coordinates. The formal procedure is described in Algorithm 1.

Algorithm 1. Block coordinate DCA

Input: A starting point α^0, a distribution $\mathcal{P}$ over Ω; Set $k = 0$.
repeat
    1. Generate from the distribution $\mathcal{P}$ a set of coordinates S.
    2. Compute a partial subgradient $\beta^k \in \partial_{\alpha_S} H(\alpha_S^k, \alpha_{S^C}^k)$.
    3. Solve the convex problem: $\alpha_S^* \in \operatorname{argmin}_{\alpha_S} \{G(\alpha_S, \alpha_{S^C}^k) - \langle \beta^k, \alpha_S \rangle\}$.
    4. Update solution $\alpha_i^{k+1} = \begin{cases} \alpha_i^* & \text{if } i \in S, \\ \alpha_i^k & \text{otherwise.} \end{cases}$
    5. Set $k \leftarrow k + 1$.
until Stopping criterion.

For a given distribution $\mathcal{P}$, we denote $\operatorname{Supp}(\mathcal{P}) = \{A \in \Omega : \mathcal{P}(A) > 0\}$ the support of $\mathcal{P}$. We have established the following convergence results.

Proposition 1. *Assume that either G or H is strongly convex. Then, almost surely, every limit point α^* of the sequence $\{\alpha^k\}$ generated by the block coordinate DCA satisfies: $\forall S \in \operatorname{Supp}(\mathcal{P}) : \partial_{\alpha_S} G(\alpha^*) \cap \partial_{\alpha_S} H(\alpha^*) \neq \emptyset$.*

In other words, the found solution α^* is DC critical with respect to each block of coordinates that is assigned a non-zero probability. We call such a point weakly DC critical point with respect to the mentioned blocks of coordinates.

3.3 Application to Kernel SVM with LS-DC Losses

According to Zhou and Zhou [24], a loss ℓ is called an LS-DC loss if there exists a constant $A > 0$ such that the associated function ψ, i.e. $\ell(y, t) = \psi(1 - yt)$, has the following DC decomposition $\psi(u) = Au^2 - (Au^2 - \psi(u))$.

Let $\ell(y, t)$ be any LS - DC loss associated with ψ, the kernel SVM model (2) can be written as the following DC program

$$\min_{\alpha \in \mathbb{R}^m} F(\alpha) = \lambda \alpha^\top K \alpha + \frac{1}{m} \sum_{i=1}^m \psi(1 - y_i K_i \alpha) := G(\alpha) - H(\alpha) \qquad (3)$$

with the DC components being given by

$$G(\alpha) := \lambda \alpha^\top K \alpha + \frac{1}{m} A \sum_{i=1}^m (1 - y_i K_i \alpha)^2 + \frac{\rho}{2} \|\alpha\|^2, \qquad (4)$$

$$H(\alpha) := \frac{1}{m} \sum_{i=1}^m \left(A(1 - y_i K_i \alpha)^2 - \psi(1 - y_i K_i \alpha) \right) + \frac{\rho}{2} \|\alpha\|^2, \qquad (5)$$

where $\rho > 0$ is a regularization parameter to make both DC components strongly convex.

Since the DC program (3) is high dimensional, we shall employ the Block coordinate DCA to handle it. At iteration k, we choose a block of coordinates $S \in \mathcal{D} := \{1, 2, \ldots, m\}$ $(1 \leq |S| < m)$. Then, the partial subgradient of H on the set of coordinates S, $\beta \in \partial_{\alpha_S} H(\alpha_S^k, \alpha_{Sc}^k)$, is computed as

$$\beta^k = \frac{1}{m} \sum_{i=1}^m 2A(1 - y_i \mathbf{K}_i \alpha^k)(-y_i \mathbf{K}_i^{[S]\top})$$
$$- \frac{1}{m} \sum_{i=1}^m \left(\psi' \left(1 - y_i \mathbf{K}_i \alpha^k\right) \left(-y_i \mathbf{K}_i^{[S]\top}\right) \right) + \rho \alpha_S^k,$$

where $\psi'(u)$ denotes a subgradient of ψ at u. To further reduce the computational cost, we approximate the two large sums above (each with m components) by a minibatch of data. For convenience, the minibatch index set is chosen to be the same as S. So β^k is approximated by:

$$\tilde{\beta}^k = \frac{1}{|S|} \sum_{i \in S} 2A(1 - y_i \mathbf{K}_i \alpha^k)(-y_i \mathbf{K}_i^{[S]\top})$$
$$- \frac{1}{|S|} \sum_{i \in S} \left(\psi' \left(1 - y_i \mathbf{K}_i \alpha^k\right) \left(-y_i \mathbf{K}_i^{[S]\top}\right) \right) + \rho \alpha_S^k. \tag{6}$$

Then, we solve the following convex subproblem

$$\min_{\alpha_S} G(\alpha_S, \alpha_{Sc}^k) - \langle \tilde{\beta}^k, \alpha_S \rangle. \tag{7}$$

We write the problem (7) in detail as follows. The first term of $G(\alpha)$ in (4) can be expanded:

$$[\alpha_S, \alpha_{Sc}^k]^\top K [\alpha_S, \alpha_{Sc}^k] = \alpha_S^\top K_{SS} \alpha_S + 2\alpha_S^\top K_{SSc} \alpha_{Sc}^k + \alpha_{Sc}^\top K_{ScSc} \alpha_{Sc}^k \tag{8}$$

The second term of $G(\alpha)$ is as follows:

$$-2 \left[\sum_{i=1}^m y_i \mathbf{K}_i^S \right] \alpha_S + \alpha_S^\top \left[\sum_{i=1}^m y_i^2 (\mathbf{K}_i^S)^\top \mathbf{K}_i^S \right] \alpha_S + 2\alpha_S^\top \left[\sum_{i=1}^m y_i^2 (\mathbf{K}_i^S)^\top \mathbf{K}_i^{Sc} \right] \alpha_{Sc}^k + C \tag{9}$$

where C is a constant which does not depend on α.

The optimization problem (7) can be written as follows:

$$\min_{\alpha_S} \lambda \left(\alpha_S{}^\top K_{SS}\alpha_S + 2\alpha_S^\top K_{SSc}\alpha_{Sc}^k \right)$$

$$+ \frac{A}{|S|} \left(-2(\sum_{i\in S} y_i K_i^S)\alpha_S + \alpha_S^\top(\sum_{i\in S} y_i^2 (K_i^S)^\top K_i^S)\alpha_S + 2\alpha_S^\top(\sum_{i\in S} y_i^2 (K_i^S)^\top K_i^{Sc})\alpha_{Sc}^k \right)$$

$$+ \frac{\rho}{2}\|\alpha_S\|^2 - \langle \beta^k, \alpha_S \rangle$$

$$= \min_{\alpha_S} \alpha_S{}^\top \left(\lambda K_{SS} + \frac{A}{|S|}\sum_{i\in S} y_i^2(K_i^S)^\top K_i^S + \frac{\rho}{2}I \right) \alpha_S \tag{10}$$

$$+ \alpha_S^\top \left(2\lambda K_{SSc}\alpha_{Sc}^k - \frac{2A}{|S|}\sum_{i\in S} y_i(K_i^S)^\top + \frac{2A}{|S|}(\sum_{i\in S} y_i^2(K_i^S)^\top K_i^{Sc})\alpha_{Sc}^k - \beta^k \right).$$

This is a positive definite quadratic program, which results in a system of linear equations being solved at each iteration. Because α_S has a relatively small dimension, the solution can be efficiently solved using existing packages.

Block Selection Rule. Given a set of possible blocks, the block selection rule is used to identify which block of the optimization variable to update. In our proposed method, we examined the random strategy for selecting a block at each iteration. On the other hand, Lee and Wright [12] provided an analysis to show that the random permutations cyclic selection (RPCD) is slightly better than the random strategy (RCD) in terms of convergence rate. Therefore, we consider two strategies for selecting a block of variables S at each iteration: Random selection and cyclic selection with random permutations. For the random strategy, the term *iteration* refers to the number of times a block of variables passes through the algorithm. For the cyclic strategy, the number of times the algorithm will run over the full training dataset is represented by the term *epoch*.

Our proposed algorithm is referred to as BC-DCASVM, and is presented in Algorithm 2.

Algorithm 2. BC-DCASVM

Input: Given a training set $\mathcal{D} = \{(x_i, y_i)\}_{i=1}^m$ with $x_i \in \mathbb{R}^d$ and $y_i \in \{-1, +1\}$; Kernel matrix K satisfying $K_{i,j} = \kappa(x_i, x_j)$; Any LS-DC loss function $\psi(u)$ with parameter $A > 0$; Set $e = 0$, $\alpha = 0$, $M > 0$

repeat

    for $k = 1 \ldots M$ **do**

        1. Pick a block S cyclically or randomly.

        2. Compute $\tilde{\beta}^k$ in (6).

        3. Solve (10) to obtain α_S^*.

        4. Update α^{k+1}.

    end for

    5. Set $e \leftarrow e + 1$.

until Stopping criterion.

---

4   Numerical Experiments

In this section, we analyze the performance of our proposed algorithm BC-DCASVM with two state-of-the-art SVM algorithms, including UniSVM [24] and LibSVM [2] on some large datasets. To evaluate the two unified models: BC-DCSVM and UniSVM, four LS-DC loss functions (for both convex and non-convex) and their corresponding subdiferentials will be used in our experiments:

1. Least squares: $\psi(u) = u^2$ is a convex loss function; $\nabla\psi(u) = 2u$.

2. Truncated-least-squares: $\psi(u) = \min\{u^2, a\}$, with $a > 0$ is a nonconvex function; $\partial\psi(u) = \begin{cases} 2u, & |u| < \sqrt{a} \\ 0, & |u| \geq \sqrt{a} \end{cases}$.

3. Squared Hinge: $\psi(u) = u_+^2$ with $A \geq 1$ is a convex function; $\nabla\psi(u) = 2u_+$.

4. Truncated squared Hinge: $\psi(u) = \min\{u_+^2, a\}$ with $A \geq 1$ and the truncated parameter $a > 0$ is a nonconvex function; $\partial\psi(u) = \begin{cases} 2u, & 0 < u < \sqrt{a}, \\ 0, & \text{others} \end{cases}$.

For each $\psi(u)$, we replace a concrete subgradient as given above to (6) to get the corresponding algorithm.

4.1   Datasets

We perform the related algorithms on ten well-known benchmark datasets: Five datasets [NEWS20, RCV1, GISETTE, MNIST, CIFA10] are from the LIBSVM website[1]. MNIST-17 (Dataset consists of labels: 1 and 7), MNIST-38 (Labels: 3 and 8), CIFA10-CP (Labels: Car and Plane) and CIFA10-TS (Labels: Truck and Ship) are the sub-datasets which extracted from two image datasets MNIST and CIFA10. DEXTER is a text classification dataset from UCI Machine Learning repository[2]. PCMAC dataset (PC vs Mac) is a subset of the 20 Newsgroups[3] used in [23]. GLI-85 is a microarray-bio dataset[4]. Table 1 summarizes the information included in the datasets.

Table 1. Datasets, samples (m), features (n) are used in our experiments.

Dataset	Name	m	n	Dataset	Name	m	n
D1	GLI-85	85	22,283	D2	DEXTER	600	20,000
D3	PCMAC	1,943	3,289	D4	GISETTE	7,000	5,000
D5	MNIST-17	15,170	784	D6	MNIST-38	13,728	784
D7	CIFA10-TS	12,000	3,072	D8	CIFA10-CP	12,000	3,072
D9	RCV1	20,242	47,236	D10	NEWS20	19,996	1,355,191

---

[1] https://www.csie.ntu.edu.tw/~cjlin/libsvm/.

[2] https://archive.ics.uci.edu/.

[3] http://qwone.com/~jason/20newsgroups/.

[4] https://www.ncbi.nlm.nih.gov/geo/query/acc.cgi?acc=gse4412.

For model selection purposes, we use the 5-fold cross-validation strategy to search for the best parameters (grid search). The binary datasets have the labels in $\{+1, -1\}$ will be split into two subsets of the labels $[+1]$ and $[-1]$. To avoid overfitting and preserve the proportions of the classes, each subset will be divided into 5 equal-sized subfolds, and then the subfolds of the label $[+1]$ will be merged with the corresponding subfolds of the label $[-1]$ to produce 5 folds for training and testing. For evaluation, each fold will serve in turn as the testset, while the remaining four folds will serve as the trainset. Before feeding the training data into the learning models, the whole data will be shuffled, and then scaled by the median absolute deviation in the range of $[0, 1]$ by using the function *normalize*[5] in MATLAB 2021a to avoid one feature having a greater influence than the others in the Gaussian kernel values. The same process is applied to the test data. Finally, mean accuracy is obtained by averaging the results. The best model is the one that achieves the highest average accuracy on the testset.

4.2 Set up Experiments and Parameters

The two algorithms BC-DCASVM and UniSVM are implemented in MAT-LAB. The source-code of UniSVM[6] is from the authors in [24]. The LibSVM model is compiled from the LibSVM C++ source-code (see Footnote 1) as MEX-files and run in MATLAB. All algorithms are performed on a PC with an Intel Core i7-8700 CPU @3.20GHz×6 with a memory of 16GB. The computer runs Windows 10 with the MATLAB-2021a version. For all algorithms, we particularly consider the Gaussian kernel: $\kappa(x, z) = \exp\left(-\gamma\|x - z\|^2\right)$ and used the following sets of candidate values: $\{2^{-10}, 2^{-8}, 2^{-6}, 2^{-4}, 2^{-2}, 2^0, 2^2\}$ and $\{2^{-2}, 2^0, 2^2, 2^4, 2^6, 2^8, 2^{10}\}$ respectively of the parameter γ (for the Gaussian kernel) and λ (the regularization parameter) in our experiments. For the proposed algorithm, α_0 is set as a vector with all zeros, ρ is set with value 10^{-5}. To solve the system of linear equations in (10), we use the function **linsolve**[7] in MAT-LAB. The block-sizes are set with different values depending on the number of samples of datasets as follows:

GLI-85	(32)	PCMAC	(128)	MNIST-38	(1024)	MNIST-17	(1024)	RCV1	(1024)
GISETTE	(128)	DEXTER	(128)	CIFA10-CP	(1024)	CIFA10-CP	(1024)	NEWS20	(1024)

4.3 Experiments on Large Benchmark Datasets

We use three criteria for evaluating the performances of the comparative algorithms: the train accuracy (TRAIN: in %), the test accuracy (TEST: in %) and CPU runtime (CPU: in seconds). After tuning, we assess the models using

---

[5] www.mathworks.com/help/releases/r2021a/matlab/ref/double.normalize.html.
[6] https://github.com/stayones/code-unisvm.
[7] www.mathworks.com/help/releases/r2021a/matlab/ref/linsolve.html.

the mean and the standard deviation of each evaluation criteria in Table 2 and Table 3. The bold values in the two tables are the best results. For any algorithm that is unable to complete tasks due to the long training period (exceeding 1800 s seconds), we denote the outcomes as N/A. Three experiments will be conducted to comprehensively analyze the proposed approach.

Experiment 1: We evaluate the performances of BC-DCASVM, UniSVM and LibSVM on 10 datasets (as described in Table 1). The BC-DCASVM and UniSVM models are trained with the Least square loss function, which produced the best experimental results in terms of runtime, as Zhou and Zhou [24] stated in their experiment. For our proposed algorithm, testing indicates that just going over all of the data once is sufficient to get comparable results. Therefore, we use a single epoch with the random permutations cyclic technique for BC-DCASVM in this experiment. The results of the experiment are in Table 2.

Table 2. Performances of the related algorithms on 10 benchmark-datasets. All results are averaged over 5 folds with the standard deviations.

Dataset	Metric	BCDCASVM	UniSVM	LibSVM	Dataset	Metric	BCDCASVM	UniSVM	LibSVM
D1	TRAIN	**100(0.00)**	**100(0.00)**	100(0.00)	D2	TRAIN	**100(0.00)**	99.25(0.00)	100(0.00)
	TEST	**90.00(0.00)**	**90.00(0.00)**	83.75(0.08)		TEST	93.89(0.01)	**94.00(0.01)**	94.00(0.02)
	CPU	**0.05(0.00)**	0.06(0.00)	0.19(0.00)		CPU	**0.13(0.00)**	1.38(0.01)	0.33(0.01)
D3	TRAIN	**99.25(0.00)**	94.83(0.01)	96.10(0.01)	D4	TRAIN	**100(0.00)**	98.45(0.00)	100(0.00)
	TEST	**90.82(0.01)**	**90.82(0.02)**	88.87(0.01)		TEST	**98.29(0.00)**	97.54(0.00)	97.96(0.01)
	CPU	**0.30(0.00)**	1.80(0.08)	1.27(0.02)		CPU	**3.13(0.01)**	10.60(0.19)	176.60(1.37)
D5	TRAIN	**100(0.00)**	**100(0.00)**	100(0.00)	D6	TRAIN	**100(0.00)**	99.84(0.00)	100(0.00)
	TEST	**99.84(0.00)**	99.62(0.00)	99.75(0.01)		TEST	**99.77(0.00)**	99.63(0.00)	99.75(0.00)
	CPU	**2.01(0.03)**	5.22(0.04)	196.47(2.42)		CPU	**2.10(0.17)**	5.80(0.01)	165.48(2.03)
D7	TRAIN	**99.77(0.00)**	87.39(0.00)	99.77(0.01)	D8	TRAIN	98.51(0.00)	88.57(0.01)	100(0.00)
	TEST	**88.48(0.00)**	86.81(0.01)	88.28(0.02)		TEST	88.34(0.00)	87.36(0.01)	**89.05(0.02)**
	CPU	**5.36(0.08)**	10.68(0.08)	762.84(4.85)		CPU	**5.21(0.07)**	9.81(0.03)	685.26(5.01)
D9	TRAIN	99.38(0.02)	92.83(0.02)	**99.81(0.00)**	D10	TRAIN	**98.45(0.00)**	84.02(0.00)	N/A
	TEST	**96.94(0.02)**	92.61(0.01)	96.65(0.00)		TEST	**95.83(0.00)**	83.87(0.01)	N/A
	CPU	**7.08(0.06)**	8.80(0.16)	1035.27(3.48)		CPU	**18.04(0.14)**	39.12(0.11)	N/A

Experiment 2: This experiment is designed to validate our hypothesis on the proposed algorithm: The more training epochs, the higher accuracy of the model. We conduct the experiment with ten runs of the BC-DCASVM algorithm with numbers of epochs in $\{1, 2, 3, 4, 5, 6, 7, 8, 9, 10\}$ respectively on two datasets: CIFA10-CP and NEWS20. The optimal hyperparameters obtained from the model selection process in **Experiment 1** are used for training. Also, the Least square loss function is utilized to assess the influence of increasing the number of epochs on accuracy. The cyclic strategy is used for block selection rule and the metrics: Accuracies on the trainset and on the testset are used as evaluation criteria. Figure 1 illustrates the results of this experiment.

Experiment 3: To determine the effectiveness of the unified scheme, we compare the two unified algorithms BC-DCASVM and UniSVM using different loss functions. Three additional loss functions are investigated: One convex loss

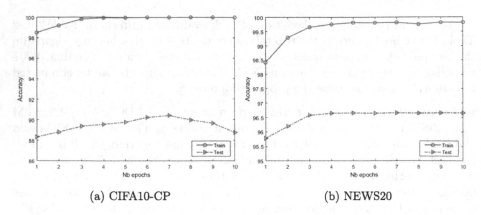

(a) CIFA10-CP   (b) NEWS20

Fig. 1. Performances of BC-DCASVM on CIFA10-CP (1a) and NEWS20 (1b) as the number of epochs increases.

function-squared Hinge loss and two non-convex loss functions: Truncated least square loss (a = 2) and truncated squared Hinge loss (a = 2). Three metrics: Train accuracy, test accuracy, and runtime are evaluated on five datasets with the random selection strategy (Number of iterations $M = \left\lceil \frac{m}{block\_size} \right\rceil$. Table 3 summarizes the experimental outcomes.

Table 3. Performances of the two unified algorithms: BC-DCASVM and UniSVM with three loss functions: Truncated least square (Trunc-Least-Square), truncated squared Hinge (Trunc-Squared-Hinge) and Squared Hinge.

Dataset	Metric	Trunc-Least-Square		Trunc-Squared-Hinge		Squared-Hinge	
		BC-DCASVM	UniSVM	BC-DCASVM	UniSVM	BC-DCASVM	UniSVM
D2	TRAIN	100(0.00)	100(0.00)	100(0.00)	100(0.00)	100(0.00)	100(0.00)
	TEST	94.00(0.01)	94.00(0.01)	94.67(0.01)	94.83(0.00)	94.00(0.00)	94.00(0.00)
	CPU	0.20(0.02)	1.28(0.03)	0.18(0.01)	1.13(0.01)	0.24(0.01)	1.34(0.01)
D4	TRAIN	99.89(0.00)	98.60(0.00)	100(0.00)	98.45(0.00)	100(0.00)	99.52(0.00)
	TEST	97.81(0.00)	97.27(0.00)	98.21(0.00)	97.50(0.00)	98.06(0.00)	98.00(0.00)
	CPU	3.25(0.07)	9.13(0.15)	3.37(0.09)	14.68(0.20)	3.11(0.05)	11.87(0.03)
D6	TRAIN	100(0.00)	99.84(0.00)	100(0.00)	99.95(0.00)	100(0.00)	99.98(0.00)
	TEST	99.77(0.00)	99.65(0.00)	99.75(0.00)	99.71(0.00)	99.77(0.00)	99.77(0.00)
	CPU	2.04(0.02)	5.42(0.02)	2.01(0.07)	5.33(0.09)	2.01(0.02)	6.22(0.06)
D8	TRAIN	96.57(0.02)	89.91(0.00)	99.84(0.02)	91.53(0.01)	99.84(0.00)	91.53(0.00)
	TEST	87.22(0.03)	87.06(0.01)	89.36(0.03)	87.84(0.02)	89.36(0.00)	87.84(0.00)
	CPU	5.78(0.05)	10.90(0.09)	5.83(0.15)	12.97(0.25)	5.75(0.18)	12.98(0.15)
D10	TRAIN	99.70(0.00)	87.28(0.01)	99.58(0.00)	92.93(0.00)	99.58(0.00)	93.98(0.01)
	TEST	96.61(0.00)	86.58(0.01)	96.63(0.00)	91.98(0.00)	96.63(0.00)	92.15(0.00)
	CPU	18.97(0.08)	39.73(1.37)	18.08(0.15)	45.37(0.64)	18.33(0.17)	41.56(0.34)

Comments on Experimental Results: According to Table 2, our approach outperforms the comparative algorithms on almost all benchmark datasets. BC-DCASVM is much faster than UniSVM, and greatly outperforms LibSVM in terms of runtime. In some cases, BC-DCASVM is 5 times faster than UniSVM (for example, on D2 and D3) and 100 times faster than LibSVM (on D7, D8, D9 and D10). As the dataset size increases, while the classic SVM becomes slower (or even fails to handle), and UniSVM appears to make a trade-off between accuracy and runtime, our method shows efficiency by working on smaller data blocks. It is also important to note that, even though our approach is trained with only one epoch, it outperforms the two state-of-the-art algorithms in terms of accuracy in most datasets. That is, if runtime is not critical and accuracy is the primary concern, the algorithm can be trained with more epochs to achieve higher accuracy. However, without contradicting machine learning theory, Fig. 1 demonstrates that if training takes an excessive number of epochs, the performance does not improve (even decreases) due to the model overfitting. The last experiment shows that with three additional loss functions, our method outperforms UniSVM in most of the evaluation criteria, while remaining consistent performance with the first experiment. That means, our technique can be effectively applicable to a variety of LS-DC loss functions.

5   Conclusion and Future Work

To conclude, we propose a new approach for solving the large-scale kernel SVM, which applies DCA efficiently in combination with the block coordinate technique. Owing to the block coordinate approach with a nice DC decomposition, the proposed algorithm can both efficiently handle datasets with rich dimensionality and a large number of instances, while maintaining competitive performance. Thus, our method can overcome the storage and computation bottlenecks of classic SVM when dealing with big-data. Despite the noisy and partial updates of the block coordinate approach, our research shows that the power of DCA still remains. With the unified scheme, like UniSVM, BC-DCASVM can apply to most of the existing loss functions. However, while UniSVM uses the low-rank method for approximation, which may be a limitation when dealing with non-strongly correlated datasets, our solution employs the block coordinate approach that is independent of data correlation. The experimental results on ten real-world datasets show that our algorithm is more effective than the two mentioned methods.

Nonetheless, the proposed method has the following shortcomings that will be addressed in our future research. First, there is a gap between theory and practice, as the approximation errors caused by the use of mini-batch gradient have not been quantified. In addition, when the overlap occurs in computing the kernel matrix over multiple epochs (iterations), our implementation has not been able to reuse the calculations from the previous iteration in the current iteration. Moreover, there are aspects of the proposed algorithm that need to be further studied, such as investigating better strategies for block selection rule and evaluating the effectiveness of nonconvex losses in handling noisy data.

References

1. Boser, B.E., Guyon, I.M., Vapnik, V.N.: A training algorithm for optimal margin classifiers. In: Proceedings of COLT 1992, pp. 144–152 (1992)
2. Chang, C.C., Lin, C.J.: LIBSVM: a library for support vector machines. ACM Trans. Intell. Syst. Technol. (TIST) **2**(3), 1–27 (2011)
3. Chou, H.Y., Lin, P.Y., Lin, C.J.: Dual coordinate-descent methods for linear one-class SVM and SVDD. In: Proceedings SIAM International Conference Data Mining, pp. 181–189. SIAM (2020)
4. Cortes, C., Vapnik, V.: Support-vector networks. Mach. Learn. **20**(3), 273–297 (1995)
5. Hsieh, C.J., Chang, K.W., Lin, C.J., Keerthi, S.S., Sundararajan, S.: A dual coordinate descent method for large-scale linear SVM. In: Proceedings of the 25th International Conference on Machine Learning, pp. 408–415 (2008)
6. Le, H.M., Le Thi, H.A., Nguyen, M.C.: Sparse semi-supervised support vector machines by dc programming and DCA. Neurocomputing **153**, 62–76 (2015)
7. Le Thi, H.A., Le, H.M., Nguyen, V.V., Pham Dinh, T.: A dc programming approach for feature selection in support vector machines learning. Adv. Data Anal. Classif. **2**(3), 259–278 (2008). https://doi.org/10.1007/s11634-008-0030-7
8. Le Thi, H.A., Le, H.M., Pham Dinh, T.: Feature selection in machine learning: an exact penalty approach using a difference of convex function algorithm. Mach. Learn. **101**(1), 163–186 (2015)
9. Le Thi, H.A., Pham Dinh, T.: The DC (difference of convex functions) programming and DCA revisited with dc models of real world nonconvex optimization problems. Ann. Oper. Res. **133**(1), 23–46 (2005)
10. Le Thi, H.A., Pham Dinh, T.: DC programming and DCA: thirty years of developments. Math. Program. **169**(1), 5–68 (2018)
11. Lee, C.P., Roth, D.: Distributed box-constrained quadratic optimization for dual linear SVM. In: ICML, pp. 987–996. PMLR (2015)
12. Lee, C.P., Wright, S.J.: Random permutations fix a worst case for cyclic coordinate descent. IMA J. Numer. Anal. **39**(3), 1246–1275 (2019)
13. Lu, Z., Xiao, L.: On the complexity analysis of randomized block-coordinate descent methods. Math. Program. **152**, 615–642 (2014). https://doi.org/10.1007/s10107-014-0800-2
14. Nutini, J., Laradji, I., Schmidt, M.: Let's make block coordinate descent go fast: faster greedy rules, message-passing, active-set complexity, and superlinear convergence. arXiv preprint arXiv:1712.08859 (2017)
15. Pham Dinh, T., Le Thi, H.A.: Convex analysis approach to DC programming: theory, algorithms and applications. Acta Math. Vietnam **22**(1), 289–355 (1997)
16. Pham Dinh, T., Le Thi, H.A.: A DC optimization algorithm for solving the trust-region subproblem. SIAM J. Optim. **8**(2), 476–505 (1998)
17. Pham Dinh, T., Le Thi, H.A.: Recent advances in DC programming and DCA. In: Nguyen, N.T., Le-Thi, H.A. (eds.) Transactions on Computational Intelligence XIII. LNCS, vol. 8342, pp. 1–37. Springer, Heidelberg (2014). https://doi.org/10.1007/978-3-642-54455-2_1
18. Phan, D.N., Le Thi, H.A.: Group variable selection via $l_p,0$ regularization and application to optimal scoring. Neural Netw. **118**, 220–234 (2019)
19. Qin, Z., Scheinberg, K., Goldfarb, D.: Efficient block-coordinate descent algorithms for the group lasso. Math. Program. Comput. **5**(2), 143–169 (2013)

20. Schölkopf, B., Herbrich, R., Smola, A.J.: A generalized representer theorem. In: Helmbold, D., Williamson, B. (eds.) COLT 2001. LNCS (LNAI), vol. 2111, pp. 416–426. Springer, Heidelberg (2001). https://doi.org/10.1007/3-540-44581-1_27

21. Shalev-Shwartz, S., Ben-David, S.: Understanding machine learning: from theory to algorithms. Cambridge University Press (2014)

22. Vapnik, V.: The Nature of Statistical Learning Theory. Springer Science & Business Media. Springer, New York (1999).https://doi.org/10.1007/978-1-4757-3264-1

23. Zhao, Z., Zhang, R., Cox, J., Duling, D., Sarle, W.: Massively parallel feature selection: an approach based on variance preservation. Mach. Learn. **92**(1), 195–220 (2013). https://doi.org/10.1007/s10994-013-5373-4

24. Zhou, S., Zhou, W.: Unified SVM algorithm based on LS-DC loss. Mach. Learn. 1–28 (2021). https://doi.org/10.1007/s10994-021-05996-7

Knowledge Engineering and Semantic Web

Hybrid Approach to Designating Ontology Attribute Semantics

Bogumiła Hnatkowska[1] , Adrianna Kozierkiewicz[1] , Marcin Pietranik[1(✉)] ,
and Hai Bang Truong[2]

[1] Faculty of Computer Science and Management, Wroclaw University of Science and
Technology Wybrzeze, Wyspianskiego 27, 50-370 Wroclaw, Poland
{bogumila.hnatkowska,adrianna.kozierkiewicz,marcin.pietranik}@pwr.edu.pl
[2] Faculty of Information Technology, Nguyen Tat Thanh University, Ho Chi Minh,
Vietnam
thbang@ntt.edu.vn

Abstract. In our previous works, we have developed a novel approach
to ontologies that provides a notion of attributes semantics. We have
noticed that attributes by themselves contain no explicit meaning besides
being a carrier of values, and gain such only if included within a concept.
The biggest difficulty while creating and maintaining ontologies using
our formal framework is asserting the consistency of vocabulary used
to express the aforementioned semantics. The following article presents
the method for automatic designating of attributes semantics in ontologies. We extend our previous work where a semi-automatic method has
been proposed. The new approach utilizes Word2Vec similarity (incorporating the Genism library) and the WordNet lexical database. The
experiments confirmed the usefulness of the framework by comparing
attribute semantics created by experts manually and using the proposed
solution.

1 Introduction

Ontologies are a widely accepted and utilized method of formal knowledge representation. By providing a flexible and expressive approach to modeling some
domain of knowledge, they are used in a plethora of different applications, span-
ning from biomedical informatics to geographic information systems.

Concepts are the basic building blocks of ontologies. They can be treated
as a description of objects taken from the real world. These concepts are then
decomposed into attributes that describe their internal properties. Furthermore,
concepts can be connected with other concepts via relationships, which describe
how they interact with each other. Eventually, ontologies can contain instances of
concepts that are materializations of concepts. In other words, instances describe
particular elements of the real world, while concepts describe classes of objects.
Such an approach entails a layered definition of ontologies, which consists of a
level of concepts, a level of relations, and a level of instances.

N. T. Nguyen et al. (Eds.): ICCCI 2022, LNAI 13501, pp. 351–363, 2022.
https://doi.org/10.1007/978-3-031-16014-1_28

To enrich the above approach to ontologies, in our previous work [11], we have developed a framework that provides a notion of attribute semantics. We have noticed that an attribute by itself contains no explicit meaning besides being a carrier of values. However, in the real world attributes may have many different explicit and implicit meanings. For example, the date of birth of some person can be treated only as a date, or as a date and a method of determining someone's age or zodiac sign. To achieve such flexibility, we have introduced a function that assigns to every inclusion of an attribute within a concept a logic sentence built from a set of symbols and basic logic operators.

Such an approach allowed to not only express detailed knowledge about attributes but also to track relationships between them. However, the biggest difficulty while creating and maintaining ontologies using our formal framework is asserting the consistency of vocabulary used in the aforementioned logic sentences. For example, if there are three classes with three attributes each, then there are nine logic formulas to be provided. Manually asserting their consistency may be at least annoying and for large-scale ontologies, with hundreds of concepts and attributes, the process may be so time-consuming and error-prone that the whole method may become unusable.

To remedy this situation, we proposed to incorporate WordNet [4], an online lexical database, that organizes words into sets of synonyms (so-called synsets) together with their meanings and lexical relationships between them. These relationships form a graph, which is a foundation of WordNet. This entails that for almost every pair of words there exists at least one path in this hierarchy.

The developed solution aids ontology developers who need to select synsets for words extracted from names of concepts and attributes. The method eventually designates the shortest path between the chosen synsets in the WordNet graph. Synsets from this path can be then combined using logic operators eventually forming the desired attribute's semantics.

In [6] we described and experimentally proved the usefulness of the proposed approach to utilizing WordNet. The only flaw of this solution appears when the name of some selected attribute has a few different matching synsets in WordNet. The proposed solution is only semi-automatic and serves as an aid during the ontology creation process, not as a fully automatic tool. Therefore, if such a situation occurs, then the ontology developer must make a decision about which synset is the most accurate and will be used in designating attribute's semantics. This decision may be difficult for one person, or if few people work on the same ontology, different selections can be made. In other words, their choices may lead to another inconsistency – by remedying one issue, a different one is introduced.

Let us consider the leading example presented in Table 1. We asked five human experts to choose the definition for the indicated attributes. The experts have been previously informed about a concept to which these attributes will be belonging to. As we can see, the attribute *gender*, which refers to the concept *Person*, has been interpreted differently by different experts. One of them chose the first synset for *gender* which is understood as *a grammatical category in inflected languages governing the agreement between nouns and pronouns and adjectives; in some languages, it is quite arbitrary but in Indo-European languages, it is usually based on sex or animateness).* Another expert decided to assign the second synset of *sex: either of the two categories (male or female) into which most organisms are divided.* Most of the experts choose the fourth synset for *sex: the properties that distinguish organisms based on their reproductive roles.* Experts had a bigger problem in choosing a definition for an attribute *has_short_title* belonging to the *Social_Event* concept. Most of them could not completely define this attribute. One expert chosen *title- a general or descriptive heading for a section of a written work* which is not adequate. Only one expert was intuitively closer than others. He chose the synset *abbrevation: a shortened form of a word or phrase.* The third case caused even more confusion. Experts were not unanimous in their responses. *Has_postal_code* belonging to the *Organization* concept was interpreted vaguely as: post.n.11- *the delivery and collection of letters and packages,* mail.n.04- *any particular collection of letters or packages that is delivered* or using very general approach: *address- the place where a person or organization can be found or communicated with.* Only one expert could find the precise synset: zip_code.n.01- *a code of letters and digits added to a postal address to aid in the sorting of mail.*

The example described above clearly illustrates the ambiguity that appears while choosing appropriate synset, which eventually makes it difficult to assert consistency of attributes semantics. Different experts selected different synsets for the same attributes (e.g. *has_postal_code*), so the necessity of further aiding them during the ontology development process is obvious. Therefore, the main goal of the following article is extending the framework proposed in [6] with an automatic method of choosing synsets that would be suited best for attribute semantics.

Table 1. Leading example

Attribute name	Expert 1	Expert 2	Expert 3	Expert 4	Expert 5
has_gender	gender.n.01	sex.n.04	sex.n.04	sex.n.02	sex.n.04
has_short_title	abbreviation.n.01	title.n.03	?	?	?
has_postal_code	post.n.11	?	zip_code.n.01	mail.n.04	address.n.02

The article is structured as follows. In the next section, a selection of related works is provided. Section 3 contains basic notions and definitions used in the remainder of the paper. Section 4 presents the proposed approach to designating attributes semantics. The experimental procedure is described in Sect. 5. A summary and an overview of our research plans are given in Sect. 6.

2 Related Works

WordNet and ontologies are two research topics that are both similar and dissimilar and it is not completely clear how strictly to distinguish the difference between them. It is very simple to find multiple publications concerning using WordNet in ontology applications and vice versa. For example, in [7] authors noticed that despite being a very large lexical database, WordNet focuses on a generic vocabulary, and frequently it is impossible to use it in applications where very specific, technical phrases are used. On the other hand, such phrases can be easily structured using ontologies. Therefore, the authors of [7] propose to extend WordNet by adding words and relationships derived from students' class notes stored as wikidata. The obtained knowledge base includes both common phrases and technical terms, which in consequence improve the quality of different tasks like text summarization. Similar remarks can be found in [5].

Other research where these two topics overlap concerns various tasks related to ontology alignment [2] and integration [1], where WordNet is treated as a source of background knowledge. For example, the authors of [13] use Word-Net to detect semantic relationships between concepts in two ontologies that are aligned. Such a matching task is defined in this context as the creation of mappings between semantically related nodes of two ontologies. The authors offer a collection of element-level semantic matchers that use WordNet to broaden the scope of semantic similarity measurements. Authors of [8] took a different approach and based their approach to ontology alignment on using lexical relationships between words (hyponymy, holonymy, meronymy).

Incorporating WordNet resources in the process of ontology development is not a completely new idea. For example, in [9] authors developed a novel computational model that utilizes data mining mechanisms, Natural Language Processing, WordNet, and a class-based n-gram model for automatic ontology discovery and recognition from the given set of patent documents. WordNet itself was used to generate class labels.

What mainly distinguishes the ideas presented in the following article from previous WordNet applications are the base ontology definitions. In [11] we demonstrated that a method to ontology alignment based on analyzing attribute semantics yields good results. Manually specifying semantics, on the other hand, is extremely error-prone, time-consuming, and costly. For this reason we aimed to incorporate WordNet as a technique of strengthening base definitions and making them actually useful. In other words, to fill the gap which appears when applying the theoretical framework in practical applications.

To the best of our knowledge, only a handful of similar approaches to extending ontology definition exist. The closest one can be found in [12] which describes a procedure for coupling ontology concepts with corresponding WordNet entries. These correspondences are then used to generate a collection of virtual documents representing various ontology concepts, which can then be incorporated during similarity calculations.

In [3], the authors propose to use a strongly typed first-order logic language that is eventually translated to the OWL - the most popular ontology representation format - to conduct the merging of two related ontologies. This approach may appear similar to the one considered in the following article, but the aforementioned logic clauses are not part of the processed ontologies; rather, they are inferred during the runtime of an ontology integration process. This feature is a significant difference between the presented approach and the ideas proposed in the following paper.

3   Basic Notions

At the beginning, we need to define the ontology in a formal way. For this task, we define a pair (A, V) which is so-called "closed world". By A we denot a set of attributes describing objects and V is a set of valuations of such attributes (their domains), where: $V = \bigcup_{a \in A} V_a$. The (A, V)-based ontology as a quintuple:

$$O = (C, H, R^C, I, R^I) \tag{1}$$

where C is a finite set of concepts, H is a concepts' hierarchy, a distinguished relation between concepts, R^C represents a set of concepts relations $R^C = \{r_1^C, r_2^C, ..., r_n^C\}$, $n \in N$, such that every $r_i^C \in R^C$ ($i \in [1, n]$) is a subset of a cartesian product, $r_i^C \subset C \times C$, I is a set of instances' identifiers, and $R^I = \{r_1^I, r_2^I, ..., r_n^I\}$ is a set of relations between concepts' instances.

Each concept c belonging to the set C is defined as:

$$c = (id^c, A^c, V^c, I^c) \tag{2}$$

where id^c is an identifier of the concept c, A^c denotes a set of its attributes, $(A^c \subset A)$, V^c represents a set of attributes domains, where $V^c = \bigcup_{a \in A^c} V_a$, and I^c is a set of concepts' c instances. For simplicity, we can write $a \in c$ and it is interpreted that an attribute a is a part of the concept c.

In this paper, the most important remark refers to the lack of semantics for all attributes from set A. They can be only interpreted if they are part of the chosen concept. Let us consider attribute *title*. If it is part of concept *Book* it is understand as the name given to a literary work, however attribute *title* belonging to concept *Person* may describes a person's job in a company or organization.

For better distinction of different meanings of attributes we introduce a set D_A which contains atomic descriptions of them. We also assume the existence of a sub-language of the sentence calculus, denoted as (L_S^A). The L_S^A is composed of D_A elements and logical operators of conjunction, disjunction, and negation. Formally, we define a function, which allow us to assigns a logical sentence from L_S^A to attributes within a specific concept:

$$S_A : A \times C \to L_S^A \tag{3}$$

For better understanding of the above definition let us consider attribute *birthday* within a concept *Person*. The following semantics can be determined: $S_A(birthday, Person) : day\_of\_birth \land month\_of\_birth \land year\_of\_birth \land age$.

4   Generating Attribute Semantics

A simplified version (which skips all the edge cases) of an algorithm broadly described in [6] for designating attribute's semantics in the context of a given concept is presented on Algorithm 1. The procedure is straightforward and starts with selecting the first synset for the given input concept c among synsets found in WordNet based on the concept's name. We assume that the name of the concepts is unique, and according to Eq. 1 stored as a value of its identifier id^c. Then the algorithm uses a different procedure *select_attribute_synset* presented on Algorithm 2 to select the most suitable synset for the given attribute and concept names. Eventually, for synsets chosen for the attribute a and the concept c, the shortest path within WordNet between them is found and its elements' names are concatenated using conjunction symbol forming the final attribute semantics. For clarity, we assume that WordNet can be formally treated as a finite set of synsets. Each synset $syn \in WordNet$ is a pair $syn = (name, definition)$, where *name* is a unique synset identifier and *definition* is an informal description of the synset. Within the algorithm, to refer to the value of a name or a definition of a particular synset, we use the dot notion (e.g. *syn.name*). The *shortest_path* procedure returns a subset of synsets from WordNet, each being connected with another one, together forming a path between two given synsets.

Algorithm 1. Designating attribute's semantics

Input: $c \in C$, $a \in A^c$
Output: $S_A(a, c)$ (semantics of attribute a in the concept c according to Eq. 3)
 1: select first synset for c based on the value of id^c and store it as $syn(c)$
 2: $syn(a) := select\_attribute\_synset(a, c)$
 3: $S_A(a, c) := ''$
 4: designate $shortest\_path(syn(a), syn(c))$
 5: **for** $node \in shortest\_path(syn(a), syn(c))$ **do**
 6:      $S_A(a, c) := S_A(a, c) + ' \wedge ' + node.name$
 7: **end for**
 8: **return** $S_A(a, c)$

The aforementioned *select_attribute_synset* procedure is the main contribution of the following article. It takes as an input an attribute and a concept to which it belongs and returns the most appropriate synset that can semantically represent the attribute's inclusion within the concept. It is presented on Algorithm 2.

Algorithm 2. Select attribute synset

Input: $c \in C$, $a \in A^c$

Output: $syn \in WordNet$ (synset best representing attribute a in the concept c)

1: **function** $select\_attribute\_synset(a, c)$
2:     $tagged\_concept\_name := tokenize\_and\_tag(id^c)$
3:     $tagged\_attribute\_name := tokenize\_and\_tag(a)$
4:     $max := 0$
5:     **for** $candidate \in get\_candidate\_synsets(tagged\_attribute\_name)$ **do**
6:         $pairs = tagged\_concept\_name \times tokenize\_and\_tag(candidate.definition)$
7:         $partial\_sim := \frac{\sum_{pair \in pairs} sim_{Word2Vec}(pair)}{|pairs|}$
8:         **if** $partial\_sim > max$ **then**
9:             $max := partial\_sim$
10:            $syn := candidate$
11:        **end if**
12:    **end for**
13:    **return** syn
14: **end function**

15: **function** $get\_candidate\_synsets(tagged\_attribute\_name)$
16:     $previous\_iteration :=''$
17:     $mutations := \emptyset$
18:     **for** $attr\_part \in tagged\_attr\_name$ **do**
19:         **if** $previous\_iteration =''$ **then**
20:             $current\_iteration := attr\_part$
21:         **else**
22:             $current\_iteration := previous\_iteration +' \_' + attr\_part$
23:             $previous\_iteration := current\_iteration$
24:             $mutations := mutations \cup \{current\_iteration\}$
25:         **end if**
26:     **end for**
27:     $candidates := \{\}$
28:     **for** $mut \in mutations$ **do**
29:         $candidates := candidates \cup WordNet.synsets\_for\_word(mut)$
30:     **end for**
31:     **if** $candidates = \emptyset$ **then**
32:         **for** $attr\_part \in tagged\_attribute\_name$ **do**
33:             $candidates := candidates \cup WordNet.synsets\_for\_word(attr\_part)$
34:         **end for**
35:     **end if**
36:     **return** $candidates$
37: **end function**

The procedure starts with preprocessing a name of a given attribute and a name of a given concept (Line 2–3). This is done using the *tokenize_and_tag* function which utilizes Spacy[1] library to discard any appearing stop words preserving only nouns, verbs, pronouns, adjectives, and adverbs in their base forms.

---

[1] https://spacy.io/.

Then, the algorithm uses *get_candidate_synsets* to select from WordNet candidate synsets (Line 6). This is done by concatenating the elements of the processed attribute's name with the underscore symbol, eventually creating a set of mutations of such attribute's name. Subsequently (Line 29) the algorithm checks if there exists a matching synset for mutations which include the underscore symbol. If no synset is found (Line 32), the algorithm checks if there are any synsets matching with unmutated elements of the attribute's name. We favor mutations containing underscores (e.g. a synset *first_name* should be chosen over the synset *name*) over base elements due to the fact, that in WordNet more specific synsets are usually named with an underscore.

For every candidate synset, the algorithm performs the same preprocessing of its definition using the *tokenize_and_tag* function. Then, for each combination of words from the processed concept name and processed synset definition the algorithm calculates Word2Vec similarity, incorporating the Gensim library[2]. Eventually, the average similarity value (Line 8) is calculated for each selected candidate synset. Finally, the algorithm returns the synset which scored the highest value (Line 14).

5   Experimental Verification

In our experiment, we engaged 12 human experts. All participants are familiar with object-oriented programming, and that metaphor was used for the concept of ontology explanation (if it was required). They all work in the area of IT and have different ages (24–65, average about 40).

We choose 4 ontologies: Edas, Sigkdd, ConfTool, Sofsem provided by OAEI organization [10]. The experiment is based on selecting attribute synset with the purpose of attribute semantic designating. The choice of the synset has been done by Algorithm 2 and manually by the independent group of experts. Each synset has been determined six times by randomly chosen 6 experts (from the total 12). The main purpose of our experimental verification is to demonstrate the usefulness of our method for attribute synset choice confronted to the manual approach. Below, in the Table 3, 4, 5, 6 we present results of our algorithm (column *Synset*) in comparison with a choice made with the majority of experts' decision (column *Majority choice of experts*). The last column contains a synset chosen by six experts in a democratic way. The *lack of decisiveness* means that experts select different synsets or the majority of final decision is missing. The *lack of choice* refers to the situation in which experts couldn't select any synset definition from WordNet. All of the results can be found in [14]

In previous sections, we mentioned that our semi-automatic approach for determining attribute's semantic [6] has a main flaw which occurs when the name of an attribute has a few different matching synsets in WordNet. Then, the choice of synset is done manually by experts. Our experiment showed that selections of synsets done by human experts are inconsistent, choosing them is error-prone and difficult.

---

[2] https://radimrehurek.com/gensim_3.8.3/models/word2vec.html.

Table 2. The summary results of experiment

Ontology	Sofsem	Edas	Sigkdd	Conftool	**Summary**
Total number of expected synsets	22	20	11	32	**85**
Total number of no decisiveness	0	3	1	5	**9**
Total number of no choice	12	11	4	22	**49**
Total number of synsets chosen by human experts	10	6	6	5	**27**
Total number of common synsets	4	2	1	1	**8**

In total, experts have been asked to select 85 synsets defining attributes (Table 2). In 49 cases (this is more than 57%) experts have not been able to choose any synset. In 9 cases (more than 10%) their decisions have been inconsistent and the final selection has not been done. Only for 27 attributes (less than 32%), a synset has been assigned. Our Algorithm 2 has been able to find a synset for attributes in 82 cases (more than 96%). The choice of common synset chosen by experts and our Algorithm 2 is equal to 8 (less than 30%).

Table 3. The results of Algorithm 2 for Sigkdd ontology

Concept	Attribute	Synset	Majority choice of experts
Conference	City_of_conference	city.n.02	lack of decisiveness
Registration_fee	Currency	currency.n.02	lack of choice
Deadline	Date	date.v.02	lack of choice
Person	E-mail	mail.v.02	electronic_mail.n.01
Conference	End_of_conference	end.n.03	end.n.02
Person	Name	name.n.02	name.n.01
Conference	Name_of_conference	name.v.03	name.n.01
Sponsor	Name_of_sponsor	name.v.05	lack of choice
Person	Nation	nation.n.02	nation.n.02
Registration_fee	Price	price.n.06	lack of choice
Conference	Start_of_conference	start.n.01	beginning.n.02

Sometimes, the difference between the chosen synsets (by experts and our algorithm) is very ambiguous, and therefore, it is difficult to tell which one is better (from a human perspective). For example, both synsets: *e-mail.v.01: communicate electronically on the computer* and *electronic_mail.n.01: a system of worldwide electronic communication in which a computer user can compose a message at one terminal that can be regenerated at the recipient's terminal when the recipient logs in* of the attribute *has_an_email* for the *Person* concept seem to be correct.

Synsets selected by our Algorithm 2 are better than synsets chosen by experts if the context of the concept to which that attribute belongs is taken into consideration. Let us consider Table 4. Human experts have chosen the same synset for two attributes: *has_a_name* and *has_the_first_name*. The chosen definition is very general, so it is applicable, however, it lacks nuances. Our approach distinguishes the notion of publisher's name, conference proceeding's name, topic's name, and conference's name from person's first name.

Table 4. The results of Algorithm 2 for Sofsem ontology

Concept	Attribute	Synset	Majority choice of experts
Conference_document	has_a_date of_issue	date.n.05	lack of choice
Review_preference	has_a_degree	degree.n.02	lack of choice
Person	has_a_gender	sex.n.04	sex.n.04
Conference_volume	has_a_location	localization.n.01	localization.n.01
Conference	has_a_name	name.v.03	name.n.01
Topic	has_a_name	name.n.06	name.n.01
Publisher	has_a_name	name.n.01	name.n.01
Conference_part	has_a_name	mention.v.01	name.n.01
Conference_proceedings	has_a_name	name.v.03	name.n.01
Conference_www	has_a_URL	url.n.01	lack of choice
Conference_proceedings	has_a_volume	volume.n.04	lack of choice
Person	has_an_email	e-mail.v.01	electronic_mail.n.01
Review_expertise	has_an_expertise	lack of choice	lack of choice
Conference_proceedings	has_an_ISBN	lack of choice	lack of choice
Person	has_the first_name	first_name.n.01	name.n.01
Person	has_the last_name	surname.n.01	surname.n.01
Important_dates	is_a_date_of acceptance announcement	announcement.n.02	lack of choice
Important_dates	is_a_date_of camera_ready paper_submission	ready.s.04	lack of choice
Important_dates	is_a_full paper_submission date	full.a.01	lack of choice
Important_dates	is_a_starting date	originate.v.02	lack of choice
Important_dates	is_an_abstract submission_date	abstract.v.04	lack of choice
Important_dates	is_an_ending date	end.n.02	lack of choice

Table 5. The results of Algorithm 2 for Edas ontology

Concept	Attribute	Synset	Majority choice of experts
Conference	endDate	date.n.05	lack of decisiveness
Person	hasBiography	biography.n.01	biography.n.01
ContactInformation	hasCity	city.n.02	lack of choice
Sponsorship	hasCostAmount	come.v.15	lack of choice
Sponsorship	hasCostCurrency	cost.v.01	lack of choice
Person	hasEmail	e-mail.v.01	electronic_mail_n.01
ConferenceEvent	hasEndDateTime	date.n.05	end.n.02
Person	hasFirstName	first_name.n.01	name.n.01
Person	hasLastName	surname.n.01	surname.n.01
Conference	hasName	name.v.03	lack of decisiveness
ContactInformation	hasPhone	call.v.03	lack of choice
ContactInformation	hasPostalCode	zip_code.n.01	lack of choice
ConferenceEvent	hasStartDateTime	date.n.05	beginning.n.02
ConferenceEvent	hasStreet	street.n.04	lack of choice
Call	hasSubmissionDeadline	deadline.n.01	lack of choice
Call	hasSubmisssionInstruction	direction.n.06	lack of choice
Conference	manuscriptDueOn	due.s.02	lack of choice
Conference	paperDueOn	due.s.02	lack of choice
Conference	registrationDueOn	due.s.02	lack of choice
Conference	startDate	date.n.05	lack of decisiveness

Table 6. The results of Algorithm 2 for Conftool ontology

Concept	Attribute	Synset	Majority choice of experts
Social_event	defaultChoice	default.n.01	lack of choice
Working_event	defaultChoice	default.n.01	lack of choice
Participant	earlyRegistration	registration.n.02	lack of choice
Event	ends_on	end.n.03	lack of choice
Social_event	has_short_title	short.r.06	lack of choice
Working_event	has_short_title	short.r.06	lack of choice
Social_event	has_title	claim.n.04	lack of choice
Working_event	has_title	claim.n.04	lack of choice
Social_event	has_Vat	tub.n.02	lack of choice
Working_event	has_Vat	tub.n.02	lack of choice
Person	hasEmail	e-mail.v.01	electronic_mail.n.01
Person	hasFax	fax.v.01	facsimile.n.02
Person	hasFirstName	first_name.n.01	name.n.01
Person	hasHomePage	home_page.n.01	lack of decisiveness
Contribution	hasKeyword	lack of choice	lack of choice
Person	hasPhone	phone.n.02	phone_number.n.01
Person	hasPostalCode	zip_code.n.01	lack of decisiveness
Organization	hasPostalCode	zip_code.n.01	lack of decisiveness
Person	hasStreet	street.n.05	lack of decisiveness
Organization	hasStreet	street.n.04	lack of decisiveness
Person	hasSurname	surname.n.01	surname.n.01
Contribution	hasTitle	title.n.02	lack of choice
Social_event	location	localization.n.01	lack of choice
Working_event	location	localization.n.01	lack of choice
Social_event	maxChoice	choice.n.01	lack of choice
Working_event	maxChoice	option.n.02	lack of choice
Social_event	minChoice	choice.n.01	lack of choice
Working_event	minChoice	option.n.02	lack of choice
Contribution	remark	note.v.01	lack of choice
Event	starts_on	start.n.01	lack of choice

However, the biggest advantage of our algorithm is its 96% efficiency. Our automatic approach is able to select a synset for almost all attributes. The good example are synsets not identified by human experts like: *zip_code.n.01:a code of letters and digits added to a postal address to aid in the sorting of mail* for attriubte *hasPostalCode, currency.n.02: general acceptance or use* for attribute *Currency, deadline.n.01: the point in time at which something must be completed* for attribute *hasSubmissionDeadline* or *end.n.02: the point in time at which something ends* for attribute *is_ an_ ending_ date*. The human experts yield good results only if an attribute is unambiguous, however. Out Algorithm 2 can deal with more non-obvious situations.

6   Summary and Future Works

In recent years ontologies become expressive and flexible knowledge structures. However, the process of creating ontology still requires human participation. Both this and our previous works focus on reducing human engagement in the process of ontology creation and integration.

This paper extends the framework proposed in [6] by developing an automatic method for choosing WordNet synset describing attribute meaning. To the best of our knowledge, there is no research addressing the mentioned problem. We have proposed an easy approach utilizing Word2Vec similarity (incorporating the Genism library) between each candidate synset definition selected from WordNet and concept name. The experiments confirmed the usefulness of the proposed approach. Our method is able to choose synset in more than 96%, where human experts only in less than 32%. The human expert cannot select any definition if the attribute name is complex, not obvious, or is somehow nuanced. Our automatic approach deals with all, even non-intuitive cases.

In the future, we plan to further verify our ideas by engaging human experts for the evaluation of the selected attribute synset. Furthermore, we would like to prepare a tool for creating, storing, and processing ontologies that would support or even replace human experts in each mentioned task. The implemented framework for ontology integration should be further verified using benchmark datasets provided by Ontology Alignment Evaluation Initiative. Due to the limitation of this paper, we presented only a solution where synset are selected based on the biggest average similarity value. Therefore, we plan to experiment with different strategies.

References

1. Chen, R.C., Bau, C.T., Yeh, C.J.: Merging domain ontologies based on the Word-Net system and fuzzy formal concept analysis techniques. Appl. Soft Comput. **11**(2), 1908–1923 (2011)
2. Cross, V., Hu, X.: In Proceedings of the 6th International Conference on Ontology Matching - Volume 814 (OM'11). CEUR-WS.org, Aachen, DEU, pp. 61–72 (2011)
3. Dou, D., McDermott, D., Qi, P.: Ontology translation on the semantic Web. In: Spaccapietra, S., Bertino, E., Jajodia, S., King, R., McLeod, D. (eds.) Journal on Data Semantics II, pp. 35–57. Springer, Berlin, Germany (2005)
4. Fellbaum, C.: WordNet. In: Poli, R., Healy, M., Kameas, A. (eds.) Theory and Applications of Ontology: Computer Applications, pp. 231–243. Springer, Dordrecht (2010). https://doi.org/10.1007/978-90-481-8847-5_10
5. Fellbaum, C., Hicks, A.: When WordNet met ontology. Ontology Makes Sense 136–151 (2019). https://doi.org/10.3233/978-1-61499-830-3-30

6. Hnatkowska, B., Kozierkiewicz, A., Pietranik, M.: Semi-automatic definition of attribute semantics for the purpose of ontology integration. IEEE Access **8**, 107272–107284 (2020). https://doi.org/10.1109/ACCESS.2020.3000035

7. Kanika, C.S., Chakraborty, P., Aggarwal, A., Madan, M., Gupta, G.: Enriching WordNet with subject specific out of vocabulary terms using existing ontology. In: Nanda, P., Verma, V.K., Srivastava, S., Gupta, R.K., Mazumdar, A.P. (eds.) Data Engineering for Smart Systems. LNNS, vol. 238. Springer, Singapore (2022). https://doi.org/10.1007/978-981-16-2641-8_19

8. Kwak, J., Yong, H.S.: Ontology matching based on hypernym, hyponym, holonym, and meronym sets in WordNet. Int. J. Web Semantic Technol. **1**(2), 1–14 (2010)

9. Li, Z., Tate, D.: Automatic ontology generation from patents using a pre-built library, WordNet and a class-based n-gram model. Int. J. Prod. Dev. **20**(2), 142–172 (2015)

10. http://oaei.ontologymatching.org

11. Pietranik, M., Nguyen, N.T.: A multi-attribute based framework for ontology aligning. Neurocomputing **146**, 276–290 (2014). https://doi.org/10.1016/j.neucom.2014.03.067

12. Schadd, F.C., Roos, N.: Coupling of word net entries for ontology mapping using virtual documents. In: Proceedings of the 7th International Conference on Ontology Matching, vol. 946, pp. 25–36 (2012)

13. Yatskevich, M., Giunchiglia, F.: Element level semantic matching using WordNet. In: Proceedings of the Meaning Coordination Negotiation Workshop at ISWC, pp. 37–48 (2004)

14. http://github.com/radioarm/wordnet-attributes

A New Approach of Morphological Analysis of Arabic Syntagmatic Units Based on a Linguistic Ontology

Mariem El Abdi[1(✉)], Boutheina Smine Ben Ali[1], and Sadok Ben Yahia[2]

[1] Faculty of Sciences of Tunis, Department of Computer Science,
Tunis El Manar University, LIPAH-LR 11ES14, 2092 Tunis, Tunisia
elabdi.mariem@gmail.com
[2] Tallinn University of Technology, Tallinn, Estonia
http://www.utm.rnu.tn/utm/fr/, https://taltech.ee/en/

Abstract. For a natural language, morphology is the basic layer over which the higher syntactic and semantic layers are built. Several works relating the Arabic language morphology have been proposed to produce a practical morphological analyzer. However, the latter doesn't consider the words-agglutination in the same syntagmatic unit. This paper attempts to remedy these constraints using the richness of the diacritized Arabic language and its derivational morphology. So, we introduce a morphological analysis method of Arabic syntagmatic units based on a linguistic ontology. The output system named ARAMO offers the user the possibility of management of the ontology and the morphological analysis of the syntagmatic units. The evaluation results are encouraging compared to other systems.

Keywords: Ontology · Syntagmatic unit · Arabic language

1 Introduction

For a natural language, morphology is the basic layer over which the higher syntactic and semantic layers are built. There has been much work on Arabic morphology as Shaalan et al. [11], Gridach and Chenfour [13]. However, there are a few current initiatives towards the morphological analysis of the diacritized Arabic language. Moreover, the Arabic language is considered complex due to his words agglutination. Nevertheless, this agglutination reflects a strong cohesion of some text constituents, justifying their relation in the same syntagmatic unit taken into account and eventually constituting an entire sentence. The challenges of Arabic Natural Language Processing are discussed in Farghaly and Shalaan [1] as its morphological richness, diacritization in Arabic and word agglutination, etc. In this paper, we are paying heed to two of these challenges. The first one concerns the consideration of Arabic as a diacritized language. The second challenge is to handle the complexity of the Arabic morphology by exploiting

N. T. Nguyen et al. (Eds.): ICCCI 2022, LNAI 13501, pp. 364–377, 2022.
https://doi.org/10.1007/978-3-031-16014-1_29

an ontology. So, we introduce a method of morphological analysis of Arabic syntagmatic units using a linguistic ontology developed within this work, which reflects the constituents of verbal and prepositional syntagmatic units. This work was created in a system named ARAMO.

The process of our method takes into account a syntagmatic unit that is compounded of a single entity, as well as of several entities. It is worth mentioning that the degree of granularity of a morphological analysis process depends on the extension of the syntagmatic unit taken into account, to wit the lower extent of the syntagmatic unit is, the less precise the morphological analysis requirements are. This task of morphological analysis is often an intermediate step taken as part of a solution to a more significant, more complex NLP problem. For this reason, the carried out experiments on our system ARAMO showed that it is scalable, accurate, and easily extensible. Moreover, our ontology can be reused as a basis for other NLP applications. The paper is organized as follows: Sect. 1 gives some background about the Arabic morphology of syntagmatic Units. Then, in Sect. 2, we list some existing works on morphological analysis of Arabic. Section 3 introduces our ontology of the syntagmatic unit components that are exploited in the morphological analysis process, which is described in Sect. 4 Finally, the results of the evaluation process are described in Sect. 5.

2   The Arabic Syntagmatic Unit Morphology

The morphology of any natural language is the linguistic system that governs how the words of this language are built [9]. It focuses on the word's grammatical category, such as nouns, verbs, and case, gender, number, tense, person, etc. In Arabic language, words are classified into three types: verbs, nouns, and prepositions, and the structure of any syntagmatic unit is presented below:

1. The syntagmatic unit's central part, a verb, a noun, or a preposition, occurs in the middle. Let us call this part the **Base**.
2. The Base may be prefixed by an **Ant-Fix** like conjunction, a particle, or some combination of them.
3. The Base may be suffixed by a **Post-Fix** such as a pronoun.

In this paper, we focus on verbal and prepositional syntagmatic units: أَمَام، وَرَاء،
فَوْق، تَحْت، بَعْد، قَبْل، فِي، عَن، عَلَى،حَتَّى، مِن، إِلَى. However, Arabic verbs have
the following grammatical categories: tense (past, present, imperative, and future), number (singular, dual, and plural), person (first, second and third), mood (indicative, subjunctive), gender (masculine and feminine) and voice (active and passive) [6].Arabic verbs are mainly characterized by their rich derivational morphology, where almost all of the verbs are derived from basic patterns. These patterns can correspond to triliteral verbs whenever the number of consonants is three (فعل) and to quadriliteral verbs, as for as the number of consonants is four (فعلل). Many derivatives are produced from these basic patterns by adding diacritized consonants to them. There are twelve derivations from triliteral verbs and four derivations from quadriliteral ones.

3   Scruting of the Related Work

A lot of interest in studying the Arabic language and especially its morphological analysis has been shown. Applications have taken this study, e.g., Information Retrieval and Question Answering Systems [7], to name but a few. Studies saw the derivational and inflexional aspects of the language and its diacritics as a shortage rather than an advantage whenever it comes to the automatic analysis of the Arabic language. They did not use the specificities of the diacritized Arabic language but used approaches that were successful with Latin languages. These studies lead to systems that can be split into two categories:

1. Systems implemented by individuals as part of their academic activities such as the system of Xerox Arabic Morphological Analysis and Generation [10] which uses morphological rules to obtain stems for nouns and verbs based on a table of thousands of roots. Khoja's stemmer [17] and Buckwalter morphological analyzer [18] are other analyzers that rely on tables of valid combinations between prefixes, suffixes, and stems. The work of Yousfi. [3] is also worthy of mention, proposing a morphological analysis of Arabic verbs by using the degree of similarity between the word and the surface patterns to find the correct pattern. All the cited systems used a table of thousands of data to process the morphological analysis process.
2. The second category of systems is proposed by commercial organizations for realizing market applications, such as the morphological Analyzer DIINAR (DIctionnaire INformatisé de l'ARabe) [8]. The latter proposes for each word morphological specification structured in a database. SALMA [14] is a system that adds the appropriate linguistic information to each part of the word. The project MADA [15] uses a morphological analyzer to produce all possible morphological features of the word. MADA was then included in a larger and faster system, called MADAMIRA [2] for Arabic morphological analysis and disambiguation.

All these systems proceed with the morphological analysis of diactiritzed and non-diacritized Arabic language. However, the non-diacritized Arabic language generates many ambiguities that most of the cited systems partially treat. Moreover, these systems use data sets stored in files or tables which can affect the analysis process. Thus, we propose a morphological analysis method of Arabic syntagmatic units using not tables of data but an ontology where the linguistic data are organized and which can be reused by other systems.

4   Ontology Engineering

Recently, several works related to ontology engineering have been proposed to support Arabic in the semantic web as the work of Hakkoum et al. [21]. The latter proposed a natural language Interface to Arabic ontologies. In the remainder of this paper, we introduce a linguistic ontology to assist the morphological analysis of Arabic verbal and prepositional syntagmatic units. Exploiting an ontology in our morphological analysis method allows us to avoid using dictionaries and to treat ambiguities in the analysis process. Thus, for the development of our ontology, we have followed an ontological engineering approach based on the WSMO framework [20]. It is a formal, explicit description of concepts in a domain of discourse, properties of each concept describing various features and attributes of the concept, and relationships between classes. We build the ontology using the Protégé-5.2.0 tool, a free, open-source platform used to describe ontologies. Our ontology represents a hierarchy of 209 classes with a set of instances and properties which constitute a knowledge base. We implemented an interface within our system ARAMO for the end-user to facilitate the extension and the management of our ontology. All the constituents of our ontology are detailed in the following.

4.1   Classes

A class represents a group of different instances sharing common characteristics that may be more or less specific. It can contain another class (a subclass of), instances, or a combination of both [4]. As already underscored in Sect. 2, an Arabic verbal or prepositional syntagmatic unit can be composed of Ant-Fixes, Base, and Post-Fixes. These elements represent the classes of the First level of our ontology. In the second level, these classes are extended into sub-classes to specify their components (see Fig. 1).

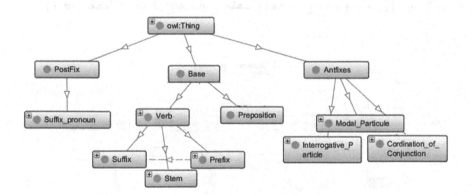

Fig. 1. The first and second Level classes of our ontology

- The class *AntFix* is divided into three subclasses: *ConjunctionOfCoordination, InterrogativeParticle and ModalParticle.*
- The class *PostFix* has only one subclass *SuffixPronoun*, which contains the list of suffix pronouns.
- The class *Base* is divided into two subclasses:
  ° The class *Preposition* corresponds to the list of Prepositions in Arabic

° The class Verb is detailed into three subclasses: *Prefix, Stem and Suffix*, which correspond respectively to the components Prefix, Stem, and Suffix of a conjugated verb. The subclass *Suffix* represents the suffix of the conjugated verb and is divided into three sub-classes:

* The sub-class *Past* contains the instances of the verb suffixes conjugated in the past;
* The sub-class *Present* for the instances of the suffixes of a verb conjugated in the present;
* The sub-class *Imperative* for the instances of the suffixes of a verb conjugated in the imperative.

4.2   Instances and Properties

Instances in the Ontology are objects of predefined classes. The developed ontology contains 140 instances. They have 72 features or properties that describe the object itself. The characteristics of a verb, as shown in Fig. 2, are:

- its Structure{trilateral, quadrilateral},
- its Category{augmented, unaugmented},
- its Person متكلم،مخاطب،غائب,
- its Subject-gender{Masculine, Feminine, Common},
- its Subject-number{Singular, Dual, Plural},
- its Mode{active, Passive},
- its Tense {{ماضي،مضارع مرفوع،مضارع منصوب،مضارع مجزوم،أمر}}.

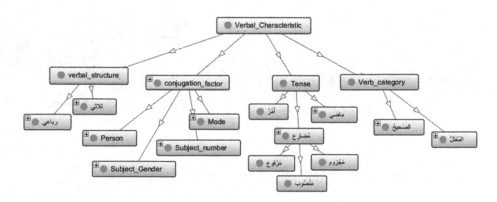

Fig. 2. Characteristics of a verb in our ontology

4.3   Relationships

Relationships in an ontology describe how objects interact with each other. Relationships can usually be expressed directly between instances or classes. In the latter case, this represents a relationship between all the instances of the classes. These relationships are described in the following:

- The simplest relationship which appears in any ontology is the inheritance. It relates concepts in generalization and specialization relation. The inheritance relationship usually organizes concepts in taxonomy from where child nodes are connected to parent nodes employing unidirectional *"is-a"* relationships. For instance, *SuffixPronuoun is a subclass of PostFix*.
- The relationship between the classes and the instances to represent specific rules of the Arabic language morphology. These relationships will help us optimize our morphological analysis process of syntagmatic units.
- The relationships between instances in our ontology. In Arabic, the prefix and the suffix of a conjugated verb must be compatible with each other (see Fig. 3).
- The relationship between the instances of the class *Stem* and those of the class *Scheme* (see Fig. 4).

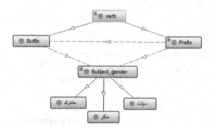

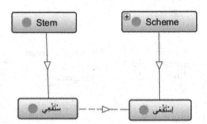

Fig. 3. The compatibility relationship between the prefix and the suffix of a conjugated verb

Fig. 4. The bonding relationship between the stem and the scheme of the verb

To ensure the effective use of our ontology, we validated it using the reasoner HermiT[1] included in the platform Protégé[2]. Furthermore, ontology management constitutes a part of our system ARAMO. So, we offer an end-user interface to facilitate the manipulation, the extension, or the reuse of the different components of our ontology in other applications.

---

[1] http://www.hermit-reasoner.com/.
[2] https://protege.stanford.edu/.

5   The Proposed Method for Morphological Analysis of Arabic Syntagmatic Units

In Arabic, a syntagmatic unit can be composed of a verb and a pronoun or a preposition and a pronoun. It can express an entire sentence. The different eventual components of a syntagmatic unit according to our ontology are:

- *AntFix*: contains all the instances of these lists:
  - ° *ConjC*: the conjunctions of coordination ˙و and ﻑ;
  - ° *PartInt*: the interrogative particle ﺃ;
  - ° *PartMod*: the other particles which are ﻝ, ﺱ and ﻑ.
- *Base*: this string can be:
  - ° *Preposition*: the list of Arabic prepositions is finite;
  - ° *ConjV*: the conjugated verb of the verbal syntagmatic unit and is composed of these three elements:
    - * *Pref*: the list of the instances of verbal prefixes;
    - * *Stem*: the stem of the conjugated verb (ConjV);
    - * *Suff*: the list of instances of verbal suffixes.
- *ProS*: the pronouns succeed a verb or a preposition by a syntagmatic unit.

We propose an approach called ARAMO to analyze the syntagmatic units using the ontology presented above. Its architecture is presented in Fig. 5.

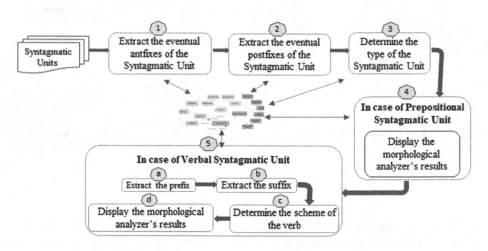

Fig. 5. ARAMO system general architecture as a galance

5.1   Extraction of the Eventual Antfixes of the Syntagmatic Unit

To perform this step, our system ARAMO proceeds as follows:

- Match all possible antfixes of the syntagmatic unit against the list *AntFix* of the ontology. It begins with the longest combination of antfixes as the string فَ which the concatenation of the conjunction فَ and the particle فَ.
  If the match fails, then the system tries to match again with the instances of the list *AntFix*
- Extract the antfix, which matches against one of the different possibilities of antfixes.

To determine whether a substring is an antfix or a part of a conjugated verb, some verification rules are implemented based on the number of characters and the position of diacritics that remained after the extraction of the antfix. For example, the substring وَ is a conjunction in the syntagmatic unit وَكَتَب and it can be a substring of the verb وَقَف. After its extraction from the latter verb, we have the string قَف composed of 4 letters (two consonants and two vowels). Moreover, the first vowel is a *"Fetha"* which can not correspond to any of the schemes of verbs in the ontology. Then, the extracted substring وَ is a part of the conjugated verb. For example, the syntagmatic unit وَيُخْبِرُهُم considered at the beginning of this section, the antFix is the conjunction وَ.

5.2 Extraction of the Eventual Postfix of the Syntagmatic Unit

After the extraction of the eventual antfixes, the system will proceed to the extraction of an eventual postfix, which corresponds to a pronoun suffix at the end of the syntagmatic unit:

- It matches all possible postfixes of the syntagmatic unit with the list *ProS*. It is the same process of matching the antfixes except that the order of the match process begins at the end of the syntagmatic unit.
- Extract the postfix which matches with an instance of the list *ProS*.

For the example, "وَيُخْبِرُهُم" the postfix is the pronoun suffix هُم, which is extracted, and the remaining string is يُخْبِر.

5.3 Determination of the Type of the Syntagmatic Unit

After the extraction of the antfix and postfix, the system will match the remaining substring (*Base*) to the list *Preposition* of the ontology:

- **if** the substring equals one of the instances of *Preposition*, **then** the *Base* is a preposition, and the output of this step is the morphological features of the prepositional syntagmatic unit. As for the example فَإِلَيْهَا, the displayed features are the folowingg:
  - فَ: Conjunction of coordination
  - إِلى: a particle

- هَا: a pronoun suffix (singular, feminine)
- **Other while, if** the *Base* is a conjugated verb and a morphological analysis process is applied to this *Base* **then:**
  - ° Extract the prefix of the conjugated verb that matches the instances of the list *Pref*.

    For the example, وَيُخْبِرُهُم, the Base is the string يُخْبِرُ and the Prefix is the substring يـ expressing the conjugation of the verb in the present.
  - ° Extract the suffix of the conjugated verb that matches the instances of the list *Suff*, which is the diacritic " ضَمّة ".
  - ° Check the concordance between the prefix and the suffix of the conjugated verb to validate the analysis process.
  - ° Match the remaining substring against the instances of the list *Stem*. This matching is based on the position of the fixed characters such as the diacritics in the stem.

    For our example, the stem is the string خْبِرُ:
  - ° Determine the scheme of the verb related to the stem according to the ontology, which is in the case of our example the scheme أَفْعَل of the verb أَخْبَر.
  - ° Display of the morphological analysis results: For a given syntagmatic unit, our system enables the identification of the different components associated with their morphosyntactic features.

Concerning the morpho-syntactic features given by our morphological analysis approach, they are wealthy regarding the information provided to the user. The system displays several morphological features relative to the syntagmatic unit components as the component type (preposition, verb, pronoun, etc.). In the case of the *Base* of the syntagmatic unit is a verb, these features are displayed to the use: its tense (past, present, future, and imperative), a gender (feminine or masculine), and a number (singular, dual, plural) and its scheme. We note that the position of the diacritics in an Arabic word and the relations established in the ontology allow us to resolve several ambiguities related to each step of our process. The morphosyntactic features are then inserted in a TXT file. These features of the syntagmatic unit وَيُخْبِرُهُم are the following:

- وَ: a conjunction of coordination
- يُخْبِرُ: a verb conjugated in the present with the masculine singular person
  - أَخْبَر: the infinitive form of the verb
  - أَفْعَل: the scheme of the verb (a trilateral augmented verb)
- هُم: a pronoun suffix (masculine, plural)

Table 1 presents the notation's description used in the ARAMO main algorithm. The pseudo code is depicted by the following Algorithm 1.

Table 1. The notation's description used in ARAMO Algorithm

Notation	Description
SU	*Syntagmatic unit*
su	*Element of Syntagmatic unit*
SU_{ANT}	*Syntagmatic unit's* Antifix
SU_{POST}	*Syntagmatic unit's* Postfix
SU_{PRE}	*Syntagmatic unit's* Prefix
SU_{SUF}	*Syntagmatic unit's* Suffix
SU_{SV}	*Syntagmatic unit's* Schema Verb

Algorithm 1: Aramo's Algorithm

Data:
- SU : *Syntagmatic unit*

Result:

- *Type of the Syntagmatic unit {feature, value}*

```
begin
1    SU_ANT ← ExtractAntfixes(SU);
2    SU_POST ← ExtractPostFix(SU_ANT);
     feature = "", value = "";
3    foreach (SU_POST) do
         if (IsPreposition(SU_POST) = True) then
4            foreach (su) do
5                feature ← su;
6                value ← Type;
         else if (IsConjugatedVerb(SU_POST = True) then
7            foreach (su) do
8                SU_PRE ← ExtractPrefix(SU);
9                SU_SUF ← ExtractSuffixe(SU_PRE);
10               SU_SV ← DetermineSchemaVerb(SU_SUF);
11               feature ← su;
12               value ← Type;
13       emit(feature, value) ;
```

6 Evaluation

In this section, we start by describing the data set that we used for the evaluation of the morphological analysis module of our system and the experiments that we conducted. It is worthy of mention that a standard corpus for Arabic syntagmatic units is not yet available, which would make the evaluation process more tricking. Therefore, we used the corpus Tashkeela [19], which stands for a collection of Arabic vocalized texts on subjects such as history, grammar, economics, and geography that covers modern and classical Arabic language. It contains over 75 million fully vocalized words obtained from 97 books. We select more than 55 000 verbal and prepositional syntagmatic units from this corpus. We note that the number of prepositional syntagmatic units is limited to 152 due to the finite number of prepositions in Arabic To evaluate the performance of our system, we compare it versus two other systems. The first of them is the one introduced in Smine and Mankai paper. [5], which is denoted by SYSTEM 1 in our evaluation. This comparison will allow us to assess the contribution of our ontology and the developments carried out by our system. The second system is MADAMIRA [2], since it is one of the best known morphological analyzers and it is well documented. We thus analyzed our corpus's verbal and prepositional syntagmatic units using the three systems. In addition, we were interested in the common shared outputs (morphosyntactic features): the type of the syntagmatic unit components. For example, in the case of a verb, we are interested in its tense, number, gender, and scheme. For the evaluation process, we consider two alternatives relative to the morphosyntactic features displayed to the user.

- The morphosyntactic features relative to a syntagmatic unit are correct;
- The morphosyntactic features relative to a syntagmatic unit are false.

The metrics Precision, Recall, and F-measure are the most used to evaluate the quality of such systems. As the first step of our evaluation process, the syntagmatic units of our corpus were annotated manually by linguists assisted by the dictionary of Ammar and Dichy [16]. It contains an index of 10, 000 Arabic verbs conjugated in the past, present, and Imperative tenses. The obtained result is considered the reference files containing the annotated syntagmatic units by linguists. We compared these results with those obtained by the system's SYSTEM 1, MADAMIRA, and ARAMO, and we compute three sets which are: the false-negative F_n, the true positive T_p and the false-positive F_p.

Consequently, the precision is computed to identify how many annotated syntagmatic units are relevant. Indeed, it is the ratio of the number of correctly annotated syntagmatic units by the total number of syntagmatic units annotated by the system. It assesses the ability of the system to provide correctly morphosyntactic features [12].

The recall is identified to how many syntagmatic units are annotated. Indeed, it is the ratio of the number of correctly annotated syntagmatic units by the total number of syntagmatic units which must be annotated. The recall metric indicates the part of the correctly annotated syntagmatic units [12].

$$Precision = \frac{T_p}{T_p + F_p} \ , \ Recall = \frac{T_p}{T_p + F_n}$$

Both metrics are combined together in the F-measure metric. It measures the ability of the system to provide all relevant solutions and to deny others. We also assess the scalability of each system by counting the number of the analyzed syntagmatic units per second, and we note the *Performance* of a system. We present in Table 2 the values of the metrics Precision, Recall, F-measure, and Accuracy of the system's SYSTEM 1, MADAMIRA, and ARAMO.

Table 2. Evaluation of ARAMO compared to the SYSTEM 1 and MADAMIRA

	SYSTEM 1	MADAMIRA	ARAMO
Precision	70,56%	83,32%	**88,22%**
Recall	62,12%	75,15%	**78,14%**
F-measure	65,33%	78,45%	**82,15%**
Performance	26	383	**360**

We note that the best results are obtained with our system ARAMO. Indeed, this system was able to analyze correctly 88% of the syntagmatic units returned against 83% for MADAMIRA analyzer and a lower rate for the SYSTEM 1. This underscores to the sharp improvement made on the SYSTEM 1 [5] and that is largely due to the introduction of the ontology. Our system achieves a performance close MADAMIRA (360 syntagmatic units per second versus 383 for MADAMIRA). We analyzed the reasons of failure for syntagmatic units that our system could not analyze correctly and they are mainly the lack of some diacritics in several syntagmatic units which can embarrass the analysis process an the ambiguities related to the concordance between letters of the different components of the syntagmatic unit.

7 Conclusion

In this paper, we introduced a new morphological analysis method of verbal and prepositional Arabic syntagmatic units based on a linguistic ontology of their components. The originality of our approach remains in the use of ontology instead of a dictionary or a database, which offers many advantages such as the separation between the linguist and the developer task and the possibility to extend the system with some new morphological rules and features. The experimental results confirm the success fullness of our approach. We consider, as future work, the extension of our approach to include morphological analysis of nominal syntagmatic units.

References

1. Farghaly, A., Shalaan, K.: Arabic natural language processing: challenges and solutions. ACM Trans. Asian Language Inf. Process. (TALIP) 8(4), 1–22 (2009)

2. A. Pasha, et al.: MADAMIRA: a fast, comprehensive tool for morphological analysis and disambiguation of Arabic. In: Proceedings of the Ninth International Conference on Language Resources and Evaluation (LREC 2014), 26–31 May 2014
3. Yousfi, A.: The morphological analysis of Arabic verbs by using the surface patterns. Int. J. Comput. Sci. **7**(3 No 11), 254–258 (2010)
4. Belkredim, F.Z., El Sebai, A.: An ontology based formalism for the Arabic language using verbs and their derivatives. Commun. IBIMA **11**, 44–52 (2009)
5. Smine, B., Mankai, Ch.: تركيبة المركب الفعلي و طريقة تحليله مرفولوجيا In: The Proceedings of the Third International Conference of Computer Science Practices in Arabic (CSPA 2006), 10–11 March 2006, Sharjah, UAE (2006)
6. Mubarak, H.: Build fast and accurate lemmatization for Arabic. arXiv preprint arXiv:1710.06700 (2017)
7. Samy, H., Hassanein, E., Shaalan, K.: Arabic question answering: a study on challenges, systems, and techniques. Int. J. Comput. Appl. **181**(44), 6–14 (2019)
8. Dichy, J., Braham, A., Ghazali, S., Hassoun, M.: La base de connaissances linguistiques DIINAR. 1 (DIctionnaire INformatisé de l'Arabe, version 1). In Braham, A. (Ed.), Proceedings of the International Symposium on the Proceeding of Arabic, University of Manouba, Tunisia (2002)
9. Dichy, J., Farghaly, A.: Grammar-lexis relations in the computational morphology of Arabic. In: Soudi, A., Bosch, A.V., Neumann, G. (eds.) Arabic Computational Morphology, vol. 38, pp. 115–140. Springer, Dordrecht (2007). https://doi.org/10.1007/978-1-4020-6046-5_7
10. Beesley, K.R.: Arabic finite-state morphological analysis and generation. In: Proceedings of the 16th Conference on Computational Linguistics- Volume1. Association for Computational Linguistics:Copenhagen, Denmark (1996)
11. Shaalan, K., Magdy, M., Fahmy, A.: Morphological analysis of IL-formed Arabic verbs for second language learners. In: McCarthy, P., Boonthum, C. (eds.), Applied Natural Language Processing: Identification, Investigation and Resolution, pp. 383–97. Hershey (2012)
12. Elabdi, M., Smine, B., Ben Yahia, S.: DFBICA: a new distributed approach for sentiment analysis of bibliographic citations. In: International Conference on Research Challenges in Information Science (RCIS 2018), Nantes, France, 29–31 May 2018. IEEE (2018)
13. Gridach, M., Chenfour, N.: Developing a New Approach for Arabic Morphological Analysis and Generation, CoRR abs/1101.5494 (2011)
14. Sawalha, M., Atwell, E., Abushariah, M.A.M.: SALMA: standard Arabic language morphological analysis, pp. 1–6. In: Proceedings ICCSPA International Conference on Communication Signal Process. Their Appl. Sharjah, UAE (2013)
15. Habash, N., Rambow, O., Roth, R.: MADA + TOKAN: a toolkit for Arabic tokenization, diacritization, morphological disambiguation, POS tagging, stemming and lemmatization. In: Choukri, K., Maegaard, B., (eds.) Proceedings of the Second International Conference on Arabic Language Resources and Tools. The MEDAR Consortium, April 2009
16. Ammar, S., Dichy, J.: الشامل في تصريف الأفعال العربية. Hatier, 1999, Paris, 273p (1999)
17. Khoja, S.: APT: Arabic part-of-speech tagger. In: Proceedings of the Student Workshop at the Second Meeting of the North American Chapter of the Association for Computational Linguistics, Carnegie Mellon University, Pennsylvania (2001)

18. Buckwalter, T.: Issues in Arabic orthography and morphology analysis. In: Proceedings of the Workshop on Computational Approaches to Arabic Script-Based Languages (CAASL 2004), pp. 31–34 (2004)
19. Zerrouki, T., Balla, A.: Tashkeela: novel corpus of Arabic vocalized texts, data forauto-diacritization systems. Data Brief **11**, 147 (2017)
20. Keller, U., Lausen, H., Fensel, D., Lara, R., Lausen, H., Fensel, D.: Semantic web service discovery in the WSMO framework, Semantic Web Services: Theory, Tools and Applications, pp. 1–44, April 2006
21. Hakkoum, A., Kharrazi, H., Raghay, S.: A portable natural language interface to Arabic ontologies. Int. J. Adv. Comput. Sci. Appl. **9**(3), 69–76 (2018)

Collinear Data Structures and Interaction Models

Leon Bobrowski[1,2](✉) (iD)

[1] Faculty of Computer Science, Bialystok University of Technology,
Wiejska 45A, Bialystok, Poland
l.bobrowski@pb.edu.pl
[2] Institute of Biocybernetics and Biomedical Engineering, PAS, Warsaw, Poland

Abstract. Models of interactions between multiple fetaures (genes) can be obtained from collinear data sets consisting of multivariate feature vectors. Such models can be designed by minimizing the collinearity criterion function with the basis echange algorithm.

The collinearity criterion functions are defined on learning data subsets representing selected categories (e.g. diseases). Based on the minimization of the collinearity functions, interaction models specific to each category can be defined.

Keywords: Collinear data sets · Interaction models · Convex and piecewise linear criterion functions · Basis exchange algorithm

1 Introduction

Data mining tools are used to discover useful patterns in large data sets [1]. Typically, data mining procedures operate on datasets that consist of a large number of feature vectors with small or medium dimensions. A given feature vector represents various characteristics (features) of a specific patient or object [2].

In practice, data sets consisting of a small number of multidimensional feature vectors are often encountered [3]. Genetic data sets are a characteristic example of such a data structure. Discovering important patterns from small samples of multidimensional vectors is actually a challenge due to, among other things, the large number of potentially important solutions [4]. In such a case, efficient and precise calculation based on vertices in parameter space are useful [5].

Complex layers of linear classifiers were designed on the basis of data sets composed of a small number of multidimensional feature vectors [5]. In this approach, the multidimensional feature space is decomposed into a number of feature subspaces with a dimension not greater than the number of patients represented in a given data set.

The presented work takes into account the situation in which the same data set has been repeatedly divided into subsets related to different categories (diseases, problems). A method of designing collinear interaction models characteristic for particular categories is proposed.

N. T. Nguyen et al. (Eds.): ICCCI 2022, LNAI 13501, pp. 378–387, 2022.
https://doi.org/10.1007/978-3-031-16014-1_30

2 High-Dimensional Learning Sets

Consider the data set C, composed of m feature vectors $\mathbf{x}_i = [x_{i,1}, \ldots, x_{j,n}]^T$ belonging to the n-dimensional feature space $F[n] (\mathbf{x}_j \in F[n])$ [2]:

$$C = \{\mathbf{x_j} : j = 1, \ldots, m\} \tag{1}$$

We assume that feature vectors $\mathbf{x}_j$ in the data set C (1) are high-dimensional. This means that the number m of feature vectors $\mathbf{x}_j$ in the data set C (1) is much smaller than the dimension n of these vectors ($m << n$) [6].

Consider a family of K pairs of learning sets $G_k^+[n_k]$ and $G_k^-[n_k]$ ($k = 1, \ldots, K$). The k-th pair of learning sets $G_k^+[n_k]$ and $G_k^-[n_k]$ in this family consists of m_k positive and m_k negative examples of feature vectors $\mathbf{x}_i[n_k]$ belonging to n_k-dimensional feature space $F_k[n_k] (\mathbf{x}_j[n_k] \in F_k[n_k])$:

$$(\forall k \in \{1, \ldots, K\}$$
$$G_k^+[n_k] = \{\mathbf{x}_j[n_k] : j \in J_k^+\}, \text{ and } G_k^-[n_k] = \{\mathbf{x}_j[n_k] : j \in J_k^-\} \tag{2}$$

where J_k^+ and J_k^- are disjoint sets of indices $j (J_k^+ \cap J_k^- = \emptyset)$ of feature vectors $\mathbf{x}_j[n_k]$.

We assumed that the feature vectors $\mathbf{x}_i[n_k] = [x_{i,1}, \ldots, x_{i,nk}]^T$ belonging to the k-th pair of learning sets $G_k^+[n_k]$ and $G_k^-[n_k]$ have the same dimension n_k. Feature vectors $\mathbf{x}_j[n_k]$ from the learning set $G_k^+[n_k]$ represent objects (patients, images, events,...) P_j related to the k-th category (class, property, concept, disease, ...) $\omega_k (k = 1, \ldots, K)$.

The *positive* learning set $G_k^+[n_k]$ contains m_k of feature vectors $\mathbf{x}_j[n_k]$ of dimension n_k representing objects P_j with the k-th property ω_k. The *negative* learning set $G_k^-[n_k]$ can be used as an alternative to the set $G_k^+[n_k]$ and contains m_k feature vectors $\mathbf{x}_j[n_k]$ representing objects P_j without the k-th property ω_k. The *negative* learning set $G_k^-[n_k]$ can be chosen randomly from a greater number of objects P_j not belonging to the k-th class ω_k.

The learning sets $G_k^+[n_k]$ and $G_k^-[n_k]$ (2) are constituted by m_k different feature vectors $\mathbf{x}_j[n_k]$ (2). We assume that the learning sets $G_k^+[n_k]$ and $G_k^-[n_k]$ are formed by high-dimensional feature vectors $\mathbf{x}_j[n_k]$. It means that:

$$(\forall k \in \{1, \ldots, K\} \quad m_k << n_k \tag{3}$$

Acording to the inequalities (3), the number m_k of feature vectors $\mathbf{x}_j[n_k]$ in each learning set $G_k^+[n_k]$ (2) is much smaller than the dimension n_k of these vectors. The components $x_{j,i}(x_{j,i} \in R^1$ or $x_{j,i} \in \{0, 1\})$ of the feature vector $\mathbf{x}_j[n_k]$ (1) are numerical values of n_k features (attributes, measurements, genes,...) $X_i (i = 1, \ldots, n_k)$ of the j-th object (patient) P_j with the k-th property ω_k.

Pattern recognition methods often examine the possibility of separating learning sets $G_k^+[n_k]$ and $G_k^-[n_k]$ (2) by a certain hyperplane $H(\mathbf{w}_k, \theta_k)$ in the feature space $F_k[n_k] (\mathbf{x}[n_k] \in F_k[n_k])$ [7]. The hyperplane $H(\mathbf{w}_k, \theta_k)$ is defined as follows:

$$H(\mathbf{w}_k, \theta_k) = \left\{\mathbf{x}[n_k] : \mathbf{w}_k^T \mathbf{x}[n_k] = \theta_k\right\} \tag{4}$$

where $\mathbf{w}_k = [w_{k,1}, \ldots, w_{k,nk}]^T \in R^{nk}$ is the weight vector the dimension n_k, $\theta_k \in R^1$ is the threshold, and $\mathbf{w}_k^T \mathbf{x}[n_k] = \Sigma_i w_{k,i} x_i$ is the inner product.

3 Dual Hyperplanes and Vertices in the Parameter Space

Each feature vector $\mathbf{x}_j$ of dimension n_k, from the positive learning set $G_k^+[n_k](\mathbf{x}_j \in G_k^+[n_k])$ (2), defines the following dual hyperplane h_j in the parameter space $\mathbf{R}^{nk}$ [7]:

$$(\forall \mathbf{x}_j \in G_k^+[n_k]) \quad h_j = \left\{ \mathbf{w} \in R^{nk} : \mathbf{x}_j^T \mathbf{w} = 1 \right\} \tag{5}$$

The dual hyperplanes $h_i{}^0$ in the parameter space R^{nk} are defined by unit vectors $\mathbf{e}_i$ [7]:

$$(\forall i \in I_k) h_i^0 = \left\{ \mathbf{w} \in R^{nk} : \mathbf{e}_i^T \mathbf{w} = 0 \right\} = \left\{ \mathbf{w} \in R^{nk} : w_i = 0 \right\} \tag{6}$$

It is assumed that each unit vector $\mathbf{e}_i$ is related in a fixed manner to one feature (gene) X_i. $(i = 1, \ldots, n)$.

Definition 1: The vertex $\mathbf{w}_k$ of rank r in the parameter space $\mathbf{R}^{nk}$ $(r \leq m_k$ (2)) is located at the intersection of r dual hyperplanes h_j (5) and $n_k - r$ hyperplanes $h_i{}^0$ (6), where $i \in I_k$.

The vertex $\mathbf{w}_k$ of rank $r = m_k$ (2) is defined by the following system of n_k linear equations:

$$\begin{align} (\forall \mathbf{x}_j \in G_k^+[n_k]) \quad \mathbf{x}_j^T \mathbf{w}_k &= 1 \\ (\forall i(l) \in I_k) \quad \mathbf{e}_{i(l)}^T \mathbf{w}_k &= 0 \end{align} \tag{7}$$

where $I_k = \{i(1), \ldots, i(n_k - r)\}$ is the k-th subset of indices $i(l)$ defining the $n_k - r$ unit vectors $\mathbf{e}_{i(l)}$ related to the vertex $\mathbf{w}_k$.

The linear Eqs. (7) can be given in the following matrix form [8]:

$$\mathbf{B}_k(r)\mathbf{w}_k = \mathbf{1}_k \tag{8}$$

where $\mathbf{1}_k = [1, \ldots, 1, 0, \ldots, 0]^T$ is a vector in which the first r components are equal to one and the remaining $n_k - r$ components are zero.

Assuming the linear independence of $r = m_k$ feature vectors $\mathbf{x}_j$ (2) in the set $G_k^+[n_k]$, the square matrix $\mathbf{B}_k(r)$ in Eq. (8) may have the following structure:

$$\mathbf{B}_k(r) = \left[\mathbf{x}_1, \ldots, \mathbf{x}_r, \mathbf{e}_{i(r+1)}, \ldots, \mathbf{e}_{i(nk)} \right]^T \tag{9}$$

where the symbol $\mathbf{e}_{i(l)}$ denotes the unit vector which forms the l-th row $(l = r + 1, \ldots, n_k)$ of the matrix $\mathbf{B}_k(r)$.

The non-singular matrix $\mathbf{B}_k(r)$ (9) formed by r linearly independent feature vectors $\mathbf{x}_j (j \in J_k)$ from the positive learning set $G_k^+[n_k]$ (2), and $n_k - r$ unit vectors $\mathbf{e}_i$ $(i \in I_k)$ is the *basis* of n_k - dimensional feature space $F[n_k]$ $(\mathbf{x}_j \in F[n_k])$ related to vertex $\mathbf{w}_k(r)$ [7]:

$$\mathbf{w}_k(r) = \mathbf{B}_k(r)^{-1} \mathbf{1}_r = \mathbf{r}_1 + \ldots + \mathbf{r}_r \tag{10}$$

where $\mathbf{B}_k(r)^{-1}$ is the inverse matrix:

$$\mathbf{B}_k(r)^{-1} = \left[\mathbf{r}_1, \ldots, \mathbf{r}_r, \mathbf{r}_{r+1}, \ldots, \mathbf{r}_{nk} \right] \tag{11}$$

Lemma 1: The last n_k - r components $w_{k,i}$ of the vector $\mathbf{w}_k(r) = \left[W_{k,1}, \ldots, W_{k,nk}\right]^T$ (10) are equal to zero

$$(\forall l \in \{r+1, \ldots, n_k\}) w_{k,l} = 0 \tag{12}$$

This lemma results directly from the system of equations $\mathbf{w}_k(r)^T \mathbf{e}_{i(l)} = 0$ (7).

4 Collinearity Criterion Function

The collinearity criterion function $\Phi_k(\mathbf{w})$ was introduced to detect collinear subsets in data sets C (1) [9]. For this purpose, the collinearity penalty functions $\varphi_j(\mathbf{w})$ are defined on elements $\mathbf{x}_j$ of the positive learning set $G_k^+[n_k]$ (2) (or $G_k^-[n_k]$ if needed):

$$\left(\forall \mathbf{x}_j \in G_k^+[n_k]\right) \quad \varphi_j(\mathbf{w}) = \left|1 - \mathbf{x}_j^T \mathbf{w}\right| \tag{13}$$

where $\mathbf{w} = [w_1, \ldots, w_{nk}]^T \in \mathbf{R}^{nk}$.

The penalty function $\varphi_j(\mathbf{w})$ (13) is zero if and only if the weight Vector $\mathbf{w} = [w_1, \ldots, w_{nk}]^T$ lies on the dual hyperplane h_j (5) in the parameter space $\mathbf{R}^{nk}$.

The collinearity criterion function $\Phi_k(\mathbf{w})$ is defined as the sum of the penalty functions $\varphi_j(\mathbf{w})$ (13) based on the elements $\mathbf{x}_j$ of the positive learning set $G_k^+[n_k]$ (2) [9]:

$$\Phi_k(\mathbf{w}) = \Sigma_j \varphi_j(\mathbf{w}) \tag{14}$$

The collinearity criterion function $\Phi_k(\mathbf{w})$ (14) is convex and piecewise linear (*CPL*). It has been shown that the minimum value $\Phi_k(\mathbf{w}_k^*)$ of the *CPL* criterion function $\Phi_k(\mathbf{w})$ (14) can be found at one of the vertices $\mathbf{w}_k$ (10) in the parameter space $\mathbf{R}^{nk}$ [7]:

$$(\exists \mathbf{w}_k^*)(\forall \mathbf{w}) \Phi_k(\mathbf{w}) \geq \Phi_k(\mathbf{w}_k^*) \geq 0 \tag{15}$$

The basis exchange algorithm allows for efficient and precise finding of the optimal vertex $\mathbf{w}_k^*$ (15) that is the minimum of the collinearity criterion functions $\Phi_k(\mathbf{w})$ (14) [7]. Basis exchange algorithms use the Gauss-Jordan transformation and are therefore similar to the *Simplex* algorithm used in linear programming [10].

Theorem 1: The minimum value $\Phi_k(\mathbf{w}_k^*)$ (15) of the collinearity criterion function $\Phi_k(\mathbf{w})$ (14) defined on the m_k elements $\mathbf{x}_j$ of the learning set $G_k^+[n_k]$ (2) is equal to zero $(\Phi_k(\mathbf{w}_k^*) = 0)$, if all feature vectors $\mathbf{x}_j$ from this set are located on a certain hyperplane $H(\mathbf{w}_k, \theta_k)$ (4) with the threshold θ_k different from zero ($\theta_k \neq 0$).

Proof of a similar theorem can be found in [7]. From the definition of the collinearity criterion function $\Phi_k(\mathbf{w})$ (14) it follows that the minimum value $\Phi_k(\mathbf{w}_k^*)$ (15) is equal to zero $(\Phi_k(\mathbf{w}_k^*) = 0)$ if and only if each of the dual hyperplanes h_j (5) passes through the optimal vertex $\mathbf{w}_k^*$.

The minimum value $\Phi_k(\mathbf{w}_k^*)$ (15) of the collinearity criterion function $\Phi_k^+(\mathbf{w})$ (14) defined on the m_k elements $\mathbf{x}_j$ of the learning set $G_k^+[n_k]$ (2) is equal to zero $(\Phi_k(\mathbf{w}_k^*) = $

0) if the all the vectors $\mathbf{x}_j$ from this set are located on the following hyperplane $H(\mathbf{w}_k^*, 1)$ (4) defined by the optimal vertex $\mathbf{w}_k^*[5]$:

$$H(\mathbf{w}_k^*, 1) = \left\{ \mathbf{x} \in F[n_k] : (\mathbf{w}_k^*)^T \mathbf{x} = 1 \right\} \tag{16}$$

The regularized criterion function $\Psi_k(\mathbf{w}; \lambda)$ is defined as the weighted sum of the collinearity criterion function $\Phi_k(\mathbf{w})$ (14) and the cost functions $\lambda |w_i|$ []:

$$\Psi_k(\mathbf{w}; \lambda) = \Phi_k(\mathbf{w}) + \lambda \Sigma |w_i|$$
$$i \in \{1, \ldots, n\} \tag{17}$$

where $\lambda \geq 0$ is the *cost level*.

Like the function $\Phi_k(\mathbf{w})$ (14), the regularized function $\Psi_k(\mathbf{w}; \lambda)$ (17) is convex and piecewise linear (*CPL*). The optimal vertex $\mathbf{w}_k^*(\lambda)$ can be found by minimizing the function $\Psi_k(\mathbf{w}; \lambda)$ (17):

$$(\forall \lambda \geq 0)(\exists \mathbf{w}_k^*(\lambda))(\forall \mathbf{w}) \Psi_k(\mathbf{w}; \lambda) \geq \Psi_k(\mathbf{w}_k^*(\lambda)) \tag{18}$$

The minimizing of the criterion function $\Psi_k(\mathbf{w}; \lambda)$ (17) makes it possible to form collinear patterns from learning sets $G_k[n_k]$ (2) [9].

Definition 2: The collinear (flat) pattern $P_k(\mathbf{w}_k^*(\lambda))$ in the set $G_k^+[n_k]$ (2) consists of such feature vectors $\mathbf{x}_j$ from this set ($\mathbf{x}_j \in G_k^+[n_k]$), which are located on the hyperplane $H(\mathbf{w}_k^*(\lambda), 1)$ (16):

$$P_k(\mathbf{w}_k^*(\lambda)) = \left\{ \mathbf{x}_j \in G_k^+[n_k] : \mathbf{w}_k^*(\lambda)^T \mathbf{x} = 1 \right\} \tag{19}$$

Flat patterns $P_k(\mathbf{w}_k^*(\lambda))$ (19) make it possible to design linear models of interactions between features X_i, e.g. between selected genes on the basis of the positive learning set $G_k^+[n_k]$ (2) [5].

5 Bases with a Small Number of Feature Vectors

We consider the situation (3) when the learning sets $G_k^+[n_k]$ (2) are formed by high-dimensional feature vectors $\mathbf{x}_j[n_k]$. In this case, the number m_k of feature vectors $\mathbf{x}_j[n_k]$ in the set $G_k^+[n_k]$ is much smaller than the dimension n_k of these vectors ($m_k << n_k$). The basis $\mathbf{B}_k(r)$ (9) of the feature space $F[n_k]$ related to the vertex $\mathbf{w}_k(r)$ (10) of the rank r (*Definition 1*) is formed by r linearly independent feature vectors $\mathbf{x}_j$ ($j \in J_k$) from the learning set $G_k^+[n_k]$ (2), and $n_k - r$ vectors $\mathbf{e}_i$ ($i \in I_k$).

The basis exchange algorithm finds the optimal vertex $\mathbf{w}_k^*$ representing the global minimum $\Phi_k(\mathbf{w}_k^*)$ (15) of the collinearity criterion function $\Phi_k(\mathbf{w})$ (14) [7]. In this approach, the optimal vertex $\mathbf{w}_k^*$ is reached after a finite number L of steps between vertices $\mathbf{w}_k(l)$ (10) [5]:

$$\mathbf{w}_k(0) \to \mathbf{w}_k(1) \to \ldots \ldots \to \mathbf{w}_k(L) = \mathbf{w}_k^* \tag{20}$$

The sequence of vertices $\mathbf{w}_k(l)$ (20) is related by the Eq. (10) to the following sequence of the inverse matrices $\mathbf{B}_k(l)^{-1} = [\mathbf{r}_1(l), \ldots, \mathbf{r}_{nk}(l)]$:

$$\mathbf{B}_k(0)^{-1} \to \mathbf{B}_k(1)^{-1} \to \ldots \to \mathbf{B}_k(L)^{-1} \tag{21}$$

The first vertex $\mathbf{w}_k(0)$ in the sequence (20) can be equal to the vertex $\mathbf{w}_k(0) = [0, \ldots, 0]^T$ based on the identity matrix $\mathbf{B}_k(0) = [\mathbf{e}_1, \ldots, \mathbf{e}_n]^T$ [7].

In step $l + 1$. One of the unit vectors $\mathbf{e}_i$ contained in the matrix (basis) $\mathbf{B}_k(l) = [\mathbf{x}_1, , \mathbf{x}_l, \mathbf{e}_{i(l+1)}, \ldots, \mathbf{e}_{i(nk)}]^T$ (9) is replaced by the feature vector $\mathbf{x}_{l+1}$ and the matrix $\mathbf{B}_k(l + 1) = [\mathbf{x}_1, \ldots, \mathbf{x}_{l+1}, \mathbf{e}_{i(l+2)}, \ldots, \mathbf{e}_{i(nk)}]^T$ related to the vertex $\mathbf{w}_k(l + 1)$ (20) appears:

$$(\forall l \in \{0, 1, \ldots, L - 1\})\mathbf{B}_k(l) \to \mathbf{B}_k(l + 1). \tag{22}$$

According to the vector Gauss-Jordan transformation, replacing in the basis $\mathbf{B}_k(l) = [\mathbf{x}_1, \ldots, \mathbf{x}_l, \mathbf{e}_{i(l+1)}, \ldots, \mathbf{e}_{i(nk)}]^T$ (9) the unit vector $\mathbf{e}_{i'(l)}$ with the feature vector $\mathbf{x}_{l+1}(\mathbf{x}_{l+1} \in G_k^+[n_k]$ (2)) results in the following modifications of the columns $\mathbf{r}_i(l)$ of the inverse matrix $\mathbf{B}_k(l)^{-1} = [\mathbf{r}_1(l), \ldots, \mathbf{r}_{nk}(l)]$ during step $l+1$ [11]:

$$\mathbf{r}_{i'(l)}(l + 1) = (1/\mathbf{r}_{i'(l)}(l)^T\mathbf{x}_{l+1})\mathbf{r}_{i'(l)}(l) and$$

$$(\forall i \neq i'(l))\mathbf{r}_i(l + 1) = \mathbf{r}_i(l) - (\mathbf{r}_i(l)^T\mathbf{x}_{l+1})\mathbf{r}_{i'(l)}(l + 1)$$

$$= \mathbf{r}_i(l) - (\mathbf{r}_i(l)^T\mathbf{x}_{l+1}/\mathbf{r}_{i'(l)}(l)^T\mathbf{x}_{l+1})\mathbf{r}_{i'(l)}(l) \tag{23}$$

where $i'(l)$ is the index of the unit vector $\mathbf{e}_{i'(l)}$ leaving the basis $\mathbf{B}_k(l) = [\mathbf{x}_1, \ldots, \mathbf{x}_l, \mathbf{e}_{i(l+1)}, \ldots, \mathbf{e}_{i(nk)}]^T$ (9) during step $l + 1$.

The vector Gauss-Jordan transformation (23) is determined at each step l by an *entry criterion*, an *exit criterion*, and a *stop criterion* [10]. The entry criterion adopted here is such that in step $l + 1$ the feature vector $\mathbf{x}_{l+1}$ will enter the basis $\mathbf{B}_k(l) = [\mathbf{x}_1, \ldots, \mathbf{x}_l, \mathbf{e}_{i(l+1)}, \ldots, \mathbf{e}_{i(nk)}]^T$ (9). The exit criterion based on the following inequalities is proposed here:

$$(\forall i(l) \in \{l + 1, \ldots, n_k\})$$
$$\mathbf{r}_{i'(l)}(l)^T\mathbf{x}_{l+1}| / ||\mathbf{r}_{i'(l)}(l)||\,|\mathbf{r}_{i(l)}(l)^T\mathbf{x}_{l+1}| / ||\mathbf{r}_{i(l)}(l)|| \tag{24}$$

The unit vector $\mathbf{e}_{i'(l)}$ leaving the basis $\mathbf{B}_k(l) = [\mathbf{x}_1, \ldots, \mathbf{x}_l, \mathbf{e}_{i(l+1)}, \ldots, \mathbf{e}_{i(nk)}]^T$ (9) during step $l + 1$ is determined by the inequalities (24) (*exit criterion*). The exit criterion based on the inequalities (24) can be associated with the steepest descent strategy of minimizing the *CPL* criterion function $\Phi_k(\mathbf{w})$ (14) [7].

The exit criterion (24) results in reducing the value of the criterion function $\Phi_k(\mathbf{w})$ (14) in successive vertices $\mathbf{w}_k(l)$ (20) [5]:

$$\Phi_k(\mathbf{w}_k(0)) > \Phi_k(\mathbf{w}_k(1)) > \ldots > \Phi_k(\mathbf{w}_k(L)) = \Phi_k(\mathbf{w}_k^*).$$

The multi-stage minimization (25) is stopped at the vertex $\mathbf{w}_k(l)$ (20) if the condition $\Phi_k(\mathbf{w}_k(L)) > \Phi_k(\mathbf{w}_k(L + 1))$ cannot be satisfied (*stop criterion*).

The optimal vertex $\mathbf{w}_k^*(\lambda)$ representing the global minimum (18) of the regularized criterion functions $\Psi_k(\mathbf{w}; \lambda)$ (17) can also be identified by the basis exchange algorithm with the same entry criterion, exit criterion and the stop criterion mentioned above.

6 Properties of Collinear Patterns

The collinear (flat) pattern $P_k\left(\mathbf{w}_k^*(\lambda)\right)$ (19) in the set $G_k^+[n_k]$ (2) is formed by the feature vectors $\mathbf{x}_j$ from this set $(\mathbf{x}_j \in G_k^+[n_k])$, which are located on the hyperplane $H(\mathbf{w}_k^*(\lambda),\ 1)$ (16). The flat pattern $P_k\left(\mathbf{w}_k^*(\lambda)\right)$ (19) is determined by the optimal vertex $\mathbf{w}_k^*(\lambda)$ (18) which depends on the cost level $\lambda(\lambda \geq 0)$ in the regularized criterion function $\Psi_k(\mathbf{w}; \lambda)$ (17). The flat pattern $P_k\left(\mathbf{w}_k^*(0)\right)$ (19) with $\lambda = 0$ is defined by the optimal vertex $\mathbf{w}_k^*$, which represents the minimum $\Phi_k\left(\mathbf{w}_k^*\right)$ (15) of the collinearity criterion function $\Phi_k(\mathbf{w})$ (14).

Theorem 2: If the feature vectors $\mathbf{x}_j$ making up the learning set $G_k^+[n_k]$ (2) are linearly independent then the value $\Phi_k(\mathbf{w}_k(L))$ of the collinearity criterion function $\Phi_k(\mathbf{w})$ (14) in the final vertex $\mathbf{w}_k(l)$ (20) is equal to zero $(\Phi_k(\mathbf{w}_k(L)) = 0)$.

The proof of this theorem can be based on the multi-step minimization procedure (25) described in the previous paragraph. Feature vectors $\mathbf{x}_j$ forming the learning set $G_k^+[n_k]$ (2) are usually linearly independent in the case when the number m_k of vectors $\mathbf{x}_j$ is much smaller than the dimension n_k of these vectors $(m_k << n_k$ (3)) [5]. Consequently, it can be expected that all feature vectors $\mathbf{x}_j$ from the learning set $G_k^+[n_k]$ $(\mathbf{x}_j \in G_k^+[n_k]$ (2)) belong to the flat pattern $P_k\left(\mathbf{w}_k^*(\lambda)\right)$ (19). Increasing the value of the cost level λ makes it possible to eliminate vectors $\mathbf{x}_j$ that are weakly related to the pattern $P_k\left(\mathbf{w}_k^*(\lambda)\right)$ (19).

The final vertex $\mathbf{w}_k(l)$ in the sequence (20) is equal to the optimal vertex $\mathbf{w}_k^*(\lambda)$ (18) of the rank L (*Definition* 1). The basis $\mathbf{B}_k(L)$ (9) connected to the optimal vertex $\mathbf{w}_k^*(\lambda)$ (18) contains L linearly independent vectors $\mathbf{x}_j$ from the learning set $G_k^+[n_k]$ (2) [12].

Lemma 2: The rank L of the optimal vertex $\mathbf{w}_k^*(\lambda)$ (18) can be arbitrarily reduced even to zero by increasing the cost level λ in the criterion function $\Psi_k(\mathbf{w}; \lambda)$ (17).

This lemma reflects properties of multi-stage minimization (18) that the rank L of the optimal vertex $\mathbf{w}_k^*(\lambda)$ (18) can be controlled by the parameter λ (17). The optimal vertex $\mathbf{w}_k^*(0)$ with $\lambda = 0$ represents the minimum $\Phi_k\left(\mathbf{w}_k^*\right)$ (15) of the collinearity criterion function $\Phi_k(\mathbf{w})$ (14). The rank L of the vertex $\mathbf{w}_k^*(0)$ (15) is equal to the number of linearly independent vectors $\mathbf{x}_j$ in the learning set $G_k^+[n_k]$ (2). The maximal rank L is equal to the number m_k of elements $\mathbf{x}_j$ of the learning set $G_k^+[n_k]$ $(L \leq m_k)$. A sufficiently high cost level λ (17) results in an optimal vertex $\mathbf{w}_k^*(\lambda) = [0,..., 0]^T$ of zero rank $(L = 0)$ related to the basis $\mathbf{B}_k^* = [\mathbf{e}_1, \dots, \mathbf{e}_{nk}]^T$ determined by unit vectors $\mathbf{e}_i$ of dimension n_k.

7 Interaction Models Based on Collinear Patterns

The collinear pattern $P_k\left(\mathbf{w}_k^*(\lambda)\right)$ (19) is defined by the optimal vertex $\mathbf{w}_k^*(\lambda)$ (18) which is the minimum $\Psi_k(\mathbf{w}_k^*(\lambda))$ (18) of the regularized criterion function $\Psi_k(\mathbf{w}; \lambda)$ (17). The optimal vertex $\mathbf{w}_k^*(\lambda)$ (18) of the rank L is the final vector $\mathbf{w}_k(L)$ $(\mathbf{w}_k^*(\lambda) = \mathbf{w}_k(L))$ in the sequence (20) based on the function $\Psi_k(\mathbf{w}; \lambda)$ (17). The vertex $\mathbf{w}_k(l)$ is related to the basis $\mathbf{B}_k(L)$ (9):

$$\mathbf{B}_k(L) = [\mathbf{x}_1, \ldots, \mathbf{x}_L, \mathbf{e}_{i(L+1)}, \ldots, \mathbf{e}_{i(nk)}]^T \tag{26}$$

According to Lemma 1, the last $n_k - L$ components $\mathrm{w}_{k,i}$ of the vector $\mathbf{w}_k(L) = [w_{k,1}, \ldots, w_{k,nk}]^T$ (20) related to unit vectors $\mathbf{e}_i$ in the matrix $\mathbf{B}_k(L)$ (26) are equal to zero $(w_{k,i} = 0)$ (12). Hence the corresponding components $\mathrm{x}_{j,i}$ of feature vectors $\mathbf{x}_j[n_k] = [x_{j,1}, \ldots, x_{j,nk}]^T$ $(\mathbf{x}_j[n_k] \in G_k^+[n_k]$ (2)), and features $X_i (i \in I_k(L)$ (7)) are omitted [12]:

$$(\forall i = 1, \ldots, n_k) if (\mathbf{e}_i \in \mathbf{B}_k(L)\ (26)), \ then$$
$$i - th\ component\ \mathrm{x}_{j,i}\ of\ the\ vector\ and \tag{27}$$
$$i - th\ feature\ X_i (i \in I_k(L)(7))\ are\ omitted$$

The k-th *vertexical feature subset* $R_k(L)$ of L not omitted features X_i is formed in the optimal vertex $\mathbf{w}_k^*(L)$ (20):

$$R_k(L) = \{X_{i(1)}, \ldots, X_{i(L)}\} = \{X_i : i \notin I_k(L)\}. \tag{28}$$

The k-th *vertexical feature subspace* $F_k[L]$ $(F_k[L] \subset \mathbf{F}[n_k])$ based on the optimal vertex $\mathbf{w}_k^*(\lambda) = [w_{k,1}^*, \ldots, w_{k,L}^*]^T$ (18) contains m_k reduced vectors $\mathbf{x}_j[L] = [x_{j,1}, \ldots, x_{j,L}]^T$ $(\mathbf{x}_j[L] \in F_k[L])$ with L components $x_{j,i}$ related to weights $w_{k,i}^*$ different from zero $(w_{k,i}^* \neq 0)$. The reduced vectors $\mathbf{x}_j[L]$ fulfil the following equation in the vertex $\mathbf{w}_k^*(\lambda) = \mathbf{w}_k(L)$ (20):

$$(\forall j \in \{1, \ldots, m_k\})\mathbf{w}_k^*(\lambda)^T \mathbf{x}_j[L] = 1 \tag{29}$$

or

$$(\forall \mathbf{x}_j[L] \in P_k(\mathbf{w}_k^*(\lambda))\ (19))\ w_{k,1}^* x_{j,i(1)} + \ldots + w_{k,L}^* x_{j,i(L)} = 1 \tag{30}$$

The following collinear model of interaction between L selected features $X_{i(l)} (X_{i(l)} \in R_k(L)$ (28)) is based on the set of Eqs. (30) [5]:

$$w_{k,1}^* X_{i(1)} + \ldots + w_{k,L}^* X_{i(L)} = 1 \tag{31}$$

The collinear interaction model (31) allows for the formulation and application of a regression model for various dependent features $X_{i'}$ [9]:

$$(\forall X_{i'} \in R_k(L)\ (28)) X_{i'} = a_{i',0} + a_{i',1} X_{i(1)} + \ldots + a_{i',rk} X_{i(L)} \tag{32}$$

where $\alpha_{i',0} = 1 / \mathrm{w}_{k,i'}^*$, $\alpha_{i',i'} = 0$, and $(\forall(l) \neq i')) \alpha_{i',i(l)} = \mathrm{w}_{k,i(l)}^* / \mathrm{w}_{k,i'}^*$.

The interaction model (31) is defined by the optimal vertex $\mathbf{w}_k^*(\lambda)$ (18). The optimal vertex $\mathbf{w}_k^*(\lambda)$ can be obtained by minimizing the regularized criterion function $\Psi_k(\mathbf{w}; \lambda)$ (17) using the basis exchange algorithm [7]. The criterion function $\Psi_k(\mathbf{w}; \lambda)$ (17) is the sum of the collinearity criterion function $\Phi_k(\mathbf{w})$ (14) and the regulating part $\lambda \Sigma_i |w_i|$.

Feature vectors $\mathbf{x}_j$ forming the learning set $G_k^+[n_k]$ (2) are usually linearly indepen-dent in the case when $m_k \ll n_k$ (3). It can be shown that the minimum value of the collinearity criterion function $\Phi_k(\mathbf{w})$ (14) defined on the linearly independent feature vectors $\mathbf{x}_j$ (2) is equal zero [5].

In this case, the minimization of the criterion function $\Psi_k(\mathbf{w}; \lambda)$ (17) is based on the the minimization of the regulating part $\Sigma_i |w_i|$. Minimizing *the regulating part* $\Sigma_i |w_i|$ (17) can be related to *better conditioning* of the base matrix $\mathbf{B}_k(L)$ (26). The model of interaction (31) is based on the optimal vertex $\mathbf{w}_k^*(\lambda)$ related (10) to the well-conditioned basis $\mathbf{B}_k(L)$ (26) [5]. Well-conditioned matrices $\mathbf{B}_k(L)$ (26) give better interaction models (31).

8 Concluding Remarks

We assumed that learning set $G_k^+[n_k]$ (2) represents objects (patients) P_j having the k-th property (disease) $\omega_k (k = 1, \ldots, K)$. The k-th learning set $G_k^+[n_k]$ (2) is a long when consists of m_k feature vectors $\mathbf{x}_j[n_k]$ with a large dimension $n_k (m_k \ll n_k)$ (3) [6].

Repeated minimization of the regularized criterion function $\Psi_k(\mathbf{w}; \lambda)$ (17) deter-mined on a long learning set $G_k^+[n_k]$ (2) gives possibility to extract many collinear patterns $P_k(\mathbf{w}_k^*(\lambda))$ (19) from this set (2). Optimal vertices $\mathbf{w}_k^*(\lambda)$ (15) allow to build collinear models of interaction (31) between selected features X_i related to individual vertices.

The proposed design procedure may discover a family of L linear interaction models (31) specific for specific for each category (disease) ω_k represented by the positive learning sets $G_k^+[n_k]$ (2). In this way, disease-specific models of interaction (31) between genes can be designed.

Changes in the interaction models (31) make it possible to assess the influence of a given therapy on the course of the disease ω_k. This possibility is especially important in the case of rare diseases [13].

Acknowledgments. The presented study was supported by the grant WZ/WI-IIT/3/2020 from the Bialystok University of Technology and funded from the resources for research by the Polish Ministry of Science and Higher Education.

References

1. Hand, D., Smyth, P., Mannila, H.: Principles of Data Mining. MIT Press, Cambridge (2001)
2. Duda, O.R., Hart, P.E., Stork, D.G.: Pattern classification. J. Wiley, New York (2001)
3. Bishop, C.M.: Pattern Recognition and Machine Learning. Springer Verlag (2006)
4. Johnson, R.A., Wichern, D.W.: Applied Multivariate Statistical Analysis. Prentice- Hall Inc, Englewood Cliffs (2002)
5. Bobrowski, L.: Computing on vertices in data mining. In: Data Mining – Concepts and Applications, Ed. by Ciza Thomas, INTECH OPEN 2021. ISBN 978-1-83969-267-3
6. Bobrowski, L.: Small samples of multidimensional feature vectors. In: Hernes, M., Wojtkiewicz, K., Szczerbicki, E. (eds.) ICCCI 2020. CCIS, vol. 1287, pp. 87–98. Springer, Cham (2020). https://doi.org/10.1007/978-3-030-63119-2_8

7. Bobrowski, L.: Data Exploration and Linear Separability, pp. 1–172, Lambert Academic Publishing (2019)
8. Bobrowski, L.: Complexes of low dimensional linear classifiers with L_1 margins. In: Nguyen, N.T., Chittayasothorn, S., Niyato, D., Trawiński, B. (eds.) ACIIDS 2021. LNCS (LNAI), vol. 12672, pp. 29–40. Springer, Cham (2021). https://doi.org/10.1007/978-3-030-73280-6_3
9. Bobrowski, L., Zabielski, P.: Flat patterns extraction with collinearity models. In: 9th EUROSIM Congress on Modelling and Simulation, EUROSIM 2016 , 12–16 September 2016, Oulu Finland, IEEE Conference Publishing Services (CPS)
10. Simonnard, M.: Linear Programming, Prentice – Hall. Englewood Cliffs, New York (1966)
11. Bobrowski, L., Bołdak, C.: Stepwise inversion of large matrices with the Gauss-Jordan vector transformation. J. Adv. Math. Comput. Sci. (2022)
12. Bobrowski, L., Łukaszuk, T.: Relaxed Linear Separability (*RLS*) Approach to Feature (Gene) Subset Selection, p. 103 – 118 in: Selected Works in Bioinformatics, Edited by: Xuhua Xia, INTECH OPEN 2011
13. Bobrowski, L., et al.: Separating gene clustering in the rare mucopolysaccharidosis disease. J. Appl. Genet. **63**(2), 361–368 (2022). https://doi.org/10.1007/s13353-022-00691-2

Competency Management Model for a Team of Trainers

Jarosław Wikarek and Paweł Sitek[✉]

Department of Control and Management Systems, Kielce University of Technology, Kielce,
Poland
{j.wikarek,sitek}@tu.kielce.pl

Abstract. The paper proposes a model of management and configuration of competences of a team conducting advanced training in the field of IT, electronics, robotics and other advanced technologies. The model enables decision support in managing the training team and finding answers to numerous questions in this area. The most important questions include: *Does the team have the appropriate composition and competences to conduct a training cycle in accordance with a given schedule? What competences are missing in the team to conduct the training cycle? What composition of the team of trainers ensures that the trainings can be conducted as scheduled in the absence of any trainer?* etc. The model was formulated as a set of questions and a set of constraints. An approach that integrates mathematical programming and constraint logic programming was used to implement the model. The data has been saved in the form of facts, which enables their storage in both SQL and NoSQL databases and easy integration with decision support systems.

Keywords: Competency management · Personnel assignment problem (PAP) ·
Decision support · Mathematical programming · Constraint logic programming

1 Introduction

In the era of dynamic development of modern technologies in the field of IT, electronics, automation and robotics, there is a great demand for specialist training for users, designers and developers working in these areas. Very often trainings have to be carried out under temporal, financial and personnel limitations. The basic issue when conducting this type of training is gathering a team of trainers having adequate competences and being available on a given date. Because of the often imposed training schedule, availability of trainers with relevant competences, the necessity of conducting an entire training cycle, possible absences, etc., the problem of completing a team of trainers becomes non-trivial.

Therefore, organizers of this type of training must address several key questions before the training begins. The questions concern the composition and competences of the training team, the ability to meet the time schedule, etc.

For the purpose of automating and optimizing the process of answering these and similar questions, a model for managing and configuring the competences of the team of

© The Author(s), under exclusive license to Springer Nature Switzerland AG 2022
N. T. Nguyen et al. (Eds.): ICCCI 2022, LNAI 13501, pp. 388–395, 2022.
https://doi.org/10.1007/978-3-031-16014-1_31

trainers was proposed. It was formulated as a set of questions (both proactive and reactive) and a set of constraints. In order to implement it, an approach was used which integrates constraint logic programming and mathematical programming. The parameters of the model were saved in the form of facts which makes it possible to store them in any database system (SQL, NoSQL, XML). The proposed model can serve as the basis for a decision-support system for the organization of trainings in the field of selection of the training team.

The discussed problem of managing and configuring the competences of the training team can be qualified as a certain variant and extension of the personnel assignment problem (PAP), which is a class of generalized assignment problem (GAP). The GAP is defined using the knapsack or the scheduling terminology [1]. Problems related to assignment arise in a number of areas such as transport, education, healthcare, sport, distribution, etc. In practice, this is a well-studied problem in combinatorial optimization with constraints. PAP refers to the research on how to assign n objects (personnel, teachers, students, workers, etc.) to m objects (projects, courses, tasks, etc.) in the best possible way (cheapest cost, fastest, etc.) [2]. In classical approach the key question in PAP is: *How to carry out an assignment with optimal objective while at the same time fulfilling all the related constraints?* Several methods have been proposed in the literature to answer such a question [2]. The most important ones include the exact methods [1], heuristic methods, the population search methods, the local search methods and the hybrid techniques. PAPs are particularly evident in the field of education, where they most often appear as timetable problems or allocation problems. As far as the timetable problem is concerned, one can find in the literature many of its variants in the area of education [3–5], e.g. the examination timetabling problem (ETP) [3], course timetabling problem (CTP) [4], school timetabling problem (STP) [5], etc. As for the allocation problem, the following variants dominate the literature: student-project allocation (SPAP) [6], space allocation problem (SAP), etc. What differentiates the approach proposed in the paper and is our contribution is the proposal of an original problem model that allows to find answers not to one general question as in the PAP but many, both general and specific questions. Additionally, the model allows to obtain feedback on what assignments we fail to make and why, which is crucial in managing the training cycle. We also suggest an original method of implementing the model in the form of a hybrid approach [7], which integrates the mathematical programming (MP) and constraint logic programming (CLP) methods.

2 Problem Description

The problem is defined as follows. Given is a set L (l – single training index) of trainings to be carried out according to a given schedule H. Each training requires that the trainer who conducts it has appropriate qualifications. These shall be denoted by C – the set of all competences (c – competency index), and by Cz_l – the set of competences needed to carry out training l, with $Cz_l \subseteq C$. For each training there is a known date of its delivery (when it begins and how long it lasts) and the profit earned for conducting it h_l. Given is a set of trainers P (p – trainer index). Each trainer p has a set of specific competences Cd_p, with $Cd_p \subseteq C$. A trainer can conduct a given training if they have all the competences needed to do so, that is $Cz_l \subseteq Cd_p$. For each trainer there is a minimum and maximum working time and a unit cost of work. The problem takes into account the unavailability of trainers with certain competences by introducing the so-called unavailability states W (w – unavailability state index). For instance w_1 – trainer p_1 is unavailable, w_2 – trainer p_2 and p_4. Are unavailable, etc. For a problem formulated in this way, it is crucial to find answers to several key questions. The most important of them are: *Is the available team of trainers sufficient to conduct all trainings (taking into account their competences, working time and schedule)?(Q1), Which trainer should conduct which training so that the cost of work is as low as possible? (Q2), What composition of the team of trainers ensures that the trainings can be conducted as scheduled in the absence of any trainer? (Q3).* It should be emphasized that questions $Q1$, $Q2$, are reactive, while question $Q3$ is a proactive question.

3   Problem Formalization

The problem model is formulated as a $Q1..Q3$ set of questions and a (1)...(12) set of constraints. The individual questions are modeled as a combination of the constraints and, in some cases, the objective function and additional quantities (Table 2). Depending on the nature of the question, the model is either a CSP (Constraint Satisfaction Problem) or a BILP (Binary Integer Linear Programing) model. Indices, parameters and decision variables of the model presented in Table 1. The meaning of constraints (1)...(12) are as follows: ensuring training delivery (1), the training can be conducted only by a trainer with appropriate qualifications (2), calculation of the cost of conducting trainings *cost_1* (3), the trainer works for the time permitted (4), how many trainings cannot be conducted/completed *count_1* (5). If the trainer conducts the training using a certain skill, they conduct the training (combination of variables) (6–7), one trainer cannot conduct two trainings at the same time (8), calculation of the profit for conducting trainings *cost_2* (9), additional constraints related to the presolving of the modeled problem-exclude Trainers who do not have the appropriate qualifications to conduct adequate training (10–11), binarity of variables (12).

Table 1.   Indices, parameters, and decision variables of the model

Symbol	Description
Parameters	
sp, c	If a trainer p has the competency c then $s_{p,c} = 1$, otherwise $s_{p,c} = 0$
t_l	Duration of the training l
hl	Profit from the training l
rp	Cost of work of the trainer p per time unit
n_p	Minimum working time of the trainer p

(continued)

Table 1. (*continued*)

Symbol	Description
m_p	Maximum working time of the trainer p
fl, c	If conducting the training l requires the competency c then $f_{l,c} = 1$, otherwise $f_{l,c} = 0$
aw, p	If the trainer p is available in the state w then $a_{w,p} = 1$, otherwise $a_{w,p} = 0$
bp, l	If the trainer p has the competences required for conducting the training l then $b_{p,l} = 1$, otherwise $b_{p,l} = 0$
$ell, l2$	If the schedule assumes the implementation of training $l1$, which coincides with the implementation of training $l2$ then $e_{l1,z2} = 1$ otherwise $e_{l1,z2} = 1$
con	Arbitrarily large constant
Decision variables	
Xw, p, l, c	If, in the unavailability state w, the trainer p using competency c conducts the training l then $X_{w,p,l,c} = 1$ otherwise $X_{w,p,lc} = 0$
Zw, p, l	If, in the unavailability state w, the trainer p conducts the training l $Z_{w,p,l} = 1$ otherwise $Z_{w,p,l} = 0$
Yw, l, c	If the training l cannot be conducted due to the impossibility of obtaining competency c in the unavailability state w then $Y_{w,l,c} = 0$ (decision variable introduced only to achieve a solution in each case – so that the NFSF/No Feasible Solution Found situation/state does not appear), otherwise $Y_{w,l,c} = 1$

What is unique in the structure of the proposed model is such a choice of decision variables that the modelled problem will always have a solution i.e. there will be no NFSF situation (No Feasible Solution Found). This is guaranteed by the introduction of the decision variable $Y_{w,l,c}$. The second unique feature of the model is the introduction of additional constraints (10), (11). These constraints do not arise from the properties of the problem being modeled but are the result of presolving with CLP predicates and appear at the model generation stage in the form of MPS (Mathematical Programming System).

Table 2. Question modelling method

Question	Problem	Constrains	Objective	Solution
Q1	CSP	1..12, Count_1 = 0	---	$X_{w,p,l,c}$
Q2	BILP	1..12, Count_1 = 0	Min (Cost_1)	$X_{w,p,l,c}$
Q3	BILP	Analogous to Q2 only with a change in the values of parameters concerning the availability of the trainers		

$$\sum_{p\in P} X_{w,p,l,c} = (1 - Y_{w,l,c}) \cdot f_{l,c} \forall l \in L, c \in C, w \in W \tag{1}$$

$$X_{w,p,l,c} \le b_{p,l} \forall w \in W, p \in P, l \in L, c \in C \tag{2}$$

$$\text{Cost\_1} = \sum_{w\in W} \sum_{p\in P} \sum_{l\in L} t_l \cdot r_p \cdot Z_{w,p,l} \tag{3}$$

$$n_p \le \sum_{l\in L} (t_l \cdot Z_{w,p,l}) \le m_p \forall w \in W, p \in P \tag{4}$$

$$\text{Count\_1} = \sum_{w\in W} \sum_{l\in L} \sum_{c\in C} Y_{w,l,c} \tag{5}$$

$$\sum_{c\in C} X_{w,p,l,c} \le con \cdot Z_{w,p,l} \forall w \in W, p \in P, l \in L \tag{6}$$

$$\sum_{c\in C} X_{w,p,l,c} \ge Z_{w,p,l} \forall w \in W, p \in P, l \in L \tag{7}$$

$$Z_{w,p,l1} + Z_{w,p,l2} \le 1 \forall w \in W, p \in P, l1, l2 \in L, e_{l1,l2} = 1 \tag{8}$$

$$\text{Cost\_2} = \sum_{w\in W} \sum_{l\in L} h_l \cdot (\sum_{p\in P} Z_{w,p,l}) \tag{9}$$

$$X_{w,p,l,c} = 0 \forall w \in W, p \in P, l \in L, c \in C \wedge b_{p,l} = 0 \tag{10}$$

$$X_{w,p,l,c} = 0 \forall w \in W, p \in P, l \in L, c \in C \wedge a_{w,p} = 0 \tag{11}$$

$$X_{w,p,l,c} \in \{0, 1\} \forall w \in W, p \in P, l \in L, c \in C; Z_{w,p,c} \in \{0, 1\} \forall w \in W, p \in P, c \in C \tag{12}$$

4 Implementation

The data of the modelled problem were stored as facts [8]. This form enables their further storage in both SQL and NoSQL databases and easy integration with decision support systems. The implementation of the proposed model (Sect. 3) was performed using an original hybrid approach, which is based on the integration of CLP and MP. Different variants of this approach were used by the authors to model and solve numerous problems in the field of manufacturing, distribution and logistics [9]. In the presented variant, the CLP predicates [8] where used for the generation of facts defining the possibility of specific trainers to conduct specific trainings and possible exclusions. The predicates used [8] in the generation of these facts are based on a set of basic facts in which information about trainers, training, competences, etc. are stored. The use of these CLP predicates presents a presolving problem based on data instances. In the next step, based on the set of all facts, constraints (1)…(12) and questions $Q1..Q3$, another set of CLP predicates allows to generate a problem implementation model in the MPS (Mathematical Programming System) format, which contains only non-zero parameter values in effect reducing its size and thus significantly shortens the computation time. The model so generated can be solved using any MP solver. The implementation presented here uses the Gurobi solver [10]. The general implementation scheme is shown in Fig. 1.

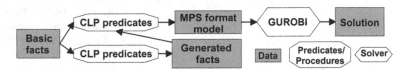

Fig. 1. Implementation scheme of the modelled problem

5 Computational Experiments

Computational experiments using the proposed model were carried out for the case where the organizer has to deliver 10 trainings $l = \{l1..l10\}$. Conducting a given training requires certain competences of trainers $c = \{c1..c5\}$. The training schedule is given and shown in Fig. 2. Each training should be conducted by one of the 5 trainers $p = \{p1..p5\}$. The trainer conducting the training should have all required qualifications. The qualifications that the individual trainers have are shown graphically in Fig. 3. Detailed numerical data of the parameters of the model used in the experiment are presented in the form of facts in [8]. In the first stage of the experiments, the answer to question $Q1$ was sought. This was accomplished in two ways. The first consisted in manually assigning the trainers to the courses. The result of such an allocation can be seen in Fig. 4. The cost of delivering the trainings in this case was 6400. Then the answer to this question was found using the proposed model (Sect. 3). The result obtained is shown in Fig. 5 and the corresponding cost is 5800. The next stage was to seek an answer to question $Q2$, which requires determining the optimal assignment of trainers to courses in relation to the costs. The optimal allocation of trainers to courses/trainings is shown in Fig. 6. In view of the data in the experiments [8]. This question only serves a purpose if the answer to $Q1$ or $Q2$ is negative. Next, the answer to question $Q3$ was sought. This question deals with the situation when one of the trainers is unavailable. Figure 7 illustrates the allocation of the trainers to trainings in the absence of trainer p_1. In this case it was possible to conduct the training according to the specified schedule (Fig. 2) with the cost 5800. Other experiments concerning question $Q3$ in case of unavailability of other trainers were carried out.

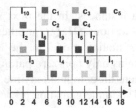

Fig. 2. Training schedule

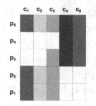

Fig. 3. Competences
of trainers

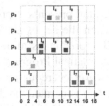

Fig. 4. Allocation for an
answer to question Q1
(cost1 = 6400 – the result
was obtained manually)
Computation time 300 s.

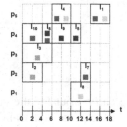

Fig. 5. Allocation for an
answer to question Q1 (cost1
= 5800 – acceptable solution).
Computation time 5 s.

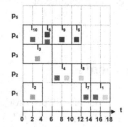

Fig. 6. Optimal allocation
for an answer to
question Q2 (cost1 =
5000 – optimal solution)
Computation time 17 s.

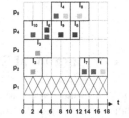

Fig. 7. Optimal allocation
for an answer to question Q3
in the case of unavailability
of trainer p_1 (cost1 =
5800 – optimal solution).
Computation time 21 s.

6   Conclusions

The analyzed problem of management of competences of a training team is extremely
important in the context of organization of trainings. The proposed model (Sect. 3) can
serve as a basis for building a decision support system for selecting the staff of trainers
and carrying out the training cycle. This is due to the fact that the application of the model
allows for automatic finding of answers to key questions concerning the possibility of
delivering the training according to the set schedule with the available trainers, what kind
of competences of the trainers are missing in order to deliver the training, the possibility
of delivering the training in case of absence of a particular trainer, etc. Additionally, the
model enables determining acceptable and optimal allocations of trainers to particular
trainings so that the cost/profit of conducted trainings was the lowest/the highest. In this
case, being proactive allows you to conduct the courses in the absence of any trainer. The
proposed model can be implemented in any mathematical programming environment.
The hybrid approach [7, 9] to its implementation proposed in the paper allows presolving
the model and thus reducing its size. This is of great importance due to the combinatorial

nature of the problem. In further works, it is expected to integrate the proposed model with the training planning and scheduling system [11]. Such integration will provide an opportunity to develop or find an optimal training schedule that can be carried out based on the existing team of trainers, without the need to supplement it and/or their competencies which is especially important in reconfigurable manufacturing systems [12].

References

1. Qu, R., Burke, E.K., McCollum, B., Merlot, L.T.G., Lee, S.Y.: A survey of search methodologies and automated system development for examination timetabling. J. Schedul. **12**(1), 55–89 (2009)
2. Singh, S.: A comparative analysis of assignment problem. IOSR J. Eng. **2**(8), 1–15 (2012)
3. Burke, E., Elliman, D., Ford, P., Weare, R.: Examination timetabling in British universities: a survey. In: Burke, E., Ross, P. (eds.) PATAT 1995. LNCS, vol. 1153, pp. 76–90. Springer, Heidelberg (1996). https://doi.org/10.1007/3-540-61794-9_52
4. Obit, J.H.: Developing Novel Meta-Heuristic. University of Nottingham, Hyper-Heuristic and Cooperative Search for Course Timetabling Problems (2010)
5. Cerdeira-Pena, A., Carpente, L., Farina, A., Seco, D.: "New" approaches for the school timetabling problem. In: Proceedings of the 7th Mexican International Conference on Artifcial Intelligence, MICAI 2008, pp. 261–267, mex, October 2008
6. Manlove, D.F., O'Malley, G.: Student-project allocation with preferences over projects. J. Discrete Algor. **6**(4), 553–560 (2008)
7. Sitek, P., Wikarek, J.: A multi-level approach to ubiquitous modeling and solving constraints in combinatorial optimization problems in production and distribution. Appl. Intell. **48**(5), 1344–1367 (2017). https://doi.org/10.1007/s10489-017-1107-9
8. ICCCI_PAPER_309. https://drive.google.com/drive/folders/1l9Ns1kLwRyDvAyietTI6zE5 mqpSHLGQn. Accessed 30 Jan 2022
9. Sitek, P., Wikarek, J., Grzybowska, K.: A multi-agent approach to the multi-echelon capacitated vehicle routing problem. In: Corchado, J.M., et al. (eds.) PAAMS 2014. CCIS, vol. 430, pp. 121–132. Springer, Cham (2014). https://doi.org/10.1007/978-3-319-07767-3_12
10. Gurobi, http://www.gurobi.com/. Accessed 30 Jan 2022
11. Bocewicz, G., Szwarc, E., Wikarek, J., Nielsen, P., Banaszak, Z.: A competency-driven staff assignment approach to improving employee scheduling robustness. Eksploatacja i Niezawodność, **23**(1), 117–131 (2021). https://doi.org/10.17531/ein.2021.1.13
12. Gola, A., Pastuszak, Z., Relich, M., Sobaszek, Ł., Szwarc, E.: Scalability analysis of selected structures of a reconfigurable manufacturing system taking into account a reduction in machine tools reliability. Eksploatacja i Niezawodnosc – Mainten. Reliabil. **23**(2), 242–252 (2021). https://doi.org/10.17531/ein.2021.2.4

Querying and Reasoning in Paraconsistent Rule-Object Languages with Inheritance Expressions

Andrzej Szałas[1,2](✉) [ID]

[1] Institute of Informatics, University of Warsaw, Warsaw, Poland
andrzej.szalas@mimuw.edu.pl
[2] Department of Computer and Information Science, University of Linköping, Linköping, Sweden
andrzej.szalas@liu.se

Abstract. Inheritance has intensively been investigated during the past decades in object-oriented programming and knowledge representation and reasoning areas. In the paper we focus on recently introduced inheritance expressions that allow one to represent dynamic concept hierarchies as well as fuse and disambiguate beliefs acquired by the objects involved. We focus on querying and reasoning about inheritance expressions using a four-valued paraconsistent formalism that has been developed over the last ten years. In particular, we show that querying inheritance expressions and formulas can be efficiently implemented. In addition, we provide tableaux for general reasoning purposes. Complexity of the investigated tools is also analyzed.

Keywords: Tableaux · Paraconsistent reasoning · Rule-object query languages · Inheritance expressions · Belief fusion

1 Introduction and Motivations

Fusing and disambiguating beliefs from heterogeneous sources is one of the key mechanisms of collective intelligence. In the paper we approach these methods using rule-object languages equipped with inheritance expressions. While rule-based languages are the major logic-based tool for expressing and reasoning about beliefs, objects provide a useful machinery for organizing belief bases in a distributed and heterogeneous manner. Inheritance expressions, on the other hand, allow one to dynamically structure objects in concept-subconcept hierarchies at the same time providing means for fusing and disambiguating conflicting or complementary beliefs. Inheritance expressions formalism, IEF, has been introduced in [21] and further developed in [20]. In the current paper we investigate its properties related to querying and reasoning.

Supported by the Polish National Science Centre grant 2017/27/B/ST6/02018.

Though the IEF formalism is defined in [21] for arbitrary many-valued logics, we focus on a paraconsistent four-valued logic $\mathcal{L}_4$ with truth values $\mathbb{T}$ (true), $\mathbb{F}$ (false), $\mathbb{I}$ (inconsistent), $\mathbb{U}$ (unknown). $\mathcal{L}_4$ is a minimalistic logic that allows us to illustrate and address the involved phenomena. As emphasized already in [2], collective beliefs from a variety of sources may be:

- $\mathbb{T}$: when a source claims that the belief is true and no source denies it;
- $\mathbb{F}$: when a source claims that the belief is false and no source denies it;
- $\mathbb{I}$: when a source claims that the belief is true and a source claims its falsity;
- $\mathbb{U}$: when no source claims its truth nor falsity.

Inheritance has intensively been investigated during the past decades in object-oriented programming (see [4,7,8,17,23,25] and references there), as well as in knowledge representation and reasoning [5,6,14,18], [12, Chapter 9]. In particular, a mechanism for combining methods from multiply inherited classes is presented in [4,23]. The IEF formalism is simpler to use and focused on query languages what, among others, simplify the querying and reasoning methods. IEF can be used to complement rule-object languages by providing inheritance expressions as a convenient tool that may be used in applications where objects serve as knowledge providers. In particular, IEF can extend the approach to rule-object fusion provided in [19], where rule-based languages are embedded in object-oriented tools but miss an inheritance mechanism.

The original contents of this paper include:

- sound and complete tableau rules for inheritance expressions and formulas;
- an analysis of complexity of querying and reasoning about inheritance expressions;
- examples and discussions of investigated concepts.

The paper is structured as follows. In Sect. 2 we present a paraconsistent four-valued logic underlying the IEF formalism, discuss the understanding of classes and objects, and recall inheritance networks. In Sect. 3 we summarize inheritance expressions. Section 4 is devoted to querying and reasoning about objects embedded in inheritance expressions. Finally, Sect. 5 concludes the paper with final remarks and possible directions for further research.

2 Preliminaries and Background

2.1 Four-Valued Logic Used in the Paper

While classical logic deals with two truth values, $\mathbb{T}$ and $\mathbb{F}$, many-valued logics assume additional truth values [16,22]. As mentioned in the introduction, in the paper we will deal with a four-valued logic $\mathcal{L}_4$ [1,24], extended in [11] by doxastic connectives. $\mathcal{L}_4$ is used as a basis for the paraconsistent 4QL rule language [15] enjoying tractable model and query evaluation. In addition to the classical truth values, in $\mathcal{L}_4$ we use $\mathbb{U}$ and $\mathbb{I}$.

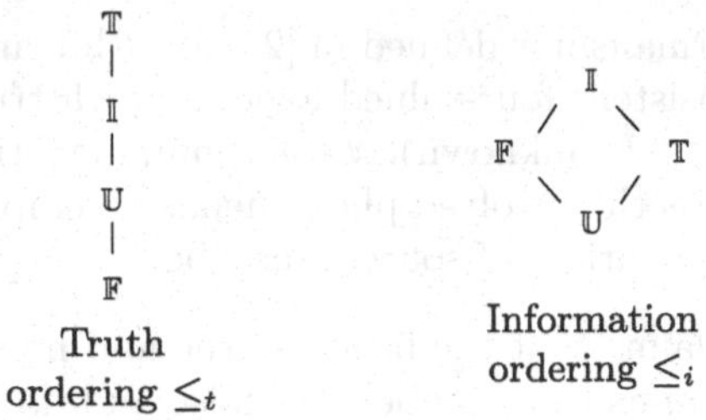

$$
\begin{array}{c}
\mathrm{T} \\
| \\
\mathrm{I} \\
| \\
\mathrm{U} \\
| \\
\mathrm{F}
\end{array}
\qquad
\begin{array}{c}
\mathrm{I} \\
\diagup \quad \diagdown \\
\mathrm{F} \qquad \mathrm{T} \\
\diagdown \quad \diagup \\
\mathrm{U}
\end{array}
$$

Truth
ordering $\leq_t$
                Information
                ordering $\leq_i$

Fig. 1. Orderings on truth values used in the paper.

For $k \geq 0$, by $\mathcal{R}_k$ we denote a set of *k-argument relation symbols*. By $\mathcal{R}$ we mean the set of all relation symbols, $\mathcal{R} \overset{\text{def}}{=} \bigcup_{k \geq 0} \mathcal{R}_k$. Let $\mathcal{C}$ be a finite set of constants. A *positive ground literal over* $\mathcal{C}$ is an expression of the form $r(c_1, \ldots, c_k)$, where $r \in \mathcal{R}_k$ and $c_1, \ldots, c_k \in \mathcal{C}$. A *negative ground literal over* $\mathcal{C}$ is an expression of the form $\neg \ell$, where ℓ is a positive ground literal. A *ground literal over* $\mathcal{C}$ is a positive or a negative ground literal.[1]

The following BNF grammar defines the syntax of $\mathcal{L}_4$, where non-terminal symbols $\langle \mathcal{T} \rangle$, $\langle \mathcal{G} \rangle$ and $\langle \mathcal{F} \rangle$ respectively represent truth values, ground literals, and formulas:

$$
\begin{aligned}
\langle \mathcal{F} \rangle :: = \ & \langle \mathcal{T} \rangle \mid \langle \mathcal{G} \rangle \mid \neg \langle \mathcal{F} \rangle \mid \langle \mathcal{F} \rangle \vee \langle \mathcal{F} \rangle \mid \langle \mathcal{F} \rangle \wedge \langle \mathcal{F} \rangle \mid \\
& \langle \mathcal{F} \rangle \mathbin{\dot{\vee}} \langle \mathcal{F} \rangle \mid \langle \mathcal{F} \rangle \mathbin{\dot{\wedge}} \langle \mathcal{F} \rangle \mid (\langle \mathcal{F} \rangle).
\end{aligned}
\tag{1}
$$

In addition to traditional connectives $\neg$ (negation), $\vee$ (disjunction) and $\wedge$ (conjunction), we consider *doxastic disjunction* $\dot{\vee}$ and *doxastic conjunction* $\dot{\wedge}$ that allow one to compose objects in a doxastic (belief-like) fusion manner. For the sake of simplicity we restricted the set of connectives to a reasonable subset. It can, of course, be arbitrarily extended. For example, one can define implication traditionally:

$$
\tau \to \tau' \overset{\text{def}}{\equiv} \neg \tau \vee \tau',
\tag{2}
$$

or in any other suitable way.

The semantics of $\mathcal{L}_4$ is defined as follows, where $\tau, \tau' \in \mathcal{T}$ are truth values and orderings $\leq_t, \leq_i$ are shown in Fig. 1, and lub, glb denote respectively the least upper bound and the greatest lower bound:

$$
\neg \mathrm{F} \overset{\text{def}}{=} \mathrm{T}, \quad \neg \mathrm{U} \overset{\text{def}}{=} \mathrm{U}, \quad \neg \mathrm{I} \overset{\text{def}}{=} \mathrm{I}, \quad \neg \mathrm{T} \overset{\text{def}}{=} \mathrm{F};
\tag{3}
$$

$$
\tau \vee \tau' \overset{\text{def}}{=} \max{}_{\leq_t}(\tau, \tau'), \quad \tau \wedge \tau' \overset{\text{def}}{=} \min{}_{\leq_t}(\tau, \tau');
\tag{4}
$$

$$
\tau \mathbin{\dot{\vee}} \tau' \overset{\text{def}}{=} \mathrm{lub}_{\leq_i}(\tau, \tau'), \quad \tau \mathbin{\dot{\wedge}} \tau' \overset{\text{def}}{=} \mathrm{glb}_{\leq_i}(\tau, \tau').
\tag{5}
$$

---

[1] We don't employ function symbols, which is a standard in rule-based query languages. We also omit variables for the sake of presentation simplicity, what does not affect complexity results.

Truth ordering $\leq_t$ serves traditional evaluation of truth values of disjunctions and conjunctions. It generalizes classical ordering on $\mathbb{T}$, $\mathbb{F}$: after removing non-classical truth values, $\leq_t$ becomes classical, where simply $\mathbb{F} \leq \mathbb{T}$. Information ordering $\leq_i$ reflects the process of information gathering and fusing:

- initially there may be no evidence about a given fact what is represented by the bottom value $\mathbb{U}$;
- then evidences are being collected, supporting the fact (represented by the value $\mathbb{T}$) or against it (represented by the value $\mathbb{F}$);
- finally, evidences for as well as against the fact may be collected, what is represented by $\mathbb{I}$.

Remark 1. Notice that the Kleene 3-valued logic, $\mathcal{K}_3$ is a sub-logic of $\mathcal{L}_4$: when the value $\mathbb{I}$ is removed, the resulting logic is $\mathcal{K}_3$, frequently used in computer science, e.g., providing the semantics of SQL queries when tables may contain 'null' values.

When one removes the value $\mathbb{U}$, the resulting logic is compatible with $\mathcal{K}_3$ what reflects the idea that inconsistency is a kind of lack of knowledge, indicating that there are contradictory information sources and it is currently unknown which one is right.   □

Of course, other orderings may be considered here, as investigated in the area of paraconsistent reasoning [3].

2.2   Classes and Objects

We follow the ideas of [19], where object-rule fusion formalism, $\mathrm{o}^n\mathrm{QL}$, has been developed for many-valued rule-based query languages using n-valued logics. $\mathrm{o}^n\mathrm{QL}$ employs the correspondence between rule-based programs and their models, being sets of ground literals. Roughly speaking,

- classes contain relations defined by means of rules;
- objects are instances of classes, containing ground literals and serving as query answerers.

The net result is that any object can be seen as a set of ground literals representing a model of a logic program specified by facts and rules of the class the object instantiates. In the paper we consider $\mathrm{o}^4\mathrm{QL}$ with the logic $\mathcal{L}_4$ recalled in Sect. 2.1. The corresponding rule language is 4QL [15].[2]

In what follows, by $o.\ell$ we denote the truth value of ground literal (method) ℓ returned by the object o. An expression of the form $o.\ell$ or $\neg o.\ell$ is respectively called a *positive* or *negative object literal*.

Example 1. As an example, consider the class shown in Table 1. When an object instantiating 'car_model' class is created, 'car_model(hybx)', representing a concrete car model, say 'hybx', rules are evaluated by querying an external object

---

[2] For open-source implementation of 4QL, inter4ql, see **4ql.org**.

Table 1. Specification of the class 'car_model'.

```
class car_model(M);            % represents car model M
{   ...
        ctax :- env.polluting(M).      % subject to car environmental tax
                                        % when the model M is polluting
        ¬ctax :- ¬env.polluting(M).  % not subject to car environmental tax
                                        % when the model M is not polluting
        ...
}
```

'env' whether 'hybx' is polluting the environment. The query is formulated using a literal 'polluting(hybx)'. For a query 'car_model(hybx).ctax',[3]

- the value $\mathbb{T}$ is returned when 'env.polluting(hybx)' is $\mathbb{T}$;
- the value $\mathbb{F}$ is returned when 'env.polluting(hybx)' is $\mathbb{F}$;
- the value $\mathbb{U}$ is returned when 'env.polluting(hybx)' is $\mathbb{U}$;
- the value $\mathbb{I}$ is returned when 'env.polluting(hybx)' is $\mathbb{I}$.   □

For the rest of the paper we will assume that:

- the contents of objects is computed, regardless of when and how their methods (literals) were acquired;
- semantically each object is identified with a set of ground literals.

2.3 Inheritance Networks

Inheritance networks have been intensively studied in the KRR area (see, e.g., [5,6,14,18] and numerous references there). An *inheritance network* is a finite directed graph with two types of edges, $o_1 \dashrightarrow o_2$ and $o_1 \not\dashrightarrow o_2$. The '$\dashrightarrow$' arrow indicates the inheritance, while the crossed '$\not\dashrightarrow$' arrow prevents it.

One of the major problems in inheritance networks depends on disambiguating beliefs when a node inherits from multiple parent nodes. In such cases inherited beliefs may be complementary or contradictory. Also, while inheritance is transitive, in some cases one would like to break transitivity. The next example illustrates these problems.

Example 2. Consider the inheritance net shown in Fig. 2(a), where we assume that 'gasoline', 'hybrid', 'electric' and 'car' are classes parameterized by 'M' representing car models, and 'polluter' is a non-parameterized class representing objects that pollute the environment. We further assume that:

- 'hybrid' inherits from 'gasoline' as well as from 'electric';
- both 'gasoline' and 'electric' inherit from 'car_model' which inherits from 'polluter';

---

[3] We use the semantics of 4QL here.

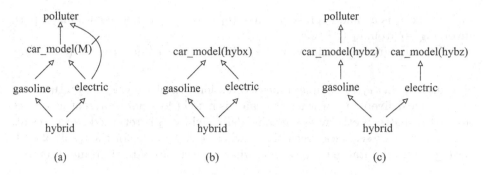

Fig. 2. Inheritance network involving the 'car_model' class (a) and sample object inheritance hierarchies (b)–(c) instantiating and resolving (a).

– 'electric' does not inherit from 'polluter' though transitivity of inheritance 'electric' $\dashrightarrow$ 'car_model' $\dashrightarrow$ 'polluter' would otherwise make 'electric' a subclass of 'polluter'.

Given that the class 'polluter' contains a literal 'tax' $(= \mathbb{T})$, indicating that inheriting classes represent objects that are subject to a general environmental tax, the question would be whether a particular hybrid car should or should not inherit 'tax'$= \mathbb{T}$. Indeed, in Fig. 2(a), the lefthand inheritance path suggests that this inheritance occurs, whereas the righthand path prevents it.   □

We address these issues by considering *dynamic* rather than *static* inheritance: objects are dynamically assigned appropriately modified inheritance nets. Possible instantiations of the net shown in Fig. 2(a) are shown in Fig. 2(b)–(c). Given a particular car model, it may be a polluter or not what may depend on the proportion of electricity versus gas consumption. The object inheritance hierarchy shown in Fig. 2(b) is adequate for a non-polluting car model 'hybx', and the one shown in Fig. 2(c) is adequate for a polluting car model 'hybz'.

3   Inheritance Expressions

Syntax. In their essence, objects deliver truth values of literals (methods) via their interfaces. In the IEF framework we focus on dynamic knowledge processing and reasoning objectives. We will deal with a finite set of objects identified by names/references gathered in a set $\mathcal{O}$. To avoid ambiguities, we assume that each element in $\mathcal{O}$ identifies an object in a one-to-one manner. The essence of the IEF framework are *inheritance expressions over* $\mathcal{O}$, denoted by $\mathcal{E}(\mathcal{O})$, as defined by the following BNF grammar, where $\circ \in \{\vee, \wedge, \dot{\vee}, \dot{\wedge}\}$:

$$\langle \mathcal{E}(\mathcal{O}) \rangle :: = \langle \mathcal{O} \rangle \mid \neg \langle \mathcal{E}(\mathcal{O}) \rangle \mid \langle \mathcal{E}(\mathcal{O}) \rangle \circ \langle \mathcal{E}(\mathcal{O}) \rangle \mid \langle \mathcal{E}(\mathcal{O}) \rangle \dashrightarrow \langle \mathcal{E}(\mathcal{O}) \rangle \mid (\langle \mathcal{E}(\mathcal{O}) \rangle), \quad (6)$$

assuming *acyclicity* wrt $\dashrightarrow$ in the sense that there is no path in the expression tree through $\dashrightarrow$, leading from an element of $\mathcal{O}$ to itself. For example,

$(o_1 \vee o_2) \dashrightarrow o_3$ is a valid expression while $(o_1 \vee o_2) \dashrightarrow o_1$ is not, containing a path involving $\dashrightarrow$ from o_1 to itself.

We assume right-associativity of $\dashrightarrow$, i.e., $e \dashrightarrow e' \dashrightarrow e''$ denotes $e \dashrightarrow (e' \dashrightarrow e'')$.

Semantics. Let e_1, e_2 be inheritance expressions, Intuitively, $e_1 \dashrightarrow e_2$ returns the truth value delivered by e_1 when the value is not $\mathbb{U}$ (does not represent ignorance about the matter); otherwise the value delivered by e_2 is returned as the result.

We define the semantics recursively, where $\varrho(e.\ell)$ stands for the result of evaluating ℓ wrt inheritance expression e, where objects are sets of ground literals:

$$\varrho(o.\ell) \stackrel{\text{def}}{=} \begin{cases} \mathbb{T} \text{ when } \ell \in o \text{ and } \neg \ell \notin o; \\ \mathbb{F} \text{ when } \neg \ell \in o \text{ and } \ell \notin o; \\ \mathbb{I} \text{ when } \ell \in o \text{ and } \neg \ell \in o; \\ \mathbb{U} \text{ when } \ell \notin o \text{ and } \neg \ell \notin o; \end{cases} \tag{7}$$

$$\varrho(\neg(e.\ell)) \stackrel{\text{def}}{=} \neg(\varrho(e.\ell)); \tag{8}$$

$$\varrho((e_1 \circ e_2)).\ell) \stackrel{\text{def}}{=} \varrho(e_1.\ell) \circ \varrho(e_2.\ell)), \text{ where } \circ \in \{\vee, \wedge, \dot{\vee}, \dot{\wedge}\}; \tag{9}$$

$$\varrho((e_1 \dashrightarrow e_2).\ell) \stackrel{\text{def}}{=} \begin{cases} \varrho(e_1.\ell) \text{ when } \varrho(e_1.\ell) \neq \mathbb{U}, \text{ i.e.,} \\ \qquad \text{when } e_1 \text{ is not ignorant about } \ell; \\ \varrho(e_2.\ell) \text{ otherwise.} \end{cases} \tag{10}$$

Notice that clauses (7)–(10) handle all alternatives listed in (6), so they recursively cover all inheritance expressions.

Let us illustrate the use of inheritance expressions in the following example.

Example 3. As an example consider expressions related to inheritance nets shown in Fig. 2(b). For the sake of illustration assume that:

- 'electric' contains the literal '¬ctax' (making 'ctax'=$\mathbb{F}$), indicating that electric cars are not subject to car environmental tax;
- 'hybrid' and 'gasoline' contain no literals involving 'ctax', so 'hybrid.ctax' = 'gasoline.ctax' = $\mathbb{U}$;
- 'env.polluting(hybx)' is $\mathbb{T}$, so 'car_model(hybx).ctax'=$\mathbb{T}$ (see Table 1).

Since 'gasoline' inherits 'ctax'=$\mathbb{T}$ from 'car_model(hybx)', there is a conflict between 'ctax' inherited by 'hybrid' from 'gasoline' and from 'electric'. Consider the following inheritance expressions as candidates for resolving the conflict:

$$(\text{hybrid} \dashrightarrow (\text{gasoline} \vee \text{electric}) \dashrightarrow \text{car\_model(hybx)}).\text{ctax}; \tag{11}$$

$$(\text{hybrid} \dashrightarrow (\text{gasoline} \dot{\vee} \text{electric}) \dashrightarrow \text{car\_model(hybx)}).\text{ctax}. \tag{12}$$

The expression (11) returns the value $(\mathbb{U} \dashrightarrow (\mathbb{T} \vee \mathbb{F}) \dashrightarrow \mathbb{T}) = \mathbb{T}$, and the expression (12) returns the value $(\mathbb{U} \dashrightarrow (\mathbb{T} \dot{\vee} \mathbb{F}) \dashrightarrow \mathbb{T}) = \mathbb{I}$. Assuming that the object 'env' is better informed than more general object 'electric', the expression (11) is more appropriate to resolve the conflict.

Recall that 'polluter' contains the literal 'tax'. Therefore, in the case of Fig. 2(c), 'gasoline' inherits 'tax' from 'polluter'. However, 'tax' in 'electric' is $\mathbb{U}$.

Assuming that in this case one would like to receive the value $\mathbb{U}$ for 'tax', the following expression could be used:

$$\left(\text{hybrid} \dashrightarrow \left(\begin{array}{c}(\text{gasoline} \dashrightarrow \text{car\_model}(\text{hybz}) \dashrightarrow \text{polluter}) \wedge \\ (\text{electric} \dashrightarrow \text{car\_model}(\text{hybz}))\end{array}\right)\right).\text{tax.} \qquad \square$$

4 Querying and Reasoning with Inheritance Expressions

4.1 Querying Inheritance Expressions

Let a finite set of objects $\mathcal{O}$ be fixed. Recall that each object in $\mathcal{O}$ is identified with a finite set of ground literals. Let $e \in \mathcal{E}(\mathcal{O})$ be a given inheritance expression and ℓ be a ground literal. Evaluating $e.\ell$ requires, in the worst case, to query all objects involved in e. During the evaluation the contents of objects is not changed. The worst case complexity of computing the values of inheritance expressions $e.\ell$ is then:

$$\mathcal{O}\big(|e| * c(\ell, e)\big), \tag{13}$$

where $|e|$ denotes the number of objects' occurrences in e and $c(\ell, e)$ is the maximal complexity of computing the truth value of ℓ in objects in e.

Since the size of inheritance expressions is typically rather small, the main source of worst-case complexity is the factor $c(\ell, e)$. It involves searching for ℓ and $\neg\ell$ in objects occurring in e. When organized in data structures such as B-tree, the complexity is $\mathcal{O}(\log(m))$, where m is the maximal cardinality of objects (being sets of ground literals). When hash tables are used, the average complexity becomes $\mathcal{O}(1)$ but the worst-case complexity worsens to $\mathcal{O}(m)$.

When a query is expressed by an inheritance formula, $\mathcal{O}$ serves as the underlying database. Let A be a given query. Assuming that objects occurring in A are directly referenced by pointers, the worst case complexity of a query expressed by A is:

$$\mathcal{O}\big(|A| * d(A)\big), \tag{14}$$

where $|A|$ is the length of A and $d(A)$ is the maximal complexity of of computing the values of inheritance expressions $e.\ell$ occurring in A, given by (13). When objects are not referenced directly but have to be searched in the $\mathcal{O}$ database, they can also be organized in a B-tree. In this case (14) should additionally involve a factor $\log(|\mathcal{O}|)$, where $|\mathcal{O}|$ is the number of objects in $\mathcal{O}$.

4.2 Signed Tableaux for Inheritance Formulas

Let $\mathcal{O}$ be a fixed set of objects. By *inheritance formulas* we understand expressions defined by extending the syntax clauses of $\mathcal{L}_4$ provided in (1) with an additional clause, stating that $e.\ell$ is also a formula, where $e \in \mathcal{E}(\mathcal{O})$ is an inheritance expression and ℓ is a positive ground literal.

For defining signed tableaux we need signed formulas being expressions of the form $\tau : A$, where $\tau \in \{\mathbb{T}, \mathbb{F}, \mathbb{I}, \mathbb{U}\}$ and A is an inheritance formula. The intuitive meaning of $\tau : A$ is that formula A obtains the truth value τ. A signed tableau is a rooted tree with nodes labeled by sets of formulas. The root of the tree is labeled by a single signed formula. The tree is then expanded according to rules shown in Table 2 and Table 3. The following types of rules are used, where ',' and '|' represent (classical) conjunction and disjunction, respectively:

$$\text{(a)} \ \frac{\tau : A}{\tau' : B} \quad \text{(b)} \ \frac{\tau : A}{\tau_1 : A_1, \ldots, \tau_k : A_k} \quad \text{(c)} \ \frac{\tau : A}{\tau_1 : A_1 \mid \ldots \mid \tau_k : A_k}. \tag{15}$$

Table 2. Tableau rules for $\mathcal{L}_4$ connectives, where A, B are inheritance formulas.

$(\neg)$	$\dfrac{T : \neg A}{F : A} \quad \dfrac{F : \neg A}{T : A} \quad \dfrac{I : \neg A}{I : A} \quad \dfrac{U : \neg A}{U : A}$
$(\vee)$	$\dfrac{T : A \vee B}{T : A \mid T : B} \quad \dfrac{I : A \vee B}{I : A, \{I, U, F\} : B \mid \{I, U, F\} : A, I : B}$
	$\dfrac{F : A \vee B}{F : A, \ F : B} \quad \dfrac{U : A \vee B}{U : A, \{U, F\} : B \mid \{U, F\} : A, \ U : B}$
$(\wedge)$	$\dfrac{T : A \wedge B}{T : A, \ T : B} \quad \dfrac{I : A \wedge B}{I : A, \{T, I\} : B \mid \{T, I\} : A, I : B}$
	$\dfrac{F : A \wedge B}{F : A \mid F : B} \quad \dfrac{U : A \wedge B}{U : A, \ \{T, I, U\} : B \mid \{T, I, U\} : A, \ U : B}$
$(\dot\vee)$	$\dfrac{T : A \dot\vee B}{T : A \mid \{T, U\} : B \mid \{T, U\} : A, T : B}$
	$\dfrac{I : A \dot\vee B}{I : A \mid I : B \mid T : A, F : B \mid F : A, T : B}$
	$\dfrac{F : A \dot\vee B}{F : A, \ \{F, U\} : B \mid \{F, U\} : A, F : B} \quad \dfrac{U : A \dot\vee B}{U : A, U : B}$
$(\dot\wedge)$	$\dfrac{T : A \dot\wedge B}{T : A \mid \{T, I\} : B \mid \{T, I\} : A, T : B} \quad \dfrac{I : A \dot\wedge B}{I : A, I : B}$
	$\dfrac{F : A \dot\wedge B}{F : A, \ \{F, I\} : B \mid \{F, I\} : A, F : B}$
	$\dfrac{U : A \dot\wedge B}{U : A \mid U : B \mid T : A, F : B \mid F : A, T : B}$

The provided rules preserve equivalence between input formulas and the results of rules. That is, referring to rule types (15), we will have:

$$\begin{array}{ll} \text{(a)} \ \tau{:}A \equiv \tau'{:}B, & \text{(b)} \ \tau{:}A \equiv (\tau_1{:}A_1 \wedge \ldots \wedge \tau_k{:}A_k), \\ & \text{(c)} \ \tau{:}A \equiv (\tau_1{:}A_1 \vee \ldots \vee \tau_k{:}A_k), \end{array} \tag{16}$$

where $\wedge, \vee, \equiv$ are classical conjunction, disjunction and equivalence.[4]

---

[4] Notice that signed formulas only have the value T or F, so classical connectives can be used.

Table 3. Tableau rules for inheritance expressions, where $e, e' \in \mathcal{E}(\mathcal{O})$ and ℓ is a ground literal.

$(\neg), (\vee), (\wedge), (\dot{\vee}), (\dot{\wedge})$: by analogy to rules given in Table 2, e.g.,

$$(\neg) \; \frac{\mathbb{T} : (\neg e).\ell}{\mathbb{F} : e.\ell} \quad (\vee) \; \frac{\mathbb{T} : (e \vee e').\ell}{\mathbb{T} : e.\ell \mid \mathbb{T} : e'.\ell} \quad (\wedge) \; \frac{\mathbb{T} : (e \wedge e').\ell}{\mathbb{T} : e.\ell, \; \mathbb{T} : e'.\ell}$$

$$(\dot{\vee}) \; \frac{\mathbb{F} : (e \dot{\vee} e').\ell}{\mathbb{F} : e.\ell, \; \{\mathbb{F}, \mathbb{U}\} : e'.\ell \mid \{\mathbb{F}, \mathbb{U}\} : e.\ell, \mathbb{F} : e'.\ell} \quad (\dot{\wedge}) \; \frac{\mathbb{I} : (e \dot{\wedge} e').\ell}{\mathbb{I} : e.\ell, \mathbb{I} : e'.\ell}$$

$$(\rightarrow) \; \text{for } \tau \in \{\mathbb{T}, \mathbb{F}, \mathbb{I}\} : \quad \frac{\tau : (e \rightarrow e').\ell}{\tau : e.\ell \mid \mathbb{U} : e.\ell, \tau : e'.\ell} \qquad \frac{\mathbb{U} : (e \rightarrow e').\ell}{\mathbb{U} : e.\ell, \mathbb{U} : e'.\ell}$$

The tree branches are indicated by the vertical bar '|'. To simplify rules we use notation $T : A$, where $\emptyset \neq T \subseteq \{\mathbb{T}, \mathbb{F}, \mathbb{I}, \mathbb{U}\}$ meaning that formula A may obtain any truth value from the set T. For example, the rule:

$$\frac{\mathbb{U} : A \vee B}{\mathbb{U} : A, \{\mathbb{U}, \mathbb{F}\} : B \mid \{\mathbb{U}, \mathbb{F}\} : A, \mathbb{U} : B} \tag{17}$$

abbreviates:

$$\frac{\mathbb{U} : A \vee B}{\mathbb{U} : A, \mathbb{U} : B \mid \mathbb{U} : A, \mathbb{F} : B \mid \mathbb{U} : A, \mathbb{U} : B \mid \mathbb{F} : A, \mathbb{U} : B} . \tag{18}$$

Of course, a duplicated occurrence of '$\mathbb{U} : A, \mathbb{U} : B$' can be removed, so the rule (18) can be simplified to:

$$\frac{\mathbb{U} : A \vee B}{\mathbb{U} : A, \mathbb{U} : B \mid \mathbb{U} : A, \mathbb{F} : B \mid \mathbb{F} : A, \mathbb{U} : B} .$$

Comma in the removed sequences represents conjunction, so the order of signed formulas in the sequences is irrelevant.

A branch leading from the root to a leaf of a tableau is *closed* when it contains signed formulas of the form $\tau : A$ and $\tau' : A$ with $\tau \neq \tau'$. In this case two distinct truth values are being assigned to A, leading to a contradiction. A branch is *open* when it is not closed and no rule is applicable to its leaf. A tableau is *completed* when all its branches are open or closed. A completed tableau is *closed* when all its branches are closed.

Observe that each rule in Tables 2–3 eliminates a connective or inheritance operator $\rightarrow$. Therefore, for any inheritance formula A and $\tau \in \{\mathbb{T}, \mathbb{F}, \mathbb{I}, \mathbb{U}\}$, the construction of each completed tableau for $\tau : A$ stops after a finite number of steps.

If a branch in a tableau for $\tau : A$ is open then by $\mathcal{B}$ we denote the set of signed formulas of the form $\tau_i : \delta_i$ occurring in the branch, where δ_i is a positive ground literal or a positive object literal. The set $\mathcal{B}$ provides a (partial) assignment of truth values to object/ground literals under which A evaluates to τ. If a ground literal or an object literal occurring in A is not in $\mathcal{B}$ then it can be assigned an arbitrary truth value from $\{\mathbb{T}, \mathbb{F}, \mathbb{I}, \mathbb{U}\}$.

Example 4. To illustrate the use of tableau rules, let us verify whether the expression (12) can be assigned the value $\mathbb{I}$. We then construct a tableau for the signed formula:

$$\mathbb{I} : \big(h \dashrightarrow (g \mathbin{\dot\vee} e) \dashrightarrow c\big).ct, \tag{19}$$

where h, g, e, c, ct abbreviate 'hybrid', 'gasoline', 'electric', 'car_model(hybx)' and 'ctax', respectively. Let us construct a tableau for (19):

$$\mathbb{I} : \big(h \dashrightarrow (g \mathbin{\dot\vee} e) \dashrightarrow c\big).ct$$

$\mathbb{I} : h.ct \mid$	$\mathbb{U} : h.ct,\ \mathbb{I} : \big((g \mathbin{\dot\vee} e) \dashrightarrow c\big).ct$	
$\mathbb{I} : (g \mathbin{\dot\vee} e).ct$		$\mid \quad \mathbb{U} : (g \mathbin{\dot\vee} e).ct, \mathbb{I} : c.ct$
$\mathbb{I}{:}g.ct \mid \mathbb{I}{:}e.ct \mid \mathbb{T}{:}g.ct, \mathbb{F}{:}e.ct \mid \mathbb{F}{:}g.ct, \mathbb{T}{:}e.ct$		$\mathbb{U} : g.ct, \mathbb{U} : e.ct$

There are six branches in the tableau, respectively containing:

$\mathcal{B}_1 = \{\mathbb{I} : h.ct\}$, $\mathcal{B}_2 = \{\mathbb{U} : h.ct, \mathbb{I} : g.ct\}$, $\mathcal{B}_3 = \{\mathbb{U} : h.ct, \mathbb{I} : e.ct\}$,
$\mathcal{B}_4 = \{\mathbb{U} : h.ct, \mathbb{T} : g.ct, \mathbb{F} : e.ct\}$, $\mathcal{B}_5 = \{\mathbb{U} : h.ct, \mathbb{F} : g.ct, \mathbb{T} : e.ct\}$,
$\mathcal{B}_6 = \{\mathbb{U} : h.ct, \mathbb{I} : c.ct, \mathbb{U} : g.ct, \mathbb{U} : e.ct\}$.

Each branch provides a (partial) assignment satisfying the signed formula (19). For example,

- $\mathcal{B}_1$ assigns $\mathbb{I}$ to 'h.ct', what suffices to make the formula $\big(h \dashrightarrow (g \mathbin{\dot\vee} e) \dashrightarrow c\big).ct$ inconsistent, regardless of the values of other components it includes;
- $\mathcal{B}_5$ assigns $\mathbb{U}$ to 'h.ct', $\mathbb{F}$ to 'g.ct' and $\mathbb{T}$ to 'e.ct'. Under this assignment, the value of $(g \mathbin{\dot\vee} e).ct$ is $\mathbb{I}$. Since the value of 'h.ct' is $\mathbb{U}$, $\mathbb{I}$ is inherited from $(g \mathbin{\dot\vee} e).ct$.

If a software designer wishes to block inconsistencies in expression (19), (s)he can, e.g., change 'h.ct' to $\mathbb{T}$ or $\mathbb{F}$ by adding a literal 'ct' or '¬ct' to 'h'. This would close all branches since the first branch forces '$\mathbb{I}$: h.ct' and all other branches start with '$\mathbb{U}$: h.ct'. Of course, given the contents of objects in $\mathcal{O}$, many branches may become closed. For example, assuming that 'electric' is not subject to car environmental tax, i.e., $\mathbb{F}$: e.ct, one could close branches (e) and (f). □

The following theorem provides soundness and completeness of the provided tableaux.

Theorem 1. *There is a completed tableau for $\tau : A$ containing an open leaf if and only if there is an assignment of truth values to object/ground literals for which the truth value of A is τ.* □

Notice that from Theorem 1 it follows that whenever all tableaux for $\tau : A$ are closed then there is no assignment of truth values to literals for which the truth value of A is τ.

Since $\mathcal{L}_4$ contains classical propositional logic and the length of each branch of an arbitrary tableau for $\tau : A$ is linear in the number of connectives and inheritance operators occurring in A, we have the following theorem.

Theorem 2. *For every inheritance formula A, checking whether A can be assigned a truth value $\tau \in \{\mathbb{T}, \mathbb{F}, \mathbb{I}, \mathbb{U}\}$ is NP-complete.* □

One of potential complexity sources of tableau-based reasoning with inheritance expressions is the database containing values of literals in objects in $\mathcal{O}$. However, given these values and an input signed formula $\tau : A$ it suffices to construct a tableau for:

$$\tau_1 : o_1.\ell_1, \ldots, \tau_m : o_m.\ell_m, \tau : A, \tag{20}$$

where $o_1.\ell_1, \ldots, o_m.\ell_m$ are all object literals occurring in A, and $\tau_1, \ldots, \tau_m$ are truth values of $o_1.\ell_1, \ldots, o_m.\ell_m$, respectively. In any tableau for (20), the object literals $o_1.\ell_1, \ldots, o_m.\ell_m$ appear only in the root node. No rule is applicable to them, so they do not participate in further construction of tableau branches, except for perhaps closing them.

5   Conclusions

In the paper we have focused on inheritance expressions that can be used in object-rule query languages. We have analyzed the complexity of querying and reasoning with inheritance expressions in the context of a paraconsistent four-valued logic. Time complexity of queries is logarithmic in the size of objects and linear in the size of inheritance expressions. Generalized satisfiability is shown to be NP-complete.

The presented formalism can be both restricted and extended. For example, one can remove the truth value $\mathbb{I}$, reducing $\mathcal{L}_4$ to Kleene logic $\mathcal{K}_3$. The querying machinery and tableau rules provided in the paper are easily adaptable to $\mathcal{K}_3$. Also, the framework can be adjusted to arbitrary finitely-valued extensions of $\mathcal{K}_3$, while keeping the complexity results. Indeed, $\mathbb{U}$ is the only non-classical truth value needed for IEF to work and well serves paracomplete forms of reasoning. We used $\mathcal{L}_4$ to address phenomena related to paraconsistency. Other forms of reasoning many times use additional truth values, too [16,22].

The presented tableaux technique can be optimized along the lines of [9,10, 13]. A promising future research could also depend on embedding inheritance expressions to description logics and investigate their use and reasoning complexity. Rules ($\rightarrow$) shown in Table 3 provide a good starting point towards that direction.

References

1. Amo, S., Pais, M.: A paraconsistent logic approach for querying inconsistent databases. Int. J. Approximate Reason. **46**, 366–386 (2007)
2. Belnap, N.: A useful four-valued logic. In: Eptein, G., Dunn, J. (eds.) Modern Uses of Many Valued Logic, pp. 8–37. Reidel (1977)
3. Béziau, J.Y., Carnielli, W., Gabbay, D. (eds.): Handbook of Paraconsistency. College Publications (2007)
4. Bobrow, D., Kahn, K., Kiczales, G., Masinter, L., Stefik, M., Zdybel, F.: CommonLoops: Merging Lisp and object-oriented programming. In: Cardenas, A., McLeod, D. (eds.) Research Foundations in OO and Semantic Database System, pp. 70–90. Prentice-Hall (1990)
5. Bonatti, P., Petrova, I., Sauro, L.: Defeasible reasoning in description logics: an overview on DLN. In: Cota, G., Daquino, M., Pozzato, G. (eds.) Applications and Practices in Ontology Design, Extraction, and Reasoning, Studies on the Semantic Web, vol. 49, pp. 178–193. IOS Press (2020)
6. Casini, G., Straccia, U.: Defeasible inheritance-based description logics. J. Artif. Intell. Res. **48**, 415–473 (2013)
7. Corradi, A., Leonardi, L.: Static vs. dynamic issues in object-oriented programming languages. JOOP - J. Object-Orient. Program. **13**, 11–64 (2000)
8. Dingle, A.: Object-Oriented Design Choices. Taylor & Francis (2021)
9. Doherty, P.: A constraint-based approach to proof procedures for multi-valued logics. In: Proceedings of the 1st World Conference on Fundamentals of Artificial Intelligence (WOCFAI). Springer, Heidelberg (1991)
10. Doherty, P., Szałas, A.: Signed dual tableaux for Kleene answer set programs. In: Golińska-Pilarek, J., Zawidzki, M. (eds.) Ewa Orłowska on Relational Methods in Logic and Computer Science. OCL, vol. 17, pp. 233–252. Springer, Cham (2018). https://doi.org/10.1007/978-3-319-97879-6_9
11. Dunin-Kęplicz, B., Szałas, A.: Shadowing in many-valued nested structures. In: 50th IEEE International Symposium on Multiple-Valued Logic, ISMVL. pp. 230–236. IEEE (2020)
12. Gabbay, D., Schlechta, K.: Logical Tools for Handling Change in Agent-based Systems. Cognitive Technologies, Springer, Heidelberg (2009). https://doi.org/10.1007/978-3-642-04407-6
13. Hähnle, R.: Tableaux for many-valued logics. In: D'Agostino, M., Gabbay, D., Hähnle, R., Posegga, J. (eds.) Handbook of Tableau Methods, pp. 529–580. Springer, Netherlands (1999). https://doi.org/10.1007/978-94-017-1754-0_9
14. Haugh, B.: Tractable theories of multiple defeasible inheritance in ordinary nonmonotonic logics. In: Shrobe, H., Mitchell, T., Smith, R. (eds.) Proceedings of the AAAI, 7th National Conference on AI, pp. 421–426. AAAI Press/The MIT Press (1988)
15. Małuszyński, J., Szałas, A.: Partiality and inconsistency in agents' belief bases. In: Barbucha, D., Le, M., Howlett, R., Jain, L. (eds.) KES-AMSTA. Frontiers in AI and Applications, vol. 252, pp. 3–17. IOS Press (2013)
16. Rescher, N.: Many-Valued Logic. McGraw Hill, New York (1969)
17. Salus, P. (ed.): Handbook of Programming Languages. Object-Oriented Languages, vol. 1. Macmillian Technical Publishing (1998)
18. Sandewall, E.: Defeasible inheritance with doubt index and its axiomatic characterization. Artif. Intell. **174**(18), 1431–1459 (2010)

19. Szałas, A.: Revisiting object-rule fusion in query languages. In: Cristani, M., Toro, C., Zanni-Merk, C., Howlett, R., Jain, L. (eds.) Proceedings of the 24th International Conference on KES-2020. Procedia Computer Science, vol. 176, pp. 50–59. Elsevier (2020)
20. Szałas, A.: Inheriting and fusing beliefs of logically heterogeneous objects. In: Proceedings of the 26th International Conference on KES-2022. Procedia Computer Science, Elsevier (2022, to appear)
21. Szałas, A.: Many-valued dynamic object-oriented inheritance and approximations. In: Ramanna, S., Cornelis, C., Ciucci, D. (eds.) IJCRS 2021. LNCS (LNAI), vol. 12872, pp. 103–119. Springer, Cham (2021). https://doi.org/10.1007/978-3-030-87334-9_10
22. Urquhart, A.: Many-valued logic. In: Gabbay, D., Guenthner, F. (eds.) Handbook of Philosophical Logic, vol. 3, pp. 71–116. Reidel (1986)
23. Veitch, J.: A history and description of CLOS. In: Salus, P. (ed.) Handbook of Programming Languages. Functional, Concurrent & Logic Programming Languages, vol. 4, pp. 107–158. Macmillian Technical Publishing (1998)
24. Vitória, A., Małuszyński, J., Szałas, A.: Modeling and reasoning with paraconsistent rough sets. Fundamenta Informaticae 97(4), 405–438 (2009)
25. Wegner, P.: Concepts and paradigms of object-oriented programming. OOPS Messenger 1(1), 7–87 (1990)

Fundamental Formal Language

Marek Krótkiewicz[✉][ID]

Faculty of Information and Communication Technology, Wrocław University of Science
and Technology, Wrocław, Poland
marek.krotkiewicz@pwr.edu.pl

Abstract. The article presents a proposal of the formal symbolic notation operate for basic mathematical concepts. This notation is distinguished by its unam-
biguousness in terms of key terms used in computer science. This notation defines
many concepts such as entity, type, structure definition, compositional relationship and aggregation relationship, references, features related to the admission of
variation, ordering, uniqueness, generalisation-specialisation relationship, inheritance, and polymorphism mechanism. Purely mathematical notation operates on
concepts that are blurry in the sense of computer science. Moreover, in mathematics, there are no direct mechanisms such as inheritance or polymorphism.
They can be defined mathematically in many ways, which can sometimes make it
difficult to understand such formalisms in the context of computer science solutions. The proposed solution is a response to a research problem defined in this
way. The article also presents a case study illustrating how to apply the proposed
method.

Keywords: Formal language · Meta-model · Formalisation

1 Introduction

Scientific issues in the area of computer science are presented in various ways of expression. Natural language is the least formal way. It gives a lot of freedom, which is an
advantage, but also poses a significant risk of ambiguity. It is also relatively unclear,
i.e. requires a large number of sentences, often with a complicated structure. It is
suitable for explaining a research problem, but it is not a good way of presenting a
solution of it. Semi-formal languages such as *Semantics of Business Vocabulary and
Business Rules*(SBVR) are very well suited to formalising some elements while allowing great freedom of expression. SBVR focuses on expressions rather than diagrams,
although the language also has a graphical representation for creating diagrams. It is
a semi-formal language, it has a grammar that allows you to create expressions with
well-defined semantics. This is because the expression elements are: term, **Name**, *verb*
and keyword. SBVR contains many keywords with specific semantics in this language,
included related to logic. This makes it possible to express the rules relatively precisely.
The most accurate and concise way of writing is a symbolic notation based on concepts
known in mathematics. There are, for example, set theory, logic, relational algebra and
other formalisms ensuring high accuracy of the notation. Concepts in mathematics are

© The Author(s), under exclusive license to Springer Nature Switzerland AG 2022
N. T. Nguyen et al. (Eds.): ICCCI 2022, LNAI 13501, pp. 410–422, 2022.
https://doi.org/10.1007/978-3-031-16014-1_33

abstract concepts, which is a great advantage to allow the problem to be expressed at a higher level of abstraction. Breaking away from a specific domain of discourse gives the opportunity to express research problems and solutions in a general way. However, this type of formalisation also has disadvantages. It is a notation that requires knowledge of many mathematical concepts and the relationships between them. A high level of abstraction can sometimes make it difficult to find a proper reference of the formal structure to entities from the described domain of discourse. The way of representing the problems and their solutions should take into account both the nature of the described domain, the degree of its complexity and the ease of using formalisms by the author of the description.

The scientific contribution of this article is a proposal of a formalism that combines certain features. It is a symbolic formalism. It is based on basic mathematical concepts, but at the same time it does not require knowledge of complex mathematical concepts. Although it is a formalism based on mathematical concepts, it defines concepts specific to computer science. It greatly facilitates its use when defining problems and solutions, as it is conceptually similar to computer science, while maintaining its formal and symbolic character. It is an open solution, i.e. it can be easily expanded with new concepts or even entire trends.

The article was built as follows. In the Sect. 2, related works will be presented, where alternative solutions are presented and briefly characterised. In the Sect. 3, a research problem is defined. The Sect. 4 describes the proposed solution. The Sect. 5 presents a case study, and the following sections contain summarization, conclusions and a description of the future work.

2   Related Works

Since the beginning of information systems sciences, people tend to use formal and semi-formal notations to describe universe of discourse. Some formal systems include logic systems of different expressive power [9], including first-order logic (FOL) [10] and higher-order logic [6]. The formal foundation for ontology languages and tools is description logic [11], which gathers a family of logic-based knowledge representation formalisms, well-suited for the representation of Semantic Web [3] and performing reasoning.

Formal systems are well-founded and useful, but for practitioners tend to find them too difficult and too strict from the mathematical point of view to describe more complex universes of discourse. Thus, semi-formal tools and solutions like Unified Modeling Language (UML) [2,7] have been invented. An interesting standard for defining terminology and business rules is so-called SBVR released by Object Management Group (OMG) [8]. SBVR enables to define vocabularies and rules for business domains using controlled natural language. SBVR defines itself as a dictionary, specifying semantics of internal concepts. Some parts of SBVR are conforming to Common Logic (CL) [1], which is a recently-accepted ISO standard based on FOL. SBVR has been proven to be useful for defining some concept systems like e.g. Conceptual Layer of Metamodels (CLoM) [4].

3   Research Problem

The undertaken research problem concerns the need to formalise the notation of issues and their solutions. Descriptions expressed in natural language are too long and ambiguous. Therefore, their verification and implementation may create real problems. This is mainly due to the ambiguity of the definitions of the concepts represented by the terms used in natural language. Semi-formal languages like SBVR are definitely better solution and in many cases it is perfectly adequate. Sometimes, however, more formalisation is required. The language of mathematics based on set theory, logic, relational algebra, etc. is strict, but also very abstract. Therefore, far from domain-based solutions. In the context of computer science, some mathematical concepts do not fit the implementation issues as if they could. For example, for obvious reasons, the concept of infinity or a continuous plane in computer science is impossible to implement without simplifications and additional assumptions. On the other hand, the concept of variation over time is not something natural in mathematics as it has different conventions and approaches. The classical mathematical concept of a set assumes that there is no operation to add an element to the set. Two sets can be summed to produce a third set: $C = A \cup B$, which means, that $x \in (A \cup B) \Leftrightarrow (x \in A) \vee (x \in B)$ or otherwise: $A \cup B = \{x \in C : x \in A \vee x \in B\}$. It is unnatural to create a new structure by adding two others together. If you wanted to iteratively add n elements to the set, you would have to create a new set each time, then sum the two sets, which in effect generates a new set with each iteration. In an abstract sense, the concept is flawless, but it is quite far from thinking in computer science terms. In computer science, firstly, we do not need to generate a new entity (collection of items) to add something to it, and secondly, we do not have to "wrap" it in structures to perform addition with its elements. Moreover, the set as such does not have an order relation, and in computer science everything has a place or order assigned to it. The set cannot have two of the same elements. In computer science, the concept of the same elements is not so simple. One can consider the identity of beings in the sense of memory space. Then one cannot speak of the same entities at all. Information equivalence can also be considered, which is definitely more natural. However, the issue arises when to consider that entities (e.g. objects in the object-oriented paradigm) are information identical, and when to recognise that they are the same being. Formally, each object is a separate an entity, regardless of its informational content, similar to e.g. references to a entity. It is hard to conclude that two references pointing to the same entity (e.g. an object) are the same, they simply point to the same, but are not essentially the same.

There are many issues of this type, where the perception of mathematics and information technology is very different. There is also a very important issue of distinguishing between an entity and reference to it. Since a mathematical set contains elements, it is impossible for it to contain the same two elements, or for two sets to have the same element. It would have to occur in duplicate, but then it would be two different items and not one belonging to two sets. Therefore, from the computer science point of view, mathematical sets really group references to entities, not entities themselves. Only then does it make sense to speak from the elements that are unique in the set. So a set in the category of computer science is something that groups references to entities, and no pair of these references can point to the same element. The lack of ordering of the set can be easily achieved by ignoring the order that will undoubtedly occur during the implementation.

The set itself is something very abstract and detached from computer science. There are also such computer science concepts as entity, type, structure definition, compositional relationship and aggregation relationship, references, features related to the admission of variation, ordering, uniqueness, generalisation-specialisation relationship, inheritance and polymorphism mechanism. All these elements are important for building formalisms in computer science. Direct use of mathematical concepts, without defining the above-mentioned concepts in the context of computer science, may not only be difficult to interpret, but also ambiguous in implementation. In relation to this, a research problem was identified, consisting in the definition of symbolic formalism on the study of the concept of the domain of computer science, the solution to this problem is the scientific contribution presented in this article.

4 Solution

Fundamental Formal Language (FFL) is a symbolic formal language used to define a meta-models. When referring to more than one meta-model or modelling language, it is assumed that the prefix is used: $metamodel :: category$, denoting the context in which the given metamodel category name is used. For the sake of legibility, the prefixes should be used only when there is ambiguity or it increases the level of readability. An example of using a prefix: $FFL :: comp$ denoting the relationship of the composition in context FFL.

4.1 Basic Abstract Concepts and Structures

Basic Concepts

entity is a concept representing any existence of the modelled fragment of reality. Entities can be complex structures, i.e. have an internal structure. Each entity represents a unique entity. Regardless of the internal structure and the current state of an entity[1]. An entity exists only in one instance[2].

reference entity (reference) this concept refers to the way in which entity are interpreted. A reference is some kind of entity, except that the value of that entity is interpreted as pointing to the entity of the modelled slice of reality. Potentially, all CRUD[3] operations are allowed on reference to an entity and the entity itself. You can create multiple references to a given entity, but each reference is a separate entity. The reference to the entity does not have any direct impact on the entity it points to, i.e. any CRUD operation on the reference does not cause any changes in the entity

---

[1] *state of an entity* is determined by the set of values it has.

[2] Creating a new entity on the basis of an existing one (copying an entity) creates a new, independent entity. An entity created as a result of copying another entity may be identical with the original entity or not, it all depends on how the relation operator identity is defined, and this in turn must be embedded in context of the type for which it was defined.

[3] CRUD – *create, read, update, delete.*

it points to, because the indicated entity and the entity being the reference to it are independent entities. They are independent, however, deleting the entity indicated by the reference entity causes that the reference entity points to a non-existent entity, which should be taken into account when performing operations on entities.

type is a concept that represents a description of the kind, structure, and range of values that a literal, variable, constant, argument, function result, or value can potentially have.

Symbol and Semantics.

$e : t$ means that the e entity is of the t type, in the case of a greater number of entities of the same type, the following form can be used: $e_1, e_2, e_3 : t$.

$t^{\varnothing}$ stands for an abstract type named t which means there are no entities (instances) of this type.

$\&x$ stands for a reference to x, but the reference may point to specific entities or refer to the definition of the reference type[4], e.g. $\&int$, and in the case of an entity with a specific type as reference, the phrase, e.g. $x : \&int$, means that the x entity is a reference type referring to an entity of type int.

$*y$ stands for the y dereference, which means that if y was a reference, the expression $*y$ refers to the value indicated by y. For example, if y is a reference to the integer type[5] $y : \&int$, i.e. in other words y points to int entities, then $*y$ refers to this entity, which is a value of type int indicated by y.

$\sigma(t) =$ stands for the definition of a type with name t.

$e =$ stands for assigning a value to a specific entity.

Ownership Relationship and Aggregate Entities. In order to define the concept of *aggregate entity*, you must first define the concept of *ownership relationship (own)*.

Ownership Relationship (own). Ownership relationship is a binary directed relationship $whole \xrightarrow{own} part$ between two entities: the *whole* and *part*. The *whole* element must be *aggregate entity* and the *part* element can be: *entity, entity reference* or *aggregate entity*. *Part* is contained in *whole* such that when *whole* is deleted, all of its *parts* also cease exist. *Part* cannot belong to more than one *total (whole)*. If two *reference entities* have *reference entities* and both point to the same entity, both *reference entities* are still separate and independent entities.

The Compositional and Reference Character of the Ownership Relationship. Although there is only one type of relationship in FFL, i.e. *part-whole*, it is conceptually necessary to separate them. This is because the two compounds have different properties. The reason for this is that the type of the bonded element differs in both cases. This issue concerns a reference property, which can be a *part ownership relationship* element.

---

[4] *reference type* i.e. it is a reference entity, but it points to entities of a specific type.

[5] this applies to the intensional aspect.

Compositional Relationship. If the *part* element is a *entity* or *aggregate entity*, in other words it is a specific entity and not a reference to it, then *ownership relationship* is compositional, i.e. the *part* element is *owned* exclusively by *whole* and deletion of *whole* consequently deletes all parts *part* – this is the *existance dependency*. *Compositional Relationship* will be denoted as:

$$whole \xrightarrow{comp} part \tag{1}$$

In the case of more compounds, the notation can be used for one *whole* element:

$$whole \xrightarrow{comp} \{part_1, part_2, \ldots, part_n\} \equiv whole \xrightarrow{comp} part_i \mid i = 1, 2, \ldots, n. \tag{2}$$

Reference Relationship. If the *part* element is a *reference entity*, then this relationship can be considered *reference* because the element pointed to by this reference is not related to the lifetime relationship and is not owned exclusively. *Reference relationship* will be denoted as

$$whole \xrightarrow{ref} part \tag{3}$$

In the case of more than one relationship, the following notation can be used for one *whole* element:

$$whole \xrightarrow{ref} \{part_1, part_2, \ldots, part_n\} \equiv whole \xrightarrow{ref} part_i \mid i = 1, 2, \ldots, n. \tag{4}$$

Summary of the Compositional and Referential Relationship. The Table 1 shows a comparison of the properties of the compositional relationship and the reference relationship

Table 1. Comparison of the properties of the *compositional relationship* and the *reference relationship*

Properties of relationships		Relationships	
Name	Formula	$\xrightarrow{comp}$	$\xrightarrow{ref}$
Reflexive	$x\ R\ x$	–	–
Nonreflexive	$\neg(x\ R\ x)$	✓	–
Symmetric	$x\ R\ y \implies y\ R\ x$	–	–
Asymmetric	$x\ R\ y \implies \neg(y\ R\ x)$	✓	–
Antisymmetric	$x\ R\ y \wedge y\ R\ x \implies x = y$	–	–
Transitive	$x\ R\ y \wedge y\ R\ z \implies x\ R\ z$	✓	–
Conncex	$x\ R\ y \vee y\ R\ x$	–	–
Semi-connex	$x\ R\ y \vee y\ R\ x \vee x = y$	–	–
Acyclicity	$\neg\exists_{x_1, x_2, \ldots, x_n} (x_1\ R\ x_2, \ldots, x_{n-1}\ R\ x_n, x_n\ R\ x_1)$	✓	–
Exclusivity	$\neg\exists_{i,j} (x_i\ R\ y \wedge x_j\ R\ y \wedge i \neq j)$	✓	–

Aggregate Entity. Aggregate entity consists of two kinds of elements: *whole* and *parts*. *Whole* is always one and *part* can be zero or more: $part_i \mid i = 0, 1, \ldots, n;\ n \geq 0$. The important *aggregate entity* is that all the elements constituting *part* are owned by *whole*:

$$\forall_{i=1,2,\ldots,n} \left(whole \xrightarrow{own} part_i \right) \tag{5}$$

Various types of *aggregate entities* have been defined. Their distinguishing features are the following features:

Exterior mutability the ability to modify the number of components of an aggregate entity (*add* and *delete* operation), values: $E \in \{\top, \bot\}$;

Interior mutability the ability to modify the value of the components of an *aggregate entity* (value modification operation), values: $I \in \{\top, \bot\}$;

Order fixed order of *aggregate entity* elements, values: $O \in \{\top, \bot\}$;

Uniqueness the need for no duplicates in the *aggregate entity*, value: $U \in \{\top, \bot\}$.

The uniqueness trait is considered in the context of defined for a given type of identity relation operator, which specifies the conditions that must be met by certain two elements to be considered identical. In particular, it can be defined in such a way that two elements, although there are some differences in the values they have, are considered the same, on the other hand, two elements having identical values can be considered different because they occupy different place in the[6]. In this regard, it all depends on how this operator is defined, which has a strong relationship with data types, since it is within them that the identity relationship should be defined. The Table 2 presents the properties for each type of aggregate entity.

Table 2. Properties of the predefined types of aggregate entities in FFL

Type of aggregate entities	Symbol	Generalised symbol	E	I	O	U
multiset	$\lvert \cdot \rvert$	$\lvert \cdot \rvert$	–	–	–	–
set	$\{\cdot\}$	$\lvert \cdot \rvert_U$	–	–	–	✓
tuple	$(\cdot)$	$\lvert \cdot \rvert_O$	–	–	✓	–
vector	$[\cdot]$	$\lvert \cdot \rvert_{IO}$	–	✓	✓	–
list	$\langle \cdot \rangle$	$\lvert \cdot \rvert_{EIO}$	✓	✓	✓	–

For the expression of the type of *aggregate entity* with specific properties[7], the following notation was used: $\lvert t \rvert_f$, where: t – type of structure elements, f – the configuration of the aggregate structure features consisting of set elements $\{E, I, O, U\}$. For multiset, set, tuple, vector, and list, the notation is as follows:

$$\lvert t \rvert, \{t\}, (t), [t], \langle t \rangle \tag{6}$$

---

[6] data space The concept of *data space* has been used informally, without being defined, and only as some kind of intuition related to the data allocation mechanism and its consequent consequences.

[7] *Properties* are understood as specific values of the features, in which case all features take the logical values *true* or *false*: $E, I, O, U \in \{\top, \bot\}$.

In order to build a new type of aggregate entity on the basis of the existing ones, you can activate *true* value a specific property: (E, I, O, U) or deactivate it *false* value. Adding a symbol in the subscript will activate the selected feature, while adding a symbol of the selected feature with a horizontal line above this symbol will deactivate that feature.

For example:

$\langle t \rangle_U$ – list with additionally activated *uniqueness* feature,

$[t]_{E\bar{O}}$ – vector with additionally activated *interior mutability* feature and deactivated *order*.

Optionally, a restriction can be made on the lower bound and upper bound of the cardinality of a particular *aggregate entity*. Notation is used for this purpose:

$$|t|_f^{n..m}, n \leq m \tag{7}$$

where:

n – the lower bound of the cardinality of an *aggregate entity* as a natural number or $*$ symbol with no constraint,

m – the upper bound of the cardinality of the *aggregate entity* as a natural number or $*$ symbol with no constraint,

where $n \leq m$. The $*..*$ designation can be omitted as it does not introduce any cardinality limitation. For multiset, set, tuple, vector, and list, the notation is as follows:

$$|t|^{n..m}, \{t\}^{n..m}, (t)^{n..m}, [t]^{n..m}, \langle t \rangle^{n..m}. \tag{8}$$

The current cardinality of an *aggregate entity* is marked with the notation: $\#|t|_f^{n..m}$. The example expression $\#\langle int \rangle^{1..*}$ represents the current cardinality of the list of integer elements with a minimum size of 1.

To indicate that the e entity is an element (*part*), the *aggregate entity* uses notation for multiset, set, tuple, vector, and list, respectively:

$$e \in |t|, e \in \{t\}, e \in (t), e \in [t], e \in \langle t \rangle. \tag{9}$$

If the example type t has been defined as a vector of three numbers of type int as follows:

$$\sigma(t) = [a : \texttt{int}, b : \texttt{int}, c : \&W] \tag{10}$$

is an example, a specific instance of this vector in the form of the entity $e : t$ may look like this:

$$e = [2, 3, \&w_1], \tag{11}$$

where: $w_1 : W$.

The reference to a component on the name a for this type of structure t can be done after the name as follows: $e.a$ or explicitly by specifying a type:

$$(e : t).(a : \texttt{int}), \tag{12}$$

where:

e – *aggregate entity* (in the extensional sense),
t – entity type,
a – name of a element of an *aggregate entity* (in the intensional sense).

If the aggregate entity has a fixed order of elements, it is also possible to refer via the index[8]. For example:

$$e\,[1] \; \equiv \; e.a \; \equiv \; (e:t).(a:\texttt{int}) \tag{13}$$

stands for the first element of the e *aggregate entity*. If v is defined as the following vector:

$$\sigma(v) = [a:\texttt{int}, b:\texttt{int}, c:\&W]\,, \tag{14}$$

that is, there are relationships within it:

$$v \xrightarrow{\;comp\;} \{a,b\}\,, v \xrightarrow{\;ref\;} c \tag{15}$$

i.e. v has two compositional entities: a and b, and has reference one element: c. In the following example there are only types without names of elements:

$$v \xrightarrow{\;comp\;} \{\texttt{int},\texttt{int}\}\,, v \xrightarrow{\;ref\;} W, \tag{16}$$

which should be interpreted that v has[9] two values of the type $\texttt{int}$ and one reference to the type in. Both names and types of members can be denoted as:

$$v \xrightarrow{\;comp\;} \{a:\texttt{int}, b:\texttt{int}\}\,, v \xrightarrow{\;ref\;} c:W. \tag{17}$$

The Relationship of Generalisation-Specialisation. The *generalisation-speciali sation* relationship is related to two mechanisms: *inheritance* and *polymorphism*. It includes the following variants:

≻ denotes a full generalisation-specialisation relationship, i.e. taking into account both the mechanism of inheritance and polymorphism,
·≻ denotes a generalisation-specialisation relationship that takes into account only the inheritance mechanism,
o≻ denotes a generalisation-specialisation relationship that takes into account only the mechanism of polymorphism.

The Mechanism of Inheritance. The mechanism of inheritance is based on copying the components of a base type to a derived type. Inheritance can only occur within the same type of aggregate entity.

$t \prec \{k_1, k_2, k_3\}$ and $t \prec\cdot \{k_1, k_2, k_3\}$ means that the type t is a specialisation of the types k_1, k_2 and k_3 and thus the types k_1, k_2 and k_3 are generalisations of the t type, which in effect causes that all elements components of the type k_1, k_2 and k_3 become components of the type t;

---

[8] The smallest index value is 1.
[9] in other words: "consists of".

$t \succ \{k_1, k_2, k_3\}$ and $t \cdot \succ \{k_1, k_2, k_3\}$ means that the type t is a generalisation of the types k_1, k_2 and k_3 and thus the types k_1, k_2 and k_3 are specialisations of the t type, which in effect causes that all components of type t become components of types k_1, k_2 and k_3.

For example, if the following types and the generalisation-specialisation relationship are defined:

$$\sigma(t) = [a : \text{int}, b : \text{int}, c : \text{int}]$$
$$\sigma(k) = [x : \text{byte}, y : \text{real}] \tag{18}$$
$$t \prec\cdot k,$$

then as a result of the inheritance mechanism, the type t will have the following structure:

$$\sigma(t) = [a : \text{int}, b : \text{int}, c : \text{int}, x : \text{byte}, y : \text{real}]. \tag{19}$$

Mechanism of Polymorphism. The mechanism of polymorphism consists in the possibility of replacing elements which are generalisations with any elements which are specialisations. For example, if the following types and the generalisation-specialisation relationship are defined:

$$\sigma(t) = [a : \text{int}, b : \text{int}, c : \text{int}]$$
$$\sigma(k) = [x : \text{byte}, y : \text{real}]$$
$$s \diamond\!\!\succ t, k \tag{20}$$
$$\sigma(r) = [z : \text{int}, v : \&s],$$

then the $r.v$ component can be a reference pointing to entities of the type t or entities of the type k.

5   Case Study

5.1   Abstract Syntax of EGG, Expressed in FFL

This section introduces the main components of abstract syntax of the *Extended Generalized Graph* (EGG) [5], defined by grammar rules expressed in FFL.

Basic EGG Concepts.   The basic concept and at the same time the aggregating structure (in the extensional sense) of all other elements is *Container*. Additionally, the following concepts exist in EGG: grouping structure – *Egg, Vertex, Edge, Label*.

Relationships.   The following relationships exist in EGG: composition – *comp*, aggregation – *aggr*, *connection* (the relationship with the ability to determine *navigability*), description – *descr*.

Main Definition

1. The extensional aspect EGG
   (a) *Container* it is a vector that is a composition of four elements:

$$Container = \begin{bmatrix} G : \langle Egg \rangle^{1..*}, \\ V : \langle Vertex \rangle, \\ E : \langle Edge \rangle, \\ L : \langle Label \rangle \end{bmatrix}, \tag{21}$$

representing a list of entities of the following types: *Egg*, *Vertex*, *Edge* and *Label*, where *Container* must consist of a non-empty list of *Egg* type entities.

2. Intensional aspect EGG
   (a) The abstract concept of an element ($Element^{\varnothing}$) is a vector of three references:

$$\sigma(Element^{\varnothing}) = \begin{bmatrix} connby : \langle \& Edge \rangle, \\ aggrby : \langle \& Egg \rangle, \\ descr : \langle \& Label \rangle \end{bmatrix}, \tag{22}$$

where: *connby* – is responsible for the fact that the $Element^{\varnothing}$ can be bound by any number of *Edges*, *aggrby* – is responsible for the fact that the $Element^{\varnothing}$ may belong to any number of entities of the *Egg* type.

   (b) The abstract element concept ($Element^{\varnothing}$) generalises the *Egg*, *Vertex* and the *Edge*: $Element^{\varnothing} \succ \{Egg, Vertex, Edge\}$.

   (c) The *Egg* grouping structure is a single-element vector containing a list of references to abstract elements ($Element^{\varnothing}$). This relationship is aggregation, i.e. it has a reference character and does not have the property of transitivity: $\sigma(Egg) = [aggr : \langle \& Element^{\varnothing} \rangle]$. The *Egg* is a specialisation of the abstract element ($Element^{\varnothing}$): $Egg \prec Element^{\varnothing}$, which means that considering the inheritance mechanism, the *Egg* structure has the form:

$$\sigma(Egg) = \begin{bmatrix} aggr : \langle \& Element^{\varnothing} \rangle, \\ connby : \langle \& Edge \rangle, \\ aggrby : \langle \& Egg \rangle, \\ descr : \langle \& Label \rangle \end{bmatrix}. \tag{23}$$

   (d) The node (*Vertex*) does not have a specific internal structure, so it is formally represented as an empty vector: $\sigma(Vertex) = [\,]$. *Vertex* is the specialisation of the abstract element ($Element^{\varnothing}$): $Vertex \prec Element^{\varnothing}$, which means that taking into account the inheritance mechanism, the node (*Vertex*) looks like:

$$\sigma(Vertex) = \begin{bmatrix} connby : \langle \& Edge \rangle, \\ aggrby : \langle \& Egg \rangle, \\ destr : \langle \& Label \rangle \end{bmatrix}. \tag{24}$$

   (e) *Edge* is a one-element vector consisting of a list of *connections*, the elements of which are two-element vectors consisting of a *navigability* definition and a list of references to abstract elements ($Element^{\varnothing}$):

$$\sigma(Edge) = [connection : \langle [navigability, \langle \& Element^{\varnothing} \rangle] \rangle] \tag{25}$$

The *Edge* is the specialisation of the abstract element ($Element^{\varnothing}$): $Edge \prec Element^{\varnothing}$, which means that considering the inheritance mechanism, the *Edge* has the form:

$$\sigma(Edge) = \begin{bmatrix} connection : \left\langle \begin{bmatrix} navigability, \\ \langle \& Element^{\varnothing} \rangle \end{bmatrix} \right\rangle, \\ connby \quad : \langle \& Edge \rangle, \\ aggrby \quad : \langle \& Egg \rangle, \\ descr \quad : \langle \& Label \rangle \end{bmatrix}, \tag{26}$$

wherein: $navigability \in \{not\ defined, left, right, bidirectional\}$.

(f) A *Label* is a description. Within the definition of EGG, the internal structure of a *Label* is not restricted, so it is formally represented as an empty vector: $\sigma(Label) = [\,]$.

The formal definition of the EGG includes limitations, extensions and generalisations, but they are not essential to represent this use case in the FFL.

6   Summarization

The article presents a proposal of a symbolic language (FFL) in which the most important basic concepts used in computer science are concisely and unequivocally defined. To these concepts, among others belongs: entity, type, structure definition, compositional relationship and aggregation relationship, references, features related to the admission of variation, ordering, uniqueness, generalisation-specialisation relationship, inheritance and polymorphism mechanism. These formalisms are based on very basic mathematical concepts that do not require knowledge of advanced aspects of set theory, logic, or relational algebra or type theory. The presented case study shows the usefulness of the proposed solution.

7   Conclusions and Future Work

The proposed solution seems to be useful due to the combination of the brevity of the symbolic notation and the uniqueness in the computer science domain. An important feature of the proposed formalism is predefining concepts that are very often used when defining problems, mechanisms or meta-models. From the point of view of applications related to the construction of meta-models, complex concepts of inheritance are important. The separation of the mechanism of inheritance and polymorphism allows for a fairly free approach to defining various types of solutions. Further work will focus on developing this formalism to encompass a possible wide range of basic concepts from the computer science domain.

References

1. Delugach, H.S.: Towards conceptual structures interoperability using common logic. In: CS-TIW, pp. 13–21 (2008)

2. Evans, A., France, R., Lano, K., Rumpe, B.: The UML as a formal modeling notation. In: Bézivin, J., Muller, P.-A. (eds.) UML 1998. LNCS, vol. 1618, pp. 336–348. Springer, Heidelberg (1999). https://doi.org/10.1007/978-3-540-48480-6_26

3. Hitzler, P.: A review of the semantic web field. Commun. ACM **64**(2), 76–83 (2021)

4. Jodłowiec, M., Krótkiewicz, M.: An approach to expressing metamodels' semantics in a concept system. In: Fujita, H., Selamat, A., Lin, J.C.-W., Ali, M. (eds.) IEA/AIE 2021. LNCS (LNAI), vol. 12798, pp. 274–282. Springer, Cham (2021). https://doi.org/10.1007/978-3-030-79457-6_24

5. Jodłowiec, M., Krótkiewicz, M., Zabawa, P.: The extended graph generalization as a representation of the metamodels' extensional layer. In: Fujita, H., Selamat, A., Lin, J.C.-W., Ali, M. (eds.) IEA/AIE 2021. LNCS (LNAI), vol. 12798, pp. 369–382. Springer, Cham (2021). https://doi.org/10.1007/978-3-030-79457-6_32

6. Leivant, D.: Higher order logic. Handbook of Logic in Artificial Intelligence and Logic Programming **2**, 229–322 (1994)

7. OMG: Object Management Group, Unified Modeling Language (UML) superstructure version 2.5 (2015). http://www.omg.org/spec/UML/2.5/

8. OMG: Object Management Group, Semantics Of Business Vocabulary And Rules 1.5 (2019). http://www.omg.org/spec/SBVR/1.5/

9. Orłowska, E., Pawlak, Z.: Expressive power of knowledge representation systems. Int. J. Man-Mach. Stud. **20**(5), 485–500 (1984). https://doi.org/10.1016/s0020-7373(84)80023-1

10. Schirrmacher, N., Siebertz, S., Vigny, A.: First-order logic with connectivity operators. In: Manea, F., Simpson, A. (eds.) 30th EACSL Annual Conference on Computer Science Logic (CSL 2022). Leibniz International Proceedings in Informatics (LIPIcs), vol. 216, pp. 34:1–34:17. Schloss Dagstuhl - Leibniz-Zentrum für Informatik, Dagstuhl, Germany (2022). http://drops.dagstuhl.de/opus/volltexte/2022/15754

11. Turhan, A.Y.: Description logic reasoning for semantic web ontologies. In: Proceedings of the International Conference on Web Intelligence, Mining and Semantics. WIMS 2011, New York, NY, USA. Association for Computing Machinery (2011). https://doi.org/10.1145/1988688.1988696

Computer Vision Techniques

Deep Learning for Robust Information Retrieval System

Achref Ouni[✉], Eric Royer, Thierry Chateau, Marc Chevaldonné,
and Michel Dhome

Université Clermont Auvergne, CNRS, SIGMA Clermont, Institut Pascal,
63000 Clermont-Ferrand, France
Achref.EL_OUNI@uca.fr

Abstract. In this paper we address the problem of localizing a query image in a 3D map obtained using a Structure From Motion (SfM) or a visual SLAM algorithm. Many situations, such as lighting or viewpoint changes, make the estimation process very difficult. In this paper, we have tried to increase the pose accuracy by integrating semantic information in the matching step. The classical output in semantic segmentation is a single label l for each pixel. We propose either to assign more than one label to each keypoint by two different ways. We compare the proposed methods with the state of the art. For this, we use two public datasets (Dubrovnik, Rome). We show that by incorporating visual and semantic information, the pose estimation can be improved in terms of time and precision.

Keywords: Deep learning · Semantic segmentation · Image localization · Pose estimation · SFM

1 Introduction

Vision Based Localization (VBL) is the process of finding the pose (orientation, translation) of a query image relative to a 3D model of the environment. Furthermore, estimating the pose is a fundamental key step in computer vision algorithms for many applications such as SLAM [3], SFM [2].

Semantic segmentation is an image processing operation that aims to attribute each pixel to a class with a label (road, building, car ...) and is an important task in computer vision. Moreover, semantic segmentation has been widely used and has proven useful in VBL problems. The semantic information given by applying a trained deep learning network [27] on millions of manually annotated images can improve the visual localization process. It is thus possible to find precisely the pose in difficult situations and when the matching performance suffers due to (**1**) hard conditions (various weather conditions, day/night, ...) (**2**) viewpoint changes (**3**) presence of dynamic objects obscuring parts of the scene.

© The Author(s), under exclusive license to Springer Nature Switzerland AG 2022
N. T. Nguyen et al. (Eds.): ICCCI 2022, LNAI 13501, pp. 425–436, 2022.
https://doi.org/10.1007/978-3-031-16014-1_34

Even with the increase of the performance of semantic segmentation algorithms, the output of the segmented image presents imprecise inter-class boundaries, noisy segmentation, which require the smoothing of the segmentation.

Inspired by previous research, we propose in this paper a robust visual localization framework that incorporates both standard local features extracted from images and semantic information in an effective and efficient way. Our method is able to handle a large number of outliers and to precisely and quickly find the relative pose in a large scale 3D map. We show experimentally that adding semantic information to features for both the query and 3D map clearly improves the accuracy of the retrieved pose. We tested with 2D-3D association strategy and we limited the matching only between the query features and the features extracted using visibility information from the global 3D point cloud thanks to the discriminative nearest neighbors. Traditionally, semantic segmentation gives us the opportunity to assign a class label to each pixel kp. Our approach completes image features with semantic information in order to make the feature matching procedure more robust.

In this paper we suggest and evaluate two different ways to improve the keypoints labelisation. The description of the labeling methods is below.

- Fully depending on the information given from the network based semantic segmentation, we improve the labelisation based on the output of the SoftMax layer. A keypoint is associated to more than one label if the probability of the major class is not decisive. Otherwise, the pixel is associated with a single label.
- We combine the output of two convolutional neural networks to generate a set of labels for each pixel. The first network is a classical semantic segmentation network. The second one is a semantic edge detector which gives a set of labels for the pixel at the boundary between two or more classes. Then, depending on the output of these networks, We keep either a single label from the first network or a set of labels from the second one.

In addition, we exploit the semantic information to: Delete the dynamic or non-stationary classes that are considered as noise such as person, car, bus, animal... with the aim of reducing the outliers during the matching step. Select the discriminative nearest neighbors by incorporating the standard matching between two images and the semantic information.

The remainder of this paper is structured as follows: we provide a brief overview of visual localization methods related studies in Sect. 2. We explain our approach in Sect. 3. We present the experiments on different datasets in Sect. 4. Conclusion of our work and experiments are presented in Sect. 5.

2   Related Work

Visual localization. Traditionally, in image visual localization there are two different approaches for estimating the relative pose (Rotation, Translation): (1) Direct method (2) Indirect method. In addition, there are also two main strategies for matching the features. Features to Points (F2P or 2D-3D) [11]: this strategy matches the query features against the features of the 3D point cloud. Points to Features strategy (P2F or 3D-2D) matches the features of a global model against the features of the query image. Let's start with direct methods. These methods are based on the correspondences found by directly matching the features from the query with the points from the 3D point cloud. Sattler et al. [15] improve the 2D-3D matching strategy based on visual vocabulary and a prioritized correspondence search. Also Sattler et al. [17] propose a framework based on a bag of visual words method that matches the query features and the 3D features that share the same visual word index. [16] increase the number of inliers by applying two different strategies (features to query, query to features) between the input query and the 3D cloud. Zeisl et al. [25] present an outlier rejection algorithm based on a voting system with low complexity $O(n)$. Graph and co-visibility [12, 20] have been widely used in visual localization: Raul et al. [5] exploit co-visibility and introduce two ratio tests that are used to select the distinct matches. Indirect methods have also have been shown to be effective. These methods are based on two key steps: first, finding the nearest neighbors using CBIR (Content Based Image Retrieval) algorithm; then, matching the query features and the 3D point cloud which belongs to the retrieved key images. We can mention two main approaches from the state of the art to retrieve the closest image: BoVW (Bag of visual words) and CNN descriptors for image retrieval. Song et al. [19] propose a fast algorithm able to quickly find the relative pose without using a PnP solver with the assignment of the relative pose of the most similar key image to the input query. Based on a voting system, Sattler et al. [18] propose an efficient algorithm that selects the discriminative nearest neighbors to compute the 6-DoF (Degrees of Freedom) pose. Moreover, deep learning architecture [9] has shown its effectiveness and robustness in pose estimation context.

Semantic Segmentation Improves Visual Localization. Semantic segmentation has been widely used in different contexts and has proven useful in VBL problems. Larsson et al. [10] improve the matching step by training the CNN on the 2D-2D correspondence between a pair of images taken during favourable conditions and challenging conditions; then enforce the class labels to be the same. This idea increases the number of inliers for pose estimation when the query or key image was taken in poor conditions. Taira et al. [22] present a pose verification approach composed by two steps for pose estimation and targeted to indoor scenes. In the first stage, they estimate the relative pose using indirect methods; then, during the verification stage, it exploits geometric and semantic information from the set of retrieved poses. Toft et al. [23] propose an outlier rejection approach that assigns a score for each correspondence by incorporating both semantic information and feature matching between the input image and the 3D model.

3   The Proposed Method

Figure 1 illustrates our labellisation framework for improving visual localization. Our approach exploits the power of the semantic segmentation algorithm by

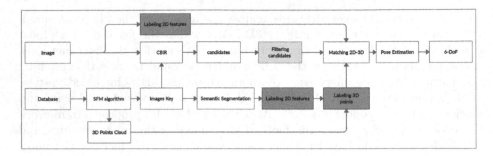

Fig. 1. Global labelisation framework proposed in this paper for efficient Visual Based Localization

incorporating both standard local features extracted from the images and their semantic information in an effective and efficient way for an accurate pose. Our framework is composed of a set of key steps. In the first, we compute the closest key images to an input query using CBIR (Content Based Image Retrieval) with the algorithm described in [14]. Our goal is to utilize the nearest neighbors (KNN) to extract a region from the global model based on the shared list of visibility in which the query is probably seen. But, the list of KNN contains a set of images that are not necessarily similar to the query input due to the limit of CBIR algorithm. To select the most similar ones in a robust way, we add the semantic information to both the query and key images and we match them by assigning a score to each pair according to the number of inliers with removing the images which have fewer inliers. We obtain a list of keyframes that we augment with the neighbors in the pose graph of the SFM map. As a reminder, two poses are connected in the pose graph if they share some 3D points. Then we consider all the 3D points visible in this new list of keyframes. The next step is matching the features using 2D-3D strategy and by taking the semantic information into account. The final step is computing the relative pose.

Semantic segmentation doesn't always produce perfect segmentation and we often find some overfilling at the boundaries of some classes and a border-blur effect. Most of the time, the keypoint detector produces a lot of features on or near the borders of objects because these regions in the image satisfy the detectors constraints. We then try to reduce the semantic segmentation error at the frontier by two different robust labeling methods.

In the following sections we will explain each one in more depth.

3.1   Method 1: Multiple-label Based on Semantic Segmentation

Affecting a label to each pixel is still a hard challenge for many to many reasons such as imperfect semantic segmentation algorithms, overfilling in border regions which generates a wrong class label... The keypoints, which are related to the visual localization problem, are widely used in VBL and the detection algorithm focuses on specific points of an image selected according to specific criteria like

Fig. 2. (a) Key images used to build the SFM model (b) key images segmented using EncNet [26] algorithm trained on ADE20K [28] datasets (c) Detect the pixels with low probability using deep learning

corners and points with strong variations of texture. Usually, the positions of the detected points are around and within the object. When the segmented image contains more than one class (sky, building, ...), we can't take the class label obtained by the detected point at the frontier into consideration for two main reasons **(1)** the probability of the major class of the detected point is not decisive **(2)** the overlapping prediction between two classes forces to produce an inaccurate class label as shown in Figs. 2 and 3.

The standard output in semantic segmentation is a single label l for each pixel. In this paper, we compare different ways of using the semantic information. In the first method called mono label we assign to each keypoint kp the label of the underlying pixel. Just before the final output the network contains the SOFTMAX layer. This layer is the same size as the input image with each pixel containing a vector of probabilities $y = [y_1, .., y_N]$. This vector of size N corresponding to the number of classes on which the network was trained. In the mono label method the label of each pixel is given by

$$l = \mathrm{argmax}(y_i) \tag{1}$$

To improve the labellisation at the borders we use the SoftMax Layer of the network to extract multiple-labels for the keypoints. We also take the neighboring pixels into account to reduce the noise given by the semantic segmentation. First we apply a mean filter to the SoftMax layer with window size ranging from 3×3 to 7×7 in experiments. For one pixel of this filtered layer we keep the label with the highest probability p^* then we add all the labels with probability p so that

$$p/p^* > \epsilon \tag{2}$$

$\epsilon = 0.3$ in experimentation.

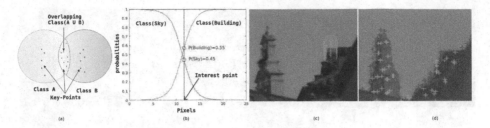

Fig. 3. (a) Overlapping between two classes (b) The blue curve presents the probabilities of the Sky class and the red curve presents the probabilities of the Building class (c) Image contains two classes (Sky, Building) and shows the sampled points according to the curve represented in (b). (d) The segmented image shows the overlapping between two classes at the frontier. Also, the figure shows the detected keypoints: (1) keypoints with false class label (red symbol), (2) keypoints with true class label (green symbol). (Color figure online)

3.2 Method 2: Multiple-label Based on a Combination of Semantic Segmentation and Semantic Edge

Semantic edge detection [1,8,24] is a new field in computer vision. It is based on convolutional neural network (CNN) to detect pixels situated in contours between two or more semantic classes (Fig. 4). The network takes an image as input and outputs N 2D-maps where N is the number of semantic classes. Each 2D map is a matrix of probabilities of pixels belonging to a specific semantic class. In Fig. 6, we present an example of semantic edge detection [8] output for the principal classes existing in the image. For each semantic class, we present its 2D map (in the bottom) and the corresponding pixels in the image (in the top).

Fig. 4. Examples of global semantic edge map detected using DFF [8] algorithm trained on Ade20k and their corresponding pixels.

At that point, in the yield of semantic edge detector just the pixels at boundary have a rundown of labels. Each pixel is characterized by a vector of 150 probabilities. The index whose probabilities are above zero correspond to the labels of the pixel. In Fig. 6, we present two examples: (A) the pixel is assigned to three labels (Building, Sky, Vegetation) (B) the pixel is assigned to two labels (Building, Person).

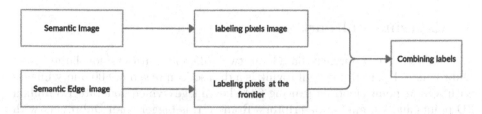

Fig. 5. Labeling pixels between semantic segmentation and edge semantic segmentation.

The difference between the previous method and this one that the border pixels are labeled using a semantic edge detector. So given an image, we start by detecting the labelisation using two neural networks(see Fig. 5). The first network assigns to each pixel a label (semantic segmentation). The second network assigns a set of labels for the pixels located on the edge (semantic edge detector).

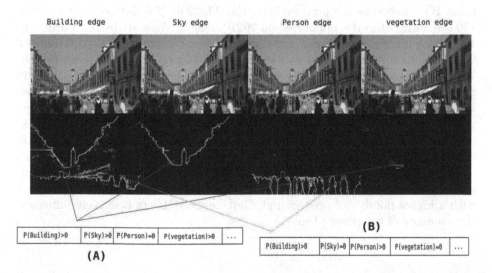

Fig. 6. Semantic Edge detection for each semantic class predicted using DFF [8] algorithm trained on Ade20k. In button figure, we take two pixel (A, B) as example. Depending to the probabilities extracted from all edges output the first pixel (A) has three labels (Sky, Building, Vegetation) and the second (B) has two labels (Building, Person).

We combine the two deep networks results with the intend to improve the labelisation. We assign several labels to the pixel if it was detected by the semantic edge detector. Otherwise, the pixel is assigned to a single label obtained using the semantic segmentation algorithm. The advantage of using an edge detector is to increase the precision of assignment of labels to pixels between semantic classes. After assigning labels to the keypoints, the 3D point label is the mixture of all the keypoints labels.

4   Experimental Part

We evaluate our approach based on two different datasets for large scale: Dubrovnik [11] and Rome. Dubrovnik is a dataset composed of 800 query images with a SFM point cloud built using 6044 key images which generate 1.8 million 3D points and 9.6 million descriptors. Rome [11] is bigger than Dubrovnik with 1000 query images and the SFM point cloud is built using 15176 key images which generates 4.3 million 3D points and 21.5 million descriptors. To estimate the relative pose, we have used the P3P solver inside RANSAC [7] (4096 iteration) on the set of correspondences obtained by matching the features query against the 3D points with a maximum reprojection error $\epsilon \leq 6$ pixel. Following [11,15], we consider a query is successfully registered only if the number of inliers is higher than 12 after the filtering step. To obtain the semantic information, we use in this work two different convolutional neural networks. The first network EncNet [26] is used to extract a class label by pixel and the SoftMax layer. The second network, DFF [8] is used to detect the pixels at class boundaries. Both networks are pretrained on the ADE20K [28] dataset that contains 150 semantic categories annotated on 20210 images. We start by computing the 100 closest images to the input query, using a recent improvement on Resnet [14] CNN architecture used to generate the signatures for both query and key images. We compute the similarity between the images using the FLANN [13] library to construct a KDtree for each input and we stop after finding 100 candidates. We apply a filter with the aim of removing the wrong images: first, we compute the score for each pair based on semantic matching and we remove the nearest neighbors with zero inliers. In most cases, we noticed that the remaining candidates are connected in the pose graph which means they have many 3D points in common. We use the Features to points (F2P) strategy for testing the performance of our approach. Our contribution clearly increases the number of inliers with a higher number of poses found. Getting more inliers positively influences the accuracy of the poses (Table 1).

Table 1. Detailed results for the multiple-label method for Dubrovnik dataset with different window sizes. Q1, Q2 and Q3 are the quartiles of the localization error.

Window size (pixel)	# reg images	Q1(m)	Q2(m)	Q3(m)	Images with error < 18.3 m	Images with error > 400 m
1*1	797	0.35	0.92	2.86	727	7
3 * 3	**798**	**0.25**	**0.78**	**2.35**	**734**	**6**
5 * 5	796	0.34	0.96	2.75	729	9
7 * 7	797	0.37	1.01	2.96	725	13

Table 2. Comparison results on our framework between mono label and multiple label. Q1, Q2 and Q3 are the quartiles of the localization error.

Labeling pixel	# reg images	Q1(m)	Q2(m)	Q3(m)	Images with error < 18.3 m	Images with error > 400 m
Mono-label	791	0.45	1.22	3.78	715	9
Ours(method 1)	797	0.35	0.92	2.86	727	7
Ours(method 2)	**799**	**0.22**	**0.81**	**2.29**	**738**	**6**

The accuracy can be evaluated by looking at Q1, Q2, Q3 which represent the quartiles of the localization errors. We show experimentally that sharing information between neighbors and the target pixel increases the number of registered queries. Keeping the same settings, we set the window size to 3×3 we show that the labelling of the pixels in the borders with more than one class label reduces the error rate and increases the number of registered query images, the number of inliers and the accuracy of the computed poses (Table 2).

Table 3. Comparison of our approach with methods from the state of the art for Dubrovnik Dataset. Q1, Q2 and Q3 are the quartiles of the localization error.

Methods	# reg images	Q1(m)	Q2(m)	Q3(m)	Images with error <18.3 m	Images with error >400 m	Time (s)
Without a priori information							
Ours (method 2)	798	**0.24**	**0.78**	**2.35**	**734**	6	0.72
Sattler [15]	783	0.40	1.40	5.90	685	16	0.31
Sattler [16]	795	0.40	1.40	5.30	704	9	**0.25**
Raul [5]	**800**	1.09	7.92	27.76	550	10	0.62
Youji [6]	781	0.42	1.28	4.67	–	12	0.46
Li [11]	753	7.50	9.30	13.40	655	–	–
Choudhary [4]	788	0.88	3.10	11.83	–	–	–
With a priori information							
(direction verticale et la hauteur de la caméra sont connue)							
Zeisl [25]	796	0.19	0.56	2.09	744	7	3.78
Svarm [21]	798	–	0.56	–	771	3	5.06

Table 4. Comparison of our approach with methods from the state of the art for Rome Dataset

Methods	# reg images	Inliers	Time
Sattler [15]	977	100	0.29
Sattler [16]	991	200	**0.28**
Youji [6]	985	–	0.33
Li [11]	924	–	0.87
Ours(method 1)	995	346	0.96
Ours(method 2)	**997**	**387**	0.89

Comparison with State-of-the-Art. In Table 3 we compare our results with the state of the art. Two methods use a priori information [21,25](known vertical direction and bounded camera height). Their retrieval results with error ≤ 18.3 m is the best. Our methods without priori information achieves slightly lower results. Now we compare our approach to methods without priori information [4,5,11,16,17]. We obtained the higher number of poses with error lower than 18.3 m. Table 4 shows additional results on the Rome datasets.

5 Conclusion

In this paper, we have presented a novel framework based on deep learning for camera pose estimation. Two different deep learning approach have been used in this paper: semantic segmentation algorithm and semantic edge detection. We compared our proposals on several data sets. Thanks to the use of a multiple-label scheme, our algorithm shows state of the art results. We retrieve more poses than with a mono-label strategy and the retrieved poses are more accurate.

References

1. Acuna, D., Kar, A., Fidler, S.: Devil is in the edges: learning semantic boundaries from noisy annotations. In: Proceedings of the IEEE Conference on Computer Vision and Pattern Recognition, pp. 11075–11083 (2019)
2. Bao, S.Y., Savarese, S.: Semantic structure from motion. In: CVPR 2011, pp. 2025–2032. IEEE (2011)
3. Bowman, S.L., Atanasov, N., Daniilidis, K., Pappas, G.J.: Probabilistic data association for semantic slam. In: 2017 IEEE International Conference on Robotics and Automation (ICRA), pp. 1722–1729. IEEE (2017)
4. Choudhary, S., Narayanan, P.J.: Visibility probability structure from SfM datasets and applications. In: Fitzgibbon, A., Lazebnik, S., Perona, P., Sato, Y., Schmid, C. (eds.) ECCV 2012. LNCS, vol. 7576, pp. 130–143. Springer, Heidelberg (2012). https://doi.org/10.1007/978-3-642-33715-4_10
5. Díaz, R., Fowlkes, C.C.: Cluster-wise ratio tests for fast camera localization. In: Proceedings of the IEEE Conference on Computer Vision and Pattern Recognition Workshops, pp. 19–28 (2017)

6. Feng, Y., Fan, L., Wu, Y.: Fast localization in large-scale environments using super-vised indexing of binary features. IEEE Trans. Image Process. **25**(1), 343–358 (2015)
7. Fischler, M.A., Bolles, R.C.: Random sample consensus: a paradigm for model fitting with applications to image analysis and automated cartography. Commun. ACM **24**(6), 381–395 (1981)
8. Hu, Y., Chen, Y., Li, X., Feng, J.: Dynamic feature fusion for semantic edge detection. arXiv preprint arXiv:1902.09104 (2019)
9. Kendall, A., Grimes, M., Cipolla, R.: Posenet: a convolutional network for real-time 6-dof camera relocalization. In: Proceedings of the IEEE International Conference on Computer Vision, pp. 2938–2946 (2015)
10. Larsson, M., Stenborg, E., Hammarstrand, L., Pollefeys, M., Sattler, T., Kahl, F.: A cross-season correspondence dataset for robust semantic segmentation. In: Proceedings of the IEEE Conference on Computer Vision and Pattern Recognition, pp. 9532–9542 (2019)
11. Li, Y., Snavely, N., Huttenlocher, D.P.: Location recognition using prioritized feature matching. In: Daniilidis, K., Maragos, P., Paragios, N. (eds.) ECCV 2010. LNCS, vol. 6312, pp. 791–804. Springer, Heidelberg (2010). https://doi.org/10.1007/978-3-642-15552-9_57
12. Liu, L., Li, H., Dai, Y.: Efficient global 2D–3D matching for camera localization in a large-scale 3D map. In: Proceedings of the IEEE International Conference on Computer Vision, pp. 2372–2381 (2017)
13. Muja, M., Lowe, D.: Flann-fast library for approximate nearest neighbors user manual. Computer Science Department, University of British Columbia, Vancouver, BC, Canada (2009)
14. Radenović, F., Tolias, G., Chum, O.: Fine-tuning CNN image retrieval with no human annotation. IEEE Trans. Pattern Anal. Mach. Intell. **41**(7), 1655–1668 (2018)
15. Sattler, T., Leibe, B., Kobbelt, L.: Fast image-based localization using direct 2D-to-3D matching. In: 2011 International Conference on Computer Vision, pp. 667–674. IEEE (2011)
16. Sattler, T., Leibe, B., Kobbelt, L.: Improving image-based localization by active correspondence search. In: Fitzgibbon, A., Lazebnik, S., Perona, P., Sato, Y., Schmid, C. (eds.) ECCV 2012. LNCS, vol. 7572, pp. 752–765. Springer, Heidelberg (2012). https://doi.org/10.1007/978-3-642-33718-5_54
17. Sattler, T., Leibe, B., Kobbelt, L.: Towards fast image-based localization on a city-scale. In: Dellaert, F., Frahm, J.-M., Pollefeys, M., Leal-Taixé, L., Rosenhahn, B. (eds.) Outdoor and Large-Scale Real-World Scene Analysis. LNCS, vol. 7474, pp. 191–211. Springer, Heidelberg (2012). https://doi.org/10.1007/978-3-642-34091-8_9
18. Sattler, T., Weyand, T., Leibe, B., Kobbelt, L.: Image retrieval for image-based localization revisited. In: BMVC, vol. 1, p. 4 (2012)
19. Song, Y., Chen, X., Wang, X., Zhang, Y., Li, J.: Fast estimation of relative poses for 6-dof image localization. In: 2015 IEEE International Conference on Multimedia Big Data (BigMM), pp. 156–163. IEEE (2015)
20. Stumm, E., Mei, C., Lacroix, S., Nieto, J., Hutter, M., Siegwart, R.: Robust visual place recognition with graph kernels. In: Proceedings of the IEEE Conference on Computer Vision and Pattern Recognition, pp. 4535–4544 (2016)
21. Svarm, L., Enqvist, O., Oskarsson, M., Kahl, F.: Accurate localization and pose estimation for large 3D models. In: Proceedings of the IEEE Conference on Computer Vision and Pattern Recognition, pp. 532–539 (2014)

22. Taira, H., et al.: Is this the right place? geometric-semantic pose verification for indoor visual localization. arXiv preprint arXiv:1908.04598 (2019)

23. Toft, C., et al.: Semantic match consistency for long-term visual localization. In: Ferrari, V., Hebert, M., Sminchisescu, C., Weiss, Y. (eds.) ECCV 2018. LNCS, vol. 11206, pp. 391–408. Springer, Cham (2018). https://doi.org/10.1007/978-3-030-01216-8_24

24. Yu, Z., Feng, C., Liu, M.Y., Ramalingam, S.: Casenet: deep category-aware semantic edge detection. In: Proceedings of the IEEE Conference on Computer Vision and Pattern Recognition, pp. 5964–5973 (2017)

25. Zeisl, B., Sattler, T., Pollefeys, M.: Camera pose voting for large-scale image-based localization. In: Proceedings of the IEEE International Conference on Computer Vision, pp. 2704–2712 (2015)

26. Zhang, H., et al.: Context encoding for semantic segmentation. In: The IEEE Conference on Computer Vision and Pattern Recognition (CVPR), June 2018

27. Zhao, H., Shi, J., Qi, X., Wang, X., Jia, J.: Pyramid scene parsing network. In: Proceedings of the IEEE conference on computer vision and pattern recognition, pp. 2881–2890 (2017)

28. Zhou, B., Zhao, H., Puig, X., Fidler, S., Barriuso, A., Torralba, A.: Scene parsing through ade20k dataset. In: Proceedings of the IEEE Conference on Computer Vision and Pattern Recognition, pp. 633–641 (2017)

A New CBIR Model Using Semantic Segmentation and Fast Spatial Binary Encoding

Achref Ouni[✉], Thierry Chateau, Eric Royer, Marc Chevaldonné,
and Michel Dhome

Université Clermont Auvergne, CNRS, SIGMA Clermont, Institut Pascal,
63000 Clermont-Ferrand, France
`Achref.EL_OUNI@uca.fr`

Abstract. Content Based Image Retrieval (CBIR) is the task of finding
similar images from a query one. Since the term similar means here "with
the same semantic content", we propose to explore in this paper, a framework that uses Deep Neural Networks based semantic segmentation networks, coupled with a binary spatial encoding. Such simple representation
has several relevant properties: 1) It takes advantage of the state of the
art semantic segmentation networks and 2) the proposed binary encoding
allows a Hamming distance that requests a very low computation budget
resulting to a fast CBIR method. Several experiments achieved on public datasets show that our binary semantic signature leads to increase the
CBIR accuracy and reduce the execution time. We study the performance
of the proposed approach on six different public datasets: Wang, Corel 10k,
GHIM-10K, MSRC-V1, MSRC-V2, Linnaeus.

Keywords: CBIR · Deep learning · Semantic segmentation · Image
retrieval

1 Introduction

CBIR is the task of retrieving the images similar to the input query from the
dataset based from their contents. State of the art mentions two main contributions used for image similarity: BoVW [12] (Bag of visual words) and CNN
descriptors [17]. For retrieval, images must be represented as numeric values.
Both contributions represents images as vector of valued features. This vector
encodes the primitive image such as color, texture, and shape. BoVW encode
each image by a histogram of the frequency of the visual words in the image.
Deep learning is a set of machine learning methods attempting to model with
a high level of data abstraction. Deep learning, learn features from an input
data (image in our case) using multiple layers for a specified task. Furthermore, deep learning used to solve many computer vision problem such as image
and video recognition, image classification, medical image analysis, natural language processing.... Particularly Convolutional Neural Network (CNN) have

N. T. Nguyen et al. (Eds.): ICCCI 2022, LNAI 13501, pp. 437–449, 2022.
https://doi.org/10.1007/978-3-031-16014-1_35

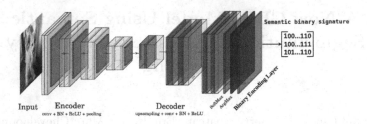

Fig. 1. Illustrate a general semantic segmentation architecture with an additional layer (Binary Encoding Layer). This layer transforms the output (2D-map) to a semantic binary signature.

met with great success for image processing. In deep learning (CNN), the image signature is a vector (feature map) of N floats extracted from the feature layer (Example Fc7 layer for AlexNet [17]). Then computing the distance between the input query and dataset using L2 metric or approximate nearest neighbor (ANN) search methods to find the closest images. CNN based features used in existing CBIR works have been trained for classification problems. It is therefore invariant to spatial position of objects. However CBIR applications should take care of spatial position of semantic objects. We propose, in this paper to study how recent semantic segmentation networks can be used in CBIR context. Deep Learning based semantic segmentation networks output a 2D-map that associates a semantic label (class) to each pixel. This is a high level representation suitable for encoding a feature vector for CBIR that also encodes roughly spatial position of objects. Semantic segmentation is a key step in many computer vision applications such as Traffic control systems, Video surveillance, Video object co-segmentation and action localization, Object detection and Medical imaging. In CBIR models, the raw image should be transformed in a high level presentation. We argue that semantic segmentation network, originally designed for other application can also be used for CBIR.

Then, by classifying all the pixels of an image, it is then possible to construct abstract representations focusing on objects and their forms. Our approach transforms the semantic 2D-map into binary semantic descriptor. Our descriptor encode the object and forms with their semantic proportion and spatial position in the image. The proposed signature can be localized at the output of the CNN architecture as seen in Fig. 1. Our results on six different database highlight the power of our approach.

This article is structured as follows: we provide a brief overview of convolutional neural networks descriptors and bag of visual words related works in Sect. 2. We explain our proposals in Sect. 3. We present the experimental part on six different datasets and discuss the results of our work in Sect. 4. Section 5 conclusion.

2   State of the Art

Many CBIR systems have been proposed in the last years [1, 7, 11, 14, 25, 34]. The content based image retrieval system (Fig. 2) receives as input a query image and

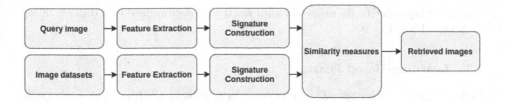

Fig. 2. General CBIR system architecture

returns a list of the most similar images in the database. The framework start with the detection and extraction of the features then the signature construction step. Finally, the closest images to the input query found by the similarity measures between the images signature using dL2 distance. We present a brief overview of approaches based on either visual and learning features.

2.1   Local Visual Feature

Bag of Visual Words proposed by [12] is one of the most model used to classify the images by content. This approach is composed of three main steps: (i) Detection and Feature extraction (ii) Codebook construction (iii) Vector quantization. Detection and extraction features in an image can be performed using extractor algorithms. Many descriptors have been proposed to encodes the images into a vector. Scale Invariant Feature Transform (SIFT) [21] and Speeded-up Robust Features (SURF) [6] are the most used descriptors in CBIR. Interesting work from Arandjelović and Zisserman [4] introduces an improvement by upgrading SIFT to RootSift. In other side, binary descriptors has proven useful [27] proposes ORB (Oriented FAST and Rotated BRIEF) to speed up the search. An other work [19] combines two aspects: precision and speed thanks to BRISK (Binary Robust Invariant Scalable Keypoints) descriptor. [15] present a discriminative descriptor for image similarity based on combining contour and color information. Then, creation of clusters from descriptors with K-Means, DBSCAN or another clustering algorithm. The center of each group will be used as the visual word. Finally, creation for each image the histograms of the frequency of vocabularies or visual words, i.e. the image signature. Due the limit of bag of visual words model many improvement have been proposed for more precision. Bag of visual phrases (BoVP) [23] is a high-level description using a more than word for representing an image. Formed a phrases using a sequence of n-consecutive words regrouped by L2 metric [26]. Build an initial graph then split the graph into a fixed number of sub-graphs using the N-Cut algorithm. Each histogram of visual words in a sub graph forms a visual phrases [10]. Groups visual words in pairs using the neighbourhood of each point of interest. The pairs words are chosen as visual phrases. Perronnin and Dance [24] applies Fisher Kernels to visual words represented by means of a Gaussian Mixture Model (GMM). Similar approach, introduced a simplification for Fisher kernel. Similar to bag of visual words, vector of locally aggregated descriptors (VLAD) [16] assign each feature or keypoint to its nearest visual word and accumulate this difference for each visual word.

2.2 Learning-Based Feature

Deep learning particularly Convolutional Neural Network have met with great success and in many situation CNN replace local detectors and descriptors. Extracting features using CNN models from images has proven a best result for retrieval. Before, the prediction and extraction features steps the CNN must be trained on large-scale datasets like ImageNet [13]. Neural network training is the process in which the configuration of a neural network determines and calculates the value of each of its weights until the network is able to make correct predictions on images. CNN architecture is composed by a set of layers. The major layers for CNN are: the input layer, hidden layers and the output layer. In CNN the input layer is an image with three dimensional reshaped according to the model. In CNN three applications can be applied on image: Classification, Object detection and Segmentation. Related to CBIR context, in classification category we are interest to extract the vector features from fully connected layer. Many CNN models used for extracting features, including AlexNet [17], VGGNet [29], GoogleNet [32] and ResNet [31]. For example, in AlexNet the size of descriptor from the layer fc7 is 4,096-dim. Similar to Local visual Feature approaches, after extracting all descriptors the retrieval accuracy computed using Euclidean distance between the images. NetVLAD [3] inspired from VLAD is a CNN architecture used for image retrieval. [5] reduce the training time and provides an average improvement in accuracy. Using ACP is frequently in CBIR application thanks to his ability to reduce the descriptor dimension without losing its accuracy. [28] use convolution neural network (CNN) to train the network and support vector machine (SVM) to train the hyerplane then compute the distance between the features image and the trained hyper-plane.

3 Contributions

Encoding is the process of converting the data into a specified format for a specific task. In CBIR, encoding image content have met with great success. In addition, encoding images offers many advantages and benefits in terms of searching, retrieving and increasing the accuracy of CBIR system. Many approach based encoding such as BoVW [12], Fisher vector encoding [24], VLAD [16], CNN [17] achieves excellent performance. Consequently, encoding image content is a key element leads to increase the CBIR system performance. Inspired by recent successes of deep learning, we propose a CNN-based model by encoding the output of semantic segmentation architecture for CBIR. So, given a semantic 2D-map, our method (Fig. 3) transforms the semantic prediction into a semantic binary signature. The signature construction comprises of two main unsupervised processing units: (i) Encoding of spatial information (ii) Encoding of proportion. As shown in above of Fig. 3, given a query image I_q, we obtained the prediction I_{seg}

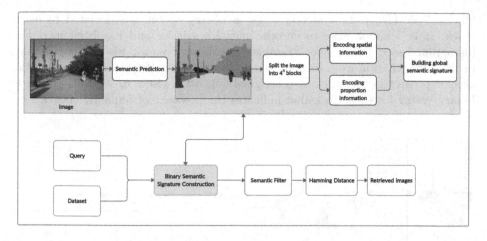

Fig. 3. Global framework

using semantic segmentation algorithm [30] in offline stage. Then, we split the predicted I_{seg} into 4^n blocks I_{sub}. For each block, we encode both spatial and proportion information into a binary matrix. In order to obtain the two main components, we concatenate them to perform a discriminative semantic signature. The similarity between the images signatures are computed by $Hamming$ metric because this distance is fast for the comparison of binary data.

3.1 Encoding of Spatial Information

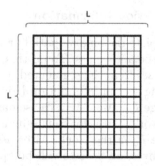

Fig. 4. Illustration of the spatial division. The semantic image divided into 4^n blocks

We propose to encode spatial information using a binary encoding. In a first stage, the image is divided in a recursive way (see Fig. 4). For level one, the image is split into 2×2 spatial areas without overlap that are denoted as blocks. The same operation is then achieved for each block (level 1), and so on. It results that for L levels, the recursive splitting process generates a set of $n_b = \sum_{n \in \{1,..,L\}} 4^n$

blocks $\mathcal{B} \doteq \{B_{n_b}\}$. In a second stage, a binary vector is associated to each block. It is a simple way to encode spatial statistics and has been used for histogram based features for example. The binary vector we propose should provide information from existing semantic classes in the block: if a semantic class is present in the block, it is assigned a 1, otherwise a 0. We thus obtain a binary vector for each block that indicates the presence of semantic classes.

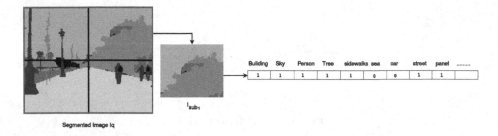

Fig. 5. An example of converting a semantic block to a semantic binary vector.

Figure 5 shows a spatial division into four blocks of the semantic image. A binary vector is assigned to each block to indicate the presence of semantic classes. Our example here shows by value 1 the presence of semantic classes such as sky, building, person, ... and by 0 the missing classes. The process of creating binary vectors stops when we obtain four vectors corresponding to the four blocks. Finally, we concatenate the binary vectors of all blocks to obtain the global signature S_s from an input image.

3.2   Encoding of Proportion Information

In the second step, we complete the binary spatial presentation with information on the proportion of each semantic class. To do this, we propose to encode the proportion of semantic classes from the segmented image using the same spatial division used when encoding spatial information (Fig. 6).

Given a segmented image I_{seg}, we detect the semantic classes present in each block using the neural network. Then, for each semantic class C we calculate its proportion as a percentage P_c in the block. After assigning the percentages of all the classes, a binary conversion process will be applied to each P_c indicated in the Eq. (1) in order to create a binary signature per block named B_{Pc}.

$$\begin{cases} \text{if} \quad 0 < P_c <= 0.25 \quad \text{then} \quad B_{Pc} = 0001 \\ \text{if} \quad 0.25 < P_c <= 0.5 \quad \text{then} \quad B_{Pc} = 0011 \\ \text{if} \quad 0.5 < P_c <= 0.75 \quad \text{then} \quad B_{Pc} = 0111 \\ \text{if} \quad\quad\quad P_c > 0.75 \quad \text{then} \quad B_{Pc} = 1111 \end{cases} \tag{1}$$

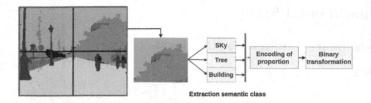

Extraction semantic class

Fig. 6. Example of encoding the proportion information. Given an image divided into 4 blocks, we iteratively select each block to calculate the proportion of the semantic class inside.

For cases where the semantic class C_i is not present in the block, an assignment is automatically assigned to it in the block $B_{Pc} = [0000]$. In order to keep all the scores, we collect them together in the B_{Sub-Pc} matrix. This matrix is a binary description of the proportion of a block.

$$B_{Sub-Pci} = \begin{bmatrix} B_{Pc1} \\ B_{Pc2} \\ ...... \\ B_{PcM-1} \\ B_{PcM} \end{bmatrix}$$

where M is the number of classes that the network has learned to detect. Finally, we concatenate all the binary conversions $B_{Sub-Pci}$ to obtain a signature of global proportion S_P corresponding to the segmented input image I_{seg} where $S_P = \{B_{Sub-Pc_1}. B_{Sub-Pc_2} ..... B_{Sub-Pc_M}\}$. We start the tests with large blocks, then we repeat them with smaller to more smaller blocks. When $n_b = 1$ it means that no spatial division was applied on the image. Therefore, we only encode the semantic proportion information B_{Sub-Pc}.

Table 1. Database used to evaluate of approach

Name	Size DB/Queries	Ground Truth	Query mode
Corel 1K [33] (Wang)	1000/1000	100	Query-in-ground Truth
Corel 10K [33]	10.000/10.000	100	Query-in-ground Truth
GHIM-10K [33]	10.000/10.000	500	Query-in-ground Truth
Linnaeus [9]	6000/2000	400	Queries/ Dataset are disjoint
MSRC v1	241/241	–	Query-in-ground Truth
MSRC v2	591/591	–	Query-in-ground Truth

4   Experimental Setup

4.1   Benchmark Datasets for Retrieval.

See Table 2

Fig. 7. From different categories selected from different datasets, we show the queries with their corresponding predictions and the three nearest neighbors selected by our method using HRNet-W48 [30] trained on Mseg dataset

Table 2. Details about semantic dataset used to predict the images

Dataset	Images	Merged classes	All classes	Stuff/Thingclasses	Year
Mseg [18]	220K	194	316	102/94	2020

Table 3. MAP evaluations using Coco-stuff datasets

Semantic Dataset: Mseg [18]				
Retrieval Dataset	Size of blocks			
	$4^0 = 1$	$4^1 = 4$	$4^2 = 16$	$4^3 = 64$
MSRC v1	0.79	0.89	0.83	0.81
MSRC v2	0.64	0.73	0.71	0.67
Linnaeus [9]	0.71	0.77	0.78	0.73
Corel 1K (Wang) [33]	0.77	0.86	0.81	0.80
Corel 10K [20]	0.53	0.55	0.56	0.55
GHIM-10K [20]	0.53	0.52	0.53	0.51

4.2   Results on Benchmark Datasets for Retrieval

We conducted our experimentation on two different semantic prediction datasets [8,18] and six retrieval datasets (Table 1). Table 3 presents the mean average precision (MAP) [2] scores for dataset per size of blocks. We start the tests with large blocks to small blocks. When the parameter $n = 1$ then the encoding of semantic spatial information not exist and we encode only the semantic proportion information. Figure 7 clearly indicates that our method capable to select the similar images to input query based on semantic content. The selection is based hamming distance between the query and the images dataset. Experiments with a single thread for each image, the descriptor requires 9 ms on average (Table 4). For [17, 29, 31] we extract from their architectures the features vector from the features layer for evaluating their performance on the datasets using L2 distance.

Table 4. Execution time on milliseconds (**ms**) per image (using a single thread) for all datasets

Retrieval dataset	Size of blocks			
	$4^0 = 1$	$4^1 = 4$	$4^2 = 16$	$4^3 = 64$
MSRC v1	8.8	9.1	12.8	28.1
MSRC v2	8.5	9.8	13.6	30.6
Linnaeus [9]	9.1	11.3	18.6	37.6
Corel 1K (Wang) [33]	10.1	14.3	29.5	41.6
Corel 10K [20]	10.4	14.5	28.9	42.1
GHIM-10K [20]	11.2	15.4	30.1	44.2

4.3   Comparison with State-of-the-Art

Table 5. Comparison of the accuracy of our approach with methods from the state of the art (best scores in bold)

Methods	MSRC v1	MSRC v2	Linnaeus	Wang	Corel-10K	GHIM-10K
BoVW [12]	0,48	0.30	0,26	0.48	0.30	0.39
n-BoVW [22]	0.58	0.39	0.31	0.60	0.34	0.41
VLAD [16]	0.78	0.41	–	0.74	0.38	0.44
N-Gram [23]	–	–	–	0.37	–	–
AlexNet [17]	0.81	0.58	0,47	0.68	0.40	0.41
VGGNet [29]	0.76	0.63	0,48	0.76	0.45	0.43
ResNet [31]	0.83	0.70	0,69	0.82	**0.59**	0.49
SaCoCo [15]	–	–	–	0.54	0.17	0.15
Ruigang [28]	–	–	0.70	–	–	–
Ayan [7]	–	–	–	0.79	0.52	–
Chu [11]	–	–	–	0.80	0.45	0.51
Ours	**0.89**	**0.73**	**0.78**	**0.86**	0.55	**0.53**

We compare our results against two main categories: (i) Local visual Feature: methods that based on local features like Surf, Sift included the inherited methods such as BoVW, Vlad, Fisher. (ii) Learning based features: methods that based on learning the features using deep learning algorithms. *Hamming* distance is the similarity metric used to compute the similarity between the query and dataset. In Table 5 we compare our results with a large state of the art methods. As indicate the results our proposed present good performance for all datasets. In Table 6, we compare the precision of the top 20 retrieved image for all categories for Wang dataset. In Fig. 8 we show the precision performance of top 20 retrieved image for 10 category compared to [1,14,25,34] methods. The second objective desired in this work is to reduce and minimize the execution time of CBIR system. For any CBIR the execution time depends to time of signature construction. Then, we compare only the time taken by each method to build its signature. We explain here that the extraction, detection and prediction time are not taken into consideration. Table 4 and Fig. 9 present a comparison time of signature construction for the state of the art methods and our method. Its clearly the interest of our approach in the terms of time against the state of the art methods.

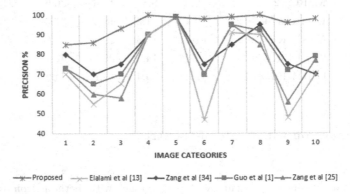

Fig. 8. comparison of precision for top 20 retrieved images for all categories (Corel 1K (Wang) dataset)

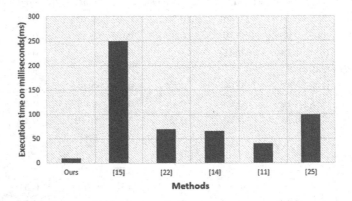

Fig. 9. Comparison of execution time against the state of the art

Table 6. comparison of precision for top 20 retrieved images (Wang dataset)

Methods	Top 20
ElAlami [14]	0.76
Guo and Prasetyo [1]	0.77
Zeng et al. [34]	0.80
Jitesh Pradhan [25]	0.81
Proposed method	0.94

5   Conclusion

We present in this paper a fast and efficient CBIR approach based on semantic segmentation prediction to improve the image similarity. We have shown that by encoding the image information as binary leads to increase the CBIR accuracy. Two gain well shown in our work (i) Time saving (ii) Robust signature based on CNN. Experimental evaluation indicates that our approach achieve a better results in terms of accuracy and time against the state of the art methods.

References

1. Admile, N.S., Dhawan, R.R.: Content based image retrieval using feature extracted from dot diffusion block truncation coding. In: 2016 International Conference on Communication and Electronics Systems (ICCES), pp. 1–6. IEEE (2016)
2. Chatzichristofis, S.A., Iakovidou, C., Boutalis, Y.S., Angelopoulou, E.: Mean Normalized Retrieval Order (MNRO): a new content-based image retrieval performance measure. Multimedia Tools and Appl. **70**(3), 1767–1798 (2012). https://doi.org/10.1007/s11042-012-1192-z
3. Arandjelović, R., Gronat, P., Torii, A., Pajdla, T., Sivic, J.: NetVLAD: CNN architecture for weakly supervised place recognition. In: IEEE Conference on Computer Vision and Pattern Recognition (2016)
4. Arandjelovic, R., Zisserman, A.: All about vlad. In: Proceedings of the IEEE conference on Computer Vision and Pattern Recognition, pp. 1578–1585 (2013)
5. Balaiah, T., Jeyadoss, T.J.T., Thirumurugan, S.S., Ravi, R.C.: A deep learning framework for automated transfer learning of neural networks. In: 2019 11th International Conference on Advanced Computing (ICoAC), pp. 428–432. IEEE (2019)
6. Bay, H., Tuytelaars, T., Van Gool, L.: SURF: speeded up robust features. In: Leonardis, A., Bischof, H., Pinz, A. (eds.) ECCV 2006. LNCS, vol. 3951, pp. 404–417. Springer, Heidelberg (2006). https://doi.org/10.1007/11744023_32
7. Bhunia, A.K., Bhattacharyya, A., Banerjee, P., Roy, P.P., Murala, S.: A novel feature descriptor for image retrieval by combining modified color histogram and diagonally symmetric co-occurrence texture pattern. Pattern Analysis and Applications, pp. 1–21 (2019)
8. Caesar, H., Uijlings, J., Ferrari, V.: Coco-stuff: thing and stuff classes in context. In: Proceedings of the IEEE Conference on Computer Vision and Pattern Recognition, pp. 1209–1218 (2018)

9. Chaladze, G., Kalatozishvili, L.: Linnaeus 5 dataset for machine learning. Technical report (2017)
10. Chen, T., Yap, K.-H., Zhang, D.: Discriminative soft bag-of-visual phrase for mobile landmark recognition. IEEE Trans. Multimedia **16**(3), 612–622 (2014)
11. Chu, K., Liu, G.-H.: Image retrieval based on a multi-integration features model. Mathematical Problems in Engineering (2020)
12. Csurka, G., Dance, C., Fan, L., Willamowski, J., Bray, C.: Visual categorization with bags of keypoints. In: Workshop on Statistical Learning in Computer Vision, ECCV, vol. 1, pp. 1–2. Prague (2004)
13. Deng, J., Dong, W., Socher, R., Li, L.-J., Li, K., Fei-Fei, L.: Imagenet: a large-scale hierarchical image database. In: 2009 IEEE Conference on Computer Vision and Pattern Recognition, pp. 248–255. IEEE (2009)
14. Esmel ElAlami, M.: A new matching strategy for content based image retrieval system. Appl. Soft Comput. **14**, 407–418 (2014)
15. Iakovidou, C., Anagnostopoulos, N., Lux, M., Christodoulou, K., Boutalis, Y., Chatzichristofis, S.A.: Composite description based on salient contours and color information for CBIR tasks. IEEE Trans. Image Process. **28**(6), 3115–3129 (2019)
16. Jégou, H., Douze, M., Schmid, C., Pérez, P.: Aggregating local descriptors into a compact image representation. In: 2010 IEEE Computer Society Conference on Computer Vision and Pattern Recognition, pp. 3304–3311. IEEE (2010)
17. Krizhevsky, A., Sutskever, I., Hinton, G.E.: Imagenet classification with deep convolutional neural networks. In: Advances in Neural Information Processing Systems, pp. 1097–1105 (2012)
18. Lambert, J., Zhuang, L., Sener, O., Hays, J., Koltun, V.: MSeg: a composite dataset for multi-domain semantic segmentation. In: Computer Vision and Pattern Recognition (CVPR) (2020)
19. Leutenegger, S., Chli, M., Siegwart, R.Y.: Brisk: binary robust invariant scalable keypoints. In: 2011 IEEE International Conference on Computer Vision (ICCV), pp. 2548–2555. IEEE (2011)
20. Li, J., Wang, J.Z.: Automatic linguistic indexing of pictures by a statistical modeling approach. IEEE Trans. Pattern Anal. Mach. Intell. **25**(9), 1075–1088 (2003)
21. Lindeberg, T.: Scale invariant feature transform (2012)
22. Ouni, A., Urruty, T., Visani, M.: A robust CBIR framework in between bags of visual words and phrases models for specific image datasets. Multimedia Tools Appl. **77**(20), 26173–26189 (2018)
23. Pedrosa, G.V., Traina, A.J.M.: From bag-of-visual-words to bag-of-visual-phrases using n-grams. In: 2013 XXVI Conference on Graphics, Patterns and Images, pp. 304–311. IEEE (2013)
24. Perronnin, F., Dance, C.: Fisher kernels on visual vocabularies for image categorization. In: 2007 IEEE Conference on Computer Vision and Pattern Recognition, pp. 1–8. IEEE (2007)
25. Pradhan, J., Kumar, S., Pal, A.K., Banka, H.: Texture and color visual features based CBIR using 2D DT-CWT and histograms. In: Ghosh, D., Giri, D., Mohapatra, R.N., Savas, E., Sakurai, K., Singh, L.P. (eds.) ICMC 2018. CCIS, vol. 834, pp. 84–96. Springer, Singapore (2018). https://doi.org/10.1007/978-981-13-0023-3_9
26. Ren, Y., Bugeau, A., Benois-Pineau, J.: Visual object retrieval by graph features (2013)
27. Rublee, E., Rabaud, V., Konolige, K., Bradski, G.: Orb: an efficient alternative to sift or surf. In: 2011 IEEE international conference on Computer Vision (ICCV), pp. 2564–2571. IEEE (2011)

28. Fu, R., Li, B., Gao, Y., Wang, P.: Content-based image retrieval based on CNN and SVM. In: 2016 2nd IEEE International Conference on Computer and Communications (ICCC), pp. 638–642 (2016)
29. Simonyan, K., Zisserman, A.: Very deep convolutional networks for large-scale image recognition. arXiv preprint arXiv:1409.1556 (2014)
30. Sun, K., et al.:. High-resolution representations for labeling pixels and regions. arXiv preprint arXiv:1904.04514 (2019)
31. Szegedy, C., Ioffe, S., Vanhoucke, V., Alemi., A.A.:Inception-v4, inception-resnet and the impact of residual connections on learning. In: Thirty-first AAAI Conference on Artificial Intelligence (2017)
32. Szegedy, C.: Going deeper with convolutions. In: Proceedings of the IEEE Conference on Computer Vision and Pattern Recognition, pp. 1–9 (2015)
33. Wang, J.Z., Li, J., Wiederhold, G.: Simplicity: semantics-sensitive integrated matching for picture libraries. IEEE Trans. Pattern Anal. Mach. Intell. **23**(9), 947–963 (2001)
34. Zeng, S., Huang, R., Wang, H., Kang, Z.: Image retrieval using spatiograms of colors quantized by gaussian mixture models. Neurocomputing **171**, 673–684 (2016)

Temporal Segmentation of Basketball Continuous Videos Based on the Analysis of the Camera and Player Movements

Kazimierz Choroś[(✉)] [iD]

Faculty of Information and Communication Technology, Department of Applied Informatics,
Wrocław University of Science and Technology, Wyb. Wyspiańskiego 27, 50-370 Wrocław,
Poland
kazimierz.choros@pwr.edu.pl

Abstract. Sports video segmentation is a very useful process in video indexing, video summarization, or video highlight detections. For continuous videos when the full game is recorded the segmentation cannot be based on the detection of cuts or cross-dissolve transitions as it is the case of edited videos like sports news or other short sports coverages. One basketball game usually lasts even for around two hours including play parts as well as breaks. In the paper the approach of a basketball game segmentation is presented and examined. The proposed method is based on the analysis of the camera and player movements. The tests performed in the AVI Indexer showed that the analysis of the camera and player movements leads to the correct detection of segments with game breaks but also segments with the interesting highlights in continuous basketball videos.

Keywords: Content-Based video analysis · Continuous video segmentation · Sports videos · Highlight detection methods · Basketball video segmentation · Automatic video summarization · Camera movements · Basketball player movements · Automatic video indexer AVI

1 Introduction

Videos presenting sports games are often recordings of large length. In many sports disciplines such as soccer, football, volleyball, basketball, cycling or car race, ice hockey, and others sports competitions may last several dozen minutes or even several hours. The analysis of such recordings is easier if the video is segmented. However, such recordings are of continuous nature. Video cut effects are observed only if the transmission is realized using more than one camera. But even then the video is composed of very long parts. Moreover these camera changes do not correspond to the real partition of actions in a sports game. Very often the players are simply shown from other perspective and a given sports action continues. So, the camera change is not a good criterion for segmentation of such continuous sports videos.

The main goal of content-based analysis of sports videos is to automatically detect the highlights in analyzed videos, such as goals scored, free kicks or penalties, corners,

© The Author(s), under exclusive license to Springer Nature Switzerland AG 2022
N. T. Nguyen et al. (Eds.): ICCCI 2022, LNAI 13501, pp. 450–463, 2022.
https://doi.org/10.1007/978-3-031-16014-1_36

fouls, volleyball spikes, tennis winner balls, cycling race finishes, very nice ski jumping, etc. In the case of basketball these are usually shots with slam dunks as well as quick actions after interceptions (picks). When the ball is passed as intended for a player of the same team it happens that the ball is caught by a player of the team on defense. Then the other team gains possession and control of the ball and in consequence it makes an opportunity to quickly counter the opposing team. Such fast action after the ball is intercepted by the opposing team and scored is a nice individual video segment we would like automatically extract as a potential highlight of a basketball competition.

The goal of this paper is to present a method of detecting individual basketball actions extracted from continuous basketball videos. The proposed method is based on the analysis of the camera and player movements in basketball videos. This method can be similarly used for the video analysis of other team games.

The paper is structured as follows. The next section describes related work on the basketball video analysis and the segmentation of continuous videos. The third section discusses the structure of basketball continuous videos. The next section describes the data used in the experiments. Whereas the fifth section presents the results of the tests showing how the analysis of camera and player movements can be applied to segment continuous basketball videos. The final conclusions are presented in the last section.

2 Related Work

Basketball videos have been frequently examined in experimental research concerning content sports video analysis. In the previous works in this area several goals have been set, among them are: highlight detection, player tracking and identification, scoring identification, shot class recognition, and event classification.

In earlier research a basketball video structure was studied and then categorized into different classes according to visual and motional features using rule-based classifier [1]. The general features were: motion features, color features, and edge features. In the experiments the objects were not tracked because it was computationally complex and time consuming. To find the motion patterns for basketball videos, the authors focused on the direction and magnitude of video sequence motion flows by examining only predictive frames in MPEG-1 videos. A basketball video was classified into nine major meaningful events: team offense at left court, team offense at right court, fast break (a swift attack from a defensive position) to left, fast break to right, dunk (score by shooting the ball down through the basket with the hands above the rim) in left court, dunk in right court, score in right court, score in left court, and close-ups for audience or players. In the experimental results of using the trained rules to classify events in a basketball game video the accuracies were from 70% to 82% and recall rate from 76% to 89% for nine defined basketball classes.

In many sports video analysis the main goal is to identify meaningful segments in a game which are segments that show a shooter scoring a goal. It is a case of soccer [2] but also of basketball [3]. In this last paper the goal segments were identified by assuming that every goal in a basketball game is followed by crowd cheer within three seconds, and by a scoreboard display within seven seconds after the crowd cheer. The next examined solution was to identify an applause that appears within 10 s of a change in direction players' movements or a scoreboard appears within 10 s of a change in direction. These features including energy levels of audio signals, embedded text regions, and change in direction of motion were automatically derived from MPEG videos. Unfortunately, feature extraction algorithms used for scoreboard did not detected only scoreboards but also other texts such as team coach or player names as well as the number of fouls committed by a player. It increased the number of false positive results. Also the analysis of crowd cheer is possible when a game took place with a large audience what is not a case for example in the COVID pandemic period.

The basketball parts can be also classified into three kinds of shots depending on the focal length of a camera and the field of view: close-up view, medium view, or full court view shot. In [4] scene changes were detected in MPEG videos in the compressed domain. The full court view shots were chosen for further processing. The ball was tracked and then possible shooting positions were extracted.

Whereas in [5] the basketball video shots were classified into such three categories as close-up views, far views, and replays. Close-up and far views were detected basing on the percentage of edge pixels. Replay segments were identified by detecting logos. The experiments were conducted on two real-world Olympic and one NBA basketball games.

In the paper [6] three basic visual cues were found to be helpful to segment events on basketball broadcasting videos: camera movement, shot class, and clock digits. The camera panning movement was estimated by the optical flow estimation and flow segmentation algorithm. To determine shot class and to detect clock digits in the image convolutional neural network (CNN) was applied. The performed experiment showed that such an approach was simple and fast but at the same time reliable to give useful information for the event segmentation.

The goal of the approach presented in [7] was to detect the shots and the scoring of the shot in the basketball video and then to determine the shooter of the corresponding shot. In the shot detection procedure and the determination of the result of the shot the ball tracking and the detection of hoop was applied. Whereas to identify the shooter for each shot, an unsupervised player re-identification method was used. The player re-identification process was performed on the basis of feature vectors of each player by finding the Euclidean distance between them.

An automatic generation method of basketball continuous pitching motion based on multi-objective machine vision was proposed in [8]. The method was based on the feature extraction of fuzzy images of basketball continuous pitching motion. The feature segmentation was used to carry out the adaptive enhancement processing of the fuzzy image of the basketball.

In other research performed not only with basketball sports videos also continuous videos were examined. The goal of [9] was to compare several feature extraction methods and classifiers for the sports video classification. The methods were applied to continuous videos, without a priori knowledge about the moments when the topic changes. The classification was based on the SVM classifier and convolutional neural networks to extract high level features from the image.

In [10] a long continuous video containing several social human activities was divided into individual labeled pieces of a single action. The recognition of human's various actions in videos is extremely important in security or monitoring systems and also for example in human-robot interaction. The authors proposed a simultaneous segmentation of continuous videos and human action recognition method. Action recognition method was based on the locality preserving projections and bag of words.

Also in [11] temporal segmentation and recognition of team activities in sports videos was discussed. The method based on a new activity feature extraction was proposed for handball and field hockey videos. The continuous videos sequences were tested. However, it was also observed that in handball there are also time-out segments which occur when the ball is out or when the play is stopped. During the breaks teams do not move and then start to perform the next activity. It resulted in both segmentation and classification of continuous videos.

Video recording systems are frequently used for monitoring construction activities. Unfortunately such monitoring generates the huge amount of video data. On the other hand the relatively slow pace of construction activities results in a significant amount of the redundant and useless recorded video data. The solution suggested by the authors of [12] was based on the automatic processing of construction continuous videos including the selection of video features, scene segmentation, and key frame extraction. The proposed technique was used to develop a construction video summary system.

Basketball videos were analyzed for different purposes. The goal of the studies presented in [13] was to develop an algorithm to analyze a basketball training in real time, mainly to detect the players and scores for each player. First, the shots were detected and then it was determined whether they were successful or missed.. To detect the position of the hoop a deep learning model was applied and to detect the shot background subtraction was used. Then, scoring was determined using a classification method based on neural network. Finally, the player who sent the shot was identified.

Whereas in [14] the problem of the selection of multiple actions in an unsegmented continuous video stream was discussed. The solution was to detect the transitions between actions. A semi-supervised action model was defined for action segmentation. In this model the long-term dependencies among frames were found, as well as the relationships among consecutive action sequences.

Much research has been performed on the analysis of basketball videos mainly to extract meaningful segments, i.e. segments that show a shooter scoring a goal. Different temporal models were developed in [15] helping to identify such segments based on key events that were defined as common repetitive events present throughout the game. In the proposed model the following basic assumptions were tested: a loud cheer follows every legal goal within 3 s and a loud cheer only occurs after a legal goal, a scoreboard display appears (usually as embedded text) within 10 s of scoring a legal goal, and every goal is followed by crowd cheer within 3 s and by a scoreboard displayed within 7 s after the crowd cheer – it is a temporal combination of two first key events, then the union of loud cheer and scoreboard display, and finally a crowd cheer appears within 10 s of a change in direction of players or a scoreboard appears within 10 s of a change in direction of players. The experimental results were promising but some obstacles were also observed, such as: lack of supporters for a team among the spectators or generally even lack of spectators (it was frequent nowadays in pandemic times) and in consequence the lack of crowd cheer, and also free throws are not often accompanied by scoreboard displays.

Content analysis of basketball sports videos can also be applied to generate video summaries composed of the most interesting parts of the streams provided by several cameras. The process can take into account individual user preferences, making the process adaptive and personalized [16].

Recently software for automatic processing of basketball videos has been used for evaluating teams and players [17]. Such a complex analysis enables the basketball team coach to recognize the strengths and weaknesses in the game, to better evaluate opponent teams, to see how to optimize performance indicators, to use them for team and player forecasting, and finally to make better choices for team composition.

Much present research is based on the application of machine learning techniques to determine strategies in basketball derived from player or ball tracking data [18].

3 Structure and Segmentation of Basketball Videos

Such processes of video content analysis as highlight detection, shot class recognition, and event classification would be easier performed if the basketball videos were temporally segmented. Unfortunately, many basketball as well as many other team games, mainly local and or lower league competitions, are frequently recorded using one or only two cameras. It results in recording very long segments of a given game. In such one segment several actions, several scores, shooting, rebounds, nice dribbling or blocking, free throw, slam dunk, etc. are included.

Some research has attempted to propose solutions to segment continuous videos, not only sports videos.

How to divide a long segment into shorter parts if there is no cuts or any other transitions being usually natural points for segmentation processes? The segmentation should be performed not on the basis of technical features of basketball videos but on the basis of some critical moments such as breaks, free throws, fouls, or ball interception by the opposing team and carrying out a counterattack. The goal of this paper is to verify whether the analysis of camera and player movements enables us to segment continuous parts of a basketball video that are between two consecutive game breaks.

Break segments seem to be natural boundaries in continuous basketball videos. Play and break segments in basketball videos can be automatically detected basing for example on the analysis of the slope of the basketball court boundary [19]. However, it is normal and frequent that several player actions are recorded between two consecutive breaks in a game. Our assumption is that these parts between two breaks can be further segmented into individual actions by analyzing the camera and player movements. Individual single action is an action of one team till the ball is caught by a player of the other team on defense or the ball is thrown into the basket, so in consequence the ball passes to the other team. However, if the opposing team reached to prevent from shooting through their own hoop, the new action starts or in the case of a foul committed, timed play stops and we have a break, frequently free throws are then performed.

4 Basketball Videos Used in the Tests

To illustrate the proposed procedure the basketball match recorded during the XXXI Olympic Games in Rio de Janeiro was used in the experiment performed in the AVI Indexer [20]. Table 1 presents the characteristics of the chosen part of the recorded game and used in the experiment. The description of the special events in this part of the video shows the potential segments for automatic detection between two breaks in the match (Fig. 1).

Table 1. Events in the analyzed part of the basketball video.

Event symbol	Time	Description
P_1	04:32.00	close-up view of the player
B_1	04:34.45	break, camera change, view on the right side of the playing field, referee with a ball
P_2	04:41.40	close-up view of the player
L_1	04:44.15	long view of the playing field, game starts from the right basket, offence at the left side
L_2	04:45.46	centre of the playing field, camera is moving to the left
A_1	04:54.46	ball throw into the basket
P_3	04:57.11	play, close-up view of the player running to the right
R_1	05:00.17	view on the playing field, team running to the right
R_2	05:01.42	centre of the playing field, camera is moving to the right
A_2	05:12.08	taking over the ball near right basket
L_3	05:14.11	centre of the playing field, camera is moving to the left
A_3	05:18.09	taking over the ball near left basket
R_3	05:20.44	centre of the playing field, camera is moving to the right
B_2	05:30.06	break, referee whistled foul, view on the playing field
P_4	05:34.05	close-up view of the player

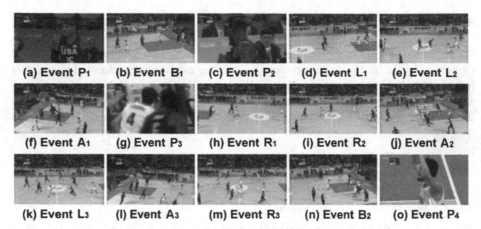

Fig. 1. Examples of basketball events in the analysed part of the basketball video. A – action near the basket, B – break in the game, P – view of the player, L – player or camera movement to the left, R – player or camera movement to the right.

5 Camera or Player Movements

The course of a basketball game can be analyzed – as it was shown in [19] – by examining the plot of the values of slope of the basketball top court boundary. The positive value in the plot is observed when the game is played on the left part of the basketball court and the negative value when on the right part of the court. Whereas the curve passes the horizontal axis when the camera is directed exactly to the center of the court, because the main camera is always placed just in front of the center of the basketball court.

Table 2. The accuracy of the break detection process based on the analysis of the differences of the values of slope of the basketball top court boundary.

	Number of frames	Ratio [%]	Length of time
Whole basketball video	263161	100	01:27:43.11
BREAKS			
Real breaks	141638	53.8218	00:47:12.38
Frames detected as breaks	121920	46.3291	00:40:38.20
Accuracy of break detection	112543	79.4582	00:37:30.43
Negative predictive value	112543	92.3089	00:37:30.43

The process of the break detection based on the analysis of the differences of the values of slope of the basketball top court boundary is successful (Table 2). The accuracy of play detections has been achieved on the level of 92%. The accuracy of break detections has been slightly lower (almost 80%) comparing to play detections. However in average the accuracy of this process was over 85%.

It would be desirable to extract individual game actions recorded between two consecutive breaks. The assumption is that it can be done by analyzing the camera or player movements.

The detection of camera and player movements has been performed using the well-known and widely applied algorithm of Lucas, Kanade and, Tomasi [21–24]. It defines motion vectors for selected feature points. The motion vectors represent the distances the object has shifted between two consecutive frames. Figure 2 illustrates an example of the set of points on the field trucked in the algorithm.

Fig. 2. Detection of camera movements.

The camera movements can be perceived as chaotic, mainly during the breaks but also in the case of close-up views of the players (Fig. 3 and Fig. 4). However, in many situations we can observed a series of movements to the left or to the right side of a basketball field. In the case when the movement of the camera is not observed or the movement is relatively small it means that the same part of the basketball field is shown, usually it happens for a long view of the basketball field.

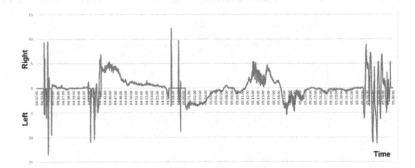

Fig. 3. Camera movements detected in the analyzed part of the basketball video.

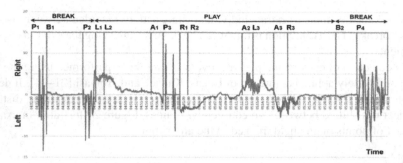

Fig. 4. Events observed in the analyzed part of the tested basketball video placed on the curve of camera movements.

Instead of absolute values of camera movements the differences between camera movements in consecutive video frames can be analyzed (Fig. 5 and Fig. 6). These differences signal much more information.

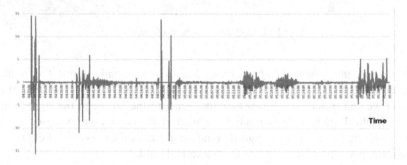

Fig. 5. Differences of camera movements detected in the analyzed part of the basketball video.

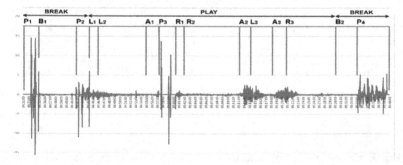

Fig. 6. Events observed in the analyzed part of the tested basketball video placed on the curve of differences of camera movements.

It is a little surprising but the most differentiated values of differences of camera movements are observed for player close-up views. Whereas for break as well as play segments these differences of camera movements are relatively very small.

The player movements have been next similarly analyzed. Figure 7 illustrates an example of the set of points for moving objects, in this case for players moving during the game and trucked in the algorithm.

Fig. 7. Detection of player movements.

The results of player movements are very interesting for temporal segmentation of basketball videos because to shot the ball into the hoop the players need to advance the ball usually walking or running (dribbling) or by passing it to another teammate. So, the single action starts near the end of the court and ends near another end of the court of the opposing team. The detected direction of player movements can be used as a criterion for the detection of the beginning of the action as well as of its end in the temporal segmentation of continuous basketball videos.

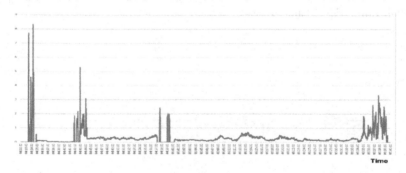

Fig. 8. Player movements detected in the analyzed part of the basketball video.

Similarly to camera movements we observe that the most differentiated values of differences of player movements are observed for player close-up views (Fig. 8 and Fig. 9). Whereas for break as well as play segments these differences of movements are relatively very small. These differences are relatively small and adequate for the running speed of players shown usually as long-view shots, so the movements in such kind of views are not great when comparing to the movements observed in close-up views of players and close-up views during the breaks.

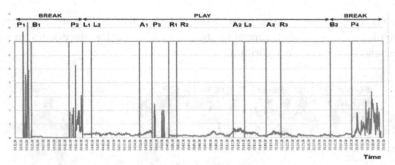

Fig. 9. Events observed in the analyzed part of the tested basketball video placed on the curve of player movements.

The change in the direction of player movements happens when the defense team collects a rebound, that is, a missed shot that bounces from rim or backboard and also when the ball is simply caught by a player of the team on defense. The team till now on defense goes to attack and the new action starts. At that moment we are observing the change of the direction of player movements.

These moments when one team is successfully shooting and is scoring the points or when the ball is caught by the defense team seem to be very natural boundaries of play segments and in consequence the detection of breaks and the analysis of camera and player movements lead to the segmentation of continuous sports videos. The individual segments present breaks during the game or basketball actions which can be included in the video summary or news presenting the most interesting highlights of a reported basketball game (Fig. 10 and Fig. 11).

Fig. 10. Differences of player movements detected in the analyzed part of the basketball video.

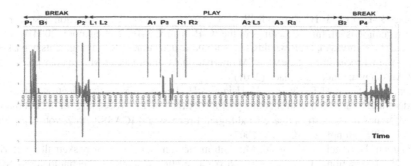

Fig. 11. Events observed in the analyzed part of the tested basketball video placed on the curve of differences of player movements.

6 Conclusions

Sports video segmentation is one of the basic process in video indexing, video summarization, or video highlight detections. The temporal segmentation is nowadays well performed in the case of edited videos. The automatic detection of cuts and of other video transitions [25] as well as the structure of edited videos like sports news or other short sports coverages [26] is efficient although all the time new techniques are proposed, developed, tested, and improved.

The problem is different in the case of sports videos which are not edited but continuous. One basketball game usually lasts even for around two hours including play parts as well as game breaks. Such videos when several cameras where used have also cuts but many parts of videos include several highlights which should be separated. The approach of a basketball game segmentation is presented and examined in the paper. The proposed method is based on the analysis of the camera and player movements. The performed tests showed that the analysis of the camera and player movements leads to the correct detection of segments with game breaks but also segments with the interesting highlights in continuous basketball videos.

The further experimental research will be undertaken on a long whole recorded basketball game to verify the efficiency of the proposed technique. Moreover, the observations have shown that close-up views have specific characteristics when analyzing camera and player movements. These movements seem chaotic, much more varied. It may suggest that this technique can be also used to detect such segments which are parts of break or play scenes depending on which segment they are adjacent to. Another question arises whether this approach is also appropriate for videos of other sports genres? It is very probable that for example handball games can be also analyzed using the proposed approach.

References

1. Zhou, W., Vellaikal, A., Kuo, C.J.: Rule-based video classification system for basketball video indexing. In: Proceedings of the ACM Multimedia Workshop, pp. 213–216. Los Angeles, California, USA (2000)

2. Kang, Y.-L., Lim, J.-H., Kankanhalli, M.S., Xu, C., Tian, Q.: Goal detection in soccer video using audio/visual. In: Proceedings of the ICIP, pp. 1629–1632. Singapore (2004)
3. Nepal, S., Srinivasan, U., Reynolds, G.: Automatic detection of 'Goal' segments in basketball videos. In: Proceedings of the 9th ACM International Conference on Multimedia, pp. 261–269. ACM, Ottawa, Ontario, Canada (2001)
4. Tien, M.C., Chen, H.T., Chen, Y.W., Hsiao, M.H., Lee, S.Y.: Shot classification of basketball videos and its application in shooting position extraction. In: Proceedings of the International Conference on Acoustics, Speech and Signal Processing – ICASSP 2007, vol. 1, pp. 1085–1088. IEEE, Honolulu, HI, USA (2007)
5. Chauhan, D., Patel, N.M., Joshi, M.: Automatic summarization of basketball sport video. In: 2nd International Conference on Next Generation Computing Technologies – NGCT, pp. 670–673. IEEE, India (2016)
6. Park, J.H., Cho, K.: Extraction of visual information in basketball broadcasting video for event segmentation system. In: International Conference on Information and Communication Technology Convergence – ICTC, pp. 1098–1100. IEEE, Jeju Island, Korea (2016)
7. Teket, O.M., Yetik, I.S.: A fast deep learning based approach for basketball video analysis. In: Proceedings of the 4th International Conference on Vision, Image and Signal Processing – ICVISP, pp. 1–6. Bangkok, Thailand (2020)
8. Qiaomei, L., Yi, X.: Automatic generation method of basketball continuous pitching action based on multi-objective machine vision. In: Proceedings of the 3rd International Conference on Information Systems and Computer Aided Education – ICISCAE, pp. 241–245. IEEE, Dalian, China (2020)
9. Campr, P., Herbig, M., Vaněk, J., Psutka, J.: Sports video classification in continuous TV broadcasts. In: Proceedings of the 12th International Conference on Signal Processing – ICSP, pp. 648–652. IEEE. HangZhou, China (2014)
10. Ji, L., Xiong, R., Wang, Y., Yu, H.: A method of simultaneously action recognition and video segmentation of video streams. In: Proceedings of the International Conference on Robotics and Biomimetics – ROBIO, pp. 1515–1520. IEEE, Macau, China (2017)
11. Direkoğlu, C., O'Connor, N.E.: Temporal segmentation and recognition of team activities in sports. Mach. Vis. Appl. 29(5), 891–913 (2018). https://doi.org/10.1007/s00138-018-0944-9
12. Chen, L., Wang, Y.: Automatic key frame extraction in continuous videos from construction monitoring by using color, texture, and gradient features. Autom. Constr. 81, 355–368 (2017)
13. Teket, O.M., Yetik, I.S.: A fast deep learning based approach for basketball video analysis. In: Proceedings of the 4th International Conference on Vision, Image and Signal Processing – ICVISP, pp. 1–6. ACM, Bangkok Thailand (2020)
14. Gammulle, H., Denman, S., Sridharan, S., Fookes, C.: Fine-grained action segmentation using the semi-supervised action GAN. Pattern Recogn. 98(107039), 1–12 (2020)
15. Yuan, Y., et al.: Key frame extraction based on global motion statistics for team-sport videos. Multimedia Syst. , 1–15 (2021). https://doi.org/10.1007/s00530-021-00777-7
16. Chen, F., Delannay, D., De Vleeschouwer, C.: An autonomous framework to produce and distribute personalized team-sport video summaries: a basketball case study. IEEE Trans. Multimedia 13(6), 1381–1394 (2011)
17. Sarlis, V., Tjortjis, C.: Sports analytics – evaluation of basketball players and team performance. Inf. Syst. 93(101562), 1–19 (2020)
18. Tian, C., De Silva, V., Caine, M., Swanson, S.: Use of machine learning to automate the identification of basketball strategies using whole team player tracking data. Appl. Sci. 10(1), 24 (2020)
19. Choroś, K., Paruszkiewicz, K.: Automatic detection of play and break segments in basketball videos based on the analysis of the slope of the basketball court boundary. In: Nguyen, N.T., Chbeir, R., Exposito, E., Aniorté, P., Trawiński, B. (eds.) ICCCI 2019. LNCS (LNAI), vol. 11684, pp. 639–648. Springer, Cham (2019). https://doi.org/10.1007/978-3-030-28374-2_55

20. Choroś, K.: Video structure analysis and content-based indexing in the automatic video indexer AVI. In: Nguyen, N.T., Zgrzywa, A., Czyżewski, A. (eds.) Advances in Multimedia and Network Information System Technologies, Advances in Intelligent and Soft Computing, AISC 80, Springer, Heidelberg, pp. 79–90 (2010). https://doi.org/10.1007/978-3-642-14989-4_8

21. Lucas, B.D., Kanade, T.: An iterative image registration technique with an application to stereo vision. In: Proceedings of the 7th International Joint Conference on Artificial Intelligence – IJCAI, pp. 674–679 (1981)

22. Shi, J., Tomasi, C.: Good features to track. In: Proceedings of the Computer Society Conference on Computer Vision and Pattern Recognition, pp. 593–600. IEEE (1994)

23. Bouguet, J.Y.: Pyramidal implementation of the affine Lucas Kanade feature tracker description of the algorithm. Intel Corpor. **5**, 1–10 (2001)

24. Han, B., Paulson, C., Lu, T., Wu, D., Li, J.: Tracking of multiple objects under partial occlusion. In: Automatic Target Recognition XIX, vol. 7335. International Society for Optics and Photonics, Orlando, Florida, USA (2009)

25. Shih, H.C.: A survey of content-aware video analysis for sports. IEEE Trans. Circuits Syst. Video Technol. **28**(5), 1212–1231 (2017)

26. Choroś, K.: Video structure analysis for content-based indexing and categorisation of TV sports news. Int. J. Intell. Inf. Database Syst. **6**(5), 451–465 (2012)

Hybrid UNET Model Segmentation for an Early Breast Cancer Detection Using Ultrasound Images

Ikram Ben Ahmed[1,3]($\boxtimes$) (iD), Wael Ouarda[2], and Chokri Ben Amar[3]

[1] Higher Institute of Computer Science and Communication Technology (IsitCom),
4011, Hammam Sousse, Sousse University, Sousse, Tunisia
benahmedikram@gmail.com

[2] Digital Research Center of Sfax (CRNS), Sakiet Ezzit, Tunisia
wael.ouarda@crns.rnrt.tn

[3] ReGIM-Lab- REsearch Groups in Intelligent Machines, National School
of Engineers (ENIS), Sfax University, 3038 Sfax, Tunisia
chokri.benamar@ieee.org

Abstract. In recent years, progress in breast cancer mortality reduction has slowed. The mortality rate was increasing and Breast cancer became the first cause of death for women. The early diagnosis is crucial in a treatment process as it may avoid the complications as well as the heavy treatment of the pathology. For this purpose, a lot of CAD systems were established. However, to provide more precise results, the later still needs to improve by incorporating new techniques. In this paper, we present a deep learning framework built on the U-Net architecture. A MobileNetV2 and a VGG16 model encoder have been used to handle the semantic segmentation of a biomedical image effectively. This approach is based on the integration of these pre-trained models with the UNet and having an efficient network architecture. By transfer learning, these CNNs are fine-tuned to segment Breast Ultrasound images in normal and tumoral pixels. An extensive experiment of our proposed architecture has been done using Breast Ultrasound Dataset B. Quantitative metrics for evaluation of segmentation results including Dice coefficient, Precision, Recall, and, all reached over 80%, which proves that the method proposed has the capacity to distinguish functional tissues in breast ultrasound images. Thus, our proposed method might have the potential to provide the segmentation necessary to assist the clinical diagnosis of breast cancer and improve imaging in other modes in medical ultrasound.

Keywords: Breast cancer · Unet · MobileNetV2 · Deep learning · VGG16 · Semantic segmentation

1 Introduction

Breast cancer is considered as the world's leading cause of death among different cancer sites in women [17]. Based on statistics, it is expected that more than eight percent of women would develop it in their lifetime [7].

© The Author(s), under exclusive license to Springer Nature Switzerland AG 2022
N. T. Nguyen et al. (Eds.): ICCCI 2022, LNAI 13501, pp. 464–476, 2022.
https://doi.org/10.1007/978-3-031-16014-1_37

Because of its high mortality rate, medical researchers have paid close attention to it. Accurate and early diagnosis is the key to prevent it [15]. Ultrasound imaging is a widely employed modality for screening to characterize breast masses due to the fact that they are non-radioactive, real-time visualization, relatively inexpensive price and non-invasive diagnosis. However, ultrasound is not a standalone modality, as it requires the engagement of experienced radiologists, and, usually a biopsy and the findings from US breast imaging are used to determine the diagnosis results [5, 9].

Opportunely, in recent years, CAD has immensely progressed and could be of great help to radiologists in the ultrasound based detection of breast cancer by having a more operator-independent nature of ultrasound imaging. Different studies that investigated the influence of CAD on diagnostics has shown that CAD is an essential tool to improve the diagnostic sensitivity and specificity. It also has been useful for medical personnel to diagnose and discriminate tumors for improved diagnostic accuracy. Thus, the most critical task for a CAD program is the ability to locate the lesion when assisting the doctor in mapping the region of the tumor. Therefore, the automatic segmentation of the tumor region from the breast ultrasound images with high accuracy is of primary importance. Furthermore, a high specificity and sensitivity are expected. With the progress of computer technology, since deep-learning approaches have surpassed traditional ones and become the predominant choices for breast ultrasound image segmentation [12], researchers have employed deep learning algorithms to improve the use of ultrasound in breast cancer diagnosis [6].

Therefore Deep learning has become a strong alternative for supervised image segmentation [4, 14]. Often features extracted automatically through CNNs outperform hand-crafted and pre-defined feature sets, they have been used to handle a variety of biomedical imaging problems, including medical image segmentation. Breast cancer diagnosis is one of the many areas that has taken advantage of artificial intelligence to achieve better performance, despite the fact that obtaining adequate training image datasets for machine learning algorithms can be challenging.

Transfer learning is a phenomenon that enables deep learning algorithms to overcome the issue of shortage of training data in constructing an efficient model by transferring knowledge from a given source task to a target task [1]. Although many studies have attempted to employ transfer learning in medical image analyses. Transfer learning is based on the principle that previously learned knowledge can be exceptionally implemented to solve new problems in a more efficient and effective manner [2, 3].

In this paper, based on the U-Net architecture, we proposed an improved method, to achieve precise tumor segmentation in breast ultrasound images. To the best of our knowledge, the first hybrid method combining two transfer learning approaches based on Unet model for ultrasound breast cancer image segmentation is proposed. Two approaches of transfer Learning were used, using a pre-trained VGG16 model to build the U-Net (VGG-Unet) and a pre-trained MobileNetV2 to built the (MB-Unet). We used pre-trained MobileNetV2 and

VGG16 as the encoder for the UNet architecture. We integrate these pre-trained CNNS as the encoder for the UNet architecture and have an efficient network architecture. These CNNs are trained on the ImageNet dataset, which is one of the largest and most popular dataset commonly used. The organizational structure of this paper is as follows. The related works are depicted in Sect. 2. Section 3 elaborates on our developed approaches. The experiments are exhaustively depicted in Sect. 4. Section 5 elaborates on the ablation studies. The conclusions are presented in Sect. 6.

2   Related Work

Several papers have been written on breast cancer detection and many approaches have been proposed. We review briefly deep learning approaches: transfer learning, ResNet, Mobilnet, U-Net, imaging with CNN, and fine-tuned VGG-Net. Several deep-learning models have been proposed, such as AlexNet [10], VGG [11], DenseNet [21] and Residual network [24], and they all have excellent performance in numerous areas. But the Fully Convolutional Networks (FCN) [18] provide superior performance when compared with other deep-learning models with respect to semantic medical image segmentation.

Yu et al. [22] proposed a novel method based on U-Net to improve the tumor segmentation accuracy in breast ultrasound images. At first, they introduced Res Path into the U-Net to reduce the difference between the feature maps of the encoder and decoder. Then, in order to alleviate the vanishing gradient problem and to reduce the feature information loss, they added a new connection, dense block from the input of the feature maps in the encoding to-decoding section. For training and testing models, a breast ultrasound database, which contains 538 tumor images, was used. The results demonstrated an overall improvement by the proposed approach when compared with the U-Net in terms of true-positive rate, false-positive rate, Hausdorff distance indices, Jaccard similarity, and Dice coefficients.

Xu at al. [19] carried out to use convolutional neural networks (CNNs) for segmenting breast ultrasound images into four main tissues: skin, mass, fibroglandular tissue, and fatty tissue, on three-dimensional (3D) breast ultrasound images. For evaluating the segmentation results, quantitative metrics including Accuracy, Precision, Recall, and, all reached over 80%, which indicates that their proposed method has the capacity to distinguish functional tissues in breast ultrasound images. The Jaccard similarity index (JSI) yields an 85.1% value, outperforming their previous study using the watershed algorithm with 74.54% JSI value.

Zhang1 et al. [23] proposed a multi-task learning (SHA-MTL) model based on soft and hard attention mechanisms for breast ultrasound (BUS) image simultaneous segmentation and binary classification. Their model consists of a dense CNN encoder and an upsampling decoder, which are connected by attention-gated (AG) units with soft attention mechanism. Cross-validation experiments are performed on BUS datasets with category and mask labels, and multiple comprehensive analyses are performed on the two tasks. They assess the SHA-MTL model on a public BUS image dataset. For the segmentation task, the sensitivity and DICE of the SHA-MTL model to the lesion regions increased by 2.27% and 1.19% compared with the single task model, respectively.

3   Proposed Approach

In this part, we first introduce the overview of our combined model. Then, we first depict the designed VGG-Unet and MB-Unet in detail. Finally, we will elaborate on the overall architecture of the developed models.

Since an encoder-decoder structure is effective for the segmentation task, we chose U-Net as the network architecture framework. It has a CNN structure that is first designed and outperformed in medical image segmentation tasks. It is an end-to-end, pixel-to-pixel fully convolutional network, allowing efficient whole-image-at-a-time learning and dense prediction for per-pixel semantic segmentation. In our work, We adopted the basic U-Net architecture framework [13].We combined the idea of transfer learning like illustrated in Fig. 1 into U-Net with two approaches which are VGG-Unet and MB-Unet.

Figure 4 illustrates some images of the base B with its corresponding masks.

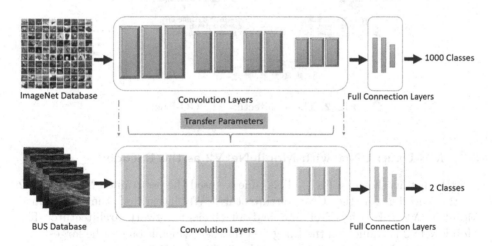

Fig. 1. Illustrations of transfer learning: The parameters are transferred in all layers from Conv1 to Conv5.

3.1   VGG-Unet: UNet with VGG16 as the Encoder

In VGG-Unet, as shown in Fig. 2 We are going to replace the UNET encoder with the VGG16 implementation from the TensorFlow library. The UNET encoder would learn the features from scratch, while the VGG16 is already trained on the Image ImageNet classification dataset. Therefore VGG16 has already learned enough features, which improves the overall performance of the network.

To resemble the VGG16 into a symmetrical U-Net structure, the last three fully connected layers were excluded and new layers for the expanding path were added. The expanding path worked reversely to the VGG16, with up-sampling through deconvolution by transposed conv layers. In order to reuse the features and retain more information from previous layers, we used Concatenated skip connections to connect blocks of the same filter size from the contracting path to expanding it.

For mapping the feature vector from 0 to 1, we used a 1×1 conv layer with sigmoid activation as the last layer. Also we used a threshold value of 0.5 to convert all pixels with values above 0.5 to 1 and pixels with values below 0.5 to 0, Due to the binary nature of the feature masks. The whole network had 25,862,337 parameters in total.

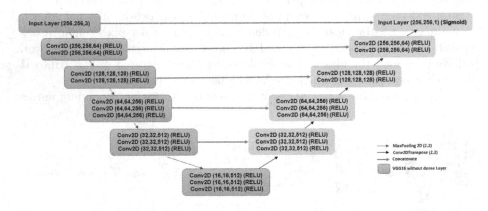

Fig. 2. The architecture of VGG-Unet.

3.2   MB-Unet: UNet with MobileNetV2 as the Encoder

In MB-Unet, as shown in Fig. 3, This time we used the pre-trained MobileNetV2 as the encoder for the UNet architecture. We integrated the pre-trained MobileNetV2 with the UNet and had an efficient network architecture. The MobileNetV2 is trained on the ImageNet dataset, which is one of the largest and most popular dataset commonly used.the MobileNetV2 consists of two types of blocks. One is residual block with stride of 1, and the other one is a block with stride of 2 for downsizing. Both blocks possess three layers .

The first layer is 1 * 1 convolution with ReLU, and the second layer is the depth-wise convolution. The third layer is another 1 * 1 convolution, but, without any non linearity. We chose MobileNetV2 since it has less parameters, due to which it is easy to train. Using a pre-trained encoder helps the model to converge much faster in comparison to the non-pretrained model. A pre-trained encoder helps the model to achieve high performance as compared to a non pre-trained model.

Type	Stride	Filter Size	Input Size
Convolution	2 × 2	3 × 3 × 3 × 32	224 × 224 × 3
Convolution dw	1 × 1	3 × 3 × 32	112 × 112 × 32
Convolution	1 × 1	1 × 1 × 32 × 64	112 × 112 × 32
Convolution dw	2 × 2	3 × 3 × 64	112 × 112 × 64
Convolution	1 × 1	1 × 1 × 64 × 128	56 × 56 × 64
Convolution dw	1 × 1	3 × 3 × 128	56 × 56 × 128
Convolution	1 × 1	1 × 1 × 128 × 128	56 × 56 × 128
Convolution dw	2 × 2	3 × 3 × 128	56 × 56 × 128
Convolution	1 × 1	1 × 1 × 128 × 256	28 × 28 × 128
Convolution dw	1 × 1	3 × 3 × 256	28 × 28 × 256
Convolution	1 × 1	1 × 1 × 256 × 256	28 × 28 × 256
Convolution dw	2 × 2	3 × 3 × 256	28 × 28 × 256
Convolution	1 × 1	1 × 1 × 256 × 512	14 × 14 × 256
5 × Convolution dw	1 × 1	3 × 3 × 512	14 × 14 × 512
5 × Convolution	1 × 1	1 × 1 × 512 × 512	14 × 14 × 512

Fig. 3. General structure and parameters of MobileNetV2 architecture

4   Experimentation

4.1   Database

The performance of our method is verified on an open public dataset of breast ultrasound images known as Dataset B. Dataset B [20] was collected in 2012 from the UDIAT Diagnostic Centre of the Parc Tauli Corporation, Sabadell (Spain) with a Siemens ACUSON Sequoia C512 system 17L5 HD linear array transducer (8.5 MHz).

The dataset consists of 163 images from different women with a mean image size of 760×570 pixels, where each of the images presented one or more lesions. Within the 163 lesion images, 53 were images with cancerous masses and 110 with benign lesions.

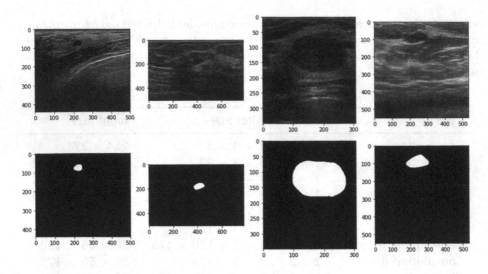

Fig. 4. Several US images and their corresponding mask From dataset B.

4.2 Experiments

The choice of evaluation metrics are very important in domain of Artificial Intelligence for Biomedical or Health Care. Considering the sensitivity of Breast Cancer research, we have evaluated our Breast Cancer Detection models efficiency by incorporating below mentioned metrics:

- True Positive (TP): The case when patient is actually suffering from the cancer and the model also classified as positive.
- False Positive (FP): The case when patient is not suffering from the cancer but the model classified as positive.
- True Negative (TN): The case when patient is not suffering from the cancer and the model also classified as negative.
- False Negative (FN): The case when patient is actually suffering from the cancer but the model classified as negative.
- Accuracy: It defines correctly identified category of Breast Cancer. It is defined as:
  Displayed equations are centered and set on a separate line.

$$Accuracy = \frac{TP + TN}{TP + FP + TN + FN} \tag{1}$$

- Recall/True-Positive Rate: It is defined as the ratio of amount of samples that have been correctly predicted corresponding all of samples in the data. It can defined as
  Displayed equations are centered and set on a separate line.

$$Recall = \frac{TP}{TP + FN} \tag{2}$$

- Precision: It is defined as the ratio of amount of samples that have been correctly predicted corresponding all samples of the particular category. It can defined as
Displayed equations are centered and set on a separate line.

$$Precision = \frac{TP}{TP + FP} \tag{3}$$

- The IOU metric: It is a measure for how close our prediction is to the true label. We'll use this value to determine whether or not our mask prediction was "successful", as defined by having an IOU score above some specified threshold.

Quantitative Evaluation: In order to find the right combination of parameters to have a good segmentation, we change each time the number of epochs and other times the batch's size. As shown in Table 1, each time the batch size is increased, the value of the loss increases and consequently the value of the precision and of the dice coefficient decreases. We then conclude after several experiments that the good combination for the two proposed models VGG-UNET and MB-UNET is 100 as number of epochs and 8 as batch size.

As shown in the Table 2, we tried each time to modify the number of epochs on the one hand and the batch size on the other hand in order to improve the segmentation of the tumor and to have a better delineation. Secondly, we tried to change the value of the alpha parameter in our proposed MB-UNET architecture. The role of the alpha parameter is controlling the width of the network. This is known as the width multiplier in the MobileNet.

- If alpha < 1.0, proportionally decreases the number of filters in each layer.
- If alpha > 1.0, proportionally increases the number of filters in each layer.
- If alpha = 1, default number of filters from the paper are used at each layer. Default to 1.0.

At first time we chooses alpha = 0.35 and second case we chooses alpha = 0.5. We obtained better results with alpha = 0.35, as shown in Table 3.

Our proposed VGG-UNET model surpasses, in terms of precision, the values given by the UNET model and other architectures such as Resnet 50, DensNet 161 and VGG-16 by a value of 0.9394. The table below (Table 4) shows the best variation's curves for the loss, recall, dice coefficient and precision values of the VGG-UNET model.

Qualitative Evaluation: In our experiments, breast ultrasound image segmentation was trained and tested using the GPU of the google collaboratory. Table 5 illustrates the segmentation results of our two proposed models which are the VGG-UNET and MB-UNET side by side with the original images, their ground truth image and the original UNET model segmentation result. As shown in the figure VGG-UNET has the better segmentation.

Table 1. Loss vs Dice coefficient and recall vs precision values in training experiments for the study of MB-UNET behavior by varying the epoch number and the batch size

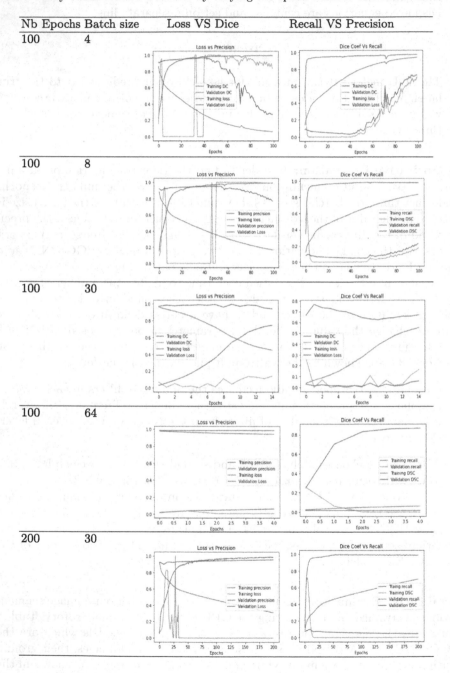

Nb Epochs	Batch size	Loss VS Dice	Recall VS Precision
100	4		
100	8		
100	30		
100	64		
200	30		

Table 2. Variation of the alpha parameter during MB-UNET training: alpha = 0.35 and alpha 0.5 for 100 epochs and batch size = 4

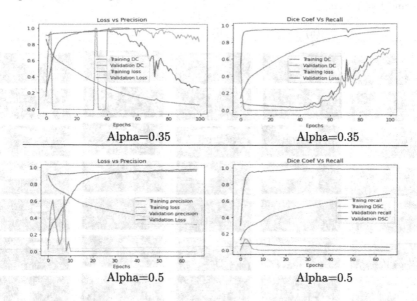

Table 3. VGG-UNET model: Best result with epochs number =100 and batch size = 8.

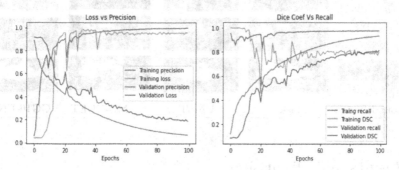

Table 4. The average result of all our models. Loss, Dice coefficient, recall and precision, for segmentation compared to [8]. Bold indicates the best result.

	Time/s	s/Step	Loss	Dice_coef	Recall	Precision
DenseNet_161	–	–	–	0.8957	0.6959	0.7833
VGG-16	–	–	–	0.9834	0.7364	0.8073
ResNet-50	–	–	–	0.8102	0.7500	0.8810
UNET	1	0.544	0.1936	0.8064	0.7288	**0.9104**
VGG_UNET	8	4	0.1902	0.8098	0.7751	**0.9384**
MB_UNET	5	1	0.3573	0.6427	0.5734	**0.8527**

Table 5. Representative segmentation results using original image (a) mask image (b), UNET (c) predicted MB-UNET image (d) and predicted VGG-UNET image for 100 epochs and batch size = 8

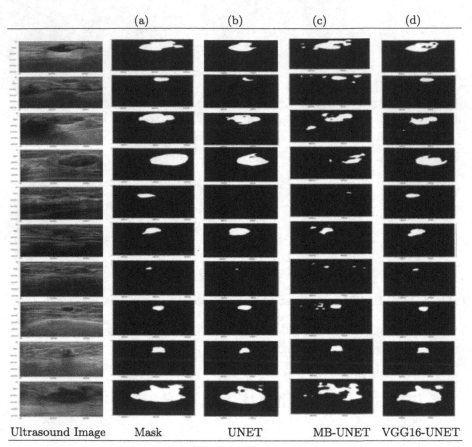

	(a)	(b)	(c)	(d)
	Ultrasound Image	Mask	UNET	MB-UNET	VGG16-UNET

5   Results and Discussion

It is evident that transfer learning has been included in various application areas of ultrasound imaging analyses [16]. Although, there still exists room for improvement. Transfer learning methods have evermore been improving the existing capabilities of machine learning in terms of different aspects for breast ultrasound analyses.

In this work, aimed at the problem that original U-Net model performed poorly with a low segmentation accuracy when used in the auxiliary diagnostic system for breast tumor segmentation, we proposed an improved model based on U-Net. The main reason for the low performance is the large semantic differences and the vanishing gradient problem of the U-Net. The Both VGG-Unet and MB-Unet exhibited the importance of transfer learning and fine tuning by having significant improvements in DICEs coefficient which can also be visualized from our two hybrid model prediction comparison of the original Unet.

However, VGG-Unet model is generally very vulnerable to artifacts and outlines that cannot be reflected from its high DICE. It may be due to the fact that an learning rate of 10–4 for transfer learning is too large in VGG-Unet, causing the model to converge too quickly without fully learning and adapting to the edge details of breast ultrasound images. Future investigation can implement adaptive learning rate through callbacks during training.

6 Conclusion

This paper uses segmentation method to detect breast cancer lesions from ultrasound images. Two variant of UNET called VGG-UNET and MB-UNET was proposed for breast tumor segmentation. The performance of our proposed method is validated on Ultrasound breast dataset B and evaluation metrics use in the segmentation method are Loss, dice coefficient, precision and recall. The obtained results shows that proposed models produces more accurate and better outputs than the UNET model.

Lesion detection is the initial step of a CAD system. Hence, future work will focus on increasing the accuracy by adding more training data, extending our works to breast ultrasound lesion segmentation and classification, and evaluate the performance of the complete CAD framework. Another modality images like mammography need to be tested, and why not combined with the ultrasound modality.

References

1. Ayana, G., Dese, K., Choe, S.W.: Transfer learning in breast cancer diagnoses via ultrasound imaging. Cancers **13**(4), 738 (2021)
2. Basly, H., Ouarda, W., Sayadi, F.E., Ouni, B., Alimi, A.M.: Lahar-CNN: human activity recognition from one image using convolutional neural network learning approach. Int. J. Biomet. **13**(4), 385–408 (2021)
3. Basly, H., Ouarda, W., Sayadi, F.E., Ouni, B., Alimi, A.M.: DTR-HAR: deep temporal residual representation for human activity recognition. Vis. Comput. **38**(3), 993–1013 (2022)
4. Ben Ayed, I., et al.: Srd5a3-CDG: 3D structure modeling, clinical spectrum, and computer-based dysmorphic facial recognition. Am. J. Med. Genet. A **185**(4), 1081–1090 (2021)
5. Boca, I., Ciurea, A.I., Ciortea, C.A., Dudea, S.M.: Pros and cons for automated breast ultrasound (ABUS): a narrative review. J. Personalized Med. **11**(8), 703 (2021)
6. Burt, J.R., et al.: Deep learning beyond cats and dogs: recent advances in diagnosing breast cancer with deep neural networks. Br. J. Radiol. **91**(1089), 20170545 (2018)
7. Cheng, H.D., Shan, J., Ju, W., Guo, Y., Zhang, L.: Automated breast cancer detection and classification using ultrasound images: a survey. Pattern Recogn. **43**(1), 299–317 (2010)

8. Dizaj, S.B., Valizadeh, P.: Breast cancer segmentation and classification in ultrasound images using convolutional neural network (2021)
9. Geisel, J., Raghu, M., Hooley, R.: The role of ultrasound in breast cancer screening: the case for and against ultrasound. In: Seminars in Ultrasound, CT and MRI, vol. 39, pp. 25–34. Elsevier (2018)
10. Ilesanmi, A.E., Chaumrattanakul, U., Makhanov, S.S.: A method for segmentation of tumors in breast ultrasound images using the variant enhanced deep learning. Biocybern. Biomed. Eng. **41**(2), 802–818 (2021)
11. Inan, M.S.K., Alam, F.I., Hasan, R.: Deep integrated pipeline of segmentation guided classification of breast cancer from ultrasound images. Biomed. Signal Process. Control **75**, 103553 (2022)
12. Liu, S., et al.: Deep learning in medical ultrasound analysis: a review. Engineering **5**(2), 261–275 (2019)
13. Ronneberger, O., Fischer, P., Brox, T.: U-Net: convolutional networks for biomedical image segmentation. In: Navab, N., Hornegger, J., Wells, W.M., Frangi, A.F. (eds.) MICCAI 2015. LNCS, vol. 9351, pp. 234–241. Springer, Cham (2015). https://doi.org/10.1007/978-3-319-24574-4_28
14. Sassi, A., Ouarda, W., Amar, C.B., Miguet, S.: Sky-CNN: a CNN-based learning approach for skyline scene understanding. Int. J, Intell. Syst. Appl. **4**, 14–25 (2019)
15. Seely, J., Alhassan, T.: Screening for breast cancer in 2018-what should we be doing today? Curr. Oncol. **25**(s1), 115–124 (2018)
16. Siddique, N., Paheding, S., Elkin, C.P., Devabhaktuni, V.: U-net and its variants for medical image segmentation: a review of theory and applications. IEEE Access (2021)
17. Siegel, R.L., Miller, K.D., Jemal, A.: Cancer statistics. CA: Can. J. Clin. **68**(1), 7–30 (2018)
18. Subuhana, N., Rega, A., Sundar, S.: Deep learning techniques for breast cancer analysis: a review. In: 2021 Fourth International Conference on Microelectronics, Signals & Systems (ICMSS), pp. 1–6. IEEE (2021)
19. Xu, Y., Wang, Y., Yuan, J., Cheng, Q., Wang, X., Carson, P.L.: Medical breast ultrasound image segmentation by machine learning. Ultrasonics **91**, 1–9 (2019)
20. Yap, M.H., et al.: Automated breast ultrasound lesions detection using convolutional neural networks. IEEE J. Biomed. Health Inform. **22**(4), 1218–1226 (2017)
21. Yifeng, D., Yufeng, Z., Bingbing, H., Zhiyao, L., Yuxin, Z.: Semantic segmentation with densenets for breast tumor detection. In: 2021 9th International Conference on Communications and Broadband Networking, pp. 54–59 (2021)
22. Yu, K., Chen, S., Chen, Y.: Tumor segmentation in breast ultrasound image by means of res path combined with dense connection neural network. Diagnostics **11**(9), 1565 (2021)
23. Zhang, G., Zhao, K., Hong, Y., Qiu, X., Zhang, K., Wei, B.: SHA-MTL: soft and hard attention multi-task learning for automated breast cancer ultrasound image segmentation and classification. Int. J. Comput. Assist. Radiol. Surg. **16**(10), 1719–1725 (2021)
24. Zhao, T., Dai, H.: Research on automatic location of seed points in ultrasound breast tumor images based on fuzzy logic algorithm. In: 2021 International Conference on Aviation Safety and Information Technology, pp. 758–762 (2021)

Multiple-criteria-Based Object Pose Tracking in RGB Videos

Mateusz Majcher and Bogdan Kwolek[✉]

AGH University of Science and Technology, 30 Mickiewicza, 30-059 Krakow, Poland
bkw@agh.edu.pl

Abstract. In this work, a multi-criteria analysis is leveraged to improve object pose tracking in RGB videos on the basis of keypoints and object shape. A quaternion representing object pose in the previous frame and RGB image in the current frame are fed to a multi-input neural network that predicts 2D locations for a set of predefined 3D object keypoints. The shape features are utilized to exclude keypoints, which are not consistent with object shape. We demonstrate experimentally that by combining shape information with sparse object keypoints considerable gains in tracking accuracy can be achieved in least-squares-based pose refinement. Owing to multiple-criteria decision-making and harnessing such object representations, the proposed method gains significant performance improvements on the OPT benchmark and achieves promising results on challenging YCB-Video dataset.

Keywords: Intelligent image processing · Machine learning · Multiple objective decision-making

1 Introduction

Estimating 6D object poses (i.e. 3D translation and 3D rotation) in cluttered scenes is an important yet challenging task. Recent methods for household objects pose estimation usually use a single RGB image [1], RGBD image [2,3], or multi-view images [4]. Depth maps simplify recovering the scale of the object. Typically, methods that employ depth information permit achieving higher accuracies in comparison to methods that are based on RGB images only. Since recovering object scale from single RGB images is not easy, 6D pose estimation from RGB images is a challenging problem. In practice, recovering the 6DoF pose from a single RGB image is an ill-posed problem. For instance, in an early work [5], an approach to marginalize object coordinate distributions over depth was proposed in order to cope with missing information about object scale. To determine the object scale without ambiguity, most RGB-based pose estimation approaches learn a prior on the basis of 3D object models, which permit leveraging the geometry in the estimation.

With the advent of deep learning approaches, rapid progress on the task of object pose estimation has been achieved [6]. Two main directions have emerged

© The Author(s), under exclusive license to Springer Nature Switzerland AG 2022
N. T. Nguyen et al. (Eds.): ICCCI 2022, LNAI 13501, pp. 477–490, 2022.
https://doi.org/10.1007/978-3-031-16014-1_38

for data-driven 6DoF object pose estimation: direct pose regression and indirect ones. Regression-based methods utilize convolutional neural networks to perform direct pose estimation from an input image, where the model is learned thanks to given mapping from the training images to their ground-truth 6DoF poses. PoseCNN [7] is a complex architecture that tackles the pose estimation problem in end-to-end manner through three related tasks: semantic labeling, prediction of translation from the estimated 2D object center, and rotation inference. There are also end-to-end methods that perform quantization of the continuous pose space and conduct classification rather than regression [1]. Indirect approaches usually determine sparse or dense 2D-3D correspondences and then leverage a variant of the RANSAC-based PnP algorithm to determine the object pose. They estimate the pose either by training a model to predict the corresponding 3D coordinates for object pixels [8] or detect some pre-defined semantic keypoints from the input image [9–12]. Object occlusions can lead to drop in accuracy of keypoint-based methods for pose estimation. In a seminal approach [10] in order to coarsely segment out the object a deep network is executed first, and then in order to establish 2D-3D correspondences another network that is responsible for prediction of 2D projections of the 3D bounding box corners is employed. Given 2D-3D correspondences, the 6DoF pose is recovered using the PnP algorithm.

Object pose tracking approaches recover object pose with the help of information from the previous frame [6]. Usually, in scenarios in which statistical properties of foreground and background are distinctively different, region-based methods are capable of achieving competing results. Since region-based approaches calculate the 3D object pose only from 2D silhouette, they suffer from pose ambiguities. In more complex scenarios with tracking heterogeneous objects in cluttered backgrounds, where the variation of foreground and background statistics takes place, their performance strongly degrades [13]. Through conditioning orientation estimation on translation, a recently proposed Rao–Blackwellized particle filter (PoseRBPF) [14] can effectively represent complex uncertainty distributions over the space of 6D object poses. The discussed PoseRBPF also delivers uncertainty information about the tracked object's pose. In a refinement-based approach [15] the object pose is refined by a neural network in a single forward pass which results in coarse pose estimates. A recently proposed DeepIM [16] exploits optical flow to adjust initial pose estimation via minimization of differences between the 2D re-projection of the 3D model and the object appearance. A pretrained FlowNet [17], which is designed for two image inputs has been utilized to determine optical flow. DeepIM gradually learns to match the pose of the object by iteratively re-rendering the target such that the two input images that are fed to the network become more and more similar. DeepIM requires a large number of real-world images for training and it has considerable computational requirements. In [18] a single neural network for a set of objects is trained to estimate the location of object keypoints using object pose from the previous frame and current RGB image. The pose is determined using keypoints that are generated on separated output maps to get corresponding 3D points and then match them by the least-squares.

As mentioned above, indirect approaches usually rely on sparse or dense keypoints, which are determined by a deep neural network. To the best of our knowledge, currently there exist almost no significant work demonstrating significant improvements as a result of using the object shape in a deep learning-based framework.

In this work, we present a shape-aware algorithm for object pose tracking in RGB videos. Given the current RGB image and the estimated rotation in the last frame, a neural network determines the 2D locations of nine object keypoints. The initial pose guess is determined by a PnP algorithm. We demonstrate experimentally that by leveraging a multi-criteria analysis on shape information and sparse object keypoints considerable gains in tracking accuracy can be achieved in least-squares-based pose refinement. By harnessing such object representations, the proposed method gains significant performance improvements on the OPT benchmark and achieves promising results on challenging YCB-Video dataset. On the OPT dataset it outperforms recently published region-based methods except one that is based on contour energy. However, such region-based methods including contour-based methods are only suitable for simpler scenarios than those in the YCB-Video dataset.

2 Method

The aim of object pose estimation is to predict the 3D position and 3D rotation of an object in camera-centered coordinates. Algorithms for object pose tracking take advantages of the temporal consistency among video frames. Given an RGB image acquired by a calibrated camera as well as object rotation determined in the previous frame, our algorithm estimates the 3D object pose. We assume that the object to be tracked is rigid and its 3D model is available. The initial object pose that is determined by a PnP is used as a starting pose guess for an optimizer responsible for refinement of the object pose. The 2D locations for a set of predefined 3D object keypoints are determined by Y-Net [18]. This mixed-input neural network operates on RGB images acquired in time t and quaternions representing object rotation in time $t - 1$. This way we utilize temporal consistency among video frames at the pose level. Information about object rotation in the previous frame permits layers in the quaternion branch to learn attention blobs representing positions of object keypoints as well as *geometry* among them. It guides the model to explicitly reason about the 2D location of sparse keypoints in the current frame. The neural network generates blobs, whose centers represent 2D positions of the object keypoints. The sparse keypoints are generated on separate output channels. Each object keypoint is generated on a specific channel to provide 2D-3D correspondences. The keypoints are then fed to a PnP that is responsible for determining the initial pose of the object, see Fig. 1. Such an initial pose of the object is refined by the Levenberg-Marguardt (LM) algorithm. The objective function of LM algorithm contains component expressing matching between the estimated keypoints and reprojected keypoints as in [18], and additionally a component expressing fitting between object shape and projected outline of the 3D model. Additionally, with the help of the object shape a multiple-criteria decision making is performed to decide which keypoints are of low confidence, i.e. should be excluded from the set of keypoints, which is then fed to the LM for extra pose refinement, see also Fig. 1. This way the 6D pose is determined via the PnP algorithm from the best set of points, which are consistent to the object shape, i.e. with reduced outliers.

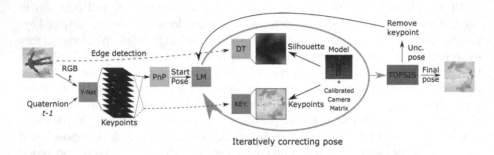

Fig. 1. Algorithm for 6D object tracking in sequences of RGB images.

Non-linear optimization-based methods allow pose refinement by optimizing the residual between reprojected 3D points on the model and corresponding points on the image. The Levenberg-Marquardt algorithm, also known as the damped least-squares is one of the most preferred methods for object pose refinement. It utilizes an adaptive parameter to switch between gradient descent and Newton - Raphson in an adaptive way, which permits convergence to a local extremum (a local minimum or local maximum). LM algorithm needs a good initial solution, otherwise a poor initialization can cause the optimization to get stuck in a local extremum. The optimization stops if the algorithm has exceeded the limit of function evaluations or has met any of the desired convergence criteria. In this work, the error is calculated on the basis of nine manually selected object keypoints and the object shape. The shape of the 3D model is projected onto the image plane and then the values of a distance transform at the projected locations are summed. The initial pose guess is determined by the EPnP algorithm [19]. The distance transform (DT) is calculated using a CUDA-based implementation [20].

The object rotations are represented by unit quaternions. A unit quaternion $\mathbf{q} \in \mathbb{R}^4$, where $\mathbf{q} = [q_0, q_1, q_2, q_3]^T = \pm[\cos\frac{\theta}{2}, \mathbf{u}^2 \sin\frac{\theta}{2}]^T = [w \ \mathbf{v}]^T$, and $\|\mathbf{q}\| = 1$ represents a rotation of angle θ around the axis $\mathbf{u}$. Since $\mathbf{q}$ and $-\mathbf{q}$ represent the same rotation, enforcing $q_0 \geq 0$ leads to one-to-one correspondence between the quaternion and the rotation matrix, and $\theta \in [0, \pi]$. Quaternion rotations do not suffer from gimbal lock. In this work, the state vector assumes the following form: $\mathbf{x} = [\mathbf{q} \ \mathbf{z}]$, where $\mathbf{q}$ is the unit quaternion representing object rotation and $\mathbf{z}$ is a 3D translation vector.

The objective function assumes the following form:

$$L_{loss} = \sum_{n=1}^{9} \|key_{Pose}^n - key_{Net}^n\|_2^2 + \gamma \Big(\frac{1}{|E|} \sum_{e \in E} D(e) \Big)^2, \qquad (1)$$

where key_{Net}^n is 2D position of n keypoint detected by the Y-Net and rescaled to a reference plane, key_{Pose}^n is a projected keypoint of the 3D model in the actual pose, rescaled to the reference plane, whereas E is a set of pixels representing the silhouette of the object in the actual pose and rescaled to reference plane and $D(e)$ is a function which returns a value of distance transform at the location e, and γ is a factor that has been determined experimentally. The aim of projecting the object shape onto the reference plane is to keep roughly the same object size despite different distances of the object to the camera and thus to normalize values of the DT transform. The projection of keypoints onto the reference plane permits the use of predefined distances to object outline for detection of keypoints protruding beyond the object. In order to cope with incorrectly predicted keypoints, which can have a significant impact on pose prediction, we have proposed multi-criteria decision-making to select the keypoints which should be skipped during additional pose refinement. This is based on multiple objective decision-making, or more precisely on a Technique for Order Preference by Similarity to an Ideal Solution (TOPSIS) [21]. In our approach each keypoint has assigned two values that indicate the uncertainty during decision-making. Firstly, using the obtained position of keypoints, we take into account the value of a pixel from the heatmap representing a particular keypoint. The higher the value, the more certain the keypoint is. Secondly, the distance from keypoint to the nearest point of the contour is determined by the distance transform. Contrary to the first value, the keypoint is more significant when the second value is lower. Then, during the decision-making, the scores for each criterion are normalized and the geometric distance is calculated between each alternative and the ideal alternative, which is the best score in each criterion. Similarly, it is done for the worst condition. Then, the keypoints are ranked according to similarity to positive and negative ideal solutions. This kind of decision-making allows for situations where a poor result in one criterion can be negated by a good result in another.

3   Experimental Results

The accuracy of 6-DoF object pose tracking has been evaluated using ADD score (Average Distance of Model Points) [2]. ADD is used to compute the averaged Euclidean distance between points transformed using the ground truth pose and the estimated pose. It is calculated in the following manner:

$$ADD = avg_{x \in M} \|(Rx + t) - (\hat{R}x + \hat{t})\|_2 \qquad (2)$$

where M is a set of all 3D object model points, t and R are the translation and rotation of a ground truth transformation, respectively, whereas $\hat{t}$ and $\hat{R}$ correspond to those of the estimated transformation. Following [2] we compute the distance between all pairs of points from the model and consider the maximum distance as the diameter d of this model. Then a pose estimation is considered to be correct if the average distance is within 10% of the model diameter.

At the beginning, we evaluated our algorithm on the freely available OPT dataset [22], which is used to benchmark algorithms for tracking the 6D pose of the objects. It includes RGB image sequences that were recorded under various lighting conditions, different motion patterns and speeds using a camera mounted on a programmable robotic arm. It contains six objects: House, Ironman, Jet, Bike, Chest, and Soda. The dataset includes seven settings: x-y translation, z translation, in-plane rotation, out-of-plane rotation, flash light, moving light, and free motion. The most challenging is the free motion scenario, in which an object moves in arbitrary directions, whereas in translation and rotation scenarios the objects move at five different speed levels, from slow to fast one. Because the discussed dataset does not contain keypoint data, for each object we added nine keypoints on the corresponding 3D models and then on the basis of the ground-truth data we generated 2D locations of the keypoints.

Table 1 presents reprojection errors in terms of 5 px scores [5] that were obtained on the OPT dataset for keypoints estimated by our network. The discussed error score expresses how close the 2D projected vertices are to the ground-truth. As we can observe, the largest reprojection error is for the House object. The errors achieved by the network with no information about object rotation in the previous frame are significantly larger.

Table 1. Reprojection error 5 px scores [%] achieved by our algorithm on the OPT dataset.

OPT obj.	House	Iron	Jet	Bike	Chest	Soda
5px score (no quat.) [%]	71.0	83.5	77.0	83.0	80.3	81.1
5px score [%]	74.8	90.2	82.9	90.0	85.9	86.7

The ADD scores that have been obtained on the OPT dataset are summarized in Table 2. As we can observe, the ADD scores for the House objects assume high values despite low 5 px scores. The discussed ADD scores have been achieved in the free motion scenario.

Next, we compared ADD scores achieved by three different modules for pose estimation on the basis of keypoints determined by our network. We compared the scores achieved by (i) PnP algorithm, (ii) LM initialized with pose determined by the PnP algorithm and fitness score calculated on the basis of keypoints fitting, and (iii) LM initialized as previously by with fitness function calculated the object shape and keypoints selected in the decision making. Experimental results are shown in Table 3. As we can observe, the algorithm using the object shape and the selected object keypoints achieves superior results for ADD 10% and ADD 20%.

Table 2. ADD scores [%] achieved by our algorithm on the OPT dataset.

ADD [%]	House	Iron	Jet	Bike	Chest	Soda
Beh., ADD 10%	76	74	63	76	76	55
Beh., ADD 20%	90	93	81	94	94	72
Left, ADD 10%	93	75	73	78	50	49
Left, ADD 20%	100	94	95	98	90	83
Right, ADD 10%	74	90	86	77	71	47
Right, ADD 20%	98	98	94	99	96	100
Front, ADD 10%	92	96	72	49	83	89
Front, ADD 20%	100	100	91	84	98	97
Avg., ADD 10%	84	84	74	70	70	60
Avg., ADD 20%	97	96	91	94	95	88

Table 3. ADD scores [%] achieved by our algorithm on the OPT dataset.

Avg. ADD [%]	House	Iron	Jet	Bike	Chest	Soda	avg.
PnP, ADD 10%	76	80	65	62	55	53	65
Key. LM, ADD 10%	81	81	71	66	59	45	67
Our alg., ADD 10%	**84**	**84**	**74**	**70**	**70**	**60**	**74**
PnP, ADD 20%	**97**	95	88	93	85	84	90
Key. LM, ADD 20%	95	95	88	93	86	84	90
Our alg., ADD 20%	**97**	**96**	**91**	**94**	**95**	**88**	**94**

Figure 2 demonstrates usefulness of object shape in estimating the 6DoF pose. As we can observe at bottom left image, due to fast motion of the robotic arm with camera mounted on it, the image is contaminated by motion blur. This in turn resulted in not enough precise localizations of keypoints and in consequence poor PnP-based object pose estimate. Through analysis of the reprojected 3D object boundary and overlaid on the image, see blue contour, it is clear that this will result in large shape-based error. As we can observe on the plot, the objective function combining both keypoints and shape permits the LM to considerably improve the accuracy of pose estimation. It is worth noting that most approaches to 6D object pose estimation neglect object shape.

Table 4 presents AUC scores (Area Under Curve) achieved on the OPT Dataset and compared against results that were achieved by recent methods. As already mentioned above, the free motion scenario is far more challenging in comparison to other scenarios. As we can observe, the algorithm [23], which is the region-based algorithm achieves superior results for three objects. The average AUC score is slightly better than AUC score achieved by our algorithm. The best AUC score is achieved by [24], which is also a region-based algorithm. As mentioned previously, the performance of region-based algorithms degrade in real-scenarios in which, usually, there are strong variations of foreground and background statistics. By including in the objective function a component expressing fitness between object shape and re-projected shape of the 3D model the AUC score is far better, c.f. results in the last two rows.

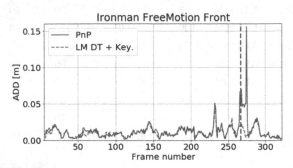

Fig. 2. ADD score [m] vs. frame number for the Ironman object in free motion scenario (top), images in frame #267 with reprojected 3D model outline for pose estimates determined on the basis of the EPnP and the LM with objective function combining keypoints and object shape (bottom).

Table 4. AUC scores on OPT Dataset [22] compared against results achieved by recent methods (best scores are in bold, second-best scores are underlined).

AUC score [%]	Scenario	House	Iron	Jet	Bike	Chest	Soda	avg.
PWP3D [25]	All tests	3.58	3.92	5.81	5.36	5.55	5.87	5.02
UDP [5]	All tests	5.97	5.25	2.34	6.10	6.79	8.49	5.82
ElasticFusion [26]	All tests	2.70	1.69	1.86	1.57	1.53	1.90	1.88
Reg. G-N. TPAMI [27]	All tests	10.15	_11.99_	_13.22_	11.90	11.76	8.86	11.31
Region-based TIP [23]	All tests	13.61	11.21	**15.44**	**12.83**	**12.24**	_9.01_	12.39
Contour energy & keyp. [24]	free M	–	–	–	–	–	–	**13.91**
ph. enh. edge [28]	free M	_13.70_	10.86	–	–	9.77	–	11.44
Quat-driven [18]	free M	12.52	11.98	12.16	10.31	8.04	8.71	10.62
Our method	free M	**13.98**	**13.99**	12.84	_12.40_	_11.77_	**10.48**	_12.58_

Data for the training of the neural network have been acquired from in-plain rotation and out-of-plane rotation scenarios. The network has been trained on such 2520 RGB images from 24 videos. Each of the four sides of each object contains 323 test frames. This means that the OPT dataset has been evaluated on $6 \times 1292 = 7752$ frames from the free motion scenario. The tracking scores that are presented in the above tables are averages of three independent runs of the algorithm with unlike initializations.

Afterwards, we evaluated our algorithm on YCB-Video dataset [7], which is a large-scale video dataset for 6D object pose estimation. It has been used also in a few recent works to track the object pose. The dataset provides accurate 6D poses of 21 objects of varying shape and texture observed in 92 videos. The videos are annotated with poses and segmentation masks. Following the evaluation protocol, we divided the dataset into 80 videos for training and 12 videos for testing. For training of the neural network, we additionally utilized 80K synthetically rendered images that are released with the dataset. Table 5 compares results achieved by our algorithm against results achieved by recent algorithms on this very challenging dataset. As we can observe, our algorithm achieves competitive results on the considered objects. It achieved better results in comparison to PoseRBPF [14] and competitive results compared to DeepIM [16], which similarly to our algorithm permit tracking of 6D object pose in sequences of RGB maps. For ten objects the results achieved by our algorithm were better than those achieved by the DeepIM algorithm. It is worth noting that DeepIM requires a pretrained model and has considerable computational overheads. Most methods estimate the object pose on single RGB images and do not take advantages of the temporal consistency among video frames. Temporal consistency is a very important cue, which is commonly observed and utilized in robotic and several relevant areas.

Figure 3 depicts qualitative results for sample objects from YCB-Video dataset. Example images depict how our algorithm handles occlusions, objects in various poses, and lighting conditions. As we can see, the algorithm permits achieving promising results.

Figure 4 contains plots of ADD scores vs. frame number that have been obtained for the considered objects from the YCB-Video dataset. As we can observe, our algorithm delivers reliable object pose estimates in sequences of RGB images.

Table 5. AUC ADD scores [%] (max. th. 10 cm) achieved by our algorithm on the YCB-Video dataset. AUC ADD is calculated for non-symmetric objects, whereas AUC ADD-S [7] is determined for symmetric objects, "-" denotes unavailable results, and '*' stands for symmetric objects.

Object	Pose recovery on single RGB images					Pose tracking		
	PoseCNN [7]	DOPE [29]	[30]	[31]	GDR-Net [32]	PoseRBPF [14]	DeepIM [16]	Our
002_master_chef_can	50.9	–	81.6	49.9	65.2	63.3	89.0	**90.2**
003_cracker_box	51.7	55.9	83.6	80.5	**88.8**	77.8	88.5	85.4
004_sugar_box	68.6	75.7	82.0	85.5	**95.0**	79.6	94.3	87.5
005_tomato_soup_can	66.0	76.1	79.7	68.5	**91.9**	73.0	89.1	82.3
006_mustard_bottle	79.9	81.9	91.4	87.0	**92.8**	84.7	92.0	90.0
007_tuna_fish_can	70.4	–	49.2	79.3	**94.2**	64.2	92.0	87.9
008_pudding_box	62.9	–	**90.1**	81.8	44.7	64.5	80.1	83.3
009_gelatin_box	75.2	–	93.6	89.4	92.5	83.0	92.0	**94.4**
010_potted_meat_can	59.6	39.4	79.0	59.6	80.2	51.8	78.0	**82.3**
011_banana	72.3	–	51.9	36.5	**85.8**	18.4	81.0	73.6
019_pitcher_base	52.5	–	69.4	78.1	**98.5**	63.7	90.4	90.7
021_bleach_cleanser	50.5	–	76.1	56.7	**84.3**	60.5	81.7	80.6
024_bowl*	69.7	–	76.9	23.5	85.7	85.6	**90.6**	87.9
025_mug	57.7	–	53.7	54.0	**94.0**	77.9	92.0	85.8
035_power_drill	55.1	–	82.7	82.8	**90.1**	71.8	85.4	79.7
036_wood_block*	65.8	–	55.0	29.6	82.5	31.4	75.4	**82.6**
037_scissors	35.8	–	65.9	46.0	49.5	38.7	70.3	**71.4**
040_large_marker	58.0	–	56.4	9.8	76.1	67.1	80.4	80.6
051_large_clamp*	49.9	–	67.5	47.4	89.3	59.3	84.1	**89.5**
052_extra_large_clamp*	47.0	–	53.9	47.0	**93.5**	44.3	90.3	91.8
061_foam_brick*	87.8	–	89.0	87.8	**96.9**	92.6	95.5	87.4
Avg.	61.3	65.8	72.8	61.0	84.4	64.4	**86.3**	85.0

The system has been implemented in Python using Tensorflow and Keras API. The neural networks have been trained in 400 epochs, batch size set to four, learning rate equal to 0.001, MSE loss function, using RMSprop. For $eps = 0.0001$ the average number of evaluations of the objective function by the LM is about eleven. The maximum number if iterations was set to twenty. The shape features have been detected using Canny edge detector.

Fig. 3. Qualitative results on YCB-Video dataset. Example images demonstrate how our algorithm handles occlusions, objects in various poses, and lighting conditions. Depicted are the following objects: 002_master_chef_can, 003_cracker_box, 008_pudding_box, 010_potted_meat_can, 035_power_drill, 040_large_marker, and 051_large_clamp. The blue bounding boxes show the ground truth poses, whereas the green ones correspond to the estimated poses. For better visualization the regions of interest were cropped. (Color figure online)

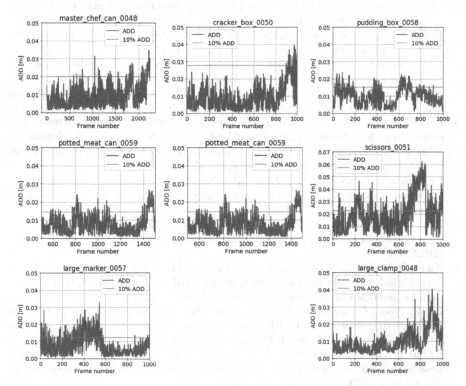

Fig. 4. ADD score [%] vs. frame number for objects from the YCB-Video dataset.

4 Conclusions

In this work we demonstrated that by combining shape information with sparse object keypoints considerable gains in tracking accuracy can be achieved in least-squares-based pose refinement. Given an initial pose guess determined by the EPnP, the object pose is refined by the Levenberg-Marquardt. The residual error depends on keypoint matching and object shape fitting. By exploiting an implicit shape representation based on distance function the algorithm achieves better results against the keypoint-based algorithm. A multiple-criteria decision making has been leveraged to decide which keypoints should be selected for the refinement of the object pose. We demonstrated experimentally that our algorithm achieves promising results on freely available OPT and YCB-Video datasets.

Acknowledgment. This work was supported by Polish National Science Center (NCN) under a research grant 2017/27/B/ST6/01743.

References

1. Kehl, W., Manhardt, F., Tombari, F., Ilic, S., Navab, N.: SSD-6D: making RGB-based 3D detection and 6D pose estimation great again. In: IEEE International Conference on Computer Vision, pp. 1530–1538 (2017)
2. Hinterstoisser, A., et al.: Model based training, detection and pose estimation of texture-less 3D objects in heavily cluttered scenes. In: Lee, K.M., Matsushita, Y., Rehg, J.M., Hu, Z. (eds.) ACCV 2012, Part I. LNCS, vol. 7724, pp. 548–562. Springer, Heidelberg (2013). https://doi.org/10.1007/978-3-642-37331-2_42
3. Brachmann, E., Krull, A., Michel, F., Gumhold, S., Shotton, J., Rother, C.: Learning 6D Object pose estimation using 3D object coordinates. In: Fleet, D., Pajdla, T., Schiele, B., Tuytelaars, T. (eds.) ECCV 2014, Part II. LNCS, vol. 8690, pp. 536–551. Springer, Cham (2014). https://doi.org/10.1007/978-3-319-10605-2_35
4. Labbé, Y., Carpentier, J., Aubry, M., Sivic, J.: CosyPose: consistent multi-view multi-object 6D pose estimation. In: Vedaldi, A., Bischof, H., Brox, T., Frahm, J.-M. (eds.) ECCV 2020, Part XVII. LNCS, vol. 12362, pp. 574–591. Springer, Cham (2020). https://doi.org/10.1007/978-3-030-58520-4_34
5. Brachmann, E., Michel, F., Krull, A., Yang, M., Gumhold, S., Rother, C.: Uncertainty-driven 6D pose estimation of objects and scenes from a single RGB image. In: CVPR, pp. 3364–3372 (2016)
6. Fan, Z., Zhu, Y., He, Y., Sun, Q., Liu, H., He, J.: Deep learning on monocular object pose detection and tracking: a comprehensive overview. ACM Comput. Surv. (2022)
7. Xiang, Y., Schmidt, T., Narayanan, V., Fox, D.: PoseCNN: a convolutional neural network for 6D object pose estimation in cluttered scenes. In: IEEE/RSJ International Conference on Intelligent Robots and Systems (2018)
8. Li, Z., Wang, G., Ji, X.: CDPN: coordinates-based disentangled pose network for real-time RGB-based 6-DoF object pose estimation. In: IEEE International Conference on Computer Vision (ICCV), pp. 7677–7686 (2019)
9. Pavlakos, G., Zhou, X., Chan, A., Derpanis, K.G., Daniilidis, K.: 6-DoF object pose from semantic keypoints. In: IEEE International Conference on Robotics and Automation (ICRA), pp. 2011–2018 (2017)

10. Rad, M., Lepetit, V.: BB8: a scalable, accurate, robust to partial occlusion method for predicting the 3D poses of challenging objects without using depth. In: IEEE International Conference on Computer Vision, pp. 3848–3856 (2017)
11. Hu, Y., Hugonot, J., Fua, P., Salzmann, M.: Segmentation-driven 6D object pose estimation. In: IEEE Conference on Computer Vision and Pattern Recognition, (CVPR), pp. 3385–3394 (2019)
12. Peng, S., Liu, Y., Huang, Q., Zhou, X., Bao, H.: PVNet: pixel-wise voting network for 6DoF pose estimation. In: IEEE Conference CVPR, pp. 4556–4565 (2019)
13. Hexner, J., Hagege, R.R.: 2D–3D pose estimation of heterogeneous objects using a region based approach. Int. J. Comput. Vis. **118**(1), 95–112 (2016). https://doi.org/10.1007/s11263-015-0873-2
14. Deng, X., Mousavian, A., Xiang, Y., Xia, F., Bretl, T., Fox, D.: PoseRBPF: a Rao-Blackwellized particle filter for 6D object pose estimation. In: Proceedings of the Robotics: Science and Systems XV, Freiburg IM Breisgau, Germany, June 2019
15. Manhardt, F., Kehl, W., Navab, N., Tombari, F.: Deep model-based 6D pose refinement in RGB. In: Ferrari, V., Hebert, M., Sminchisescu, C., Weiss, Y. (eds.) Computer Vision – ECCV 2018. LNCS, vol. 11218, pp. 833–849. Springer, Cham (2018). https://doi.org/10.1007/978-3-030-01264-9_49
16. Li, Y., Wang, G., Ji, X., Xiang, Y., Fox, D.: DeepIM: deep iterative matching for 6D pose estimation. Int. J. Comput. Vis. **128**, 657–678 (2020)
17. Dosovitskiy, A., et al.: FlowNet: learning optical flow with convolutional networks. In: Proceedings of the IEEE International Conference on Computer Vision (ICCV), pp. 2758–2766. IEEE Computer Society (2015)
18. Majcher, M., Kwolek, B.: Quaternion-driven CNN for object pose tracking. In: International Conference on Visual Communications and Image Processing (VCIP), pp. 1–4 (2021)
19. Lepetit, V., Moreno-Noguer, F., Fua, P.: EPnP: an accurate O(n) solution to the PnP problem. Int. J. Comput. Vis. **81**(2), 155–166 (2009)
20. de Assis Zampirolli, F., Filipe, L.: A fast CUDA-based implementation for the Euclidean distance transform. In: International Conference on High Performance Computing Simulation (HPCS), pp. 815–818 (2017)
21. Hwang, C.L., Lai, Y.J., Liu, T.Y.: A new approach for multiple objective decision making. Comput. Oper. Res. **20**(8), 889–899 (1993)
22. Wu, P., Lee, Y., Tseng, H., Ho, H., Yang, M., Chien, S.: A benchmark dataset for 6DoF object pose tracking. In: IEEE International Symposium on Mixed and Augmented Reality, pp. 186–191 (2017)
23. Zhong, L., Zhao, X., Zhang, Y., Zhang, S., Zhang, L.: Occlusion-aware region-based 3D pose tracking of objects with temporally consistent polar-based local partitioning. IEEE Trans. Image Process. **29**, 5065–5078 (2020)
24. Bugaev, B., Kryshchenko, A., Belov, R.: Combining 3D model contour energy and keypoints for object tracking. In: Ferrari, V., Hebert, M., Sminchisescu, C., Weiss, Y. (eds.) ECCV 2018, Part XII. LNCS, vol. 11216, pp. 55–70. Springer, Cham (2018). https://doi.org/10.1007/978-3-030-01258-8_4
25. Prisacariu, V.A., Reid, I.D.: PWP3D: real-time segmentation and tracking of 3D objects. Int. J. Comput. Vis. **98**(3), 335–354 (2012)
26. Whelan, T., Salas-Moreno, R.F., Glocker, B., Davison, A.J., Leutenegger, S.: ElasticFusion. Int. J. Robot. Res. **35**(14), 1697–1716 (2016)
27. Tjaden, H., Schwanecke, U., Schömer, E., Cremers, D.: A region-based Gauss-Newton approach to real-time monocular multiple object tracking. IEEE Trans. PAMI **41**(8), 1797–1812 (2019)

28. Valença, L., et al.: Real-time monocular 6DoF tracking of textureless objects using photometrically-enhanced edges. In: VISAPP, pp. 763–773. Scitepress (2021)

29. Tremblay, J., To, T., Sundaralingam, B., Xiang, Y., Fox, D., Birchfield, S.: Deep object pose estimation for semantic robotic grasping of household objects. In: Proceedings of the 2nd Conference on Robot Learn, Volume 87 of Proceedings of Machine Learning Research, pp. 306–316 (2018)

30. Oberweger, M., Rad, M., Lepetit, V.: Making deep heatmaps robust to partial occlusions for 3D object pose estimation. In: Ferrari, V., Hebert, M., Sminchisescu, C., Weiss, Y. (eds.) ECCV 2018. LNCS, vol. 11219, pp. 125–141. Springer, Cham (2018). https://doi.org/10.1007/978-3-030-01267-0_8

31. Zappel, M., Bultmann, S., Behnke, S.: 6D object pose estimation using keypoints and part affinity fields. ArXiv, CoRR abs/2107.02057 (2021)

32. Wang, G., Manhardt, F., Tombari, F., Ji, X.: GDR-Net: geometry-guided direct regression network for monocular 6D object pose estimation. In: CVPR, June 2021

Beyond the Visible Spectrum: Is Person Identity Well Preserved in Thermal Cameras?

Afef Ben Said[1], Hajer Fradi[1(✉)], Dorra Lamouchi[1],
and Mohamed Amine Marnissi[2,3]

[1] Université de Sousse, Institut Supérieur des Sciences Appliquées et de Technologie de Sousse, LATIS-Laboratory of Advanced Technology and Intelligent Systems, 4023 Sousse, Tunisie
hajer.fradi@issatso.rnu.tn
[2] Université de Sousse, Ecole Nationale d'Ingénieurs de Sousse, LATIS-Laboratory of Advanced Technology and Intelligent Systems, 4023 Sousse, Tunisie
[3] Université de Sfax, Ecole Nationale d'Ingénieurs de Sfax, 3038 Sfax, Tunisie

Abstract. Face recognition is a well investigated problem in the computer vision community. Beyond the visible spectrum, it is identified as an active-oriented and attractive research area. In particular, thermal cameras have recently emerged as increasingly important sensors for visual surveillance applications. In addition to the fact that these cameras operate well in challenging environments such as adverse weather and lighting conditions, they are commonly known as keystone biometric solution that preserves person identity. In this paper, we intend to prove that faces could be highly recognized from thermal cameras using a powerful generative adversarial model. This model is employed to deal with the domain shift between thermal and visible sensors. Extensive experiments of different generative models and face recognition systems demonstrate the effectiveness of the proposed pipeline to reveal the person identity even though it is acquired by different sensing modalities, with significant facial variations.

Keywords: Generative Adversarial Network · Thermal · Visible · Face recognition · Cross-spectral

1 Introduction

Face recognition represents one of the most highly accurate and minimally intrusive biometric approaches [5]. During the last decades, it has gained the interest of researchers in various fields such as defense, security, surveillance, biology and public safety [32]. Recent face recognition systems focus on addressing a number of challenges including illumination variations and unconstrained settings [2]. Despite the great success of recent deep face recognition systems acquired in the visible light domain, these systems fail to deal with challenging or adverse lighting conditions which is the major performance-limiting factor.

N. T. Nguyen et al. (Eds.): ICCCI 2022, LNAI 13501, pp. 491–503, 2022.
https://doi.org/10.1007/978-3-031-16014-1_39

Recently, the use of thermal cameras is progressively developing in multiple video surveillance applications [18]. Actually, these cameras enable to observe the invisible thermal radiation emitted or reflected by any object, whatever the lighting conditions [33]. In addition, it is commonly known that thermal cameras preserve well face identity information which represents a key advantage for privacy preservation in video surveillance systems [14]. Despite the increasing need and the relevance of these sensors to deal with different illumination and weather conditions, they remain less investigated compared to the visible spectrum. The underlying reduced focus on thermal imaging can be partly explained by the following factors: thermal cameras are much more expensive than visible ones, the mostly used thermal cameras suffer from low image resolution, noise and blurred details [17]. More importantly, thermal imaging suffers from shortage of existing datasets and models.

The impressive performance of face recognition systems together with the available deep models and facial data in the visible light domain justify the need to extend them to less studied domains as the case of near-infrared and thermal imaging. Compared to near-infrared imaging where face images are close to the visible ones, thermal face images embody more differences in terms of edges and texture information. Consequently, a face recognition model trained on visible images but applied to thermal images gets significantly worse results due to the misfit between the two domains [14,36].

Aiming to achieve a better face recognition performance in the target thermal domain, every model needs to be trained on a specific data to be accurate enough while predicting results. It would be a tough process, if we realize data collection and retrain facial recognition models, which have been already trained on visible data. To gain time and to avoid retraining existing models, transfer learning could be instead used. It aims at overcoming the limited generalization of the existing face models when training and testing images are from different domains. In particular, it is about domain adaptation that enables the use of existing models in a new target domain [37]. Once adapted, these face recognition models can be reused in the thermal domain at no additional cost.

Cross-spectral face recognition refers to the goal of identifying a person acquired beyond the visible spectrum from a gallery of visible images. Particularly in this paper, we focus on different sensing modalities, i.e. visible vs. thermal. Recent advances in cross-spectral face recognition focus on image synthesis by means of generative models. The basic idea is to generate a realistic visible image from every thermal face image in order to improve its visual quality. Although the generative process is a challenging problem to solve, its resolution can address the huge effort allocated to gather thermal data and to retrain face recognition systems. Following the same strategy, we aim in this paper to apply a thermal-to-visible domain adaptation method using a powerful generative model. The applied model that has the advantage of generating realistic and sharp looking images is considered as the main contribution of this paper. Once this adaptation is performed, the existing visible face recognition models can be reused, achieving a much better recognition performance without additional annotation cost and without re-training models.

The remainder of the paper is organized as follows: in Sect. 2, an overview of the existing face recognition systems with a focus on cross-spectral models is presented. Then, our proposed approach of visible image synthesis for face recognition is detailed in Sect. 3. The conducted experiments and the obtained results are discussed in Sect. 4. Finally, we conclude and give an outlook of possible future works in Sect. 5.

2   Related Work

In this section, we give an overview of some existing face recognition systems from traditional to deep models. This overview includes as well the existing generative models mapping from thermal to visible domains for cross-spectral face recognition.

2.1   Face Recognition Systems

Face recognition has been widely studied in the field of computer vision for various surveillance applications. The first face recognition models were developed with a set of hand-crafted feature extractors such as facial landmarks [7] that present 21 subjective facial features including hair color and lips thickness. In 1990s, the study of face recognition became popular following the introduction of Eigenfaces [31] based on Principal Component Analysis (PCA) technique. Eigenfaces aim at reducing the large dimensionality of feature spaces and at reconstructing faces from the available dataset. Other research studies were conducted including outer linear algebra techniques such as Linear Discriminant Analysis (LDA), commonly known as Fisherfaces [3]. It is a supervised learning technique that reduces the high dimensional image space and increases the class separability.

Afterwards, deep networks have promoted the research in many computer vision applications, including face recognition and verification, where compelling results in terms of accuracy have been achieved. Current face recognition systems can be categorized into single-CNN and multi-CNN based methods according to [9]. Single-CNN based methods include DeepFace [30], which is a deep CNN architecture that consists of 9 layers, as well as a pre-processing phase in which the input RGB face images are aligned using a 3D model. Also, FaceNet [27] is a popular face recognition system based on learning a mapping function from face images to a compact euclidean space that optimizes the embedding itself by a triplet loss. VGGFace [22] is another face recognition system that proposes a new concept of fine-tuning the model via a triplet-based metric similar to FaceNet.

Other existing methods conducted for face recognition incorporate more than one CNN architecture. These multi-CNN methods have witnessed a great success by extracting deep features of different regions and different aspects of a face, then concatenate them as a final face representation. Multi-CNN methods include DeepID series that extract robust features of different local face patches such as DeepID, DeepID2, DeepID2+ and DeepID3 [28, 29].

2.2   Cross-Spectral Face Recognition Systems

It is commonly known that thermal cameras are more convenient at nighttime and in adverse weather conditions compared to the conventional visible cameras. In spite of their usefulness in such conditions, only few studies have investigated the problem of face recognition in the thermal domain. That could be explained by the fact that face features are significantly altered in thermal images which justifies the drastic performance drop. The existing studies in thermal images include NIRFaceNet [23] which is a CNN-based method to recognize NIR faces. It is an extension of GoogleNet, that has much more compact structure based only on eight layers, achieving higher identification rates with much less training time. In [21], an hybrid method which combines CNN and Fact Wavelet Transform (FWT) is proposed. It is based on a set of features extractors and classifiers to minimize errors in face recognition from spoofing and adverse lighting conditions. To classify images, a deep neural network of six layers is applied; an input layer, two conv layers, two sub-sampling layers and an output layer. The corresponding classification error has been significantly reduced mainly when images were pre-processed with LDA and PCA.

It is important to highlight that for the above methods dedicated to operate in the thermal domain, data collection and annotation are required. These limitations could be catered by means of generative models. These models enable to deal with the domain shift between thermal and visible cameras. Consequently, they enable to harness the abundance of face recognition systems trained in the visible spectrum and to adapt them to the thermal domain at no additional annotation cost and without the need of retraining.

Based on the success of Generative Adversarial Networks (GANs) in synthesizing images, some methods have been proposed for thermal-to-visible face recognition. For instance, in [25] a two-step method was introduced. It firstly consists of estimating visible-like features from thermal capture, then reconstructing the new visible-like images to solve the cross-spectral problem. Related work also includes Deep Convolutional Generative Adversarial Network (DCGAN) [24], Conditional Generative Adversarial Network (CGAN) [34], and Boundary Equilibrium Generative Adversarial Network (BEGAN) [4]. DCGAN [24] introduced a Convolution Neural Network into the generator and the discriminator. CGAN [34] proposed to produce images with photo-realistic texture. BEGAN [4] controlled the training step via a balancing factor between the discriminator and generator. Although these models succeeded to improve the stability of the training process to some extent, the identity information is not yet well preserved.

[11] solves the problem of matching visible face images to thermal ones through a deep coupled learning framework called CpDCNN. It is based on learning deep global discriminative features of thermal faces in an embedding space to find their corresponding visible-like faces. This method has been extended in [26], where a multi-facial-region leveraging both global and local evidences is applied in order to improve the overall facial structure of the generated visible-like images. TV-GAN [36] is another related work that solves the problem of

transforming thermal to visible faces. It has the advantage of training the discriminator to realize both binary classification of fake or real and to realize closed-set face recognition task. SG-GAN [6] is another approach that regularizes the training of GAN architecture with semantic priors which are extracted by a face parsing network. It helps to reduce the per-pixel loss value calculated between the synthesized visible images and thermal ones. Finally, in [35] Zhang *et al.* proposed a novel face synthesis approach based on multi-stream feature-level fusion to generate high-quality visible-like images from thermal images.

3   Proposed Approach

In this paper, we propose a novel approach of image synthesis for face recognition dedicated to operate in the thermal domain at no additional annotation cost. The proposed adaptation scheme falls into the category of generative models. Precisely, we employ a powerful architecture that enables the generation of perceptually realistic and sharp looking images via adversarial learning. Once synthetic visible images are generated, a face recognition system already trained in the visible spectrum could be directly applied. The proposed pipeline is shown in Fig. 1.

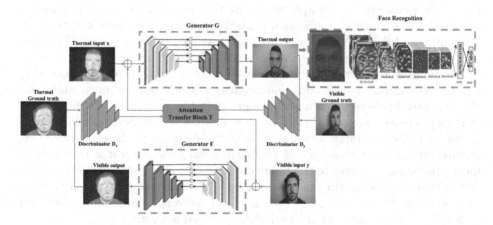

Fig. 1. The architecture of the proposed cross-spectral face recognition. DeepFace chosen for illustrative purpose can be readily replaced by other face recognition systems.

3.1   Generative Model for Visible Image Synthesis

Generative models basically consist of generating synthetic data that is similar to the target data and shares the annotations of the source domain. They are typically based on Generative Adversarial Networks, deep architectures initially introduced by Goodfellow *et al.* in [8]. These architectures are generally composed of two sub-networks: a generative sub-network G and a discriminative sub-network D. They have shown good performance in image generation, colorization and restoration [1]. The adversarial loss of these architectures can be expressed as:

$$\mathcal{L}_{gan}(G, D) = \mathbb{E}_{y \sim \mathcal{Y}}[\log D(y)] + \mathbb{E}_{x \sim \mathcal{X}}[\log(1 - D(G(x)))] \tag{1}$$

where $x \sim \mathcal{X}$ denotes the input image and $y \sim \mathcal{Y}$ is the target image.

One typical example is the generation of a visible image from an input thermal image. This transformation aims at converting thermal image to perceptually realistic RGB image in order to enable better content interpretation. Commonly known as colorization, this transformation has been mostly performed by Pix2Pix architecture [12] which is a GAN model designed for image-to image translation. It is precisely a subset of conditional Generative Adversarial Network (cGAN) [19], where the output generated image is conditioned by an input source image. The generator is trained via adversarial loss, forcing it to generate credible images in the target domain. Also, the generator is updated through the $L1$ loss calculated between the generated image and the expected output image. This extra loss stimulates the generator model to build plausible translations of the input image [12].

CycleGAN [38] is another GAN architecture, that is trained on a collection of images from the source and target domains without any need for matching examples. It is a powerful and simple technique that can provide visually stunning results in a wide range of application fields. In this paper, we specifically employ a recently published GAN architecture called Attention-based Spatial Guidance for Image-to-image Translation (ASGIT) [13]. This architecture is selected since it incorporates a powerful spatial attention mechanism to guide the generator and to consequently handle some failure cases of GAN architectures, where the discriminator becomes much more stronger than the generator. The key idea is that high-intensity areas in the attention map are more meaningful while translating, thus the generator would allocate more resources to these regions. This architecture has the advantage of explicitly forcing the generator to attribute more processing resources to the frequented areas so that it can perform a clear translation. In general, this method can be applied to any conditional translation problem. The discriminator does not only deliver the probability, but also a useful spatial attention map based on its internal activation.

As illustrated in Fig. 1, the framework is traced in an unsupervised manner through a pair of generators (G, F) and discriminators (D_y, D_x), as well as through a cycle consistency adjustment. To further stabilize the training process and to enhance the generated image quality, we use the least-square error [16] as adversarial loss function $\mathcal{L}_{gan}$. This loss is the same in both directions of our system i.e. G generates a visible synthetic image y' and F generates a thermal synthetic image x'. The adversarial loss is defined as:

$$\mathcal{L}_{gan}(G, D) = \mathbb{E}_{y \sim \mathcal{Y}}[D(y) - 1)^2] + \mathbb{E}_{x \sim \mathcal{X}}[(G(x'))^2] \tag{2}$$

where x' denotes the output of pixel-wise addition between the thermal input image x and the attention map generated by D_y. Since the missing of matched data leads to a problem in the case of unsupervised learning and the adversarial loss is insufficient to solve it, it is necessary to add a cycle consistency loss defined as:

$$\mathcal{L}_{cyc}(G, F) = \mathbb{E}_{x \sim \mathcal{X}}[\|F(G(x)) - x\|_1] + \mathbb{E}_{y \sim \mathcal{Y}}[\|(G(F(y)) - y)\|_1] \qquad (3)$$

The resulting objective loss function to train our model is defined as follows:

$$\arg\min_{G,F} \max_{D_{\mathcal{X}}, D_{\mathcal{Y}}} \mathcal{L}_{gan}(G, D_{\mathcal{Y}}) + \mathcal{L}_{gan}(F, D_{\mathcal{X}}) + \lambda \mathcal{L}_{cyc}(G, F) \qquad (4)$$

where λ is used to weight the cycle consistency loss.

3.2   Cross-spectral Face Recognition

Once the mapping function across domains is approximated, a face recognition system is applied on the generated visible images. For this goal, two state-of-the-art face recognition systems are assessed:

FaceNet. [27] is one of the most important face recognition systems that employs a deep CNN network followed by L2 normalization. This system maps face images to a compact euclidean space and uses it for clustering and face verification. FaceNet has as inputs color images and returns back embeddings as outputs which are vectors of size 128. Embeddings are followed by a triplet loss function during the training phase. This face recognition system achieved 99.63% in terms of accuracy when evaluated on LFW database [10].

DeepFace. [30] is another facial recognition system that consists of 9-layer deep neural network. It takes as input RGB face image pre-processed with 3D-alignment. Its architecture includes more than 120 million parameters using several locally connected convolutional layers without weight sharing, and every location in feature maps of these layers learns a different set of filters. DeepFace was trained on more than 4 million images and reached an accuracy of 97.35% on LFW database.

4   Experiments and Results

4.1   Dataset and Experiments

The proposed approach is evaluated on VIS-TH face dataset [15]. This dataset was acquired by FLIR Duo R camera which is designed to simultaneously capture images and videos from both visible and thermal spectra. The visible and thermal sensors have a pixel resolution of 1920×1080 and 160×120, respectively. The dataset contains 21 face images for 50 persons of different ages, genders and facial variations, resulting a total number of 4200 images. Precisely, it includes 7 expressions, 4 head poses, 5 occlusions and 5 illumination variations. In order to apply cross-validation, our experimental setting on face recognition follows the setup in [14], where face images from 45 subjects are used for training and the remaining subjects are used for testing. This split is repeated 10 times in order to synthesize all images without overlapping the test and the train images.

The performance of both face recognition systems FaceNet and DeepFace trained and tested on visible images is evaluated in terms of accuracy. These results are compared to the those obtained when tests are performed on original thermal images and on synthesized ones. Precisely, we compare our results to Pix2Pix and CycleGAN architectures. Four different configurations [20] are thereby assessed: ResNet with 6 residual blocks (denoted as ResNet-6), ResNet with 9 residual blocks (ResNet-9), Unet with 7 sub-sampling blocks (Unet-128) and Unet with 8 sub-sampling blocks (Unet-256). Since Pix2Pix runs faster than the other architectures, we choose to evaluate these configurations on it, and the best performing generator is selected for further comparisons and analysis. The training was running for 200 epochs, batch size of 2 and $2e-4$ as learning rate with Adam optimizer. For all experiments, the models are learned on NVIDIA Titan RTX GPU using Tensorflow framework.

4.2   Results and Analysis

In this section, we intend to demonstrate the effectiveness of our proposed architecture for face recognition in the thermal spectrum by realizing various experiments on VIS-TH dataset. First, we compare face recognition performance of different generators on Pix2Pix architecture in order to select the most performing one for next experiments. The results are reported in Table 1.

Table 1. Evaluation of different generators on Pix2Pix architecture for cross-spectral face recognition systems in terms of accuracy.

Recognition system	ResNet-6	ResNet-9	Unet-128	Unet-256
FaceNet	**33.55%**	31.84%	11.97%	19.07%
DeepFace	**73.66%**	71.66%	62.33%	70.00%

As shown in the table, ResNet-6 as generator gives the best accuracy for both face recognition systems FaceNet and DeepFace. For this reason, it is selected in the following experiments.

Once the most performing generator is selected, we aim to evaluate the results of face recognition systems on the generated images and compare them to the original results without generation. As depicted in Table 2, we evaluate the performance of the two face recognition systems trained on visible images and tested on thermal ones. By doing so, only 3.66% as accuracy is obtained by FaceNet compared to 97.66% if tests are performed on visible images. The same observation is made on DeepFace system, in which 90.66% is initially obtained on visible images compared to 2.66% if the tests are instead performed on thermal images.

Table 2. Evaluation of cross-spectral face recognition systems in terms of accuracy using our proposed approach, compared to other GAN architectures, and to the baseline systems in thermal and visible spectrums. All models are made on ResUnet-6 as generator.

Recognition system	Visible	Thermal	Pix2Pix	CycleGan	Ours
FaceNet	97.66%	3.66%	33.55%	20.13%	**39.86%**
DeepFace	90.66%	2.66%	73.66%	65.00%	**77.33%**

As expected, the domain gap between visible face images and thermal ones leads to a high performance drop of cross-spectrum face recognition systems, of 94%% and 88% in terms of accuracy on FaceNet and DeepFace, respectively. These results comply with our main observation stated at the beginning of the paper about the distribution shift between feature spaces of thermal and visible domains. These insufficient results justify the need for adaptation by means of generative models to synthesize visible-like images in order to enhance the recognition process in the target domain.

In the same Table 2, we additionally evaluate our results using FaceNet and DeepFace systems and compare them to other GAN architectures. From the obtained results, it is clearly shown that our proposed approach outperforms the results on the thermal spectrum with a significant margin of 36.20% using FaceNet and of 74.67% using DeepFace. Compared to other generative architectures Pix2Pix and CycleGan, we achieve the best results on both face recognition systems. These results prove the importance of the generated visible-like images in reducing the domain gap between thermal and visible spectrums. The recognition process is consequently improved if we need to utilize a face recognition system on thermal images, but initially trained in the visible domain without additional training cost. Particularly, it can be clearly noticed that our architecture shows outstanding performance in recognizing the subject identities from the new generated images using DeepFace system. The corresponding results are significantly improved from 2.66% to 77.33%. Hence, the assumption that thermal cameras preserve identity information cannot always hold true since by means of generative models trained on unseen images, we are able to reach 77.33% as accuracy for recognition.

To further prove the obtained results, we show some qualitative examples of the synthesized images in Fig. 2, where each row corresponds to an example from different facial identity. The synthesized visible-like images from thermal captures using different architectures are compared to the original thermal images, and to the ground-truth i.e. visible images.

As shown in the figure, synthesized face images using Pix2Pix and CycleGan architectures suffer from noisy details and incorrect skin colors due to the difficulty of deducing skin color tone from thermal captures. On the other hand, our proposed architecture using ResNet-6 as generator gives better visual quality from different aspects. It succeeds in giving better generated faces with clearly informative details and less noisy information compared to the other architectures.

Thermal   Pix2Pix   CycleGan   Ours   GT

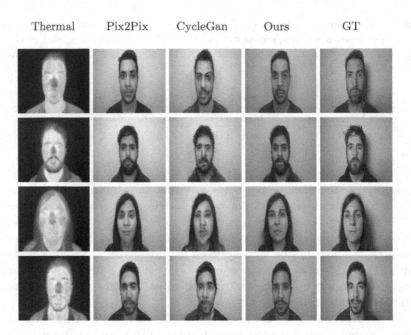

Fig. 2. Samples results of synthesized images using different architectures (Pix2Pix, CycleGan and our proposed architecture) compared to the original thermal images and to the ground-truth (visible images).

To better prove these observations, we evaluate the visual results by calculating PSNR and SSIM metrics between the original images and the generated ones. Our obtained results are reported in Fig. 3 with comparisons to the other generative architectures. As shown the results are notable, demonstrating the high visual quality of our synthesized images, mainly in terms of PSNR with a large margin compared to the other architectures.

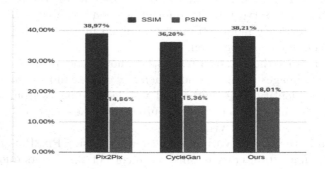

Fig. 3. Comparison of our results to Pix2Pix and CycleGan architectures in terms of PSNR and SSIM

5   Conclusion

It is commonly known that face recognition process from thermal images is a challenging task due to the fact that features are significantly altered and to the limited available data compared to visible face images. In this paper, we proposed to synthesize visible-like images from thermal spectrum in order to reduce the domain shift and to enable direct applications of existing visible face recognition systems without retraining. In the experimental results, we proved that our proposed architecture succeeds in generating realistic and sharp looking images. The effectiveness of the proposed approach has been demonstrated on face recognition by obtaining better results compared to the baseline systems and to other generative models. As perspectives, FaceNet and DeepFace recognition systems chosen for illustrative purpose can be readily replaced by other systems. Also, the domain shift between visible and thermal spectrums addressed in this paper by means of generative models can be instead addressed by non-generative models, i.e. by aligning feature spaces inside the recognition system.

Acknowledgment. The authors would like to thank A. Ayed for his important development skills.

References

1. Aghabiglou, A., Eksioglu, E.M.: MR image reconstruction based on densely connected residual generative adversarial network–DCR-GAN. In: Wojtkiewicz, K., Treur, J., Pimenidis, E., Maleszka, M. (eds.) ICCCI 2021. CCIS, vol. 1463, pp. 679–689. Springer, Cham (2021). https://doi.org/10.1007/978-3-030-88113-9_55
2. Anghelone, D., Chen, C., Ross, A., Dantcheva, A.: Beyond the visible: A survey on cross-spectral face recognition. arXiv preprint arXiv:2201.04435 (2022)
3. Belhumeur, P.N., Hespanha, J.P., Kriegman, D.J.: Eigenfaces vs. fisherfaces: Recognition using class specific linear projection. IEEE Trans. Pattern Anal. Mach. Intell. **19**(7), 711–720 (1997)
4. Berthelot, D., Schumm, T., Metz, L.: Began: boundary equilibrium generative adversarial networks. arXiv preprint arXiv:1703.10717 (2017)
5. Bourlai, T., Hornak, L.A.: Face recognition outside the visible spectrum. Image Vis. Comput. **55**, 14–17 (2016)
6. Chen, C., Ross, A.: Matching thermal to visible face images using a semantic-guided generative adversarial network. In: 2019 14th IEEE International Conference on Automatic Face & Gesture Recognition (FG 2019), pp. 1–8. IEEE (2019)
7. Goldstein, A.J., Harmon, L.D., Lesk, A.B.: Identification of human faces. Proc. IEEE **59**(5), 748–760 (1971)
8. Goodfellow, I., et al.: Generative adversarial nets. In: Advances in neural information processing systems (nips) (2014)
9. Guo, G., Zhang, N.: A survey on deep learning based face recognition. Comput. Vis. Image Underst. **189**, 102805 (2019)
10. Huang, G.B., Mattar, M., Berg, T., Learned-Miller, E.: Labeled faces in the wild: a database forstudying face recognition in unconstrained environments. In: Workshop on faces in'Real-Life'Images: detection, alignment, and recognition (2008)

11. Iranmanesh, S.M., Dabouei, A., Kazemi, H., Nasrabadi, N.M.: Deep cross polarimetric thermal-to-visible face recognition. In: 2018 International Conference on Biometrics (ICB), pp. 166–173. IEEE (2018)

12. Isola, P., Zhu, J.Y., Zhou, T., Efros, A.A.: Image-to-image translation with conditional adversarial networks. In: Proceedings of the IEEE Conference on Computer Vision and Pattern Recognition, pp. 1125–1134 (2017)

13. Lin, Y., Wang, Y., Li, Y., Gao, Y., Wang, Z., Khan, L.: Attention-based spatial guidance for image-to-image translation. In: Proceedings of the IEEE/CVF Winter Conference on Applications of Computer Vision, pp. 816–825 (2021)

14. Mallat, K., Damer, N., Boutros, F., Kuijper, A., Dugelay, J.L.: Cross-spectrum thermal to visible face recognition based on cascaded image synthesis. In: 2019 International Conference on Biometrics (ICB), pp. 1–8. IEEE (2019)

15. Mallat, K., Dugelay, J.L.: A benchmark database of visible and thermal paired face images across multiple variations. In: 2018 International Conference of the Biometrics Special Interest Group (BIOSIG), pp. 1–5. IEEE (2018)

16. Mao, X., Li, Q., Xie, H., Lau, R.Y., Wang, Z., Paul Smolley, S.: Least squares generative adversarial networks. In: Proceedings of the IEEE international conference on computer vision. pp. 2794–2802 (2017)

17. Marnissi, M.A., Fradi, H., Sahbani, A., Amara, N.E.B.: Thermal image enhancement using generative adversarial network for pedestrian detection. In: 2020 25th International Conference on Pattern Recognition (ICPR), pp. 6509–6516. IEEE (2021)

18. Marnissi, M.A., Fradi, H., Sahbani, A., Amara, N.E.B.: Unsupervised thermal-to-visible domain adaptation method for pedestrian detection. Pattern Recogn. Lett. **153**, 222–231 (2022)

19. Mirza, M., Osindero, S.: Conditional generative adversarial nets. arXiv preprint arXiv:1411.1784 (2014)

20. Morís, D.I., de Moura Ramos, J.J., Buján, J.N., Hortas, M.O.: Data augmentation approaches using cycle-consistent adversarial networks for improving covid-19 screening in portable chest x-ray images. Expert Syst. Appl. **185**, 115681 (2021)

21. Orji, C., Hurwitz, E., Hasan, A.: Thermal imaging using cnn and knn classifiers with fwt, pca and lda algorithms. In: Seventh International Conference on Computer Science, Engineering and Information Technology (CCSEIT 2017), pp. 133–143 (2017)

22. Parkhi, O.M., Vedaldi, A., Zisserman, A.: Deep face recognition (2015)

23. Peng, M., Wang, C., Chen, T., Liu, G.: Nirfacenet: A convolutional neural network for near-infrared face identification. Information **7**(4), 61 (2016)

24. Radford, A., Metz, L., Chintala, S.: Unsupervised representation learning with deep convolutional generative adversarial networks. arXiv preprint arXiv:1511.06434 (2015)

25. Riggan, B.S., Short, N.J., Hu, S., Kwon, H.: Estimation of visible spectrum faces from polarimetric thermal faces. In: 2016 IEEE 8th International Conference on Biometrics Theory, Applications and Systems (BTAS), pp. 1–7. IEEE (2016)

26. Riggan, B.S., Short, N.J., Hu, S.: Thermal to visible synthesis of face images using multiple regions. In: 2018 IEEE Winter Conference on Applications of Computer Vision (WACV), pp. 30–38. IEEE (2018)

27. Schroff, F., Kalenichenko, D., Philbin, J.: Facenet: A unified embedding for face recognition and clustering. In: Proceedings of the IEEE Conference on Computer Vision and Pattern Recognition, pp. 815–823 (2015)

28. Sun, Y., Liang, D., Wang, X., Tang, X.: Deepid3: Face recognition with very deep neural networks. arXiv preprint arXiv:1502.00873 (2015)

29. Sun, Y., Wang, X., Tang, X.: Deep learning face representation from predicting 10,000 classes. In: Proceedings of the IEEE Conference on Computer Vision and Pattern Recognition, pp. 1891–1898 (2014)
30. Taigman, Y., Yang, M., Ranzato, M., Wolf, L.: Deepface: closing the gap to human-level performance in face verification. In: Proceedings of the IEEE Conference on Computer Vision and Pattern Recognition, pp. 1701–1708 (2014)
31. Turk, M., Pentland, A.: Eigenfaces for recognition. J. Cogn. Neurosci. **3**(1), 71–86 (1991)
32. Wang, M., Deng, W.: Deep face recognition: a survey. Neurocomputing **429**, 215–244 (2021)
33. Wang, Y., Ming-Shi, C.: Human face recognition using thermal image. J. Med. Biol. Eng. **22**(2), 97–102 (2002)
34. Zhang, H., Patel, V.M., Riggan, B.S., Hu, S.: Generative adversarial network-based synthesis of visible faces from polarimetrie thermal faces. In: 2017 IEEE International Joint Conference on Biometrics (IJCB), pp. 100–107. IEEE (2017)
35. Zhang, H., Riggan, B.S., Hu, S., Short, N.J., Patel, V.M.: Synthesis of high-quality visible faces from polarimetric thermal faces using generative adversarial networks. Int. J. Comput. Vision **127**(6), 845–862 (2019)
36. Zhang, T., Wiliem, A., Yang, S., Lovell, B.: Tv-gan: generative adversarial network based thermal to visible face recognition. In: 2018 International Conference on Biometrics (ICB), pp. 174–181. IEEE (2018)
37. Zhou, S.K., Rueckert, D., Fichtinger, G.: Handbook of medical image computing and computer assisted intervention. Academic Press (2019)
38. Zhu, J.Y., Park, T., Isola, P., Efros, A.A.: Unpaired image-to-image translation using cycle-consistent adversarial networks. In: Proceedings of the IEEE International Conference on Computer Vision, pp. 2223–2232 (2017)

Social Networks and Intelligent Systems

TunTap: A Tunisian Dataset for Topic and Polarity Extraction in Social Media

Mohamed Amine Djebbi[1,2] and Riadh Ouersighni[1,2(✉)]

[1] Sciences and Technologies of Defense LR19DN01 (STD), La Marsa, Tunisia
[2] CRM Military Research Center, 2045 Taieb Mhiri street, ElAouina, Tunisia
`riadh.ouersighni@gmail.com`

Abstract. The massive usage of social networks has recently opened up new research avenues in the fields of data mining and decision-making. One of the most relevant forms of data generated by users in social media is an unstructured text that identifies their emotions on a given topic. Analyzing this new form of writing to extract valuable information is a challenging task, and could be of great interest in several fields such as healthcare, business intelligence, marketing strategies,... to name but a few. This article considers topic and polarity extraction in application to Online Social Media (OSM) analysis, in the benefit of numerous domain applications. Implementing sentiment analysis and topic extraction algorithms for the purpose of detecting the polarity of a given comment towards a certain topic requires a sophisticated machine and deep learning supervised models and, at the same time, collecting, preparing and annotating a huge amount of data to train those models.

In this paper, we propose a special dataset that can be used to extract both topic and polarity features from dialectical messages used in Tunisian daily electronic writing across the most popular OSM networks. We collected our data by crawling posts and comments' text from Facebook, Twitter and YouTube using related network graph API. In this work, we describe the whole pipeline used to prepare our corpus as well as the several extensive experiments setup and results conducted to evaluate the generated dataset. Up to our knowledge, the proposed multivariate Arabic dataset (Topic and Polarity) of Tunisian dialect is a first-time introduced in the NLP community up to now, and we made it publicly available on GitHub (https://github.com/DescoveryAmine/TunTap).

Keywords: Text-mining · Natural language processing · Social media computing · Machine learning · BERT model

1 Introduction

Today's social media offers people the opportunity to connect across the globe and express their opinions and feelings on topics as diverse as politics, music, health, retail, and more. Facebook is one of the most frequented social networking

© The Author(s), under exclusive license to Springer Nature Switzerland AG 2022
N. T. Nguyen et al. (Eds.): ICCCI 2022, LNAI 13501, pp. 507–519, 2022.
https://doi.org/10.1007/978-3-031-16014-1_40

platforms in the World Wide Web where users can post written comments and reviews. Recent statistics[1] shows that Facebook has 50 times more viewership than other OSM around the world and its huge text traffic posted online produces a massive amount of data related to opinions, news and events in trending topics. As a result, text mining processing emerged as a valuable task to detect users ideas and attitudes from their comments and posts that are generated in a variety of language forms such as the Tunisian Arabic dialect.

The studies on text mining and natural language processing made a great advance in language resource generation for almost all varieties of languages except Arabic dialects, which need more attention [14]. A huge amount of annotated datasets should be available for Arabic dialects where material resources are still scarce in several tasks such as sentiment analysis and topic mining.

In this paper, we are motivated by previous researches in the field of sentiment analysis of Tunisian dialect to address the limitation of having a corpus annotated solely for sentiments by building a corpus and annotating it simultaneously for both topic and polarity. We create our corpus from different OSM mainly from comments and posts on Facebook due to its widespread use in the world. The resulting corpus provides a resource complementary to existing Tunisian dialect resources [8,15], and opens doors to investigate in models that exploit topic identification along with sentiment analysis. The rest of this paper is organized as follows: In Sect. 2 we describe previous efforts related to the creation of various Arabic datasets in topic and sentiment mining as well as the main results discussed in the context. In the third section, we look into the creation of our corpus, its characteristics and the pre-processing steps conducted. Section 4 presents experiments setup and results to highlight the effectiveness of the new contextualized deep learning models in text understanding. In addition to that, we emphasize the impact of data representation approach in relation to the performance of the classifiers. We end the study by a conclusion and ideas for future work.

2   Related Works

Numerous studies on Arabic opinion mining, topic detection, named entity recognition (NER), information retrieval and so on, in relation to short text analysis from OSM are challenging tasks. Such tasks require the availability of large row annotated data within the target language, which is mostly absent and even time consuming, especially when dealing with low resources languages like the Arabic and its various dialects. The complexity of the text generated by Arabic users has increased because Arabic is a rich language with considerable slang varieties. Tunisian Dialect (TD) is the native language in a population of 12 million Tunisians and it is used in everyday communication. Since it is derived from Arabic, it uses the same Arabic alphabet in many ways. Tunisians are constantly adopting new words from foreign languages such as French and English and translating them into TD. Some researchers are trying to use OSM to create

---

[1] http://www.socialbakers.com/website/data/industry-report.

different datasets for different NLP tasks, but few of them are interested in TD language when considering topic extraction tasks.

In [15] the author pay special attention to electronic writing where Arabic and Latin letters are used in TD. They propose a method for constructing a TD corpus and introduce the characteristics of this new form of writing, as well as some extraction methods and filtering steps. The collected corpus initially contained more than 43K messages scraped from user-generated textual content on social media. In particular, they use Facebook and YouTube as the main OSM networks. According to this research, more than 60% of extracted messages were written in Latin characters, of which 64% contained Tunisian dialect words. After processing the data, they generated about 10K instances of Arabic and Latin characters that were cleaned and annotated. This dataset was created for a two label Opinion Mining task and consists of 9K training set with an average split of 4969 positives and 4714 negatives, and 1K test set. In the same context, the work [8] presents the TUNIZI dataset, a corpus of more than 9K Tunisian comments that are written only in the Latin alphabet and published by YouTube channels covering sports, politics, comedy, various TV shows, TV series, art and music. They get a representative and diverse dataset to train machine learning models and deploy various NLP applications such as chat-bots for the Q&A system.

Egyptian language has various original works. We can mention one such (ASTD) corpus in [12], which consists of 10K tweets manually annotated as objective, positive, negative, and neutral via the AWS Turk service. In the work [10], around 40K tweets extracted from text users' blogs build a robust corpus in the same language, manually cleaned and annotated. A large Egyptian dataset (ATSAD) has recently appeared in [1], the authors collected 59K tweets using the Twitter API and continued to label the training and testing datasets as positive and negative using automatic annotation methods. A total of 30K cleaned, validated, and annotated corpora are publicly available for research purposes.

Work related to Algerian dialects may give a little written material while reviewing the literature. A small set of linguistic resources of Algerian dialect are cited in [9] and [6]. However, in [11], the corpus generated by the TWIFIL platform in the period between 2015 and 2019 has more than 40K tweets annotated by three different annotators. TWIFIL introduces much better set of Algerian resources in term of size and quality. The work in the paper [3] introduces (AHS) as a new Arabic dataset on health services for opinion mining purposes. The data set contains 2K tweets and it is unbalanced data set with 1398 negative and 628 positive samples. The authors of this work explained the process of collecting data using the twitter API, pre-processing task for cleaning and filtering data as well as the numerous experiments with machine and deep learning algorithms used in features selection and classification. In the papers [4,5], the authors created a multi-dialect Arabic sentiment Twitter data set (ArSenti-TD) that covers four Arabic countries languages. The annotation included five topics and the overall sentiments in the tweets, the target of the comments and the way it was expressed.

In [2] authors evaluate the performance and effectiveness of topic detection in Arabic texts using a new model of Naive Bayes (NB) classifier. They conducted the experiments with their created corpus ATMC (Arabic Topic Mining Corpus). These latter contains 1897 documents belonging to three different topics; economic (625 doc), culture (639 doc) and sport (633 doc). The corpus was collected from several online newspapers in various time periods from May 2017 to June 2017. It adds more diversity to the data and provides a fair lexicon to the test and training dictionaries for the classifier. To conclude this literature review, we notice few writing materials for combining topic and sentiment analysis, such as the work of [13]. In fact, the authors in [13] considered general Maghreb dialects in corpora extracted from various Facebook pages. They implemented a supervised method to extract sentiment and an unsupervised method to extract topics. They conclude their work by proposing a new semi-supervised approach that combines topic and sentiment in a single model to extract both features and associate each topic with a specific sentiment. However, no resource material were mentioned for the task of topic detection in the TD language up to now.

This was the main purpose that encourages us to build our own corpus of Tunisian dialect language in the object of both topic and sentiment analysis tasks.

3   The Built Corpus

3.1   Presentation

The obtained dataset is referred to TunTap as Tunisian Topics and Polarities Corpus. It consists of over 17K comments collected from various OSM networks (Facebook, YouTube, and Twitter) using relevant API. The resulting corpus consists of three columns. The first column corresponds to comments, and the second column corresponds to the polarity of messages. In the third column, we label each comment with an integer from 1 to 5 for five different topics (Politics, Sports, Media, Sociology, and Health) and 0 for undefined subjects. The dataset was manually annotated by two different annotators. We collected 69772 messages listed in the Table 1. The majority of posts and comments are crawled from Facebook. Different types of pages have been used to ensure the diversity of the corpus (Arts, Sport, Media, Politics, ...) which allow us to cover the maximum of the vocabulary used and avoid imprecision errors. In fact, the author states in [7] that the collection should not take place within a limited social circle to avoid possible message reduplication issues. To increase the diversity and avoid the redundancy, we decided to collect our data in two different periods from February 2021 to July 2021. Table 1 gives information about the pages used in comment extraction.

Table 1. Number of OSM comments by type of page

Type of OSM	Type of pages	Number of extracted comments
Facebook	Sociology	21241
	Politics	7081
	Media	1815
	Sport	24320
	Total	54457
Youtube	Health	1920
	Sociology	329
	Politics	1964
	Total	4213
Twitter	Politics	2789
	Sport	460
	Media	845
	Total	4094

In fact, manual collection makes it possible to identify some filtering rules. We expect that the messages of the corpus should be written in the Tunisian dialect, using only Arabic and Latin alphabets. However, we can find links, advertisements (spam), messages in French, English and other languages. Therefore, it is necessary to identify and classify the form of each message in order to perform statistics and extract samples of our interest.

3.2 Characteristics of the Corpus

Below we briefly examine the main features of our Tunisian dialect corpus (TunTap), which is consisting of 15016 Tunisian dialect comments written in Latin characters and 47748 comments written in Arabic script.

1. Message sizes:
   In our TunTap, the shortest message consists of a single word and two characters. The longest consists of 170 words and 799 characters. We notice that the highest number of messages are a short comments consisting of a number of words varying between 1 and 10.
2. Word sizes:
   On average, a word in the TunTap corpus consists of 9 characters. The sizes were counted according to the number of letters and digits. The statistics shows that the longest word consists of 18 letters. In fact it contains a stretching character (a repeated letter).
3. Multilingualism

Spoken Tunisian can have more than three different languages in one sentence. The most common are: Dialects, Modern Standard Arabic (MSA), Standard French, and Standard English. As for the written form, it is much more complicated. Tunisian dialect words can be written in different ways. There are no special rules because it is not an official or taught language, but a native language. Based on statistics in the corpus, a mixed distribution between dialects and other languages have been identified and the large number of words were split between Tunisian Dialect and MSA. We found that 9% words in the dictionary of the corpus are ambiguous, and the rest are distributed between dialects, MSA, French and English.

3.3 Data Pre-processing and Normalisation

The number of samples collected is sufficient for subject and polarity detection experiments as it contains a wide variety of words and sentence structures. In contrast, the total number of messages contains a large number of noisy observations, making it impossible to use the data previously mentioned in the original format. The unstructured text that will later be used to feed the ML models should be cleaned up before processing the NLP task to meet the requirements. Therefore, unused and unnecessary words and characters should be removed from the corpus, as they do not add any value to the features presented in the comments. The next operation is to perform a normalization process to maintain basic patterns from words, so the feature extraction process can be more efficient. The following items are examples of noise data that has been removed.

- Spam comments which are messages that contain advertisements or harmful links
- users' name which are in the form of @user-name
- URLs which started by https://
- Hashtags topics
- Punctuation

Although, removing stop words seems to be crucial to improve the classification accuracy of the model. The limitations of this operation are related to the availability of language-specific stop words data. To this end, when running the stop word removal function in the classification algorithm, we restrict the task to the list of stop words suggested in the NLTK library for English, French, and Arabic.

In addition to these operations, we performed a normalization process of some words letters as summarized below;

1. Eliminating Arabic short vowels (diacritics) added above or below an arabic letter to indicate the particularity in its pronunciation, especialy the character < Hamzah > < ؤ,ئ > to < وى,ى > and < Alif > < أ,إ > to < ا >.
2. Normalizing any word with stretching (repeated letter) used in OSM to pump up the emotions such as < مريييييض > to < مريض >.

3. Removing the Tatwiil < ___ >   which does not affect the meaning of the word.
4. Manually fixing the spaces between words either missing or expanded.
5. Correcting words which were either missing some letters or replacing letters by other special ones.

The number of retrieved comments was massive over (69K) but it decreased to 62K after filtering and pre-processing. We were able to prepare 17k of cleaned and annotated instances and we kept an extra 45k of cleaned data to further work. Table 2 shows the number of samples of each sentiment class and Table 3 shows the number of samples in each topic.

Table 2. Cardinalities distributions of Polarity

	Neutral	Positive	Negative
Number of samples	2819	5697	9303

Table 3. Topic cardinalities distributions before and after pre-processing steps

Topic	Original data	Generated data
Undefined	21550	9898
Politic	8840	2401
Sport	2660	660
Media	3120	703
Sociology	24420	3661
Health	2174	489

According to the provided topic and polarity cardinals, it is evident that the proposed dataset is unbalanced. Thus, more current efforts in exploring the remaining data are undertaken to expand our corpus and avoid issues related to unbalanced classifications in predictive modeling, since most of the ML algorithms are designed around the assumption of an equal number of examples for each class.

4   Experiments and Results

For machine learning perspective, the Sentiment Analysis (SA) and Topic Mining (TM) could be represented as text classification problem, except some clustering tasks in Topic Modeling. In this section we present a benchmark of experiments we performed in order to find the most suitable ML model in features extraction and classification as well as evaluating the reliability of our TunTap corpus with reference to other dialects datasets.

4.1 Steps and Methods

The experiments undertaken above exploit the described datasets as follow:

First, not only we implement and test different baseline (DesicionTree and RandomForest) classifiers and complex (GaussianNB, SGDclassifier and linearSVC) models, but we also tested the recent BERT model (the UNCASED-L8-H12-BERT).

Second, Intrinsic experiments have been conducted on our TunTap corpus with different data representation (Frequency, TF-IDF and Embedding) models and several train steps on two different text mining tasks (SA and TM), in the benefit of extracting the relation existing between each task and the data representation model.

Finally, we study and evaluate the effectiveness of our corpus and discuss its limitations.

4.2 Training Data and Features Extraction

The overall data used in the experiments are described in details in Sect. 2. All experiments are undertaken for two main text mining tasks, Sentiment Analysis task (SA) and Topic Mining task (TM). We used three different training corpus for each task among SA and TM. AHS (Arabic Health Services) dataset, TSAC (Tunisian Sentiment Analysis Corpus) and TunTap (our corpus) are the three datasets used in SA experiments. ATMC (Arabic Topic Mining Corpus), ArSenTD (Multi-Dialect Arabic Sentiment Dataset) and TunTap (our corpus) are the three datasets used in TM experiments.

In order to simplify the evaluation of our dataset reliability, each sentence is considered as a document sample for all datasets and each document is vectorized using TF-IDF model in the dimention of its dictionary (dataset).

4.3 Classification

In both SA and TM, the most widely used machine learning models are MLP classifiers, Support Vector Machines (SVM) and Naive Bayes (NB). On top of these methods, we evaluated one of the most recent contextual neural language model BERT. We conducted two main intrinsic sets of experiments. The first set was performed in the benefit of Sentiment Analysis as illustrated in Table 4 and the second set was implemented to evaluate the effectiveness of our corpus in topic extraction as presented in Table 5.

Table 4. Results of SA experiments using various classifiers for each dataset including our TunTap corpus

Dataset	Number of labels	Model	Accuracy	Precision	Recall	F1
AHS 2K	2 sentiment labels	Gaussian_NB	0,79	0,71	0,74	0,72
		RandomForestClassifier	0,65	0,64	0,65	0,64
		SGDClassifier	0,71	0,70	0,73	0,71
		DecisionTreeClassifier	0,59	0,57	0,55	0,56
		LinearSVC	**0,80**	**0,81**	**0,74**	**0,77**
		Uncased_L8_H12_BERT	0,75	0,75	0,76	0,75
TSAC 10K	2 sentiment labels	Gaussian_NB	0,72	0,69	0,71	0,70
		RandomForestClassifier	0,69	0,61	0,52	0,56
		SGDClassifier	0,65	0,71	0,73	0,72
		DecisionTreeClassifier	0,39	0,67	0,55	0,60
		LinearSVC	0,67	0,71	0,74	0,72
		Uncased_L8_H12_BERT	**0,85**	**0,85**	**0,86**	**0,85**
TunTap 17K	3 sentiment labels	Gaussian_NB	0,58	0,60	0,67	0,63
		RandomForestClassifier	0,46	0,43	0,40	0,41
		SGDClassifier	0,60	0,51	0,60	0,55
		DecisionTreeClassifier	0,52	0,43	0,52	0,47
		LinearSVC	0,58	0,54	0,52	0,53
		Uncased_L8_H12_BERT	**0,81**	**0,78**	**0,81**	**0,79**

Table 5. Results of our corpus evaluations in the task of Topic extraction using various classifiers for each dataset including TunTap corpus

Dataset	Feature-EX	Model	Accuracy	Precision	Recall	F1
ATMC 2K	3 topics	Gaussian_NB	0,81	0,95	0,79	0,86
		RandomForestClassifier	0,46	0,70	0,28	0,40
		SGDClassifier	0,73	0,87	0,68	0,76
		DecisionTreeClassifier	0,53	0,33	0,41	0,37
		LinearSVC	0,85	0,71	0,94	0,81
		Uncased_L8_H12_BERT	**0,92**	**0,86**	**0,95**	**0,90**
ArSenTD 4K	5 topics	Gaussian_NB	0,49	0,63	0,62	0,62
		RandomForestClassifier	0,68	0,49	0,34	0,40
		SGDClassifier	0,65	0,64	0,62	0,63
		DecisionTreeClassifier	0,48	0,50	0,36	0,42
		LinearSVC	0,67	0,66	0,64	0,65
		Uncased_L8_H12_BERT	**0,77**	**0,76**	**0,77**	**0,76**
TunTap 17K	5 topics	Gaussian_NB	0,70	0,70	0,51	0,59
		RandomForestClassifier	0,55	0,57	0,75	0,65
		SGDClassifier	**0,85**	**0,84**	**0,57**	**0,68**
		DecisionTreeClassifier	0,81	0,83	0,78	0,80
		LinearSVC	0,80	0,61	0,57	0,59
		Uncased_L8_H12_BERT	0,65	0,65	0,66	0,65

4.4   Results and Discussion

The results of different classifiers with the given experimental datasets at hand are evaluated using 10% of test sets. The above results are illustrated using four metrics: precision (P), recall (R), F1 measure and accuracy (ACC). As mentioned in Table 4 and Table 5, multiple approaches have been investigated in the experiments, starting with traditional ML techniques, then moving to more complex approaches. As expected, the best classification performance for all datasets are obtained using SVM and BERT models. The highest and best measurements are marked by using bolt font and yellow background color in the tables. These measurements agree with the results of previous studies which found that contextualized models and transformers are good classifiers in text mining processing.

As alluded to above, we obtained a promising results in the task of sentiment analysis on our TunTap corpus being 81% with BERT, 58% with SVM, 60% with SGD classifier and 58% with NB. As shown in Table 4, BERT and SVM models obtain similar results for all datasets in solving the SA task. However, higher results are obtained with Stochastic Gradient Descent classifier in the task of topic detection.

The main two reasons are related to the limitations of our TunTap dataset regarding label distribution balancing as described in Sect. 3, as well as the size of the generated samples. Hence, much effort are in progress. Nevertheless, the results illustrated by the NB classifier in Table 5 motivated us to conduct extensive experiments using various data representation models (Frequency, TF-IDF, Embedding-encoder, ...) and different classifiers to evaluate the relation between the data presentation model and each text mining task conducted with our corpus.

As we see, both Fig. 1 and Fig. 2 highlights a special aspect related to data representation model and accuracy results. The seq2vec representation using TF-IDF vectorisation model Fig. 2 illustrates much better accuracy results than word2vec embedding representation for almost all baseline classifiers in the task of topic detection. Whereas, Fig. 1 shows that TF-IDF data representation model was tied to the worst results in the task of Sentiment Analysis. The reason is that TF-IDF model combined to some baseline classifiers holds crucial insights about existing patterns of words frequencies among sentences in respect to their relevant topics and field of interest. Thus, such configuration contributes more in several NLP and ML tasks like topic detection. However, the noise and misspelling jargon presented in social media texts, makes word2vec embedding representation model more suitable in dealing with the task of polarity detection as shown in Fig. 1.

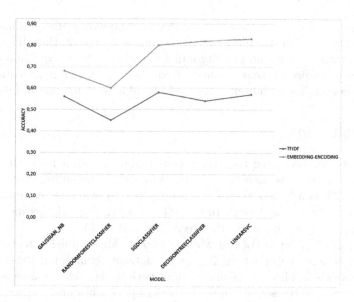

Fig. 1. Illustration of TunTap corpus accuracy results using several data representation models for Sentiment Analysis

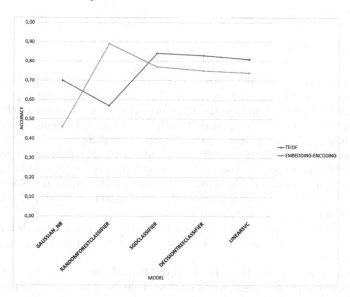

Fig. 2. Illustration of TunTap corpus accuracy results using several data representation models for Topic Detection

Considering the undertaken experiments above, there are different approaches and methods specific to each task along with the most appropriate document representation model. In addition to that, models have to be more independent from dictionary redesign and should not be sensitive strictly to tokens spelling. Each word can have different embedding under different topics and topics relation can influence on document representation. In particular, the case of tuning topic and polarity multi-model classifiers requires a new data representation approach that combines frequency document representation and document embedding technique. This could be of a great interest in future work.

5   Conclusions

In this paper, we presented the first Tunisian Dialect corpus for both sentiment analysis and topic detection tasks at the same time, including more than 17k comments. We conducted extensive experiments to evaluate our dataset. The results demonstrated that both the BERT model and SVM classifier achieved outstanding accuracy measures (between 60% and 80%)

The main contribution of this work was to enhance Tunisian resource materials on topic and sentiment mining, as no datasets combining these two variants are provided. This new Tunisian multivariate dataset opens new doors in NLP researches to investigate in multi-model approaches and techniques. More developed and concrete social media analytics systems build on top of these approaches will lead to precise and accurate semantic feature extraction and decision making.

References

1. Abu Kwaik, K., Chatzikyriakidis, S., Dobnik, S., Saad, M., Johansson, R.: An arabic tweets sentiment analysis dataset (ATSAD) using distant supervision and self training. In: Proceedings of the 4th Workshop on Open-Source Arabic Corpora and Processing Tools, with a Shared Task on Offensive Language Detection, pp. 1–8. European Language Resource Association (05 2020)
2. Al-khurayji, R., Sameh, A.: An effective Arabic text classification approach based on kernel Naive Bayes classifier (2017). https://doi.org/10.5121/IJAIA.2017.8601
3. Alayba, A.M., Palade, V., England, M., Iqbal, R.: A combined CNN and LSTM model for Arabic sentiment analysis. arXiv:1807.02911 [cs] 11015, 179–191 (2018). https://doi.org/10.1007/978-3-319-99740-7_12
4. Baly, R., et al.: Comparative evaluation of sentiment analysis methods across arabic dialects. Procedia Comput. Sci. **117**, 266–273 (2017). https://doi.org/10.1016/j.procs.2017.10.118
5. Baly, R., Khaddaj, A., Hajj, H., El-Hajj, W., Shaban, K.B.: ArSentD-LEV: a multi-topic corpus for target-based sentiment analysis in Arabic levantine tweets. arXiv:1906.01830 [cs, stat], 25 May 2019
6. Cotterell, R., Callison-Burch, C.: A multi-dialect, multi-genre corpus of informal written Arabic. In: Proceedings of the Ninth International Conference on Language Resources and Evaluation (LREC 2014), pp. 241–245. European Language Resources Association (ELRA), May 2014
7. Fairon, C., Klein, J., Sébastien, P.: Le langage SMS : révélateur d'1compétence, 01 January 2006
8. Fourati, C., Messaoudi, A., Haddad, H.: TUNIZI: a tunisian arabizi sentiment analysis dataset. arXiv:2004.14303 [cs] (2020-04-29)

9. Meftouh, K., Bouchemal, N., Smaïli, K.: A study of a non-resourced language: an Algerian dialect. In: SLTU (2012)
10. Mohammed, A., Kora, R.: Deep learning approaches for Arabic sentiment analysis. Soc. Netw. Anal. Min. **9**(1), 1–12 (2019). https://doi.org/10.1007/s13278-019-0596-4
11. Moudjari, L., Aklii Astouati, K.: An experimental study on sentiment classification of Algerian dialect texts. Procedia Comput. Sci. **176**, 1151–1159 (2020). https://doi.org/10.1016/j.procs.2020.09.111
12. Nabil, M., Aly, M., Atiya, A.: ASTD: Arabic sentiment tweets dataset. In: Proceedings of the 2015 Conference on Empirical Methods in Natural Language Processing, pp. 2515–2519. Association for Computational Linguistics, September 2015. https://doi.org/10.18653/v1/D15-1299
13. Taoufiq, Z., Chiheb, R., Moumen, R., Faizi, R., El Afia, A.: Topic and sentiment model applied to the colloquial Arabic: a case study of Maghrebi Arabic, 21 June 2017. https://doi.org/10.1145/3128128.3128155
14. Wahdan, A., Hantoobi, S., Salloum, S., Shaalan, K.: A systematic review of text classification research based on deep learning models in Arabic language, pp. 6629–6643, 12 January 2020. https://doi.org/10.11591/ijece.v10i6.pp6629-6643
15. Younes, J., Hadhémi, A., Souissi, E.: Constructing linguistic resources for the Tunisian dialect using textual user-generated contents on the social web. vol. 9396, pp. 3–14, 23 June 2015. https://doi.org/10.1007/978-3-319-24800-4_1

An Adaptive Social Network Model
for Expatriate Integration Based on Bonding
by Homophily and Interaction Connects

Kamiel Gülpen[1], Dante de Lang[1], and Jan Treur[2(✉)]

[1] Computational Science, University of Amsterdam, Amsterdam, The Netherlands
{k.gulpen,d.c.c.de.lang}@student.vu.nl
[2] Social AI Group, Vrije Universiteit Amsterdam, Amsterdam, The Netherlands
j.treur@vu.nl

Abstract. This paper introduces a new view on modelling expatriate integration by mapping connections between expats and between expats and the local community. The proposed adaptive social network model differs from existing integration models in that it considers both the bonding by homophily principle together with the interaction connects principle to model the adaptivity of the strength of social connections. In the results it was found that both principles have different influences on how well expats integrate with the local community; a combination of both principles showed to be stronger than their sum.

1 Introduction

Although in recent years there has been a surge in interest in the literature about expatriate integration, the quantity of literature available on the subject is relatively limited [5]. More research in this area would be preferable as the amount of expatriates rises. Finaccord [9] reports that the number of expatriates increased by 15% between 2013 and 2017 and they expect the increasing trend to continue.

Expatriate integration is an important topic of study since it aids to improving the well-being of expatriates. According to [3] feeling alone is a regular phenomenon that expats and their partners cope with when moving to their host country. In addition to improving their well-being, job performance of expatriates can improve by being more integrated. Despite a paucity of empirical data, there is a favorable association between expatriate social relationships to host country nationals and job performance [15].

In this study, we provide a computational model of the integration between expatriates and the local community in their host country. The modeling techniques used in this study have already been demonstrated to be applicable in a different social situation, as demonstrated in the paper of Kappert et al. [13], which looked at how segregation emerges, using friendship homophily in a network of immigrants. For our model we have chosen a two leveled adaptive network approach in which social connections are determined by weights. These weights cover the connections between expats and between expats and the local community. Furthermore, we focus on two important principles that drive integration, namely bonding by homophily [2, 16, 17] and the interaction connects [11, 18] principle.

Together with more background knowledge, these principles will be explained further in the next section. Following the background, the model will be explained in detail in Sect. 3. In Sect. 4 the simulation results will be discussed for four different scenarios. These results will be verified, validated and discussed in Sects. 5 and 6.

2 Background Knowledge

According to van Houdt [27], citizenship is no longer something that a person acquires just by housing within a country, an individual must also be able to integrate economically, socially and culturally. Although expatriates are already economically integrated upon arrival, they do not seem to be interested in the long commitment of integrating socially and culturally [7]. Because of their movements, expats frequently reside in a globalized culture distinct from the local culture in which they live; they have access to different government programs, expat groups, and other services during the time they are in one location [7]. Expats are therefore the fraction of individuals who feel strongly affiliated with the global cosmopolitan culture that exists inside the worldwide networks in which they operate, as opposed to the majority of the rest of the population, who feel strongly identified with their regional identities [4].

Expatriates feel most at home in their expatriate 'bubble', which means that expats prefer to engage with fellow expatriates rather than with local inhabitants [6, 8]. At the same time, expatriates can be viewed as cosmopolitans who desire to bridge the gap between themselves and local inhabitants [12]. Moreover van Bochove and Engbersen [26] show in their study an example of expatriates who wish to be more active in the local community but find it difficult to do so owing to the lack of effort that local inhabitants put into integration. This is consistent with previous studies [20, 21] and Weiner's [28] hypothesis, which states that one of the three crucial aspects of effective integration is the is willingness of the society to absorb the immigrant.

Governmental organizations may play an important role in integrating expats into the local population. However, expats are regarded differently than other immigrants since they are typically well educated and as such valuable to the state in which they relocate [22]. This difference in treatment results in the fact that it is not required for expats to attend language classes or take the civic exam, which might lead to the expats failing to integrate properly. Another way the state can improve the integration of the expats is by influencing the interaction the expats have with the local citizens, for example by organising nonseparated housing and education [28]. In contrast to the expat bubble, there are family members or partners of expats who do not necessarily reside in the expat bubble, partially because they cannot find work in the place of arrival [7, 19]. As a result, these individuals are more likely to form social relationships outside of the expat bubble and feel a greater need to learn the host language and integrate.

For these social relationships we have focused on two connection principles, namely bonding by homophily and interactions connects. The bonding by homophily principle relies on the similarity between individuals and states that the higher this similarity is, the stronger the connection will become: 'birds of a feather flock together' [2, 16, 17]. The second principle, Interaction Connects, addresses how the weights of connections can be affected by the actual interaction taking place. This effect is based on the assumption that the more frequent and intense the interaction is between two persons, the stronger their connection will become. This effect is found within musical settings [11, 18] but also has shown to increase the willingness of expats to communicate in a foreign language [23]. For some further discussion of the Interaction Connects principle in relation to the neural and social psychological domains (in particular, involving interpersonal synchronisation), see the last paragraph in the discussion of Sect. 6.

3   The Social Network Model of Expatriate Integration

This section will first give a general description of the designed adaptive network model. In relation to Sect. 2, the corresponding rationale behind it will be indicated.

Temporal-causal network models can be represented at two levels, namely conceptually, by graphical network images, and numerically, by formulae [25]. Furthermore, they can be quantitatively examined and confirmed by comparing simulation findings to actual data. They often contain a number of parameters for different domain-, human-, or social context-specific traits. In the first place, a declarative representation of a temporal-causal network model entails describing states X, Y and connections $X \to Y$ between them that indicate (causal) impacts of states on each other, as assumed within the application area that is being addressed. The states have the possibility to contain varying (activation) levels $X(t)$, $Y(t)$ throughout time. In addition, as not all causal relationships are equally strong, a weighted connection is used, indicated by weight $\omega_{X,Y}$. Furthermore, when more than one causal link affects a state, a method is needed to aggregate various causal influences on a state. Additionally, a concept of the speed factor of a state is employed in order to simulate process timing.

In order for these states to have a causal relation the model relies on combination functions and weights. A certain state Y can be impacted by a connecting state X, this impact is defined as $\mathbf{impact}_{X,Y}(t) = \omega_{X,Y} X(t)$ where $\omega_{X,Y}$ represents the weight of the connection from X to Y. For simple connections state values change according to these weights and the speed factors, which are commonly denoted by η_Y. In order to aggregate the impact of multiple incoming states X_i on Y, combination functions (available in a library) are used, denoted by $c_Y(..)$. Using these network characteristics $\omega_{X,Y}$ for connectivity, $c_Y(..)$ for aggregation, and η_Y for timing, we can formulate the following difference (or differential) equations in a standard numerical format:

$$\mathbf{aggimpact}_Y(t) = c_Y(\mathbf{impact}_{X_1,Y}(t),...,\mathbf{impact}_{X_k,Y}(t)) = c_Y(\omega_{X_1,Y}X_1(t),...,\omega_{X_k,Y}X_k(t))$$

Based on this, the standard difference and differential equation used here, is obtained by adding the speed factor η_Y to gradually (in proportion with this speed factor) get the impact (represented by $\mathbf{aggimpact}_Y(t)$) on Y:

$$\mathbf{d}Y(t)/\mathbf{d}t = \eta_Y[\mathbf{aggimpact}_Y(t) - Y(t)] = \eta_Y[c_Y(\omega_{X_1,Y}X_1(t),...,\omega_{X_k,Y}X_k(t)) - Y(t)]$$

or as difference equation:

$$Y(t + \Delta t) = Y(t) + \eta_Y [\mathbf{c}_Y (\omega_{X_1,Y} X_1(t), ..., \omega_{X_k,Y} X_k(t)) - Y(t)] \Delta t$$

For adaptive network models, self-model states are used that represent some network characteristics $\omega_{X,Y}$, $\mathbf{c}_Y(..)$, η_Y. For example, a self-model state $\mathbf{W}_{X,Y}$ can be (and has been) used to represent the connectivity characteristic $\omega_{X,Y}$.

As shown below, the designed adaptive temporal-causal adaptive network model consists of 17 base states and 36 (first-order) self-model states, which function as adaptive weights for the connections of the base states; see Tables 1 and 2 for an overview of all states. The base level contains 5 expat states (X_1 to X_5), one local citizen state (L), one government state (G) and 10 interaction connects states (I) specifying the amounts of interaction they have, for example, by working together. Of the 36 self-model states there are 20 connection weight self-model states (also called **W**-states) from which 10 states are model bonding by homophily ($\mathbf{W}_{X-X/LH}$) and 10 states model the interaction

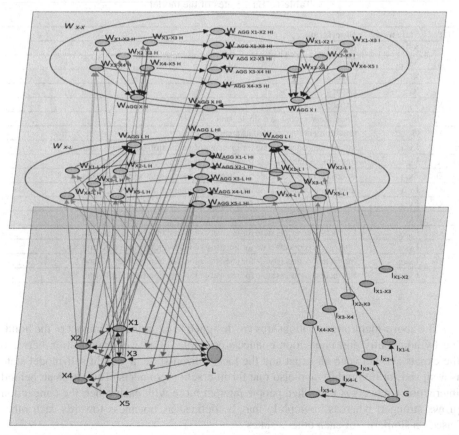

Fig. 1. Graphical representation of the adaptive network with a base level (pink) and a (first-order) self-model level (blue). (Color figure online)

connects principle ($\mathbf{W}_{X-X/LI}$) [24]. The remaining 16 states are used to aggregate these adaptive weights ($\mathbf{W}_{AGG}$).

Within the five expat states there are only bidirectional connections, three of the five expats $X_1 - X_3$ are fully connected in a triangle, this cluster of connected states is based on the expat 'bubble' [6, 8]. Although each expats connection weight varies, the expats within this 'bubble' have a reasonably high connection weight with one another while maintaining a comparatively low connection weight with local inhabitants L. Expats X_4 and X_5 are connected sequentially to X_3. Expat X_4 is based on the idea that although expats tend to connect to one another they also desire to bridge the gap between themselves and local inhabitants [12]. Based on this assumption, the X_4 state has a bigger interaction weight with the local states than the expat cluster does, while still maintaining a connection with the expats. Expat X_5 is based on the premise that partners of expats do not necessarily reside in the expat bubble [7, 19]. As a result, X_5 has one link to expat X_4 and no linkages to the expat cluster, while maintaining stronger relationships with the local citizen state L than the other X states.

Table 1. Base states of the model

ID	State name	Description
X_1	X_1	Expat 1
X_2	X_2	Expat 2
X_3	X_3	Expat 3
X_4	X_4	Expat 4
X_5	X_5	Expat 5
X_6	L	Locals represented as a single state
X_7	G	Government represented as a single state
X_8	$\mathbf{I}_{X_1\text{-}L}$	Interaction connects state for intensity of interaction between X_1 and L
X_9	$\mathbf{I}_{X_2\text{-}L}$	Interaction connects state for intensity of interaction between X_2 and L
X_{10}	$\mathbf{I}_{X_3\text{-}L}$	Interaction connects state for intensity of interaction between X_3 and L
X_{11}	$\mathbf{I}_{X_4\text{-}L}$	Interaction connects state for intensity of interaction between X_4 and L
X_{12}	$\mathbf{I}_{X_5\text{-}L}$	Interaction connects state for intensity of interaction between X_5 and L
X_{13}	$\mathbf{I}_{X_1\text{-}X_2}$	Interaction connects state for intensity of interaction between X_1 and X_2
X_{14}	$\mathbf{I}_{X_1\text{-}X_3}$	Interaction connects state for intensity of interaction between X_1 and X_3
X_{15}	$\mathbf{I}_{X_2\text{-}X_3}$	Interaction connects state for intensity of interaction between X_2 and X_3
X_{16}	$\mathbf{I}_{X_3\text{-}X_4}$	Interaction connects state for intensity of interaction between X_3 and X_4
X_{17}	$\mathbf{I}_{X_4\text{-}X_5}$	Interaction connects state for intensity of interaction between X_4 and X_5

The above-mentioned relationships are designed to examine the impact of the bonding by homophily and interaction connects principles. For every connection between the expats and between an expat and the local citizen state, a weight self-model state is assigned for homophily and also one for interaction connects. The rationale behind interaction connects is that when people interact more with each other, the connection grows stronger, whereas homophily may be defined as openness towards each other based on similarity of each other's states.

As we modeled only bidirectional connections between the expats and between the expats and the native citizen state L, the aggregated weight self-model states are used as adaptive weights for both directions of the connection. In combination with the other aggregated states this enables us to create insights in the strength of integration.

The mathematical formulations of the four functions in our network are provided in Table 3. The identity function, the first and most basic function in this table, is used

Table 2. The self-model states of the model

ID	State name	Description
X_{18}	$W_{X_1\text{-}L\,I}$	Interaction connects weight self-model state between X_1 and L
X_{19}	$W_{X_2\text{-}L\,I}$	Interaction connects weight self-model state between X_2 and L
X_{20}	$W_{X_3\text{-}L\,I}$	Interaction connects weight self-model state between X_3 and L
X_{21}	$W_{X_4\text{-}L\,I}$	Interaction connects weight self-model state between X_4 and L
X_{22}	$W_{X_5\text{-}L\,I}$	Interaction connects weight self-model state between X_5 and L
X_{23}	$W_{X_1\text{-}X_2\,I}$	Interaction connects weight self-model state between X_1 and X_2
X_{24}	$W_{X_1\text{-}X_3\,I}$	Interaction connects weight self-model state between X_1 and X_3
X_{25}	$W_{X_2\text{-}X_3\,I}$	Interaction connects weight self-model state between X_2 and X_3
X_{26}	$W_{X_3\text{-}X_4\,I}$	Interaction connects weight self-model state between X_3 and X_4
X_{27}	$W_{X_4\text{-}X_5\,I}$	Interaction connects weight self-model state between X_4 and X_5
X_{28}	$W_{X_1\text{-}X_2\,H}$	Homophily weight self-model state between X_1 and X_2
X_{29}	$W_{X_1\text{-}X_3\,H}$	Homophily weight self-model state between X_1 and X_3
X_{30}	$W_{X_2\text{-}X_3\,H}$	Homophily weight self-model state between X_2 and X_3
X_{31}	$W_{X_3\text{-}X_4\,H}$	Homophily weight self-model state between X_3 and X_4
X_{32}	$W_{X_4\text{-}X_5\,H}$	Homophily weight self-model state between X_4 and X_5
X_{33}	$W_{X_1\text{-}L\,H}$	Homophily weight self-model state between X_1 and L
X_{34}	$W_{X_2\text{-}L\,H}$	Homophily weight self-model state between X_2 and L
X_{35}	$W_{X_3\text{-}L\,H}$	Homophily weight self-model state between X_3 and L
X_{36}	$W_{X_4\text{-}L\,H}$	Homophily weight self-model state between X_4 and L
X_{37}	$W_{X_5\text{-}L\,H}$	Homophily weight self-model state between X_5 and L
X_{38}	$W_{Agg\,X_1\text{-}X_2\,HI}$	Aggregate weight state for Homophily and Interaction connects between X_1 and X_2
X_{39}	$W_{Agg\,X_1\text{-}X_3\,HI}$	Aggregate weight state for Homophily and Interaction connects between X_1 and X_3
X_{40}	$W_{Agg\,X_2\text{-}X_3\,HI}$	Aggregate weight state for Homophily and Interaction connects between X_2 and X_3
X_{41}	$W_{Agg\,X_3\text{-}X_4\,HI}$	Aggregate weight state for Homophily and Interaction connects between X_3 and X_4
X_{42}	$W_{Agg\,X_4\text{-}X_5\,HI}$	Aggregate weight state for Homophily and Interaction connects between X_4 and X_5
X_{43}	$W_{Agg\,X_1\text{-}L\,HI}$	Aggregate weight state for Homophily and Interaction connects between X_1 and L
X_{44}	$W_{Agg\,X_2\text{-}L\,HI}$	Aggregate weight state for Homophily and Interaction connects between X_2 and L
X_{45}	$W_{Agg\,X_3\text{-}L\,HI}$	Aggregate weight state for Homophily and Interaction connects between X_3 and L
X_{46}	$W_{Agg\,X_4\text{-}L\,HI}$	Aggregate weight state for Homophily and Interaction connects between X4 and L
X_{47}	$W_{Agg\,X_5\text{-}L\,HI}$	Aggregate weight state for Homophily and Interaction connects between X_5 and L
X_{48}	$W_{Agg\,L\,I}$	Aggregate weight state for Interaction connects between L and all X's
X_{49}	$W_{Agg\,X\,I}$	Aggregate weight state for Interaction connects between all X's
X_{50}	$W_{Agg\,X\,H}$	Aggregate weight state for Homophily between all X's
X_{51}	$W_{Agg\,X\,HI}$	Aggregate weight state for Interaction connects and Homophily between all X's
X_{52}	$W_{Agg\,L\,H}$	Aggregate weight state for Homophily between L and all X's
X_{53}	$W_{Agg\,L\,HI}$	Aggregate weight state for Interaction connects and Homophily between L and all X's

for the interaction and government beginning states, I states and G state, in order for them to continue feeding the network. The scaled sum function is used to aggregate and normalize input connections for state L for locals and the expat base states $X_1 - X_5$. The incoming connections for the interaction connects weight self-model states $\mathbf{W}_I$, are modeled by an advanced logistic function. For the homophily connection weight self-model states $\mathbf{W}_H$, the simple linear homophily function is used. The full specification of the model can be found in the Appendix available as Linked Data at https://www.res earchgate.net/publication/357340188.

Table 3. Combination functions used and their formulation.

Name	Function	Formula	Parameters
Identity	$\mathbf{id}(V)$	V	–
Scaled sum	$\mathbf{ssum}_\lambda(V_1, ..., V_k)$	$\frac{V_1+\cdots+V_k}{\lambda}$	Scaling factor λ
Advanced logistic sum	$\mathbf{alogistic}_{\sigma,\tau}(V_1, ...,V_k)$	$[\frac{1}{1+e^{-\sigma(V_1+\cdots+V_k-\tau)}} - \frac{1}{1+e^{\sigma\tau}}](1+e^{-\sigma\tau})$	Steepness σ Threshold τ
Simple linear homophily	$\mathbf{slhomo}_{\alpha,\tau}(V_1, V_2,W)$	$W+\alpha(\tau-|V_1-V_2|)(1-W)W$ V_1, V_2 state values; W connection weight	Modulation factor α Tipping point τ

4 Simulation Scenarios and Results

The simulations have been obtained using the dedicated software environment (see ch 9 of [25]); all graphs were generated from this. For our results we will focus on the values of the aggregated weight reification states between the expats and the local community. These states, e.g. $\mathbf{W}_{AGG\ X1\ L\ HI}$, represent the overall connection between an expat and the L state and can be seen as a representation of integration. We will also discuss the expat state values on base level while this can be seen as some sort of opinion value. In both cases a value closer to 1 represents a higher level of integration. A detailed representation of the scenario's can be found in the Appendix mentioned above.

In the first scenario all principles are already present between the expats and between the expats (X-) states and the local citizen (L-) state. However, the connections between the expats are in this base scenario stronger then those between them and the L-state. This ensures we start with an situation were the expats are more prone to stick with each other instead of mixing with the local population. As shown in graph in Fig. 2 only the connection weight between X_5 and L reaches the value of 1.

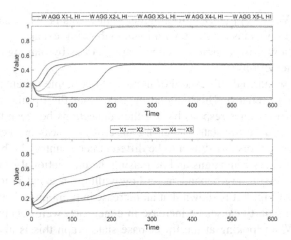

Fig. 2. Simulation results for Scenario 1

This is as expected since we have constructed the model as such that X_5 is the most prone to connecting to the local community by symbolizing the partner of X_4. In addition the $X_1 - L$ aggregated weight remains at the lowest level showing no integration at all. When inspecting the base states in the lower graph it can also be observed that the states remain divided between the value range 0.3–0.8.

In the second scenario we focus on the interaction connects principle by increasing the speed factors of the interaction (I-) states driven by the government (G-) state. This will result in an increase of interaction between the X-states and L-state. This symbolizes a government taking action by for instance actively mixing expats with the local community or by expats working together with local inhabitants in a diverse work environment. In the above graph in Fig. 3 it is shown that increasing the interaction between locals and expats causes all weight reification states to increase quicker while

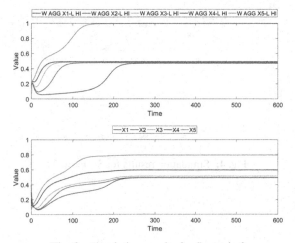

Fig. 3. Simulation results for Scenario 2

also pulling the $\mathbf{W}_{\text{AGG X1-L HI}}$ state to a higher value. This is also visible in the lower base state graph as X_1 clusters more with its neighbouring expats $X_2 - X_3$. This give some insight in how it is possible to connect both parties by playing an active role in increasing the interactions.

For the third scenario the threshold of homophily principle is being decreased with respect to the first scenario. This is done by increasing the tipping point values for the weight reification states responsible for the connections between the X-states and the L-state. This can be translated as an increase of openness or acceptance in both directions. In practice this has shown to be different per country [1], but could also be increased by awareness campaigns and increasing the international status of a country. It is however, also still very dependent on how willing an expat is to integrating. In the above graph of Fig. 4 it is shown that an increase in homophily between the expats and the local community causes an increase in connection weight between X_3, X_4 and the L − state. When looking at the lower base state graph this is also visible as the X_3 and X_4 end at a higher value then in the first scenario. This is interesting since it shows that the least interconnected expats seem to be more susceptible for small changes that influence homophily. This behaviour is also translated to the base states as shown in the lower graph were all states also reach a value close to 1. This shows that the combination of both principles has a stronger effect than their sum. For the last scenario the parameter changes of Scenario 2 and 3 are combined. This creates a combination of both governmental actions for increasing interaction and an increase in openness and willingness. The results for this scenario are shown in Fig. 5. In the top graph it is shown how all of the connection weight self-model states reach a value close to 1 within a relatively short time span.

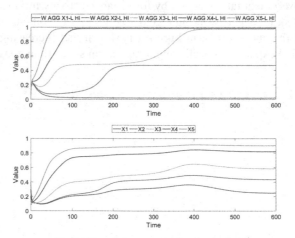

Fig. 4. Simulation results for Scenario 3

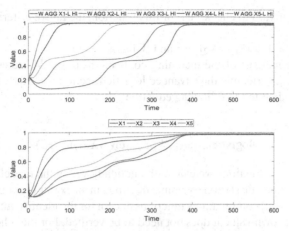

Fig. 5. Simulation results for Scenario 4

5   Mathematical Analysis of the Model

From a dynamical perspective, a temporal-causal network model can be defined using its mathematical representations. This section will elaborate on the mathematical combination functions that play a main role in the model. These functions handle multiple incoming impact from other states. The state values from the connected states are multiplied with their corresponding connection weights to obtain (multiple) single impacts upon which the combination function is applied to get the aggregated impact. For mathematical formulation behind this we rely on previous work [24, 25].

When looking at the definitions stated in this work a certain state Y, has a time-dependent value denoted by $Y(t)$, mostly has a real number value in the interval $[0, 1]$. In order to analyse the model it is useful to determine stationary points or equilibria. An equilibrium is found when every state of the model is in a stationary point. A stationary point occurs if $\mathbf{d}Y(t)/\mathbf{d}t = 0$. The stationary points can be determined using the difference or differential equations as formulated in Sect. 3. In order for this equation to adhere to the definition for a stationary point, it should hold that $Y(t + \Delta t) = Y(t)$. For nonzero speed factors, this is equivalent to the following criterion in terms of the network characteristics:

$$\mathbf{aggimpact}_Y(t) = Y(t)$$
$$\text{where } \mathbf{aggimpact}_Y(t) = \mathbf{c}_Y(\mathbf{impact}_{X_1,Y}(t),....,\mathbf{impact}_{X_k,Y}(t))$$

For the homophily principle the combination function is used by the $\mathbf{W}_H$-states is (see Table 1):

$$\mathbf{slhomo}_{\alpha,\tau}(V_1,...,V_k) = W + \alpha(\tau - |V_1 - V_2|)(1 - W)W$$
$$\text{where } V_1, V_2 \text{ are state values and } W \text{ is the connection weight}$$

It is straightforward to check that for this function, the above criterion is equivalent to

$W = 0$ or $W = 1$ or $|V_1 - V_2| = \tau$ and W has any value.

(note that the weights of the incoming connections to the **W**-states are 1). For the interaction connects principle the advanced logistic function is used. For this, the above criterion is equivalent to the following equation:

$$\mathbf{alogistic}_{\sigma,\tau}(\omega_{X_1,Y}X_1(t),...,\omega_{X_k,Y}X_k(t)) = Y(t)$$

Using the above equations we can mathematically verify the model by filling in the needed values for specific stationary points obtained in an example simulation. This was done separately for all combinations functions except for the identity function, since this function copies its own value it does not need to be verified. For the other functions, the results of this verification can be found in Tables 4, 5 and 6. As shown the error values are well below the accepted accuracy.

Table 4. Verification of states using the scaled sum combination function.

ssum	X_1	X_2	X_3	X_4	X_5
timepoint	284.50	290.25	301.25	346.00	243.25
state value	0.27550	0.38850	0.42050	0.55450	0.76950
aggimpact	0.27528	0.38852	0.42052	0.55450	0.76956
deviation	0.00023	0.00002	0.00002	0.000003	0.00005

Table 5. Verification of states using the simple linear homophily combination function

slhomo	X_{30}	X_{33}	X_{36}
timepoint	256.5	500	88.25
state value	0.99950	0.00000	0.00049
W	1.0	0.0	0.0
deviation	0.0005	0.00000	0.00049

Table 6. Verification of states using the advanced logistic combination function.

alogistic	X_{18}	X_{24}	X_{27}
timepoint	212.75	110.5	65
state value	0.040	0.997	0.99852
aggimpact	0.040	0.99651	1
deviation	0.00008	0.00001	0.00148

6 Discussion and Conclusion

Concluding our research we can state that we have added novel view on modelling expatriate integration by mapping connections between expats and between expats and the local community. The proposed model differs from existing integration models, such as [13], in that it considers both the bonding by homophily principle together with the interaction connects principle to simulated the strength of social connections, which is more in accordance with reality. In our results we have found that both principles have different influences on how well expats integrate with the local community. Furthermore, a combination of both principles showed to be stronger than their sum. In the Appendix available as Linked Data at URL https://www.researchgate.net/publication/357340188 further validation of the model has been performed and the full specification of the model is shown. In this validation it was also confirmed that both principles did not overrule each other when fitting to data.

For future research this model could function as a bases for mapping and analyzing different social situations regarding integration. It should also be noted that this research was conducted within a limited time span and as such still has a large parameter space that is not yet discovered fully. Furthermore, the chosen combination functions can also be differentiated in order to create more complex social structures. This could also be done by changing the higher order states or even add extra levels in order to add accelerations or adaptive speed factors.

Regarding the validation it should also be noted that collecting data on expat integration showed to be a challenging task. For future research this could be improved by taking this into account when setting up the model. It would also be possible to change the method used for tuning to a computationally more efficient method.

The Interaction Connects principle for bonding used in the current computational analysis has also some further connections to the notion of interpersonal synchronising of actions and emotions known in psychology; e.g., [29–31]. When persons interact often some forms of synchronisation take place. Much literature studies the perspective that such synchronisation indeed occurs and under what circumstances. However, part of the literature also studies what the effects are of being synchronized. It has been found that synchronisation leads to more closeness, mutual coordination, alliance, or affiliation between the synchronized persons; e.g., [30–34]. For example, this may be a main reason to let soldiers march. This literature outlines a causal pathway from interpersonal interaction to interpersonal synchronisation to interpersonal bonding and thus provides an additional (and more detailed) scientific justification of the Interaction Connects principle. The connection of the principle to this area of synchronisation may be another interesting application domain for the type of adaptive social network model introduced here.

References

1. Expat insider 2021: The best and worst places to feel at home abroad (2021)
2. Byrne, D., Clore, G.L., Smeaton, G.: The attraction hypothesis: do similar attitudes affect anything? J. Pers. Soc. Psychol. **51**(6), 1167–1170 (1986)

3. Cangia, F.: (Im) mobility and the emotional lives of expat spouses. Emot. Space Soc. **25**, 22–28 (2017)
4. Castells, M.: The Rise of the Network Society, vol. 12. Wiley, Hoboken (2011)
5. Clarivate: Times cited and publications over time (2021)
6. Cuperus, R.: Wiardi Beckman Stichting: de wereldburger bestaat niet: waarom de opstand der elites de samenleving ondermijnt. Bakker (2009)
7. DeVries, M.M.: Integration, mobility and connection: an anthropological study of expat communities in the Netherlands. Master's thesis (2017)
8. Fechter, A.M.: Transnational Lives: Expatriates in Indonesia. Routledge (2016)
9. Finaccord: Global expatriates: size, segmentation and forecast for the worldwide market (2018). Accessed 12 July 2018
10. Harder, N., Figueroa, L., Gillum, R.M., Hangartner, D., Laitin, D.D., Hainmueller, J.: Multi-dimensional measure of immigrant integration. Proc. Natl. Acad. Sci. **115**(45), 11483–11488 (2018)
11. Hove, M.J., Risen, J.L.: It's all in the timing: Interpersonal synchrony increases affiliation. Soc. Cogn. **27**(6), 949–960 (2009)
12. Kanter, R.: World Class: Thriving Locally in the Global Economy. Simon & Schuster, New York (1995)
13. Kappert, C., Rus, R., Treur, J.: On the emergence of segregation in society: network-oriented analysis of the effect of evolving friendships. In: Nguyen, N.T., Pimenidis, E., Khan, Z., Trawiński, B. (eds.) ICCCI 2018. LNCS (LNAI), vol. 11055, pp. 178–191. Springer, Cham (2018). https://doi.org/10.1007/978-3-319-98443-8_17
14. Kirkpatrick, S., Gelatt, C.D., Vecchi, M.P.: Optimization by simulated annealing. Science **220**(4598), 671–680 (1983)
15. Mahajan, A., Toh, S.M.: Facilitating expatriate adjustment: the role of advice-seeking from host country nationals. J. World Bus. **49**(4), 476–487 (2014)
16. McPherson, M., Smith-Lovin, L., Cook, J.M.: Birds of a feather: homophily in social networks. Ann. Rev. Sociol. **27**(1), 415–444 (2001)
17. Mislove, A., Viswanath, B., Gummadi, K.P., Druschel, P.: You are who you know: inferring user profiles in online social networks. In: Proceedings of the third ACM International Conference on Web Search and Data Mining, pp. 251–260 (2010)
18. Pearce, E., Launay, J., Dunbar, R.I.M.: The ice-breaker effect: singing mediates fast social bonding. R. Soc. Open Sci. **2**(10), 150221 (2015)
19. Plas, S.: The butterfly: a sense of home, community and integration for expat families in Amsterdam (2018)
20. Portes, A., Böröcz, J.: Contemporary immigration: theoretical perspectives on its determinants and modes of incorporation. Int. Migr. Rev. **23**(3), 606–630 (1989)
21. Rumbaut, R.G., Gonzales, R.G., Golnaz, K., Morgan, C.V., Tafoya-Estrada, R.: Immigration and incarceration. Immigr. Crime Ethnicity Race Violence **64** (2006)
22. Salt, J.: Migration processes among the highly skilled in Europe. Int. Migr. Rev. **26**(2), 484–505 (1992)
23. Tarp, G.: Building dialogue between cultures: expats' way of coping in a foreign country and their willingness to communicate in a foreign language. In: Zarrinabadi, N., Pawlak, M. (eds.) New Perspectives on Willingness to Communicate in a Second Language. Second Language Learning and Teaching, pp. 55–84. Springer, Cham (2021). https://doi.org/10.1007/978-3-030-67634-6_4
24. Treur, J.: Network-Oriented Modeling. Springer, Cham (2016). https://doi.org/10.1007/978-3-319-45213-5
25. Treur, J.: Network-Oriented Modeling for adaptive Networks: Designing Higher-Order Adaptive Biological, Mental and Social Network Models. Springer, Cham (2020). https://doi.org/10.1007/978-3-030-31445-3

26. Van Bochove, M., Engbersen, G.: Beyond cosmopolitanism and expat bubbles: challenging dominant representations of knowledge workers and trailing spouses. Popul. Space Place **21**(4), 295–309 (2015)
27. Van Houdt, F., Suvarierol, S., Schinkel, W.: Neoliberal communitarian citizenship: current trends towards 'earned citizenship' in the united kingdom, France and the Netherlands. Int. Sociol. **26**(3), 408–432 (2011)
28. Weiner, M.: Determinants of immigrant integration: an international comparative analysis. In: Carmon, N. (eds.) Immigration and Integration in Post-Industrial Societies. Migration, Minorities and Citizenship, pp. 46–62. Palgrave Macmillan, London (1996). https://doi.org/10.1007/978-1-349-24945-9_4
29. Hendrikse, S.C.F., Treur, J., Wilderjans, T.F., Dikker, S., Koole, S.L.: On the same wavelengths: emergence of multiple synchronies among multiple agents. In: Van Dam, K.H., Verstaevel, N. (eds.) Multi-Agent-Based Simulation XXII, MABS 2021. LNCS (LNAI), vol. 13128, pp. 57–71. Springer, Cham (2022). https://doi.org/10.1007/978-3-030-94548-0_5
30. Koole, S.L., Tschacher, W.: Synchrony in psychotherapy: a review and an integrative framework for the therapeutic alliance. Front. Psychol. **7**, 862 (2016)
31. Koole, S.L., Tschacher, W., Butler, E., Dikker, S., Wilderjans, T.F.: In sync with your shrink. In: Forgas, J.P., Crano, W.D., Fiedler, K. (eds.) Applications of Social Psychology, pp. 161–184. Taylor and Francis, Milton Park (2020)
32. Hove, M.J., Risen, J.L.: It's all in the timing: Interpersonal synchrony increases affiliation. Soc. Cognit. **27**(6), 949–960 (2009)
33. Tarr, B., Launay, J., Dunbar, R.I.M.: Silent disco: dancing in synchrony leads to elevated pain thresholds and social closeness. Evol. Hum. Behav. **37**(5), 343–349 (2016)
34. Valdesolo, P., Ouyang, J., DeSteno, D.: The rhythm of joint action: Synchrony promotes cooperative ability. J. Exp. Soc. Psychol. **46**(4), 693–695 (2010)

A Reinforcement Learning and Transformers Based Intelligent System for the Support of Alzheimer's Patients in Daily Life Activities

Ahmed Snoun[✉], Tahani Bouchrika, and Olfa Jemai

Research Team in Intelligent Machines (RTIM), National Engineering School of Gabes (ENIG), University of Gabes, Gabes, Tunisia
ahmed.snoun.3@gmail.com, olfa.jemai@isimg.tn

Abstract. Alzheimer's disease is one of the most well-known diseases among the elderly. It is a neuro-degenerative and irreversible brain disease that gradually erodes memory, thinking skills, and, eventually, the capacity to do even basic daily activities. Therefore, patients should be aided at all times in carrying out their daily tasks. In this study, we propose a new assistance system for Alzheimer's patients to help them performing daily life activities independently. The proposed assistance system is composed of a human activity recognition module, based on 3D skeletons data and transformer encoder, in order to monitor the patient behavior and an assistance module, based on reinforcement learning (RL), to detect anomalies in the patient behavior and provide alerts accordingly. Experiments carried out on the DemCare dataset proved the effectiveness of our RL-based assistance system compared to state-of-the-art methods.

Keywords: Alzheimer · Reinforcement learning · Transformer · Assistance · 3D skeletons

1 Introduction

According to [4], elderly people are becoming a higher share of the global population. Several recent studies predict that the proportion of seniors in the population would more than double in the near future affecting a variety of aspects of our communities [3]. Indeed, as people age, they are more likely to face a number of difficulties, such as cognitive impairment, memory loss, chronic disease, sight and hearing issues, and a variety of other disorders. They may also have difficulty interacting with others. All of these issues limit their capacity to perform daily tasks and lower their quality of life, forcing them to rely on caregivers.

One of the most well-known disorders among the elderly is Alzheimer's disease. It's a neuro-degenerative and irreversible brain illness that erodes memory, reasoning skills, and eventually the ability to perform even simple tasks.

N. T. Nguyen et al. (Eds.): ICCCI 2022, LNAI 13501, pp. 534–547, 2022.
https://doi.org/10.1007/978-3-031-16014-1_42

According to the world health organization (WHO), Alzheimer's disease is the most common type of dementia, accounting for 60 to 80% of all cases [5]. Alzheimer's disease has terrible effects on the patient, his family, and society overall. Thus, the patients cognitive capacities deteriorate to the point that they are unable to carry out their activities of daily life (ADLs) independently. Therefore, Alzheimer's patients should be aided at all times in carrying out their daily tasks. As a result, the necessity for an effective, dynamic, and friendly support system for Alzheimer's patients has become critical. This has become possible in recent years, thanks to technological advancements.

Through the last several years, few systems were studied to assist Alzheimer's patients performing their activities of daily life. For example, in [8], the COACH (Cognitive Orthosis for Assisting aCtivities in the Home) assistance system for older people was designed. It was used to assist older persons with moderate-to-severe dementia, as well as their caregivers. In fact, COACH is a machine learning system that uses voice and/or audio-video instructions to guide a dementia-affected older adult through the handwashing process. It was based on the use of a markov decision process (MDP) in order to provide the right alert according to the hands positions which are detected using a background subtraction technique. Another assistance system for elderlies was proposed in [11]. This system is known as TEBRA (TEeth BRushing Assistance), and it is a technology that helps people with mild cognitive impairment brush their teeth. The TEBRA system monitors users with an instrumented toothbrush and cameras. A bayesian network classifier is used in the TEBRA system to address spatial variance in a behavior recognition component. Furthermore, the work in [2] proposed a cooking support system that leads patients through the process of preparing spaghetti. To provide support to the patient throughout the cooking task, this system used a reinforcement learning (RL) technique as a decision making system. In addition, RL was proven successful in many other healthcare applications, such as, dynamic treatment regimes (DTR) [15] and medical diagnosis [10].

However, all of the previous systems are restricted to one activity. They all designed to assist the patient in one specific daily activity. Also, the monitoring of the patient in these systems was limited to a specific location such as the sink in the COACH system [8]. To overcome these constraints, we propose, in this paper, a support system based on a human activity recognition (HAR) module to monitor the entire behavior of an Alzheimer's patient. Surveillance cameras can be placed anywhere in the patient's environment, not only in one spot, to monitor the patient's actions. In addition, the HAR module, which is based on 3D skeletons data and transformer encoder, allows us to identify the majority of the patient's activities and provide him with support in a wide range of tasks. Finally, assistance will be provided only when it is required, and only when anomalous behavior is observed, using a module based on reinforcement learning (RL). The proposed assistance system is an improvement of our previous developed assistance system [7], which is based on bidirectional long-short term memory

(Bi-LSTM) as a HAR module and a simple conditional structure methodology as an assistance module.

The remainder of this paper will be as follows: Sect. 2 will be reserved to explain the different parts of the proposed assistance system for Alzheimer's patient. In Sect. 3, we will discuss the experimental results on a public dataset as well as a comparative study with the literature works. Finally, Sect. 4 presents the conclusion and future works.

2   Architecture of the Proposed Assistance System

We designed an assistance system to reduce the need for a caregiver to assist Alzheimer's patients in daily activities, in order to lessen the difficulties they face.

The designed assistance system, as depicted in Fig. 1, is composed of two parts. First, a human activity recognition (HAR) module is applied on the video stream in order to monitor the patient behavior during performing a daily activity. After that, an assistance module exploits the output of the HAR system in order to provide assistance in form of alerts to the Alzheimer's patient when it is needed. Therefore, this module detects the anomalies in the patient's behavior and provides alerts based on the current state of the patient.

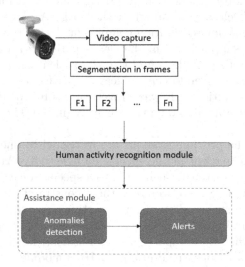

Fig. 1. Overview of the assistance system for Alzheimer's patient

An anomaly in the patient's behavior can be recognized when the patient misses a step in the activity or takes longer or shorter than the required time to complete a certain step. In this scenario, the patient must be alerted in order to assist him in correctly completing the task.

2.1   Human Activity Recognition Module

To recognize and monitor the behavior of Alzheimer's patients, we used our previous developed human activity recognition (HAR) system based on 3D skeletons data and transformer encoder [13].

The developed HAR system, as shown in Fig. 2, is composed of two steps. The first step consists in generating a set of view-invariant and spatio-temporal features from the 3D skeletons provided by a depth sensor like Microsoft's Kinect. The second step consists in analyzing the extracted features using a Transformer encoder in order to recognize the performed activity.

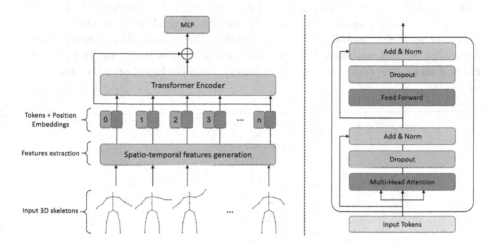

Fig. 2. Overview of the used HAR system (left) and transformer encoder layer architecture (right) [13]

To extract the set of view-invariant and spatio-temporal features from the 3D skeletons, we start by relocating the origin of the coordinate system from the camera's center to the head and spine of the skeleton in order to prevent the view variance problem, which can have a negative impact on the recognition process. Then, for the spatial features, we computed the euclidean distances between each joint and the head and spine. For the temporal features, we computed the movement angle and type of each joint between two consecutive frames. Finally, the extracted features were fed into a typical transformer encoder, where the architecture is illustrated by the right part of Fig. 2, in order to recognize the ongoing activity.

For more details about the used HAR system based on 3D skeleton data and transformer encoder, refer to [13].

2.2   Assistance Module Based on Reinforcement Learning

A daily life activity might be regarded as a sequence of successive actions or steps. As a result, in order to complete an activity successfully, the subject must do all of the steps that make up the activity in the correct order and at the correct time. This can be difficult for Alzheimer's patients, especially those who are in the later stages of the disease. In fact, the patient can take a longer time to finish a step or action or he can skip a step while performing the activity.

In order to assist the Alzheimer's patient to perform daily life activities in the correct order and at the correct time, we propose in this paper a new assistance system based on reinforcement learning (RL), which is a machine learning methodology that allows an agent to learn in an interactive environment by trial and error using feedback from its own actions and experiences. This method is an enhancement of our previous assistance system based on simple conditional structure [7]. The proposed method begins by detecting the patient's actions in a video stream using the HAR system, described in previous section, based on 3D skeletons and transformer encoder. Then, using RL, an agent detects anomalies in the patient's behavior and sends alarms based on the patient's current state. The process of the assistance mechanism based on RL is illustrated in Fig. 3.

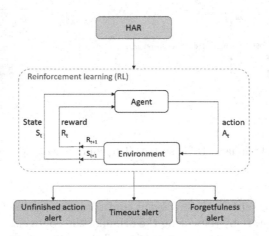

Fig. 3. Overview of our assistance system based on reinforcement learning (RL)

As shown in Fig. 3, the proposed assistance system can provide three types of alerts:

- **Timeout alert:** triggered when the patient exceeds the time limit for a specific action.
- **Unfinished action alert:** triggered when the patient moves to a new action without finishing the previous one.
- **Forgetfulness alert:** triggered when the patient misses a specific action.

Reinforcement learning (RL) is one of the most popular artificial intelligence research topics, and its popularity is growing. It is a machine learning training technique that promotes good behavior while punishing bad one. In general, a reinforcement learning agent can observe and grasp its environment, act, and learn through trial and error. Although both supervised and reinforcement learning involve mapping between input and output, reinforcement learning uses rewards and punishments as signals for positive and negative behavior, unlike supervised learning, which provides the agent with a right set of behaviors for executing a task. Therefore, for a changing behavior like in the case of Alzheimer's patient, RL seems to be more suitable than supervised learning.

Reinforcement learning, on the other hand, differs from unsupervised learning in terms of goals. The purpose of unsupervised learning is to find similarities and differences between data points, whereas the goal of reinforcement learning is to create an optimal action model that maximizes the agent's total cumulative reward. Figure 3 depicts the action-reward feedback loop of a generic RL model.

Reinforcement Learning's Components. Reinforcement learning is a technique for learning how to behave in a given situation by taking actions and seeing the results. Reinforcement learning is used in applications where the algorithm must make decisions with consequences. The goal is to increase the expected cumulative reward as much as possible.

Depending on the input data, the algorithm provides a state in which the user rewards or punishes the algorithm for the action it took. This cycle continues as the algorithm learns from the reward/punishment and adjusts itself. Therefore, as shown in Fig. 3, the main components of a RL system are as follows:

- **State:** the observation conducted by the agent on the environment after performing an action.
- **Action:** the decision taken by the agent based on the state.
- **Reward:** the feedback given to the agent based on the action it took. It receives a reward if the feedback is positive, and it receives a punishment if the feedback is negative.

In addition, there is an agent as well as an environment. The agent's state is dictated by the environment. The agent choose an action and is rewarded by the environment who sends the new state afterwards. This learning process continues until the goal is reached or another condition is met.

Formalising the RL Problem. The purpose of the agent in our RL-based assistance system is to deliver alerts to the Alzheimer's patient in the correct context and at the right time. As a result, the environment in which the agent acts is represented by the patient's behavior. In this scenario, the agent is rewarded if he sends the correct alert at the exact time and punished if he sends a false alert. The states are the patient's current activity and the amount of time it takes him to perform it, as well as the patient's previous activity.

A markov decision process (MDP) is commonly used to mathematically represent the RL problem. MDPs are mathematical frameworks for defining an environment in RL, and they can be applied to almost any RL problem. An MDP model consists of a set of finite environment states S, a set of feasible actions $A(s)$ in each state, a real valued reward function $R(s)$, and a transition model $P(s', s|a)$.

We applied the Q-learning algorithm to train the agent, which is a widely used off-policy approach for creating a good agent capable of making proper decisions [6]. In fact, the Q-learning technique uses a Q-table containing State-Action values (also known as Q-values), as shown in Fig. 4. In this Q-table, each state has its own row, and each action has its own column. Each cell contains the estimated Q-value for the corresponding state-action pair.

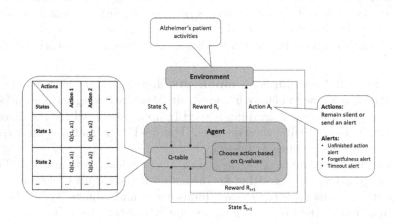

Fig. 4. Flowchart of RL system based on Q-learning algorithm

Q-table. The Q-table is a data structure that is used to determine the maximum future expected rewards for each state's taken action. Essentially, this assists the agent in determining the appropriate course of action for each state. The Q-learning algorithm is used to learn each value of the Q-table (also known as Q-value). Therefore, we start by initializing all of the Q-values to zero. As the agent interacts with the environment and receives feedback, the method iteratively improves these Q-values until they converge to the ideal Q-values. To update them, the Bellman equation (Eq. 1) is employed.

$$Q(S, A) \leftarrow Q(S, A) + \alpha(R + \gamma \max Q(S', A) - Q(S, A)) \tag{1}$$

where $Q(S, A)$ is the current Q-value (or old value), $Q(S', A)$ is the target Q-value (or future value), α is the learning rate, R is the reward and γ is a discount factor.

Q-learning Algorithm Process. By learning the optimal Q-values for each state-action pair, the Q-learning algorithm seeks to identify the best policy. To do so, the agent initially chooses actions randomly. However, the agent learns which actions are more useful based on the rewards it receives as it interacts with its environment. Based on this knowledge, it incrementally adjusts the Q-values. The Q-learning algorithm's process is depicted in Fig. 5.

The Q-learning algorithm continues to follow this four-step pattern until the end of the episode. Then it starts over with a new episode and repeats the same process.

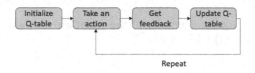

Fig. 5. Q-learning algorithm process

3 Experimental Results

In this section, we provide an experimental study of the different parts of our proposed assistance systems. The evaluation will be done in terms of performance and time complexity. Note that all experiments were carried out on a Google Colab environment which is a hosted Jupyter notebook service that requires no installation and offers free access to computing resources such as GPUs. Also, all the codes were written using Python language and Keras library which is a library based on Python used to develop deep learning applications.

3.1 Used Dataset

In order to assess the effectiveness of our proposed assistance system for Alzheimer's patients, we conducted experiments on the DemCare dataset[1] [9], which is frequently used in the literature in the field of daily activities of Alzheimer's patients. The dataset includes video sequences of 32 persons with mild cognitive impairments (MCI) performing five distinct activities of daily living (ADLs), including drinking, making a phone call, eating, communicating, and reading. Each activity is broken down into 2 to 3 sub-activities or steps.

For the rest of our experiments, we used, as a use case, the drinking activity. This activity is composed of 3 sub-activities, which are, Serve Beverage (SB), Drink Beverage (DB) and Clean Up (CU) as shown in Fig. 6.

---

[1] https://demcare.eu/datasets/.

Fig. 6. Samples of the drinking activity of the DemCare dataset. (a) Serve Beverage, (b) Drink Beverage and (c) Clean Up

3.2 Evaluation of HAR System

In this section, we present the results obtained by the previously explained HAR system, based on 3D skeletons and transformer encoder, on the drinking activity of the DemCare dataset. Here, in order to extract 3D skeletons from the images provided by the DemCare dataste, we applied an algorithm called ONNX[2] to extract 3D skeletons from the drinking activity videos. An example of 3D skeleton extracted from a video frame is shown in Fig. 7. Then, we applied the steps explained in Sect. 2.1 to extract the view-invariant and spatio-temporal features from the extracted 3D skeletons. Finally, we trained the transformer encoder, as reported in Sect. 2.1, using the extracted set of features.

Fig. 7. 3D pose estimation using ONNX algorithm applied on Clean Up video frame of the DemCare dataset

To evaluate our method, we used a 5-fold cross-validation evaluation protocol. Figure 8 illustrates the confusion matrix of our HAR system on the drinking activity of the DemCare dataset. According to the reported results, our HAR system reached an accuracy equals to 99.7%. We notice that the transformer encoder using the 3D skeletons features was able to discriminate between the three sub-activities as shown by the confusion matrix.

Also, we carried out a comparison between our HAR system and other systems in the literature that used the DemCare dataset. Therefore, the work reported in [1] proposed a local/global representation approach in which points of interest are detected and sampled on dense grids, tracked over time using

---

[2] https://github.com/ibaiGorordo/ONNX-Mobile-Human-Pose-3D.

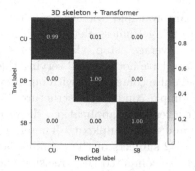

Fig. 8. Confusion matrix of the proposed HAR system

a Kanade-Lucas-Tomasi (KLT) tracker, and represented by local HOGHOF (Histograms of Oriented Gradients, Histograms of Optical Flow) descriptors. A multi-class support vector machine (SVM) model was used to perform the recognition task in this study. The work in [12], on the other hand, is based on the extraction of motion vectors from video sequences. For action classification, an SVM model with a linear kernel was used. Finally, in our previous work [7], we used a bidirectional long-term short memory (Bi-LSTM) to analyze a set of 2D skeletons extracted from RGB images. According to the results shown in Table 1, our suggested HAR system 3D skeletons and transformer encoder outperforms the approaches of the literature.

Table 1. Comparison of proposed HAR systems with state-of-the-art methods on the DemCare dataset

Method	Accuracy
Avgerinakis et al. (2016) [1]	90.8%
Poularakis et al. (2017) [12]	83.3%
Jarray et al. (2020) [7]	98.06%
Transformer + 3D skeletons (ours)	**99.7%**

3.3 Evaluation of the RL-based Assistance System

In this section, we evaluate our proposed assistance system for Alzheimer's patients based on reinforcement learning (RL). The evaluation was done, as mentioned before, on the drinking activity of the DemCare dataset. Therefore, to be considered a successful completion of the drinking activity, the patient must complete all three steps in the correct order and at the appropriate time interval. The steps are in the following order: 1. Serving Beverage (SB), 2. Drinking Beverage (DB), and 3. Cleaning Up (CU).

Three sorts of alerts are available from the support system (timeout alert, incomplete action alert and forgetfulness alert). For instance, If the patient does not complete the "Serve beverage" step, the system sends out an incomplete action alert that says, "You have not finished serving the drink!".

In addition, we carried out a comparison with our previous assistance system based on BiLSTM and simple conditional structure [7]. To determine which system is most suited for a real-time application, the evaluation was conducted in terms of performance and time complexity. Therefore, we evaluated the two assistance systems on the 32 subjects of the drinking activity of the DemCare dataset. For each subject, we computed the precision and recall of each system to provide alerts as well as the processing time. The precision and recall are computed using the following equations:

$$\text{Precision} = \frac{\text{nb. of correct alerts}}{\text{nb. of correct alerts} + \text{nb. of alerts triggered in a wrong time}} \quad (2)$$

$$\text{Recall} = \frac{\text{nb. of correct alerts}}{\text{nb. of correct alerts} + \text{nb. of false alerts}} \quad (3)$$

Table 2 reports the results in terms of precision and recall of our RL-based assistance system compared to our previous work reported in [7]. According to the obtained results, we notice that our RL-based system outperform our previous work [7] in terms of precision and recall, which proves the efficiency of 3D skeletons compared to 2D skeletons used in our previous work [14], as well as the superiority of the transformer encoder compared to BiLSTM in the task of HAR. In addition, reinforcement learning (RL) seems to be more accurate than a simple conditional structure in the decision making task.

Table 2 presents, as well, a comparison in terms of time complexity between our RL-based assistance system and our previous system based on conditional structure [7]. The obtained results prove the superiority of our RL-based system in term of execution time. The RL-based system's better processing time can be explained by the fact that the agent is trained offline, which reduces the online processing time when compared to the conditional structure method employed in [7]. To summarize, our suggested system, which is based on 3D skeleton data and uses a transformer encoder as a classifier for activity recognition and reinforcement learning (RL) for assistance, is the best fit for a real-time application.

Table 2. Precision, recall and processing time of our RL-based system compared to our previous work [7]

Subject	Nb. frames	RL-based system (ours)			Jarray et al. [7]		
		Precision (%)	Recall (%)	Processing time (s)	Precision (%)	Recall (%)	Processing time (s)
S1	330	100	100	0.623	100	100	3.692
S2	270	100	100	0.338	100	100	0.612
S3	870	93.333	100	1.104	93.336	80	2.029
S4	780	92.308	100	1.002	100	100	1.802
S5	390	100	100	0.511	100	83.336	0.924
S6	360	100	100	0.456	100	100	0.82
S7	210	100	100	0.258	75	80	0.477
S8	570	100	100	0.748	100	100	1.298
S9	360	100	100	0.469	100	100	0.819
S10	240	100	100	0.309	100	100	0.548
S11	240	100	100	0.325	80	100	0.594
S12	330	100	100	0.429	100	100	0.746
S13	630	100	100	0.82	100	100	1.415
S14	210	100	100	0.276	75	83.336	0.491
S15	240	100	50	0.344	100	100	0.551
S16	330	100	100	0.433	100	100	0.741
S17	300	100	100	0.394	83.33	93.336	0.661
S18	270	100	100	0.343	100	100	0.611
S19	270	100	100	0.354	100	100	0.6
S20	240	100	66.557	0.306	100	83.333	0.545
S21	240	100	100	0.304	80	100	0.541
S22	360	100	100	0.463	88.889	75	1.161
S23	360	100	100	0.456	100	100	0.828
S24	330	100	100	0.43	100	100	0.82
S25	570	100	100	0.733	100	100	1.291
S26	300	100	100	0.389	83.333	75	0.709
S27	270	100	100	0.341	80	100	0.611
S28	390	100	100	0.518	75	80	0.9
S29	270	100	100	0.34	100	100	0.638
S30	300	100	100	0.384	80	93.336	0.688
S31	300	100	100	0.404	100	100	0.731
S32	300	100	100	0.646	100	100	0.713
Average	357.18	99.55	97.39	0.477	93.559	94.583	0.925

4   Conclusion

In this study, we suggested a new assistance system for Alzheimer's patients that will assist them in performing daily activities independently. To begin, we developed a human activity recognition (HAR) system to track the patient's actions, which is based on a transformer encoder that analyzes a set of view-invariant and spatio-temporal features retrieved from 3D skeletons. Then, to detect anomalies in the patient's behavior and offer alerts as needed, we implemented a reinforcement learning (RL) system. The two components of the system were tested on the Demcare dataset, and the outcomes demonstrated that our system outperformed state-of-the-art methods in terms of performance and time complexity.

As part of our future work, we plan to incorporate an augmented reality module to provide more interactive guidance to Alzheimer's patients, as well as, deep Q-learning instead of Q-learning which is more suitable for more complex and stochastic environment.

Acknowledgements. The authors would like to acknowledge the financial support of this work by grants from General Direction of Scientific Research (DGRST), Tunisia, under the ARUB program.

References

1. Avgerinakis, K., Briassouli, A., Kompatsiaris, Y.: Activity detection using sequential statistical boundary detection (SSBD). Comput. Vis. Image Underst. **144**, 46–61 (2016)
2. Chen, H., Soh, Y.: A cooking assistance system for patients with Alzheimers disease using reinforcement learning. Int. J. Inf. Technol. **23**(2) (2018)
3. Chernbumroong, S., Cang, S., Atkins, A., Yu, H.: Elderly activities recognition and classification for applications in assisted living. Expert Syst. Appl. **40**(5), 1662–1674 (2013). https://doi.org/10.1016/j.eswa.2012.09.004
4. Division, U.: World population ageing, 2019: highlights, p. 37 (2019)
5. Dua, T., Seeher, K., Sivananthan, S., Chowdhary, N., Pot, A., Saxena, S.: World health organization's global action plan on the public health response to dementia 2017–2025. Alzheimer's & Dementia 13, P1450–P1451, June 2017. https://doi.org/10.1016/j.jalz.2017.07.758
6. Jang, B., Kim, M., Harerimana, G., Kim, J.W.: Q-learning algorithms: a comprehensive classification and applications. IEEE Access **7**, 133653–133667 (2019). https://doi.org/10.1109/ACCESS.2019.2941229
7. Jarray, R., Snoun, A., Bouchrika, T., Jemai, O.: Deep human action recognition system for assistance of Alzheimer's patients. In: HIS (2020)
8. Jean-Baptiste, E., Mihailidis, A.: Benefits of automatic human action recognition in an assistive system for people with dementia. In: 2017 IEEE Canada International Humanitarian Technology Conference (IHTC), pp. 61–65 (2017)
9. Karakostas, A., Briassouli, A., Avgerinakis, K., Kompatsiaris, I., Tsolaki, M.: The dem@care experiments and datasets: a technical report, December 2016
10. Ling, Y., et al.: Diagnostic inferencing via improving clinical concept extraction with deep reinforcement learning: a preliminary study. In: Proceedings of the 2nd Machine Learning for Healthcare Conference. Proceedings of Machine Learning Research, vol. 68, pp. 271–285. PMLR, 18–19 August 2017
11. Peters, C., Hermann, T., Wachsmuth, S., Hoey, J.: Automatic task assistance for people with cognitive disabilities in brushing teeth - a user study with the tebra system. ACM Trans. Access. Comput. **5**(4) (2014). https://doi.org/10.1145/2579700. https://doi.org/10.1145/2579700
12. Poularakis, S., Avgerinakis, K., Briassouli, A., Kompatsiaris, Y.: Efficient motion estimation methods for fast recognition of activities of daily living. Signal Process. Image Commun. **53**, 1–12 (2017)
13. Snoun., A., Bouchrika., T., Jemai., O.: View-invariant 3d skeleton-based human activity recognition based on transformer and spatio-temporal features. In: Proceedings of the 11th International Conference on Pattern Recognition Applications and Methods - ICPRAM, pp. 706–715. INSTICC, SciTePress (2022). https://doi.org/10.5220/0010895300003122

14. Snoun, A., Jlidi, N., Bouchrika, T., Jemai, O., Zaied, M.: Towards a deep human activity recognition approach based on video to image transformation with skeleton data. Multimed. Tools Appl. **80**(19), 29675–29698 (2021). https://doi.org/10.1007/s11042-021-11188-1
15. Zhang, J., Bareinboim, E.: Designing optimal dynamic treatment regimes: a causal reinforcement learning approach. In: Proceedings of the 37th International Conference on Machine Learning, ICML 2020, JMLR.org (2020)

Multi-task Learning Dataset for the Development of Remote Patient Monitoring System

Firas Khlil[1]([✉]) [iD], Sami Naouali[1] [iD], Awatef Raddadi[2,3] [iD],
Sameh Ben Salem[1] [iD], Hedi Gharsallah[3,4,5] [iD],
and Chihebeddine Romdhani[2,3,4] [iD]

[1] Laboratory of Science and Technology for Defense STD, Military Research Center,
Tunis, Tunisia
firas.khlil@ept.u-carthage.tn
[2] Department of the Anesthesiology Intensive Care medicine at Military Hospital
of Gabes, Gabes, Tunisia
[3] Research Unit UR17DN05 Medical Support to the Armed Forces in Operations
and Disaster Situations, Tunis, Tunisia
[4] Faculty of Medicine of Tunis, University Tunis El Manar, Tunis, Tunisia
[5] Military Hospital of Tunis, Department of Anaesthesiology and Intensive Care,
Tunis, Tunisia

Abstract. The COVID-19 pandemic caused havoc on the world, infecting more than 3.5 billion people and resulting in over 15 million deaths, and overwhelmed existing healthcare infrastructures around the world, as announced by the World Health Organization (WHO). We propose in this work an effective and low-cost strategy for collecting, pre-processing, and extracting meaningful information from different types of patient data that may be useful for statistics and training of Machine Learning (ML) models to respond to pandemics such as COVID-19. Information like medical history, clinical examination, para-clinical testing, and patient RGB videos are collected This achievement will enable further studies to train, test, and deploy on-device decentralized ML models to monitor patients at home.

Keywords: Data science · Artificial intelligence · COVID-19

1 Introduction

Technological advancements have transformed the healthcare field. It have made significant contributions to enhancing millions of people's lives, since ever the discovery of antibiotics and vaccines to the digital revolution which, again, transformed healthcare field once more today through the development and deployment of computational intelligence systems to provide smart and rapid health services to combat pandemics like COVID -19. Billions of dollars have been spent

Supported by the Military Research Center and the Military Hospital of Tunis.

to collect massive amounts of Electronic Health Records (EHR) data, patients' vital signs measurements, and imaging data. For instance, the National Institutes of Health (NIH) has announced a new program called the "All of Us" formerly known as the "Precision Medicine Cohort Program". This program aims to collect data such as EHR, genetic, imaging, socio-behavioral, and environmental data[1] from about a one million sample of patients over the next few years. Thus, the collection of such data seeks to design and develop smart systems and applications that help healthcare professionals with patient monitoring and early mortality prediction [1] and making critical decisions in a short time. Our study was launched since September 2021, proposes a new approach to collecting and preprocessing a useful dataset for statistics and training ML models to monitor isolated patients. The process of data collection must go along with the goals and challenges of our research perspectives. Indeed, the created dataset must include patients' information, their vital signs, and recorded videos. Patients data collection and processing is a major challenge wherein researchers must deal with a variety of issues, especially in hospitals without EHR infrastructure including (i) Privacy and security within patients data collection, (ii) Data cleaning, preprocessing and meaningful information extracting, and (iii) Data augmentation techniques.

2   Related Works

The increased interest in applying AI to address COVID-19 concerns has sped up research in the field of artificial intelligence, resulting in an exponential growth in articles and review studies in a short time. Many research topics were proposed to deal with the pandemic (diagnosis, progression, treatment, and patient monitoring) [2]. However, there is one task that all of these issues have in common, that is the collection of patient data and the corresponding analytic strategy. For example, a study was conducted on the design of a minimum dataset (MDS) for the COVID-19 registry system [3]. From 2020 to 2021, Ahvaz University of Medical Sciences conducted a qualitative study to build an MDS for the COVID-19 registration system in five-phases. The information requirements for the COVID-19 registry system were assessed in the first phase. In the second phase, data elements were discovered. The MDS was chosen in the third phase, and the COVID-19 registration system was developed as a pilot study to test the MDS in the fourth phase. In the final phase, the MDS were analyzed and corrected based on the COVID-19 registry system deployment lessons. Another dataset called MIMIC III (Medical Information Mart for Intensive Care) [2], publicly available by request single-center database that contains deidentified health-related data for approximately 40,000 patients [4], MIMIC III consisted of 26 tables associated by IDs provided as a collection of comma-separated value (CSV) files containing vital signs, medications, laboratory measurements, observations and notes charted by care providers, fluid balance, procedure codes, diagnostic codes, imaging reports, hospital length of stay, survival data, and more. In addition,

---

[1] https://allofus.nih.gov/.
[2] https://github.com/MIT-LCP/mimic-code.

other types of datasets were proposed essentially for patients' vital signs monitoring using computer vision algorithms one of them is COHFACE dataset [5] where subjects were asked to look into an RGB webcam connected to a laptop for approximately 60 s. The dataset includes 160 one-minute video sequences of 40 subjects (12 females and 28 males) under different conditions (lighting, respiration pattern, etc.) synchronized with their heart rate and breathing rate as physiological signals obtained using devices from Tought Technologies and using the provided BioGraph Infiniti software suite. The video sequences were captured with a Logitech HD C525 at a resolution of 640×480 pixels and a frame rate 20 Hz.

3   The Proposed Dataset

Our goal is to create an intelligent system to assist healthcare providers in monitoring patients at home and detecting respiratory distress. This study focuses on collecting, preprocessing, and extracting meaningful information from patients' data, respecting the privacy and security of this information. So with the help of the Intensive Care Unit (ICU) of two public hospitals in Tunisia, we developed a low-cost strategy for collecting patients' general information, like their medical histories, and vital signs. In addition, patients' face and profile videos are taken with their official consent.

3.1   Data Collection

This paper suggests an easy and secure strategy for gathering data from patients admitted to the ICU between February 2021 and January 2022. At first place, healthcare personnel fill up a form in a desktop program to prepare for the patient-doctor consultation. These information consists the patient's name, medical history (hypertension, diabetes, ischemic heart disease, heart failure, etc.), lifestyle habits (smoking, alcoholism, etc.), and present symptoms (fever, rhinorrhea, pharyngitis, cough, dyspnea, chest pain, etc.), and also the result and the date of realization of the Covid-19 test if it was done. Then, they mention the medical examination including Body Mass Index (BMI), temperature (T), blood pressure (BP), heart rate (HR), Respiratory Rate (RR), Pulse oximeter level (Spo2), Glasgow Coma Scale (GCS), symptoms and signs of respiratory distress if existing as it is shown in Fig 1 below:

```
Index(['id', 'Age', 'Sexe', 'IMC', 'HTA', 'Insuffisance cardiaque',
       'tbc péritonéale', 'SAOS', 'Asthme', 'Diabète', 'hypothyroidie',
       'Fumer', 'Traitement en cours', 'Fièvre', 'Toux', 'Asthénie',
       'Arthralgies', 'Myalgies', 'Rhinorrhée', 'Pharyngite', 'Céphalées',
       'Anosmie', 'Agueusie', 'Diarrhées', 'Douleurs thoraciques',
       'Vomissements', 'Anorexie', 'Odynophagies', 'Dyspnée', 'Covid_test',
       'Température', 'Pression artérielle systolique',
       'Pression artérielle diastolique', 'Fréquence cardiaque',
       'Fréquence respiratoire ', 'Saturation pulsée en oxygène', 'Detresse'],
      dtype='object')
```

Fig. 1. Patient informations in the first set of data

Next, healthcare professionals ask the patient or his legal representative for his consent to take two videos face and profile in different positions (lying down or sitting) on the doctor's smartphone. The face, thorax, abdomen, and hands should be visible in each of these sequences to determine the respiratory rate and detect signs of respiratory distress if present. Then, the videos are encrypted, kept on a protected hard drive, and removed from the smartphone, with access to these computers protected by a two-factor authentication procedure. To comply with the Health Insurance Portability and Accountability Act (HIPAA) rules, data is deidentified using structured data cleansing before being sent to the analytic process. The anonymization process for collected data required removing all eighteen of the identifying data elements from the Comma-separated values (CSV) file, including fields such as patient name and phone number, address, and dates. In addition, all the contributors in the collection and analysis of this dataset were asked to sign a Dataset License Agreement containing the license, and rules to respect the security and privacy of patients' data. Moreover, building an ethical dataset is critical when it comes to AI systems used in healthcare and one of ethics' challenges is gender imbalance, especially for computer vision and deep learning algorithms [6]. That's why we have collected data with as much gender diversity as possible.

3.2 Data Annotation

In our dataset, annotation was performed manually with the help of medical experts. In this process, each patient was annotated after the physical examination by the existence or not of signs of respiratory distress associated with the respiratory rate (RR) value for the videos dataset. In Table 1, we provide the cardinality of each class in the first dataset:

Table 1. Class cardinality

Class	Cardinality
Distress	118
NoDistress	160

3.3 Data Preprocessing

Preprocessing of the First Set of Data

Data Cleansing: Observations are not recorded in specific fields due to healthcare professionals or patient mistakes and the values may not be recorded correctly and breakdown or unavailability of measuring equipment in the acquisition of vital signs values. To know how to handle missing and/or inaccurate data, we need to carefully analyze each column. In our case, the best solution to handle this data is to eliminate the rows containing null or erroneous values, which are less than 20%, since replacing these values with the mean or other values may affect our learning process

Data Transformation: The first step is the transformation of categorical values. For example, The symptoms and medical history were written as a list. A patient can have several symptoms 'symptom 1', 'symptom 2', etc. In addition, the same categorical values can be written differently (health professionals may report the same word with an uppercase or a lowercase), so we should fix this issue. Also, we have to convert categorical values to numerical form using the one-hot encoding technique since our categories are not ordinal.

Preprocessing of the Second Set of Data: After viewing the collected videos, we notice that there are many issues associated with the quality and other properties related to the loss of visual quality caused by smartphone camera shaking and irregular camera motions, the movement of the patient during the video recording, the brightness level in recorder videos and the videos are from various periods, quality levels, and frame rates. Thus, the first step of preprocessing this dataset sample is to split those videos into smaller chunks equal to 15 s. Indeed, the respiration rate is the number of breaths a person takes per minute, so to improve deep learning algorithm performance applied to this dataset and to normalize the training data, we reduce the duration of each video to 15 s and then multiplied the output value of breaths count by 4 [7]. Then, we reduced the videos' resolution to 640 * 352 which is the minimal resolution in our dataset. In addition, we normalized the frame rates of all the videos to 30 fps. The second step aimed to improve videos' quality and reduce the camera shake using a stabilizer predefined function looped over all of this dataset. Finally, we extract frames from videos and reduce their size according to our computer vision model.

4   The Experiments

The patients' ages in this dataset ranged from 18 years to 87 years, with a median equal to 47 years. In addition, 53.3 % of patients had negative PCR tests, 40.5 % positive, and 6.2 % had not taken the PCR test. Also, the participants' temperature is between 36° and 40°, with a mean of 37° and 40°, with a mean of 37°, the Systolic Blood Pressure measurement range is from 80 to 190, with an average of 125, and the Diastolic Blood Pressure minimum is 45, and the maximum is 110, with a mean of 69.72. The patients' heart rates range from 45 to 133, with an average of 80, while their respiratory rates range from 11 to 60, with a mean of 21.63. Finally, the Pulse Oximeter reading ranges from 67 to 100, with an average of 94. In the experiments, many data visualization techniques are used to visualize the distribution, correlations, and proportions of collected data. After this step, we notice that:

- The number of respiratory distress cases increases with advancing age
- Almost all patients with respiratory distress tested positive for Covid-19.
- Patients with a high-value BMI are more vulnerable to distress

We create also a correlation heatmap that shows the 2D connection between all the features in our dataset as is shown in the following figure and we notice that the highly correlated features with distress labels are: 'Respiratory Rate', 'Spo2', 'Covidtes', and 'dyspnea' (Fig. 2).

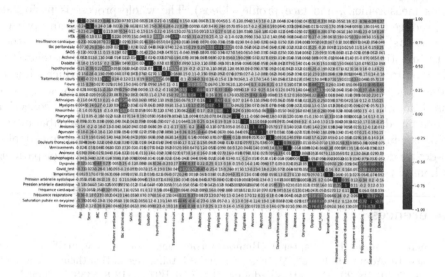

Fig. 2. Correlation Heatmap

The second group of data is composed of 462 videos collected from 199 patients. These videos dataset are related to a CSV file which contains information about each one (video-name, patient-id, view, nframe, resolution, duration, size) associated with RR and distress class label as it is shown in the Fig. 3

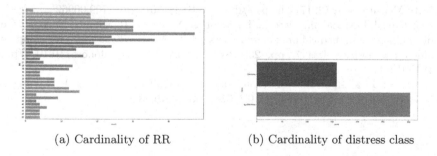

(a) Cardinality of RR   (b) Cardinality of distress class

Fig. 3. Cardinality of the two labels in the videos dataset

5   Conclusions and Perspectives

In this paper, we proposed a low-cost strategy to collect and preprocess a medical dataset from patients admitted to the ICU. This dataset was decomposed into two groups containing a variety of patients' data (General information, Vital Signs measurement, and face/profile videos). The whole process is performed to produce and preprocess the dataset with respect to the security and privacy of patients' data as described previously. The main contribution of this study is to investigate the collection and preprocessing of healthcare data related to the monitoring of patients at home using artificial intelligence which aims to reduce the number of hospitalized patients. To the best of our knowledge, and based on a review of the literature, no previous works addressed the collection of combined healthcare data with videos which makes our work valuable in this field. So, future work will include using this dataset to train, test and deploy on-device decentralized Machine and Deep Learning Models to monitor patients at home.

References

1. Zineb, J., Adam, B.: Chapter 9 - Remote patient monitoring using artificial intelligence, In: Adam, B., Kaveh, M. (eds.) Artificial Intelligence in Healthcare, Academic Press 2020, pp. 203–234. https://doi.org/10.1016/B978-0-12-818438-7.00009-5
2. Rohmetra, H., Raghunath, N., Narang, P. et al. AI-enabled remote monitoring of vital signs for COVID-19: methods, prospects and challenges. Computing (2021). https://doi.org/10.1007/s00607-021-00937-7
3. Zarei, J., Badavi, M., Karandish, M., et al.: A study to design minimum dataset of COVID-19 registry system., vol. 773, pp. 13. BMC Infect Dis (2021). https://doi.org/10.1186/s12879-021-06507-8
4. Pollard, T., Shen, L., et al. : MIMIC-III, a freely accessible critical care database., vol. 160035, pp. 9. Sci Data 3 (2016). https://doi.org/10.1038/sdata.2016.35
5. Guillaume, H., Andr´e, A., Sebastien, M.: A Reproducible Study on Remote Heart Rate Measurement (2017) . https://doi.org/10.48550/arxiv.1709.00962
6. Agostina, J. Larrazabal., Victoria, P., Nicol´as, N., Diego, H. Milone., Enzo, F.: Gender imbalance in medical imaging datasets produces biased classifiers for computer-aided diagnosis. vol. 117, pp. 23. PNAS (2020). https://doi.org/10.1073/pnas.1919012117
7. Rolfe, S.: The importance of respiratory rate monitoring. British J. Nursing **28**, 504–508 (2019). https://doi.org/10.12968/bjon.2019.28.8.504

Developing a Student Monitoring System for Online Classrooms Based on Face Recognition Approaches

Trong-Nghia Pham[1,2]([⊠]) [iD], Nam-Phong Nguyen[1,2] [iD],
Nguyen-Minh-Quan Dinh[1,2] [iD], and Thanh Le[1,2] [iD]

[1] Faculty of Information Technology, University of Science,
Ho Chi Minh city, Vietnam
{ptnghia,lnthanh}@fit.hcmus.edu.vn
[2] Vietnam National University, Ho Chi Minh city, Vietnam

Abstract. One of the primary activities that lectures usually do is to take a roll call. This activity not only helps lecturers determine the participation of students but also detect strangers in the classroom. When the number of students increases, lectures take more time to monitor and check students' attendance. We propose a student monitoring system based on facial recognition approaches to tackle that problem. With the recent development of deep learning techniques, many new approaches have made remarkable progress in face recognition. However, most of those approaches only focus on improving accuracy, while a practical end-to-end face recognition system demands good accuracy and reasonable runtime. We make adjustments and apply CenterFace for the face detection task and ArcFace for extracting embedding features from images to achieve high efficiency in both accuracy and speed. In addition, our proposed system is designed to be lightweight and scalable, capable of running in various environments, especially in a web browser. The results show that the system takes an average of 0.22 s to register a new face and 4.3 s for identifying a face in a database of 500 samples. Experiments also indicate that the system was less likely to misrecognize faces in most of our tests.

Keywords: Face recognition · Student monitoring system · CenterFace · FaceNet · ArcFace

1 Introduction

The online classroom has been on the trend in recent years, especially when the Covid pandemic has prevented students from going to school. It offers many advantages such as we can study from anywhere, the number of participants can be extended up to hundreds without limited space like a traditional classroom. Besides the benefits that online classroom offers, there are issues that lecturers have to deal with, like strangers appearing in the classroom, checking students'

N. T. Nguyen et al. (Eds.): ICCCI 2022, LNAI 13501, pp. 555–567, 2022.
https://doi.org/10.1007/978-3-031-16014-1_44

attendance becomes more challenging. We propose an end-to-end face recognition system to tackle those problems and improve the online teaching/studying experience.

Face recognition is a branch of study in the field of biometrics along with fingerprint recognition, iris recognition. Although face recognition is less reliable than fingerprint or iris recognition, it does not require specialized device or hardware. In addition, face recognition has a richer data source and requires less interaction to perform. That is why a face recognition system is easier and cost less to deploy.

Many current face recognition systems need high processing power hardware to perform [18,25]. However, those systems are deployed on a single machine and could encounter overload when there are many students to identify. Therefore, we aim to develop a face recognition system that can be deployed across machines that do not have powerful hardware. Furthermore, in real life scenario where only a fraction of probe sample identities is enrolled in the database, the system should be able to reject or ignore those that correspond to unknown identities. Moreover, the ability to quickly identify and export the results are other objectives of the system. We review the state-of-the-art approaches to choose the most suitable models for the proposed system. We also make adjustments to meet the reality of the context.

To sum up, the contributions of this paper are as follows:

- We analyze the main components of an end-to-end face recognition system and compare them under different conditions.
- We point out the effect of different components on the overall system's performance.
- We propose a face recognition system that has a good trade-off between accuracy and execution time can perform on hardware that does not have high processing power.

We organize the paper into six sections. The first section introduces an overview of the motivation and the requirements of the problem. The following section describes the related work and the components of a typical end-to-end face recognition system. The architecture and core elements applied to our system are introduced in Sect. 3. Section 4 describes parameters, datasets, and settings for evaluation. In Sect. 5, we present and analyze the results obtained. Finally, the conclusion and the future work are given.

2   Related Work

In this section, we describe the primary components of an end-to-end face recognition system and review some promising approaches.

A facial recognition system has three basic components (shown in Fig. 1): face detection, feature extraction, and face recognition. There are many factors such as pose, age, glasses, hairstyle, facial expression, and lighting conditions which may have significant impact on discrimination ability of a facial recognition system. Many developed methods have focused on addressing these challenges in order to enhance robustness of facial recognition systems. However, they require high processing time, consume a lot of memory, and are relatively complex. Therefore, we conduct research and evaluate different methods to check the suitability of the system we intend to build.

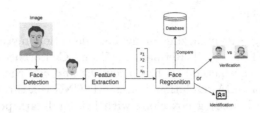

Fig. 1. Three basic steps of face recognition

The purpose of face detection is to assess whether or not the input image contains human faces. Some classics face detection methods such as Haar Cascade [20], Histograms of Oriented Gradients (HOG) [4] can perform fast. However, these methods do not archive good result when it comes to different light angles, face poses. There are many current methods have been developed that have good performance like Single-Shot Detector (SSD) [12] with ResNet 10 as the foundation, Multi-task Cascaded Convolutional Networks (MTCNN) [24], RetinaFace [5], CenterFace [23].

Feature extraction's primary role is to extract the characteristics of the face found in the detection step. The major aspects of the face image, such as the eyes, nose, and mouth, as well as their geometric distribution is represented by a collection of features vector. Some well-known methods for carrying out this work are linear discriminant analysis (LDA) [10], principal component analysis (PCA) [15] and local binary sampling method (LBP) [14]. With the recent development of deep learning techniques, many state-of-the-art methods such as FaceNet [19], CosFace [21], ArcFace [6] have achieved high performance while still having reasonable execution time.

Face recognition step compares the features extracted from the feature extraction step to known faces stored in databases. Face recognition has two general applications, one is identification and the other is verification. In the identification process, an input face is compared to a collection of faces in order to find the most likely match. In the verification process, an input face is compared to a known face in the database to determine if it should be accepted or rejected. Some of classic methods to solve this task are support vector machine (SVM) [3], softmax classifier [8], and k-nearest neighbors (K-NN) [2].

3   The Proposed Student Monitoring System

In this section, we introduce architecture of our face recognition system and core components that match the system's criteria including high accuracy, reasonable runtime, scalability.

3.1   Face Detection

Through surveying and analyzing many face detection methods, we selected three methods: MTCNN [24], RetinaFace [5] and CenterFace [23]. The reason for choosing these two methods is high accuracy and can run on a single CPU core in real-time for VGA resolution images. MTCNN is a three-stage algorithm used to detect the bounding box along with five landmark points on the face. RetinaFace is designed based on the feature pyramids with independent context modules. Following the context modules, a multi-task loss is calculated for each anchor. CenterFace is a one-stage, anchor-free approach for predicting facial box and landmark position in real-time with high accuracy.

MTCNN is composed of three stages corresponding to three convolutional neural networks which are P-Net, R-Net and O-Net. Before being fed into P-Net, the input image is scaled down to several sizes. Each scaled image is an input to this network. This operation aims to find many faces of different sizes in the input image. For each scaled image, a 12×12 kernel slides over its surface to find the face with a stride of 2 pixels. After each convolution layer, the PReLU activation function is applied. Output is the coordinates, the probability that a face exists and does not exist in each frame. After collecting all outputs, the model discards all frames with low confidence and merges high-overlapped frames into an unique frame using NMS (non-maximum suppression). Because some frames may grow out of the image boundary when we convert them to square, it is necessary to buffer them to get enough input value. Then, all frames are converted to 24×24 size and fed into the R-net. After each convolution layer, the PReLU activation function is applied. One output is the coordinates of the more precise frames and the confidence of that frame.

O-Net and R-NET are structurally similar, differing only in-depth. The results of R-Net after employing NMS are resized to 48×48, then fed into O-Net as its input. O-Net outputs not only the coordinates of the bounding boxes, but also the coordinates of the five landmarks on the face.

RentinaFace is a single-stage face detector that uses a multi-task learning strategy to predict face score, face box, five facial landmarks, and dense facial landmark at the same time.

The loss function for an anchor i is presented follow:

$$L = L_{cls}(p_i, p_i^*) + \lambda_1 p_i^* L_{box}(t_i, t_i^*) + \lambda_2 p_i^* L_{pts}(l_i, l_i^*) + \lambda_3 p_i^* L_{pixel} \qquad (1)$$

This multi-task loss function consists of four parts.

- The first part is face classification loss, $L_{cls}(p_i, p_i^*)$, where p_i is the predicted probability of anchor i being a face and p_i^* is 1 for the positive anchor and 0 for the negative anchor. The classification loss L_{cls} is the softmax loss for binary classes.
- The second part is face box regression loss, $\lambda_1 p_i^* L_{box}(t_i, t_i^*)$, where $t_i = \{t_x, t_y, t_w, t_h\}_i$ and $t_i^* = \{t_x^*, t_y^*, t_w^*, t_h^*\}_i$ represents the predicted and ground-truth box location corresponding with the positive anchor and $L_{box}(t_i, t_i^*) = R(t_i - t_i^*)$, where R is the robust loss function (smooth-L1) defined in [7].
- Facial landmark regression loss, L_{pts}, represent the predicted five facial landmarks and groundtruth associated with the positive anchor.
- The last part is dense regression loss, L_{pixel} (refer to Eq. 2).

$$L_{pixel} = \frac{1}{W \times H} \sum_i^W \sum_j^H \| R(D_{P_{ST}}, P_{cam}, P_{ill})_{i,j} - I_{i,j}^* \|_1 \tag{2}$$

where W and H are the width and height of the anchor crop $I_{i,j}^*$, respectively.

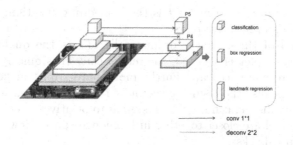

Fig. 2. The Architecture of CenterFace

One of the severe downsides of the anchor-based method is to require a large dense of anchors to attain a good recall rate to improve the overlap between anchor boxes and ground truth. As a result, the models implemented using this approach are rather heavy and sluggish. CenterFace is a lightweight and effective anchor-free face detection method, thereby avoiding the downsides of the anchor-based method.

For the subsequent detection, CenterFace used MobileNetV2 [17] as the backbone and Feature Pyramid Network (FPN) [11] as the neck. In general, FPN builds a feature pyramid from a single scale input using a top-down architecture with lateral connections. CenterFace represents the face by using the face box's center point. The box size and placement of the face are then regressed to image features at the central location. As a result, just one layer of the pyramid is employed for face detection and alignment. The architecture of CenterFace is shown in Fig. 2.

3.2   Feature Extraction

We focus on FaceNet [19] and Arcface [6] because of the good capabilities. FaceNet is an algorithm introduced in 2015 by Google that uses deep learning to extract features on human faces. FaceNet takes an image of a person's face and returns a vector containing 128-dimensional important features.

In FaceNet, the CNN network helps encode the input image into a 128-dimensional vector and then input the triplet error function to evaluate the distance. To use the triplet loss function, three images are required, of which one is selected as the landmark. The landmark photo (A) must be fixed first of the three. The remaining two images include an image labeled Negative (N) (object different from the original image subject) and an image labeled Positive (P) (same object as the original image). The objective of the error function is to minimize the distance between two images if it is negative and maximize the distance when the two images are positive. The loss function is as follows:

$$L(A, P, N) = \sum_{i=0}^{n} \max(\| f(A_i) - f(P_i)\|_2^2 - \| f(A_i) - f(N_i)\|_2^2 + \alpha, \ 0) \quad (3)$$

where n is the number of triplets; f is the embedding function; α is a margin between positive and negative pairs.

The selection of three images dramatically affects the quality of FaceNet model. If a good triplet is selected, the model converges quickly, and the prediction results are more accurate. Furthermore, hard triplet makes the training model smarter because the resulting vector is a vector representing each image. These vectors can distinguish negatives (similar to positives). As a result, images with the same label are closer together in Euclidean space. However, the triplet loss has some drawbacks:

– Combinatorial explosion in the number of face triplets especially for large-scale datasets, creating an increase in iteration steps.
– For effective model training, semi-hard sample mining is a difficult task.

To avoid these problems, some methods use the solfmax-loss. However, the softmax loss function does not explicitly optimise the feature embedding to enforce higher similarity for intraclass samples and diversity for inter-class samples, which results in a performance gap for deep face recognition under large intra-class appearance variations. To boost the discriminative ability of the face recognition model and stabilize the training process, Arcface introduces an additive angular margin loss, is presented as follows:

$$L = -\frac{1}{N} \sum_{i=1}^{N} \log \frac{e^{s(\cos(\theta_{y_i} + m))}}{e^{s(\cos(\theta_{y_i} + m))} + \sum_{j=1, j \neq y_i}^{n} e^{s \cos \theta_j}} \quad (4)$$

where m is an angular margin penalty, s is feature scale, N is the batch size, n is the number of classes (identities), and y_i is the ground-truth label of sample x_i.

After the last convolutional layer, the BN - Dropout - FC - BN structure is applied to get the final 512-D embedding feature.

3.3   Classifiers

There are two strategies to build a classifier in a face recognition system. The first approach is to use closed set classifier such as support vector machine (SVM), Bayesian classification. However, when an unknown object is added, the closed set classifiers misclassify it as a known class. To solve this problem, we can periodically retrain classifiers, but it still takes more time and resource. The second approach is to use open set classifiers based on the distance between two feature vectors. Then we can set a threshold to classify unknown objects.

Cosine Similarity: is a method of measuring the similarity between two non-zero vectors in an inner product space. It is calculated by taking the cosine of the angle formed by two vectors. Therefore, it depends on vectors' orientation, not magnitude. The formula for cosine similarity is:

$$cosine\_similarity(x, y) = \frac{x \cdot y}{\|x\|\|y\|} \tag{5}$$

Based on cosine similarity, the cosine distance between two vectors can be easily inferred as follows:

$$cosine\_distance(x, y) = 1 - cosine\_similarity(x, y) = 1 - \frac{x \cdot y}{\|x\|\|y\|} \tag{6}$$

where x, y are feature embeddings extracted from face images in our system.

3.4   The Architecture System

Attendance and student monitoring system should have a high accuracy rate while maintaining a reasonable runtime. In addition, the system need to be able to detect unknown identities in classroom.

To register, student faces are collected then use CenterFace to detect and extact face region from original images. Detected faces go through Arcface model to extract features. The feature vectors are labeled by the system and stored in the database (Fig. 3). The lecturer only need to do this register step once during the first lecture. Whenever the lecturer want to check student's attendance, the system detects the face from photo captured from student's camera. The detected face then go through the feature extraction step, return a 512-dimensional vector. Finally, the system calculates and compares the cosine distance between the feature vector with other feature vectors stored in the database to determine face's identity. If the face matches the known identity, the system makes a record on student's attendance. Otherwise, the system informs the lecturer about unknown identities (Fig. 4).

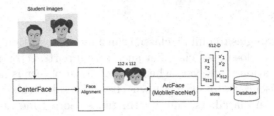

Fig. 3. An illustration of the student registration

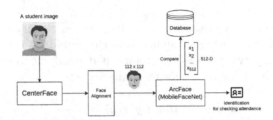

Fig. 4. The architecture of the attendance checking

We trained Arcface model from scratch using MobileFaceNet [1] as backbone on the MS1MV2 dataset with more than 5.8 million photos of nearly 85,000 identities. The input is a 112 × 112 pixels color image normalized on all three color channels.

In real-life scenarios, the face obtained after the detection step can have different angles, which impact the system's accuracy. The work in [22] shows that moderate alignment can boost the recognition accuracy. Therefore, We apply 2D affine transformation to align face in prior to feature extraction step.

4   Datasets and Experiment Settings

4.1   Datasets

Face datasets have grown in size and variety in recent years, and the testing scene has been approaching the real-world unconstrained condition. We evaluate the proposed face recognition system on several well-known datasets:

- Labeled Faces in the Wild (LFW) [9]: contains 13,233 images of 5,749 individuals collected from the web; this is one of the most popular benchmark datasets for face verification with 6,000 pairs.
- AgeDB-30: The subset of AgeDB [13] contains 12,240 images of 570 famous people. There are 6,000 pairs in this dataset; the age difference of each pair's faces is equal to 30 years.
- Celebrities in Frontal-Profile in the Wild (CFPW) [16] includes frontal and profile images of 500 celebrities' faces with ten frontal and four profile images per person. This dataset has two verification protocols: one compares just

frontal faces (CFP-FF), and the other compares frontal and profile faces (CFP-FP) with 7,000 pairs for each protocol.

For face identification task, we generate four mini versions of LFW, AgeDB-30, CFP-FF and CFP-FP to simulate the student attendance check process. For each dataset, we randomly select 500 individuals with two images apiece, then we divide them into two different classrooms (250 individuals each) and register their first image in database. The remaining 500 images are used as data to evaluate our system's performance when taking a roll call.

Furthermore, we also evaluate our system in an online class of 17 students on the Google Meet platform in unconstrained environments. We focus on testing our system with various poses, light conditions, glasses, and mask.

4.2 Experiment Settings

Experimental configuration includes computers equipped with Intel Core i5 8400. To make experiments closer to real-life scenarios, we conduct experiments on CPU only because most clients' machines do not support GPU. The validation method utilized is k-fold cross-validation, with $k = 10$. The integrated librares have OpenCV and Scikit-learn to support preprocessing images. We use MySQL database to store and manage embedding vectors.

5 Experiments and Result Analysis

Face detection is the initial step of an end-to-end face recognition system, and serves as input towards face alignment and feature extraction. The quality of detection bounding box has a direct impact on the performance of the subsequent steps. As shown in Table 1, the system that uses MTCNN detector achieves lowest accuracy compare to CenterFace and RentinaFace detector. The results indicate that a robust face detector can boost face recognition accuracy.

Table 1. Accuracy of verification task of our system with different face detectors and feature extraction models on LFW dataset

	ArcFace	Facenet
MTCNN	0.955	0.948
CenterFace	**0.996**	**0.992**
RentinaFace	0.995	0.984

Figure 5 shows average time our system takes to perform verification task with a pair of 250 × 250 pixels input images. Overall, systems use Arcface as feature extraction model take less time than Facenet to perform. There is a significant gap in execution time when we apply different face detectors. The system

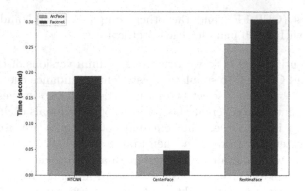

Fig. 5. Average time to verify a pair of face

that uses CenterFace achieves impressive results compares to other detectors. Our final system applies CenterFace to detect face and Arcface to extract embedding vector because it achieves not only high accuracy but also fast execution time.

In the identification task, the proposed system takes an average of 0.22 s to register a new face and 4.3 s to identify a face in a database of 500 samples. The highest accuracy rate our proposed system achieve on LFW, AgeDB-30, CFP-FF, CFP-FP is 0.996, 0.968, 0.995, 0.925 respectively. As shown in Fig. 6, we recommend the threshold should be in range from 0.6 to 0.75 so that the system has best performance. If we set the threshold too small, the system tends to be too sensitive and it is pointless if the system can not recognize most registered member. On the other hand, if the threshold is too high, the system is likely to misrecognize. We also notice that our system is more sensitive to data from cfp-fp when the profile and the frontal images are mixed.

Figure 7 shows the results of the identification task performed by the proposed system under various settings. We do not show all of the volunteers due to paper length constraints and we have to blur their face because of the policy on privacy protection. As a result, instead of all 17, we only show 6 of them in Fig. 7. We use cosine distance in these tests and set the threshold to 0.6. In Fig. 7, the red highlights represent students that our system labels Unidentified because the value of cosine distance is greater than the threshold. On the other hand, the green highlights represent students that are correctly identified by the system. In the Different light conditions and Without glasses test, our system correctly identifies all 17 students. Only 2 out of 17 students are labeled Unidentified in the Do not look at camera test as shown in Fig. 7. With the threshold set to 0.6, our system can only successfully identify 4 students in the Mask test. To overcome this problem, we try to increase the threshold to 0.7 and the system can now correctly identify 12 out of 17 students.

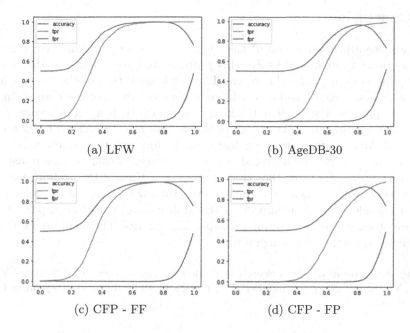

(a) LFW

(b) AgeDB-30

(c) CFP - FF

(d) CFP - FP

Fig. 6. The accuracy, the true positive rate, the false positive rate of the identification task under different thresholds

Fig. 7. Results of the identification task in an online classroom

6   Conclusion

The face identification is one of the highly applicable problems. We focus on deep learning approaches to solve this problem and apply them to the student monitoring system in the classroom. The implementation of the system helps lecturers track students and detect intruders, especially in online classes. In this work, we propose the student tracking system which has good accuracy and real-time execution time. The cores of the system are CenterFace for detecting faces and ArcFace for extracting features. To improve the ability to identify unknown objects, we also adjusted and added measures such as cosine distance. Experimental results show that the accuracy and time of the system meet the requirements for practical implementation. Moreover, some issues need to be further considered, such as improving the ability to recognize when parts of the face are obscured and preventing anti-spoofing attacks. They will be interesting challenges to continue working on in the future.

Acknowledgements. This research is funded by the University of Science, VNU-HCM, Vietnam under grant number CNTT 2021-14 and Advanced Program in Computer Science.

References

1. Chen, S., Liu, Y., Gao, X., Han, Z.: MobileFaceNets: efficient CNNs for accurate real-time face verification on mobile devices. In: Zhou, J., Wang, Y., Sun, Z., Jia, Z., Feng, J., Shan, S., Ubul, K., Guo, Z. (eds.) CCBR 2018. LNCS, vol. 10996, pp. 428–438. Springer, Cham (2018). https://doi.org/10.1007/978-3-319-97909-0_46
2. Chen, Y., Garcia, E.K., Gupta, M.R., Rahimi, A., Cazzanti, L.: Similarity-based classification: Concepts and algorithms. J. Mach. Learn. Res. **10**(3) (2009)
3. Cortes, C., Vapnik, V.: Support-vector networks. Mach. Learn. **20**(3), 273–297 (1995)
4. Dalal, N., Triggs, B.: Histograms of oriented gradients for human detection. In: 2005 IEEE Computer Society Conference on Computer Vision and Pattern Recognition (CVPR 2005), vol. 1, pp. 886–893. IEEE (2005)
5. Deng, J., Guo, J., Ververas, E., Kotsia, I., Zafeiriou, S.: Retinaface: single-shot multi-level face localisation in the wild. In: Proceedings of the IEEE/CVF Conference on Computer Vision and Pattern Recognition, pp. 5203–5212 (2020)
6. Deng, J., Guo, J., Xue, N., Zafeiriou, S.: Arcface: Additive angular margin loss for deep face recognition. In: Proceedings of the IEEE/CVF Conference on Computer Vision and Pattern Recognition, pp. 4690–4699 (2019)
7. Girshick, R.: Fast R-CNN. In: Proceedings of the IEEE International Conference on Computer Vision, pp. 1440–1448 (2015)
8. Gupta, P., Saxena, N., Sharma, M., Tripathi, J.: Deep neural network for human face recognition. Int. J. Eng. Manuf. (IJEM) **8**(1), 63–71 (2018)
9. Huang, G.B., Mattar, M., Berg, T., Learned-Miller, E.: Labeled faces in the wild: a database for studying face recognition in unconstrained environments. In: Workshop on faces in'Real-Life'Images: Detection, Alignment, and Recognition (2008)
10. Jolicoeur, P.: Fisher's linear discriminant function, pp. 303–308. Springer, US, Boston, MA (1999)

11. Lin, T.Y., Dollár, P., Girshick, R., He, K., Hariharan, B., Belongie, S.: Feature pyramid networks for object detection. In: Proceedings of the IEEE Conference on Computer Vision and Pattern Recognition, pp. 2117–2125 (2017)
12. Liu, W., Anguelov, D., Erhan, D., Szegedy, C., Reed, S., Fu, C.-Y., Berg, A.C.: SSD: single shot MultiBox detector. In: Leibe, B., Matas, J., Sebe, N., Welling, M. (eds.) ECCV 2016. LNCS, vol. 9905, pp. 21–37. Springer, Cham (2016). https://doi.org/10.1007/978-3-319-46448-0_2
13. Moschoglou, S., Papaioannou, A., Sagonas, C., Deng, J., Kotsia, I., Zafeiriou, S.: Agedb: the first manually collected, in-the-wild age database. In: Proceedings of the IEEE Conference on Computer Vision and Pattern Recognition Workshop, vol. 2, p. 5 (2017)
14. Ojala, T., Pietikäinen, M., Harwood, D.: A comparative study of texture measures with classification based on featured distributions. Pattern Recogn. 29(1), 51–59 (1996)
15. Pearson, K.: Liii. on lines and planes of closest fit to systems of points in space. The London, Edinburgh Dublin Philosophical Mag. J. Sci. 2(11), 559–572 (1901)
16. S. Sengupta, J.C. Cheng, C.C.V.P.R.C.D.J.: Frontal to profile face verification in the wild. In: IEEE Conference on Applications of Computer Vision, February 2016
17. Sandler, M., Howard, A., Zhu, M., Zhmoginov, A., Chen, L.C.: Mobilenetv 2: Inverted residuals and linear bottlenecks. In: Proceedings of the IEEE Conference on Computer Vision and Pattern Recognition, pp. 4510–4520 (2018)
18. Sardar, S., Babu, K.A.: Hardware implementation of real-time, high performance, RCE-NN based face recognition system. In: 2014 27th International Conference on VLSI Design and 2014 13th International Conference on Embedded Systems, pp. 174–179. IEEE (2014)
19. Schroff, F., Kalenichenko, D., Philbin, J.: Facenet: a unified embedding for face recognition and clustering. In: Proceedings of the IEEE Conference on Computer Vision and Pattern Recognition, pp. 815–823 (2015)
20. Viola, P., Jones, M.: Rapid object detection using a boosted cascade of simple features. In: Proceedings of the 2001 IEEE Computer Society Conference on Computer Vision and Pattern Recognition, CVPR 2001, vol. 1, p. I. IEEE (2001)
21. Wang, H., Wang, Y., Zhou, Z., Ji, X., Gong, D., Zhou, J., Li, Z., Liu, W.: Cosface: large margin cosine loss for deep face recognition. In: Proceedings of the IEEE Conference on Computer Vision and Pattern Recognition, pp. 5265–5274 (2018)
22. Wei, H., Lu, P., Wei, Y.: Balanced alignment for face recognition: a joint learning approach. arXiv preprint arXiv:2003.10168 (2020)
23. Xu, Y., Yan, W., Yang, G., Luo, J., Li, T., He, J.: Centerface: joint face detection and alignment using face as point. Scientific Programming 2020 (2020)
24. Zhang, K., Zhang, Z., Li, Z., Qiao, Y.: Joint face detection and alignment using multitask cascaded convolutional networks. IEEE Signal Process. Lett. 23(10), 1499–1503 (2016)
25. Zhang, Y., Cao, W., Wang, L.: Implementation of high performance hardware architecture of face recognition algorithm based on local binary pattern on FPGA. In: 2015 IEEE 11th International Conference on ASIC (ASICON), pp. 1–4. IEEE (2015)

Cybersecurity and Internet of Things

Towards a Webshell Detection Approach Using Rule-Based and Deep HTTP Traffic Analysis

Ha V. Le[1], Hoang V. Vo[1], Tu N. Nguyen[2], Hoa N. Nguyen[1(✉)], and Hung T. Du[1]

[1] Department of Information Systems, VNU University of Engineering and Technology, Hanoi, Vietnam
levietha@chinhphu.vn, {hoa.nguyen,thanhhung82}@vnu.edu.vn
[2] Department of Computer Science, Kennesaw State University, Marietta, USA
tu.nguyen@kennesaw.edu

Abstract. Web applications are highly vulnerable to injecting malicious code (webshell) attacks. The static analysis is considered the best method to detect webshells. However, this method consumes a lot of time and hardware resources. In this work, we propose a network-based approach that combines the advantage of the rule-based intrusion detection system and deep learning algorithms for webshell detection, termed HRDWD. Specifically, we first consider our rule-based detector for early detection of known webshell and utilize it as a filter to determine HTTP traffics. Then, the HTTP traffics passed through the detector is extracted and represented by 79 features. Finally, the deep neural network model is designed to deeply analyze these features and detect the webshell traffics among the benign ones. To validate the proposed approach, we conduct rigorous experiments to test the performance of HRDWD. The results indicate that HRDWD achieves a high F1-score of 99.98%, an accuracy of 99.96%, and performs better than related models using the same dataset. We put HRDWD into practice to build an IPS system named UET.IPS, and this system has proven feasible in real-time detection and prevention of webshell attacks, including unknown types.

Keywords: Webshell detection · Hybrid rule-based and deep analysis · Intrusion detection and prevention system · Deep neural network

1 Introduction

The evolution of Web technologies has led to the fact that Web applications that are not dependent on the operating system environments are gradually replacing traditional applications. Webshell injection is a popular way for the attacker to escalate and maintain continued access to an already compromised Web application. A webshell contains a backdoor to remotely access and control an Internet-facing server at any time without having to exploit a vulnerability. High-skilled hackers will immediately patch the vulnerabilities to ensure no

N. T. Nguyen et al. (Eds.): ICCCI 2022, LNAI 13501, pp. 571–584, 2022.
https://doi.org/10.1007/978-3-031-16014-1_45

one else can detect and exploit them. Furthermore, webshells are also equipped with many modern techniques such as: using password authentication, blocking search engines, or obfuscation. They significantly reduce the effectiveness of the protection solutions.

There are two approaches to detecting webshell attacks in an organization: host-based detection and network-based detection. The former is usually scanning the Web application source code [1] by static analysis tools. This approach has the advantage of detecting webshell with high accuracy. However, their downside is that they consume a lot of time and resources, especially for large Web applications. We cannot do real-time scans of the source code. It will be too late if the hacker successfully injects the webshell into the system. Furthermore, the effectiveness of these techniques is highly dependent on the Web scripting languages. With the latter, the network flow exchanged through Web application servers is large and flexible, so it is difficult to adequately capture and analyze in real-time the features of the anomaly packets to detect the webshell. However, the malicious functionality appears in network flow when the attacker starts the HTTP communication to execute the webshell. Therefore, investigating a network-based solution that can effectively detect and prevent the free-language webshell in real-time is an exciting challenge but also tricky.

To address these challenges, we propose a hybrid approach of rule-based and deep analysis method that focuses on HTTP traffic to detect webshell, namely HRDWD. Specifically, we first analyze traffic flows using our rule-based detector, customized from an intrusion detection and prevention system (IDPS), for early detection of known attacks. The detector is also used as a filter for selecting HTTP traffic. Then, the HTTP flow that is not triggered by any signature of the rule-based detector is captured and modeled by 79 features. The deep neural network (DNN) model is then used to detect the webshell from these HTTP features. If webshell is detected, the URL corresponding to the detected Webshell traffic will be sent with the highest alert to the administrator and generate a rule to drop future requests. This combination, therefore, inherits the advantages of both methods. Which are the ability to quickly and accurately detect known webshell attacks of rule-based techniques and the ability to analyze the features of HTTP traffic to detect unknown webshell attacks of the DNN model. We summarize the main contributions of this paper as follows:

- We propose a method that extracts hundreds of millions of data packets in real-time network flow to choose webshell content features. This method reduces the number of features to increase performance while still ensuring webshell detection efficiently.
- We propose the HRDWD model that combines rule and DNN-based webshell detection methods to take their advantage. The former is the ability to detect known webshell packets quickly. It is also used to extract webshell features as input to the deep learning model to take advantage of the ability to detect unknown webshells accurately. The HRDWD method allows us to discover webshells in the system regardless of the programming language.

– We experiment to evaluate our proposed HRDWD method, and the results show that the proposed model performs high efficiency with an F1-score of 99.98% and Accuracy of 99.96%.
– We put HRDWD into practice to build an IDPS named UET.IPS. This system has proven feasible in real-time detection and prevention of webshell attacks of all kinds, including unknown attacks.

Organization: The remainder of this paper is divided into four sections. In Sect. 2, we analyze some of the research results related to webshell detection. In Sect. 3, we introduce some basic principles and describe our proposed method. In Sect. 4, we present experimental results, evaluate the proposed work, and provide benchmarks. Section 5 is dedicated to discussing some concluding remarks and future works.

2   Related Works

There are primary research works in designing malware detection techniques based on MLAs and DLAs. The authors in [2] propose a webshell detection model based on the word attention mechanism. In the model, they use Word2Vec to vectorize the words, and then they use Gated Recursive Unit and the attention mechanism to train and detect the samples. Focus on webshell detection in PHP Web applications source code, the authors in [1,3] propose methods of a deep learning model in combination with the Yara-based pattern matching technique. The authors in [4,5] propose methods to detect the various types of PHP webshell, including the one that is equipped with obfuscation techniques. Their methods use a combination of popular MLAs techniques such as XGBoost, Multilayer Perceptron, Random Forest and Naive Bayes, Gradient Boosting Decision Tree.

Realizing that the malware detection problems can be transformed into image classification problems, the authors in [6,7] take advantage of image processing techniques and other techniques to propose hybrid methods to detect and classify malware. By monitoring the network traffic to find abnormal behaviors, the authors in [8] propose an unsupervised deep neural network model called Variational Auto-Encoder to solve the problem of a large amount of labeled data applied in NetIDS. The advantage of this model is that it can work well with a large amount of training data. The authors in [9] propose a deep neural network model to solve the problem of detecting new types of network attacks. Using hyperparameter tuning with KDDCup 99 dataset, the authors develop an optimal DNN model. Having the same idea of webshell detection based on analyzing HTTP packets, the authors in [10] propose a webshell detection approach based on 'word2vec' representation and convolutional neural network (CNN). Firstly, HTTP requests are represented as vectors using the 'word2vec' tool. In this way, a Web request can be represented as a size-fixed matrix. Finally, a CNN-based model is designed to detect the webshells. However, the content of HTTP requests contains special characters and is long text with no spaces. Significantly, modern webshells are equipped with obfuscation, evasion, or encrypted techniques that can easily interfere with the content of requests, making it challenging to identify the characteristics of webshell. By deeply analyzing the log data, the authors in [11,12] succeed in applying machine learning and deep learning techniques to detect attacks in the network.

3   HRDWD for Webshell Detection and Prevention Based on Deep HTTP Traffic Analysis

In this section, to solve the problem of real-time webshell detection and prevention, we propose a model which combines the advantage of rule-based intrusion detection techniques and a Deep Learning algorithm for Webshell Detection, namely HRDWD. HRDWD is designed with the following ideas and uses the network traffics as input data:

- Network traffics is first analyzed by the rule-based detector to detect intrusion attacks. If the network flow is determined to be clean, the HTTP packets will be extracted into 79 features.
- The HTTP packets represented by 79 features will be input to the DNN to predict whether the network traffics contains webshell attacks or not.

In case of having detected webshell attacks, HRDWD alerts the system administrator and automatically updates the rule-based detector ruleset by adding the attackers' source IP addresses to block them the next time possibly.

3.1   IDPS for Webshell Detection

To detect webshell based on HTTP communications, an IDPS, namely UET.IPS, is built to perform both the signature-based and anomaly-based mechanisms. UET.IPS is implemented as a man-in-the-middle proxy in the network, so all HTTPS traffic will be decrypted to plaintext. UET.IPS has a signature database of known webshell attacks with the former. If a hacker makes any webshell HTTP communication on the network that matches the signatures, IDPS will detect and prevent intrusion activities with the anomaly-based work on the statistics of daily data. UET.IPS monitors for any anomalies in network flow compared to daily data to trigger an alert. However, in reality, webshell communications often employ encryption, encoding, and obfuscation to blend in well with legitimate traffic. Then the hackers can send commands which may appear like regular network traffic to the server over HTTP. Essentially, the advantage of IDPS is that it can quickly identify network traffic of some common webshells that have not been modified based on the signature. Suricata (https://suricata-ids. org/) is a fast and robust network IDPS using a powerful signature language to detect complex threats. Moreover, the network flow of a system contains a massive amount of data, many of which are not helpful for webshell detection. So our UET.IPS is customized from Suricata to take advantage of its features, including the network flow filtering function to select HTTP connections.

3.2   Feature Extraction

One of the most challenging problems is feature engineering to detect webshell using network-based Machine Learning Algorithms (MLAs) or Deep Learning Algorithms (DLAs) techniques. The input data is the flow of incoming and outgoing network traffic of the Web server that includes the connections between the hacker and the webshell via the HTTP protocol. However, this is raw data and cannot be used directly for machine learning or deep learning models. Some studies applied MLAs for text classification to analyze the text context of HTTP requests. However, the difficulty of this approach is because the content of HTTP requests contains special characters and is long text without spaces. Significantly, modern webshells are equipped with obfuscation, evasion, or encrypted techniques that can easily interfere with the content of requests, making it challenging to identify the characteristics of webshell. To extract features from network traffic, we use the CICFlowMeter[1] that can extract 83 HTTP data features in bidirectional flows. Using the first packet to determine the forward and backward directions, so many network traffic features such as duration, number of packets, number of bytes, length of packets, etc., can be calculated separately in the bi-direction. However, we do not use four features *'Flow ID, Src IP, Src Port, Label'*. From the remaining 79 features, *'Dst Port, Protocol'* is set as the categorical variable, 77 other features are set as continuous variables, and all this data is stored in a CSV format file. Because all the critical information to identifying a webshell attack in the network data flow is represented by these features, we can use them as input to our deep learning models described in the following subsection.

3.3   DNN Model

Because of the large number of extracted features, it is difficult and time-consuming to point out exactly which features are necessary for detecting webshell attacks. Therefore, we propose using the Deep Neural Network (DNN) model, with the advantage of comparing it with MLAs to automatically select essential features, to solve the webshell detection problem. DNN can directly use the type of data kept in tabular format. FastAI[2] is a deep learning library for Python that can quickly and easily provide state-of-the-art results in deep learning domains and outstanding support for tabular data. So we use FastAI to represent the DNN model. However, in a DNN task, we can never build an optimal model right from the start; it also needs to be turned into hyperparameters to achieve the best efficiency and performance. When designing the DNN model, we also do the process of hyperparameters turning with the Adaptive Experimentation Platform that uses Bayesian Optimization to get the optimal model, as shown in the Fig. 1. In our DNN model, there are four crucial components, including categorical embeddings, continuous variables, hidden layers, and output hidden layers with the following parameters:

---

[1] https://github.com/ahlashkari/CICFlowMeter.
[2] https://www.fast.ai/.

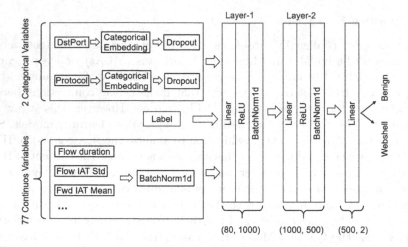

Fig. 1. Architecture of our DNN model

- Batch Normalization: Batch normalization is one of the most popular normalization methods in the deep learning model. It allows the training of deep neural networks to be faster and more stable by stabilizing the distribution of the input layers during training. Batch normalization is normalizing activation functions over a mini-batch according to a defined size. Batch normalization also serves as a regularization to help reduce overfitting. Using batch normalization, we do not need to use dropout, which makes losing too much information.
- Rectified Linear Unit (ReLU): The *ReLU* function is commonly used when training neural networks. *ReLU* filters for values less than 0, the formula is easy to understand $f(x) = max(0, x)$. It has many advantages compared to *Sigmoid* and *Tanh* such as convergence and calculation speed is much faster.

3.4 HRDWD Architecture

Our proposed HRDWD is deployed inline mode in the network for webshell detection and prevention. It uses real-time network traffic as input as described in Fig. 2. Firstly, the rule-based detector is used to capture real-time network packets and works as an IDPS with a database of signatures to detect and prevent known webshell attacks. Rule-based detector captures only HTTP traffic, while other network flows will be passed to the Traffic Out. All the HTTP traffic is compared with the signatures to detect any webshell attack on the network system. If no webshell attack is detected, the rule-based detector works as the network traffic filter to forward the temporarily considered clean HTTP connections to Deep HTTP Traffic Analysis. The CICFlowmeter works as a FeatureExtractor to extract all the HTTP connections into 79 features used as input to the trained DNN model to detect unknown or obfuscated, encrypted webshells. Suppose the DNN model detects a webshell attack, new signatures will be updated

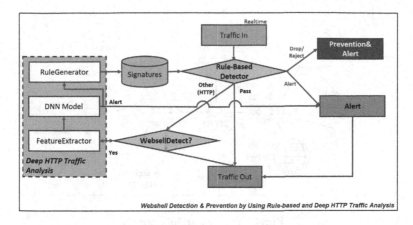

Fig. 2. Architecture of HRDWD

immediately to the rule-based detector signatures database. These signatures will request a rule-based detector to drop all network flow with the source IP and request a URL corresponding to the detected webshell. At the same time, it will send alerts to system administrators to implement system security.

4 Experiment and Evaluation

4.1 Environment Setup

This section describes the server system and the software framework libraries to demonstrate the HRDWD. We use Python version 3.6 as a programming language. For selecting and tuning hyperparameters in the DNN model, we use the Adaptive Experimentation Platform, termed Ax[3], which is a machine learning system to help automate this process. Using Bayesian optimization makes Ax suitable for a wide range of applications.

4.2 Evaluation Metrics

To evaluate the webshell detection method, we use some common evaluation metrics such as confusion matrix, F1-score that is calculated according to True Positive (TP), False Positive (FP), False Negative (FN), and True Negative (TN).

Accuracy is not a good performance measure when the number of samples being evaluated is disproportionate. Therefore, we also generate and report the F1-score, Precision, Recall, and confusion matrix to evaluate the performance of a model.

---

[3] https://ax.dev/.

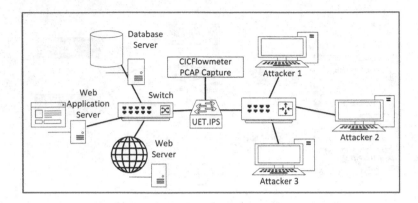

Fig. 3. Testbed architecture

4.3 Dataset

To experiment, one of the most severe difficulties we encountered was data collecting. There have been many published network flow datasets since 1998, such as DARPA (Lincoln Laboratory 1998–99), CAIDA (Center of Applied Internet Data Analysis 2002–2016), ADFA (University of New South Wales 2013), and CSE-CIC-IDS2017, CSE-CIC-IDS2018 (Canadian Institute for Cybersecurity). However, these datasets cover many types of network attacks, with very little data available about webshell attacks. So to collect data for training and testing the model, we built a testbed system as shown in Fig. 3, which is divided into two completely separated networks, namely Webserver-Network and Attack-Network. On the former, we deploy all standard and necessary equipment, including routers, firewalls, switches, and 03 servers which are a Web server, Web application server, and Web database server. On the Attack-Network, we use the Kali Linux operating system as the attacker server, which uses more than 400 types of PHP, ASP, ASPX, JS webshell. We use several craws website tools to create the normal HTTP traffic as legal clients. Besides that, we also simulate Webshell attacks by using Kali Linux to upload and execute webshell for creating intrusion traffic. UET.IPS is used as a packet capturing HTTP filtering tool, which also saves network traffic into PCAP files.

Thus, in order to validate and evaluate the effectiveness of the HRDWD method, we use two datasets:

- Dataset 1 (DS1): This is the data set that we directly build through the testbed system described above. There are two labeled data types in the data set: *Webshell* representing a flow containing a Webshell attack embedded in packets and sent directly to a Web server using the HTTP method, and *Benign* for normal HTTP flow. Data labeling is also an important step that takes a considerable amount of time and effort. In this step, we create an automatic tool by Python for automatically labeling the data. There is a total of 180,089 Benign flows and 7,310 Webshell flows. The goal of using this

Table 1. Total HTTP flows in cleaned datasets

Dataset	Benign flows	Webshell/Malicious flows
DS1	180,079	7,310
DS2	1,042,301	566

Table 2. Number of training and testing samples

Dataset	Train samples	Test samples
DS1	131,171 [126,055 B - 5,116 W]	56,218 [54,024 B - 2,194 W]
DS2	730,006 [729,610 B - 396 M]	312,861 [312,691 B - 170 M]

dataset is to verify HRDWD's ability to detect webshell attacks by analyzing the network traffic correctly.

- Dataset 2 (DS2): We use the CSE-CIC-IDS2018 [13] dataset collected on 02-23-2018 that was published by Canadian Institute for Cybersecurity. This dataset includes seven different types of attacks: brute-force, heartbleed, botnet, dos, ddos, web attacks, and infiltration of the network from inside. This is a well-known and reliable dataset and is used by many research projects [14]. Therefore, our goal when using this data set is to objectively compare the efficiency of our HRDWD method with those of other studies using the same dataset.

4.4 Data Preparation

After obtaining datasets are generated from CICFlowMeter for each label type, we aggregate them into one dataset and clean it up. There are six columns labeled for each flow, namely FlowID, SourceIP, DestinationIP, SourcePort, Destination-Port, and Protocol, with 79 network traffic features. We convert timestamps to Unix epoch numeric values and keep DestinationPort and Protocol. We parse and remove multiple column headers in some data files. We then shuffle the data before saving it into one file containing all the labels. The cleaned dataset contains 79 features, out of which two (Destination Port and Protocol) are treated as categorical. The two cleaned datasets are described in Table 1.

We divide the dataset into two parts: training and testing at the ratio of 7:3. For the training phase, we use the ratio of 9:1 for the sub-training set and validation set. The training phase use crossed data-validation iterators with stratification based on class labels. Dataset split information is presented in Table 2. Note that, in this table, the B symbol means *Benign*; W for *Webshell*; and M for *Malicious*.

4.5 Hyperparameter Optimization

We select model parameters based on a technique called Hyperparameter Optimization. We use Ax for the selection of optimal parameters. Ax is a platform for

Table 3. Hyperparameter optimization value

Hyperparameter	Value	Type	Optimal value
Learning rate	[0.001, 1.0]	Range	0.003
Batch size	[32, 64, 96, 128]	Choice	64
Epochs	[8, 10, 16, 24, 32]	Choice	24
Layers	[[200, 100], [400, 200],[800, 400], [1000, 500]]	Range	[400, 200]

Table 4. Result of hyperparameter optimization with 5-fold cross validation for DS1

Epoch	Accuracy	Recall	F1-score	FPR	Prediction time (s)
1	99.99	100	100	0.2	0.90
2	100	100	100	0.0	1.35
3	99.98	99.99	99.99	0.34	1.96
4	99.99	100	99.99	0.2	0.98
5	99.98	99.99	99.99	0.34	1.00
Average	99.99	100	99.99	0.216	1.238

optimizing any experiment, including machine learning experiments, A/B tests, and simulations. We use a technique called Bayesian Optimization. It starts by building a smooth surrogate model of the outcomes using Gaussian processes based on the observations available from previous rounds of experimentation.

There are four hyperparameters that can be turned, and they take two types of values that are range and choice. Table 3 shows information of hyperparameters. We generate the learning rate from the interval 0.003, batch size from 64, the total number of epoch runs 24, and [400, 200] for the range number of layers. To ensure the hyperparameters are optimized, we perform k-fold cross-validation with the DS1 and also measure the prediction time.

We chose the number of folds as 5, and Table 4 shows our cross-validation results. The results of 5-fold cross validation are almost perfect with an average accuracy of 99.99%, F1-score of 99.99%, FPR ratio 0.216%, and execution time are also very short, under two seconds.

4.6   Experiment Results

Based on the proposed method, we built the tool to evaluate our method with the cleaned datasets mentioned above. We implement HRDWD based on the FastAI framework. The experimental results, especially the accuracy, precision, F1-score of HRDWD with the two datasets DS1 and DS2, are described in detail below.

DS1 Results. Based on the test part of DS1, we evaluated the effectiveness of HRDWD and obtained the results shown as the confusion matrix illustrated in Table 5a. Thus, we compute the accuracy, precision, F1-score, recall, false

Table 5. Experiment results for DS1

	TrueBenign	TrueWebshell
Predicted Benign	54,022	2
Predicted Webshell	2	2,192

(a) Confusion matrix

Metric	Value(%)
Accuracy	99.99
Precision	99.99
F1-score	99.99
Recall	100
FNR	0.00
FPR	0.09

(b) Performance indicators

Table 6. Experiment results for DS2

	TrueBenign	TrueMalicious
Predicted Benign	312,557	2
Predicted Malicious	134	168

(a) Confusion matrix

Metric	Value (%)
Accuracy	99.96
Precision	100
F1-score	99.98
Recall	99.96
FNR	0.04
FPR	1.18

(b) Performance indicators

negative rate (FNR), false positive rate (FPR). It can be seen in Table 5b that our method gives a very high F1-score of 99.99%. With the dataset used for the test, HRDWD detects Webshells with an accuracy of 99.99%. Moreover, the false positive/negative rates of HRDWD are also tiny: only 0.09% and 0.00%, respectively. This means our method allows us to reduce the rate of webshell false detection as well as reduce the rate of missing webshell flows.

DS2 Results. As mentioned above, the purpose of using this DS2 set is to objectively compare the effectiveness of the HRDWD with methods in other studies that also use this dataset. However, one of the disadvantages of this dataset is that the amount of data related to a webshell attack is relatively low. To evaluate effectiveness, we also use a confusion matrix to calculate the accuracy, precision, F1-score metrics as shown the in Table 6a and 6b.

From the results, we can see that HRDWD only mistakenly identified 2 out of 170 accurate webshell attacks, resulting in a relatively low FPR value of 1.18%. The high-value accuracy of 99.96% and low False Negative Rate of 0.04% means that the rate of benign flow misclassified to a webshell flow is low.

The source code and the dataset used in our experiment can be freely accessed from the GitHub link: https://github.com/levietha0311/HRDWD/.

Table 7. Comparision of HRDWD with other methods

Method	Accuracy (%)	F1-score (%)
HRDWD	99.96	99.98
Artificial Intelligence IDS [16]	99.97	100.00
FastAI [15]	99.92	–
Keras-TensorFlow [15]	99.94	–
Keras-Theano [15]	99.95	–

4.7 Comparison

To objectively evaluate the effectiveness of the HRDWD method, we experiment and compare the results with a number of other studies that also use the same dataset CSE-CIC-IDS2018. The authors in [15] propose three models using fast.ai, Keras-TensorFlow, and Keras-Theano applied on the CSE-CIC-IDS2018 dataset on 02-23-2018. The authors in [16] use Hyper-Parameter Optimization Tuning to build an Artificial Intelligence IDS system and experiment with it on the CSE-CIC-IDS2018 dataset.

The results in Table 7 show that the accuracy of the HRDWD method reaches 99.96%, higher than the accuracy of three models using fast.ai, Keras-TensorFlow, and Keras-Theano, which are of 99.92%, of 99.94% and 99.95% respectively. The result of Artificial Intelligence IDS is the highest with accuracy of 99.97% and F1-score of 100% because in their study the authors used Hyper-Parameter Optimization Tuning technique to select the best fit model for the CSE-CIC-IDS2018 dataset. However, this does not confirm that this model will have good results for other datasets because, in fact, the HRDWD model, when experimenting with our data set built by testbed can achieve accuracy up to 99.99% and F1-score up to 99.99%.

5 Conclusions

In this work, we have proposed the HRDWD method to real-time detection and prevention of webshell in Web applications based on network traffic analysis. Our main idea is to use a combination of rule-based and DNN webshell detection. First, a rule-based detector analyzes the network flows for early detection of abnormal packets, and it is also used as a filter for selecting only HTTP traffic. Then the HTTP network flow passed through the rule-based detector will be extracted into 79 features. Finally, from extracted feature HTTP data, the DNN model is adopted to detect the webshell. If webshells are detected, the result will be sent back to IPS for blocking. In terms of evaluation, to demonstrate the effectiveness and performance of our HRDWD method, extensive simulations have been conducted. The obtained results validate that it achieves an excellent F1-score of 99.98% and accuracy of 99.96%, showing that our model is better than the other models on the same dataset. Finally, we applied HRDWD to a practice of the UET.IPS system that enables real-time detection and prevention of webshell attacks.

For future works, we will continue to improve and expand the application range of HRDWD. Firstly, we plan to apply MLA to feature engineering before using deep learning models to increase the efficiency of HRDWD. Secondly, we will expand the model to be able to detect and classify more types of cyberattacks (as in the CIC dataset, there are 12 types of attacks). Finally, we also plan to apply this model to static analysis code sources of many kinds of languages such as PHP, ASP, Golang, Python, etc.

References

1. Nguyen, H.N., Le, H.V., Phung, O.V., Du, H.P.: Toward a deep learning approach for detecting PHP webshell. In: Proceedings of the Tenth International Symposium on Information and Communication Technology, ser. SoICT 2019, pp. 514–521. Association for Computing Machinery, New York (2019)
2. Li, T., Ren, C., Fu, Y., Xu, J., Guo, J., Chen, X.: Webshell detection based on the word attention mechanism. IEEE Access **7**, 185 140–185 147 (2019)
3. Le, H.V., Nguyen, T.N., Nguyen, H.N., Le, L.: An efficient hybrid webshell detection method for webserver of marine transportation systems. IEEE Trans. Intell. Transp. Syst. Early Access, pp. 1–13 (2021)
4. Tianmin, G., Jiemin, Z., Jian, M.: Research on webshell detection method based on machine learning. In: 2019 3rd International Conference on Electronic Information Technology and Computer Engineering (EITCE), 2019, pp. 1391–1394 (2019)
5. Cui, H., Huang, D., Fang, Y., Liu, L., Huang, C.: Webshell detection based on random forest-gradient boosting decision tree algorithm. In: IEEE Third International Conference on Data Science in Cyberspace (DSC) 2018, pp. 153–160 (2018)
6. Makandar, A., Patrot, A.: Malware class recognition using image processing techniques. In: 2017 International Conference on Data Management, Analytics and Innovation (ICDMAI), 2017, pp. 76–80 (2017)
7. Vinayakumar, R., Alazab, M., Soman, K.P., Poornachandran, P., Venkatraman, S.: Robust intelligent malware detection using deep learning. IEEE Access **7**, 46 717–46 738 (2019)
8. Osada, G., Omote, K., Nishide, T.: Network intrusion detection based on semi-supervised variational auto-encoder. In: Foley, S.N., Gollmann, D., Snekkenes, E. (eds.) ESORICS 2017. LNCS, vol. 10493, pp. 344–361. Springer, Cham (2017). https://doi.org/10.1007/978-3-319-66399-9_19
9. Vinayakumar, R., Alazab, M., Soman, K.P., Poornachandran, P., Al-Nemrat, A., Venkatraman, S.: Deep learning approach for intelligent intrusion detection system. IEEE Access **7**, 41 525–41 550 (2019)
10. Tian, Y., Wang, J., Zhou, Z., Zhou, S.: CNN-webshell: malicious web shell detection with convolutional neural network. In: Proceedings of the 2017 VI International Conference on Network, Communication and Computing (2017)
11. Landauer, M., Höld, G., Wurzenberger, M., Skopik, F., Rauber, A.: Iterative selection of categorical variables for log data anomaly detection. In: Bertino, E., Shulman, H., Waidner, M. (eds.) ESORICS 2021. LNCS, vol. 12972, pp. 757–777. Springer, Cham (2021). https://doi.org/10.1007/978-3-030-88418-5_36

12. Daihes, Y., Tzaban, H., Nadler, A., Shabtai, A.: MORTON: detection of malicious routines in large-scale DNS traffic. In: Bertino, E., Shulman, H., Waidner, M. (eds.) ESORICS 2021. LNCS, vol. 12972, pp. 736–756. Springer, Cham (2021). https://doi.org/10.1007/978-3-030-88418-5_35
13. Ayachi, Y., Mellah, Y., Berrich, J., Bouchentouf, T.: Increasing the performance of an ids using ANN model on the realistic cyber dataset CSE-CIC-IDS2018. In: International Symposium on Advanced Electrical and Communication Technologies (ISAECT) 2020, pp. 1–4 (2020)
14. Leevy, J., Khoshgoftaar, T.: A survey and analysis of intrusion detection models based on CSE-CIC-IDS2018 big data. J. Big Data **7**, 11 (2020)
15. Atefinia, R., Ahmadi, M.: Network intrusion detection using multi-architectural modular deep neural network. J. Supercomput. **77**, 3571–3593 (2021)
16. Kanimozhi, V., Jacob, T.P.: Artificial intelligence based network intrusion detection with hyper-parameter optimization tuning on the realistic cyber dataset CSE-CIC-IDS2018 using cloud computing. In: International Conference on Communication and Signal Processing (ICCSP) 2019, pp. 0033–0036 (2019)

Security Consideration of BIA Utilization in Smart Electricity Metering Systems

Vladimir Sobeslav[✉] [iD], Josef Horalek[iD], Tomas Svoboda[iD], and Hana Svecova[iD]

Faculty of Management and Informatics,
University of Hradec Kralove, Hradec Kralove, Czech Republic
{vladimir.sobeslav,josef.horalek,tomas.svoboda,
hana.svecova}@uhk.cz

Abstract. Smart electricity metering is a modern component of distribution networks, whereby it enables efficient management of the distribution system based on actual requirements and reporting of actual electricity consumption to the customer and the market regulator. It is a relatively complex issue encompassing wide range of technologies, business processes and legislative requirements. In order to create an effective Smart Metering System, it is advisable to use Business impact analysis to analyse the efficiency of data usage and the impacts of non-availability or loss of data in the power system. By implementing a BIA, distribution companies operating in the EU market reduce the risk of financial losses caused by non-compliance with regulatory requirements. An integral part of this is the establishment of security and mitigation measures to ensure a non-penalizing system of data transfer to the regulatory authorities in the energy sector. The main objective of the paper is to establish a model for data classification and its use in the BIA in the field of smart metering.

Keywords: BIA · Confidentiality · Availability · Integrity · Analysis

1 Introduction

The national and international legislative framework defining the data transfer obligations between the entities providing electricity sales and the distributor has a significant impact on the area of electricity metering. In the environment of the Czech Republic as a member of the European Union, it is the state administration authorities in the form of the Ministry of Industry and Trade and the Energy Regulatory Office that provide the regulatory and normative framework in the energy sector, implement market supervision, price and non-price regulation, sub-competition or provide dispute resolution. In addition to these two governmental bodies, there is the Czech electricity and gas market operator (OTE), which is separated from all energy companies so as not to compromise its independence and whose role is to deal with commercial and operational matters such as the organisation of markets and the assessment of energy metering deviations. For the actual distribution of consumption and generation plants according to importance, a division into different types of metering has been introduced and is defined by legislation.

N. T. Nguyen et al. (Eds.): ICCCI 2022, LNAI 13501, pp. 585–597, 2022.
https://doi.org/10.1007/978-3-031-16014-1_46

This is metering type A, which includes the largest electricity consumers with a reserved power of over 250 kW inclusive, or when connected to the grid with a voltage of over 52 kV inclusive, and generators that are connected to the distribution or transmission system with a voltage of over 1 kV. It also includes transfer points between different systems of other countries or between different national systems with a voltage above 1 kV. For Metering Type A, metering is only performed using static meters with GPRS and GSM modem and point-to-point remote communication due to legislative requirements for daily transmission of meter data to OTE. It is a remote continuous measurement with daily data transmission and a measurement interval of 15 min. The possibility of using surrogate values and guesses is supported. Another type of metering is type B metering, which includes medium power consumption realized by indirect metering up to 52 kV and reserved power up to 250 kW, or when there is some production connected to the grid with voltage up to 1 kV and take forward points with voltage up to 1 kV.

1.1 Principle of Aggregation

If OTE has metered data for generation and consumption, it then performs aggregation, a process whereby the deviations from the agreed values are calculated for the balance groups of the individual settlement entities and used as the basis for the settlement of deviations. A clearing entity's deviation is defined as the difference between the actual supply and actual electricity consumption on the one hand and the total agreed supply and total agreed electricity consumption on the other hand. Supply production is always marked with a positive sign and consumption is marked with a negative sign. The deviation is always set in MWh with a resolution of three decimal places.

$$D_{SS} = E_{ss}^{act} - E_{ss}^{agre}$$

DSS - deviation subject of settlement [MWh]
Ess act - actually delivered / collected energy [MWh]
Ess egre - agreed energy [MWh]

OTE determines the subject of settlement the value of actual electricity supply and actual electricity consumption as the sum of electricity supply to the electricity system and the sum of electricity consumption from the electricity system at supply and delivery points (SDP) [1].

$$E_{ss}^{act} = \sum\nolimits_{SDP \in SS} E_{sup,ss}^{mea} - \sum\nolimits_{SDP \in SS} E_{con,ss}^{mea}$$

Index SDP $\in$ SS - expresses the set of all SDPs that the OTE has registered in the system to a particular clearing entity. $E_{sup,ss}^{mea}$ resp. $E_{con,ss}^{mea}$ – the measurement value of the supply, respectively consumption [MWh] in the given domestic SDP (SDP for measurement of cross-border electricity transfers is assigned by the transmission system operator) [MWh], this value includes also positive, respectively negative control energy, which was actually produced/not produced/consumed, respectively not produced/consumed, and therefore must be measured. According to the legislation, the actual quantity of electricity of the clearing entity in the trading hour is the sum of the quantity of electricity based on the data obtained from measurements and using type diagrams at the points of consumption or transmission of the clearing entity and at the points of consumption or transmission of the electricity market participants for which the clearing entity has assumed responsibility for the deviation. The contracted quantity of electricity shall be the sum of the quantity of electricity contracted by that clearing entity with other clearing entities in a given trading hour, including the quantity of contracted control energy. [1]

$$E_{ss}^{agre} = \sum_{RD \in SS} E_{sup,ss}^{agre} - \sum_{RD \in SS} E_{con,ss}^{agre} + \sum_{RD \in SS} E_{imp,ss}^{agre}$$
$$- \sum_{RD \in SS} E_{exp,ss}^{agre} + \sum_{RD \in SS} E_{reg,ss}^{mes}$$

Index $\Sigma_{RD \in SS}$ expresses the set of all (realisation diagrams) realisation diagrams negotiated by a given clearing entity (or market participants for which it has assumed responsibility for a deviation) with other clearing entities. $E_{sup,ss}^{agre}$ respectively $E_{con,ss}^{agre}$ the commercially negotiated resulting value of the clearing entity's obligation to deliver or withdraw electricity to/from the EC based on the registration of negotiated values on organised markets and from the registration of domestic bilateral trades [MWh]. $E_{imp,ss}^{agre}$ respectively $E_{exp,ss}^{agre}$ the commercially agreed value of the clearing entity's obligation to deliver or withdraw electricity to/from the EC based on the registration of cross-border bilateral trades [MWh]. $E_{reg,ss}^{agre}$ the total value of the contracted control energy [MWh].

1.2 Significance and Purpose of BIA

In order to ensure the above requirements, arising from international and national legislatives determining the framework of regulated business in the energy sector, it is essential to ensure procedural and technical measures that will enable its implementation. The implementation of procedural and technical measures must be systematic, controlled and economically realistic. In order to establish these measures, generally defined within the framework of ISO/IEC 27001, it is necessary to know the importance and value of the individual data assets to be protected and their impact on the business and security of the entire data acquisition, evaluation and transmission system.

To ensure the systematic nature of individual activities, it is then advisable to use one of the generally accepted sets of practice-tested concepts and procedures that allow better planning, use and improvement of the use of information technology, both from the side of IT service providers and from the perspective of customers, such as ITIL, which in the first phase of the Plan sets out the principles and procedures for the analysis of a given system as a whole. One of the most used approaches is Business Impact Analysis (BIA) aiming to evaluate the impact on an organization when there is a failure in the supply of products or services that are important to its operations as defunct in the asset-impact relationship [1, 2]. The overlap of BIA to the energy issue at hand has then been published in [3] and in the Smart Cities volume. Related to the issue of impact assessment using BIA is the issue of remote readings using wireless technologies in electricity metering, the results of which have been published in [4] and similarly in [5].

The BIA results are then used to determine Business Continuity Management (BCM) [6, 7]. An essential part of BIA is the determination of the minimum levels of resources required to restore critical activities within specified times and at specified levels. BIA analysis must also include an assessment from a Con-identity Integrity Availability (CIA) perspective, which focuses on the data or information as a whole and the options for selecting the level of protection [8]. The analysis was created for one of the most important distribution companies in Czech Republic (DC).

Based on the above information, it can be concluded that the use of BIA in the field of power systems using wireless technologies with possible impacts of power outages has hardly been addressed so far. Therefore, the assessment of impacts using BIA can be stated as desirable, since by using BIA the overall impacts during possible power outages can be eliminated.

The first step is to determine the security classification (SC) to specify the security requirements for the data sent from the metering equipment to the OTE (Czech electricity and gas market operator). The classification system enables the process of designing, implementing and controlling security measures to be simplified and made more transparent and sets parameters for the selection of the service provision model. SC is also used to determine the severity level of security incidents. The BIA identified the impact of each asset on DC business processes in terms of confidentiality, integrity and availability. The impacts were then used to determine a security classification class for each identified information asset.

1.3 Security Considerations for CIA

This section presents the setting of security considerations and metrics on information assets within the data sent to OTE for daily market and billing purposes. First, a classification is established for each of the security aspects that we will use for the SC of each data to determine their significance. The rating is made A, B, C, D, where the letters denote each security level from highest to lowest. The classification is given in Table 1, 2 and 3.

Table 1. Availability criteria

Class	Marking	Description
A	[A; *; *]	Disruption of the availability of the information asset is not acceptable and it is necessary to start solving even short-term unavailability without delay. Recovery is required within minutes, otherwise the interests of Distribution System Operator (DSO) may be critically compromised
B	[B; *; *]	The unavailability of the information asset must be restored within hours, otherwise the interests of DSO may be significantly compromised
C	[C; *; *]	The unavailability of a system information asset should not exceed a period of one day. A longer outage may result in a partial compromise of DSO's interests
D	[D; *; *]	The unavailability of the information asset system affects the interests of DSO on an insignificant scale

Table 2. Confidentiality criteria

Class	Marking	Description
A	[*; A;*]	Information assets are highly confidential and if disclosed could have fatal consequences for DSOs and possibly the operation of distribution systems (DS)
B	[*; B; *]	Information assets are confidential and their protection is mandated by law, civil code or GDPR
C	[*; C; *]	Information assets are not public and their disclosure would violate unbundling rules
D	[*; D; *]	Information assets may only be disclosed under certain conditions set out by law or DSO's internal regulations

Table 3. Integrity criteria

Class	Marking	Description
A	[*; *; A]	The information asset integrity breach could ultimately have a significant impact on the functioning of DS and the interests of DSO
B	[*; *; B]	The information asset integrity breach could limit the important interests and objectives of DSO
C	[*; *; C]	The information asset integrity breach could partially limit the interests and objectives of DSO
D	[*; *; D]	The information asset integrity breach does not significantly limit the interests and objectives of DSO

The input metrics will be used to assess data unavailability, data loss and data disclosure or modification from the perspective of the system user. The impact rating scale is on a scale of 1 - none, 2 - low, 3 - medium, 4 - high, 5 - critical. Furthermore, BIA evaluation metrics were determined in the parameters of data unavailability in time intervals of 15 min (15M), 1 h (1H), 5 h (5H), 12 h (12H), 1 day (1D), 1 week (1W), more than 1 week (1WW). Another parameter is missing backup 1 h (1B), missing backup 24 h (24B), missing backup a week (WB), missing backup a month (MB), and complete loss of data (ALLB). In addition, the metrics evaluated are unauthorized disclosure to outsiders (UD), minor errors (ME), major errors (LE), and intentional data modification error (IME).

1.4 BIA/CIA at the Distribution Company

For DC, it is first necessary to determine what systems and information assets will be involved in the analysis. Then, according to the specified guidelines and the specified scale, the evaluation is carried out.

1.5 Data Communication Model

For a relevant BIA determination, it was necessary to analyse and classify the data occurring in the power distributor's systems designed to handle and process the metering data. Some of the systems, and the data contained in them, are designed to communicate remotely with the meters while others process the data for billing or sending to the on-national electricity and gas market operator (OTE). For some, the impact on operation is negligible, while others must not be out of service for more than an hour. Therefore, for the purpose of creating BIA, the systems and data were divided into individual blocks.

Reading system is an application designed for the reading system administrator and is used to read meters from the points of consumption remotely. If necessary, it can receive data from handheld terminals from the field worker. Terminal reading is mainly used during meter installation or dismantling and in case of unavailability of signal at the supply point (SP).

The accounting system is used for invoicing production and consumption. The system contains data about customers and all installed devices. The system validates the type C readings and sends some data to OTE, in particular to DUFMO. The accounting system is divided into so-called transactions, which allow different operations to be carried out independently in the system. The user of the accounting system is mainly responsible for invoicing data, dealing with reporting, contractual matters, creating and recording field worker orders. The field worker ensures the operation of remotely read meters based on orders sent from the accounting system.

The OTE messaging system is an application designed to send data to OTE and is used in conjunction with the reading system. It is an intermediate link between the reading system and OTE to which the LP60 forwards data. The OTE messaging system is populated with data from the reading system. This application is then the responsibility of OTE communication administrator, who by default also has access to other systems in the measurement chain.

Customer data portal is designed as an interface to the customer, to which it displays the data from the continuous measurement and the data downloaded from the LP15 meter and converted to LP 60. It is primarily a supplementary service for customers with continuous metering. The application is the responsibility of the data provision portal administrator responsible for user registration and data currency.

Base Transceiver Station operated (BTS) as a third party that can affect the meter reading is the operator's BTS listed here. It can potentially arrange not to read meters in a certain area. Occasionally, a BTS may lose the signal from some sim cards due to some parameter reconfiguration or BTS failure. The operator is bound by certain service standard agreements, so whenever there are any modifications to its equipment that could affect remote communication via sims set to GPRS readout and in exceptional cases GSM, it should give timely notice. Such an outage has the greatest impact on the Field Personnel (Installer) (TPM) who must carry out any SIM replacement or modem reconfiguration at these sites.

1.6 Information Assets

For the purpose of the analysis, the information asset that comes from the remote meter reading data or, alternatively, the information asset for which the remote reading is the basis will be used. In ČEZd, the following is used as an information asset for electricity metering and subsequent remote communication with the system:

LP15 (Last-profile 15 min), is the average of the maximum measured energy at an interval of 15 min, which is successively stored in the memory of the instrument. This makes it possible to observe the evolution of the active and reactive energy components of consumption or production over time. BV (Billing value) is a register of the meter in which the current state of the dial of the active or reactive energy consumed/delivered is written. In addition, the register is used to record data on the active energy consumed from the meter register, among other things, for billing purposes to the accounting system.

For the purpose of Electricity Billing, the following information assets are also used, which are used, for example, for settlement of deviations or other billing. **P60** (Last-profile 60 min) is a 60-min profile, which is calculated as the arithmetic average of the sum of the four values from LP15, thus obtaining a profile in a 60-min interval. This profile is subsequently used for daily dispatch and aggregation see Sect. 1.2. The Supplementary Finding for Billing (known as DUF) is used as the basis for the billing for the distribution of electricity sent by DSO, either to the trader or to other electricity billing entities. DUF is further divided into **DUF VO** - it is the billing data for the distribution of electricity at the points of consumption connected to the HV or VVN network. The second type is **DUF MO**, i.e. the billing data for the distribution of electricity at consumption points connected to the LV (Low Voltage) network.

1.7 BIA Evaluation

Evaluation of input data used from remote power metering in terms of availability, loss, disclosure or error. This evaluation is carried out by interviewing individual users:

- Metering system administrator (MSA) – readout system user.
- Administrator of communication with OTE (AC_OTE) – the user of an application designed to send data to OTE.
- Provisioning portal manager (PPM) – customer service portal user.
- Field worker (fitter) (FW) – the user depending mainly on the functioning of the reading system, partly on the functioning of the BTS and the accounting system.
- Accounting system user (ASU) – accounting system user.

The initial evaluation of Table 4 clearly demonstrates that the users of the metering and accounting system would be the most affected by the outage, which is quite understandable, as the data in this system is used for billing or daily dispatch and many other tasks, therefore, its prolonged unavailability may lead to violation of ordinances, laws or possible penalties. The least vulnerable are the users of the portal through which the data is provided to customers, which are practically only control data for them, but their unavailability may lead to more work in terms of handling customer requests. Backups in the accounting system should preferably be hourly, as a lot of data is processed and entered every minute, not only on customers but also on contracts, invoices and orders for field staff, and any measurement data would have to be re-uploaded. Which would be very laborious for the users of the system. For a meter reading system, a weekly backup would be sufficient. If there was a complete loss of data in one week, then it would be

Table 4. BIA evaluation criteria by the user

User	Impact														
	15M	1H	6H	12H	1D	1W	1WW	1B	24B	VB	MB	ALLB	UD	ME	LE	IME
ASU	1	2	3	4	4	5	5	3	4	5	5	5	5	3	4	5
MSA	1	2	3	4	4	5	5	2	3	4	5	5	5	3	4	5
AC	1	1	3	4	4	5	5	1	1	2	3	2	5	2	3	5
PPM	1	1	2	2	2	3	4	1	1	3	4	4	5	2	3	5
FW	1	1	2	3	3	4	5	2	3	4	5	5	3	2	3	5

BIA evaluation scale: 1 – none; 2 – low; 3 – medium; 4 – high; 5 – critical.

possible to read the data from the memory of all meters in the event of a restore, but this process ultimately leads to increased costs for data transmission and provisioning and increased labour for system users and field workers at sites without a signal. For the application designed to send data to OTE, no data backup is necessary as it downloads all data from the meter reading system and is only used to send the data, the workload for the users of this application is not particularly increased. For users of the data provisioning portal application, in the event of a complete loss of data, a lengthy and laborious upload of data from the readout system and possible re-establishment of access to the customer application must be performed. In terms of disclosure, all users are equally affected except the field worker. For the field worker, the risk is lower because the worker always has the data of the customer sites only for a specific day and sends the measured data they read from the meter at the customer site immediately to the system. In contrast, other users have access to personal data and measurement data from the system and applications on a large number of customers. Therefore, the risk of disclosure is critical for all these users. Most large errors can occur in the readout and accounting systems, due to their size and the large amount of heterogeneous data they contain. Therefore, also if users of these systems create relatively small errors, they can do a lot of damage in these systems, whereas other applications are not so susceptible, so the users are not as much at risk. However, when it comes to deliberate errors, all users are the same, because it is always possible to make a deliberate error that can affect the functioning of part or all of the system.

1.8 CIA Evaluation of ČEZd Measured Data

CIA analysis is used to assess how important an information asset is to a company. In this analysis, the information assets associated with the measured data are considered. Each flow meter measures LP15 and BW but for some of them the importance of these information assets varies for this reason the distribution of Table 5 is made with respect to the importance of the information asset for each type of measurement. Another specificity is the measurement type B where DUF and LP60 are sent for OM at two different voltage levels.

   LP15 - as far as LP15 metering data is concerned, type A metering is the most risky because it has to be sent to OTE every day and billing data (DUF VO) is calculated from it, moreover type A metering has large consumption points. For type B metering at the

Table 5. Evaluation of information assets

Class Information asset	A	B Voltage level HF	B Voltage level LV	C (TDD)
LP 15	[B; B; A]	[C; B; A]	[C; B; A]	[D; B; B]
BW	[C; B; B]	[C; B; B]	[B; B; A]	[D; B; D]
LP60	[B; B; B]	[B; B; B]	[C; B; B]	[D; C; B]
DUF VO	[B; B; B]	[B; B; B]	–	–
DUF MO	–	–	[B; B; A]	[B; B; B]

HV voltage level the situation is similar, except that the metering data is sent once a month and they do not mind if communication goes down for a day. In the case of a meter type B at LV voltage level, the LP15 profile is not used for billing, it is only used for monthly billing of deviations and possible control, it is also important, but if it does not communicate for a day, it does not matter so much. For the TDD samples of meter type C, the data is not sent to OTE and is not used for billing, but is only provided to EGU Brno for calculations, if a meter of a TDD sample has frequent communication failures, it is always replaced.

BW - for meter registers the situation is reversed, where the data from the meter register on OM connected at the HV level are only control and are important for verification in AMS, but the data from them are not sent anywhere. At LV voltage level for type B metering, the registers are important for billing and the consumption taken from them is billed. For metering type C TDD, the consumption is billed from the registers that are physically read at the meter at the OM by a field worker.

LP60 - LP 60 data are calculated from LP15, thus they are evaluated in the same way as LP 15 to the respective measurement types and voltage levels. However, LP60 is rated lower in terms of consistency because LP60 can always be recalculated in case of error.

DUF VO - it is calculated from LP15 and contains minimum data compared to DUF MO, but it is important for billing of consumption at HV voltage level. So if we have LP15 available, it is not a problem to find out or calculate from it all the items listed in the DUF VO.

DUF MO - is created by copying invoice items from the accounting system. It lists all charges and payments for individual invoice items and the amount of electricity consumed for a specific period.

1.9 BIA Results for Selected Systems

BIA results (Table 6) have impacts on individual systems of the data communication model, the consideration of which is the basis for determining security mitigation measures for their elimination.

Reading system - in the area of legal obligations, a failure of the meter reading system can cause a violation of virtually all laws and decrees related to the transmission

Table 6. Risk assessment

System	Legal obligations	Control and operation	Loss of confidence	Financial burden	Essential services restrictions	MTPD	MIDP	MTDL
Reading system	High	High	Critical	Critical	High	16 H	6 H	24B
Accounting system	Critical	Critical	Critical	Critical	Critical	16 H	6 H	1B
OTE messaging system	Medium	High	Medium	Medium	High	16 H	6 H	1BM
Customer data portal	Medium	Medium	Medium	Low	Medium	1W	1WW	1BM
Base Transceiver Station operated (BTS)	Medium	Medium	Low	Low	Low	1W	1WW	1M

of electricity metering data to OTE. For this reason, the risk assessment of a breach of a legal obligation is rated as high, as in many cases it may lead to major litigation. However, this should not be liquidating for the distributor. In the area of management and operation, the extent of the failure of the meter reading system is significant. If metering data from more than 85,000 m cannot be obtained in any way in time, either for sending to OTE or for billing purposes, the impact on the distributor's operations is high.

Accounting system - The failure of the accounting system may cause a violation of decrees and laws that are related to the metering of electricity and the distributor's customers, namely Act No. 458/2000 § 11 [9], Decree No. 540/2005 Coll. From § 12 to § 20 [10] and Decree No. 408/2015 Coll. § 41 [11]. In particular, contracts and supplier changes, which would also be affected by this non-compliance, are not counted in the impact of compliance with the legal obligations. Given the extent and number of decrees that would be violated, the impact on the energy system is described as critical. In the area of management and operations, it can be noted that if there were a major failure of the accounting system for a prolonged period of time, this would not compromise the daily dispatch to OTE in any way. However, it will stop the billing of all electricity, not only from continuous metering. Therefore, the outage would impact hundreds of thousands of customers and many other customer-targeted operations (complaints, connections, installation, disconnections, etc.). If there is a prolonged system outage, the risk of loss of trust would be at a critical level, as virtually all requests from customers could not be resolved, and this could lead to media coverage.

OTE messaging system - in the area of legal obligations, the failure of the messaging application may cause a violation of decrees that are somehow related to the transmission of electricity metering data to OTE, namely Act No. 458/2000 § 11, Decree No. 408/2015 Coll. § 20, § 22. For this reason, the risk assessment of violation of a legal obligation is rated as medium, because in the event of the system being inoperable for a longer period of time, a possible fine from ERU could be imposed. This application has a high impact on the management and operation in the event of an outage. If the application were to be down for a longer period of time, there could be a problem with sending daily data to OTE, but also monthly data which is important for the billing of deviations and then possibly more staff would need to be involved to ensure that the data is sent by an alternative route. The risk of loss of confidence was assessed as medium, as in the event of an application failure, the limitation will only affect the daily market traders.

Customer data portal - this application is designed to provide measurement data to customers free of charge. If it were to fail, it could violate Decree No. 82/2011 Coll., § 8 in terms of legal requirements. In the area of management and operation, it is expected that in the event of an outage there will be an increased workload for the operator who accesses and uploads data from the meter reading system to the application, due to the increased number of data queries from customers. The impact on the operation of its non-functionality is approximately medium.

Base Transceiver Station operated (BTS) - in the event of an outage of one or more BTSs, the Decree (Decree No. 408/2015 Coll., § 20, § 22) may be violated in the area of compliance with the legal obligation to send monthly deviation settlement data. Should there be a failure at the end of the month, communication with BTS at the beginning of the month may fail, in which case communication must be restored as soon as possible. This could result in unavailability of data for billing and thus a violation of Decree No. 408/2015 Coll. § 41. For these reasons, the risk has been assessed as medium. In the area of management and operation, in the event of a single BTS outage, this could have low impacts on operations, as only connectivity could be impaired and the meter could be read somehow after a longer period of time.

2 Conclusion

For the CIA analysis, the information assets related to meter reading and the data underlying the meter reading were primarily considered. The CIA analysis suggests that the greatest emphasis should be placed on the source data for billing, particularly its consistency so that its accuracy cannot be questioned. The individual information assets here differ mainly in terms of how often they need to be available. The confidentiality is the same for all information assets, as they are always customer data and can be misused in some way. The most confidential invoice data is in DUF MO, where all item and payment information is also included as in the invoice. In contrast, confidentiality is least at risk in LP60 Type C Measurement Data (TDD), which does not provide enough detail to be misused for anything. With regard to information assets, there is no way to differentiate security according to the importance of the information asset, on the grounds that this would add cost and complexity to the system for the distributor to operate.

For the input metric of the BIA analysis, applications and systems were evaluated in terms of their impact on users. In this case, the largest impact on users was on the Reading System and the Accounting System; for these systems, it would be appropriate to focus on operational security. If one of them were to go down it would stop the activities of most users who consider them central to their work. The other applications tend to complement the functions of the individual systems and are in many cases not needed for their core activities. When evaluating the systems according to the individual guidelines, it is clear that the greatest impact on the company would be in the case of a non-functioning Accounting System. This is because of the large number of tasks involved in meeting legislative requirements, this system should not be down for more than a few hours. In the case of this system, an hourly backup would be appropriate.

Acknowledgement. This work and the contribution were supported by the project "Use of artificial intelligence to ensure cyber security in Smart Cities" - VJ02010016, granted by Ministry of Defence of the Czech Republic and also by the project of Specific Research Project, Faculty of Informatics and Management, University of Hradec Kralove, Czech Republic. We would like to thank Mr. R. Werner, a graduate of Faculty of management and informatics, University of Hradec Kralove, for the practical verification of the proposed solutions and close cooperation in the solution.

References

1. Bolla, R., Davoli, F., Bruschi, R., Christensen, K., Cucchietti, F., Singh, S.: The potential impact of green technologies in next-generation wireline networks: is there room for energy saving optimization? IEEE Commun. Mag. **49**(8), 80–86 (2011). https://doi.org/10.1109/MCOM.2011.5978419
2. Specht, J.M., Madlener, R.: Energy supplier 2.0: a conceptual business model for energy suppliers aggregating flexible distributed assets and policy issues raised. Energy Policy **135**(C) (2019). https://econpapers.repec.org/article/eeeenepol/v_3a135_3ay_3a2019_3ai_3ac_3as0301421519304896.htm. Accessed 09 Nov 2021
3. Barreto, A.B., Tavares Santos, R.A., Ubaldino De Souza, P.E., Abrunhosa, M., Dominice, A., De Souza, J.D.: Smart-grid assets inspections - enabling the smart cities infrastructure. In: 2018 International Conference on Computational Science and Computational Intelligence (CSCI), pp. 531–536 (2018). https://doi.org/10.1109/CSCI46756.2018.00108
4. Mu, Y., Wu, J., Jenkins, N., Jia, H., Wang, C.: A spatial–temporal model for grid impact analysis of plug-in electric vehicles. Appl. Energy **114**, 456–465 (2014). https://doi.org/10.1016/j.apenergy.2013.10.006
5. Business impact analysis for business continuity: Evidence from Romanian enterprises on critical functions - ProQuest. https://www.proquest.com/docview/2167937255?fromopenview=true&pq-origsite=gscholar&accountid=58905. Accessed 08 Nov 2021
6. Torabi, S.A., Rezaei Soufi, H., Sahebjamnia, N.: A new framework for business impact analysis in business continuity management (with a case study). Saf. Sci. **68**, 309–323 (2014). https://doi.org/10.1016/j.ssci.2014.04.017
7. Herbane, B., Elliott, D., Swartz, E.M.: Business continuity management: time for a strategic role? Long Range Plan. **37**(5), 435–457 (2004). https://doi.org/10.1016/j.lrp.2004.07.011
8. Cyber intrusion of wind farm SCADA system and its impact analysis | IEEE Conference Publication | IEEE Xplore. https://ieeexplore.ieee.org/abstract/document/5772593. Accessed 08 Nov 2021
9. A. C.-info@aion.cz, "458/2000 Sb. Energetický zákon", Zákony pro lidi. https://www.zakonyprolidi.cz/cs/2000-458. Accessed 07 Nov 2021
10. A. C.-info@aion.cz, "540/2005 Sb. Vyhláška o kvalitě dodávek elektřiny a souvisejících služeb v elektroenergetice", Zákony pro lidi. https://www.zakonyprolidi.cz/cs/2005-540. Accessed 07 Nov 2021

11. A. C.-info@aion.cz, "408/2015 Sb. Vyhláška o Pravidlech trhu s elektřinou", Zákony pro lidi. https://www.zakonyprolidi.cz/cs/2015-408/zneni-20210401. Accessed 07 Nov 2021
12. 82/2011 Sb. Vyhláška o měření elektřiny a o způsobu stanovení náhrady škody při neoprávněném odběru, neoprávněné. https://www.zakonyprolidi.cz/cs/2011-82. Accessed 09 Nov 2021

Towards Optimizing Malware Detection: An Approach Based on Generative Adversarial Networks and Transformers

Ayyub Alzahem[1] , Wadii Boulila[2,4]([✉]) , Maha Driss[3,4] , Anis Koubaa[2] , and Iman Almomani[3,5]

[1] Deanship of Information Technology, Taibah University,
Medina 42353, Saudi Arabia
[2] Robotics and Internet-of-Things Lab, CCIS, Prince Sultan University,
Riyadh 12435, Saudi Arabia
wboulila@psu.edu.sa
[3] Security Engineering Lab, CCIS, Prince Sultan University,
Riyadh 12435, Saudi Arabia
[4] RIADI Laboratory, University of Manouba, Manouba 2010, Tunisia
[5] CS Department, King Abdullah II School of Information Technology,
The University of Jordan, Amman 11942, Jordan

Abstract. Nowadays, cybercriminals are carrying out many forms of cyberattacks. Malware attacks, in particular, have emerged as one of the most challenging concerns in the cybersecurity area, as well as a key weapon used by cybercriminals. Malware is a term used to describe harmful software. Malware can be used to modify or destroy data on target computers, steal private information, control systems to attack other devices, host and disseminate illicit material, and disrupt vital infrastructures. As a result, many tools and approaches for detecting and mitigating malware attacks have been developed. Despite the improvement and rapid expansion of malware defense techniques, cybercriminals are able to develop more sophisticated and advanced malware that can defeat state-of-the-art security and anti-malware solutions. This paper proposes a novel approach based on generative adversarial networks and transformers to improve malware detection performance. By using generative adversarial transformers, the proposed approach aims to increase the malware data size and solve the data imbalance distribution issue. Promising experimental results showed an improved accuracy of malware detection of 3% using several pre-trained models when solving the problem of unbalanced data.

Keywords: Malware analysis · Generative adversarial networks · Transformers · Data augmentation · Deep learning

1 Introduction

Malware is a term commonly used to describe a variety of undesirable, harmful software applications with malicious and destructive intentions [6,13,23].

This work is supported by Prince Sultan University in Saudi Arabia.

Malware attacks aim to compromise an information system's or computer device's security policies involving data integrity, confidentiality, and availability when they are running [9,17]. Malware is produced or utilized by cybercriminals who want to exhibit their skills by wreaking havoc and stealing information for financial gain. Malware can be used to modify or destroy data on target computers, steal private information, hijack systems to attack other devices, transmit spam, host and disseminate illicit material, bring servers down, infiltrate networks, and disrupt vital infrastructures [18,22,25,26]. Malware is becoming increasingly sophisticated and diverse in recent years. For example, the authors in [2,3] managed to hide malware (specifically ransomware) using cryptography and steganography in high-resolution video streams. As a result, they successfully bypassed 70 famous antivirus engines without being detected. Even though, such antivirus systems are equipped with advanced malware detection solutions. Consequently, many tools and approaches for detecting and mitigating malware attacks have been developed. However, a number of significant concerns (e.g., newer versions of malware families that behave completely differently from their predecessors) still have to be remedied appropriately. As a result, typical detection technologies have significant limitations in detecting these recent malware samples. This is confirmed by the work of Baig et al. [7], which provides an overview of malware developers' tactics to avoid typical static detection methods. As proven in [8,19], deep learning (DL) approaches are more efficient than static code analysis techniques. The detection of malware using DL follows a particular learning methodology. The data must first be classified by features, which may be performed using custom feature selection methods or predefined algorithms; after that, this data is fed into the DL algorithm with the selected optimal feature set. Before proceeding to the testing phase, this algorithm will be trained. To accomplish malware detection, a training set of both goodware and malware data samples will be required so that the algorithm can learn to differentiate between the two classes. One of the most frustrating aspects of real-world malware data is that it might be unbalanced. This entails creating detection models with unequal class distributions. Furthermore, large amounts of data are required in certain circumstances to effectively train detection/classification models, which is not the case with commonly used intrusion detection applications [1,20]. These two issues can significantly impact the learning process and result in a poor detection rate. To deal with these challenges, we propose to apply the Generative Adversarial Network (GAN) and the Transformer classifier to perform data augmentation that leads us to efficient training for vision-based malware detection using deep convolutional neural networks. Recently, GANs have received much traction in the computer vision field, and several variants have been proposed for producing high-fidelity natural images [27]. Besides, Transformer networks' recent advances in natural language processing have piqued the computer vision community's interest in adapting these models to different multimodal vision, and learning tasks, including image generation [14]. The main contributions of the proposed study are summarized in the following points:

- To the best of the authors' knowledge, the proposed study constitutes the first work that proposes to combine GANs and transformers classifiers to generate plausible image outputs for performance enhancement of malware detection. The primary goal of combining these two classifiers is to enhance the training of commonly used CNN models by offering large amounts of data. The proposed DL model is named GANformer. The generated samples demonstrate GANformer's capabilities to recognize spatial relationships between pixels and high-level features.
- The use of GANs and iterative transformers to increase the malware data size and solve the data imbalance problem leads to better performances of the classification models. Combining GANs and transformers enhances the generation process's capacity and captures the dependencies between patterns in the images leading to closer generative modeling. The main advantage of using this technique is that no information from the original malware dataset is lost, as all observations from the different classes are kept.
- Several experiments have been conducted to evaluate the performances of the proposed approach using seven pre-trained CNN models: MobileNetV2, ResNet50, ResNet50V2, ResNet152V2 DenseNet121, DenseNet201, and EfficientNetV2L. Performance metric values show an increase in malware detection accuracy for the previous TL techniques when applying GANformer to the data.

This paper is organized as follows. Section 2 discusses recent relevant works about using DL for malware detection. The proposed approach is described in depth in Sect. 3. Section 4 summarizes and analyzes the results of the experiments. Finally, in Sect. 5, our conclusions are drawn and recommendations for future research directions are highlighted.

2   Related Works

For various contexts, several analytical techniques have been utilized for malware detection. Recently, DL and vision-based methods have been employed to conduct extensive research on malware detection [19,31]. This section provides a comprehensive overview of recent and relevant malware detection approaches that make use of these two techniques.

In [28], Vinayakumar et al. compared and contrasted traditional machine learning and DL architectures for malware detection and classification by using a variety of public and private datasets. They proposed a new framework named ScaleMalNet for detecting, classifying, and categorizing zero-day malware. This framework used DL techniques to analyze malware gathered from end-user hosts in a two-step approach. Malware categorization was done in the first step using a static and dynamic analysis combination. The malware was classified into corresponding malware categories in the second step, which involved the application of image processing techniques.

DL-Droid, an automated dynamic analysis system for Android malware detection, was proposed in [4]. DL-Droid integrated DL with dynamic analysis and stateful input generation techniques. This research aimed to improve the detection of zero-day Android malware. The performance of the proposed DL-based system is compared to that of prominent machine learning classifiers in a series of tests utilizing real devices.

The prospect of identifying cryptomining malware using AI-based static and dynamic analysis methods of Portable Executable (PE) samples was examined in [16]. On sequences of opcodes and system call events, Darabian et al. employ DL models such as Long Short-Term Memory (LSTM), Attention-based LSTM (ATTLSTM), and Convolutional Neural Networks (CNN).

The study presented in [12] focused on metamorphic malware. The primary purpose of this study is to provide a classification approach for malware types that takes into account malware behavior. One of the contributions provided in this study was the proposal of a new dataset including API calls performed on the Windows operating system, which simulated malicious software behavior. Adware, Backdoor, Downloader, Dropper, spyware, Trojan, Virus, and Worm were among the malware types contained in the proposed dataset. The LSTM (Long Short-Term Memory) classifier was utilized in this study.

In [15], the authors propose a malware detection strategy based on ensemble classification. A stacked ensemble of dense (fully connected) and CNN networks performed the first-stage classification, while a meta-learner carried out the final-stage classification. In this paper, 14 classifiers were examined and compared. The findings of this study on the Classification of Malware with PE Headers (ClaMP) dataset demonstrated that an ensemble of five dense and CNN neural networks and the ExtraTrees classifier as a meta-learner provide the highest results in terms of performance indicators.

By correlating the distribution of known and unknown malware, an Unsupervised Domain Adaptation (UDA)-based malware detection approach was presented in [29]. In the first stage, symmetric adversarial learning was used to learn common feature representations, which reduced the distribution divergence between the source and target domains. In the second stage, to get more semantic information from unlabeled target domain data, the proposed approach aligned the class centers of labeled source and pseudo-labeled target domain data to decrease class-level distribution divergence. Finally, a residual network with a self-attention mechanism was employed to extract more accurate feature information.

In [30], a DL-based malware detection methodology was proposed. This methodology combined a greyscale image representation of malware with an autoencoder network. It examined the effectiveness of the greyscale image representation of malware based on the autoencoder's reconstruction error. The autoencoder's dimensionality reduction features were utilized to realize malware classification from benign software.

A vision-based approach for IoT-malware detection and multi-classification is suggested in [9]. This approach benefited from the advantages of deep transfer learning and integrates the fine-tuning technique as well as other ensembling strategies to improve detection and classification performance without having to create new training models. It used a random forest voting technique to combine three CNNs: ResNet18, MobileNetV2, and DenseNet161.

In the studies stated above, several enhancements were performed to improve the detection of malware attacks. Traditional DL and vision-based malware detection systems, on the other hand, still face various intrinsic limitations. In the following, we will discuss the main points about the use of GANs.

- Data labeling is a time-consuming and expensive process. Most existing DL algorithms require proper and large data labeling to generate accurate decisions. Among the main DL strengths is its ability to handle more complex data and relationships. However, this also means that DL algorithms will be more complex. GANs can play an important role in generating synthetic data that can help improve DL performances.
- Dataset balancing is often encountered when solving real-world classification tasks. In this case, the main problem is that ML models may focus on learning the characteristics of specific classes and neglect the other classes. The main advantage of using GANs for data balancing is that no information from the original dataset is lost, as all observations from the different classes are kept.
- GANs are unsupervised, so no labeled data is required to train them. In addition, GANs are currently the sharpest image generators. This is made possible via adversarial training. Mean Squared Error-generated fuzzy images have no chance against GANs. On the other hand, using a vision transformer will help capture relationships between patterns in images thanks to the attention mechanism. Combining GANs and transformers will help tackle many image-vision challenges.

3   Proposed Approach

In this study, we propose to improve the detection and analysis of malware. The main components of the proposed approach, as depicted in Fig. 1 are:

- Data generation using GANformer: the main objective of this module is to increase the size of the malware data to create a balanced dataset. This will improve the performance of the pre-trained models in detecting malware.
- Pre-trained CNNs: transfer Learning (TL) is a machine learning method that aims to reuse prior knowledge as a starting point for a model on a new task. In general, TL techniques are trained on a large dataset to serve as a generic model in image classification. Reusing the network layers' weights of pre-trained models contributes in the enhancement of the learning process instead of developing a classification model from scratch, which requires considerable time, big resources, and large data. The effectiveness of this method has been proven in several case studies [9–11]

3.1   Generative Adversarial Transformers

The Generative Adversarial Transformer (GANformer) was proposed by [5,21] as a type of GAN that consists of a generator network (G) that maps a sample

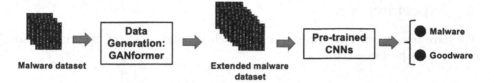

Fig. 1. Architecture of the proposed approach.

from the latent space to the output space and a discriminator network (D) that attempts to distinguish between real and fake samples. The two networks G and D are composed of many layers of convolution using a Bipartite Transformer. G translates a partitioned latent into an image, and D seeks to differentiate between real and fake images.

A bipartite attention operation transfers information from the latent to the image grid, followed by convolution and upsampling in the GANformer layer. These are stacked several times, beginning with a 4×4 grid and progressing to a final high-resolution image.

GANformer includes bipartite-transformer layers in the generator, which calculate attention between the k latents and the image features. Equation 1 depicts the attention, whereas Eq. 2 refers to modulation between the latents and the image. $\mathcal{I}$ is the image, $\mathcal{S}$ an intermediate space created by the feed-forward network, $q(),k(),v()$ are the query, key, and value functions and $\gamma(),\beta()$ calculate multiplicative and additive styles of $Attention(\mathcal{I},\mathcal{S})$.

$$Attention(\mathcal{I},\mathcal{S}) = softmax(\frac{q(\mathcal{I})k(\mathcal{S})^{\mathcal{T}}}{\sqrt{d}})v(\mathcal{S}) \qquad (1)$$

$$u(\mathcal{I},\mathcal{S}) = \gamma(\mathcal{I},\mathcal{S}) \odot LayerNorm(\mathcal{I}) + \beta(\mathcal{I},\mathcal{S}) \qquad (2)$$

Figure 2 describes the architecture of the GANformer. Information is propagated from latents to images using the bipartite attention operation (simplex or duplex), convolution, and upsampling. The main advantage of this architecture is the ability of pixels in images to interact with distant pixels in a moderated manner. The information is propagated in two directions (top-down/bottom-up), from the local pixel to the high-level representation.

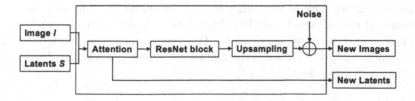

Fig. 2. Architecture of the generative adversarial transformers.

4   Experiments

We have investigated the proposed approach through a set of experiments to evaluate its performance.

4.1   Dataset Description

The dataset used in this study consists of a raw PE byte stream that has been rescaled to a 32 × 32 greyscale image using the Nearest Neighbor Interpolation algorithm. Images have two classes: malware (collected from virusshare.com) and goodware (collected from portableapps.com) [24]. Figure 3 depicts a sample of the dataset considered in this study.

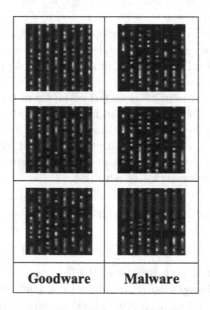

Fig. 3. Sample of the dataset.

The dataset contains 51892 images (49376 malware and 2516 goodware) as shown in Table 1. The main observation for the considered dataset is that it is unbalanced; we have a very high number of malware samples compared to goodware. However, most ML/DL algorithms are designed on problems that assume an equal distribution of classes. This means that these models may focus on learning the characteristics of the malware class only, neglecting the examples from the goodware class.

4.2   Hardware Specifications

In this study, all experiments were conducted on Google Colab (an online browser-based platform) with a Pro+ subscription. It does not support dis-

Table 1. Dataset description.

Label	Number of images
Malware	49376
Goodware	2516
Total	51892

tributed training on multiple GPUs. We used just one GPU at a time in each experiment, and that was a bit challenging due GANformer training (Table 2).

Table 2. Hardware specifications.

Feature	Value
GPUs	K80, P100, and T4
CPUs	2 x vCPU

4.3   Results

The first step is to apply the GANformer module to generate good-quality data for the goodware class. This will help resolve the unbalanced-class problem. We start by dividing images belonging to the goodware class into multiple folders based on the image size. The GANformer module is trained using the specifications depicted in Table 3; where total kimg denotes the training length in thousands of images. We achieved a value of 28.5 for Frechet Inception Distance (FID) over 50k samples as our best results on the considered data after three days of training. Lower FID values mean better-generated image quality. Equation 3 depicts how FID is calculated.

$$FID(\mathcal{I}, \mathcal{I}') = \parallel \mu_{\mathcal{I}} - \mu_{\mathcal{I}'} \parallel^2 + Tr\left(\sum_{\mathcal{I}} + \sum_{\mathcal{I}'} - 2 * \sqrt{\left(\sum_{\mathcal{I}} * \sum_{\mathcal{I}'}\right)}\right) \quad (3)$$

where $\mathcal{I}$ and $\mathcal{I}'$ are the real and generated images, Tr sums up all the diagonal elements of the square matrix. $\mu_{\mathcal{I}}$, $\mu_{\mathcal{I}'}$, $\sum_{\mathcal{I}}$ and $\sum_{\mathcal{I}'}$ denotes the feature-wise mean and covariance matrix of the real and generated images. $\parallel \mu_{\mathcal{I}} - \mu_{\mathcal{I}'} \parallel^2$ denotes the sum squared difference between the two mean vectors.

Table 4 depicts that 46860 new images for the class goodware were generated using GANformer to make each class has the same number of images.

To evaluate the efficiency of the GANformer in generating images, the MobileNetV2 was applied to the two datasets (Tables 1 and 4) with a batch size of 64, learning rate of 0.0001, 100 epochs, (32, 32, 3) input shape, and binary cross-entropy loss function. The primary goal of the proposed approach

Table 3. Training specifications of GANformer.

Number of threads	4
Global batch size	32
Batch size per GPU	4
Total kimg	4000
Gamma	10
Generator learning rate	0.002
Discriminator learning rate	0.002

Table 4. Dataset description after applying GANformer.

Label	Number of images
malware	49376
goodware	49376
Total	98752

is to improve malware detection by resolving the problem of unbalanced data. As it is demonstrated in Table 5, an improvement of 3% in test accuracy is recorded after applying the GANformer to increase the size of the data.

Table 5. Test accuracy and loss results before and after applying GANformer.

Experiment	Test accuracy	Test loss
Before GANformer	0.95	0.49
After GANformer	0.98	0.10

Figure 4 describes the confusion matrix results before and after applying GANformer. As we can note, after applying the GANformer, the MobileNetV2 was able to identify the class goodware better. After balancing the number of images in each class, the discovered patterns will divide fairly between the two classes, improving accuracy (Figs. 5 and 6).

4.4   Evaluation

In order to evaluate the performances of the proposed approach, several TL techniques, namely: ResNet50, ResNet50V2, ResNet152V2, DenseNet121, DenseNet201, and EfficientNetV2L have been applied to the two datasets (before and after applying the proposed approach). All models are evaluated under the same conditions of the training scheme, model size, and optimization details. Table 6 depicts the validation accuracy obtained while training the six CNNs models. The evaluation is based on the accuracy defined in Eq. 4 and the loss.

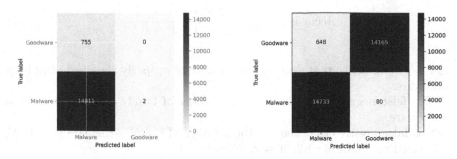

(a) Before applying GANformer   (b) After applying GANformer

Fig. 4. Confusion matrix results before and after applying GANformer.

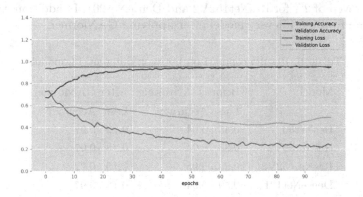

Fig. 5. Accuracy and loss visualization before applying GANformer.

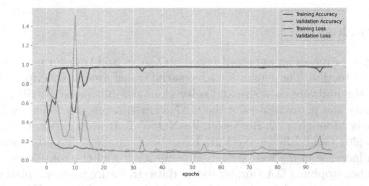

Fig. 6. Accuracy and loss visualization after applying GANformer.

$$Accuracy = \frac{TP + TN}{TP + TN + FP + FN} \tag{4}$$

where

- TP is true positive that denotes the number of properly classified samples as malware.
- FN is false negative that denotes the number of falsely detected samples as goodware.
- FP is false positive that denotes the number of samples that are incorrectly classified as malware while it is goodware.
- TN is true negative that denotes the number of properly classified samples as goodware.

We note that applying the GANformer helps improve the validation accuracy for all models. For example, the validation accuracy for ResNet50, ResNet50V2, DenseNet121, and EfficientNetV2L has been improved of 3%; where it is has been improved of 2% for ResNet152V2 and DenseNet201. In addition, the losses have been improved in every model after applying GANformer.

Table 6. Results comparison between different TL models.

Model	Before GANformer		After GANformer	
	Loss	Accuracy	Loss	Accuracy
ResNet50	0.43	0.94	0.22	0.97
ResNet50V2	0.33	0.94	0.18	0.97
ResNet152V2	0.33	0.95	0.19	0.97
DenseNet121	0.39	0.94	0.18	0.97
DenseNet201	0.37	0.95	0.20	0.97
EfficientNetV2L	0.24	0.94	0.21	0.97

5   Conclusion

This paper proposes an approach based on GANs and transformers to improve malware detection. The generative adversarial transformers (GANformer) aim to increase the malware data size and solve the data imbalance distribution issue. To evaluate the performances of the GANformer, seven pre-trained CNN models, namely MobileNetV2, ResNet50, ResNet50V2, ResNet152V2, DenseNet121, DenseNet201, and EfficientNetV2L have been applied. Experimental results show an increase in malware detection accuracy for all the considered TL techniques when applying GANformer to the data. In future work, we plan to evaluate the performance of the proposed approach on other datasets. We also plan to propose a GAN-based approach to improve the image quality in the considered dataset, which can help improving the accuracy of malware detection.

References

1. A Ghaleb, F., et al.: Misbehavior-aware on-demand collaborative intrusion detection system using distributed ensemble learning for vanet. Electronics **9**(9), 1411 (2020)
2. Almomani, I., AlKhayer, A., El-Shafai, W.: Novel ransomware hiding model using HEVC steganography approach. CMC-Comput. Mater. Continua **70**(1), 1209–1228 (2021)
3. Almomani, I., Alkhayer, A., El-Shafai, W.: A crypto-steganography approach for hiding ransomware within hevc streams in android iot devices. Sensors **22**(6), 2281 (2022)
4. Alzaylaee, M.K., Yerima, S.Y., Sezer, S.: Dl-droid: deep learning based android malware detection using real devices. Comput. Secur. **89**, 101663 (2020)
5. Arad Hudson, D., Zitnick, L.: Compositional transformers for scene generation. Advances in Neural Information Processing Systems 34 (2021)
6. Aslan, Ö.A., Samet, R.: A comprehensive review on malware detection approaches. IEEE Access **8**, 6249–6271 (2020)
7. Baig, M., Zavarsky, P., Ruhl, R., Lindskog, D.: The study of evasion of packed PE from static detection. In: World Congress on Internet Security (WorldCIS-2012), pp. 99–104. IEEE (2012)
8. Bello, I., et al.: Detecting ransomware attacks using intelligent algorithms: recent development and next direction from deep learning and big data perspectives. J. Ambient. Intell. Humaniz. Comput. **12**(9), 8699–8717 (2021)
9. Ben Atitallah, S., Driss, M., Almomani, I.: A novel detection and multi-classification approach for IoT-malware using random forest voting of fine-tuning convolutional neural networks. Sensors **22**(11), 4302 (2022)
10. Ben Atitallah, S., Driss, M., Boulila, W., Ben Ghezala, H.: Randomly initialized convolutional neural network for the recognition of covid-19 using x-ray images. Int. J. Imaging Syst. Technol. **32**(1), 55–73 (2022)
11. Ben Atitallah, S., Driss, M., Boulila, W., Koubaa, A., Ben Ghezala, H.: Fusion of convolutional neural networks based on dempster-shafer theory for automatic pneumonia detection from chest x-ray images. Int. J. Imaging Syst. Technol. **32**(2), 658–672 (2022)
12. Catak, F.O., Yazı, A.F., Elezaj, O., Ahmed, J.: Deep learning based sequential model for malware analysis using windows exe API calls. PeerJ Comput. Sci. **6**, e285 (2020)
13. Chakkaravarthy, S.S., Sangeetha, D., Vaidehi, V.: A survey on malware analysis and mitigation techniques. Comput. Sci. Rev. **32**, 1–23 (2019)
14. Chen, H., et al.: Pre-trained image processing transformer. In: Proceedings of the IEEE/CVF Conference on Computer Vision and Pattern Recognition, pp. 12299–12310 (2021)
15. Damaševičius, R., Venčkauskas, A., Toldinas, J., Grigaliūnas, Š: Ensemble-based classification using neural networks and machine learning models for windows PE malware detection. Electronics **10**(4), 485 (2021)
16. Darabian, H., et al.: Detecting cryptomining malware: a deep learning approach for static and dynamic analysis. J. Grid Comput. **18**(2), 293–303 (2020)
17. Driss, M., Hasan, D., Boulila, W., Ahmad, J.: Microservices in IoT security: current solutions, research challenges, and future directions. Procedia Comput. Sci. **192**, 2385–2395 (2021)

18. Dutta, N., Jadav, N., Tanwar, S., Sarma, H.K.D., Pricop, E.: Introduction to malware analysis. In: Cyber Security: Issues and Current Trends. SCI, vol. 995, pp. 129–141. Springer, Singapore (2022). https://doi.org/10.1007/978-981-16-6597-4_7

19. Fernando, D.W., Komninos, N., Chen, T.: A study on the evolution of ransomware detection using machine learning and deep learning techniques. IoT 1(2), 551–604 (2020)

20. Ghaleb, F.A., Maarof, M.A., Zainal, A., Al-rimy, B.A.S., Alsaeedi, A., Boulila, W.: Ensemble-based hybrid context-aware misbehavior detection model for vehicular ad hoc network. Remote Sens. 11(23), 2852 (2019)

21. Hudson, D.A., Zitnick, L.: Generative adversarial transformers. In: International Conference on Machine Learning, pp. 4487–4499. PMLR (2021)

22. Melhim, L.K.B., Jemmali, M., Alharbi, M.: Network monitoring enhancement based on mathematical modeling. In: 2019 2nd International Conference on Computer Applications & Information Security (ICCAIS), pp. 1–4. IEEE (2019)

23. Melhim, L.K.B., Jemmali, M., AsSadhan, B., Alquhayz, H.: Network traffic reduction and representation. Int. J. Sensor Networks 33(4), 239–249 (2020)

24. Oliveira, A.: Malware analysis datasets: Raw pe as image. IEEE dataport (2019)

25. Roseline, S.A., Geetha, S.: A comprehensive survey of tools and techniques mitigating computer and mobile malware attacks. Comput. Electr. Eng. 92, 107143 (2021)

26. Sarhan, A., Jemmali, M., Ben Hmida, A.: Two routers network architecture and scheduling algorithms under packet category classification constraint. In: The 5th International Conference on Future Networks & Distributed Systems, pp. 119–127 (2021)

27. Shamsolmoali, P., et al.: Image synthesis with adversarial networks: a comprehensive survey and case studies. Inf. Fusion 72, 126–146 (2021)

28. Vinayakumar, R., Alazab, M., Soman, K., Poornachandran, P., Venkatraman, S.: Robust intelligent malware detection using deep learning. IEEE Access 7, 46717–46738 (2019)

29. Wang, F., Chai, G., Li, Q., Wang, C.: An efficient deep unsupervised domain adaptation for unknown malware detection. Symmetry 14(2), 296 (2022)

30. Xing, X., Jin, X., Elahi, H., Jiang, H., Wang, G.: A malware detection approach using autoencoder in deep learning. IEEE Access (2022)

31. Zhao, J., Masood, R., Seneviratne, S.: A review of computer vision methods in network security. IEEE Commun. Surv. Tutorials (2021)

An XGBoost-Based Approach for an Efficient RPL Routing Attack Detection

Faicel Yaakoubi[1] , Aymen Yahyaoui[1,2] , Wadii Boulila[3,4]($\boxtimes$) ,
and Rabah Attia[1]

[1] SERCOM Lab, Polytechnic School of Tunisia, University of Carthage,
Carthage, Tunisia
[2] Military Academy of Fondouk Jedid, Nabeul, Tunisia
[3] RIOTU Lab, Prince Sultan University, Riyadh, Saudi Arabia
[4] RIADI Laboratory, National School of Computer Sciences, University of Manouba,
Manouba, Tunisia
wboulila@psu.edu.sa

Abstract. Routing Protocol for Low Power and Lossy Networks (RPL) is characterized by a reliable routing functionality compared with traditional protocols in IoT domains. However, it has basic security functionalities; therefore, many hackers exploit this characteristic to make various attacks. Extending RPL security presents a challenge, mainly due to the constrained devices and connectivity to unsecured Internet. In this paper, several routing attacks in RPL such as hello flood, decreased rank, and version number modification have been analyzed in different scenarios. In addition, an anomaly-based intrusion detection system using the XGBoost algorithm has been proposed. Several simulations have been conducted to generate normal and attack data. Results demonstrate a high detection accuracy of the XGBoost for the three considered types of attacks compared to Naive Bayes, Stochastic Gradient Descent, Multilayer Perceptron, and Support Vector Machines.

Keywords: Intrusion detection · IoT · RPL · Routing attacks · Machine learning · XGBoost

1 Introduction

The Internet Of Things represents the new generation of the internet [6,13]. It often relies on popular technologies such as Wireless Sensor Networks (WSN) to collect and forward data from zones of interest. Actually, IoT is widely used in several domains such as e-health, smart cities, smart agriculture, and smart environment [1,2,7,8]. We focus in this work, especially on using IoT for border control to detect illegal physical intrusions and terrorist attack risks. In

This work is supported by Prince Sultan University in Saudi Arabia.

N. T. Nguyen et al. (Eds.): ICCCI 2022, LNAI 13501, pp. 611–623, 2022.
https://doi.org/10.1007/978-3-031-16014-1_48

these kinds of environments, we usually need to use contained devices with optimal energy consumption in order to avoid sending troops to exchange batteries. Therefore, persevering nodes energy is a high priority in order to prevent the risk of military troops being detected and save their lives.

The use of IoT devices complies correctly with energy, processing, and memory [27] constraints. Therefore, using traditional protocols may not be suitable [14] in constrained environments. The ROLL group of IETF designed the new protocol called RPL for routing in WSN and IoT in general. This protocol is Distance-Vector (DV) based and designed to work on top of different link-layer mechanisms such as MAC Layers and IEEE 802.15.4 PHY.

RPL was designed considering two issues. The first one is prospective low data rate, and the second is high error rate communication. Its design contains three basic modes of security: unsecured mode, pre-installed mode, and authenticated mode. These modes are generally limited and do not have sufficient mechanisms to mitigate all types of attacks.

In this work, an intrusion detection system is designed based on machine learning techniques to detect three types of well-known RPL attacks. Its contribution is mainly related to the dataset of benign and attack collection and preparation as well as the chosen ML algorithm (XGBoost) accuracy in detecting attacks compared to other related works.

The main contributions of the proposed study are:

1. Several simulations were performed for IoT-network attacks with different scenarios containing up to 1000 nodes using Contiki cooja simulator [19]. This will generate a large dataset that constitutes a perfect scenario for real-world applications. Most existing related works are based on a small number of notes up to 50 nodes [22]. The generated dataset contains benign and malicious nodes.
2. Pertinent features are extracted and normalized using marginal values negative effects minimization.
3. The main challenge of the implementation of our algorithm is detecting malicious nodes. For this purpose, the XGBoost algorithm was utilized to detect malicious nodes and identify the type of attack. Pertinent features are extracted and fed to the algorithm for prediction. The results exhibit a high prediction accuracy (up to 98%).

In the following, we describe the paper's organization. Section 2 presents an overview and classification of routing attacks on RPL and mechanisms for intrusion detection. Section 3 presents related works. Section 4 depicts the proposed system for detecting hello flood, decreased rank, and version number attacks. It also provides details on data collection and feature extraction, normalization, and selection. Section 5 is dedicated to simulation, experimentation, and evaluation. Finally, in Sect. 6, a conclusion is provided with perspectives for future works.

2   Background

In this section, we present the concepts of RPL, routing attacks, and intrusion detection.

2.1   RPL Routing Protocol

RPL stands for Routing Protocol for Low-Power and Lossy Networks, a proactive routing protocol (LLNs). It supports multi-point-to-point traffic from LLN devices to a central control point and point-to-multi-point traffic from the main control point to LLN devices [24,25]. RPL incorporates several ideas that make it a versatile protocol and the industry standard for low-power, lossy networks:

– DODAG (Destination Oriented Directed Acyclic Graph) is a topology that optimizes traffic pathways between the sink and other nodes (collect and distribute). Each node in the network has a rating assigned to it. As the node moves away from the sink, this rank rises. The nodes use the lowest range as route selection criteria when resending packets.
– DIS (DODAG Informational Solicitation): used to ask RPL nodes for a DODAG Information Object.
– DIO (DODAG Information Object) item: used to build and maintain the DODAG, as well as to update the information of the nodes on the network topology regularly.
– DAO (Destination Advertisement Object): used by nodes to convey destination information upstream via the DODAG to distribute their parents' information.

2.2   RPL Routing Attacks

In [17], IoT routing attacks are classified into three categories:

– Attacks on network resources: to exhaust the network resources (energy, memory, and power).
– Attacks on network topology: to disrupt the RPL network topology.
– Attacks on network traffic: to attack the network traffic.

According to [23], RPL routing attacks can be classified into two categories:

– Attacks which are inherited from the use of WSNs and internet based networks like black-hole, selective forwarding, sinkhole, wormhole, cloneID, sybil and hello flood attacks.
– Attacks specific to RPL protocol like Rank attacks, Version attacks, local Repair attacks, DIS attacks, Neighbor attacks and DODAG Inconsistency attacks.

3   Related Work

We present related works for IoT intrusion detection in terms of placement strategies and the knowledge-driven approach.

– **Placement strategies**: The physical, network, and application domains can be used in different placement strategies. The physical domain concerns the sensors for collecting data and actuators for providing the response. The transmission phase concerns the network domain. It is considered the bridge between the physical and application domains. The users manage the objects by application domain. There are three strategies for IDS placement: distributed, centralized, and hybrid. The comparison of IDS placement strategies is presented in Table 1.

Table 1. Attack detection placement strategies

Intrusion detection system	Works	Details/Limitations
Distributed IDS	Cervantes et al. [3] proposed an intrusion detection system for sink hole attacks	It consumes resources. The impact of proposed solutions for low power devices is not studied
Centralized IDS	Lee et al. [15] proposed a solution of Dos attack. It is based on nodes energy consumption analysis	Only one parameter for anomaly detection is used
	Wallgren et al. [26] proposed a heartbeat protocol for sinkhole attack detection	Detection accuracy is relatively low, and there are overhead in 6BR
	Kasinathan et al. [9] proposed a framework for flood attack detection. The framework includes a monitoring system and a detection engine	
Hybrid IDS	Bhosale et al. [5] proposed Real Time IDS for the detection of wormhole attack	These work can be extended to other attacks such sybil, blackhole attack, selective forwarding attack and not be detailed
	Midi et al. [18] proposed knowledge driven intrusion detection system for detecting attacks in real time scenarios of IoT	
	Pongle et al. [12] proposed real time IDS. It is used for detecting wormhole attacker who performs the attacks	The proposed method yields 94% of detection rate

– **Knowledge Driven Approach**. It is used for the detection of malicious traffic. The proposed system provides security as a service. There are two types in this category: machine learning and deep learning [11]. Different works in this domain are depicted in Table 2. In these works, we can note that several techniques have been used. However, XGboost has not received much interest as a technique for detecting malicious traffic.

4   Proposed Approach

The proposed system is described in Fig. 1. It has three main steps: data generation, data preprocessing, and routing attack detection.

Table 2. Table of knowledge driven approaches

Knowledge driven approach	Works	Limitations
Deep learning	Geethapriya et al. [16] proposed deep learning-based IDS for IoT networks. It is used for the detection of malicious traffic	Requires large processing power
Machine learning	Verma et al. [21] proposed Machine Learning Based NIDS on RPL	Time consuming and needs larger dataset to train
	Kfoury et al. [10] proposed a Self-Organizing Map (SOM) neural network for clustering routing attacks	Requires intensive computations

4.1   Data Generation

For data generation, the Contiki's cooja environment with different simulation scenarios is used: 100 nodes, 300 nodes, and 1000 nodes, as shown in Fig. 2. Malicious nodes account for 20% of the total number of nodes. We modified the simulator source code to simulate the attacks. The dataset used for intrusion detection training, validation, and test is built from these files, which are stored in pcap format.

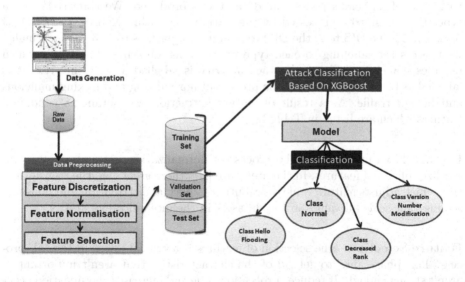

Fig. 1. The design of proposed system.

For each situation, multiple simulations were run. Table 3 shows simulation attributes.

Table 3. Simulation attributes

Attributes	Values
Type de fonction objective	OF0, ETX
Send interval	10 s
RX ratio	100%
TX ratio	100%
Interference range	100 m
Temps de simulation	3 h
Number of node's sink	1
Number of node's sender	100, 300, 1000
Number of malicious nodes	10, 30, 100
Node's type	Zolertia Z1
Wireless channel model	(UDGM)
Network layer	μIPv6 + 6LowPAN
MAC layer	ContikiMAC
PHY+ Radio layer	IEEE 802.15.4 CC2420

4.2 Data Preprocessing

After generating various attack scenarios at a wide-scale number of IoT nodes with 20% of malicious nodes, the dataset was produced. We convert the data types that cannot be processed by the learning algorithm XGBoost. The DAO packet to 1, The DIS to 2, the DIO to 3, and data packets to 5, 6, and 7. Finally, we process the labelling to each type of traffic as following: The traffic which includes malicious nodes and attack activity is labelled as 1. Otherwise, it is labelled as 0. Finally, we apply the process of normalizing and mixing malicious and benign traffic. As a result of feature extraction, we obtain 18 candidate features which are listed in Table 4.

Feature Normalization: The process of normalization is necessary to standardize collecting features. In the literature [20], there are a quantile transformation which adjusts feature value distribution to normal distribution and min-max scaling that scale all values in the datasets in the interval range [0–1].

Feature Selection: The selection of features is a crucial phase in the ML process. This phase aims to get rid of the characteristics that aren't important or aren't strong enough. It reduces processing time and increases classification accuracy. The filter, wrapper, and embedding methods are the three most frequent selection methods. CFS is the algorithm that is employed (Correlation-based Feature Selection). It uses the heuristic search approach to couple the feature evaluation formula by measuring the proper correlation between the features

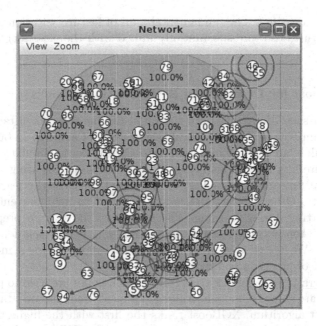

Fig. 2. Scenario of 100 normal nodes.

Table 4. Table of candidate features for extraction

Number	Abbrs	Description	Formule
1	No	Packet .seq. nr	
2	Time	Simulatiion Time	
3	Source	Source node IP	
4	Destination	Destination Node IP	
5	Length	Packet Length	
6	Info	Packet Information	
7	TR	Transmission Rate	TPC/1000
8	RR	Reception Rate	RPC/1000
9	TAT	Transmission Avg. Time	TTT/TR
10	RAT	Reception Avg. Time	TTT/RR
11	TPC	Transmitted Packets	
12	RPC	Received Packets	
13	TTT	Total Transmission time	
14	TRT	Total Reception Time	
15	DAO	DAO Packets	
16	DIS	DIS Packets	
17	DIO	DIO Packets	
18	Label	Label: Benign/Malicious	

and the class identifier. The fundamental goal of feature selection is to locate a subset of features that are substantially linked with the class identifier but not each other.

4.3   XGBoost for Detection of RPL Routing Attacks

In recent years, XGBoost has been the main driving force for attack detection. This algorithm is used to solve classification tasks of attacks. In our methodology, we simulate an IoT network using the Contiki cooja simulator. The traffic packet capture files for various benign and attack scenarios are generated. The pertinent features are extracted and normalized to make the learning process more accurate. Other characteristics are dropped to help prevent over-fitting and under-fitting during learning. The output of the feature preprocessing is ready to be taken into the learning algorithm. The IoT attack detection model is generated. We tested it against the dataset validation for a more accurate measurement of precision and recall.

In the literature, machine learning-based techniques are used to predict cyber attacks that are going to happen. Among the most used ones are Random Forest and XGBoost algorithm. XGBoost ranks the first with the highest accuracy in many studies [4,28]. For this reason, we choose the XGBoost algorithm as the detection technique.

The pseudo-code of our XGBoost algorithm used in our dataset is given in Algorithm 1.

Algorithm 1. XGBoost Algorithm for IoT Detection

1: **Data:** Dataset and hyperparameters
2: **Initialise:** $f_0(x)$
3: **for** $k = 1, 2..., M$ **do**
4:      Calculate $g_k = \frac{\partial L(y,f)}{\partial f}$;
5:      Calculate $h_k = \frac{\partial^2 L(y,f)}{\partial f}$;
6:      Determine the structure by choosing splits with maximized gain
7:      $A = \frac{1}{2}[\frac{G_L^2}{H_L} + \frac{G_L^2}{H_R} - \frac{G^2}{H}]$
8:      Determine the leaf weights $\mathcal{W}^* = -\frac{G}{H}$;
9:      Determine the base learner $\hat{b}(x) = \sum\limits_{j-1}^{T} WI$;
10:      **Add trees** $\mathcal{F}_k(x) = f_{k-1}(x) + \hat{b}(x)$
11: **end for**
12: **Result:** $f(x) = \sum\limits_{k=0}^{M} f_k(x)$;

---

5   Experimentation and Discussion

5.1   Simulation Setup

Contiki 3.2 system and cooja simulator, which implements the RPL IPv6 protocol, are used for our experiments. Many scenarios are simulated to evaluate the effectiveness of our approach. In each scenario, a set of parameters and features is chosen. Also, there are common properties for all the simulation scenarios, such as:

- The node use of the beaconless IEEE 802.15.4 MAC/PHY operating with a default configuration in the 2.4 GHz range.
- The communication range of each node is 100 m, and the interference range is 50 m.
- Every node can communicate with the sink (multi-hop).
- There is no external noise to eliminate the effects of the environment on the outcomes.
- Every 10 s, each node sends one packet to the sink.

5.2   Dataset Description

The simulation scenarios generated 510000 packets for the hello flood attack, 540000 packets for the decreased rank attack, and 503326 packets for version number attacks. The total number of normal packets was 530000.

5.3   Attack Classification Based on XGBoost

The main goal of the proposed approach is to detect RPL routing attacks using the XGBoost method. To evaluate the performance of the proposed approach, precision, recall, F1-score, and accuracy metrics were computed according to the following Eqs. 1–4.

$$Precision = \frac{TP}{TP + FP} \tag{1}$$

$$Recall = \frac{TP}{TP + FN} \tag{2}$$

$$F1 - score = \frac{2 * Precision * Recall}{Precision + Recall} \tag{3}$$

$$Accuracy = \frac{TP + TN}{TP + TN + FP + FN} \tag{4}$$

where:

- TP describes the number of samples that are correctly identified as a given class C.
- TN describes the number of samples that are correctly identified as other classes.

- FP denotes the number of samples predicted as the considered class while they belong to other classes.
- FN denotes the number of samples predicted as other classes while they belong to the considered class.

The XGBoost algorithm achieved 98.66% for the accuracy of classification, the F1-score, the recall, and the precision. Figure 3 illustrates the confusion matrix of the XGBoost algorithm. Rows represent the predicted class, while columns represent the actual class. 0, 1, 2, and 3 denote the classes normal, hello flooding attack, decreased rank attack, and version number attack, respectively.

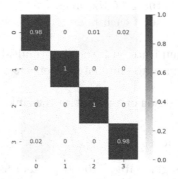

Fig. 3. The confusion matrix obtained using the XGBoost method.

5.4   Evaluation

Several experiments were conducted using other ML techniques, namely, Naive Bayes (NB), Stochastic Gradient Descent (SGD), Multilayer Perceptron (MLP), and Support Vector Machines (SVM). We note that the XGBoost has improved the detection of RPL attacks. XGBoost has achieved 98.66%, whereas the accuracies of NB, SGD, MLP, and SVM are 51.71%, 53.32%, 59.36%, and 61.94% respectively.

Table 5. Comparison of performances of different ML techniques.

Method	Accuracy	Precision	Recall	F1-score
NB	51.71	48.89	51.71	53.45
SVM	61.94	61.85	61.95	65.31
SGD	53.32	48.15	53.33	58.84
MLP	59.36	58.48	59.36	61.08

Table 5 depicts a comparison of performances of different ML techniques according to accuracy, recall, f1-score, and precision. The best performances of

NB, SGD, MLP, and SVM were achieved by SVM with 61.94% for the accuracy, 61.85% for the precision, 61.95% for the recall, and 65.31% for the F1-score.

Figure 4 describes the confusion matrix results of the RPL attack classification using the three ML techniques NB, MLP, SGD, and SVM. The best classification accuracy is achieved using SVM with 61.94% and the worst one using NB with 51.71%.

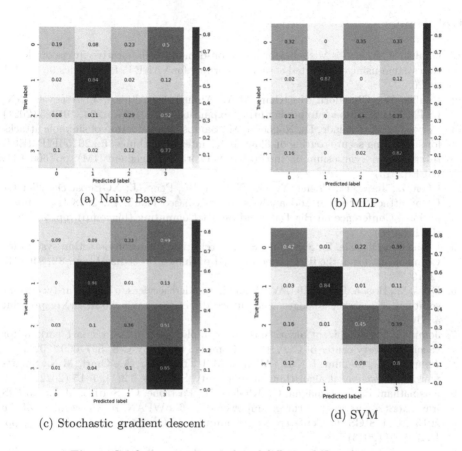

(a) Naive Bayes

(b) MLP

(c) Stochastic gradient descent

(d) SVM

Fig. 4. Confusion matrix results of different ML techniques.

6   Conclusions

In this paper, an approach for the detection of RPL routing attacks in IoT platforms is proposed. The proposed approach is based on three main steps, namely data generation, data preprocessing, and routing attack detection. Three types of attacks are considered, which are decreased rank attacks, hello flood attacks, and version number attacks. In this paper, a complete scenario is described for data generation using Contiki's cooja environment. Several experiments have been conducted to evaluate the performances of different machine learning in detecting RPL routing attacks. Results show high performances of the XGBoost method compared to state-of-the-art techniques. In future work, the introduction of additional attack types will be planned. The dataset will be increased by other types of attacks. Deep learning techniques known for high detection accuracy will be tested as well.

References

1. Ghaleb, A.F., et al.: Misbehavior-aware on-demand collaborative intrusion detection system using distributed ensemble learning for VANET. Electronics 9(9), 1411 (2020)
2. Boulila, W., Ghandorh, H., Khan, M.A., Ahmed, F., Ahmad, J.: A novel CNN-LSTM-based approach to predict urban expansion. Ecol. Inform. 64, 101325 (2021)
3. Cervantes, C., Poplade, D., Nogueira, M., Santos, A.: Detection of sinkhole attacks for supporting secure routing on 6lowpan for internet of things. In: 2015 IFIP/IEEE International Symposium on Integrated Network Management (IM), pp. 606–611. IEEE (2015)
4. Chen, Z., Jiang, F., Cheng, Y., Gu, X., Liu, W., Peng, J.: XGBoost classifier for DDoS attack detection and analysis in SDN-based cloud. In: 2018 IEEE International Conference on Big Data and Smart Computing (bigcomp), pp. 251–256. IEEE (2018)
5. Deshmukh-Bhosale, S., Sonavane, S.S.: A real-time intrusion detection system for wormhole attack in the RPL based internet of things. Procedia Manuf. 32, 840–847 (2019)
6. Driss, M., Hasan, D., Boulila, W., Ahmad, J.: Microservices in IoT security: current solutions, research challenges, and future directions. arxiv 2021. arXiv preprint arXiv:2105.07722
7. Jemmali, M.: Intelligent algorithms and complex system for a smart parking for vaccine delivery center of COVID-19. Complex Intell. Syst. 8, 597–609 (2021)
8. Jemmali, M., Melhim, L.K.B., Alharbi, M.T., Bajahzar, A., Omri, M.N.: Smart-parking management algorithms in smart city. Sci. Rep. 12(1), 1–15 (2022)
9. Kasinathan, P., Costamagna, G., Khaleel, H., Pastrone, C., Spirito, M.A.: An IDS framework for internet of things empowered by 6LoWPAN. In: Proceedings of the 2013 ACM SIGSAC Conference on Computer & Communications Security, pp. 1337–1340 (2013)
10. Kfoury, E., Saab, J., Younes, P., Achkar, R.: A self organizing map intrusion detection system for RPL protocol attacks. Int. J. Interdiscip. Telecommun. Netw. (IJITN) 11(1), 30–43 (2019)
11. Khan, M.A., et al.: Voting classifier-based intrusion detection for IoT networks. In: Saeed, F., Al-Hadhrami, T., Mohammed, E., Al-Sarem, M. (eds.) Advances on Smart and Soft Computing. AISC, vol. 1399, pp. 313–328. Springer, Singapore (2022). https://doi.org/10.1007/978-981-16-5559-3_26
12. Kumar, A., Matam, R., Shukla, S.: Impact of packet dropping attacks on RPL. In: 2016 Fourth International Conference on Parallel, Distributed and Grid Computing (PDGC), pp. 694–698. IEEE (2016)
13. Latif, S., et al.: Deep learning for the industrial internet of things (iiot): a comprehensive survey of techniques, implementation frameworks, potential applications, and future directions. Sensors 21(22), 7518 (2021)

14. Le, A., Loo, J., Luo, Y., Lasebae, A.: Specification-based ids for securing RPL from topology attacks. In: 2011 IFIP Wireless Days (WD), pp. 1–3. IEEE (2011)
15. Lee, T.-H., Wen, C.-H., Chang, L.-H., Chiang, H.-S., Hsieh, M.-C.: A lightweight intrusion detection scheme based on energy consumption analysis in 6LowPAN. In: Huang, Y.-M., Chao, H.-C., Deng, D.-J., Park, J.J.J.H. (eds.) Advanced Technologies, Embedded and Multimedia for Human-centric Computing. LNEE, vol. 260, pp. 1205–1213. Springer, Dordrecht (2014). https://doi.org/10.1007/978-94-007-7262-5_137
16. Levis, P., Clausen, T., Hui, J., Gnawali, O., Ko, J.: The trickle algorithm (rfc 6206). Internet Eng. Task Force (IETF) 1, 13 (2011)
17. Mayzaud, A., Badonnel, R., Chrisment, I.: A taxonomy of attacks in RPL-based internet of things. Int. J. Netw. Secur. 18(3), 459–473 (2016)
18. Midi, D., Rullo, A., Mudgerikar, A., Bertino, E.: Kalis-a system for knowledge-driven adaptable intrusion detection for the internet of things. In: 2017 IEEE 37th International Conference on Distributed Computing Systems (ICDCS), pp. 656–666. IEEE (2017)
19. Osterlind, F., Dunkels, A., Eriksson, J., Finne, N., Voigt, T.: Cross-level sensor network simulation with COOJA. In: Proceedings. 2006 31st IEEE Conference on Local Computer Networks, pp. 641–648. IEEE (2006)
20. Pedregosa, F., et al.: Scikit-learn: machine learning in python. J. Mach. Learn. Res. 12, 2825–2830 (2011)
21. Perrey, H., Landsmann, M., Ugus, O., Schmidt, T.C., Wählisch, M.: Trail: topology authentication in RPL. arXiv preprint arXiv:1312.0984 (2013)
22. Pongle, P., Chavan, G.: Real time intrusion and wormhole attack detection in internet of things. Int. J. Comput. Appl. 121(9) (2015)
23. Raoof, A., Matrawy, A., Lung, C.H.: Routing attacks and mitigation methods for RPL-based internet of things. IEEE Commun. Surv. Tutor. 21(2), 1582–1606 (2018)
24. Sarhan, A., Jemmali, M., Ben Hmida, A.: Two routers network architecture and scheduling algorithms under packet category classification constraint. In: Proceedings of the 5th International Conference on Future Networks & Distributed Systems, pp. 119–127 (2021)
25. Sobral, J.V., Rodrigues, J.J., Rabêlo, R.A., Al-Muhtadi, J., Korotaev, V.: Routing protocols for low power and lossy networks in internet of things applications. Sensors 19(9), 2144 (2019)
26. Wallgren, L., Raza, S., Voigt, T.: Routing attacks and countermeasures in the RPL-based internet of things. Int. J. Distrib. Sens. Netw. 9(8), 794326 (2013)
27. Winter, T., et al.: RPL: ipv6 routing protocol for low-power and lossy networks. rfc 6550, 1–157 (2012)
28. Zhang, X., Li, T., Wang, J., Li, J., Chen, L., Liu, C.: Identification of cancer-related long non-coding RNAs using XGBoost with high accuracy. Front. Genet. 10, 735 (2019)

An Automatic Refinement for Event-B Through Annotated Temporal Logic Patterns

Badr Siala[(⊠)] and Mohamed T. Bhiri

MIRACL, FSS, University of Sfax, Sfax, Tunisia
badr.siala@gmail.com

Abstract. Traditionally, formal methods have been mostly concerned by producing correct and certified code. Recently, the use of formal methods has shifted to requirements. Actually, formal methods are more and more used to formalize as well high level requirements as well as domain specific skills. In this paper, we investigate how patterns could be used in order to generate Event-B refinements automatically through DSL(s) for temporal, timed or distribution patterns. We are interested in behavioural patterns formalized as Büchi automata. One of our major concern is to produce Event-B machines such that the user can refine them further. Our ultimate goal is to produce certified code for distributed platforms starting from high level requirements.

Keywords: Correct by construction · Event-B · BIP · Temporal patterns · Timed patterns · Formal methods · Distributed systems

1 Introduction

In the realm of software engineering, formal methods have become a must for the development of systems and software correct by construction. In the beginning, they have been mostly focused on software steps concerned with code generation. As a matter of fact, the B method has been used [17] to produce the actual C code that was downloaded on some control equipments. Then, the use of formal methods has shifted to requirements. Actually, the use of formal methods is more and more used to formalize as well high level requirements [4] as well as domain specific skills. Event B, the successor of the B method, has the objective to address these new goals which are mainly concerned by requirements. Similarly to GoF design patterns in the object-oriented development, we aim at assisting developers in modelling and design by increasing automation of development steps. For example, BART tool [16] supports automatic refinement guided by a catalogue of well formalized refinement patterns (data refinement). Furthermore, the work described in [2,12] provides refinement patterns for reactive systems.

© The Author(s), under exclusive license to Springer Nature Switzerland AG 2022
N. T. Nguyen et al. (Eds.): ICCCI 2022, LNAI 13501, pp. 624–637, 2022.
https://doi.org/10.1007/978-3-031-16014-1_49

In this paper, we are interested by the construction of distributed systems. Indeed, we propose temporal and timed refinement patterns. Their formal semantic is described within LTL and timed automata formalism. These patterns are expressed by the specifier via a DSL. Likewise, we provide a method for the automatic use of temporal and timed patterns proposed. For the latter, we propose a transformation from timed automata to Event-B. For the former, we suggest two transformations: LTL to Büchi automata and Büchi automata to Event-B.

The rest of the paper is organized as follows. Section 2 gives an overview of the Event-B language. Section 3 outlines the proposed development method and a case study. Section 4 details the proposed refinement patterns that support our method. Section 5 applies some of our proposals to the case study. After discussing about some related work, we conclude by sketching future issues.

2   Event B: A Brief Overview

Event-B is a formal method that allows the development of correct by construction systems and software [2]. Indeed, it uses mathematical techniques based on set theory and first order logic for modelling discrete systems. Event-B supports natively a formal development process based on a refinement mechanism with mathematical proofs.

2.1   Machines and Contexts

Models in Event-B are described in terms of the two basic constructs: contexts and machines. The latter contains the dynamic part of a model whereas contexts contain the static part. Indeed, contexts define abstract data types through sets, constants, axioms and theorems while machines define symbolic labelled transition systems through variables (state) and events specifying their evolution while preserving invariant properties. Events can be parameterized (local variables) and occur when enabled by their guards (predicate) being true and as a result actions (assignment to a state variable) are executed. Moreover, an Event-B machine includes a mandatory event called INITIALISATION, with TRUE as guard, which defines the initial state.

As a running example, we will consider the controller for pedestrian crossing and traffic lights as a case study (see Sect. 3.1). The context (Listing 1.1) describes the roles played by the actors of the system as a so-called enumerated set. The set Role models the two roles (Vehicle and Pedestrian) and the fact that Role contains only these two elements.

```
context roles
sets
  Role
constants
  Vehicle
  Pedestrian
axioms
  @r partition(Role,
      {Vehicle}, {Pedestrian})
end
```

Listing 1.1. Roles context

```
machine turns
sees roles
variables turn
invariants
  @turn_ty turn    Role
events
  event INITIALISATION
  then
    @t_init turn    Vehicle
  end
  event switch
  then
    @t turn {Vehicle ↦ Pedestrian,
        Pedestrian ↦ Vehicle}(turn)
  end
end
```

Listing 1.2. Turn machine

In order to reason about our system in a simple way, we start by building an abstract model which takes account of only very few constraints. The **turns** machine (Listing 1.2) defines one state variable **turn** in the **variables** clause. This variable is typed by the invariant, labelled turn_ty, and initialised in the **INITIALISATION** event. The **switch** event allows to give an access right to each role in turn. The next value of the **turn** variable is obtained by applying the function defined as an enumerated set of source-target ordered pairs on the current value of **turn**.

2.2   Refinements

Refinement is at the core of Event-B modelling [2]. It is a process allowing the construction of a model in a gradual way, making it more and more accurate and closer to an implementation. In each step of the stepwise refinement, further details are added to elaborate a concrete model. This consists of constructing an ordered sequence of models where each one is a refinement of the previous model in the sequence. One starts by an abstract model which specifies the system at an abstract level. A refinement step must guarantee that every behaviour of the concrete model is allowed by the abstract model. In Event-B, we can distinguish two types of refinement [2]: horizontal refinement and vertical refinement (or data refinement). The first one, can be used to subsequently add complexity to the model by introducing further requirements of the system and the second one is used to transform and enrich the state of the abstract model.

Event-B refinement can be applied separately to a machine and to a context. Indeed, it is possible to extend contexts by adding new sets, constants or axioms to an existing context while respecting abstract context properties. Also, a machine can refine at most one other machine by enriching its state and its behaviour. We can remove some state variables or add new ones. This requires the introduction of gluing invariants that relate abstract and concrete states. Moreover, an event can refine one or more events of an abstract machine and new events can be introduced refining an implicit event which does nothing (skip). These kind of events require a variant to ensure non-divergence. They can be marked as convergent (the event makes the variant strictly decrease) or anticipated (the event does not make the variant increase).

3   Development Method

Our aim is to enhance the refinement-based development method. We are interested in high level specifications in terms of the so-called patterns. One important aspect of our proposal is that we generate Event-B machines that can be further refined. It follows that the user must be able to read the generated machines. For such a purpose, key identifiers of the generated machines are given through a Domain Specific Language (DSL). Also, since we consider patterns dedicated to behavioral aspects rooted in temporal logics, we are also interested in automating (more or less) the proposed transformations. Actually, the studied transformations are based on tools which generate Büchi automata from temporal logics formulas[1].

In this paper, we present a work which is a continuation of a previous one [18] where we were mainly concerned by the construction of distributed systems specified initially as Event-B models. The studied construction suggests successive steps in order to split and schedule the computation of complex events and then to map them on subcomponents. The specification of these steps is done through two domain specific languages. From these specifications, two *refinements* are generated. Eventually, a distributed code architecture is also generated. Our distributed code generator targets the distributed BIP framework [6,19].

3.1   Case Study

A pedestrian crossing light is a road signals system which gives priority to vehicles. Pedestrians are allowed to cross only when the signals halt vehicle traffic on the road. This system consists of a set of traffic lights for drivers, a set of light signals for pedestrians and a push button. The latter is used by pedestrians to change traffic signal to give pedestrians long enough to complete their crossing before the signals change to allow vehicle traffic again. In this paper, we show how such a system can be built by using problem requirements incrementally by applying refinement patterns. The following subset of requirements is taken into account:

1. The system switches between pedestrian crossing and vehicle traffic.
2. Pedestrian should ask for crossing right before being allowed to cross.
3. Demands done when pedestrian have already the crossing right are ignored.
4. Pedestrian can cross 30 time units after their first valid demand.

---

[1]   As we will see, this translation is not automatic since Event-B machines are event based while most of the tools are state based.

4   Refinement Patterns

4.1   Temporal Logic Patterns

In Event B and more generally within the practice of any formal method, the transition from informal requirements to formal specifications is a crucial step. The use of patterns can be considered as a first response to alleviate such a step. Actually, patterns try to capture usual problem formulations and give them an intuitive syntax while hiding their precise (and may be intricate) semantics. Then, in order to express his requirements, a user has a catalogue of requirement patterns. Recently, the DSL technology has popularized such practice. In this paper, we are especially interested in patterns related to behavior requirements which are very common in embedded systems for instance. Dwyer et al. [10] have been among the first to identify well known temporal patterns in order to capture the knwoledge of expert system designers: this knowledge consisted in as well the requirements expression *as well as* solutions to software design problems. [10] have elaborated a specification pattern system for describing the relationships between events or states. LTL (Linear Temporal Logic) is one of the logics, used by [10], for specifying unambiguously the desired behavior of a system. LTL extends propositional logic with two basic modal connectives: $\circ$ and $\mathbf{U}$. $\circ\varphi$ (**next** φ) holds if φ holds at *the* next step. $\varphi\ \mathcal{U}\ \psi$ (φ **until** ψ) holds if ψ holds in the future and φ keeps holding until the moment in the future where ψ holds. The auxiliary modalities: $\Diamond, \Box$ and $\mathbf{W}$ are also used. $\Diamond\varphi$ (φ holds **eventually** in the future), $\Box\varphi$ (φ holds **always** in the future) and $\varphi\ \mathbf{W}\ \psi$ (φ **weak until** ψ) holds if φ holds until ψ holds in the future (unlike **until**, ψ is not required to hold in the future.) An original proposal of [10] has been to introduce relationships between events/states within the so called *pattern scopes* which delimit where the pattern must hold. Examples of such scopes are `Global`, `Before`, ...

4.2   Extracting Refinement Patterns

In this paper, we propose to use temporal patterns as a way to specifiy a refinement of a given Event-B machine. A new machine will be generated. It should refine the original one by adding new events and constraining the execution in order to satisfy the logical property expressed by the pattern. Given a temporal pattern and an Event-B machine, the generation process will be guided by the following steps:

- Expression of the semantics of the pattern as an LTL formula
- Generation of the Büchi automaton associated to the LTL formula
- Definition of the refined machine as a superposition [13] of the orginal machine and the automaton derived from the logical specification.

Semantics of Patterns. The considered set of patterns is defined as a fixed number of property schemas parameterized by a fixed number of events. Thus patterns cannot be composed (except by an implicit conjunction). Their semantics are directly given by an LTL formula. So this step is only an expansion of the pattern definition. As an example, we consider the pattern e1 **precedes** e2 **initially** which means that the first occurrence of e_2 must be preceded by e_1. Its semantics is given by the LTL formula $\neg e_2 \mathbf{W} e_1$.

Generation of the Büchi Automaton. As the patterns are known, their LTL definition are also statically known. Thus, this step is performed offline using one of the existing LTL to Büchi tools [5,9]. Actually, these tools do not take into account that events are exclusive. Since in our patterns, we reason about events, we formalize the exclusiveness property of events as follows

$$(\Box(\bigvee_{i\in\mathcal{E}} e_i \wedge \bigwedge_{\substack{i,j\in\mathcal{E}\times\mathcal{E}\\i\neq j}} \neg(e_i \wedge e_j))) \wedge f$$

where f is the basic temporal logic property associated to the pattern and $\mathcal{E}$ is the set of events of the formula and the machine we reason about. In the following examples we define $\mathcal{E}$ as the set of the events of the pattern and a special event o representing all the other events. Thanks to [9], we obtain the automaton (see Fig. 1) for the LTL formula $\neg e_2 \mathbf{W} e_1$.

- its set of states is $\{0, 1\}$.
- its initial state is 0.
- its set of labels is $\{e_1, e_2\}$.
- its set of labeled transitions is
$\{e_1 \mapsto \{0 \mapsto 1, 1 \mapsto 1\}, e_2 \mapsto \{1 \mapsto 1\}\}$.

Generation of the Event-B Refined Machine.
The refined machine restricts the set of behaviors of the given abstract machine by adding a control variable specifying a Büchi state. In order to help the user guide the process, the name of this variable is attached to the pattern. Then, each event is extended

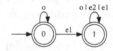

Fig. 1. Büchi automaton

by adding a guard specifying allowed start states and an action updating the control variable. In the general case, given a control variable st and the set of transitions $(S_i \xrightarrow{e} D_i)_{i\in 1..n}$ where e is an event and S_i and D_i the source and destination states, we get the following non deterministic event which assigns to st any element in the image by the enumerated relation of the singleton $\{st\}$:

```
event e extends e
when
    @g st ∈ {S₁, ..., Sₙ}
then
    @a st :∈ {S₁ ↦ D₁,..., Sₙ ↦ Dₙ}[{st}]
end
```

As the set of LTL formula is statically known, some simplifications have been manually performed during plugin development, such as deleting useless guards or actions. Furthermore, some events can be declared as new and thus do not extend existing ones.

Most patterns lead to two-states deterministic automata. The control variable is then a boolean variable. For the considered example, using the boolean variable b to represent the state ($b = \perp$ for 0 and $b = \top$ for 1), we have:

```
event INITIALISATION then @b b := FALSE end
event e1 extends e1 then @b b := TRUE end
event e2 extends e2 when @b b = TRUE end
```

It has to be noted that recurrent states of the Büchi automaton are not considered. They would lead to the introduction of a variant. Its definition should be provided by the user as it could be data dependent. Furthermore, dedicated proof obligations should be added to the model as theorems, as Event-B does not allow variants on existing events. The timed variants of the patterns solve this problem by providing a bound to the waiting time.

Extension to Timed Constraints. It is tempting to apply the same method to build Event-B machines from timed linear specifications. Several timed extensions of LTL exist such as MTL [14] where temporal operators are indexed with time intervals or TLTL [15] where explicit clocks are introduced. However, even if some proposals to convert timed temporal logic in timed automata variants exist, to the best of our knowledge, no tool is available. Furthermore, the number of clocks needed to convert a timed property into a timed automaton may be infinite (in a continuous time setting: each p must be followed by a q within exactly one time unit) or hard to master. With respect to timed patterns, one can also consider a timed process algebra as the semantic domain. [8] propose to transform timed process algebra to timed automata. Such a method is better suited to a composition-based approach while we are interested in a refinement-based approach.

Thus, we consider here that the semantics of a timed pattern is given by a timed automaton and we will select patterns so that the corresponding semantics is readable, our objective being that the corresponding Event-B machine should be refined further by the user.

As an example, we consider the timed response pattern e_2 **responds to each** e_1 **within less than** N which should constrain each e_1 to be followed by an e_2 within less than N time units. This pattern is defined by the following timed automaton using clock c:

$with \; \mathrm{inv}(1) \equiv c \leq N$

In order to express this automaton in Event-B, we introduce a boolean variable b with $b = \perp$ for state 0. The clock variable is supposed to be incremented by the *tick* event while preserving the invariant ($c \leq N$ in state 1, i.e. when b is TRUE). The `extends` construct is used to express superposition, thus ensuring the refinement property with respect to the user-provided machine.

```
invariant                                    event e2 extends e2
  @i b = TRUE ⇒ c ≤ N                           when @c b = TRUE ⇒ c = N
event INITIALISATION then @b b := FALSE end     then @b b := FALSE end
event e1 extends e1                          event tick
  then @b b := TRUE                             when @cN b = TRUE ⇒ c < N
      @c c := {TRUE ↦ c, FALSE ↦ 0}(b) end   then @c c := c + 1 end
```

The verification of the timed automaton to B conversion is left for future work, as well as the link with a timed linear logic-based specification.

Towards a Domain Specific Language. The previous patterns together with extra-logical annotations define a domain specific language that governs the automatic generation of a refinement of a given Event-B machine. Additional information include:

- the names of the original and refined machines
- the names of the events introduced by the refinement
- the names of control or clock variables to be introduced
- the names of control variables that should be used to represent the state of the Büchi automaton associated to the pattern
- the name of the event supposed to model discrete time advance in the Event-B model being refined

We will not detail the syntax of the language here. However, we give an example of what can be specified using our DSL to generate a refinement constrained by an annotated pattern:

```
refinement M1 refines M0
  new event e1 responds to each event e2
    (using new status b);
  ... other temporal constraints
```

We remark that the control of the automatically generated machines is expressed in terms of the variables of the pattern annotation. Thanks to the name of these variables given by the user, unlike usual code generation, we do not use internally generated names. This is the main motivation of our pattern annotations. It follows that such a machine is easier to read and, we believe, it is possible to refine it further.

4.3 Supported Patterns

In the following, we propose untimed and timed patterns in the spirit of Dwyer patterns. Precedence patterns require that an event precedes another one in a particular context. Response patterns require that an event occurs after another one in a particular context. Timed variants add time bounds to these requirements. For each pattern, we give its LTL (or timed automaton) semantics and its Event-B semantics. We do not claim here that Event-B and automata-based semantics match. This is left for future work and requires a deep analysis of the management in Event-B of the Büchi condition for untimed patterns and of non Zeno behaviors for timed patterns.

Untimed Patterns. The following patterns differ from Dwyer patterns by the context part. Except for the first one, we give their LTL and Event-B semantics.

– e_1 **precedes** e_2 **initially**
  This pattern has been studied in the previous section.
– e_1 **precedes** e_2 **within scope** e
  This pattern states that in segments delimited by the event e, the event e_1 should precede the first occurrence of e_2. Its LTL semantics is defined by:

$$(\neg e_2 \ \mathbf{W} \ (e_1 \vee e)) \ \wedge \ \Box(e \Rightarrow \mathbf{X}(\neg e_2 \ \mathbf{W} \ (e_1 \vee e)))$$

This LTL formula is automatically transformed into the following two-states deterministic automaton:

In order to generate the event B refinement, we annotate the pattern with a boolean variable b supposed to be true in state 0:

```
e1 precedes e2 within scope e
  (using status b)
```

Given this annotation, the automaton is translated into the following Event-B machine:

```
event INITIALISATION then @b b := FALSE end
event e1 extends e1 then @b b := TRUE end
event e2 extends e2 when @b b = TRUE end
event e extends e then @b b := FALSE end
```

– e_1 **responds to each** e_2 **globally**
  This pattern states that each event e_2 should be followed by an event e_1, implicitly before the next occurrence of e_2, if any. Its semantics is defined in LTL as follows:
$$\Box(e_2 \rightarrow \mathbf{X}(\neg e_2 \ \mathbf{U} \ e_1))$$

This formula is automatically transformed into the following Büchi automaton (see Fig. 2) where state 0 is marked as recurrent: an accepted execution should visit this state infinitely often.

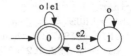

Fig. 2. Response pattern.

For the moment, the acceptance condition is ignored. It would require managing variants to ensure that the set of non accepting states is left within a finite number of steps. We annotate the pattern by declaring one boolean variable supposed to be false in state 0. We obtain the following machine:

```
e1 responds to each e2 globally
  (using new status st)

variables st
invariants @st st ∈ 𝔹
event INITIALISATION then @st st := FALSE end
event e1 extends e1
  when @sf st = FALSE then @st st := TRUE end
event e2 extends e2 then @sf st = FALSE end
```

Timed Patterns. In this paragraph, we consider a timed version of a precedence pattern. Timed patterns are more complex as we must specify between which occurrences of repeated events time is measured. As previously, we suppose that all mentioned events are different and thus cannot occur simultaneously.

first e_1 precedes first e_2 within scope e, delay N.

This state-event precedence pattern specifies that between occurrences of e, the first occurrence of event e_2 should occur N time units after the first occurrence of event e_1. Its semantics is given by the following timed automaton which differs from the previous one by the fact that e_1 cannot occur in state 1:

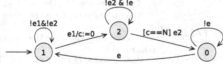

$$with \ \text{inv}(2) \equiv c \leq N$$

In order to generate the Event-B refinement, we annotate the pattern with three variables: b1 is true in state 2, b2 is false in state 1 and c is a clock.

```
first e1 precedes first e2 (using status b1)
  within
    scope e (using status b2),
    delay N (using event tick, clock c).
```

Given these annotations, the timed automaton is translated into the following Event-B machine. Compared to the automaton, one simplification has been done: as the contents of the clock variable c is not significant in states 0 and 1, it is silently reset by the event e_2. Furthermore, the tick event is added. It is supposed to increment all the clocks while preserving the invariant.

```
invariant                             when @c b1 = TRUE ⇒ c = N
  @i b1 = TRUE ⇒ c ≤ N                     @b2 b2 = TRUE
event INITIALISATION then             then @b1 b1 := FALSE end
  @b1 b1 := FALSE @b2 b2 := FALSE end  event e extends e
event e1 extends e1                     when @b1 b1 = FALSE
  then @c c := {TRUE ↦ c, FALSE ↦ 0}(b1)  then @b2 b2 := FALSE end
       @b1 b1 := {FALSE↦TRUE,TRUE↦b1}(b2)  event tick extends tick
       @b2 b2 := TRUE end               when @bc b1 = TRUE ⇒ c < N
event e2 extends e2                     then @c c := c + 1 end
```

5   Case Study Illustrations

In this section, we illustrate our proposed patterns through examples taken from the case study of Sect. 3.1.

5.1   Event Splitting

The first step aims at splitting the event *switch* depending on *pedestrian_path* value: when false, *switch* corresponds to giving crossing authorization to pedestrian; otherwise, it corresponds to *end_of_auth*. Refinement is guaranteed. Absence of deadlock introduction comes from the fact that conditions are complementary. As a result, we get the machine given in Listing 1.4 where the **switch** event as been split.

```
                                  machine Crossing_auth refines Crossing
                                  variables vehicle_path pedestrian_path
                                  events
                                    event authorization refines switch
                                      where
                                        @gw pedestrian_path = FALSE
 event splitting Crossing_auth         then
 refines Crossing                          @av vehicle_path := FALSE
 split switch into                         @aw pedestrian_path := TRUE
    authorization                      end
      when @gw pedestrian_path = FALSE, event end_of_auth refines switch
    end_of_authorization                 where
      when @gw pedestrian_path = TRUE      @gw pedestrian_path = TRUE
                                         then
      Listing 1.3. Roles context             @av vehicle_path := TRUE
                                              @aw pedestrian_path := FALSE
                                      end
                                  end
```

Listing 1.4. Introducing the *authorization* event

5.2   Introduction of the Request Event

This step adds a new event allowing the pedestrian to ask for the authorization. This event is supposed to be uncontrollable and thus not guarded. It should have no effect if pedestrians are already allowed to cross. It is introduced by generating a refinement from the following specification:

```
refinement Crossing_request          within scope end_of_auth
refines Crossing_auth                (using new status authorization_req)
  new request precedes authorization
```

5.3   Adding Timed Constraints

This step adds timing constraints between existing events. The authorization should be given 30 time units after the first occurrence of a request in each segment delimited by the `end_of_authorization` event. We reuse the existing status variable `authorization_req` and introduce a new status variable `is_waiting` and a clock variable (`waiting`) incremented by a new `tick` event. This specification can be written as follows:

```
refinement Crossing_request
  refines Crossing_auth
  sees cTiming
 first request precedes first authorization
  (using new status is_waiting)
  within
    scope end_of_authorization
      (using status authorization_req),
    delay WaitingTime
      (using new clock waiting, new event tick)
```

The application of this pattern to the previously obtained machine generates a refinement with the two newly introduced variables and the new event `tick` managing the discrete advance of time. The control variable `authorization_req` is reused. The generator should check that its usage conforms to the pattern. Existing events are extended so that the refinement property is satisfied by construction.

The ultimate step is builds a distributed model from a centralized one. Four subcomponents are introduced: controller, vehicle lights `VLights`, pedestrian lights `PLights` and sensors. Then, variables are mapped to components and the obtained refined machine is projected on the components. A BIP model is generated in order to be executed on a distributed platform.

6   Related Work

Several researchers have studied how to enhance the basic refinement-based development method. Especially, [11] have generalized the so-called atomicity decomposition technique for events. As they notice, such a technique has made the standard refinement more systematic and visual. With respect to our work, we remark that in [11], the authors are mainly concerned by sequential decomposition patterns of a unique event[2]. We believe that temporal logic-based patterns

---

[2] In the sense that they concern a unique process.

are richer with respect to behavioral concerns. Moreover, the automata based approach to generate correct refinements is generic. Last, the annotation of patterns is essential to obtain readable models that can be refined further.

With respect to time, timed patterns have been studied by [8]. They propose to transform timed process algebra to timed automata. [1] propose timed patterns as a beahvioral specification language for FIACRE models. Their semantics is Time Petri Nets-based. These two proposals are not concerned by refinements.

7   Conclusion

In this paper, we have presented a work which aims at promoting formal methods for the development of distributed systems. One of our concerns was to integrate some usual temporal patterns within an Event-B development. For such a purpose, we have used and adapted well known tools which translate LTL formulas to Büchi automata. We generate Event-B machines which can be refined further. We use a DSL to express patterns and a plugin to generate a refinement of a given Event-B machine. It is defined as a superposition of the input machine and the automaton associated to the pattern.

As future work, we envision two research directions concerning temporized patterns and parameterized systems. With respect to temporized patterns, we have to look for a better integration of the usual operational devices, e.g., timed automata [3] and time Petri nets [7], within Event-B. With respect to parameterized systems, although already sketched in [10], we have to deepen their theoretical basis.

References

1. Abid, N., Dal Zilio, S., Le Botlan, D.: Real-time specification patterns and tools. In: Stoelinga, M., Pinger, R. (eds.) FMICS 2012. LNCS, vol. 7437, pp. 1–15. Springer, Heidelberg (2012). https://doi.org/10.1007/978-3-642-32469-7_1
2. Abrial, J.R.: Modeling in Event-B: System and Software Engineering, 1st edn. Cambridge University Press, New York (2010)
3. Alur, R., Dill, D.: A theory of timed automata. Theor. Comput. Sci. **126**(1), 183–235 (1994)
4. Aziz, B., Arenas, A., Bicarregui, J., Ponsard, C., Massonet, P.: From goal-oriented requirements to Event-B specifications. In: First NFM Symposium 2009, USA, 6–8 April 2009, pp. 96–105 (2009)
5. Babiak, T., Křetínský, M., Řehák, V., Strejček, J.: LTL to Büchi automata translation: fast and more deterministic. In: Flanagan, C., König, B. (eds.) TACAS 2012. LNCS, vol. 7214, pp. 95–109. Springer, Heidelberg (2012). https://doi.org/10.1007/978-3-642-28756-5_8
6. Basu, A., et al.: Rigorous component-based system design using the BIP framework. IEEE Softw. **28**(3), 41–48 (2011)
7. Berthomieu, B., Diaz, M.: Modeling and verification of time dependent systems using time Petri nets. IEEE Trans. Softw. Eng. **17**(3), 259–273 (1991)
8. Dong, J.S., Qin, S., Yi, W., Sun, J., Hao, P.: Timed automata patterns. IEEE Trans. Softw. Eng. **34**, 844–859 (2008)

9. Duret-Lutz, A., Lewkowicz, A., Fauchille, A., Michaud, T., Renault, É., Xu, L.: Spot 2.0 – a framework for LTL and ω-automata manipulation. In: Artho, C., Legay, A., Peled, D. (eds.) ATVA 2016. LNCS, vol. 9938, pp. 122–129. Springer, Cham (2016). https://doi.org/10.1007/978-3-319-46520-3_8

10. Dwyer, M.B., Avrunin, G.S., Corbett, J.C.: Patterns in property specifications for finite-state verification. In: Proceedings of the ICSE 1999, Los Angeles, CA, USA, 16–22 May 1999, pp. 411–420 (1999)

11. Salehi Fathabadi, A., Butler, M., Rezazadeh, A.: Language and tool support for event refinement structures in Event-B. Formal Aspects Comput. 27(3), 499–523 (2014). https://doi.org/10.1007/s00165-014-0311-1

12. Hoang, T.S., Fürst, A., Abrial, J.: Event-B patterns and their tool support. Softw. Syst. Model. 12(2), 229–244 (2013)

13. Jonsson, B.: On decomposing and refining specifications of distributed systems. In: de Bakker, J.W., de Roever, W.-P., Rozenberg, G. (eds.) REX 1989. LNCS, vol. 430, pp. 361–385. Springer, Heidelberg (1990). https://doi.org/10.1007/3-540-52559-9_71

14. Koymans, R.: Specifying real-time properties with metric temporal logic. Real-Time Syst. 2(4), 255–299 (1990)

15. Raskin, J.-F., Schobbens, P.-Y.: State clock logic: a decidable real-time logic. In: Maler, O. (ed.) HART 1997. LNCS, vol. 1201, pp. 33–47. Springer, Heidelberg (1997). https://doi.org/10.1007/BFb0014711

16. Requet, A.: BART: a tool for automatic refinement. In: Börger, E., Butler, M., Bowen, J.P., Boca, P. (eds.) ABZ 2008. LNCS, vol. 5238, pp. 345–345. Springer, Heidelberg (2008). https://doi.org/10.1007/978-3-540-87603-8_33

17. Sabatier, D., Lartigue, P.: The use of the B formal method for the design and the validation of the transaction mechanism for smart card applications. Formal Methods Syst. Des. 17(3), 245–272 (2000)

18. Siala, B., Bodeveix, J.P., Filali, M., Bhiri, M.: An Event-B development process for the distributed BIP framework, pp. 283–307 (2021)

19. Sifakis, J., Bensalem, S., Bliudze, S., Bozga, M.: A theory agenda for component-based design. In: De Nicola, R., Hennicker, R. (eds.) Software, Services, and Systems. LNCS, vol. 8950, pp. 409–439. Springer, Cham (2015). https://doi.org/10.1007/978-3-319-15545-6_24

Xtend Transformation from PDDL to Event-B

Farah Fourati[1(✉)], Mohamed Tahar Bhiri[1], and Riadh Robbana[2]

[1] Faculty of Science of Sfax, Sfax, Tunisia
farah.fourati@ymail.com
[2] National Institute of Applied Science and Technology, Tunis, Tunisia

Abstract. PDDL is a de facto standard language for formally describing planning problems. It is equipped with dynamic tools for executing PDDL descriptions. But, it is not equipped with static tools allowing to reason a priori on the correction of the PDDL descriptions. To remedy this shortcoming, we have designed, produced and tested a tool called PDDL2EventB in order to automate the approach and the systematic translation rules from PDDL to Event-B. This allows a formal static verification of PDDL descriptions and exploit the static tools associated with Event-B. To achieve this, we successfully used the Xtext MDE tool creating an integrated development environment specific to the PDDL language, and the Xtend tool to implement our transformation and produce the Event-B models according to a top-down approach.

Keywords: Event-B · Transformation · MDE plugin · Static verification

1 Introduction

The PDDL language (Planning Domain Definition Language) [7] is a formal language dedicated to the description of planning problems in the broad sense. It relies on first-order predicate logic and pre/post specification of actions. PDDL descriptions are difficult to write and a fortiori to formally validate. Event-B is a formal method based on the correct-by-construction paradigm [1] with mathematical proofs.

Given the semantic proximity between PDDL and Event-B [1], we recommend opening the PDDL on Event-B in order to check the consistency of the initial PDDL descriptions.

In this paper, we propose a transformation tool from PDDL to Event-B: PDDL2Event-B (See Sect. 3) and we describe an approach allowing to reason on the Event-B models obtained (See Sect. 4).

2 Motivations

The PDDL language is a de facto standard language used to formally describe planning problems. It has tools called planners [5] to solve planning problems

© The Author(s), under exclusive license to Springer Nature Switzerland AG 2022
N. T. Nguyen et al. (Eds.): ICCCI 2022, LNAI 13501, pp. 638–644, 2022.
https://doi.org/10.1007/978-3-031-16014-1_50

described in PDDL and automatic plan validation [4] to test a posteriori PDDL descriptions. But the a posteriori use of dynamic tools -after describing the PDDL models- are insufficient for the verification and validation of PDDL descriptions. In fact, PDDL descriptions are often difficult to write and easily lead to errors, even those which are considered benchmarks to test planners [6]. Therefore, we propose a **formal static approach** (**a priori**) for the verification and validation of PDDL descriptions. To achieve this, we propose to translate the PDDL description into the Event-B formal method [1]. This allows the use of the **correct-by-construction** paradigm [1] and static tools associated with Event-B such as provers, model checkers, animators and simulators [8]. In our opinion, the opening of the PDDL on Event-B is motivated by the semantic proximity between these two formal languages. In fact, PDDL and Event-B have the same operational semantics defined by a system of labeled transitions.

3   PDDL2Event-B Tool

3.1   Proposed Approach from PDDL to Event-B

A PDDL "domain" is translated into an abstract model described by "context" and "machine" Event-B that respectively have the static and the dynamic parts of the domain. The c_domain context includes translations of the types, constants and static predicates from the domain of the PDDL file description concerned. Knowing that a static predicate appears only in the preconditions of PDDL action. The Event-B machine m_domain includes translations dynamic predicates and actions from the domain of the concerned PDDL file. Knowing that a predicate is called dynamic if it is in the postcondition part "effect" of a PDDL action. Equally, a PDDL problem is translated into a refined Event-B model with a c_problem context and m_problem machine. The c_problem concrete context that extends c_domain includes the translation of objects from the problem file. The m_problem concrete machines that refines m_domain. In the m_problem machine, the initial state "init" is translated by INITIALISATION event that refines the m domain abstract machine and introduces a new event "GOAL" in order to translate the state "goal" of the planning problem. The Table 1 illustrate our approach for translating PDDL constructs into Event-B.

   We have designed, realized and tested a tool called PDDL2EventB. This automates the proposed approach and systematic translation rules from PDDL to Event-B. Such intuitive rules have been realized thanks to our good knowledge of two languages PDDL and Event-B. Our PDDL2EventB plugin, integrable into the Eclipse platform, built components of two kind context and machine from a file that contains a domain construction and zero or more problem construction. PDDL2EventB tool generates as output a textual representation of Event-B system accepted by Camille editor of Event-B. To achieve this, we have successfully used the MDE approach and available plugins of EMF Eclipse and oAW platform (Xtext [2] and Xtend [3]).

Table 1. General layout of the translation from PDDL to Event-B

PDDL	Event-B
define	CONTEXT c_domain_<nameD> END
(domain <nameD>)	MACHINE m_domain_<nameD> SEES c_domain_<nameD> END
define (problem <nameD>)	CONTEXT c_problem_<nameP> EXTENDS c_domain_<nameD>END
(:domain <nameP>)	MACHINE m_problem_<nameP> REFINES m_domain_<nameD> SEES c_problem_<nameP>END

The Xtext framework (See Sect. 3.2) develops programming languages and domain-specific languages from a grammar described in Xtext. The Xtend language is a language based on Java, it provides the possibility to use Java libraries. In addition, it offers other means such as extensions methods, template expressions. They are used to implement our Xtend transformation and produce the Event-B models by a top-down approach.

```
5 System. dom Domain  prob+ (Problem) ,
6
7 Domain:'(' 'define'
8          '(' 'domain' name=ID ')'
9          ('(' ':requirements' (requireKey+=Requirement)*')')?
10         ('(' ':types' ((typesA+=Type)*|(typesH+=HierType)*)')')?
11         ('(' ':constants' (constants+=ListConstants)*')')?
12         ('(' ':predicates' (predicates+=Predicate)*')')?
13         (actions+=Action)*
14         ')';
15 HierType: (subtypes+=Type)* '-'superType=Type;
16 Type: name=ID ;
17 ListConstants: (cons+=Constant)* '-' type=[Type];
18 Constant: name=ID;
19 Predicate: '('name=ID (parameters+=Variable)* ')';
20 Action: '(' ':action' name=ID
21         ':parameters' '(' (parameters+=Variable)* ')'
22         ':precondition' (pre+=conGD)*
23         ':effect' (eff+=conGD)* ')';
24 Variable:'?'name=ID '-' type=[Type];
25 conGD:Assertion|NotAssertion|And|Or|Implication|Forall|Exists|
   Equality|NotEquality;
26
27
```

Fig. 1. Extract of the Xtext code related to PDDL domain

3.2 DSL for PDDL Language via Xtext

A grammar written wih Xtext is composed of a set of rules. A rule can be terminal rule or non-terminal. The ID rule can be cited as a terminal rule. While the domain rule is a non-terminal rule. The Domain entity (See figure Fig. 1) is the host entity of a PDDL domain. A domain must begin with "define" and "domain" keywords, it can contain atomic or hierarchical types. In addition, it may contain constants, our tool only accepts typed constants. Then, the domain contains a set of predicates followed by actions. The symbol "+ =" means that the variable contains a set of corresponding type. The symbol "*" is the cardinality zero or more. The symbol "?" is the cardinality zero or one. The Xtext tool use the ANTLR parser. The generator of ANTLR is based on LL (*) algorithms, a left factorization is sometimes necessary. Through the Xtext description of the PDDL language (See Fig. 1), the Xtext framework produces a syntax editor for PDDL. Such user-friendly editor can check the entered PDDL code.

3.3   Transformation and Code Generation via Xtend

After developing our DSL, we treat the transformation and code generation step. In fact, Xtend allows to treat transformation and code generation phases.

The domain is transformed into a context and an abstract machine. Similarly, any problem is transformed into a context and a concrete machine (See Table 1). The context and the corresponding machine take respectively the name assigned to the corresponding instance of domain or problem with uppercase first letter preceded by "C_" for context and "M_" for the machine. The templates are used as the host structure for the generation of the abstract context, the abstract machine, the concrete contexts and the concrete machine.

```
def  genDomM(Domain d)'''
machine M_«d.name.toFirstUpper»  sees C_«d.name.toFirstUpper»
variables
«FOR p:d.predicates»
    «p.name»
«ENDFOR»
invariants
«FOR p:d.predicates»
@inv_«p.name» «p.name» : «FOR pa:p.parameters SEPARATOR ' ** '»
 «pa.type.name» «ENDFOR» --> BOOL
«ENDFOR»
events

event INITIALISATION
then
«FOR p:d.predicates»
@act_«p.name» «p.name» :: «FOR pa:p.parameters SEPARATOR ' ** '»
 «pa.type.name» «ENDFOR» --> BOOL
«ENDFOR»
end
«FOR a:d.actions»
event evt_«a.name»
any «FOR pa:a.parameters» «pa.name» «ENDFOR»
where
«var int i=1»
«FOR pa:a.parameters»
    @grd«i++» «pa.name» : «pa.type.name»
«ENDFOR»
«FOR ga:a.pre»
    «ga.getPrecondition(i++,false)»
«ENDFOR»

then
```

Fig. 2. Extract from the genDomM template

Figure 2 present an extract from the genDomM template that allows the generation of the concrete machine. Dynamic predicates and actions constitutes the Event-B machine associated with the domain PDDL. It is translated into Event-B by a variable. INITIALISATION event has no antecedent in the PDDL description. It is added to initialize a dynamic predicates forming the state of the domain machine.

A PDDL action is translated into Event-B by an event. The template expressions allow for readable string concatenation (it can contain conditional structures, loops, ..), the corresponding string is automatically inserted in its position. We also used the concept of polymorphic templates "dispatch template", these templates are called according to context of their execution, for example the getPrecondition template is called polymorphic template. It can be called accordance to one of the conGD entity context of the Xtext file presented in Fig. 1.

```
def  genProbM(Problem p)'''
machine M_«p.name.toFirstUpper» refines M_«p.domain.name.toFirstUpper»
sees C_«p.name.toFirstUpper»
variables
«FOR v:p.domain.predicates»
     «v.name»
«ENDFOR»
events

event INITIALISATION
«var int i=1»
then
«FOR v:p.domain.predicates»
     @act«i++»  «v.name» := («FOR pa:v.parameters SEPARATOR ' ** '»
       «pa.type.name» «ENDFOR» ** {FALSE}) <+{«p.init.getElem(v.name as String)»}
«ENDFOR»
end

event GOAL
«var int j=1»
where
«FOR v:p.domain.predicates»
     @grd«j++»  «v.name» = «v.name» <+{«p.goal.getElem(v.name as String)»}
«ENDFOR»
end
«FOR a:p.domain.actions»
event evt_«a.name» extends evt_«a.name»
end
«ENDFOR»
end'''
```

Fig. 3. Extract from the genProbM template

Figure 3 present an extract from the genProbM template that allows the generation of the abstract machine. A machine that define the dynamic part of the PDDL problem, it refines the machine of the PDDL domain. The dynamic predicates, they are initialized by the INITIALISATION event into the machine associated with the construction problem. The goal state "goal" translate into Event-B by a new event "GOAL". Such an event has a guard translated from formula that specifies the goal action of PDDL problem. GOAL is an event with no parameters and does nothing.

The activity of proof and validation of Event-B model generated are performed through the Rodin platform.

4   Consistency of Generated Event-B Models

The PDDL2EventB tool produces Event-B models from PDDL descriptions. We can make formal reasoning on the Event-B models generated. These reasonings concern the abstract Event-B model as well as the refined Event-B model. Such reasoning aimed at formal verification of several types of properties. These include safety properties, deadlock-free and liveness properties.

Reasonings on the Obtained Abstract Model

The Event-B abstract model produced by our PDDL2EventB tool corresponds to the domain PDDL. It comprises Event-B context and Event-B machine. According to our experiments the Event-B abstract model meets the safety properties: the invariant is established by the INITIALISATION event and it is preserved by the others events. In general, the deadlock-free property is not formally verified on Event-B abstract models produced by our PDDL2Event-B tool, particularly for models with multiple events (greater than 10). But using ProB and reducing the size of abstract sets, the ProB model checker does not detect deadlocks. Finally, liveness properties specific to each PDDL domain can be described using the great possibilities of LTLe language (extended Linear Temporal Logic) and formally verified by ProB.

Strengthening Invariant

The abstract model in Event-B streamed from the PDDL domain includes the invariant relating to typing properties of Event-B variables corresponding to the dynamic predicate of PDDL domain concerned. Such invariant can be strengthened by properties describing constraints within or between variables. These constraints could be established by animation of Event-B models using ProB. Also, they can be obtained by further analyzing the specifications related to treated PDDL domain. The addition of these constraints can promote mathematical proof of deadlock-free and the verification and the validation of Event-B events corresponding to PDDL actions.

Reasoning About Refined Model Obtained

The refined model generated by our PDDL2EventB tool is expected to produce an automatic refinement of the abstract model. According to the experiments and to the use of the internal and the external provers of the Rodin platform, the refinement relation between the two models produced by PDDL2EventB is formally proven.

Through the use of ProB animator, we can validate plan solutions. Unlike the VAL tool associated with PDDL, the animation with ProB allows locating errors of an incorrect plan solution.

Axioms Associated with Static Predicates

Static predicates of a PDDL description are translated into Event-B by typed constants. Following the constraints within and between variables it is often useful to add constraints related to constants. This allows a consistent initialisation of the initial state and identification of the inherent properties of the treated planning issues.

5   Conclusion

In this work, we described our MDE tool for transforming PDDL to Event-B: PDDL2EventB written in Xtend. PDDL2EventB is validated according a syntax-oriented functional testing approach. Finally, we have explored the consistency of the generated Event-B models. Currently, we are using our PDDL2EventB tool on real case studies in the areas of web services composition and software reconfiguration.

References

1. Abrial, J.R.: Modeling in Event-B: System and Software Engineering. Cambridge University Press, Cambridge (2010)
2. Efftinge, S., Völter, M.: oAW xText: a framework for textual DSLs. In: Workshop on Modeling Symposium at Eclipse Summit, vol. 32, p. 118 (2006)
3. Haase, A., Völter, M., Efftinge, S., Kolb, B.: Introduction to openarchitectureware 4.1. 2. In: MDD Tool Implementers Forum (2007)
4. Howey, R., Long, D., Fox, M.: Val: Automatic plan validation, continuous effects and mixed initiative planning using PDDL. In: 16th IEEE International Conference on Tools with Artificial Intelligence. ICTAI 2004, pp. 294–301. IEEE (2004)
5. ICAPS: International Conference on Automated Planning and Scheduling (2022, Online)
6. Long, D., Fox, M., Howey, R.: Planning domains and plans: validation, verification and analysis. In: Proceedings of Workshop on V&V of Planning and Scheduling Systems (2009)
7. McDermott, D., et al.: PDDL-the planning domain definition language (1998)
8. Voisin, L., Abrial, J.R.: The Rodin platform has turned ten. In: Ait Ameur, Y., Schewe, K.D. (eds.) Abstract State Machines, Alloy, B, TLA, VDM, and Z. ABZ 2014. LNCS, vol. 8477, pp. 1–8. Springer, Heidelberg (2014). https://doi.org/10.1007/978-3-662-43652-3_1

Cooperative Strategies for Decision Making and Optimization

An Integrated Artificial Bee Colony Algorithm for Scheduling Jobs and Flexible Maintenance with Learning and Deteriorating Effects

Nesrine Touafek[1(✉)], Fatima Benbouzid-Si Tayeb[1], Asma Ladj[2],
Alaeddine Dahamni[1], and Riyadh Baghdadi[3]

[1] Laboratoire des Méthodes de Conception de Systèmes (LMCS), Ecole nationale
Supérieure d'Informatique (ESI), 68M-16270 Oued Smar, Algiers, Algeria
en_touafek@esi.dz
[2] Railenium Research and Technology Institute, 59540 Valenciennes, France
[3] New York University Abu Dhabi, Abu Dhabi, UAE

Abstract. In this paper, we address two versions of the permutation
flowshop scheduling problem (PFSP) with makespan minimization under
availability constraints with learning and deteriorating effects. Availability constraints are due to flexible maintenance activities scheduled based
on prognostics and health management (PHM) results. In the first study,
human learning effect is considered and position-dependent model is
applied to generate variable maintenance processing times. In the second
one, besides learning effect, time-dependent machine deteriorating jobs
are assumed. Since the PFSP is proven to be NP-complete, improved
artificial bees colony algorithms were proposed. Intense computational
experiments are carried out on Taillard's well known benchmarks, to
which we add both PHM and maintenance data. The results of comparison and experiments show the efficiency of our algorithms.

Keywords: Permutation flowshop scheduling problem · Learning
effect · Deteriorating effect · Flexible maintenance · PHM · Artificial
bee colony

1 Introduction

The permutation flowshop scheduling problem (PFSP) is an attractive combinatorial problem in the field of scheduling, encountered in many real world
applications given its practical relevance [30]. Classical PFSP problems assumed
a stable and deterministic context. In such context, all machines are supposed
to be continuously available throughout the scheduling horizon and job processing times are assumed to be constant and independent of human factor impact.
However, in real industry settings, these hypotheses fail. Indeed, machines can be
unavailable for multiple reasons, such as inspections, maintenance interventions,

© The Author(s), under exclusive license to Springer Nature Switzerland AG 2022
N. T. Nguyen et al. (Eds.): ICCCI 2022, LNAI 13501, pp. 647–659, 2022.
https://doi.org/10.1007/978-3-031-16014-1_51

sudden breakdowns, etc. [20]. Moreover, job processing times may be extended due to machine deterioration effects [13] caused by the increased usage and time, or shortened as a result of the human learning effects [10] caused by frequent repetition of identical tasks. Regarding these features and to deal with more realistic environment, recent research works are focusing on extending classical models to include practical constraints. Therefore, machines unavailability constraints, learning as well as deteriorating effects are recently introduced in the study of scheduling problems.

In industries, equipment maintenance is an important key factor, and affects the operation time of equipment and its efficiency. Thus, equipment faults need to be identified and solved, avoiding shutdown in the production processes. The evolution of modern techniques (e.g., Internet of things, sensing technology, artificial intelligence, etc.) reflects the transition of maintenance strategies from Corrective Maintenance (CM) to Preventive Maintenance (PvM) to the more advanced Predictive Maintenance (PdM) based on prognostic health management (PHM) [8]. PdM is performed based on an online estimate of the "health" status of the machine and can achieve timely pre-failure interventions. PdM allows the maintenance frequency to be as low as possible to prevent unplanned CM, without incurring costs associated with doing too much PvM.

In almost studies dealing with the joint optimization of production and maintenance, the maintenance duration is assumed to be constant regardless the current condition of the machine or operator. However, this assumption fails in real industry settings due to the uncertainty of the machine or the operator condition. Indeed, the maintenance duration may be affected by the machine deteriorating effect in that the later maintenance is planed, the worse the machine conditions are, hence, a longer time is needed to perform the maintenance. On the other hand, the learning effect of the operator may shorten the maintenance duration by repeating the same operating processes frequently. Scheduling problems with variable maintenance times are studied in the literature. While deteriorating maintenance activities are most often considered [17,19,31]. Nonetheless, variable maintenance durations due to the learning effect are scarcely studied.

To the best of authors' knowledge, the joint scheduling problem of production and PHM-based predictive maintenance with learning and deteriorating effects, was never studied in the literature. In this context, we propose to first study the PFSP with flexible maintenance and variable maintenance duration due to the learning effect, and then with deteriorating jobs and variable maintenance duration due to the learning effect simultaneously, with makespan minimization. When maintenance activities and production jobs are scheduled simultaneously, the problem becomes NP-hard in strong sense [22]. In this paper, the formulated joint scheduling problem is even more complex. As well as allocating jobs and maintenance activities to machines, the learning and deteriorating effects on processing times are also considered. Therefore, metaheuristics seem to be the most promising resolution approach given their ability to provide near optimal solutions with reasonable computational times.

In recent decades, the popularity of swarm intelligence algorithms has increased. Complex problems are solved using the behavior of living swarms such birds, bees, and ants. In this regard, the artificial bee colony (ABC) is a recently introduced swarm knowledge based algorithm to formulate NP-Hard problems [14]. It is inspired by the intelligent, self-organizing and aggregated behavior of bee colonies when searching for promising food sources associated to higher nectar amount. Motivated by its high efficiency in solving many variants of the flowshop scheduling problems such as the PFSP [2], the hybrid flowshop [18] and the flexible flowshop [28] it was adapted to solve the studied problems. So improved and adapted ABC algorithms were developed, according to the problem constraints and objectives. The main features of the proposed ABC algorithms are: (1) To get a population with a certain level of quality and diversity, we generated an initial population of integrated candidate solutions that were generated at random and "seeded" with some good solutions. This strategy not only provides a high level of diversity in the population, but it also outperforms the approach where the initial population consisted of only randomly generated integrated solutions; (2) Five local search operators to generate new neighbourhood solutions for employed bees; (3) A local search method with destruction and construction procedures to enhance the best individuals by the onlooker bees. Finally, to prove the effectiveness of our proposed algorithm, it is first compared to a variable neighborhood search (VNS) algorithm [16]. Then, intensive computational experiments are carried out on well-known Taillard's benchmarks enhanced with both PHM and maintenance data.

The rest content of the paper is structured as follows. A literature review is presented in Sect. 2. Section 3 describes the tackled scheduling problems. Section 4 is devoted to presenting the proposed ABC algorithms. Finally, Sect. 5 compares and analyses the performances of the newly designed algorithms. A general conclusion and perspectives of the work are drawn in Sect. 6.

2 A Brief Review of Scheduling Problems with Learning/Deteriorating Effects

Scheduling problems with the learning or the deteriorating effect considerations have received a lot of attention in recent years and many models were proposed in the literature which can be either time-dependent or position dependent [6]. In the former models, variable processing times of jobs depend on their processing times, while in the later, variable processing times of jobs depend on their scheduled position in the sequence. For details on this research topic, time-dependent scheduling problems are discussed in comprehensive reviews of [11] and [7], while position-dependent scheduling problems are studied in surveys of [4,6]. More recently, [29] addressed the flowshop scheduling problem under time-dependent learning effect to minimize the makespan. To solve this problem, a Branch and Bound (B&B) algorithm and heuristics were proposed. [9] studied the flowshop scheduling problem under position-dependent learning effect. They proposed a B&B algorithm and four metaheuristics to minimize the total completion time. [3] investigated the PFSP under position-dependent learning effect and time-dependent deteriorating effet. A Population-based Tabu search algorithm is proposed for its resolution.

The integrated production and maintenance scheduling problems with learning and/or deteriorating effects have been widely studied in literature. Recently, [1] addressed the integrated scheduling problem in a parallel machines configuration under position-dependent deteriorating effect to minimize makespan. To solve large-size problems, six heuristic solution methods are developed. [27] investigated the integrated single machine scheduling problem under a time-dependent deteriorating effect. To minimize the makespan and the total completion time, polynomial algorithms were proposed. [12] considered the makespan single machine scheduling problem with time-dependent deteriorating effect. Two batch-based heuristics and a iterated greedy algorithm were developed to solve the problem.

3   Problem Statement

The PFSP is a well-known scheduling problem that can be described as follows. A set J of n independent jobs $J = \{J_1, J_2, ..., J_n\}$ has to be processed on a set M of m independent machines $M = \{M_1, M_2, ..., M_m\}$ in the same order on the m machines. We assume that all jobs are available at time zero and no preemption is allowed. In order to ensure the system reliability and to prevent the occurrence of fatal breakdowns during the processing horizon, machines are monitored continuously by a PHM module. This module is able to predict, for each machine M_i, the relative time before fail after processing a job J_j, noted RUL_{ij}. This value is used to estimate the corresponding degradation of the machine M_i caused by processing the job J_j. Let σ_{ij} be this degradation, and σ_{ij}=f(RUL$_{ij}$). We fix $\sigma_{ij} = p_{ij}/RUL_{ij}$, where $0 < \sigma_{ij} < 1$. Let Δ be the maximal authorized degradation of a machine. We fix $\Delta = 1$ for all machines. When the accumulated degradation ($\sum_{j=1}^{l} \sigma_{ij}$) of a machine M_i after processing l jobs sequentially reaches this threshold, a predictive maintenance intervention (PM) should be planned. During the maintenance, the machine is not available for processing jobs and it will be restored to *"As good as new"* state after the end of the maintenance intervention. We assume also, that at least one predictive maintenance intervention is performed on each machine and no predictive maintenance operation is performed after the processing of the last job. In order to make the model more realistic, we further assume, in a first time, variable maintenance duration due to the learning effect, then variable job processing times due to the deterioration effect, besides.

Let S_i denotes a schedule of n jobs and k_i (≥ 1) predictive maintenance on machine M_i. Then S_i can be seen as a succession of $k + 1$ blocks of jobs (B_{il}) separated by predictive maintenance operations (PM_{ix}):
$S_i = \{B_{i1}, PM_{i1}, B_{i2}, PM_{i2}, ..., B_{ik}, PM_{ik}, B_{i(k+1)}\}$, where $\cup_{l=1}^{k+1} B_{il} = J$.

We use the following notations to formulate the production and the maintenance data, as well as, the problem assumptions:

p_{ij}: the normal processing time of job j on machine i.
p_{ij}^A: the actual processing time of job j on machine i.
t_{ij}: the processing time of job j on machine i.
PM_{il}: the basic processing time of the lth maintenance on machine i.
PM_{il}^A: the actual processing time of the lth maintenance on machine i.
α: the learning index.
β: the deteriorating index.

For the first scheduling problem with variable maintenance duration due to the learning effect, the actual maintenance duration are defined by the following position-dependent learning model:

$$PM_{il}^A = PM_{ij}.l^{\alpha}, -1 < \alpha < 0 \tag{1}$$

For the second scheduling problem with variable maintenance duration due to the learning effect and variable job processing times due to the deterioration effect, the actual maintenance duration are defined by Eq. (1), while the actual job processing times are defined by the following time-dependent deteriorating model:

$$P_{ij}^A = P_{ij} + \beta.t_{ij}, \beta > 0 \tag{2}$$

The objective of this study is to propose an integrated solution that combines production schedule and flexible maintenance planning so that the total completion time of the schedule after maintenance operations insertion, noted C_{max}, is minimized. Under the learning and the deteriorating effects, C_{max} depends mainly on the sum of actual processing times of maintenance operations and those of production jobs. The C_{max} of the first and the second problem respectively are calculated using formula 3 and 4 respectively, where IT refers to the total idle time of the last machine m, waiting jobs arrival and k is the number of inserted maintenance activities on the last machine m.

$$C_{max} = IT + \Sigma_{j=1}^{j=n} P_{mj}^A + \Sigma_{l=1}^{l=k} PM_{ml}^A = IT + \Sigma_{j=1}^{j=n} P_{mj} + \Sigma_{l=1}^{l=k}(PM_{mj}.l^{\alpha}) \tag{3}$$

$$C_{max} = IT + \Sigma_{j=1}^{j=n} P_{mj}^A + \Sigma_{l=1}^{l=k} PM_{ml}^A = IT + \Sigma_{j=1}^{j=n}(P_{mj} + \beta.t_{ij}) + \Sigma_{l=1}^{l=k} PM_{mj}.l^{\alpha} \tag{4}$$

4   Proposed Solving Approach

An improved and adapted artificial bee colony (ABC) algorithms are proposed to solve the two problems. In the ABC algorithm [14], candidate solutions to the problem are represented as food sources and their quality or fitness corresponds to the nectar amount. The ABC algorithm starts from previous generated solutions, and applies an iterated search process to approach the optimal solution. Each iteration of the search process consists of three main phases: employed and onlooker bees local search phases, for exploitation and scout bees global search phase, for exploration. In the employed bees phase, each food source is associated to an artificial employed bee, which generates new solutions by a neighborhood search approach. Then, the solution with the higher fitness value replaces the current one. In order to enhance the local search of optimal solution, onlooker bees apply a probability selection of the best candidate solutions and then generate new neighboring solutions using similar method as employed bees. In the scout bees phase, if a solution cannot be further improved through a limited number of iterations *limit*, then the solution is assumed to be abandoned and a new solution is generated randomly. The search process is iterated till the termination condition is met. Main steps of the proposed ABC algorithms, starting by solution representation and initial population generation, then the iterated process of employed, onlooker and scout bees phases, and finally the termination condition, are detailed in the following sub-sections.

4.1   Encoding Scheme and Solution Representation

In the proposed ABC algorithms, a food source (solution) is represented by a two-field structure corresponding each to production and predictive maintenance. For production part, a sequence S represents the execution order of production jobs by machines. For maintenance part, a $m * (n - 1)$ binary matrix PM that represents the positions of predictive maintenance on the m machines is used [5]. If an element $M[i, j]$ is set to 1 value, then a predictive maintenance is scheduled on the ith machine after the jth job. Otherwise $M[i, j] = 0$.

For instance, let S=(1 9 3 8 5 6 7 4 2 0), and M=$\begin{pmatrix} 0 1 0 0 1 0 0 0 1 \\ 0 0 1 0 0 1 0 0 0 \\ 0 1 0 0 0 1 0 0 0 \end{pmatrix}$, represent a solution of an integrated flowshop scheduling problem with $m = 3$ machines and $n = 10$ jobs. Then, the execution order of the ten jobs and predictive maintenance operations on the three machines is the following:

Machine 1: j_1, j_9, PM_{11}, j_3, j_8, j_5, PM_{12}, j_6, j_7, j_4, j_2, PM_{13}, j_0
Machine 2: j_1, j_9, j_3, PM_{21}, j_8, j_5, j_6, PM_{22} j_7, j_4, j_2, j_0
Machine 3: j_1, j_9, PM_{31}, j_3, j_8, j_5, j_6, PM_{32}, j_7, j_4, j_2, j_0

4.2   Initial Population Generation

In order to generate an initial population of *PopSize* complete integrated solutions (S, PM), we propose a two-step initialization procedure as follows:

- **Step 1.** Firstly, we generated a mixed initial production population which comprises: (1) one production sequence generated using the well-known NEH heuristic [21] ; (2) α%PopSize production sequences generated using the modified NEH [23]; (3) the remaining part, and the largest one, consists of $(100 - \alpha)$%PopSize randomly generated production sequences. Thus, we ensure quality and diversity of the research space.
- **Step 2.** After generating production sequences in Step 1, predictive maintenance activities are scheduled using the PHM-based greedy heuristic of [15].

In this heuristic, maintenance operations are inserted according to the current accumulate degradation of machine estimated by the PHM module, starting from the first machine M_1 to the last one M_m.

4.3   Employed Bees Phase

Each artificial employed bee is placed on a complete integrated solution (S, M) and performs a local search, based either on the production sequence S or on the maintenance matrix M, for an improved one through the local neighborhood. If the fitness of the generated solution is higher, then the current one is replaced and the *nb_trails* counter is reset. Otherwise, the *nb_trails* counter of the current solution is incremented. From prior literature, we learn that two common operators, insert and swap, are commonly used to generate neighboring solutions [24]. Therefore, these neighborhoods are applied in this paper. These neighborhood structures allow to create new solutions by changing the execution order of production jobs. Besides, a third type of neighborhood structure by shifting predictive maintenance tasks, is used. In each iteration of the employed bees phase, one of these operators is chosen randomly with a uniform distribution. Based on these neighborhoods, five local search operators are described as follows:

1. **Swap move on production jobs.** it consists in swapping the positions of two production jobs selected randomly from the production sequence.
2. **Double swap move on production jobs.** It consists of making two consecutive swap moves on the production sequence.
3. **Insert move on production.** it consists in selecting a production job randomly and then inserting it into another selected position in the production sequence.
4. **Double insert move on production jobs.** It consists of making two consecutive insert moves.
5. **Right/Left shift move on maintenance activities.** it consists in choosing a maintenance intervention in a selected machine and randomly shifting it to the left, i.e. before the previous job in the sequence, or to the right, i.e. after the next one.

After generating a new solution by the employed bee, the positions of PM operations may be perturbed. Therefore, the maintenance insertion heuristic should be applied again to re-adjust the PM positions.

4.4   Onlooker Bees Phase

In order to enhance the intensification of promising food sources, the onlooker bees use the roulette wheel selection where solutions with higher fitness value have higher probability to be selected. Probability value for each solution is given by Eq. 5. Then a local search method borrowed from the iterated local search (ILS) algorithm [26] with destruction and reconstruction procedures is applied on selected solutions to explore possible promising neighbors.

$$p(sol_i) = \frac{fitness(sol_i)}{\sum_{k=1}^{n} fitness(sol_k)} \tag{5}$$

4.5 Scout Bees Phase

In order to escape from local optima and to allow diversification, the food sources whose *nb_trials* is greater than the limited number of iterations *limit* are abandoned and their associated employee bees become scout bees. Subsequently, they randomly generate new food sources.

4.6 Termination Condition

The termination condition of the proposed ABC is a maximum number of iterations of the algorithm or when the limit of the number of iterations without improving the best solution is reached.

5   Experimental Testing and Analyses

In this section, we present the results of computational experiments we conducted to test the newly proposed ABC algorithms on Microsoft Azure NC6 Promo virtual machine with six cores and 6 GB RAM. Firstly, details on test environment and data generation are given. Then, a performance comparison of the proposed ABC algorithms against the VNS algorithm of [16] is conducted, where joint scheduling problem of production and PHM-based predictive maintenance without effects of learning and deteriorating, is considered. Finally, computational results testing the performances of our algorithms to resolve the two studied problems are analysed and CPU times are discussed.

5.1 Data Generation

The test instances are generated using the well-known Taillard's benchmark instances [25] comprising 120 instances with different size of jobs and machines (n × m) where n ∈ {20, 50, 100, 200} and m ∈ {5, 10, 20}, to which we add PHM and maintenance data For PHM data, we consider three kinds of jobs according to their processing times intervals as follow:

1. Jobs with processing times < 20 inducing small machine degradation σ_{ij} generated from a uniform distribution $\mathcal{U}[0.02; 0.03]$.
2. Jobs with processing times between 20 and 50 inducing medium machine degradation σ_{ij} generated from a uniform distribution $\mathcal{U}[0.03; 0.06]$.
3. Jobs with processing times > 50 inducing big machine degradation σ_{ij} generated from a uniform distribution $\mathcal{U}[0.06; 0.1]$.

For maintenance data, two levels of maintenance durations are separately considered as follow:

1. First level with medium maintenance durations generated from a uniform distribution $\mathcal{U}[50, 100]$.
2. Second level with long maintenance durations generated from a uniform distribution $\mathcal{U}[100, 150]$.

The performance of the proposed ABC algorithm to solve the different problems is evaluated based on the following metrics:

1. P_RPD : the relative percentage deviation of the returned C_{max} over the best known solution C_{max}^{best} (upper bound) for each instance as described in Eq. 6.

$$P\_RPD = \frac{C_{max} - C_{max}^{best}}{C_{max}^{best}} \times 100. \tag{6}$$

2. CPU: computational time of the proposed algorithm.

5.2 Performance Analysis of the Proposed ABC Without Effects

The first set of tests is conducted to evaluate the performances of the ABC algorithm when comparing to a VNS algorithm [16]. ABC parameters are set as follow: $PopSize = 70$, $Max\_iterations = 200$, $limit = 5$, $onlooker\_bees\% = 40\%$. For a fair comparison, the VNS algorithm was re-executed on the same machine and instances as the ABC algorithm. The results of comparison based on the P_RPD and CPU values are listed in Table 1, for the two levels of maintenance durations.

One can notice that best P_RPD values are provided by the ABC algorithm for almost the instances except instances (50×5, 50×10, 50×20). The mean difference between the two algorithms is 02.29%, which can go up to 10.19% for the 20×20 benchmark for the first level of maintenance and it is of 0.93% for the second level of maintenance. This enhance the efficiency of our ABC algorithm with its embedded local search methods for solution intensification and global search approach for diversification throughout an iterated process. On the other hand, comparing the computational times (CPU) of the two algorithms, we notice that, for small instances (20×5, 20×10, 20×20, 50×5) VNS is faster than ABC. For the other instances, ABC is faster than VNS with a mean difference of 2915.51 s which can go up to 05.07 h for the 200×20 benchmark. We note that we did not could run VNS tests for instances of size 500×20 because of too long execution times.

5.3 Performance Analysis of the Proposed ABC with Learning Effects

In this section, we report experiment results evaluating the performance of the ABC algorithm to solve the integrated scheduling problem with variable maintenance durations due to the learning effect. For each instance described in Sect. 5.1, we generate The learning indexes of the maintenance processing times randomly from a uniform distribution within three different modes, as follow:

1. Mode 1: small common learning index in [0, 0.20] reflecting low learning rate among maintenance operators.
2. Mode 2: large common learning index in [0.80, 1] reflecting high learning rate among maintenance operators.

Table 1. P_RPD and CPU results for ABC and VNS.

Instance	P_RPD for level 1		P_RPD for level 2		CPU time (s)	
	VNS	ABC	VNS	ABC	VNS	ABC
20 × 5	11.52	4.62	10.617	3.68	0.85	15.94
20 × 10	23.01	12.82	24.199	14.05	1.97	22.47
20 × 20	28.19	25.03	32.982	27.52	5.54	34.38
50 × 5	1.72	1.94	1.933	3.03	19.32	29.56
50 × 10	8.24	9.8	9.955	12.39	55.93	50.32
50 × 20	18.50	19.69	19.276	24.9	198.85	72.73
100 × 5	1.35	1.17	1.463	1.47	178.05	53.2
100 × 10	5.09	4.37	5.483	6.23	569.9	103.36
100 × 20	15.00	13.47	15.614	16.43	2375.4	166.37
200 × 10	3.13	1.75	3.429	2.52	10116	234.4
200 × 20	11.21	7.25	12.549	9.64	20808	262.61
500 × 20		3		3.04		1761.34
Average	11.55	9.26	12.50	11.57	3149.40	233.89

3. Mode 3: different learning indexes per machine in $[0, 1]$ reflecting dependency of the learning rate on machine characteristics.

Results of the execution of the ABC algorithm on the different instances with the two levels of maintenance durations and the three modes of learning indexes (LE_M1, LE_M2, LE_M3) are given in Table 2.

For small size instances ($n = 20$), we notice equivalent C_{max} deviation values for the ABC algorithm in the two cases where the learning effect is considered (see Table 2) or no (see Table 1). While a significant decrease of P_RPD can be noticed when the learning effect is considered in case of large size instances and high learning indexes. Consequently, we can deduce that the learning effect has no significant impact on the P_RPD when few maintenance interventions are inserted (the case of small size instances) as well as in case of low learning rate among maintenance operators. On the other hand, the learning effect manifests clearly when an important number of maintenance interventions are inserted (the case of large size instances) as well as in case of high learning rate.

5.4 Performance Analysis of the Proposed ABC with Learning and Deteriorating Effects

In this section, experiment results evaluating the performance of the ABC algorithm to solve the integrated scheduling problem with both deteriorating jobs and variable maintenance durations due to the learning effect, are listed in Table 2 for the two levels of maintenance (LDE columns). We used the instances described in Sect. 5.1, to which we added learning and deteriorating indexes generated for each machine, randomly from a uniform distribution in $[0, 1]$.

Table 2. P_RPD results for first and second problems

Instance	P_RPD for level 1				P_RPD for level 2			
	LE_M1	LE_M2	LE_M3	LDE	LE_M1	LE_M2	LE_M3	LDE
20×5	4.47	4.73	4.4	13.04	3.35	3.29	3.38	12.45
20×10	12.81	13.34	13.69	23.66	14.44	14.22	14.2	23.02
20×20	24.76	25.1	25.11	37.3	27.2	26.95	27.28	36.17
50×5	1.87	0.21	0.76	11.3	2.24	−0.43	1.24	12.09
50×10	8.98	6.85	7.63	18.49	12.26	8.15	9.86	19.32
50×20	19.43	16	17.66	28.54	23.37	18.69	20.96	30.06
100×5	0.39	−2.82	−1.47	10.84	0.38	−4.3	−1.55	11.45
100×10	3.7	−0.4	1.84	13.29	4.93	−1.62	1.52	13.32
100×20	12.39	7.71	9.9	21.41	14.46	6.52	9.3	20.32
200×10	0.43	−3.84	−1	12.86	0.74	−6.36	−2.1	8.91
200×20	6.31	0.7	3.45	17.69	7.16	−1.36	3.19	15.01
500×20	1.26	−4.39	−0.52	13.04	0.23	−8.17	−2.49	12.45
Average	8.69	6.14	7.45	23.66	10.05	5.80	7.93	23.02

We notice a significant increase of C_{max} deviations values in this case where the deteriorating effect on job processing times is considered comparing to those of the first problem where no deteriorating effect is considered. Therefore, we can conclude that the deteriorating effect has a negative impact on the makespan because of the insertion of additional delays.

An important note to highlight is that, high C_{max} deviations do not reflect bad solution quality since they are calculated relatively to Taillard best known solutions with no consideration of maintenance operations and learning/deteriorating effects. Therefore, the presented P_RPD deviations (for all the experiments) are much higher than it should be if they were calculated with respect to a more precise lower bound which takes into account maintenance tasks and learning/deteriorating effects, as reported in [16].

6   Conclusion

In this paper, two makespan minimization flowshop scheduling problems under flexible maintenance activities with learning and deteriorating effects, are investigated. The maintenance activities are scheduled based on PHM post decision approach. Motivated by the complexity of the presented problems, an improved and adapted ABC algorithm is developed for their resolution. To prove the high performances of the ABC algorithm, a total of 3600 executions of the ABC algorithms is conducted on different combinations of problems data and constraints. The ABC algorithm is also compared to a VNS algorithm developed for the same problem in literature. All the experiment results show the efficiency of our proposed algorithm with its embedded local search methods for solution intensification and global search approach for diversification throughout an iterated process. As perspective of this work and given the lack of suitable test benchmarks, we propose to extend the taillard well-known benchmark with maintenance, learning and deteriorating effects data for a standard comparison study. Furthermore, it will be interesting to use the Machine learning algorithms to calibrate the ABC algorithm parameters and to propose ideal learning/deteriorating effects' indexes.

References

1. Alfares, H., Mohammed, A., Ghaleb, M.: Two-machine scheduling with aging effects and variable maintenance activities. Comput. Ind. Eng. **160**, 107586 (2021)
2. Arık, O.A.: Artificial bee colony algorithm including some components of iterated greedy algorithm for permutation flow shop scheduling problems. Neural Comput. Appl. **33**(8), 3469–3486 (2020). https://doi.org/10.1007/s00521-020-05174-1
3. Arık, O.A.: Population-based tabu search with evolutionary strategies for permutation flow shop scheduling problems under effects of position-dependent learning and linear deterioration. Soft Comput. **25**(2), 1501–1518 (2021)
4. Bachman, A., Janiak, A.: Scheduling jobs with position-dependent processing times. J. Oper. Res. Soc. **55**(3), 257–264 (2004)
5. Benbouzid-Sitayeb, F., Guebli, S.A., Bessadi, Y., Varnier, C., Zerhouni, N.: Joint scheduling of jobs and preventive maintenance operations in the flowshop sequencing problem: a resolution with sequential and integrated strategies. Int. J. Manuf. Res. **6**(1), 30–48 (2011)
6. Biskup, D.: A state-of-the-art review on scheduling with learning effects. Eur. J. Oper. Res. **188**(2), 315–329 (2008)
7. Blazewicz, J., Ecker, K.H., Pesch, E., Schmidt, G., Sterna, M., Weglarz, J.: Time-dependent scheduling. In: Handbook on Scheduling, pp. 431–474. Springer, Heidelberg (2019). https://doi.org/10.1007/978-3-540-69446-5
8. Bougacha, O., Varnier, C., Zerhouni, N., Hajri-Gabouj, S.: Integrated production and predictive maintenance planning based on prognostic information. In: 2019 International Conference on Advanced Systems and Emergent Technologies (IC_ASET), pp. 363–368. IEEE (2019)
9. Wu, C.C., et al.: A branch-and-bound algorithm and four metaheuristics for minimizing total completion time for a two-stage assembly flow-shop scheduling problem with learning consideration. Eng. Optim. **52**(6), 1009–1036 (2020)
10. Biskup, D.: Single-machine scheduling with learning considerations. Eur. J. Oper. Res. **115**, 173–178 (1999)
11. Gawiejnowicz, S.: A review of four decades of time-dependent scheduling: main results, new topics, and open problems. J. Schedul. **23**(1), 3–47 (2020). https://doi.org/10.1007/s10951-019-00630-w
12. Xu, H., Li, X., Ruiz, R., Zhu, H.: Group scheduling with nonperiodical maintenance and deteriorating effects. IEEE Trans. Syst Man Cybern Syst. **51**, 1–13 (2019). https://doi.org/10.1109/tsmc.2019.2917446
13. Gupta, J.N., Gupta, S.K.: Single facility scheduling with nonlinear processing times. Comput. Ind. Eng. **14**, 387–393 (1988). https://doi.org/10.1016/0360-8352(88)90041-1

14. Karaboga, D., et al.: An idea based on honey bee swarm for numerical optimization. Technical report, Technical report-tr06, Erciyes University, Engineering Faculty, Computer (2005)

15. Ladj, A., Varnier, C., Tayeb, F.S.: IPRO-GA: an integrated prognostic based GA for scheduling jobs and predictive maintenance in a single multifunctional machine. IFAC-PapersOnLine **49**(12), 1821–1826 (2016)

16. Ladj, A., Tayeb, F.B.S., Varnier, C., Dridi, A.A., Selmane, N.: A hybrid of variable neighbor search and fuzzy logic for the permutation flowshop scheduling problem with predictive maintenance. Procedia Comput. Sci. **112**, 663–672 (2017)

17. Li, X.J., Wang, J.J.: Parallel machines scheduling based on the impact of deteriorating maintenance. J. Interdisc. Math. **21**(3), 729–741 (2018)

18. Li, Y.: A discrete artificial bee colony algorithm for distributed hybrid flowshop scheduling problem with sequence-dependent setup times. Int. J. Prod. Res. **59**(13), 3880–3899 (2021)

19. Lu, S., Liu, X., Pei, J., Thai, M.T., Pardalos, P.M.: A hybrid abc-ts algorithm for the unrelated parallel-batching machines scheduling problem with deteriorating jobs and maintenance activity. Appl. Soft Comput. **66**, 168–182 (2018)

20. Ma, Y., Chu, C., Zuo, C.: A survey of scheduling with deterministic machine availability constraints. Comput. Ind. Eng. **58**(2), 199–211 (2010)

21. Nawaz, M., Enscore, E.E., Jr., Ham, I.: A heuristic algorithm for the m-machine, n-job flow-shop sequencing problem. Omega **11**(1), 91–95 (1983)

22. Qi, X., Chen, T., Tu, F.: Scheduling the maintenance on a single machine. J. Oper. Res. Soc. **50**(10), 1071–1078 (1999)

23. Ruiz, R., Maroto, C., Alcaraz, J.: Two new robust genetic algorithms for the flowshop scheduling problem. Omega **34**(5), 461–476 (2006)

24. Ruiz, R., Stützle, T.: A simple and effective iterated greedy algorithm for the permutation flowshop scheduling problem. Eur. J. Oper. Res. **177**(3), 2033–2049 (2007)

25. Taillard, E.: Benchmarks for basic scheduling problems. Eur. J. Oper. Res. **64**(2), 278–285 (1993)

26. Tasgetiren, M.F., Pan, Q.K., Suganthan, P., Oner, A.: A discrete artificial bee colony algorithm for the no-idle permutation flowshop scheduling problem with the total tardiness criterion. Appl. Math. Model. **37**(10–11), 6758–6779 (2013)

27. Sun, X., Geng, X.N.: Single-machine scheduling with deteriorating effects and machine maintenance. Int. J. Prod. Res. **57**, 3186–3199 (2019). https://doi.org/10.1080/00207543.2019.1566675

28. Xuan, H., Zhang, H., Li, B.: An improved discrete artificial bee colony algorithm for flexible flowshop scheduling with step deteriorating jobs and sequence-dependent setup times. Math. Prob. Eng. **2019** (2019)

29. Zou, Y., et al.: Two-stage three-machine assembly scheduling problem with sum-of-processing-times-based learning effect. Soft Comput. **24**(7), 5445–5462 (2019). https://doi.org/10.1007/s00500-019-04301-y

30. Yenisey, M.M., Yagmahan, B.: Multi-objective permutation flow shop scheduling problem: literature review, classification and current trends. Omega **45**, 119–135 (2014)

31. Zhang, X., Wu, W.H., Lin, W.C., Wu, C.C.: Machine scheduling problems under deteriorating effects and deteriorating rate-modifying activities. J. Oper. Res. Soc., 1–10 (2017)

Chaotic Dingo Optimization Algorithm: Application in Feature Selection for Beamforming Aided Spectrum Sensing

Sarra Ben Chaabane[1(✉)], Kais Bouallegue[2], Akram Belazi[3],
Sofiane Kharbech[1], and Ammar Bouallegue[1]

[1] Laboratory Sys'Com-ENIT (LR-99-ES21), Tunis El Manar University,
Tunis 1002, Tunisia
sarra.benchaabane@enit.utm.tn
[2] Laboratory IETR-UMR (CNRS-6164), University of Rennes, Rennes, France
[3] Laboratory RISC-ENIT (LR-16-ES07), Tunis El Manar University,
Tunis 1002, Tunisia

Abstract. Spectrum sensing based on Beamforming, like others classification problem, require feature selection to perform learning algorithms and enhance the classification task. This paper proposes a novel version of the Dingo Optimization Algorithm (DOA) to optimize feature selection for a Deep Neural Network (DNN) classifier. Two improvements are introduced to avoid the premature convergence problem and stagnation in the local optima of the original DOA. First, the chaos strategy is executed to produce a high level of diversification in the algorithm, which improves its ability to escape from potential local optimums. Second, the weight factor is introduced to boot up the search process to the global optima. Here, the aim is to improve the DOA for feature selection in the deep learning approach in order to enhance the performance of blind spectrum sensing based on Beamforming in the context of cognitive radio (CR). Through simulations results, we illustrate that our algorithm, called Chaotic Dingo Optimization Algorithm (CDOA), outperforms the original one and a set of state-of-the-art optimization algorithms (i.e., HS, BBO, PSO, and SA) for feature selection in the learning approach.

Keywords: DOA optimization algorithm · Deep learning · Feature selection · Cognitive radio · Spectrum sensing · Beamforming

1 Introduction

Nowadays, dimensionality reduction has become the most common preprocessing step to prepare the dataset for machine learning algorithms. Dimensionality reduction helps machine learning and data mining algorithms be faster and more efficient. The feature selection approach is a critical pre-processing step to eliminate the irrelevant, redundant, and noisy data and find a set of

N. T. Nguyen et al. (Eds.): ICCCI 2022, LNAI 13501, pp. 660–673, 2022.
https://doi.org/10.1007/978-3-031-16014-1_52

informative features [19]. Feature Selection algorithms are classified into two main categories: filter-based algorithms and wrapper-based algorithms [4]. Filter-based algorithms depend on statistical methods to calculate the relation between features and find optimal parameters. On the other hand, Wrapper-based algorithms are based on machine learning algorithms to find near-optimal features. Although Wrapper-based algorithms are computationally expensive, they obtain better results than filter-based algorithms in selecting features, as shown in the results in [13]. Meta-heuristic algorithms have been well applied as wrapper methods for feature selection in machine learning [5,10,18,27]. They are divided into three basic categories: physics-based [6], evolutionary-based [16], and swarm-based [25]. Thus, many studies have been presented to improve the performance of meta-heuristic algorithms and overcome this problem. Most of these studies used chaotic theory in their system [3,11,15,29]. Chaos is one of the most common mathematical approaches recently employed to boost the performance of meta-heuristic algorithms. It is defined as the simulation of the dynamic behavior of nonlinear systems [28]. In this work, a novel hybridization approach based on Dingo Optimization Algorithm (DOA) and chaos theory are proposed, referred to as CDOA, that later on will be utilized for the feature selection. DOA is a recent swarm algorithm presented by Hernan and Adrian, imitating the hunting behavior of the dingoes [26].

The main contributions of this paper are two-fold: (i) We introduce chaos theory to control the main parameter of DOA, which helps in balancing exploration and exploitation and enhancing the solution precision; (ii) inertia weight is added to tune the influence on the current best solution, improving convergence speed and avoiding the entrapment in local optima.

To validate its performance, the proposed algorithm is compared first, with a variety of most popular optimization algorithms, the original version, i.e., DOA, Particle Swarm Optimization (PSO) [14], Biogeography-Based Optimization (BBO) [30], harmony search (HS) [2], and Simulated Annealing (SA) [1] on common benchmark functions before evaluating them for feature selection example to give a better misclassification rate for the studied classification problem. The classification problem aborded in this paper is blind spectrum sensing based on Beamformer Receiver for Cognitive Radio, using a deep learning model. Indeed, the CR is exploited in many applications, as e-Health in Wireless Sensor Network (WBSN) or in Structural Health Monitoring (SHM). The CR network is also used for safety and civil use in smart city and home, and also in military domain and satellite [12,24]. Spectrum Sensing (SS) is the process of monitoring a distinct wireless communication frequency band, aiming to detect the presence or absence of primary users [21]. Beamforming is a signal processing technique used for directional signal transmission or reception in sensor arrays [20]

This paper is structured as follows. In Sect. 2, we formulate the optimization problem. Section 3 illustrates the original DOA algorithm and introduces our motivation and improvements. The proposed algorithm is evaluated by twelve optimization benchmark functions in Sect. 4. In Sect 5, the performance of the

CDOA algorithm in feature selection is discussed. Finally, Sect 6 summarizes the main concluding remarks and suggests new directions for future research.

2 Problem Formulation

In order to highlight the performance of the contribution for feature selection, the SS for CR represents the most suitable paradigm for classification task. The SS method is based on beamforming combined with the ratio of the maximum energy among different directions to the mean one of the received signal. The system model is the one described in [7]. Here, we assume a SU as a CR system with M ($M > 1$) linear antennas. In the CR context, we define two main hypotheses noted H1 when the PU is present and H0 when the frequency resource is vacant. DNN is performed for binary classification, making it a good candidate for the SS paradigm (H0 or H1). We applied the Deep Feed-forward Neural Network [13]. The feed-forward model always pushes in one direction and never backward, while the data may give through multiple hidden nodes.

The inputs of the DNN are the statistical tests of different SS based on beamforming approach using normalized received energy from different sectors. The layers include three hidden layers and two outputs representing H1 and H0 hypotheses. The tenfold cross-validation method has also been preferred in classification and feature selection phases to increase the reliability of the result. Hence, the fundamental objective is to find the optimal feature set denoted $\{\mathcal{F}\}^*$ that provides the minimum misclassification rate. It can be formulated as the optimization problem shown as:

$$\{\mathcal{F}\}^* = \underset{F \in \mathbb{R}^{(1 \times nf)+}}{\arg \min} \frac{1}{|\mathcal{F}|} \sum_{i \in \mathcal{F}} \left(\mathbf{Y}_i \neq \tilde{\mathbf{Y}}_i\right), \tag{1}$$

where $\{\mathcal{F}\}$ is the set of the selected features and $|\mathcal{F}|$ is its cardinality, nf is the number of features. $\mathbf{Y}$ and $\hat{\mathbf{Y}}$ present the true class and DNN output (predicted class), repectivelly, used in classification problems.

3 Improvements on Dingo Optimization Algorithm

3.1 DOA, the Basic Algorithm

The dingo optimization algorithm (DOA) is a recent swarm algorithm proposed for global optimization. It is inspired by the hunting strategies of Dingoes, which are attacking by persecution, grouping tactics, and scavenging behavior developed using (2), (3), and (4), respectively. The optimization algorithm is inspired by the dog Dingo, living in The Australia, which faces possible extinction. So, in this algorithm, the survival probability of dingoes is also considered, as in (5).

$$\mathbf{x}_i[k+1] = \beta_1 \sum_{j=1}^{n} \frac{(\varphi[j] - \mathbf{x}_i[k])}{n} - \mathbf{x}^*[k], \tag{2}$$

$$\mathbf{x}_i[k+1] = \mathbf{x}^*[k] + \beta_1 e^{\beta_2} \left(\mathbf{x}_1^r[k] - \mathbf{x}_i[k]\right), \tag{3}$$

$$\mathbf{x}_i[k+1] = \frac{1}{2} \left(e^{\beta_2} \mathbf{x}_1^r[k] - (-1)^\sigma \mathbf{x}_i[k]\right), \tag{4}$$

$$\mathbf{x}_i[k+1] = \mathbf{x}^*[k] + \frac{1}{2} \left(\mathbf{x}_1^r[k] - (-1)^\sigma \mathbf{x}_2^r[k]\right), \tag{5}$$

where $\mathbf{x}_i[k]$ is the position of a search agent at iteration k, The set $\{\mathbf{x}_i\}_{i=1}^{n}$ is identified as the dingoes' population, n is the number of search agents. $\mathbf{x}_1^r$ and $\mathbf{x}_2^r$ are a random vector selected from the current population. , $\varphi[j]$ is a sub-set of search agents, $\mathbf{x}^*[k]$ is the best search agent found from the previous iteration, and β_1 and β_2 are a random number uniformly generated in the interval of $[-2, 2]$, and σ is a binary number randomly generated. Figure 1 depicts the flowchart of DOA algorithm.

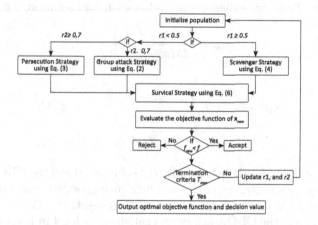

Fig. 1. Flowchart of the DOA algorithm.

3.2 Motivation and Improvements

Using the survival strategy, DOA is very competitive in exploiting the search space. However, like many other optimization algorithms, it still suffers from the problem of stagnation in local optima and low convergence rate. Figure 2(a) and Fig. 3(a) show the evaluated solutions using the DOA algorithm for optimizing f_3 and f_8 (two selected benchmark functions [26]), their corresponding convergence visualizations are plotted in Fig. 2(b) and Fig. 3(b), respectively. As observed in these figures, the algorithm fails to reach the best solution (here, the global optima, i.e., the $(0; 0)$ pair). In addition, we can note that the DOA is unable to converge to the global optima. Therefore, to overcome the mentioned issues, firstly, we apply the chaos theory. Chaotic methods have essential properties such as ergodicity, stochastically intrinsic, and showing irregular conduct [22]. These properties have been translated to various equations called "chaotic maps" for computational applications such as optimization problems. So, using these maps to replace random variables with chaotic variables can escape from local optima and attain a high- speed search than random search. The original has mainly two parameters, r_1 and r_2, which affect its performance. As seen in the flowchart of DOA, the two main parameters influence updating position of a dingo. Therefore, the tuning of these parameters using chaotic maps plays an essential role in improving the DOA mechanism to balance exploration and exploitation and avoid the stagnation problem. The Sine-Tangent chaotic mapping strategy proposed in Literature [31] is adopted in this paper. The model is as follows:

$$a_{i+1} = \sin\left(u\tan\left(\frac{3}{2a_i}\right)\right), \tag{6}$$

where $a_0 > 0$ and $u \geq 0.5$. Secondly, we involve an inertia weight w, as in (8) and (9), to provide the best solution to guide the search agents around the most optimal areas. Thus, we enhance the exploitation and solution accuracy.

$$w = \sin\left(\frac{\pi t}{2Max_{iter}} - \frac{\pi}{2}\right) + 1, \tag{7}$$

$$\mathbf{x}_i[k+1] = \beta_1 \sum_{j=1}^{n} \frac{(\varphi[k] - \mathbf{x}_i[k])}{n} - w\mathbf{x}^*[k], \tag{8}$$

$$\mathbf{x}_i[k+1] = w\mathbf{x}^*[k] + \beta_1 e^{\beta_2}\left(\mathbf{x}_1^r[k] - \mathbf{x}_i[k]\right), \tag{9}$$

Figure 2(c) and Fig. 3(c) show the evaluated solutions using the CDOA algorithm for optimizing f_3 and f_8, respectively. Their correspondent convergence visualizations are plotted in Fig. 2(d) and Fig. 3(d), respectively. As can be observed from these figures, the CDOA achieved a satisfactory level in leading to the best solution. Moreover, it is efficient in converging toward the global optima. All the above results confirm that these improvements enhance the DOA algorithm. Figure 4 illustrates the flowchart of the CDOA algorithm.

4   Benchmarking of DOA and CDOA Algorithms

The proposed CDOA is tested by solving 12 benchmark functions under dimension 30 (dimension of agent) reported in [26]. These functions are grouped into unimodal functions ($f_1 - f_6$) with one local optimum and multimodal functions ($f_7 - f_{12}$) with many local optima. The number of search agents is set to 40 for all tests. In addition to the original DOA algorithm, the proposed CDOA algorithm is compared with BBO, HS, PSO, and SA algorithms.

4.1 Comparison Based on Solution Accuracy

Table 1 depicts the performance of the CDOA via the best mean values (Mean), the standard deviations (SD), and the standard errors of means (SEM). The results for the unimodal functions ($f_1 - f_6$) indicate that CDOA is much better than the original algorithm and succeeds in reaching the global optima. Thus, we can affirm that the proposed algorithm is convenient for boosting the exploitation performance. Unlike the unimodal functions, the multimodal benchmark functions ($f_7 - f_{12}$), have many local optimums. As a result, they are suitable for testing the exploration of a given algorithm. From the reported results, CDOA outperforms DOA as well as the comparative algorithms.

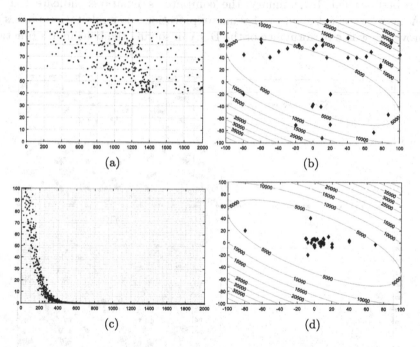

Fig. 2. Evaluated solutions, in terms of objective function #evaluations, for f_3 using (a) DOA and (c) CDOA; corresponding convergence visualizations (b) and (d) in accordance with (a) and (c).

4.2 Comparison Based on Convergence

The speed of attaining global optimum is a critical factor in estimating the performance of a given optimization algorithm. Table 2 shows this factor, expressed by the mean number of function evaluations (MeanFES) and the success rate (SR). CDOA presents the highest SR and the lowest MeanFES needed to achieve an acceptable solution for all benchmark functions. Except for f_{11}, and f_{12} functions, PSO has the best convergence speed. Similarly, the proposed algorithm reached a 100% success rate for ten test functions. To further confirm the convergence rate of the CDOA, the graphs of convergence (Fig. 5) show that CDOA converges faster than other algorithms in most test functions.

4.3   Statistical Tests

Statistical analysis is conducted to quantitatively analyze the different outcomes obtained from multiple optimization algorithms. Since the results are not based on hypotheses, we have applied the non-parametric tests, Friedman and Quade tests [17,23]. Figure 6 displays the average rankings of the tested algorithms based on the standard errors of means (SEM). As it is shown in this figure, CDOA is the best ranked. In summary, the computer simulations indicate that the DOA has an excellent ability to balance exploration and exploitation phases and improve the whole performance of the DOA in solving the benchmark functions.

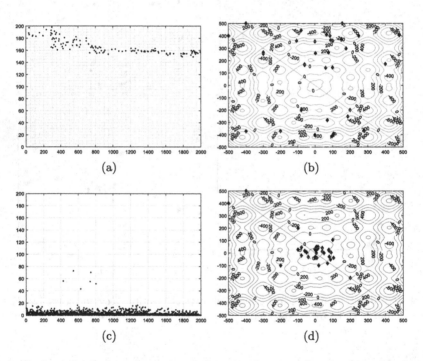

Fig. 3. Evaluated solutions, in terms of objective function #evaluations, for f_8 using (a) DOA and (c) CDOA; corresponding convergence visualizations (b) and (d) in accordance with (a) and (c).

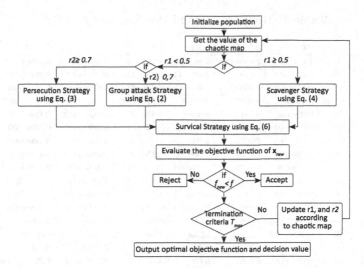

Fig. 4. Flowchart of the CDOA algorithm.

5   CDOA for Feature Selection in SS

In this section, we measure the performance of the proposed algorithm in providing the best features for SS based on beamforming, using a DNN classifier. We consider a wireless communication system with many angles of arrival. Thus, the beamforming technique exploits the energy from different angles of the received signal. The source signal from the PU is a BPSK modulated signal. For all tests, number of PU, number of antennas, the number of observed samples, and Monte Carlo are set to $P = 1$, $M = 20$, $N = 250$ and $n = 500$, respectively. Hence, the training set is set to 20 features and 1000 samples (500 for each class H1 and H0). Table 3 displays the solution accuracy for all algorithms. One can see that CDOA reaches the best mean. Table 4 reports that the proposed algorithm based on the feature selection approach remains the best misclassification the rate in differents SNR. In Fig. 7, we compare the proposed method to two recent

Table 1. Mean, SEM and SD for functions $f_1 - f_{12}$.

		BBO	HS	PSO	SA	DOA	CDOA
f_1	Mean	1.62e–01	2.193e+00	4.90e–15	3.78e–42	1.16e–306	**0.00e+00**
	SD	0.00e+00	1.128	2.07e–14	1.35e–42	0.00e+00	0.00e+00
	SEM	**0.00e+00**	0.205	3.78e–15	2.42e–43	0.00e+00	0.00e+00
f_2	Mean	0.0833	0.0517	0.0149	4.8776e–21	4.02e–187	**0.00e+00**
	SD	0.00e+00	0.046	0.0006	4.40e–22	0.00e+00	0.00e+00
	SEM	0.00e+00	0.0066	0.0084	8.04e–23	0.00e+00	0.00e+00
f_3	Mean	23.7669	2735.4	4.20e–06	1.51e–39	2.35e–292	**0.00e+00**
	SD	0.00e+00	855.06	7.30e–06	6.15e–40	0.00e+00	0.00e+00
	SEM	0.00e+00	156.11	1.33e–06	1.12e–40	0.00e+00	0.00e+00
f_4	Mean	0.561	4.92e–01	1.30e–03	5.18e–21	1.46e–184	**3.37e–271**
	SD	0.00e+00	0.88	1.34e–03	3.74e–22	0.00e+00	0.00e+00
	SEM	0.00e+00	0.162	2.40e–04	6.84e–23	0.00e+00	0.00e+00
f_5	Mean	27.8	247.8	35.8	64.56	28.9	**27.461**
	SD	**0.00e+00**	53.5	26.44	91.8	0.029	**0.5359**
	SEM	**0.00e+00**	9.77	4.82	16.7	0.0053	**0.0978**
f_6	Mean	0.0029124	0.036	0.0055	0.027	6.6139e–05	**9.7666e–06**
	SD	**0.00e+00**	0.01	0.0018	0.0092	7.1436e–05	8.1349e–06
	SEM	**0.00e+00**	0.0018	0.00034	0.0016	1.3042e–05	1.4852e–06
f_7	Mean	–8759.1	**–12568.7**	–6594.5	–10454.1	–5203.6	–4877.7
	SD	**0.00e+00**	0.66	842.04	470.2	1029.05	785.5
	SEM	**0.00e+00**	0.12	153.7	85.8	187.87	143.4
f_8	Mean	37.8	0.70	46.5	37.04	00.00e+00	0.00e+00
	SD	0.00e+00	0.54	12.51	8.25	0.00e+00	0.00e+00
	SEM	0.00e+00	is 0.099	2.28	1.50	0.00e+00	0.00e+00
f_9	Mean	0.10	0.46	0.0220	7.5199e–15	8.8818e–16	**8.8818e–16**
	SD	0.00e+00	0.19	0.87	1.2283e–15	0.00e+00	0.00e+00
	SEM	0.00e+00	0.035	0.15	2.2426e–16	0.00e+00	0.00e+00
f_{10}	Mean	0.41	0.98	0.028	0.0037	0.00e+00	0.00e+00
	SD	0.00e+00	0.051	0.031	0.0065	0.00e+00	0.00e+00
	SEM	0.00e+00	0.009	0.0058	0.0011	0.00e+00	0.00e+00
f_{11}	Mean	0.00029	0.0099	0.051	**1.57e–32**	0.49	0.39
	SD	**0.00e+00**	0.0095	0.10	5.5674e–48	0.19	0.127
	SEM	**0.00e+00**	0.0017	0.018	1.0165e–48	0.035	0.023
f_{12}	Mean	0.01	0.277	0.084	**0.00036**	2.82	2.55
	SD	**0.00e+00**	0.095	0.29	0.002	0.35	0.51
	SEM	**0.00e+00**	0.017	0.054	0.00036	0.064	0.093
Best for		0/12	1/12	0/12	2/12	2/12	**9/12**

ones based on beamforming for $SNR = -17db$: (i) maximum-to-minimum beam energy method (MMBE) [9] and (ii) maximum-to-mean energy detector method (MMED) [8]. The proposed approach for features weighting is still the most efficient method, among the compared ones, in the considered context.

Table 2. MeanFES and SR by comparative algorithms for functions $f_1 - f_{12}$.

		BBO	HS	PSO	SA	DOA	CDOA
f_1	MeanFES	89721	NaN	6311.1	22842.3	983.7	**44.5**
	SR (%)	0	100	100	100	100	100
f_2	MeanFES	NaN	68721	8459.4	33182.3	1199.2	**38.9**
	SR (%)	0	10	73.3	100	100	100
f_3	MeanFES	NaN	NaN	89325.03	45425	1591.4	**50.1**
	SR (%)	0	0	90	100	100	100
f_4	MeanFES	NaN	NaN	73289.03	33170.3	1065.4	**80.5**
	SR (%)	0	0	100	100	100	100
f_5	MeanFES	30245	NaN	14486.7	16671	683.6	**36.16**
	SR (%)	33	0	70	67	100	100
f_6	MMeanFES	NaN	NaN	NaN	NaN	1098.4	**135.3**
	SR (%)	0	0	0	0	100	100
f_7	MMeanFES	57.1	53.9	66.2	25.2	18.8	**11.7**
	SR (%)	100	100	100	100	100	100
f_8	MMeanFES	NaN	NaN	NaN	NaN	1565.03	**51.3**
	SR (%)	0	0	0	0	100	100
f_9	MMeanFES	NaN	NaN	14819.1	58019.6	1696.1	**60.3**
	SR (%)	0	0	33	60	100	100
f_{10}	MMeanFES	NaN	NaN	9956.2	42176.2	1176.6	**46.6**
	SR (%)	0	0	16.7	70	100	100
f_{11}	MMeanFES	NaN	NaN	**8921.2**	29026.3	NaN	NaN
	SR (%)	0	0	70	**100**	0	0
f_{12}	MMeanFES	NaN	NaN	**9364.3**	34256.1	NaN	NaN
	SR (%)	0	0	43	**96.7**	0	0
Best for	MeanFES	0/12	0/12	2/12	0/12	0/12	**10/12**
	SR (%)	1/12	2/12	3/12	6/12	9/12	**10/12**

When an algorithm cannot reach an acceptable solution over the fixed number
of runs, the value is marked as 'NaN'.

Table 3. MeanFES and SR comparison for differents SNR.

		DOA	CDOA
SNR $= -25$ db	Mean	7.71e–2	**9.53e–2**
	SD	3.30e–3	**2.60e–3**
	SEM	1.00e–3	**8.20e–4**
SNR $= -20$ db	Mean	3.61e–2	**3.52e–2**
	SD	1.25e–3	**1.23e–3**
	SEM	3.80e–4	**3.70e–4**
SNR $= -15$ db	Mean	6.50e–3	**4.60e–3**
	SD	2.25e–4	**1.59e–4**
	SEM	6.96e–5	**4.92e–5**
SNR $= -10$ db	Mean	3.50e–3	**1.30e–3**
	SD	1.21e–4	**4.51e–5**
	SEM	3.75e–5	**1.39e–5**

Table 4. Misclassification rate for differents SNR.

	SNR = −25	SNR = −20	SNR = −15	SNR = −10	SNR = −5
DOA	0.0953	0.0361	0.0065	0.0035	0
CDOA	**0.0771**	**0.0352**	**0.0046**	**0.0013**	0

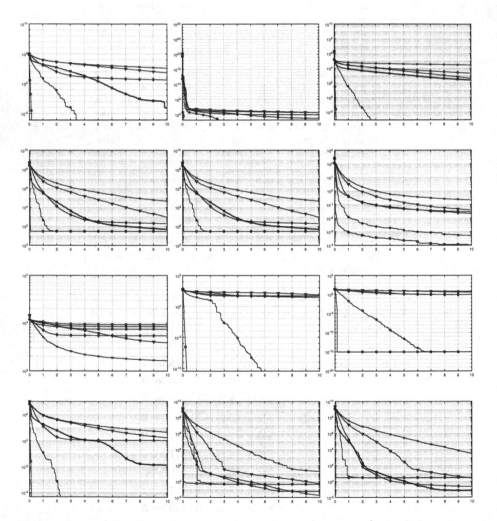

Fig. 5. Convergence results (average best solution in terms of FES[‡]) for the benchmark functions $f_1 - f_{12}$ in row-major order. BBO[◇], PSO[□], HS[×], SA[▽], DOA[⋆], and CDOA[○].]. [‡] The x-axis values are to be multiplied by 10^3.

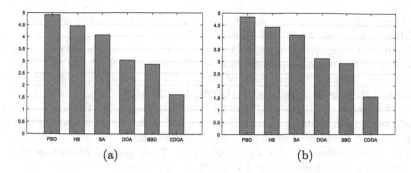

(a)   (b)

Fig. 6. Average ranking of comparative algorithms by Friedman test (a), and Quade test (b).

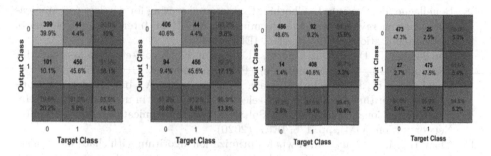

Fig. 7. Confusion matrices given by MMBE (a), MMED (b), DOA (c), and CDOA (d) for SNR = −17 db

6   Conclusion

In this work, we proposed an improved version of DOA called CDOA by incorporating chaos strategy to optimize feature selection in spectrum sensing for CR in wireless communication networks, using a deep learning method. The CDOA relies mainly on the excellent balance between local and global searches. Simulation results on benchmarking functions and feature selection in SS, as a case study, illustrated that the proposed algorithm outperforms the other approaches used for comparison in terms of solution accuracy and convergence. Due to its reliability, the proposed approach can be exploited in many applications such as e-Health, smart city and home or in military domain. In future work, we will focus on the proposed model for pattern recognition under non-Gaussian noise.

References

1. Aarts, E., Korst, J., Michiels, W.: Simulated annealing. ek burke y g. kendall, editores, search methodologies (2005)
2. Alatas, B.: Chaotic harmony search algorithms. Appl. Math. Comput. **216**(9), 2687–2699 (2010)

3. Arora, S., Singh, S.: An improved butterfly optimization algorithm with chaos. J. Intell. Fuzzy Syst. **32**(1), 1079–1088 (2017)

4. Awad, A.A., Ali, A.F., Gaber, T.: Feature selection method based on chaotic maps and butterfly optimization algorithm. In: Hassanien, A.-E., Azar, A.T., Gaber, T., Oliva, D., Tolba, F.M. (eds.) AICV 2020. AISC, vol. 1153, pp. 159–169. Springer, Cham (2020). https://doi.org/10.1007/978-3-030-44289-7_16

5. Ben Chaabane, S., Belazi, A., Kharbech, S., Bouallegue, A., Clavier, L.: Improved salp swarm optimization algorithm: application in feature weighting for blind modulation identification. Electronics **10**(16), 2002 (2021)

6. Biswas, A., Mishra, K., Tiwari, S., Misra, A.: Physics-inspired optimization algorithms: a survey. J. Optim. **2013** (2013)

7. Bouallegue, K., Crussiere, M., Kharbech, S.: SVM assisted primary user-detection for non-cooperative cognitive radio networks. In: 2020 IEEE Symposium on Computers and Communications (ISCC), pp. 1–5. IEEE (2020)

8. Bouallegue, K., Dayoub, I., Gharbi, M.: Spectrum sensing for wireless communications using energy ratio and beamforming. In: 2017 IEEE International Conference on Communications (ICC), pp. 1–6. IEEE (2017)

9. Bouallegue, K., Dayoub, I., Gharbi, M., Hassan, K.: A cost-effective approach for spectrum sensing using beamforming. Phys. Commun. **22**, 1–8 (2017)

10. Chaabane, S.B., Kharbech, S., Belazi, A., Bouallegue, A.: Improved whale optimization algorithm for SVM model selection: application in medical diagnosis. In: 2020 International Conference on Software, Telecommunications and Computer Networks (SoftCOM), pp. 1–6. IEEE (2020)

11. Chen, H., Li, W., Yang, X.: A whale optimization algorithm with chaos mechanism based on quasi-opposition for global optimization problems. Expert Syst. Appl. **158**, 113612 (2020)

12. Dolinina, O., Pechenkin, V., Mansurova, M., Tolek, D., Ixsanov, S.: Algorithmic approach to building a route for the removal of household waste with associated additional loads in the "Smart Clean City" project. In: Nguyen, N.T., Iliadis, L., Maglogiannis, I., Trawinski, B. (eds.) ICCCI 2021. LNCS (LNAI), vol. 12876, pp. 745–755. Springer, Cham (2021). https://doi.org/10.1007/978-3-030-88081-1_56

13. Dutta, S., Jha, S., Sankaranarayanan, S., Tiwari, A.: Output range analysis for deep feedforward neural networks. In: Dutle, A., Muñoz, C., Narkawicz, A. (eds.) NFM 2018. LNCS, vol. 10811, pp. 121–138. Springer, Cham (2018). https://doi.org/10.1007/978-3-319-77935-5_9

14. Eberhart, R., Kennedy, J.: A new optimizer using particle swarm theory. In: MHS 1995: Proceedings of the Sixth International Symposium on Micro Machine and Human Science, pp. 39–43. IEEE (1995)

15. Farah, A., Belazi, A.: A novel chaotic Jaya algorithm for unconstrained numerical optimization. Nonlinear Dyn. **93**(3), 1451–1480 (2018)

16. Fonseca, C.M., Fleming, P.J.: An overview of evolutionary algorithms in multiobjective optimization. Evol. Comput. **3**(1), 1–16 (1995)

17. García, S., Fernández, A., Luengo, J., Herrera, F.: Advanced nonparametric tests for multiple comparisons in the design of experiments in computational intelligence and data mining: Experimental analysis of power. Inf. Sci. **180**(10), 2044–2064 (2010)

18. Ghaemi, M., Feizi-Derakhshi, M.R.: Feature selection using forest optimization algorithm. Pattern Recogn. **60**, 121–129 (2016)

19. Hernes, M., Wojtkiewicz, K., Szczerbicki, E. (eds.): ICCCI 2020. CCIS, vol. 1287. Springer, Cham (2020). https://doi.org/10.1007/978-3-030-63119-2

20. Hussein, A.H., Fouda, H.S., Abdullah, H.H., Khalaf, A.A.: A highly efficient spectrum sensing approach based on antenna arrays beamforming. IEEE Access **8**, 25184–25197 (2020)
21. Koçkaya, K., Develi, İ.: Spectrum sensing in cognitive radio networks: threshold value optimization and analysis (2020)
22. Li, M.W., Wang, Y.T., Geng, J., Hong, W.C.: Chaos cloud quantum bat hybrid optimization algorithm. Nonlinear Dyn. **103**(1), 1167–1193 (2021)
23. Liu, Z., Blasch, E., John, V.: Statistical comparison of image fusion algorithms: recommendations. Inf. Fusion **36**, 251–260 (2017)
24. Morozkin, P., Swynghedauw, M., Trocan, M.: Neural network based eye tracking. In: Nguyen, N.T., Papadopoulos, G.A., Jedrzejowicz, P., Trawinski, B., Vossen, G. (eds.) ICCCI 2017. LNCS (LNAI), vol. 10449, pp. 600–609. Springer, Cham (2017). https://doi.org/10.1007/978-3-319-67077-5_58
25. Parpinelli, R.S., Lopes, H.S.: New inspirations in swarm intelligence: a survey. Int. J. Bio-Inspired Comput. **3**(1), 1–16 (2011)
26. Peraza-Vázquez, H., et al.: A bio-inspired method for engineering design optimization inspired by dingoes hunting strategies. Math. Prob. Eng. **2021** (2021)
27. Pourbahrami, S.: Improving PSO global method for feature selection according to iterations global search and chaotic theory. arXiv preprint arXiv:1811.08701 (2018)
28. dos Santos Coelho, L., Mariani, V.C.: Use of chaotic sequences in a biologically inspired algorithm for engineering design optimization. Expert Syst. Appl. **34**(3), 1905–1913 (2008)
29. Sayed, G.I., Khoriba, G., Haggag, M.H.: A novel chaotic SALP swarm algorithm for global optimization and feature selection. Appl. Intell. **48**(10), 3462–3481 (2018)
30. Simon, D.: Biogeography-based optimization. IEEE Trans. Evol. Comput. **12**(6), 702–713 (2008)
31. Zhu, H., Qi, W., Ge, J., Liu, Y.: Analyzing devaney chaos of a sine-cosine compound function system. Int. J. Bifurcation Chaos **28**(14), 1850176 (2018)

Multi-start Tabu Agents-Based Model for the Dual-Resource Constrained Flexible Job Shop Scheduling Problem

Farah Farjallah[1,4]($\boxtimes$), Houssem Eddine Nouri[2,4], and Olfa Belkahla Driss[3,4]

[1] Ecole Nationale des Sciences de l'Informatique ENSI,
Université de la Manouba, Manouba, Tunisia
`farah.farjallah1@gmail.com`
[2] Institut Supérieur de Gestion de Gabes, Université de Gabes, Gabes, Tunisia
[3] Ecole Supérieure de Commerce de Tunis, Université de la Manouba, Manouba, Tunisia
[4] LARIA La Recherche en Intelligence Artificielle, ENSI,
Université de la Manouba, Manouba, Tunisia

Abstract. Typically, processing jobs on a production floor require both machines and human resources. However, most classical scheduling problems ignore possible constraints caused by the availability of workers and treat machines only as limited resource. This paper presents a Multi-Start Tabu Agents-based Model (MuSTAM) for Dual-Resource Constrained Flexible Job shop Scheduling Problem (DRCFJSP). It considers a set of initial solutions running in parallel using the intensification technique. It has a single objective which is to minimize the maximum completion time (makespan) due to its importance in research workshops. The proposed model consists of two classes of agents: MainAgent and TabuAgents. The MainAgent receives inputs, generates the initial population, creates TabuAgents based on the number of solutions in the initial population PopSize, launches the system and finally displays the best solution. Each TabuAgent takes a solution from the created initial population and applies Tabu Search using the technique of concentrated intensification to neighborhood search. TabuAgents cooperate and communicate between them in order to improve the search quality. In experimental phase, numerical tests are performed to evaluate our MuSTAM model compared to ITS based on FJSPW benchmark instances of Gong. The obtained results show the efficiency of the Multi-Start Tabu Agents-based Model in terms of makespan and CPU time.

Keywords: Flexible job shop · Single objective · Tabu search · Multi-agent · Workers flexibility · Dual-resource · Makespan

1 Introduction

Scheduling problems are present in all sectors of the economy, from manufacturing to IT. One of the most well-known production scheduling problems is the Job shop Scheduling Problem (JSP). It has several application fields such as airport scheduling, port scheduling, railway train scheduling. An important objective of this problem is how to find a sequence of operations which minimizes the maximum completion time

N. T. Nguyen et al. (Eds.): ICCCI 2022, LNAI 13501, pp. 674–686, 2022.
https://doi.org/10.1007/978-3-031-16014-1_53

(makespan) of the last one. In addition to the classical Job shop Scheduling Problem there are several generalizations [1] such as the Flexible Job shop Scheduling Problem (FJSP) proposed by Brucker and Schlie [2], which considers the flexibility of machines. The Flexible Job shop Scheduling Problem with Worker flexibility (FJSPW) according to Zheng and Wang [3] is an extension of the classical Job shop Scheduling, due to the importance of human factors in real world manufacturing systems which is commonly named as Dual-Resource Constrained Job shop Scheduling Problem (DRCJSP).

DRCFJSP was introduced by Nelson [4] and has three sub-problems: (i) machine selection, (ii) worker assignment, (iii) operation sequencing on the machines with workers constraint in order to minimize the end date of the last operation on all jobs which is known as makespan.

Figure 1 shows an example of a Dual-Resource Constrained Flexible Job shop Scheduling Problem. There are three jobs, six machines and five workers. Job1 is composed of three operations $O_{1,1}$, $O_{1,2}$ and $O_{1,3}$, job2 contains of two operations $O_{2,1}$ and $O_{2,2}$, Job3 is composed of two operations $O_{3,1}$ and $O_{3,2}$. $O_{1,1}$ can be executed by M_1 or M_2. $O_{1,2}$ can be processed on M_2 or M_5. $O_{1,3}$ can be operated on M_4 or M_6. $O_{2,1}$ may be executed by M_3 or M_6. $O_{2,2}$ can be processed on M_4 or M_5. $O_{3,1}$ can be operated on M_1 or M_3. $O_{3,2}$ can be executed by M_2 or M_6. The worker W_1 can operate on M_2 or M_3. W_2 can operate on M_1 or M_2. W_3 can operate on M_1 or M_5 or M_6. W_4 can operate on M_3 or M_5. W_5 can operate one of these machines: M_4, M_5 or M_6.

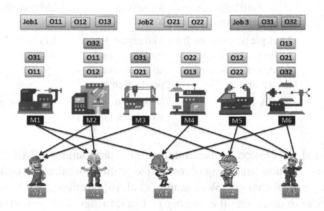

Fig. 1. Example of a practical dual-resource constrained flexible job shop scheduling problem

In this paper, we present a new multi-start tabu search algorithm based on a multi-agent model named MuSTAM for solving the Dual-Resource Constrained Flexible Job shop Scheduling Problem (DRCFJSP), where we detail the global process of the multi-agent system and then, each agent is described by its different operators.

The rest of the paper is organized as follows:

In Sect. 2, we present a state-of-the-art for solving the Dual-Resource Constrained Flexible Job shop Scheduling Problem (DRCFJSP), where we detail the different studies proposed for this problem and we propose a classification according to three criteria. In Sect. 3, we define the mathematical formulation of the DRCFJSP with its objective function. Then, in Sect. 4, we detail the Multi-Start Tabu Agents-based Model. The experimental and comparison results are provided in Sect. 5. Finally, Sect. 6 ends the paper with a conclusion and future works.

2   State-of-the-Art

In this section, we present a study of the literature for solving DRCFJSP. Then, we classify this study according to three criteria: (1) Used method type (exact, meta-heuristic), (2) Implemented method (tabu search, genetic algorithm, mixed integer programming,...) and (3) Optimization criteria (makespan, cost...) as shown in Table 1.

Table 1. Classification of the most recent papers studying the DRCFJSP

Used method type	Implemented approaches	Optimization criteria	Authors
Exact	Mixed-integer linear programming	Profit, late orders and workforce	Da Silva et al. 2006
	Integer programming model	Total cost	Wirojanagud et al. 2007
	Variable neighborhood search	Makespan	Lei and Guo 2014
Metaheuristic	Hybrid artificial bee colony algorithm	Makespan	Gong et al. 2020
	Multiple populations for multiple objectives framework based genetic algorithm	Makespan, tardiness, total advance time, production cost	Liu et al. 2021
	NSGA-II	Makespan, worker workload, tardiness	Vital-soto et al.2022

Da Silva et al. [5] created a mixed integer linear programming (MILP) model with multi objectives function consisting of maximize profit, minimize late orders, and minimize work force level changes. Wiriojangud et al. [6] developed a mixed integer programming model to determine the number of hires, firings, and cross-training at each General Cognitive Ability (GCA) level to minimize total costs, including training costs, salary costs, firing costs, and missed production costs over multiple time periods.

Lei and Guo [7] presented an effective variable neighbourhood search (VNS), where the solution is a quadruple string of the ordered operations and their resources. Two neighbourhood search procedures are executed to generate new solutions for two sub-problems of the problem. Gong et al. [8] presented a Hybrid Artificial Bee Colony Algorithm (HABCA), were the goal was to minimize the makespan. A comparative study showed that the proposed algorithm was more effective than hybrid GA [9] and improved ABCA [10]. Vital-soto et al. [11] developed an elitist Non-dominated Sorting Genetic Algorithm (NSGA-II) with an innovative operator to solve DRCFJSP where the multi-objective functions are (1) makespan, (2) worker workload, (3) tardiness. A novel Multiple Populations for Multiple Objectives (MPMO) framework-based Genetic Algorithm

(GA) approach (MPMOGA) was proposed by Liu et al. [12] to optimize five objectives simultaneously. Firstly, MPMOGA used five populations to optimize the five goals. Then, Secondly, an archive sharing technique was proposed to avoid that each population can be concentrated only on its corresponding mono objective. Therefore the populations can get optimization informations about the other goals according to the archive.

3   Mathematical Model of the DRCFJSP

3.1   Problem Description

The proposed DRCFJSP is illustrated by Gong et al. [8]: There are a set of n jobs, a set of m machines, and a set of l workers. Each job has a sequence of r_i operations to be processed one after another according to the precedence constraint. Each operation must be processed by one selected worker from the worker set on one selected machine from the machine set. The processing time of each operation, which is operated by one worker on a selected machine, is fixed. Table 2 shows an example of DRCFJSP as a demonstration case. There are two jobs, three machines, and three workers. Job 1 and Job 2 have two operations. The jobs are listed in column 1. Each set of job's operations is listed in column 2. The machines that process the appropriate operations are listed in column 3. Column 4 shows the appropriate worker for each machine operations. Finally, the processing time of the operations performed by the corresponding workers is shown in column 5.

Table 2. Sample instance of the DRCFJSP

Jobs	Operations	Machines	Workers	Time
J1	$O_{1,1}$	M1	W1	10
			W3	20
		M2	W2	10
	$O_{1,2}$	M2	W1	10
			W2	15
J2	$O_{2,1}$	M2	W1	20
			W2	10
		M3	W3	15
	$O_{2,2}$	M1	W1	15
		M2	W3	20
			W1	10

The objective of this paper is to minimize makespan. Some assumptions are considered:

- Each machine can process only one selected operation from its corresponding operation set at any given time.
- Each worker can operate on only one machine at a time, selected from the appropriate machine set.

- Each operation can only be processed once by one machine from the corresponding machine set, and must satisfy the operation constraints of all jobs.
- Each operation can be operated only once by a worker chosen from the corresponding worker set and operation constraints of all jobs should be satisfied.
- There are no precedence constraints among the operations of different jobs.
- preemption is not permitted.
- An operation of any job cannot be processed until its preceding operations are completed.
- The processing time is known in advance.

3.2   Problem Formulation

The concepts used in this article are as follow:

Indices	
i, h	Index of jobs, $i,h= 1, 2, \ldots,n$
j, g	Index of operations, $j,g=1,2,\ldots r_i$
k	Index of machines, $k = 1, 2, \ldots, m$
s	Index of worker, $s = 1, 2, \ldots, l$

Parameters	
n	Total number of job
m	Total number of machine
l	Total number of workers
r_i	Total number of operations in job i
$O_{i,j}$	The jth operation of job i
$T_{i,j,k,s}$	Processing time of O_{ij} by worker s on machine k
$CO_{i,j}$	Completion time of operation $O_{i,j}$
C_i	Completion time of job i

Decision variables

$$X_{ijks} = \begin{cases} 1 & \text{if worker s is selected to operate on machine k for operation } O_{i,j} \\ 0 & \text{otherwise} \end{cases}$$

The mathematical model used in this article is as follows:
The objective function:

$$minf = max_{1 \leq i \leq n} (C_i) \tag{1}$$

Subject to :

$$CO_{ij} - CO_{ij-1} \geq T_{ijks}X_{ijks} \quad \forall i = 1,...,n; j = 2,...,r_i; k = 1,...,m; s = 1,...l \tag{2}$$

$$(CO_{hg} - CO_{ij} - T_{hgks})X_{ijks}X_{hgks} \geq 0 \vee (CO_{ij} - CO_{hg} - T_{ijks})X_{ijks}X_{hgks} \geq 0$$
$$\forall i = 1,...,n; j = 1,...,r_i; k = 1,...,m; s = 1,...,l \tag{3}$$

$$\sum_{j=1}^{r_i} X_{ijks} = 1 \quad \forall i = 1,...,n; k = 1,...,m; s = 1,...,l \tag{4}$$

$$\sum_{k=1}^{m} X_{ijks} = 1 \quad \forall i = 1,...,n; j = 1,...,ri; s = 1,...,l \tag{5}$$

$$\sum_{s=1}^{l} X_{ijks} = 1 \quad \forall i = 1,...,n; j = 1,...,ri; k = 1,...,m \tag{6}$$

Equation (1) for the objective function, consists on minimizing the makespan. Constraint (2) to ensure precedence constraints, constraint (3) to ensure that each machine can handle only one operation at any time, constraint (4) to ensure that an operation chosen from the operation set can only be handled once, the constraint (5) to ensure that only one machine is chosen from a corresponding machine set to process each operation. Constraint (6) to ensure that each operation can be executed by one and only one worker.

4   Multi-start Tabu Agents-Based Model (MuSTAM)

4.1   Tabu Search

Tabu Search is a metaheuristic introduced by Glover [13], it is a local search method combined with a set of techniques to avoid being trapped in a local minimum or recycling. Tabu Search (TS) has shown great efficiency for solving NP-hard problems. Recently this method is still used in the literature which explains its importance and performance in the field of research. Hajibabaei and Benhnamain [14] introduced Tabu Search (TS) algorithm for solving Flexible Job shop Scheduling Problem (FJSP) with unrelated parallel machines and sequence-dependent setup time. The results show that it performs better than Genetic Algorithm (GA) where the goal is to minimizing the costs of makespan, total weighted tardiness, delivery time and inventory.

4.2   The Basic Principle of MuSTAM

A multi-agent system composed of multiple interacting agents that cooperate, communicate and coordinate with each other to achieve a common goal [15]. We propose a Multi-Start Tabu Agents-based Model for solving Dual-Resource Constrained Flexible Job shop Scheduling Problems. It consists of two classes of agents: MainAgent and a set of PopSize TabuAgents, where PopSize is the number of solutions initially generated based on a neighborhood parameter, see Fig. 2.

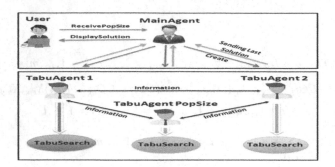

Fig. 2. Multi-start tabu agents-based model

4.3 MainAgent Process

It is the one that reacts with the user to receive the maximum number of iterations for the search operation. It is responsible for creating TabuAgents based on the size of the initial population PopSize and then provides for each TabuAgent its necessary information: agent identification (as an autonomous agent and also as a system member), its initial solution and the maximum number of instructions for the search. The MainAgent is satisfied when the stopping criterion is reached. In this case, it sorts the found solutions in terms of the makespan values and displays the best obtained solution to the user.

4.4 Initial Population

To make the individual solutions more diversified and distributed in the search space, the starting population is created at random using a uniform law based on a neighborhood parameter. In fact, to be considered as a new member of the initial solutions, each new solution should have a predetermined distance from all existing solutions. The used method based on neighborhood parameter was inspired from [16]. Equation 7 presents the formula for total distance of dissimilarity between two solutions.

$$Dist_{max} = [\sum_{i=1}^{n} \sum_{i,1}^{i,ni} M(O_{i,j})] + L \tag{7}$$

where the number of alternative machines for each operation is $M(O_{i,j})$. The total number of operations for all tasks is L. The distance between them is $Dist$ and, n_i is a total number of operations to be performed successively according to the given sequence for each sequence of job J_i. In-addition, for each case, we select a solution (i) and we verify consecutively for each next solution (j) from the remaining population, if the dissimilarity distance between solution (i) and solution (j) is less than or equal to a fixed threshold $Dist_{fix}$ (representing a percentage of difference X% relatively to $Dist_{max}$, look Eq. (8)) which is illustrated from [17]. In our case we choose the fair percentage 50%.

$$Dist_{fix} = Dist_{max} \times X\% \tag{8}$$

4.5   Representation of Solutions

The solutions are represented in three vectors, the first vector O for the operations, the second M for the machines and the third W for the workers and final vector that combines the three vectors together. Figure 3 shows an example of solution representation.

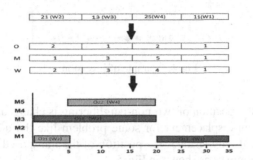

Fig. 3. Solution representation

The final vector explanation is as follows: in the first r vector, all operations are numbered as a series of consecutive integers. In this example, job 1 has operations numbered 1 and 2, and job 2 has operations numbered 1 and 2. Therefore, the indices of the vector ([2, 4, 1, 3]) represent two jobs [$(O_{11}, O_{12}, O_{21}, O_{22})$]. In the second vector, each machine selected to process the corresponding operation is numbered as an integer according to its order in the predefined set of machines. In this example, O_{11}, O_{12}, O_{21} and O_{22} are handled by machines M_3, M_1, M_1 and M_5. In the third vector, each worker selected to operate the corresponding operation is numbered as an integer according to its sequence in a predefined worker set. In this example, O_{11}, O_{12}, O_{21}, and O_{22} are processed by workers W_3, W_1, W_2, and W_4.

4.6   TabuAgents Optimization Process

The TabuAgents are created by the MainAgent each one represents a solution. All TabuAgents simultaneously start their process by performing a Tabu Search algorithm using the technique of concentrated intensification to neighborhood search to guarantee the multi-start mechanism of our model. The cooperation and communication of TabuAgents manage the sending and receiving of messages between them containing their necessary information in order to improve the search quality. The TabuAgents complete their process by sending theirs last solutions to the MainAgent, which consider the best of them as the global solution for the DRCFJSP.

4.7   Neighborhood Parameter

This parameter starts from an initial feasible solution s of the initial solutions S, to build a set of neighboring solutions of this solution, at each iteration it completely examines the neighborhood V(s) of the current solution s. Then it chooses the best solution of V(s)-s, even if it does not improve the value of the objective function. There are three possible moves on permutations as follows:

1. **Inversion:** the position of two neighboring is reversed. It gives us *n-1* possible moves. Figure 4 shows an example of permutation.

Fig. 4. Example of inversion

2. **Transposition:** the position of two non-neighboring is changed. This movement is more efficient than displacement for some problem like the quadratic assignment problem because it only changes the position of the transposed objects. It gives us *n(n-1)/2* possible moves as shown in Fig. 5.

Fig. 5. Example of transposition

3. **Shifting:** we change the position of a single box. This movement is better for sequencing problems because it is the sequencing that is important, not the individual position of the tasks. It gives us (n-1)2 possible moves. Figure 6 presents this function

Fig. 6. Example of shifting

Since the permutation movement is on three levels i.e. if there is a change in the O vector there are also changes in the M and W vectors the ITS takes the transposition for the permutation movement for decrease the number of changes.

4.8 Neighborhood Evaluation

After the generation of all neighbor solutions, the neighbor evaluation step is started. This stage takes place over two stages. The first step consists in choosing the best non-tabu neighbors among the set of neighboring solutions, this neighbor will be the current solution. The second step compares the value of makespan for the current solution with the makespan of the best solution, if it is lower, it will be the best solution.

4.9   Tabu List

An essential element of Tabu Search is the use of flexible short-term memory, which can keep track of some recent past actions. The size of the tabu list used is static "TL". If the size of the list exceeds the maximum allowed size, we remove the oldest item from this list (FIFO strategy: first in, first out: the element that arrives first is the first to be removed).

4.10   Stopping Criterion

In our model, we adopt the maximum number of iterations as the stopping criterion. The Tabu Search process tries to improve the solution after a maximum number of iterations (maxiter = 10000). Then, the best schedule found during the search and its makespan time are returned.

5   Experimental Results

To evaluate our model and to show the importance of using the multi-agent systems, we have developed an enhanced Tabu Search method named Improved Tabu Serach (ITS), which is based on an initial population of solutions. The Improved Tabu Search (ITS) and Multi-Start Tabu Agents-based Model (MuSTAM) are implemented in Java on PC with 2,50 GHz intel (core i5 vPro) and 12 GB of RAM memory, using Eclipse IDE to code these two approaches and the Jade platform to create the MuSTAM multi-agent system.

To compare and evaluate the efficiency of these approaches, numerical tests are provided in Table 3 showing results of different problem instances of Gong data [8], from the literature of the FJSPW. It consists of 13 problems (FGW01-FGW13) with a number of operations ranging from 2 to 15 for all jobs which will be processed on a number of machines ranging from 5 to 15 by a number of workers ranging from 5 to 15. FGW01-03 are smaller, while FGW04-13 are large instances.

DRCFJSP can be divided into total worker flexibility and partial worker flexibility. In this work, we consider the total worker flexibility case, which means that each machine can be operated by all workers.

The comparison experimental results are shown in Table 3, in which PopSize means the population size of initial solutions, C_{max} is the best makespan among 5 runs, Avg is the average value from the 5 runs, and CPU time is the best computation time (in seconds) for each best makespan. Best makespan and CPU values for each case of the benchmark instances are marked in bold.

The obtained results show that MuSTAM provides good results in terms of C_{max} and CPU time. For all used instances, we find the best CPU time values. Figure 7 ensures this best results for PopSize=100. While for the comparisons between the two approaches in terms of Avg makespan (C_{max}), we find for population size 25 that MuS-TAM is 69% of the instances, better than ITS. In addition, for population size 50 MuS-TAM is 53,8% of the instances, better than ITS and for population size 100 MuSTAM is 92,3% of the instances, better than ITS.

Table 3. Results of the Gong instances

Instances	ITS									MuSTAM								
	Cmax						CPU(s)			Cmax						CPU(s)		
	Best			Avg			Best			Best			Avg			Best		
	25	50	100	25	50	100	25	50	100	25	50	100	25	50	100	25	50	100
FGW01	15	**13**	13	15,2	14	14,2	96	183	362	**12**	**13**	**12**	14,4	14,4	13	7	**9**	**12**
FGW02	47	46	41	49,2	47,2	45,25	66	211	463	**45**	44	**39**	48,8	47,3	44	**13**	**18**	**18**
FGW03	**36**	36	36	28,2	38,25	35,75	123	265	1993	**36**	**34**	**31**	38,6	37,6	36,2	**8**	**10**	451
FGW04	**77**	**74**	74	80,8	78,14	75,83	253	290	607	**77**	76	**72**	79,8	77,8	77,2	**14**	**23**	**39**
FGW05	81	79	74	82	80,5	76,25	245	346	625	**73**	**70**	**72**	75,4	74	74,6	**13**	**19**	**35**
FGW06	499	485	485	508	492	491,5	680	1260	2521	**485**	**478**	**478**	497,2	495,2	496,6	65	113	**214**
FGW07	135	134	134	138,5	135,25	137,25	332	627	1311	**128**	**129**	**128**	138,75	132,66	134,75	23	**38**	**35**
FGW08	**326**	**319**	319	335,5	324	323,25	540	830	1580	327	321	**302**	331	329	316,25	26	51	**100**
FGW09	**224**	224	211	236	234,25	226,5	718	1093	3916	234	**216**	**210**	240	226,25	225,5	48	105	**212**
FGW10	389	**388**	388	398	397	393	415	742	1499	**379**	399	**376**	390,33	405,75	380,5	23	45	84
FGW11	**873**	**852**	852	896	876	859,3	1051	2279	4885	890	857	**835**	906	871,25	852	104	214	425
FGW12	809	**799**	**781**	829,6	818,4	811,8	923	1829	3700	**771**	818	796	800,5	837	810,25	118	277	554
FGW13	**614**	**614**	614	656,5	642	628	945	2049	4103	655	652	**612**	680	657,5	633	124	310	485
AVG				4253,5	4176,99	4117,88						AVG	4240,78	4205,71	4093,85			

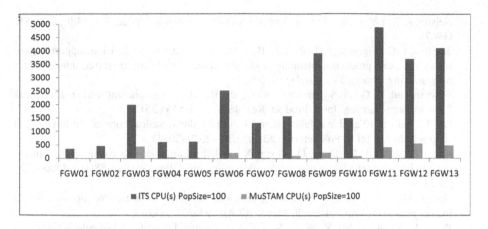

Fig. 7. Comparison results in terms of CPU time

These best results guarantee the usage of a multi-agent system, which comprises first and foremost of reducing execution time and enhancing the quality of neighborhood search, due to the cooperation and communication between TabuAgents.

6   Conclusion and Future Researches Directions

In this paper, we have proposed a new Multi-Start Tabu Agents-based Model (MuS-TAM) for the DRCFJSP with makespan objective. It is composed of two types of agents, which was the MainAgent and a set of TabuAgents, which cooperate and communicate between to improve the quality of neighborhood search to find the best solution. To determine its performance, numerical tests was created using a well-known data set from literature of the DRCFJSP. The experimental results showed that our MuSTAM obtained the best set of solutions in comparison to ITS in terms of makespan and CPU time.

In the future works, we will be able to adapt our work to a multi-objective case of the solved problem. Thereby, we will compare the generated results by our work with other approaches from the literature. Also, it will be possible to add new constraints such as workers age which will present the real effect of the human energy on the production process.

References

1. Dhiflaoui, M., Nouri, H.E., Driss, O.B.: Dual-resource constraints in classical and flexible job shop problems: a state-of-the-art review. Procedia Comput. Sci. **126**, 1507–1515 (2018)
2. Brucker, P., Schlie, R.: Job-shop scheduling with multi-purpose machines. Computing **45**(4), 369–375 (1990)
3. Zheng, X.L., Wang, L.: A knowledge-guided fruit fly optimization algorithm for dual resource constrained flexible job-shop scheduling problem. Int. J. Product. Res. **54**(18), 5554–5566 (2016)

4. Nelson, R.T.: Labor and machine limited production systems. Manag. Sci. **13**(9), 648–671 (1967)
5. da Silva, C.G., Figueira, J., Lisboa, J., Barman, S.: An interactive decision support system for an aggregate production planning model based on multiple criteria mixed integer linear programming. Omega **34**(2), 167–177 (2006)
6. Wirojanagud, P., Gel, E.S., Fowler, J.W., Cardy, R.: Modelling inherent worker differences for workforce planning. Int. J. Product. Res. **45**(3), 525–553 (2007)
7. Lei, D., Guo, X.: Variable neighbourhood search for dual-resource constrained flexible job shop scheduling. Int. J. Product. Res. **52**(9), 2519–2529 (2014)
8. Gong, G., Chiong, R., Deng, Q., Gong, X.: A hybrid artificial bee colony algorithm for flexible job shop scheduling with worker flexibility. Int. J. Product. Res. **58**(14), 4406–4420 (2020)
9. Gao, J., Gen, M., Sun, L.Y.: Scheduling jobs and maintenances in flexible job shop with a hybrid genetic algorithm. J. Intell. Manuf. **17**(4), 493–507 (2006)
10. Wang, L., Zhou, G., Xu, Y., Wang, S., Liu, M.: An effective artificial bee colony algorithm for the flexible job-shop scheduling problem. Int. J. Adv. Manuf. Technol. **60**(1–4), 303–315 (2012)
11. Vital-Soto, A., Baki, M.F., Azab, A.: A multi-objective mathematical model and evolutionary algorithm for the dual-resource flexible job-shop scheduling problem with sequencing flexibility. Flex. Serv. Manuf. J., 1–43 (2022)
12. Liu, S.C., Chen, Z.G., Zhan, Z.H., Jeon, S.W., Kwong, S., Zhang, J.: Many-objective job-shop scheduling: a multiple populations for multiple objectives-based genetic algorithm approach. IEEE Trans. Cybern. (2021)
13. Glover, F.: Future paths for integer programming and links to artificial intelligence. Comput. Oper. Res. **13**(5), 533–549 (1986)
14. Hajibabaei, M., Behnamian, J.: Flexible job-shop scheduling problem with unrelated parallel machines and resources-dependent processing times: a tabu search algorithm. Int. J. Manag. Sci. Eng. Manag. **16**(4), 242–253 (2021)
15. Xiong, W., Fu, D.: A new immune multi-agent system for the flexible job shop scheduling problem. J. Intell. Manuf. **29**(4), 857–873 (2015). https://doi.org/10.1007/s10845-015-1137-2
16. Bożejko, W., Uchroński, M., Wodecki, M.: The new golf neighborhood for the flexible job shop problem. Procedia Comput. Sci. **1**(1), 289–296 (2010)
17. Nouri, H.E., Driss, O.B., Ghédira, K.: A holonic multiagent model based on a combined genetic algorithm–tabu search for the flexible job shop scheduling problem. In: Bajo, J., et al. (eds.) PAAMS 2015. CCIS, vol. 524, pp. 43–54. Springer, Cham (2015). https://doi.org/10.1007/978-3-319-19033-4_4

Segment Based Approach to Travelling Salesman Problem

Andrzej Siemiński[✉]

Department of Applied Informatics, Faculty of Information and Communication Technology,
Wrocław Technical University, Wrocław, Poland
Andrzej.Sieminski@pwr.edu.pl

Abstract. The paper presents the Segment Based Approach (SBA) - a novel
technique to solve the Traveling Salesman Problem. In this technique, the path
is constructed from segments, which are sequences of adjacent edges. Although
the approach is memory extensive, it has built-in measures for identifying useful
segments and controlling its memory requirements. The paper contains a detailed
description of the SBA operation and an analysis of the impact that its parameters
have on the obtained results. The SBA has some advantages over solutions of
the TSP that are inspired by Ant Colony System. It is capable of finding shorter
paths than the ACO methods but its main advantage is low computational complexity and the superiority of SBA over the ACO grows with the increase of the
distance matrice size. The parallelization of its operation is also possible in a more
straightforward manner than in the case of the ACO.

Keywords: Travelling Salesman Problem · Segment Based Approach · Ant
Colony Optimization

1 Introduction

The aim of the paper is to present the Segment Based Approach (SBA) - a new technique
to solve the Traveling Sales Problem (TSP). The TSP is a well-known problem of finding
the shortest possible route that connects a number of cities under the constraint that each
one of them should be visited exactly once. This is one of the classical NP-hard problems of Artificial Intelligence. Its solution space is staggering large even for relatively
small number of cities. The number of all possible different routes for just 50 cities is
approximately equal to 3,04141 E+64. The distances between the cities are represented
by nodes of a weighted, symmetric graph.

Due to the size of the solution space, the brute-force approach is not feasible. There
are algorithms for providing an exact solution for real life problems but they are extremely
time consuming. The cumulative CPU time used for solving the TSP for all cities in
Sweden (17,180 nodes and 85,900 vertices) required 84.8 CPU years on a single Intel
Xeon 2.8 GHz processor [1]. Therefore, a number of metaheuristics have been proposed.
One of them, the popular Ant Colony Optimization (ACO) technique was originally
developed to solve exactly the TSP [2]. In this approach, a solution is constructed by

© The Author(s), under exclusive license to Springer Nature Switzerland AG 2022
N. T. Nguyen et al. (Eds.): ICCCI 2022, LNAI 13501, pp. 687–700, 2022.
https://doi.org/10.1007/978-3-031-16014-1_54

attaching connections that are deemed useful to the already constructed path. It suffers from extensive computational effort and has problems with parallel work. The ACO mimics the foraging behavior of real world ants. The proposed SBA also creates the solution by attaching connections between cities. It has a different sort of inspiration namely, the organization of long-term memory [3].

The paper is organized as follows. The second Section presents the basic version of the ACO used to solve the Travelling Salesman Problem. Section 3 discusses the intu-itions that lead to the concept of the SBA and confronts it with the ACO. It describes also in detail the SBA building blocks and its operation. Section 4 is devoted to presentation of the experimental results. The next Sect. 5 discusses possible enhancement of the SBA, especially with respect to solving of the DTSP – Dynamic Traveling Sales Problem. The paper concludes with the sixth Section, which summarizes the obtained so far, results.

2   Using Ant Colony Optimization to Solve the TSP

ACO is a popular meta-heuristic for solving complex combinatorial optimization prob-lems of large complexity. Its inspiration was the foraging behavior of ants. TSP was the ACO first application. The concept proved to be very fruitful and its' applications include such diverse tasks as image retrieval [4], Portfolio Optimization [5] or Bankruptcy Pre-diction [6] to name just a few. The paper [7] contains a comprehensive presentation of the ACO state of art and its potentials.

2.1   Operation of ACO

An Ant Colony consists of a number of ants that are extremely simple agents. They move from one node to another laying a pheromone trail on their way. The pheromone evaporates in time. The pseudocode for ACO is relatively simple:

```
BEGIN
Initialize colony and the pheromone matrice
WHILE stopping criteria have not been satisfied DO
       Select a starting position for each ant
       FOR EACH ant IN colony DO
              Select next node using the transition rule
              Update pheromone matrice
       END FOR
       Update the best solution so far
       Apply the pheromone evaporation rule
END WHILE
RETURN best solution found
```

The specific formulas used for the selection of edges, deposition, and evaporation of pheromone could be found e.g. in [2]. The formulas use several parameters, see Table 1.

Table 1. ACO parameter description with recommended values

Name	Description	Value
Q0	Probability of selecting exploitation over exploration	0.8
α	Aging factor used in the global updating rule	0.1
β	Moderating factor for the cost measure function	2.0
ρ	Aging factor in the local updating rule	0.1

In the construction of a path the following probabilistic equation for the selection of the next node c_{ij} is used [X1]:

$$
p(c_{ij}|s_k^p) = \begin{cases} \dfrac{\tau_{ij}^\alpha \cdot \eta_{ij}^\beta}{\sum_{c_{il} \in N(s_k^p)} \tau_{il}^\alpha \cdot \eta_{il}^\beta} & \text{if } j \in N(s_k^p), \\ 0 & \text{otherwise,} \end{cases}
$$

where:

$N(s_k^p)$ is a set of edges, not yet visited in a tour
α and β are pheromone and heuristic weight parameters respectively, both are real and positive
$\eta_{ij} = 1/d_{ij}$, where d_{ij} is the length of edge connecting i and j
τ_{ij} is the pheromone level on the edge connecting edge i and j

The probabilities have to be calculated constantly as the pheromone levels change during the optimization process. The calculations require many floating point operations including the time consuming power function.

2.2 Parameter Analysis

The operation of ACO is controlled by several parameters. As always in such a case the problem of a proper if not even optimal selection of their values arises. The descriptions of these parameters in the section clearly describe their expected impact on the operation of the algorithm. It does not mean, however, that the expected action is actually observed.

The analysis of the effect of parameters is hampered by the intrinsic indeterminism of ACO. The obtained result is an effect of the collaboration of often several hundred autonomous agents. Agents are usually implemented as separate threads making the contents of the pheromone array unpredictable. Moreover, each of the agents selects the next node using a pseudorandom number generator. As a result, the values of parameters are set by performing a number of experiments [8].

An extensive analysis of the impact of individual parameters is presented in a recent work [9]. The results are not very encouraging. Experiments show that parameters linked with the algorithm mechanics (α, β, q0, and ρ) do not influence the performance in an easily noticeable fashion. The performance does not seem to follow any clear pattern. Even when we compare the results for strikingly different parameter values, there is no easily detectable relationship between their values and the performance. It should be stressed, however, that the differences in performance are not great and usually the observed route lengths are only a few percent longer than the best-recorded results.

The only certain way to reduce the path length is to intensify the computational effort by increasing the number of ants and/or the number of iterations. Results presented in [10] suggest that within certain limits increasing the number of ants maybe more productive than increasing the number of iterations. As the number of cities grow just increasing the computational effort is less and less productive. Parallel operation with several distinct processes running concurrently seems to be an obvious way of mitigating the problem [11]. The solution has however some difficulties with synchronizing the content of pheromone matrice [12].

To sum up: the ACO is computationally extensive and hard to optimize approach to solve TSP. Its operational rules are pretty much complex. The SBA attempts to alleviate at least to some degree these deficiencies.

3   Description of the Segment Based Approach

Human beings can more easier memorize facts that are firmly embedded in a memory structure than isolated facts. To remember a given fact we have to entangle it with old and newly acquired facts. Paradoxically remembering more is easier than remembering less. Neuroscientists explain that the more connections between two neurons are activated, the easier it is to get access to them. This phenomena is used in the popular memory palace technique. In the SBA approach there is no pheromone matrice. All connections have the same priority. The more useful ones are simply more numerous. The approach uses also other techniques inspired by the way human memory operates: storing useful sequences of connections (declarative memory) and reorganizing those sequences – memory consolidation.

Let d denote a N * N matrix of floating point values in the range [0..1]. The matrice represents the distances between the nodes. In the following, n_x denotes the x node and $d_{k,j}$ represents the distance between the nodes n_k and n_j. We assume that the matrice is symmetric, that is $d_{jk} = d_{kj}$. A segment s(k, k + 1, ... m) is a sequence of edges connecting nodes leading with n_{k1}, through n_{k+1}, and finally n_m. Let size(s) denote the number of nodes in the sequence s and len(s) its total length:

$$len(s(n_1, \ldots, n_k)) = \sum_{x=1}^{k-1} d_{x,x+1}.$$

3.1   SBA Basic Operational Principle

The operation of SBA and ACO are have some similarities. In both of them, the optimization process consist of several iterations. In each of them starting from a randomly selected node a complete path is constructed by attaching not used so far nodes. There are however some differences.

The SBA tries to address the deficiencies of Ant based approaches by using a memory-extensive algorithm. The basic operational principle is simple. The path is built up from segments selected from a pool of productive segments in a random order. A segment could connect just 2 nodes or could be much longer. In short, the process of path construction differs from the Ant based algorithms in four major aspects:

- The path is constructed not from matrice edges but from segments that could connect many edges.
- There are no complex formulas for the evaluation of evaluation of usefulness of edges and finally their selection. The selection process is a simple operation of selecting at random a segment from a pool of matching segments.
- There is no pheromone matrice to represent the cumulative knowledge about the usefulness of edges. The number of copies of a segment is proportional to its estimated usefulness.
- The rules for accepting segments to enter the segment store and for their elimination from it are the replacement of the pheromone deposit/evaporation process.

The above description rises hope that the computational complexity of the SBA should be much smaller than ACO leading to a much shorter execution time. This is due to the following facts:

- The segments may consist of many edges and therefore the path building process requires substantially fewer steps.
- A random selection of a segment from a pool of suitable segments replaces the complex selection mechanism that needs many time consuming floating-point operations.
- ACO relies on the cooperation of many ants, in SBA we have only one agent constructing the road.

3.2 Used Notation

Let:

- BsF denote the best so far path, that is the shortest constructed path in any of previous iterations
- AccLev (Acceptance Level) which decides whether the current solution is good enough to update the Segment Pool.
- RejLev (Rejection Level): is used to prematurely abort the generation of a solution. This happens when the length of path built so far is so long that most probably Acclev would reject it. Therefore, there is no need to continue the path generation
- MaxSplit: is a small integer number. The paths exceeding the AccLev are cut into sub segments with lengths of up to MaxSplit. These sub-segments re are then passed to the Segment Pool.
- MaxSize: is used to control the size of the Segment Pool. It prevents the Segment Pool from being unacceptably large. It is the maximal allowed number of elements that are kept in a single glue node, see Sect. 3.5.

- Benefit: it is a small integer number that specifies how many copies of a sub-segment of the BsF solution are stored in Segment Pool.

3.3   Overview of Path Building Process

All two-node segments are always stored in the Segments Pool. The SBA works in iterations. Each iteration starts with a randomly selected segment. Iterations consist of a sequence of steps. In each step, we select a set of matching segments. A segment matches a path if:

- It has a glue node so one can connect it to the path. The glue node is either a staring or ending node that is identical to the stating or ending node of the path
- With the exception of the glue node, all segments' and paths' nodes must be distinct.

Next, a randomly selected segment from the set of matching segments is attached to the path. It may be necessary to reverse the order of nodes. This is possible as the distance matrice is symmetrical.

Example:
For the path [1, 5, 7] the matching segments are e.g. [9, 2, 1] or [4, 7]:

- Attaching the first segment to the front of a path: [9, 2, 1] ➜ [9, 2, 1, 5, 7]
- Appending the second segment to the path requires reversing it: [4, 7] ➜ [1, 5, 7, 4]// reversing the segment and then appending it to the end of a path

The following segments are not appropriate:

- [9, 2, 1, 5] // the node 5 is not a glue node and it is present both in the path and the segment
- [2, 9, 11] // there is no glue node.

The process of attaching new segments could result in:

1. Completing of a path. If its length is shorter than that of the BsF then it replaces the old BsF. Its sub-segments are loaded to the Segment Store, see Sect. 3.4. The Benefit parameter specifies how many copies of a sub-segment are loaded.
2. Acceptance of the path. The length of the complete path is above acceptance level threshold (ALev). The path looks promising so a single copy of all its sub-segments is loaded to the Segment Store.
3. Rejection of a path. The path is complete but its length is too long, the ALev criterion is not met. There is a good reason to reject to path.
4. Termination: the SBA at each step of path construction constantly evaluates its length. If the Rejection Level (RLev) is exceeded then it is highly likely that after completion, the path will be too long and therefore the path construction is immediately terminated. The algorithm proceeds to another iteration see next Sect. 3.5 for the details.

3.4   Operation of Segment Pool

All selected and accepted paths are split into segments. The minimal number of such nodes in a segment is equal to 3 and the maximal number of nodes in a segment is equal to MaxSplit.

Example:
Assuming that the MaxSplit is 4 then the path [1, 6, 4, 3, 2, 5] would be the source of the following sequences:

[1, 6, 3]; [6 4 3]; [4, 3, 2], [3, 2, 5]
[1, 6, 4, 3]; [6, 4, 3, 2]; [4, 3, 2, 5]

The Segment Store tries to optimize the segments it receives. For each segment, the permutations of all its nodes, with the exemption of the glue node, are generated and their lengths are calculated. Only the shortest one is stored in the Segment Store. It could well be, that the segment is already there. Therefore, the Segment Store could contain many instances of the same segment. The rationale is that the more useful segments are, the more copies of them should be stored so to increase their chances for selection. This mimics the feature of long-term memory: vivid recollections are heavily entangled within the memory structure.

3.5   Details of Path Building Process

There are two problems that have to be addressed. The first is the selection of matching segments. It is a very frequent operation. Therefore, the Store is implemented as a mapping where the key is the potential glue node and the value is a collection of its segments. As described above, the path can be extended at its beginning as well as at its end. As a consequence, each segment has two entries in the Store: one in which the key is the last node of a path and second where the key is the first node.

The second problem is the need to control the Store size. If the number of elements in the set exceeds the MaxSize parameter for a glue node, then the newly added segment replaces a randomly selected segment already in the set, provided it contains at least 3 nodes. The pseudocode for the SBA is presented below.

Input: symmetric distance matrice with N nodes
1. Store all two node segments in the Segment Store
2. Initialize BsF with an empty path
3. Initialize SOLUTION with a randomly selected segment
4. While number of nodes in SOLUTION <N
    a. Choices= selectMatchingSegments(SegmentStore, SOLUTION)
    b. Select sg: a random segment from Choices
    c. Attach sg to SOLUTION
    d. If q(SOLUTION) ==REJECT the abandon the iteration
5. If q(SOLUTION) is BEST:
    a. Update the Segment Store with BENEFIT copies of all sub -
       segments of SOL
    b. Store SOL in BsF
    c. Stop the iteration
6. If q(SOLUTION) is ACCEPT:
    a. Update the Segment Store with one copy of all sub -segments of
       SOL
    b. Stop the iteration

The SBA evaluates the potential usefulness of a constructed solution constantly, as it is built. Therefore the quality function q(Sol) has to take into account the number of nodes in the solution: $size(Sol)/N$.

$$q(SOL) = \begin{cases} BEST: size(SOL) == N \text{ and } len(SOL) < len(BSF) \\ ACCEPT: size(SOL) == N \text{ and } len(SOL) * ALev < len(BsF) \\ REJECT: \frac{size(SOL)}{N} * len(SOL) > \frac{size(Sol)}{N} * len(BsF) \text{ otherwize } CONTINUE \end{cases}$$

The most complex operation is updating the Segment Store. The operation calculates the distances of all possible permutations of sub-segments of a segment destined for storage in the Store. Note, that the glue nodes keep their position. This looks like a potential computational trap. In practice, however the PA performs well when the number nodes n < 7 and it turned out that the computational burden is not that significant.

4   SBA in Action

This Section contains a rudimentary discussion of the performance of SBA. It starts with an analysis of the impact some parameters have on the resulting path length. Next there is the comparison of SBA with ACO. The comparison takes into account the paths' lengths and required processing time. In the experiments, we used two matrices: 50 × 50 and 200 × 200. All reported below values are averages of 50 optimization runs, which gives us a reasonable confidence as to the statistical validity of the reported mean values. The maximal number of iterations for an optimization run was 500.

4.1   Parameter Analysis

As stated in Sect. 3.2 the operation of the SBA is controlled by just five parameters: Acceptance Level (AccLev), Rejection Level (RejLev), Benefit, Maximal Segment Length (MaxSplit), and Memory Size (MaxSize).

Table 2. Average path length for matrice 50×50, AccLevel $= 0.01$, RejLev $= 0.01$

MaxSize	Benefit2	Benefit3	Benefit4	Benefit5	Benefit6
100	2,507	2,52	2,51	2,518	2,528
200	2,519	2,509	2,522	2,523	2,522
300	2,518	2,51	2,516	2,515	2,503
400	2,532	2,521	2,524	2,515	2,503
500	2,519	2,518	2,517	2,517	2,508
600	2,51	2,513	2,516	2,516	2,505

The SBA uses heavily memory. The first set of experiments was to find out what is the impact of used memory on the path length. The Acceptance level and Rejection level have a very low value: 0.01. This means that only the best solution was used for Storage Store enhancement. Additionally different Benefit Factors were used. These are presented in the Table 2 and Table 3. The values do not differ much, which means that contrary to initial expectations, the SBA is resilient to even substantial changes in the memory-based parameters.

Table 3. Average path length for matrice 200×200, AccLevel $= 0.01$, RejLev $= 0.01$

MaxSize	Benefit2	Benefit3	Benefit4	Benefit5	Benefit6
300	3,716	3,745	3,755	3,699	3,761
200	3,695	3,752	3,706	3,753	3,775
400	3,75	3,742	3,763	3,713	3,749
600	3,755	3,703	3,766	3,744	3,725
500	3,754	3,716	3,788	3,769	3,785

Increasing substantially the value of AccLevel to 0.95 does not change the performance very much. The path lengths are more stable but not much shorter than in the previous case, see Fig. 1.

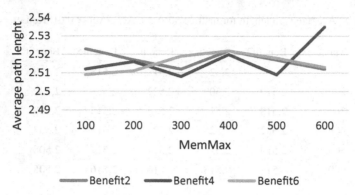

Fig. 1. Average path length for 50 × 50 matrice, MaxSplit = 2, AccLevel = 0.95, RejLevel = 0.05

However, after increasing both the MaxSplit and the AccLevel the shortening of paths is clearly visible, see Fig. 2. The data shown there are for the 200 × 200 matrice, AccLevel = 0.95 and MaxSplit = 5.

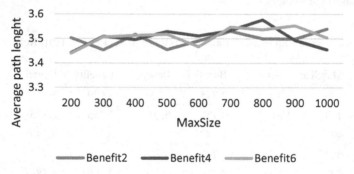

Fig. 2. Average path length for 50 × 50 matrice, MaxSplit = 5, AccLevel = 0.9, RejLevel = 0.05

There is no clear relationship between path length and MaxSize but the change has some advantages:

- the average path length has decreased (from ca. 3,716 to ca. 3,439)
- The results are stable
- The increase in MaxSplit results in the generation of many segments but increasing the MaxSize is not necessary.

These above results are just preliminary but they give us some insight into the operation of the SBA. The optimization of the parameter values must involve more than one parameter. Some of them like Benefit and especially MaxSize do not seem to have much influence on the path length.

4.2 Comparison with ACO

In order to identify the set of parameter values that provide short paths a substantial number of test runs were executed. The aim was to find out whether the SBA is capable of outperforming the ACO. The ACO version used in experiments was the JAWS framework described in. [X] with recommended there set of parameters:

Number of ants equal to the number of nodes, $Q0 = 0.8$, $\alpha = 0.1$, $\beta = 2$, $\rho = 0.1$.

Table 4 contains data on the path length for the matrices with 50 and 200 nodes. The values shown in the tables are average value from 50 individual runs. For the ACO the Table 4 contains also the range of values for the 0.95 confidence level. The number of iterations was equal to 500 for both algorithms.

Table 4. Comparing average path length of SBA and ACO

Distance matrice	SBA	ACO Avg.	ACO from	ACO to
Matrice 50 × 50	2,341	2,396	2,37	2,420
Matrice 200 × 200	3,434	3,440	3,40	3,475

As you can see, the values for the SBA are significantly lower for the ACO. In both cases, they are below the 0.95 confidence level. Although statistically valid, the difference is in the length is not large.

More detailed data illustrating the behavior of SBA is contained in the Table 5 and Table 6.

Table 5. SBA detailed data for matrice 50 × 50

meanBSF	bsfspan	lastiter	Storage
2,341	0,021	240,52	50
2,422	0,036	212,62	70
2,466	0,038	214,2	90
2,497	0,042	238,88	110
2,508	0,037	250,36	130
2,548	0,036	280	150

Table 6. SBA detailed data for matrice 200 × 200

meanBSF	bsfspan	lastiter	Storage
3,434	0,048	249,7	200
3,461	0,045	275,2	300

(continued)

Table 6. (*continued*)

meanBSF	bsfspan	lastiter	Storage
3,514	0,043	296,6	600
3,519	0,046	291,82	500
3,527	0,049	251,58	400

The tables indicate three interesting features:

- The variance in the path lengths is remarkably small, which indicates the ability of the SBA to deliver consistent results.
- The average iteration number that delivered the best result exceeds slightly 250 that is half of the iteration count used in the experiment. It means, that there is no need to run the thousands of iterations as it were reported in some studies on ACO. Note, that although the LastIter for matrice 200 × 200 is greater than for matrice 50.50 but the difference is not significant.
- The average path length decreases with the available memory size. This indicates that keeping in memory not frequently used segments is counterproductive.

The Table 7 compares the average time used to run a optimization process.

Table 7. Comparing execution time of the SBA and ACO

Distance matrice	SBA duration	ACO duration
Matrice 50	0,638075	9,70265
Matrice 200	15,68875	562,650725

The difference in the duration of the optimization run between the SBA and ACO is very large. The duration of an optimization run is more stable for the ACO as the computational complexity of each iteration is the same. In the case of the SBA it differs to some extent because some iterations could be terminated before completing a full route. The difference is staggering. For the Matrice 50 the SBA is 15 times faster and for the Matrice 200 the value rises to more than 35. The ability of the SBA to increase the difference with the increase of problem complexity is definitely a welcome feature.

It is possible that some optimization techniques and/or careful selection of parameters could improve the performance of the ant based approaches. It is however unlikely, that results could change it by such a large degree measure. Therefore, it is possible to argue with a significant level of certainty that the SBA is capable of delivering paths of roughly the same length as the ACO based algorithms but in a time at least an order of magnitude shorter than ACO.

The memory size necessary to run the SBA is much larger than that required for the ACO. With the constant increase in the availability of memory, this is not a compromising factor.

5 Possible Enhancements to the SBA

The presented above version of the SBA is a preliminary one. Experimental results strongly suggest, that playing with parameter values does not produce significant changes in the performance as in the case of ACO.

A more promising path is to devise more elaborate methods for the updating of Segment Store. Up to now, the segments are replaced in a random manner. The Benefit Factor is supposed to ensure that useful segments are more numerous. It is however worth considering whether older, not recently used segments, should not be eliminated more often than newer ones. After all it is easier to be the BsF, solution in the earlier iterations than at the end of optimization process. There is obviously more than a one strategy of doing this. As criteria for the elimination, one could name e.g. the time of entering the Segment Store, the number of times it was used to produce a solution, or a weighted combination of these two.

As described in Sect. 2.2, in order to speed up the optimization process parallelization is advocated. In ACO the agents have to work upon a common pheromone matrice. One has to balance the burden of its synchronization with the advantages resulting from the ant or ant cooperation. The parallelization of the SBA is much more easy. Many instances of the algorithm could work concurrently sharing the same Segment Store. The tasks of segment selection/optimization/replacement could be centralized and executed as local service of the Segment Store. Speeding-up the optimization offered by parallelization is always welcome and offers a chance to adopt to even fast changing environments.

For the Dynamic TSP one should consider introducing an individual process or maybe even processes which are responsible for optimizing the arrangement of nodes making up segments in the Store. This could be done separately from the regular operations of the Store. The elimination of not recently used segments also seems a reasonable procedure.

6 Conclusions

The Segment Building Approach is a novel heuristic to find solutions in large solution space. Reusing partial, locally optimized sub-solutions enables it to achieve good quality results in a relatively short time. Especially valuable is that the time necessary to find a solution increases in an acceptable manner with the increase of a problem's complexity. The conducted experiments clearly indicate that SBA shares with ACO robustness to changes in parameter values. In order to improve the SBA performance one should concentrate upon the modifications of its operation rather than adjusting its parameter values. Compared to the ACO based algorithm, preliminary version the SBA is capable of delivering paths of roughly the same length but the time in of at least one order of a magnitude shorter. The SBA achieves its efficiency through intensive usage of memory.

The experiments clearly show that memory consumption could be kept within reasonable limits and actually, at some point increasing the available memory is counterproductive.

An initial analysis indicates that the parallelization of its operation is much easier than for the ACO. The hard problem of shared access to common data simply does not exit. This opens the way to apply the proposed approach to solve the Dynamic Traveling Salesman Problem. The next step in the study is to verify that assumption.

References

1. Tinós, R., Helsgaun, K., Whitley, D.: Efficient recombination in the Lin-Kernighan-Helsgaun traveling salesman heuristic. In: Auger, A., Fonseca, C., Lourenço, N., Machado, P., Paquete, L., Whitley, D. (eds.) PPSN 2018. LNCS, vol. 11101, pp. 95–107 (2018). Springer, Cham. https://doi.org/10.1007/978-3-319-99253-2_8
2. Dorigo, M.: Optimization, learning and natural algorithms, Ph.D. thesis, Politecnico di Milano, Italie (1992)
3. Klimesch, M.: The Structure of Long-Term Memory. A Connectivity Model of Sementic Processing. Psychology Press (2013). ISBN 9781138876385. Accessed 8 May 2015
4. Picard, D., Cord, M. Revel, A.: Image retrieval over networks : active learning using ant algorithm. IEEE Trans. Multimedia 10(7), 1356–1365 (2008)
5. Abolmaali, S., Roodposhti, F.R.: Portfolio optimization using ant colony method a case study on Tehran stock exchange. J. Account. Finance Econ. 8(1), 96–108 (2018)
6. Zhang, Y.: A rule-based model for bankruptcy prediction based on an improved genetic ant colony algorithm. Math. Probl. Eng., 753251 (2013). https://doi.org/10.1155/2013/753251
7. Dorigo, M., Stuetzle, T.: Ant colony optimization: overview and recent advances, IRIDIA – Technical report series, Technical report No. TR/IRIDIA/2009-013, May 2009
8. Chirico, U.: A Java Framework for ant colony systems. In: Ants2004: Forth International Workshop on Ant Colony Optimization and Swarm Intelligence, Brussels (2004)
9. Pytka, M.: Parameter optimization for ant colonies for dynamic environments, Msc thesis, Wrocław Technical University, Wrocław (2020)
10. Siemiński, A.: Using hyper populated ant colonies for solving the TSP. Vietnam J. Comput. Sci. 3(2), 103–117 (2016). https://doi.org/10.1007/s40595-016-0059-z
11. Bullnheimer, B., Kotsis, G.: Parallelization strategies for the ant system, high performance algorithms and software in nonlinear. Optimization 24, 87 (2013)
12. Siemiński, A., Kopel, M.: Comparing efficiency of ACO parallel implementations. J. Intell. Fuzzy Syst. 32(2), 77–88 (2017)

A Second-Order Adaptive Network Model for Organizational Learning and Usage of Mental Models for a Team of Match Officials

Sam Kuilboer[1], Wesley Sieraad[2], Gülay Canbaloğlu[3], Laila van Ments[4], and Jan Treur[2(✉)]

[1] Computational Science, University of Amsterdam, Amsterdam, The Netherlands
`s.m.m.kuilboer@student.vu.nl`
[2] Social AI Group, Department of Computer Science, Vrije Universiteit Amsterdam, Amsterdam, The Netherlands
`w.r.sieraad@student.vu.nl, j.treur@vu.nl`
[3] Department of Computer Engineering, Koç University, Istanbul, Turkey
`gcanbaloglu17@ku.edu.tr`
[4] AutoLeadStar, Jerusalem, Israel
`laila@autoleadstar.com`

Abstract. This paper describes a multi-level adaptive network model for mental processes making use of shared mental models in the context of organizational learning in team-related performances. The paper describes the value of using shared mental models to illustrate the concept of organizational learning, and factors that influence team performances by using the analogy of a team of match officials during a game of football and show their behavior in a simulation of the shared mental model. The paper discusses potential elaborations of the different studied concepts, as well as implications of the paper in the domain of teamwork and team performance, and in terms of organizational learning.

Keywords: Shared mental model · Network model · Organizational learning · Teamwork · Match officials

1 Introduction

It has generally been found that team performance is affected by shared cognition of the task (Salas et al. 2008). Teams that are aware of the objective and difficulties of a task at hand are performing better than teams that are not aware of their shared responsibilities (Katz-Navon and Miriam Erez 2005). The construction of a shared mental model can help explain team functioning and the underlying processes that are in force during team performances. Such theory, stemming from social psychology, can be used to help improve the teamwork of teams. A shared mental model is basically about concurrence. Inside the setting of collaboration, the shared mental model describes the different roles and responsibilities of each team member and how they connect with one another based on each member's ability and preference. We preserve the notion that the shared mental

© The Author(s), under exclusive license to Springer Nature Switzerland AG 2022
N. T. Nguyen et al. (Eds.): ICCCI 2022, LNAI 13501, pp. 701–716, 2022.
https://doi.org/10.1007/978-3-031-16014-1_55

model is not only highly relevant in relation to the theoretical framework of team-based collaboration, but also in the context of human-agent teams.

Furthermore, mental models can be used to emulate the mental processes that are at play during the relevant tasks and can help describe the internal mental simulation and decision making based on their outcomes; e.g. (Craik 1952). Moreover, by making the connections and relevant factors of such a mental model adaptive, forms of learning and control can be applied; the relevant factors at play and the behavior of the agent can be learned or forgotten. Working in teams generates yet another process, namely that of creating, retaining, and transferring knowledge within an organization. Based on this, an organization is able to grow in knowledge and experience over time, and members within this organization can both learn from this cumulative knowledge and contribute to this knowledge of the organization. This process is known as organizational learning.

This dynamic multilevel type of learning involves different individuals and combines their different pieces of knowledge as a team. The dynamic factor is represented by the people, which adapt over time, the multilevel type stems from the fact that organizational learning is different from individual learning. Both types of learning interact with one another but evolve differently. The modeling of all the different processes that occur at different levels during the different stages of organizational learning can be shown by feedback learning mechanisms, which show to what extent and how exactly individuals share knowledge and learn from the organization's shared mental model and eventually bring this knowledge into practice. This complex interplay of different types of mechanisms is a vital part of understanding the learning process of organizations (Canbaloğlu et al. 2022a, 2022b, 2022c; Kim 1993; Crossan et al. 1999; Wiewiora et al. 2019) and the usage of such learned knowledge.

The current paper addresses these aspects of a shared mental model. The focus of the paper is put on the mental processes of members of a team of referees during a football match. The goal is to show (1) how the members of the team learn before the match by organisational learning to get rid of imperfections in their mental models (2) how exactly the organization's shared mental model affects and directs the individual mental models, (3) the ways in which the members are influenced by the actual contextual states of the match, possibly resulting in errors and other imperfections, and (4) how the team acts during such cases. The contribution of this paper is that it integates models that were separately available from two sides, (1) learning a shared ment model, and (2) using a shareld mental model, and evaluates this in a new case study.

Some background knowledge is described in Sect. 2; an example scenario of the referees in action during a football match is given. Moreover, in Sect. 3, the background information of the network-oriented modeling approach is described in detail. Section 4 elaborates on the design of the adaptive network model and shows how it is able to model the organizational learning processes, with the underlying characteristics and models of the individuals' behavior. Simulations of the example scenario are provided in Sect. 5, which is followed by mathematical analysis of the model in Sect. 6. This is all concluded by a discussion of the network model, its behavior and possible extensions, and the relevancy of the model to support the referee process during football matches in Sect. 7.

2 Background

The problem at hand involves a number of processes and concepts, such as individual and shared mental models, and organizational learning. A mental model is of particular importance when people are performing team-related work. In most cases, team members have a shared task, but also have underlying individual subtasks, therefore each individual usually has their own individual mental model. In order to have a properly working team, the individual mental models must be aligned in such a way, that a universally team-based shared mental model emerges from the merging of the individual mental models, which is called the organization's or team's shared model. It has been found that errors in the team process have been linked to problems stemming from the shared mental model, and its lack of adaptivity (Mathieu et al. 2000). The second-order adaptive network model that will be used to describe the underlying processes of the refereeing process in this paper combines information from computational (modeling) science, psychology, social sciences and stress-related behavior, and integrates information from the physiological and psychological states of referees during a football game (Boyko et al. 2007; Gomez-Carmona and Pino-Ortega 2016). In this section, these processes and concepts along with respective previous literature that exists about these topics will be briefly discussed. This stage provides a basis of the underlying workings of the models and serves as a scientific rationale for the design choices.

Organizational Learning. In the case study that is addressed in this paper, the mental models of three football match officials (referee R and his two assistants A1 and A2) are not interlinked well just yet. Initially, they are based on weak connections. The officials can not use a shared mental model, as its connections have not materialized, meaning that it does not exist yet. Organizational learning is used to create such a shared mental model. This form of learning covers the following (Crossan et al. 1999; Kim 1993; Wiewiora et al. 2019): (1) individual learning by the officials takes place, which generates stronger individual mental models, (2) there is a creation of an organization's shared mental model, by combination of the individual mental models, (3) a learning process of the individuals from the shared mental model takes place thus improving their individual mental models, (4) the creation and learning from the shared mental model creates stronger connections and makes it possible to create the complete individual mental models. So, the following levels of the organizational learning are considered (Canbaloğlu et al. 2022a; Kim 1993):

- **Individual level.** Individual mental models are created, which are subject to internal simulation and individual mental model learning based on the context.
- **Organizational level.** The creation of the organization-level model, which is obtained by institutionalising the shared mental model.
- **From individual level to organizational level (feed forward learning).** Handles the creation of a shared mental model by aggregating the developed individual mental models.
- **From organizational level to individual level (feedback learning).** Deals with how individuals adopt the shared mental model by learning from it.

Case Description. The setting of the case is that of an official football match. A team of officials (the Referee and his or her assistants) is assigned to officiate a match between two rival clubs. Both clubs are still running to become the league champion, so the match is clouded by tension. In addition to this, one of the regular senior assistants feels ill and is replaced by an inexperienced junior assistant (A2).

To be adequately prepared for the match, the referee (R) and the assistants come together before the match. They walk through multiple scenarios of which one is high-lighted in this paper. This scenario refers to a situation where a player of rival team 1 is offside. The senior assistant (A1) will immediately be aware of this and will flag for offside and subsequently communicate this to the referee. In this case, the referee has two options, he can validate the decision of the assistant; e.g., because the player does not come into possession of the ball the referee can ignore his assistant. If the referee positively validates the call of the assistant, the referee will give a free kick to the opponent team and resume the game and if ignored, the game will resume without the intervention of a free kick. As the senior assistant and the referee reach a consensus on how to appropriately handle the offside situation, the junior referee listens and takes it all in. At the end of the meeting, the officials have a shared mental model when it comes to this particular situation.

During the match, the offside situation as described above happens twice. Once at the side of the senior assistant referee (A1) and once at the side of the junior assistant referee. As it happens on the side of the senior assistant referee, everything goes down as planned. The assistant flags for offside, communicates it to the referee, the referee whistles, gives a free kick and the game resumes. The second time, it happens on the side of the junior assistant referee (A2) and a couple of things go wrong. The tension of the game has led to a huge amount of stress for the junior assistant referee. As a consequence, he does observe that the striker might have been in a possible offside position, but fails to judge whether there is actually a case of punishable offside. Moreover, the assistant forgets to communicate this to the referee and the other assistant. Thankfully, they did observe the situation and found that the offside was punishable, therefore they take the appropriate actions.

3   The Modeling Approach Used

The modeling approach to model the different mental models and their organisational learning is described in this section. In general, a network-oriented modeling app-roach can be seen as a unification of the causal modeling tradition and the perspectives described by philosophy of mind; e.g. (Heil 1998). A network-oriented modeling app-roach (Treur 2020) is suitable to model causal relationships among states and can be used to emulate the creation process of shared mental models by an adaptive network. The network uses a dynamic (and possibly adaptive) time-related perspective on the states, their behavior, and the causal relations that play a role in the situation. Therefore, such network models can represent mental states and the (social) interactions occurring between the members of the network.

The modeling approach used is a widely usable generic dynamic AI modeling approach that distinguishes itself by incorporating a dynamic and adaptive temporal perspective, both on states and on causal relations. This dynamic perspective enables the modeling of cyclic and adaptive networks, and also of timing of causal effects. This enables modeling by adaptive causal networks for connected mental states and for evolving social interaction. In general, according to (Treur 2020) the conceptualization of a network model involves the declaration of all states X and Y (with values $X(t)$, $Y(t)$ over time t), connections between the states, the weights $\omega_{X,Y}$ of these connections, the single impacts $\omega_{X,Y} X(t)$ and aggregated impacts $c_Y(\omega_{X_1,Y} X_1(t), ..., \omega_{X_k,Y} X_k(t))$ by combination functions $c_Y(..)$ that these states have, and the way states can change over time using speed factors η_Y.

The concepts $\omega_{X,Y}$, $c_Y(..)$, η_Y are the network characteristics that define a network model. For specification of a network model, they are indicated in a standard format by a handful of tables. The connectivity between the states is indicated by a table (called role matrix) **mb** that shows the incoming connections for every state in the model. The strength of these connections is indicated by the connection weights assigned to each individual connection in another table (role matrix) **mcw**. Moreover, speed factors are capable of regulating the timing of the states and their respective values; they are represented in a table **ms**. Lastly, combination functions represent the impact that other states have on a particular state. There are different ways one can model the combination of the multiple impacts; such methods incorporate a function that specifies how to combine (aggregate) multiple incoming connection effects. These are specified in tables **mcfw** and **mcfp**. The way in which these network characteristics define the dynamics of a network model is explained as follows:

$$\mathbf{impact}_{X_i,Y}(t) = \omega_{X_i,Y} X_i(t)$$

$$\mathbf{aggimpact}_Y(t) = c_Y\left(\mathbf{impact}_{X_1,Y}(t), ..., \mathbf{impact}_{X_k,Y}(t)\right) \tag{1}$$

Here $X_1,..,X_k$ are the states from which state Y gets incoming connections. This is assembled in the following canonical differential equation used for all states:

$$dY(t)/dt = \eta_Y\left[\mathbf{aggimpact}_Y(t) - Y(t)\right] \tag{2}$$

This differential equation can be rewritten into difference equation format to determine the state values with regard to the change in time Δt:

$$Y(t + \Delta t) = Y(t) + \eta_Y[\mathbf{aggimpact}_Y(t) - Y(t)]\Delta t$$
$$= Y(t) + \eta_Y[c_Y(\omega_{X_1,Y} X_1(t), ..., \omega_{X_k,Y} X_k(t)) - Y(t)]\Delta t \tag{3}$$

As can be seen in the equations, the speed factor η stretches the impact over time, the connection weight ω, together with the aggregated impact determines the impact of the connected states to Y on the activation value of state Y. This type of difference equation is already available in the dedicated software environment, together with a library (of more than 50 functions) from which combination functions can be selected. So, a modeler does not need to deal with these equations themselves, only with the choice of the network characteristics $\omega_{X,Y}$, $c_Y(..)$, η_Y (via the role matrices **mb**, **mcw**, **ms**, **mcfw**, **mcfp** that are inserted as tables in the software environment) so that the software environment can automatically instantiate the difference equations in the intended manner. In (Treur 2021) it is shown by Theorem 1 that format (3) enables to model any dynamical system.

The combination functions that are used in the model are the advanced logistic sum, scaled maximum, steponce, and complemental identity function, as shown in the Table 1. As the model introduced in Sect. 4 has states X_1 to X_{88}, during simulation the software environment runs a system of 88 instances of (coupled) difference equations of the type indicated in (3); the functions used for these instantiations for the 88 states are found in the last column of Table 1.

In the case of modeling adaptive networks, some of these network characteristics $\omega_{X,Y}$, $c_Y(..)$, η_Y are subject to change over time. This is defined by self-model states added to the network; for example:

- For any adaptive connection from state X to state Y, there is a self-model state $\mathbf{W}_{X,Y}$ (also called a $\mathbf{W}$-state) representing the connection weigh $\omega_{X,Y}$
- For any adaptive speed factor η_Y there is a self-model state $\mathbf{H}_Y$ (also called an $\mathbf{H}$-state) representing η_Y

Table 1. The combination functions used

Name	Formula	Parameters	Used for states
$\text{alogistic}_{\sigma,\tau}(V_1,...,V_k)$	$[\dfrac{1}{1+e^{-\sigma(V_1+\cdots+V_k-\tau)}} - \dfrac{1}{1+e^{\sigma\tau}}]\,(1+e^{-\sigma\tau})$	Steepness $\sigma > 0$, excitability threshold τ	X_1–X_{24}, X_{32}–X_{52}, X_{59}–X_{61}, X_{86}
$\text{smax}_\lambda(V_1,...,V_k)$	$\max(V_1,...,V_k)/\lambda$	Scaling factor λ	X_{25}–X_{31}, X_{53}–X_{58}
$\text{steponce}_{\alpha,\beta}(V_1,...,V_k)$	1 if $\alpha \le t \le \beta$, else 0 (time t)	Start time α, end time β	X_{83}–X_{85}, X_{87}–X_{88}
$\text{compid}(V)$	$1 - V$	–	X_{62}–X_{82}

This self-modeling concept can also be applied iteratively to model multiple orders of adaptation. For example, the adaptation speed $\eta_{\mathbf{W}_{X,Y}}$ (learning rate) of a (first-order) self-model state $\mathbf{W}_{X,Y}$ for an adaptive connection can be made adaptive, thus modeling a form of plasticity. This can be modeled by a second-order self-model state $\mathbf{H}_{\mathbf{W}_{X,Y}}$ (also called an $\mathbf{H_W}$-state). Such second-order self-model states create second-order adaptivity, which can be used to model metaplasticity (Abraham and Bear 1996; Treur 2019). Another form of second-order adaptivity can be modeled by a second-order $\mathbf{W_W}$-state (also called a higher-order $\mathbf{W}$-state) controlling the weight of a connection connecting two $\mathbf{W}$-states. In (Treur 2021) it is shown by Theorem 2 that the format defined by (3) together with the concept of self-modeling is able to model any adaptive dynamical system. To model mental models, their adaptation, and the control of this adaptation, the three-level cognitive architecture, as shown in Fig. 1, can be used (Treur and Van Ments 2022; Van Ments and Treur 2021; see also (Van Ments et al. 2021a, 2021b):

- **The base level** models the internal simulations of the mental models.

- **The middle level** describes the adaptation of the mental models, this concerns learning and forgetting of a mental model.
- **The highest level** models the control over these processes.

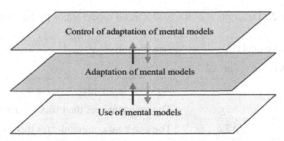

Fig. 1. Cognitive architecture for mental models; adopted from (Treur and Van Ments 2022; Van Ments and Treur 2021)

4   The Introduced Adaptive Network Model

The adaptive mental and social processes of the team of match officials are modeled by the second-order adaptive network model introduced in this section. A picture of the connectivity of the model is shown later in this section; it takes the three-level network structure shown in Fig. 1 as point of departure. An overview of all states with their examplanation can be found in Sect. 7. The full specification by role matrices is defined in the Appendix (see Linked Data at https://www.researchgate.net/publication/357622527). An example simulation for the scenario as described in the case description in Sect. 2 is shown in Sect. 5.

In the **base plane**, the mental model states of referee and assistants and the shared mental model are modeled (see Fig. 2). The shared mental model is represented in the dark-colored rectangle, while the three individual mental models are covered in the oval forms. The officials are represented by the letters R, A1, and A2 for the Referee, Assistant 1, and Assistant 2, respectively. These mental models represent knowledge of the individual referee and assistants and of the shared mental model. Within each mental model, the tasks are represented by nodes; they represent the states of the mental

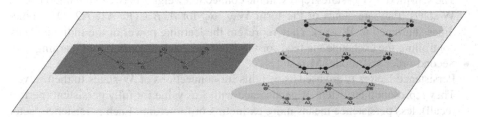

Fig. 2. Base level of model. The thickened lines are the connections which are initially part of the mental model of the corresponding official (R/A1/A2).

model. For an explanation of these states, see Table 2. The mental states of every person are connected by using links. These links represent the fact that the persons know the temporal order of the multiple tasks. The first mental model state for every person, is activated by external activation states (not shown in Fig. 2).

Table 2. Description of the base mental model states in the scenario.

States of the mental models			Description
For R	For A1	For A2	
R_a	$A1_a$	$A2_a$	A player is offside
R_b	$A1_b$	$A2_b$	The assistant sees the offside situation and flags
R_c	$A1_c$	$A2_c$	The assistant communicates this to the referee
R_d	$A1_d$	$A2_d$	The referee whistles for offside
R_e	$A1_e$	$A2_e$	The referee gives a free kick
R_f	$A1_f$	$A2_f$	The match continues

To model multi-order adaptivity in the network model, a number of first- and second-order self-model states were created for the mental models; see Fig. 3. The first-order adaptivity is modeled in the **middle plane**, and addresses the adaptivity of the mental models. The middle plane solely consists of such **W**-states; they represent all the weights of the connections between the base level mental model states. Some arrows are omitted due to clarity.

A full overview of the connections can be found in the **mcw** matrix in the Appendix. Next to the influence on the base-level states, there are intralevel (coloured black) connections from all **W**-states of individual mental models to their equivalent **W**-states of the shared mental model and back. These connections represent parts where the individual team members contribute to the formation of the shared organization mental model (feed forward learning) and vice versa (feedback learning).

To be able to control the first-order adaptation processes in a context-dependent manner a third level was created. In this **upper plane** five types of states are shown (see Fig. 3):

- Second-order self-model $\mathbf{W_W}$-states
  The self-model $\mathbf{W_W}$-states represent the connection weights between the middle level **W**-states; they are states of the form $\mathbf{W_{W_A,W_B}}$ for $A, B \in \{R, A1, A2, O\}$ (sometimes shortened to $\mathbf{W_{W_{A,B}}}$). They represent the learning power of the individuals by controlling the exchange via feed forward and feedback organisational learning.
- Second-order self-model $\mathbf{M_W}$-states
  Persistence factors μ are used as weights for connections of **W**-states to themselves. They represent their extent of persistence with 1 as value for fully persistent (perfect recall); less persistence means more extinction or forgetting. Each persistence factor μ is made adaptive (depending on circumstances) by adding a corresponding $\mathbf{M_W}$-state to the upper plane: a control state representing the persistence factor, affecting the

memory of the individuals. The M_W-states are affected by the stress state. Note that, as the persistence factors are modeled in the middle plane as weights of connections from W-states to themselves, M_W-states can be considered a special case of W_W-states: higher order W-states of the form W_{W_A,W_A} for $A \in \{R, A1, A2, O\}$.

- Second-order self-model H_W-states
  The self-model H_W-states represent the adaptive speed factors η_W for W-states (their learning rate); these H_W-states regulate the timing of the W-states when receiving an impact.
- Stress state
  The stress state influences other second-order self-model states, in particular the M_W-states. By doing so, they influence the memory of the individuals. If the stress level is 0, perfect recall takes place ($\mu = 1$), if the stress level is >0, then some extinction or forgetting takes place, depending on how high the stress level is.
- Activation-states
  The activation states are responsible for the start of the different phases as explained in the case description in Sect. 2.

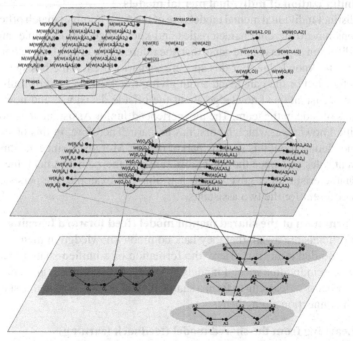

Fig. 3. The connectivity of the full model depicted in a base-level, adaptation of mental models and control of adaptation of mental model. The black arrows represent intralevel influences, the red lines represent interlevel influences and the blue lines represent the influence from the phases. (Color figure online)

Figure 3 the connectivity of the full model depicted in a base-level, adaptation of mental models and control of adaptation of mental model. The black arrows represent intralevel influences, the red lines represent interlevel influences and the blue lines represent the influence from the phases.

5 Simulation of the Scenario Case

The case scenario from Sect. 2 was simulated with a multi-phase approach, such that the different occurring phases can be observed. Note that in practice, these processes can, and often do, take place simultaneously; the model can also do that but for reasons of presentation the different phases were used. First, the individual models can be observed, some of the officials hold information about certain parts of the processes, while others do not. Therefore, the formation and the effects of the shared mental model for the team are shown. Both the feedforward learning from the different individuals to the shared organizational network and the feedback learning of individuals from the shared mental model, occur. In short, the following phases are shown.

Phase 1: Initialization of individual mental models
The three distinct individual mental models are of the three Football match officials. Since these persons have different characteristics and knowledge (for example, an Assistant deals with different aspects of the game than the referee), the officials have both common and role-specific knowledge. For this specific scenario, the referee has specific knowledge about the start of the game, and about giving free kicks in case of fouls, while the experienced Assistant has knowledge about the offside decisions, and how they communicate this offside in the team. The inexperienced Junior Assistant does not have any team-specific knowledge, which he first has to learn. Therefore, in this phase, A2 does not have knowledge about this specific part of the job. Moreover, since the three officials have different roles and since they react differently to their environment, they also have different characteristics that govern their learning. For example, the persistence of the learning is different for the two assistants.

Phase 2: Formation of the shared mental model (feed forward learning)
The match officials are aware that they lack common knowledge in their new team, so they have scheduled a meeting. Here, the formation of a unified shared mental model takes place. The individual mental models are merged, using the aggregation function, through the process of learning to form a shared mental model. Within this shared mental model, each connection strengthens.

Phase 3: Learning from the shared model (feedback learning)
Since the connections from the weight states stemming from the shared mental model are activated, knowledge is extracted from the shared mental model, the so-called instructional learning from the meeting. In this scenario, the officials learn from the organization's shared mental model.

Phase 4: Using (and forgetting) the learned individual mental models
In the last phase of the case simulation, the match officials officiate the game to which they were assigned. The highly stressful environment, make the officials more prone to

forget certain rules and/or to make mistakes. This additional stress component makes the connections in their own mental models weaker. During this stage, the effect of the previous learning, the organization's shared mental model, and the individual mental models along with the added stress factor all have their influences on the decisions made by the match officials.

Figure 4 shows the results of the simulation for the entire model. In the subsequent subsections, the behavior of the different match officials is shown in more detail. During the first stage of the simulation, the individual mental models are formed. The $\mathbf{W_W}$-states of the match officials towards the organization ($\mathbf{W_{W_R, W_O}}$, $\mathbf{W_{W_{A1}, W_O}}$, $\mathbf{W_{W_{A2}, W_O}}$ or, shorter, $\mathbf{W_{W_{R,O}}}$, $\mathbf{W_{W_{A1,O}}}$, $\mathbf{W_{W_{A2,O}}}$) are active during this stage, as can be seen in Fig. 4, allowing for the transfer (feed forward learning), of the individual mental models towards the organization's shared mental model. It can be seen that during this stage, only the $\mathbf{W}$-states for the connections which the respective match official has knowledge about are active, while the others are not. During the second stage of the organizational learning, feedback learning takes place in which the individual mental models can learn from the constructed organization's shared mental model.

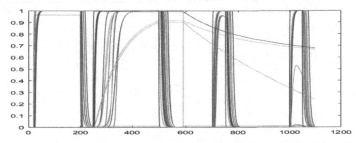

Fig. 4. Result of the full simulation: feed forward learning 20–200, feedback learning 250–500, usage and forgetting during match 590–1100.

During this stage, the $\mathbf{W_W}$-states representing the feedback learning ($\mathbf{W_{W_{O,R}}}$, $\mathbf{W_{W_{O,A1}}}$, $\mathbf{W_{W_{O,A2}}}$) are active while also the speed factors associated with the $\mathbf{W}$-states for the weights of the connections of the three officials ($\mathbf{H_{W_R}}$, $\mathbf{H_{W_{A1}}}$, and $\mathbf{H_{W_{A2}}}$) allow the learning to take place during this stage. It can clearly be seen that the weights of the previous unlearned connections are starting to become active as time progresses, in other words, the match officials are learning from the organization's shared mental model. Note that a distinction is made in terms of weight activation processes for previously unlearned states and between the three different match officials. Roles of the officials which were previously not known, do not have as strong a connection as states which were already known before the organization's mental model was constructed, which models a less perfect learner. Moreover, the Referee and Assistant 1 reach slightly higher values for their newly formed connections, since they have experience in officiating a match together. In other words, newly learned roles and behavior are not as strong as ones that were already known, which accurately depicts learning in real life. The results of some of the second-order self-model states ($\mathbf{W_W}$-states and $\mathbf{H_W}$-states) are shown in Fig. 5(a)(b) and for some of the first-order self-model states ($\mathbf{W}$-states) in Fig. 5(c)(d). In this figure it can be seen that the $\mathbf{W}$-states of the referee are subject to learning. Initially, the referee is proficient only in possibly detecting offside, whistling for a foul, and letting the game continue after interruptions. Therefore, the **W**-states for these connections ($\mathbf{W}_{R_a,R_d}$, $\mathbf{W}_{R_d,R_e}$, $\mathbf{W}_{R_d,R_f}$, $\mathbf{W}_{R_e,R_f}$) have value 1 at the start of the briefing at time 20. During this stage, the Referee transfers his knowledge to the organization's shared mental model. However, the other **W**-states of the Referee ($\mathbf{W}_{R_a,R_b}$, $\mathbf{W}_{R_b,R_c}$) which deal with the communication between the assistant and the referee concerning an offside position are initially of value 0 and thus have to be learned by the referee from the organization's shared mental model in the next (feedback) stage of the organizational learning. This follows intuitively since this it is the first time the three officials officiate a match together. It can be seen that these **W**-states are increasing once the second stage of the model takes place, during this stage the organizational learning takes place.

Assistant 1 initially is proficient in detecting the offside, and communicating this with the referee, **W**-states $\mathbf{W}_{A1_a,A1_b}$ and $\mathbf{W}_{A1_b,A1_c}$ therefore have value 1 from the start. The Assistant will transfer this knowledge to the organizational model during the feed forward learning stage of the organization's shared mental model.

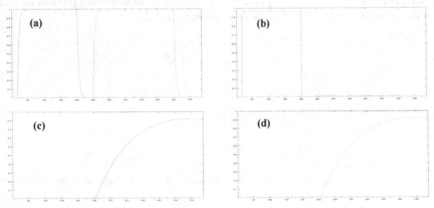

Fig. 5. The results of the simulation for some first- and second-order self-model states: **(a)** $\mathbf{W_W}$-states **(b)** $\mathbf{H_W}$-states **(c)** **W**-states Referee **(d)** **W**-states Assistant 1

The other stages, which are not fully developed yet, have to be learned by the assistant. These other weight states $\mathbf{W}_{A1_a,A1_d}$, $\mathbf{W}_{A1_d,A1_e}$, $\mathbf{W}_{A1_d,A1_f}$, $\mathbf{W}_{A1_e,A1_f}$ have an initial value of 0 and should thus be learned from the organizational model. One can see that this does indeed happen during the second stage of the organizational learning, once the weight states of the connections from the organization's shared mental model towards those of the match officials become active.

As opposed to the Referee and Assistant 1, the newly joined Assistant A2 does not have any knowledge within this team. Therefore, the Assistant is not yet proficient in any of the tasks. Consecutively, all **W**-states for A2 ($\mathbf{W}_{A2_a,A2_b}$, $\mathbf{W}_{A2_b,A2_c}$, $\mathbf{W}_{A2_a,A2_d}$, $\mathbf{W}_{A2_d,A2_e}$, $\mathbf{W}_{A2_d,A2_f}$, $\mathbf{W}_{A2_e,A2_f}$) are having a value of 0 at the start and have to be learned first during the second stage (feedback learning) of the organizational learning. The weights corresponding to A2's learning from the organization's mental model start to increase in that phase. During this stage, the assistant learns, although the obtained weights are not as strong as those of the Referee and the Assistant because they are more experienced.

During the match two instances of offside are taking place. It can be seen in Fig. 4 that when the match (a derby) starts (time 590), via the **M**-states the induced stress causes the **W**-states representing the weights of the match officials to decline, with different intensities based on their experience and role. During the first possible offside offense, all three match officials are aware of the offside position of the striker and handle the situation appropriately. The chronological nature of the infringement and the match official's subsequent behavior is clearly visible. First, the striker moves into the offside position, which is then registered and communicated by the match officials, after which a free kick is given, and the game continues. Later in the game, the striker moves into an offside position again. This time, the inexperienced assistant, who is overloaded with stress and induced forgetting via the **M**-states, has much lower **W**-states and therefore fails to communicate the offside position correctly with the other match officials. Thankfully, because the referee and the other assistant validated the offside position themselves, the appropriate measures could be taken by the match officials and the game could continue. For more graphs, see the Appendix.

6 Mathematical Analysis of the Network Model

Any given network node can find itself in one of three states. It is either at a stationary point and if not, its level is increasing or decreasing. The following definition is given for these three states:

- Y is stationary point at t if $dY(t)/dt = 0$
- Y is increasing at t if $dY(t)/dt > 0$
- Y is decreasing at t if $dY(t)/dt < 0$

The model is in equilibrium at t if and only if every state Y of the model is a stationary point. To test whether the implemented model described in this paper satisfies these equations and therefore is implemented correctly with respect to its design, some states will be analyzed. This will be done for stationary points of these states.

For a network node Y, by (1) and (2) from Sect. 3 it is found that having a stationary point is expressed in terms of network characteristics by the following criterion:

$$\eta_Y = 0 \quad \text{or} \quad \mathbf{c}_Y(\omega_{X_1,Y}X_1(t), ..., \omega_{X_k,Y}X_k(t)) = Y(t) \tag{4}$$

The **W**-states in the middle-level make use of the advanced logistic sum function given in Table 1. It can be observed that for example $\mathbf{W}_{R_c,R_d}$ has a stationary point at $t = 450$. This is a consequence of the (adaptive) speed factor being zero: $\mathbf{H}_{W_R} = 0$ due to activation state 2. The model follows in this Eq. (4). Secondly, the stationary point of X_{21} at $t = 740$ is investigated. At $t = 740$, Fig. 3 shows that X_{21} reaches a maximum. The speed factor is fixed and is 0.2, which is non-zero. The advanced logistic sum parameters are given and are respectively 20 and 0.5 for σ and τ. The state at $t = 740$ can be calculated using only X_{20} with connection weight X_{47}, being:

$$X_{21} = 0.998828 \qquad X_{47} = 0.654299$$

If these values are substituted in advanced logistic sum function, we get:

$$\textbf{alogistic}_{20,0.5}(0.654299 * 0.998828) = 0.95566 \tag{5}$$

According to the simulation X_{21} at $t = 740$ is 0.955735, which compared to the value from (5) only deviates 0.000075, which is $< 10^{-4}$. This is a good approximation of the actual simulated value, meaning the model was implemented correctly. A second stationary point for X_{20} can be found at $t = 1028$. At this t, the same calculation can be performed for X_{20}, which solely depends on X_{19} and its corresponding connection weight X_{46}. Substituting this leads to the following aggregated impact:

$$\textbf{alogistic}_{20,0.3}(0.306668 * 0.997255) = 0.527931 \tag{6}$$

According to the simulation, the value of X_{19} at $t = 1028$ is 0.530266. The deviation is therefore just 0.0023, which is in the order of 10^{-3}, which is again a good approximation. Similarly, a third verification was done for X_{23} at $t = 450$; this provided a deviation of 0.000194. Which is $< 10^{-3}$. A last calculation was performed for X_{34} at $t = 495$. Here a deviation of 0.000460 is found, which is also $< 10^{-3}$. These verification instances all provide evidence that the implemented model is correct with respect to its design.

7 Discussion

Computational analysis of organisational learning can offer quite an interesting insight in addition to the mainstream literature within the organizational learning field. By using individual mental models, a shared mental model on the organizational level is formed: feed forward learning. Once formed, the shared mental model can be used to teach the individuals who do not have knowledge of certain parts. To be able to analyse this in a computational manner the underlying conceptual and computational mechanisms have to be identified (Canbaloğlu et al. 2022a, 2022b, 2022c; Wiewiora et al. 2019). The computational model introduced in this paper is a second-order adaptive network model integrating parts described separately in (Canbaloğlu et al. 2022a) for organisational learning and (Treur and Van Ments 2022) for usage of a mental models. These sources themselves did not yet address in a detailed manner the integration of formation (by organisational learning) and usage (where also world states and their dynamics play a role) of the (shared) mental models. This paper follows a team which comes together to line-up their thoughts and bring them into reality in a match in the world within one model. In addition, a totally unaware teammate is introduced and he is able to learn from the shared mental model. To demonstrate such, the second junior assistant was introduced, which was unaware of all his tasks. The organization's shared mental model was learned using the knowledge of both the referee and the first assistant, and subsequently used to teach the second assistant.

The model provides a strong basis for computational analysis. However, many improvements and extensions can still be made. For example, currently, it is explicitly stated that the Referee and Assistant 1 both have half of the knowledge, meaning they want to learn from each other. However, one can think of situations of where two individuals have different, conflicting looks on a situation. The model has not been designed or tested to cope with this kind of situations. Another possible extension is to further optimize the **M**-states. Currently, the states follow a likewise trajectory. By implementing differences for states that are more likely to react on certain stress-full situations an even more realistic model can be created. Further extensions could be considered taking into account context-sensitive aggregation of mental models by controlling the type of aggregation (Canbaloğlu and Treur 2022a, 2022b) and also a distincition may be added between shared mental models at the team level and at a higher organisation level covering more teams; e.g., as addressed in (Canbaloğlu et al. 2022b).

References

Abraham, W.C., Bear, M.F.: Metaplasticity: the plasticity of synaptic plasticity. Trends Neurosci. **19**(4), 126–130 (1996)

Boyko, R.H., Boyko, A.R., Boyko, M.G.: Referee bias contributes to home advantage in English premiership football. J. Sports Sci. **25**(11), 1185–1194 (2007)

Canbaloğlu, G., Treur, J.: Context-sensitive mental model aggregation in a second-order adaptive network model for organisational learning. In: Benito, R.M., Cherifi, C., Cherifi, H., Moro, E., Rocha, L.M., Sales-Pardo, M. (eds.) COMPLEX NETWORKS 2021. SCI, vol. 1015, pp. 411–423. Springer, Cham (2022a). https://doi.org/10.1007/978-3-030-93409-5_35

Canbaloğlu, G., Treur, J.: Using boolean functions of context factors for adaptive mental model aggregation in organisational learning. In: Klimov, V.V., Kelley, D.J. (eds.) BICA 2021. SCI, vol. 1032, pp. 54–68. Springer, Cham (2022b). https://doi.org/10.1007/978-3-030-96993-6_5

Canbaloğlu, G., Treur, J., Roelofsma, P.H.M.P.: Computational modeling of organisational learning by self-modeling networks. Cognit. Syst. Res. J. **73**, 51–64 (2022a)

Canbaloğlu, G., Treur, J., Roelofsma, P.: An adaptive self-modeling network model for multilevel organizational learning. In: Yang, XS., Sherratt, S., Dey, N., Joshi, A. (eds.) ICICT 2022. LNNS, vol. 448, pp. 179–191 (2022b). Springer, Singapore. https://doi.org/10.1007/978-981-19-1610-6_16

Canbaloğlu, G., Treur, J., Wiewiora, A.: Computational modeling of multilevel organisational learning: from conceptual to computational mechanisms. In: Proceedings of Computational Intelligence: Automate Your World. The Second International Conference on Information Technology, InCITe 2022. Lecture Notes in Electrical Engineering, Springer (2022c)

Craik, K.J.W.: The nature of explanation. CUP Archive, vol. 445 (1952)

Crossan, M.M., Lane, H.W., White, R.E.: An organizational learning framework: From intuition to institution. Acad. Manag. Rev. **24**, 522–537 (1999)

Gomez-Carmona, C., Pino-Ortega, J.: Kinematic and physiological analysis of the performance of the referee football and its relationship with decision making. J. Hum. Sport Exerc. **11**(4), 397–414 (2016)

Heil, J.: Philosophy of Mind. Routledge (1998)

Katz-Navon, T.Y., Erez, M.: When collective-and self-efficacy affect team performance: the role of task interdependence. Small Group Res. **36**(4), 437–465 (2005)

Kim, D.H.: The link between individual and organizational learning. Sloan Manag. Rev. **33**(1), 37–50 (1993)

Mathieu, J.E., et al.: The influence of shared mental models on team process and performance. J. Appl. Psychol. **85**(2), 273 (2000)

Salas, E., Cooke, N.J., Rosen, M.A.: On teams, teamwork, and team performance: discoveries and developments. Hum. Factors **50**(3), 540–547 (2008)

Treur, J.: A modeling environment for reified temporal-causal networks: modeling plasticity and metaplasticity in cognitive agent models. In: Baldoni, M., Dastani, M., Liao, B., Sakurai, Y., Zalila Wenkstern, R. (eds.) PRIMA 2019. LNCS, vol. 11873, pp. 487–495. Springer, Cham (2019). https://doi.org/10.1007/978-3-030-33792-6_33

Treur, J.: Network-Oriented Modeling for Adaptive Networks: Designing Higher-Order Adaptive Biological, Mental and Social Network Models. Springer, Cham (2020). https://doi.org/10.1007/978-3-030-31445-3

Treur, J.: On the dynamics and adaptivity of mental processes: relating adaptive dynamical systems and self-modeling network models by mathematical analysis. Cogn. Syst. Res. **70**, 93–100 (2021)

Van Ments, L., Treur, J., Klein, J., Roelofsma, P.H.M.P.: A computational network model for shared mental models in hospital operation rooms. In: Mahmud, M., Kaiser, M.S., Vassanelli, S., Dai, Q., Zhong, N. (eds.) BI 2021. LNCS, vol. 12960, pp. 67–78. Springer, Cham (2021a). https://doi.org/10.1007/978-3-030-86993-9_7

Van Ments, L., Treur, J., Klein, J., Roelofsma, P.H.M.P.: A second-order adaptive network model for shared mental models in hospital teamwork. In: Nguyen, N.T., Iliadis, L., Maglogiannis, I., Trawiński, B. (eds.) ICCCI 2021. LNCS (LNAI), vol. 12876, pp. 126–140. Springer, Cham (2021b). https://doi.org/10.1007/978-3-030-88081-1_10

Treur, J., Van Ments, L. (eds.): Mental Models and their Dynamics, Adaptation, and Control: a Self-modeling Network Modeling Approach. Springer, Cham (2022). https://doi.org/10.1007/978-3-030-85821-6

Van Ments, L., Treur, J.: Reflections on dynamics, adaptation, and control: a cognitive architecture for mental models. Cogn. Syst. Res. **70**, 1–9 (2021)

Wiewiora, A., Smidt, M., Chang, A.: The 'how' of multilevel learning dynamics: a systematic literature review exploring how mechanisms bridge learning between individuals, teams/projects and the organization. Eur. Manag. Rev. **16**, 93–115 (2019)

Computational Intelligence for Digital Content Understanding

Speech Representation Using Linear Chirplet Transform and Its Application in Speaker-Related Recognition

Hao D. Do[1,2,3]($\boxtimes$) (iD), Duc T. Chau[1,2], and Son T. Tran[1,2]

[1] University of Science, Ho Chi Minh City, Vietnam
{ctduc,ttson}@fit.hcmus.edu.vn
[2] Vietnam National University, Ho Chi Minh City, Vietnam
[3] FPT University, Ho Chi Minh City, Vietnam
haodd3@fpt.edu.vn

Abstract. Most speech processing models begin with feature extraction and then pass the feature vector to the primary processing model. The solution's performance mainly depends on the quality of the feature representation and the model architecture. Much research focuses on designing robust deep network architecture and ignoring feature representation's important role during the deep neural network era. This work aims to exploit a new approach to design a speech signal representation in the time-frequency domain via Linear Chirplet Transform (LCT). The proposed method provides a feature vector sensitive to the frequency change inside the human speech with a solid mathematical foundation. This is a potential direction for many applications, such as speaker gender recognition or emotion recognition. The experimental results show the improvement of the feature based on LCT compared to MFCC or Fourier Transform. Particularly, the proposed method gains 95.56% and 97.28% in term of accuracy for speaker gender recognition in English and Vietnamese, respectively. This result also implies that the feature based on LCT is independent of language, so it can be used in a wide range of applications.

Keywords: Speech representation · Feature extraction · Time-frequency plane · Linear chirplet transform · Speaker gender recognition

1 Introduction

During the development of the speech processing field, many methods for speech representation are proposed. A wide range of applications, from speech recognition, speaker authentication, and emotion recognition, use many forms of speech representation as to the input for the model. The methods for representing human speech mainly were researched and designed a long time ago and not a hot topic after 2010. Many states of the art models in speech processing are

© The Author(s), under exclusive license to Springer Nature Switzerland AG 2022
N. T. Nguyen et al. (Eds.): ICCCI 2022, LNAI 13501, pp. 719–729, 2022.
https://doi.org/10.1007/978-3-031-16014-1_56

mainly based on the deep learning approach, which requests many data for training and powerful computing resources. Our main question in this research is how to design a more meaningful form for speech representation to loosen the data and computing resource requirements.

In the past, many feature extraction approaches were proposed to represent human speech into new spaces, which are easier to solve speech-related recognition problems. There are two groups with the root ideas to design the representation space. The first group of speech signals features relates to stationary analysis, while the second one uses the strength of a deep neural network to model the feature space.

The first group originates from the phenomenon that the vibration of two vocal tracks creates human speech. This fact shows that speech signals can be seen as stationary signals. So most of the acoustics properties, including content, prosody, emotion, can be analyzed in the frequency domain. On the other hand, this stationary nature of speech signals impacts many hierarchical levels of spoken language such as phonemes, words, phrases, or whole sentences. In this group, the earlier sub-group with stationary features includes the pitch or frequency f_0, energy, and duration of the signal [1]. These features reflect the speech behaviours merely in a less meaningful space. The second sub-group includes many methods that use the integral transform to represent the data into a new space with a more informative form. Some representatives in this group can be listed as Fourier Transform, Wavelet Transform, and their extensions [2].

Integral transforms use a new space named the frequency domain, or spectrum space, to present the speech feature. Because of the creation of speech, a speech signal is nearly the stationary signal, which is analyzed effectively in the frequency domain. Analyzing the speech in this domain emphasizes the process of modelling and exploiting the speech data. Conventional transform such as Fourier Transform can be applied first to convert the speech into the spectrum. Then many post-processing techniques are proposed including Mel Frequency Cepstral Coefficients (MFCC) [2], Envelope Subtraction [3], Linear Prediction Cepstral Coefficients (LPCC), Log-Frequency Power Coefficients (LFPC), or Gammatone Frequency Cepstral Coefficients (GFCC) [4]. These features are the stronger forms of the spectrum with some differences in design. Each of them is established to emphasize other aspects of a speech signal, corresponding with different applications.

The second group uses a deep neural network such as AutoEncoder [5], which receives raw speech signal and then propagates to reach the final result [6]. In this approach, the feature vector with its pure meaning does not exist [7,8]. A deep neural network is a black box so that there is no pure algorithm for speech feature vector implemented. On the other hand, all layers in the network can also be seen as feature vectors with different meaningful levels. Although its meaning is unclear, hidden layers in neural networks play a positive role in improving the whole model's performance. The reason here is that a neural network can extract the idiosyncratic vector in a hidden space. Although the feature is not visible in our observable space, it is separable in the latent space.

Because the model's output comes from the computing process in these latent spaces, separation ability in the hidden space yields good results.

The two groups below include many advantages and also disadvantages. This motivates us to design a new feature to strengthen the feature vector in particular cases. The first group exploits the periodic features, while the second group uses the power of a deep neural network. We aim to establish a more meaning-richer feature extraction algorithm than the first group and more apparent and interpretable than the second group.

Many applications, including speaker authentication, gender recognition, emotion recognition, dialect recognition, Etc., relates to the trend and change in speech frequency. The values of f_0, energy, silence, or spectrum and its extensions concentrate on the aspect stationary of speech, so they are not good enough for the recognition tasks mentioned above. While speech recognition needs the stationary of the signal to form the phoneme, emotion or dialect is defined based on the change during the pronunciation process. Traditional Fourier Transform and their variances can show the signal properties in the statics frequency domain. The coefficients of their representation reflect the contribution of each particular frequency element to the whole signal. We need a better design to gain a better feature vector encoding the signal change.

Linear Chirplet Transform (LCT), proposed at the same time by Mann et al. [9,10] and Mihovilovic et al. [11], provides a fundamental method to exploit the change in the general signal, including human speech. Chirplet is a piece of chirp, a signal with frequency increases or decreases. LCT can become a potential approach for speech representation related to many applications requiring frequency change from its idea and origin. Compared with conventional Fourier Transform, LCT models the signal more flexibly. While Fourier Transform uses the basis vector set with a fixed instantaneous frequency, LCT builds a basis vector set with a time-linear function for instantaneous frequency. This linear function can be described with a new parameter called chirp rate. With this parameter, the transform can emphasize every grade of change in frequency during the time.

Within this research, what we contribute includes these aspects:

- Explaining the limit of traditional spectrum using Fourier Transform in many applications relating to speech frequency change.
- Designing a new algorithm via LCT operator for speech representation to emphasize the frequency change in the human speech signal.
- Proving the advantages of the proposed feature experimentally via speaker gender recognition.

The remaining of the paper is organized as follow. Section 2 briefly introduces the LCT. We present the linear form of this transform because this approach is the most suitable choice for the case in which the signal is modelled as a linear chirp. Section 3 is the application of LCT into speech processing. This section presents this research's most important contribution: an algorithm for speech feature extraction using LCT. The experiment is shown in Sect. 4. We validate our proposed algorithm using LCT into speaker gender recognition.

Experimental result shows that LCT is a potential approach for speech feature extraction. The paper ends with the section conclusion, where the contributions are summarized.

2   Linear Chirplet Transform

The LCT was first introduced in 1991 by Mann et al. [9] and Mihovilovic et al. [11] to model the chirp signal. With signal $s(t) \in L^2(R)$, in the first step, its analytical form is established using Hilbert transform [12] as follow:

$$z(t) = s(t) + j\mathcal{H}[s(t)] \tag{1}$$

with $\mathcal{H}$ denotes Hilbert transform. This process is used to remove all negative frequency components in the signal. Next, the original form of LCT is defined as:

$$CT_s(t_0, \omega, \alpha, \sigma) = \int_{-\infty}^{+\infty} z(t)\Psi_{t_0,\alpha,\sigma}^*(t)exp(-j\omega t)dt \tag{2}$$

with $\Psi_{t_0,\alpha,\sigma}^*$ is the complex window described by:

$$\Psi_{t_0,\alpha,\sigma}(t) = w_{(\sigma)}(t - t_0)exp\left(-j\frac{\alpha}{2}(t - t_0)^2\right) \tag{3}$$

In the Eq. 3, t_0 denotes time, real number α denotes chirp rate, and w denotes the window function with parameter σ. The chirp rate α is one of the most important parameters which is used to control the slope of the basic vector in the time-frequency plane.

The window $w \in L^2(R)$ is a normalized real window, which identify and normalize the range in the signal used to compute the coefficients. Normally, Gaussian window, one of the most common choice, is defined as:

$$w_{(\sigma)}(t) = \frac{1}{\sqrt{2\pi}\sigma}exp\left(-\frac{1}{2}\left(\frac{t}{\sigma}\right)^2\right) \tag{4}$$

with σ is the standard deviation for the Gaussian function.

With the original form in the Formula 2, it is not easy to compute the result of the transform. This leads the LCT to be interpreted as an extension of STFT of the analytical signal. So Formula 2 can be re-written as:

$$CT_s(t_0, \omega, \alpha, \sigma) = A(t_0) \int_{-\infty}^{+\infty} \bar{z}(t)w_{(\sigma)}(t - t_0)exp(-j\omega t)dt \tag{5}$$

with:

$$\bar{z}(t) = z(t)\Phi_\alpha^R(t)\Phi_\alpha^M(t, t_0) \tag{6}$$

Function $\Phi_\alpha^R(t)$ presents for frequency operator in the time-frequency plane:

$$\Phi_\alpha^R(t) = exp\left(-j\alpha\frac{t^2}{2}\right) \tag{7}$$

This operator rotates the analytical signal $z(t)$ by θ. This angle satisfies the constrain that $\theta = Acrtan(-\alpha)$.

Function $\Phi_\alpha^M(t, t_0)$ is the shifting operator. It relocates the frequency component from ω to $\omega + \alpha t_0$:

$$\Phi_\alpha^M(t, t_0) = exp(j\alpha t_0 t) \tag{8}$$

The analytical signal can be transformed via LCT using STFT as the fundamental technique with the rotating and shifting operators above.

The remaining factor in the Eq. 5 is the amplitude, which is defined by:

$$A(t_0) = exp\left(-jt^2\frac{\alpha}{2}\right) \tag{9}$$

To simplify the computing process, because the amplitude has the modulus $|A(t_0)| = 1$, it should be removed out of the Formula 5. So the final form for the LCT is described by:

$$CT_s(t_0, \omega, \alpha, \sigma) = \int_{-\infty}^{+\infty} \bar{z}(t)w_{(\sigma)}(t - t_0)exp(-j\omega t)dt \tag{10}$$

From these analyses, there are three main stages to implement the LCT as follow:

– Step 1: Rotating the analytical signal by the angle $\theta = Arctan(\alpha)$.
– Step 2: Shifting the output of step 1 with an increment of αt_0 in the direction of frequency.
– Step 3: Applying STFT with the signal received after step 2, with Gaussian window $w_{(\sigma)}$.

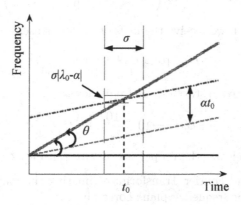

Fig. 1. Illustration of the Linear Chirplet Transform with three main steps (Color figure online)

These three steps are illustrated in the Fig. 1 [13]. Assuming the objective signal has the instantaneous frequency trajectory as the blue line, which is identified as:

$$\omega = \omega_0 + \lambda_0 t \tag{11}$$

This function is purely linear, or the most simple function to represent the trajectory for instantaneous frequency. After step 1, the signal rotates and becomes the green line. As in the Fig. 1, the rotating angle is θ, which is defined by $\theta = Arctan(-\alpha)$. Next, the signal is increased with a distance αt_0 in the direction of frequency and return the red line. Finally, the red signal is normalized with a Gaussian window and then passed into STFT to compute the coefficient corresponding with time t_0 and frequency ω.

3   Speech Representation with Linear Chirplet Transform

3.1   The Difference Between Linear Chirplet Transform and Short-time Fourier Transform

Linear Chirplet Transform and Fourier Transform share the same idea about converting the signal from the time domain into another domain. While Fourier Transform uses the basis vector with a fixed frequency, LCT processes the input signal with a dynamic-frequency basis vector. In the time-frequency plane, the basis vectors used in Fourier Transform are presented as horizontal lines and are difficult to modify. On the other hand, the LCT provides the parameter called chirp rate α to control the slope of the instantaneous frequency trajectory. In a particular problem, with a particular type of data, the parameter of LCT can be adjusted flexibly to capture the meaningful information from data.

To illustrate the different between LCT and Fourier Transform, let us consider a signal component signal as follow:

$$s(t) = sin\left(2\pi\left(10t + \frac{5}{4}t^2 + \frac{1}{9}t^3 - \frac{1}{160}t^4\right)\right) \tag{12}$$

So, using FM model, we receive the instantaneous phase:

$$\phi(t) = 10t + \frac{5}{4}t^2 + \frac{1}{9}t^3 - \frac{1}{160}t^4 \tag{13}$$

and then the objective instantaneous frequency is:

$$\omega = \phi'(t) = 10 + \frac{10}{4}t + \frac{1}{3}t^2 - \frac{1}{40}t^3 \tag{14}$$

Figure 2 shows clearly the properties of two transforms:

- Both of LCT and Fourier Transform: estimating the main trajectory of the signal in the time-frequency plane correctly
- Fourier Transform: focusing on the stable area of in the plane or the stationary properties of the signal. In Fig. 2a, the value at the top of the curve is red, presenting for big values, while the remaining in the curve is green, meaning smaller values.
- LCT with positive chirp rate: painted red, emphasizing the range with a significant increase. The other ranges in the curve, which are stable or decreasing, are not highlighted and are painted green.

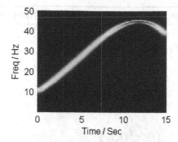

(a) Linear Chirplet Transform with chirp rate $\alpha = 0$

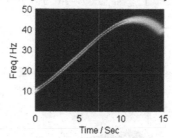

(b) Linear Chirplet Transform with chirp rate $\alpha = 5$

Fig. 2. Instantaneous frequency trajectory returned by Linear Chirplet Transform with different chirp rate. Sub figure (a) presents the trajectory with $\alpha = 0$, which is corresponding with Fourier Transform. Sub figure (b) shows the trajectory with a chirp rate $\alpha > 0$. These illustrations mean that Fourier Transform is a special case of LCT with zero chirp rate. (Color figure online)

3.2 Feature Design for Speech Using the Linear Chirplet Transform

The algorithm to extract the speech feature include two important stages: defining the hyperparameters and running the transform to get the feature representation. The hyperparameters for LCT includes:

- T: a set of time points that the features will be taken. In practice, one second of a signal with sample-rate 16000 Hz is usually divided to get 40 time points. Each time point corresponds with 400 samples in the time domain.
- Ω: a set of frequency. In range [1 Hz, 8000 Hz] or [1 Hz, 16000 Hz], Ω usually contains 256 or 512 values.
- α: chirp rate
- σ: standard deviation of the Gaussian window

After defining the hyperparamers, the feature extraction stage is processed as in the Algorithm 1 with $w_{(\sigma)}(t)$, $\Phi_\alpha^R(t)$, and $\Phi_\alpha^M(t, t_0)$ are defined in Sect. 2.

Algorithm 1 is sensitive to the frequency change in the speech signal. If the chirp rate $\alpha > 0$, this method can capture so well the moment that the speech tone increases. Figure 3 shows a 3D illustration of a speech signal after processed by our proposed algorithm.

Algorithm 1. Speech feature extraction using Linear Chirplet Transform

1: **procedure** FEATURE-EXTRACTION$(T, \Omega, \alpha, \sigma, s(t))$
2:     $z(t) \leftarrow s(t) + j\mathcal{H}[s(t)]$
3:     $Feature \leftarrow [,]$
4:     **for** $t_0 \in T$ **do**
5:         **for** $\omega \in \Omega$ **do**
6:             $z_{t_0,\omega}(t) \leftarrow z(t)w_{(\sigma)}(t - t_0)$
7:             $z_{t_0,\omega}^{R}(t) \leftarrow z_{t_0,\omega}(t)\Phi_{\alpha}^{R}(t)$
8:             $z_{t_0,\omega}^{R,M}(t) \leftarrow z_{t_0,\omega}^{R}(t)\Phi_{\alpha}^{M}(t, t_0)$
9:             $Feature[t_0, \omega] \leftarrow \int_{-\infty}^{+\infty} z_{t_0,\omega}^{R,M}(t)exp(-j\omega t)dt$

10:     **return** $Feature$

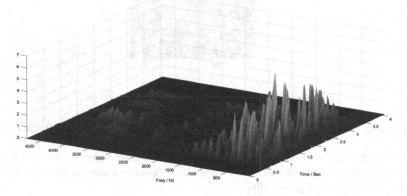

Fig. 3. Illustration of 3D time-frequency representation returned by Linear Chirplet Transform (Color figure online)

In Fig. 3, the valuable information concentrates mainly in the frequency range [50 Hz, 1200 Hz], or human voice band. The top coefficients, highlighted with yellow and green, occur sparsely in the representation. In this speech signal, the speaker increases their tone significantly at these positions. This information could become the key for identification or recognition tasks.

4   Experiment

4.1   Gender Recognition: Problem and Dataset

Gender recognition is an essential task in many speech-related application systems. In Apple Siri, Amazon Echo or Google Assistant, if the system identifies the speaker's gender, it can respond or provide the appropriate answer. For example, if a male user asks the virtual assistant "play music", it should return a song that is liked or highly scored by men, not by women. When the system serves the users with correct information, users' experiments become pretty.

This task is modelled as a binary classification. The input is an audio signal containing a single utterance from one person. The objective is to identify that voice belongs to a man or a woman. In this work, we use accuracy measures to evaluate the quality of methods.

Dataset used in this research include Timit [14] and Vivos [15]. Timit contains 630 English speakers, including male and female, while Timit collects voice from 46 Vietnamese speakers. We aim to verify whether our proposed speech representation method is good or not and language-dependent or independent during this experiment.

4.2 Experimental Result

In the experiment, with each dataset, we create training and testing data as follow:

- Using the default partition for training and testing of each dataset.
- With each audio file, dividing it into many 1-second audio chunks and removing the final chunk is its length is less than 1 s.
- Extracting speech feature of chunks using different methods presented in the Table 1.
- Tagging each chunk with the gender label of the corresponding audio file.

To recognize the speaker's gender, we use a simple model Lenet [16], proposed by Yann Lecun. The model contains two pairs of convolutional layer and pooling layer and three FC layers. During the operation of the model, it works as follow:

- Training phase: repeating the process below
  - Receiving feature of a speech chunk.
  - Straight forwarding to get the output.
  - Comparing the output with the training label to get loss value.
  - Doing backpropagation to adjust the parameters in the whole network.
- Testing phase: receiving a feature vector computed from a chunk, feeding the network and getting the label.

Table 1 shows the recognizing results of Lenet to gender recognition task via four features. It is easy to identify that the highest score in terms of accuracy is the LCT. The difference between LCT and the others is not significant but clear and observable. The improvement is nearly 1%, which is a significant number.

The reason for the difference among features in Table 1 could become inside the gender recognition problem. A piece of speech from a man is distinguished with once from a woman at least two aspects. The first is the frequency domain's range and shape of speech signal distribution. Furthermore, which is more important, is the increasing and decreasing tone or frequency. The styles of pronunciation, man and woman, are different. These properties are mined and exploited via the LCT, a tool sensitive to frequency change during time.

On the other hand, the results in English via Timit and Vietname via Vivos dataset imply that LCT is an approach independent of language. This means that our approach can be extended and applied in many other languages.

Table 1. Speaker gender recognition for English and Vietnamese with different features

Feature	Feature size	English accuracy(%)	Vietnamese accuracy(%)
Spectrum	512	92.41	94.01
Mel-spectrum	512	91.38	96.49
MFCC	39	94.90	96.39
LCT (proposed method)	512	95.56	97.28

5   Conclusion

In this work, we have presented a new approach for speech signal representation in the time-frequency domain via Linear Chirplet Transform (LCT). Our approach creates a new feature for speech processing which is very sensitive with increment and decrement in the frequency domain. This LCT feature is a potential choice for speech-related applications such as speaker gender recognition, speaker age prediction, dialect prediction, or emotion prediction. These problems can be solved based on the change of tone or up and down prosody, which are so appropriate with the properties of LCT.

Our experiment with speaker gender recognition demonstrates our hypothesis about the strength of LCT. Experimental result shows that our proposed feature performs so well and yields a better result than the conventional features, including MFCC and spectrum. On the other hand, because the transform in this research is a mathematical tool that transforms the data from one space to another space, the proposed feature depends on the speakers' language. This is another advantage of the feature designed with LCT. After all, we conclude that our new design for speech representation in the time-frequency domain could bring better results for speech processing, and this approach should be extended to exploit more aspects of the transforms.

Acknowledgement. Hao D. Do was funded by Vingroup JSC and supported by the PhD Scholarship Programme of Vingroup Innovation Foundation (VINIF), Institute of Big Data, code VINIF.2021.TS.120. The authors would like to thank OLLI Technology JSC for their support.

References

1. Cowie, R., Douglas-Cowie, E.: Automatic statistical analysis of the signal and prosodic signs of emotion in speech. In: Fourth International Conference on Spoken Language Processing (1996)
2. Koolagudi, S.G., Rao, K.S.: Emotion recognition from speech: a review. Int. J. Speech Technol. **15**(2), 99–117 (2012)

3. Do, H.D., Chau, D.T., Nguyen, D.D., Tran, S.T.: Enhancing speech signal features with linear envelope subtraction. In: Wojtkiewicz, K., Treur, J., Pimenidis, E., Maleszka, M. (eds) Advances in Computational Collective Intelligence. Communications in Computer and Information Science, vol. 1463. Springer, Cham. https://doi.org/10.1007/978-3-030-88113-9_25(2021)

4. Nwe, T.L., Foo, S.W., De Silva, L.C.: Detection of stress and emotion in speech using traditional and FFT based log energy features. In: Joint Conference of the Fourth International Conference on Information, Communications and Signal Processing and Fourth Pacific Rim Conference on Multimedia, pp. 1619–1623 (2003)

5. Do, H.D., Tran, S.T., Chau, D.T.: Speech separation in the frequency domain with autoencoder. J. Commun. **15**(11), 841–848 (2020). https://doi.org/10.12720/jcm.15.11.841-848

6. Tzirakis, P., Zhang, J., Schuller, B.W.: End-to-End speech emotion recognition using deep neural networks. In: IEEE International Conference on Acoustics, Speech and Signal Processing (ICASSP), pp. 5089–5093. (2018). https://doi.org/10.1109/ICASSP.2018.8462677

7. Do, H.D., Tran, S.T., Chau, D.T.: A variational autoencoder approach for speech signal separation. In: Nguyen, N.T., Hoang, B.H., Huynh, C.P., Hwang, D., Trawiński, B., Vossen, G. (eds.) Computational Collective Intelligence. Lecture Notes in Computer Science, vol. 12496. Springer, Cham. https://doi.org/10.1007/978-3-030-63007-2_43(2020)

8. Do, H.D., Tran, S.T., Chau, D.T.: Speech source separation using variational autoencoder and bandpass filter. IEEE Access **8**, 156219–156231 (2020). https://doi.org/10.1109/ACCESS.2020.3019495

9. Mann, S., Haykin, S. : The Chirplet transform: a generalization of Gabor's logon transform. In: Proceedings Vision Interface, pp. 205–212 (1991)

10. Mann, S., Haykin, S.: The Chirplet transform: physical considerations. IEEE Trans. Signal Process. **43**(11), 2745–2761 (1995). https://doi.org/10.1109/78.482123

11. Mihovilovic, D., Bracewell, R.N.: Adaptive Chirplet representation of signals in the time-frequency plane. Electron. Lett. **27**(13), 1159–1161 (1991)

12. Liu, Y., An, H., Bian, S.: Hilbert-Huang transform and the application. In: IEEE International Conference on Artificial Intelligence and Information Systems (ICAIIS), pp. 534–539 (2020). https://doi.org/10.1109/ICAIIS49377.2020.9194944

13. Yang, Y., Peng, Z.K., Dong, X.J., Zhang, W.M., Meng, G.: General parameterized time-frequency transform. IEEE Trans. Signal Process. **62**(11), 2751–2764 (2014). https://doi.org/10.1109/TSP.2014.2314061

14. Garofolo, J.S., et al.: TIMIT acoustic-phonetic continuous speech corpus. In: Linguistic Data Consortium (1993)

15. Luong, H.T., Vu, H.Q.: A non-expert Kaldi recipe for Vietnamese speech recognition system. In: Proceeding of WLSI/OIAF4HLT at COLING, pp. 51–55 (2016)

16. LeCun, Y., et al.: Backpropagation applied to handwritten zip code recognition. Neural Comput. **1**(4), 541–551 (1989). https://doi.org/10.1162/neco.1989.1.4.541

Towards Making University PDFs Conform to Universal Accessibility Standard

Marek Kopel[✉][iD]

Faculty of Information and Communication Technology, Wroclaw University of Science and Technology, wybrzeze Wyspiańskiego 27, 50-370 Wroclaw, Poland
marek.kopel@pwr.edu.pl

Abstract. This paper reports on the findings of the research aiming at changing public document authoring process to support publishing only accessible documents. The main contribution is finding the most commonly invalidated rule checks of legally enforced standard PDF/UA in PDF files from university websites and analysis of the authoring errors that rendered the public documents inaccessible for people with disabilities, usually visual impairments. For most popular failed check rules author proposes recommendations how to avoid non-accessibility in the future. Based on the popularity of invalidated PDF/UA rules, proposed recommendations and their mutual relations a significance method for scoring and thus ranking the rules is proposed. Conclusions are drawn and some ideas for future works are outlined.

Keywords: Accessibility · PDF/UA · Validation rule · Conformance · Standard · Scoring method

1 Introduction

Accessibility in the context of information technologies means avoiding the discrimination of users with specific needs, like people with physical disabilities, situational disabilities, and socio-economic restrictions. That includes visual, auditory and motor impairments. To overcome the disabilities assistive technologies can be used, like screen magnifiers and readers using speech synthesis, Braille terminals, speech recognition, joysticks and keyboard overlays. Accessibility in the context of content means creating documents which the assistive technologies can use. A document is accessible when it is readable by assistive technologies, which means e.g. a computer can present or read the content of such document aloud to anyone who depends on assistive technologies. Another form of accessible documents may be subtitled or sign language videos.

One of the main requirements of an accessible document is that it provides a *logical reading order*. This means that a screen reader should be able to determine the correct order in which the document text must be presented, i.e. read aloud,

© The Author(s), under exclusive license to Springer Nature Switzerland AG 2022
N. T. Nguyen et al. (Eds.): ICCCI 2022, LNAI 13501, pp. 730–743, 2022.
https://doi.org/10.1007/978-3-031-16014-1_57

so the content is understandable. Another common requirement is an *alternative description*, which is a human-readable text that could be used for example with text-to -speech engine for the benefit of users with visual impairment. Both of the above requirements can be met using tagged content. The most common document format using tags is HTML. So HTML, being the default format for Web documents, gives a natural way for efforts to make Web documents accessible. The first such effort was *Web Accessibility Initiative* (WAI). It was formed by W3C in 1997. Its main outcome was the *W3C Recommendation: The Web Content Accessibility Guidelines 1.0* (WCAG) released in 1999 [4]. The 1.0 version was strongly based on HTML and CSS. In 2008 the WCAG 2.0 [3] was released with two main differences from 1.0: the guidelines are technology-neutral (so in particular applicable also to PDFs) and the guidelines became testable statements instead of instructions to authors. In 2018 WCAG 2.1 [12] was published, which focused on adding accessibility recommendations for mobile devices and low vision users.

Another popular document format used not only on the Web, but anywhere in digital communication is PDF. This document format, being developed in 1992 and first standardized as ISO 32000 in 2008, also soon became a subject to accessibility. First PDF accessibility standards concern archiving and long-term preservation. ISO 19005, also known as PDF/A [5], aims at uniform representation of documents across time and platforms. Since PDF was created as a format that provides interoperability across different software and hardware, PDF/A extends the idea across time: it ensures that PDF documents can be opened in the future. PDF/A comes in 4 conformance parts, which are, basically, format evolution stages. They refer correspondingly to PDF v.1.4, v. 1.7, v. 1.7, and v. 2.0. The latest, PDF/A-4 was published in 2020 as ISO 19005-4. Also with each part of PDF/A more capabilities are permitted in a PDF/A-compliant document. Each part can be used with one of three conformance levels: b (basic), u (unicode) or a (accessible). The conformance increases in exactly this order: from b that ensures the least, to a that requires all possible conformance according to PDF/A specification.

The accessibility of PDFs meant for people with disabilities and assistive technologies is *PDF/Universal Accessibility*. PDF/UA [11] standardized as ISO 14289 was initially released in 2012. The connection between PDF/A and PDF/UA is well put by [7]: a really good PDF/A-1a file is one that also complies with PDF/UA. And furthermore: A PDF/A-1a conforming file is not just visually reproducible, it's logically reproducible as well. So, extending the two aforementioned accessibility requirements, when validating for PDF/A-1a conformance, three main questions are:

1. Is the semantic content tagged in correct logical order?
2. Are the headings, lists and tables and other tags in the tags tree correctly structured?
3. Is the non-semantic content marked as artifact?

The connection between PDF/UA and WCAG is also explained by [7]: PDF/UA provides a means of making PDF files that conform to WCAG by defining the correct use of features in PDF.

Document accessibility is enforced by law [6]. *The UN Convention on the Rights of People with Disabilities* defined the general human rights including accessibility, in effect since 2008. In the United States, *Section 508 Amendment to the Rehabilitation Act* of 1973 requires federal government IT services be accessible for people with disabilities and *Title III of the Americans with Disabilities Act (ADA)* forbids discrimination of the disabled. A European Commission Communication on eAccessibility from 2005 tasked standardization organizations "to harmonise and facilitate the public procurement of accessible ICT products and services". In 2016 the European Parliament approved the *Web Accessibility Directive* (standard EN 301 549), which requires that the websites and mobile apps of public sector bodies be accessible. In 2019 the European Union introduced the *European Accessibility Act* and aims to improve the trade between members of the EU for accessible products and services, by removing country specific rules. Right now in EU and in Poland in particular there are fines for public institutions for not conforming to accessibility standards.

This research is a staring point in a EU funding programme towards making the authors workplace, i.e. Wrocław University of Technology compliant with aforementioned laws and avoid paying fines. The compliance concerns the university departments websites and all the published document's accessibility. The goal of the first stage is to assess the accessibility of PDF documents in the *pwr.edu.pl* domain (domain for the university websites) by conformance to PDF/UA standard. Based on that further actions can be planned, which are briefly outlined in Sect. 5.

1.1 Related Works

Many similar studies have been published since the introduction of the accessibility standards and laws enforcing conformance to them. Many of them are for a specific organization document collections. Authors of [10] describe how they managed to make accessible the papers submitted to the conference DSAI 2016 using .docx format and PDF checker. In [9] authors run validation of 200 selected journal articles published 2014-2018 in PDF and used manual inspection with Adobe Acrobat Pro, PDF Accessibility Checker and NVDA screen reader. A case study of accessibility conformance of PDF publication applied to the universities in Latin America with the highest academic prestige is described in [2]. In [1] authors show a case study for a random sample of 10 documents related to the modern architectural heritage of Quito with PDF Accessibility Checker. All the aforementioned studies show that there is still plenty of space for improvement and a long way to full accessible Web and its documents.

There are also more general publications on explaining how the accessibility guidelines shall be used. In [11] authors claim the need for conforming to the standards and authoring accessible documents, while explaining what would be the benefits for that. In [5] the author focuses more on technical aspects of authoring tools that support creating accessible content.

Since authors of aforementioned publications could not use veraPDF (it didn't exist at that time as in current form) they used PDF Accessibility Checker and manual inspection. In result their research was based on a limited amount of test files. Their data sets consisted of correspondingly: [9] - 200, [10] - 59, and [1,2] - only 10 randomly selected documents has been validated. In this experiment all the university PDFs that could be download are validated. In total they amount to 24366 files.

Also veraPDF check rules are much more granulated. While authors of [1, 2, 9, 10] has checked and discussed less than a dozen of accessibility aspects, in this research 17 most invalidated rules (of total 89) are given an insightful analysis.

2 Experiment

The idea of the experiment is to download all "attachment documents" from WUST websites and check the PDFs against PDF/UA conformance. Then find the standard rules that are invalidated by the highest percentage of PDFs and explain what the accessibility problems are to eventually propose and implement some solutions to improve accessibility of WUST web publications.

2.1 Dataset

The "attachment documents" from WUST websites are all files that are published by administration and faculty staff usually in the form of office files, often exported to PDFs. From 46 websites of WUST structure units 24.5k documents of weight 28.5 GB were downloaded. 3,6k files of weight 2GB are non-PDF files (.doc(x), .xls(s), .ppt(x), .odt and .csv). It clearly proves that PDF is most popular and - apart from HTML - it is the first format to start the accessibility investigation.

2.2 Procedure

For the validation process tool veraPDF [8] was chosen because of the Linux platform and command line support. This allowed easy script and test the initial trial run only for the PDFs from ICT department (wit.pwr.edu.pl). Later similar scripts were run for the entire collection of PDFs.

VeraPDF allows checking PDF files against test rules of accessibility standards. In this research PDF/UA was used. For each file each failed rule was logged. Finally all failed test rules were aggregated and sorted by their popularity in failing against the highest number of files. Files that could not be tested as not being valid PDF (marked broken on diagram) stated about 1% of all files. All rules with number of files that failed the rule test are shown in Fig. 1.

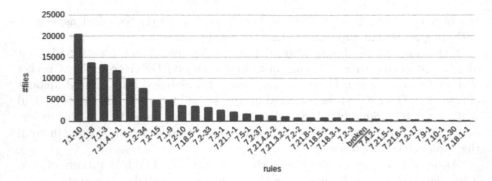

Fig. 1. Number of files failing each PDF/UA Universal Accessibility rule test. Broken files, i.e. invalid PDF files are underlined with red. The rest of rules on the right that are not shown on the diagram were invalid in less that 1% of the files inspected. (Color figure online)

The diagram shows that number of files invalidating most popular rules drop quickly. Only 28 rule tests were failed by more than 1% and only 15 - by more that 5% of the PDF files. If show that in percentage of all files (as in Fig. 2), the statistics would be as follows: the average fail percentage of all failed rules is only 7,53%; and the median - 0,39%. This statistics tell that only a small number of most popular rules impact hugely the overall accessibility of the PDF collection. This is why the following discussion shall only concern those most popular rules invalidated by documents from the ICT department and WUST university.

3   Results

Only 27 out of 89, which is hardly 30%, rules of the PDF/UA standard are not invalidated by the collection of all WUST university public PDFs. Out of 24366 PDF files 23855 are invalidated by at least one rule. 551 files are broken, meaning they are not valid PDF files, so could not be inspected. This means that not a single PDF file in the university websites is fully accessible!

On diagram Fig. 2 number of whole WUST PDF files that failed for most popular rules are compared with those from ICT dept. For the first 6 rules results are similar for WUST and ICT. There are about putting the most important metadata into document, like document title or language of the text and embedding used font files into document file. Only the second rule, 7.1-8 is much less popular in ICT than in WUST. But on the other hand 2 more less popular rules in WUST (7.2.33 and 7.21.7.1), below 10% are highly popular in ICT (above 60%). These rules treat about specifying natural language and Unicode mapping.

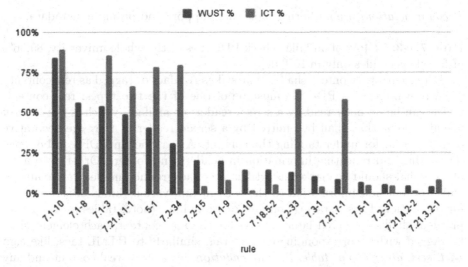

Fig. 2. The percentage of all public WUST University PDFs that failed PDF/UA - Universal Accessibility validation tests for specific rules versus the percentage of those PDFs only from Computer Science department. (Color figure online)

In the following subsections all most popular failed PDF/UA check rules are described in detail and analyzed for the reason the errors were made and a recommendation on how to avoid them in the future.

Rule 7.1-10: 84,35% of all failed check PDF files of the whole university, 89,54% of failed check files only in ICT dept.

Requirement: "The document catalog dictionary shall include a ViewerPreferences dictionary containing a DisplayDocTitle key, whose value shall be true."

If the key DisplayDocTitle is not set true then usually the filename is displayed instead of the actual title of the document. This was also the case when PDF files were created from an Office file, (e.g. .doc or .xls). When creating an Office file, the original filename would have been set as the title of the document. And then when exporting the file as PDF, the original filename - unless changed in Office document properties - was displayed in the viewer window bar. *Recommendation:* always set the docTitle to be displayed.

Rule 7.1-8: 56,71% of all failed check PDF files of the whole university, 17,99% of failed check files only in ICT dept.

Requirement: "The Catalog dictionary of a conforming file shall contain the Metadata key whose value is a metadata stream as defined in ISO 32000-1:2008, 14.3.2."

Not specifying the mandatory metadata is an invalidation. And when the document catalog dictionary doesn't even contain a metadata key, then a red flag shall be raised before any going further and checking specific metadata values.

Recommendation: use authoring tools that support and promote metadata.

Rule 7.1-3: 54,45% of all failed check PDF files of the whole university, 85,56% of failed check files only in ICT dept.

Requirement: "Content shall be marked as Artifact or tagged as real content"

Any content of a PDF file must be of one of the two types: real content, which can be actually read by a screen reader; or artifact, which is the type of visual content that shall be omitted by a screen reader as they are decorative or not crucial for understanding the content. An artifact in PDF can be: page numbering and repeating information in headers and footers. Other decorative objects that should be marked as artifact are: background and decorative images which do not add information to the content and various kinds of strokes, i.e.: for decoration, for separating columns or table lines (note: tables as a separate problem shall be covered later on).As for the real content, each element shall be tagged with a corresponding content tag, similarly to HTML tags, like e.g.: *part, sect, div, h1, p* or *table. Recommendation:* always tag real content and any other mark as Artifact.

Rule 7.21.4.1-1: 49,16% of all failed check PDF files of the whole university, 66,53% of failed check files only in ICT dept.

Requirement: "The font programs for all fonts used for rendering within a conforming file shall be embedded within that file, as defined in ISO 32000-1:2008, 9.9."

ISO32000-1:2008, 9.9 tells how to embed font files within a PDF document. Since fonts are usually a subject to copyright, they are not allowed to be distributed along with the document. This specific test checks 4 alternatives: whether the used font is of Type3 or Type0 . Then, whether renderingMode is set to 3, which means font rendering is "neither fill nor stroke text" which makes the text invisible and so irrelevant for the reader. And the last checked alternative is whether there was embedded at least one font file.

Rule 5-1: 41,19% of all failed check PDF files of the whole university, 78,45% of failed check files only in ICT dept.

Requirement: "The PDF/UA version and conformance level of a file shall be specified using the PDF/UA Identification extension schema."

The very first thing to create a conforming document is to declare to what standard the document conforms to. If the document metadata stream doesn't contain PDF/UA Identification Schema then the reader would not know which level of accessibility to expect from the document. The Information Schema shall include three fields: *part* - stating version id of PDF/A family standards, *amd* - optional PDF/A amendment identifier and *conformance* - stating a corresponding conformance level. *Recommendation:* use authoring tool that can set properly identification metadata.

Rule 7.2-34: 31,56% of all failed check PDF files of the whole university, 79,71% of failed check files only in ICT dept.

Requirement: "Natural language for text in page content shall be determined"

Natural language for text in page content is not set then a screen reader would not know which voice with a corresponding pronunciation and accent should be used, which is crucial information in case of any TTS (text-to-speech) procedure. *Recommendation:* always set natural language explicitly for each text element.

Rule 7.2-15: 20,65% of all failed check PDF files of the whole university, 4,81% of failed check files only in ICT dept.

Requirement: "Tables shall be regular, that is have the same number of cells in each row after accounting for rowspan and colspan attributes."

Each table should contain columns x rows number of cells, unless multi-column (colspan) or multi-row (rowspan) cells are declared. Any other case with the number of cells not matching earlier assumptions makes the table irregular and is treated as broken. *Recommendation:* be sure that your tool supports generating a proper table or check it yourself before publishing.

Rule 7.1-9: 20,47% of all failed check PDF files of the whole university, 8,37% of failed check files only in ICT dept.

Requirement: "The Metadata stream in the document's catalog dictionary shall contain a dc:title entry, where dc is the recommended prefix for the Dublin Core metadata schema as defined in the XMP specification, which clearly identifies the document."

When 7.1-8 is valid then the validator can go further and check all the necessary metadata in the Metadata stream, like the title from the Dublin Core - the most popular ontology from XMP specification. *Recommendation:* Use tools that takes care of title metadata properly.

Rule 7.2-10: 15,04% of all failed check PDF files of the whole university, 2,09% of failed check files only in ICT dept.

Requirement: "TR element may contain only TH and TD elements"

A standard rule for a table. Works the same way as in HTML: for any table row (tagged as TR), its children only element types are either standard (TD) or header cells (TH). Of course cells themselves can have children of many types - inside of the cell can be formatted with different elements, but the core structure at a table row level contains only the cell elements. *Recommendation:* same as for 7.2-15.

Rule 7.18.5-2: 14,73% of all failed check PDF files of the whole university, 5,65% of failed check files only in ICT dept.

Requirement: "Links shall contain an alternate description via their Contents key as described in ISO 32000-1:2008, 14.9.3."

Similar to 7.3-1 above for Figure tags, this rule enforces that links must contain an alternative description in the form of an annotation through a Contents entry. *Recommendation:* always use alternative descriptions if an element cannot be presented another way, e.g. only by text-to-speech.

Rule 7.2-33: 13,49% of all failed check PDF files of the whole university, 64,85% of failed check files only in ICT dept.

Requirement: "Natural language for document metadata shall be determined"

This is a twin rule for 7.2-34 (covered earlier), but for the whole document instead of just a text object. *Recommendation:* same as for 7.2-34.

Rule 7.3-1: 10,77% of all failed check PDF files of the whole university, 4,18% of failed check files only in ICT dept.

Requirement: "Figure tags shall include an alternative representation or replacement text that represents the contents marked with the Figure tag as noted in ISO 32000-1:2008, 14.7.2, Table 323"

Similarly to HTML attribute ALT, when the image is not visible to the reader then an alternative way for giving its content must be available. ISO 32000-1:2008 provides for that either an alternative description (14.9.3) or a replacement text (14.9.4). *Recommendation:* same as for 7.18.5-2.

Rule 7.21.7-1: 9,10% of all failed check PDF files of the whole university, 58,37% of failed check files only in ICT dept.

Requirement: "The Font dictionary of all fonts shall define the map of all used character codes to Unicode values, either via a ToUnicode entry, or other mechanisms as defined in ISO 14289-1, 7.21.7."

When a glyph can not be mapped to Unicode then there will be a problem with interpreting text in any language using non-latin, diacritic characters. While Unicode has been widely adopted in operating systems for over 20 years now (since Windows NT) and in the Web (since HTML 4.0), there are still problems with the proper encoding in PDF document creation. *Recommendation:* make sure you tool properly embeds and maps Unicode font files.

Rule 7.5-1: 7,32% of all failed check PDF files of the whole university, 5,23% of failed check files only in ICT dept.

Requirement: "If the table's structure is not determinable via Headers and IDs, then structure elements of type TH shall have a Scope attribute"

When a table is not organized with Headers attributes and IDs to uniquely connect headers to columns or rows, then a Scope attribute must be used. Similar to HTML attribute Scope, it has no visual effect, but is used by screen readers. *Recommendation:* same as for 7.2-15.

Rule 7.2-37: 5,64% of all failed check PDF files of the whole university, 4,81% of failed check files only in ICT dept.

Requirement: "TBody element may contain only TR elements"

Another rule of 7.2, which deals with proper table construction. This one checks whether the body of the table does not contain anything but table rows. *Recommendation:* same as for 7.2-15.

Rule 7.21.4.2-2: 4,89% of all failed check PDF files of the whole university, 1,67% of failed check files only in ICT dept.

Requirement: "If the FontDescriptor dictionary of an embedded CID font contains a CIDSet stream, then it shall identify all CIDs which are present in the font program, regardless of whether a CID in the font is referenced or used by the PDF or not."

Since all CIDs present in an embedded font file shall be addressed, if a CID Font subset does not define a CIDSet entry in its Descriptor dictionary - a red flag is raised. *Recommendation:* same as for 7.21.7-1.

Rule 7.21.3.2-1: 4,60% of all failed check PDF files of the whole university, 8,37% of failed check files only in ICT dept.

Requirement: "ISO 32000-1:2008, 9.7.4, Table 117 requires that all embedded Type 2 CIDFonts in the CIDFont dictionary shall contain a CIDToGIDMap entry that shall be a stream mapping from CIDs to glyph indices or the name Identity, as described in ISO 32000-1:2008, 9.7.4, Table 117."

A Type 2 CIDFont dictionary entry CIDToGIDMap is mandatory and shall allow mapping the CIDFont to a True Type font embedded in the PDF file. This mapping is only needed for Type 2 CIDFont. *Recommendation:* same as for 7.21.7-1.

4 Severity of Non-accessibility Scoring Method

The next step for improving the PDF accessibility situation in the university is to improve the PDF creation process, so newly published PDF shall have a better accessibility - ideally be completely conformant to PDF/UA. The least invasive method for that is giving PDF authors hints where a part of the created document is non- accessible (i.e. failing a certain PDF/UA rule check). This hint might be given the author as a summary check before publishing or even in an interactive way while invalidating a certain rule while creating the document - the same way spell checking works. The hints shall be ranked to show the most severe accessibility check failures first. For this kind of ranking we need to propose a scoring method for each rule's failed check.

There are 21 subsections of Sect. 7 of the PDF/UA ISO document covering different aspects of document format accessibility requirements. Subsections 7.4 (Headings), 7.18 (Annotations) and 7.21 (Fonts) are divided into more subsections. Each subsection has corresponding veraPDF rule checks, which makes 87 rules from 7.1-1 to 7.21.8-1, plus rules 5.1 and 5.2 covering the ISO's Sect. 5: version identification.

The starting point is to make the score proportional (e.g. a normalized version) to the popularity of each invalidated rule. Of course then the score must be specific to a certain group of authors. As can be seen on diagram Fig. 2, different rules have different popularity based on different subsets. But this popularity is not the only aspect that can be taken into account while creating such scores. Since the rules are not testing aspects mutually exclusive, on the contrary: the same second number in the rule numbering groups the rules by the aspect covered in ISO in the corresponding subsection of Sect. 7. But inside of the groups some rules may be even more related, by checking different effects of the same editorial errors.

The first 3 rules of 7.1 state that real content must be tagged and cannot be contained by Artifact (7.1-2), decorative - must be marked as Artifact and cannot be inside tagged content (7.1-1) and there should not be any content unmarked or marked otherwise (7.1-3). So proper tagging and marking can fix all the three rule checks.

Similar situation is with the last 3 rules of 7.1. They require that a metadata stream is present in catalog dictionary (7.1-8) and it contains proper dc:title entry (7.1-9) and it should be set to display in ViewerPreferences dictionary (7.1-10). So properly adding the title to be visible for the viewer can again fix all the three rule checks.

The same way rules 7.2-3 to 7.2-15 and 7.2-36 to 7.2-36 to 7.2-38 and 7.5-1 concern the construction of a proper table, rules 7.2-17 to 7.2-20 - a proper list, rules 7.2-21 to 7.2-25 - and rules 7.2-26 to 7.2-27 - a proper table of content. Rules 7.2.-29 to 7.2-34 check the proper specification for natural language for different elements of the document.

So usually fixing an issue causing failed checking of one rule of an aspect, probably other failed check rules of the aspect (from a rule group like the aforementioned ones) will in effect also be fixed. This shall give those rules a higher score, because fixing one of the group rules can automatically fix the rest of the group rules. This can be also more evident when considering the proposed recommendations for each rule.

One more thing that could be taken into account is the number of fails of a certain rule per file. For instance rule 5-1 fails only once for each file, in which it is invalid and number of fails per file for rule 7.1-3 ranges from a few to a few thousands. That makes considering what the rules test. Rule 5-1 tests whether PDF/UA version and conformance level was set properly for the document. It can be set once and it is either done properly or not, so the rule check can only fail once. Rule 7.1.-3 on the other hand can check marking of real-content or Artifact for each element of a document, so it can fail multiple times depending on the length of a document. This characteristic makes it hard to objectively use for scoring and that is why it is not included in the scoring method.

Using the knowledge about rule's mutual relations and similar recommendations the score method can be constructed to promote (score better) rules of the same group, the more the higher they are in the ranking. So the score value R_C for each rule r_i considering the collection C can be calculated using formula 1.

$$R_C(r_i) = fp_C(r_i) + \sum_{r_j \in G(r_i)} \alpha * fp_C(r_j) \qquad (1)$$

where: $fp_C(r_i)$ - percentage of documents that failed the rule r_i checking in collection C, $\alpha = 0.1$ - arbitrary coefficient, $G(r_i)$ - group of rules mutually related with r_i.

Table 1. Score values and ranking for PDF/UA rules calculated for 2 collections: WUST and ICT

Rule	Group	WUST %	Score	Rank	ICT %	Score	Rank
7.1-10	A	0,84	0,92	1	0,90	0,92	1
7.1-8	A	0,57	0,67	2	0,18	0,28	8
7.1-3		0,54	0,54	3	0,86	0,86	3
7.21.4.1-1		0,49	0,49	4	0,67	0,67	6
5-1		0,41	0,41	5	0,78	0,78	4
7.1-9	A	0,20	0,35	6	0,08	0,19	9
7.2-34	B	0,32	0,33	7	0,80	0,86	2
7.2-15	C	0,21	0,23	8	0,05	0,06	12
7.2-10	C	0,15	0,18	9	0,02	0,04	16
7.2-33	B	0,13	0,17	10	0,65	0,73	5
7.18.5-2		0,15	0,15	11	0,06	0,06	14
7.5-1	C	0,07	0,11	12	0,05	0,13	10
7.3-1		0,11	0,11	13	0,04	0,04	15
7.2-37	C	0,06	0,10	14	0,05	0,06	13
7.21.7-1		0,09	0,09	15	0,58	0,58	7
7.21.4.2-2		0,05	0,05	16	0,02	0,02	17
7.21.3.2-1		0,05	0,05	17	0,08	0,08	11

In Table 1 the score values and final rankings are calculated for $\alpha = 0.1$ and for 2 collections: WUST - the entire set of university PDFs and ICT - the PDFs published only by the ICT dept. It shows how the rule ranking based on the scoring method can differ for different collections, probably created by different authors or/and using different templates and tools. In this case *Pearson Correlation Coefficient* equals 0.652.

5 Conclusions

The experiment of this study shows that for PDF files published on WUST university websites only a few PDF/UA rules are highly invalidated, i.e. by more than 25% of the files. This is promising, because it means that by avoiding a small number of common mistakes, the PDF authors can create documents with much better accessibility conformance score. Additionally a scoring method was proposed to rank the severity/significance of the errors causing the PDF documents are not accessible. The method was tested for two document collection and will be verified empirically during next stages of the process of making WUST university websites accessible, i.e. implementing guidelines and tools aiding the creation of accessible PDFs and other content forms. Eventually university's public files should be accessible, so the university can avoid potential fines imposed by law for not conforming to the accessibility standards.

This analysis is the first step towards healing the document accessibility situation in WUST university. After understanding the common author mistakes while preparing an accessible document a scoring method was proposed allowing to determine which errors shall be fixed first to maximise accessibility improvement. The next step might be an editor plugin that check PDF/UA or other accessibility conformance before publication and informs the author about the problems ordered by the proposed scoring method. Going even further the plugin might hint the author about how to fix the document part that invalidates accessibility rules or even try to apply the fix automatically. At that point fixing automatically the legacy documents published at the university websites would not pose a challenge any more.

References

1. Acosta-Vargas, P., Gonzalez, M., Zambrano, M.R., Medina, A., Zweig, N., Salvador-Ullauri, L.: The portable document format: an analysis of PDF accessibility. In: Nunes, I.L. (ed.) AHFE 2020. AISC, vol. 1207, pp. 206–214. Springer, Cham (2020). https://doi.org/10.1007/978-3-030-51369-6_28
2. Acosta-Vargas, P., Luján-Mora, S., Acosta, T.: Accessibility of portable document format in education repositories. In: Proceedings of the 2017 9th International Conference on Education Technology and Computers, pp. 239–242 (2017)
3. Caldwell, B., Cooper, M., Reid, L.G., Vanderheiden, G., Chisholm, W., Slatin, J., White, J.: Web content accessibility guidelines (WCAG) 2.0. WWW Consortium (W3C) 290, pp. 1–34 (2008)
4. Consortium, W.W.W., et al.: Web content accessibility guidelines 1.0 (1999)
5. Darvishy, A.: PDF accessibility: tools and challenges. In: Miesenberger, K., Kouroupetroglou, G. (eds.) ICCHP 2018. LNCS, vol. 10896, pp. 113–116. Springer, Cham (2018). https://doi.org/10.1007/978-3-319-94277-3_20
6. Drümmer, O., Chang, B.: PDF/UA in a Nutshell: Accessible documents with PDF. Satzweiss. com (2014)
7. Johnson, D.: Accessibility: What pdf/a-1a really means, October 2010. https://www.pdfa.org/accessibility-what-pdf-a-1a-really-means/
8. McGuinness, R., Wilson, C., Johnson, D., Doubrov, B.: veraPDF: open source pdf/a validation through pragmatic partnership. In: iPRES (2017)
9. Nganji, J.T.: An assessment of the accessibility of pdf versions of selected journal articles published in a WCAG 2.0 era (2014–2018). Learned Publishing 31(4), 391–401 (2018)
10. Ribera, M., Pozzobon, R., Sayago, S.: Publishing accessible proceedings: the DSAI 2016 case study. Univ. Access Inf. Soc. 19(3), 557–569 (2020)

11. Spencer, A., McCall, K.: A strategic approach to document accessibility: integrating PDF/UA into your electronic content. In: Miesenberger, K., Fels, D., Archambault, D., Peňáz, P., Zagler, W. (eds.) ICCHP 2014. LNCS, vol. 8547, pp. 202–204. Springer, Cham (2014). https://doi.org/10.1007/978-3-319-08596-8_32
12. Spina, C.: WCAG 2.1 and the current state of web accessibility in libraries. Weave: J. Libr. User Exper. 2(2) (2019)

Table Recognition in Scanned Documents

Takwa Kazdar[1,2(✉)], Marwa Jmal[1], Wided Souidene[1], and Rabah Attia[1]

[1] SERCOM Laboratory, Ecole Polytechnique de Tunisie,
Université de Carthage, La Marsa, Tunisie
{takwa.gazdar,wided.souidene}@ept.rnu.tn, rabah.attia@ept.u-carthage.tn
[2] Telnet Holding, Telnet Technocentre, Les berges du Lac, Tunisia

Abstract. Invoices are so vastly used in business. For each invoice, an employee has to verify carefully written data including date, legal, and the courtesy amount present in each table. However, this task is not only time-consuming but also prone to inaccuracies and errors, especially when it comes to processing a massive amount of invoices. A smart capture system is required to facilitate processing invoices automatically and it is more challenging since relevant data are not narrative but arranged in tables. Although it is true that OCR (Optical Character Recognition) is able to read and capture data, it suffers from inefficiency in table locating and loses structural features of tabular data. Table recognition is widely carried out using deep learning and heuristics and a better result was reached as humans would. In this paper, we present a part of a smart capture system for invoices which is based on table recognition workflow for scanned invoices. This workflow consists of three main steps: the first step is a prepossessing step which is used to enhance the quality of scanned invoices. The second step is a deep learning-based table detection approach where we use DocCutout and DocCutmix for data augmentation. The third step is a heuristic-based table structure recognition approach. The presented approaches are evaluated on public data sets.

Keywords: Table detection · Table structure recognition · Scanned document · Faster R-CNN · Heuristics

1 Introduction

Extraction and recognition of relevant data from invoices is an interesting field of research. Traditionally, the manual processing of invoices is time consuming and prone to inaccuracies. For each invoice, an employee has to verify carefully written information including date, legal and courtesy amount present in each table which is a time-consuming task, especially when it comes to treat a massive amount of invoices. That's why many organizations across the world, try to capture and process scanned document's content through smart capture systems, in order to reduce human efforts [2].

Tables, as data containers, are used in order to present essential information to the reader in a structured manner. Automatically extract data from tables is

N. T. Nguyen et al. (Eds.): ICCCI 2022, LNAI 13501, pp. 744–754, 2022.
https://doi.org/10.1007/978-3-031-16014-1_58

required but what create various challenges is table understanding. Table under standing plays important roles in understanding the structure of documents [15]. Many competitions were, indeed, organized for table understanding such [8,9]. The most first one was on 2013 [12] which defined the table detection as a three tasks: 1) table localization: locating the regions of a document with tabular content. In [25] also, it has been reported that table detection task deals with the problem of finding boundaries of tables in a documment image. It is performed similarly to the object detection in natural scene images [24]. The next challenge in 2013 ICDAR competition, 2), is table structure recognition which consist on locating the rows and columns which make up the physical structure of the table. Finally, 3) table interpretation consists of recovering the meaning of the tabular structure.

In [16], it was suggested to detect tables basing not only on the lines but also on their building blocks which are ruling and fields. In other words, the structure of tables is built on the basis of those building blocks, considered as features. The most classical features that helped in both localization and recognition of tables are text blocks, recognized word and characters by Optical Character Recognition (OCR) algorithms, ruling intersections and terminal points [4]. By 2017, researchers started to use a number of efficient developed algorithms in the field of deep learning to solve table detection related problems. When reviewing deep learning based-table detection papers, we found that many researchers [1,9,10,21,26,27] leveraged the power of Faster R-CNN [23] in locating the table and reached better result when compared to hand-crafted based approaches. However, Faster R-CNN failed to recognize table structure recognition in [26]. When training a deep neural network for table detection with small amount of data like UNLV [25], the risk of over-fitting is increased. To avoid over-fitting, many researchers used to take advantage from regularization techniques, namely data augmentation [6]. Data augmentation allows for enlarging data set with geometrical transformations where transformed images are produced from the original images and will not be stored on disk [19]. In this context, the used transformations are flip, rotation, etc. contribute at improving generalization accuracy and avoiding over-fitting. It should be noted that Cutout [6] and Cutmix [31] were proposed as new trends in data augmentation. However, they cannot be directly applied for a task such table detection where semantic features of text are necessary in discriminating tables from other objects such charts and figures. But, when it comes to crop tables or hide some regions of that tables, consequently the model could lose the valuable features. That's why authors in [20] adapt Cutout [6] and Cutmix [31] to document images focusing on textual features so that DocCutout and DocCutmix contribute to enhance the capablity of generalisation.

Table structure recognition focuses on analyzing a detected table by finding its rows and columns and tries to extract the structure of the table [18,25] by analyzing the geometric arrangement of table blocks and in order to determinate tables cells. What make this task more challenging than table detection that rows and columns are located in very close proximity [5,24]. Tables were defined in

[4] as an assembly of 2D cells where data type is determined by either horizontal or vertical indexes. In [32], authors consider a table like a hierarchy of columns, rows, boxhead, stub, headers and nested columns, headers and nested rows. Traditionally, these elements were used by numerous researchers that made lots of efforts towards locating and recognizing tables [22]. Kieninger et al. [17] proposed the known T-recs system which rely on word grouping into columns to identify table cells. The first learning-based approach was introduced by [3] where authors represented a document by an MXY tree from which they identified blocks surrounded by horizontal and vertical lines. Later, the table structure recognition is solved using machine learning techniques like in [28] where the hidden state in the Hidden-Markov-Models belonging to a table or not. Tran et al. [29] define a set of heuristics in order to detect a table in bottom-up way. They began by locating text component and explore the spatial arrangement of extracted text blocks: the algorithm locates the text components and extracts text blocks. After that, text blocks are studied and if they satisfy a series of rules, the region of interest is regarded as a table. In our work, and following the same logic of [29], we propose a workflow for table recognition in invoices that starts by finding the table and than understanding the structure of the table. Our method includes the following steps: Firstly, we use OCR on a prepossessed image in order to get the text bounding box in the whole document. Then, we feed the prepossessed invoice to the Faster R-CNN (Region based CNN) and get the table region(s) in the the invoice. These are called region of interest (ROI). In each ROI, detected text blocks are called cells. Then, we check cells if they are arranged horizontally and vertically using heuristics. If text blocks are arranged horizontally, the boxes of text are merged to form a row, else, they are merged to form a column. We evaluate our approaches on public data sets.

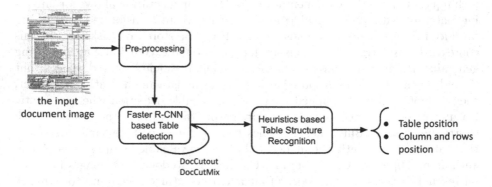

Fig. 1. An overview of our proposed table recognition workflow

The paper is organized as follows. Section 2 define our methodology and its main steps. Section 3, shows the experiments, data and results. Finally Sect. 4 concludes the work and provides future guidelines.

2   Methodology

Let's consider an invoice. At first glance, the reader sees the table as a whole. He, then, focuses on its content to read relevant information which are arranged into rows and columns. Regardless its layout, it is quite easy for humans to find and read table in a document. But, for an algorithm, it is more difficult [7]. It is in fact hard to process a document with a sophisticated template where all of the relevant data are organized in tables. Following the same logic, we propose in this paper a table recognition workflow for invoices that starts by finding the table and than understanding the structure of the table. Our method is illustrated in Fig. 1 and includes the following steps: Firstly, we use morphological operations to enhance the quality of the scanned document. Than, we apply OCR in order to get the text bounding box in the whole document. The prepossessed document is feeded to the Faster R-CNN to locate the table regions. These are called region of interest (ROI). The Faster R-CNN is trained using data augmentation techniques which are DocCutout and DocCutmix. In each ROI, detected text blocks are called cells. Then, we check cells if they are arranged horizontally and vertically using heuristics. If text blocks are arranged horizontally, the boxes are merged to form a row, else, they are merged to form a column.

2.1   Pre-processing and Table Detection

Scanning document may produce a low quality image and thus affect the clearance of objects, namely texts and tables. Then, the system will not be able to accurately localize or even recognize tabular structure. Thus, we transform the input document using a dilation operation followed by an erosion with 2×2 kernel. Therefore, the small scale details in the document are removed, in our case, the noise.

After processing the input document and applying Tesseract OCR to obtain bounding boxes of words, the image is fed to the second stage which is Faster R-CNN based table detection. Faster R-CNN [23] have been proposed and promote the development of general object detection by a large margin. Faster R-CNN is a Region based CNN variant composed of two stages: While the first stage consist on the region proposal network (RPN), the second stage is Fast R-CNN [11]. An RPN is a fully convolutional network that predicts positions and probability scores for each region proposal [23]. RPN and Fast R-CNN [11] are merged into a single network so that the RPN component tells the Fast R-CNN where to look. Instead of traditional data augmentation techniques, we train our model on table detection task using DocCutout and DocCutmix in order to not only prevent overfitting but also improve the generalization capability of the model. Different data augmentation techniques are illustrated in Fig. 2. As Cutout, DocCutout, randomly hide some regions of an input image region and in addition [20], it retains the text shape in words during augmentation. In the other hand, Cutmix mix training samples by simply hide an image region with patches from another training images.

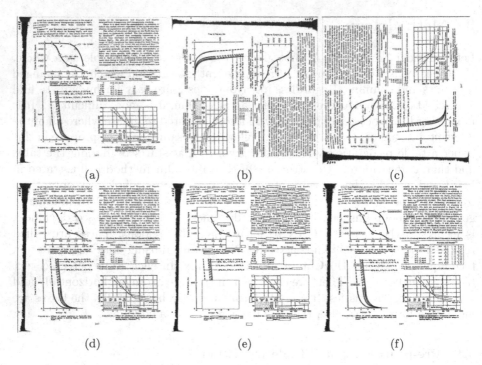

(a)   (b)   (c)

(d)   (e)   (f)

Fig. 2. Data augmentation effects on document image from UNLV: from left to right:(a) and (d) original images, (b) rotated image, (c) flipped image, (e) DocCutouted image, (f) DocCutmixed image. Blue boxes indicate the effect of DocCutout and Docutmix on the image (Color figure online)

2.2   Table Structure Recognition

The table structure recognition step is performed on a bottom-up way. In other words, we check the arrangement of cells and find rows and columns. To this end, we start by filtering the obtained bounding boxes to get those only inside the ROI (table region) predicted by the Faster R-CNN. After applying OCR on transformed image, we observed that morphological operations contribute in making words so close. Than, we merge those close bounding boxes into a single one to form a unified text block. Once we get text blocks, we considered them as cells and for each cell we first group the cells forming each column, and then these boxes will be merged into a single bounding box for the column. At this step, we regroup the cells of each column in one array with the help of vertical arrangement formulas proposed in [29]. For each text blocks, the algorithm have to find the aligned blocks that belong to the same row using the horizontal arrangement of [29]. If two consecutive text blocks are horizontally aligned, so they are merged to form a unified bounding boxes of the row.

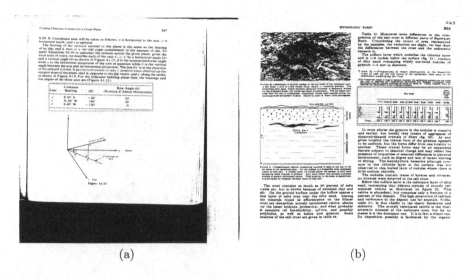

(a)   (b)

Fig. 3. Some sample images from UNLV where red bounding box describe the ground truth and the blue bounding box describe the predicted one: (a) True Positive (b) example of false positive where a figure is detected as table and a true positive (Color figure online)

3   Experiments and Results

3.1   Data Sets

To evaluate the performance of our approaches on scanned documents with noise, we have manually extracted and annotated some invoices from the RVL-CDIP dataset for both table detection and table structure recognition [14]. RVL-CDIP contains 400,000 grayscale images, which are categorized into 16 classes with 25,000 images per class. We extract about 500 invoices images and annotated tables and backgrounds. But also, we used the public dataset UNLV [25] which is comprised of a variety of documents including technical reports, business letters, newspapers and magazines etc. The dataset contains a total of 2889 scanned documents where only 424 documents contains a tabular region. We only used the images containing a tabular region in our experiments.

For table structure recognition, we used ICDAR 2013 dataset and our annotated set from RVL-CDIP. ICDAR 2013 dataset was presented for a competition on table detection and structure recognition [12]. Authors used digital-born PDF documents collected in [13] from the European Union and US Government websites. The dataset contains structure information for either table detection and structure recognition tasks. There are 238 images in total where 128 contains tables only. Our approach is implemented using python and OpenCV.

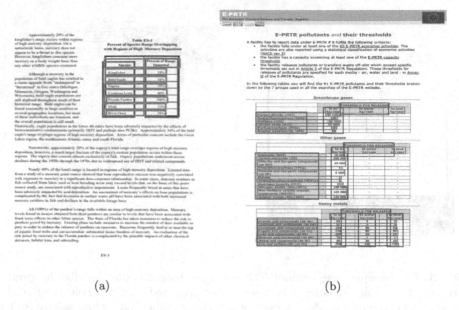

(a)   (b)

Fig. 4. Some sample images from ICDAR 2013 showing: (a) rows and columns are well recognized (b) spanned columns are not recognized and some rows lack text blocks like in first and second table

3.2   Table Detection

In this paper, the baseline is the Faster R-CNN with a pretrained ResNeXt-152 [30] on ImageNet. In all our experiments, training and testing were performed on Google Colaboratory Pro platform, using Tesla P100 GPU. The model was trained on 80000 steps with a momentum of 0.9 and learning rate of 0.00001. For DocCutout and DocCutmix we used the default parameters as detailed in the original paper [20]. In Table 1, we compare the impact of data augmentation and preprocessing on table detection in terms of precision, recall and F1-score for both UNLV and RVL CDIP. In the experiments, we begin by training the baseline on the set composed of RVL CDIP and UNLV using the most used data augmentation techniques which are rotation and horizontal flips to avoid overfitting as in [10]. Than, we apply prepossessing step to enhance the quality of input images and retrain the model using the same data augmentation techniques. It is obvious on Table 1 that the prepossessing step have a great impact in improving the accuracy of the model and increase the F1-score from 74.06% to 88.35% with UNLV as well as with RVL CDIP. Furthermore, using data augmentation techniques devoted to documents images contribute in not only avoiding over-fitting but also improving the performance of the Faster R-CNN. Compared to horizontal flip and rotation, training the baseline with prepossessed images and using DocCutout contribute in achieving a better F1-score which is about 92.55% on UNLV and 95.72% on RVL CDIP. Faster R-CNN with DocCutmix perform well also and outperform traditional data augmentation techniques.

Those latter results showed that DocCutmix is more suitable data augmentation technique for table detection task than DocCutout and even horizontal flip and rotation. It should be noted that Cutout [20] was firstly proposed to improve the robustness of the model against occluded objects which is generally dominated in case of person detection. When combining DocCutmix and DocCutout, the F1-score slightly decreased, indeed, from 93.18% to 92.24% on UNLV. In Fig. 3, we present examples of table detection on UNLV.

Table 1. Performance comparison on UNLV and RVL CDIP with data augmentation techniques and preprocessing

Baseline	ICDAR2013			RVL CDIP		
	Precision	Recall	F1-score	Precision	Recall	F1-score
FR-CNN-Resnext152						
+ Horizontal flip + rotation	0.7470	0.7345	0.7406	0.7093	0.7689	0.7378
+ Pre+horizontal flip + rotation	0.8961	0.8714	0.8835	0.8260	0.8531	0.8393
+ Pre+DocCutout	0.9145	0.9368	0.9255	0.9647	0.95	0.9572
+ Pre+DocCutmix	0.9227	0.9412	0.9318	0.9736	0.9647	0.9691
+ Pre+DocCutout + DocCutmix	0.9166	0.9283	0.9224	0.9481	0.9644	0.9561

3.3   Table Structure Recognition

Experiments results on ICDAR 2013 are reported in Table 2 where precision, recall and, F1 scores are calculated. Our approach is proposed for document images. However, ICDAR 2013 is composed of PDF files. Thus, we convert the document of the set to images. Also, those documents are not noisy, like RVL CDIP and UNLV. So we apply directly OCR without any prepossessing step. We used the ground truth table regions provided in the annotation file and we suppose that the table detection is initially performed. Our approach achieve an F1-score of 52.27% for rows and 46.38% for columns on ICDAR 2013 set. However, F1-score is about 85.44% for rows and 79.67% for columns on RVL CDIP. This difference could be explained by the fact that tables in ICDAR 2013 contains more spanned columns and rows compared to tables in RVL CDIP. Unfortunately, our approach do not treat that special case. Some results of our table structure recognition approach on ICDAR 2013 are represented in Fig. 4. It is obvious in this figure that in some other cases, our approach fail to recognize the whole row because of missing text blocks like in Fig. 4.b which affect directly the precision. In Fig. 5, we present some images from RVL CDIP where we applied the whole workflow starting with prepossessing til table structure recognition. In this set, our approach achieve a good result but with some missing rows and columns. The used rules may need further revision in order to enhance the prediction.

Table 2. Table structure recognition on ICDAR2013 and RVL CDIP

Objects	ICDAR2013			RVL CDIP		
	AP	AR	F1-score	AP	AR	F1-score
Rows	0.5725	0.4809	0.5227	0.8703	0.8391	0.8544
Columns	0.4480	0.4809	0.4638	0.8184	0.7763	0.7967

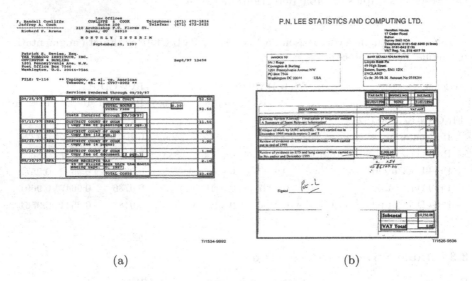

(a)   (b)

Fig. 5. Examples of images from RVL CDIP where the whole workflow is applied: red bounding box describes the predicted table, the blue describes the predicted columns and the green describes the predicted rows (a) most of the rows and columns are predicted but there is some missed rows (b) example of some columns that miss cells (Color figure online)

4   Conclusion

The primary purpose of our paper is to present a part of a smart document capture system developed to prevent errors and inaccuracies during extracting data from scanned documents. Our contribution consist on a table recognition workflow composed mainly of three steps. The system prepossesses the received invoice and enhance its quality. Than, we trained Faster R-CNN with ResneXt152 to the table detection task using new data augmentation techniques which are DocCutout and DocCutmix. Once table regions are located in the invoice, the system find and predict the rows and columns using vertical and horizontal arrangement rules. Experiments showed that DocCutmix is more suitable for the table detection task. Experiments on public data sets showed also that our model generalized well with the variety of tables. As future work, we will pursue the search for improving especially table structure recognition to get more accurate rows and columns prediction.

Acknowledgments. This research and innovation work is supported by MOBIDOC grants from the EU and National Agency for the Promotion of Scientific Research under the AMORI project and in collaboration with Telnet Innovation Labs from Telnet Holding.

References

1. Arif, S., Shafait, F.: Table detection in document images using foreground and background features. In: 2018 Digital Image Computing: Techniques and Applications (DICTA), pp. 1–8 (2018)
2. Boals, S.: The Value of Smart Capture in Digital Transformation. https://ephesoft.com/blog/the-value-of-smart-capture-in-digital-transformation/ (2020)
3. Cesarini, F., Marinai, S., Sarti, L., Soda, G.: Trainable table location in document images. In: Object Recognition Supported by User Interaction for Service Robots, vol. 3, pp. 236–240. IEEE (2002)
4. Coüasnon, B., Lemaitre, A.: Recognition of tables and forms (2014)
5. Deng, Y., Rosenberg, D., Mann, G.: Challenges in end-to-end neural scientific table recognition. In: International Conference on Document Analysis and Recognition (ICDAR), pp. 894–901. IEEE (2019)
6. DeVries, T., Taylor, G.W.: Improved regularization of convolutional neural networks with cutout. arXiv preprint (2017)
7. Embley, D., Hurst, M., Lopresti, D., Nagy, G.: Table-processing paradigms: a research survey. IJDAR **8**, 66–86 (2006)
8. Gao, L., et al.: ICDAR 2019 competition on table detection and recognition (CTDAR). In: International Conference on Document Analysis and Recognition (ICDAR), pp. 1510–1515 (2019)
9. Gao, L., Yi, X., Jiang, Z., Hao, L., Tang, Z.: ICDAR 2017 competition on page object detection. In: 14th IAPR International Conference on Document Analysis and Recognition (ICDAR), vol. 1, pp. 1417–1422 (2017)
10. Gilani, A., Qasim, S.R., Malik, I., Shafait, F.: Table detection using deep learning. In: 14th IAPR International Conference on Document Analysis and Recognition (ICDAR), vol. 01, pp. 771–776 (2017)
11. Girshick, R.: Fast R-CNN. In: Proceedings of the IEEE International Conference on Computer Vision, pp. 1440–1448 (2015)
12. Göbel, M., Hassan, T., Oro, E., Orsi, G.: ICDAR 2013 table competition. In: 12th International Conference on Document Analysis and Recognition, pp. 1449–1453 (2013)
13. Göbel, M., Hassan, T., Oro, E., Orsi, G.: A methodology for evaluating algorithms for table understanding in pdf documents. In: Proceedings of the ACM Symposium on Document Engineering, pp. 45–48 (2012)
14. Harley, A.W., Ufkes, A., Derpanis, K.G.: Evaluation of deep convolutional nets for document image classification and retrieval. In: International Conference on Document Analysis and Recognition (ICDAR)
15. He, D., Cohen, S., Price, B., Kifer, D., Giles, C.L.: Multi-scale multi-task FCN for semantic page segmentation and table detection. In: 14th IAPR International Conference on Document Analysis and Recognition (ICDAR), vol. 1, pp. 254–261 (2017)
16. Jahan, M.A.C.A., Ragel, R.G.: Locating tables in scanned documents for reconstructing and republishing. In: 7th International Conference on Information and Automation for Sustainability, pp. 1–6 (2014)

17. Kieninger, T., Dengel, A.: The T-Recs table recognition and analysis system. In: International Workshop on Document Analysis Systems, pp. 255–270 (1998)
18. Kieninger, T.G.: Table structure recognition based on robust block segmentation. In: Document Recognition V, vol. 3305, pp. 22–32 (1998)
19. Krizhevsky, A., Sutskever, I., Hinton, G.E.: ImageNet classification with deep convolutional neural networks. Commun. ACM **60**, 84–90 (2012)
20. Lee, Y., Hong, T., Kim, S.: Data augmentations for document images. In: SDU@ AAAI (2021)
21. Li, M., Cui, L., Huang, S., Wei, F., Zhou, M., Li, Z.: TableBank: table benchmark for image-based table detection and recognition. arXiv preprint (2019)
22. Lopresti, D., Nagy, G.: A tabular survey of automated table processing. In: Chhabra, A.K., Dori, D. (eds.) Graphics Recognition Recent Advances, pp. 93–120. Springer, Berlin Heidelberg (2000). https://doi.org/10.1007/3-540-40953-X_9
23. Ren, S., He, K., Girshick, R., Sun, J.: Faster R-CNN: towards real-time object detection with region proposal networks. In: Advances in Neural Information Processing Systems 28, pp. 91–99 (2015)
24. Schreiber, S., Agne, S., Wolf, I., Dengel, A., Ahmed, S.: DeepDeSRT: deep learning for detection and structure recognition of tables in document images. In: 2017 14th IAPR International Conference on Document Analysis and Recognition (ICDAR), vol. 1, pp. 1162–1167 (2017)
25. Shafait, F., Smith, R.: Table detection in heterogeneous documents, pp. 65–72. New York, NY, USA (2010)
26. Siddiqui, S.A., Fateh, I.A., Rizvi, S.T.R., Dengel, A., Ahmed, S.: DeepTabStR: deep learning based table structure recognition. In: International Conference on Document Analysis and Recognition (ICDAR), pp. 1403–1409 (2019)
27. Siddiqui, S.A., Malik, M.I., Agne, S., Dengel, A., Ahmed, S.: DeCNT: deep deformable CNN for table detection. IEEE Access **6**, 74151–74161 (2018)
28. e Silva, A.C.: Learning rich hidden Markov models in document analysis: table location. In: The 10th International Conference on Document Analysis and Recognition, pp. 843–847 (2009)
29. Tran, D.N., Tran, T.A., Oh, A., Kim, S.H., Na, I.S.: Table detection from document image using vertical arrangement of text blocks. Int. J. Contents **11**(4), 77–85 (2015)
30. Xie, S., Girshick, R., Dollár, P., Tu, Z., He, K.: Aggregated residual transformations for deep neural networks (2017). https://doi.org/10.1109/CVPR.2017.634
31. Yun, S., Han, D., Oh, S.J., Chun, S., Choe, J., Yoo, Y.: CutMix: regularization strategy to train strong classifiers with localizable features. In: Proceedings of the IEEE/CVF International Conference on Computer Vision, pp. 6023–6032 (2019). https://doi.org/10.1109/ICCV.2019.00612
32. Zanibbi, R., Blostein, D., Cordy, J.: A survey of table recognition: models, observations, transformations, and inferences. Online: https://www.cs.queensu.ca/~cordy/Papers/IJDAR_Tables.pdf, Last Checked pp. 12–01 (2007)

TT-ViT: Vision Transformer Compression Using Tensor-Train Decomposition

Hoang Pham Minh[1,2](✉), Nguyen Nguyen Xuan[1,2], and Son Tran Thai[1,2](✉)

[1] Faculty of Information Technology, University of Science,
VNU-HCM, Ho Chi Minh City, Vietnam
{pmhoang,ttson}@fit.hcmus.edu.vn
[2] Vietnam National University, Ho Chi Minh City, Vietnam

Abstract. Inspired by Transformer, one of the most successful deep learning models in natural language processing, machine translation, etc. Vision Transformer (ViT) has recently demonstrated its effectiveness in computer vision tasks such as image classification, object detection, etc. However, the major issue with ViT is to require massively trainable parameters. In this paper, we propose a novel compressed ViT model, namely Tensor-train ViT (TT-ViT), based on tensor-train (TT) decomposition. Consider a multi-head self-attention layer, instead of storing whole trainable matrices, we represent them in TT format via their TT cores using fewer parameters. The results of our experiments on CIFAR-10/Fashion-MNIST dataset reveal that TT-ViT achieves outstanding performance with equivalent accuracy to its baseline model, while total parameters of TT-ViT are just half of those of the baseline model.

Keywords: Vision transformer · Tensor decomposition · Tensor-train decomposition · Model compression

1 Introduction

In recent years, deep learning models such as CNN [12], RNN [22], Transformer [25], etc. have emerged as tremendous successes of neural networks, and they are widely used structures in computer vision, natural language processing, automatic speech recognition,... However, one of the most significant issues facing deep learning models is the massive amount of memory usage required. Modern devices tend to reduce the size of models while preserving their performance. For mobile applications, training networks is performed on a powerful server before applying trained parameters to execute these applications on mobile devices. To address this problem, our work is to propose an equivalent alternative by using a compressed representation to minimize the number of parameters while maintaining reliable performance.

This research is funded by University of Science, VNU-HCM under grant number CNTT 2020-09.

Currently, Transformer model has been demonstrated to be a breakthrough for processing sequence-to-sequence data. Transformer leverages the multi-head self-attention mechanism for connecting relevant information from a very long input sequence. One of the advantages of the transformer is that this model is capable of processing input sequences in parallel. Some of the most notable Transformer models [25] including BERT [3], GPT [21], RoBERTa [14] have been incredibly common in natural language processing, text classification, machine translation, and question answering,... Researchers from Google have introduced the Vision Transformer architecture [4], a Transformer architecture version for images, as a new direction for computer vision tasks. This architecture has achieved outstanding results for image classification tasks on ImageNet [2]/CIFAR-100 [10] compared to state-of-the-art CNN. Vision Transformer (ViT), on the other hand, has to be pre-trained on larger-scale datasets such as JFT300M before being fine-tuned on the ImageNet-1k dataset to improve its performance. DeiT [24] proposed a convolution-free transformer network with high top-1 accuracy on ImageNet using no external data, also provides a novel teacher-student technique that transfers knowledge from the teacher model to the student with distillation token. Pyramid Vision Transformer (PVT) [26] is introduced as a pure Transformer model to address many difficulties for dense prediction. PVT developed a progressive shrinking pyramid and a self-attention called Spatial-Reduction Attention (SRA) to reduce computations and make PVTs flexible for learning multi-scale and high-resolution features. SWIN transformer [16] introduced a hierarchical transformer whose representation is generated by shifting windows, to address the issues of transferring Transformers from language to vision. The shifted windowing approach improves efficiency by restricting self-attention computation to non-overlapping local windows while allowing for cross-window interaction.

Recently, tensor decomposition methods are applied to many supervised learning tasks such as image classification, data compression,... [13]. Tensor decomposition is an approach for factorizing weights into an undirected graph where each node is represented by a high-order tensor. The number of parameters can be significantly reduced because the principle of tensor decomposition is to enhance the correlation and entanglement between nodes in networks [1]. Some of the best-known applications of tensor networks are image super-resolution [28], image recovery [15],...

A lot of researchers concentrate on deep learning model compression using tensor decomposition as a new approach for representing the trainable weights. For instance, some compressed CNN decompose the fourth-order convolutional tensor W of size $L \times L \times C \times S$ into other forms with low order tensors requiring fewer parameters. Jaderberg et al. [8] approximated the convolutional tensor W by stacking two convolutional tensor of size $1 \times L \times S \times M$ and $L \times 1 \times M \times S$. The approach of [9] used Tucker decomposition to compress the convolutional kernel tensor by factorizing a $N-$order tensor into a core tensor and N factor matrices. Kim et al. [9] represents a fourth-order tensor in compressed form containing a smaller four-order core tensor and two factor matrices. A standard convolutional layer with kernel tensor of size $D \times D \times S \times T$ is replaced by 3 different convolutional layers with kernel of size $1 \times 1 \times S \times R_3$, $D \times D \times R_3 \times R_4$, and $1 \times 1 \times R_4 \times T$ where R_3, R_4 are Tucker ranks. The basic idea of [11] [23] is to split the kernel tensor using CP decomposition, which is a special case of Tucker decomposition where the core tensor is sparse. The initialized kernel of size $D \times D \times S \times T$ is split into 5 new kernel tensors of size $1 \times 1 \times S \times R$, $D \times 1 \times 1$, $1 \times D \times 1$, $1 \times 1 \times R \times T$, respectively.

Novikov et al. [18] use Tensor Train (TT) [20] to represent the weight matrix of a fully connected layer via a set of TT cores and replace the matrix-vector product with a TT matrix-vector product. Garipov et al. [5] augment the 4-order kernel tensor $\mathcal{K}$ into a $(2D+1)-$ order tensor, which is compressed by $(D+1)$ TT cores. Yang et al. [29] used TT decomposition to factorize weight matrices into TT-cores using fewer parameters. Tensorized Transformer [17] is a pioneering study that uses tensor decomposition Block-Term Tensor Decomposition (BTD) to compress the self-attention layer, namely Multi-linear attention by combining two compression ideas: parameter sharing and low-rank approximation. Another method [6], known as a low-rank transformer, employs matrix decomposition to improve the self-attention module based on two linguistic constraints: low-rank and locality.

In this work, our major contributions are as follows

- We propose the new compressed Vision Transformer (ViT) framework, namely tensor-train vision transformer (TT-ViT), based on Tensor-train decomposition that factorizes trainable matrices into TT cores with fewer parameters and replaces all of the matrix products with TT matrix-by-vector products with lower computational complexity.
- We evaluate our proposed method for image classification on two datasets: CIFAR-10 [10] and Fashion-MNIST [27]. Our experimental results show that the accuracy of compressed models TT-ViT approximates or even surpasses that of their baseline models while just half of the parameters are used.

The paper is structured as follows. Section 2 introduces some basic concepts of tensor such as definition, Tensor-train decomposition, and TT matrix-by-vector product. Section 3 presents our proposed TT-based compressed ViT (TT-ViT). All of the experiments for the image classification task on CIFAR10 [10] and Fashion-MNIST [27] are described in Sect. 4. Section 5 concludes the paper.

2   Tensor Foundation

In this section, we introduce fundamental concepts in tensor processing, such as tensor definition, Tensor-train (TT) decomposition, and Tensor-train (TT) matrix-vector product.

2.1   Definition

A tensor $\mathcal{X} \in \mathbb{R}^{I_1 \times I_2 \times \cdots \times I_N}$ is defined as a multidimensional array with the number of dimensions N as its **mode** or **order**, and I_k $(k = 1, \ldots, N)$ as the size of k-th mode. Scalars, vectors, and matrices are all generalized into tensors. A scalar is a zero-order tensor denoted by a lowercase letter, such as x. A vector is a first-order tensor denoted by a boldface lowercase letter such as $\mathbf{x}$, whereas a matrix is a two-order tensor denoted by capital letters, e.g. $\mathbf{X} \in \mathbb{R}^{I_1 \times I_2}$. A higher order tensor is denoted by a calligraphic letter, e.g. $\mathcal{X} \in \mathbb{R}^{I_1 \times I_2 \times \cdots \times I_N}$.

2.2   Tensor Train Decomposition

Tensor train (TT) [20] is a method of factorizing a high order tensor $\mathcal{W} \in \mathbb{R}^{I_1 \times I_2 \times \cdots \times I_C}$ into C third-order tensors $\{\mathcal{G}_c\}_{c=1}^{C} \in \mathbb{R}^{I_c \times r_{c-1} \times r_c}$ where each element $\mathcal{X}(i_1, i_2, \ldots, i_C)$ is computed by

$$
\mathcal{W}(i_1, i_2, \ldots, i_C) = \sum_{\alpha_1=1}^{r_1} \sum_{\alpha_2=1}^{r_2} \cdots \sum_{\alpha_{C-1}=1}^{r_{C-1}} \mathcal{G}_1(i_1, \alpha_1)\mathcal{G}_2(i_2, \alpha_1, \alpha_2) \cdots
$$
$$
\mathcal{G}_{C-1}(i_{C-1}, \alpha_{C-1}, \alpha_C)\mathcal{G}_C(i_C, \alpha_{C-1}), \qquad (1)
$$

The tuple of $(r_1, r_2, \ldots, r_{C-1})$ is called TT-ranks with r_0 fixed as 1, r_C fixed as 1, and third-order tensors $\{\mathcal{G}_c\}_{c=1}^{C}$ are referred to TT-cores. In addition to the TT representation in scalar form as (1), we can express a C-th order tensor in TT format using matrix form

$$
\mathcal{W}(i_1, i_2, \ldots, i_C) = \mathcal{G}_1[i_1]\mathcal{G}_2[i_2] \ldots \mathcal{G}_C[i_C]. \qquad (2)
$$

where $\mathcal{G}[i_c] \in \mathbb{R}^{r_{c-1} \times r_c}$ denotes the c-th slice of $\mathcal{G}_c$. The objective of TT decomposition is to find TT cores $\{\mathcal{G}_c\}_{c=1}^{C}$ for approximating $\mathcal{W}$ according to (2). To perform this, TT-SVD [20] leverages a truncated SVD of unfolding matrices from $\mathcal{W}$ to determine TT cores. The TT ranks $\{r_c\}_{c=1}^{C}$ can be thought of as parameters for adjusting model sizes. By encoding $\mathcal{W}$ with a set of third-order TT cores, TT decomposition is particularly effective in reducing the number of elements of the C-th order tensor $\mathcal{W}$ if the TT ranks are small enough.

2.3   TT Matrix-Vector Product

Consider a matrix-by-vector product $\mathbf{y} = \mathbf{Wx}$ where $\mathbf{W}$ is a matrix of size $M \times N$, and $\mathbf{x}$ is a vector of size N. Firstly, we apply tensor augmentation [7] to transform $\mathbf{W}$ into $2C$-th order tensor $\mathcal{W}$ of size $m_1 \times n_1 \times m_2 \times n_2 \times \cdots \times m_C \times n_C$ with $M = \prod_{c=1}^{C} m_c$ and $N = \prod_{c=1}^{C} n_c$. By encoding indices (i, j) using $2C$-digit words $(i_1 j_1 i_2 j_2 \ldots i_C j_C)$, tensor augmentation allows us to express a matrix into a high-order tensor, which is a flexible structure capable of enhancing all correlations and entanglements between matrix entries [7]. Secondly, using the matrix form as (2), the high order tensor $\mathcal{W}$ is then factorized by TT decomposition into a set of TT cores $\{\mathcal{G}_c\}_{c=1}^{C}$ of size $m_c \times n_c \times r_{c-1} \times r_c$ where $\{r_c\}_{c=1}^{C}$ are

TT ranks ($r_0 = r_C = 1$), so that each of element $\mathcal{W}(i_1, j_1, i_2, j_2, \ldots, i_C, j_C)$ is written in TT format as follows

$$\mathcal{W}(i_1, j_1, i_2, j_2, \ldots, i_C, j_C) = \mathcal{G}_1[i_1, j_1]\mathcal{G}_2[i_2, j_2] \cdots \mathcal{G}_C[i_C, j_C] \tag{3}$$

where $\mathcal{G}_c[i_c, j_c]$ is a matrix of size $r_{c-1} \times r_c$. Similarity, we also reshaped the input vector $\mathbf{x} \in \mathbb{R}^N$ into a C-th order tensor $\mathcal{X}$ of size $m_1 \times m_2 \times \cdots \times m_C$. The TT matrix-by-vector product, which replaces the matrix-vector product $\mathbf{y} = \mathbf{Wx}$, is defined as a new multiplication between a sequence of TT-cores $\{\mathcal{G}\}_{c=1}^C$ and a high order tensor $\mathcal{X}$.

$$\mathcal{Y}(i_1, \ldots, i_C) = \sum_{j_1=1}^{n_1} \cdots \sum_{j_C=1}^{n_C} \mathcal{W}(i_1, j_1, i_2, j_2, \ldots, i_C, j_C)\mathcal{X}(j_1, j_2, \ldots, j_C) \tag{4}$$

$$= \sum_{j_1=1}^{n_1} \cdots \sum_{j_C=1}^{n_C} \mathcal{G}_1[i_1, j_1]\mathcal{G}_2[i_2, j_2] \cdots \mathcal{G}_C[i_C, j_C]\mathcal{X}(j_1, \ldots, j_C) \tag{5}$$

Finally, the C-th order output tensor $\mathcal{Y}$ of size $m_1 \times m_2 \times \cdots \times m_C$ is transformed to one dimensional vector $\mathbf{y} \in \mathbb{R}^M$. According to [19], the TT matrix-by-vector product is performed by a recursive algorithm described in Algorithm 1.

Algorithm 1: How to perform a TT matrix-by-vector product

1: **Input:** TT-cores $\{\mathcal{G}_c\}_{c=1}^C \in \mathbb{R}^{m_c \times n_c \times r_{c-1} \times r_c}$, TT ranks $\{r_c\}_{c=1}^C$, $M = \prod_{c=1}^C m_c$,
   $N = \prod_{c=1}^C n_c$, vector $\mathbf{x} \in \mathbb{R}^N$.
2: **Output:** vector $\mathbf{Y} \in \mathbb{R}^M$ vector $\mathbf{Y} \in \mathbb{R}^M$
   ◇ Reshape $\mathbf{x}$ into tensor $\mathcal{X}$ of size $n_1 \times n_2 \times \cdots \times n_C$
   ◇ $\mathcal{Y}_1(j_1, \ldots, j_C) = \mathcal{X}(j_1, \ldots, j_C)$
   ◇ $\mathcal{Y}_2(\alpha_1, i_1, j_2, \ldots, j_C) = \sum_{j_1=1}^{n_1} \mathcal{G}_1[i_1, j_1](\alpha_1)\mathcal{Y}_1(j_1, \ldots, j_C)$
   ◇ For $c = 2, \ldots, C-1$

$$\mathcal{Y}_{c+1}(\alpha_c, i_1, \ldots, i_c, j_{c+1}, \ldots, j_D) = \sum_{j_c=1}^{n_c} \sum_{\alpha_{c-1}=1}^{r_{c-1}} \mathcal{G}_c[i_c, j_c](\alpha_{c-1}, \alpha_c) \tag{6}$$

$$\mathcal{Y}_c(\alpha_{c-1}, i_1, \ldots, i_{c-1}, j_c, \ldots, j_C)$$

   ◇ $\mathcal{Y}(i_1, \ldots, i_C) = \sum_{j_C=1}^{n_C} \sum_{\alpha_{C-1}=1}^{r_{C-1}} \mathcal{G}_C[i_C, j_C](\alpha_{C-1})\mathcal{Y}_C(\alpha_{C-1}, i_1, \ldots, i_{C-1}, j_C)$
   ◇ Reshape tensor $\mathcal{Y}$ to vector $\mathbf{y} \in \mathbb{R}^M$
3: **Return:** $\mathbf{y}$.

All of the equations used to compute tensors $\{\mathcal{Y}_c\}_{c=1}^C$ in Algorithm 1 can be expressed in tensor contraction form [13], which is a basic tensor operation and implemented in deep learning framework such as Pytorch, Tensorflow. The computational cost of the TT matrix-by-vector product, according to Novikov et al. [18], is $\mathcal{O}(Cr^2m\max(M, N))$, where $m = \max(m_1, \ldots, m_C)$ and $r = \max(r_1, \ldots, r_{C-1})$. For small TT ranks $\{r_c\}_{c=1}^C$, total parameters $\sum_{c=1}^C n_c r_{c-1} r_c m_c$ of TT-cores are less than total elements MN of the matrix $\mathbf{W}$, indicating the efficient memory usage of representing $\mathbf{W}$ in TT format.

3   TT-ViT: A TT-Based Compressed ViT

A vision transformer model (ViT) [4] is made up of three primary modules: a linear projection for patch embedding, a sequence of transformer blocks, and several fully connected layers for the classification head. Firstly, ViT takes an input image of size $W \times H \times U$ where W, H are the spatial sizes, U is the number of channels. After that, we split the input image into a sequence of $2D$ patches, each of which is of size $WH/P^2 \times UP^2$ where P is the patch size. Secondly, these patches are linearly transformed into a D-dimensional space to produce N patch embeddings $\mathbf{z}_n \in \mathbb{R}^D$, where D is the embedding dimension. To capture positional information, positional encoding is added to $\mathbf{z}_n$. Consequently, we collect N embedding patches $\mathbf{z}_n$ to generate a matrix $\mathbf{Z} \in \mathbb{R}^{N \times D}$ before feeding it into transformer blocks, each of which is composed of a multi-head self-attention layer (MSA) and multi-layer perceptron blocks (MLP). Suppose $\mathbf{Z}^{\prime l}$ and $\mathbf{Z}^l$ respectively be the output of MSA and MLP in l-th transformer block, we have

$$\mathbf{Z}^{\prime l} = \text{MSA}(\text{LN}(\mathbf{Z}^{l-1})) + \mathbf{Z}^{l-1} \tag{7}$$

and

$$\mathbf{Z}^l = \text{MLP}(\mathbf{Y}^{(l)}) + \mathbf{Z}^{\prime l} \tag{8}$$

where LN(.) is the layer normalization, MSA(.) can be seen as a function mapping the input $\text{LN}(\mathbf{Z}^{l-1})$ to attention map, and MLP(.) denote multi-layer perceptron blocks. The output of l-th transformer block becomes the input of $(l+1)$-th transformer block with the embedding dimension D remaining constant throughout all transformer blocks. Finally, a sequence of fully connected layers is applied to the class token to calculate the prediction score for classification.

Multi-head Self-attention. Assume that $\mathbf{Z} \in \mathbb{R}^{N \times D}$ is the input sequence after patch embedding and layer normalization step, we calculate three matrices Query $\mathbf{Q}$, Key $\mathbf{K}$, and Value $\mathbf{V}$ by following linear transformations.

$$\mathbf{Q} = \mathbf{Z}\mathbf{W}^Q \tag{9}$$

$$\mathbf{K} = \mathbf{Z}\mathbf{W}^K \tag{10}$$

$$\mathbf{V} = \mathbf{Z}\mathbf{W}^V \tag{11}$$

where $\mathbf{W}^Q \in \mathbb{R}^{D \times S}$, $\mathbf{W}^Q \in \mathbb{R}^{D \times S}$, and $\mathbf{W}^Q \in \mathbb{R}^{D \times S}$ are their trainable weights for learning. The output of MSA layer is computed by

$$\text{Att}(\mathbf{Q}, \mathbf{K}, \mathbf{V}) = \text{softmax}(\frac{\mathbf{Q}\mathbf{K}^T}{\sqrt{S}})\mathbf{V} \tag{12}$$

where $\sqrt{S}$ is a scaling factor based on the number of hidden dimension S. Instead of computing the attention once, the multi-head mechanism divides the matrices $\mathbf{Q}, \mathbf{K}$, and $\mathbf{V}$ into H heads $\mathbf{Q}_h, \mathbf{K}_h$, and $\mathbf{V}_h$ and computes the scaled dot-product attention in parallel. The attention map of each head is concatenated to obtain the final output

$$\text{Multihead}(\mathbf{Q}, \mathbf{K}, \mathbf{V}) = [\text{Att}_1, \text{Att}_2, \dots, \text{Att}_H]\mathbf{W}^O \qquad (13)$$

where $\text{Att}_h = \text{Att}(\mathbf{Q}_h, \mathbf{K}_h, \mathbf{V}_h)$ and $\mathbf{W}^O \in \mathbb{R}^{S \times D}$ is the matrix to be learned.

Compressing MSA Using TT Decomposition. In this section, we propose a method for compressing the multi-head self-attention (MSA) based on TT decomposition. To begin, let C be the number of TT-cores, we reshape the input matrix $\mathbf{Z} \in \mathbb{R}^{N \times D}$ into the tensor $\mathcal{Z}$ of size $N \times d_1 \times d_2 \times \cdots \times d_C$ with $D = \prod_{c=1}^{C} d_c$. For $S = \prod_{c=1}^{C} s_c$, the trainable weight matrices $\mathbf{W}^K$, $\mathbf{W}^Q$, $\mathbf{W}^V$, and $\mathbf{W}^O$ are expressed in TT format using four sets of TT cores $\{\mathcal{G}_c^Q\}_{c=1}^{C}$, $\{\mathcal{G}_c^K\}_{c=1}^{C}$, $\{\mathcal{G}_c^V\}_{c=1}^{C}$, and $\{\mathcal{G}_c^O\}_{c=1}^{C}$, respectively. We can rewrite the linear transformations (9) as

$$\mathbf{Q} = \mathbf{Z}\mathbf{W}^Q = (\mathbf{W}^Q)^T\mathbf{Z}^T = [(\mathbf{W}^Q)^T\mathbf{z}_1^T; (\mathbf{W}^Q)^T\mathbf{z}_2^T; \dots; (\mathbf{W}^Q)^T\mathbf{z}_N^T] \qquad (14)$$

where $\mathbf{z}_i$ are i-th rows of the matrix $\mathbf{Z}$ ($i = 1, 2, \dots, N$). Rather than calculating $(\mathbf{W}^Q)^T\mathbf{z}_i^T$ with full matrix $\mathbf{W}^Q$ of size $D \times S$, we substitute all of matrix-by-vector product $(\mathbf{W}^Q)^T\mathbf{z}_i^T$ with a sequence of N TT matrix-by-vector products between a set of TT cores $\{\mathcal{G}_c^Q\}_{c=1}^{C}$ and the high order tensor $\mathcal{Z}[i] \in \mathbb{R}^{d_1 \times d_2 \times \cdots \times d_C}$. In the previous section, we provide all steps for performing a TT matrix-by-vector product in Algorithm 1. For simplification, we use the notation $\text{TTP}(\mathbf{Z}, \{\mathcal{G}_c^Q\}_{c=1}^{C})$ to denote a sequence of TT matrix-by-vector products for computing the Eq. (14). As a result, the linear transformations (10), (11) and (13) can be computed using TTP products, and the complete compressed MSA algorithm using TT decomposition can be described as follows.

Algorithm 2: How to compute the MSA layer output when representing trainable weights in TT format

---

Input : input $\mathbf{Z} \in \mathbb{R}^{N \times D}$, number of TT-cores C, TT-ranks $\{r_c\}_{c=1}^{C}$,
$\qquad\quad D = \prod_{c=1}^{C} d_c$, $S = \prod_{c=1}^{C} s_c$, number of heads H
Weight: TT-cores $\{\mathcal{G}_c^Q\}_{c=1}^{C}$, $\{\mathcal{G}_c^K\}_{c=1}^{C}$, $\mathcal{G}_c^V\}_{c=1}^{C}$, $\{\mathcal{G}_c^O\}_{c=1}^{C}$
Output: Mutihead$(\mathbf{Q}, \mathbf{K}, \mathbf{V})$
Compute $\mathbf{Q}$, $\mathbf{K}$, $\mathbf{V}$ using TTP
$\mathbf{Q} = \text{TTP}(\mathbf{Z}, \{\mathcal{G}_c^Q\}_{c=1}^{C})$
$\mathbf{K} = \text{TTP}(\mathbf{Z}, \{\mathcal{G}_c^K\}_{c=1}^{C})$
$\mathbf{V} = \text{TTP}(\mathbf{Z}, \{\mathcal{G}_c^V\}_{c=1}^{C})$
Divide $\mathbf{Q}$, $\mathbf{K}$, $\mathbf{V}$ into H heads $\{\mathbf{Q}_h\}_{h=1}^{H}$, $\{\mathbf{K}_h\}_{h=1}^{H}$, $\{\mathbf{V}_h\}_{h=1}^{H}$
for $h = 1$ **to** H **do**
$\qquad \text{Att}_h(\mathbf{Q}_h, \mathbf{K}_h, \mathbf{V}_h) = \text{softmax}(\frac{\mathbf{Q}_h\mathbf{K}_h^T}{\sqrt{S}})\mathbf{V}_h$
end
Mutihead$(\mathbf{Q}, \mathbf{K}, \mathbf{V}) = \text{TTP}([\text{Att}_1, \text{Att}_2, \dots, \text{Att}_H], \{\mathcal{G}_c^O\}_{c=1}^{C}))$
return Mutihead$(\mathbf{Q}, \mathbf{K}, \mathbf{V})$

The process for computing the MSA output using TT decomposition is performed by Algorithm 2 and illustrated as Fig. 1. There are two advantages when representing weight matrices in TT format.

- If the TT ranks $\{r_c\}_{c=1}^C$ are small enough, total parameters of TT cores $\{\mathcal{G}_c^Q\}_{c=1}^C, \{\mathcal{G}_c^K\}_{c=1}^C, \{\mathcal{G}_c^V\}_{c=1}^C$, and $\{\mathcal{G}_c^O\}_{c=1}^C$ reduce rapidly comparing with total parameters of full matrices $\mathbf{W}^K, \mathbf{W}^Q, \mathbf{W}^V$, and $\mathbf{W}^O$. To demonstrate that, we compute the compression rate as the ratio between the number of parameters in MSA and that of its compressed form $c_r = \frac{\sum_{c=1}^C d_c s_c r_{c-1} r_c}{DS}$
- Apparently, substituting all matrix-by-vector products with $\mathsf{TTP}(.)$ products allows us to save computational costs efficiently. As aforementioned, the computational cost of a TT matrix-by-vector is just $\mathcal{O}(Cr^2 d \max(D, S)))$ with $r = \max(r_1, \ldots, r_C)$ and $d = \max(d_1, \ldots, d_C)$ less than $\mathcal{O}(DS)$ of a matrix-by-vector product. Thus, the computational cost of a TTP product consisting of N TT matrix-by-vector products is $\mathcal{O}(NCr^2 d \max(D, S))$, which is less than the computational cost of a matrix-by-matrix product $\mathcal{O}(NDS)$.

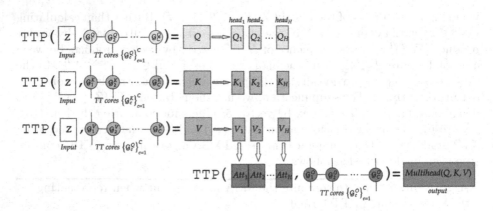

Fig. 1. The illustration of Algorithm 2 for computing the MSA output using TT decomposition

4   Experiments

In this section, we present the results of our experiments for the image classification task on two datasets. The first one is CIFAR-10 [10], which comprises 60,000 color images size of $32 \times 32 \times 3$ from 10 distinct classes (frogs, birds, cats,...). This dataset is divided into two sections: 50,000 samples for training and 10,000 samples for testing. The other is Fashion-MNIST [27], which has 70,000 images of size 28×28 from 10 categories like dresses, coats, shirts, bags,... This dataset is also partitioned into two parts: 60,000 training samples and 10,000 testing samples. We build two vision transformers as baseline models, which are respectively called ViT-A and ViT-B. Their architectures are depicted in Table 1, where their hyper-parameters include the patch size P, number of transformer blocks L, fully connected layer (FC) dimension for classification head, and hyper-parameters for each transformer block such as number of attention heads H, embedding dimension D, the number of hidden dimension S, and MLP layer dimensions. To compress the MSA layer, we first choose two tuples $(d_1, d_2, \ldots, d_C)$ and $(s_1, s_2, \ldots, s_C)$ that satisfy $D = \prod_{c=1}^{C} d_c$ and $S = \prod_{c=1}^{C} s_c$, respectively. Following that, the trainable weight matrices $\mathbf{W}^Q \in \mathbb{R}^{D \times S}$, $\mathbf{W}^K \in \mathbb{R}^{D \times S}$, $\mathbf{W}^Q \in \mathbb{R}^{D \times S}$, and $\mathbf{W}^O \in \mathbb{R}^{S \times D}$ are compressed by representing them in TT format using four sets of TT cores $\{\mathcal{G}_c^Q\}_{c=1}^{C} \in \mathbb{R}^{d_c \times s_c \times r_{c-1} \times r_c}$, $\{\mathcal{G}_c^Q\}_{c=1}^{C} \in \mathbb{R}^{d_c \times s_c \times r_{c-1} \times r_c}$, and $\{\mathcal{G}_c^Q\}_{c=1}^{C} \in \mathbb{R}^{d_c \times s_c \times r_{c-1} \times r_c}$ where $\{r_c\}_{c=1}^{C}$ are TT ranks. Using notations $vec(D) = (d_1, \ldots, d_C)$, $vec(S) = (s_1, \ldots, s_C)$, and $vec(R) = (1, r_1, \ldots, r_{C-1}, 1)$, we describe the parameters of compressed ViT-A and ViT-B, which are referred to as TT-ViT-A and TT-ViT-B, in Table 2.

Table 1. Hyper-parameters of two baseline models: ViT-A and ViT-B

Hyper-parameters	ViT-A	ViT-B
Patch size	4	6
#transformer block	8	6
#attention heads	16	4
Embedding dimension	64	64
The number of hidden dimension	64	64
MLP dimensions	[128,64]	[128,64]
FC dimensions for classification head	[128,10]	[128,64,10]

Table 2. Hyper-parameters of TT-ViT-A and TT-ViT-B including the number of TT-cores C, $vec(D) = (d_1, \ldots, d_C)$, $vec(S) = (s_1, \ldots, s_C)$, and $vec(R) = (1, r_1, \ldots, r_{C-1}, 1)$

Hyper-parameters	TT-cores	$vec(D)$	$vec(S)$	$vec(R)$
TT-ViT-A (R = 2)	3	(4,4,4)	(4,4,4)	(1,2,2,1)
TT-ViT-A (R = 4)				(1,4,4,1)
TT-ViT-A (R = 6)				(1,6,6,1)
TT-ViT-A (R = 8)				(1,8,8,1)
TT-ViT-B (R = 2)	3	(4,4,4)	(4,8,4)	(1,2,2,1)
TT-ViT-B (R = 4)				(1,4,4,1)
TT-ViT-B (R = 6)				(1,6,6,1)
TT-ViT-B (R = 8)				(1,8,8,1)

To evaluate the performance of TT-ViT-A and TT-ViT-B with TT ranks $r_c \in \{2, 4, 6, 8\}$, we compute the accuracy as the ratio between the number of samples correctly predicted and total samples

$$\text{accuracy} = \frac{\#\text{samples correctly predicted}}{\#\text{total samples}} \tag{15}$$

To demonstrate the effectiveness of our proposed TT-ViT models in terms of saving parameters, we define the compression rate as the ratio between total parameters of the compressed model and total parameters of its baseline

$$\text{compression rate} = \frac{\#\text{params of the compressed model}}{\#\text{params of the baseline model}} \tag{16}$$

Table 3. The results on CIFAR-10 using baseline models (ViT-A, ViT-B) and our compressed models (TT-ViT-A, TT-ViT-B) with varying TT ranks $R \in \{2, 4, 6, 8\}$

Models	#params	Compression rate	Accuracy (%)
ViT-A (baseline)	284,746	1.0	71.82
TT-ViT-A (R = 2)	157,770	0.55	69.48
TT-ViT-A (R = 4)	165,962	0.58	70.52
TT-ViT-A (R = 6)	178,250	0.62	71.20
TT-ViT-A (R = 8)	**194,634**	**0.68**	**72.72**
ViT-B (baseline)	325,898	1.0	79.91
TT-ViT-B (R = 2)	230,666	0.70	78.51
TT-ViT-B (R = 4)	236,810	0.73	79.66
TT-ViT-B (R = 6)	246,026	0.75	79.75
TT-ViT-B (R = 8)	**258,314**	**0.79**	**80.42**

Note that, in these experiments, we just mention training configurations for baseline models, because each baseline model (ViT-A or ViT-B) and its corresponding compressed models (TT-ViT-A or TT-ViT-B) share the same configurations. Specifically, both ViT-A and ViT-B are trained for 100 epochs with Adam optimizer. We use a batch size of 64 for ViT-A and 256 for ViT-B, learning rate of 0.001 for both ViT-A and ViT-B. We train ViT-A on CIFAR-10 with an input image of size $32 \times 32 \times 3$ and Fashion-MNIST with an input image of size 28×28. When ViT-B is trained, the input image is scaled to $72 \times 72 \times 3$ for CIFAR-10 and 72×72 for Fashion-MNIST.

The results shown in Table 3 for CIFAR-10 and Table 4 for Fashion-MNIST include accuracy, the number of parameters, and compression rate. We observe that

- In terms of CIFAR-10, all compression models have approximately the same accuracy when compared to their baseline. Specifically, in the case of ViT-A, the performance of the compressed model TT-ViT-A reduces by at most 2.34% with $R = 2$, and in the case of ViT-B, TT-ViT-B with $R = 2$ also decreases by no more than 1.4%. Meanwhile, total parameters of compressed models account for only 55% ($R = 2$) to 68% ($R = 8$) for ViT-A and 70% ($R = 2$) to 79% ($R = 8$) for ViT-B. Even with $R = 8$, TT-ViT-A and TT-ViT-B are more accurate than the baseline (72.72% of TT-ViT-A vs. 71.82% of ViTA and 80.42% of TT-ViT-B vs. 79.91% of ViT-B).
- In terms of Fashion-MNIST, all compressed models TT-ViT-A ($R \in \{2, 4, 6, 8\}$) have better accuracy than ViT-A. The accuracy of TT-ViT-A with $R = 2$ is 89.02%, which is the lowest among all TT-ViT-A models but still higher than the baseline of 0.3%. All of TT-ViT-B models have the equivalent accuracy as the baseline ViT-B while using only 75% to 82% total parameters. With the lowest accuracy of 89.41%, TT-ViT-B ($R = 2$) only decreased 1% compared to the baseline accuracy of 90.41% although it only uses 75% of parameters, which is the lowest compression rate among TT-ViT-B.

Table 4. The results on Fashion-MNIST using baseline models (ViT-A, ViT-B) and our compressed models (TT-ViT-A, TT-ViT-B) with varying TT ranks $R \in \{2, 4, 6, 8\}$

Models	#params	Compression rate	Accuracy (%)
ViT-A (baseline)	281,738	1.0	88.84
TT-ViT-A ($R = 2$)	154,762	0.55	89.40
TT-ViT-A ($R = 4$)	162,954	0.58	89.46
TT-ViT-A ($R = 6$)	**175,242**	**0.62**	**89.51**
TT-ViT-A ($R = 8$)	191,626	0.68	89.37
ViT-B (baseline)	**383,498**	**1.0**	**90.68**
TT-ViT-B ($R = 2$)	288,266	0.75	89.68
TT-ViT-B ($R = 4$)	294,410	0.77	90.04
TT-ViT-B ($R = 6$)	303,626	0.79	89.76
TT-ViT-B ($R = 8$)	315,914	0.82	90.41

5 Conclusion

This work introduces TT-ViT, a novel compressed vision transformer model based on TT decomposition. By representing trainable weight matrices in TT format using four sets of TT cores, we minimize the total parameters of TT-ViT while preserving accuracy. Simulations on datasets such as CIFAR-10 and Fashion-MNIST demonstrate its efficacy in addressing the problem of requiring a large number of parameters. When compared to baseline models, the accuracy of

TT-ViT reduces at most about 2% despite requiring half of the total parameters. TT-ViT opens some interesting and potential approaches in the future. The first one is to express the weight matrices using some common alternative tensor decomposition methods such as Tucker, CP, or MIRA... Other research focuses on quantum-classical machine learning models, which are created by encoding input data into quantum circuits.

Acknowledgement. This research is funded by University of Science, VNU-HCM under grant number CNTT 2020-09.

References

1. Cichocki, A., Lee, N., Oseledets, I., Phan, A.H., Zhao, Q., Mandic, D.P.: Tensor networks for dimensionality reduction and large-scale optimization: part 1 low-rank tensor decompositions. Found. Trends Mach. Learn. **9**(4–5), 249–429 (2016)
2. Deng, J., Dong, W., Socher, R., Li, L.J., Li, K., Fei-Fei, L.: ImageNet: a large-scale hierarchical image database. In: 2009 IEEE Conference on Computer Vision and Pattern Recognition, pp. 248–255 (2009)
3. Devlin, J., Chang, M., Lee, K., Toutanova, K.: BERT: pre-training of deep bidirectional transformers for language understanding. In: Proceedings of the 2019 Conference of the North American NAACL-HLT 2019, Minneapolis, MN, USA, 2–7 June 2019, vol. 1 (Long and Short Papers), pp. 4171–4186. Association for Computational Linguistics (2019)
4. Dosovitskiy, A., et al.: An image is worth 16 × 16 words: transformers for image recognition at scale. In: International Conference on Learning Representations (2021)
5. Garipov, T., Podoprikhin, D., Novikov, A., Vetrov, D.P.: Ultimate tensorization: compressing convolutional and FC layers alike. CoRR abs/1611.03214 (2016)
6. Guo, Q., Qiu, X., Xue, X., Zhang, Z.: Low-rank and locality constrained self-attention for sequence modeling. IEEE/ACM Trans. Audio Speech Lang. Process. **27**(12), 2213–2222 (2019)
7. Hoang, P.M., Tuan, H.D., Son, T.T., Poor, H.V.: Qualitative HD image and video recovery via high-order tensor augmentation and completion. IEEE J. Sel. Topics Signal Process. **15**(3), 688–701 (2021)
8. Jaderberg, M., Vedaldi, A., Zisserman, A.: Speeding up convolutional neural networks with low rank expansions. In: Valstar, M.F., French, A.P., Pridmore, T.P. (eds.) British Machine Vision Conference, BMVC 2014, Nottingham, UK, 1–5 September 2014. BMVA Press (2014)
9. Kim, Y., Park, E., Yoo, S., Choi, T., Yang, L., Shin, D.: Compression of deep convolutional neural networks for fast and low power mobile applications. In: Bengio, Y., LeCun, Y. (eds.) 4th International Conference on Learning Representations, ICLR 2016, San Juan, Puerto Rico, 2–4 May 2016, Conference Track Proceedings (2016)
10. Krizhevsky, A., Hinton, G.: Learning multiple layers of features from tiny images. Technical Report 0, University of Toronto, Toronto, Ontario (2009)
11. Lebedev, V., Ganin, Y., Rakhuba, M., Oseledets, I.V., Lempitsky, V.S.: Speeding-up convolutional neural networks using fine-tuned CP-decomposition. In: 3rd International Conference on Learning Representations, ICLR 2015, San Diego, CA, USA, 7–9 May 2015, Conference Track Proceedings (2015)

12. Lecun, Y., Bottou, L., Bengio, Y., Haffner, P.: Gradient-based learning applied to document recognition. Proc. IEEE **86**(11), 2278–2324 (1998)
13. Lee, N., Cichocki, A.: Fundamental tensor operations for large-scale data analysis in tensor train formats (2016)
14. Liu, Y., et al.: Roberta: a robustly optimized BERT pretraining approach. CoRR abs/1907.11692 (2019)
15. Liu, Y., Long, Z., Huang, H., Zhu, C.: Low CP rank and Tucker rank tensor completion for estimating missing components in image data. IEEE Trans. Circ. Syst. Video Techn. **30**(4), 944–954 (2020)
16. Liu, Z., et al.: Swin transformer: hierarchical vision transformer using shifted windows. In: Proceedings of the IEEE/CVF International Conference on Computer Vision (ICCV), pp. 10012–10022, October 2021
17. Ma, X., et al.: A tensorized transformer for language modeling. In: Wallach, H., Larochelle, H., Beygelzimer, A., d' Alché-Buc, F., Fox, E., Garnett, R. (eds.) Advances in Neural Information Processing Systems, vol. 32. Curran Associates, Inc. (2019)
18. Novikov, A., Podoprikhin, D., Osokin, A., Vetrov, D.P.: Tensorizing neural networks. In: Advances in Neural Information Processing Systems, vol. 28. Curran Associates, Inc. (2015)
19. Oseledets, I.V.: Approximation of $2^d \times 2^d$ matrices using tensor decomposition. SIAM J. Matrix Anal. Appl. **31**(4), 2130–2145 (2010)
20. Oseledets, I.V.: Tensor-train decomposition. SIAM J. Sci. Comput. **33**(5), 2295–2317 (2011)
21. Radford, A., Narasimhan, K.: Improving language understanding by generative pre-training (2018)
22. Sherstinsky, A.: Fundamentals of recurrent neural network (RNN) and long short-term memory (LSTM) network. Physica D **404**, 132306 (2020)
23. Song, D., Zhang, P., Li, F.: Speeding up deep convolutional neural networks based on tucker-CP decomposition. In: Proceedings of the 2020 5th International Conference on Machine Learning Technologies, pp. 56–61. Association for Computing Machinery, New York, NY, USA (2020)
24. Touvron, H., Cord, M., Douze, M., Massa, F., Sablayrolles, A., Jegou, H.: Training data-efficient image transformers & distillation through attention. In: International Conference on Machine Learning, vol. 139, pp. 10347–10357, July 2021
25. Vaswani, A., et al.: Attention is all you need. In: Advances in Neural Information Processing Systems, vol. 30. Curran Associates, Inc. (2017)
26. Wang, W., et al.: Pyramid vision transformer: a versatile backbone for dense prediction without convolutions. In: Proceedings of the IEEE/CVF International Conference on Computer Vision (ICCV), pp. 568–578, October 2021
27. Xiao, H., Rasul, K., Vollgraf, R.: Fashion-MNIST: a novel image dataset for benchmarking machine learning algorithms (2017)
28. Xing, Y., Yang, S., Jiao, L.: Hyperspectral image super-resolution based on tensor spatial-spectral joint correlation regularization. IEEE Access IEEE, vol. 8, pp. 63654–63665, 2020 8, 63654–63665 (2020)
29. Yang, Y., Krompass, D., Tresp, V.: Tensor-train recurrent neural networks for video classification. In: Proceedings of the 34th International Conference on Machine Learning, vol. 70, pp. 3891–3900. ICML 2017, JMLR.org (2017)

Medical Prescription Recognition Using Heuristic Clustering and Similarity Search

Ngoc-Thao Nguyen[1,2](✉)(iD), Hieu Vo[1,2](iD), Khanh Tran[1,2](iD), Duy Ha[1,2](iD), Duc Nguyen[1,2](iD), and Thanh Le[1,2](iD)

[1] Faculty of Information Technology, University of Science,
Ho Chi Minh city, Vietnam
{nnthao,lnthanh}@fit.hcmus.edu.vn
[2] Vietnam National University, Ho Chi Minh city, Vietnam

Abstract. The necessity to convert printed documents to facilitate the storage and retrieval of information is growing, particularly in the medical and healthcare industries. In our last work, we presented a method to extract prescriptions from images using CRAFT and TESSERACT so that patients could quickly save and check up on their pharmaceutical use information. However, the slow processing speed and the limited number of medication names lead to it being impractical. Based on this model structure, a new system is introduced, using bounding box clustering heuristics to detect the featured text areas, before employing VietOCR tool to identify the texts in prescription images. Simultaneously, a fast and accurate technique for extracting prescriptions is developed, utilizing word embedding and the vector search algorithm. The experiment results reveal that the proposed model significantly reduces the error of the retrieved data on the two standard measures, WER and CER, prominently with CER lowered to 26.95. Furthermore, the execution time decreases from 17.81 s to an average of 3.64 s, demonstrating the great effectiveness of our effort to improve the prior system.

Keywords: Document layout analysis · Optical character recognition · Word embedding · Approximate nearest neighbor

1 Introduction

In the advanced development of science and technology in 4.0 revolutionary, information technology is applied in many fields: economics, education, medical, transportation. In health, the application of information technology contributes much to enhancing system quality, improving care quality, and early detection of infectious disease outbreaks. To a study [1] by RAND Health, the US healthcare system could save more than 81$ billion annually if health information technology (HIT) were taken on. In 2019, the Vietnamese Ministry of Health approved the project on the Application of Health Information technology in 2019–2025

N. T. Nguyen et al. (Eds.): ICCCI 2022, LNAI 13501, pp. 768–780, 2022.
https://doi.org/10.1007/978-3-031-16014-1_60

about principal policies such as investment in infrastructure technology, application development, healthcare, hospital management system, and health administration. The primary purpose is that by 2030, 95% of the population can manage their health, and all medical facilities around the country use electronic medical records. Besides, people control their personal health information through electronic applications. Furthermore, pharmacological records, a list of drugs used need to be managed closely. This kind of information has features of sciences and unpopularity, is stored through prescription. It includes a variety of words/subwords that could be localized or not, leading to difficulty remembering precisely the name and ingredient ratio. In the 2016 and 2017 medicine error reports from Norway's incident reporting system [2] of more than 64 hospitals, the wrong dosage accounted for 38%, wrong medication 15%, missed medication 23%, causing 0.8% of deaths. In addition, information digitalization also takes a lot of time to manually enter each field, which may lead to potential errors.

There have been some studies that help to process these tasks, such as an automatic prescription recognition system developed for the visual system of pharmacy robotic technology, the handwritten prescription converter using electronic tablet, or an application extracting medicine information from a prescription. In this paper [3], a basic structure is developed which allows user obtains pharmacological names from printed prescription images to store, control dosage, compare information, avoid overdose cases or active ingredient conflicts. However, it has contained limitations in the database, running time, accuracy and multilingual processing. Through the analysis and synthesis of documents, the prescription is evaluated as a type of text with a particular layout and content. By adopting neural network models and analyzing layout, we propose an improved system that enhances accuracy to 76%, speeds up information extraction and can be used in prescriptions including both Vietnamese and English medicine names. In the following part, some common issues of Optical Character Recognition (OCR), Natural Language Processing (NLP) and Information extraction are discussed to provide definitions to comprehend structure. Section 3 shows a complete system and involving problems. Experimental results and conclusions are given in Sects. 4 and 5, respectively.

2 Related Work

This section addresses related techniques and work relevant to the proposed system's construction.

2.1 Optical Character Recognition

The character recognition problem is the first and indispensable step in the field of identifying and extracting information from digital content. OCR tasks are often divided into two parts: text detection and text recognition. Besides, the post-processing step also plays an important role in ensuring the results of OCR. Text detection is the process of determining the position of the text from the original image. With the advent of deep neural networks, many techniques based on deep learning methods have come into use, such as semantic segmentation or object recognition in images. These techniques use Fully Convolutional Networks (FCNs) [4] to extract blocks of text, then generate the corresponding bounding boxes. This survey covers and explains related techniques in depth [5]. CTPN [6], CRAFT [7], EAST [8], and SegLink [9] are prominent approaches that perform well on natural photos. Post-processing is essential for ensuring the correctness of the OCR system. Each sort of data typically have its unique features depending on the intended purpose of OCR. Hence, there are numerous techniques to tackle this issue, as discussed in the survey [10]. The spell checker is one of the simplest method to check whether a word is in a dictionary. Thompson et al. [11] expand this approach by limiting the dictionary to a lexicon. In this way, only terms relating to the text field are retrieved to save matching costs while improving the post-processing system's accuracy.

2.2   Natural Language Processing Tasks

The output of the OCR step is "free text". After that, NLP models are employed to extract the desired entities from the text. An NLP task typically consists of multiple steps, beginning with sentence segmentation and ending with word tokenization. The tokens are then labeled (Part-of-Speech tagging) to generate distinct groups of entities in the text, from which the necessary information could be retrieved. This process is carried out using a variety of state-of-the-art approaches which are explained in Sonit Singh et al.'s work [12]. Pattern matching is the most basic method, which uses RegEx rules to define and extract structured information from text. This method is quick to implement, but it is still unable to locate important entities in the text without a predefined structure. In addition, the methods based on Machine Learning is the next prominent approaches discussed.

2.3   Information Extraction

With the combination of two parts, OCR and NLP, we can build a method to help extract information from text images into valuable information, suitable for modern information mining needs. In the ICDAR2019 competition [13], many solutions were presented to extract information from scanned receipt. The method named "Ping An Property and Casualty Insurance Company" uses a set of lexicons for error correction and then feeds into RegEx to extract information This method gives quite satisfactory results with H-mean score 90.49%. The "H&H Lab" method uses the same architecture as BiGRU-CNNs-CRF [14] and then adds some rules to correct errors, thereby obtaining a H-mean score of 89.63%.

In the previous model [3], a drug extraction system was built, including two stages: (1) Converting prescription images to text using CRAFT and Tesseract OCR tools, (2) Extracting drug names from texts by matching terms with medicine dictionaries using Levenshtein distance. The model achieves 98% of matching results for text detection, but the execution time is relatively high and the number of drugs in the dictionary is limited. In this work, a new framework is proposed to introduce a larger medical dictionary besides utilizing new word embedding and vector search algorithm to improve the speed and accuracy of the model's performance.

3 The Proposed System

The enhanced system includes three primary stages: text detection, text recognition, and extraction, which is expressed in Fig. 1

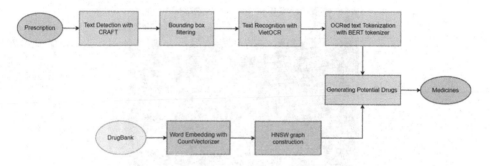

Fig. 1. Architecture of the proposed recognition system

3.1 Text Detection

CRAFT [2] has a fundamental structure of VGG-16 that acts as feature extraction for the input. Then it is represented as feature matrices combining batch normalization and skip connections (similar to U-net networks) to associate with low-level features. It links recognized characters with specific character areas, allowing these text detected regions to be associated with one another. As a result, some regions are closely linked to others. CRAFT is currently regarded as one of the most effective text detection models. To detect text regions, Fatih Cagatay Akyon's craft-text-detector framework[1] has been implemented.

3.2 Bounding Box Filter

As mentioned, the prescription is one of a particular layout text types. A medicine often consists of information about facility, patient, diagnosis, and list of drugs. A list of drugs is commonly columned, including name, actives, dosage, and quantity. Each text region or bounding box would be specified by column label and row label. Firstly, text regions are columnedly labeled by dividing coordinate x of the left top vertices of them to a constant (default 100). Secondly, in every group of regions having the same column label, distances between

---

[1] https://pypi.org/project/craft-text-detector/.

them are calculated. Then outliers detection is applied to find out the threshold (minimum of outliers). They are figured out by the IQR-score equation[2]. If the distance between two bounding boxes is bigger than the threshold, their row label is updated, then they are separated into two different groups. After this stage, regions are set up basically. Next, regions are checked whether they are in the columned text. This means regions' s centroids are in the same virtual line relatively. If any, they could contain drug names. Finally, distances from the image's centroid to columned regions are computed and the nearest is chosen. Bounding boxes belonging to selected regions are adopted for the next stage, which is different from the previous version (Fig. 2).

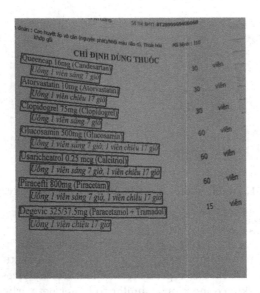

Fig. 2. Selected bounding boxes

3.3   Text Recognition with VietOCR

The bounding boxes selected from the previous stage are converted into small PIL images and taken to the text recognition engine named VietOCR. This model is an example of integrating NLP language models into the text recognition system to produce significantly better results than traditional methods. Meticulously, the CNN model is combined with Transformer or Seq2Seq model to form a model that could solve OCR problems better. VietOCR could be retrained with the new dataset. However, because this model is trained on a large dataset of 10 million samples, including real-world images and autogenerated images, it is not necessary to retrain VietOCR in our case.

---

[2] https://en.wikipedia.org/wiki/Interquartile_range.

3.4   Medicine Extraction

Converting Drug Names into Vectors Using N-Grams Bag of Words.
As computers can only process numeric data, drug names need to be converted
into a set of numbers before being input into machine learning models. The
proposed system uses the Countvectorizer model installed in the sklearn library
to perform Word Embedding on the Drugbank dictionary. In the Countvectorizer model, N-grams Bag of Words is supported by adjusting *ngram_range*
parameter. The N-grams approach is considered to provide a solution for calculating potential spelling errors and derivatives of a word. In addition, the
char_wb option in the analyzer parameter allows characters to be encoded inside
the bounds of a word while producing less noise than encoding with the *char*
option, making it a good choice for languages with a space-separated vocabulary like Vietnamese. The result of the model is a sparse matrix of vectors,
which contains the frequency of each N-gram of drug names in the Drugbank
dictionary.

Build the Vector Database. Constructing vector space is critical for conducting an effective search and comparison between vectors. The introduced
approach employs the Hierarchical Navigable Small World Graph (HNSW) [15]
to construct the vector database. HNSW is an Approximate Nearest Neighbors
search algorithm, which is a proximity graph with two main components: a
probabilistic skip list and a navigable small world network (NSW) (Fig. 4). The
arrangement of NSW into multiple layers assists HNSW in lowering the number
of intermediary nodes while moving from one node to another. Besides, it also
allows HNSW to demonstrate optimization in the query search task.

The sparse matrix, which is the result of Word Embedding model, is used
to create the Approximate Nearest Neighbor Index. Each vector is entered one
by one. The probability function determines in which layer the vector should
be placed. Vector insertion begins at the top layer both in the construction and
searching stages. When there are no neighbor nodes closer to the inserted vector
than the current node or the local maximum is reached, the search proceed to
the next layer. The process stops when the layer chosen for insertion is reached.
The inserted vector would be added to the selected layer and the ones below it.
At the end, an index with nodes representing drug name embedded vectors is
constructed.

'Đi', 'Ch', '##ọ', 'chỗ', 'cây', 'tr', '##e', 'Thú', '##y', 'nh', '##á'

Fig. 3. BERT tokenizer ability to capture Vietnamese subwords

Text Tokenizations. Since the input request of the HNSW search graph is a
list of queries, splitting the text into tokens is necessary. The obtained OCR text
is divided into tokens using the BERT [16] tokenizer model in this stage. BERT's

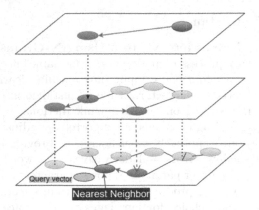

Fig. 4. Hierarchical navigable small world graph

Tokenizer model employs the WordPiece algorithm, which can acquire a limited vocabulary and use the characters "##" to indicate subwords that are part of a whole word. Using this approach, BERT may represent a non-vocabulary term as meaningful subwords without needing to expand the vocabulary.

Although BERT's vocab incorporates Vietnamese characters, BERT's outcomes in this language are often ineffective. In our proposed system, the BertTokenizerFast model is used to fine-tune the dataset of articles on pharmaceutical information crawled from the Vinmec.com website. The goal is to augment BERT's vocabulary with single Vietnamese terms relating to pharmacology. As a result, BertTokenizerFast could detect single words rather than tokenizing them to the character level as the original BERT model. At the same time, BERT demonstrates the capacity to catch common Vietnamese subwords such as "ch, nh, tr" (Fig. 3).

Drug names in the being resolved problem are a collection of terminologies that includes both English and Vietnamese drug names, in which the length of Vietnamese drug names varies greatly. Accordingly, the approach of extracting medication names based on fixed templates is not optimum and may miss some of the names in the prescriptions with unusual formats. To enrich BERT's vocabulary with domain-specific words, we use the *add_tokens* function to add a list of drug names from the DrugBank dictionary to the Word Embedding matrix of the BERT tokenizer. Since drug names have no contextual qualities and are entirely independent of edge words, our technique is able to extract the medication's name fast and reliably, without requiring any additional data or resources to retrain the model on the medical datasets.

Candidate Generation. The second step's output contains medicine names and certain chunk words unrelated. Therefore, there is a need to filter out specific medicine names from a list of tokens. Each token is turned into a vector using the CountVectorizer model and searched in the HNSW graph. Before generating candidates, the parameters k and *threshold* are defined, where k indicates the

Table 1. An illustration of generated candidates

Text	Candidate	Similarity
Cefuroxim	Cefuroxime	0.8838
Paracetamol	Paracetamol	1.0
Cetamin	Cetamin	1.0

maximum number of candidates to return for each query and the *threshold* indicates candidates' minimal similarity to the query text. The search function may even return the desired medicine names for misspelled drug names queries by utilizing the approximate nearest neighbors search approach. Nonetheless, there is a reduction in the similarity between misspelled query text and its candidates. By establishing the proper *threshold* value, candidates of these misspelled words are not rejected. The final results are a list of pharmaceutical names comparable to the query text, with absolute similarity being 1.0. Table 1 shows an example of generated candidates.

4 Experiment

4.1 Datasets

Prescription. A dataset of 1500 prescription photos was collected from the Facebook group named "Kho don thuoc"[3]. It is various in terms of format, order of prescriptions and active ingredients, tabular form, the layout of medications, and types of drugs. Besides, there has distorted samples such as tilted images, unevenly lit or blurred ones. The image's source concealed the patient's personal information before publishing it on the social network.

Pharmaceutical Documents from Vinmec. The dataset includes 2009 documents crawled from the Vinmec pharmaceutical information website[4]. These texts are in Vietnamese, describe the drug's details, such as name, ingredients, uses, user indications, some side effects (if any), and instructions with many specialized words. The dataset is used to train the BERT Tokenizer model with default parameters in order to expand BERT's vocabulary with common Vietnamese health terms.

Drug Dictionary from Drugbank. A drug vector database is build based on drug names obtained from a website called DrugBank[5] of the Ministry of Health. This website has about 41,000 elements of English and Vietnamese names that have been registered to circulate in the Vietnam market, as well as detailed information about drug brand names and chemical compounds for each medicine.

---

[3] https://www.facebook.com/khodonthuoc.

[4] https://www.vinmec.com/vi/thong-tin-duoc/.

[5] https://drugbank.vn/.

4.2   Metrics

WER and CER metrics are employed to evaluate the disparity between extracted drugs and labels. Their formulas are:

$$CER = \frac{S + I + D}{N} \tag{1}$$

$$WER = \frac{S_w + I_w + D_w}{N_w} \tag{2}$$

where S, I, D is the number of substitution, insertion and deletion operations. Recall is also used to calculate the number of medication names accurately recognized (TP) out of the entire drug names contained in 200 prescriptions (TP + FN) in order to evaluate the overall system's performance. The Recall formula is as follows:

$$Recall = \frac{TP}{TP + FN} \tag{3}$$

The Average Prescription Recognition (APR) is calculated as follows:

$$H = \frac{\sum_{i=0}^{n} \frac{x}{X}}{N} \tag{4}$$

where x and X is respectively the number of extracted drugs and labels in a prescription, N is the number of samples in data set:

4.3   Environment and Parameters

The experiment is conducted on Kaggle with kernels of NVidia K80 GPUs, CUDA version 11.0, and parameters at stages are set up as follows:

- For framework craft-text-detector: $text\_threshold = 0.6$ and $link\_threshold = 0.4$, $low\_text = 0.4$
- For VietOCR engine: $config['name'] =' vgg\_transformer'$
- CounVectorizer model: $ngram\_range = (1, 4)$, $analysis =' char\_wb'$
- For HNSW graph construction: $M = 128$, $efSearch = 200$, $efConstruction = 2000$
- At extraction stage: $k = 1$, $threshold = 0.8$

4.4   Results and Analysis

The histogram (Fig. 5) illustrates that a prescription's processing time mainly ranges from 2 to 5 s, with 3 s being the most typical. Notably, there are approximately 150 prescriptions with less than 2 s of processing time. The presented system takes an average of 3.73 s to process, approximately five times faster than our prior model. This indicates that the proposed method outperforms the prior system in terms of execution time.

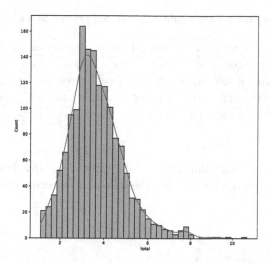

Fig. 5. Distribution of processing time for each prescription

Table 2 expresses records of execution time at stages. The quickest overall processing time per prescription was 1.092 s, while the longest was 10.691 s, compared to 3.808 s and 51.240 s, respectively, in the previous model. The recognition stages turn out to require the most time, with the average time to recognize the image being 2.6466 s seconds. In the worst-case scenario, the value increases to 8.725 s, which may be attributed to the impacts of input image distortion such as noise, and too blurry text creating trouble for the OCR engine. Additionally, the average recognition time has been lowered by around 6 times when compared to the prior method. This might be due to three factors. Firstly, VietOCR was trained primarily on Vietnamese datasets and partially in English texts, therefore VietOCR's recognition capability in Vietnamese is robust . Secondly, in the last work, Tesseract tool's Connected Component Analysis phase generates duplication by performing text detection on regions that the CRAFT detector has already spotted, which unnecessarily increases recognition time. Finally, the proposed model's bounding box filter stage eliminates redundant bounding boxes that do not include the content to be retrieved, greatly lowering the number of bounding boxes as input to the recognition model. As a result, the time required for text recognition is greatly reduced. In general, it is noticeable that the modified system takes significantly less time than the last work at most stages. The overall system's average recognition time is 3.6407 s which is nearly 5 times faster than our previous system.

Table 2. Execution time of proposed system at each stage

	Filtering		Detection		Recognition		Extraction		Total	
	Old	New	Old	New	Old	New	Old	New	Old	New
Min	–	0.004	0.0466	0.074	3.3381	0.387	0.0003	0.434	3.8076	1.092
Mean	–	0.0147	0.4336	0.38	15.8426	2.6466	1.5386	0.5748	17.8149	3.6407
Max	–	0.055	2.046	1.086	46.2663	8.725	5.1112	1.278	51.2404	10.691

Due to resource limitations, we could only manually label 200 prescriptions. These 200 prescriptions yielded the following experimental CER and WER results.

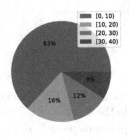

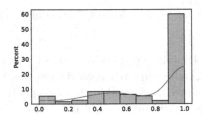

(a) The ratio of CER errors on drug names   (b) The distribution of APR score

Fig. 6. The performance of recognition system

Because the extracted text is short strings of less than four words in most cases, the assessment based on the CER metric is more relevant and applicable. The WER metric is used as a reference point and compared with the prior model. The achieved average CER and WER errors of the extraction are 26.95 and 38.68, respectively. (Table 3). For a more comprehensive view of the results, the pie chart (Fig. 6a) expresses the distribution of CER values across extracted drug names. The under 20% error rate accounted for 79%. A number of prescriptions with at least 40% error rate accounts for a relatively small proportion, only about 9% of the total drugs. This might be due to the significant prescription image distortion, which makes OCR challenging and, in the worst-case situation, results in substantial CER errors. Furthermore, discrepancies between the actual prescription drug name and the drug name stored in the Drug Bank can increase errors. For example, the drug name in the actual prescription is "Gloversin 4mg"; however, in the collected Drug Bank, the medicine is stored as "Gloversin 4", i.e., without the unit part. This effects CER results to some extent even though the drug names extracted by the system are entirely correct.

Table 3. Comparison Average Word and Character Error Rate and Recall score of two version system

	CER	WER	Recall
Old version	93.93	96.30	0.17
New version	26.95	38.68	0.8

APR efficiency is 0.78 and Recall of 0.8 for the total amount of pharmaceuticals extracted in the whole system. The histogram (Fig. 6b) shows the distribution of the APR score on the test set. Most prescriptions have approximately from 80% to 100% recognition efficiency. Through the manual inspection process, poor image quality and unusual text patterns are identified as factors for low performance. Besides, experiments are also conducted on the last system. As the prior system's vocabulary included a limited number of drug names, roughly 100 drug names, and did not contain Vietnamese medicine names, which omitted many medication names in the test set and led to poor performance on all three metrics CER, WER and Recall. Therefore, expanding the drug names dictionary size to 41,000 drugs and adding multilingual drugs is critical in significantly enhancing the model's performance.

5   Conclusion

This work is an endeavor to integrate heuristic clustering, word embedding, and similarity search to improve the last work on extracting drug names from printed prescriptions. We use the new text recognition model VietOCR in order to solve the problem of multilingualism. Besides, BERT Tokenizer and approximately nearest neighbor search are also employed to better information extraction results. The experiment results show that the enhanced model has solved the issues: Vietnamese and English drugs are recognized and recorrect (if any); the database is tuned and enlarged; running time is about 3.64 s; Recall is up to 0.8. However, through the layout analysis, the results still depend on the prescription structure. If it has a complex structure, the system might give out an incorrect result. In the future, we desire to construct a more comprehensive layout analysis method that could be applied to more type of structures and execute faster. Additionally, the work of pre-processing and extracting information could be enhanced even further.

Acknowledgements. This research is funded by the University of Science, VNU-HCM, Vietnam under grant number CNTT 2021-12 and Advanced Program in Computer Science.

References

1. Hillestad, R., et al.: Health information technology: can HIT lower costs and improve quality? Santa Monica, CA: RAND Corporation; 2005. RB-9136-HLTH. RAND Corporation research briefs (2005)
2. Mulac, A., Taxis, K., Hagesaether, E., Granas, A.G.: Severe and fatal medication errors in hospitals: findings from the Norwegian Incident Reporting System. Eur. J. Hosp. Pharm. **28**(e1), e56–e61 (2021)
3. Nguyen, T.T., Nguyen, D.V.V., Le, T.: Developing a prescription recognition system based on CRAFT and tesseract. In: International Conference on Computational Collective Intelligence, pp. 443–455. Springer, Cham, September 2021. https://doi.org/10.1007/978-3-030-88081-1_33
4. Long, J., Shelhamer, E., Darrell, T.: Fully convolutional networks for semantic segmentation. In: Proceedings of the IEEE Conference on Computer Vision and Pattern Recognition, pp. 3431–3440 (2015)
5. Ye, Q., Doermann, D.: Text detection and recognition in imagery: a survey. IEEE Trans. Pattern Anal. Mach. Intell. **37**(7), 1480–1500 (2014)
6. Tian, Z., Huang, W., He, T., He, P., Qiao, Y.: Detecting text in natural image with connectionist text proposal network. In: European Conference on Computer Vision, pp. 56–72. Springer, Cham, October 2016. https://doi.org/10.1007/978-3-319-46484-8_4
7. Baek, Y., Lee, B., Han, D., Yun, S., Lee, H.: Character region awareness for text detection. In: Proceedings of the IEEE/CVF Conference on Computer Vision and Pattern Recognition, pp. 9365–9374 (2019)
8. Zhou, X., et al.: East: an efficient and accurate scene text detector. In: Proceedings of the IEEE Conference on Computer Vision and Pattern Recognition, pp. 5551–5560 (2017)
9. Nguyen, T.T.H., Jatowt, A., Coustaty, M., Doucet, A.: Survey of post-OCR processing approaches. ACM Comput. Surv. (CSUR) **54**(6), 1–37 (2021)
10. Shi, B., Bai, X., Belongie, S.: Detecting oriented text in natural images by linking segments. In: Proceedings of the IEEE Conference on Computer Vision and Pattern Recognition, pp. 2550–2558 (2017)
11. Thompson, P., McNaught, J., Ananiadou, S.: Customised OCR correction for historical medical text. In: 2015 Digital Heritage, vol. 1, pp. 35–42. IEEE, September 2015
12. Singh, S.: Natural language processing for information extraction. arXiv preprint arXiv:1807.02383 (2018)
13. Huang, Z., et al.: ICDAR 2019 competition on scanned receipt OCR and information extraction. In: 2019 International Conference on Document Analysis and Recognition (ICDAR), pp. 1516–1520. IEEE, September 2019
14. Ma, X., Hovy, E.: End-to-end sequence labeling via bi-directional LSTM-CNNS-CRF. arXiv preprint arXiv:1603.01354 (2016)
15. Malkov, Y.A., Yashunin, D.A.: Efficient and robust approximate nearest neighbor search using hierarchical navigable small world graphs. IEEE Trans. Pattern Anal. Mach. Intell. **42**(4), 824–836 (2018)
16. Tenney, I., Das, D., Pavlick, E.: BERT rediscovers the classical NLP pipeline. arXiv preprint arXiv:1905.05950 (2019)

Employing the Google Search and Google Translate to Increase the Performance of the Credibility Detection in Arabic Tweets

Rabeaa Mouty[(✉)] [iD] and Achraf Gazdar

Software Engineering Department, College of Computer and Information Sciences,
King Saud University, Riyadh, Saudi Arabia
443204492@student.ksu.edu.sa, agazdar@ksu.edu.sa

Abstract. Many studies have been proposed to discover the deceptive information on different social networking sites, especially on Twitter, and in many languages. For the disclosure of credibility in Arabic publications, few works have been published. In this paper, we propose a smart classifier that determines the credibility of Arabic "tweets" posted on Twitter. This classifier integrates social mining and natural language processing techniques. Several (user- and content-related) features have been used in the training and testing phases for the proposed model. We have added the ability to check for tweets by comparing them to Google search results. We have also developed an algorithm to check the similarity of the user's screen and his/her official name on Twitter. By combining these new features with the most common features of credibility detection, our proposed classifier identifies the credibility of the tweets in the dataset we are utilizing and outperforms similar works in the field associated with the detection of the credibility of Arabic tweets in terms of accuracy.

Keywords: Credibility detection · Data mining · Machine learning natural language processing · Social media mining · Text mining · Twitter

1 Introduction

Twitter is one of the most important social media networks for the circulation of news and information, and it has a clearly influential impact on the Arabic Street [9]. Currently, many researchers have conducted studies toward several languages—especially English—whereas credibility detection in the Arabic language is still fresh and needs great effort. Therefore, we have built a smart analyzer model that reveals the facts of Arabic tweets. We propose two newly added features employed to compare the content of the tweet with the first page of Google's search results and find the relationship between the two names of the user (username and display name).

The remaining of this paper is organized as follows: in Sect. 2, we study the related works. Then, in Sect. 3, we present the credibility detection model details, and we evaluate it. Finally, in Sect. 4 we conclude our paper and cite future works.

© The Author(s), under exclusive license to Springer Nature Switzerland AG 2022
N. T. Nguyen et al. (Eds.): ICCCI 2022, LNAI 13501, pp. 781–788, 2022.
https://doi.org/10.1007/978-3-031-16014-1_61

2 Related Works

Different approaches were followed to detect deceptive information from Twitter:

The Feature-based Approach depends on extracting special characteristics from social media sites [12]. In the Arabic studies, El-ballouli et al. [17], Alrubaian et al. [5–8] and Amal AlMansour [3] proposed several techniques related to Arabic tweets. The recently proposed models in [11, 22, 23] and [25] used the feature-based model to enhance the performance of fake news detection. Features and Source-based Approaches take advantage of real time and add the method of source validation to the traditional feature-based approach [1] and [13]. This approach was investigated recently in detecting fake news concerning COVID-19 tweets [16, 19]. Real-Time Credibility Detection Approach was applied to detect the credibility of tweets in real-time [6, 20].

3 Credibility Detection Model

The proposed model for detecting the credibility of Arabic tweets is shown in Fig. 1. Our model consists of five steps to detect the credibility of Arabic tweets: 1) Twitter-Data-Collection, 2) Data Pre-processing, 3) Features Extraction, 4) Mining Algorithm, and finally 5). The next subsections describe systematically the proposed model in order to detect the credibility of Arabic tweets with high accuracy.

3.1 Twitter Data Collection

An appropriate amount of data should be collected for the training and testing of the model. After collecting the dataset, Data Labeling is started. Many researchers have published the datasets they used in their studies for the purpose of developing scientific research. In 2017, a set of 9,000 tweets was collected and annotated by El-ballouli et al. [17][1]. This dataset is the one we depend on it for our research.

3.2 Data Pre-processing

During this step, the raw data will be transformed into a suitable format for the next processing steps. For some features, we need to eliminate the" Tashkeel" ("تشكيل"). Regular expressions were used in our work in order to remove special symbols, non-Arabic letters, or URLs. Natural Language ToolKit "NLTK"[2] and ISRIStemmer"[3] were used for stemming, tokenizing, matching sentences, and then comparing sentences.

---

[1] https://www.oma-project.com.
[2] https://www.nltk.org/.
[3] https://kite.com/python/docs/nltk.stem.ISRIStemmer.

3.3   Features Extraction and Selection

In order to input data into a classifier, it must be formed as a vector, which contains many features that provide enough information to make the classification process accurate" [10]. We depend on known user- and content features. More explanations about the code related to feature extraction and selection can be found on this GitHub project[4].

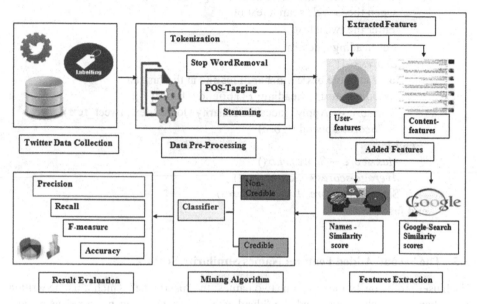

Fig. 1. Credibility detection model

3.4   The First Added Feature: Google Similarity Feature

When someone reads a news item, he/she may then turn to Google and look for the same news text. Observing that the first Google search results page is the most relevant to the searching sentence [19], we conduct experiments by adding new features, comparing the tweet text with only the top, basic search results on Google's first result page (if any—excluding advertisements). We take the average of the similarity between the text of the tweet and these results (the heading and lines below it without opening the links) as well as the top result possessing the closest similarity to the tweet text. An "**Algorithm I**" was proposed to calculate the Google Search Similarity. To match the two sentences, we used the Jaccard Index [2].

---

[4] https://github.com/rabeaamuty/Extracting-Features-for-Credibility-detection-in-Arabic-tweets.

Algorithm I Google Search Similarity Calculation
Start
    Importing Selenium.webdriver. Nltk, RE, and other needed libraries
    for tweet in tweets dataset **do**
        Get tweet text
        Preprocess (tweet text)
        Open the driver (Chrome path, Google URL)
        Open the Google search text box
        Enter the tweet text
        Get headings, details
        Scores ←[]
        for i in range basic number of results in the first **do**
            Joined-text ←heading[i].append (Details[i])
            score ← Apply (Jaccard-similarity (Joined-text, tweet_text))
            Scores-append (*score*)
    end for
        Max-score ←*Scores.max*()
        Average-scores ←*Scores.avg*()
        Save (*Max-score, Average-scores)*
    end for

3.5   The Second Added Feature: Names Similarity Feature

Each user profile on Twitter contains two names; the "username" which must be written in alphanumeric characters, and the "display name", which can be typed using any combination of letters and/or symbols. We conducted experiments to estimate the effect of the Names Similarity percentage on user credibility considering the cases of using the Arabic Chat Alphabet (ACA) [14, 15] in detail in our previous work Mouty and Gazdar [18]. Google Translator "GT" was chosen because it is "One of the most popular translation services is services offered by Google that has been improving in recent years" [26]. GT is immediately able to translate ACA into English [21]. We proposed **Algorithm II**, which calculates comparison scores between the username and the display name.

Algorithm II Names Similarity Score Calculation
Importing fuzzywuzzy and googletrans
    function Translate word (*word*)
        return (*translator.translate(word)*)
    end function
    function Translate_letter(*word*)
        Text ←""
        for *j* in word **do**
            w ←translator.translate(*j*)
            Text= Text + w.text
        end for
        return *text*
    end function
    function Comp_word(*display-name,username*)
        return(fuzz.ratio(Translate_word(*display-name*),Translate_word(*username*))
    end function
    function Comp_letter(*display-name, username*):
        return (fuzz.ratio(translate_letter(*display-name*),translate_letter(*username*))
    end function
    word comp score ←Comp word(*display-name,username*)
    letter comp score ←Comp letter(*display-name,username*)
    return (max (*word comp score, letter comp score*)).

3.6 Mining Algorithm

Through this step, the dataset will be divided into a training set and a testing set. Each tweet from the used dataset is presented as a group of 43 features. Many of the classification methods are applied in our model using the "Weka" tool [24]. K-fold cross-validation [4] is applied to obtain a fair measurement of performance. A total number of 9,000 feature vectors were used to train and test the classifiers.

3.7 Evaluation

We evaluate our model, before and after adding the proposed features. Next, we compare the performance of our model with the performance of the baseline models.

3.8 Evaluation of the Proposed Model

Four experiments "E1-E4" were conducted to evaluate the performance of the proposed model. The results are presented in Table 1. The first experiment "E1" where we used 40 features (18 user-based, 22 content-based), before adding the new proposed features. For the second experiment "E2", we added the Google Search Similarity features. Third experiment "E3", we added a similarity score feature between the username and screen name. In the fourth experiment "E4" we added the new added features. The highest-obtained accuracy, using the random forest classifier, equals 78.71%.

Table 1. Results of evaluation of the proposed model.

Classifier	E1	E2	E3	E4
Random Forest	**76.17%**	**78.71%**	**77.81%**	**78.61%**
SVM	66.56%	70.97%	67.51%	71.13%
DT	72.47%	74.21%	74.22%	73.97%
Naïve Bayes	54.71%	58.60%	57.45%	58.71%

3.9 Comparing Our Model with Baseline Models

Three of the previous works were concerned with exposing the general credibility of the Arabic tweets, used features related to the user and content and their used dataset was from the general tweets (El-ballouli et al. [17], Amal AlMansour [3], and the work of AlRubaian et al. [6]). Table 2 presents the results of the compression between the performance of our model and the base-line studies. As we can conclude, the new added features, in addition to the old features, have enhanced classification accuracy.

Table 2. Comparison between the results from our proposed model and the baseline models.

Model	Precision	Recall	F-measure	Accuracy
CAT	76.1%	76.3%	75.8%	-
AlMansour (2016)	0.766	0.774	0.766	77.44%
AlRubaian et al. Aug 18 (2016)	–	–	–	77.71%
Proposed model	**0.785**	**0.787**	**0.785**	**78.71%**

4 Conclusion and Future Work

Many studies have investigated Twitter's publishing credibility—especially in English. We have proposed a model that reveals the credibility of Arabic tweets and consists of five stages. To improve the accuracy of credibility detection in regard to Arabic tweets, we have proposed two additional new features. The first feature was calculated by comparing the tweet text with the main search results on the first Google search page. The second feature, which was related to the user, the measurement of how the user's username is related to his/her display name. We conducted several experiments to determine the contribution of the model as a whole and the added features specifically. Then, we compared our model with baseline models. The best result (accuracy of 78.71%) was obtained using the random forest classifier. The results of our work reveal that our model outperformed the baseline works in terms of accuracy and F-measure.

In the future, we plan to collect and label a huge dataset from daily tweets such that it will be available for scientific research. we plan to study the credibility of the user by evaluating his/her history and network and assigning him/her a degree of credibility.

References

1. Al-Khalifa, H.S., Al-Eidan, R.M.: An experimental system for measuring the credibility of news content in Twitter. Int. J.Web Inf. Syst.(2011)
2. Shi, R., Ngan, K.N., Li, S.: Jaccard index compensation for object segmentation evaluation. In: 2014 IEEE International Conference on Image Processing (ICIP), pp. 4457–4461 (2014)
3. Almansour, A.: Credibility assessment for arabic micro-blogs using noisy labels. Ph.D. thesis, King's College London (2016)
4. Rodriguez, J.D., Perez, A., Lozano, J.A.: Sensitivity analysis of k-fold cross validation in prediction error estimation. IEEE Trans. Pattern Anal. Mach. Intell. 32(3), 569–575 (2010)
5. Alrubaian, M., Al-Qurishi, M., Al-Rakhami, M., Alamri, A.: A credibility assessment model for online social network content. In: Kaya, M., Erdoğan, Ö., Rokne, J. (eds.) From Social Data Mining and Analysis to Prediction and Community Detection. LNSN, pp. 61–77. Springer, Cham (2017). https://doi.org/10.1007/978-3-319-51367-6_3
6. AlRubaian, M., Al-Qurishi, M., Al-Rakhami, M., Hassan, M.M., Alamri, A.: Credfinder: a real-time tweets credibility assessing system. In: Proceedings of the 2016 IEEE/ACM International Conference on Advances in Social Networks Analysis and Mining, ASONAM 2016, pp. 1406–1409. IEEE Press (2016)
7. Alrubaian, M., Al-Qurishi, M., Al-Rakhami, M., Hassan, M.M., Alamri, A.: Reputation-based credibility analysis of Twitter social network users. Concur. Comput. Pract. Exp. 29(7), e3873 (2017)
8. Alrubaian, M., Al-Qurishi, M., Hassan, M.M., Alamri, A.: A credibility analysis system for assessing information on Twitter. IEEE Trans. Dependable Secure Comput. 15(4), 661–674 (2018)
9. Althiabi, S.: The emergence of social media networks and their impacts of professional journalism practices in Saudi Arabia. Ph.D. thesis, Nottingham Trent University (2017). http://irep.ntu.ac.uk/id/eprint/34881/
10. Mouty, R., Gazdar, A.: Survey on steps of truth detection on Arabic tweets. In: 2018 21st Saudi Computer Society National Computer Conference (NCC), pp. 1–6 (2018)
11. Al-Yahya, M., Al-Khalifa, H., Al-Baity, H., AlSaeed, D., Essam, A.: Arabic fake news detection: comparative study of neural networks and transformer-based approaches. Complexity 2021 (2021)
12. Castillo, C., Mendoza, M., Poblete, B.: Information credibility on Twitter. In: Proceedings of the 20th International Conference on World Wide Web, WWW 2011, pp. 675–684. Association for Computing Machinery, New York (2011)
13. Chen, C., Wang, Y., Zhang, J., Xiang, Y., Zhou, W., Min, G.: Statistical featuresbased real-time detection of drifted Twitter spam. IEEE Trans. Inf. Forensics Secur. 12(4), 914–925 (2016)
14. Yaghan, M.A.: "Arabizi": a contemporary style of Arabic slang. Des. Issues 24(2), 39–52 (2008)
15. Zhao, Z., Resnick, P., Mei, Q.: Enquiring minds: early detection of rumors in social media from enquiry posts. In: Proceedings of the 24th International Conference on World Wide Web, WWW 2015, pp. 1395–1405 (2015)
16. Qasem, S.N., Al-Sarem, M., Saeed, F.: An ensemble learning based approach for detecting and tracking COVID19 rumors. Comput. Mater. Continua, 1721–1747 (2021)

17. El Ballouli, R., El-Hajj, W., Ghandour, A., Elbassuoni, S., Hajj, H., Shaban, K.: Cat: credibility analysis of Arabic content on Twitter. In: Proceedings of the Third Arabic Natural Language Processing Workshop, pp. 62–71 (2017)
18. Mouty, R., Gazdar, A.: The effect of the similarity between the two names of Twitter users on the credibility of their publications. In: 2019 Joint 8th International Conference on Informatics, Electronics Vision (ICIEV) and 2019 3rd International Conference on Imaging, Vision Pattern Recognition (icIVPR), pp. 196–201 (2019)
19. Mahlous, A.R., Al-Laith, A.: Fake news detection in Arabic tweets during the COVID-19 pandemic. Int. J. Adv. Comput. Sci. Appl. (2021)
20. Gupta, A., Kumaraguru, P., Castillo, C., Meier, P.: TweetCred: real-time credibility assessment of content on Twitter. In: Aiello, L.M., McFarland, D. (eds.) SocInfo 2014. LNCS, vol. 8851, pp. 228–243. Springer, Cham (2014). https://doi.org/10.1007/978-3-319-13734-6_16
21. Wu, Y., et al.: Google's neural machine translation system: bridging the gap between human and machine translation. CoRR abs/1609.08144 (2016)
22. Thaher, T., Saheb, M., Turabieh, H., Chantar, H.: Intelligent detection of false information in Arabic tweets utilizing hybrid harris hawks based feature selection and machine learning models. Symmetry 13(4), 556 (2021)
23. Alzanin, S.M., Azmi, A.M.: Rumor detection in Arabic tweets using semi-supervised and unsupervised expectation–maximization. Knowl. Based Syst. 185, 104945 (2019)
24. Srivastava, S.: Article: Weka: A tool for data preprocessing, classification, ensemble, clustering and association rule mining. Int. J. Comput. Appl. 88(10), 26–29 (2014)
25. Gumaei, A., Al-Rakhami, M.S., Hassan, M.M., De Albuquerque, V.H.C., Camacho, D.: An effective approach for rumor detection of Arabic tweets using extreme gradient boosting method. In: Transactions on Asian and Low-Resource Language Information Processing, vol. 21, no. 1, pp. 1–16 (2022)
26. Thamrin, H., Ariyanto, G., Pamungkas, E.W., Sulistyono, Y.: User participation in building language repository: the case of google translate. IOP Conf. Ser. Mater. Sci. Eng. 403, 012072 (2018)

Applications for Industry 4.0

RF-Based Mini-Drone Detection, Identification & Jamming in No Fly Zones Using Software Defined Radio

Feten Slimeni[✉], Tijeni Delleji, and Zied Chtourou

Science and Technology for Defense Laboratory, Center for Military Research,
Aouina, Tunis, Tunisia
feten.slimeni@gmail.com

Abstract. Recently, mini-drone exploitation is rising in diverse domains such as recreation, commerce and defense. It serves to save human lives, protect country borders and carry urgent deliveries. Given the use of inexpensive components, mini-drones are within every one's reach. Therefore, malicious mini-drone users are able to threaten sensitive areas and to do illegal acts. Hostile applications endanger critical airspace like above nuclear sites, official buildings and military institution. Countermeasures are an imminent require to ensure individual privacy, secure government institutions and track mini-drone misusers. However, effective anti-drone technologies are expensive and depends on the target drone characteristics and the protected area sensitivity.

In this paper, we develop an RF-based countermeasure that is able to detect, identify and disrupt the communication link between the mini-drone and its remote controller. The proposed solution is implemented in a Software Defined Radio (SDR) platform which enables adapting the countermeasure to future attacks and the drone market evolution in view of protecting a No Fly Zone such as airports, public events and military installations. We detail the conducted experiments and provide results proving the efficiency of the developed solution.

Keywords: Mini-drone · Attacks · Countermeasures · RF-based method · SDR · Detection · Identification · Jamming

1 Introduction

Nowadays, research and everyday services are more and more interested in UAVs due to its continuous development and falling cost. It is ubiquitous today from educational to commercial applications [1]. Among personal services, it is used by photography fans and film makers. The common commercial applications are surveillance, geographical mapping, agriculture, healthcare, weather forecasting, delivery and disaster management. Moreover, military usage of UAVs is in continuous rise for research and development, supervision and diverse military missions that are characterized by time sensitivity and high risks.

© The Author(s), under exclusive license to Springer Nature Switzerland AG 2022
N. T. Nguyen et al. (Eds.): ICCCI 2022, LNAI 13501, pp. 791–798, 2022.
https://doi.org/10.1007/978-3-031-16014-1_62

While receiving a great deal of attention in a variety of civilian and commercial applications, mini-UAVs, especially the Commercial-Off-The-Shelf (COTS) 'mini-drones' undoubtedly pose a number of threats to airspace security that could endanger people and property. While these threats can vary widely in terms of intent and attacker sophistication, ranging from pilot recklessness to deliberate attacks, they all have the potential to produce serious disruption. Their frequency is also increasing: in the past three years, for example, various airports in the United States, the United Kingdom, Ireland, and the United Arab Emirates have experienced significant disruptions to their operations as a result of mini-drone sightings [2].

The need to mitigate disruptive and destructive COTS mini-drones misuses has given rise to the investments in counter-UAV technologies. A crucial and common first step consists in rogue mini-UAV detection. It presents an interesting challenge to researchers. A following function consists in mini-UAV identification before going through alerting, tracking and neutralization. Among mini-drone detection techniques, visual awareness can be accomplished using camera sensors and computer vision algorithms. However, this technique is hindered by the image background, the weather conditions and the drone similarity to other flying objects like planes and birds [3]. The speed of visual detection is also limited compared to the speeds that can be reached by drones [4]. Another detection technique deals with pre-programmed drones, that follow a flight plan based on aboard GPS navigation system, can be done by Radars. However, this technique is hampered by the high miss detection of small drones made of low-reflective plastic materials capable of flying at low levels [5,6]. Differently, RF based methods are characterized by low hardware and software cost with the deployment flexibility [7]. These techniques are based on the detection and prevention of the mini-drone wireless communication links. Given the variety of frequency bands and communication protocols, the reconfigurability and cognitive abilities of SDR platforms enable the adaptation of the proposed countermeasure accordingly to the drone market evolution and threats adaptation.

In this paper, we leverage a low cost SDR board to implement an RF-based drone detection, identification and jamming technique. The target link can be used either for uplink drone command or downlink video streaming or telemetry information. The proposed solution consists in disrupting the drone-ground wireless link over the commonly used frequency band of 2.4 GHz. This work focuses in practically evaluating the feasibility of the complete RF solution going through detection, identification and neutralization. This paper is organized as follows. Section 2 presents the proposed RF solution, followed by the experimental setup in Sect. 3. The experimental results are detailed in Sect. 4. Finally, conclusions and future work axis are provided.

2   RF-Based Mini-Drone Countermeasure

In this work, we provide an RF-based countermeasure that goes through the following steps of Fig. 1: RF detection, identification and neutralization.

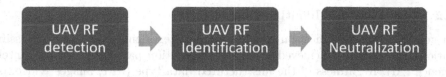

Fig. 1. RF-based mini-UAV countermeasure

2.1 Mini-UAV RF Detection

SDR platforms are low cost commercial off the shelf (COTS) equipments that replace the radio functions of signal processing from hardware components to software techniques. Due to its abilities of high precision measurements and digital processing reconfigurability, it can be used for detecting RF communications and replacing expensive spectrum analyzers [8]. To accomplish the detection step, we have implemented energy detection (ED) technique on SDR platform. This is the common approach to spectrum sensing due to its low computational and execution complexity compared to cyclostationary based techniques. Also, unlike matched filter detector, prior knowledge on the transmitted incumbent signal is not required.

An energy detector sets a threshold according to the noise floor and compares it with the energy of the data stream in input.

Digitally implementation of this method uses the Fast Fourier Transform (FFT), then the absolute value of the samples is squared and integrated over the observation band.

Otherwise, ED technique consists in measuring the received energy during the observation interval. If the energy is less than certain threshold value then it declares it as spectrum hole. The detection is achieved (i.e. the detection flag is set to high) when the Received Signal Strength Indicator (RSSI) of the detected signal exceeds a certain threshold, in our case the threshold is set to -82dBm (which was measured in absence of transmission) and can be configured to an other value. The three main steps followed to build this code are:

Step 1: The SDR platform configuration and the threshold declaration.

Step 2: Start sensing in order to capture the signal samples. This phase continues until the detection flag is high, when this condition is valid the phase of storing samples starts. These samples are stored in memory until the requested number (or the maximum number according to the memory size) of samples is reached. After that, the reception module returns to idle state and stops listening in order to avoid overwriting the already captured data. Finally, these samples can be extracted from the memory.

Step 3: The final step is the spectral representation of these collected data using FFT.

2.2   Mini-UAV RF Identification

In general, data identification consists in its categorizing into specific classifications which can be achieved using the recognition pattern of artificial intelligence (AI). Regardless of the unstructured data type (text, images, video, or other), machines based on cognitive technology and implementing machine learning (ML) become able to perceive it.

In our context, the mini-drone signal, wifi and bluetooth signals operate in the same frequency band which require their classification. The objectif is to distinguish the UAV communication link among the other coexisting signals.

The data collected during the detection step constitute the input of the identification step which provide in output the class to which it belongs among the three classes: UAV signal, wifi or bluetooth signal.

In order to perform this classification step, a prestored dataset of measurements associated to the IQ samples of the three considered signal categories is used to train a ML algorithm. It consists of 60 rows for each of the RF signal wifi and bluetooth along with 120 rows associated to a Parrot drone2 which give a total of 240 rows. For each measurement row, we have the following statistical features.

Signal Features

- The mean of a set of N observations is the average, we consider the means of both the I and Q values (I_mean and Q_mean).
- The median absolute deviation (I_mad, Q_mad) of a set of observations consists in selecting the median as a reference point and then reporting the deviations from that reference point. The median is the middle value got after sorting the values into ascending order.
- The standard deviation σ (I_std, Q_std) is the square root of the variance that is used to calculate the mean squared deviations from the mean.
- The kurtosis of a set of data observations (I_kurt, Q_kurt) is a measure of the pointiness of this data. It is flatter (less pointed) than the normal distribution when the kurtosis value is negative. The data distribution has almost the same shape as the normal distribution if the kurtosis is almost null, and it is too pointed when the kurtosis is positive.

2.3   Mini-UAV RF Neutralization

The phase of neutralization consists in jamming the frequency band 2.4 GHz. It results in shutting down or disrupting the wireless connections in this band. Therefore, we identify the signal class (wifi, bluetooth, drone) in order to generate the jamming signal when a drone signal is detected. The developed jamming code is based on these steps:

Step1: Generating a continuous long training sequence (LTS), which is defined with a preamble similar to the 802.11a standard.

Step2: Enabling the FrontEnd of the MRP and setting it to Tx mode.

Step3: Setting the sampling rate of the FrontEnd.

Step4: Configuring the hopping pattern of the selected Frontend.

3   Experimental Setup

In this section, we present the experimental setup including mainly the SDR plateform and the mini-drones.

3.1   The Modular Radio Platform (MRP)

MRP-A200 or Modular Radio Platform-A200 is a full duplex board based on high performance System On a Chip (SoC), two flexible RF interfaces and Ethernet connection. It is designed to define radio transmitter/receiver by software based on its FPGA and micro-controller Microsemi SoC. Its high rate Full duplex RF transceiver operates at 5 GHz unlicensed band. We have used the MRP-A200 board, which is developed by CODINTEK. This society is a provider of innovative RF broadband product design services and solutions, it offers a family of synthesizable programmable DSP IP cores [9].

3.2   Mini-drones Under Analysis

Mini-drones use diverse RF signals which can be exploited for detection and identification. The following is an initial selection of the commercial mini-drones used in our experimental tests.

Parrot Drone2.0: The Parrot Drone2.0 is a plastic quad-copter essentially composed of four plastic rotors. These drones are the innovation of the version Parrot1.0.

AR Drone2.0: The AR Drone2.0 is similar to the earlier version 1.0. It has four propellers which helps it to navigate in the air.
These mini-drones has two cameras: front camera (extremely powerful) and a less powerful camera located at the lower part of the drone adjacent to the pressure detector. This type of drone is easy to control with any mobile device, by installing an application like "FreeFlight2.0 app".

Custom-Made Drone. This drone is fabricated at CODINTEK company, it is a quad-copter controlled via a professional command named "TURNIGY 9X".

4   Experiments Results

Our proposed approach is divided in three main phases; the first is detecting the existence of a wireless communication in a specific zone followed by the step of mini-UAV control signal identification. The last step is jamming the frequency band 2.4 GHz to shut down or disrupt the mini-drone wireless connection.

In this work, two different experiences were realized using the MRP platform and the considered commercial and custom drones.

4.1   Mini-UAV RF Detection Results

In this phase we tried to detect the wireless connections in the band 2.4 GHz–2.5 GHz. In our case we study three types of wireless connections: bluetooth, wifi and drone command signal.

In first time, we have used the HP8562A spectrum analyzer to analyze the spectrum related to each wireless connection. Then, we have executed our ED-based sensing code to detect and draw the spectrum using the MRP-A200.

Signal Detection Using the Spectrum Analyzer. We visualized the different spectral figures of bluetooth, wifi and the command link of the drone using the spectrum analyzer.

Signal Detection Using MRP and ED Based Sensing. After installing the test equipment and executing our sensing code, we obtain spectral results similar to those of the spectrum analyzer.

4.2   Mini-UAV RF Identification Results

To classify this labeled data, we can rely on supervised learning algorihtms like Support vector machines (SVMs) and k nearest neighbors (KNN). After being fitted, the model can then be used to predict new values.

The KNN classifier is robust to noisy training data. The parameter k is an integer number of the nearest neighbors that should be specified. $k = 3$ gives the higher accuracy. The considered data was splitted into 70% as training and 30% as testing sets. Training and testing the KNN model with the specified k value gives an accuracy score of almost $90,28\%$. Then, we have tested it on a new set of values that was measured using MRP platform during the previous detection step. The model predicts correctly the associated class which allows going to the next step of RF neutralization when the identification step gives drone class.

4.3   Mini-UAV RF Jamming Results

In order to validate the jamming attack, we have considered the following tests.

Jamming Results with Custom Drone: The connection of the custom drone receiver with its controller is successful when the red light of the receiver is on. After launching the jammer this connection is interrupted, the red light is off until stopping the jamming signal. The jamming signal is a continuous signal sent from the MRP's transmitter and engrossed the full 2.4 GHz bandwidth.

Jamming Results with the Parrot Drone: We have commanded the Parrot drone using the smatphone FreeFlight2.0 application. As a first test of the link, the application enables commanding the drone until a distance of almost 50 m. But after launching the jammer this distance decreases reaching 9 m. When the connection is interrupted, a message indicating loss connection is displayed. The problem here is that the output power is too low which limits the jammer range and efficiency. To solve this limitation, we have used a preamplifier.

It has a gain of 20 dB which helps to increase the output power of the MRP from 1 mW to 100 mW. Repeating the test after adding the preamplifier, results in decreasing the distance corresponding to the loss of connection to 2.5 m.

To summarize, the results prove the success of the proposed RF system to jam rogue mini-drones.

5   Conclusion

In this paper, we have developed an RF-based mini-drone detection, identification and jamming system using MRP software defined radio platform. We have trained an artificial intelligence algorithm to differentiate the received mini-drone signals from wifi and bluetooth that use the same 2.4 GHz frequency band. We have detailed the steps along with the environment work. We have provided the detection and identification results. Moreover, we have proved the success of the jamming phase that limits the range of the command link. As extension of this work, we will ameliorate the detection step through adaptive threshold, the identification step through learning over larger dataset of diverse mini-UAVs and adapt the jamming signal to the hopping pattern of each mini-UAV class. Moreover, the proposed SDR-based RF system can be embedded on a drone that tries to detect malicious drones to avoid ground detection limits due to multipath and coexisting wireless transmitters.

References

1. Finn, R., Scheding, S.: Developments and Challenges for Autonomous Unmanned Vehicles: A Compendium, vol. 3. Springer, Heidelberg (2010). https://doi.org/10.1007/978-3-642-10704-7
2. McFarland, M.: Airports scramble to handle drone incidents
3. Coluccia, A., et al.: Drone-vs-bird detection challenge at IEEE AVSS 2019. In: 2019 16th IEEE International Conference on Advanced Video and Signal Based Surveillance (AVSS), pp. 1–7. IEEE (2019)

4. Seidaliyeva, U., Akhmetov, D., Ilipbayeva, L., Matson, E.T.: Real-time and accurate drone detection in a video with a static background. Sensors **20**(14), 3856 (2020)
5. Coluccia, A., Parisi, G., Fascista, A.: Detection and classification of multirotor drones in radar sensor networks: A review. Sensors **20**(15), 4172 (2020)
6. de Quevedo, Á.D., Urzaiz, F.I., Menoyo, J.G., Asensio, A.: Drone detection and radar cross-section measurements by RAD-DAR. IET Radar Sonar Navig. **13**, 1437–1447 (2019)
7. Lv, H., Liu, F., Yuan, N.C.: Drone presence detection by the drone's RF communication. J. Phys. Conf. Ser. **1738**, 012044 (2021)
8. Wright, D., Ball, E.: Highly portable, low cost SDR instrument for RF propagation studies. IEEE Trans. Instrum. Meas. **69**(8), 5446–5457 (2020)
9. CodinTek. Codintek communications (2018)

A New 3D-Regular Shaped Geometry-Based MIMO Channel Model for Vehicle-to-Vehicle Communications in Rectangular Tunnel

Jalel Chebil[1], Hanene Zormati[2(✉)], Ali Mansour[3], Ismail Ben Mabrouk[4], and Jamel Bel Hadj Tahar[2]

[1] Department of Technology and Transport Engineering, ISTLS, NOCCS Laboratory, University of Sousse, Sousse, Tunisia

[2] Department of Electric Engineering, ENISO, NOCCS Laboratory, University of Sousse, Sousse, Tunisia
zormati.hanen@hotmail.fr

[3] ENSTA Bretagne, Brest, France

[4] Department of Engineering, Durham University, Durham, UK

Abstract. The intelligent transportation systems have attracted the attention of many researchers and developers in the last few decades in order to make the exploitation of transportation networks be safer, more coordinated, and smarter. Channel modeling for vehicle-to-vehicle (V2V) communication is one of the related research topics that are being investigated in this field. In this paper, a three-dimensional wideband regular shaped geometry based channel model for multiple-input and multiple-output V2V communication channel is proposed for rectangular tunnel environments. A two semi-circular geometry is adopted to describe moving vehicles around transmitter and receiver, and a cuboid model is employed to depict scatterers located on internal surfaces of the tunnel walls. Using this channel model, the channel characteristics including space time correlation function, frequency correlation function and auto-correlation function are determined and simulated numerically. Then, the results are compared with the derived statistics from Avazov *et al.* and Zhou *et al.* methods to prove the efficiency of the proposed model.

Keywords: Channel model · MIMO channel · Rectangular tunnel · Vehicle-to-vehicle communication

1 Introduction

Vehicle-to-Vehicle (V2V) communications are one of the central part of Intelligent Transport System (ITS) which uses this evolving technology to improve traffic management by allowing vehicles to communicate with one another [1, 2]. V2V communications enable automobiles to exchange wirelessly real-time information such as speed, braking, stability, direction of travel and so on. This technology allows vehicles to receive multi-directional messages from all other vehicles within proximity from which potential

© The Author(s), under exclusive license to Springer Nature Switzerland AG 2022
N. T. Nguyen et al. (Eds.): ICCCI 2022, LNAI 13501, pp. 799–808, 2022.
https://doi.org/10.1007/978-3-031-16014-1_63

threats of crashes or incidents can be detected [1, 3]. The importance of this technology will enhance road safety by alerting the driver of any dangerous incidents before it can be seen or detected. Thus it facilitates crash avoidance. Therefore, V2V communications can reduce the number of road accidents and fatalities which is quite vital for saving lives and minimizing damages to vehicles and road infrastructures. However, this new technology is still evolving and more research is required in this area. One of the challenges of V2V communications is the modeling of the communication channel especially for complex environment such as curved roads, bridges, intersections, highway, tunnels, etc.

V2V require an accurate communication channel models for different environments which should be validated under various scenarios since the modeling of radio wave propagation channels is very important in the design and optimal operation of any wireless communication systems [4]. Major channel models proposed in the literature can be divided into two dominant classes: deterministic or stochastic models [5]. Deterministic channel models are based on Maxwell's equations and ray tracing method which applies geometric optics and uniform theory of diffraction. However, these models require detailed and precise information of the V2V communication environment, such as: number of buildings, the dimensions of the buildings, the materials of these buildings, number of scatterers along the roadsides, number of moving vehicles and their speeds, size and type of moving vehicles, positions of the transmitter and receiver etc. Although, the obtained results reflect the reality, they are site specific and cannot be generalized to other scenarios with different environment [6]. Moreover, these deterministic models generally require high computational time. Since V2V communication is characterized by high mobility of the transmitter and receiver and dynamic non-stationary environments, then deterministic models are not favored for such applications [4]. On the other hand, stochastic channel modeling approaches are preferred in many applications, since it is faster in generating a realistic channel with considerably fewer input parameters [7]. Stochastic channel models are based on channel statistics obtained from large numbers of measurements conducted at various communication environments. From these statistics, propagation path parameters are derived and used to describe the properties of stochastic channel models. These types of models can be classified as Non-Geometrical Stochastic Channel Models (NGSM) and Geometry-Based Stochastic Channel Models (GBSM) [5]. For the NGSM, the physical parameters of a V2V channel are derived in a completely stochastic manner without any geometrical assumptions or details, while GBSM is determined from predefined stochastic distribution of effective scatterers and by using the fundamental laws of wave propagation [5]. In addition, the GBSM model can be easily adapted to different scenarios by altering the shape of the scattering region. So it can be simple for useful theoretical investigation of channels or can be rendered relatively complex for simulating real channels [8–10]. For this reason, this study will focus on the GBSM modeling technique applied to rectangular tunnel environment using regular shape scattering region.

Few channel models were proposed for rectangular tunnel environment. In [11], Avazov et al. have proposed a 3D Multiple-Input Multiple-Output (MIMO) V2V channel model inside a rectangular tunnel, the model considers a random distribution of the scatterers on the tunnel wall. It analyzes the impact of various model parameters on the V2V channel statistics such as antenna element spacing and tunnel width. Similarly,

Zhou *et al.* [12] presents a 3D MIMO channel model for V2V communication system in a rectangular tunnel environment. The model considers the single-bounced scattering propagation path of electromagnetic signals and also assumes that the scatterers are randomly distributed on the rectangular tunnel wall. Both papers consider only static scatterers located on the internal walls of the tunnel, while moving scatterers between transceivers are not considered.

This paper proposes a new regular shaped GBSM applied to MIMO channel model for V2V communication inside rectangular tunnels. The contributions of this paper are:

(i) Proposing a new three Dimensional (3D) Regular-Shaped Geometry-Based Stochastic Model (RS-GBSM) for V2V communication inside rectangular tunnels and providing the expressions of channel impulse response.

(ii) Determining the expressions of Space Time Correlation Function (STCF), Frequency Correlation Function (FCF) and Auto-Correlation Function (ACF).

(iii) Evaluating the new model in terms of FCF and ACF by comparing them with other models dealing with rectangular tunnels.

The rest of this paper is organized as follows. The new RS-GBSM channel model is presented in Sect. 2. In Sect. 3 general expressions of STCF, FCF and ACF are determined. Then, the proposed model is tested and evaluated in Sect. 4. Finally, Sect. 5 concludes the paper.

2   Proposed Model

This section describes the proposed RS-GBSM for a MIMO V2V channel inside a rectangular tunnel with length L, height H and width W. It is assumed that there are two lanes of traffic moving in opposite directions inside the tunnel as shown in Fig. 1. The movement between the mobile transmitter and mobile receiver results in time-varying geometric statistics that make the channel non-stationary.

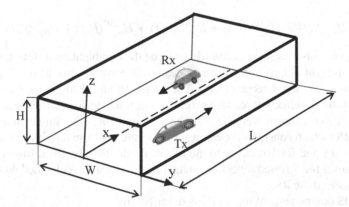

Fig. 1. Typical propagation scenario in a two-way rectangular tunnel.

Scatterers inside the tunnel can be classified into two types: static and moving. Static scatterers are assumed to be randomly distributed on the wall of the tunnel, whereas, moving scatterers are moving vehicles located around the transmitter and the receiver. A two semi-circular geometry is adopted to describe the moving scatterers, while a cuboid model is employed to depict the static scatterers as shown in Fig. 2. In this work, (m, n, o) are considered to be the coordinates used to represent the position of the scatterers $S^{(mno)}$ where $m = 1, 2, ... M; n = 1, 2, ... N$ and $o = 1, 2, ... O$.

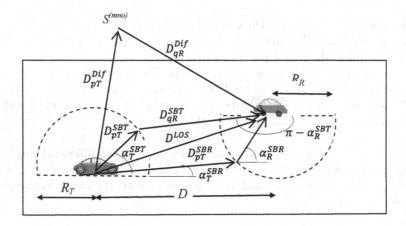

Fig. 2. Geometrical model for V2V channel in rectangular tunnel environment.

The MIMO V2V channel can be characterized by a channel matrix $H(t, \tau) = [h_{pq}(t, \tau)]$ of size $M_R \times M_T$ where $h_{pq}(t, \tau)$ is the channel impulse response, CIR, between the pth (1, 2, ..., M_T) transmit antenna and the qth (1, 2, ..., M_R) receive antenna. For simplifying the analysis, the Fourier transform of $h_{pq}(t, \tau)$ is used and is commonly known as the Time-Variant Transfer Function (TVTF). It can be expressed as

$$H_{pq}(f, t) = H_{pq}^{LOS}(f, t) + H_{pq}^{SBT}(f, t) + H_{pq}^{SBR}(f, t) + H_{pq}^{Dif}(f, t) \tag{1}$$

The channel impulse response is considered to be the combination of four components. The Line-Of-Sight (LOS) component represents the waves that travel directly from the transmitter (Tx) to the receiver (Rx). The Single-Bounced component at the Tx side (SBT) stands for the effects of scatterers from moving clusters located between the Tx and Rx but closer to the transmitter side. The third component is the Single-Bounced at the Rx side (SBR) which considers the effects of the scatterers from moving clusters located between the Tx and Rx but closer to the receiver side. Finally, the diffuse component (Dif) represents the diffused reflection emanating from scatterers located on the wall of the tunnel toward the Rx.

The LOS components of the TVFT is described by

$$H_{pq}^{LOS}(f, t) = \sqrt{\frac{K}{K+1}} e^{-j\frac{2\pi}{\lambda}D^{LOS}} e^{j[2\pi t(f_T^{LOS} + f_R^{LOS}) + \theta^{LOS} - 2\pi\tau^{LOS}f]} \tag{2}$$

where

K represents the Rice distribution factor,

D^{LOS} is the distance from the transmitter to the receiver for LOS path, it can be written as:

$$D^{LOS} = D - (M_T - 2p + 1)\frac{\delta_T}{2}\cos\phi_T\cos\gamma_T - (M_R - 2q + 1)\frac{\delta_R}{2}\cos\phi_R\cos\gamma_R \quad (3)$$

τ^{LOS} is the propagation delay of the LOS component and is related with D^{LOS} and the free space speed of light c by $\tau_{pq}^{LOS} = D^{LOS}/c$,

θ^{LOS} is the initial phase of the LOS path,

f and t denotes the frequency and time respectively,

λ corresponds to the wavelength, and

f_T^{LOS} and f_R^{LOS} refer to the transmitter and receiver frequencies in the LOS path and are defined as

$$f_T^{LOS} = f_{Tmax}\cos(\alpha_T^{LOS} - \varphi_T)\cos(\beta_T^{LOS}) \quad (4)$$

$$f_R^{LOS} = f_{Rmax}\cos(\alpha_R^{LOS} - \varphi_R)\cos(\beta_R^{LOS}) \quad (5)$$

where α_T^{LOS}, β_T^{LOS}, α_R^{LOS} and β_R^{LOS} refer to the Azimuth Angle Of Departure (AAOD), Elevation AOD (EAOD), the Azimuth Angle Of Arrival (AAOA), and Elevation AOA (EAOA) of the LOS component, respectively. The angles φ_T and φ_R are the angles of motion for the transmitter and the receiver respectively.

The frequencies f_{Tmax} and f_{Rmax} represent the maximum Doppler frequencies associated with the transmitter and receiver, respectively, i.e. $f_{Tmax} = v_T/\lambda$ and $f_{Rmax} = v_R/\lambda$.

The SBT component of the TVFT is expressed as

$$H_{pq}^{SBT}(f, t) = \frac{1}{\sqrt{N_T(K + 1)}} \sum_{n=1}^{N_T} e^{-j\frac{2\pi}{\lambda}D_{pq}^{SBT}} e^{j[2\pi(f_T^{SBT} + f_R^{SBT})t + \theta^{SBT} - 2\pi\tau_{pq}^{SBT}]} \quad (6)$$

where

N_T is the number of vehicles existing on the semi-circular surface around the Tx,

f_T^{SBT} and f_R^{SBT} refer to the transmitter and receiver frequencies in the SBT path and they are defined as

$$f_T^{SBT} = f_{Tmax}\cos(\alpha_T^{SBT} - \varphi_T)\cos(\beta_T^{SBT}) \quad (7)$$

$$f_R^{SBT} = f_{Rmax}\cos(\alpha_R^{SBT} - \varphi_R)\cos(\beta_R^{SBT}) \quad (8)$$

θ^{SBT} is the initial phase of the SBT path,

D_{pq}^{SBT} is the distance from the transmitter to the receiver via the SBT path,

τ_{pq}^{SBT} is the propagation delay of the SBR path and is defined by $\tau_{pq}^{SBT} = D_{pq}^{SBT}/c$,

α_T^{SBT}, β_T^{SBT}, α_R^{SBT} and β_R^{SBT} are respectively the AAOD, EAOD, AAOA, and EAOD.

Similarly, the SBR component of the TVFT is expressed as

$$H_{pq}^{SBR}(f,t) = \frac{1}{\sqrt{N_R(K+1)}} \sum_{n=1}^{N_R} e^{-j\frac{2\pi}{\lambda}D_{pq}^{SBR}} e^{j[2\pi(f_T^{SBR}+f_R^{SBR})t+\theta^{SBR}-2\pi\tau_{pq}^{SBR}]} \quad (9)$$

where
N_R is the number of vehicles existing on the semi-circular surface around the Rx,
f_T^{SBR} and f_R^{SBR} refer to the transmitter and receiver frequencies in the SBR path and they are defined as

$$f_T^{SBR} = f_{Tmax}\cos(\alpha_T^{SBR} - \varphi_T)\cos(\beta_T^{SBR}) \quad (10)$$

$$f_R^{SBR} = f_{Rmax}\cos(\alpha_R^{SBR} - \varphi_R)\cos(\beta_R^{SBR}) \quad (11)$$

θ^{SBR} is the initial phase of the SBR path,
D_{pq}^{SBR} is the distance from the transmitter to the receiver via the SBR path,
τ_{pq}^{SBR} is the propagation delay of the SBR path and is defined by $\tau_{pq}^{SBR} = D_{pq}^{SBR}/c$,
α_T^{SBR}, β_T^{SBR}, α_R^{SBR} and β_R^{SBR} are respectively the AAOD, EAOD, AAOA, and EAOD.
Finally, the diffuse component of the TVFT is determined from

$$H_{pq}^{Dif}(f,t) = \lim_{\substack{M \to \infty \\ N \to \infty \\ O \to \infty}} \frac{1}{\sqrt{(K+1)MNO}} \sum_{m,n,o=1}^{M,N,O} e^{-j\frac{2\pi}{\lambda}D_{pq}^{Dif}}$$

$$\times e^{j[2\pi(f_T^{Dif}+f_R^{Dif})t+\theta^{(m,n,o)}-2\pi\tau_{pq}^{Dif}f]} \quad (12)$$

where

$$D_{pq}^{Dif} = D_{pT}^{Dif} + D_{qR}^{Dif} \quad (13)$$

$$f_T^{Dif} = f_{Tmax}\cos(\alpha_T^{Dif} - \varphi_T)\cos(\beta_T^{Dif}) \quad (14)$$

$$f_R^{Dif} = f_{Rmax}\cos(\alpha_R^{Dif} - \varphi_R)\cos(\beta_R^{Dif}) \quad (15)$$

D_{pq}^{Dif} is the distance which the radiated wave travels from the pth transmitter antenna element to the qth receiver antenna element via the scatterer $S^{(mno)}$,
D_{pT}^{Dif} and D_{qR}^{Dif} denote the distances from the transmitter to scatterer located on the wall of the tunnel and from the latter to the receiver respectively,
τ_{pq}^{Dif} is the propagation delay of the diffused path, and is defined by $\tau_{pq}^{Dif} = D_{pq}^{Dif}/c$,
$\theta^{(m,n,o)}$ is the initial phase,
f_T^{Dif} and f_R^{Dif} refer to the transmitter and receiver frequencies in the diffused path,
α_T^{Dif}, β_T^{Dif}, α_R^{Dif} and β_R^{Dif} are respectively the AAOD, EAOD, AAOA, and EAOD.
It is assumed that each of the initial phases $\theta^{LOS}, \theta^{SBT}, \theta^{SBR}$ and $\theta^{(m,n,o)}$ follows a uniform distribution over the interval $(0, \pi]$.

3 Statistical Characteristics of the Proposed Model

In this section, the analytical expressions of the STCF, the temporal ACF, and the FCF are derived based on the analytical solution described in [11]. Using (1) the STCF between $H_{pq}(f, t)$ and $H_{pq}(f + v, t + \tau)$ can be expressed as

$$\rho_{pq,p'q'}(\delta_T, \delta_R, \tau, v) = E\left[H_{pq}^*(f, t)H_{pq}(f + \tau, t + v)\right] \tag{16}$$

$$= \rho_{pq,p'q'}^{LOS}(\delta_T, \delta_R, \tau, v) + \rho_{pq,p'q'}^{SBT}(\delta_T, \delta_R, \tau, v)$$

$$+ \rho_{pq,p'q'}^{SBR}(\delta_T, \delta_R, \tau, v) + \rho_{pq,p'q'}^{Dif}(\delta_T, \delta_R, \tau, v) \tag{17}$$

where δ_T and δ_R are the spacing between the antenna elements at the transmitter and the receiver respectively, v represents the frequency separation, (*) is the complex conjugate operator, and $E[\cdot]$ denotes the expectation operator.

The FCF can be obtained by setting δ_T, δ_R and τ to zero

$$FCF = \rho_{pq,p'q'}(0, 0, 0, v) \tag{18}$$

Similarly, the ACF is determined by setting δ_T, δ_R and v to zero

$$ACF = \rho_{pq,p'q'}(0, 0, \tau, 0) \tag{19}$$

4 Numerical Results

This section presents numerical results obtained by evaluating FCF and ACF. The parameters of the simulation are set as in Table1.

Table 1. Simulation parameters

Parameter	value
L	100 m
H	5m
W	8 m
$\phi_T = \phi_R$	$\pi/4$
f	5.9 GHz
$R_T = R_R$	5m

Figure 3 shows the behavior of the absolute value of FCFs for different values of the K factor for both LOS and NLOS cases. According to the obtained results, the FCF for the proposed model decreases when frequency separation increases. Similar characteristics can be seen in [11] and [12]. In addition, the coherence bandwidth of the proposed channel model, corresponding to the frequency according to which the value of the FCF drops to 0.5, is less than the coherence bandwidth corresponding to [11] and [12]. For example, for K = 0 the coherence bandwidth of the proposed model is equal to 10 MHz whereas for [11] and [12] the coherence bandwidth is 35 MHz and this proves the effectiveness of the proposed model. In addition, when K increases the coherence bandwidth increases for the referenced models while it remains almost constant for the proposed model.

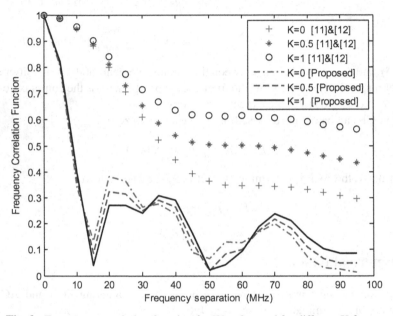

Fig. 3. Frequency correlation function for W = 8 m and for different K factors.

In the second part of this study, the ACF was simulated in terms of time delay when both transmitter and receiver are travelling in the same direction and the results are shown in Fig. 4. The ACF decreases when time delay increases and tends to be around zero for the proposed model when K = 0. Moreover, the ACF behavior is comparable to that of [12]. Similar ACF distribution can also be seen in the V2V communication channel model of Jiang *et al.* [13], which validates the feasibility of the proposed channel model to describe the vehicle communication environments. In addition, the obtained results show that the ACF increases when K factor increases and the ACF of the proposed model is generally lower than the one in [12]. It is also noted that the obtained coherence time is lower than the one in [12] which prove the effectiveness of the model proposed in this paper.

5 Conclusion

In this paper, a 3D RS-GBSM channel model for MIMO V2V communications in rectangular tunnel environment was proposed. General expressions of characteristics have been derived including the STCF, FCF and ACF under the considerations of both LOS and NLOS propagations. In addition, channel characteristics were simulated numerically and compared with statistics derived by Avazov et al. and Zhou et al. to prove the efficiency of the proposed model. Results demonstrate that coherence bandwidth and coherence time for proposed model are lower than those of reference papers. Moreover, the impact of K factor on channel statistics was studied. Functions developed in this work will enable system designers to analyze the performance of various vehicular communication systems. Validation of results with measurements was not possible due to the scarcity of the V2V channel measured data.

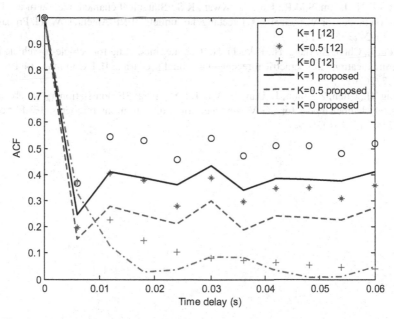

Fig. 4. Autocorrelation function for W = 8 m and for different values of K factor.

References

1. Zadobrischi, E., Dimian, M.: Vehicular communications utility in road safety applications: a step toward self-aware intelligent traffic systems. Symmetry **13**(3), 438 (2021)
2. Arena, F., Giovanni, P.: An overview of vehicular communications. Future Internet **11**(2), 27 (2019)
3. Matolak, D.W.: Modeling the vehicle-to-vehicle propagation channel: a review. Radio Sci. **49**(9), 721–736 (2014)

4. El Zorkany, M., et al.: Vehicle to vehicle communication: scope, importance, challenges, research directions and future. Open Transp. J. **14**(4), 86–98 (2020)
5. Chebil, J., Zormati, H., Taher, J.B.H.: Geometry based channel modeling for V2V communication: a review. Int. J. Antennas Propag. **2021**, 1–10 (2021)
6. Karedal, J., et al.: A geometry-based stochastic MIMO model for vehicle-to-vehicle communications. IEEE Trans. Wirel. Commun. **8**(7), 3646–3657 (2009)
7. Dreyer, N., et al.: A comparison of stochastic and deterministic channel models for V2V applications. In: Proceedings of the 2020 EuCNC, Dubrovnik, Croatia, pp. 79–83 (2020)
8. Yin, X., Cheng, X.: Propagation Channel Characterization, Parameter Estimation, and Modeling for Wireless Communications. Wiley, Singapore (2016)
9. Jiang, H., Zhang, Z., Gui, G.: A novel estimated wideband geometry-based vehicle-to-vehicle channel model using an AoD and AoA estimation algorithm. IEEE Access **7**, 35124–35131 (2019)
10. Wu, S., Wang, C.-X., Aggoune, e.-H.M, Alwakeel, M.M., You, X.: A general 3-D non-stationary 5G wireless channel model. IEEE Trans. Commun. **66**(7), 3065–3078 (2018)
11. Avazov, N., Islam, S.M.R., Park, D., Kwak, K.S.: Statistical characterization of a 3-D propagation model for V2V channels in rectangular tunnels. IEEE Antennas Wirel. Propag. Lett. **16**, 2392–2395 (2017)
12. Zhou, J., Chen, Z., Jiang, H., Kikuchi, H.: Channel modelling for vehicle-to-vehicle MIMO communications in geometrical rectangular tunnel scenarios. IET Commun. **14**(19), 3420–3427 (2020)
13. Jiang, H., Chen, Z., Zhou, J., Dang, J., Wu, L.: A general 3D non-stationary wideband twin-cluster channel model for 5G V2V tunnel communication environments. IEEE Access **7**, 137744–137751 (2019)

Avoiding Hazardous Color Combinations in Traffic Signs on STN Based Model for Autonomous Vehicles

Sagdat Okimbek[1](✉) [iD], Nurlan Razak[1](✉) [iD], Iskander Akhmetov[1,2](✉) [iD], and Alexandr Pak[1](✉) [iD]

[1] Kazakh-British Technical University Almaty, Almaty, Kazakhstan
s_okimbek@kbtu.kz
[2] Institute of Information and Computational Technologies, Almaty, Kazakhstan
i.akhmetov@ipic.kz
http://iict.kz

Abstract. The future in which autonomous vehicles will become commonplace is very near. The biggest companies around the world are testing autonomous vehicles. But despite the rapid progress in this area, there are still unresolved technical problems that prevent the spreading of self-driving vehicles. As a result, we are still quite far from "self-driving" cars, even though marketing is the opposite of us. Of course, driver assistance technologies capable of keeping the lane, braking, and following the road rules (under human supervision) are entering the market thanks to Tesla.

Nowadays, there is a problem; an autonomous car may suddenly stop. Some colors cause panic in self-driving vehicles, becoming a safety threat. This research paper approached a model using a deep neural network that identifies color combinations to prevent panic in autonomous cars by combining outputs from event-based cameras. Finally, we show the advantages of using event-based vision, and this approach outperforms algorithms based on standard cameras.

1 Introduction

There is a total system failure, an autonomous vehicle may leave the lane or suddenly stop. Sample of color combinations that cause a state of panic in a self-driving vehicle, and this becomes a safety threat. The pattern of color combinations can be easily applied to T-shirts or stickers on road signs or shopping bags. Hackers can take advantage of this, too.

The problem lies in the imperfection of artificial intelligence, which comes out in image recognition. The algorithm uses a camera to identify the environment, such as the road, and to detect obstacles [4]. If recognition fails, the car stops for safety reasons. The camera in the car sees the same spot several times, its reaction will be unique each time. In addition to real barriers, the article [7] describes the Unified Map, which depicts the outputs of numerous detection systems as fictitious obstacles. Autonomous driving technologies are projected

N. T. Nguyen et al. (Eds.): ICCCI 2022, LNAI 13501, pp. 809–822, 2022.
https://doi.org/10.1007/978-3-031-16014-1_64

to dramatically increase driving safety and convenience by relieving a driver's strain, especially in hazardous conditions. Nevertheless, another highly regarded work [4] has demonstrated that using geometric cues alone is insufficient in the situation of recognizing things that cover only limited visual areas and appear in all possible shapes and dimensions. To find traffic information, color-based detectors for artificial road markings and obstruction detectors based on Light Detection, also Ranging sensors are proposed, as well as pedestrian and vehicle detectors. If the road is assumed to be flat, any object spotted by a single LiDAR sensor that is a given height is simply classified as an obstacle. The problem with technology is computing. In order to simplify the computing, in contrast to typical cameras, event cameras, including the Dynamic Vision Sensor (DVS) article [9], are bio-inspired sensors that do not acquire entire images at a fixed frame rate but instead feature autonomous pixels that output only intensity changes asynchronously at the time they occur. Event cameras, when linked with specially built neural networks, can detect the dynamics of a scene with low latency, outperforming state-of-the-art systems based on ordinary cameras (Fig. 1).

The writers of the paper [1] demonstrated that in the sphere of autonomous vehicles, there are issues with updating cycles. Over-the-air updates, as used by Tesla, are a means of distributing new models from a company's servers to consumers' automobiles. According to Consumer Reports, Tesla's Autopilot semi-autonomous driving functions have experienced modest gains in terms of safety and dependability with recent updates. Unfortunately, significant data transfers may be required for these over-the-air upgrades of existing CNN/DNN models. Larger models, like as AlexNet, would require 240MB of data to be transferred to the vehicle from the server. A smaller model would necessitate less communication, which would allow for more frequent updates.

Detection of tiny and unforeseen traffic hazards, such as misplaced cargo and color combinations that could provide a safety risk. As a result, self-driving automobiles on public highways must be capable of avoiding hazards. This endeavor is difficult because of the resulting demand for environment perception systems. It is necessary to find a precise solution to these challenges in order to fix them.

This article has used STN based model for object detection. Spatial Transformer Networks rotate the original image so that the main classifier network can more easily identify the desired object. Spatial transformers can be used in CNN to tackle a variety of issues, such as: (i)image classification: a CNN model has been trained to recognize the multifarious classification of images, such as whether they contain a digit - and if so, what position, shades of different colors and the size of the digit can differ dramatically for each instance; (ii) a spatial transformer that cuts and normalizes the scale in the corresponding area can make the subsequent classification task easier and result in better classification performance, co-localization: given a large number of images containing various cases of the very same unfamiliar class, a spatial transformer can be used to distinguish them in each image; (iii) The spatial transformer is used for tasks that require attention, although it is more flexible and can only be

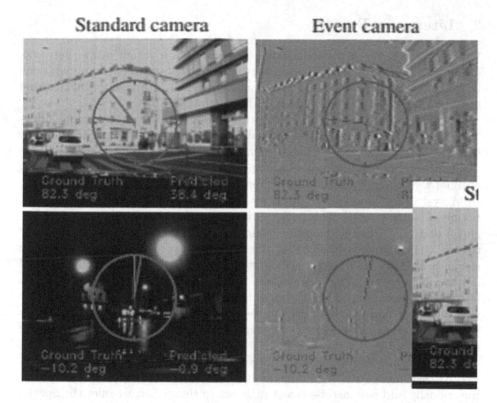

Fig. 1. Performance of steering angle regression on grayscale frames and event camera data in the first and second columns respectively. Visual features can be retrieved from grayscale frames in the first row, which depict a sunny day. The network, however, predicts an incorrect steering angle due to camera saturation and a lack of temporal information. When using grayscale frames, the network struggles to anticipate the correct steering angle in the second row, which depicts a night scene.

trained through error backpropagation rather than reinforcement learning. One of the main advantages of employing a model is that the transformed input at a lower resolution can be used instead of the raw data at a higher resolution, which improves computing efficiency. This paper has been organized in the following way to present our work: Sects. 2 and 3 summarize the methodologies in this field; Sect. 4 presents our experiments and results; Sect. 5 examines our conclusions and future work.

According to research, we offer a basic and easy-to-implement form detection-based approach for traffic sign identification. To reduce classification time, the proposed technique can be parallelized.

2   Literature Review

We cover the key notions of modeling transformations using neural networks [4–6,10,12,13], learning and analyzing transformation-invariant representations [1,2,7,11], as well as how deep learning has ushered in a new era of machine learning outside of computer vision in this section [3,8,9].

Current Transformer Neural Network architecture has a tremendous drawback in terms of its attention mechanism computational complexity, namely being $O(N^2)$. This causes Transformers inefficiency while working with long sequences. Therefore, lots of researchers turn towards solving this problem in an optimal way using stochastic and heuristic approaches [13].

A system for autonomous driving was presented built on the idea of overtaking and following [4]. This policy directs the vehicle to follow an automobile ahead of it, and when it gets near enough, it performs an overtaking maneuver to pass the car and then return to the lane. This work took advantage of the strength of CNN for object tracking, which was used to keep driving behind our autonomous car. The pixel location of the tracker, as well as data from a laser scanning sensor, are employed as input signals in a PID controller, which is in charge of independently driving the vehicle. In addition, we evaluated our proposed strategy in the Gazebo simulator, with the results indicating that the method is feasible.

Convolutional Neural Networks are a powerful type of model, but they're limited by their incapacity to be dimensionally unchangeable input data in a computationally and parameter-efficient manner. In this paper, we offer the Spatial Transformer, a new learnable module that explicitly permits spatial data manipulation within the network. This new module may be added to existing convolutional architectures to allow neural networks to proactively spatially adjust feature maps based on the feature map itself without requiring further training or changing the optimization process. We show that utilizing spatial transformers results in models that learn invariance to translation, scaling, rotation, and so more generic warping, ending in best-in-class performance on a variety of benchmarks and transformation classes.

We suggest employing a Convolutional Neural Network for visual recognition of places. The research focuses on automatically detecting and extracting interesting parts from a query image. These areas are utilized to generate an image encoding from a vector of locally aggregated descriptors, which is then used to recover the image. Unlike other methods, which use the complete image to construct the encoding, we just use the most essential image interest sections in our approach. This improves invariance to changes in lighting, occlusions, and extreme viewpoints of view. The incorporation of a completely convolutional spatial transformer based on the convolutional neural network architecture is another contribution of the work [6].

The ability to recognize minor road hazards, such as misplaced luggage, is critical for self-driving automobiles. With a vision system, we tackle this difficult and rarely handled subject, [10]. Convolutional Neural Networks are a powerful class of models, but they are hampered by their inability to be spatially invariant to the input data while remaining computationally and parameter economically. In this paper, we offer the Spatial Transformer, a new learnable module that explicitly permits spatial data manipulation within the network. This differentiable module can be added to present convolutional architectures, letting neural networks dynamically spatially modify feature maps based on the feature map itself, without the need for additional training or changes to the optimization process [5].

Many end-to-end tasks involving autonomous driving have been successfully implemented using CNN. Previous end-to-end steering control approaches used an image or an image sequence as input and used CNN to directly forecast steering angle. Despite the fact that learning a single task on steering angles has produced significant results, vehicle control cannot be obtained only through steering angles. We present an end-to-end multi-task learning system for predicting steering angle and speed control at the same time in this study. Because predicting precise speed values with only visual inputs is difficult, we first propose a technique to estimate the speed of discrete orders and steering angles with image sequences. Furthermore, researchers provide a multi-modal multi-task network that uses prior feedback speeds and visual records as inputs to forecast speed values and steering angles. The public Udacity dataset and a newly collected SAIC dataset are used in the experiments. The suggested model accurately predicts steering angles and speed values, according to the results. In addition, we improve failure data synthesis methods to address the issue of error accumulation in real-world road tests [12].

Clustering techniques are used to divide an existing set of items into groups based on their attribute similarity. The authors present mathematical procedures for determining beginning points (centroids) and subsequent cluster propagation. The competitive expansion of clusters is based on the absorption of boundary (contiguous) objects. If the object maximizes the cluster's total energy, it is absorbed by that cluster or moved from a neighboring cluster. Noise is made up of the leftover objects that haven't been grouped. The algorithm's parameter identification problem is next considered. On numerous publicly available test data sets, preliminary results on clustering and parameter identification have been obtained [1].

An excellent approach has been proposed for assisting a driver in making overtaking judgments in bad nighttime dark conditions on a two-lane single carriageway road. A tough road situation is presented here, in which an automobile is moving in the same side as the test vehicle and another vehicle is approaching from the other side. Due to the darkness of the environment, only the headlights and taillights of any vehicle are visible. It's tough to estimate distance and speed with more accuracy, at nighttime when vehicles aren't visible. The proposed assistance system can assess the actual and slow car's related distance and speed in front of the test car and the vehicle arriving from the other direction by observing taillights and headlights. The necessary spacing, level of condition of the road, speed, and acceleration for safely passing is then computed. Eventually, the decision to overtake is made in such a way that no vehicle collisions occur. In terms of accuracy and safety, several real-time investigations show that the estimation surpasses state-of-the-art methodologies utilizing a low-cost 2D camera [7].

Self-driving cars have made great progress recently, and they will play a major part in future intelligent transportation systems. Driverless vehicles would have to be able to navigate along collision-free paths while complying with traffic laws in order to be successful on real roads. In contrast to many existing approaches that employ preconfigured maps of highways and traffic signals, we describe algorithms and systems that use Unified Map generated using numerous on-board sensors that detect objects, other autos, traffic signs, and pedestrians. The suggested map includes not just information on surrounding real impediments, but also virtual obstacles such as traffic signals and pedestrians. The path planner can find collision-free paths while adhering to traffic restrictions using this map. The proposed algorithms were tested in a variety of situations, including the 2012 Hyundai Autonomous Ground Vehicle [11].

Due to [2] ability to measure distances and perform 3D surface mappings, laser imaging detection and ranging (LiDAR) sensors can be employed in a variety of applications. LiDAR sensors, on the other hand, require a stabilizing platform in certain conditions, such as in a moving vehicle, to prevent terrain imperfections from distorting their results. Furthermore, precise platform control is one of the most difficult problems in modern control engineering. Despite the fact that numerous methods for this problem have been proposed, the high computational cost of control algorithms remains their most significant limitation.

At the global, regional, and national levels, road safety is a serious concern, both in terms of the number of road fatalities and the economic impact of these incidents. Combating road insecurity is a top issue for all countries, as traffic continues to rise and, despite many countries' efforts to improve road safety, much more has to be done to reduce the number of deaths and injuries. In this work, we examine the most widely used methods for detecting driver distractions. Furthermore, in the framework of intelligent transportation, we suggest a novel technique for reducing road crashes. The proposed methodology appears to be efficient and accurate based on preliminary results [3].

Apart from computer vision, deep learning has ushered in a new era of machine learning. Image categorization, segmentation, and object detection have all used convolutional neural networks. Despite recent development, network architecture is still in its early phases, and optimum experiences in the area of deep design, modest size, and rapid training time have yet to be established. Residual Squeeze VGG16, a compressed convolutional neural network model which tackles the issue of speed and size, is proposed in this research. The suggested model compresses the previously successful VGG16 network and improves on the following aspects: (a) reduced model size, (b) faster velocity, (c) consuming knowledge for convergence rate, stronger adaptation, and degradation resolution, and (4) on the extremely large-scale grand challenge, equals the recognition the non-compressed model's accuracy of MIT 365-Standard picture dataset of places VGG16 is 88.4%smaller and takes 23.86% longer to train than the proposed model. This supports our assertion that the current proposal improves on the best characteristics of VGG16 (citeQassim2018) [9].

One of the bio-inspired vision event camera devices captures the natural rhythms of a scene while filtering out extraneous information. The goal of this study is to use a deep neural network to maximize the power of event cameras for a tough movement estimation task steering angle prognostication. To build the most out of this sensor algorithm combination, we adapt state-of-the-art neural networks to the result of occasion sensors and comprehensively examine the performance of our method on an available public large-scale event-camera dataset is about 1000 km [8]. We provide theoretical and practical arguments into why event cameras may accurately anticipate steering in conditions where ordinary cameras can't, like weak lighting and fast motion.

3 Data

In the project we create folder with three sub-folders: train, test, and meta. Each of the 43 folders in our 'train' folder represents a different class. The folder's size ranges from 0 to 42. Using the OS module, we iterate over all of the classes, inserting images and labels into the data and labels array. Meanwhile, we've created lists for whole pictures and labels. The data has the shape 39209, 30, 30, 3, suggesting that there are 39,209 30 pixel images in total, with the final three showing that the data contains colored.

4 Methods

The model could be incorporated into a typical CNN architecture that allows for spatial transformation [5]. Individual input samples determine the action, whereas the accompanying behavior is determined during the problem's training. The spatial transformer modules are a dynamic process that may effectively spatially modify a picture by implementing processing and management for each example, unlike many other layers where the receptive fields are stable and local. Dynamic analysis takes the opposite approach and is performed while the program is running. The dynamic test will monitor system memory, functional behavior, response time, and overall system performance. This method is similar to the way a malicious third party can interact with an application. Rotations, non-rigid deformations, cropping, and scaling, are all possible transformations for the full feature map see Fig. 2.

It is a differentiable module that applies a spatial transform to a characteristic map during a single forward pass where the transformation is driven by a specific input, creating a single output characteristic map. For multichannel inputs, the same distortion is applied to each channel. The spatial transformation consists of three parts, shown in Fig. 5. First, the localization network receives the input feature map and through a series of hidden layers outputs the spatial transformation parameters that must be applied to the feature map - this gives

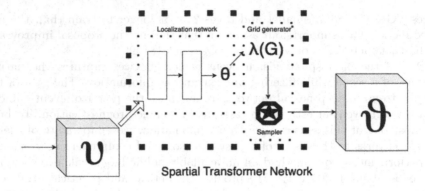

Fig. 2. The architecture of a spatial transformer module.

the transformation at the input. Then, in the second part, the predicted transform parameters are used to create a sampling grid, which is a set of points at which the input map must be sampled to obtain the transformed output. This is done by the grid generator. Finally, the feature map and the sample grid are taken as input to the sampler, creating an output map sampled from the input at the grid points.

4.1 Evaluation

The formulas of precision, recall, F1 measure are following:

$$Precision = \frac{TP}{TP + FP} \tag{1}$$

where TP - true positive, FP - false positive, FN - false negative.

$$Recall = \frac{TP}{TP + FN} \tag{2}$$

$$F1 = 2 * \frac{Precision * Recall}{Precision + Recall} \tag{3}$$

4.2 Localization Network

The localization network receives feature map $U \epsilon R^{H x W x C}$ which includes width, height, channel and the parameters T_θ applied to the feature map $\Theta = f_{loc}(U)$.

4.3 Grid Generator

The grid applies a sample kernel that is focused at a given place mostly on input for every output pixel. The output pixels are arranged on a regular grid $G = G_i$ of pixels $G_i = (x_i, y_i)$, then it creates an output feature map $V \epsilon R^{H' x W' x C'}$ where

H is height and W is width, and C is number of channels. For example, assume T_θ is two dimensional transformation A_θ. The transformation is in (4).

$$\begin{pmatrix} x_i^s \\ y_i^s \end{pmatrix} = T_\theta(G_i) = A_\theta \begin{pmatrix} x_i^t \\ y_i^t \\ 1 \end{pmatrix} = \begin{bmatrix} \theta_{11} & \theta_{12} & \theta_{13} \\ \theta_{21} & \theta_{22} & \theta_{23} \end{bmatrix} \begin{pmatrix} x_i^t \\ y_i^t \\ 1 \end{pmatrix} \tag{4}$$

where (x_i^t, y_i^t) are needed coordinates of regular grid in output map, and (x_i^s, y_i^s) are the source coordinates in the feature map which defines points, A_θ is transformation matrix. With the transform we can crop, rotate, and scale in the input map, it requires six parameters of A_θ to be created by localization network Fig. 3.

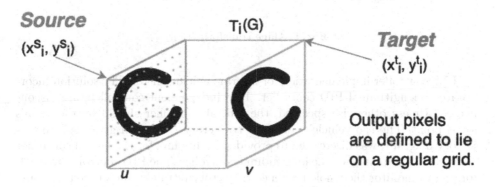

Fig. 3. Identity Transformation

4.4   Sampler

A sampler takes the set of points $T_\theta(G)$, with feature map U and creates the output map V. Each (x_i^s, y_i^s) coordinate in $T_\theta(G)$ finds spatial location in input and aim is to find the value in output V. The formula: (5)

$$V_i^c = \sum_n^H \sum_m^W U_{nm}^c k(x_i^s - m; \Phi_x) k(y_i^s - n; \Phi_y) \tag{5}$$

$$\forall i \in [1...H'W'], \forall c \in [1...C] \tag{6}$$

where Φ_x and Φ_y are the parameters of the generic sampler kernel $k()$ which defines interpolation of image, U_{nm}^c is a value at the location (n, m) in channel c in input and V_i^c is value in output at pixel i in channel c Fig. 4.

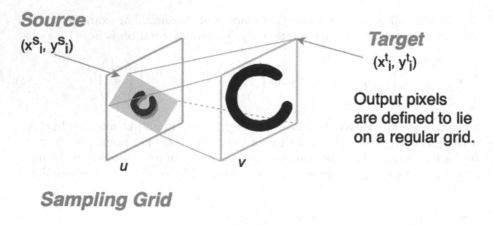

Fig. 4. Affine transformation

PID controller implementation for lateral vehicle control. The solution incorporates a longitudinal PID controller. Two independent controllers are disconnected. Unless otherwise specified, the lateral controller should be the issue's focus point. The ego vehicle's reference trajectory (shown in green on the trajectory diagram) was discretized to provide touchpoints for the lateral controller and velocity setpoints for the longitudinal controller. The PID controller was calibrated to monitor the whole reference trajectory (straight and curved sections) at varying longitudinal speeds. Even if the controller doesn't compromise comfort or safety, tracking accuracy is limited, especially on steeper bends. A single PID controller is a "sufficient" method for handling lateral vehicle dynamics, although more sophisticated approaches (such as gain scheduling) and/or better controllers are preferable. With the embedded disturbance observer, the vehicle model acts like its nominal model within its bandwidth. Delay in the actual vehicle's "steer-by-wire" system may create stability concerns by destabilizing the plant frequency response. A communication disturbance observer (CDOB) is introduced into the steering actuation loop to compensate for this delay.

5   Experiment Setup

We'll use a CNN model to classify the photos into their appropriate groups (Convolutional Neural Network). For picture categorization, CNN is the best option. Although, the train test split() method in the sklearn package is used to split training and testing data. We utilize the to categorical method from the keras.utils package to transform the labels in y_train and t_test into one-hot encoding. Cause of that we have several classes to categorize, we compile the model with Adam optimizer, which performs well, and the loss is "categorical cross-entropy." After constructing the model architecture, we use model.fit() to train the model. And tested batch sizes of 32 and 64 were with 64 batches, our model fared better. The accuracy was stable after 15 epochs. With a test folder and the details tied to the photo locations and their associated class labels in a test.csv file, we may test our model. We retrieve the image path and labels using pandas. Then, in order to take decisions the model, we must scale our photographs to 3030 pixels and create a NumPy array with all of the image data. We used the accuracy score from sklearn.metrics to see how our model predicted the real labels. Eventually, we will save the model that we have trained with the Keras model. The function save() is used to save data.

6 Results

Totally 16 attempts were made from different angles. 11 of them were true positive, algorithm recognized road signs with the sample color combinations even from the left edge, 2 of them were false positive - when signs did not have hazardous colors but were placed in a place where the algorithm could not identify them, 3 times were false negative - when traffic signs have dangerous colors on them but did not recognize, and 1 true negative - when sign did not even have those colors (7).

Calculation:

$$Precision = \frac{11}{11+2} = 0.85 \tag{7}$$

$$Recall = \frac{11}{11+3} = 0.78 \tag{8}$$

$$F1 = 2 * \frac{0.85 * 0.78}{0.85 + 0.78} = 0.81 \tag{9}$$

Model was tested in complex conditions like in poorly lighted apartment. After calculation accuracy, which is weighted average of Precision and Recall, F1 equal to 0.81. That is not bad for sign recognition with sample of colors, but there is a room to grow.

After these test, I have made another model testing with library TrafficSign-Net, model was passed almost 300 epochs in Fig. 5.

Test	Test accuracy	Train accuracy	Validation accuracy
1	87.324%	97.324%	93.367%
2	87.645%	97.645%	94.367%

Fig. 5. Testing with library TrafficSignNet

where test accuracy in first test was equal to 87.324, in second test almost the same 87.645. However, in train dataset model had shown good accuracy 97.324. Validation accuracy also was not bad 93.367. In TrafficSignNet we have small amount of signs with dangerous color combinations, which is not good for our condition. But, model was trained good enough for recognizing the rest of signs on road. We successfully identified the traffic signs classifier with 95% accuracy in this project using source code, and we also visualized how our accuracy and loss increases over time, which is really excellent for a simple CNN model. The proposed solution in this work has low accuracy but the proposed solution has following advantages over other deep learning models. Deep learning models with CNN can achieve about 98% accuracy but they are computationally complex and require costly resources to train. They cannot be parallelized and classification time is high.

7   Conclusion

Spatial Transformer Network is used to minimize a set of colors that could be hazardous to autonomous cars. The model's findings teach interpretability to translations, scale, rotation, and additional genetic warping, resulting in numerous of benchmarks and transformation categories. With this work, we were able to achieve a 95/100 test accuracy in a controlled setting. We present the spatial transformer, a confidence level module for neural networks, throughout this investigation. This module can really be added to a network to perform explicit features' spatial transformations, permitting neural networks to model data in novel ways. It can be learned from start to finish without compromising the loss function.

In future works, there is plan to using STN model for various things on the road to avoid panic of self-driving car.

Acknowledgments. This research is conducted within the Committee of Science of the Ministry of Education and Science of the Republic of Kazakhstan under the grant number AP09260670 "Development of methods and algorithms for augmentation of input data for modifying vector embeddings of words".

References

1. Ahmad, W., Sahil, S., Mughal, A.: Predicting solar intensity using cluster analysis. In: Nguyen, N.T., Pimenidis, E., Khan, Z., Trawiński, B. (eds.) ICCCI 2018, Part I. LNCS (LNAI), vol. 11055, pp. 549–560. Springer, Cham (2018). https://doi.org/10.1007/978-3-319-98443-8_50

2. Antonio, J., Gutiérrez, T., Villalobos, P.Q.: Design and implementation of an automatic control system using motors and control sensors to stabilize a horizontal platform with a LiDAR sensor. Computación y Sistemas 26(1), 389–397 (2022). https://doi.org/10.13053/CyS-26-1-3906

3. Bekka, R., Kherbouche, S., Bouhissi, H.E.: Distraction detection to predict vehicle crashes: a deep learning approach. Computación y Sistemas **26**(1), 373–387 (2022). https://doi.org/10.13053/CyS-26-1-3871

4. Campos, R.L., Perez, L.O.R., Carranza, J.M.: Following and overtaking: a policy for autonomous car driving. Computacion y Sistemas **24**(3), 1149–1157 (2020). https://doi.org/10.13053/CYS-24-3-3475

5. Jaderberg, M., Simonyan, K., Zisserman, A., Kavukcuoglu, K.: Spatial transformer networks. In: Cortes, C., Lawrence, N., Lee, D., Sugiyama, M., Garnett, R. (eds.) Advances in Neural Information Processing Systems, vol. 28. Curran Associates, Inc. (2015)

6. Lugo Sánchez, O.E., Sossa, H., Zamora, E.: Robust place recognition using convolutional neural networks. Computacion y Sistemas **24**(4), 1589–1605 (2020). https://doi.org/10.13053/CYS-24-4-3340

7. Mandal, G., Bhattacharya, D., De, P.: Real time vision based overtaking assistance system for drivers at night on two-lane single carriageway. Computacion y Sistemas **25**(2), 403–416 (2021). https://doi.org/10.13053/CyS-25-2-3783

8. Maqueda, A.I., Loquercio, A., Gallego, G., Garcia, N., Scaramuzza, D.: Event-based vision meets deep learning on steering prediction for self-driving cars. Proceedings of the IEEE Computer Society Conference on Computer Vision and Pattern Recognition June 2018, pp. 5419–5427 (2018). https://doi.org/10.1109/CVPR.2018.00568

9. Qassim, H., Verma, A., Feinzimer, D.: Compressed residual-VGG16 CNN model for big data places image recognition. In: 2018 IEEE 8th Annual Computing and Communication Workshop and Conference, CCWC 2018 January 2018, pp. 169–175 (2018). https://doi.org/10.1109/CCWC.2018.8301729

10. Ramos, S., Gehrig, S., Pinggera, P., Franke, U., Rother, C.: Detecting unexpected obstacles for self-driving cars: fusing deep learning and geometric modeling. In: IEEE Intelligent Vehicles Symposium, Proceedings 2017-July–December, pp. 1025–1032 (2017). https://doi.org/10.1109/IVS.2017.7995849

11. Shim, I., et al.: Self-driving-car Boss. IEEE Trans. Intell. Transp. Syst. [11] **16**(4), 1–15 (2015)

12. Yang, Z., Zhang, Y., Yu, J., Cai, J., Luo, J.: End-to-end multi-modal multi-task vehicle control for self-driving cars with visual perceptions. In: Proceedings - International Conference on Pattern Recognition 2018 August–January 2018), pp. 2289–2294 (2018). https://doi.org/10.1109/ICPR.2018.8546189
13. Ziyaden, A., Yelenov, A., Pak, A.: Long-context transformers: a survey. In: 2021 5th Scientific School Dynamics of Complex Networks and their Applications (DCNA), pp. 215–218 (2021). https://doi.org/10.1109/DCNA53427.2021.9587279

Feasibility of RSS Measurements for Smartphone-Based Indoor Acoustic Localization

Veronika Hromadova[iD], Peter Brida[✉][iD], Roman Jarina[iD], and Juraj Machaj[iD]

University of Zilina, Zilina, Slovakia
{veronika.hromadova,peter.brida,roman.jarina,
juraj.machaj}@feit.uniza.sk

Abstract. Mobile smartphones' potential for usage in innovative localization systems based on audio signal processing is limited due to a lack of technical specifications on audio input sensitivity in the upper limit of the audio range when the embedded microphone is considered as an acoustical sensor. Acoustical intensity may change with distance as well as rotation of the smartphone, however, there is a lack of information on essential characteristics of microphones implemented in smartphones. In this paper, tests are performed to investigate the feasibility of smartphones for acoustic localization. The objective was to evaluate the impact of the movement in a complex room on the RSS (Received Signal Strength) acoustic signal received by the smartphone. Experiments were performed under the worst-case scenario, in which both receiver and transmitter of acoustic signals were represented by smartphones.

Keywords: Smartphones · Indoor localization · Acoustical measurements · Frequency response · Received signal strength

1 Introduction

Location services are becoming increasingly important and widely used in a variety of applications. One of the placement options we address in our research is the implementation of audio signals, which is aimed at developing an acoustic location system that can be used with standard smartphones. Several papers on acoustic sensing-based indoor location systems have recently been published [1–5]. Since smartphones are always on hand, they represent attractive candidates for use as sound sensors with built-in microphones.

However, to avoid bothering the user and their surroundings, signals for the acoustic location must utilize the inaudible frequency range. Because of smartphone hardware restrictions, these systems use acoustic waves that are close to or slightly above the upper limit of audible frequencies, the available bandwidth is typically below 22 kHz. When setting up a localization system, it's important to understand the degree of signal drop based on the environment, distance, architecture, and hardware used.

Before proceeding with any additional scientific study, we must first verify whether commercially available smartphones fulfil the required technical specifications. This

© The Author(s), under exclusive license to Springer Nature Switzerland AG 2022
N. T. Nguyen et al. (Eds.): ICCCI 2022, LNAI 13501, pp. 823–835, 2022.
https://doi.org/10.1007/978-3-031-16014-1_65

study is focused on smartphones and their embedded input/output acoustical transducers in a frequency range of around 20 kHz. The main goal was to find the decrease in RSS (Received Signal Strength) depending on the rotation of the smartphone and the dependence of RSS on distance. Standardly, the human ear can hear frequencies ranging from 20 Hz up to 20 kHz. On the other hand, as people get older, their ability to perceive higher frequencies decreases. Hearing frequencies above 18 kHz is difficult for anyone above the age of eighteen [6–10]. Moreover, according to studies on the effects of airborne ultrasonography on human hearing, an inaudible sound played on typical computer hardware has no health hazards [6, 7, 11–13].

Because RSS data are related to the distance between a transmitter and a receiver through an appropriate propagation model, they represent valuable source of information in localization systems [14–16]. Although acquiring RSS measurements is very simple, obtaining an appropriate propagation model is more difficult. The acoustic signal propagation model is not uniform; it is affected by parameters of the acoustic transducer, i.e. frequency response, directivity, etc., as well as environmental factors such as absorption, temperature, and humidity.

The paper is organized as follows, Sect. 2 provides an overview of indoor localization using sound, measurement scenarios are presented in Sect. 3, in Sect. 4 achieved results are presented and discussed and Sect. 5 concludes the paper.

2   Related Work

Based on the frequency band used for the acoustic signal for localization, we can divide the systems into two basic groups, namely the frequency band in ultrasound, above 20 kHz [1, 17, 18] and the frequency band below 20 kHz [5, 18, 19]. The problem with frequencies below 20 kHz is that their use can be sensed as noise by some users and therefore such systems are not widely popular.

The localization system proposed in [1] employs two scenarios. The first scenario was a receiver localization system: the system includes MS (Mobile Station) and reference nodes. The acoustic signal is transmitted by reference nodes and is received by the localized MS through its microphone. The authors created and designed the reference nodes which transmit a signal at a different time and interval than the others. The communications use two OFDM carrier frequencies, at 38.3 kHz and 40 kHz, with the signal comprising the node identification number.

The data gathered by MS was used to estimate position using a variation of the UKF (Unscented Kalman Filter) and the PF (Particle Filter). The outcomes were nearly the same in both cases, however, PF requires more computing resources. When using UKF the achieved error was 0.061 m with a standard deviation of 0.064 m. In the second scenario, the speaker localization system was tested. The localized MS in this case transmits an acoustic signal which is received by static reference nodes. The MS is not synchronized with the receiver, however, receivers share a common time base. In the experiment, a fusion of data from the IMU (Inertial Measurement Unit) and REKF (Robust Extended Kalman Filter) was used and achieved localization error was 0.13 m with a standard deviation of 0.08 m.

The location system in [17] consists of independent reference nodes that contain a radio transmitter, a receiver, and an ultrasound signal transmitter. The system combines the use of radio and acoustic signals. The reference node sends both signals at the same time, due to the different propagation speeds of the individual signals, the radio signal comes first and triggers the MS speaker to receive the acoustic signal. Positioning is performed using TDoA between acoustic and signals. The system operates in the 40 kHz frequency band, so both reference nodes and MS require special hardware. The achieved accuracy of the system was 12 cm. Subsequently, the authors supplemented the system with an ultrasonic compass which was added to the MS and reached an accuracy of 3° [20].

The localization system in the work [18] is called the Active Bat system, which is based on transmitting a short acoustic signal with a frequency of 40 kHz. The user wears a wireless badge called Bat, hence the name. The Bat can also be attached to a specific device. The system works by activating Bat via a radio signal, then sends an acoustic signal lasting 50 μs. This signal is then received by reference nodes that are mounted on the wall. These nodes measure the ToA of the acoustic signal and the position of the Bat is determined by circular lateration.

Because all the above-mentioned solutions use high frequencies it is required to develop special hardware solutions, thus increasing the cost of the localization system. However, when developing low-cost audio localization systems smartphones are widely considered mobile stations. Therefore, the frequency response of the built-in microphone in smartphones in the spectrum around 20 kHz [1–4] has to be considered in the design of the localization system. Therefore this paper is focusing on the evaluation of smartphone audio characteristics in the area of 20 kHz.

3 Measurement Scenarios

When deploying a sound-based localization system, it is necessary to know the degree of signal drop depending on the environment, distance, architecture of the building, and employed hardware. Therefore, in this paper measurements aimed to gain this information were performed.

The frequency response of a microphone is an essential property since it indicates how sensitive it is to various frequencies. The frequency response graph may be used to determine the range of frequencies that the microphone can pick up as well as the frequencies it is most sensitive to. At all the frequencies, a microphone with a flat frequency response gathers sound at the same volume. Because creating a completely flat frequency response is extremely difficult, the term "flat" is occasionally used to describe a frequency response with small variations over the frequency range [14]. The frequency response is typically measured in an anechoic room with a one-meter gap between the sound source and the microphone. For each frequency, the sound pressure level (SPL) is measured in dB on the reference as well as the measured microphone. The frequency response of the employed sound source (e.g. loudspeaker) is then used for correction.

The focus of this study is to carry out initial experiments on the frequency response and directivity of input/output acoustic transducers (i.e. microphones and speakers) implemented in commonly used smartphones as well as the upper-frequency range sound intensity variations in an indoor environment. Detailed specifications of the measurement setup are summarised in Table 1. The experiments were carried out in a recording studio at the Studio of Multimedia Creation, Department of Multimedia and Information-Communication Technology, University of Zilina.

Table 1. Specifications of hardware and software.

Device		Specification
Reference device	Norsonic Nor140 with Nor1225 condenser microphone [21]	Freefield sensitivity: 50 mV/Pa Frequency response: 3.15 Hz to 22 kHz Measurement range: −10 to 137 dB
Sound source	Samsung Galaxy A20	Year of release: 2019 Informative price: 150€
	OnePlus 7T PRO	Year of release: 2019 Informative price: 600€
Receiver	Huawei P20 PRO	Year of release: 2018 Informative price: 400€
	Honor 8	Year of release: 2016 Informative price: 250€
Recording software	WaveEditor [22]	WAV or MP3 recording formats

The experiments were performed in the following scenarios:

- Sound source calibration
- Impact of smartphone manipulation/rotation on RSS
- Impact of distance from the sound source on RSS
- Walking in a damped room
- Walking in an ordinary room

Description of the individual scenarios can be found in Subsects. 3.1–3.5 below.

3.1 Sound Source Calibration

In the first scenario, the sound source's frequency response was evaluated for calibration of the equipment. As reference measurement equipment, the calibrated Norsonic Nor140 sound level meter [21] was employed, it is a "class 1" sound analyser. The measurement arrangement is depicted in Fig. 1. The frequency responses of the Samsung Galaxy A20 and OnePlus 7T PRO smartphones, which were both considered as sound sources, were incorporated. The devices were positioned on microphone stands with smartphone holders at a distance of 1 m between the reference equipment and the smartphone speaker. Foam absorption panels were installed behind the stands, the floor was carpeted and the entire space was muted. The reverberation time in the measured zone was less than 0.2 s. The temperature during the experiments was 23 °C and the humidity was 34%. The audio volume of the smartphones has been set to maximum.

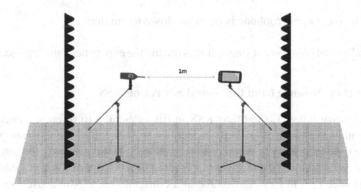

Fig. 1. Measurement scheme with the reference device.

3.2 Impact of Smartphone Manipulation/Rotation on RSS

The second scenario was performed to determine the effect of different rotations of the smartphone on the received signal strength (RSS) of an audio signal. The experimental measurements were performed at frequencies between 15 kHz and 22 kHz with a step of 1 kHz up to 20 kHz and a step of 0.2 kHz above 20 kHz. The testing frequencies were chosen this way since the main interest is in the use of the upper part of the spectrum for localization purposes. Pure tones were generated at the mentioned frequencies and radiated from the reference sound source (Galaxy A20) and recorded by the receiver represented by the Huawei P20 PRO smartphone.

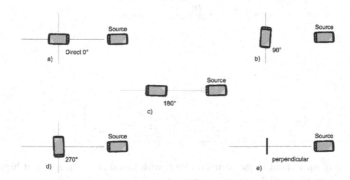

Fig. 2. Measurement scheme with the reference device.

Each tone lasted 25 ms, with a 50-ms gap between each generated tone. The rotation of the smartphone's body (and thus of a microphone, which is positioned at the bottom of the device) was as follows:

- direct, i.e. angle 0°, thus the microphone and speaker point towards each other,
- rotation 90°,
- rotation 180°, i.e. microphone and speaker point in the same direction
- rotation 270°,

• perpendicular, i.e. microphone is pointing down to the floor.

The individual positions of smartphones during the experiment are depicted in Fig. 2.

3.3 Impact of Distance from the Sound Source on RSS

It is obvious that the SPL (and thus RSS in dB calculated to reference energy 10^{-4}) declines with the distance, therefore, measurements in the third scenario are performed to estimate the dependency between distance and RSS. In this scenario, the sound source was placed on a stand, and the receiver represented by a smartphone was gradually moved up to a distance of 6 m from the source at a constant speed. An acoustic signal (pure tone) with a frequency of 20 kHz was generated by the source.

3.4 Random Walking in a Damped Room

The purpose of the fourth scenario was to find out how RSS changes as a user with a smartphone in hand is moving around the damped room. The measurement was done in two setups: In the first case, the sound source was put in the centre of the room, while in the second case, the sound source was placed on the perimeter of the room. The experiment was carried out in the acoustically damped room of the area 7×4 m. The user was moving in the room in the given trajectory, which can be seen in Fig. 3, with a speed of 1.2 m/s.

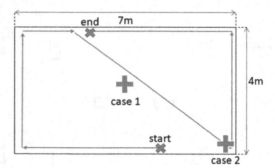

Fig. 3. Scheme of movement in the damped room, with sound source placement highlighted by green + sign in both cases (Color figure online)

3.5 Random Walking in the Ordinary Room

In the last scenario, the measurement with the sound source in the middle of a room was repeated in a room without acoustic damping. The trajectory of the user is shown in Fig. 4. The user starts in the corner of the room then walks around the perimeter of the room, and finally headed to the source of the acoustic signal.

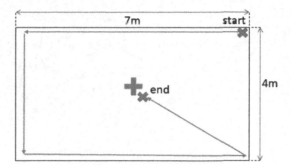

Fig. 4. Scheme of movement in the ordinary room, a sound source in the middle

4   Achieved Results

The results of the frequency response measured in the first scenario are presented in Fig. 5. From the achieved results it is clear that Samsung Galaxy A20 achieved more stable results (i.e. flatter characteristic), while the OnePlus 7T Pro had greater variations in SPL in the audio range above 15 kHz. Thus, the Samsung Galaxy A20 was chosen to serve as the reference acoustic source for the subsequent experiments.

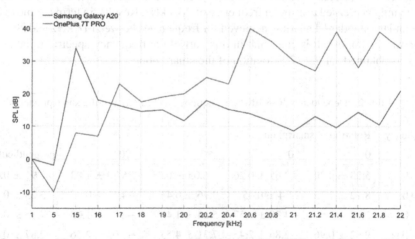

Fig. 5. Standard frequency response of speakers of the OnePlus 7T Pro and Samsung Galaxy A20 smartphones.

The measured frequency response of the smartphone receiver for each rotation in the second scenario is depicted in Fig. 6. Since inaudible audio signals are utilized in localization systems measurements were focused on frequencies above 18 kHz. It is important to find the highest possible frequency up to which smartphones can operate reliably. It can be concluded that the useable limit was 20.2 kHz in the worst-case scenario, which represents the transmission and reception of an acoustic signal by the smartphone's speaker and the smartphone's microphone, respectively.

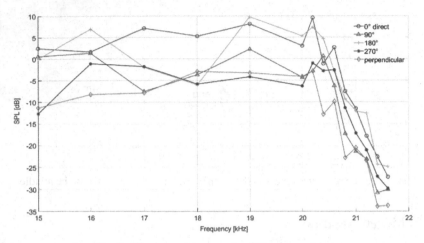

Fig. 6. Frequency response for different rotations.

We used the median of the measured values at 15 kHz as a reference value for evaluating frequency response for different rotations, therefore measured SPL [dB] values in the graph and table acquired both positive and negative values when SPL was higher and lower than reference value, respectively. From the results, it is clear that RSS is significantly decreased at a signal frequency of 20.4 kHz. Results, in terms of mean RSS value and the standard deviation, achieved for frequencies between 18 kHz and 20.2 kHz are shown in Table 2. It is clear that in this part of the frequency spectrum, the lowest RSS was obtained for the 270° rotation of the smartphone.

Table 2. Dependency RSS [dB] on frequency and rotation of the smartphone

Frequency	Rotation of smartphone				
	0°	90°	180°	270°	perpendicular
18 kHz	5.28 ± 0.30	−3.65 ± 0.26	−6.05 ± 0.38	−5.79 ± 1.83	−2.91 ± 0.63
19 kHz	8.12 ± 1.13	2.24 ± 0.45	9.76 ± 0.43	−4.17 ± 0.48	−3.25 ± 0.92
20 kHz	2.98 ± 0.66	−4.38 ± 2.57	5.24 ± 1.45	−6.31 ± 1.03	−4.15 ± 0.62
20.2 kHz	9.52 ± 0.96	−2.86 ± 2.45	7.31 ± 4.55	−1.03 ± 2.36	−2.87 ± 0.41

As one can see, the average RSS gradually decreased at the end of the observed frequency range, while its standard deviation was increased. From the results, it is clear that different rotations have a significant impact on readings and should be considered while developing the localization system based on acoustic signals.

The results achieved in the third scenario for the transmitter at the frequency of 20 kHz placed are shown in Fig. 7. The waveform of the received acoustic signal is represented by the first curve. The second curve represents normalized energy, which was created by squaring and averaging in a 1-s sliding window (1 s of movement corresponds with the distance change of approx. 0.24 m). The third curve shows normalized RSS, which declines with distance. Fluctuations in the graph are caused by wave interference due to partial reflections from walls. It is important to note that some reflections occurred although the room was highly damped.

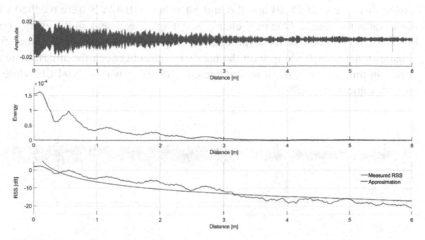

Fig. 7. Dependency of the received audio signal on distance. (Color figure online)

The red line in the figure shows an approximation of the dependency of the RSS samples on distance using the following logarithmic function:

$$RSS = -6.58 - 5.83 \log_{10}(d). \tag{1}$$

The approximation was performed on the measured data using the least square method with the resulting RMSE of 2.8 dB.

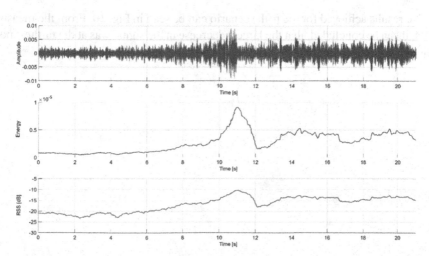

Fig. 8. Scenario 4 case 1 - moving around the damped room with the sound source in the middle.

The results achieved for the fourth scenario in a case when the sound source at a frequency of 20 kHz is placed in the middle of the room and in the corner of the room are shown in Fig. 8 and Fig. 9, respectively.

The maximum RSS that we can see as a peak in Fig. 8 corresponds to the smallest distance from the source, which was during the crossing of the room, while the lowest RSS was in this case −23.95 dB and the highest value −10.42 dB were reached when walking towards the source. One may clearly see it again as a peak in the energy curve (see Fig. 9). It was found that the largest signal drop was at the greatest distance from the acoustic signal source, along with the user's position between the smartphone and the source. In this scenario, the lowest detected RSS value was −23.94 dB while the highest RSS value was −7.85 dB.

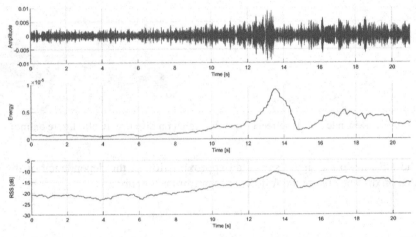

Fig. 9. Scenario 4 case 2 – moving around the damped room with the sound source at the edge.

The results achieved for the fifth scenario can be seen in Fig. 10. From the measurements, it can be concluded, that the largest decrease in the signal was at the farthest point while the user was blocking the direct signal with his body.

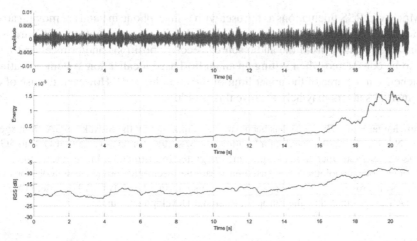

Fig. 10. Moving around an ordinary (undamped) room with the sound source is in the middle.

The lowest RSS value in this scenario was −21.77 dB while the highest value was −7.85 dB. From the presented results it is clear that RSS of the audio signal may be considered for positioning using smartphones when frequencies around 20 kHz are used. These frequencies are inaudible for humans, therefore audio signals used in a localization system will not cause any problems with audio noise. Moreover, it is clear that the majority of the off-the-shelf smartphone devices can operate (transmit and receive) signals up to 20.2 kHz. One of the main challenges may be additional attenuation caused by the orientation of the device, however, this problem may be compensated by utilizing data from inertial sensors implemented in smartphones.

5   Conclusion

In this paper, we first investigate the behaviour of the audio signal in the upper limit of the audible range. The goal was to prove that smartphones can be used to radiate as well as receive signals in the upper limit of the audible range and thus such signals can be used for positioning applications. The experiments were focused on the evaluation of the impact of distance and rotation of smartphones on intensity as well as fluctuations. The objective of the experimental scenarios was to evaluate signal characteristics during complex movement across the damped and ordinary room and its impact on the RSS of the acoustic signal.

It can be concluded that the attenuation of the propagated sound is around 3.89 dB per meter at 20 kHz in the damped room. In the worst-case scenario, both the source and receiver of the acoustic signal are smartphones that are not primarily designed to work in such high acoustic frequencies. Changes in received signal strength (RSS) due to rotation are around 14 dB for spectrum in the range of 18 to 20.2 kHz. We explored the highest frequency at which smartphones could be utilized for positioning applications using audio signals. Based on the achieved results can be concluded that 20.2 kHz is the maximum feasible frequency since RSS drops significantly at 20.4 kHz.

Moreover, RSS fluctuations as the user with a smartphone in hand are moving around the damped and ordinary rooms were examined. It is important to note that RSS drops and fluctuations resulting from the audio source-receiver positions and/or receiver rotation have to be considered when setting up an audio-based localization system operating at frequencies in the area of the upper limit of the audible range. However, the use of data from inertial sensors may help to solve this problem.

Acknowledgement. This work has been partially supported by the Slovak VEGA grant agency, Project No. 1/0588/22 "Research of a location-aware system for achievement of QoE in 5G and B5G networks", and Operational Programme Integrated Infrastructure: Independent research and development of technological kits based on wearable electronics products, as tools for raising hygienic standards in a society exposed to the virus causing the COVID-19 disease, ITMS code 313011ASK8, co-funded by the European Regional Development Fund.

References

1. Bordoy, J.: Acoustic localization in mixed environments with line-of-sight and non-line-of-sight, p. 139, July 2020
2. Cai, C., Zheng, R., Li, J., Zhu, L., Pu, H., Hu, M.: Asynchronous acoustic localization and tracking for mobile targets. IEEE Internet Things J. **7**(2), 830–845 (2020). https://doi.org/10.1109/JIOT.2019.2945054
3. Li, S., Rashidzadeh, R.: Hybrid indoor location positioning system. IET Wirel. Sens. Syst. **9**(5), 257–264 (2019). https://doi.org/10.1049/iet-wss.2018.5237
4. Qiu, C., Mutka, M.W.: Silent whistle: effective indoor positioning with assistance from acoustic sensing on smartphones. In: 2017 IEEE 18th International Symposium on a World of Wireless, Mobile and Multimedia Networks (WoWMoM), pp. 1–6, June 2017. https://doi.org/10.1109/WoWMoM.2017.7974312
5. Hiroaki, M.: Indoor Acoustic Localization using Reflected Signals, 25 March 2021. https://doi.org/10.14943/doctoral.k14584. Accessed 24 May 2021
6. Ashihara, K.: Threshold of hearing for pure tones between 16 and 30 kHz. J. Acoust. Soc. Am. **120**(5), 3245 (2006). https://doi.org/10.1121/1.4788280
7. Ashihara, K., Kurakata, K., Mizunami, T., Matsushita, K.: Hearing threshold for pure tones above 20 kHz. Acoust. Sci. Technol. **27**(1), 12–19 (2006). https://doi.org/10.1250/ast.27.12
8. Sakamoto, M., Sugasawa, M., Kaga, K., Kamio, T.: Average thresholds in the 8 to 20 kHz range in young adults. Scand. Audiol. **27**(3), 169–172 (1998). https://doi.org/10.1080/010503998422674
9. Sakamoto, M., Sugasawa, M., Kaga, K., Kamio, T.: Average thresholds in the 8 to 20 kHz range as a function of age. Scand. Audiol. **27**(3), 189–192 (1998). https://doi.org/10.1080/010503998422728
10. Stelmachowicz, P.G., Beauchaine, K.A., Kalberer, A., Jesteadt, W.: Normative thresholds in the 8- to 20-kHz range as a function of age. J. Acoust. Soc. Am. **86**(4), 1384–1391 (1989). https://doi.org/10.1121/1.398698
11. Fletcher, M.D., Lloyd Jones, S., White, P.R., Dolder, C.N., Lineton, B., Leighton, T.G.: Public exposure to ultrasound and very high-frequency sound in air. J. Acoust. Soc. Am. **144**(4), 2554–2564 (2018). https://doi.org/10.1121/1.5063817
12. Fletcher, M.D., Lloyd Jones, S., White, P.R., Dolder, C.N., Leighton, T.G., Lineton, B.: Effects of very high-frequency sound and ultrasound on humans. Part I: adverse symptoms after exposure to audible very-high frequency sound. J. Acoust. Soc. Am. **144**(4), 2511–2520 (2018). https://doi.org/10.1121/1.5063819

13. Lopes, S.I., Vieira, J.M.N., Albuquerque, D.F.: Analysis of the perceptual impact of high frequency audio pulses in smartphone-based positioning systems. In: 2015 IEEE International Conference on Industrial Technology (ICIT), pp. 3398–3403, March 2015. https://doi.org/10. 1109/ICIT.2015.7125603

14. Górak, R., Luckner, M.: Modified random forest algorithm for Wi–Fi indoor localization system. In: Nguyen, N.-T., Manolopoulos, Y., Iliadis, L., Trawiński, B. (eds.) ICCCI 2016. LNCS (LNAI), vol. 9876, pp. 147–157. Springer, Cham (2016). https://doi.org/10.1007/978-3-319-45246-3_14. springerprofessional.de. https://www.springerprofessional.de/en/modified-random-forest-algorithm-for-wi-fi-indoor-localization-s/10714596. Accessed 18 June 2022

15. Drozdova, M., Bridova, I., Uramova, J., Moravcik, M.: Private cloud security architecture. In: 2020 18th International Conference on Emerging eLearning Technologies and Applications (ICETA), pp. 84–89, November 2020. https://doi.org/10.1109/ICETA51985.2020.9379217

16. Torres-Sospedra, J., Lohan, E.S., Molinaro, A., Moreira, A., Rusu-Casandra, A., Smékal, Z.: Applications and innovations on sensor-enabled wearable devices. Sensors **22**(7), Art. no. 7 (2022). https://doi.org/10.3390/s22072599

17. Priyantha, N.B., Chakraborty, A., Balakrishnan, H.: The Cricket location-support system. In: Proceedings of the 6th Annual International Conference on Mobile Computing and Networking, New York, NY, USA, pp. 32–43, August 2000. https://doi.org/10.1145/345910. 345917

18. Woodman, O.J., Harle, R.K.: Concurrent scheduling in the Active Bat location system. In: 2010 8th IEEE International Conference on Pervasive Computing and Communications Workshops (PERCOM Workshops), pp. 431–437, March 2010. https://doi.org/10.1109/PER COMW.2010.5470631

19. Mandal, A., Lopes, C.V., Givargis, T., Haghighat, A., Jurdak, R., Baldi, P.: Beep: 3D indoor positioning using audible sound. In: Second IEEE Consumer Communications and Networking Conference, CCNC 2005, pp. 348–353, January 2005. https://doi.org/10.1109/CCNC. 2005.1405195

20. Priyantha, N.B., Miu, A.K.L., Balakrishnan, H., Teller, S.: The cricket compass for context-aware mobile applications. In: Proceedings of the 7th Annual International Conference on Mobile Computing and Networking, New York, NY, USA, pp. 1–14, July 2001. https://doi. org/10.1145/381677.381679

21. Sound Analyser Nor140. https://web2.norsonic.com/product_single/soundanalyser-nor140/. Accessed 29 June 2021

22. Sound-Base Audio, LLC: WaveEditor for Android^{TM} Audio Recorder & Editor. https://play. google.com/store/apps/details?id=io.sbaud.wavstudio&hl=sk&gl=US. Accessed 28 June 2021

Cognitive Load Measurement Using Arithmetic and Graphical Tasks and Galvanic Skin Response

Patient Zihisire Muke⬭, Zbigniew Telec⬭, and Bogdan Trawiński$^{(\boxtimes)}$⬭

Department of Applied Informatics, Wrocław University of Science and Technology, Wrocław, Poland
{patient.zihisire,zbigniew.telec,bogdan.trawinski}@pwr.edu.pl

Abstract. The results of an experiment to measure cognitive load using arithmetic and graphical tasks and galvanic skin response (GSR) biometric technique are presented in this paper. 62 volunteers were recruited to take part in a laboratory experiment conducted with the integrated iMotions biometric platform. Data were collected using observations, Single Ease Question (SEQ) and NASA Task Load Index (NASA-TLX) self-report questionnaires, and GSR measurements. The 18 performance, subjective, and psychophysiological indicators were calculated from the collected data to measure the cognitive load associated with arithmetic and graphical tasks. Nonparametric tests of statistical significance of differences between individual metrics were made for the easy, medium, and hard arithmetic and graphical tasks. The conducted research proved the usefulness of most measures in the analysis of the cognitive load associated with arithmetic and graphical tasks.

Keywords: Cognitive load · Arithmetic tasks · Graphical tasks · Galvanic skin response · NASA-TLX questionnaire

1 Introduction

Cognitive load in cognitive psychology has been be described as the load imposed on a person's working memory by a specific (learning) task [1]. In relation to HCI (Human Computer Interaction), cognitive load is described as the quantity of mental effort that is used from the working memory while performing cognitive tasks and interacting with the computer system [2]. Assessing the cognitive load could be useful in designing user interfaces and user experience evaluation. Data from biosensors could provide the possibility to qualify the behavioral responses caused by given software, insight into missing information, or lack of understanding. A significant number of diverse biometric techniques such as electroencephalography (EEG), eye tracking, facial expression analysis, galvanic skin response (GSR), electrocardiography (ECG) and electromyography (EMG), allow researchers to perform comparative analysis, which can determine the reflection of cognitive load levels [3].

© The Author(s), under exclusive license to Springer Nature Switzerland AG 2022
N. T. Nguyen et al. (Eds.): ICCCI 2022, LNAI 13501, pp. 836–850, 2022.
https://doi.org/10.1007/978-3-031-16014-1_66

The aim of the research presented in this paper was to explore cognitive load while participants completed arithmetic and graphical matrix reasoning tasks. A multimodal approach to measurement was applied which included performance measurements, subjective self-reports with Single Ease Question (SEQ) and NASA Task Load Index (NASA-TLX) and Single Ease Question (SEQ) questionnaires, and biometric measurements using several metrics based on psychophysiological data from the GSR sensor.

The iMotions biometric research platform [4] was used to conduct an experiment on 62 participants, mostly young people with a university education. The designed stimuli were consistent with standard tests used to measure cognitive workload. Arithmetic and graphical tasks of low, medium, and difficult difficulty were used as the stimuli. The arithmetic task involved mentally calculating mathematical expressions involving addition and subtraction of numbers with varying numbers of digits. Graphical tasks, on the other hand, were a type of graphical matrix reasoning in which the participant's task was to find a missing element in a matrix containing abstract shapes. The collected data was analyzed using non-parametric tests in order to determine the statistical significance of the differences between the individual measurements.

As part of this research, three Master's theses were completed and they contain a detailed description of the experiment presented in this paper [5–7]. Due to the limited space in the paper, we present here only a part of the results. The first part of the research on impact of the Stroop effect on cognitive load was presented by the authors in [8]. The experiment was conducted during the COVID-19 pandemic period, therefore, the participants and research team had to observe strict laboratory hygienic rules. The study was approved by the Research Ethics Committee at the Wroclaw University of Science and Technology, Poland.

2 Background and Related Works

2.1 Cognitive Load

The concept of cognitive load arises from the early work done in the area of education including teaching and was expressed in the cognitive load theory (CLT) designed in the late 1980s by the psychologist John Sweller to describe how human short and long-term memory works and how the human brain processes and stores information [9, 10].

CLT was constructed based on the human memory model that includes the sensory, working and long-term memory subsystems [11]. The sensory memory holds the correct sensory information of what is briefly presented (i.e., <0.25 s). They come from the five senses: smell, vision, taste, touch and hearing. On the other hand, the working memory is only able to process certain pieces of information and retains the more processed input information for a short period of time (i.e., <30 s). At last, the long-term memory is a repository of all the knowledge of a learner for a long period of time. This model prove that CLT can be utilized to limit unnecessary effort in this area [12].

To fully understand the theory of cognitive load, in connection with the instructional area, it is essential to classify knowledge in two categories. The first one is called the biologically primary knowledge and defined as the basic knowledge that can be acquired naturally and effortlessly by living beings through evolution for many generations. Learning a first language as a child is a great example of biologically primary knowledge, and both speaking and hearing do not require teaching. The second one is named the biologically secondary knowledge and describe as the knowledge acquired through intellectual effort, which must be learned through explicit instructions. A good example of this are writing skills, which require awareness and demanding continuous work [13, 14].

Furthermore, in CLT, three types of cognitive load can be distinguished: intrinsic, extraneous and germane load. The intrinsic cognitive load refers to the inherent difficulty or complexity of a task or material. Activities vary depending on the level of difficulty. If the task is too complex or difficult, it overloads the working memory and makes it too tough to process. A great example is an equation containing derivatives or integrals which is more difficult to solve than the simple task of adding two numbers [15, 16].

The extraneous load is a subset of cognitive load which is generated by the presence of irrelevant information that distracts people from the normal learning process. For example, if a graphic and text are not properly combined, the learner will spend more time switching from graphics to text. This information overloads the working memory and produces extraneous cognitive load [15, 16].

The germane load, on the other hand, is defined as the "effective cognitive load". This is the result of properly representing information in working memory and organizing it into schemas. For example, someone creates flowcharts that will be more helpful to learners than plain text with steps to be followed. Systematic ordering of information accelerates its memorization [15, 16].

2.2 Cognitive Load Measurements

Cognitive load can be measured using two approaches. The first is an analytical technique where the main emphasis is on assessing mental load and collecting analytical metrics based on tasks, as well as analyzing mathematical models and subjective measures, more specifically expert opinions. The second is the empirical technique that focuses on subjective measures, which include a self-rating approach, and objective measures, which consist of a performance or task based approach, physiological approach and behavioral approach. The empirical method is more often used by researchers than the analytical method [17].

Regarding the empirical technique, methods based on subjective evaluation rely on participants' own judgment of their task performance efforts. The user evaluates his own cognitive processes and the mental effort required for a given task. In this method, there are two types of rating scales: the unidimensional scales, which measure the overall cognitive load, e.g. the Paas' nine-point mental effort rating scale [18] and the multidimensional scales, which focus on different components of workload, e.g. one of the most commonly used is NASA-TLX (NASA-Task Load Index) with six dimensions: mental demand, physical demand, time pressure, mental effort, performance satisfaction, and frustration level [19]. Another used subjective rating scale measure especially in user experience testing and usability, is the Single Ease Question (SEQ). It is a 7-point rating scale to evaluate how difficult participants find a task [20]. NASA-TLX and SEQ were used in this study.

In terms of objective measures, the performance-based approach is often used in dual-task environments to measure a user's workload based on their own performance in secondary tasks compared to primary tasks, e g. task completion times, completion rates, error rates and test scores [17]. In this study performance metrics were as well measured. On the other hand, the behavioral approach implicitly and objectively records the subjects' actions, e.g. eye activity like fixation duration and blink frequency, mouse usage, speech features and head movements [21].

Finally, the psychophysiological approach based on neuroscience is an effective strategy for measuring cognitive load with the advantages of real-time, objectivity and low data reading invasiveness. Examples are: EEG, ECG, EMG, GSR, facial expression analysis and eye tracking [3].

2.3 Cognitive Load and Arithmetic Tasks

Applying mental arithmetic tasks in research is quite common in the study of the mechanisms of human cognitive activity because of its complex mental function. Mental arithmetic appears to engage the memory processes in retrieving arithmetic facts from the long-term memory and can be considered as a standardized stress-inducing experimental protocol [22].

Thus, many researchers in the literature used arithmetic tasks to measure cognitive load. In [23] six metrics of GSR were studied in the perception of four levels of cognitive load with emotional interference. Data were derived from two arithmetic experiments and emotions were elicited by displaying unpleasant and pleasant images in the background. Two classifiers were used to detect the level of cognitive load. The results showed that the identified metrics were able to detect four and two levels of cognitive load with high accuracy, even in the case of emotional changes.

In addition, the study in [24] presented and evaluated several metrics from blink and GSR signals to classify levels of cognitive stress. The experiment included four levels of difficulty with the use of arithmetic tasks, and two types of machine learning algorithms were used for classification. The results obtained showed that the blink and GSR metrics tested could reasonably differentiate the levels of cognitive load, and the combination of the metrics could improve the accuracy of the cognitive load classification.

Moreover, in [25] participants were classified as bad and good counting based on their performance while performing mental arithmetic tasks. Mathematical calculations actively engaged participants in mental work. In this study, the mental load concept was used with the EEG to classify signals. As a result, the participants were successfully classified into classes with 80% accuracy.

2.4 Cognitive Load and Graphical Matrix Reasoning Tasks

The concept of matrix reasoning evokes the measurement of visual and fluid intelligence through a series of incomplete visual matrices. The participants of an experiment or test have to choose one pattern from the five suggested options that best complete the matrix [26].

Raven's Advanced Progressive Matrices is one of the most widely used measures of visual and fluid intelligence. This measure is a matrix reasoning test in which subjects are given a matrix of 3×3 with patterns representing a figure lacking the bottom right pattern. The patterns form a figure, and participants have to choose the appropriate pattern to fill in the missing space with one of eight suggested options [27].

In [27] it was stated that the Raven's matrices is a task designed to answer the question of whether matrix reasoning problems requiring new rule combinations correspond more closely to fluid intelligence and working memory capacity than problems requiring repetitive rule combinations.

In the same perspective, [28] presents a study where a multimodal sensing approach was used (GSR, ECG, blood oxygen content saturation and respiration) and three cognitive tests were performed, consisting of a Raven's matrices reasoning test, a numerical test, and a video game to induce cognitive workload in 12 subjects on the easy and hard levels of task difficulty. This research presents preliminary results in which a set of cognitive workload indicators is identified.

Another measure of the working memory capacity is the Matrix Reasoning Item Bank (MaRs-IB) which contains graphical tasks very similar to Raven's matrices. A description of the MaRs-IB can be found in [29]. Our study employed the same type of matrix reasoning to access cognitive load.

2.5   Galvanic Skin Response

The galvanic skin response (GSR) is part of the electrodermal activity measurement that tracks the activity of the sweat glands. Its measures can be divided into two groups that are tonic and phasic. The skin's conductance level is a good example of tonic responses and is thought to reflect changes in arousal. The phasic reactions include the skin conductivity response, which is a change in electrical conductivity. Positive and negative stimuli can increase arousal. An increase in the level of excitation causes an increase in skin conductivity [30, 31].

An increase in the difficulty level of a task intensifies cognitive load. Previous studies show a link between stress and cognitive load. Therefore, the number of GSR peaks could also be a determinant of cognitive load, which tends to increase with the cognitive load level. Researchers list further GSR measures used to measure cognitive load such as accumulative and mean galvanic skin response. The accumulative GSR is the summation of GSR values over the time of the ongoing task, from the first occurrence of the stimulus till its end. On the other hand, the mean GSR is the value of the GSR data divided by the average from the entire session [32–34].

3   Experiment Setup

The experiment was conducted on the iMotions biometric platform [4] using a variety of stimuli and biometric techniques. Due to the limited space, in this paper we present only a part of the results concerning human cognitive load associated with arithmetic and graphical tasks using a single biosensor technique GSR along with other subjective and performance measurements.

Based on the literature, we formulated three main hypotheses. First, the values of the GSR psychophysiological metrics increase with increasing cognitive load levels in both arithmetic and graphical tasks (*H1*). Second, the subjective ratings based on the NASA-TLX and SEQ self-report questionnaires increase with increasing cognitive load levels in both arithmetic and graphical tasks (*H2*). Third, the values of the performance metrics are good supplementary indicators of the level of cognitive load (*H3*).

3.1 Participants

62 volunteers took part in the experiment, including 14 females and 48 males. Most of the respondents had higher education, which guaranteed that they would be able to solve the tasks. 39 people were university students, 6 PhD students, 9 IT specialists, one high school student and 6 other professions. 53 were right-handed, 6 were left-handed, and 3 were without a dominant hand. 42 respondents had good eyesight, 15 wore glasses and 5 wore contact lenses. They were between the ages of 20 and 38. 26 participants came from Poland, 24 from India, 10 from Indonesia and 2 from other countries. Before starting the experiment, participants signed their consent to participate in the study. They were instructed on the course of the experiment.

3.2 Arithmetic and Graphical Tasks

In our experiment, we used two types of stimuli in the form of arithmetic and graphical tasks. Each type consisted of three groups of five tasks at easy, medium and hard levels.

The arithmetic tasks consisted in mentally calculating a set of four equations with unknowns and determining the value of the last variable. The participant chose the correct answer from among four options. Each difficulty level differed in the size of numbers added and subtracted as well as partial results and the complexity of logical reasoning. At the easy level, the arguments were single-digit numbers and the partial scores were greater than zero. At the medium level, the arguments were two-digit numbers between 10 and 29 and the partial scores were greater than 10 and less than 100. On the hard level, on the other hand, the arguments were two-digit numbers between 41 and 99 and the calculated variables were larger than 100 and smaller than 300. Similar calculations were used in [35]. An example of an arithmetic task on the hard level is shown in Fig. 1. In the rest of the article, the arithmetic tasks are denoted as *ArL*, *ArM*, and *ArH*, respectively, for tasks on the low, medium, and hard difficulty levels.

Graphical tasks were developed based on the Matrix Reasoning Item Bank (MaRs-IB) [29]. The questions were in the form of a 3×3 matrix containing eight abstract graphics. The participants deduced relations between graphics that could differ in four dimensions: color, size, position and shape, and then selected the missing ninth graphics from four options. Difficulty levels were based on the dimensionality of individual tasks, which represented the number relation changes in the matrix. Tasks on the easy, medium, and hard levels had dimensions of 1, 2 and 3, and 4 to 6, respectively. An example of a graphical task on the medium level is presented in Fig. 2. In the further part of the paper, the graphical tasks are marked as *GrL*, *GrM* and *GrH*, which means tasks on the low, medium and hard difficulty level, respectively.

The time limit for solving arithmetic and graphical tasks on the easy, medium, and hard levels was 25, 40, and 50 s, respectively.

Calculate mentally

48 + 69 = X
X + 86 = Y
Y − 47 = Z
Z + 72 = W
W = ?

○ 228   ○ 238   ○ 248   ○ 258   ● I don't know

Fig. 1. An example of an arithmetic task on the hard level.

Select a suitable figure from the four alternatives that would complete the figure matrix

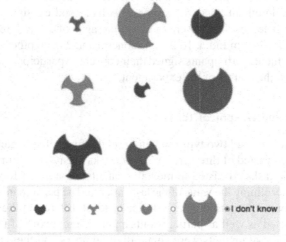

Fig. 2. An example of a graphical task on the medium level.

3.3 Measurement of Cognitive Load

For subjective measurement, we applied two types of self-report questionnaires that participants completed after finishing each group of tasks. A modified version of the NASA TLX questionnaire was used in this study because we did not use a weighting scheme in calculating the total score. Also, instead of the original scale, we used a 7-point Likert scale to score each question. We hypothesized that this scale might make it easier for participants to make a more reliable assessment in less time. The second questionnaire was the Single Ease Question (SEQ). The SEQ is a 7-point rating scale that was used to determine participants' perceived level of task difficulty.

A Shimmer GSR device was used to measure the electrodermal activity. The GSR electrodes were placed on the index and middle fingers of the participants' non-dominant hand. The participants used their dominant hand to operate the mouse.

In total, 18 performance, subjective and psychophysiological metrics were defined and calculated on the basis of the collected data. They are presented in Table 1.

Due to incorrect GSR measurements, we rejected the results of 5 participants. Consequently, all metrics were calculated from the data collected for 57 respondents. Moreover,

Table 1. Metrics used to measure cognitive load

Type	Metrics	Denotation
Performance metrics	Task completion rate	Tcr
	Task completion time	Tct
Subjective metrics	Task difficulty (SEQ)	Seq
	NASA-TLX - Overall	NXo
	NASA-TLX - Complexity	NXc
	NASA-TLX - Physical demand	NXp
	NASA-TLX - Time pressure	NXt
	NASA-TLX - Performance satisfaction	NXs
	NASA-TLX - Mental effort	NXm
	NASA-TLX - Frustration	NXf
Psychophysiological metrics	GSR Peak count	Gpc
	GSR Peaks per minute	Gpm
	GSR Mean value	Gmv
	GSR Mean value (normalized)	Gmn
	GSR Max value	Gxv
	GSR Max value (normalized)	Gxn
	GSR Accumulative value	Gav
	GSR Accumulative value (normalized)	Gan

taking into account that the participants performed five tasks on each difficulty level, the results are the average value of the measurements of the five tasks. Only, the task completion rate was calculated as the percentage of successfully completed tasks. Scores for each question from the SEQ and NASA-TLX questionnaires were a separate metric and they ranged from 1 to 7. The overall NASA-TLX score was calculated as the average of the scores for the six survey questions.

Psychophysiological metrics were calculated for the data collected from the GSR sensor using two algorithms implemented in the iMotions platform, namely GSR Peak Detection [36] and GSR Epoching Pre-processing [37]. The Gmn, Gxn, and Gan values were normalized for individual participants by dividing Gmv, Gxv, and Gav by the baseline values determined when filling in the personal questionnaires. A detailed description of the GSR metrics is contained in our previous paper presenting the first part of the results of our experiment [8].

4   Analysis of Experiment Results

The mean and median values of individual performance, subjective, and psychophysiological metrics are presented in Figs. 3, 4 and 5, respectively.

Prevailing majority of the results produced by the performance, subjective and psychophysiological metrics did not have a normal distribution according to the Shapiro-Wilk test. Therefore, the nonparametric Friedman test was applied, followed by the post-hoc Nemenyi test for multiple comparisons. The null hypotheses assumed that there were no significant differences in the values of individual metrics between the tasks. The significance level for rejecting the null hypothesis was set at 0.05. The results of the Nemenyi test for individual metrics are presented in Table 2, where the + sign means that the value of a given metric is statistically significantly larger for the task on the higher difficulty level compared to the task on the lower difficulty level. Sign – indicates that the value of the metric is statistically significantly smaller for the task on the higher difficulty level compared to the task on the lower difficulty level. The ≈ sign, on the other hand, denotes that the null hypothesis was not rejected.

For the psychophysiological measurements the values of the *Gpc*, *Gav*, and *Gan* metrics for hard tasks (*ArH* and *GrH*) were significantly greater than the values for medium tasks (*ArM* and *GrM*), and these, in turn, were significantly greater than the values for easy tasks (*ArE* and *GrE*). The values of the *Gmv*, *Gmn*, *Gxv*, and *Gxn* metrics were consistent with this observation for arithmetic tasks except for *ArE* and *ArM*, between which no statistically significant differences occurred. Also, the Gpm metric values for graphical tasks were in line with the main observation. In turn, the results provided by the *Gmv*, *Gmn*, *Gxv*, and *Gxn* metrics for graphical tasks were inconsistent.

In the case of subjective measurements, the values of the seven *Seq*, *Nxo*, *NXc*, *NXp*, *NXt*, *NXm*, and *NXf* metrics for hard tasks (*ArH* and *GrH*) were significantly higher than the values for medium tasks (*ArM* and *GrM*), and these, in turn, were significantly greater than the values for easy tasks (*ArE* and *GrE*). Only for the *NXs* metrics there were no significant differences between all arithmetic and graphical tasks.

Among performance metrics, the task completion time *Tct* increased significantly with increasing difficulty of arithmetic and graphical tasks. In turn, the task completion rate *Tcr* significantly decreased with increasing difficulty of arithmetic and graphical tasks, except for arithmetic easy and medium tasks. There were no significant differences in *Tcr* between the *ArE* and *ArM* tasks.

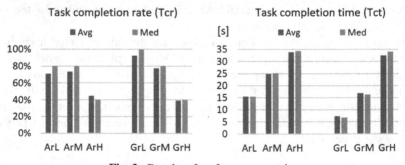

Fig. 3. Results of performance metrics

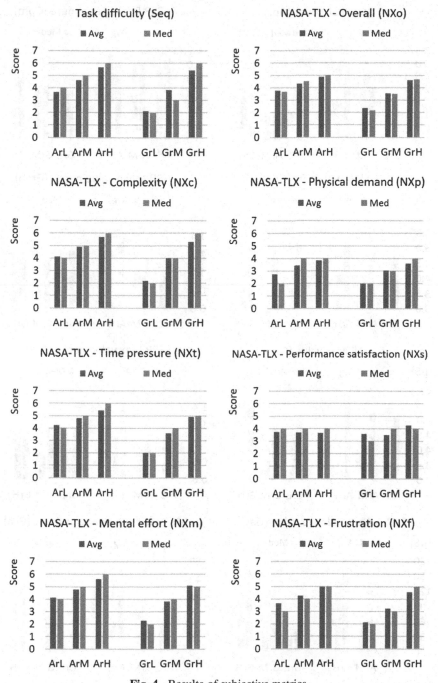

Fig. 4. Results of subjective metrics

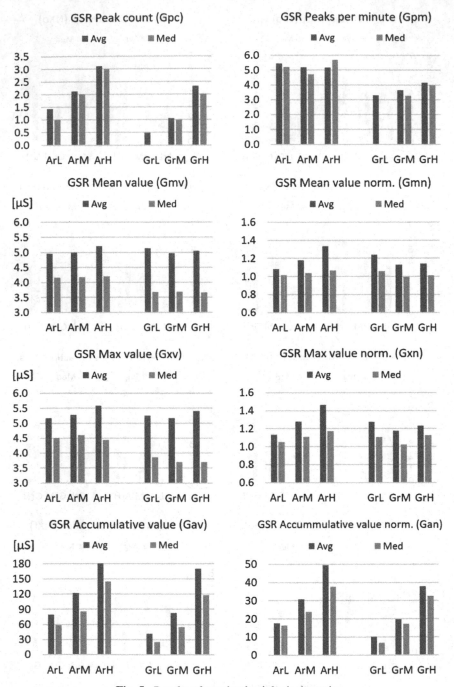

Fig. 5. Results of psychophysiological metrics

Table 2. Nemenyi test results for comparing the arithmetic and graphical tasks

Metrics	ArL vs ArM	ArL vs ArH	ArM vs ArH	Metrics	GrL vs GrM	GrL vs GrH	GrM vs GrH
Tcr	≈	−	−	*Tcr*	−	−	−
Tct	+	+	+	*Tct*	+	+	+
Seq	+	+	+	*Seq*	+	+	+
NXo	+	+	+	*NXo*	+	+	+
NXc	+	+	+	*NXc*	+	+	+
NXp	+	+	+	*NXp*	+	+	+
NXt	+	+	+	*NXt*	+	+	+
NXs	≈	≈	≈	*NXs*	≈	≈	≈
NXm	+	+	+	*NXm*	+	+	+
NXf	+	+	+	*NXf*	+	+	+
Gpc	+	+	+	*Gpc*	+	+	+
Gpm	≈	≈	≈	*Gpm*	≈	+	+
Gmv	≈	+	+	*Gmv*	−	≈	≈
Gmn	≈	+	+	*Gmn*	−	≈	≈
Gxv	≈	+	+	*Gxv*	−	≈	+
Gxn	+	+	+	*Gxn*	−	≈	+
Gav	+	+	+	*Gav*	+	+	+
Gan	+	+	+	*Gan*	+	+	+

5   Conclusions

The experiment in this study was conducted under laboratory conditions for one month with 62 participants who followed strict sanitary procedures. Age and education restrictions were also taken into account when recruiting participants, so that age and prior knowledge did not affect the results. The stimulus design was based on standardized tests that were validated to measure cognitive load. They consisted of 15 arithmetic and 15 graphical reasoning tasks of easy, medium and hard difficulty levels, with 5 tasks at each difficulty level. All tasks were implemented in a standalone application developed in Python. Biometric data collection was done using several biosensors from the iMotions platform. However, due to the limitation of the paper volume, among biometric data, only GSR metrics are presented, calculated with the use of algorithms built into the iMotions platform.

The collected biometric data was also normalized with baseline data in order to eliminate subjective dependencies. Apart from biometric data, subjective and performance measures were also analyzed. The calculated measures were visualized in graphs and tables to facilitate review of the experimental data and to compare the level of cognitive load based on the two designed stimuli. Moreover, statistical tests were performed to determine the impact of each stimulus on the measurements.

Based on statistical tests, the most common observations were as follows: the values of the metrics for the hard tasks (*ArH* and *GrH*) were significantly greater than the values for the medium tasks (*ArM* and *GrM*), and these in turn were significantly greater than the values for the easy tasks (*ArE* and *GrE*). This occurred for the performance metrics: *Tct*, subjective metrics: *Seq, Nxo, NXc, NXp, NXt, NXm,* and *NXf*, and psychophysiological metrics: *Gpc*, *Gav*, and *Gan*. The task completion rate Tcr changed significantly in an inverse manner, except for the arithmetic tasks *ArE* and *ArM*, between which no significant differences were observed..

Regarding biometric data, eight GSR metrics were calculated to provide insight into the experienced level of cognitive load. The results show that the *H1* hypothesis is supported in the case of the *Gpc*, *Gav* and *Gan metrics* which increase when task difficulty is increasing for both arithmetical and graphical tasks. Whereas, for the *Gpm*, *Gmv*, *Gmn*, *Gxv* and *Gxn* metrics *H1* was not confirmed. The exceptions were *Gpm* metrics for graphical tasks as well as for *Gmn* and *Gxn* for arithmetic tasks, where the increase in GSR values with increasing difficulty levels occured for either arithmetic tasks or for graphical tasks.

Concerning subjective measurements, eight metrics were analysed. The results indicate that *Seq*, *Nxo*, *NXc*, *NXp*, *NXt*, *NXm*, and *NXf* metrics support the *H2* hypothesis where the obtained values increased significantly with the difficulty of the tasks for both arithmetic and graphical tasks In contrast, *H2* was not proved for the *NXs* performance satisfaction metrics.

In the case of performance measurements, two metrics were examined. The results show that *Tct* increased significantly with increasing difficulty of arithmetic and graphical tasks, thus supporting the *H3* hypothesis. *Tcr*, which changes in the opposite direction, i.e. decreases with the difficulty of the task, for graphical tasks also supports *H3*. *Tcr* did not reveal significant differences only for the *ArE* and *ArH* tasks. This indicates that *Tcr* requires larger differences in the difficulty levels for the arithmetic tasks to distinguish them.

In conclusion, our study demonstrated the usefulness of both arithmetic and graphical tasks as stimuli and the performance, subjective, and psychophysiological metrics we used to measure cognitive load. The following metrics are most appropriate for measuring cognitive load when participants perform arithmetic and graphical tasks: *Tct*, *Seq*, *Nxo*, *NXc*, *NXp*, *NXt*, *NXm*, *NXf*, *Gpc*, *Gav*, and *Gan*.

Other types of graphical reasoning tasks can be considered to ensure deep involvement in memory processes. In addition, a greater variety of difficulty levels of arithmetic tasks can be provided.

The future work will concentrate on including HCI stimuli in the study such as mobile and web applications along with different biometric techniques using multiple machine learning algorithms to predict the level of users' cognitive load from the human-computer interaction perspective.

References

1. Van Gog, T., Paas, F.: Cognitive load measurement. In: Seel, N.M. (ed.) Encyclopedia of the Sciences of Learning. Springer, Boston (2012). https://doi.org/10.1007/978-1-4419-1428-6_412
2. Kumar, N., Kumar, J.: Measurement of cognitive load in HCI systems using EEG power spectrum: an experimental study. Procedia Comput. Sci. **84**, 70–78 (2016). https://doi.org/10.1016/j.procs.2016.04.068

3. Zihisire Muke, P., Trawinski, B.: Concept of research into cognitive load in human-computer interaction using biometric techniques. In: Proceedings of the PP-RAI 2019 Conference, Wrocław, Poland, pp. 78–83 (2019). http://pp-rai.pwr.edu.pl/PPRAI19_proceedings.pdf. Accessed 01 June 2022
4. iMotions Biometric Research Platform (8.1): iMotions A/S, Copenhagen, Denmark (2020)
5. Bresso, P.: Study of the impact of various stimuli on human cognitive load using electroencephalography and other biometric techniques. Master's thesis, Wroclaw University of Science and Technology, Wrocław (2020)
6. Desai, H.: Study of the impact of various stimuli on human cognitive load using eye tracking and other biometric techniques. Master's thesis, Wroclaw University of Science and Technology, Wrocław (2021)
7. Maharani, P.A.: Study of the impact of various stimuli on human cognitive load using facial expression analysis and other biometric techniques. Master's thesis, Wroclaw University of Science and Technology, Wrocław (2020)
8. Zihisire Muke, P., Piwowarczyk, M., Telec, Z., Trawiński, B., Maharani, P.A., Bresso, P.: Impact of the Stroop effect on cognitive load using subjective and psychophysiological measures. In: Nguyen, N.T., Iliadis, L., Maglogiannis, I., Trawiński, B. (eds.) ICCCI 2021. LNCS (LNAI), vol. 12876, pp. 180–196. Springer, Cham (2021). https://doi.org/10.1007/978-3-030-88081-1_14
9. Sweller, J.: Cognitive load during problem solving: effects on learning. Cogn. Sci. 12(1), 257–285 (1988). https://doi.org/10.1016/0364-0213(88)90023-7
10. Sweller, J.: Cognitive load theory, learning difficulty, and instructional design. Learn. Instr. 4(4), 295–312 (1994). https://doi.org/10.1016/0959-4752(94)90003-5
11. Young, J.Q., Van Merrienboer, J., Durning, S., Ten Cate, O.: Cognitive Load Theory: Implications for medical education: AMEE Guide No. 86. Med. Teach. 36(5), 371–384 (2014). https://doi.org/10.3109/0142159X.2014.889290
12. McLeod, S.A.: Multi store model of memory. Simply Psychology (2017). https://www.simplypsychology.org/multi-store.html
13. Sweller, J., Ayres, P., Kalyuga, S.: Cognitive Load Theory. Explorations in the Learning Sciences, Instructional Systems and Performance Technologies, vol. 1. Springer, New York (2011). https://doi.org/10.1007/978-1-4419-8126-4
14. Geary, D.: An evolutionarily informed education science. Educ. Psychol. 43(4), 179–195 (2008). https://doi.org/10.1080/00461520802392133
15. Orru, G., Longo, L.: The evolution of cognitive load theory and the measurement of its intrinsic, extraneous and germane loads: a review. In: Longo, L., Leva, M.C. (eds.) H-WORKLOAD 2018. CCIS, vol. 1012, pp. 23–48. Springer, Cham (2019). https://doi.org/10.1007/978-3-030-14273-5_3
16. Sweller, J., van Merriënboer, J.J.G., Paas, F.: Cognitive architecture and instructional design: 20 years later. Educ. Psychol. Rev. 31(2), 261–292 (2019). https://doi.org/10.1007/s10648-019-09465-5
17. Paas, F., Tuovinen, J., Tabbers, H., Van Gerven, P.: Cognitive load measurement as a means to advance cognitive load theory. Educ. Psychol. 38(1), 63–71 (2003)
18. Paas, F.: Training strategies for attaining transfer of problem solving skills in statistics: a cognitive load approach. J. Educ. Psychol. 84, 429–434 (1992)
19. Rubio, S., Diaz, E., Martin, J., Puente, J.M.: Evaluation of subjective mental workload: a comparison of SWAT, NASA-TLX, and workload profile methods. Appl. Psychol. 53(1), 61–86 (2004). https://doi.org/10.1111/j.1464-0597.2004.00161
20. Gibson, A., et al.: Assessing usability testing for people living with dementia. In: REHAB 2016: Proceedings of the 4th Workshop on ICTs for improving Patients Rehabilitation Research Techniques, pp. 25–31 (2016). https://doi.org/10.1145/3051488.3051492

21. Chen, F., et al.: Robust Multimodal Cognitive Load Measurement. Springer, Cham (2016). https://doi.org/10.1007/978-3-319-31700-7
22. Zyma, I., et al.: Electroencephalograms during mental arithmetic task performance. Data **4**(1), 2–7 (2019). https://doi.org/10.3390/data4010014
23. Nourbakhsh, N., Chen, F., Wang, Y., Calvo, R.A.: Detecting users' cognitive load by galvanic skin response with affective interference. ACM Trans. Interact. Intell. Syst. **7**(3), 1–12 (2017). https://doi.org/10.1145/2960413. Article 12
24. Nourbakhsh, N., Wang, Y., Chen, F.: GSR and blink features for cognitive load classification. In: Kotzé, P., Marsden, G., Lindgaard, G., Wesson, J., Winckler, M. (eds.) INTERACT 2013. LNCS, vol. 8117, pp. 159–166. Springer, Heidelberg (2013). https://doi.org/10.1007/978-3-642-40483-2_11
25. Rai, A.A., Ahirwal, M.K.: Electroencephalogram-based cognitive load classification during mental arithmetic task. In: Patgiri, R., Bandyopadhyay, S., Borah, M.D., Emilia Balas, V. (eds.) Edge Analytics. LNEE, vol. 869, pp. 479–487. Springer, Singapore (2022). https://doi.org/10.1007/978-981-19-0019-8_36
26. Kievit, R.A., et al.: Mutualistic coupling between vocabulary and reasoning supports cognitive development during late adolescence and early adulthood. Psychol. Sci. **28**(10), 1419–1431 (2017). https://doi.org/10.1177/0956797617710785
27. Harrison, T.L., Shipstead, Z., Engle, R.W.: Why is working memory capacity related to matrix reasoning tasks? Mem. Cogn. **43**(3), 389–396 (2014). https://doi.org/10.3758/s13421-014-0473-3
28. Hirachan, N., Mathews, A., Romero, J., Rojas, R.F.: Measuring cognitive workload using multimodal sensors, pp. 2–5 (2022). http://arxiv.org/abs/2205.04235
29. Chierchia, G., Fuhrmann, D., Knoll, L.J., Pi-Sunyer, B.P., Sakhardande, A.L., Blakemore, S.J.: The matrix reasoning item bank (MaRs-IB): novel, open-access abstract reasoning items for adolescents and adults. Roy. Soc. Open Sci. **6**(10), 1–13 (2019). https://doi.org/10.1098/rsos.190232
30. Braithwaite, J., Watson, D., Jones, R., Rowe, M.: A guide for analysing electrodermal activity (EDA) skin conductance responses (SCRs) for psychological experiments. Technical report, 2nd version. University of Birmingham, UK (2015)
31. Farnsworth, B.: What is GSR (galvanic skin response) and how does it work? (2018) https://imotions.com/blog/gsr/
32. Yoshihiro, S., Takumi, Y., Koji, S., Akinori, H., Koichi, I., Tetsuo, K.: Use of frequency domain analysis of skin conductance for evaluation of mental workload. J. Physiol. Anthropol. **27**(4), 173–177 (2008)
33. Shi, Y., Ruiz, N., Taib, R., Choi, E., Chen, F.: Galvanic skin response (GSR) as an index of cognitive load. In: CHI 2007 Extended Abstracts on Human Factors in Computing Systems, pp. 2651–2656 (2007). https://doi.org/10.1145/1240866.1241057
34. Nourbakhsh, N., Wang, Y., Chen, F., Calvo, R.: Using galvanic skin response for cognitive load measurement in arithmetic and reading tasks. In: 24th Australian Computer-Human Interaction Conference (OzCHI), Melbourne, Australia, pp. 420–423. ACM Press (2012). https://doi.org/10.1145/2414536.2414602
35. Sinharay, A., Chatterjee, D., Sinha, A.: Evaluation of different onscreen keyboard layouts using EEG signals. In: IEEE International Conference on Systems, Man, and Cybernetics, pp. 480–486 (2013). https://doi.org/10.1109/SMC.2013.88
36. GSR R-Notebooks: Processing in iMotions and algorithms used (Latest Version) (2021). https://help.imotions.com/hc/en-us/articles/360010312220-GSR-R-Notebooks-Processing-in-iMotions-and-algorithms-used-Latest-Version. Accessed 6 Jan 2021
37. R Notebooks (EDA): GSR Epoching (2021). https://help.imotions.com/hc/en-us/articles/360013685940-R-Notebooks-EDA-GSR-Epoching. Accessed 6 Jan 2021

Author Index

Printed in the United States
by Baker & Taylor Publisher Services